THE CONTESTED PLACE OF RELIGION IN FAMILY LAW

Like many beliefs, religious views matter across an individual's life and the life cycle of a family – from birth to marriage, through child-rearing, and, eventually, death. This volume examines clashes over religious liberty within the personal realm of the family. Against swirling religious beliefs, secular values, and legal regulation, this volume offers a forward-looking examination of tensions between religious freedom and the state's protective function. Contributors unpack some of the Court's recent decisions and explain how they set the stage for ongoing disputes. They evaluate religious claims around birth control, circumcision, modesty, religious education, marriage, polygamy, shared parenting, corporal punishment, faith healing, divorce, and the end of life. Authors span legislators, attorneys, academics, journalists, ministers, physicians, child advocates, and representatives of minority faiths. *The Contested Place of Religion in Family Law* begins an overdue conversation on questions dividing the nation.

Robin Fretwell Wilson is the Roger and Stephany Joslin Professor of Law and Director of the Program in Family Law and Policy at the University of Illinois College of Law.

The Contested Place of Religion in Family Law

Edited by

ROBIN FRETWELL WILSON

University of Illinois College of Law

CAMBRIDGE
UNIVERSITY PRESS

CAMBRIDGE
UNIVERSITY PRESS

University Printing House, Cambridge CB2 8BS, United Kingdom

One Liberty Plaza, 20th Floor, New York, NY 10006, USA

477 Williamstown Road, Port Melbourne, VIC 3207, Australia

314-321, 3rd Floor, Plot 3, Splendor Forum, Jasola District Centre, New Delhi - 110025, India

79 Anson Road, #06-04/06, Singapore 079906

Cambridge University Press is part of the University of Cambridge.

It furthers the University's mission by disseminating knowledge in the pursuit of education, learning and research at the highest international levels of excellence.

www.cambridge.org
Information on this title: www.cambridge.org/9781108405508
DOI: 10.1017/9781108277976

First published 2018
First paperback edition 2019

A catalogue record for this publication is available from the British Library

Library of Congress Cataloging in Publication data
NAMES: Wilson, Robin Fretwell, editor.
TITLE: The contested place of religion in family law / edited by Robin Fretwell Wilson.
DESCRIPTION: Cambridge,UK; New York, NY, USA : Cambridge University Press, 2018.
IDENTIFIERS: LCCN 2017043605 | ISBN 9781108417600 (hardback)
SUBJECTS: LCSH: Domestic relations – United States. | Freedom of religion – United States. | Religious minorities – Legal status, laws, etc. – United States. |
BISAC: LAW / Family Law / General.
CLASSIFICATION: LCC KF505 .C657 2018 | DDC 346.7301/5–dc23
LC record available at https://lccn.loc.gov/2017043605

ISBN 978-1-108-41760-0 Hardback
ISBN 978-1-108-40550-8 Paperback

To The Honorable E. Grady Jolly

For opening a window to me on what it means to be a scholar of the law and the value of a life spent in service.

Contents

Notes on Contributors

Senator J. Stuart Adams is Senate Majority Whip in the Utah State Senate. Elected to the Utah Senate in 2009, Senator Adams also served in the Utah House of Representatives and on the Layton City Council. During the 2015 legislative session, Senator Adams was the sponsor and lead negotiator of the three religious liberties bills that together formed the landmark Utah Compromise. The former chairman of the Utah Transportation Commission, Senator Adams currently chairs the Military Installation Development Authority. A graduate of the University of Utah, Senator Adams is a partner in the Adams Company, a real estate, construction, and development firm.

Arianne Renan Barzilay is Assistant Professor of Law at the University of Haifa Faculty of Law. She earned her JSD and LLM from New York University School of Law and LLB from Tel Aviv University Faculty of Law *magna cum laude* after clerking for the Israeli Supreme Court. Her research focuses on the regulation of families, sex discrimination, and feminism. She uses historical, socio-legal, and gender analysis in her work to explore the myriad and intricate ways in which the law influences the construction of families, the power dynamics within them, and gender inequality. Her work has been published in leading journals; recently, the Israeli Ministry of Justice adopted her proposals for addressing economic abuse in intimate partner relationships. She has won several prestigious research grants, scholarships and awards, including the Israeli Ministry of Science Grant to evaluate legal mechanisms for the promotion of women, the Harry and Michael Sacher Institute Award for Legislative Research and Comparative Law, the Bar-Ilan University Gender Studies Award for Young Scholars, the New York University School of Law JSD fellowship, the Israeli Council on Higher Education fellowship, and the Israeli Returning Scientist fellowship; she was voted Outstanding Teacher at the University of Haifa.

Brian H. Bix is Frederick W. Thomas Professor of Law and Philosophy at the University of Minnesota. He received his JD from Harvard University and his DPhil from Oxford University. Professor Bix works in family law, contract law, and legal philosophy. He is a member of the American Law Institute and was the Reporter for the Uniform Premarital and Marital Agreements Act. His publications include OXFORD INTRODUCTIONS TO US LAW: FAMILY LAW (2013) and JURISPRUDENCE: THEORY AND CONTEXT (7th ed., 2015). Professor Bix is a past Chair of the Section on Family and Juvenile Law of the Association of American Law Schools.

Margaret "Peg" Brinig is Fritz Duda Family Chair in Law at the Notre Dame Law School. Professor Brinig is best known for her empirical studies of families, social capital, and social welfare legislation. In 2000, she published FROM CONTRACT TO COVENANT: BEYOND THE LAW AND ECONOMICS OF THE FAMILY. In 2010, Professor Brinig published LAW, FAMILY AND COMMUNITY: SUPPORTING THE COVENANT, and in 2014 she published LOST CLASSROOM, LOST COMMUNITY: CATHOLIC SCHOOLS' IMPORTANCE FOR URBAN AMERICA (with Nicole Garnett). Professor Brinig is a past chair of the AALS Section on Family and Juvenile Law, sits on the Executive Council of the International Society of Family Law, and is a member of the American Law Institute. Her books include monographs, treatises, practitioner manuals, and casebooks on family law. She has also published more than a hundred articles in law reviews and peer-reviewed journals.

James G. Dwyer is Arthur B. Hanson Professor of Law at William & Mary Law School, where he has taught Family Law and Youth Law since 2000. He is the author of RELIGIOUS SCHOOLS V. CHILDREN'S RIGHTS (1998), which argues for greater regulation of religious schools, and of VOUCHERS WITHIN REASON: A CHILD-CENTERED APPROACH TO EDUCATION REFORM (2001), which argues (on the surface, paradoxically) for state financial support of religious schools. He is also the coauthor of HOMESCHOOLING: AN HISTORICAL AND PHILOSOPHICAL ANALYSIS (forthcoming). His other publications theorize children's rights in relation to unfit parents and dysfunctional communities and topics of religiously motivated parenting and the position of children in liberal political theory. Dwyer is the past chair of and currently serves on the Executive Committee of the AALS Section on Children and the Law.

Naomi Cahn is Harold H. Greene Professor at the George Washington University Law School, where she teaches family law, feminist jurisprudence, trusts and estates, and elder law, and she has written numerous law review articles and books in those areas. She is the author of several books, including THE NEW KINSHIP: CONSTRUCTING DONOR-CONCEIVED FAMILIES (2013) and TEST TUBE FAMILIES: WHY THE FERTILITY MARKET NEEDS LEGAL REGULATION (2009); she has coauthored HOMEWARD BOUND: MODERN FAMILIES, ELDER CARE, & LOSS (2017) (with Amy Ziettlow); RED FAMILIES V. BLUE FAMILIES: LEGAL POLARIZATION AND THE CREATION OF CULTURE (2010); and MARRIAGE MARKETS: HOW INEQUALITY IS REMAKING THE AMERICAN FAMILY (2014) (both with Professor June Carbone); and she has co-written casebooks in the fields of family law and trusts and estates. Her work has been featured in the *New York Times, Washington Post, Christian Science Monitor, The New Yorker*, NPR, and MSNBC. Professor Cahn is a member of the American Law Institute and the American College of Trust and Estate Counsel, and a Fellow of the American Bar Foundation.

William N. Eskridge, Jr., is John A. Garver Professor of Jurisprudence at Yale Law School. He has authored dozens of articles and several books on statutory interpretation; the most recent is INTERPRETING LAW: A PRIMER ON HOW TO READ STATUTES AND THE CONSTITUTION (2016). Professor Eskridge has also written dozens of articles and several books on the rights of sexual and gender minorities, including DISHONORABLE PASSIONS: SODOMY LAW IN AMERICA, 1861–2003 (2008); GAY MARRIAGE: FOR BETTER OR FOR WORSE? WHAT WE HAVE LEARNED FROM THE EVIDENCE (2006) (with Darren Spedale); EQUALITY PRACTICE: CIVIL UNIONS AND THE FUTURE OF GAY RIGHTS (2002); GAYLAW: CHALLENGING THE APARTHEID OF THE CLOSET (1999); and SEXUALITY, GENDER, AND THE LAW (1997, 2003, 2005) (with Nan Hunter). His current project (with Christopher Riano) is a study of the marriage equality debate, 1967–2017. In 2015, Professor Eskridge received the inaugural Harry Krause Lifetime Achievement Award in Family Law.

Michele Goodwin is Chancellor's Professor of Law at the University of California, Irvine, where she is Founder and Director of the Center for Biotechnology and Global Health Policy. She is also Founder of the Institute for Global Child Advocacy. Professor Goodwin's research concerns the role of law in the promotion and regulation of medicine, science, and biotechnology. Her scholarship defines new ways of thinking about supply, demand, and access to sophisticated medical technologies, spanning assisted reproductive technology to genetics (human and modified organisms), organ transplantation, and creation of families. She is a prolific author and public voice on civil liberties and human rights, with editorials and commentaries appearing in the *Los Angeles Times, New York Times, Gene Watch, Christian Science Monitor, Cleveland Plain Dealer, Houston Chronicle, Chicago Sun Times, Washington Post, AlterNet*, and *Forbes Magazine*.

Senator Orrin Hatch is President Pro Tempore of the United States Senate, sworn in on January 6, 2015. Senator Hatch has served during the administrations of six Presidents and alongside nine Senate Majority Leaders. One of the most effective and bipartisan lawmakers of all time, Senator Hatch has authored 112 bills, and cosponsored 638 bills that have become law. Senator Hatch is responsible for many of the most consequential laws of the modern era on religious liberty, including the Religious Freedom Restoration Act of 1993 – a bill he coauthored with the late Senator Ted Kennedy – and the Religious Land Use and Institutionalized Persons Act. These landmark pieces of legislation prohibit substantial government burdens on the free exercise of religion, allowing Americans of all faiths to live, work, and worship in accordance with their deeply held personal beliefs. Senator Hatch recently delivered a series of speeches on the Senate floor on the subject of religious liberty – its origins, its meaning, and its status in modern society – reproduced in his newly published book, PROTECTING OUR RELIGIOUS LIBERTIES. Senator Hatch has also long been on the front lines of legislative battles to protect our vulnerable Americans. Senator Hatch authored the recently passed Amy and Vicky Act, which created an effective, balanced restitution process for victims of child pornography.

Michael Helfand is Associate Professor of Law at Pepperdine University School of Law and Co-Director of the Diane and Guilford Glazer Institute for Jewish Studies. His research considers how US law treats religious law, custom, and practice, focusing on the intersection of private law and religion in contexts such as religious arbitration, religious contracts, and religious torts. His academic articles have appeared in numerous law journals, including the *Yale Law Journal, New York University Law Review*, and *Duke Law Journal*, and they have twice been selected for presentation at the Harvard-Stanford-Yale Junior Faculty Forum. In addition, Professor Helfand frequently provides commentary on clashes between law and religion, and his writing has appeared in the *Wall Street Journal, Los Angeles Times*, and *USA Today*. Prior to joining the Pepperdine Law faculty, Professor Helfand was an associate at Davis Polk & Wardwell LLP and a law clerk for the Honorable Julia Smith Gibbons of the United States Court of Appeals for the Sixth Circuit.

Kari Hong is Assistant Professor of Law at Boston College Law School. An expert in immigration law, criminal law, and family law, Professor

Hong's scholarship focuses on the immigration consequences of criminal convictions, the intersection of family law and immigration law, and contemporary matters in criminal law. Prior to academia, Professor Hong owned her own firm with offices in California and Oregon. In private practice, Professor Hong prepared nearly 100 actions in the United States Court of Appeals for the Ninth Circuit, representing noncitizens in asylum, removal defense, and citizenship claims. At Boston College Law School, she founded a clinic supervising law students who represent noncitizens with criminal convictions before the Ninth Circuit. Before entering private practice, she clerked for the Honorable Jeremy Fogel, United States District Court of the Northern District of California, and the Honorable Sidney Thomas, United States Court of Appeals for the Ninth Circuit.

Richard L. Kaplan is Guy Raymond Jones Chair in Law at the University of Illinois College of Law, specializing in federal income taxation and elder law. In addition to numerous books and articles involving taxation and tax policy, he is the coauthor of ELDER LAW IN A NUTSHELL (2014), as well as articles on various elder law topics, including Social Security, Medicare, long-term care financing, and retirement funding. He has served as the faculty advisor to *The Elder Law Journal*, the oldest scholarly publication devoted to this subject, since that publication was created in 1992. He was a congressionally designated delegate to the National Summit on Retirement Savings and is an elected member of the National Academy of Social Insurance.

Robin Bradley Kar is Professor of Law and Philosophy at the University of Illinois, Urbana-Champaign. He is a graduate of Harvard College; Yale Law School, where he edited the *Yale Law Journal*; and the University of Michigan, where he completed a PhD in moral, legal, and political philosophy. His work is highly interdisciplinary, but one major strand is devoted to studying the evolution of moral and legal systems. As a part of this project, Professor Kar recently began writing on the evolution of marital practices both domestically and within the larger world historical record, including two articles in the *Illinois Law Review*. His articles have appeared in the *University of Chicago Law Review*, *Law & Social Inquiry*, and the *Texas Law Review*.

Anthony Michael Kreis is Visiting Assistant Professor of Law at the Illinois Institute of Technology's Chicago-Kent College of Law. He earned his PhD from the University of Georgia's School of Public and International Affairs in 2016. His dissertation, *The Capital of Trust*, examines the significance of judicial institutions in the movement to advance same-sex marriage. A graduate of Washington and Lee University School of Law, Professor Kreis's research focuses on historical development of civil rights law, the rights of LGBT persons, and contemporary religious liberty controversies.

Gregory M. Lipper is a partner at Clinton Brook & Peed in Washington, DC; his trial and appellate practice includes criminal defense, civil rights cases, and commercial disputes. He previously served as Senior Litigation Counsel at Americans United for Separation of Church and State, where he represented Notre Dame students who intervened in federal court to protect their access to contraceptive coverage under the Affordable Care Act and wrote amicus briefs in the Supreme Court contraception cases of *Burwell v. Hobby Lobby Stores* and *Zubik v. Burwell*. He also served as co-counsel in a class action challenge to Alabama's ban on marriage by same-sex couples and was part of the team that represented the respondents before the Supreme Court in *Town of Greece v. Galloway*. In 2013 Super Lawyers named Lipper a "Rising Star" in Washington, D.C. Lipper received his JD, *magna cum laude*, from Harvard Law School, where he was Notes Editor of the *Harvard Law Review* and an oralist on the winning team in the Ames Moot Court Competition. After law school, he clerked for Judge R. Guy Cole, Jr., on the United States Court of Appeals for the Sixth Circuit and then practiced at Covington & Burling.

Paul A. Offit, M.D., is Director of the Vaccine Education Center at the Children's Hospital of Philadelphia as well as the Maurice R. Hilleman Professor of Vaccinology and Professor of Pediatrics at the Perelman School of Medicine at the University of Pennsylvania. He received a Research Career Development Award from the National Institutes of Health, the Luigi Mastroianni and William Osler Awards from the University of Pennsylvania School of Medicine, Maxwell Finland award for Outstanding Scientific Achievement, and the Charles Mérieux Award from the National Foundation for Infectious Diseases. Bill and Melinda Gates honored him during the launch of their Foundation's Living Proof Project for global health. Dr. Offit has published more than 160 papers in medical and scientific journals and is a member of the National Academy of Medicine, the American Academy of Arts and Sciences, and the Advisory Committee on Immunization Practices to the Centers for Disease Control and Prevention. He is also the author of six medical narratives, including THE CUTTER INCIDENT: HOW AMERICA'S FIRST POLIO VACCINE LED TO TODAY'S GROWING VACCINE CRISIS (2005); VACCINATED: ONE MAN'S QUEST TO DEFEAT THE WORLD'S DEADLIEST DISEASES (2007), for which he won an award from the American Medical Writers Association; AUTISM'S FALSE PROPHETS: BAD SCIENCE, RISKY MEDICINE, AND THE SEARCH FOR A CURE (2008); DEADLY CHOICES: HOW THE ANTI-VACCINE MOVEMENT THREATENS US ALL (2011), which was selected by Kirkus Reviews and Booklist as one of the best nonfiction books of the year; and BAD FAITH: WHEN RELIGIOUS BELIEF UNDERMINES MODERN MEDICINE (2015), selected by the *New York Times Book Review* as an "Editor's Choice" book in April 2015.

Patrick N. Parkinson is Professor of Law at the University of Sydney. He was president of the International Society of Family Law from 2011 to 2014. He served from 2004 to 2007 as chairperson of the Family Law Council, an advisory body to the Australian attorney-general, and he also chaired a review of the Child Support Scheme in 2004–05, which led to the enactment of major changes to the child support system. He is a member of the Order of Australia. His books include FAMILY LAW AND THE INDISSOLUBILITY OF PARENTHOOD (Cambridge University Press, 2011); AUSTRALIAN FAMILY LAW IN CONTEXT (2015); THE VOICE OF A CHILD IN FAMILY LAW DISPUTES (2008) (with Judy Cashmore); and CHILD SEXUAL ABUSE AND THE CHURCHES: UNDERSTANDING THE ISSUES (2003).

Eric Rassbach has been Deputy General Counsel at the Becket Fund for Religious Liberty since 2004. He has represented Buddhists, Christians, Hindus, Jains, Jews, Muslims, Santeros, and Sikhs, among many others. He represented the winning parties in several pathbreaking religious liberty cases at the United States Supreme Court, including *Hosanna-Tabor Evangelical Lutheran Church and School v. EEOC*, *Burwell v. Hobby Lobby Stores*, and *Holt v. Hobbs*. He has also represented clients at the European Court of Human Rights in Strasbourg, France. He is a well-known commentator on church-state issues and has been quoted in the *New York Times*, *Washington Post*, *Times of India*, *Wall Street Journal*, and other publications. Before joining the Becket Fund, Rassbach served as a law clerk to United States District Judge Lee Rosenthal in Houston, Texas, and worked in private practice. Rassbach is a graduate of Harvard Law School.

Mark L. Rienzi is Professor of Law at The Catholic University of America, Columbus School of Law, Senior Counsel at the Becket Fund for Religious Liberty, and Visiting Professor at Harvard Law School. Professor Rienzi teaches constitutional law, religious liberty, torts, and evidence. His litigation and research interests focus on the First and Fourteenth Amendments, with an emphasis on free speech and the free exercise of religion. His scholarship on these issues has appeared in a variety of prestigious journals, including the *Harvard Law Review*, *Fordham Law Review*, *Emory Law Review*, *Notre Dame Law Review*, and *George Mason Law Review*. At the Becket Fund, Professor Rienzi has successfully represented a variety of parties at the Supreme Court, including in *Little Sisters of the Poor v. Sebelius* (emergency order, 2014); *Burwell v. Hobby Lobby* (2014); *Wheaton College v. Burwell* (emergency order, 2014); *Holt v. Hobbs* (2015); and *McCullen v. Coakley* (2014). Professor Rienzi represented the Little Sisters of the Poor and other religious petitioners in *Zubik v. Burwell*.

Shaakirrrah R. Sanders is Associate Professor of Law at the University of Idaho College of Law, where she teaches constitutional law, criminal procedure, and the First Amendment. After earning a JD from Loyola University New Orleans College of Law, Professor Sanders clerked for Ivan L.R. Lemelle in the United States District Court for the Eastern District of Louisiana and Chief Judge Lavenski R. Smith of the United States Court of Appeals for the Eighth Circuit. She also practiced law in New Orleans at Locke Lorde and in Seattle at K&L Gates and the Public Defender Association. Her current scholarship encompasses jury trial rights, criminal sentencing, and the First Amendment. Her forthcoming scholarship explores how the US Constitution applies to family law. She has discussed this issue on national media outlets, including Al Jazeera America, Associated Press, the *New York Times*, and the *Washington Post*, as well as local and regional public television and radio stations and news affiliates for ABC, CBS, NBC, and Fox.

Elizabeth Sepper is Professor of Law at Washington University School of Law. She is a recognized expert in health law and religious liberty law. Professor Sepper has written extensively on conscientious refusals to provide reproductive and end-of-life care, objections to the contraceptives coverage mandate, and conflicts between religion and gender and sexual orientation nondiscrimination laws. Her recent articles have appeared in top law journals, including the *Columbia Law Review*, *Virginia Law Review*, *Indiana Law Journal*, and *Harvard Law Review Forum*. She received her JD and LLM in International Legal Studies from New York University School of Law and her BA in History from Boston University. She is currently an Executive Committee member of the AALS Section on Law and Religion.

Maura Strassberg is Professor of Law at Drake University Law School. She is a graduate of Columbia University Law School, where she was a member of the *Law Review*. After clerking for United States Court of Appeals for the First Circuit Judge Hugh H. Bownes, she practiced law as a commercial litigator in

Boston, Massachusetts. She inaugurated a course in Sexuality and the Law at Drake in addition to teaching Contracts, Legal Ethics, and Sales. Professor Strassberg first addressed the legal status of polygamy in her 1997 article "Monogamy, Polygamy and Same-Sex Marriage: Distinctions of Form or Substance" in the *North Carolina Law Review*. She has contributed book chapters on polygamy and polyamory most recently to Families: Beyond the Nuclear Ideal (Daniela Cutas and Sarah Chan, eds., 2014) and The Polygamy Question (Janet Bennion and Lisa Fishbayn Joffe, eds., 2016) and a symposium on polygamy in the *Emory Law Journal*.

Asma T. Uddin is a Fellow in the Initiative on Security and Religious Freedom at the UCLA Burkle Center for International Relations. She is also the Director of Strategy for the Center for Islam and Religious Freedom (CIRF), a Washington, DC–based nonprofit engaging in research, media, education, and advocacy at the intersection of Islam and religious freedom in both the West and Muslim-majority countries. She is also the founder and editor in chief of *altmuslimah.com* and a research fellow at Georgetown University's Berkley Center. Prior to joining CIRF, Uddin served as counsel with Becket Law, a nonprofit law firm specializing in religious freedom cases in the United States and abroad. Her scholarly work has been published by numerous law reviews and prominent university presses. She also serves on the Organization for Security and Co-Operation in Europe's Office for Democratic Institutions and Human Rights Panel of Experts on Freedom of Religion or Belief and the advisory council for the Institute for Global Engagement's Center for Women, Faith & Leadership. Uddin is a graduate of the University of Chicago Law School, where she was a staff editor at the *University of Chicago Law Review*.

Merle H. Weiner is Philip H. Knight Professor of Law at the University of Oregon School of Law, where she is the faculty director and co-founder of the Domestic Violence Clinic, now in its eighteenth year. Professor Weiner is a member of the American Law Institute, the International Society of Family Law, and the Executive Committee of the Section on Family Law of the American Association of Law Schools. She also sits on the National Executive Committee for the Order of the Coif. Professor Weiner coauthored the first US casebook on comparative and international family law, now in its third edition, and has written extensively on the topic of international child abduction. Professor Weiner's book, A Parent-Partner Status for American Family Law, was published by Cambridge University Press in 2015.

Robin Fretwell Wilson is Roger and Stephany Joslin Professor of Law and Director of the Family Law and Policy Program at the University of Illinois College of Law, where she also directs the Epstein Health Law and Policy Program. She is the author of eleven books, including RECONCEIVING THE FAMILY: CRITICAL REFLECTIONS ON THE AMERICAN LAW INSTITUTE'S PRINCIPLES OF THE LAW OF FAMILY DISSOLUTION (Cambridge University Press, 2006, ed.); THE HANDBOOK OF CHILDREN, CULTURE & VIOLENCE (2006, with Nancy Dowd and Dorothy Singer, eds.); SAME-SEX MARRIAGE AND RELIGIOUS LIBERTY (2008, with Douglas Laycock and Anthony Picarello, eds.); RELIGIOUS FREEDOM, LGBT RIGHTS AND THE PROSPECTS FOR COMMON GROUND (2018, with William N. Eskridge, Jr. eds., Cambridge University Press) (in press); and DOMESTIC RELATIONS: CASES AND MATERIALS, 8th ed. (2017, with Walter Wadlington and Raymond C. O'Brien). Professor Wilson has been consistently ranked as one of the top ten scholars in family law in the United States in terms of scholarly impact. Her work has been featured in the *New York Times, Washington Post, Los Angeles Times, Wall Street Journal, Good Morning America*, and *Essence* magazine, among others. A member of the American Law Institute and the Executive Council of the International Society of Family Law, Professor Wilson is presently the chair of the Section on Law and Religion of the Association of American Law Schools and past chair of the AALS Section on Family and Juvenile Law. In 2018, Professor Wilson received the Thomas L. Kane Religious Freedom Award, presented annually to an individual who has contributed in significant ways to the defense of religious freedom in the public square.

John Witte, Jr., is Robert W. Woodruff University Professor of Law, McDonald Distinguished Professor, and Director of the Center for the Study of Law and Religion at Emory University School of Law. A specialist in legal history, marriage law, and religious liberty, he has published 230 articles, 15 journal symposia, and 30 books. Recent book titles include SEX, MARRIAGE AND FAMILY LIFE IN JOHN CALVIN'S GENEVA, 2 vols. (2005, 2018); MODERN CHRISTIAN TEACHINGS ON LAW, POLITICS, AND HUMAN NATURE, 3 vols. (2006); GOD'S JOUST, GOD'S JUSTICE: LAW AND RELIGION IN THE WESTERN TRADITION (2006); THE REFORMATION OF RIGHTS: LAW, RELIGION, AND HUMAN RIGHTS IN EARLY MODERN CALVINISM (Cambridge University Press, 2007); CHRISTIANITY AND LAW: AN INTRODUCTION (Cambridge University Press, 2008); THE SINS OF THE FATHERS: THE LAW AND THEOLOGY OF ILLEGITIMACY RECONSIDERED (Cambridge University Press, 2009); CHRISTIANITY AND HUMAN RIGHTS: AN INTRODUCTION (Cambridge University Press, 2010); RELIGION AND HUMAN RIGHTS: AN INTRODUCTION (2012); FROM SACRAMENT TO CONTRACT: MARRIAGE, RELIGION, AND LAW IN THE WESTERN

TRADITION (2012); NO ESTABLISHMENT OF RELIGION: AMERICA'S ORIGINAL CONTRIBUTION TO RELIGIOUS LIBERTY (2012); THE WESTERN CASE FOR MONOGAMY OVER POLYGAMY (Cambridge University Press, 2015); and RELIGION AND THE AMERICAN CONSTITUTIONAL EXPERIMENT (4th ed., 2016). Professor Witte received the 2016 Harry Krause Lifetime Achievement Award in Family Law and the National Religious Freedom Award. Professor Witte's writings have appeared in fifteen languages. With major funding from the Pew, Ford, Lilly, Luce, and McDonald foundations, he has directed twelve major international projects on democracy, human rights, and religious liberty, and on marriage, family, and children. He edits EMORY UNIVERSITY STUDIES IN LAW AND RELIGION and CAMBRIDGE LAW AND CHRISTIANITY SERIES (Cambridge University Press).

Karin Carmit Yefet is Associate Professor at the University of Haifa Faculty of Law. She earned her LLM and JSD from Yale Law School and completed the LLB and LLM Honors program in Bar-Ilan University *summa cum laude* (valedictorian). Her award-winning scholarship on family law and feminist legal theory focuses on the impact of religion on various dimensions of women's lives and legal status from feminist, comparative, and constitutional perspectives. Dr. Yefet was recently nominated by the Israeli government as a chief consultant to the Public Commission on international humanitarian law issues; clerked in the Israeli Supreme Court; and won several prestigious research grants, scholarships, and awards, including the Israeli Parliament prize, the Cegla Prize for the Best Article of junior scholars in Israel, the Justice Cheshin Prize for Scholarly Excellence in Law, the Dasti and Etti Miller Prize for Best Junior Scholar in the University of Haifa, the Israeli Sociology Society Prize, the Israeli Association of Public Law Prize, the BIU Rector Prize, the Israeli Science Foundation grant, the Israeli Ministry of Science grant, and the Fischman excellence scholarship, the HSBC fellowship, and the Fulbright fellowship.

Amy Ziettlow is Pastor of Holy Cross Lutheran Church (ELCA) & former COO of Hospice of Baton Rouge. She is ordained in the Evangelical Lutheran Church in America and currently serves at Holy Cross Lutheran. Her recent publications include HOMEWARD BOUND: MODERN FAMILIES, ELDER CARE & LOSS (with Naomi Cahn) published in 2017; "The Honor Commandment: Law, Religion, and the Challenge of Elder Care" (with Naomi Cahn) in the *Journal of Law and Religion*; and "Making Things Fair: An Empirical Study of How People Approach the Wealth Transmission System" (with Naomi Cahn) in *The Elder Law Journal*. She is a contributor to the *Huffington Post*, Institute for Family Studies blog, and *The Atlantic* Health section.

Foreword

We live in a critical time for religious liberty. This fundamental freedom – so esteemed by our forebears that they enumerated it in the First Amendment – is now in danger both at home and abroad. Threats to free exercise are proliferating across America as courts narrow religious liberty protections and new laws restrict the ability of believers to express views or practice their faith when out of step with prevailing orthodoxy.

At the core of these attacks is a fundamental misunderstanding of the nature and substance of religious liberty. Religious liberty is not an ancillary freedom in service to our other rights and privileges; it is the foundation of freedom itself. Indeed, the ability to think, speak, and act in accordance with one's conscience is preliminary to the exercise of all other liberties – including freedom of speech and the rights of assembly and petition. In this regard, religious liberty is indispensable to the future of our Republic.

Perhaps this is why, of all the rights delineated in the Constitution, the Framers chose to list religious freedom first. This priority of place suggests that religious exercise has particular significance and merits special protection. Indeed, freedom of conscience deserves preeminence because it goes to the very heart of who we are as human beings and how we make sense of our world. It implicates duties that transcend mere personal choice and become obligatory in the life of the believer.

No decision is more fundamental to human existence than the decision we make regarding our relationship to the divine. It follows, then, that no act of government can be more intrusive or more invasive of individual autonomy and free will than the act of compelling a person to violate his or her sincerely chosen religious beliefs.

When government denies religious freedom, it forces believers to choose between duty to God and duty to man – duty to man backed by threat of force.

No government that values its citizens' agency, and certainly no limited government that exists at the suffrage of the people, should put its citizens to such an impossible choice.

Yet today, with respect for religious liberty eroding in the wake of rising secularism, the role of faith in public life faces unprecedented scrutiny. Even in the private sphere, religion is under attack. The sacred rights of conscience, once held to be inviolable, are increasingly subordinated to the demands of a progressive political agenda. Nowhere is the assault on religious belief more apparent than in our courts.

Landmark Supreme Court cases, such as *Obergefell v. Hodges*, have called into question the special solicitude traditionally given to religion in family law. In the aftermath of these momentous decisions, the boundaries between church and state are being tested anew. Much as *Burwell v. Hobby Lobby Stores, Inc.* disturbed what some saw as a settled understanding of the relationship between the state and its citizens, *Obergefell* reimagined the nature of what many Americans believe to be a fundamentally religious institution: marriage. Such decisions tear at the seams of a delicate social fabric.

In the ongoing debate over the government's authority to effect change across religious institutions, protecting the family is of paramount importance. The family plays an indispensable role in preserving religious freedom by serving as the primary buffer between the state and the individual. While historically the courts have treated the family as "an entity which has a claim against legal intrusion,"[1] that claim has been weakened in the aftermath of recent court decisions. As a consequence, the status of religion in the legal landscape of the family is more contested today than perhaps ever before.

Protecting the rights of religious individuals from further intrusion requires a keen understanding of the current legal environment. In answering the myriad questions raised by *Obergefell*, *Hobby Lobby*, and *Zubik v. Burwell*, The Contested Place of Religion in Family Law offers the most comprehensive analysis to date. Contributors to this volume include leading scholars in both family law and religious liberty law – two areas of legal scholarship that significantly overlap, yet all too infrequently interact.

Perhaps the most remarkable aspect of this volume is the diversity of perspectives contained within it. The authors include journalists, academics, ordained ministers, feminists, child advocates, physicians, social conservatives, liberals, and moderates. In conducting their research, contributors have utilized a wide range of analytical tools, including economic theory, constitutional law, social science analysis, empirical methods, historical

[1] Lee E. Teitelbaum, *Family History and Family Law*, 197 Utah Law Review 237 (2006).

examination of the law's development, and comparative perspectives from outside the United States.

The Contested Place of Religion in Family Law is distinct from other publications because it includes voices missing in many academic works, such as federal and state legislators – the groups that principally decide how much protection governments accord religion in the sphere of the family – as well as litigators at the forefront of legal battles to preserve religious autonomy in family life.

Safeguarding the right to worship amid growing hostility requires steadfast vigilance and determination. I am confident that the superlative scholarship of this volume will guide individuals of faith, and all Americans, as we chart a new path forward to restore religious liberty to its rightful place in the American legal system.

Senator Orrin G. Hatch
President Pro Tempore
United States Senate

Acknowledgements

I am indebted to the Epstein Health Law and Policy Program and the Family Law and Policy Program at the University of Illinois College of Law and to DePaul University College of Law and Professor Zoë Robinson for their generous support of the conference that preceded this book, out of which came the corpus of chapters.

I am especially grateful for our contributors and their professionalism and insight. Special thanks to Senator Hatch and Senator Adams, Dr. Paul Offit, Reverend Amy Ziettlow, and the litigators at the forefront of the religious liberty struggles—Greg Lipper, Mark Rienzi, Eric Rassbach, and Asma Uddin—for making time in busy schedules to ground this discussion with real-world perspectives.

Special thanks to the University of Illinois College of Law's Law Library for partnering to produce timely, relevant scholarship. Heather Simmons and Michelle Dewey provided excellent research advice and citation assistance throughout the project. Michelle, you will be sorely missed. Thanks to Stephanie Davidson and Amy Tomaszewski for painstaking work on the Index. Natalie Ellis (J.D. 2017) and Karla Geanina Bayas Salinas (J.D. expected 2018) assisted with research on corporal punishment laws in the 50 states.

Most, I am grateful to William Duncan and Jessica Roberts for pouring themselves into refining the final manuscript, and to my research assistants for extensive citation work, legal research, and input into the framing of the book and building cross-talk between authors: Kaylyn Belcher (J.D. 2016), Rachel Bernal (J.D. 2017), Laura Buecker (J.D. 2017), Jessica Diedrich (J.D. expected 2018), Craig Foster (J.D. 2017), Anna Gotfryd (J.D. 2016), Dmitri Kachan (J.D. expected 2018), Catrina Miksis (J.D. 2016), Robert J. Morse (J.D. 2016), Philip Pence (J.D. 2016), Paul Schmitt (J.D. 2017), Ahad Syed (J.D. 2016), Collin Stich (J.D. expected 2018), Breanna Taylor (J.D. 2016), and Elaina Valtierra

(J.D. 2017). Really, every one of your names belong on the cover, thank you for being wonderful colleagues.

Finally, I am thankful for John Berger's advice in the formative stages of this project and for Rebecca Jackaman, Allan Alphonse, and Linda Benson's care in preparing this book for publication.

Introduction

The Contested Place of Religion in Family Law

Robin Fretwell Wilson

Roger and Stephany Joslin Professor of Law University of Illinois College of Law

This volume comes at an important moment. In the space of three years, the United States Supreme Court decided cases about marriage equality, the government's ability to require contraceptives as part of employer health policies, and the ability of religious actors to step aside from duties that otherwise apply.[1] The cases ranked among the most closely watched of each term. Two of them captured the nation's attention and highlighted the sharp divide on the Court – and among Americans – as to these issues.

In a 5–4 decision, *Obergefell v. Hodges*, the Court recognized same-sex marriage – reimagining the boundaries of marriage, an institution most Americans still see as fundamentally religious.[2] In *Burwell v. Hobby Lobby*, the Court again split 5–4 and breathed new life into religious claims not to be burdened by government regulation. In both cases, the dissenters questioned not only the validity but also the legitimacy of the majority's reasoning.[3] And so did Americans.

[1] Burwell v. Hobby Lobby Stores, Inc., 134 S. Ct. 2751 (2014) (holding that closely held corporations could not be made to provide contraceptive coverage under the Patient Protection and Affordable Care Act because it would substantially burden their religious exercise and the Obama Administration had a less restrictive means available to it, requiring an insurer provide the contraceptives rather than the employer as it did with objecting religious nonprofit employers); Obergefell v. Hodges, 135 S. Ct. 2584 (2015) (establishing the right to marry for same-sex couples in all U.S. states); Zubik v. Burwell, 136 S. Ct. 1557 (2016) (remanding to allow parties to find an accommodation that accomplishes government's interests in contraceptive coverage for women while respecting objectors' religious liberty claims).

[2] *Marriage Update*, Rasmussen Reports (June 25, 2015), www.rasmussenreports.com/public_content/politics/current_events/marriage/marriage_update (finding that 50% of Americans "consider marriage a religious institution").

[3] Burwell, *supra* note 1, at 2793 (Ginsburg, J., dissenting) ("Misguided by its errant premise that [the Religious Freedom Restoration Act] moved beyond the pre-[Employment Division v. Smith] case law, the Court falters at each step of its analysis."); Obergefell *supra* note 1, at

Hobby Lobby "sent shock waves through America. It seemed to signal that the legal system would side with religious interests in a very broad range of ideological clashes among private parties."[4] In the post–*Hobby Lobby* world, free exercise of religion suddenly carried the power to "punch a large hole in the government's power to enact all kinds of federal social, economic, and welfare programs."[5] For *Hobby Lobby*'s critics, "[a]t stake is no less than the social progress made on 'contraception and abortion, sexual freedom and choice, women's rights, gay rights, [and] racial discrimination.'"[6] Especially when social change runs counter to deeply held religious understandings, the fear is that "a stringent interpretation" of statutory protections for religious liberty, such as the federal Religious Freedom Restoration Act ("RFRA") at the heart of *Hobby Lobby*, would "bring religious objectors 'out of the woodwork.'"[7]

Obergefell drew equally vocal critics. The decision, religious thought-leaders said, tore at the seams of an "already volatile social fabric."[8] For Kentucky Senator Rand Paul, like many Americans, *Obergefell* highlighted the "danger that a government that involves itself in every nook and cranny of our lives [may] now enforce definitions that conflict with sincerely felt religious convictions of others."[9] Although a slight majority of Americans support same-sex marriage, the country remains divided on the matter.[10] Some are so

2612 (Roberts, C.J., dissenting) ("The majority's decision is an act of will, not legal judgment. The right it announces has no basis in the Constitution or this Court's precedent."). *See also* Kar, this volume, for a close reading of *Obergefell*; Helfand, Chapter 2, this volume, and Sepper, Chapter 1, this volume, for close readings of *Hobby Lobby*.

4 Dwyer, Chapter 8, this volume.

5 Garrett Epps, *The U.S. Supreme Court's Nonsense Ruling in Zubik*, ATLANTIC, May 16, 2016, www.theatlantic.com/politics/archive/2016/05/the-supreme-courts-non-sensical-ruling-in-zubik/482967/.

6 Emma Long, *How Bad Is the Hobby Lobby Ruling?*, HISTORY NEWS NETWORK (July 14, 2014), historynewsnetwork.org/article/156320.

7 Eugene Volokh, *Prof. Michael McConnell (Stanford) on the Hobby Lobby Arguments*, WASH. POST (Mar. 27, 2014), www.washingtonpost.com/news/volokh-conspiracy/wp/2014/03/27/prof-michael-mcconnell-stanford-on-the-hobby-lobby-arguments/ (quoting Justice Elena Kagan).

8 *Here We Stand: An Evangelical Declaration on Marriage*, THE ETHICS & RELIGIOUS LIBERTY COMMISSION (June 26, 2015), http://erlc.com/resource-library/statements/here-we-stand-an-evangelical-declaration-on-marriage.

9 Rand Paul, *Government Should Get Out of the Marriage Business Altogether*, TIME (June 28, 2015), http://time.com/3939374/rand-paul-gay-marriage-supreme-court/.

10 *See Changing Attitudes on Gay Marriage*, PEW RESEARCH CENTER (May 12, 2016), www.pewforum.org/2016/05/12/changing-attitudes-on-gay-marriage/ (reporting that a majority of Americans in 2016, 55%, supported same-sex marriage compared to more than a third, 37%, who opposed it and that support for same-sex marriage tipped over to a slim majority only in 2011).

bitterly opposed to it that they publicly dissented, as Kentucky clerk Kim Davis did when she refused to perform any marriages and blocked others in her office from doing so.[11]

These divides carried into the 2016 presidential election. Wide swaths of the country felt disenfranchised by the remainder. Trump voters believed "nobody's listening to us."[12] Those disappointed by Donald Trump's election felt equally lost, "waking up to a whole new world," a "nightmare," one father said, for his family.[13]

The struggle for religious liberty animated the 2016 election. With a vacancy on the U.S. Supreme Court after Justice Antonin Scalia's sudden death six months before, a centerpiece of Trump's appeal was the ability to name justices who would "uphold[] not only this freedom, but all that [emanates] from it," as Hobby Lobby CEO David Green explained in *USA Today*.[14] In a speech to the Iowa Faith and Family Coalition in September 2015, then-candidate Trump said: "The first priority of my administration will be to preserve and protect our religious liberty."[15]

Although Trump shrugged off *Obergefell*'s reverberations – saying it's "been settled, and I'm fine with that"[16] – his base hoped to overturn *Obergefell* and

[11] For analysis and reactions, see Adams, Chapter 21, this volume; Goodwin, Chapter 3, this volume; Kar, Chapter 15, this volume; Wilson, Chapter 16, this volume.

[12] *See* Jeff Guo, *A New Theory for Why Trump Voters Are So Angry – That Actually Makes Sense*, WASH. POST (Nov. 8, 2016), www.washingtonpost.com/news/wonk/wp/2016/11/08/a-new-theory-for-why-trump-voters-are-so-angry-that-actually-makes-sense/?utm_term=.c437e2701b56 (reporting findings by a political science professor that Trump supporters felt "they were not getting their fair share of decision-making power").

[13] Matea Gold, Mark Berman, & Renae Merle, *"Not My President": Thousands Protest Trump in Rallies Across the U.S.*, WASH. POST (Nov. 11, 2016), www.washingtonpost.com/news/post-politics/wp/2016/11/10/not-my-president-thousand-protest-trump-in-rallies-across-the-u-s/?utm_term=.f9ce9a422d83.

[14] David Green, *One Judge Away from Losing Religious Liberty: Hobby Lobby CEO*, USA TODAY (Sep. 1, 2016), www.usatoday.com/story/opinion/2016/09/01/hobby-lobby-religious-freedom-liberty-obamacare-christian-david-green/89597214/?hootPostID=2a2ad7db1f58238473e45a42809 59e65.

[15] Bradford Richardson, *Trump Stance on Religious Liberty Leaves Social Conservatives Nervous*, WASH. TIMES (Feb. 19, 2017), www.washingtontimes.com/news/2017/feb/19/trump-stance-on-religious-liberty-leaves-social-co/.

[16] Ariane de Vogue, *Trump: Same-Sex Marriage Is "Settled," but Roe v. Wade Can Be Changed*, CNN (Nov. 15, 2016), www.cnn.com/2016/11/14/politics/trump-gay-marriage-abortion-supreme-court/index.html.

the Supreme Court's landmark abortion decision, *Roe v. Wade*.[17] Opponents believed a Trump presidency would mean exactly that.[18]

Trump's naked appeal to religious liberty and the U.S. Supreme Court's composition appears to have made a difference. In exit polls, white Evangelical voters went for Trump by a margin of 80% to 16%, as did a majority of Catholic voters.[19]

UNCERTAINTY AROUND MARRIAGE

Even before the election, however, the country witnessed considerable push-back over *Obergefell*'s implementation. State legislators introduced bills to end state-recognized marriage as a way to "get back to government being in its role and religion being in its role."[20] Some legislators proposed scrapping marriage as a legal category in favor of private contracts; others proposed redubbing marriages as domestic partnerships. As this volume shows, changing the state's relationship to marriage raises a thicket of questions about how already married couples will fare and whether couples would take the relationship "as seriously" if the state replaced marriage.[21] Drawing on Israel's

[17] Mark Berman, *Trump Promised Judges Who Would Overturn Roe v Wade*, WASH. POST (March 21, 2017), www.washingtonpost.com/politics/2017/live-updates/trump-white-house/neil-gorsuch-confirmation-hearings-updates-and-analysis-on-the-supreme-court-nominee/trump-promised-judges-who-would-overturn-roe-v-wade/?utm_term=.07124697546d; Carlos Santoscoy, *FRC's Peter Sprigg Hopeful Trump's Justices Will Overturn Gay Marriage Ruling*, ON TOP MAGAZINE (Dec. 20, 2016), www.ontopmag.com/article/24733/FRCs_Peter_Sprigg_Hopeful_Trumps_Justices_Will_Overturn_Gay_Marriage_Ruling.

[18] Jay Michaelson, *Donald Trump's Supreme Court Won't Just Overturn Gay Marriage and Abortion Cases, It Will Strangle the Federal Government*, DAILY BEAST (Nov. 9, 2016), www.thedailybeast.com/donald-trumps-supreme-court-wont-just-overturn-gay-marriage-and-abortion-cases-it-will-strangle-the-federal-government.

[19] Sarah Pulliam Bailey, *White Evangelicals Voted Overwhelmingly for Donald Trump, Exit Polls Show*, WASH. POST (Nov. 9, 2016), www.washingtonpost.com/news/acts-of-faith/wp/2016/11/09/exit-polls-show-white-evangelicals-voted-overwhelmingly-for-donald-trump/?utm_term=.54af2de3a219. *But see* Alec Tyson & Shiva Maniam, *Behind Trump's Victory; Divisions by Race, Gender, Education*, PEW RESEARCH CENTER (Nov. 9, 2016), www.pewresearch.org/fact-tank/2016/11/09/how-the-faithful-voted-a-preliminary-2016-analysis/ (documenting differentials in support for Clinton versus Obama).

[20] Alisa Nelson, *Missouri Legislator Says His Bill Would Defuse Some Controversy in Gay Weddings Resolution*, MISSOURINET (Dec. 1, 2016), www.missourinet.com/2016/12/01/missouri-legislator-says-his-bill-would-diffuse-some-controversy-in-gay-weddings-resolution/; Wilson, Chapter 16, this volume (cataloging state law proposals to divorce the state from marriage); H.B. 62, 99th Gen. Assemb., 1st Reg. Sess. (Mo. 2017).

[21] Wilson, this volume; Summer Ballentine, *A Lawmaker's Solution for Marriage Debate: Remove the State*, AP NEWS (Dec. 30, 2016), https://apnews.com/efcdc917b4d04b2ba05126c7557d1bf2/lawmakers-solution-marriage-debate-remove-state.

fragmented system around religious marriage and civil divorce, Professors Karin Yefet and Arianne Barzilay (Chapter 25) probe the workability of unwinding religious and civil marriage as it has been understood in the United States.

What *Obergefell* portended for other claims to marry was not long in coming. Within a week of *Obergefell*, Nathan Collier of *Sisters Wives* fame applied for a marriage license to "legally wed his second wife" – exactly as Chief Justice John Roberts predicted.[22] Although Collier claimed no religious affiliation, he claimed a religious conviction: as Professor Robin Kar (Chapter 15) urges, marriage alone holds the transformative power to bind individuals to one another and to bring them into conversation with God. Collier's religious claim ultimately failed, but only because he could not show that Montana would prosecute him.[23] In a reversal of course for Utah,[24] the state has said it will not enforce its constitutional ban on polygamy, absent some other crime or malfeasance.[25]

Despite parallels drawn by Justice Roberts between polygamy and same-sex marriage, Professor John Witte (Chapter 17) believes the line can be held against polygamy: only polygamy was viewed as a *malum in se* in Western culture. Professor Maura Strassberg (Chapter 18) mounts a modern harm-based case against polygamy's recognition, showing how the practice harms women and children. She believes those harms would likely suffice to sustain marriage bans on polygamy, if not polygamy as a crime, against challenges under state RFRAs – laws patterned on, but not identical to, the federal RFRA, as Utah Senator Stuart Adams (Chapter 21) explains – which twenty-two states have enacted. Professor Patrick Parkinson (Chapter 24) evaluates the status of

[22] Obergefell, *supra* note 1, at 2621 (Roberts, C.J., dissenting) ("[I]t is striking how much of the majority's reasoning would apply with equal force to the claim of a fundamental right to plural marriage . . . If a same-sex couple has the constitutional right to marry because their children would otherwise 'suffer the stigma of knowing their families are somehow lesser,' why wouldn't the same reasoning apply to a family of three or more persons raising children?"); Cheryl Wetzstein, *"Sister Wives." Polygamist Nathan Collier Cites Gay Marriage Ruling in Legal Fight*, WASH. TIMES (July 1, 2016), www.washingtontimes.com/news/2015/jul/1/nathan-collier-sister-wives-polygamist-cites-gay-m/.

[23] Collier et al. v. Fox et al., No. 15-CV-83-BLG-SPW-CSO, at *3 (D. Mont. Dec. 8, 2015).

[24] In 2006, the Utah Supreme Court sustained a man's conviction for polygamous cohabitation over Justice Christine Durham's strident dissent that criminalizing polygamy allows "the state to conduct a fishing expedition for evidence of other crimes." State v. Holm, 137 P.3d 726, 775 (Utah 2006) (Durham, C.J., dissenting in part).

[25] Sean Reyes, *Attorney General Statement on U.S. Tenth Circuit Court of Appeals Dismissal of* Brown v. Buhman (Apr. 11, 2016), http://attorneygeneral.utah.gov/tag/polygamy (describing his office's policy as "only prosecut[ing] bigamy crimes against those who induce marriage under false pretenses or if there is a collateral malfeasance, such as fraud, domestic abuse, child abuse, sex abuse, or other abuse").

secular marriage after same-sex marriage legislation and case law in Australia and Europe. He believes that the lack of "any convincing narrative about what marriage *is*" presages not only credible claims to polygamy but, worse, marriage's increasing irrelevance.

In this push-and-pull over the state's authority to police the outlines of marriage as an institution, and to prop it up, Professor Kari Hong (Chapter 14) reminds us that marriage historically conferred a right to be let alone, an essential protection for citizens and democracy. Professor Merle Weiner (Chapter 11) observes, however, that the absence of law can be just as profound as legal regulation itself. When no law encourages romantically involved parents to be supportive hands-on co-parents, whether or not married, they often are not – to the detriment of their children.[26]

BEYOND MARRIAGE

Far more looms on the horizon than just who may marry. *Obergefell* and *Hobby Lobby* may spur flashpoints over other matters that are core to persons but also impinge on religious beliefs or religious communities. These tensions may extend to matters such as end-of-life decision making, religiously educating children, childrearing decisions involving corporal punishment, treating childhood illnesses by faith alone,[27] the ability to structure divorce to reflect religious values,[28] circumcision practices, birth control practices,[29] modest dress,[30] and shared parenting.[31]

The family is the place where we experience the most intimate parts of our lives. As U.S. Senator Orrin Hatch notes in his *Foreword*, the family acts as the bulwark between the state and the individual, serving an "indispensable role in preserving religious freedom." Within the family, people of faith care deeply about having the autonomy to practice their faith and instill it in their children.[32] As the Court recognized in *Obergefell*, decisions concerning

[26] A record number of Americans have never married, making the absence of regulation especially problematic. Wendy Wang & Kim Parker, *Record Share of Americans Have Never Married*, Pew Research Center (Sep. 24, 2014), www.pewsocialtrends.org/2014/09/24/record-share-of-americans-have-never-married/; Weiner, Chapter 11, this volume.

[27] Offit, Chapter 12, this volume; Wilson & Sanders, Chapter 13, this volume.

[28] Bix, Chapter 9, this volume; Brinig, Chapter 10, this volume.

[29] Goodwin, Chapter 3, this volume; Lipper, Chapter 5, this volume; Rienzi, Chapter 4, this volume.

[30] Uddin, Chapter 26, this volume.

[31] Weiner, Chapter 11, this volume.

[32] Pope John Paul II, *Familiaris Consortio* (1981) ("In matrimony and in the family a complex of interpersonal relationships is set up – married life, fatherhood and motherhood, filiation and fraternity – through which each human person is introduced into the 'human family' and into the 'family of God,' which is the Church.").

"family relationships, procreation, childrearing . . . [and] marriage are among the most intimate that an individual can make."[33]

In the legal regulation of the family, the place of religion, which is now contested, spans every stage of an individual's life and the life cycle of a family: from birth to marriage, family formation, childrearing, and the end of life. The ability to circumcise a child,[34] for instance, or to school a child in one's faith,[35] or to respect (or override) a loved one's religious values in end-of-life care[36] reflect and shape a person's religious identity. The choices made also shape relationships within the family – affecting parental autonomy, child well-being, the protection of vulnerable adults, and society's interest in the family separate and apart from its interests in the individuals involved. Thus, for many Americans, the family is the crucible where the limits of the state's power to intervene get worked out.

The U.S. Supreme Court has long acknowledged a "private realm of family life which the state cannot enter[,]"[37] where the "custody, care and nurture of the child reside first in the parents, whose primary function and freedom include preparation for obligations the state can neither supply nor hinder."[38] When state regulation threatens to encroach on religious practice, moreover, the family's already strong claims against legal intrusion thicken. As the Court remarked in *Prince v. Massachusetts*:

> To make accommodation between these freedoms and an exercise of state authority always is delicate . . . On one side is the obviously earnest claim for freedom of conscience and religious practice. With it is allied the parent's claim to authority in her own household and in the rearing of her children. The parent's conflict with the state over control of the child and his training is serious enough when only secular matters are concerned. *It becomes the more so when an element of religious conviction enters.* Against these sacred private interests, basic in a democracy, stand the interests of society to protect the welfare of children.[39]

Professor James Dwyer (Chapter 8) questions the wisdom of conferring on parents an "other-determining" power over their children. Protecting parental decisions to homeschool children, for example, saddles some children with state-sanctioned disabilities, especially girls who may be straightjacketed into "conventional and severely limited social roles." Despite the Supreme Court's

33 Obergefell, *supra* note 1, at 2599 (2015).
34 Rassbach, Chapter 7, this volume.
35 Dwyer, Chapter 8, this volume.
36 Cahn & Ziettlow, Chapter 20, this volume; Kaplan, Chapter 19, this volume.
37 Smith v. Organization of Foster Families, 431 U.S. 816, 862–63 (1977) (Stewart, J., concurring).
38 Prince, 321 U.S. at 166.
39 *Id.* at 165 (emphasis added).

nominal respect for families making internal decisions, its constitutional jurisprudence is more nuanced: parental authority does not extend to causing harm to their children.[40]

Like Dwyer, feminists and others have long recognized that the marital family is "a sphere divorced from the legal order[,]" inviting the "subordination of women."[41] Professor Michele Goodwin (Chapter 3) and attorney Gregory Lipper (Chapter 5) extend this critique to a metastasizing number of conscience claims by pharmacists and other providers that impede women from purchasing emergency contraceptives. In Goodwin's words, conscience slips over from asking to be left alone to operating as a "mighty sword," prevailing over secular interests including access to healthcare and nondiscrimination.[42] And as Professor Richard Kaplan (Chapter 19) shows, "conscience" clauses operate not just at the beginning of life but also at the end, allowing physicians *not* to follow a patient's desires about end-of-life care for any reason, including the *provider's* own religious views.[43] Pushing back, Professor Mark Rienzi (Chapter 4), senior counsel for Little Sisters of the Poor in *Zubik v. Burwell*, maintains that the state's interests can be accomplished without encroaching on providers' beliefs.

Within the family, the human costs of religious conviction are often borne by children. As Dr. Paul Offit (Chapter 12) documents in this volume, across the U.S., "parents are legally empowered to rely upon their religious beliefs and 'faith-healing' practices as an antidote to when their children contract preventable and treatable illnesses." In this respect, the family encapsulates in miniature the driving concern after *Hobby Lobby* and *Zubik*: the potential for harm to others when society gives thick protection to religion.

That said, legislators have given wide berth to religious practices in the family. Forty-seven states have exempted parents from duties to vaccinate children against wholly preventable diseases if vaccinating conflicts with the parents' religious beliefs or philosophical views.[44] Legislators have largely not scaled back these laws despite their tragic consequences. For example, children have died in fundamentalist communities from Pennsylvania to Idaho; in Idaho, child mortality rates are ten times greater than rates in the rest of the state.[45]

40 Wilson & Sanders, Chapter 13, this volume (analyzing Meyer v. Nebraska, 262 U.S. 390 (1923); Pierce v. Society of the Sisters of the Holy Names of Jesus & Mary, 268 U.S. 510 (1925); Prince v. Massachusetts, 321 U.S. 158 (1944); Wisconsin v. Yoder, 406 U.S. 205, 230–234 (1972)).

41 Elizabeth M. Schneider & Nadine Taub, *Perspectives on Women's Subordination and the Role of Law, in* The Politics of Law (David Kairys, ed., 1982).

42 Goodwin, Chapter 3, this volume.

43 Kaplan, Chapter 19, this volume.

44 Offit, Figure 12.1, this volume.

45 Wilson & Sanders, Chapter 13, this volume.

Faith-healing practices have contributed to a resurgence of once-eradicated diseases including measles, leading California and Vermont in 2016 to repeal their religious or personal belief exemptions to vaccination requirements.[46]

States have, however, moderated the latitude given to parents in the realm of corporal punishment. In the late 1990s, forty-eight states authorized parents to discipline children in accordance with biblical passages instructing them to not withhold "correction from the child: for if thou beatest him with the rod, he shall not die."[47] In a description of the law that has been sorely missing in recent national discussions, this volume shows that by 2017, forty-four states and the District of Columbia allowed corporal punishment. These states generally bracket acceptable discipline to not using "excessive force" or causing "substantial injury."[48]

In one sense, continuing solicitude for religious practices is not surprising. Even as religiosity in the U.S. ebbs,[49] America remains deeply spiritual. More than 75% of Americans identify with a faith tradition.[50] More than half say religion is "very important" in their own lives.[51] But contributors to this volume ask whether governments have gotten it right.

The idea that individuals can hold religious liberty claims against society, or the application of laws, is difficult for many; it becomes even harder to swallow when it comes to religious groups. In *Hobby Lobby*, arguably the claim that most exercised the public was that a corporation could even have

46 California S.B. 277 (2015); Vt. Legis. Serv. 98 (West); VT. STAT. ANN. tit 18 § 1122 (West 2016) (retaining a religious exemption); *see also* Sarah Breitenbach, *States Make It Harder to Skip Vaccines*, VALLEY NEWS (May 29, 2016), www.vnews.com/To-combat-disease-states-make-it-harder-to-skip-vaccines-2486243.

47 Proverbs 23:13 (King James version); Susan H. Bitensky, *Spare the Rod, Embrace Our Humanity: Toward a New Legal Regime Prohibiting Corporal Punishment of Children*, 31 U. MICH. J.L. REFORM 353 (1997–1998). *See also* Proverbs 29:15 (King James version) ("The rod and reproof give wisdom: but a child left to himself bringeth his mother to shame."); Proverbs 13:24 (King James version) ("He that spareth his rod hateth his son: but he that loveth him chasteneth him betimes.").

48 Wilson & Sanders, Figure 13.4, this volume; Appendix 1.

49 Individuals with no religious affiliation, or "nones," comprise nearly a quarter of our population, 23%, up from 16% in 2007. Michael Lipka, *A Closer Look at America's Rapidly Growing Religious "Nones,"* PEW RESEARCH CENTER (May 13, 2015), www.pewresearch.org/fact-tank/2015/05/13/a-closer-look-at-americas-rapidly-growing-religious-nones/.

50 *Religious Landscape Study*, PEW RESEARCH CENTER (2014), www.pewforum.org/religious-landscape-study/#religions. Religious communities have become less homogenous as members fragment in their views of contraceptives, same-sex marriage, abortion, and other matters; Michael Likpa, *10 Facts About Religion in America*, PEW RESEARCH CENTER (Aug. 27, 2015), www.pewresearch.org/fact-tank/2015/08/27/10-facts-about-religion-in-america/.

51 In a 2016 Gallup poll from 2016, 53% of people said they would consider religion to be "very important" in their own lives. *Religion*, Gallup (2016), www.gallup.com/poll/1690/religion.aspx.

a religious belief worthy of legal protection – a skepticism that runs across this volume.[52] As is true of the litigation over contraceptive coverage, religious communities assert a distinct claim to perpetuate their norms and identities, whether in childrearing, by mediating disputes using religious norms, or circumcising male children as a symbol of belonging in the community.[53] Once-uncontroversial questions have become controversial. As attorney Eric Rassbach (Chapter 7) shows, the New York City Health Department, like grassroots movements in Massachusetts and California, has sought to ban certain forms of male circumcision, a religious practice important to both the Jewish and Muslim faiths.

The question of group rights is hard. The state's regulation of the family may be seen as stamping out practices core to a community's identity or beyond the state's competence to decide. This can extend to matters as mundane as modest dress or as central to religious belonging as male circumcision.[54] Whether and how to regulate are further complicated by the fact that what is seen as acceptable within the family may differ not just by religion but also by race, upbringing, and ethnic identity.[55] How parents resolve disputes, bring up their children, or baptize or fold their children into the community are not mere cultural and religious expressions. Like other practices that foster intentional communities of believers,[56] these religious practices operate as a kind of priming of receptivity to the community's particular worldview, making the ability to follow one's convictions about parenting not just a difference of opinion but also an existential concern.[57]

These questions are made all the more difficult by the fact that faith communities can undergo a renaissance in their own thinking. The Scottish

[52] *See, e.g.*, Sepper, Chapter 1, this volume ("Despite claims to the contrary, resistance to corporate exemption does not mean Americans have rejected religious accommodation, religious liberty, or religion itself."); Lipper, Chapter 5, this volume; *see generally* THE RISE OF CORPORATE RELIGIOUS LIBERTY (Micah Schwartzman et al., eds., 2016).

[53] Bix, Chapter 9, this volume; Brinig, Chapter 10, this volume.

[54] Rassbach, Chapter 7, this volume; Uddin, Chapter 26, this volume.

[55] Bix, Chapter 9, this volume; Brinig, Chapter 10, this volume; Uddin, Chapter 26, this volume; Wilson & Sanders, Chapter 13, this volume.

[56] Steve Weatherbe, *Is This the Solution Christians Need to Survive the Collapse of the West?* LIFE SITE NEWS (Mar. 9, 2017), www.lifesitenews.com/news/interview-author-rod-dreher-explains-why-we-need-benedict-option-to-survive (quoting Rod Dreher, author of THE BENEDICT OPTION: A STRATEGY FOR CHRISTIANS IN A POST-CHRISTIAN NATION, as urging Christians to "hold on even more strongly to the truths of the faith because there will be even more pressure in the public square to conform to this post-Christian orthodoxy, to abandon our faith, to apostatize").

[57] *See* Binyamin Appelbaum, *What the Hobby Lobby Ruling Means for America*, N.Y. TIMES MAG. (July 22, 2014), www.nytimes.com/2014/07/27/magazine/what-the-hobby-lobby-ruling-means-for-america.html?mcubz=0.

Episcopal Church and the Norwegian Lutheran Church decided in 2017 to perform same-sex marriages.[58] Faith communities can also hold nuanced positions. In this volume, Professor William Eskridge (Chapter 23) shows that the Church of Jesus Christ of the Latter-day Saints, commonly known as the Mormon Church, opposed same-sex marriage during California's Proposition 8. The Church later became a driving force behind Utah's landmark nondiscrimination protections for the LGBT community.

The Mormon Church's approach to two related, but distinct questions – marriage and LGBT nondiscrimination protections – is an important example of the ongoing dialogue between faith communities, cultural norms, and the law. Professor Weiner (Chapter 11) points to numerous examples of religious stakeholders engaging the political process to influence the legal regulation of the family. As Senator Adams (Chapter 21) chronicles, religious stakeholders played a crucial role in helping Utah's legislature chart the uncharted territory left by *Obergefell* and lower court decisions preceding it, which granted the right to marry but did *not* resolve a host of downstream questions. Echoing Adams, Professor Anthony Kreis (Chapter 22) gives a careful historical account of the dismantling of interracial marriage bans in the U.S., showing that court decisions work in tandem with legislation to propel civil rights movements.

LOOKING FORWARD

Against this swirling mix of religious beliefs, secular values, and legal regulation of the family, this volume steps back to provide a comprehensive look at the tensions between religious freedom, equal rights, and the state's protective function. Contributors explain how the U.S. Supreme Court's decisions about marriage equality, contraception, the parent-child relationship, and religious exercise set the stage for ongoing disputes.

The volume's contributors straddle two fields, (1) law and religion and (2) family law. PART I opens with religious liberty scholars Professors Elizabeth Sepper (Chapter 1) and Michael Helfand (Chapter 2) unpacking insights from *Hobby Lobby* and *Zubik* for the questions explored in the remainder of the book. PARTS II–V evaluate religious claims at various

[58] *Scottish Episcopal Church to Allow Same-Sex Marriage*, AP NEWS (June 9, 2017), https://apnews.com/788ec9bbdf334e88af93ccedb67b617c/Scottish-Episcopal-Church-to-allow-same-sex-weddings; Gwladys Fouche, *Norway's Lutheran Church Embraces Same-Sex Marriage*, REUTERS (Jan. 31, 2017), www.reuters.com/article/us-norway-gaymarriage-idUSKBN15E1O2.

junctures in the life of a family: at birth, during childrearing, at marriage, and at the end of life. PART VI takes a wider lens to the evolution of the law, showing how the foundational views of marriage, family, and equal rights in faith traditions have influenced, and been influenced by, the wider culture. This part shows that neither legislatures nor courts act in isolation, a phenomenon that has deeper implications for the protection of sexual minorities and other vulnerable populations. PART VII offers international perspectives on the sustainability of marriage, respect for minority cultures, and the workability of proposals to fundamentally transform the state's relationship to marriage.

The voices collected here are a microcosm of the country. Represented are longtime advocates of religious freedom: Professors Rienzi (Chapter 4) and Helfand (Chapters 2 and 6); Senator Hatch (Foreword) who, together with Senator Edward Kennedy, co-sponsored RFRA in 1993; the Deputy General Counsel to the Becket Fund for Religious Liberty, Eric Rassbach (Chapter 7); and the director of strategy for the Center for Islam and Religious Freedom, Asma Uddin (Chapter 26). They are equally matched by vigorous opponents of special accommodations for religion: Dr. Paul Offit (Chapter 12), author of the *New York Times* bestseller *Bad Faith: When Religious Belief Undermines Modern Medicine*; Professors Goodwin (Chapter 3), Sepper (Chapter 21), and Dwyer (Chapter); and Greg Lipper (Chapter 5), formerly senior litigation counsel at Americans United for Separation of Church and State.

In addition to those at the forefront of legal battles to expand (or contract) religious autonomy, the volume includes important voices missing in many academic works: federal and state legislators, the groups that principally decide how much solicitude governments accord religion. Serious scholars of the family round out the book, together with a number of rising stars: journalist and Reverend Amy Zeittlow (Chapter 20) and Professors Barzilay (Chapter 25), Bix (Chapter 9), Brinig (Chapter 10), Cahn (Chapter 20), Eskridge (Chapter 23), Kreis (Chapter 22), Parkinson (Chapter 24), Sanders (Chapter 13), Strassberg (Chapter 18), Wilson (Chapter 16), Witte (Chapter 17), and Yefet (Chapter 25). Comparative perspectives from Israel, Australia, France, and Europe underscore that tensions between religious and secular values cross international boundaries.

Each chapter stands alone. But unlike other volumes, dialogue – and sometimes pointed debate – runs throughout, surfacing differences between thinkers who have sometimes litigated against one another or intersected in other ways. Many chapters react to the Trump Administration's early indications about how it will resolve questions impinging on religious freedom, not least of which are the claims by the Little Sisters of the Poor and others to step aside from the contraceptive coverage mandate.[59]

A number of chapters also offer initial observations about the recent confirmation of Justice Neil Gorsuch to the U.S. Supreme Court. The composition of the Supreme Court obviously matters to the resolution of cases, especially if President Trump makes additional replacements during his presidency.[60] Still, the Supreme Court does not overturn precedents lightly, and it is hard to predict which cases might be trimmed as a result of new facts before the Court.[61] Paring seems a far more likely outcome than overturning binding precedent such as *Obergefell*, as Justice Gorsuch indicated in his confirmation hearings.[62]

In short, *The Contested Place of Religion in Family Law* begins a long-overdue conversation on questions that have rippled across the nation.

[59] President Trump's Executive Order on Religious Freedom provides scant detail, so it remains unclear whether religious objectors such as the Little Sisters will be wholly exempted – meaning their employees receive no coverage from anyone – or if, now that the Little Sisters "have won," the Trump Administration will direct insurers or another group to pay for employees' contraceptive coverage, as the Obama Administration did. *See* Amber Athey, *Trump to Little Sisters of the Poor: "Long Ordeal" Is Over*, DAILY CALLER (May 4, 2017), http://dailycaller.com/2017/05/04/trump-to-little-sisters-of-the-poor-long-ordeal-is-over-video/; White House, *Presidential Executive Order Promoting Free Speech and Religious Liberty* (May 4, 2017), www.whitehouse.gov/the-press-office/2017/05/04/presidential-executive-order-promoting-free-speech-and-religious-liberty; Group Health Plans and Health Insurance Issuers Relating to Coverage of Preventive Services Under the Patient Protection and Affordable Care Act, 76 Fed. Reg. 149, 46621, (August 3, 2011) (exempting churches entirely); Sarah Posner, *Leaked Draft of Trump's Religious Freedom Order Reveals Sweeping Plans to Legalize Discrimination*, THE NATION (Feb. 1, 2017), www.thenation.com/article/leaked-draft-of-trumps-religious-freedom-order-reveals-sweeping-plans-to-legalize-discrimination/.

[60] Lawrence Hurley & Andrew Chung, *Fearing Trump's Next Move, Liberals Urge Supreme Court Conservative Kennedy to Stay*, REUTERS (Jun. 1, 2017), www.reuters.com/article/us-usa-court-kennedy-idUSKBN18S4LT; Paul Bedard, *Source: Trump "Expects" Four More Supreme Court Picks*, WASH. EXAMINER (Apr. 7, 2017), www.washingtonexaminer.com/trump-expects-to-name-5-supreme-court-justices/article/2619660.

[61] Lee Epstein, William M. Landes, & Adam Liptak, *The Decision to Depart (or Not) from Constitutional Precedent: An Empirical Study of the Roberts Court*, 90 N.Y.U. L. REV. 1115, 1122–27 (2015) (reviewing studies on various issues related to overruling precedent that demonstrate that overruling Court decisions is extremely rare).

[62] Jacob Pramuk, *Neil Gorsuch: Supreme Court Has Said Same-Sex Marriage Is "Protected by the Constitution,"* CNBC (Mar. 21, 2017), www.cnbc.com/2017/03/21/neil-gorsuch-supreme-court-has-said-same-sex-marriage-is-protected-by-the-constitution.html.

PART I

THE FOUNDATIONS AND BOUNDARIES OF RELIGIOUS LIBERTY

1

The Risky Business of RFRAs After *Hobby Lobby*

Elizabeth Sepper

Professor of Law, Washington University School of Law

Today's conflicts over law and religion implicate central issues of family law – how to constitute a family, whether to bear children, how to define marriage, and when to limit decision making about death. Corporations demand the right to withhold contraceptive coverage from health plans. Healthcare institutions decline to follow patients' wishes for end-of-life care. Parents claim religion entitles them to neglect or beat their children. Inns refuse to lodge same-sex couples. Employers resist including domestic partners within employees' benefit plans. In response to the United States Supreme Court's recognition of same-sex marriage, state legislatures rush to pass religious freedom restoration acts that might allow businesses to avoid such applications of nondiscrimination laws.[1]

These contests arise at a moment when religious liberty doctrine stands at a critical juncture. In particular, the Supreme Court's decision in *Burwell v. Hobby Lobby* marks a shift in religious liberty jurisprudence with obvious resonance for family law.[2] In that case, closely held, for-profit corporations sought exemption under the Religious Freedom Restoration Act ("RFRA")[3] from the Affordable Care Act's contraceptive rule, which required large employers with employee health insurance plans to cover contraception. The Court determined that for-profit corporations had a right to bring RFRA claims, just as individuals do – an open and much-contested question. It ultimately concluded that for-profit employers merited the same accommodation that the government had made available to nonprofit religious organizations. Under this accommodation, employers must notify their insurer or the

[1] Don Byrd, *State RFRA Bill Tracker*, Baptist Joint Committee for Religious Liberty (Mar. 4, 2015), bjconline.org/state-rfra-tracker-2015/ (tracking state RFRAs).

[2] Burwell v. Hobby Lobby Stores Inc., 134 S. Ct. 2751, 2759–60 (2014).

[3] Religious Freedom Restoration Act of 1993, 42 U.S.C. § 2000bb(b) (2012).

government of their objections. The employers may then exclude contraceptive coverage from their employee insurance plans, but employees will still have access to contraceptive coverage through separate payments from the insurers.[4] The *Hobby Lobby* Court, however, refused to confirm that the accommodation "complies with RFRA for purposes of all religious claims."[5] As a result, litigation continued, challenging the accommodation itself as an infringement on religious exercise.

This chapter examines the critical doctrinal questions and emerging tensions in the Supreme Court's approach to religious liberty protections. There are various constitutional and statutory protections for religious liberty at both the federal and state levels, including the Free Exercise Clause of the First Amendment to the U.S. Constitution. From 1963 to 1990, the Supreme Court interpreted the Free Exercise Clause as offering relatively extensive protection where a law imposed a substantial burden on free exercise of religion. Under this standard, the government had to demonstrate that the law was *necessary* to advance a *compelling* government interest; if it failed on either prong, the law would be declared unconstitutional.[6] In 1990, however, the Supreme Court held in *Employment Division v. Smith* that neutral laws of general applicability – those that do not specifically target religion and apply equally to believers and nonbelievers – do not require mandatory religious accommodation even when they burden free exercise, so long as they bear a *rational* relationship to a *legitimate* government interest.[7] Under the *Smith* standard, religious objectors could only prevail in a constitutional Free Exercise challenge with great difficulty.

In response to *Smith*, Congress passed the Religious Freedom Restoration Act of 1993. The law's stated purpose was to restore pre-*Smith* Supreme Court precedent and standard of review. As Michael Helfand notes in Chapter 6, the law was motivated in part by a desire to safeguard religious minorities. Because religious objector plaintiffs face a lower burden under RFRA than the Constitution (where the *Smith* standard holds), it is RFRA – and not the First Amendment – that is central to most relevant litigation today.

Under RFRA, if (1) a person (2) shows that a law substantially burdens his or her exercise of religion, the federal government must demonstrate that the law (3) furthers a compelling governmental interest and (4) is the least restrictive means of furthering that interest.[8] At each step of the analysis, *Hobby Lobby* laid out new, broad interpretations of doctrine that potentially destabilize

4 Hobby Lobby, *supra* note 2, at 2782. 5 *Id.* at 2782.

6 See Sherbert v. Verner, 374 U.S. 398 (1963); Wisconsin v. Yoder, 406 U.S. 205 (1972).

7 494 U.S. 872 (1990). 8 42 U.S.C. § 2000bb-1(b) (2012).

religious liberty and undermine the regulatory state. Three developments in particular risk rendering exemptions deregulatory: the introduction of a new category of litigants for religious liberty claims, the reduction of the substantial burden showing for litigants, and the heightening of scrutiny of regulation of commercial activities. This chapter takes each of these developments in turn, examining *Hobby Lobby*, its progenitors, and litigation in its wake, including *Zubik v. Burwell*.

The chapter demonstrates that, with a potentially expansive religious exemption doctrine in disarray, RFRAs are a risky business. With regard to the family, religious claims by others may profoundly affect the decision whether and when to bear children, the ability to die in the manner of one's choosing, or the choice of how one's child is educated. The negative effects of religious exemptions for businesses and institutions will fall particularly hard on vulnerable religious minorities, who frequently do not share the religious perspective of powerful institutions.

THE RISE OF CORPORATE RELIGIOUS LIBERTY

The litigation against the ACA's contraceptive mandate shows how RFRA has morphed into a tool of economically powerful entities that stand in stark contrast to the individuals of minority faiths of the pre-*Smith* era. In the contraceptive litigation, for-profit employers prevailed with arguments that combined free market ideology and Christian dogma.[9] They invoked "our free enterprise system,"[10] adopted the rhetoric of limited (federal) government,[11] and described commercial regulation as intrusion into private life.[12]

9 *See generally* PIPPA NORRIS & RONALD INGLEHART, SACRED AND SECULAR (2004) (connecting religious fundamentalism and attacks on social welfare); KEVIN M. KRUSE, ONE NATION UNDER GOD: HOW CORPORATE AMERICA INVENTED CHRISTIAN AMERICA (2015) (tracing the idea that America is a Christian nation to corporations' enlistment of members of the clergy to counter the New Deal); Elizabeth Sepper, *Free Exercise Lochnerism*, 115 COLUM. L. REV. 1457 (2015) (arguing that business religious liberty claims and their successes revive reasoning of the pre–New Deal *Lochner* era).

10 Petition for Writ of Certiorari at 29, Conestoga Wood Specialties Corp. v. Burwell, 134 S. Ct. 2751 (2014) (No. 13–356), 2013 WL 5291412, at *29.

11 Irin Carmon, *Eden Foods Doubles Down in Birth Control Flap*, SALON (Apr. 15, 2013), www.salon.com/2013/04/15/eden_foods_ceo_digs_himself_deeper_in_birth_control_outrage/ ("I don't care if the federal government is telling me to buy my employees Jack Daniel's or birth control. What gives them the right to tell me that I have to do that?") (quoting Michael Potter).

12 Petition for Writ of Certiorari at 29, Conestoga Wood Specialties Corp. v. Burwell, 134 S. Ct. 2751 (2014) (No. 13–356), 2013 WL 5291412, at *29 (calling the contraceptive mandate "one of the most sweeping and intrusive laws ever enacted" with potential to subject "all private conduct ... to federal control").

The libertarian ethos of the contraceptive cases found a receptive audience in the increasingly pro-business federal courts.[13] Courts across the country granted exemptions to for-profit employers at substantial cost to their employees.[14] And, of course, in *Burwell v. Hobby Lobby*, the Court sided with the for-profit corporate challengers.[15] For the first time, the Court held that for-profit corporations possessed the right to exercise religion. It concluded that closely held, secular for-profit corporations "further[] individual religious freedom" just as religious nonprofits do, and were "persons" eligible for accommodation under RFRA.[16]

In her dissent, Justice Ruth Bader Ginsburg expressed concern that the majority's acceptance of corporate religious exercise had broad implications. She warned that the contraceptive challengers "surely do not stand alone as commercial enterprises seeking exemptions from generally applicable laws on the basis of their religious beliefs."[17] She argued that the Court's reasoning could equally apply to cases like *Elane Photography, LLC v. Willock*,[18] in which a business did not want to photograph a lesbian couple's commitment ceremony, and *Minnesota ex rel. McClure*,[19] in which a chain of for-profit health clubs would not hire LGBT people.[20]

These corporations are not the minority individuals of past accommodations, but politically powerful religious and commercial entities – the very centerpiece of regulatory efforts. While the Court emphasized that only

[13] Lee Epstein, William M. Landes, & Richard A. Posner, *How Business Fares in the Supreme Court*, 97 MINN. L. REV. 1431, 1471 (2013) ("Whether measured by decisions or Justices' votes, a plunge in warmth toward business during the 1960s (the heyday of the Warren Court) was quickly reversed; and the Roberts Court is much friendlier to business than either the Burger or Rehnquist Courts, which preceded it, were.").

[14] *See, e.g.*, Newland v. Sebelius, 881 F. Supp. 2d 1287, 1298 (D. Colo. 2012); Korte v. Sebelius, Nos. 12–3841 & 13–1077, 2013 WL 5, at *2 (7th Cir. Nov. 8, 2013). For examples of courts enjoining the mandate in its entirety vis-à-vis not-for-profit employers, see Eternal Word Television Network, Inc. v. Burwell, 756 F.3d 1339, 1340 (11th Cir. 2014) (enjoining enforcement of nonprofit accommodation); Archdiocese of St. Louis v. Burwell, No. 4:13-CV-2300-JAR, 2014 WL 2945859, at *10 (E.D. Mo. June 30, 2014) (enjoining the mandate, including the nonprofit accommodation, in its entirety).

[15] Hobby Lobby, *supra* note 2, at 2759–60; *see also* Nelson Tebbe, Richard Schragger & Micah Schwartzman, *Hobby Lobby's Bitter Anniversary*, BALKINIZATION (June 30, 2015), balkin.blogspot.com/2015/06/hobbylobbys-bitter-anniversary.html (noting that a year after the Supreme Court's decision, Hobby Lobby's employees lacked full contraceptive coverage).

[16] Hobby Lobby, *supra* note 2, at 2759.

[17] *Id.* at 2751 (Ginsburg, J., dissenting).

[18] Elane Photography v. Willcock, 309 P.3d 53 (N.M. 2013), *cert. denied*, 134 S. Ct. 1787 (2014).

[19] Minnesota *ex rel.* McClure v. Sports & Health Club, Inc., 370 N.W.2d 844 (Minn. 1985).

[20] Hobby Lobby, *supra* note 2, at 2804.

closely held, religious for-profit corporations can claim exemptions,[21] no such category of corporation exists in state or federal law. In response to *Hobby Lobby*, the U.S. Department of Health and Human Services (HHS) extended the same accommodation available to eligible religious nonprofits to eligible closely held for-profits – defined in accordance with federal tax law as not publicly traded and with an ownership structure in which more than 50% of the corporation is owned by five or fewer individuals (all members of a single family are treated as a single individual).[22]

With the rise of corporate religious exemption, businesses may now resist once-settled statutory duties to provide Social Security, unemployment insurance, and workers' compensation as infringements on religious liberty. For at least thirty years, courts have faced claims from employers for exemption under the First Amendment (and sometimes RFRA) from the Fair Labor Standards Act, the Equal Pay Act, Title VII of the Civil Rights Act, workers' compensation statutes, and unemployment insurance obligations.[23] By the 1980s, religious nonprofit employers objected with some frequency to sex nondiscrimination requirements.[24] Outside the special context of narrow exemptions for houses of worship and their ministers, these employers lost. Notably, the highest courts of New York and California upheld the application of state contraceptive mandates to religiously affiliated employers.[25] Infrequent claims by for-profit corporations were always denied.[26] What

[21] *Id.* at 2769 ("No known understanding of the term 'person' includes *some* but not all corporations.").

[22] Coverage of Certain Preventive Services Under the Affordable Care Act, 80 Fed. Reg. 41318, 41343 (July 14, 2015).

[23] *See* United States v. Lee, 455 U.S. 252, 261 (1982) (refusing to exempt employer from Social Security obligations); Droz v. Commissioner, 48 F.3d 1120, 1121–23 (9th Cir. 1995) (rejecting similar claim under the Religious Freedom Restoration Act); Tony & Susan Alamo Found. v. Sec'y of Labor, 471 U.S. 290, 306 (1985) (same for federal wage requirements); Swaggart Ministries v. Bd. of Equalization of Cal., 493 U.S. 378, 399 (1990) (same for state sales and use taxes); United States v. Indianapolis Baptist Temple, 224 F.3d 627, 631 (7th Cir. 2000) (same for unemployment insurance); EEOC v. Fremont Christian School, 781 F.2d 1362, 1366 (9th Cir. 1986) (prohibiting religious employer from sex discrimination in employee benefits); Victory Baptist Temple, Inc. v. Indus. Comm'n of Ohio, 442 N.E.2d 819, 822 (Ohio Ct. App. 1982) (refusing to exempt defendant from workers' compensation requirements); St. John's Lutheran Church v. State Comp. Ins. Fund, 830 P.2d 1271, 1278 (Mont. 1992) (same); Dayton Christian Sch., Inc. v. Ohio Civil Rights Comm'n, 766 F.2d 932 (6th Cir. 1985) (asserting First Amendment claim against employment sex nondiscrimination obligation).

[24] Ira C. Lupu, *Free Exercise Exemption and Religious Institutions: The Case of Employment Discrimination*, 67 B.U.L. Rev. 391, 395–96 (1987) (discussing such claims).

[25] *See* Catholic Charities of Diocese of Albany v. Serio, 859 N.E.2d 459, 461 (N.Y. 2006); Catholic Charities of Sacramento, Inc. v. Super. Ct., 85 P.3d 67, 94–95 (Cal. 2004).

[26] *See, e.g.*, Newman v. Piggie Park Enters., Inc., 390 U.S. 400, 402 n.5 (1968) (calling for-profit corporations' claims to religious liberty "patently frivolous").

distinguishes today's resistance to contraceptive coverage and sexual orientation nondiscrimination laws from yesteryear is not the type of claim that religious objectors are making, but their success in the courts.

While *Hobby Lobby*'s recognition of corporate practice of religion grabbed headlines, the decision also shifted doctrine in several significant ways. As the following shows, the Court diluted plaintiffs' obligation to demonstrate a on religion. It simultaneously fortified the showing required of the government for laws to survive RFRA scrutiny.

INSUBSTANTIAL BURDENS AND *HOBBY LOBBY* 2.0

In a change that alone could hobble the regulatory state's efforts to protect vulnerable persons within the family, *Hobby Lobby* lowered the threshold for plaintiffs to make RFRA claims. The government argued that the burden of the contraceptive mandate was insubstantial, because the connection between the employer's offering a comprehensive health plan covering contraceptives and an employee's ultimate use of contraceptives was too attenuated – a legal issue, rather than a religious question.[27] Writing for the majority, Justice Samuel Alito disagreed. Such analysis, he said, involved "a difficult and important question of religion and moral philosophy" – not law.[28] In answering the question, he said, the government took upon itself to "tell plaintiffs their beliefs are flawed."[29] Because plaintiffs believed their connection to immorality was direct, the courts, Justice Alito wrote, could only determine whether this belief was sincere: "It was not for us to say that their religious beliefs are mistaken or insubstantial."[30] Besides, Justice Alito noted, "[b]ecause the contraceptive mandate forces them to pay an enormous sum of money [for providing noncompliant plans] . . . if they insist on providing insurance coverage in accordance with their religious beliefs, the mandate clearly imposes a substantial burden on those beliefs."[31]

Following *Hobby Lobby*, the meaning of RFRA's substantial burden standard remains contested. In short order, the courts confronted claims by nonprofit employers that the very process of requesting a religious accommodation imposes a substantial burden on religious beliefs.[32] Though their insurance policies omitted contraceptive coverage, they said they remained complicit in the purported wrongdoing in two ways. First, plaintiffs argued, by submitting notice to their insurance issuer, their company's claims manager

27 Hobby Lobby, *supra* note 2, at 2777–78. 28 *Id.* at 2778. 29 *Id.* 30 *Id.* at 2779.
31 *Id.* at 2778.
32 Univ. of Notre Dame v. Sebelius, 743 F.3d 547, 557 (7th Cir. 2014) (describing claim as "paradoxical and virtually unprecedented").

known as a "third-party administrator," or the government, the plaintiffs had to facilitate (or "trigger") contraceptive coverage by other actors.[33] Second, the plaintiffs said, the government "hijacks" the religious employer's own relationship (or plan) with a particular insurance company to provide free coverage for contraceptives services, again involving it in the objectionable behavior through its relationship with an insurer or third-party administrator.[34] Thus, these employers sought an outright exemption, rather than an accommodation.

Eight out of nine courts of appeals to hear the issue rejected these arguments.[35] They did not defer to litigants but instead analyzed the degree to which the law burdened religious exercise and concluded that no substantial burden exists. The accommodation, they decided, excused objecting employers from any involvement – that private insurance companies complied with their own legal obligations to offer contraceptive coverage could not substantially burden the plaintiffs.[36] The courts, in effect, determined that *Hobby Lobby* cannot mean what it says.

In its October 2015 term, the Supreme Court took up a number of these nonprofit cases, consolidated under the name *Zubik v. Burwell.*[37] After oral argument, however, having taken the unusual step of proposing a possible alternative process for accommodation from the mandate and requesting supplemental briefing on that alternative, the Court remanded the cases to the appellate courts with the instruction to afford the parties "an opportunity to arrive at an approach going forward that accommodates petitioners' religious exercise while at the same time ensuring that women covered by petitioners' health plans 'receive full and equal health coverage, including contraceptive coverage.'"[38] The Court explicitly did not decide "whether petitioners' religious exercise has been substantially burdened, whether the Government has a compelling interest, or whether the current regulations are the least restrictive

33 *See, e.g.*, Priests for Life v. U.S. Dep't of Health & Human Servs., 772 F.3d 229, 237 (D.C. Cir. 2014).

34 *See, e.g.*, Univ. of Notre Dame v. Burwell, 743 F.3d 547, 557 (7th Cir. 2014).

35 *See* Eternal Word Television Network, Inc. v. Sec'y of U.S. Dep't of Health & Human Servs., No. 14–12696, 2016 WL 659222 (11th Cir. Feb. 18, 2016); Catholic Health Care Sys. v. Burwell, 796 F.3d 207 (2d Cir. 2015); Little Sisters of the Poor Home for the Aged, Denver, Colo. v. Burwell, 794 F.3d 1151 (10th Cir. 2015); E. Texas Baptist Univ. v. Burwell, 793 F.3d 449 (5th Cir. 2015); Geneva Coll. v. Sec'y U.S. Dep't of Health & Human Servs., 778 F.3d 422, 427 (3d Cir. 2015); Priests for Life v. U.S. Dep't of Health & Human Servs., 772 F.3d 229, 252–53 (D.C. Cir. 2014); Mich. Catholic Conference & Catholic Family Servs. v. Burwell, 755 F.3d 372, 389 (6th Cir. 2014); Univ. of Notre Dame v. Burwell, 743 F.3d 547 (7th Cir. 2014). Only the Eighth Circuit decided a substantial burden exists. Sharpe Holdings, Inc. v. U.S. Dep't of Health & Human Servs., 801 F.3d 927 (8th Cir. 2015).

36 *See, e.g.*, Wheaton College v. Burwell, 791 F.3d 792, 795 (2015) (making this point).

37 136 S. Ct. 444 (2015). Hobby Lobby, *supra* note 2.

38 Zubik v. Burwell, 136 S. Ct. 1557 (2016) (per curiam).

means of serving that interest."[39] Months after the remand, the government announced that the parties had found no ground for compromise and that, based on public comments, it had concluded that no feasible approach would satisfy the religious objectors.[40] The cases – and the issues of substantial burden, compelling interest, and potential alternatives – seemed likely return to the Court in the same, or similar, posture. But in October 2017, the Trump Administration released a new rule granting a total exemption from the contraceptive mandate to any employer with a religious or moral objection – and thus put to rest the question of substantial burdens in the contraceptive context.

At some point, however, the Supreme Court will be called upon to return to the substantial burden standard and answer the questions raised by its *Hobby Lobby* decision. It will have two paths before it. First, it could take a deferential approach as nonprofit plaintiffs, influential advocacy groups, and some scholars advocate.[41] Deference comes in two flavors. Some urge total deference according to which a religious objector's *ipse dixit* establishes that the burden of compliance with a regulation (or requesting an accommodation thereunder) is substantial and shifts the burden of proof to the government. Others bifurcate the analysis of substantial burden. Religious adherents receive deference as to whether their religious exercise is substantially burdened by compliance with law – the purported "religious costs." Courts, however, can consider the severity of penalties for failure to comply – the "secular costs." Defending this approach in his chapters (Chapters 2 and 6, this volume), Michael Helfand points to Justice Alito's opinion, which took a hands-off approach to questions of the corporation's proximity to and responsibility for wrongdoing, but emphasized the tax penalties that the corporations would face if they offered insurance that failed to comply with the ACA. While nominally different, both forms of the deferential approach lead to the same result, for "[i]t is the rare law whose violation triggers only trivial sanctions."[42]

39 *Id.*

40 U.S. Dep't of Labor, Employee Benefits Security Administration, FAQs About Affordable Care Act Implementation Part 36, Jan. 9, 2017, www.dol.gov/sites/default/files/ebsa/about-ebsa/our-activities/resource-center/faqs/aca-part-36.pdf.

41 Steven D. Smith & Caroline Mala Corbin, *Debate: The Contraception Mandate and Religious Freedom*, 161 U. Pa. L. Rev. Online 261, 263 (2013), https://www.pennlawreview.com/online/Steven-DSmith-Caroline-Mala-Corbin-161-U-Pa-L-Rev-261.pdf (Smith: "What matters, under both the Free Exercise Clause and RFRA, is whether a person – or in this case an employer – sincerely believes that compliance with the Mandate would violate religious duties.").

42 Frederick Mark Gedicks, *"Substantial" Burdens: How Courts May (and Why They Must) Judge Burdens on Religions under RFRA*, 85 Geo. Wash. L. Rev. 94 (2017). At the margins, differences might emerge. For example, looking to penalties of noncompliance should cause courts to reject RFRA claims to exemption from the contraceptive mandate by small

Second and alternatively, the Court could evaluate the substantiality of the burden that the law imposes by considering the link between the act demanded of the objector and the purported wrongdoing. Under this attenuation analysis, it could weigh the burden of regulatory compliance in light of proximity, necessity, and intervening actors as courts historically have done. In her *Hobby Lobby* dissent, Justice Ginsburg took this tack.[43] Separating the religious question of what faith requires from the legal question of what burdens are substantial under RFRA, she concluded that "the connection between the families' religious objections and the contraceptive coverage requirement is too attenuated to rank as substantial."[44] She noted three factors: first, the law imposed no direct requirement on employers to "purchase or provide the contraceptives they find objectionable"; second, the employer's connection to the use of contraceptives was indirect through contributions to insurance plans that finance a variety of medical care; third, independent intervening acts and actors interrupted the linkage between employer and contraceptive use.[45] Justice Ginsburg concluded that "the connection between the families' religious objections and the contraceptive coverage requirement is too attenuated to rank as substantial."[46]

While the majority opinion in *Hobby Lobby* now renders both deferential approaches plausible, the attenuation analysis is textually, doctrinally, and practically superior. Consider RFRA's text: the federal government may "substantially burden a person's exercise of religion only if it demonstrates that application of the burden to the person – (1) is in furtherance of a compelling governmental interest; and (2) is the least restrictive means of furthering that compelling governmental interest."[47] To defer entirely to plaintiffs reads "substantially" out of the statute altogether. As one court said, this converts "substantial" burden to "any burden."[48] To consider the size of the penalty gives some content to "substantially," but it makes little sense of the statute as a whole. RFRA requires that the "application of the burden" furthers a compelling interest and be a least restrictive means. The question is whether the "application" of the law – not the application of a penalty for noncompliance – satisfies these tests. Thus, in *Hobby Lobby*, the Court did not consider whether the tax penalty met the compelling interest and least-restrictive-means prongs of RFRA, as this interpretation of the statute would

employers, which are not subject to any penalty (or obligation to offer insurance). Total deference presumably would require courts to accept their claims.

43 134 S. Ct. at 2787 (Ginsburg, J., dissenting). 44 *Id.* at 2799. 45 *Id.* at 2798–99.

46 *Id.* at 2798. 47 42 U.S.C. § 2000bb-1(b) (2012).

48 Gilardi v. Sebelius, 926 F. Supp. 2d 273, 282 (D.D.C. 2013).

seem to require. Instead, the Court asked whether the requirement to provide contraceptive coverage – that is, the application of the law – did so.

RFRA's drafting history also confirms the importance of substantiating the burden of compliance. While "burden" went unmodified in RFRA's initial drafts, the word "substantial" was added to the text to ensure that the government did not have "to justify every action that has some effect on religious exercise."[49] As Professor Frederick Gedicks explains, the addition addressed fears of litigation over policies affecting (and imposing significant punishment on) prison inmates and schoolchildren, claims where if the penalty sufficed, a "claim of burden is always a claim of 'substantial' burden."[50]

As is relevant to interpretation of a statute that restores precedent under the First Amendment, courts in past free exercise cases inquired into the substantiality of burdens and did not accept every assertion of religious burden based on an objector's say-so. For example, in *Bowen v. Roy*, Native American parents asserted a religious belief that obtaining and using a Social Security number for their two-year-old daughter to access government programs would "rob" her spirit and "prevent her from attaining greater spiritual power."[51] The Supreme Court ruled that the government's use of the child's Social Security number to administer benefits did not substantially burden her or her parents' free exercise of religion.[52] While the religious believer might perceive the government to inflict substantial harms, the Court said, "for the adjudication of a constitutional claim, the Constitution, rather than an individual's religion, must supply the frame of reference."[53]

Prior to *Hobby Lobby*, courts regularly assessed the substantiality of burdens according to what the law requires of objectors.[54] RFRA specifically references *Wisconsin v. Yoder* – a canonical case in both family law and religious liberty law – that looked to the burden of compulsory school attendance on the religious exercise of the Amish community, not the fine for truancy.[55] It also lists *Sherbert v. Verner*, an unemployment case in which the Court examined both religious and secular burdens.[56] While *Sherbert* does not fit cleanly into the substantial burden framework, the cost of

49 Gedicks, *supra* note 42, at 121 (quoting Senator Hatch).

50 *Id.* at 121–22 (reviewing legislative history of RFRA's substantial burden standard).

51 476 U.S. 693, 696 (1986). 52 *Id.* at 700. 53 *Id.* at 700–701 n.6.

54 Kent Greenawalt, *Hobby Lobby: Its Flawed Interpretative Techniques and Standards of Application*, 115 Colum. L. Rev. Sidebar 153, 167 (2015) ("In past cases, the Court has assessed burdens in terms of the basic requirements, not the penalties."); Gedicks, *supra* note 42, at 121 (documenting Court's practice of adjudicating burdensome laws in terms of direct interference with a claimant's religious exercise rather than the sanction on the claimant for violating them).

55 406 U.S. 205 (1972). 56 374 U.S. 398 (1963).

compliance with the requirements to qualify for unemployment insurance was hefty, because it would have required the plaintiff to abandon her religious precepts.[57] To be eligible for unemployment compensation, Ms. Sherbert could not refuse to work on her Sabbath day. In cases involving employers in particular, the Supreme Court routinely evaluates the costs of compliance. In *Jimmy Swaggart Ministries v. Board of Equalization*, it inquired into and found "the economic cost . . . of *complying* with a generally applicable sales and use tax . . . no different from other generally applicable laws and regulations – such as health and safety regulations."[58] Similarly, *Tony and Susan Alamo Foundation v. Secretary of Labor* considered the effect of requirements under the Fair Labor Standards Act on a religious foundation's activities and its employees.[59] In these cases, the consequences of failing to collect taxes or pay wages were not discussed.[60]

Nor have courts in past RFRA cases merely assessed the penalties for failure to comply with law. Indeed, when individuals contested the ACA's individual mandate under RFRA, the existence of a tax penalty showed the *absence* of a substantial burden, not its existence. The United States Court of Appeals for the Fourth Circuit concluded, "[T]he option of paying a tax to avoid the mandates' requirements certainly imposes no substantial burden. On the contrary, this option underscores the 'lawful choice' Plaintiffs have to avoid any coverage they might consider objectionable."[61] As a D.C. district court said in a related case, given the choice, plaintiffs bore only a minimal burden and did not have to "modify their behavior and to violate their beliefs."[62]

Courts have similarly interpreted RFRA's sister statute, the Religious Land Use and Institutionalized Persons Act, which allows churches to challenge zoning decisions and prisoners to seek accommodation of their religious practices.[63] The impact of not being able to expand a church, add a wing to a school, or build a parking lot may prove a substantial burden.[64] The existence of fines for violating zoning ordinances does not suffice.

57 *Id.* at 404 ("The ruling forces her to choose between following the precepts of her religion and forfeiting benefits, on the one hand, and abandoning one of the precepts of her religion in order to accept work, on the other hand.").

58 493 U.S. 378, 391 (1990). 59 471 U.S. 290 (1985). 60 *Id.*

61 Liberty University, Inc. v. Lew, No. 10–2347, 2013 WL 3470532, *8–9 (4th Cir. July 11, 2013).

62 Mead v. Holder, 766 F.Supp.2d 16, 42 (D.D.C. 2011), aff'd by Seven-Sky v. Holder, 661 F.3d 1 (D.C. Cir. 2011).

63 42 U.S.C. § 2000cc (2012).

64 *See, e.g.*, Westchester Day Sch. v. Vill. of Mamaroneck, 504 F.3d 338, 349 (2d Cir. 2007) ("[W]here a school could easily rearrange existing classrooms to meet its religious needs in the face of a rejected application to renovate . . .[,] there would be no substantial burden, even

A deferential approach to substantial burden instead takes the novel perspective that the burden on religion is determined by the penalties for noncompliance. By conceptualizing burdens in the dollars and cents imposed on violators, this approach fails to capture the burden of regulation itself. Under the penalty approach, an objector who had to do little to comply with a law or was not bothered much by compliance would be substantially burdened by the mere existence of high penalties.[65] At the same time, a statute imposing small or nominal tax for noncompliance would prove an insubstantial burden, even where a religious objector had to assume heavy burdens to comply with it.[66] For example, if it imposed a one dollar fine on parents, a city ordinance prohibiting infant circumcision could not be challenged as a substantial burden on religious exercise. Likewise, families could not contest a minimal penalty for sending their children to a religiously affiliated school as a burden on religious exercise.

More fundamentally, if one differentiates between so-called religious and secular costs, it is not clear why the secular costs of noncompliance, rather than compliance, matter. In Helfand's view, the "secular – and civil – impact" of the contraceptive mandate on the nonprofit employers alone is cognizable, namely, the penalty for failing to offer an insurance plan covering contraception. But after the Obama Administration extended its religious accommodation, nonprofit employers bear a "secular" compliance cost of forty-nine cents, the price of a stamp. Dwelling on penalties for noncompliance obscures the vanishingly small "secular" burden of regulatory compliance. To take another example, a religiously affiliated hospital must file an application for tax-exempt status with the IRS to exempt itself from paying taxes. If one tallies only penalties, the burden of IRS regulation on religion amounts to the substantial taxes that the hospital would pay if it failed to avail itself of the tax exemption – rather than the cost of submitting an application for exemption.

Despite claims to the contrary,[67] the Supreme Court's decision in *Thomas v. Review Board of the Indiana Employment Security Division* in no way

though the school was refused the opportunity to expand its facilities."); Midrash Sephardi, Inc. v. Town of Surfside, 366 F.3d 1214, 1228 (11th Cir. 2004) (focusing on effect of permit denial and concluding that it imposed insubstantial burdens on synagogues and their members).

65 Greenawalt, *supra* note 54, at 167 ("If compliance bothered someone only a little, his doing so would not involve a substantial burden no matter how severe were the penalties for violations.").

66 Abner S. Greene, *Religious Freedom and (Other) Civil Liberties: Is There a Middle Ground?* 9 Harv. L. & Pol'y Rev. 161, 181 (2015).

67 *See* Helfand, Chapter 6 this volume; *see also* Hobby Lobby, *supra* note 2, at 2778 (referring to Thomas as "nearly identical").

prevents substantiating the burdens of legal compliance.[68] In *Thomas*, the Court was reviewing the denial of unemployment benefits to a Jehovah's Witness on the basis that his reasons for quitting were inconsistent with beliefs of other Witnesses and thus not truly religious. In rejecting this view, the Court stated that "Thomas drew a line, and it is not for us to say that the line he drew was an unreasonable one."[69] That "line" referred to determinations of what his religion required, not how substantial the burden was.[70] To resolve the case by answering a question of theology, as the state court had done, was barred to the courts by the religious question doctrine.

Under the religious question doctrine, however, courts may proceed so long as they rely on secular legal principles. Shortly following *Thomas*, the Supreme Court made clear that the substantial burden standard allowed for reliance on legal principles; it distinguished between inquiry into the centrality of belief – prohibited to the courts – and analysis of the substantiality of the burden – required of the courts when analyzing constitutional free exercise claims.[71] With regard to RFRA as well, courts have taken this approach.[72] In the contraceptive cases, this basic rule means that judges cannot second-guess plaintiffs' conclusion that, for example, Catholic teachings prohibit their involvement in the use of contraceptives, but they may employ legal analysis to examine the extent to which a law burdens plaintiffs' exercise of religion.

Assessing the substantiality of burdens – which sometimes will mean assessing the connection between the requirement imposed on an objector and the ultimate act to which he or she objects – need not lead courts into thickets of theological inquiry. While they lack expertise in religious studies, courts regularly apply principles of proximity, causation, and attenuation in a variety of First Amendment contexts.[73] They differentiate between direct

68 450 U.S. 707 (1981). 69 *Id.* at 715.

70 Greenawalt, *supra* note 54, at 170 (critiquing Justice Alito's reliance on *Thomas* as unpersuasive).

71 *See* Hernandez v. Comm'r, 490 U.S. 680, 699 (1989).

72 *See, e.g.*, Kaemmerling v. Lappin, 553 F.3d 669, 679 (D.C. Cir. 2008) (accepting plaintiffs' beliefs as sincere and religious but "not the legal conclusion, cast as a factual allegation, that his religious exercise is substantially burdened").

73 Smith & Corbin, *supra* note 41, at 271 (Corbin arguing that free exercise exemptions to the mandate should be analyzed like government endorsement of religion in school voucher cases, separated by intervening individual decisions and not seen as endorsement); Greene, *supra* note 78, at 185 (demonstrating that indirectness and generality "are of critical importance in at least three areas of First Amendment law," including school vouchers; religious groups' use of spaces in public schools open to the public; and compulsion of private parties to host the speech of others, as in shopping malls or where military recruiters are on campus).

and remote support.[74] With regard to insurance in particular, courts have distinguished between requirements to contribute to insurance (an indirect and remote burden) and requirements to accept or use it (a more direct burden).[75] Courts also examine whether objective observers might attribute a regulated act to the objector. For example, courts have reasoned that requiring recipients of city funds to extend the same health and fringe benefits to employees with domestic partners as to employees with spouses does not demand their endorsement of those relationships.[76] Tort and criminal law similarly require analysis of the connection between a person and the resulting injury/crime.[77]

As a practical matter, the attenuation inquiry that courts have long performed has shielded the government – as Congress intended – from having to justify any and all incidental effects on religious exercise. If the Supreme Court were to reject this inquiry in favor of deference to religious objectors,[78] it would remove the primary limiting mechanism for RFRA claims.[79] Religious burdens considered insubstantial would become entitled to relief under RFRA.

74 Bernstein v. Ocean Grove Camp Mtg. Ass'n, N.J. Office of Admin. L. ALJ Decision, OAL DKT. NO. CRT 6145-09, at 6 (Jan. 12, 2012), www.adfmedia.org/files/OGCMA-BernsteinRuling.pdf (noting that wedding venue objecting to renting to same-sex couples did not control or sponsor the weddings and "[t]he arm's length nature of the transactions gave respondent a comfortable distance from notions incompatible with its own beliefs" and rejecting venue's claims that nondiscrimination law violated its freedom of religion, association, and speech).

75 *See, e.g.*, Erzinger v. Regents of Univ. of Cal., 137 Cal. App. 3d 389, 392-93 (1983) (rejecting objection to student registration fee for health insurance because students were not forced "to use the student health service programs, receive pregnancy counseling, have abortions, perform abortions or endorse abortions"); South Ridge Baptist Church v. Ind. Comm'n of Ohio, 911 F.2d 1203, 1211 n.6 (6th Cir. 1990) (distinguishing employer paying into workers' compensation from compelling "an employee of the church who entertains similar views as a matter of personal conviction to accept any of the benefits conferred by the workman's compensation law").

76 Catholic Charities of Me., Inc. v. City of Portland, 304 F. Supp. 2d 77, 95 (D. Me. 2004) ("Providing benefits to domestic partners does not represent an endorsement of non-family relationships any more than providing benefits to unmarried pregnant women represents an endorsement of single parenthood.").

77 Gedicks, *supra* note 42, at 28–29 (drawing principles from tort such as factual causation, products liability, and intervening causes); Ira C. Lupu, Hobby Lobby *and the Dubious Enterprise of Religious Exemptions*, 38 HARV. J. L. & GENDER 35, 82 (2015) (suggesting that the question of "the degree of involvement of an insurance policy purchaser in the conduct of the insured employees" more closely resembles "accomplice liability in criminal law" than "Bible study").

78 Gilardi v. Sebelius, 926 F. Supp. 2d 273, 282 (D.D.C. 2013).

79 *See* Ira C. Lupu, *The Failure of RFRA*, 20 U. ARK. LITTLE ROCK L.J. 575, 594 n.86 (1998) (concluding, based on systematic review of first years of RFRA, that substantial burden requirement "accounted for over 70% of the RFRA defeats in court"); Lupu, *supra* note 89, at n.118 (compiling decisions rejecting RFRA claims for lack of substantial burdens).

Take tax objections. Courts historically turned away tax objectors, not because the amount of taxes paid is small, but because "there are too many steps in the causal chain between the taxpayer's payment of taxes and pursuit of the activity she deplores."[80] A deferential approach instead would require all tax schemes to undergo strict scrutiny. Indeed, because laws frequently are enforced through the tax system, focusing on the penalty of noncompliance converts many objections to regulatory compliance into tax objections. For example, under this approach, contraceptive challengers are burdened for purposes of RFRA analysis, not by their responsibility to provide a plan that covers contraception, but by the taxes they must pay for refusing to do so.

Granting religious exemptions to some in the face of such insubstantial burdens would inevitably interfere with the private and family lives of others. As Professor Caroline Corbin has noted, in the absence of inquiry into substantial burden, "if an institution considers it 'cooperation with evil' to allow its employees to use their salary to purchase contraception, buy alcohol, or see a movie celebrating same-sex marriage, then we … should defer to its sincere claims, and permit it to impose conditions on its employees' salaries unless laws that prohibit such conditions pass strict scrutiny."[81] Employees' decisions about family formation and private life would be subject to veto by their religious employer.

Deference to objectors' sense of connectedness to what they see as wrongdoing would invite claims from actors remote from responsibility in ways that harm others. For example, based on *Hobby Lobby*, Missouri state representative Paul Wieland filed suit, arguing that his state employer-provided health insurance plan cannot cover contraception for his daughters without violating the family's religious beliefs contrary to RFRA.[82] The Court of Appeals for the Eighth Circuit concluded that the Wielands could proceed with their suit – even though the regulations to which they object do not even apply to the Wielands, but to their employer-based plan.[83] On remand, the district court granted summary judgment in Wieland's favor, allowing him to seek insurance plans that omit contraceptive. Having prevailed, he will deprive his daughters of the benefits due to them under law.

* * *

80 Amy J. Sepinwall, *Conscience and Complicity: Assessing Pleas for Religious Exemptions in Hobby Lobby's Wake*, 82 U. Chi. L. Rev. 1897, 1940–41 (2015).

81 Smith & Corbin, *supra* note 41, at 271.

82 Wieland v. U.S. Dep't of Health & Hum. Serv., 793 F. 3d 949, 952 (8th Cir. 2015).

83 *Id.* at 957.

If in the future, the Supreme Court were to adopt this approach and conclude that a religious accommodation is itself a substantial burden on religion, every regulation (or exemption therefrom) could count. Even if religious objectors ultimately lose on the basis that an accommodation constitutes the least restrictive means to further a compelling government interest, the damage will have been done. All federal law could have to survive strict scrutiny in order to apply to religious objectors – whether they are individuals of disfavored faiths or craft stores aligned with Evangelicals.

"THE MOST DEMANDING" OF SCRUTINY IN THE ABSENCE OF A THRESHOLD

In his chapter, Helfand assures our readers not to fret, that exposing all federal regulation to strict scrutiny will be of little import. In his view, the courts will ratchet down their level of scrutiny to a balancing test sensitive to all interests at stake. Perhaps, but to assume so requires a leap of faith.

Previously, religious liberty cases under both the First Amendment and RFRA involved something short of strict scrutiny. Courts' analysis of constitutional free exercise claims was "strict in theory, but feeble in fact."[84] While RFRA requires that a law substantially burdening religion be justified by a compelling governmental interest and be the least restrictive means to satisfy that interest, courts applied a standard more deferential to the government. As a result, the government prevailed in nearly 60% of religious liberty cases, even as only 24% of laws survived in most areas of strict scrutiny.[85]

Ignoring this history, the *Hobby Lobby* Court stated unequivocally that RFRA requires "the most demanding test known to constitutional law."[86] It then applied this exacting scrutiny to the contraceptive coverage mandate. Indeed, the majority conducted scrutiny under RFRA that seems even more demanding than that used in other areas of constitutional law where strict scrutiny applies.

84 Christopher L. Eisgruber & Lawrence G. Sager, *The Vulnerability of Conscience: The Constitutional Basis for Protecting Religious Conduct*, 61 U. CHI. L. REV. 1245, 1247 (1994); *see also* Adam Winkler, *Fatal in Theory and Strict in Fact: An Empirical Analysis of Strict Scrutiny in the Federal Courts*, 59 VAND. L. REV. 793, 857–58 (2006) ("[T]he religious liberty category had the highest survival rate of any area of law in which strict scrutiny applies: 59 percent, more than double the mean of the other doctrinal categories.").

85 Winkler, *supra* note 84, at 796–97.

86 134 S. Ct. at 2780 (citing *City of Boerne*, 521 U.S. at 532).

Prior to *Hobby Lobby*, courts accepted that the government had a wide variety of compelling interests, including the eradication of discrimination and the preservation of health. In religious liberty cases, courts were particularly likely to accept the government's interest in regulation. As Professor Kent Greenawalt has observed, whereas other First Amendment cases require "an extremely powerful interest," "such a high bar has not typically been employed for religious exemption claims."[87] Those extremely powerful interests have long included sex equality and public health, allowing for infringement of rights to association, privacy, and bodily autonomy.[88] Sex equality, in turn, depends on women's "ability to control their reproductive lives," as the Supreme Court has recognized.[89]

Yet, even as it assumed, without deciding, that the governmental interest in guaranteeing cost-free access to contraceptives was compelling,[90] the *Hobby Lobby* Court questioned whether sex equality and public health could ever be compelling interests for RFRA purposes. The majority described interests in public health and sex equality as "couched in very broad terms."[91] In responding to the dissent's examples of cases involving discrimination on the basis of religion, sex, sexual orientation, marital status, and race,[92] it acknowledged only the compelling nature of norms against race discrimination. It rejected the possibility that its decision might shield "discrimination in hiring, for example on the basis of race," because "[t]he Government has a compelling interest in providing an equal opportunity to participate in the workforce without regard to race."[93] In cabining its response in this way, the Court called into question whether preventing discrimination on any other basis represents a compelling interest.

Quoting its previous decision in *Gonzales v. O Centro Espírita Beneficente União do Vegetal*, the Court instructed the lower courts to "loo[k] beyond broadly formulated interests [and] to scrutinize[] the asserted harm of granting specific exemptions to particular religious claimants."[94] If taken literally, this

87 Greenawalt, *supra* note 54, at 160.

88 Roberts v. U.S. Jaycees, 468 U.S. 609, 625 (1984) (recognizing the government's "compelling interest in eradicating discrimination against its female citizens"); *see also* Bd. of Dirs. of Rotary Int'l v. Rotary Club of Duarte, 481 U.S. 537, 549 (1987) (same); State v. Musser, 721 N.W.2d 734, 742–45 (Iowa 2006) (holding that compulsion of speech under state mandatory HIV-status reporting law survived strict scrutiny to further the state's compelling interest in protection of public health).

89 Planned Parenthood of Southeastern Pa. v. Casey, 505 U.S. 833, 856 (1992).

90 Hobby Lobby, *supra* note 2, at 2780.

91 *Id.* at 2779.

92 *Id.* at 2804–05 (Ginsburg, J., dissenting).

93 *Id.* at 2783.

94 *Id.* at 2779 (quoting Gonzales v. O Centro Espírita Beneficente União do Vegetal, 546 U.S. 418, 431 (2006)).

instruction would require the government to justify application of any law with regard to the particular objector. It is difficult, however, to imagine that the enforcement of a law against any single employer – let alone any individual – could rise to the level of a compelling interest. The more narrowly the interest is defined, the less compelling it will seem. For example, the government would seem to have a compelling interest in preventing spread of highly communicable and potentially deadly diseases like measles. But the government would seem to lack a compelling interest in ensuring John Smith is vaccinated.[95]

As Professor Greenawalt has argued, a better interpretation of *O Centro* would conclude that "the government has a compelling interest in applying the law to the particular 'person,' if nonenforcement against all others who are not distinguishable under RFRA would sacrifice that interest."[96] Instead of considering the governmental interest in applying the contraceptive mandate to Hobby Lobby, a court would weigh the government's interest in compliance by all closely held for-profit corporations. Rather than scrutinize the government's interest in John Smith's immunity, a court would take the vaccination of the public at large as a compelling goal. Whether courts will take this approach is uncertain.

Finally, *Hobby Lobby* indicated that the existence of exceptions may render a governmental interest less than compelling.[97] The majority opinion questioned whether the interest furthered by the contraceptive mandate could be compelling due to limitations on the scope of the Affordable Care Act ("ACA"). The employer mandate to provide insurance does not apply to businesses with fewer than fifty employees. And employer-based plans that existed when the ACA was passed were grandfathered, that is, exempted from the preventive care requirement including contraceptive coverage, until the levels of coverage provided or costs for employees change.[98]

If exceptions support claims for religious exemptions, as *Hobby Lobby* suggests, few federal statutes may come to apply to religious objectors. Federal laws typically include exceptions, as do state laws. Due to constitutional concerns about Congress's power and in recognition of compliance burdens, federal laws frequently do not apply to smaller businesses. New legislation often allows for incremental implementation through grandfathering. Indeed, grandfathering under the ACA was designed, not to

95 *See* Paul Offit, Chapter 12, this volume. 96 Greenawalt, *supra* note 54, at 171–72.

97 Hobby Lobby, *supra* note 2, at 2780 (describing grandfathering of plans and inapplicability to small employers as "features of ACA that support [the] view" that the mandate does not serve a compelling interest).

98 See Michele Goodwin, Chapter 3, this volume.

exempt plans, but to ease the shock of rapid change. Congress acted with the understanding that the number of grandfathered plans would decline each year, as indeed it has.[99]

Hobby Lobby sends the message that the government's burden of showing a compelling interest in regulation may be heightened in future cases. If the Court means what it says, the standard of scrutiny for religious exemption claims under RFRA has radically changed.

Hobby Lobby, however, renders it particularly difficult to predict the course future decisions will take. The Court read the Religious Freedom Restoration Act as "an obvious effort to effect a complete separation from First Amendment case law."[100] It instructed that "nothing in the text of RFRA as originally enacted suggested that the statutory phrase 'exercise of religion under the First Amendment' was meant to be tied to this Court's pre-*Smith* interpretation of that Amendment."[101] The relevance of constitutional Free Exercise precedent to emerging doctrinal questions remains unclear.

CONCLUSION: MITIGATING THE RISKY BUSINESS OF RFRAs

The claims now capturing the headlines go far beyond anything our legal system has accepted. Wedding vendors refuse to serve same-sex couples lest they facilitate same-sex marriage. Employers resist notifying their insurance companies (or the government) of their objections to contraception on the ground that they might form a pipeline to contraceptive use. In other cases, employees object to their employer providing an insurance plan that their family members or other employees might use to purchase contraceptives.[102] Small employers, exempt from any obligation to provide insurance, demand that insurers offer them contraceptive-free plans.[103] These objectors play little to no causal role in the alleged wrongdoing, are distant from it, and perform a task whose morality (on their own account) is unquestioned.

99 Employer Health Benefits Survey 233, Kaiser Family Found. (2016), files.kff.org/attachment/Report-Employer-Health-Benefits-2016-Annual-Survey (23% of offering firms had at least one grandfathered plan in 2016, down from 35% in 2015, 37% in 2014, 54% in 2013, 58% in 2012, and 72% in 2011).

100 Hobby Lobby, *supra* note 2, at 2751, 2761–62.

101 *Id.* at 2772 (quoting 42 U.S.C. § 2000bb–2(4) (2012)).

102 Wieland v. United States Dep't of Health & Human Servs., No. 4:13-CV-01577-JCH, 2016 WL 98170, at *2 (E.D. Mo. Jan. 8, 2016); *see also* March for Life v. Burwell, No. 14-cv-1149, 2015 WL 5139099, at *7 (D.D.C. Aug. 31, 2015).

103 Annex Med., Inc. v. Burwell, 769 F.3d 578, 581 (8th Cir. 2014).

While *Hobby Lobby* has immediate relevance only for the federal RFRA, which applies to federal laws and regulations, many states are now proposing the expansion or adoption of state RFRAs with *Hobby Lobby* and same-sex marriage in mind. With the doctrine teetering on the precipice, RFRAs create serious risks for disadvantaged groups and religious minorities in particular. They set powerful religious and economic actors against individuals dependent upon them for employment and services. In embracing religious libertarianism, *Hobby Lobby* sets up a collision between, on the one hand, rights to religious exercise for institutions and, on the other, rights to family formation, insurance benefits, and equal treatment that benefit people of all faiths. Families are at the forefront as religious objectors resist decisions that others make about not just how to define their families but also how to support, feed, clothe, heal, and educate them across the generations.

Under such circumstances, the public is right to be skeptical of the new batch of state RFRAs. Despite claims to the contrary, resistance to corporate exemption does not mean Americans have rejected religious accommodation, religious liberty, or religion itself.[104] Indeed, many opponents of corporate religious exemption (and the new batch of state RFRAs) would likely support traditional religious liberty claims from minority individuals, such as those that today take the form of litigation over, for example, restrictions on eagle feathers that form part of a Native American religious ritual;[105] U.S. Army grooming standards that bar a Sikh from serving as a chaplain due to his religious beliefs related to grooming,[106] and restrictions on beard length that prevent a Muslim prisoner from growing a half-inch beard.[107] As a rule, such claims do not pit institutional religion against individuals. Nor do they impose significant burdens on employees and consumers who do not share institutional religious priors.

Viewed in this way, public concern over religious exemptions for businesses reflects a core constitutional principle that prohibits the government from shifting significant costs onto some citizens to grant religious accommodations to others. Grounded in both the Free Exercise Clause and the Establishment Clause, this principle guards against government imposition of the beliefs of some citizens on others to the detriment of their own religious freedom.[108]

104 Elizabeth Sepper, *Reports of Accommodation's Death Have Been Greatly Exaggerated*, 128 Harv. L. Rev. F. 24 (2014) (refuting these claims).

105 McAllen Grace Brethren Church v. Salazar, 764 F.3d 465, 468 (5th Cir. 2014).

106 Singh v. McHugh, 2015 U.S. Dist. LEXIS 76526 (D.D.C. June 12, 2015).

107 Holt v. Hobbs, 135 S. Ct. 853 (2015).

108 For background, see Frederick Mark Gedicks & Rebecca G. Van Tassell, *RFRA Exemptions from the Contraception Mandate: An Unconstitutional Accommodation of Religion*, 49 Harv. C.R.-C.L. L. Rev. 343 (2014); Kara Lowentheil, *Where Free Exercise Is a Burden: Protecting*

In the leading case *Estate of Thornton v. Caldor*, the Supreme Court explained that "[t]he First Amendment gives no one the right to insist that in pursuit of their own interests others must conform their conduct to his own religious necessities."[109] *Caldor* involved a Connecticut statute that provided employees with an absolute right not to work on their Sabbath day and thus required either that employers assume "substantial economic burdens" of offering premium pay to attract volunteers to cover weekend shifts or that employees bear "significant burdens" of covering these shifts irrespective of their seniority or personal preferences.[110] Imposing these burdens, the Court held, violated the Establishment Clause.

Aversion to burdening third parties animates many of the Court's religious exemption decisions.[111] In *United States v. Lee*, for example, the Court refused a free exercise exemption to an Amish employer who objected to the payment of Social Security taxes for his employees, reasoning that "[g]ranting an exemption from social security taxes to an employer operates to impose the employer's religious faith on the employees."[112] In *Tony & Susan Alamo Foundation*, the Court similarly construed the Fair Labor Standards Act to require a nonprofit religious organization to pay the minimum wage to its employees, again based on the burdens that a free exercise exemption otherwise would have inflicted on employees and competitors.[113] In *Hobby Lobby* as well, the Supreme Court affirmed the importance of avoiding burden shifting under RFRA.[114] While the majority opinion contains some troubling language

"Third Parties" in Religious Accommodation Law, 62 DRAKE L. REV. 433 (2014); Micah Schwartzman, Richard Schragger, & Nelson Tebbe, *The Establishment Clause and the Contraception Mandate*, BALKINIZATION BLOG, Nov. 27, 2013, http://balkin.blogspot.com/2013/11/the-establishment-clause-and.html.

109 472 U.S. 703, 710 (1985); *see also* Cutter v. Wilkinson, 544 U.S. 709, 722 (2005) (reaffirming that to avoid violating the Establishment Clause "courts must take adequate account of the burdens a requested accommodation may impose on nonbeneficiaries").

110 472 U.S. at 709–11.

111 Wisconsin v. Yoder, 406 U.S. 204, 208 (1972) (observing that exemption of Amish children from school attendance would not cause "harm to the physical or mental health of the child or to the public safety, peace, order, or welfare"); Sherbert v. Verner, 374 U.S. 398, 409 (1963) (noting that exemption of Sabbatarian from Saturday work requirement of unemployment compensation law would not "abridge any other person's religious liberties").

112 455 U.S. 252, 261 (1982).

113 471 U.S. 290, 302 (1985) (reasoning that such an exemption "would be likely to exert downward pressure on wages in competing businesses" and thereby compromise the right of workers to earn the minimum wage).

114 134 S. Ct. 2751, 2781 n.37 (2014). The Court's unanimous decision in Holt v. Hobbs, granting a prisoner of faith an exemption under RLUIPA from a prison no-beard policy because his sincerely held religious beliefs required him to wear a short beard, further affirmed the fundamental nature of the no-third-party harms principle. 135 S. Ct. 853 (2015).

in this regard, it ultimately recognized that "[i]t is certainly true that in applying RFRA 'courts must take adequate account of the burdens a requested accommodation may impose on nonbeneficiaries.'"[115] Justice Kennedy, concurring, and four justices, dissenting, agreed.[116]

Wisconsin v. Yoder can also be read to acknowledge concern for third-party burdens within the context of the family.[117] There, the Yoders, a family of Amish, challenged the requirement that their children attend school until age sixteen, seeking to keep them home once they completed eighth grade. In accordance with their religion, they considered exposure to secular education beyond the eighth grade potentially corrupting of their children and detrimental to their vocational education in the agricultural and artisanal pursuits necessary to success in the Amish community.[118] Granting the exemption, the Court distinguished cases in which "any harm to the physical or mental health of the child or to the public safety, peace, order, or welfare has been demonstrated or may be properly inferred."[119] Whereas Justice William Douglas expressed concern in dissent that "[i]f the parents in this case are allowed a religious exemption, the inevitable effect is to impose the parents' notions of religious duty upon their children,"[120] the majority made clear that the case did not present such a conflict between the children and the parents.[121] Justices Potter Stewart and William Brennan wrote a concurrence specifically to note that what evidence there was in the record indicated that the teenage children shared their parents' beliefs and themselves sought not to attend school.[122]

The accommodation of many religious beliefs and practices in the family arguably results in immaterial third-party burdens. For example, religious rites might involve serving alcohol to minors, an act otherwise prohibited in many states. Honoring Jehovah's Witnesses' refusals to accept blood or religious beliefs around end-of-life care or autopsy similarly invite accommodation without much concern. Religious communities might object to corporal punishment in public schools without imposition of any burden. One might similarly argue that exemptions to

115 Hobby Lobby, *supra* note 2, at 2781 n.37 (quoting Cutter v. Wilkinson, 544 U.S. 709, 720 (2005)).

116 *Id.* at 2786–87 (Kennedy, J., concurring) (writing religious exemptions may not "unduly restrict other persons, such as employees, in protecting their own interests, interests the law deems compelling"); *id.* at 2801 (Ginsburg, J., dissenting) ("No tradition, and no prior decision under RFRA, allows a religion-based exemption when the accommodation would be harmful to others.").

117 406 U.S. 205 (1972). 118 *Id.* at 209–10. 119 *Id.* at 230.

120 *Id.* at 240 (Douglas, J., dissenting). 121 *Id.* at 230–31.

122 *Id.* at 237 (Stewart, J., concurring).

vaccine mandates for school attendance for good-faith religious objectors result in insignificant burdens.

Consideration of third-party burdens cannot replicate the gatekeeper role that the substantial burden standard performs. It nonetheless forms a constitutional barrier that courts must take seriously. As institutions – with economic and political power – resist legislation protective of individuals and fundamental to the modern state, this requirement should safeguard those who do not share the beliefs of the institutions that employ them or provide them with goods and services – religious minorities in particular. It suggests a path forward that preserves religious liberty for people of all faiths and ensures equality across family and socioeconomic statuses.

2

Religion and the Family in the Wake of *Hobby Lobby*

Michael A. Helfand

Associate Professor, Pepperdine University School of Law; Co-Director, Diane and Guilford Glazer Institute for Jewish Studies

Much of our doctrine surrounding religious liberty comes from our legal system's attempt to navigate questions of religious liberty within the family.[1] The contours of that doctrine have certainly varied over time, leading to repeated clashes within courthouses around the United States over the scope of the religious liberty protected by the law.

But in recent years, there is a new dimension to these debates. While many of the recent Supreme Court decisions continue to cement the constitutional status of religious liberty,[2] something profound has changed about the public's perception of it. Religious liberty is no longer viewed by the public as a hallowed constitutional principle, deserving of unwavering support as the Bill of Rights' "first freedom."[3] Increasingly, religious liberty is viewed with skepticism by the public – and as less deserving of increased legal protections.[4]

1 *See, e.g.*, Reynolds v. United States, 98 U.S. 145 (1878); Wisconsin v. Yoder, 406 U.S. 205 (1972).

2 *See, e.g.*, Burwell v. Hobby Lobby Stores, Inc., 134 S. Ct. 2751, 2759 (2014); Holt v. Hobbs, 135 S. Ct. 853 (2015).

3 *See, e.g.*, Thomas J. Curry, The First Freedoms: Church and State in America to the Passage of the First Amendment (1986); Nat Hentoff, The First Freedom (1980); Michael W. McConnell, *Religion and Constitutional Rights: Why Is Religious Liberty the "First Freedom"?* 21 Cardozo L. Rev. 1243, 1243 (2000) ("Studies of religious liberty under the American Bill of Rights often take inspiration from the fact that the Free Exercise Clause and the Establishment Clause are the first clauses of our First Amendment, making them our 'first freedoms.'").

4 *Do You Want a Religious Freedom Law in Your State?* Rasmussen Reports (Apr. 1, 2015), www.rasmussenreports.com/public_content/politics/general_politics/march_2015/do_you_want_a_religious_freedom_law_in_your_state ("Fifty-three percent (53%) of voters are concerned that religious freedom laws will lead to widespread discrimination against gays and lesbians, including 30% who are Very Concerned. Forty-three percent (43%) don't share this concern, with 22% who are Not At All Concerned."). It is worth noting that the *Rasmussen Reports*' survey question of "How concerned are you that religious freedom laws will lead to

At the core of this dramatic change in U.S. public perception is a shift in the religious liberty narrative over the past thirty years. In many ways, the contemporary fluctuations in the religious liberty narrative began with the U.S. Supreme Court's 1990 seminal decision *Employment Division v. Smith*.[5] At issue in *Smith* was the First Amendment claim of Al Smith and Galen Black, both of whom had been terminated from their employment for ingesting peyote. When Smith and Black attempted to collect their unemployment benefits, they were informed that they were not eligible because they had been terminated for cause.[6] Smith and Black, however, countered that they had ingested peyote as part of a sacramental Native American ceremony – and therefore denying their request for unemployment benefits violated their rights under the First Amendment's Free Exercise Clause.[7] In ruling against the plaintiffs, the Court held that they were not entitled to a constitutionally mandated religious exemption. In so doing, the Court held that the Free Exercise Clause only protects against laws that target or discriminate against religion. By contrast, the Free Exercise Clause does not provide any protection against laws that are "facially neutral" and "generally applicable" – that is, those that have legitimate secular objectives and only unintentionally burden religion.[8]

The Supreme Court's interpretation of the Free Exercise Clause represented somewhat of a departure from prior Supreme Court precedent.[9] While the Court's free exercise precedent had been doctrinally uneven,[10] its overall framework prior to *Smith* afforded far broader religious liberty protections. Thus, under prior decisions, the Free Exercise Clause required courts to grant exemptions from laws that substantially burdened religiously motivated

widespread discrimination against gays and lesbians?" was asked after the following question was posed to those surveyed: "A number of states have adopted or are considering laws that prohibit the government from forcing businesses to provide services they find objectionable on religious grounds. Do you favor or oppose a law in your state that would allow businesses to refuse service to customers for religious reasons?" *Questions – Religious Freedom Laws – March 30–31, 2015*, Rasmussen Reports (Apr. 1, 2015), www.rasmussenreports.com/public_content/politics/questions/pt_survey_questions/march_2015/questions_religious_freedom_laws_march_30_31_2015.

5 Employment Div. v. Smith, 494 U.S. 872 (1990). 6 *Id.* at 874. 7 *Id.* 8 *Id.* at 901–02.

9 For commentary soon after the *Smith* decision, see Michael W. McConnell, *Free Exercise Revisionism and the* Smith *Decision*, 57 U. Chi. L. Rev. 1109 (1990); William P. Marshall, *In Defense of* Smith *and Free Exercise Revisionism*, 58 U. Chi. L. Rev. 308 (1991). While McConnell and Marshall take opposing views with respect to religious exemptions, they both agree that *Smith* itself represented a change in free exercise doctrine.

10 *See* Michael A. Helfand, *Religious Institutionalism, Implied Consent and the Value of Voluntarism*, 88 S. Cal. L. Rev. 539, 556–63 (2015).

conduct, unless applying the law was necessary to achieve a compelling government interest.[11] The Court's new jurisprudence discarded this more protective framework, only providing constitutional protection against laws that targeted religiously motivated conduct.[12] Under such a framework, a law riddled with many exceptions – and none for religion – might still be seen as targeting a religion, but laws that are largely uniform with few exceptions would pass constitutional muster irrespective of whether or not the laws substantially burdened religion.

From the Court's vantage point, those seeking religious exemptions still had a viable alternative, even though they were not constitutionally entitled to an exemption. They could simply request their legislature to incorporate a religious exemption into the relevant law.[13] Indeed, this has been an approach to resolve issues of religion within the family, such as statutory protections that authorize homeschooling, certain child-rearing and medical treatment practices, and religiously guided end-of-life care discussed throughout this volume.[14] But this alternative provided cold comfort to the growing legion of *Smith* critics. Petitioning a legislature might serve as a viable alternative for more well-established and better-organized religious communities. But minority religious communities or practices would be far less likely to successfully secure the legislative exemptions necessary to protect their religious practices from legal burdens. Justice Harry Blackmun expressed this central worry in his dissent to the Court's *Smith* opinion:

[11] *See, e.g.*, Yoder, *supra* note 1. Sherbert v. Verner, 374 U.S. 398 (1963). Again, as noted earlier, Supreme Court decisions were not wholly consistent on this issue, especially in the decade prior to the *Smith* decision.

[12] *See, e.g.*, Alan E. Brownstein, *Constitutional Wish Granting and the Property Rights Genie*, 13 Const. Commentary 7, 45 (1996) ("In *Smith*, the Court drastically reduced the protection the Free Exercise Clause provided to religious minorities by limiting the application of this constitutional provision to only those laws that deliberately and exclusively burden religious practices. Neutral laws of general applicability cannot violate the Free Exercise Clause under this analysis regardless of how debilitating they may be to the ability of individuals to obey the tenets of their faith."). To be sure, the constitutional standard pre-*Smith* was far from uniform in application. *See, e.g.*, Helfand, *supra* note 10.

[13] Smith, *supra* note 5, at 890 ("Values that are protected against government interference through enshrinement in the Bill of Rights are not thereby banished from the political process. Just as a society that believes in the negative protection accorded to the press by the First Amendment is likely to enact laws that affirmatively foster the dissemination of the printed word, so also a society that believes in the negative protection accorded to religious belief can be expected to be solicitous of that value in its legislation as well. It is therefore not surprising that a number of States have made an exception to their drug laws for sacramental peyote use.").

[14] See Dwyer (Chapter 8), Kaplan (Chapter 19), Cahn and Zietlow (Chapter 20), this volume.

> [T]he Court today suggests that the disfavoring of minority religions is an "unavoidable consequence" under our system of government and that accommodation of such religions must be left to the political process. In my view, however, the First Amendment was enacted precisely to protect the rights of those whose religious practices are not shared by the majority and may be viewed with hostility. The history of our free exercise doctrine amply demonstrates the harsh impact majoritarian rule has had on unpopular or emerging religious groups such as the Jehovah's Witnesses and the Amish.[15]

As Professor Christopher Lund points out, "statutes burdening small religious minorities are disproportionately likely to be uniform ones, immune to challenge under the *Smith* rule" because "[s]mall religious minorities often want idiosyncratic things –they demand rights that no one else wants" and for which special statutory concessions are not given.[16] These worries over the limited political power of religious minorities formed the primary catalyst behind the Religious Freedom Restoration Act ("RFRA"), which aimed – as a matter of federal legislation – to undo *Smith* and restore the prior applicable free exercise standard. RFRA prohibits laws that substantially burden a person's religious exercise, unless imposing that burden is necessary to achieve a compelling government interest.[17] Not surprisingly, the hearings on RFRA conducted before the Senate's Committee on the Judiciary put a spotlight on testimony from members of religious minorities[18] – and the potential impact

[15] Smith, *supra* note 5, at 902 (Blackmun, J. dissenting).

[16] Christopher Lund, *Exploring Free Exercise Doctrine: Equal Liberty and Religious Exemptions*, 77 TENN. L. REV. 351 (2010) ("As a result of their nonmainstream beliefs, they are often burdened by laws that burden no one else. Because no significantly sized group is burdened, no exceptions to the law ever develop.").

[17] 42 U.S.C. § 2000bb-1 (2012) ("Government shall not substantially burden a person's exercise of religion even if the burden results from a rule of general applicability . . . [unless government] demonstrates that application of the burden to the person – (1) is in furtherance of a compelling governmental interest; and (2) is the least restrictive means of furthering that compelling governmental interest.").

[18] *See* Testimony of Willian Nouyi Yang, S. 2969, at 5 (Sept. 18, 1992), www.justice.gov/sites/default/files/jmd/legacy/2014/02/13/hear-j-102–82-1992.pdf (describing the inadequacies of legal protections for the Hmong community); Testimony of Dallin Oaks, S. 2969, at 5 (Sept. 18, 1992), www.justice.gov/sites/default/files/jmd/legacy/2014/02/13/hear-j-102–82-1992.pdf (describing historical persecution of the Church of Jesus Christ of Latter Day Saints and emphasizing that "[t]he worshippers who need [the Bill of Rights] protections are the oppressed minorities, not the influential constituent elements of the majority."); *see also* Testimony of Douglas Laycock, S. 2969, at 64 (Sept. 18, 1992), www.justice.gov/sites/default/files/jmd/legacy/2014/02/13/hear-j-102–82-1992.pdf (explaining that without RFRA "the mainstream faiths would not always win, but they would at least be advantaged and the minority faiths would be terribly disadvantaged").

of *Smith* on their religious practices.[19] As Professor Michael McConnell explains,

> Prior to *Smith*, the Free Exercise Clause functioned as a corrective for [the] bias [against minority religions], allowing the courts, which are institutionally more attuned to the interests of the less powerful segments of society, to extend to minority religions the same degree of solicitude that more mainstream religions are able to attain through the political process. The Free Exercise Clause, prior to *Smith*, was an equalizer.[20]

In this way, RFRA hoped to provide the type of blanket religious liberty protections that would not leave the reach of safeguards afforded religious minorities to the vicissitudes of the political process. Thus, RFRA provided religious freedom protections to religiously motivated conduct irrespective of whether or not the affected religious community had the political power to secure an exemption from the legislature. And while the Supreme Court invalidated RFRA's applicability to state law as beyond Congress's constitutional authority,[21] many states enacted their own versions of RFRA or interpreted state constitutional provisions that protected religious liberty to provide analogous RFRA protections against state law.[22] In this way, state legislatures advanced this same impulse to protect the religious liberty of minority religious communities.

But the narrative around RFRA – originating in a commitment to protect vulnerable religious minorities – has morphed radically in recent years. Nowhere was the shift more evident than in the recent attempts to enact

[19] This same perspective has been echoed throughout the secondary literature as well. *See, e.g.*, Steven H. Shiffrin, *The Pluralistic Foundations of the Religion Clauses*, 90 CORNELL L. REV. 9, 32 (2004) ("The Smith case thus reeks of insensitivity to the plight of a religious minority."); Kent Greenawalt, *Religion and the Rehnquist Court*, 99 NW. U. L. REV. 145, 155 (2004) ("The rule of Smith risks legislative indifference to the plight of unfamiliar minority religions."); Douglas Laycock, *The Religious Freedom Restoration Act*, 1993 B.Y.U. L. REV. 221, 224 ("Formally neutral laws can lead to persecution for a simple reason: Once government demands that religious minorities conform their behavior to secular standards, there is no logical stopping point to that demand. Conscientious resistance by religious minorities sometimes inspires respectful tolerance and exemptions, but sometimes it inspires religious hatred and determined, systematic efforts to suppress the religious minority."); Kathleen M. Sullivan, *Religion and Liberal Democracy*, 59 U. CHI. L. REV. 195, 216 (1992) (describing the "big flaw" of *Smith* as "entrench[ing] patterns of de facto discrimination against minority religions").

[20] McConnell, *supra* note 9. [21] City of Boerne v. Flores, 521 U.S. 507 (1997).

[22] *See* Eugene Volokh, *What Is the Religious Freedom Restoration Act?* VOLOKH CONSPIRACY (Dec. 2, 2013), http://volokh.com/2013/12/02/1a-religious-freedom-restoration-act/; *see also* David Johnson, *This Map Shows Every State with Religious Freedom Laws*, TIME (Apr. 2, 2015), http://time.com/3766173/religious-freedom-laws-map-timeline/.

a new version of RFRA in Indiana. Like many states before, the Indiana legislature enacted a parallel version of RFRA.[23] But unlike previous state RFRAs, the national backlash against Indiana was swift, overwhelming, and ubiquitous.[24] Actors, CEOs, athletes, pop stars, and politicians all decried Indiana's new "religious liberty law," characterizing it as driven by antigay discrimination.[25] The timing of Indiana's religious liberty initiative fueled this perception. It came on the heels of a handful of prominent cases around the United States where various business owners, including a florist, a baker and a photographer, had refused to provide their services for same-sex weddings or commitment ceremonies, each explaining that doing so would violate his or her religious conscience.[26] But refusing to provide these services violated state nondiscrimination laws that prohibited public accommodations from discriminating on the basis of sexual orientation; courts therefore levied significant penalties on these business owners for their conduct.[27] Indeed, some supporters of the Indiana bill claimed the new legislation was needed to protect business owners from liability under nondiscrimination laws, leading to the rank condemnation of the new law across the United States. The Indiana legislature hurriedly amended the law in an attempt to quell the growing outrage.[28]

Indiana has turned out to be just the beginning. Others states have also introduced bills with new wrinkles to the RFRA framework.[29] Each has

23 Associated Press, *Indiana Enacts Religious-Objections Law* (Mar. 26, 2015), www.wsj.com/articles/indiana-enacts-religious-objections-law-1427383220.

24 *See, e.g.*, Mark Peters & Jack Nicas, *Indiana Religious Freedom Law Sparks Fury*, WALL ST. J. (Mar. 27, 2015), www.wsj.com/articles/indiana-religious-freedom-law-sparks-fury-1427491304.

25 *Celebs Respond to Indiana's Religious Freedom Law*, CNN.COM (Mar. 30, 2015), www.cnn.com/2015/03/30/politics/celebrities-indiana-religious-freedom-response/.

26 Elane Photography, LLC v. Willock, 2013-NMSC-040 (N.M. 2013); Craig v. Masterpiece Cakeshop, CR 2013–0008 (Colo. Dec. 6, 2013), www.aclu.org/sites/default/files/assets/initial_decision_case_no._cr_2013–0008.pdf; State v. Arlene's Flowers, Inc., No. 13–2-00871–5, at 26–37 (Wash. Sup. Ct. Feb. 18, 2015) (granting summary judgment as to liability in favor of plaintiffs).

27 *See supra* note 22.

28 Mark Peters & Ana Campoy, *"Religious Freedom" Measures Revamped*, WALL ST. J. (Apr. 2, 2015), www.wsj.com/articles/indiana-lawmakers-unveil-changes-to-religious-freedom-law-1427981035; Monica Davey, Campbell Robertson, & Richard Perez-Pena, *Indiana and Arkansas Revise Rights Bills, Seeking to Remove Divisive Parts*, N.Y. TIMES (Apr. 2, 2015), www.nytimes.com/2015/04/03/us/indiana-arkansas-religious-freedom-bill.html.

29 For a collection of attempts to enact state Religious Freedom Restoration Acts in 2015 and 2016, *see* National Conference of State Legislatures, *2015 State Religious Freedom Restoration Legislation* (Sept. 3, 2015), www.ncsl.org/research/civil-and-criminal-justice/2015-state-rfra-legislation.aspx; National Conference of State Legislatures, *2016 State Religious Freedom*

similarly faced significant criticism. And in light of that criticism, some of these bills have been amended[30] and some vetoed.[31]

That RFRA is now the object of such scorn – after being originally embraced across the political spectrum – typifies the extraordinary shift in the broader religious liberty narrative.[32] As RFRA has been invoked in the current culture wars over same-sex marriage, the public perception of RFRA has now been radically reformulated. This new narrative no longer sees RFRA as primarily in the service of vulnerable religious minorities, but primarily as a tool deployed by far more secure religious majorities.[33]

To be sure, this oft-invoked characterization grossly oversimplifies the demographic dynamics at work. Indeed, to lump together all "Christians" and then describe them as a majority misses the way in which "Christian" as a category encapsulates a wide range of denominations that differ in innumerable ways on matters of religious doctrine. Indeed, the fact that subsets of Christians are also minorities, themselves at times victims of majoritarian oppression, is shown all too often by recent events

Restoration Legislation (Apr. 5, 2016), www.ncsl.org/research/civil-and-criminal-justice/2016-state-religious-freedom-restoration-act-legislation.aspx.

30 *See, e.g.*, Eric Bradner, *Arkansas Governor Signs Amended "Religious Freedom" Measure*, CNN (Apr. 2, 2015), www.cnn.com/2015/03/31/politics/arkansas-religious-freedom-anti-lgbt-bill/.

31 *See, e.g.*, Sandhya Somashekhar, *Georgia Governor Vetoes Religious Freedom Bill Criticized as Anti-Gay*, Wash. Post (Mar. 28, 2016), www.washingtonpost.com/news/post-nation/wp/2016/03/28/georgia-governor-to-veto-religious-freedom-bill-criticized-as-anti-gay/?utm_term=.85a716f3c87e.

32 Indiana is not the only state to face significant backlash of late when attempting to enact or modify a state RFRA. *See, e.g.*, Tamara Audi, *Arizona Vetoes Religious Bill Criticized as Anti-Gay*, Wall St. J. (Feb. 27, 2014), www.wsj.com/articles/SB10001424052702304255604579407784144050074; Laura Meckler & Ana Campoy, *Arkansas Governor Call for Change to "Religious Freedom" Bill* Wall St. J. (Apr. 1, 2015), www.wsj.com/articles/arkansas-governor-calls-for-changes-to-religious-freedom-bill-1427904740.

33 *See, e.g.*, Josh Eidelson, *Conservative Regroup on Religious Freedom Bills*, Bloomberg (Apr. 14, 2015), www.bloomberg.com/politics/articles/2015-04-14/conservatives-regroup-on-religious-freedom-bills (quoting Adam Talbot, spokesman of the Human Rights Campaign, as saying "[RFRAs are] being used as a cudgel by religious majorities to evade the enforcement of civil rights law"); Meredith Somers, *Religious Freedom Cases to Fill Supreme Court Docket*, Wash. Times (July 7, 2014), www.washingtontimes.com/news/2014/jul/7/religious-freedom-cases-to-fill-supreme-court-dock/?page=all (quoting Alex Luchenitser, associate legal director at Americans United for the Separation of Church and State, arguing that the *Hobby Lobby* ruling "allow[s] religious majorities to impose their religious beliefs on people who don't follow those beliefs"); Dahlia Lithwick & Mark Joseph Stern, *The 10 Worst Civil Liberties Violations of 2014*, Slate (Dec. 29, 2014), www.slate.com/articles/news_and_politics/jurisprudence/2014/12/civil_liberties_violations_of_2014_civil_forfeiture_grand_juries_religion.html ("Increasingly, to the conservatives of the Roberts court, 'religious liberty' means the freedom of religious majorities to push their religious beliefs on the rest of us.").

abroad.[34] On that count, the categories of religious majority and minority are deeply fraught, raising serious doubts about how these narratives actually align with the demographics on the ground – as well as the political and legal implications of those demographics.

And yet, notwithstanding these complexities, it seems fair to say that the recent high-profile debates between the demands of law and aspirations of religion have implicated more well-established religious groups then earlier religious liberty flashpoints. In addition to clashes between Christian businesses and same-sex marriage customers, recent religious liberty litigation has also focused in large part on the Affordable Care Act's contraceptive coverage mandate, which requires covered employers to provide their employees with health insurance that includes coverage for contraception.[35] For-profit companies immediately challenged the mandate, arguing that the law substantially burdens their Christian faith commitments, thereby violating the protections afforded by RFRA.[36]

In its blockbuster 2014 decision, *Burwell v. Hobby Lobby*, the Supreme Court held in favor of these companies, concluding that closely held for-profit corporations were indeed entitled to RFRA's protections – and that the government had alternative means to ensure that women had access to contraception without substantially burdening the religious exercise of those businesses.[37] While the decision provided important religious liberty protections to for-profit companies, the Court's opinion further bolstered the perception that religious liberty generally, and RFRA in particular, had become a tool that more well-established religions could utilize against minority groups – or groups with more limited political power. Or, put differently, religious liberty bills originally seen by the public as protecting small Native American churches that wanted to ingest peyote are now seen as wielded in broader debates over religion, sex, and the 21st century family by far more well-established religious groups against minorities – minorities who themselves are in need of protection in the workplace and the marketplace.

What should we make of this new narrative? Is RFRA no longer a viable legislative response to the post-*Smith* religious liberty vacuum? Should we embrace this new narrative and its strong criticism of RFRA as providing

34 Jonathan Merritt, *Persecution of Christians Reached Historic Levels in 2014. Will 2015 Be Worse?* Religion News Service (Jan. 7, 2015), www.religionnews.com/2015/01/07/persecution-christians-reached-historic-levels-2014-will-2015-worse/.

35 *See* Hobby Lobby, *supra* note 2.

36 *See* Becket, *HHS Mandate Information Central*, www.becketfund.org/hhsinformationcentral.

37 *Id.* at 2775–83.

medicine that is far too strong given its potential to impose on the civil liberties of others?

While critics of RFRA raise legitimate worries,[38] discarding RFRA is the wrong response. First, despite recent clashes, RFRA continues to play a key role in protecting religious minorities that all too often lack the political numbers and power to otherwise secure legislative accommodations. Indeed, recent events and litigation demonstrate that religious minorities will need RFRA – and its parallel statute the Religious Land Use and Institutionalized Persons Act (" RLUIPA"), which provides analogous protections with respect to land use and prisons[39] – if their practices are to receive protection from government overreach.

Religious minority concerns persist. Consider:

- the proposed circumcision ban in San Francisco, which explicitly rejected religious exemptions for the religious ritual circumcisions of Jews and Muslims;[40]
- the government's refusal to return confiscated bald and gold eagles' feathers, necessary for a religious ritual, to the members of a Native American tribe, returned only after litigation;[41]
- the government's refusal to allow a Sikh to become an army chaplain on account of his inability to conform to army grooming standards on account of his contrary religious grooming standards;[42] and
- Arkansas prison officials' refusal to allow a Muslim prison to grow a ½-inch beard because of unsubstantiated fears that the beard would threaten security.[43]

More generally, the persistence of anti-Muslim sentiment in the United States – a phenomenon that may extend to the judiciary[44] – raises significant

38 Adding to the growing numbers of RFRA critics, the ACLU recently announced that, notwithstanding its original endorsement, it could no longer support RFRA. *See* Louise Melling, *ACLU: Why We Can No Longer Support the Federal "Religious Freedom" Law*, Wash. Post (June 25, 2015), www.washingtonpost.com/opinions/congress-should-amend-the-abused-religious-freedom-restoration-act/2015/06/25/ee6aaa46-19d8-11e5-ab92-c75ae6ab94b5_story.html.

39 42 U.S.C.§ 2000cc (2012).

40 Jennifer Medina, *Efforts to Ban Circumcision in California Gain Traction*, N.Y. Times (June 4, 2011), www.nytimes.com/2011/06/05/us/05circumcision.html?_r=0. For the text of the proposed ban, *see* www.mgmbill.org/san-francisco-mgm-bill.html.

41 Mc Allen Grace Brethren Church v. Salazar, 764 F.3d 465, 468 (5th Cir. 2014).

42 Singh v. McHugh, 2015 U.S. Dist. LEXIS 76526 (D.D.C. June 12, 2015).

43 Holt, *supra* note 2.

44 Gregory C. Sisk & Michael Heise, *Muslims and Religious Liberty in the Era of 9/11: Empirical Evidence from the Federal Courts*, 98 Iowa L. Rev. 232 (2012).

concerns about the law's ability to protect some of its most vulnerable religious citizens.[45]

Second, with respect to religious liberty generally, RFRA can be properly calibrated to simultaneously provide meaningful protection without threatening the civil liberties of others. To do so, courts should leverage the express balancing features of the RFRA framework, evaluating claims for religious liberty in light of the consequences of such claims for other important government interests. RFRA, it must be recalled, does not simply provide exemptions for all religiously motivated conduct. It employs a balancing framework whereby laws that substantially burden religious exercise can still be enforced if they are narrowly tailored to achieve a compelling government interest.[46] If taken seriously by courts, RFRA's balancing features can provide a meaningful backstop to religious liberty protections, ensuring that a commitment to religious liberty will not run roughshod over other important civil rights or the state's ability to protect vulnerable people.

Moreover, reliance on balancing alleviates the increasing pressure on courts to use alternative front-end doctrinal arguments to short-circuit religious liberty claims before they can be substantively considered alongside their potential consequences for others. For instance, many critics contend that religious liberty claims cannot be reviewed or are not cognizable unless they cross a threshold – a device to shrink the number of instances whereby religious liberty might clash with other important values. For example, during the raging debates and litigation over the mandate, the government,[47] some scholars, and courts argued that religiously motivated for-profit corporations cannot "exercise religion" and therefore should be denied religious liberty protections.[48] Others said the companies' "raison d'être is profit, not

[45] Gallup, *Muslim Americans: Faith, Freedom and the Future* 39 (2011), virtuecenter.s3.amazonaws.com/files/2012-08-27-17/MAR_Report_ADGC_Bilingual_072011_sa_LR_web.pdf (noting that "[a]t 48%, Muslim Americans are by far the most likely of major faith groups surveyed to say they have personally experienced racial or religious discrimination in the past year").

[46] 42 U.S.C. § 2000bb–1 (2012).

[47] For examples of the government articulating this argument about the mandate, *see* Defendants' Memorandum in Opposition to Plaintiffs' Motion for Preliminary Injunction at 2-3, Hobby Lobby Stores, Inc. v. Sebelius, 870 F. Supp. 2d 1278 (W.D. Okla. 2012) (No. CIV-12-1000-HE) ("Hobby Lobby is a for-profit, secular employer, and a secular entity by definition does not exercise religion."); Defendants' Opposition to Plaintiffs' Motion for Preliminary Injunction at 2, Tyndale House Publrs., Inc. v. Sebelius, 2012 WL 5817323 (D.D.C. Oct. 22, 2012) (No. 12-1635 RBW) ("Tyndale is a for-profit employer that cannot 'exercise religion' under RFRA and the Free Exercise Clause.").

[48] *See, e.g.*, Conestoga Wood Specialties Corp. v. Sebelius, 917 F. Supp. 2d 394, 411 (E.D. Pa. 2013) ("[W]e have determined that a for-profit, secular corporation cannot exercise religion.") *aff'd sub nom.* Conestoga Wood Specialties Corp. v. Sec'y of U.S. Dep't of Health & Human

faith,"[49] and therefore it "is not reasonable to embody them with the personal attributes of their shareholders, even if the shareholders are few and closely related, and even if they themselves consider their commercial activity to constitute the practice of their faith."[50] The objective is clear. If for-profit entities cannot, by their nature, exercise religion, then there is no need to apply RFRA's balancing framework to such religious liberty claims. The net result: courts would reject out of hand the religious liberty claims of religiously motivated for-profit entities *instead of* balancing those religious liberty interests against other important government objectives, such as the civil rights of other citizens.

This legal gambit carries a significant cost. Such arguments fail to consider the ways in which some religious institutions and denominations expressly encourage the incorporation of religious belief and practice into the commercial sphere. In so doing, these arguments flatten the categories of religious experience and practice in an attempt to limit the scope of available religious liberty claims.

In reality, the relationship between for-profit entities and religious aspiration is far more varied and multifarious. For many faith traditions, commercial objectives are inextricably intertwined with religious doctrines.[51] And for others, the opportunity to inject religious aspirations into the for-profit sphere is to bring the very best of their ethical commitments into the marketplace.[52]

Servs., 724 F.3d 377 (3rd Cir. 2013), *cert granted*, 134 S. Ct. 678 (2013) and *rev'd and remanded sub nom.* Burwell v. Hobby Lobby Stores, Inc., No. 13-354 (U.S. June 30, 2014); Caroline Mala Corbin, Corporate Religious Liberty, 30 *Const. Commentary* 277, 280 (2015) ("There is no principled basis for corporate religious liberty. For-profit corporations lack the inherently human characteristics that justify religious exemptions for individuals. They cannot, for example, be said to possess either a relationship with God or inherent dignity. Nor do they possess the unique qualities that arguably justify exemptions for churches. Unlike churches, for-profit corporations are not sacred, primarily religious, or the source of theological truth.").

49 Zoe Robinson, *The Contraception Mandate and the Forgotten Constitutional Question*, 2014 Wis. L. Rev. 749, 793. ("While it seems clear that many of the owners of the for-profit businesses that have filed challenges to the Contraception Mandate have strong faith-based commitments, it is difficult to claim that these businesses have any jurisgenerative role. It may be that the ethos of the business is based on faith principles, but for-profit businesses, because of their internal structures and social role, are ill-suited to the function of a facilitator of collective belief. In other words, for-profit businesses do not meet the faith-principle, not because they are not guided by faithful persons, but because they should not be in the businesses of faith-promotion at all.").

50 Frederick Mark Gedicks, *Large For-Profit Corporations Do Not Exercise Religion*, ACS Blog (Dec. 9, 2013), www.acslaw.org/acsblog/large-for-profit-corporations-do-not-exercise-religion (arguing that "large" for-profit corporations cannot exercise religion).

51 *See* Michael A. Helfand & Barak D. Richman, *The Challenge of Co-Religionist Commerce*, 64 Duke L.J. 769 (2015).

52 *See* Alan J. Meese & Nathan B. Oman, Hobby Lobby, *Corporate Law, and the Theory of the Firm: Why For-Profit Corporations Are RFRA Persons*, 127 Harv. L. Rev. F. 273, 296 (2014)

It is true that a *per se* rule that rejects the possibility of for-profit entities exercising religion makes policing the borders of religious exercise less complicated. But, as the Supreme Court in *Hobby Lobby* recognized,[53] establishing *per se* rules that eliminate all for-profit entities from the religious liberty conversation fosters a more impoverished marketplace, banishing important religious contributions from the commercial sphere.

The push for threshold tests has not only come in the context of debates over the religious rights of for-profit entities. RFRA critics have also advocated for more robust threshold tests when evaluating the burden necessary to trigger a RFRA claim.[54] By its terms, the protections afforded by RFRA come into play when government "substantially burden[s] a person's exercise of religion."[55] However, RFRA provides little guidance as to what makes a burden *substantial*, raising significant questions over the scope of RFRA's protections.[56]

Debate over substantial burdens emerged, for example, as one of the central questions in the second wave of litigation over the mandate, which eventually

("One might object that by definition people create for-profit corporations to make a profit and thus such corporations cannot be instrumentalities for religious exercise. As noted above, as an empirical matter this claim is false. A moment's reflection also reveals its impoverished psychology. People's motives are mixed. Entrepreneurs wish to earn a profit, but they often have more grandiose ambitions to change the world. It's unsurprising that some people pursue a religious mission as part of their business. One might object that if profits are involved, the exercise cannot 'really' be religious. After all, didn't Jesus declare, 'You cannot serve God and mammon'?"); *see also* Michael A. Helfand, *Obamacare and Religious Rights in a For-Profit World*, L.A. TIMES (Mar. 18, 2014), articles.latimes.com/2014/mar/18/opinion/la-oe-helfand-hobby-lobby-supreme-court-religious-20140319.

53 Hobby Lobby, *supra* note 35, at 2771 (2014) ("HHS [The U.S. Department of Health and Human Services] would draw a sharp line between nonprofit corporations (which, HHS concedes, are protected by RFRA) and for-profit corporations (which HHS would leave unprotected), but the actual picture is less clear-cut. Not all corporations that decline to organize as nonprofits do so in order to maximize profit. For example, organizations with religious and charitable aims might organize as for-profit corporations because of the potential advantages of that corporate form, such as the freedom to participate in lobbying for legislation or campaigning for political candidates who promote their religious or charitable goals. In fact, recognizing the inherent compatibility between establishing a for-profit corporation and pursuing nonprofit goals, States have increasingly adopted laws formally recognizing hybrid corporate forms. Over half of the States, for instance, now recognize the 'benefit corporation,' a dual-purpose entity that seeks to achieve both a benefit for the public and a profit for its owners.").

54 *See, e.g.*, Sepper, Chapter 1, this volume; Elizabeth Sepper, *Free Exercise Lochnerism*, 115 COLUM. L. REV. 1453, 1509-10 (2015); *see also* Kara Loewentheil, *When Free Exercise Is a Burden*, 62 DRAKE L. REV. 433, 497 (2014).

55 42 U.S.C. § 2000bb-1(b)(1)-(2) (2012).

56 *See, e.g.*, Michael C. Dorf, *Incidental Burdens on Fundamental Rights*, 109 HARV. L. REV. 1175, 1213 (1996) ("Neither the text nor the legislative history of RFRA provides any clear indication of how courts ought to determine whether an incidental burden on religion is in fact substantial.").

made it to the Supreme Court in *Zubik v. Burwell*.[57] At issue in *Zubik* was the government's process for accommodating religiously motivated nonprofit entities seeking an exemption from the mandate.[58] To get the exemption, nonprofits could fill out a form notifying their insurance provider of their religious objections to providing their employees with insurance coverage for contraception. Under such circumstances, the health insurance company would provide the insurance on its own,[59] ensuring that the objecting nonprofit would not have to pay for contraception while still giving employees access to cost-free contraception.[60]

But many nonprofit companies objected to filling out the form – known as Form 700 – and sending it to their health insurance companies; they believed doing so still made them complicit in the eventual provision of contraception, which violated their faith. On the whole, the federal courts of appeals – with the exception of the Eighth Circuit[61] – cut these claims off on the front-end, holding that the requirement to submit the form could not constitute a substantial burden under RFRA.[62] The judicial skepticism – as well as scholarly criticism – of the claim largely rejected the assertion that filing the requisite paperwork could constitute a substantial burden on religious

57 *See* Order Granting Certiorari, Zubik v. Burwell, 136 S. Ct. 444 (Nov. 6, 2015) (No. 14-1418).

58 Zubik v. Burwell, 136 S. Ct. 1557 (2016).

59 As the regulations currently stand, nonprofit companies may also give written notice of their religious objection to the company that processes claims for its health plan, known as a third-party administrator, or directly to the government. 26 C.F.R. § 54.9815-2715A(b)-(c) (2017).

60 Hobby Lobby, *supra* note 2, at 2782 & n.38 (2014).

61 *See, e.g.*, Sharpe Holdings, Inc. v. United States HHS, 801 F.3d 927, 935-36 (8th Cir. 2015).

62 *See, e.g.*, Little Sisters of the Poor Home for the Aged v. Burwell, 794 F.3d 1151, 1192 (10th Cir. 2015) ("The notification to HHS is especially minimal, as it requires Plaintiffs only to register their objection with HHS and does not require any contact with their health insurance issuers or TPAs [third-party administrators]. Although Plaintiffs must tell HHS which health insurance issuer or TPA they use to opt out of the Mandate, this is not a substantial burden on religious exercise."); Mich. Catholic Conf. v. Burwell, 755 F.3d 372, 386 (6th Cir. 2014) (noting that complying with the terms of the accommodation could not constitute a substantial burden because merely submitting the form is "the entirety of the conduct that the objecting organization must engage in to obtain the accommodation"); Priests for Life v. United States HHS, 772 F.3d 229, 253 (DC Cir. 2014) ("Accurately understood, the opt-out mechanism imposes on Plaintiffs only the de minimis administrative burden associated with completing the self-certification form or the alternative notice."). This logic was also echoed by Justice Sotomayor in her dissent to the Supreme Court's grant of Wheaton College's requested injunction against submitting Form 700 to the Department of Health and Human Services. *See* Wheaton College v. Burwell, 134 S. Ct. 2806, 2812 (2014) (Sotomayor, J. dissenting) ("Wheaton is mistaken – not as a matter of religious faith, in which it is undoubtedly sincere, but as a matter of law: Not every sincerely felt 'burden' is a 'substantial' one, and it is for courts, not litigants, to identify which are ... [T]hinking one's religious beliefs are substantially burdened – no matter how sincere or genuine that belief may be – does not make it so.").

exercise. It was either simply too attenuated from the actual theologically objected-to conduct[63] – the use of contraception – or it was simply too insignificant to register on the RFRA scale – it was, after all, just paperwork.[64] In Professor Elizabeth Sepper's words, it is just a 44-cent stamp.[65]

Instead of addressing the merits of the case, the Court, down to eight justices after the death of Justice Antonin Scalia, chose to vacate the decisions of all the federal courts of appeals and remand for further consideration.[66] This left courts without any guidance on how to evaluate the substantiality of burdens under RFRA. Indeed, the majority of the federal courts of appeals remain free on the heels of *Zubik* to once again interpret the category of substantial burdens narrowly, erecting more threshold requirements for what kinds of burdens can trigger the balancing framework of RFRA.

Taking such an approach, however, would be a significant mistake. Burdens should not be deemed insubstantial because a court sees them as theologically insubstantial. It may be true that to those outside a particular faith that filling out the requisite paperwork seems unremarkable and wholly attenuated from conduct understood to be religiously objectionable. But government should not require claimants to clear theological bars of substantiality in order to trigger the protections of RFRA. And when courts conclude the burden imposed by filling out Form 700 – as opposed to burdens imposed on other religiously significant acts – is *de minimis*, they can do so only by placing a theological value on the contested religious exercise. But the text of RFRA

63 Geneva Coll. v. Sec'y U.S. Dep't of Health & Human Servs., 778 F.3d 422, 442 (3d Cir. 2015) ("[C]an the submission of the self-certification form, which relieves the appellees of any connection to the provision of the objected-to contraceptive services, really impose a 'substantial' burden on the appellees' free exercise of religion? We think not ... [W]here the actual provision of contraceptive coverage is by a third party, the burden is not merely attenuated at the outset but totally disconnected from the appellees."); Mich. Catholic Conference & Catholic Family Servs. v. Burwell, 755 F.3d 372, 388 (6th Cir. 2014) ("The government's imposition of an independent obligation on a third party does not impose a substantial burden on the appellants' exercise of religion ... [T]he Government's instruction to insurance issuers and third-party administrators to provide contraceptive coverage does not force the appellants to provide, pay for, and/or facilitate access to the coverage.").

64 Priests for Life v. U.S. Dep't of Health & Human Servs. 772 F.3d 229, 253 (D.C. Cir. 2014) ("Accurately understood, the opt-out mechanism imposes on Plaintiffs only the de minimis administrative burden associated with completing the self-certification form or the alternative notice."); *see also* Caroline Mala Corbin, *Paperwork as a Substantial Burden*, JURIST (May 22, 2015), jurist.org/forum/2015/05/Caroline-Corbin-Religious-Burden.php.

65 Sepper, Chapter 1, this volume.

66 Zubik, *supra* note 58, at 1560. ("The Court expresses no view on the merits of the cases. In particular, the Court does not decide whether petitioners' religious exercise has been substantially burdened, whether the Government has a compelling interest, or whether the current regulations are the least restrictive means of serving that interest.").

itself, and of RLUIPA, seems to reject such an approach by defining religious exercise as "includ[ing] any exercise of religion, whether or not compelled by, or central to, a system of religious belief."[67]

And there is good reason for that. Interrogating the religious substantiality of conduct on a theological metric runs afoul of core Establishment Clause prohibitions. As the Supreme Court noted in *Thomas v. Review Board*, "it is not for us to say that the line [the petitioner] drew was an unreasonable one. Courts should not undertake to dissect religious beliefs . . . because his beliefs are not articulated with the clarity and precision that a more sophisticated person might employ."[68] Indeed, the Supreme Court expressed a similar concern about the potential for judicial incursion into the prohibited sphere of theology in its seminal decision *Employment Division v. Smith*: "Repeatedly and in many different contexts, we have warned that courts must not presume to determine . . . the plausibility of a religious claim."[69]

To interrogate the religious substantiality of burdens would amount to government allocating legal burdens on the basis of which religious claims it found more appealing, more important – and potentially more in keeping with its own notions of morality and ethics.[70] Such an approach is likely to lead to unequal application of RFRA, by favoring religious majorities, whose religious practices are more well known and respected, as opposed to religious minorities, whose religious practices are more obscure. Under a regime wherein courts evaluate the theological substantiality of religious burdens, the impact of laws on religious minorities is likely to be underestimated and underappreciated, unfairly circumscribing the protections afforded by RFRA. Such a result would be the height of irony as it would invert RFRA's core commitment to protecting religious minorities.

67 *See* 42 U.S.C. § 2000bb–2(4); 42 U.S.C. § 2000cc–5(7)(A) (2012).

68 Thomas v. Review Bd. of Ind. Employment Sec. Div., 450 U.S. 707, 715 (1981).

69 Smith, *supra* note 5, at 887.

70 Indeed, a number of authors have argued that either moral norms or secular legal norms – instead of the claimant's internal theology – should provide the relevant guide to courts when determining the substantiality of a burden. *See, e.g.*, Amy J. Sepinwall, *Conscience and Complicity: Assessing Pleas for Religious Exemptions After Hobby Lobby*, 82 U. Chi. L. Rev. 1897, 1933 (2015) ("Our enlightenment ethos has anointed certain methodologies as truth-conferring: Observation, the scientific method, certain theoretical constructs, and so on have all been identified as reliable methods for capturing what the world is like. The state need not have a role in discovering and promoting moral truth, and by the lights of some versions of liberalism it should not have such a role. But it does need to have a role in policing empirical truth, at least in the areas where it is permitted to regulate."); Frederick Mark Gedicks, *"Substantial" Burdens: How Courts May (and Why They Must) Judge Burdens on Religion Under RFRA*, 85 Geo. Wash. L. Rev. 94, 132 (2017) (proposing that courts "enlist common law tort principles as secular sources for measuring the substantiality or religious costs in complicity cases").

Courts should instead adopt a far more theologically generous interpretation of RFRA and not establish religious threshold questions to allow claims to go forward. Attempts to paint burdens as religiously *de minimis* or attenuated seek to short circuit RFRA claims before they get started, just as claims that for-profit entities cannot exercise religion sought to do.

Of course, courts must remain true to the text of RFRA and evaluate the substantiality of burdens; to do otherwise would simply read the substantiality requirement out of the statute. But they should do so by assessing the secular substantiality of civil costs. Thus, courts should ask whether the sanctions, fees, or penalties triggered by exercising religion are sufficiently substantial to trigger RFRA's protections. By contrast, to reject RFRA claims on the basis of insufficient religious substantiality represents a narrow view of how religious claimants understand their own religious burdens. And it also dismisses RFRA claims without ever undertaking the balancing RFRA both affords and demands.[71]

A renewed focus on the balancing framework of RFRA provides a blueprint for how to address one of the central worries about RFRA's religious accommodation regime – that religious liberty will trump other important interests. Arguably the clearest statement of this worry came from Justice Ruth Bader Ginsburg who, in her *Hobby Lobby* dissent, wondered skeptically where future courts would draw the line in terms of providing religious accommodations under RFRA:

> Would the exemption the Court [orders] extend to employers with religiously grounded objections to blood transfusions (Jehovah's Witnesses); antidepressants (Scientologists); medications derived from pigs, including anesthesia, intravenous fluids, and pills coated with gelatin (certain Muslims, Jews, and Hindus); and vaccinations (Christian Scientists, among others)?[72]

These conflicts might very well implicate growing tensions between religious groups and same-sex couples, Justice Ginsburg intimated, citing the photographer who, in contravention of the state's public accommodations law, refused for religious reasons to photograph a same-sex commitment ceremony.[73] Indeed, as noted earlier, other similar cases have cropped up around the country,[74] leading some to read much of the debate in *Hobby*

[71] For more on how courts can take such a position while still giving the statutory requirement of substantiality some teeth, see Helfand, Chapter 6, this volume.

[72] Hobby Lobby, *supra* note 2, at 2805 (Ginsburg, J. dissenting).

[73] *Id.* (citing, among other conflicts over the rights of religious for-profit corporations, Elane Photography, LLC v. Willock, 309 P. 3d 53 (2013)).

[74] Craig v. Masterpiece Cakeshop, CR 2013-0008 (Colo. Dec. 6, 2013), www.aclu.org/sites/default/files/assets/initial_decision_case_no._cr_2013-0008.pdf; State v. Arlene's Flowers, Inc.,

Lobby as an attempt to stake a ground in the ongoing debate between religious and LGBT groups.[75]

All told, from litigation over the mandate to litigation over same-sex marriage, many see RFRA as in tension with evolving family structures, rights, and values. With the rise of complicity claims, a growing number of RFRA claims may be leveled by religious persons who want not only for their own family life to be governed by religious norms and values, but they also want not to be implicated in family values that they find religiously sinful.[76] For this reason, RFRA – if broadly interpreted – may precipitate exponential growth in religious liberty conflicts, especially as family structures and values evolve in the United States.

Rejecting threshold requirements under RFRA does not mean conceding that all RFRA claims must win. RFRA requires that all substantial burden claims be subjected to strict scrutiny – if the law is the least restrictive means for achieving a compelling government interest, then a court cannot provide a religious exemption.[77] Therefore, when laws meet vital public interests, courts must resist providing exceptions, thereby ensuring that the parade of horribles posited by RFRA critics does not become a reality.

This is particularly true within the family where courts frequently play the role of protecting vulnerable citizens. Thus, when petitioners assert that conduct such as torture[78] or child abuse[79] is justified by religious values, courts can and must use RFRA's safeguards to swiftly reject such claims.

RFRA critics find this approach insufficient. It puts far more pressure on the back end of the RFRA inquiry, they say, and it does so by invoking RFRA's strict scrutiny standard.[80] Thus, once a court grants that a law substantially

No. 13-2-00871-5, at 26–37 (Wash. Sup. Ct. Feb. 18, 2015) (granting summary judgment as to liability in favor of plaintiffs).

75 Paul Horwitz, *The* Hobby Lobby *Moment*, 128 Harv. L. Rev. 154, 154 (2014).

76 *See* Douglas NeJaime & Reva B. Siegel, *Conscience Wars: Complicity-Based Conscience Claims in Religion and Politics*, 124 Yale L.J. 2516 (2015).

77 42 U.S.C. § 2000bb–1(b) (2012).

78 *See, e.g.*, United States v. Epstein, 91 F.Supp.3d 573 (2015) (rejecting the RFRA claim of defendant who had tortured husbands refusing to grant their wives a Jewish divorce). For more on this case and its treatment under RFRA, *see* Michael A. Helfand, *How to Limit Accommodations: Wrong Answers and Right Answers*, 5 J. L. Rel. & State 1 (2017).

79 Amanda Terkel, *Woman Charged with Child Abuse Uses Indiana Religious Freedom Law as Defense*, The Huffington Post, Aug. 31, 2016, www.huffingtonpost.com/entry/indiana-religious-freedom-child-abuse_us_57c724e7e4b0a22de093b67c; Vic Ryckaert, *Son Had 36 Bruises. Mom Quoted the Bible as Defense*. Indy Star, Oct. 4, 2016, www.indystar.com/story/news/crime/2016/08/31/son-had-36-bruises-mom-quoted-bible-defense/88998568/.

80 Sepper, Chapter 1, this volume.

burdens a person's religious exercise, then the only way to limit the claim for accommodation is to find that the law is the least restrictive means for achieving a compelling government interest.

In other constitutional contexts, satisfying strict scrutiny is often characterized as all but impossible; indeed, in the context of the equal protection doctrine,[81] strict scrutiny has been described as "strict in theory, but fatal in fact."[82] Accordingly, critics might rightfully worry that grounding limitations on RFRA claims in strict scrutiny is an exercise in futility.

Understandable though it is, this worry is exaggerated. First, as Professor Sepper acknowledges in this volume, as a statistical matter, strict scrutiny has proven to be far less of a "deadly test" than popular rhetoric might otherwise lead us to believe.[83] Furthermore, the appropriate response to the challenges of strict scrutiny is not to proliferate threshold tests but to lower the scrutiny when applying it to claims for religious accommodation.[84] In contrast to other contexts where courts use strict scrutiny to smoke out invidious discrimination,[85] strict scrutiny serves in the RFRA context as a doctrinal standard to balance competing claims – those of the religious claimant and those of society – that are both legitimate.[86]

In balancing those claims, courts are tasked with a willingness to identify civil interests that are too important to grant exemptions for religious exercise. Our inability, in some circumstances, to craft exemptions for particular forms of religious exercise may be regrettable. But embracing RFRA's balancing framework means recognizing that while some religious liberty claims will be strong enough to secure accommodation, others will have to yield to important government interests.

81 *See, e.g.*, Fisher v. Univ. of Tex., 631 F.3d 213, 248 (5th Cir. 2011) (Garza, J., specially concurring) ("[S]ince the Court began applying strict scrutiny to review governmental uses of race in discriminating between citizens, the number of cases in which the Court has permitted such uses can be counted on one hand. The Court has rejected numerous intuitively appealing justifications offered for racial discrimination.").

82 Gerald Gunther, *The Supreme Court, 1971 Term – Foreword: In Search of Evolving Doctrine on a Changing Court: A Model for a Newer Equal Protection*, 86 HARV. L. REV. 1, 8 (1972); *see also* Fullilove v. Klutznick, 448 U.S. 448, 507 (1980) (Powell, J., concurring).

83 Sepper, Chapter 1, this volume. *See also* Adam Winkler, *Fatal in Theory and Strict in Fact: An Empirical Analysis of Strict Scrutiny in the Federal Courts*, 59 VAND. L. REV. 793, 795, 833–67 (2006) (providing empirical evidence from judicial decisions that strict scrutiny "is far from the inevitably deadly test").

84 *See* Helfand, *supra* note 10.

85 For a broader discussion of the uses of strict scrutiny in the equal protection context, see Michael A. Helfand, *How the Diversity Rationale Lays the Groundwork for New Discrimination*, 17 WM. & MARY BILL RTS. J. 607 (2009).

86 *See* Helfand, *supra* note 10.

Of course, evaluating which laws – driven by which values – constitute a sufficiently important government interest will require judges to take account of a wide range of considerations, including the particular moral, social, and historical context of any particular case. And in this analysis, judges will be playing a prominent role in the future of religious liberty, taking our society's collective temperature when it comes to balancing competing values.

These challenges, in many ways, will be most complex within the family. It is within the family that faith communities frequently express their more deeply held religious values. But at the same time, it is within the family that the law often bears the responsibility of protecting vulnerable citizens from abuse. Leaning on courts to navigate these tensions will put judges on the front line of the next wave of the culture wars. But institutionalizing religious liberty in this way provides a workable mechanism for interpreting and applying some of our deepest political commitments. Embracing competing values, and allowing courts to balance our conflicting commitments, may very well provide our best hope for navigating these tensions going forward.

PART II

RELIGIOUS CLAIMS AT BIRTH

3

Religious Exceptionalism and Religiously Motivated Harm

Michele Goodwin

Chancellor's Professor of Law, University of California, Irvine, and Founder, The Institute for Global Child Advocacy

Unlike anytime in recent history, religion strategically influences American politics and governance. Concerns regarding the influence of religion in American politics are particularly timely given a problematic trend that has emerged in broader society, namely: religion being used to justify harming women,[1] people of color,[2] members of the LGBTQ community,[3] and even inflicting injury on children.[4] Frequently, those who wish to (or do) impose harms on others in the name of religion assert an exception granted by

[1] *See* Burwell v. Hobby Lobby Stores, Inc., 134 S. Ct. 2751, 2765 (2014) (featuring plaintiffs "seeking to enjoin application of ACA's contraceptive mandate" under the Religious Freedom Restoration Act and the Free Exercise Clause); *see also* Stormans, Inc. v. Wiesman, 794 F.3d 1064, 1084–85 (9th Cir. 2015) (upholding Washington statute requiring pharmacists to provide certain contraceptives against Free Exercise Clause challenge).

[2] *See, e.g.*, Alon Harish, *Mississippi Church Refuses to Marry Black Couple*, ABC News (July 28, 2012), abcnews.go.com/US/mississippi-church-rejects-black-wedding/story?id=16878536; John Holland, *Pastor Won't Wed Interracial Couple*, Sun–Sentinel (July 11, 2000), articles.sun-sentinel.com/2000-07-11/news/0007110116_1_bumgardner-s-brother-wedding-nondenominational-church; *Interracial Couple Spurned*, ABC News, abcnews.go.com/US/story?id=96577&page=1 (Jan. 30, 2016); Kunbi Tinuoye, *Kentucky Church Denies Racism After Vote to Ban Interracial Couples*, The Grio (Dec. 1, 2011, 1:11 PM), thegrio.com/2011/12/01/kentucky-church-denies-racism-ban-interracial-couples.

[3] *See, e.g.*, Craig v. Masterpiece Cakeshop, Inc., No. 14CA1351, 2015 WL 4760453, at *21 (Colo. App. Aug. 13, 2015) (rejecting the free exercise argument of baker refusing customers due to religious views against same-sex marriage); Goodridge v. Dep't of Pub. Health, 798 N.2d 941, 1000 n.29, (Mass. 2003) (holding, *inter alia*, application of religious marriage's gender requirements to civil marriage irrational under state Due Process and Equal Protection clauses).

[4] *See, e.g.*, Workman v. Mingo Cty. Bd. of Educ., 419 Fed. App'x 348, 355 (4th Cir. 2011) (rejecting mother's claim that her religious beliefs against vaccinating her child as required by state law trigger the Equal Protection Clause); Boone v. Boozman, 217 F. Supp. 2d 938 (E.D. Ark. 2002) (featuring constitutional challenge to Arkansas' Child Immunization statute as applied to religiously opposed parent); Walker v. Super. Ct., 763 P.2d 852, 866 (Cal. 1988)

statute[5] or claim the Constitution gives them the capacity to do so. Problematically, from time to time, courts and legislatures grant legitimacy to these beliefs. As noted in the opening chapters of this volume, *Hobby Lobby* subjected the Obama Administration's contraceptive coverage mandate under the Patient Protection and Affordable Care Act ("ACA") to a more exacting scrutiny than that given in other areas of constitutional law.[6] The Trump Administration is poised to undo the careful weighing of benefits and harms that extended contraceptive coverage to women under the ACA without copays, at least when a person or religious organization, whether closely held or for-profit, objects "for religious or moral reasons."[7]

This is part of a larger trend: when individuals and groups believe that they do not need to conform to general principles and laws of nondiscrimination and accommodation in the United States, U.S. courts and legislatures from

(holding prayer-treatment exception to child neglect statutes inapplicable to involuntary manslaughter and felony child endangerment charges); State v. Neumann, 2013 WI 58, 348 Wis. 2d 455, 832 N.W.2d 560 (Wis. 2013) (holding, *inter alia*, treatment-through-prayer defense to child abuse statute inapplicable to reckless homicide).

5 Offit, Chapter 12, this volume; *Religious Exemptions to Child Neglect*, Nat'l D. Att'ys Ass'n, www.ndaa.org/pdf/2–11-2015%20Religious%20Exemptions%20to%20Child%20Neglect.pdf (last updated Feb. 2015) (discussing that thirty-nine states have laws exempting parents or guardians from criminal liability for failure to provide medical assistance to their children on the basis of religious beliefs); Aleksandra Sandstorm, *Nearly All States Allow Religious Exemptions for Vaccinations*, Pew Res. Ctr. (July 16, 2015), www.pewresearch.org/fact-tank/2015/07/16/nearly-all-states-allow-religious-exemptions-for-vaccinations (noting only California, West Virginia, Mississippi, and Minnesota lack religious exemptions to vaccination requirements); *see also* Ark. Code Ann. § 5–10-101(9)(B) (2015) (providing religious defense to capital murder); Idaho Code Ann. § 18–1501(4) (West 2015) (providing religious defense to criminal injury to children); Iowa Code § 726.6 (2016) (providing religious defense to felony child endangerment); La. Stat. Ann. § 14:93(3)(B) (2015) (providing religious defense to criminal neglect); Miss. Code. Ann. § 43–21-105(l)(i) (2015) (providing religious defense to child neglect); Ohio Rev. Code Ann. § 2919.22(a) (West 2015) (providing religious defense to child neglect); Or. Rev. Stat. § 163.115 (2013) (providing religious defense to homicide of child); W. Va. Code § 61-8D-2(d) (2015) (providing religious defense to murder of child); *infra* note 50.

6 Sepper, Chapter 1, this volume.

7 A rumored draft of an Executive Order being considered by the Trump Administration would require federal agencies that enforce the ACA to "immediately issue an interim final rule that exempts from the preventative-care mandate set forth in 42 U.S.C. 300gg-13(a)(4) all persons and religious organizations that object to complying with the mandate for religious or moral reasons." It defines a "person" as RFRA did and defines religious organization "broadly" to include closely held corporations and companies that are "operated for a religious purpose, even if its purpose is not exclusively religious," without limitation to "houses of worship or tax-exempt organizations" or organizations controlled by or associated with houses of worship. *See* Sarah Posner, *Leaked Draft of Trump's Religious Freedom Order Reveals Sweeping Plans to Legalize Discrimination*, The Nation (Feb. 1, 2017), www.thenation.com/article/leaked-draft-of-trumps-religious-freedom-order-reveals-sweeping-plans-to-legalize-discrimination/.

time to time affirm such beliefs through judicial opinions or the creation of new laws.[8] Sometimes legislatures advance religiously motivated laws with scant support from voters for such legislation.[9] In those cases, legislators appeal to strategically powerful, religiously based interest groups. Such groups may lack a broad swell of public support for their initiatives, such as when they seek to prohibit abortion, but over the years they have become politically and strategically adept at maneuvering in the political process.

In an article tellingly entitled "The Rage of White Christian America," a *New York Times* commentator reminded readers that although White Protestants are a "waning" minority who believe the United States is worse off than in 1950; they nonetheless "rage" against their marginalization by stealthy and strategic political participation. The author even attributed Donald Trump's 2016 presidential win to religious mobilization inspired by fear of a changing society.

In most instances, individuals who desire to discriminate against others based on religious beliefs claim a right to free exercise of religion based on the First Amendment *right* to do so. Business owners who shun gay men and women intending to marry and purchase services or goods,[10] clerks who refuse to issue marriage licenses to interracial or gay couples,[11] doctors who deny medical care to children of gay couples,[12] or parents who claim a religious right to pray rather than provide healthcare to their

[8] *See* Hobby Lobby, *supra* note 1, at 2785 (holding the ACA's contraception mandate contrary to the Religious Freedom Restoration Act as applied to closely held corporations).

[9] *See* Douglas Laycock, *A Syllabus of Errors*, 105 MICH. L. REV. 1169, 1173 (2007) (arguing that "[l]egislators have exempted harmful religious behavior that no judge would ever exempt under a generally applicable standard – most notably, parents refusing to provide medical care for their children" and that "preserving the life and health of children is clearly a compelling interest, because a child may suffer irreparable harm before it is old enough to decide for itself").

[10] Sarah Larimer, *Colorado Court Sides Against Baker Who Cited Religious Beliefs, Refused Same-Sex Marriage Cake Order*, WASH. POST (Aug. 13, 2015), www.washingtonpost.com/news/acts-of-faith/wp/2015/08/13/colorado-court-sides-against-baker-who-cited-religious-beliefs-refused-same-sex-couple ("Phillips cited his Christian beliefs as justification for the decision, and contended that creating the cake would violate his right to free speech, as well as his religious freedom.").

[11] A North Carolina law permits magistrates and clerks to reject issuing licenses and marrying any couple they find objectionable to their sincerely held religious beliefs but must then not marry anyone for a period of six months. *See* Mark Joseph Stern, *North Carolina May Soon Let Clerks Refuse Marriage Licenses to Gay and Interracial Couples*, SLATE (June 2, 2015, 2:39 PM), www.slate.com/blogs/outward/2015/06/02/north_carolina_law_lets_magistrates_refuse_marriage_licenses_to_gay_and.html.

[12] Abby Phillip, *Pediatrician Refuses to Treat Baby with Lesbian Parents and There's Nothing Illegal About It*, WASH. POST (Feb. 19, 2015), www.washingtonpost.com/news/morning-mix/wp/2015/02/19/pediatrician-refuses-to-treat-baby-with-lesbian-parents-and-theres-nothing-illegal-about-it.

children[13] claim that the First Amendment's Free Exercise Clause not only tolerates these forms of discrimination and harms but presumptively creates a hierarchy among legal rights with religious exercise always trumping.[14]

The costs of religion embedding in American politics or religion being granted broad credence are clearly exemplified in the abortion context. In the period between 2010 and 2013, more antiabortion legislation was enacted at the state level in the United States than in the prior thirty years combined.[15] This type of aggressive lawmaking stems primarily from influential religious lobbies in the United States.[16]

However, the fallout or costs for families when religion is granted legislative credence may be less obvious. For example, the inability to control childbearing extends beyond abortion and relates to family planning and the use of basic contraceptives.[17] In addition, religiously based lawmaking too frequently creates a bigger buffer between the state and its protections of traditionally vulnerable populations, including women and children. Indeed, religion has been used to justify in the not so distant past denying women the right to marry whom they choose, to vote, to become lawyers, and to maintain custody of their children.[18]

According to Adam Sonfield of the Guttmacher Institute, "[t]here are pharmacists who will only give birth-control pills to a woman if she is married."[19] In fact, "[t]here are pharmacists who mistakenly believe contraception

[13] Caroline Fraser, *Suffering Children and the Christian Science Church*, ATL. MONTHLY (Apr. 1995), www.theatlantic.com/past/docs/unbound/flashbks/xsci/suffer.htm; Tamara Jones, *Prayers, Parental Duty: Child Deaths Put Faith on Trial*, L.A. TIMES (June 27, 1989), articles.latimes.com/1989–06-27/news/mn-4359_1_christian-science-child-abuse-parents (noting that in the five years before the article's publication, "seven cases ... have come under public scrutiny").

[14] *See, e.g., Preserve Freedom, Reject Coercion*, THE COLSON CENTER FOR CHRISTIAN WORLDVIEW, www.colsoncenter.org/freedom.

[15] *More State Abortion Restrictions Were Enacted in 2011–2013 Than in the Entire Previous Decade*, GUTTMACHER INSTITUTE (Jan. 2, 2014), www.guttmacher.org/article/2014/01/more-state-abortion-restrictions-were-enacted-2011–2013-entire-previous-decade.

[16] Jeff Smith, *New Report on Religious Groups and Political Lobbying*, GRAND RAPIDS INSTITUTE FOR INFORMATION DEMOCRACY (Nov. 22, 2011), griid.org/2011/11/22/new-report-on-religious-groups-and-political-lobbying/ (analyzing a study from the Pew Forum, "The United States Conference of Catholic Bishops is the second largest source of religious lobbying. The $26 million plus the Catholics spent to lobby Congress has been for a variety of issues, but the top two have been to advocate for anti-abortion laws and anti-marriage equality.").

[17] Rienzi, Chapter 4, this volume; Lipper, Chapter 5, this volume.

[18] *See* Erwin Chemerinsky & Michele Goodwin, *Religion Is Not a Basis for Harming Others*, 104 GEO. L.J. 1111 (2016).

[19] Rob Stein, *Pharmacists' Rights at Front of New Debate: Because of Beliefs, Some Refuse to Fill Birth Control Prescriptions*, WASH. POST (Mar. 28, 2005), www.washingtonpost.com/wp-dyn/articles/A5490-2005Mar27.html.

is a form of abortion and refuse to [dispense] to anyone . . . [and] there are even cases of pharmacists holding prescriptions hostage, where they won't even transfer it to another pharmacy when time is of the essence"[20] – as it is for emergency contraceptives, which must be taken within 72 hours or 120 hours after unprotected sex, depending on the specific method used.[21] The scale and scope of this problem may be difficult to measure; however, cases in California, Georgia, Washington, Louisiana, Illinois, Massachusetts, Texas, Ohio, New Hampshire, Wisconsin, North Carolina, and Pennsylvania where women have been denied emergency contraceptives indicate a troubling trend.[22]

Medical providers sometimes wish to only provide the services tolerable to their personal religious beliefs or the doctrines or teachings of their faith. As Erwin Chemerinsky and I show in other work, parents refuse to provide medical care to their children, choosing instead to defer to their religious tenets, ideologies, and beliefs even when doing so will inflict injuries and death on their children.[23]

The costs of conscience are no small issue, as Steven H. Aden of the Christian Legal Society's Center for Law and Religious Freedom explained to the *Washington Post*: "[T]his is a very big issue that's just beginning to surface."[24] Aden went on to explain, "[m]ore and more pharmacists are becoming aware of their right to conscientiously refuse to pass objectionable medications across the counter," predicting that "[w]e are on the very front edge of a wave that's going to break not too far down the line."[25]

[20] *Id.* (quoting Sonfield).

[21] The three types of emergency contraceptive pills are: ulipristal sold commercially under the name ella, progestin (only) sold commercially under the name Plan B, and combination pills. A fourth emergency contraceptive, a copper intrauterine device, is a small medical device inserted into the uterus where it remains to prevent pregnancies. *See Frequently Asked Questions, Contraception*, AM. COLL. OBSTETRICIANS & GYNECOLOGISTS (Oct. 2013), www.acog.org/-/media/For-Patients/faq114.pdf?dmc=1&ts=20150907T1821589791 [hereinafter ACOG Fact Sheet]. The IUD is also used as a long-acting reversible contraceptive. *See* Peter Beldin, Cynthia C. Harper, and J. Joseph Speidel, *The Copper IUD for Emergency Contraception, A Neglected Option*, 85 CONTRACEPTION 338 (2012). Plan B is effective up to 72 hours following unprotected sex, while ella is effective up to 120 hours following unprotected sex. *See* Cameron O'Brien Flynn and Robin Fretwell Wilson, *Speaking Candidly about EC and Abortion: What Should Guide Disclosure*, 43 JOURNAL OF LAW, MEDICINE, & ETHICS 72 (Spring 2015).

[22] Rob Stein, *Pharmacists' Rights at Front of New Debate: Because of Beliefs, Some Refuse to Fill Birth Control Prescriptions*, WASH. POST, Mar. 28, 2005, at A1, www.washingtonpost.com/wp-dyn/articles/A5490-2005Mar27.html.

[23] Chemerinsky & Goodwin, *supra* note 18. *See also* Offit, Chapter 12, this volume.

[24] Stein, *supra* note 19.

[25] *Id.* For a survey of claims, see generally LAW, RELIGION, AND HEALTH IN AMERICA (Holly Fernandez Lynch, I. Glenn Cohen, & Elizabeth Sepper, eds. 2017).

Substantively, however, state deference to religious exceptions and exemptions in women's reproductive medical care reveal hostility to women's healthcare, particularly that of low-income women and those living in rural areas where medical providers and institutions may be limited. The cases described later call attention to painful realities for women patients: obtaining not just appropriate reproductive care but also ordinary medical care may not be possible in their local communities. Obtaining services guaranteed by law, such as access to civil marriage after *Obergefell v. Hodges*, which legalized gay marriage, may not be possible.[26] Moreover, the cases underscore a trend that extends beyond specific geographic regions in the United States.

Consider Cheryl Bray's case. After undergoing the extensive and sometimes arduous process to adopt, one last hurdle involved a routine medical examination to confirm her physical fitness to parent. She did not anticipate a problem with this routine physical exam, because she was healthy and forty-one years of age. However, Dr. Fred Salley, who was recommended by a friend, asked, "So, your husband is in agreement with your decision to adopt?"[27] When Bray explained that she was not married, Salley told her "[t]hen I'm not comfortable continuing this exam."[28] Salley later told a reporter that Bray's recalling of their interaction was not accurate. According to Salley, his decision not to examine Bray and complete the necessary paperwork "was not because she was unmarried; rather, it was based on my moral belief that a child should have two parental units," and "such religious beliefs are a fundamental right guaranteed by the Constitution of the United States."[29]

In some instances, those claiming religious constitutional protections for their actions work for the government. Consider the 2015 case of Kim Davis, a county clerk in Kentucky who refused to issue marriage licenses to gay couples even after the U.S. Supreme Court legalized gay marriage.[30] In that case, her attorney issued a statement noting that Ms. Kim Davis, an Apostolic Christian, "holds an undisputed sincerely held religious belief that marriage is a union between a man and a woman only."[31] In that religious-refusal case, the clerk defiantly maintained her opposition to issuing marriage licenses to gay couples (and continued in her job) despite the fact that the Supreme Court denied her petition to reject gay applicants from receiving marriage

26 Obergefell v. Hodges, 135 S. Ct. 2584, 2607 (2015). *See* Wilson, Chapter 16, this volume; Adams, Chapter 21, this volume.

27 Obergefell, *supra* note 26, at 2607. 28 *Id.* 29 *Id.*

30 Pete Williams, *Supreme Court Rules Against Kentucky Clerk in Gay Marriage Case*, NBC News.com (Sept. 1, 2015, 8:03 AM), www.nbcnews.com/news/us-news/supreme-court-rules-against-kentucky-clerk-gay-marriage-case-n419191.

31 *See id.*

licenses.[32] She issued a statement explaining, "I . . . am requesting what our Founders envisioned – that conscience and religious freedom would be protected."[33]

In Alabama, former Chief Justice Roy Moore of the Alabama Supreme Court defied the U.S. Supreme Court after it struck down gay marriage bans. Moore told judges, "no (probate judge) has to issue a marriage license to a same-sex couple" for twenty-five days.[34] Moore's illegal decree carried more than symbolic weight[35] – the message was clear to his subordinates. Moore compared magistrates who dared to abide by the Supreme Court's ruling to Nazi soldiers during the Third Reich: "[S]ay that I was following the orders of the highest authority to kill Jews . . . Could I say I was ordered to do so?"[36] When pushed by a reporter on the absurdity of the comparison, the chief justice retorted, "Is there a difference?"[37]

In North Carolina, more than a dozen magistrates officially refused to perform gay marriages by recusing themselves under a North Carolina statute permitting them to do so.[38] The magistrates cited a "sincerely held religious objection."[39] In other words, private citizens as well as government employees, and even judges, may hold irrational beliefs that the Free Exercise Clause grants a right or exception to inflict injury on others, particularly if their religious beliefs are "sincere."[40]

The Supreme Court attempted to address this concern, at least within the context of gay marriage, in *Obergefell*. In that case, the Court reasoned that "the

32 Sarah Kaplan & James Higdon, *The Defiant Kim Davis, the Ky. Clerk Who Refuses to Issue Gay Marriage Licenses*, WASH. POST (Sept. 2, 2015), www.washingtonpost.com/news/morning-mix/wp/2015/09/02/meet-kim-davis-the-ky-clerk-who-defying-the-supreme-court-refuses-to-issue-gay-marriage-licenses.

33 *Id.* (quoting Kim Davis).

34 Charles J. Dean, *Roy Moore: Alabama Judges Not Required to Issue Same-Sex Marriage Licenses for 25 Days*, AL.COM (Jan. 6, 2016) (emphasis omitted), www.al.com/news/index.ssf/2015/06/roy_moore_gay_marriage.html; in this case, Justice Moore claimed that gay marriage was inconsistent with Alabama's constitution. This may have been cover or obfuscation for religious beliefs, as Moore is quoted saying that marriage and the "pursuit of happiness is given by God under our law." Charles J. Dean, *Alabama Chief Justice Moore: Gay Marriage "Not in Accordance with Constitution,"* AL.COM (June 30, 2015), www.al.com/news/index.ssf/2015/06/alabama_chief_justice_moore_ga.html.

35 Shannon Minter of the National Center for Lesbian Rights stated that Moore's order had "no practical effect," because a federal judge ordered Alabama judges to ignore the state's marriage ban in the wake of *Obergefell*. Dean, *supra* note 35.

36 *Id.* 37 *Id.*

38 *14 NC Magistrates Use Recusal Law Focusing on Gay Marriage*, WSOCTV.COM (July 8, 2015), www.wsoctv.com/news/news/local/14-nc-magistrates-use-recusal-law-focusing-gay-mar/nmtHg.

39 *Id.* 40 *See* Williams, *supra* note 31.

Constitution . . . does not permit the State to bar same-sex couples from marriage on the same terms as accorded to couples of the opposite sex," despite "sincere conviction[s]" in their religious beliefs.[41] As I emphasize here, the Court made clear in its ruling that "those who adhere to religious doctrine[s] may continue to advocate with utmost, sincere conviction that ... same-sex marriage should not be condoned."[42] In fact, people may hold whatever religious views they desire. The right, however, to hold beliefs, even bigoted convictions, is quite distinct from expecting the law to condone the infliction of injuries on others or to grant a right to do so, as some statutes do.[43]

Despite the landmark ruling in *Obergefell*, the Supreme Court has not always been clear or consistent in its nondiscrimination approach when it comes to religion – and neither has Congress or state legislatures. For instance, consider *Burwell v. Hobby Lobby*.[44] At issue in that case was whether the federal Religious Freedom Restoration Act of 1993[45] ("RFRA") permitted the U.S. Department of Health and Human Services ("HHS") to require "closely held corporations" to provide their employees with health insurance coverage for contraceptives that violate the corporation owners' sincerely held religious beliefs.[46] In a sharply divided 5–4 opinion written by Justice Samuel Alito, the Court held that "[a]s applied to closely held corporations, the HHS regulations imposing the contraceptive mandate *violate* RFRA."[47]

The Supreme Court's ruling in *Burwell v. Hobby Lobby* resurfaces important questions related to reproductive rights. Does the U.S. Constitution's recognition of religious rights or the protection of those rights [for religious minorities] in RFRA infer a hierarchy among rights? Are religious interests among groups and individuals so vitally distinct that their protection permits harm against all other citizens, as Rienzi (Chapter 4, this volume) and Rassbach (Chapter 7, this volume) both seem to suggest in this volume? Do religious protections or rights under the U.S. Constitution and RFRA outweigh all other? Despite the flurry of news articles published in the wake of the Court's *Hobby Lobby* ruling, legal scholarship on these and related questions remains surprisingly thin. This volume rectifies that omission.

Further, the judicial record on these issues remains confusing and discordant. The Supreme Court rejected the Kentucky county clerk's insistence that her religious beliefs provide her a right to discriminate against gay men and

[41] Obergefell *supra* note 26, at 2607. [42] *Id.* [43] *See infra* note 50 (citing state laws).
[44] Hobby Lobby, *supra* note 1. [45] 42 U.S.C. §§ 2000bb-4 (2012).
[46] Hobby Lobby, *supra* note 1, at 2759. [47] *Id.* at 2785 (emphasis added).

women in her official capacity.[48] Yet, the Court reasoned only a year before that corporations may have religious beliefs and freely exercise their religion. The Court ruled that companies whose religious beliefs conflict with federal law may be exempt from duties to provide needed health benefits to female employees even if their conduct violates congressional mandates. If President Trump acts on plans to "exempt" all moral and religious objectors from the Patient Protection and Affordable Care Act's ("ACA") contraceptive coverage mandate – without imposing a duty to pay for those covered drugs onto someone else, such as an insurer – women will in fact be injured.

This chapter examines the harms inflicted by religiously based lawmaking, particularly in the contexts of women's health and reproductive decision making. It queries whether judicial deference to religiously based discrimination misreads free exercise of religion and expands the doctrine beyond its reasonable and legitimate limits. Under the premise of protecting religious groups, some legislatures and courts grant individuals and groups authority to inflict dignitary, and even physical, harms on others.[49] In *Hobby Lobby*,

[48] Title VII of the Civil Rights Act of 1964 requires employers, including the government, to provide "reasonable" accommodations of an employee's religious practice or belief unless the employer, or a coworker, will experience an "undue hardship." 42 U.S.C. § 2000e-2(a)(1) (2012); Trans World Airlines v. Hardison, 432 U.S. 63, 74–76 (1977). For an argument that the public must have access to civil marriage, see Wilson, Chapter 16, this volume.

[49] *See, e.g., id.*; ALA. CODE § 13A-13-6 (2015) (providing religious exemption to endangering the welfare of a child when parents use religious practices in lieu of medical treatment); GA. CODE ANN. § 49-5-180 (West 2015) ("No child who in good faith is being treated solely by spiritual means through prayer . . . shall, for that reason alone, be considered to be an abused child."); 325 ILL. COMP. STAT. 5/3 (2015) ("A child shall not be considered neglected or abused for the sole reason that such child's parent or other person responsible for his or her welfare depends upon spiritual means through prayer alone for the treatment or cure of disease."); IOWA CODE § 232.68(2)(4)(c) (2015) ("A parent or guardian legitimately practicing religious beliefs who does not provide specified medical treatment for a child for that reason alone shall not be considered abusing the child."); MO. REV. STAT. § 210.115.4 (2015) (providing religious exemption to child abuse and to being entered in the state abuse registry where parents deny medical care on the basis of religious beliefs); MONT. CODE ANN. § 41-3-102 (2015) (denying medical care for religious reasons does not constitute child abuse); N.H. REV. STAT. ANN. § 639:3 (2015) ("A person who pursuant to the tenets of a recognized religion fails to conform to an otherwise existing duty of care or protection is not guilty of an offense under this section."); N.J. STAT. ANN. § 9:6–8.21 (West 2015) (providing religious exemption from child abuse in treatment by spiritual means); 23 PA. CONS. STAT. § 6304(b) (2014) (providing that failure to provide medical treatment to child for religious reasons does not constitute child abuse); 11 R.I. GEN. LAWS § 11–9-5 (West 2015) (providing that failure to provide medical care to child for religious reasons does not constitute child abuse); TENN. CODE ANN. § 39–15-402 (West 2015) (providing that denial of medical care for religious reasons is not child abuse in and of itself); UTAH CODE ANN. § 76–5-109 (LexisNexis 2015) (providing that there is no offense of child abuse where parents withhold necessary medical treatment from their children for religious reasons); VA. CODE ANN. § 63.2–100(2) (2015)

Justice Alito emphasized that federal law protecting religious freedom "applies to regulations that govern the activities of closely held for-profit corporations like Conestoga, Hobby Lobby, and Mardel."[50] If that is so, what if the owners of Hobby Lobby refused to provide health insurance to lesbian spouses based on religious beliefs? Or refused to provide medical treatment to a transgendered adult or dependent seeking to undergo needed medical therapies?[51] Arguably, *Hobby Lobby* makes a strong case for supporting that type of discrimination.

Section I of this chapter examines how medical science is distorted, mischaracterized, and rejected by policy makers and objectors to justify religiously based objections to legal rights. Section II offers a narrative case study to highlight examples where religion is deployed to justify harming women in efforts to control and restrict their reproductive healthcare decision making and rights. Cases across the U.S. illustrate how physicians, hospital staff, and other healthcare professionals including pharmacists believe they have a right to refuse to provide medical services to their female patients, even in emergency situations where the patients suffer injuries or may die. Section III concludes.

I RELIGION, LAW, AND THE DISTORTION OF SCIENCE: THE CONTRACEPTIVE CONTEXT

Many of the entanglements about women's legal rights in the reproductive context rest on disputes about science. Concerns over fetal health and well-being dominate political discourse about reproduction. Although trust has ebbed in claims made by politicians in a progressively "post-truth" world, politicians still speak with authority on issues that some in the news media and the public take for granted as accurate and reliable.[52] Rarely is the science

(providing that there is no criminal offense where parent withholds medical treatment from child for religious reasons).

50 Hobby Lobby, *supra* note 1, at 2775.

51 Complaint, Conforti v. St. Joseph's Healthcare System, Inc. et al., Docket No. 2:17-cv-00050 (D.N.J. filed Jan. 05, 2017); Jessica Schladebeck, *Transgender Man Sues New Jersey Catholic Hospital for Refusing to Perform Hysterectomy*, New York Daily News (Jan. 6, 2017), www.nydailynews.com/news/national/transgender-man-sues-hospital-refusing-hysterectomy-article-1.2937202. In 2016, HHS Office for Civil Rights issued a final rule defining discrimination in the provision of medical services "on the basis of sex" under Section 1557 of the ACA to include "discrimination on the basis of . . . gender identity." *See* 45 C.F.R. § 92.4 (2017).

52 Brian Kennedy, *Most Americans Trust the Military and Scientists to Act in the Public's Interest*, Pew Research Center (Oct. 18, 2016), www.pewresearch.org/fact-tank/2016/10/18/most-americans-trust-the-military-and-scientists-to-act-in-the-publics-interest/. *See also Yes, I'd Lie*

challenged or fact-checked, particularly within the legal discourse. The circulation of "fake news" further exacerbates this problem.[53] In recent years, blatant falsehoods regarding contraception and abortion dominate political discourse, shaping media coverage, public understanding, and ultimately law. For example, few would know that legal abortions are safer for women than carrying pregnancies to term. Research shows that a woman is fourteen times more likely to die during her pregnancy and childbirth than when having an abortion.[54]

One glaring example of a myth persuasively substituting for science is found in the confusion between contraception and abortifacients. In *Hobby Lobby*, its owners claimed religious opposition to abortion. The subject of their lawsuit, however, was the ACA's federal contraceptive coverage mandate. The difference is important. Contraceptives prevent pregnancies. Abortifacients terminate pregnancies. The drugs and procedures function distinctly and differently. By definition and how they function as described later, contraceptives are not abortifacients because they prevent pregnancies from occurring. A logical comparative would be vaccines. Vaccines function to prevent diseases and illnesses. A vaccine, however, is not an antibiotic or medication to be used after the illness has embedded in the body. In other words, abortifacients work only to terminate pregnancies; they cannot prevent a pregnancy from establishing in a woman's uterus. Why does this matter?

In a disturbing trend, pharmacists are refusing to dispense or prescribe birth control and emergency contraception ("EC") based on religious or moral objections.[55] Pharmacists ground their justifications in the belief that such hormonal contraceptives, particularly emergency contraception, cloak the true purpose of that medicine. They believe this type of contraception will

to You, THE ECONOMIST (Sep. 10, 2016), www.economist.com/news/briefing/21706498-dishonesty-politics-nothing-new-manner-which-some-politicians-now-lie-and.

53 By "fake news" I mean completely fabricated stories, not reporting with which someone disagrees. Callum Borchers, *"Fake News" Has Now Lost All Meaning*, WASH. POST (Feb. 9, 2017), www.washingtonpost.com/news/the-fix/wp/2017/02/09/fake-news-has-now-lost-all-meaning/?utm_term=.562a5c78597d.

54 E. G. Raymond & D. A. Grimes, *The Comparative Safety of Legal Induced Abortion and Childbirth in the United States*, 119 OBSTETRICS & GYNECOLOGY 215, 215–19 (Feb. 2012), www.ncbi.nlm.nih.gov/pubmed/22270271.

55 *See* Alex Barker, *Pharmacists Refusing to Fill Spark National Controversy*, PHARMACY TIMES (Aug. 11, 2015), www.pharmacytimes.com/contributor/alex-barker-pharmd/2015/08/pharmacists-refusing-to-fill-spark-national-controversy (reporting that reports of "[p]harmacists' refusal to fill prescriptions for birth control and emergency contraception … have surfaced in at least 25 states," and that many are "based on personal beliefs, rather than medical or professional concerns").

abort a fetus or destroy a fertilized egg.[56] This belief persists and is used successfully to sway judges, legislators, and the public despite significant evidence that emergency contraception prevents pregnancy primarily, if not *exclusively*, by delaying or inhibiting ovulation rather than destroying an already fertilized egg.[57] In reading hundreds of political statements and articles quoting politicians, it is clear that many lawmakers responsible for crafting legislation that impacts women's lives lack basic awareness and understanding of women's health and reproduction – they lack a basic grasp of ovulation, fertilization, and pregnancy. For too many, these are all blurred lines.[58]

The scope of this problem is significant. According to the Center for Reproductive Rights, "every 10.5 seconds an unplanned pregnancy occurs in the U.S."[59] This results in about 3 million unplanned pregnancies per year.[60] Not all of these pregnancies will result in births; about 1.29 million will terminate in abortions.[61] Over the span of a decade, this could mean 30 million unintended pregnancies and almost 13 million abortions. Emergency contraceptives can play a significant role by considerably reducing the number of unplanned pregnancies – if women have access to them. Access to contraceptives influences not only the families that women form but also how they care for the children and families they already have.[62] Thus, how politicians and regulators label these drugs may significantly impact women's lives.

56 Mary K. Collins, *Conscience Clauses and Oral Contraceptives: Conscientious Objection or Calculated Obstruction?* 15 Annals Health L. 37, 37 (2006).

57 *See* Gabriela Noe et al., *Contraceptive Efficacy of Emergency Contraception with Levonorgestrel Given Before or After Ovulation*, 81 Contraception 486, 492 (2010) (concluding that levonorgestrel is "highly effective for preventing unintended pregnancy when it is used *before* ovulation, but when used after ovulation, it is completely unable to prevent pregnancy because it had no effect on subsequent reproductive processes") (emphasis added); Natalia Novikova et al., *Effectiveness of Levonorgestrel Emergency Contraception Giving Before or After Ovulation – A Pilot Study*, 75 Contraception 112, 117 (2007). *See generally* Ryan M. Hrobak & Robin Fretwell Wilson, *Emergency Contraceptives or "Abortion-Inducing" Drugs?: Empowering Women to Make Informed Decisions*, 71 Washington & Lee L. Rev. 1385 (2014) (reviewing evidence on the mechanism of action of Plan B and *ella*).

58 Amanda Marcotte, *Idaho Lawmaker Who Doesn't Understand Female Anatomy Knows What's Good for Women*, Slate (Feb. 24, 2015), www.slate.com/blogs/xx_factor/2015/02/24/vito_barbieri_anti_abortion_idaho_republican_asks_if_you_can_reach_the_vagina.html (reporting on Idaho lawmaker who queried whether gynecological exams could be performed by a woman swallowing a camera).

59 Press Release, Ctr. for Reprod. Rights, Center for Reproductive Rights Questions Timing of FDA Plan B Announcement (July 31, 2006), www.reproductiverights.org/press-room/center-for-reproductive-rights-questions-timing-of-fda-plan-b-announcement.

60 *Id.* 61 *Id.*

62 For a review of contraceptive policy on family formation, including by already married women with children, *see* June Carbone & Naomi R. Cahn, Red Families v. Blue Families: Legal Polarization and the Creation of Culture (2010).

The scientific community and federal law have long defined a pregnancy by the status of a fertilized egg implanted in the wall of a woman's uterus.[63] That is, pregnancy begins when a fertilized egg is implanted in the uterus. Conception is an essential step toward pregnancy, but *a fertilized egg is not a pregnancy*. Rather, conception is a fertilized egg in need of a home in the uterine wall – without that, a woman's body will terminate it during her monthly menstrual cycle.[64] The basic laws of biology dictate that not only will a pregnancy *not* develop from a hovering fertilized egg, it cannot develop without implantation.[65]

How pregnancy is defined becomes "critical to distinguishing between a contraceptive that prevents pregnancy and an abortifacient that terminates it."[66] Nevertheless, state definitions of pregnancies vary, and the sharp divide as to what a pregnancy is impacts law and ultimately women's healthcare and medical access. As noted by the Guttmacher Institute in a 2005 report, some states define a pregnancy at the point of "conception,"[67] which is scientifically imprecise and misleading.

These facts matter for law because policies, legislation, and judicial opinions derive from these understandings. Moreover, because appointments to federal agencies, such as the Food and Drug Administration ("FDA"), can be and have been politicized in the reproductive context,[68] safe contraceptives can be delayed coming onto the market or inaccurately labeled in the process.[69] In 2009, U.S. District Court Judge Edward R. Korman ruled that the

63 Allen J. Wilcox et al., *Time of Implantation of the Conceptus and Loss of Pregnancy*, 340 NEW ENG. J. MED. 1796 (1999), www.nejm.org/doi/full/10.1056/NEJM199906103402304. For a historical review of definitions, *see* Hrobak and Wilson, *supra* note 58.

64 *Id.* at 1799.

65 The rare exception is an ectopic pregnancy that develops in the fallopian tubes. Such pregnancies are incredibly rare, and when they do occur, they threaten the woman's life. *Ectopic Pregnancy: Complications*, THE MAYO CLINIC (Jan. 20, 2015), www.mayoclinic.org/diseases-conditions/ectopic-pregnancy/basics/complications/con-20024262 ("When you have an ectopic pregnancy, the stakes are high. Without treatment, a ruptured fallopian tube could lead to life-threatening bleeding.").

66 Rachel Benson Gold, *The Implications of Defining When a Woman Is Pregnant*, 8 GUTTMACHER REP. PUB. POL'Y 7 (May 2005), www.guttmacher.org/pubs/tgr/08/2/gr080207.html.

67 *Id.* at 8.

68 Recently dismissed Secretary of HHS Tom Price disputed as late as 2012 whether there was a need for the contraceptive coverage mandate: "Bring me one woman who has been left behind. Bring me one. There's not one." In a confirmation hearing on January 18, 2017, Secretary Price said he would want a system where "women and all Americans have access to the care and kind of coverage they want." Kimberley Lenoard, *Obamacare Repeal Could Include End to Free Birth Control, Hearing Suggests*, U.S. NEWS & WORLD REPORT (Jan. 18, 2017), www.usnews.com/news/health-care-news/articles/2017%9601-18/tom-price-leaves-door-open-to-gutting-obamacares-free-birth-control-provision.

69 Irin Carmon, *The Myth of the "Morning After Abortion Pill,"* SALON (Apr. 26, 2012), www.salon.com/2012/04/26/the_myth_of_the_morning_after_abortion_pill (arguing that "there's a

FDA ignored science while allowing politics to dictate its decisions in 2006 to limit access to over-the-counter emergency contraceptives to women older than age eighteen. In a scathing opinion, Judge Korman wrote, "[t]he FDA repeatedly and unreasonably delayed issuing a decision on Plan B for suspect reasons."[70]

The opinion went on to say:

> Putting aside for the moment the specifics of the many claims brought by plaintiffs and the details of each of the FDA's decisions, the gravamen of plaintiffs' claims is that the FDA's decisions regarding Plan B – on the Citizen Petition and the [Supplemental New Drug Applications] – were arbitrary and capricious because they were not the result of reasoned and good faith agency decision-making . . . Plaintiffs are right.[71]

If antiabortion politicians confuse contraceptives with abortifacients, that confusion very likely will impact their legislative agendas in the reproductive health sphere, including legislation they propose and how they vote on legislation related to reproductive medicines such as contraceptives. In turn, access to *preventative* pregnancy medicines that have nothing to do with aborting a fetus – or even impairing fertilized ova – will be dramatically constrained.[72] Thus, when lawmakers ignore or neglectfully interpret science in favor of religious agendas that misread biology, their political decision making directly imposes constraints and significant costs on their constituents, including "pro-life" women who oppose abortion. For example, women who oppose abortion but do not wish to become pregnant might forgo seeking or utilizing medications such as Plan B even in cases of rape based on misleading, inaccurate information.[73]

reason why people mistake emergency contraception and abortion: The right intentionally confuses the two.").

70 Tummino v. Torti, 603 F. Supp. 2d 519, 523 (E.D.N.Y. 2009) *amended sub nom.* Tummino v. Hamburg, 2013 WL 865851 (E.D.N.Y. 2013).

71 *Id.*

72 Press Release, Ctr. for Reprod. Rights, Depositions Indicate Bush Administration Exerted Political Influence on FDA During Plan B Review Process (Aug. 30, 2006), www.reproductiverights.org/press-room/depositions-indicate-bush-administration-exerted-political-influence-on-fda-during-plan-b (noting that depositions released in the Center for Reproductive Right's lawsuit against the FDA "indicate that the Bush Administration sought to unduly influence the agency during the Plan B application review process").

73 Examining the vast number of unintended pregnancies could shed light on how misinformation may chill women's reproductive decision making. For example, twenty-five years ago, researchers predicted widespread use of emergency contraceptives would significantly reduce unintended pregnancies. Those researchers, however, now say that many women avoid or choose not to use emergency contraceptives after unprotected sex – even though access is now

If contraceptives, including emergency contraceptives, are not abortifacients, how do they work? Three emergency contraceptives are dispensed in the form of oral pills. One of the drugs, Plan B, is available over the counter while the other contraceptives require a prescription or surgical insertion.[74] Emergency contraceptives function to minimize or eliminate the risk of unplanned pregnancy in two ways. First, they work to slow ovulation, which is the release of ova from the ovaries.[75] If the ova are not present, a pregnancy cannot take place. Second, these medications thicken the cervical wall "so sperm have trouble swimming."[76]

Sadly, some of these medications have been misunderstood as killing fetuses or terminating pregnancies. Neither is true or rooted in science and medicine.[77] However, these misunderstandings can be powerfully and cleverly leveraged in health debates. For example, former presidential candidate Mitt Romney referred to emergency contraceptives as "abortive pills" and other politicians "have made similar statements" likely in a strategic effort to connect with fundamentalist voters.[78]

Tellingly, political misstatements that conflate emergency contraception and birth control with abortion conflict with basic science: leading health authorities, including the National Institutes of Health, World Health Organization, the Cleveland Clinic, and the Mayo Clinic, among others, emphasize that a pregnancy exists only after a fertilized egg is actually implanted in the uterus. Dislodging an implanted, fertilized egg and preventing fertilization and implantation from occurring are two different things. Yet, some politicians continue to claim that to disrupt implantation is akin to abortion, or as the American Association of Pro-life Obstetricians and Gynecologists purports, preventing implantation is the "moral

available. Further research might help to explain why, including teasing out whether women's decision making has been influenced by political rhetoric and misinformation. Richard Knox, *Plan B Ruling Reveals Glimpse into Bush's FDA*, NPR (Mar. 24, 2009), www.npr.org/templates/story/story.php?storyId=102294234.

74 Plan B One Step, which is progestin-only, can be purchased over the counter as well as Next Choice One Dose. Combination pills and Ulipristal require a medical prescription. *See* ACOG Fact Sheet, *supra* note 22.

75 Progestin-only pills function to prevent pregnancy by preventing ovulation. These pills do not work if a woman is already pregnant. It is worth noting that a mature "egg is fertilizable for only a short period of time (usually between 8 and 12 hours)." *6 Things to Know About Conception*, Nat'l Inst. Health, www.nichd.nih.gov/news/resources/links/infographics/Documents/NICHD_InfoGraphic_Conception.pdf%23search=conception.

76 Pam Belluck, *Abortion Qualms on Morning-After Pill May Be Unfounded*, N.Y. Times (June 5, 2012), www.nytimes.com/2012/06/06/health/research/morning-after-pills-dont-block-implantation-science-suggests.html.

77 *See id.* 78 *Id.*

equivalent of a homicide."[79] In stark contrast to leading health authority, the organization urges that conception and fertilization are the equivalent of pregnancy.

Scientifically, however, conception is essentially fertilization – and not pregnancy. Understanding this finer point is important for law. According to the U.S. National Library of Medicine, "around half of all fertilized eggs die and are lost (aborted) spontaneously."[80] In a recent study, Professor Jan Brosens likened the process of some fertilized eggs implanting and others not implanting to an "entrance exam."[81] In other words, some fertilized eggs simply fail to thrive or implant – a woman's uterus basically rejects them. Reasons for the failure vary, including the quality of a woman's ova, chromosomal abnormalities in the embryo, and the woman's age. Romanticism about pregnancy aside, the human body experiences a pregnancy as a parasitic invasion – and for good reason, especially because women's health becomes compromised, if not endangered by pregnancy.[82] As a result, even among women who become pregnant, their bodies will attempt to reject those pregnancies, resulting in about 15% to 20% of all pregnancies ending in miscarriage.[83]

Increasingly, however, politicians in the United States argue that their religious views should be granted greater deference in courts and legislatures than peer-reviewed science. In arguing against the ACA's mandate, former presidential candidate and longtime Congresswoman Michele Bachman told national audiences on CNN and other networks that emergency contraception causes abortion.[84] She claimed that if the law passed, ten-year-old girls would acquire emergency contraceptives while on shopping and school field trips.[85] Notwithstanding the outlandishness of such claims, news media may be slow to correct the inaccuracies. For example, CNN headlined a story about emergency contraceptives with the words "abortion pills" in the title.[86]

79 *Id.* (quoting Dr. Donna Harrison, research director for the American Association of Pro-Life Obstetricians and Gynecologists).

80 MedlinePlus, *Miscarriage*, U.S. NAT'L LIBR. MED. (Nov. 16, 2014), www.nlm.nih.gov/medlineplus/ency/article/001488.htm.

81 Rachel Rettner, *Fate of a Fertilized Egg: Why Some Embryos Don't Implant*, LIVESCIENCE (Feb. 6, 2014, 10:18 AM), www.livescience.com/43157-embryo-implant-signals-pregnancy.html.

82 *Id.*

83 Catherine Pearson, *Miscarriage Causes, Rates Widely Misunderstood, Study Shows*, HUFFINGTON POST (Oct. 17, 2013 2:53 PM), www.huffingtonpost.com/2013/10/17/miscarriage-cause_n_4116712.html.

84 *Are Health Plans Forced to Cover Free Abortion Pills?* CNN (Sept. 13, 2011), www.cnn.com/2011/POLITICS/09/13/truth.squad.contraception.

85 *Id.* 86 *Id.*

Whether or not to draw in readers to their website, the scientifically and medically inaccurate headline not only grabbed attention but also miscast emergency contraception for millions of people who read the headline and nothing more.

The critical question then is whether emergency contraceptives can induce abortion and whether pharmacists would be justified in their concerns that the products are misbranded.[87] Empirical evidence shows that emergency contraception has neither medical efficacy nor benefit for pregnant patients.[88] This evidence raises questions about the validity of and authoritative weight g ranted pharmacists' religious refusals to dispense emergency contraception because they believe it is equivalent to an abortion. In such cases, religion is deployed as a prophylactic shield to counter the dispensation of medical treatments that would seem not to interfere with religious beliefs. In the *Hobby Lobby* decision, the Court bracketed the question of how objected-to contraceptives operate, relying on the parties' "honest conviction" that covering such drugs would violate their sincerely held religious beliefs that life begins at conception.[89]

Medical discrimination of that kind not only conflicts with the constitutional interests of women who seek such medical treatments but also violates medical standards and broader ethical norms. According to the American College of Obstetricians and Gynecologists ("ACOG") Committee on Ethics, "provider refusals to dispense emergency contraception based on unsupported beliefs about its primary mechanism of action should not be justified."[90] In a platform highlighting its concerns, ACOG elaborates that permissive religious discrimination in these contexts may disproportionately impact economically vulnerable women, explaining that "single, affluent [women] might experience such a refusal as inconvenient and seek out another physician, [however] a young mother of three depending on public transportation might find such a refusal to be an insurmountable barrier to medication because other options are not realistically available to her."[91] Although some barriers are informational, and can be alleviated with better information about where needed medicines and services are available or covered,[92] added cost, distance, and lost time are irreducible barriers when

87 *See supra* note 20. 88 *See* sources cited *supra* note 77.

89 Hobby Lobby, *supra* note 1, at 2767–65.

90 Comm. on Ethics, *The Limits of Conscientious Refusal in Reproductive Medicine*, Am. C. Obstetricians & Gynecologists Comm. Op. No. 385, 4 (2007) (reaffirmed 2016).

91 *Id.*

92 *See* Kinsey Hasstedt, *Abortion Coverage Under the Affordable Care Act: The Laws Tell Only Half the Story*, Guttmacher Pol'y Rev. at 15 (Winter 2014), www.guttmacher.org/pubs/gpr/17/1/gpr170115.pdf (observing that "[i]t is currently not easy for consumers to ascertain the degree to which abortion coverage is included within marketplace plans, likely in part because

women are racing against the clock, as Section II shows. ACOG persuasively argues, "[r]efusals that unduly burden the most vulnerable of society violate the core commitment to justice in the distribution of health resources."[93] The types of religious refusals described in this chapter place an undue burden on women such that they lose control of their "reproductive fate and quality of life" impacting not only themselves, but also their children and families, as the narratives that follow show.[94]

II RELIGIOUS EXCEPTIONALISM IN THE EMERGENCY CONTRACEPTIVE CONTEXT

As religious objections escalate, women suffer the consequences, because they continue to be harmed when state-licensed pharmacists refuse to dispense the medications that female patients are legally and medically entitled to receive. In racial contexts, such discrimination would no longer be tolerated, even if racial minorities could seek services elsewhere.[95] Sex discrimination of this kind is treated differently, however, in both society and law. Failure to accommodate based on racial status is understood to inflict stigma, shame, and emotional distress. Yet, law remains slow to recognize the severity and impacts of similar status-based harms when women are unjustly denied legal rights.

A *Discrimination and Reproductive Healthcare*

In the reproductive healthcare contexts, refusing women medical treatments is serious, exposing them to physical harms, infections, unintended pregnancies, and even death. These injuries may be particularly acute when medications must be sought and obtained in a timely manner for the drugs to be most effective. The following cases illustrate my point.

no specific, nationwide standards for how that information should be conveyed to the public have been established"). Religious objections also arise as to end-of-life care, where patients and families also lack good information. *See* Cahn and Zeitlow, Chapter 20, this volume; Kaplan, Chapter 19, this volume.

93 Comm. on Ethics, *The Limits of Conscientious Refusal in Reproductive Medicine*, Am. Coll. Obstetricians & Gynecologists Comm. Op. No. 385, 4 (2007) (reaffirmed 2016).

94 *Id.*

95 *See, e.g.*, Jonathan Rauch, *Gay Rights, Nondiscrimination, and Religious Liberty: Can We Avoid a Train Wreck?*, David C. Baum Memorial Lecture on Civil Liberties and Civil Rights, University of Illinois (Oct. 19, 2016), www.youtube.com/watch?v=3YezwtRX9XU.

1 Lori Boyer – Denial of Emergency Contraception After Rape

I was so vulnerable . . . I felt victimized all over again. First the rape, and then the doctor making me feel powerless.

–Lori Boyer[96]

Some doctors and pharmacists refuse to issue emergency contraception even after a woman is raped. In such traumatic instances, being denied care can be devastating and incomprehensible. Understandably, rape victims can be confounded by medical providers' refusal to provide emergency contraception – saddling them with the burden when seeking care elsewhere, if it is available at all.

Lori Boyer's rape occurred at the hands of someone she knew.[97] As she fled from her rapist, devastated and trembling, she drove to the nearest emergency room, located at Good Samaritan Hospital in Lebanon, Pennsylvania.[98] Boyer arrived bruised and in terrible pain from the sexual assault.[99] She tried to remember what women are counseled to do when raped: ask for a rape kit and to talk to a sexual assault counselor. Boyer met with the rape counselor at the hospital who informed her about the "morning-after-pill," which could help to prevent pregnancy. Boyer in turn asked Dr. Martin Gish, who performed her pelvic exam, for emergency contraceptives. Gish's response would be burned into her memory. He told her "No," looking back at her chart while saying "I can't do that."[100]

Boyer recounted that she was in disbelief, trying to "hold back tears."[101] She explained that if she didn't get the pills, she might become pregnant because she was "midcycle."[102] According to Boyer, she asked for another doctor and "Dr. Gish simply shook his head."[103] Gish replied, "It's against my religion."[104] Through the assistance of the sexual assault counselor, Boyer was able to track down a doctor who would issue the prescription. Yet, the injury of her encounter remained years later. As one reporter noted, "Boyer remained haunted by the ER doctor's refusal."[105] Her experience with Gish hobbled Boyer's ability to seek gynecological medical care – even routine preventative screenings; she hasn't seen an obstetrician in years. She explained, "I haven't gotten the nerve up to go [to a gynecologist], for fear of being judged again . . . The whole situation was traumatizing and embarrassing, and I just wanted to put it behind me."[106]

96 Sabrina Rubin Erdely, *Doctors' Beliefs Can Hinder Patient Care: New Laws Shore Up Providers' Right to Refuse Treatment Based on Values*, NBC News (June 22, 2007, 2:26 PM), www.nbcnews.com/id/19190916/ns/health-womens_health/t/doctors-beliefs-can-hinder-patient-care/%23.Ve4fgflVhBd (quoting Lori Boyer).

97 *Id.* 98 *Id.* 99 *Id.* 100 *Id.* 101 *Id.* 102 *Id.* 103 *Id.* 104 *Id.* 105 *Id.*

106 Boyer came forward with her experience after reading about another woman encountering a similar experience. *Id.*

2 Tara Harnish – Refused Emergency Contraception After Rape

He turned me away when I needed medical help. That's not what a doctor is supposed to do.

– Tara Harnish[107]

Tara Harnish suffered a similar experience to that of Lori Boyer: she was raped, sought medical attention, and was refused emergency contraceptives.[108] Also like Boyer, she sought care at Good Samaritan Hospital in Lebanon, Pennsylvania – in the same emergency room unit. She also was assigned Dr. Martin Gish – the same doctor who refused to provide Lori Boyer emergency contraceptives after she suffered a brutal sexual assault.[109] For Harnish, who was twenty-one years old at the time, the decision to obtain emergency contraception was unequivocal, as she told ABC News, "Who wants to carry their rapist's baby? Who wants to do that?"[110]

Harnish's account of Gish's treatment echoed Boyer's shocking treatment. When Harnish's mother contacted Gish's office to obtain emergency contraception for her daughter, he refused. "He seemed more concerned with saving the (potential) pregnancy than he was with my health," Harnish told a reporter.[111] Harnish was so devastated by her experience that she felt too traumatized to pursue the course of action that rape counselors recommend.[112] Not only was the hospital aware that Gish refused to provide standard, recommended care to rape victims, the hospital continued to assign him to rape victims.[113]

Gish is among a set of doctors who also refuse to refer patients to others who will provide the care their patients seek. Moreover, some doctors refuse to inform women patients about their medical options, including emergency contraceptives, leaving women with the choice of aborting or carrying an unintended pregnancy to term. Medical ethics groups draw an important line around information: at a minimum, "[a]ll health care providers must provide accurate and unbiased information so that patients can make informed decisions."[114]

107 *Id.*

108 Dan Harris, *Prescriptions Denied*, ABC News.com (Nov. 17, 2006), abcnews.go.com/WNT/story?id=2662616.

109 In July 2006, Harnish sought care at the same emergency ward where Ms. Boyer had previously sought care. Erdely, *supra* note 99.

110 Harris, *supra* note 111 (quoting Harnish).

111 Erdely, *supra* note 99 (quoting Harnish).

112 *Id.*

113 *Id.*

114 Comm. on Ethics, *The Limits of Conscientious Refusal in Reproductive Medicine* 1 Am. Cong. of Obstetricians & Gynecologists (2007), www.acog.org/-/media/Committee-Opinions/Committee-on-Ethics/co385.pdf?dmc=1&ts=20141117T2147507498. *See also* Rebecca Dresser, *Professionals, Conformity, and Conscience*, Hastings Center Report,

3 Amanda Renz – Spurned at K-Mart

Unlike the tragic cases just described, sometimes women simply need their standard birth control pill prescriptions filled and yet encounter similar hostility, shaming, embarrassment, and refusal of medical services as those who seek emergency contraceptives. On July 6, 2002, Amanda Renz went to the Menomonie, Wisconsin, K-Mart to refill her birth control prescription.[115] Pharmacist Neil Noesen was on duty that evening. Amanda, a student at the University of Wisconsin–Stout, did not know that her encounter with Noesen at K-Mart would lead to future litigation and that she would be in a legal fight regarding birth control.[116] Amanda's prescription was on file at this particular pharmacy.

After Amanda presented her prescription to Noesen, he asked her whether she intended to use the prescription for contraceptive purposes, to which she answered yes.[117] Thereafter, Noesen denied Amanda the medication she sought. The State of Wisconsin Pharmacy Examining Board found that "[a]fter inquiring whether [Amanda] was using the medication for contraception, [Noesen] did not ask her any further questions and stopped providing any professional services to her."[118] The disciplinary body also found that "[w]hen [Amanda] asked [Noesen] where she could go to have her prescription refilled, [Noesen] stated that he would not tell her because he did not want to be a part in her receiving the contraceptives."[119]

Noesen broadly defined his religious refusals to include participating in, performing, assisting, recommending, counseling in favor, making referrals for, dispensing, administering, promoting, encouraging, or aiding in the delivery of prescriptions to which he religiously objected.[120] More specifically, he objected to any "procedure involving a drug or device that may prevent the

Nov.–Dec. 2005, at 10 (arguing that all pharmacists have a duty to provide accurate information, including informing the patient where she can obtain EC).

[115] Noesen v. State Dep't of Regulation & Licensing, Pharmacy Examining Bd., 751 N.W.2d 385, 389 (Wis. Ct. App. 2008); *see also* Amy Bergquist, *Pharmacist Refusals: Dispensing (With) Religious Accommodation Under Title VII*, 90 MINN. L. REV. 1073, (2006); Martha S. Swartz, *"Conscience Clauses" or "Unconscionable Clauses": Personal Beliefs Versus Professional Responsibilities*, 6 YALE J. HEALTH POL'Y L. & ETHICS 269, (2013) (discussing the Renz case).

[116] *See In re* Disciplinary Proceedings Against Noesen, No. 01 PHM 080 (Wis. Pharmacy Examining Bd. Apr. 13, 2005), online.drl.wi.gov/decisions/2008/ls0310091phm-00077792.pdf (noting that "On Saturday, July 6, 2002, the patient, referred to hereinafter as 'AR', went to the K-Mart Pharmacy and requested a refill of her Loestrin FE 1/20 prescription. AR's prescription had been previously filled at the pharmacy and was on file there.").

[117] *Id.* ¶¶ 25–26. [118] *Id.* ¶ 27. [119] *Id.* ¶ 28. [120] Noesen, *supra* note 115, at 388 n.1.

implantation of a fertilized human ovum."[121] For him, this included "drugs which are prescribed as contraceptives."[122]

According to court documents, Noesen informed Amanda of his religious objection and refused to refill the prescription or tell her where and how she could get it refilled.[123] Timing mattered to Amanda, because she needed to begin the first dose of the refill the next day.[124] Missing that dose would require Amanda to obtain a secondary prescription for birth control and to take that alternative contraception for an entire month.[125]

Unfortunately for Amanda, there were no other pharmacists on duty at the time and the managing pharmacist was unable to come to the store.[126] The Wisconsin Court of Appeals stated, "Noesen did not know, nor did he attempt to ascertain, when [Amanda] Renz needed to start the new pack of pills or how many doses she would miss if the prescription was not filled that day."[127] Amanda then went to a Wal-Mart pharmacy to have the prescription filled.[128] However, when the Wal-Mart pharmacist called K-Mart to transfer the prescription, Noesen again refused to cooperate or provide the necessary information, stating that he believed it would "constitute participating in contraception."[129]

Amanda did not receive her prescription until two days later, after missing the first dose.[130] Not only did Noesen refuse to fill the prescription, he also refused to transfer it to a pharmacist willing to provide Amanda birth control.[131] In rural areas such as Menomonie, Wisconsin, being refused prescription medications based on religious objections can pose extreme burdens on patients. For women, it further exposes them to stigmatization, shaming, emotional distress, and the possibility of litigation to receive basic medical accommodations.

4 Married and Refused Emergency Contraception and Other Chilling Narratives

I couldn't believe it . . . how can they make that decision for us? I was outraged. – Kathleen Pulz[132]

121 *Id.* at 388 n.2. 122 *Id.* 123 *Id.* at 389.

124 *See In re* Disciplinary Proceedings Against Noesen, No. 01 PHM 080 (Wis. Pharmacy Examining Bd. Apr. 13, 2005), ¶¶ 21–25.

125 *Id.* ¶ 42. 126 Noesen, *supra* note 115, at 389. 127 *Id.* 128 *Id.* 129 *Id.*

130 *See In re* Disciplinary Proceedings Against Noesen, No. 01 PHM 080 (Wis. Pharmacy Examining Bd. Apr. 13, 2005), ¶¶ 24, 43.

131 A prescription transfer must be completed by communication between two pharmacists. *See* Wis. Admin. Code Phar § 7.055(1)(a) (2006).

132 Stein, *supra* note 11 (quoting Pulz).

The reach of religious refusals extends even to married women. For example, when Kathleen Pulz and her husband thought their regular method of birth control, a prophylactic condom, made them susceptible to an unintended pregnancy after it broke, Kathleen sought emergency contraception at the local Walgreens in Milwaukee, Wisconsin.[133] The pharmacy, however, refused to fill the emergency prescription. Pulz and her husband worried that they could not afford a fifth child. Pulz did not know that Walgreens and several other pharmacies allow their pharmacists to refuse to dispense medications based on religious objections. Pulz considered herself lucky because she ultimately obtained the medication directly from her doctor. Often patients are able to obtain their medications elsewhere, but the toll on them may be traumatizing and extreme.[134] In 2013, Walgreen executives said they would review its policy and do additional training with employees to ensure that prescriptions for birth control "are handled as efficiently as other prescriptions without imposing any burden on the customer."[135]

Sometimes, religious refusals are life and death matters. In December 2010, when Tenesha Means was eighteen weeks pregnant, her water broke and she went to Mercy Health Partners ("MHP"), a Catholic hospital and the only hospital within thirty minutes of her home.[136] Despite the urgency of her health condition, Means was sent home and told to consult with her doctor at an appointment she had scheduled for more than a week later.[137] The next day, Means returned to MHP bleeding and experiencing painful contractions but was again sent home. That night, Means again returned to MHP "in pain, in distress, and with signs of an infection."[138] MHP was preparing to send her home again when the fetus's feet breached her cervix and she began to deliver.[139] The baby died shortly after birth.[140] At no time was Means informed

133 *Id.* 134 *See, e.g., id.*

135 Tara Culp-Ressler, *Walgreens Will Update Its Contraception Policy After Pharmacists Refused To Sell Plan B To Men*, THINK PROGRESS (Jan. 24, 2013), https://thinkprogress.org/walgreens-will-update-its-contraception-policy-after-pharmacists-refused-to-sell-plan-b-to-men-f4cf6116adcc/.

136 Complaint at 2, Means v. U.S. Conference of Catholic Bishops, No. 2:13CV14916, 2013 (E.D. Mich. Nov. 28, 2013) Complaint at 2, Means v. U.S. Conference of Catholic Bishops, No. 2:13CV14916, 2013 (E.D. Mich. Nov. 28, 2013) (alleging negligence against the United States Conference for Catholic Bishops "for promulgating and implementing directives that cause pregnant women who are suffering from a miscarriage to be denied appropriate medical care"), transferred 15-CV-353, BL 208136 (W.D. Mich. June 30, 2015) (dismissing claim for failure to show a cognizable injury), *aff'd*, 836 F.3d 643 (6th Cir. 2016) (concluding that "present physical injury" to state a claim for negligence, for which "physical and mental pain, emotional injuries, a riskier delivery, shock and emotional trauma from making funeral arrangements for her dead child, and other 'discomforts and pain'" would not suffice).

137 *Id.* 138 *Id.* at 2–3. 139 *Id.* at 3. 140 *Id.*

that her fetus had no chance of surviving and that continuing her pregnancy would pose a serious risk to her health, including infection and possible death.[141] Nor was Means informed that the safest treatment option was to induce labor and terminate the pregnancy. Doctors refused to provide this information based on religious grounds, although she alleges it caused direct pain and injury to her.[142]

In Brittany Cartrett's case, at Walmart in Milledgeville, Georgia – where she previously worked – the pharmacist refused to fill a prescription for Misoprostol, a drug that causes the uterus to expel its contents and so "can be used both in abortions and to treat incomplete miscarriages."[143] Brittany's doctor prescribed the drug because she miscarried during the first trimester of her pregnancy.[144] She decided against a surgical procedure to remove the fetus, opting instead to "pass [the fetus] naturally" to avoid "the more invasive route."[145] Her doctor prescribed Misoprostol for that reason. However, the pharmacist, Cartrett said, told her, "I couldn't think of a reason why you would need that prescription."[146]

So the drug was not filled at Walmart. Brittany had to find another pharmacist to procure the drug. When one reporter contacted Walmart, she was told, "the pharmacist had a professional judgment call against filling the prescription, not any other reason. They're well within their rights, the pharmacists, to not agree that a specific prescription should be filled."[147] However, Brittany feared that if this tragic situation happened to her, there might be other women who experienced similar refusals during miscarriage. "This has to stop," she said on Facebook.[148] Upon hearing her story, other women in Georgia contacted Brittany sharing similar encounters – in one case, the woman opted for the abortion when pharmacists refused to dispense the prescription to help with her miscarriage.[149] While not all the costs imposed

141 *Id.* at 2–3. 142 *Id.* at 3.

143 Brittany Cartrett, *I Was Judged and Convicted by a Walmart Pharmacist*, Tampa Bay Times (Apr. 15, 2015), www.tampabay.com/news/humaninterest/i-was-judged-and-convicted-by-a-walmart-pharmacist/2225646. *See also Misoprostol, Uses*, WebMD, www.webmd.com/drugs/2/drug-6111/misoprostol-oral/details.

144 Noelle Kachinsky, *Milledgeville Pharmacist Refuses to Fill Prescription for Miscarriage Patient*, WGXA TV News (Apr. 10, 2015), wgxa.tv/news/local/milledgeville-pharmacist-refuses-to-fill-prescription-for-miscarriage-patient.

145 *Id.*

146 Amanda Marcotte, A *Miscarrying Woman Was Denied Medication Because of "Conscience,"* Slate (Apr. 14, 2015, 3:14 PM), www.slate.com/blogs/xx_factor/2015/04/14/miscarrying_woman_denied_medication_misoprostol_can_be_used_for_both_abortion.html.

147 Molly Redden, *The Scary Law that Allowed Pharmacists to Deny this Woman the Drugs She Needed After Her Miscarriage*, Mother Jones (Apr. 16, 2015, 10:33 AM), www.motherjones.com/politics/2015/04/pharmacists-refused-woman-drugs-miscarriage-walmart.

148 Cartree, *supra* note 146. 149 Redden, *supra* note 150.

on women have been of the same magnitude, none would be tolerated if imposed upon persons on account of their race.

B *The Legal Landscape*

Why should healthcare providers' discriminatory religious views acquire legal legitimacy and authority in the denial of women's reproductive-related healthcare services, including when a patient's life is at risk? Such discrimination would not be tolerated based on race, even though racial prejudices emerge in the medical setting. Religious exceptionalism suggests two important, but problematic ideas, which should be rejected. First, religious exceptionalism casts a hierarchy within law and establishes the ordering of legal rights. In other words, proponents of religious exceptionalism perceive it to take precedence over other fundamental rights and liberty interests. Second, as a result, religiously based rights and individuals protected by such interests need not conform to general principles, normal rules, or nondiscriminatory practices.

The First Amendment's Free Exercise of Religion Clause does not grant a constitutional right to impose harms or inflict injuries on others.[150] So where does the confusion on reproductive healthcare emerge, leading some to believe that law grants them a religious right to discriminate against women who seek to control their bodily autonomy? The answer may reside in the fact that some states and the federal government carve out religious exceptions or exemptions for individuals with sincerely held religious beliefs.[151] However, such laws should not serve as legal justification to inflict harm on women nor for permitting discrimination whether based on sex, sexual orientation, race, or other factors.

As a normative matter, states should not enforce religious exemptions in the delivery of medicine, specifically reproductive healthcare. In Chapter 2, this volume, Michael Helfand argues that RFRA will not really impose strict scrutiny but would be an exercise in weighing. However, under such an analysis, women's interests will be lost. Under what circumstances or framework then are women's interests evaluated? In Hefland's analysis, it then becomes a weighing of administrability versus religious believers – rather than women's interests in controlling reproduction, which I find problematic.

The substantial risks and undue burdens experienced by patients dictate that permitting religious exemptions in these contexts relegates women to a subordinate citizenship status. Essentially, women become second-class citizens, unable to acquire preventative medicines – sometimes even if their lives are at risk as described earlier. Instantiated in medical providers denying

[150] *See* Helfand, Chapter 2, this volume; Sepper, Chapter 1, this volume. [151] *Id.*

women reproductive health services and requiring that they seek services elsewhere are biases, stereotyping, and shaming unaccepted in the Supreme Court's jurisprudence on race, but seemingly tolerated in relation to sex.[152]

Indeed, powerful analogies in the denial of accommodations to African Americans fifty years ago offer a lens to view this type of discrimination. Washington Booker, an African American who remembers experiencing discrimination in Birmingham, Alabama, restaurants recalled to National Public Radio, "you may not remember all the other discrimination, but the fact that you couldn't go into Newberry's and sit at the counter . . . kind of bothered you."[153] Often, white Americans who sought to exempt themselves from providing accommodations to African Americans claimed that the refused services could be accommodated elsewhere or that they would suffer economic losses because white men and women would no longer patronize their establishments.[154] Importantly, the critical question here is not simply matters of convenience – although Southern segregationists and lawmakers certainly argued to local courts a half century ago – that African Americans could be schooled, fed, clothed, treated, and housed elsewhere.

In 2013, the Hurley Medical Center in Flint, Michigan, accommodated a request made by a parent that no African Americans tend to his newborn.[155] The father, who allegedly brandished a swastika tattoo, alerted a nurse that African Americans were not to touch or care for his baby. To comply with the father's request, hospital officials removed Nurse Tonya Battle, an African American, from care of the child in the Neonatal Intensive Care Unit and reassigned a white nurse.[156] Allegedly, the nurse manager claimed in a

[152] *See, e.g.*, United States v. Virginia, 518 U.S. 515 (1996).

[153] Andrew Yeager, *Forced To Seat Blacks, Ala. Restaurant Complied With History*, NPR (Dec. 13, 2014) (quoting Washington Booker).

[154] *Id.* (interviewing Ollie McClung, Jr., who recalled his father suing to keep his restaurant segregated, "McClung and his dad were concerned that seating blacks would drive away white patrons. So they sued."); Randall L. Kennedy, *Struggle for Racial Equality in Public Accommodations, in* Legacies of the 1964 Civil Rights Act (Bernard Grofman, ed., 2000); Heart of Atlanta Motel v. United States, 379 U.S. 241 (1964); Lombard v. Louisiana, 373 U.S. 267, 272 (1963) (restaurant manager informing black customers, "I am not allowed to serve you here ... We *have* to sell to you at the rear of the store where we have a colored counter."); *id.* at 275 (Douglas, J., concurring) ("But a restaurant, like the other departments of this retail store where Negroes were served, though private property within the protection of the Fifth Amendment, has no aura of constitutionally protected privacy about it. Access by the public is the very reason for its existence."); Garner v. Louisiana, 368 U.S. 157, 160 (1961) (describing how black patrons were informed that "they could be served at the counter across the aisle which served Negroes," but not the main counter).

[155] Robin Erb, *Nurse Sues After Hospital Grants Dad's Racial Request*, USA Today (Feb. 18, 2013), www.usatoday.com/story/news/nation/2013/02/18/black-nurse-lawsuit-father-request-granted/1928253/.

[156] *Id.*

meeting that she could sympathize with the father, "comparing it to a German caring for a Jew."[157] According to Battle's lawsuit, hospital staff posted a note next to the baby's name on the assignment clipboard: "NO AFRICAN AMERICAN NURSE TO TAKE CARE OF BABY."[158]

In that case, the Equal Opportunity Commission investigated, found wrongful discrimination, and settled the lawsuit, negotiating a financial settlement for the African American nurse and establishing a five-year monitoring protocol and training for hospital employees.[159] Even so, what distinguishes that case from others discussed in this chapter is that these women were all *denied* care. Unlike the father who desired to have only whites care for his child and was accommodated, the women discussed in this chapter sought medications and treatment and were all refused.

III CONCLUSION

Arguments advancing sincerely held religious beliefs can be deployed not only as mighty swords but also asserted as legally blessed means of discriminating against protected classes. To this end, constitutional and statutory rights given to objectors extend beyond legitimately protecting religious minorities from state, societal, and institutional discrimination, to granting priority in a ranking of rights. They permit even cruel discrimination in the advancement of claimed religious rights. Religious exceptionalism of this sort misreads the Constitution, exceeds what legislators should authorize, and establishes problematic norms.

Ultimately, granting healthcare providers authority to discriminate based on religion politicizes their roles and creates negative societal, legal, and medical impacts. In this context, physicians, nurses, and religious institutions wear two hats: that of healthcare providers and that of state-licensed entities entitled to discriminate. Wearing these hats, healthcare providers exercise significant authority over a decision that properly belongs to women and their partners: whether or not to conceive children and form families.

157 Katie Couric, *A Shocking Case of Racial Discrimination in a Hospital*, YOUTUBE (Mar. 6, 2013), www.youtube.com/watch?v=cwtl93lJyHM.

158 Erb, *supra* note 158 (emphasis added). Such instances of using racial preferences in the medical setting raise questions about the permissibility of such practices – not only as a legal matter, but also as matters of health and bioethics. *See generally* Kimani Paul-Emile, *Patients' Racial Preferences and the Medical Culture of Accommodation*, 60 UCLA L. REV. 462 (2012).

159 *See* Gary Ridley, *Hurley Settles Race Discrimination Complaint That Claimed Black Nurses Were Banned from Treating White Baby in Flint*, M LIVE (Sept. 27, 2013, 10:44 AM), www.mlive.com/news/flint/index.ssf/2013/09/hurley_settles_race_discrimina.html%23incart_story_package.

4

Contraceptive Access and Religious Liberty
Can We Afford to Protect Both?

Mark L. Rienzi

Professor of Law, The Catholic University of America, Columbus School of Law, and Senior Counsel at the Becket Fund for Religious Liberty, Visiting Professor, Harvard Law School

In 2005, Illinois Governor Rod Blagojevich made national news by requiring that every pharmacy in the State dispense all forms of contraception, including emergency contraception.[1] To pharmacists Luke Vanderbleek and Glenn Kosirog, the rule created a crisis.[2] Each had spent his entire adult life as a pharmacist and pharmacy owner. Vanderbleek operated several small-town pharmacies and Kosirog ran his family's pharmacy in Chicago. Each believed that emergency contraception could destroy an innocent human life, and that selling emergency contraception in his store was therefore sinful. They could not comply with the State's requirement, but failure to comply would mean losing the only career either had ever known.

The State was also quite serious about its requirement. Health officials argued that access to contraception is important for millions of women in Illinois. They explained that timely and convenient access to emergency contraception – which is most effective when taken within a few days of having sex – was particularly important.[3] In the State's eyes, pharmacists

[1] Leah Thorsen, *Druggists Suspended in Debate over Pill*, St. Louis Post-Dispatch (Nov. 30, 2005), at A1, 2005 WLNR 24319411.

[2] For a general review of the claims and case, see Deborah L. Shelton, *Appeals Court Sides with Pharmacists in Emergency Contraceptives Case: 2 Men Had Claimed Dispensing "Morning-After Pill" Violated their Religious Beliefs*, Chicago Tribune (Sept. 22, 2012), articles.chicagotribune.com/2012–09-22/news/ct-met-emergency-contraceptives-20120922_1_emergency-contraceptives-conscience-act-pharmacists.

[3] Dawn Turner Price, *Time to Revisit Health Care's Conscience Act*, Chicago Tribune (Feb. 6, 2006), articles.chicagotribune.com/2006–02-06/news/0602060173_1_emergency-contraception-health-care-health-care; U.S. Food and Drug Administration, *Birth Control Guide*, www.fda.gov/downloads/ForConsumers/ByAudience/ForWomen/FreePublications/UCM517406.pdf.

such as Vanderbleek and Kosirog posed an unfair impediment to women seeking access to lawful treatments they have every right to obtain.

Such conflicts over contraception and religious liberty can seem intractable. Both sides present claims of deeply personal rights – a believer's right to religious exercise and a consumer's right to access contraceptives – in a way that suggests one side must lose for the other to win. Similar winner-take-all claims appear on the surface of other disputes about contraception, such as the federal government's recent effort to make religious colleges and employers include free contraceptive coverage in student and employee health plans. Add in the obvious culture war heat that accompanies any dispute related to abortion, and conflicts about contraception and religious liberty would appear to be insoluble.

But it turns out these conflicts are actually rather easy to resolve. In fact, the past decade of litigation over these issues has proven, time and again, that contraceptive access and religious liberty can coexist well. While headlines might scream that it is a zero-sum game,[4] the actual facts on the ground and in court show that there is room for everyone to win. Religious liberty can be respected without creating any threat to healthcare for anyone.

Ultimately, the far greater threat to healthcare access comes not from pharmacists who cannot dispense certain contraceptives or from employers who cannot include them in a health plan, but from government policies that unwittingly reduce access rather than expand it. Experience has now taught us that forcing religious pharmacists to distribute contraceptives will not increase the supply of contraceptives – but it will decrease the supply of pharmacies and pharmacists. Similarly, forcing religious organizations to include contraceptives in student and employee health plans will not increase access to contraceptives, but rather decrease the availability of student and employee health plans and threaten the existence of religious social service organizations that often serve our most vulnerable citizens.

This chapter considers these issues in three parts. Section I briefly discusses the reasons that people on all sides of these disputes view contraception as deeply important. Section II explores what we can learn from the past decade of litigation over whether pharmacists should be forced to provide all types of contraception, including emergency contraception. Section II also discusses how that litigation demonstrates that both interests, broad contraceptive access and religious liberty, can be served simultaneously. Section III then discusses the still-ongoing litigation by groups such as the Little Sisters of the Poor over

[4] Marilyn Gardner, *Pharmacists' Moral Beliefs vs. Women's Legal Rights*, CHRISTIAN SCI. MONITOR (Apr. 26, 2004), at 11, www.csmonitor.com/2004/0426/p11s01-usju.html.

the federal government's mandate that employers provide employee health plans that include free access to all contraceptives. Although that litigation has not concluded, its progress to date, as well as the U.S. Supreme Court's recent unanimous opinion in *Zubik v. Burwell* focusing on available alternatives,[5] confirms that there are many ways that our society can have both broad access to contraceptives and healthy respect for religious diversity.

As this chapter illustrates, healthcare is not improved by demanding one moral orthodoxy or another from all those who would provide services. We need not agree about the morality of contraception to agree on a solution that protects everyone's rights. If we are serious about expanding access to healthcare of all kinds – not only contraceptives, but also heart medications, AIDS drugs, and cancer treatments – then we are best served by embracing pluralism and welcoming the contributions of a wide variety of people, including those with minority religious beliefs. People of good faith can often find ways to balance religious diversity and access to healthcare in a manner that advances both interests. The contraceptive cases demonstrate how easy it is to get that balance right, and how costly it is to get it wrong.

I THE IMPORTANCE OF CONTRACEPTION FOR ALL SIDES

It is not surprising that contraception is an issue that sometimes raises sharp disagreements. After all, people on all sides rightfully believe that conception, the event contraception is principally designed to avoid, is deeply important.

People who object to using or providing others with some or all types of contraception tend to do so because they believe that the creation of new human life is an event of enormous moral significance.[6] That is particularly true where contraceptives may act not only by preventing conception from occurring but also by interfering with the implantation of an already formed

5 On May 16, 2016, the Supreme Court issued a unanimous per curiam opinion – meaning that the court itself renders a decision as a collective, rather than an individual judge writing for a majority of the court. Zubik v. Burwell, 136 S. Ct. 1557 (2016). Justice Sonia Sotomayor also filed a concurring opinion, in which Justice Ruth Bader Ginsburg joined.

6 Little Sisters of the Poor Home for the Aged, Denver, Colo. v. Burwell, 794 F.3d 1151, 1167 (10th Cir.), *vacated and remanded sub nom*; Zubik v. Burwell, 136 S. Ct. 1557 (2016) (noting that the Little Sisters cannot "violate their public witness to the sanctity of human life and human dignity"); *see also* Burwell v. Hobby Lobby Stores, Inc., 134 S. Ct. 2751, 2765 (2014) ("It is therefore 'against [their] moral conviction to be involved in the termination of human life' after conception, which they believe is a 'sin against God to which they are held accountable.'").

embryo after conception.[7] It is on this basis that some people who do not generally object to using or providing contraceptives nonetheless object to the class of "emergency contraceptives." They believe that conception is an important enough event that it would be sinful for them to provide drugs that might work post-conception to terminate human life.[8]

On the other side of the dispute, those who seek contraceptives or argue for expanded contraceptive access tend to do so not because they think conception is unimportant, but rather because they too believe that the creation of new human life is highly significant and personal.[9] Indeed, conceiving a child is so significant and personal that contraceptive advocates seek maximal autonomy to decide when and whether to conceive.[10] Those who favor access to emergency contraceptives likewise do so because they believe it critically important to empower women to avoid or end pregnancy as early as possible.[11]

The Supreme Court was thus surely right to observe nearly forty years ago that "decisions whether to accomplish or to prevent conception" are particularly sensitive.[12] Indeed, decisions relating to procreation and contraception "involve[e] the most intimate and personal choices a person may make in a lifetime," and they certainly implicate, for all involved, "one's own concept

7 As the government acknowledged and as the Supreme Court found in Hobby Lobby, some FDA-approved methods of contraception "may have the effect of preventing an already fertilized egg from developing any further by inhibiting its attachment to the uterus." Hobby Lobby, *supra* note 6, at 2762–63 (citing brief of HHS and FDA, Birth Control: Medicines to Help You). Manufacturers of emergency contraceptives have likewise acknowledged that the drugs may work by altering the endometrium and inhibiting implantation of an already fertilized egg. *See* Ella Prescribing Information, www.accessdata.fda.gov/drugsatfda_docs/label/2010/022474s000lbl.pdf. For a summary of medical views indicating that human life begins at conception (i.e., before implantation, *contra* Goodwin, Chapter 3, this volume, at 73) *see* American College of Pediatricians, *When Human Life Begins* (March 2017), www.acpeds.org/the-college-speaks/position-statements/life-issues/when-human-life-begins.

8 Holly Lobby, *supra* note 6, at 2778 ("The Hahns and Greens believe that providing the coverage demanded by the HHS regulations is connected to the destruction of an embryo in a way that is sufficient to make it immoral for them to provide the coverage. This belief implicates a difficult and important question of religion and moral philosophy, namely, the circumstances under which it is wrong for a person to perform an act that is innocent in itself but that has the effect of enabling or facilitating the commission of an immoral act by another.").

9 For a view that creating a life together should create duties between the adults separate from child support itself, see Weiner, Chapter 11, this volume.

10 The Institute of Medicine, which originally recommended the specific drugs to be covered as preventative care services, said it premised inclusion of contraceptives on the dual goals of protecting public health and gender equity. *See, e.g.*, Coverage of Preventive Services Under the ACA, 77 Fed. Reg. 8725, 8729 (Feb. 15, 2012) (to be codified at 29 C.F.R. pt. 54) (citing Inst. of Med., Clinical Preventive Services for Women: Closing the Gaps 16 (2011)).

11 *See* Goodwin, Chapter 3, this volume.

12 Carey v. Population Servs. Int'l, 431 U.S. 678, 685 (1977).

of existence . . . and of the meaning of human life."[13] It is precisely because of this important nature of decisions about contraception that the Court found a constitutional right to use contraception in the first place,[14] and that some religious people believe they cannot use or provide certain types of contraception to others.

II CONTRACEPTION AND RELIGIOUS LIBERTY AT THE PHARMACY

The past decade of litigation over contraception and religious liberty in the pharmacy context offers several important lessons about healthcare, religious liberty, and the availability of win-win solutions that maximize both interests.

In April 2005, Illinois Governor Rod Blagojevich announced that Illinois would be the first state in the nation to require pharmacies to dispense contraception.[15] Governor Blagojevich cited reports that two women had recently been unable to fill contraceptive prescriptions at a pharmacy in Chicago.[16] Explaining that, in his view, the refusals in Chicago seemed to be "part of a concerted effort to deny women access to birth control," Governor Blagojevich said that while pharmacists "may be getting away with this in other states . . . here in Illinois, we are not going to let that happen."[17] The perceived problem focused on the need for emergency contraceptives, so the government's rule targeted pharmacies that provided standard contraception but would not carry emergency contraception.[18]

To Illinois, issuing the emergency contraception rule was simply a matter of public health.[19] Women have a lawful right to use and obtain contraceptives, including emergency contraception. Illinois viewed pharmacists and pharmacies refusing to fill lawful prescriptions in a timely fashion as making access to contraceptives more difficult, and therefore required all pharmacies to fill all contraceptive prescriptions in a timely fashion. As Governor Blagojevich explained, he wanted to ensure that contraceptive

13 Planned Parenthood of Southeastern Pennsylvania v. Casey, 505 U.S. 833, 851 (1993) (plurality).

14 Griswold v. Connecticut, 381 U.S. 479 (1965).

15 Office of the Governor, Gov. Blagojevich Takes Emergency Action to Protect Women's Access to Contraceptives (Apr. 1, 2005), www3.illinois.gov/PressReleases/pressreleaseslistshow.cfm?recnum=3805.

16 *Id.* 17 *Id.*

18 See Morr-Fitz, Inc. v. Blagojevich, 2011 WL 1338081 (Ill Cir. Ct. 2011), at *2 (charting how Illinois' rule "was drafted with the Plaintiffs in mind").

19 Press Release, *supra* note 15.

prescriptions were filled without regard to personal views, "No delays. No hassles. No lectures."[20]

Illinois made clear that it understood that some pharmacists and pharmacy owners could not dispense emergency contraceptives because of their religious beliefs. According to the government, however, "it is not the responsibility of the State of Illinois to accommodate those beliefs."[21] Instead, the State insisted that pharmacies "must fill prescriptions without making moral judgments. Pharmacists – like everyone else – are free to hold personal religious beliefs, but pharmacies are not free to let those beliefs stand in the way of their obligation to their customers."[22] Pharmacists who could not dispense emergency contraception for religious reasons were offered a simple solution: they should "find another profession."[23]

To Luke Vanderbleek and Glenn Kosirog, two pharmacy owners and pharmacists who believe selling emergency contraception is forbidden by their Christian religious beliefs, the new rule put them in what felt like an impossible position. They had practiced their professions for decades without complaint or incident. But they could not do what the government was now demanding. Because of Illinois's new law, they would have to give up their careers and close their stores, move to another state to practice, or seek protection in the courts. The pharmacists went to court, launching a lawsuit that would last eight years. While very long lawsuits are often wasteful and unproductive, this lawsuit actually yielded important results that should

[20] Monica Davey, *Illinois Pharmacies Ordered to Provide Birth Control*, N.Y. Times (Apr. 2, 2005), www.nytimes.com/2005/04/02/us/illinois-pharmacies-ordered-to-provide-birth-control.html; *see also* Press Release, Office of the Governor, Gov. Blagojevich Moves to Make Emergency Contraceptives Rule Permanent (Apr. 18, 2005), www4.illinois.gov/PressReleases/ShowPressRelease.cfm?SubjectID=3&RecNum=3862.

[21] Morr-Fitz, *supra* note 18, at *2, ("Secretary of the Illinois Department of Financial and Professional Regulation ('IDFPR') Fernando Grillo announced that the Rule would make sure the drugstore counter 'will not become a place to debate' religious beliefs, and that 'it is not the responsibility of the State of Illinois to accommodate those beliefs.'" *See* Letter to Chicago Tribune (Apr. 16, 2005) (Trial Ex. H to the Complaint filed in Morr-Fitz, Inc. v. Blagojevich) ("We are telling pharmacies ... they can't let an individual pharmacist's personal beliefs" interfere with selling contraceptives.). While at times the government suggested that pharmacies themselves could accommodate religious objections, Governor Blagojevich also applauded Walgreens for firing several pharmacists who could not dispense emergency contraception because of their religion. *See* Menges v. Blagojevich, 451 F. Supp. 2d 992, 998 (C.D. Ill. 2006).

[22] Statement of Governor Rod Blagojevich, Office of the Governor, In Response to Lawsuit Filed by Pat Robertson's American Center for Law and Justice Challenging Governor's Emergency Rule for Pharmacies (Apr. 13, 2005), www4.illinois.gov/PressReleases/ShowPressRelease.cfm?SubjectID=3&RecNum=3849&SubjectID=3&RecNum=3849.

[23] Morr-Fitz, *supra* note 18, at *2.

eliminate concerns on all sides about a perceived conflict between contraceptive access and religious liberty.[24]

First and foremost, the litigation demonstrated that women in Illinois already had broad access to emergency contraception, and that the handful of religious objectors were not stopping anyone from getting the healthcare they sought. Indeed, despite Governor Blagojevich's statements, the State had no evidence that even a single woman had been unable to obtain emergency contraception because of a religious objection. As the trial judge found, Illinois women actually had many willing sellers of emergency contraception – so many that there was "no evidence of a single person who ever was unable to obtain emergency contraception because of a religious objection."[25] Nor was there any evidence that anyone was having difficulties finding willing sellers of emergency contraceptives, either over the counter at pharmacies or on the Internet.[26]

None of this should have been surprising. The court found that the pharmacies challenging the government's rule were all "within either reasonably close walking or driving distance to emergency contraception distributors," and that "emergency contraception [wa]s also available over the internet."[27] The evidence was particularly weak regarding Kosirog, whose pharmacy was located in Chicago with "more than a dozen competitors within three miles and one within three blocks."[28] Even though Vanderbleek's stores were located in more rural areas, each store was only a few minutes' walk away from another provider and had "more than a dozen competitors within a fifteen-minute drive."[29]

The government's inability to find even a single person who was actually unable to get contraception was not for lack of effort. Across eight years of litigation, the government tried many different approaches to find women who had actually been stopped from getting the contraception they wanted because of a religious objection. Among other things, Illinois (1) sent letters to all physicians in Illinois asking them to report any pharmacy or pharmacist that failed to provide contraceptives,[30] (2) set up special websites to allow women to lodge complaints against pharmacies and pharmacists who interfered with

[24] Documents filed in connection with the lawsuit are available through Bloomberg. *See* Morr-Fitz, Inc. Dba Fitzgerald P et al. vs. Rod R. Blagojevich et al., Docket No. 2005-CH-000495 (Ill. Cir. Ct. Sept. 14, 2005).

[25] Morr-Fitz, *supra* note 18, at *2.

[26] *Id.* Although lower-income people may not have Internet access, public libraries partially fill this gap.

[27] *Id.* [28] *Id.* [29] *Id.*

[30] Dear Physician Letter from Governor Rod Blagojevich, Apr. 26, 2005 ("If you or your patients experience any problems, please let us know by calling us at 1–800-280–4149. I have also

access,[31] (3) posted signs and hotline telephone numbers in every pharmacy in the state advising women how to inform state officials of problems obtaining contraceptives,[32] and (4) provided specially trained government workers to assist women in lodging complaints.[33] However, all of these efforts to unearth real contraceptive access problems failed, forcing the government to admit that the health impact from religious objectors was at most "minimal"; the Court found "no evidence of a single person" who could not obtain the contraceptive she wanted.[34] A trial court permanently enjoined Illinois' evolving regulations as violating the Illinois Health Care Right of Conscience Act ("Conscience Act") and its state Religious Freedom Restoration Act – an injunction later affirmed because the Illinois Conscience Act "protects plaintiffs' decisions not to dispense emergency contraceptives due to their conscience beliefs."[35]

enclosed a flyer with our hotline that you can post to let your patients know that they are entitled to have their prescriptions filled.") (on file with author).

31 Press Release, Office of the Governor, Governor Blagojevich Introduces New Rule to Ensure Women's Access to Prescription Contraceptives After New Tactic to Deny Women Access to Birth Control Surfaces (Mar. 27, 2006), www4.illinois.gov/PressReleases/ShowPressRelease.cfm?SubjectID=1&RecNum=4738&SubjectID=1&RecNum=4738 (announcing new rules "that will require every drug store to post a sign . . . [including] IDFPR's toll-free pharmacy hotline number, 800–280-4149, and website, www.contraceptives.illinois.gov/complaint.cfm, where a customer can file a complaint if they believe they were treated unfairly").

32 Press Release, *supra* note 15 ("The Governor introduced a new toll-free number where women can report to state regulators if a pharmacy fails to dispense a prescription contraceptive in an appropriate and timely manner. The toll-free number is 1–800-280–4149 and the complaint unit at IDFPR has been specially trained to handle pharmacy complaints.").

33 *Id.*

34 Morr-Fitz, *supra* note 18, at *2. To be sure, opponents of allowing for religious exemptions claim that pharmacists have done more than refuse to process a prescription for contraceptives and have refused to return a prescription when asked. *See* Goodwin, Chapter 3, this volume, at 79–85. But no one has ever successfully asserted a religious right to hold a prescription hostage rather than simply return it; and the frequency and harm from such occurrences is apparently so minimal that Illinois could offer no evidence of the practice actually happening. In any case, the pharmacists at issue had a policy of politely returning prescriptions, not confiscating them. Morr-Fitz, Inc. v. Quinn, 2012 IL App (4th) 110398, ¶ 32, 976 N.E.2d 1160, 1168.

35 Morr-Fitz, Inc. v. Quinn, 976 N.E.2d 1160, 1176 (Ill. App. Ct. 2012) (affirming in part as modified and reversing in part and ultimately concluding that Illinois' rules violated Illinois' Health Care Right of Conscience Act (745 Ill. Comp. Stat. Ann. 70/1–14 (West 2010)), mooting the need to decide whether the rules violated the Illinois Religious Freedom Restoration Act (775 Ill. Comp. Stat. Ann. 35/1–99 (West 2010)), or the First Amendment's Free Exercise Clause). The state amended the Conscience Act in 2017 in an attempt to force religious objectors to give referrals to direct patients to willing providers. *See* Illinois Public Act 099–0690 (Senate Bill 1564), ilga.gov/legislation/BillStatus.asp?DocNum=1564&GAID=13&DocTypeID=SB&LegID=88256&SessionID=88&SpecSess=&Session=&GA=99. That provision has been enjoined under the First Amendment's protection against compelled speech

Both advocates of contraceptive access and advocates of religious liberty should be happy with these results. They demonstrate that there is ample room in our society for both the occasional pharmacy that will not sell every drug due to religious objections and for broad access to emergency contraception. It turns out that our pluralistic society is big enough and diverse enough that we can provide women with the contraceptives they want *and* allow a few pharmacists and pharmacies to step aside from providing a given service for religious reasons.

Nor are these results unique to Illinois. Washington State enacted a similar law and litigated the issue for many years with remarkably similar results.[36] The Washington law was actually more restrictive than Illinois' rules. While it was possible to satisfy the Illinois law through a process known as "facilitated referral," where the pharmacist essentially assists the patient in finding a nearby pharmacy that carries the same drug (something some, but not all, objecting pharmacists believe they can do),[37] Washington actually moved to forbid this practice.

Owners of a family-owned pharmacy, Stormans, at Ralph's Thriftway, together with two individual pharmacists, challenged Washington's law. Just as in Illinois, several years of litigation elapses before the case was tried.[38] And just as in Illinois, the trial court found that women already

requirements. Pregnancy Care Center of Rockford v. Rauner, No. 2016-MR-741 (Ill. Cir. Ct. 2016), www.adfmedia.org/files/OrderGrantingPrelimInjunction.pdf.

36 *See generally* Stormans, Inc. v. Selecky, 844 F. Supp. 2d 1172 (W.D. Wash. 2012), *reversed sub nom*. Stormans, Inc. v. Wiseman 794 F.3d 1064 (9th Cir. 2015).

37 Ed Whelan, *Pharmacists' Conscience Rights on Trial – The 2007 Regulations*, National Review (Dec. 15, 2011), www.nationalreview.com/bench-memos/285898/pharmacists-conscience-rights-trial-2007-regulations-ed-whelan www.nationalreview.com/bench-memos/285898/pharmacists-conscience-rights-trial-2007-regulations-ed-whelan.

38 This case followed a tortuous route before ending with the dispositive decision of the Ninth Circuit and the denial of certiorari by the Supreme Court. In 2007, the district court granted a preliminary injunction. Stormans, Inc. v. Selecky, 524 F. Supp. 2d 1245 (W.D. Wash. 2007). On appeal, the Ninth Circuit denied the stay motion. Stormans, Inc. v. Selecky, 526 F.3d 406 (9th Cir. 2008). Then, it reversed and remanded the trial court decision, finding the trial court had erroneously applied heightened scrutiny to the challenges regulation and the injunction was overbroad. Stormans, Inc. v. Selecky, 571 F.3d 960 (9th Cir. 2009). This opinion was superseded by an opinion on rehearing. Stormans, Inc. v. Selecky, 586 F.3d 1109 (9th Cir. 2009). The injunction was mooted by the parties' stipulation. Stormans, Inc. v. Selecky, 844 F. Supp. 2d 1172, 1180 (W.D. Wash. 2012). In the meantime, the agency reconsidered the underlying rule, but did not to add a conscience exception. *Id.* at 1180–81. It determined the regulation was not neutral as applied to the plaintiffs. *Id.* at 1201. The findings of fact and conclusions of law are reported at 854 F. Supp. 2d 925 (W.D. Wash, 2012). This decision was reversed on appeal, with the panel holding the plaintiffs had not established a fundamental right. Stormans, Inc. v. Wiesman, 794 F.3d 1064 (9th Cir. 2015). The Supreme Court denied certiorari in 2016. Stormans, Inc. v. 136 S. Ct. 2433 (2016).

had broad and easy access to emergency contraception despite the handful of religious objectors.[39] Like Illinois, Washington had been aggressively seeking evidence of women being unable to obtain contraceptives because of religious objectors, but had not found any.[40] Ultimately, Washington, like Illinois, had to admit that it had no evidence of even a single actual woman who was harmed.[41] And Washington, like Illinois, had been aggressively seeking evidence of problems – it just hadn't found any. The government was even ultimately forced to admit that the practice of "facilitated referral" that Washington was trying to outlaw was "often in the best interest of patients" and served to "help assure timely access" to drugs.[42]

Again, both supporters of contraceptive access and religious liberty should welcome this evidence. The experience in Washington confirms that the experience in Illinois is not unique, and that there is no reason to believe contraceptive access is inconsistent with religious liberty. Rather, both cases

39 As the Ninth Circuit found early in the case, "[t]he drug is generally available to Washington residents through pharmacies, physicians' offices, government health centers, hospital emergency rooms, Planned Parenthood, the Internet, and a toll-free hotline." Stormans, Inc. v. Selecky, 586 F.3d 1109, 1114 (9th Cir. 2009), *vacating* 571 F.3d 960 (9th Cir. 2009).

Moreover, "The record reflects that the Stormans' pharmacy at Ralph's Thriftway is located in Olympia, Washington, within a five-mile radius of approximately thirty other pharmacies." *Id.* at 991.

40 Stormans, 844 F. Supp. 2d at 1197 (noting that state "concedes that there was no evidence of a problem with access to Plan B prior to its 2007 rules.").

41 To be sure, Washington, like Illinois, allowed pharmacies and pharmacists to avoid selling emergency contraception for a whole host of *other* reasons besides religious disagreement. Indeed, the trial court found that Washington permitted pharmacies to decline to stock a drug "for a host of secular reasons," but not for "identical religiously-motivated conduct." *Stormans*, 844 F. Supp. 2d at 1190; *accord* Morr-Fitz, *supra* note 18, at *3 ("The Rule is also subject to a host of exceptions for what the government called 'common sense business realities.'"). The existence of so many secular exceptions to the rules further confirms that there was no access problem and that an additional pharmacy or two choosing not to sell emergency contraceptives would not be harmful.

42 Stormans, 794 F.3d at 1074 (government stipulated that "facilitated referrals are often in the best interest of patients, pharmacies, and pharmacists; that facilitated referrals do not pose a threat to timely access to lawfully prescribed medications[;] and that facilitated referrals help assure timely access to lawfully prescribed medications").

Some critics of allowing for religious diversity on these issues attempt to make up for the lack of an access problem by arguing that the government should punish religious objectors to spare customers from shame, stigma, or emotional distress when a pharmacy will not dispense a desired product. See Goodwin, Chapter 3, this volume, at 79–85. Such invitations for the government to punish one side or the other of a disagreement generally seem out of place in a liberal democracy – particularly one that zealously protects the right to engage in even nasty, hurtful, shaming speech. *See, e.g.* Syder v. Phelps. Furthermore, surely the "stigma, shame, and emotional distress," Goodwin, Chapter 3, this volume, at 78, of being forced out of one's profession by the government based on one's religion is both significant and harder to remedy than going to the next pharmacy.

show that even over a period of many years and with state governments actively seeking evidence that religious objectors posed a problem to contraceptive access, there simply was no evidence to be found. That is good news for all involved.

But there is bad news too – bad news that is worthy of our attention if we are serious about expanding access to healthcare. It turns out that by trying to force religious objectors to dispense emergency contraception, both Washington and Illinois actually risked making healthcare *worse* by making it harder for their citizens to obtain *all* drugs, not just contraceptives. For example, at least one pharmacy in Illinois closed because of the rule, leaving the town of Prophetstown without a pharmacy for nearly two years.[43] Several pharmacists were fired or suspended without pay from their jobs for refusing, for religious reasons, to fill prescriptions for emergency contraceptives.[44] Others chose to leave Illinois to practice their profession in friendlier states.[45] Surely others chose not to enter the profession at all after the Governor proclaimed that religious pharmacists needed to "find another profession." All of these incidents happened during a time when headlines across the country – and in Illinois – were already proclaiming a shortage of pharmacists.[46] Similar results

43 Morr-Fitz, v. Blagojevich, 901 N.E. 2d 373, 381 (Ill. 2008).

44 *See, e.g.*, Vandersand v. Wal-Mart Stores, Inc., 525 F. Supp. 2d 1052 (C.D. Ill. 2007) (denying employer's motion to dismiss in suit by employee pharmacist alleging that employer suspended the pharmacist without pay for refusing to dispense emergency contraceptives, in violation of Illinois's Conscience Act and Title VII's prohibition on religious discrimination). The parties settled. Vandersand v. Wal-Mart, Inc., Docket No. 3:06-cv-03292 (C.D. Ill. Dec 11, 2006), Court Docket, Bloomberg Law (on file with author); Menges v. Blagojevich, 451 F. Supp. 2d 992 (C.D. Ill. 2006) (alleging in suit by licensed pharmacists in Illinois that plaintiffs "lost their jobs at Walgreens because they would not comply with Illinois' new Rule"). The case was dismissed. Menges et al. v. Blagojevich et al., Docket No. 3:05-cv-03307 (C.D. Ill. Dec 21, 2005), Court Docket, Bloomberg Law (on file with author).

45 Casey Mattox, *Illinois' Illogical Attack on Conscience is Pennsylvania's Gain*, TOWNHALL (Oct. 2, 2012), townhall.com/columnists/caseymattox/2012/10/02/illinois_illogical_attack_on_conscience_is_pennsylvanias_gain (telling story of one pharmacist who left Illinois to practice elsewhere and concluding that "one pharmacist's story perfectly demonstrates the fundamental flaw at the core of any effort to deny freedom of conscience: compelled violations of conscience won't expand access, they'll reduce it").

46 Jim Ritter, *Area Nursing Shortage Keeps Getting Worse*, CHICAGO SUN-TIMES (Sept. 19, 2005), www.highbeam.com/doc/1N1-10D924AA75BDA120.html ("There's also a shortage of other health professionals . . . .There also aren't enough pharmacists . . . the Healthcare Council said."); Charlotte A. Kenreigh & Linda Timm Wagner, *The Pharmacist Shortage: Where Do We Stand*, MEDSCAPE (Jan. 13, 2006), www.medscape.com/viewarticle/521115_3 ("[C]urrent survey results indicate that the majority of the U.S. population live in areas that report at least a moderately high difficulty in filling pharmacist positions."); Margaret Stafford, *Pharmacist Shortage Worsens Nationwide*, WASH. POST (Nov. 7, 2005), www.washingtonpost.com/wp-dyn/content/article/2005/11/07/AR2005110700188.html ("The shortage of pharmacists, though, is not good for others in the medical field, or

were seen in Washington, where pharmacists were also fired or forced to relocate, and even the State acknowledged that some pharmacies would close when it enforced its rule.[47] Worse yet, despite the lack of harm, the easy availability of alternatives, and the dangers to the profession, an appeals court ultimately allowed Washington's rule to remain in force.[48]

And therein lies both the greatest irony and the greatest lesson of the Illinois and Washington pharmacist cases: in an effort to solve a problem that did not in fact exist, and in an effort to purge the pharmacy profession of pharmacists who could dispense all but a handful of drugs, these states actually pushed healthcare providers out of the field entirely. The religious pharmacist provides people with more than 99% of the drugs they seek, including most kinds of contraceptives. A closed pharmacy or a departed pharmacist gives them 0% of those drugs – no contraceptives (even those that were entirely unobjectionable), no heart medications, AIDS medications, cancer medications, or any other kinds of healthcare. Banning pharmacists from stepping aside from a small sliver of drug sales creates less healthcare for everyone.

The pharmacist cases thus demonstrate a few key truths about the intersection of religious liberty and healthcare. First, what initially seem like intractable conflicts where one side must lose for the other to win can often be resolved in ways that allow all interests to be met. Second, insisting on moral conformity from everyone who provides healthcare produces less healthcare, not more.[49] Our growing (and aging) population will be far better served if we

their patients, say those who have been watching the shortage worsen over the last decade.").

47 As the trial judge in Stormans found: "Specifically, it is undisputed that if Ralph's is forced to stock Plan B, it will have to close its pharmacy. And it is undisputed that if Thelen and Mesler are forced to dispense Plan B, they have to leave the profession or move to another state. Indeed, the Board conceded in the Final Significant Analysis that some pharmacy owners would close their business rather than violate their conscience. Thus, it is undisputed that the Regulations will force at least some pharmacies and pharmacists out of business, further reducing access to medication." District Court Findings of Fact and Conclusions of Law, Stormans, Inc. v. Selecky, 854 F.Supp.2d 925, 974–75, ¶ 211 (W.D. Wash. 2012).

48 Stormans, Inc. v. Selecky, 844 F. Supp. 2d 1172 (W.D. Wash. 2012), *reversed sub nom.* Stormans, Inc. v. Wiseman, 794 F.3d 1064 (9th Cir. 2015), *cert denied*, Stormans, Inc. v. Wiesman, 136 S. Ct. 2433, (Mem)–2440, 195 L. Ed. 2d 870 (2016).

49 Thus, when governments, accreditation organizations, and scholars (e.g., Goodwin, Chapter 3, this volume, at 87) consider forcing doctors to provide or refer for abortions, they would be foolish not to take into account the fact that the American College of Obstetricians and Gynecologists is predicting a shortage of more than 9,000 OB/GYNs in the next twenty years. Adam S. Levine, *The Best and Worst States for OB/GYN Practice: A Professional Liability Perspective*, MODERN MEDICINE NETWORK (Apr. 6, 2015), contemporaryobgyn.modernmedicine.com/contemporary-obgyn/news/best-and-worst-states-obgyn-practice-professional-liability-perspective-0?page=full. Those who seriously believe in providing healthcare equality to women should not be indifferent to the fact that trying to

welcome the healthcare contributions of all people, regardless of their religious beliefs. If a healthcare provider cannot provide emergency contraception due to his or her religious beliefs – or work on Saturday, or assist with capital punishment, or work for the military, or give out assisted suicide drugs, or provide abortions[50] – we should still welcome the contributions they can make rather than excluding them because of the few they cannot.

III CONTRACEPTIVES AND RELIGIOUS LIBERTY IN HEALTH INSURANCE

A similar story – though on a much larger scale – is unfolding in the ongoing litigation over the federal government's contraceptive mandate. On March 23, 2016, a group of Catholic nuns walked down the steps of the Supreme Court to a cheering crowd. The Little Sisters of the Poor had just watched the oral argument in their case, *Zubik v. Burwell*, and hundreds of happy supporters greeted them with shouts of encouragement and thanks. The case concerns whether the federal government can require the nuns and other religious organizations to offer employee health insurance that provides coverage for all FDA-approved contraceptives, including emergency contraceptives.[51] The Little Sisters believe offering such a health plan would violate their religion. They lost in the lower courts and sought the Supreme Court's protection from more than $70 million in annual fines they faced for refusing to comply with the law.[52]

At first glance, the question of whether employers must provide health insurance for contraceptives may seem even more intractable than whether pharmacists need to provide it. After all, many people have access to more than one pharmacy, but most people are only covered by one health insurance policy. And, at least until recently, most people obtained their health

force OB/GYNs to be involved in abortions will result in fewer healthcare providers for women, not more.

50 For instances of objections in the context of abortion and end-of-life care, *see* Cahn and Ziettlow, Chapter 20, this volume; Kaplan, Chapter 19, this volume; Goodwin, Chapter 3, this volume.

51 Final rule: February 15, 2012, by the Departments of HHS, Labor, and Treasury, 77 FR 8725 (Apr. 16, 2012). For a guide to the many guidance and proposed rules on the contraceptive coverage mandate – at least through 2013 – *see* Bernadette Fernandez & Annie L. Mach, *Adopted from Private Health Insurance Market Reforms in the Patient Protection and Affordable Care Act (ACA)*, Appendix A. Congressional Research Service (Feb. 5, 2013), www.fas.org/sgp/crs/misc/R42069.pdf.

52 Little Sisters of the Poor Home for the Aged, Denver, Colo. v. Burwell, 794 F.3d 1151, 1167 (10th Cir. 2015), *vacated and remanded sub nom.* Zubik v. Burwell, 136 S. Ct. 1557 (2016).

insurance policy from a single source, namely, their employer.[53] Thus, from the employee's perspective, an employer's refusal to include contraceptives might raise a different, far more significant barrier than a single pharmacy's or pharmacist's refusal to provide it. Despite years of litigation and purported "accommodations," the government has never yielded in its insistence that the relevant employers must either offer a benefits package that will "provide contraceptive coverage" or pay large fines for refusing to do so.[54] That is, even if the cost was covered by an insurer, the Little Sisters would still be "offering benefits that violate our religious beliefs."[55]

On the side of the religious objectors, the stakes are arguably higher than in the pharmacy context. In each case, the religious objector is being asked to do something she understands to be religiously prohibited because it may

[53] Gary Claxton et al., *Health Benefits in 2016: Family Premiums Rose Modestly, And Offer Rates Remained Stable*, 35 HEALTH AFFAIRS 1908 (Oct. 2016), content.healthaffairs.org/content/35/10/1908 (reporting that 62% of workers are covered by their employers' plan in 2015 and that 56% of employers offered healthcare coverage).

[54] 26 C.F.R. § 54.9815-2713A(b)(1) (2017).

[55] Constance Veit, *Obamacare's Birth-Control "Exemption" Still Tramples on Rights*, N.Y. TIMES (Mar. 18, 2016), www.nytimes.com/2016/03/19/opinion/obamacaresbirth-control-exemption-still-tramples-on-rights.html?_r=0. Many opponents of the Little Sisters argued that they either *should* have no religious objection to the "accommodation" or that any objection should be rejected as too "attenuated" to merit protection. *See* Lipper, Chapter 5, this volume, at 119–120 (suggesting that because some Catholic institutions found the accommodation acceptable all must), Sepper, Chapter 1, this volume, at 22 (arguing that the connection between the action required by the government and the ultimate use of abortion-inducing drugs or contraceptives is too "attenuated" to deserve protection). These critics are wrong on the law, because the government cannot force all Catholics to view contraception the same way, any more than it can force all Jehovah's Witnesses to view participation in war efforts the same way. *See* Thomas v. Review Bd. They were also wrong on the facts – obviously if the contraceptive coverage were so "attenuated" and "independent" from the Little Sisters, the government would not have fought all the way to the Supreme Court (twice) to force them to sign the papers. Ultimately, the government acknowledged to the Supreme Court that, for most employers, the coverage actually was "part of the same plan" after all. See Brief for the Respondents in Opp. at 19, E. Tex. Baptist Univ. v. Burwell, 793 F.3d 449 (No. 15–35) (emphasis added). The government likewise acknowledged in regulatory documents that it wanted to use the religious employer's health plan because other providers "may not be in the same insurance coverage network" and the employer's plan has a "coverage administration infrastructure" that can be used to "verify the identity of women in accommodated health plans and provide formatted claims data for government reimbursement." 80 Fed. Reg. 41328–29 (July 14, 2015). This is why the government essentially conceded the substantial burden argument at the Supreme Court. *See* Eugene Volokh, *Prof. Michael McConnell on Zubik Religious Freedom Restoration Act–Contraceptive Mandate Oral Argument*, WASH. POST (Mar. 24, 2016), www.washingtonpost.com/news/volokh-conspiracy/wp/2016/03/24/prof-michael-mcconnell-on-zubik-religious-freedom-restoration-act-contraceptive-mandate-oral-argument/?utm_term=.f5981992698f (describing how both Justices Anthony Kennedy and Ginsburg suggested the government was waiving the substantial burden argument).

extinguish innocent human life. A rule telling religious pharmacists they can only be in the profession if they provide emergency contraception would cordon off only one particular career to avoid: pharmacy. While that can be quite costly on a personal level – Vanderbleek and Kosirog, for example, were in their mid-40s with families to support and therefore in no position to change careers – a pharmacy mandate generally forecloses only a single profession. The contraceptive mandate, however, purports to apply to all types of enterprises: nursing homes, Christian bookstores, craft stores, universities, cabinet makers, and so. A religious person who cannot provide employees with emergency contraception would therefore be foreclosed from operating *any* enterprise with employees. Religious employers in all types of pursuits would thus be forced to choose between violating their religion (by providing coverage for drugs they believe will extinguish a human life), violating the law (and facing large fines), or going out of business.[56]

For these reasons, the mandate dispute may have seemed like a winner-take-all fight in which either religious liberty or contraceptive access must lose for the other to win. Indeed, the *Zubik* case was not the first time the issue had been to the Supreme Court – there had been already been one hotly contested merits case, *Burwell v. Hobby Lobby*, and several emergency applications by religious groups seeking protection.[57] And, despite the happy scene on the Supreme Court steps, many experts predicted after the *Zubik* argument that, particularly with Justice Antonin Scalia's death, the Justices would be deadlocked on the case.[58] A 4–4 tie at the Supreme Court would have been

56 Not surprisingly, our history shows precious few situations in which the government has tried to force for-profit employers to violate their beliefs. Part of why the contraceptive mandate cases are unique is that they were the first time the government attempted to force such broad participation in an issue as morally fraught as abortion. Even in that context, however, claims that there would be large numbers of religious exemption claims by businesses have been overblown. Compare, e.g., Goodwin and Sepper with Jennifer Haberkorn, *Two Years Later, Few Hobby Lobby Copycats Emerge*, Politico (October 11, 2016), www.politico.com/story/2016/10/obamacare-birth-control-mandate-employers-229627 ("Those fears have not been borne out."). The far more impactful fruits of Hobby Lobby have been seen in cases of Native Americans being free to possess sacred eagle feathers, McAllen Grace Brethren Church v. Salazar, 764 F.3d 465, 473–479 (5th Cir. 2014) (relying on Hobby Lobby); Muslim prisoners being allowed to wear short beards, Holt v. Hobbs, 135 S. Ct. 853, 860–863 (2015) (relying on Hobby Lobby); and Sikh soldiers being permitted to serve in our nation's armed forces, Singh v. Carter, 168 F. Supp. 3d 216, 226 (D.D.C. 2016) (relying on Hobby Lobby).

57 Hobby Lobby, *supra* note 52; Little Sisters of the Poor Home for the Aged, Denver, Colo. v. Sebelius, 134 S. Ct. 1022 (2014); Wheaton College v. Burwell, 134 S. Ct. 2806 (2014); Zubik, *supra* note 5.

58 *See, e.g.*, Adam Liptak, *Justices Seem Split in Case on Birth Control Mandate*, N.Y. Times (Mar. 23, 2016), www.nytimes.com/2016/03/24/us/politics/supreme-court-case-on-contraceptives-mandate-may-offer-little-closure.html?_r=0 (describing "an extended and

devastatingly troubling for the Little Sisters because it would have affirmed the lower court decisions and exposed them to the $70 million in fines for refusing to allow their health plan to provide contraceptives. A win-win resolution that would simultaneously preserve contraceptive access and protect religious liberty was considered unlikely.

But, much like the pharmacy cases, it turns out that win-win balances between contraceptive access and religious liberty are achievable in the employee health benefit context, too. In fact, just a few days after oral argument, the Justices issued a surprising order directing the parties to brief proposed compromise solutions.[59] In particular, the Court pushed the parties to discuss alternative ways to achieve the stated goals of both sides, that is, providing employees easy access to contraceptives without involving the nuns and their health plan.[60]

The supplemental briefs at the Supreme Court revealed a surprising fact: both sides agreed that it was possible for employees to get easy access to contraceptive coverage – even from the same insurer hired by the religious employer – without forcing the religious objectors to violate their religion. The religious petitioners said that such solutions were indeed possible – something the government did not expect they would do.[61] And while the government began its brief by arguing that no change to its policy was necessary, it ultimately acknowledged that its system could be changed to lessen the involvement of religious employers after all.[62]

animated argument that seemed to leave the Justices sharply divided" and that "A 4–4 tie appeared to be a real possibility").

59 "As a legal gesture, the order is so unusual that it may not have any parallels in the Court's history – with the possible exception of the call for expanded constitutional arguments in 1953, when the Court was reviewing the school desegregation case, *Brown v. Board of Education*." Lyle Denniston, *Did Catholic Theologians Influence the Zubik Order?*, SCOTUSBLOG (Apr. 8, 2016), www.scotusblog.com/2016/04/did-catholic-theologians-influence-the-zubik-order/.

60 Zubik, *supra* note 52, (directing the parties to explore how religious organizations can "do nothing more than contract for a plan that does not include coverage for some or all forms of contraception," while women receive seamless "cost-free contraceptive coverage from the same insurance company").

61 *Compare* Supplemental Brief of Petitioners at 1, Zubik v. Burwell, 136 S. Ct. 1557 (No. 14-1418) ("There are many ways in which the employees of a petitioner with an insured plan could receive cost-free contraceptive coverage through the same insurance company that would not require further involvement by the petitioner, including the way described in the Court's order.") *with* Supplemental Reply Brief for Respondents at 12-13, Zubik, 136 S. Ct. 1557 (No. 14-1418) ("In nearly five years of administrative proceedings and litigation, petitioners have never suggested that an arrangement like the one posited in the Court's order would allay their religious objections.").

62 Supplemental Reply Brief for Respondents at 14-15, Zubik, 135 S. Ct. 2924 (No. 14-1418) ("But the accommodation for employers with insured plans could be modified to operate in the

With the parties acknowledging that middle ground is possible after all, the Supreme Court ruled on the case a few weeks later.[63] Somewhat surprisingly, the Court's opinion was unanimous. All eight Justices agreed that it now seemed possible for the parties to reach a solution that simultaneously "accommodates petitioners' religious exercise" while achieving the government's stated goal of ensuring that women "receive full and equal health coverage, including contraceptive coverage."[64] Furthermore, the Justices vacated the lower court rulings (most of which had gone against the religious objectors) and ordered that the government could not impose fines on the religious objectors for failing to go along with the government's existing system.[65]

As of this writing, the end of the story of the mandate has not yet been written. The Supreme Court has instructed the lower courts to give the parties adequate time to work toward an agreement that allows for both broad contraceptive access and protects religious institutions such as the Little Sisters from being forced to assist in that process.[66] President Trump recently promised the Little Sisters that their "long ordeal will soon be over."[67] And HHS has recently issued an interim final rule acknowledging that it has many other ways to distribute contraceptives and that it had, in fact, burdened religious groups without a sufficiently compelling reason.[68]

However these matters finally resolve in the Trump Administration, the trip to the Supreme Court has highlighted several ways in which the supposedly irreconcilable interests in contraceptive access and religious liberty can be reconciled fairly easily. It is now clear that it is entirely possible to simultaneously expand contraceptive access and protect religious liberty.

For example, one obvious solution that arose from the parties' briefing is the possibility of allowing women who work for religious employers to purchase plans on the healthcare "exchanges" established under the Affordable Care Act.

manner posited in the Court's order while still ensuring that the affected women receive contraceptive coverage seamlessly, together with the rest of their health coverage.").

63 Zubik, *supra* note 52. 64 *Id.* at 1560.

65 *Id.* at 1561. The Court ordered that the government "may not impose taxes or penalties on petitioners for failure to provide the relevant notice." *Id.* Prior to the Zubik decision, the government had claimed that the religious petitioners should face large fines and penalties for failure to execute certain documents the government deemed necessary to allow the plan to provide contraceptives. *See, e.g.*, Brief for Respondents at 31-32, Zubik, 136 S. Ct. 1557 (No. 14-1418) (arguing that the prior system satisfied the compelling interest test as the least restrictive means of advancing a compelling government interest).

66 Zubik, *supra* note 5, at 1561.

67 The President's comments were made in a Rose Garden ceremony to commemorate National Prayer Day and to announce the signing of an executive order on religious liberty. Video of the President's speech is available here: www.youtube.com/watch?v=X9HqN-_KoMc.

68 CMS-9225-IFC, https://s3.amazonaws.com/public-inspection.federalregister.gov/2017-21852.pdf

The briefing at the Supreme Court demonstrated that allowing women whose employers do not provide contraceptive coverage to use the exchanges would fully meet the government's stated interest in ensuring that women have access to a plan with contraceptive coverage. In fact, using the exchanges – which of course the government generally praises as easy-to-use[69] and a good source of healthcare for millions of people – was just one of several solutions that the *government* told the Court were available for those who do not have employer-provided contraceptive coverage.[70] In particular, the government explained that women whose employers are exempt from the mandate "will ordinarily obtain coverage through a family member's employer, through an individual insurance policy purchased on an Exchange or directly from an employer, or through Medicaid or another government program. *All* of those sources would include contraceptive coverage."[71]

It is not surprising that the government believes there are so many existing ways to get women free access to contraceptives. Even before the government finalized the mandate, then-HHS Secretary Kathleen Sebelius acknowledged that birth control was "the most commonly taken drug in America by young and middle-aged women," and that "contraceptive services are available at sites such as community health centers, public clinics, and hospitals with income-based support."[72] Nearly 100 million people do not have a health plan covered by the mandate[73] – a gap that would be intolerable to the government and supporters of contraceptive access if there were not easy and available alternatives for those women to obtain contraceptives. Having already told the

69 *See, e.g.*, *Why Bother with Health Insurance?*, HEALTHCARE.GOV, www.healthcare.gov/young-adults/ready-to-apply/ ("Applying can be easy and fast," is "more affordable – and easier – than you might think" and comes with "complete coverage" including "free contraceptive services.").

70 Indeed, in his 2016 State of the Union address, President Obama explained that "filling gaps in employer-based care" is "what the Affordable Care Act is all about." President Barack Obama, White House, State of the Union Address as Delivered (Jan. 13, 2016), www.whitehouse.gov/the-press-office/2016/01/12/remarks-president-barack-obama-%E2%80%93-prepared-delivery-state-union-address.

71 Brief for Respondents at 65, Zubik, 136 S. Ct. 1557 (No. 14-1418) (emphasis in original). The government offered this concession while explaining to the Court that the other gaps in the law did not undermine its interest because those women "ordinarily" can get the coverage in so many other ways. *Id.*

72 *A Statement by U.S. Department of Health and Human Services Secretary Kathleen Sebelius*, FIERCEHEALTHCARE (Jan. 20, 2012), www.fiercehealthcare.com/payer/a-statement-by-u-s-department-health-and-human-services-secretary-kathleen-sebelius.

73 *See Understanding Who Is Exempted from the New HHS Mandate*, LITTLE SISTERS OF THE POOR, thelittlesistersofthepoor.com/math ("According to the government's own statistics, almost 100 million Americans don't have plans that must comply with the mandate.").

Supreme Court that these alternatives exist and are "ordinarily" used to get contraceptive coverage by millions of women without access to a healthcare plan covered by the mandate,[74] the government cannot seriously deny that the exact same solutions could not be used by employees working for religious organizations who happen to prefer a plan on the exchanges with contraceptives to the one offered by their employer without contraceptives.[75] Indeed, the government suggested that the Little Sisters simply drop their employee health plan entirely and send *all* of their employees to the exchanges, something that would only serve the government's interests if the exchanges were a viable option.[76]

Of course, the exchanges are not the only way around the conflict. As the Supreme Court recognized in its decision, the supplemental briefing demonstrated that the government did not actually need the signed forms and notices that it previously demanded of religious objectors. As a result, it seems that there might be many ways in which the government could provide contraceptive access – even contraceptive access obtained through the religious organizations' hired insurers – without involving the organizations or their plans. For example, the religious groups proposed a system in which women would receive a separate mailing from the insurer with a contraceptive benefit card that they could activate just like a credit card or ATM card by simply

74 Brief for Respondents at 65, Zubik, 136 S. Ct. 1557 (No. 14-1418).

75 Kaiser Family Foundation estimated in 2016 that the total average annual cost for healthcare coverage for a family was $18,142 with $5,277 the average portion paid by employees. Gary Claxton et al., *Employer Health Benefits: 2016 Annual Survey*, The Kaiser Family Foundation & Health Research and Educational Trust at 1 (2016), files.kff.org/attachment/Report-Employer-Health-Benefits-2016-Annual-Survey. Employers are incentivized to provide healthcare coverage benefits because they are tax-preferenced. *See* Alliance for Health Reform, *Tax Treatment of Health Insurance: A Primer* (Dec. 5, 2008), www.allhealth.org/briefing_detail.asp?bi=141.

76 *See, e.g.*, Brief of Appellees at 21 n.4, Little Sisters v. Sebelius (10th Cir. 2014) (No. 13-1540) s3.amazonaws.com/becketpdf/LSP_DOJ-Merits-Opp.pdf. At times the government has suggested that it might not be able to subsidize employees of a religious organization on the exchanges, if the employer continues offering a health plan. It is not clear why this is so. After all, the government decides what qualifies as an adequate health plan and could simply issue rules indicating that, for purposes of subsidies, it believes anyone offered a plan without contraceptives has not received an adequate plan. 26 U.S.C. §§ 4980H, 5000A (2012). Alternatively, the government has indicated its willingness to use discounts in exchange user fees paid by insurers who offer plans on the exchanges as a way to reimburse companies for the cost of contraceptives. 26 C.F.R. § 54.9815-2713A(b)(3) (2017) ("the costs of providing or arranging such payments may be reimbursed through an adjustment to the Federally-facilitated Exchange user fee for a participating issuer"). There is no reason that government could not also use the same mechanism to reimburse insurers for giving subsidized plans to employees of religious organizations on the exchanges.

calling a telephone number.[77] Alternatively, the government could allow for separate point-of-service enrollment at the doctor's office if any desired service is not covered by the employer's plan.[78] In fact, some states have decided that point-of-service enrollment is actually better than automatic enrollment because women are more likely to use a benefit they deliberately sign up for than one that is provided as an automatic benefit of their existing plan.[79] The government could also just make use of existing government programs such as Title X, which contraceptive access advocates have praised as actually *better than* insurance for providing easy access to contraceptives.[80] The government could even partner with organizations such as Nurx, which are being billed as "uber for birth control," and provide next-day birth control via a mobile app and website.[81]

The Supreme Court's order in *Zubik* thus points the way to the kind of win-win solutions that may have seemed impossible only a few months earlier. As with the pharmacist cases, people of good faith on all sides should recognize

77 Supplemental Brief of Petitioners at 10, Zubik, 136 S. Ct. 1557 (2016) (No. 14-1418) ("Like activating a credit card, [obtaining coverage] could be as simple as having the insurance company send each eligible employee a contraceptive coverage card with a sticker attached providing a telephone number to call or website portal to use should she wish to activate the coverage.").

78 *Id.* at 23.

79 *See* Adam Sonfield & Rachel Benson Gold, *Medicaid Family Planning Expansions: Lessons Learned and Implications for the Future* 3-4, GUTTMACHER INSTITUTE (2011), bit.ly/22mg O10. Research suggests that, while many states began with automatic enrollment, "[w]hen surveyed, many [auto-enrolled women] do not know or remember that they have been enrolled, or they do not understand what benefits are (and are not) available to them." *Id.* at 9. For this reason, some states have shifted to a simple opt-in process that can be completed at the doctor's office. *Id.*

80 *See* Rachel Benson Gold, *Going the Extra Mile: The Difference Title X Makes*, GUTTMACHER INSTITUTE (May 16, 2012), www.guttmacher.org/gpr/2012/05/going-extra-mile-difference-title -x-makes. According to the Guttmacher Institute, Title X is actually better than insurance at "helping clients obtain – and quickly begin using – a contraceptive method best suited to them" because Title X clinics are "more likely … to provide contraceptives on-site, rather than giving women a prescription that must be filled at a pharmacy." *Id.* "Doing so can be critically important. Giving a prescription for oral contraceptives requires a woman to make two trips – one to the family planning center and one to the pharmacy – to get the contraceptives she needs." *Id.* For an argument that contraceptive coverage could have been provided by expanding Title X, see Robin Fretwell Wilson, *The Erupting Clash between Religion and the State over Contraception, Sterilization, and Abortion*, *in* RELIGIOUS FREEDOM IN AMERICA: CONSTITUTIONAL TRADITIONS AND NEW HORIZONS (Allen Hertzke ed., University of Oklahoma Press, 2014).

81 *See Birth Control*, NURX, app.nurx.co/ ("Birth Control. Delivered to you without a visit to the Doctor. With or without insurance. Starting at $15/month."); *see also* Kristin V. Brown, *There's Finally an Uber for Birth Control*, FUSION (Jan. 19, 2016), fusion.net/story/256143/nurx-is-making-birth-control-on-demand/.

these results as pointing to obvious ways around what turns out to be an unnecessary conflict. Those in favor of broader contraceptive access should be heartened to see that there are so many ways to provide broader contraceptive access that could be implemented right away and without slogging through more years of litigation. And those in favor of religious liberty should be heartened because the existence of these alternatives makes clear that the government should not need the forced involvement of religious groups and their health plans to satisfy its policy goals of expanding access.

But, as with the pharmacist cases, there is bad news here that must be addressed, even if the *Zubik* case appears headed for a reasonable resolution. In the aggressive pursuit of victory, the government openly urged many employers to simply drop their employee health plans entirely – a result that would hardly seem to improve healthcare.[82] In fact, at least some universities stopped offering student health coverage entirely because of the mandate.[83] Moreover, many employers, like the Little Sisters, were faced with the prospect of tens of millions of dollars in annual fines – fines that would threaten the continuing existence of any nonprofit organization. The plight of the Little Sisters pales in comparison to that of Hobby Lobby, which only escaped even larger fines in 2014 because of the Supreme Court's decision.[84] The notion that the tens of thousands of women who work for Hobby Lobby would somehow be made better off by putting their employer out of business, or forcing their employer to stop offering health benefits entirely, is difficult to fathom. Likewise, the notion that shutting down the Little Sisters, who spend their lives caring for the elderly poor, would somehow improve healthcare is implausible.

For years, the government told the courts that it needed to force the Little Sisters and other groups to provide coverage under the mandate, or to pay the crippling fines. Now that the Supreme Court has pushed the government to acknowledge all of the other ways to achieve its goals, it seems clear that the conflict never needed to occur, and that the risk to healthcare and well-being for so many people was entirely unnecessary. Simply put, there is no real

82 *See, e.g.*, Gov't.Resp.Br.21 n.4, Little Sisters v. Sebelius (10th Cir. 2014) (No. 13-1540).

83 *See, e.g.*, Carol Zimmermann, *Franciscan University Drops Student Health Insurance Plan*, Catholic News Service (May 21, 2012), www.catholicnews.com/services/englishnews/2012/franciscan-university-drops-student-health-insurance-plan-cns-1202093.cfm (quoting school administrator: "We never thought we would be in the position to choose between faith and health care .... We will not participate in a plan that requires us to violate the consistent teachings of the Catholic Church on the sacredness of life.").

84 Hobby Lobby, *supra* note 52, at 2759 (noting that, if Hobby Lobby does not comply "they will pay a very heavy price – as much as $1.3 million per day, or about $475 million per year").

conflict between providing broad access to contraception and protecting religious liberty.

CONCLUSION

More than seventy years ago, the Supreme Court explained that "no official, high or petty, can prescribe what shall be orthodox in politics, nationalism, religion, or other matters of opinion or force citizens to confess by word or act their faith therein."[85] Allowing for diversity – and thwarting government efforts to impose orthodoxy – on important public questions is both good law and good policy. It is always tempting for government bureaucrats to refuse to grant religious exceptions, claiming that the sky will fall if we protect religious diversity. But the contraceptives cases show that those claims often turn out to be baseless or at least overblown when tested in the crucibles of litigation and real-world experience. In our pluralistic society, we are usually better off allowing room for religious diversity – which allows our society to benefit from the contributions of religious employers and healthcare workers of all kinds – rather than stamping it out.

[85] W. Virginia State Bd. of Educ. v. Barnette, 319 U.S. 624, 642 (1943).

5

The Contraceptive Coverage Cases and the Problem of Politicized Free Exercise Lawsuits

Gregory M. Lipper

Partner at Clinton Brook & Peed and formerly Senior Litigation Counsel for Americans United for Separation of Church and State

Lawsuits challenging the contraceptive coverage regulations under the Patient Protection and Affordable Care Act ("ACA")[1] have transformed free exercise lawsuits, including those brought under the federal Religious Freedom Restoration Act ("RFRA"),[2] into potent political tools. (Because the contraceptive coverage regulations are composed of different requirements, exemptions, and accommodations, and because in any event no employer or educational institution is ultimately required to provide health insurance at all[3], I refer to them collectively as the "regulations" rather than the "mandate," a term used elsewhere in this volume.) Current free exercise doctrine and practice inadequately address organized campaigns of free exercise litigation that often appear motivated by ideology more than sincere religious belief.

As I discuss in Section I, challenges to the contraceptive coverage regulations emerged from a broader set of political opposition to the Obama Administration and the ACA. These ideological concerns, more than genuine religious burdens, appear to have driven the lawsuits challenging the ACA's contraceptive coverage regulations – as I detail in Sections II and III. Nevertheless, as these sections describe, the Obama Administration took the plaintiffs' sincerity largely for granted, failing to grapple with (or even pursue discovery on) significant evidence that many of the asserted claims are insincere. The Administration also offered increasingly generous accommodations

[1] Pub. L. 111–148, 124 Stat. 119 (2010). [2] 42 U.S.C. §§ 2000bb–bb-4 (2012).

[3] *See* Marty Lederman, *Hobby Lobby Part III – There is no "Employer Mandate,"* Balkinization (Dec. 16, 2013), https://balkin.blogspot.com/2013/12/hobby-lobby-part-iiitheres-no-employer.html; *see also* Pema Levy, *When is a Mandate not a Mandate? Ask the Supreme Court*, Newsweek (Mar. 18, 2014), www.newsweek.com/when-mandate-not-mandate-ask-supreme-court-232336.

despite having no reason to believe that they would be accepted; those accommodations, in turn, were used as evidence (by litigants, by courts, and by Rienzi, Chapter 4, this volume) that the previous requirement violated the plaintiffs' free exercise rights. Although Rienzi maintains that "the actual facts on the ground and in court show that there is room for everyone to win,"[4] it has been the plaintiffs and their lawyers – Rienzi and his clients included – who have refused to take yes for an answer.

This, anyhow, was the story until 2017: free exercise lawsuits had become just another weapon of political warfare, and mainstream support for genuine free exercise claims and religious accommodations began to dwindle.

As I explain in Section IV, however, under the Trump Administration these circumstances will likely accelerate and intensify – with meaningful, long-term religious liberty suffering even more. First, the Trump Administration recently issued new rules allowing nonprofit and for-profit to withhold contraceptive coverage on religious grounds (and also allowing nonprofit and most for-profit entities to withhold such coverage on "moral" grounds). Second, even if challenges to the Obama-era regime somehow stay alive, parties challenging the contractive accommodation – or the coverage requirement proper – would likely win a 5–4 victory on their next trip to the now fully staffed Supreme Court. Third, below-the-radar efforts to constitutionalize RFRA – that is, to put more aggressive accommodation requirements back into the First Amendment's Free Exercise Clause – will intensify; they too will probably find a friendlier audience at the High Court. Fourth, arguments and precedents from the contraceptive coverage decisions will continue to make their way into challenges to formal nondiscrimination requirements, including and especially laws protecting LGBT individuals and couples. Fifth, these circumstances will likely spark an even more robust backlash to the use of free exercise doctrine to harm and discriminate against others – especially since the Religious Right groups leading these charges have stayed conspicuously silent about the more flagrant and fundamental threats to religious freedom provoked by the Trump campaign and Administration. The resulting blow to core religious freedom is likely to leave a mark.

I A PERFECT STORM

Challenges to the contraceptive coverage regulations emerged from a broader set of political, ideological, and religious opposition to the Obama Administration and healthcare reform. Many conservatives criticized

[4] Rienzi, Chapter 4, this volume, at 89.

President Obama for being insufficiently Christian, for supposedly waging war on religion generally or Christianity more specifically, and even for positing that the Crusades were bad.[5] And a disconcerting percentage of Republican voters (as well as a smaller proportion of Democrats and independents) incorrectly believe that President Obama is a Muslim.[6]

Other opposition, including from conservative Catholics and evangelical Christians, arose from President Obama's support for LGBT rights, abortion access, and stem-cell research.[7] Some felt insult atop injury after President Obama, who supports abortion rights, addressed graduates and received an honorary degree at the University of Notre Dame.[8]

These ideological differences converged on the ACA. Well before Congress enacted the law in 2010, it was opposed – quite viscerally – by conservatives.[9] The legislation passed without a single Republican vote and most Republicans continue to oppose it to this day.[10] The unrelenting opposition is especially noteworthy considering that Republicans for "two

[5] *See, e.g.*, Dan Balz & Robert Costa, *Gov. Scott Walker: "I Don't Know" Whether Obama is a Christian*, WASH. POST (Feb. 21, 2015), www.washingtonpost.com/politics/walker-says-he-is-unaware-whether-obama-is-a-christian/2015/02/21/6fdeobdo-ba17-11e4-bc30-a4e75503948a_story.html; Juliet Eilperin, *Critics Pounce After Obama Talks Crusades, Slavery at Prayer Breakfast*, WASH. POST (Feb. 5, 2015), www.washingtonpost.com/politics/obamas-speech-at-prayer-breakfast-called-offensive-to-christians/2015/02/05/6a15a240-ad50-11e4-ad71-7b9eba0f87d6_story.html; Rachel Weiner, *Romney: Obama Waging "War on Religion,"* WASH. POST (Aug. 9, 2012), www.washingtonpost.com/blogs/the-fix/post/romney-obama-waging-war-on-religion/2012/08/09/192c4e02-e213-11e1-a25e-15067bb31849_blog.html.

[6] CNN/Opinion Research Corporation Poll, Sept. 4–8, 2015, i2.cdn.turner.com/cnn/2015/images/09/12/iranpoll.pdf (Sept. 2015 poll reporting that 43% of Republicans, 29% of independents, and 15% of Democrats believed that Obama is Muslim); Sam Levine & Christine Conetta, *Yes, Conservatives Are Still Questioning Whether President Obama Is Really a Christian*, HUFFINGTON POST (Sept. 10, 2016), www.huffingtonpost.com/entry/barack-obama-christian-conservatives_us_57d446dee4b00642712dd499.

[7] *See, e.g.*, *U.S. Bishops Criticize Obama Administration's Decision on Marriage Law*, CATHOLIC NEWS (Feb. 24, 2011), www.catholicnews.com/services/englishnews/2011/us-bishops-criticize-obama-administration-s-decision-on-marriage-law-cns-1100769.cfm;
Jim Tankersley & Noam N. Levey, *Barack Obama Lifts Restrictions on Federal Funding for Stem Cell Research Using Human Embryos*, CHI. TRIB. (Mar. 10, 2009), http://articles.chicagotribune.com/2009–03-10/news/0903090708_1_cells-through-alternative-methods-executive-order-lifting-bush-bush-administration-set-policy.

[8] *See, e.g.*, Peter Slevin & Jacqueline L. Salmon, *Antiabortion Protesters Converge on Notre Dame Before Obama's Visit*, WASH. POST (MAY 13, 2009), www.washingtonpost.com/wp-dyn/content/article/2009/05/12/AR2009051203656.html.

[9] *See, e.g.*, Eduardo Porter, *Why the Health Care Law Scares the G.O.P.*, N.Y. TIMES (Oct. 13, 2013), www.nytimes.com/2013/10/02/business/economy/why-the-health-care-law-scares-the-gop.html?smid=tw-share&_r=1.

[10] Norm Ornstein, *The Real Story of Obamacare's Birth*, ATLANTIC (July 6, 2015), www.theatlantic.com/politics/archive/2015/07/the-real-story-of-obamacares-birth/397742/ ("[G]uerrilla efforts to undermine its implementation and disrupt the delivery of its

decades push[ed] legislation" containing many of the ACA's elements, including an individual coverage requirement.[11]

Repeal efforts continued throughout President Obama's second term[12] and intensified before dying and then resurrecting themselves – too many times to count – during the Trump Administration.[13] Even if Congress ultimately fails to repeal the ACA, several of its key provisions remain vulnerable if the Department of Health and Human Services ("HHS") declines to enforce the implementing regulations or otherwise support the insurance exchanges at the heart of the law.[14]

The ACA attracted not only chronic political opposition but also aggressive and recurring legal challenges. Several state attorneys general filed legal challenges to the ACA on the day that President Obama signed it.[15] In 2012, the Supreme Court rejected a constitutional challenge to the ACA's individual coverage requirement, with Chief Justice John Roberts joining the four more liberal justices to uphold that ACA linchpin as a valid exercise

services continue apace."); Ed O'Keefe, *The House Has Voted 54 Times in Four Years on Obamacare. Here's the Full List*, Wash. Post (March 21, 2014), www.washingtonpost.com/news/the-fix/wp/2014/03/21/the-house-has-voted-54-times-in-four-years-on-obamacare-heres-the-full-list/.

11 Ezra Klein, *Unpopular Mandate*, New Yorker (June 25, 2012), www.newyorker.com/magazine/2012/06/25/unpopular-mandate.

12 Sahil Kapur, *Senate Republicans Plan to Repeal Obamacare With 51 Votes*, Bloomberg (July 21, 2015), www.bloomberg.com/politics/articles/2015-07-28/senate-republicans-plan-to-repeal-obamacare-with-51-votes.

13 *See, e.g.*, Thomas Kaplan & Robert Pear, *McCain Announces Opposition to Republican Health Bill, Likely Dooming It*, N.Y. Times (Sept. 22, 2017), www.nytimes.com/2017/09/22/us/politics/mccain-graham-cassidy-health-care.html; Robert Pear & Thomas Kaplan, *Senate Rejects Slimmed-Down Obamacare Repeal as McCain Votes No*, N.Y. Times (July 27, 2017), www.nytimes.com/2017/07/27/us/politics/obamacare-partial-repeal-senate-republicans-revolt.html?_r=0; Robert Pear et al., *In Major Defeat for Trump, Push to Repeal Health Law Fails*, N.Y. Times (Mar. 24, 2017), www.nytimes.com/2017/03/24/us/politics/health-care-affordable-care-act.html; Osita Nwanevu, *The AHCA is Still Dead. Again*, Slate (Apr. 28, 2017), www.slate.com/blogs/the_slatest/2017/04/28/the_ahca_is_still_dead.html; Sarah Kliff, *The American Health Care Act: The Obamacare Repeal Bill the House Just Passed, Explained*, Vox (May 4, 2017), www.vox.com/policy-and-politics/2017/5/3/15531494/american-health-care-act-explained.

14 Anna Maria Barry-Jester, *The Future of Obamacare is in Trump's Hands*, FiveThirtyEight (Mar. 25, 2017), https://fivethirtyeight.com/features/the-future-of-obamacare-is-in-trumps-hands/; Nicholas Bagley & Adrianna McIntyre, *Executive Actions Trump Could Take to Change the ACA*, Incidental Economist (Jan. 23, 2017), theincidentaleconomist.com/wordpress/executive-actions-trump-could-take-to-change-the-aca/.

15 Sheryl Gay Stolberg & Robert Pear, *Obama Signs Health Care Overhaul Bill, With a Flourish*, N.Y. Times (Mar. 23, 2010), www.nytimes.com/2010/03/24/health/policy/24health.html ("Attorneys general in more than a dozen states, most Republican, filed lawsuits contending that the measure is unconstitutional.").

of Congress's taxing power; in a remarkable joint opinion, the four dissenters would have scrapped not only the individual coverage requirement but the ACA as a whole.[16] (The Court separately held that states may opt out of the ACA's Medicaid expansion without losing the rest of their Medicaid funding;[17] nineteen states inexplicably still refuse to expand that program, even though the federal government would cover virtually the entire cost.[18])

Then, in 2015, the Court (a hair more decisively) rejected a follow-up suit seeking to prevent the government from subsidizing insurance purchased on federal healthcare exchanges.[19] Afterward, other challenges pressed on in the lower courts[20] – although at least one set of partisan plaintiffs seems less enthusiastic about their case now that President Obama has left office.[21] More generally, efforts to bludgeon the ACA were part of a larger movement to use litigation to revisit policy battles lost in the political process.[22]

These circumstances combined to create a perfect storm of political and legal opposition to the ACA's contraceptive coverage regulations. Among other things, the ACA requires that insurance policies cover certain types of preventive care – including preventive care unique to women – without any cost to patients.[23] Relying on recommendations from the Institute of Medicine, HHS included all FDA-approved contraceptives in the required

[16] *See* Nat'l Fed'n of Indep. Bus. v. Sebelius, 132 S. Ct. 2566, 2580–2601 (2012) (opinion of Roberts, C.J.); *id.* at 2609–29 (Ginsburg, J., concurring in part, concurring in the judgment in part, and dissenting in part); *id.* at 2642–43 (Scalia, Kennedy, Thomas, and Alito, JJ., dissenting).

[17] Sebelius, *supra* note 16, at 2604 (opinion of Roberts, C.J.).

[18] *Status of State Action on the Medicaid Expansion Decision*, Kaiser Family Foundation (Jan. 1, 2017), kff.org/health-reform/state-indicator/state-activity-around-expanding-medicaid-under-the-affordable-care-act/?currentTimeframe=0&sortModel=%7B%22colId%22:%22Location%22,%22sort%22:%22asc%22%7D.

[19] King v. Burwell, 135 S. Ct. 2480 (2015).

[20] *See, e.g.*, Johnson v. U.S. Office of Personnel Mgmt., 783 F.3d 655 (7th Cir. 2015) (Republican Senator lacked standing to challenge ACA regulations governing health coverage for members of Congress and their staff); Sissel v. U.S. Dep't of Health & Human Servs., 760 F.3d 1 (D.C. Cir. 2014) (rejecting challenge to ACA under Origination Clause), *cert denied*, 136 S. Ct. 925 (2016); U.S. House of Representatives v. Burwell, 185 F.3d 165 (D.D.C. 2016) (sustaining congressional challenge to certain HHS Affordable Care Act spending), *appeal held in abeyance*, __ F. App'x __, 676 F. App'x 1 (D.C. Cir. 2016). (D.C. Cir. Dec. 5, 2016).

[21] Carl Hulse, *House Republicans Fret About Winning Their Health Care Suit*, N.Y. Times (Dec. 31, 2016), www.nytimes.com/2016/12/31/us/politics/house-republicans-health-care-suit.html?_r=1.

[22] *See generally* Brian Beutler, *The Rehabilitationists*, New Republic (Aug. 30, 2015), www.newrepublic.com/article/122645/rehabilitationists-libertarian-movement-undo-new-deal.

[23] 42 U.S.C. § 300gg-13 (2012) (preventive care); *id.* § 300gg-13(a)(4) (preventive care specific to women).

bundle of coverage.[24] HHS did so because women get numerous health, educational, and economic benefits from controlling their reproductive choices – indeed, the Centers for Disease Control and Prevention named family planning one of the ten most important public health advances of the 20th century.[25] As Goodwin describes in Chapter 3 in this volume, reproductive control is crucial to the lives of many women, families, and children. Yet for a conservative political movement hostile to the ACA and skeptical of the Obama Administration on issues relating to religion, the contraceptive coverage regulations became an epicenter of opposition.

Although the Obama Administration repeatedly sought to accommodate religious objectors, the lawsuits persisted. From the start, the regulations exempted houses of worship.[26] Then, in February 2012, HHS announced a plan to accommodate other nonprofit organizations asserting religious objections.[27] To take advantage of the accommodation, objecting entities would send a written notice of objection to their insurance company or plan administrator, which would then provide the required contraceptive coverage to the objector's employees or students, at no cost to either the objecting religious entity or its insureds.[28]

Despite this accommodation, dozens of challenges were filed by both for-profit corporations and nonprofit organizations. The for-profit corporations objected to including contraceptives (or certain contraceptives) in their health plans; the nonprofit organizations asserted religious objections despite the proposed accommodation.[29] The plaintiffs invoked RFRA, among other statutory and constitutional provisions; under RFRA, a religious objector must receive an accommodation from even a neutral, generally applicable law, if that law substantially burdens the objector's religious exercise and is not the least restrictive means of achieving a compelling governmental interest.[30] RFRA, enacted nearly unanimously in 1993,

[24] 76 Fed. Reg. 46,621 (Aug. 3, 2011).

[25] *See Ten Great Public Health Achievements in the 20th Century*, Ctrs. for Disease Control & Prevention (Apr. 26, 2013), www.cdc.gov/about/history/tengpha.htm.

[26] *See* Group Health Plans and Health Insurance Issuers Relating to Coverage of Preventative Services under the Patient Protection and Affordable Care Act, 45 C.F.R. § 147.130 (2017).

[27] 77 Fed. Reg. 8725 (Feb. 15, 2012). [28] *See id.* at 8727–28.

[29] *See, e.g.*, Jennifer Haberkorn, *More Challenge Contraception Rule*, POLITICO (May 21, 2012), www.politico.com/story/2012/05/more-challenge-contraception-rule-076570 ("More than 40 Catholic institutions on Monday filed lawsuits challenging the Obama administration's policy that requires employers to provide insurance coverage of contraceptives, a coordinated strategy backed by the U.S. Conference of Catholic Bishops.").

[30] 42 U.S.C. §§ 2000bb–bb-4 (2012). *See generally* Sepper, Chapter 1, this volume; Helfand, Chapter 2, this volume.

emerged as a weapon in a divisive culture war – over, of all things, birth control.[31]

II THE FOR-PROFIT CORPORATIONS REFUSE TO DO WHAT THEY ALWAYS DID

The backdrop previously described already creates doubt about the sincerity of the free exercise challenges to the contraceptive coverage regulations – especially when viewed in tandem with the plaintiffs' past coverage decisions. Many of the for-profit plaintiffs had previously covered the very drugs and devices that they now claim to oppose including in their insurance policies. The recent converts included Hobby Lobby Stores and Conestoga Wood, whose cases ultimately reached the Supreme Court, and at least a dozen other for-profit plaintiffs. In nearly every case, the explanation was the same: after the Obama Administration announced the coverage regulations, the company reviewed its healthcare plan and was shocked – shocked! – to discover that it was already covering contraceptives.[32]

The challenges brought by certain for-profit corporations waved even brighter red flags that the challenges flowed from political resistance, not sincere religious objections. While Eden Foods claimed in its court filings that contraceptives "almost always involve immoral and unnatural practices," the company's CEO told a reporter that he filed suit "[b]ecause I don't care if the federal government is telling me to buy my employees Jack Daniel's or birth control. What gives them the right to tell me that I have to do that?"[33] Hobby Lobby, meanwhile, invested and continues to invest its 401(k) plan in

[31] *See* Linda Greenhouse, Opinion, *Sex After 50 at the Supreme Court*, N.Y. Times (Nov. 26, 2015), www.nytimes.com/2015/11/26/opinion/sex-after-50-at-the-supreme-court.html ("Fifty years after the Supreme Court, in Griswold v. Connecticut, granted married couples the constitutional right to use birth control, here we are back at the court, still wrestling with contraception. Am I the only one who finds this remarkable?").

[32] *See* Complaint ¶ 55, Hobby Lobby Stores, Inc. v. Sebelius, 870 F. Supp. 2d 1278 (W.D. Okla.) (No. 12-1000-HE), *rev'd*, 723 F.3d 1114 (10th Cir. 2013) (en banc), *aff'd sub nom*; Burwell v. Hobby Lobby Stores, Inc., 134 S. Ct. 2751 (2014); *see also, e.g.*, Complaint ¶ 83, Annex Med., Inc. v. Sebelius, No. 12-2804 (DSD/SER), 2013 WL 1276025 (D. Minn. Jan. 8, 2013) (No. 12-2804 (DSD/SER)), *vacated*, 769 F.3d 578 (8th Cir. 2014); Complaint ¶ 8, Armstrong v. Burwell, 269 F.Supp.3d 1132 (D. Colo. 2014), (D. Colo. Sept. 29, 2014) (No. 13-cv-00563-RBJ); Complaint ¶¶ 45, 46, Beckwith Electric Co. v. Sebelius, 960 F. Supp. 2d 1328 (M.D. Fla. 2013) (8:13-cv-0648-T-17MAP); Complaint ¶ 27, Bick Holding, Inc. v. Sebelius, No. 13-cv-00462-AGF, slip op. (E.D. Mo. Apr. 1, 2013) (No. 13-cv-00462-AGF); Complaint ¶ 9, Briscoe v. Sebelius, No. 13-cv-00285-WYD-BNB, 2013 WL 4781711 (D. Colo. Sept. 6, 2013) (No. 13-cv-00285-WYD-BNB); and many others.

[33] Irin Carmon, *Eden Foods Doubles Down in Birth Control Flap*, Salon (Apr. 15, 2013), www.salon.com/2013/04/15/eden_foods_ceo_digs_himself_deeper_in_birth_control_outrage/.

companies that manufacture the very drugs and devices that it refuses to cover on religious grounds.[34]

Many of these plaintiffs also strained to conflate birth control and abortion. A number of the for-profit plaintiffs were owned by evangelical Protestants, who typically do not oppose using birth control.[35] But the Protestant-owned for-profit plaintiffs claimed that certain contraceptives – in particular, emergency contraceptives and the intrauterine device ("IUD") – were "abortifacients" because, these plaintiffs said, those contraceptives prevent fertilized eggs from implanting.[36] Although this claim is supported in part by long-outdated FDA labeling, and Rienzi (Chapter 4) suggests that some drugs "may" work on the implantation site itself, virtually all modern science refutes this factual premise, as Goodwin explains in Chapter 3.[37] In sum: even assuming that preventing a newly fertilized egg from implanting constitutes an abortion, most evidence suggests that the four objected-to drugs and devices (two types of emergency contraceptives and two types of IUDs) prevent fertilization, not implantation.[38] But the plaintiffs nonetheless insisted that their cases implicated religious beliefs about taking human life, and many of their lawyers claimed to be fighting an "abortion pill mandate."[39]

As observed by Wilson and Sanders (Chapter 13, this volume), scrutinizing sincerity is important for distinguishing secular opposition to secular duties from religious opposition to requirements implicating faith. Yet despite the anomalies in the for-profit plaintiffs' claims, the government conceded

[34] Molly Redden, *Hobby Lobby's Hypocrisy: The Company's Retirement Plan Invests in Contraception Manufacturers*, MOTHER JONES (Apr. 1, 2014), www.motherjones.com/politics/2014/04/hobby-lobby-retirement-plan-invested-emergency-contraception-and-abortion-drug-makers.

[35] *See* Molly Worthen, *The Complicated History of Catholics, Protestants, and Contraceptives*, SLATE (Feb. 9, 2012), www.slate.com/articles/double_x/doublex/2012/02/obama_birth_control_coverage_rules_and_the_history_of_catholics_protestants_and_contraceptives_.html.

[36] *See, e.g.*, Hobby Lobby, *supra* note 32.

[37] *See* Rienzi, Chapter 4, this volume, at 90 & n. 7 (citing no scientific studies), Goodwin, Chapter 3, this volume, at 73 nn. 63–69 (collecting scientific evidence).

[38] *See, e.g.*, Gregory M. Lipper, *Zubik v. Burwell, Part 3: Birth Control Is Not Abortion*, BILL OF HEALTH (Mar. 19, 2016) (summarizing literature on operation of Plan B, Ella, and two types of IUDs); Joerg Dreweke, *Contraception Is Not Abortion: The Strategic Campaign of Antiabortion Groups to Persuade the Public Otherwise*, 17 GUTTMACHER POL'Y REV. (2014), www.guttmacher.org/pubs/gpr/17/4/gpr170414.html.

[39] *See, e.g.*, *Defeat the Abortion-Pill Mandate, Defend Religious Liberty*, ACLJ, aclj.org/obamacare/oppose-abortion-pill-mandate-defend-religious-liberty; *No One Should Be Forced to Pay for Another Person's Abortion*, ALLIANCE DEFENDING FREEDOM, www.adflegal.org/issues/sanctity-of-life/defending-those-who-defend-life/key-issues (claiming that Affordable Care Act requires "pro-life family-owned businesses [to] pay for their employees' abortion pills").

that the plaintiffs' religious objections were sincere.[40] The government did not even pursue factual discovery, such as internal company emails – a staple of litigation involving corporations – to evince the plaintiffs' actual motives.

The government could have used an extra defense. After hearing cases brought by two sets of for-profit corporations, the Supreme Court held in a 5–4 decision that (1) for-profit corporations could pursue RFRA claims; (2) including the four objected-to contraceptives in the hundreds of other drugs and services covered by a company health plan substantially burdened the plaintiffs' religious exercise; and (3) even assuming that ensuring women's access to affordable contraception was a compelling governmental interest, the coverage regulations were not the least restrictive means of vindicating that interest, given that the government had made a less restrictive accommodation available to nonprofit organizations.[41] And while Hobby Lobby covered all but four forms of contraceptives, the Court promptly applied its decision to require exemptions for companies opposed to covering any and all contraceptives.[42]

Yet even after the Supreme Court in *Hobby Lobby* rejected the government's arguments, the Obama Administration failed to challenge the plaintiffs' sincerity – even in the case of Eden Foods, whose CEO admitted that his concerns transcended religion. In a pre–*Hobby Lobby* decision upholding the denial of Eden Foods's request for a preliminary injunction against the regulations, the United States Court of Appeals for the Sixth Circuit observed that the company CEO's "'deeply held religious beliefs' more resembled a laissez-faire, anti-government screed," before rejecting the company's claims on the ground that for-profit corporations such as Eden Foods are not "capable of 'religious exercise' as intended by RFRA."[43] After the Supreme Court decided *Hobby Lobby*, however, the Court vacated the Sixth Circuit's decision and remanded the case for reconsideration.[44] On remand, the government

40 *See, e.g.*, Brief of Petitioner at 12, Burwell v. Hobby Lobby Stores, Inc., 134 S. Ct. 2751 (2014) (describing the "sincerely held religious opposition" of Hobby Lobby's owners).

41 Hobby Lobby, *supra* note 36, at 2759–60.

42 *See, e.g.*, Patrick Caldwell, *Supreme Court Broadens Hobby Lobby Ruling to All Forms of Birth Control*, Mother Jones (July 2, 2014), www.motherjones.com/politics/2014/07/supreme-court-scotus-hobby-lobby-all-forms-contraception (the day after issuing *Hobby* Lobby, the Supreme Court "ordered lower courts to rehear any cases where companies had sought to deny coverage for any type of contraception, not just the specific types Hobby Lobby was opposed to").

43 Eden Foods, Inc. v. Sebelius, 733 F.3d 626, 629 n.3 (6th Cir. 2013) (citation omitted), *vacated and remanded*, 134 S. Ct. 2902 (2014).

44 Eden Foods, Inc. v. Burwell, 134 S. Ct. 2902 (2014).

again declined to contest Eden Foods's sincerity, instead conceding that Eden Foods should receive the injunction that it demanded.[45]

In sum, claims by many for-profit corporations smacked of political opposition rather than sincere religious concern; the government neither challenged nor pursued discovery on the question of sincerity; and the courts did not otherwise address this threshold question. As a result, the Obama Administration battled a coordinated, ideological campaign on the defensive and failed to pursue evidence that could have highlighted the plaintiffs' actual motives. Even after the Supreme Court in *Hobby Lobby* rejected the government's other arguments, the government ignored an elephant in the room.

III THE NONPROFIT ORGANIZATIONS REFUSE TO TAKE YES FOR AN ANSWER

Challenges to the contraceptive coverage accommodation brought the politics of free exercise litigation into even sharper focus. As noted earlier, in early 2012 the Obama Administration announced an accommodation: nonprofit organizations with religious objections would be exempt from covering contraceptives, so long as they sent a form to their insurance company or plan administrator asserting that they objected to providing the coverage.[46] After receiving this written opt-out notice, the insurer or plan administrator would provide the contraceptive coverage without charging either the objecting nonprofit organization or the affected employees or students.[47] But this concession begat a new round of lawsuits, and the Supreme Court in *Zubik v. Burwell* deferred resolving them.

A An Accommodation Brings More Lawsuits

From the start, reaction to the Obama Administration's proposed accommodation for objecting religious nonprofits was mixed. On the one hand, some religious organizations, such as Georgetown University and the Catholic Health Association, embraced it.[48] Before later changing course, the

[45] *See* Eden Foods, Inc. v. Burwell, No. 13-cv-11229, slip op. at 1 (E.D. Mich. Feb. 12, 2015).

[46] 78 Fed. Reg. 39,870, 39,873–76 (July 2, 2013). [47] *Id.* at 39,876.

[48] *See* Bridgette Dunlap, *For It Before They Were Against It: Catholic Universities and Birth Control*, RH Reality Check (Feb. 13, 2013), rhrealitycheck.org/article/2013/02/13/before-birth-control-before-they-were-against-it-when-georgetown-fordham-and-notre-dame-and-other-catholic-affiliated-schools-supported-access-to-contraception/; Julie Rovner, *White House Bends on Birth Control Requirement for Religious Groups*, NPR (Feb. 10, 2012),

University of Notre Dame's president initially called the accommodation a "welcome step toward recognizing the freedom of religious institutions."[49] And Professor Douglas Laycock, who filed an amicus brief supporting the challengers in *Hobby Lobby*, has called the accommodation "a serious plan to protect religious liberty without depriving women of contraception" – one that is "utterly inconsistent with the common charge that the Obama Administration is engaged in a 'war on religion.'"[50]

On the other hand, many nonprofit organizations rejected the accommodation and challenged it in court. This time, however, their judicial record was spotty: challenges to the accommodation were rejected by eight of nine federal appeals courts to consider them.[51] Even the Fifth Circuit, widely regarded as the most conservative federal appeals court in the country, upheld the accommodation, in an opinion by outspoken conservative Judge Jerry Smith.[52]

Along the way, a trio of Supreme Court interim orders, issued in response to requests for emergency relief by organizations whose claims had failed in the lower courts, raised yet more questions about whether the plaintiffs' objections were sincere.

To review: the government's original accommodation required objecting nonprofit organizations to complete a form and send it to their insurance

www.npr.org/sections/health-shots/2012/02/10/146693907/white-house-bends-on-birth-control-requirement-for-religious-groups.

49 Irin Carmon, *This is the Next Hobby Lobby*, MSNBC (July 30, 2015), www.msnbc.com/msnbc/the-next-hobby-lobby.

50 Douglas Laycock, Religious Liberty and the Culture Wars, 2014 U. ILL. L. REV. 839, 862.

51 *See* Catholic Health Care Sys. v. Burwell, 796 F.3d 207 (2d Cir. 2015) (rejecting challenge), *vacated and remanded*, 136 S. Ct. 2450 (2016); Geneva Coll. v. Sec'y U.S. Dep't of Health & Human Servs., 778 F.3d 422 (3d Cir. 2015) (rejecting challenge), *vacated and remanded*, 136 S. Ct. 1557 (2016); E. Tex. Baptist Univ. v. Burwell, 793 F.3d 449 (5th Cir. 2015) (rejecting challenge), *vacated and remanded*, 136 S. Ct. 1557 (2016); Mich. Catholic Conference & Catholic Family Servs. v. Burwell, 807 F.3d 738 (6th Cir. 2015) (rejecting challenge), *vacated and remanded*, 136 S. Ct. 2450 (2016); Univ. of Notre Dame v. Burwell, 786 F.3d 606 (7th Cir. 2015) (rejecting challenge), *vacated and remanded*, 136 S. Ct. 2007 (2016); Little Sisters of the Poor Home for the Aged v. Burwell, 794 F.3d 1151 (10th Cir. 2015) (rejecting challenge), *vacated and remanded*, 136 S. Ct. 1557 (2016); Eternal Word Television Network, Inc. v. Sec'y of U.S. Dep't of Health & Human Servs., 818 F.3d 1122 (11th Cir. 2016) (rejecting challenge); Priests for Life v. U.S. Dep't of Health & Human Servs., 772 F.3d 229 (D.C. Cir. 2014) (rejecting challenge), *vacated and remanded*, 136 S. Ct. 1557 (2016); Sharpe Holdings, Inc. v. U.S. Dep't of Health & Human Servs., 801 F.3d 927 (8th Cir. 2015) (sustaining challenge), *vacated and remanded*, 2016 WL 2842448 (May 16, 2016).

52 *See* Ian Millhiser, *Deeply Conservative Judge Rules Against Religious Employers, Affirms Right to Birth Control*, THINKPROGRESS (June 22, 2015), thinkprogress.org/deeply-conservative-judge-rules-against-religious-employers-affirms-right-to-birth-control-7d1145295a44#.ngiod103h; Patrick Gregory, *5th Cir.'s Smith Doesn't Always Fit "Conservative" Label*, BLOOMBERG NEWS (Aug. 15, 2016), www.bna.com/5th-cirs-smith-n73014446355/.

providers or third-party administrators. Through interim orders issued in January 2014, in *Little Sisters of the Poor Home for the Aged*, and June 2014, in *Wheaton College*, the Supreme Court adjusted the details of the notice procedure but also authorized the government to "rely[] on this notice, to the extent it considers necessary, to facilitate the provision of full contraceptive coverage under the Act."[53] In June 2015, the Court adopted a similar work-around, in *Zubik*, for another objecting organization, stating: "Nor does this order preclude the government from relying on information provided by [objecting nonprofits], to the extent it considers it necessary, to facilitate the provision of full contraceptive coverage under the [ACA]."[54]

After the interim order in *Wheaton College*, the Obama Administration expanded the accommodation to authorize an alternative form of notice similar to the one devised by the Supreme Court. Under this alternative, an organization may opt out of covering contraceptives by informing the government of its religious objection and the nature of its health plan (whether group insurance or self-funded) and identifying its insurer or plan administrator.[55] HHS finalized this alternative accommodation in July 2015 and extended it to closely held for-profit corporations, as required by *Hobby Lobby*.[56]

By summer 2015, then, the Supreme Court and HHS had each required objecting entities to provide written notice to either the government or their insurance company or third-party administrator – under either scheme, the government retained the right to arrange for the objectors' employees or students to receive contraceptive coverage through the objectors' insurance provider or third-party administrator. If the controversy had stemmed from genuine efforts to obtain religious accommodations from an actual burden on religious exercise, one would have expected roughly the same reaction to each work-around.

That is not what happened. Consider the conflicting responses of Rienzi's Becket Fund for Religious Liberty, which represents many of the for-profit and nonprofit plaintiffs, including Hobby Lobby, Little Sisters of the Poor, and Wheaton College. After the Supreme Court announced its interim approach in *Wheaton College* – notify the government of the objection, and the government may arrange for the objector's employees and students to receive contraceptive coverage from the objector's insurance provider or third-party administrator – the Becket Fund touted "another important victory against

[53] *See* Wheaton Coll. v. Burwell, 134 S. Ct. 2806, 2807 (2014) (interim order); *see also* Little Sisters of the Poor Home for the Aged v. Sebelius, 134 S. Ct. 1022 (2014) (interim order).

[54] Zubik v. Burwell, 135 S. Ct. 2924 (2015) (interim order).

[55] 79 Fed. Reg. 51,092, 51,094–95 (Aug. 27, 2014).

[56] 80 Fed. Reg. 41,318, 41,318 (July 14, 2015).

the HHS Mandate, [in which] Wheaton College received last minute relief from the Supreme Court today, protecting the College's right to carry out its religious mission free from crippling IRS fines."[57] Yet after the government's alternative accommodation – notify the government of the objection, and the government may arrange for the objector's employees and students to receive contraceptive coverage from the objector's insurance provider or third-party administrator – the Becket Fund complained (falsely) that "the government still won't give up on its quest to force nuns and other religious employers to distribute contraceptives."[58]

What could explain the differences in these responses? There is just one difference between the accommodation devised by the Supreme Court and the one offered by HHS: the latter required objecting organizations to identify their insurance providers or third-party administrators, so that the government would know whom to contact to arrange for coverage for the objector's employees. But the plaintiffs had already provided that information to the government – in writing, no less – in the complaints initiating their lawsuits challenging the accommodation. The two accommodations were otherwise materially the same, even though the objectors' responses to them pretended otherwise. Whether the Becket Fund and its allies were motivated by fundraising, publicity, longer-term legal or political goals, or something else, it is difficult if not impossible to see their wildly divergent responses as a good-faith attempt to relieve a genuine burden on religious exercise.

Combine these reactions with the litigation strategy employed by the University of Notre Dame, which has worn its insincerity on its sleeve. When President Obama announced the accommodation in February 2012, Notre Dame's president treated it as a "welcome step."[59] But three months later, Notre Dame filed a lawsuit challenging that very same accommodation.[60] The district court dismissed the lawsuit after the Obama Administration put the regulations on hold for objecting nonprofits pending the final accommodation.[61] But after HHS formalized the accommodation in July 2013, Notre Dame waited five months to challenge it, filing its new lawsuit

57 Press Release, Becket Fund for Religious Liberty, Supreme Court Grants Emergency Relief to Christian College (July 3, 2015), www.becketfund.org/wheaton-scotus-victory/.

58 Press Release, Becket Fund for Religious Liberty, Administration Issues Final Contraceptive Mandate Rules in Defiance of Supreme Court (July 10, 2015), www.becketfund.org/new-hhs-mandate-rules-defiance-supreme-court/.

59 Carmon, *This is the Next Hobby Lobby*, *supra* note 49.

60 *See* Univ. of Notre Dame v. Sebelius, No. 3:12CV253RLM, 2012 WL 6756332, at *1–2 (N.D. Ind. Dec. 31, 2012), *appeal dismissed* (7th Cir. July 26, 2013).

61 *See id.* at *3–4.

just weeks before the regulations were set to take effect.[62] The trial court was baffled: "Notre Dame has in many ways created its own emergency, and I am left to wonder why."[63]

The court need not have wondered. Before filing its second lawsuit in late 2013, Notre Dame had decided to take advantage of the accommodation beginning with the 2013–2014 school year.[64] But in October 2013, a powerful alumni group wrote to Notre Dame's president and urged the university to bring a new lawsuit because of the university's "symbolic importance" to the challenges; only then did Notre Dame resume its fight.[65] Even after its tardy lawsuit, Notre Dame continued to stall at nearly every stage: it declined to seek emergency relief from the Supreme Court, unlike the other nonprofit entities that had not obtained relief by the January 1, 2014, deadline;[66] took the maximum possible time to seek rehearings and further appellate review; and sought and received multiple extensions at various points in the case.[67]

These do not sound like the words and deeds of an entity with a genuine and profound religious objection to the accommodation. Indeed, in April 2014 – five months after Notre Dame filed its second lawsuit challenging the accommodation – its president stated, "I don't see this [invoking the accommodation] as a scandal because we are not giving out contraceptives."[68] His candor added yet more reason to doubt whether Notre Dame's objections were genuine. Nonetheless, the lawsuit continued, and the Obama Administration never challenged the university's sincerity.

62 Univ. of Notre Dame v. Sebelius, 988 F. Supp. 2d 912, 918–19 (N.D. Ind. 2013), *aff'd* 743 F.3d 547 (7th Cir. 2014), *vacated*, 135 S. Ct. 1528 (2015), *remanded to* 786 F.3d 606 (7th Cir. 2015), *vacated and remanded*, 136 S. Ct. 2007 (2016).

63 *Id.* at 919.

64 Univ. of Notre Dame, *Open Enrollment Decision Guide* 14 (2014 ed.), http://hr.nd.edu/assets/80205/2014_decision_guide.pdf ("New: Contraceptive Coverage – Our third party administrator, Meritain Health, will be offering coverage for these services").

65 *See* Statement of Position of Intervenor-Appellee Jane Doe 3, at 7–11, Univ. of Notre Dame v. Burwell, 786 F.3d 606 (7th Cir. 2015).

66 *See* Howard Friedman, *Justice Sotomayor and 3 Circuits Rule on Injunctions Pending Appeals by Non-Profits in Contraceptive Mandate Cases*, Religion Clause (Jan. 1, 2014), religionclause.blogspot.com/2014/01/justice-sotomayor-and-3-circuits-rule.html.

67 *See generally supra* note 65.

68 Matthew Archbold, *Notre Dame Alumni Call Out University's "Startling" Doublespeak on HHS Mandate*, LifeSite (Apr. 15, 2014), www.lifesitenews.com/news/notre-dame-alumni-call-out-universitys-startling-doublespeak-on-hhs-mandate. Fittingly, after finally receiving an outright exemption in fall 2017, see infra Section IV, Notre Dame soon decided to voluntarily comply with the accommodation to which it previously objected on religious grounds." Joan Frawley Desmond, *In Reversal, Notre Dame Now Says Employees Will Still Get Free Contraceptives*, Nat'l Catholic Register (Nov. 8, 2017), http://www.ncregister.com/daily-news/in-reversal-notre-dame-now-says-employees-will-still-get-free-contraceptive.

B The Supreme Court Prolongs the Cycle

Perhaps the Obama Administration believed that the Supreme Court would definitely and definitively uphold the accommodation, such that sincerity inquiries would ultimately prove unnecessary. Indeed, of the nine federal appeals courts to consider challenges to the nonprofit accommodation, all but the Eighth Circuit upheld it. In addition, Justice Anthony Kennedy's concurring opinion in *Hobby Lobby* suggested that he, too, viewed the accommodation as a reasonable compromise that "equally furthers the Government's interest but does not impinge on the plaintiffs' religious beliefs."[69] Finally, because Justice Antonin Scalia died before the Supreme Court heard the cases, the government's likely worst case scenario was a 4–4 split, which would have preserved the accommodation everywhere but in states (Arkansas, Iowa, Minnesota, Missouri, Nebraska, and North and South Dakota) located in the Eighth Circuit.

But after the *Zubik* oral argument, matters seemed considerably more – complicated.[70] At first the argument went as expected, with the four more liberal justices challenging the plaintiffs' argument that the accommodation created a substantial burden by "hijacking" plaintiffs' health plans to provide contraceptive coverage.[71] Even Justice Kennedy balked at the religious nonprofits' desire for the same outright exemption as houses of worship, advising that "[i]t's going to be very difficult for this Court to write an opinion which says that once you have a church organization, you have to treat a religious university the same."[72] His apparent concern resembled Professor Laycock's warning, in an amicus brief, that the plaintiffs' arguments posed a "mortal threat to thousands of specific religious exemptions enacted by the political branches."[73]

But the outlook changed when the U.S. Solicitor General stood up to argue for the government. He faced expected skepticism from Chief Justice Roberts and Justice Samuel Alito; but more importantly, the stance of swing vote Justice Kennedy seemed to have changed since his concurring opinion in *Hobby Lobby*. For one, Justice Kennedy's early question to the U.S. Solicitor

[69] Hobby Lobby, *supra* note 36, at 2786 (Kennedy, J., concurring).

[70] *See, e.g.*, Greg Lipper, *Justices Against "Hijacking," and Other Unsettling Details from the "Zubik v. Burwell" Oral Arguments*, Rewire (Mar. 24, 2016), rewire.news/article/2016/03/24/zubik-burwell-oral-arguments/.

[71] *See, e.g.*, Transcript of Oral Argument at 7–18, 22–25, Zubik v. Burwell, 136 S. Ct. 1557 (2016) (No. 14-1418).

[72] *Id.* at 27–29.

[73] Brief for Baptist Joint Committee for Religious Liberty as Amicus Curiae Supporting Respondents at 4, Zubik v. Burwell, 136 S. Ct. 1557 (2016) (No. 14-1418).

General hinted that he saw little separating a sincere religious objection from a substantial burden on religious exercise.[74] He appeared to believe that the government conceded substantiality when it declined to challenge sincerity.

Justice Kennedy was equally skeptical of the strength of the government's interest and the means used to achieve that interest. Throughout the case, the government had argued that contraceptive coverage needed to be "seamless" – that is, like any other element of medical coverage: part of a woman's regular health plan, available from her regular doctor and pharmacy, and the like. Anything less would create the type of Balkanized coverage that the ACA's women's-health provisions sought to unify. An array of studies, moreover, showed that forcing women to get contraceptive coverage through separate programs or arrangements – including the types of programs invoked by Rienzi (Chapter 4, this volume)[75] – creates barriers that reduce access and usage.[76] But in response to the government's argument that the accommodation, as opposed to the challengers' proposed alternatives, was necessary to ensure that women received seamless coverage, Justice Kennedy responded, "That's why it's necessary to hijack the plans."[77] Needless to say, by argument's end it appeared that *Zubik* would produce an evenly divided Court.

To avoid this result, the Supreme Court attempted to broker yet another compromise. In an unusual interim order, the Court asked the parties to submit supplemental briefs addressing a possible new approach: rather than submit a form to the insurance companies, objecting nonprofits would simply tell their insurance companies that they did not want to provide contraceptive coverage, and insurers would take it from there.[78] Then, it was déjà vu all over again: the government seemed cautiously open to a second round of compromise, while the objectors' tried to use that openness against the government – while reserving the right to challenge the new compromise, too.

[74] Transcript of Oral Argument at 46, *Zubik v. Burwell*, 136 S. Ct. 1557 (2016) (No. 14-1418) ("JUSTICE KENNEDY: Well, do – do you question their belief that they're complicit in the moral wrong? GENERAL VERRILLI: No, we do not. JUSTICE KENNEDY: Well, then – then it seems to me that that's a substantial burden. And then – and the next question is whether there is an accommodation and whether that's the least restrictive.").

[75] Rienzi, Chapter 4, this volume, at 105–107.

[76] *See, e.g.*, Brief for 240 Students, Faculty, and Staff at Religiously Affiliated Universities as Amici Curiae Supporting Respondents at 26–29, Zubik v. Burwell, 136 S. Ct. 1557 (2016) (No. 14-1418).

[77] Transcript of Oral Argument at 76, Zubik v. Burwell, 136 S. Ct. 1557 (2016) (No. 14-1418).

[78] *See* March 29, 2016, Order List, www.scotusblog.com/wp-content/uploads/2016/03/Zubik-order-6-29-15.pdf; *see also* Gregory M. Lipper, *About that Order for Supplemental Briefing in Zubik v. Burwell*, Bill of Health (Mar. 29, 2016), blogs.harvard.edu/billofhealth/2016/03/29/about-that-order-for-supplemental-briefing-in-zubik-v-burwell/.

The government, in its supplemental brief, pointed out that, at least for employers who receive group health plans, the Court's proposal was "very similar to the existing accommodation," but that the Court's proposed changes to the notice procedure would add "a real cost to its effective implementation" by reducing clarity about who was opting out of what.[79] Nonetheless, the government signaled that it could live with this change to the accommodation – despite its flaws – if the Court put the ongoing challenges to bed by holding that the Court's proposed modifications constituted the least restrictive alternative.[80]

The Court's proposal, the government also observed, might not resolve objections from the many plaintiffs with self-insured plans, due to the requirements of the Employee Retirement Income Security Act of 1974.[81] But the government noted that those entities could buy group health coverage if they wanted to.[82]

Most importantly, the government urged the Court to avoid prolonging a cycle in which the government agreed to yet another compromise, only to have the Court invoke the agreement as evidence of a less restrictive alternative but not actually uphold the less restrictive alternative – thereby dooming the previous accommodation and resigning the next one to yet another round of lawsuits. The government warned that "[a] decision requiring a modification to the accommodation while leaving open the possibility that even the arrangement so modified might itself be deemed insufficient would lead to years of additional litigation, during which tens of thousands of women would likely continue to be denied the coverage to which they are legally entitled."[83] Those tens of thousands of women needed a resolution, not an even longer limbo.

The challengers, on the other hand, claimed that they accepted the Court's proposal but then characterized it in a way suggesting that they contemplated something entirely different. The "truly separate" coverage contemplated by the challengers would require "separate enrollment processes, insurance cards, payment sources, and communication streams."[84] As the *Economist* put it, "[T]he insurer will have to segregate the contraceptive coverage all the way down the line. That means separate ID cards and separate accounts, along

79 Supplemental Brief for Respondents at 2, 3, Zubik v. Burwell, 136 S. Ct. 1557 (2016) (No. 14-1418); *see also id.* at 7–10 (describing advantages of current accommodation's notification requirements).

80 *See id.* at 3. 81 *See id.* at 15–17 (citing 29 U.S.C. § 1001 *et seq.*). 82 *See id.* at 17.

83 *Id.* at 3.

84 Supplemental Brief for Petitioners at 6, Zubik v. Burwell, 136 S. Ct. 1557 (2016) (No. 14-1418).

with, probably, a separate pool of participating doctors. Not just separate. Truly separate."[85]

The challengers took this dynamic a step further in their supplemental reply. According to the challengers, the government's reluctant openness to the Court's possible additional compromise meant that a less restrictive alternative necessarily existed, and "[t]hat alone" was "enough to doom its RFRA defense."[86] And while Rienzi claims that the ongoing contraceptive coverage conflict is "unnecessary,"[87] he and his colleagues in their brief actually mocked the government for "pleading with the Court to resolve this case in a way that lays to rest all future RFRA objections to the mandate"[88] – in other words, for asking the Court to take tens of thousands of women out of limbo.

Unsurprisingly, a compromise proved illusory. After reading the supplemental briefs, the Supreme Court delivered "an almost hilariously brazen punt"[89] and sent the cases back to the federal appeals courts.[90] In so doing, the Court assured readers that it was deciding nothing – absolutely nothing: "The Court expresses no view on the merits of the cases. In particular, the Court does not decide whether petitioners' religious exercise has been substantially burdened, whether the Government has a compelling interest, or whether the current regulations are the least restrictive means of serving that interest."[91] The cases would not conclude until the Court got its ninth justice.

After the Court's non-decision, HHS solicited and received tens of thousands of supplemental comments. These comments led the government to conclude that "no feasible approach has been identified at this time that would resolve the concerns of religious objectors, while still ensuring that the affected women receive full and equal health coverage, including contraceptive coverage."[92] At the very end of its second term, the Obama Administration finally stopped negotiating against itself.

85 Steven Mazie, *New Briefs Further Complicate Supreme Court Contraception Battle*, Economist (Apr. 13, 2016), www.economist.com/blogs/democracyinamerica/2016/04/losing-their-religion.

86 Supplemental Reply Brief for Petitioners at 1, Zubik v. Burwell, 136 S. Ct. 1557 (2016) (No. 14-1418).

87 Rienzi, Chapter 4, this volume, at 108.

88 Supplemental Reply Brief, *supra* note 87, at 10.

89 Mark Joseph Stern (@mjs_DC), Twitter (May 16, 2016, 10:24 AM), twitter.com/mjs_DC/status/732215137206030336.

90 Zubik v. Burwell, 136 S. Ct. 1557, 1560 (2016); *see also* Gregory M. Lipper, *What to Expect When You're Expecting at Least Another Year of Contraception Litigation*, Bill of Health (May 17, 2016), blogs.harvard.edu/billofhealth/2016/05/17/what-to-expect-when-youre-expecting-at-least-another-year-of-contraception-litigation/.

91 Zubik, *supra* note 90, at 1560.

92 U.S. Department of Labor, Employee Benefits Security Administration, *FAQs About Affordable Care Act Implementation Part* 36, at 4 (Jan. 9, 2017), www.dol.gov/sites/default/files/ebsa/about-ebsa/our-activities/resource-center/faqs/aca-part-36.pdf; *see also* Marcia Coyle,

C The Government Learns One Lesson, but Not Another

Perhaps the government finally learned that compromise offers would be rejected and then used against it. But in other contexts, such as product-liability cases, evidentiary rules ensure that concessions do not boomerang. For example, the federal evidentiary rules bar litigants from introducing evidence of "subsequent remedial measures" to prove that product-liability defendants' previous conduct was negligent:[93] "If subsequent safety improvements to a product could be used as evidence that prior models were defectively designed, this would discourage manufacturers from continuing to update and improve upon the safety features of their products after initial manufacture." [94] By ensuring that remedial measures do not increase litigation risk, this rule encourages voluntary steps to reduce risk.

Without similar protections for religious accommodations, a future administration might well take a harder line at the outset, lest early accommodations foreclose the ability to enforce regulations against other entities or in other circumstances. Indeed, one could forgive the government for concluding that its 2012 "concessionary accommodation was foolhardy"[95] and that in 2017 it should hold firm.

On the other hand, the government never came around on challenging sincerity, even when circumstances warranted doing so. In the future, government lawyers should be less sheepish about challenging plaintiffs' sincerity when appropriate. After all, insincere free exercise claims ruin religious freedom for everyone. And especially when claims are brought by for-profit businesses or other organizations that keep records, a robust paper trail may yield more concrete evidence of plaintiffs' motivations. There is already a tradition of evaluating sincerity in certain contexts – including claims asserting free exercise rights to use drugs, change prison conditions, or avoid military service; indeed, when "there is a financial or otherwise self-interested motive to lie about a religious belief, courts are willing and able to evaluate sincerity."[96] Yet in the modern political and legal environment,

54,231 *Comments Later, a Contraceptive Coverage Dispute Is Still Unresolved*, NAT'L L.J. (Jan. 10, 2017), www.nationallawjournal.com/home/id=1202776490632?kw=54%2C231%20Comments%20Later%2C%20a%20Contraceptive%20Coverage%20Dispute%20Is%20Still%20Unresolved&et&slreturn=20170212214847.

93 FED. R. EVID. 407. 94 Raymond v. Raymond Corp., 938 F.2d 1518, 1523 (1st Cir. 1991).

95 Leslie C. Griffin, *Symposium: The Missing Interest in the Contraceptive Mandate Cases – Catholic Women*, SCOTUSBLOG (Dec. 16, 2015, 11:08 AM), www.scotusblog.com/2015/12/symposium-the-missing-interest-in-the-contraceptive-mandate-cases-catholic-women/.

96 Ben Adams & Cynthia Barmore, *Questioning Sincerity: The Role of Courts After Hobby Lobby*, 67 STAN. L. REV. ONLINE 59 (2014).

people may be motivated to bring insincere claims for reasons other than money, recreation, or survival.[97] The sincerity requirement will necessarily become more important in free exercise cases, especially as the Supreme Court defers more and more to claims of substantial burden (as noted by both Sepper (Chapter 1, this volume) and Helfand (Chapter 2, this volume)).[98]

Of course, inquiring too aggressively into sincerity would raise its own concerns. Obscure beliefs or practices might draw skepticism even when entirely sincere.[99] Prior inconsistent conduct might reflect evolving beliefs rather than naked opportunism, and unforgiving inquiries into previous inconsistency might encourage gratuitous orthodoxy. Still, religious sincerity is something that courts have long considered – at least in some contexts – and courts regularly find facts and evaluate witness credibility in a range of settings.[100]

Although sincerity inquiries, like any other judicial inquiry, will be imperfect, judicial solicitude for insincere claims brings significant costs. Those costs afflict not just those protected by challenged laws and policies but also religious liberty itself. Dubious free exercise claims undermine protection of religious liberty for the same reason that the boy who cried wolf undermined protection against carnivores. So if we want genuine free exercise claims to be taken seriously, we have to filter out the dubious ones.

IV CONCLUSION: WHAT COMES NEXT?

After the 2016 election and the more existential threats to religious liberty posed by President Trump, fights over contraceptive coverage regulations and accommodations seem almost quaint. Nevertheless, under the Trump Administration religious entities are likely to demand even broader exemptions from laws designed to secure health benefits and prevent discrimination, and those exemption demands are more likely to be successful. This, in fact,

97 *See generally* Michael Hiltzik, Op-Ed, *Danger Sign: The Supreme Court Has Already Expanded Hobby Lobby Decision*, L.A. TIMES (July 2, 2014), www.latimes.com/business/hiltzik/la-fi-mh-expanded-hobby-lobby-20140702-column.html#page=1 ("claims of religious piety" are sometimes "just pretexts for some other viewpoint, such as libertarianism or misogyny").

98 Sepper, Chapter 1, this volume, at 22; Helfand, Chapter 2, this volume, at 52.

99 *Cf.* Helfand, Chapter 2, this volume, at 54 ("Under a regime where courts evaluate the theological substantiality of religious burdens, the impact of laws on religious minorities are likely to be underestimated and underappreciated, unfairly circumscribing the protections afforded by RFRA.").

100 *See* Adams & Barmore, *supra* note 97, at nn. 30–43 and accompanying text.

appears to be the tacit bargain struck by Religious Right groups, which have kept quiet about the Administration's naked embrace of Islamophobia and anti-Semitism in the apparent hope that the Trump Administration and Trump-appointed judges will side with them on other issues.

First, it quite likely that the contraceptive coverage cases will become moot because the Trump Administration has enlarged the regulations' religious exemptions. In early May 2017 – with the Little Sisters of the Poor standing by his side at the Rose Garden[101] – President Trump signed an executive order directing the Secretaries of the Treasury, Labor, and HHS to consider expanding religious exemptions to the contraceptive coverage regulations by "issuing amended regulations, consistent with applicable law, to address conscience-based objections to the preventive-care mandate promulgated under section 300gg-13(a)(4) of title 42, United States Code."[102] In October 2017, Trump Administration officials obliged: issuing a broad religious exemption for for-profit and nonprofit entities, and allowing most such entities to withhold coverage even on nonreligious "moral" grounds.[103]

Of course, HHS needed little prodding to curtail the coverage regulations. Former Secretary has long opposed the ACA and the contraceptive coverage regulations; while in Congress, he insisted that "not one" woman has struggled to pay for birth control and that the contraceptive coverage regulations were "trampling on religious freedom and religious liberty."[104] The new head of HHS's Civil Rights Division is Roger Severino, a Heritage Foundation alum and outspoken opponent of LGBT rights.[105] Another appointee, Assistant HHS Secretary Charmaine Yoest,[106] led the anti-

101 Matt Shuham, *At Religious Freedom Order Signing, Little Sisters of the Poor Join Trump*, Talking Points Memo (May 4, 2017), talkingpointsmemo.com/livewire/trump-little-sisters-of-the-poor.

102 *Presidential Executive Order Promoting Free Speech and Religious Liberty* (May 4, 2017), www.whitehouse.gov/the-press-office/2017/05/04/presidential-executive-order-promoting-free-speech-and-religious-liberty.

103 *See generally* Nicholas Bagley, *The Trump Administration and Contraception Coverage*, The Incidental Economist (Oct. 6, 2017 12:18 PM), http://theincidentaleconomist.com (citing new HHS rules).

104 Olga Khazan, *Tom Price: "Not One" Woman Struggled to Afford Birth Control*, Atlantic (Nov. 29, 2016), www.theatlantic.com/health/archive/2016/11/tom-price-not-one-woman-cant-afford-birth-control/509003/.

105 Charles Ornstein, *Heritage Foundation Alum Critical of Transgender Rights to Lead HHS Civil Rights Office*, ProPublica (Mar. 24, 2017), www.propublica.org/article/heritage-foundation-critical-transgender-rights-HHS-civil-rights-office.

106 *President Donald J. Trump Announces Key Additions to his Administration* (Apr. 28, 2017), www.whitehouse.gov/the-press-office/2017/04/28/president-donald-j-trump-announces-key-additions-his-administration.

abortion organization Americans United for Life, which has opposed the use of the morning-after pill and the IUD.[107] One of Trump's delegates to the United Nations Commission on the Status of Women has stated that access to contraception is "antithetical to the values and needs of women worldwide";[108] the other has criticized the UN for "a monomaniacal focus on such matters as sexual rights, reproductive health, contraception, and abortion."[109] Needless to say, this is not a contraception-friendly crowd.

Second, even if challenges to the Obama-era regime somehow make it back to the Supreme Court, the ninth and newest justice, former Tenth Circuit Judge Neil Gorsuch, would almost certainly rule in favor of those challenging the Obama-era accommodation. While serving on the Tenth Circuit, Justice Gorsuch voted for Hobby Lobby in its challenge to the coverage requirement and then joined a dissent from an order denying rehearing of the decision rejecting Little Sisters of the Poor's challenge to the accommodation.[110] His broader record, moreover, reflects opposition to reproductive rights and sympathy for broad religious accommodations, even if those accommodations allow members of the religious majority to deny rights or benefits to members of minority groups.[111]

Third, whether in the context of contraceptive coverage or elsewhere, the Supreme Court might eventually constitutionalize its RFRA decisions –

107 Olga Khazan, *Planning the End of Abortion*, ATLANTIC (July 16, 2015), www.theatlantic.com/politics/archive/2015/07/what-pro-life-activists-really-want/398297/ ("The group seems better versed legally than medically. They said they don't oppose birth control in general, but they have advocated against the morning-after pill and two types of IUDs.").

108 Laura Bassett, *Trump Sends Anti-Birth Control Delegates to UN Commission on Women*, HUFFINGTON POST (Mar. 17, 2017 06:27 PM), www.huffingtonpost.com/entry/trump-sends-anti-birth-control-delegates-to-un-commission-on-women_us_58cc3dcee4b00705db4f7970.

109 *Id.*

110 Hobby Lobby Stores, Inc. v. Sebelius, 723 F.3d 1114, 1152 (10th Cir. 2013) (en banc) (Gorsuch, J., concurring) (agreeing that Hobby Lobby is entitled to a preliminary injunction against contraceptive-coverage requirement and adding that "the [owners] themselves, as individuals, are also entitled to relief"), *aff'd*, 134 S. Ct. 2751 (2014); Little Sisters of the Poor Home for the Aged v. Burwell, 799 F.3d 1315, 1316–17 (2015) (Hartz, J., dissenting from order denying rehearing en banc) (panel decision upholding contraception accommodation is "clearly and gravely wrong – on an issue that has little to do with contraception and a great deal to do with religious liberty").

111 *See, e.g.*, Nina Totenberg, *Judge Gorsuch's Writings Signal He Would be a Conservative on Social Issues*, NPR (Mar. 16, 2017), www.npr.org/2017/03/16/519501771/judge-gorsuchs-writings-signal-he-would-be-a-conservative-on-social-issues; Amy Howe, *Gorsuch on Abortion, Religion, and Reproductive Rights*, SCOTUSBLOG (Mar. 9, 2017 2:18 PM), www.scotusblog.com/2017/03/gorsuch-abortion-religion-reproductive-rights/; Harsh Voruganti, *Judge Neil Gorsuch — Nominee to be Associate Justice of the Supreme Court: Part Three — Religious Liberty* (Feb. 27, 2017), VETTING ROOM, vettingroom.org/2017/02/27/judge-neil-gorsuch-nominee-to-be-associate-justice-of-the-supreme-court-part-three-religious-liberty/.

putting RFRA-like protections back into the First Amendment's Free Exercise Clause. Congress enacted RFRA in response to the 1990 decision in *Employment Division v. Smith*, in which the Supreme Court held that the Free Exercise Clause did not require religious exemptions from laws that are neutral and generally applicable.[112] In recent years, however, many religious conservatives have sought to return an aggressive exemption regime to the Free Exercise Clause – arguing that even modest exceptions to a neutral law prevent it from being considered "generally applicable," and thus requiring RFRA-like strict scrutiny under the Constitution itself. For one, several of the contraception plaintiffs brought free exercise claims in addition to their RFRA claims, including Conestoga Wood in the companion case to *Hobby Lobby*.[113] In 2016, moreover, a high-profile cert petition filed by Alliance Defending Freedom and the Becket Fund, on behalf of a Washington pharmacy, argued to the Supreme Court that a state law requiring pharmacies to stock emergency contraception violated the Free Exercise Clause because the law had too many secular exemptions.[114] The Court declined to hear the case, but Justice Alito, joined by two other justices, dissented from the denial of review, calling the Ninth Circuit's application of *Smith* and the Free Exercise Clause "an ominous sign."[115]

Justice Alito, the Court's most enthusiastic proponent of religious exemptions, has long argued for a more expansive accommodation regime under the Free Exercise Clause. While a judge on the Third Circuit, he wrote an opinion holding that the Free Exercise Clause required a police department to exempt a Muslim police officer from the department's ban on facial hair, because the department allowed beards for medical reasons and the "decision to provide medical exemptions while refusing religious exemptions is sufficiently suggestive of discriminatory intent so as to trigger heightened scrutiny."[116] Because virtually all laws, from the tax code on down, have exemptions or exceptions, then-Judge Alito's approach would gut *Smith* without overruling it. This aggressive approach could emerge more clearly

112 *See* Emp't Div., Dep't of Human Res. v. Smith, 494 U.S. 872, 878–79 (1990).

113 *See* Brief for Petitioners at 45, Conestoga Wood Specialties Corp. v. Sebelius, 134 S. Ct. 2751 (2014) (No. 13-1356) (arguing that other exemptions "for secular and religious reasons, in tandem with its arbitrary decision not to extend an exemption to Petitioners" "justifies strict scrutiny . . . under the Free Exercise Clause").

114 *See* Petition for a Writ of Certiorari at 23–32, Stormans, Inc. v. Wiesman (No. 15-862).

115 *See* Stormans, Inc. v. Wiesman, 126 S. Ct. 2433, 2433 (2016) (Alito, J., dissenting from denial of certiorari).

116 Fraternal Order of Police Newark Lodge No. 12 v. City of Newark, 170 F.3d 359, 365 (3d Cir. 1999) (Alito, J.).

from the Supreme Court this term, when it hears a Free Exercise Clause challenge to a Colorado law barring businesses from discriminating against LGBT customers.[117]

In addition, the Court's unanimous decision in *Hosanna-Tabor Evangelical Lutheran Church & School v. EEOC*, which held that the First Amendment's ministerial exception exempts houses of worship from employment discrimination law when hiring and firing ministers, opined that *Smith* did not apply there because it "involved government regulation of only outward physical acts"[118] – quite a significant limitation if the Court meant what it said. In any event, overruling *Smith* outright may be in the cards: of the justices who joined the Scalia-authored majority opinion in *Smith*, only Justice Kennedy remains on the Court.

Smith's scope and staying power are more than academic questions: if RFRA-like protections return to the Free Exercise Clause, then aggressive accommodations will become more widespread and harder to undo. They will become more widespread because unlike RFRA, which binds only to the federal government, the Free Exercise Clause applies to state and local governments as well.[119] And they will become harder to undo because RFRA can be amended by Congress, but the Free Exercise Clause cannot (at least not without going through the arduous process required by Article V of the Constitution). Accordingly, those seeking religious exemptions to state laws regulating healthcare or barring discrimination against LGBT individuals and couples would no longer need to try and enact controversial state-specific exemption regimes.

Fourth, if free exercise claims – whether under RFRA, the First Amendment, or both – become just another facet of political campaigns against birth control, LGBT rights, or other contentious aspects of modern life, political support for genuine free exercise claims and religious accommodations will drop. We have already started to see public opinion transform; as Helfand warns (Chapter 2, this volume) "RFRA is now the object of such scorn – after being originally embraced across the political spectrum."[120] The broad coalition supporting RFRA has fractured, with many progressives who

117 *See* Masterpiece Cakeshop, Ltd. v. Colo. Civil Rights Comm'n, 137 S. Ct. 2290 (2017) (granting certiorari) (argued Dec. 5, 2017); *see also* Jim Oleske, *Masterpiece Cakeshop and the Effort to Rewrite Smith and its Progeny*, TAKE CARE (Sept. 21, 2017), https://takecareblog.com/blog/masterpiece-cakeshop-and-the-effort-to-rewrite-smith-and-its-progeny.

118 565 U.S. 171, 190 (2012).

119 *See* City of Boerne v. Flores, 521 U.S. 507, 533–34 (1997) (Congress lacks authority to require state and local governments to comply with RFRA).

120 Helfand, Chapter 2, this volume, at 46.

previously supported RFRA calling for significant changes.[121] Likewise, proposed state RFRAs are now widely viewed as vehicles to facilitate discrimination and to undermine LGBT rights.[122] With *Hobby Lobby* creating serious concerns that religious exemptions will strip others of their rights, support for religious accommodations will likely continue to decline.[123]

The 2016 election and its aftermath have added gasoline to this fire. Those who have raised religious objections to contraception accommodations and nondiscrimination laws had no problem explicitly or implicitly backing Donald Trump, who was endorsed by the Klan and neo-Nazis, turned over his campaign to an anti-Semite, called for a ban on immigration by an entire religion, and otherwise trafficked in naked anti-Semitism and Islamophobia[124] – in a manner that rattled Holocaust survivors, among many others.[125] Indeed, Goodwin (Chapter 3, this volume) describes how one commentator "attributed Donald Trump's 2016 presidential win to religious mobilization inspired by fear of a changing society."[126] For example, Trump won support from Hobby

121 Louise Melling, Op-Ed, *ACLU: Why We Can No Longer Support the Federal "Religious Freedom" Law*, Wash. Post (June 25, 2015), www.washingtonpost.com/opinions/congress-should-amend-the-abused-religious-freedom-restoration-act/2015/06/25/ee6aaa46-19d8-11e5-ab92-c75ae6ab94b5_story.html.

122 Laycock, *supra* note 51, at 871; *see also* Howard Friedman, *Why Is Indiana's RFRA So Controversial? This Blogger's Analysis*, Religion Clause (Mar. 30, 2015, 09:05 PM), religionclause.blogspot.com/2015/03/why-is-indianas-rfra-so-controversial.html.

123 *See* Frank S. Ravitch, *Be Careful What You Wish For: Why Hobby Lobby Weakens Religious Freedom*, 2016 B.Y.U. L. Rev. 55 (2016).

124 *See* Peter Holley, *KKK's Official Newspaper Supports Donald Trump for President*, Wash. Post (Nov. 2, 2016), www.washingtonpost.com/news/post-politics/wp/2016/11/01/the-kkks-official-newspaper-has-endorsed-donald-trump-for-president/; Thea Glassman, *From Mushrooms to Skittles: The Anti-Semitic Source of Trump Jr.'s Analogy*, Forward (Sept. 21, 2016), forward.com/news/350442/from-mushrooms-to-skittles-the-anti-semitic-source-of-trump-jrs-analogy/; Nancy Dillon, *Anti-Semitic Trump Campaign CEO Stephen Bannon Not a Big Fan of "Whiny Brat" Jews, Ex-Wife Says*, N.Y. Daily News (Aug. 27, 2016), www.nydailynews.com/news/election/trump-campaign-ceo-bannon-complained-jews-daughters-school-article-1.2767615; Kristen East, *Trump Tweets Image Depicting Clinton, Cash and the Star of David*, Politico (July 2, 2016), www.politico.com/story/2016/07/donald-trump-hillary-clinton-star-david-225058; Peter Holley, *Top Nazi Leader: Trump Will be a "Real Opportunity" for White Nationalists*, Wash. Post (Aug. 7, 2016), www.washingtonpost.com/news/post-nation/wp/2016/08/07/top-nazi-leader-trump-will-be-a-real-opportunity-for-white-nationalists/; *Donald J. Trump Statement on Preventing Muslim Immigration*, Trump-Pence (Dec. 7, 2015), www.donaldjtrump.com/press-releases/donald-j.-trump-statement-on-preventing-muslim-immigration.

125 *See* Dana Milbank, Op-Ed, *In the Age of Trump, Grim Warnings from Holocaust Survivors*, Wash. Post (Jan. 27, 2016), www.washingtonpost.com/opinions/in-the-age-of-trump-grim-warnings-from-holocaust-survivors/2016/01/27/c65ea38c-c549-11e5-8965-0607e0e265ce_story.html?wpisrc=nl_draw2.

126 Goodwin, Chapter 3, this volume, at 63.

Lobby CEO David Green, who opined that "Donald Trump is our only hope for a Supreme Court that will protect freedom of religion."[127] Trump's election was also touted by the religious liberty groups that spearheaded the contraceptive coverage litigation, including Alliance Defending Freedom (ADF) and the American Center for Law and Justice (ACLJ).[128] Even Rienzi's Becket Fund, which sometimes represents non-Christian clients, has stayed silent on Trump's excesses while embracing the newfound opportunity to obtain broader exemptions from laws ensuring access to healthcare and barring discrimination – adding unironically that "Republicans were just handed complete control of government. The top priority for one of their largest voting blocs was religious freedom."[129] And in an especially sad moment in the annals of religious liberty, the Becket Fund's iconic clients, the Little Sisters of the Poor, recently appeared smiling with Trump at a White House ceremony.[130]

This tacit or explicit support persists even as Trump flirts with Holocaust denial,[131] detains immigrants outside churches,[132] appoints anti-Semites

[127] David Green, Op-Ed, *One Judge Away From Losing Religious Liberty: Hobby Lobby* CEO, USA Today (Sept. 1, 2016), www.usatoday.com/story/opinion/2016/09/01/hobby-lobby-religious-freedom-liberty-obamacare-christian-david-green/89597214/.

[128] Sarah Kramer, *Moving Forward Under a Trump Presidency – How Will We Respond?*, Alliance Defending Freedom (Nov. 9, 2016), adflegal.org/detailspages/blog-details/allianceedge/2016/11/09/moving-forward-under-a-trump-presidency-how-will-we-respond ("And while there are still many unknowns about what a Trump presidency will look like, we do know that we have an opportunity to move forward in our defense of religious liberty, the sanctity of life, and marriage and family in ways that we never expected 24 hours ago."); Jay Sekulow, *An Agenda for the Future: The Dangers and Opportunities of Presidential Succession*, ACLJ, aclj.org/obamacare/seven-steps-to-dismantle-obamacare-on-day-one-of-the-trump-administration (Trump administration presents "a major opportunity to put forward and support a positive proactive agenda for America – to defend our Constitution and sustain our liberty").

[129] *A Message from the Executive Director*, Becket Fund for Religious Liberty (Dec. 2, 2016), www.becketfundcommunity.org/emailviewonwebpage.aspx?erid=9044068&trid=3f1648f0-7273-4a77-8793-fb843a0cccb9 ("We are not in Kansas anymore. Americans voted for a big change. No more business-as-usual. This is the time for us at Becket to double down on our efforts to undo a bunch of bad laws and regulations (like the HHS and transgender mandates) and push for more laws that protect freedom.").

[130] *See* Shuham, *supra* note 104.

[131] Jon Sharman, *Donald Trump's White House "Blocked State Department Holocaust Memorial Statement that Mentioned Jews,"* Independent (Feb. 3, 2017), www.independent.co.uk/news/world/americas/donald-trump-white-house-block-state-department-holocaust-memorial-day-mention-jews-statement-nazis-a7560866.html; Josh Dawsey et al., *White House Nixed Holocaust Statement Naming Jews*, Politico (Feb. 2, 2017), www.politico.com/story/2017/02/white-house-holocaust-jews-234572.

[132] Donie O'Sullivan, *ICE Detains Undocumented Dad Who Took Sanctuary in a Denver Church*, CNN (Apr. 28, 2017), www.cnn.com/2017/04/27/us/undocumented-dad-detained-by-ice-trnd/; Julie Carey, *ICE Agents Arrest Men Leaving Fairfax County Church Shelter*, NBC4

and Islamophobes to high-ranking positions,[133] and seeks to exclude citizens from Muslim countries from the United States[134] – ADF and ACLJ have even defended the Muslim bans in court.[135] And it continues even as religiously motivated bullying and hate crimes spiked after Trump was elected and continue to rise, with barely a peep from the White House.[136] You might think that all "religious liberty" groups would condemn

(Feb. 15, 2017), www.nbcwashington.com/news/local/ICE-Agents-Arrest-Men-Leaving-Alexandria-Church-Shelter-413889013.html.

133 Zaid Jilani, *Trump's New State Department Spokesperson Spread Anti-Muslim Hate as Fox News Anchor*, INTERCEPT (Apr. 24, 2017), theintercept.com/2017/04/24/trumps-new-state-department-spokesperson-spread-anti-muslim-hate-as-fox-anchor/; Lily Bayer, *Controversial Trump Aide Sebastian Gorka Backed Violent Anti-Semitic Militia*, FORWARD (Apr. 3, 2017), forward.com/news/national/367937/exclusive-controversial-trump-aide-sebastian-gorka-backed-violent-anti-semi/; Bryan Schatz, *How a Crazy Idea About Islam Went From the Fringe to the White House*, MOTHER JONES (Mar. 11, 2017), www.motherjones.com/politics/2017/03/trump-gorka-islam-not-religion-islamophobia; Zack Beauchamp, *Trump's Counter-Jihad*, VOX (Feb. 13, 2017), www.vox.com/world/2017/2/13/14559822/trump-islam-muslims-islamophobia-sharia; Scott Shane et al., *Trump Pushes Dark View of Islam to Center of U.S. Policy-Making*, N.Y. TIMES (Feb. 1, 2017), www.nytimes.com/2017/02/01/us/politics/donald-trump-islam.html?_r=1.

134 *Executive Order: Protecting The Nation From Foreign Terrorist Entry Into The United States* (Jan. 27, 2017), www.whitehouse.gov/the-press-office/2017/01/27/executive-order-protecting-nation-foreign-terrorist-entry-united-states; Sunnivie Brydum, *The Deafening Silence of "Religious Freedom" Defenders on Trump's Muslim Ban*, RELIGION DISPATCHES (Jan. 31, 2017), religiondispatches.org/the-deafening-silence-of-religious-freedom-defenders-on-trumps-muslim-ban/ (trying – and failing – to get Becket Fund and ADF to comment on Trump's executive order).

135 *See, e.g.*, Brief for Alliance Defending Freedom as Amicus Curiae Supporting Appellants, Hawai'i v. Trump, No. 17-15589 (Apr. 21, 2017), cdn.ca9.uscourts.gov/datastore/general/2017/04/21/17-15589%20Alliance%20Defending%20Freedom%20Amicus%20Brief.pdf; Brief for American Center for Law and Justice as Amicus Curiae Supporting Defendants-Appellants' Motion for a Stay, Washington v. Trump, 847 F.3d 1151 (9th Cir. 2017) (No. 17-35105), media.aclj.org/pdf/E-filed-ACLJ-Amicus-9th-Cir-re-Trump-EO_Redacted.pdf

136 Press Release, Anti-Defamation League, U.S. Anti-Semitic Incidents Spike 86 Percent So Far in 2017 After Surging Last Year, ADL Finds (Apr. 24, 2017), www.adl.org/news/press-releases/us-anti-semitic-incidents-spike-86-percent-so-far-in-2017; Steven Goldstein, Opinion, *Anti-Semitism Continues in America – And Trump Is Silent Again*, FORWARD (Apr. 9, 2017), forward.com/opinion/368631/anti-semitism-continues-trump-silent/; Sarah A. Harvard, *35 Mosques Have Been Attacked so far in 2017 – and Trump Hasn't Uttered a Word*, MIC (Mar. 30, 2017), m.mic.com/articles/172295/35-mosques-have-been-attacked-so-far-in-2017-and-trump-hasnt-uttered-a-word#.7QyaIWgVU; Akinyi Ochieng, *Muslim Schoolchildren Bullied by Fellow Students and Teachers*, NPR (Mar. 29, 2017), www.npr.org/sections/codeswitch/2017/03/29/515451746/muslim-schoolchildren-bullied-by-fellow-students-and-teachers?utm_campaign=storyshare&utm_source=twitter.com&utm_medium=social (describing "Trump Effect"); Peter Beinart, *Why Is Trump Silent on Islamophobic Attacks?*, ATLANTIC (Feb. 27, 2017), www.theatlantic.com/politics/archive/2017/02/trump-should-condemn-attacks-on-muslims-too/517893/.

a president who refers to neo-Nazis as "very fine people,"[137] but you would be wrong.

Rather than resist these attacks on religious freedom, the Religious Right has bet on Trump, gaining more access to the Trump White House and influence over judicial nominations, including the appointment of Justice Gorsuch.[138] As one longtime religion reporter has put it, "[Trump will] keep evangelicals happy and unified by moving some of their key priorities forward – and use their support to push for what is ultimately an alt-right agenda."[139] The result is that "the religious right – which for decades has grounded its political appeal in moral 'values' such as 'life' and 'family' and 'religious freedom' – has effectively become a subsidiary of the alt-right, yoked to Trump's white nationalist agenda."[140] All while claiming, as ADF recently did, that Trump's first 100 days "are a stark departure from the Obama administration's indifference and at times hostility to religious freedom."[141]

These decisions reflect a cynical conception of religious liberty, in which exemptions from healthcare and nondiscrimination laws matter more than rank religious bigotry. Reverend Rob Schenck, an evangelical Christian, long-time antiabortion activist, and Religious Right leader, warns that this Trump-friendly trade-off "could be the undoing of American evangelicalism": "We could just become a political operation in the guise of a church."[142] These groups' choices will make it harder and harder to take religious freedom claims at face value – to the ultimate detriment of Americans of all faiths.

137 Rosie Gray, *Trump Defends White-Nationalist Protestors: "Some Very Fine People on Both Sides,"* ATLANTIC (Aug. 15, 2017), www.theatlantic.com/politics/archive/2017/08/trump-defends-white-nationalist-protesters-some-very-fine-people-on-both-sides/537012/.

138 Jeremy W. Peters, *For Religious Conservatives, Success and Access at the Trump White House*, N.Y. TIMES (Feb. 13, 2017), www.nytimes.com/2017/02/13/us/politics/trump-religious-conservatives.html?smprod=nytcore-iphone&smid=nytcore-iphone-share&referer=.

139 Sarah Posner, *Amazing Disgrace*, NEW REPUBLIC (Mar. 20, 2017), newrepublic.com/article/140961/amazing-disgrace-donald-trump-hijacked-religious-right.

140 *Id.*

141 Jared Dobbs, *Donald Trump: 100 Days In*, ALLIANCE DEFENDING FREEDOM BLOG (Apr. 28, 2017), www.adflegal.org/detailspages/blog-details/allianceedge/2017/04/28/donald-trump-100-days-in.

142 *Id.* (quotation marks omitted).

6

The Substantial Burden Question: Secular Tools for Secular Courts

Michael A. Helfand

Associate Professor of Law, Pepperdine University School of Law, and Co-Director, Diane and Guilford Glazer Institute for Jewish Studies

When is a burden "substantial"? This question stands at the center of recent clashes between law and religion, testing the scope and application of the Religious Freedom Restoration Act ("RFRA"). Enacted on the heels of the Supreme Court's decision in *Employment Division v. Smith*,[1] RFRA prohibits government from "substantially burden[ing] a person's exercise of religion," unless doing so is the "least restrictive means" for achieving a "compelling governmental interest."[2]

Because *Smith* limited the free exercise protections available under the First Amendment, RFRA has become *the* flashpoint as religiously motivated individuals and institutions seek exemptions from otherwise valid laws. Unfortunately, the text and legislative history of RFRA provide limited guidance for evaluating substantiality.[3] And as RFRA affords protection only against "*substantial* burdens" on religious exercise, articulating a methodology for evaluating substantiality has become the central question in many of the most important court battles over religious liberty.

Indeed, arguments over what constitutes a substantial burden emerged as a central issue in the Supreme Court's 2014 blockbuster decision, *Burwell v. Hobby Lobby Stores Inc.*, and its follow-up decision postponing a definitive analysis on the religious accommodation for nonprofits, *Zubik*

This chapter is adapted from my article *Identifying Substantial Burdens*, 2016 U. ILL. L. REV. 1771.

1 Emp't Div. v. Smith, 494 U.S. 872 (1990). 2 42 U.S.C. § 2000bb–1 (2012).

3 *See, e.g.*, Michael C. Dorf, *Incidental Burdens on Fundamental Rights*, 109 HARV. L. REV. 1175, 1213 (1996) ("Neither the text nor the legislative history of RFRA provides any clear indication of how courts ought to determine whether an incidental burden on religion is in fact substantial.").

v. Burwell.[4] In its *Hobby Lobby* opinion, the Court held that for-profit companies could assert a RFRA defense against the Patient Protection and Affordable Care Act's ("ACA") contraception coverage mandate ("mandate"), which would have otherwise required companies to include certain forms of contraception in their employee's insurance coverage.[5] The Court concluded that a requirement to provide such contraception coverage not only imposed a burden on religiously motivated employers who believed providing coverage would violate their own religious commitments but that such a burden for purposes of RFRA was *substantial*.[6]

In *Zubik*, religiously motivated nonprofit employers similarly challenged the mandate, contending that the current process for religious accommodation, which requires some nonprofits to self-certify as religious institutions, also violates RFRA. These nonprofit employers believe that filing the paperwork that confirms they are a religious institution, and thereby secures their religious exemption, will trigger contraceptive insurance coverage for their employees. In turn, triggering such coverage – even if paid for and provided by a third party, not the objecting institution – makes them complicit in conduct they believe to be sinful.[7] Thus, the process of securing the exemption itself not only burdens, but *substantially* burdens their religious exercise.

The question of substantial burden under RFRA has also emerged as a key issue in controversies over some religiously motivated refusals by businesses that serve the public, and are therefore regulated as "public accommodations," to provide their services at same-sex weddings or commitment ceremonies.[8] In three recent, separate, and highly publicized cases, a baker, a florist, and a photographer were each found liable for impermissibly discriminating on the basis of sexual orientation – in one case, over and above the defendant's attempt to assert RFRA as a defense.[9]

4 Burwell v. Hobby Lobby Stores, Inc., 134 S. Ct. 2751, 2759 (2014); Zubik v. Burwell, 136 S. Ct. 444 (2016).

5 *Id.* at 2775–85. 6 *See infra* Section I. 7 *Id.*

8 *See* Adams, Chapter 21, this volume, for state-by-state review of such laws.

9 Craig v. Masterpiece Cakeshop, Inc., No. 14CA1351, 2015 WL 4760453, at *1 (Colo. App. 2015). The U.S. Supreme Court has agreed to review this decision. Masterpiece Cakeshop, Ltd. v. Colorado Civil Rights Commission, No. 16–11. State v. Arlene's Flowers, Inc., 389 P.3d 543 (Wash. 2017). The business owner has said she will appeal the decision to the U.S. Supreme Court. Lynn Thompson, *Richland Florist Discriminated Against Gay Couple by Refusing Service, State Supreme Court Rules*, Seattle Times (Feb. 16, 2017), www.seattletimes.com/seattle-news/northwest/richland-florist-discriminated-against-gay-couple-for-refusing-service-states-highest-court-rules/. Elane Photography, LLC v. Willock, 309 P.3d 53, 60, 77 (N.M. 2013), *cert. denied*, 134 S. Ct. 1787 (2014) (rejecting RFRA defense).

In response to these cases, the Indiana legislature introduced its own version of RFRA in order to, in the words of one supporter of the bill, protect "Christian bakers, florists and photographers [who] should not be punished for refusing to participate in homosexual marriage."[10] Thus, the bill would allow commercial entities to assert that providing services at a same-sex wedding constitutes a substantial burden on their religious exercise. The bill, initially enacted by the Indiana legislature, received unrelenting criticism from around the country, eventually leading to the bill's modification.[11] And Indiana has turned out to be just the beginning. Other states have also introduced their own bills, some with new wrinkles to the RFRA framework.[12] Under intense criticism, some have been amended,[13] and some have been vetoed.[14] These controversies are unlikely to subside in coming years, especially given that numerous states have their own versions of RFRA that prohibit each state's respective laws from *substantially* burdening a person's religious exercise.[15]

[10] *See Victory at the State House! Governor Pence Signs Senate Bill 101!* ADVANCE AMERICA (Mar. 26, 2015), www.advanceamerica.com/blog/?p=1849.

[11] *See, e.g.*, Associated Press, *Indiana Enacts Religious-Objections Law*, WALL ST. J. (Mar. 26, 2015), www.wsj.com/articles/indiana-enacts-religious-objections-law-1427383220; Mark Peters & Jack Nicas, *Indiana Religious Freedom Law Sparks Fury*, WALL ST. J. (Mar. 27, 2015), www.wsj.com/articles/indiana-religious-freedom-law-sparks-fury-1427491304; *see also Celebs Respond to Indiana's Religious Freedom Law*, CNN (Mar. 30, 2015), www.cnn.com/2015/03/30/politics/celebrities-indiana-religious-freedom-response/; Monica Davey et al., *Indiana and Arkansas Revise Rights Bills, Seeking to Remove Divisive Parts*, N.Y. TIMES, Apr. 2, 2015, www.nytimes.com/2015/04/03/us/indiana-arkansas-religious-freedom-bill.html; Mark Peters & Ana Campoy, *"Religious Freedom" Measures Revamped*, WALL ST. J. (Apr. 2, 2015), www.wsj.com/articles/indiana-lawmakers-unveil-changes-to-religious-freedom-law-1427981035. Before Indiana, Arizona faced significant backlash when it attempted to modify its state RFRA. *See, e.g.*, Tamara Audi, *Arizona Vetoes Religious Bill Criticized as Anti-Gay*, WALL ST. J. (Feb. 27, 2014), www.wsj.com/articles/SB10001424052702304255604579407784144050074.

[12] For a collection of attempts to enact state Religious Freedom Restoration Acts in 2015 and 2016, *see* National Conference of State Legislatures, *2015 State Religious Freedom Restoration Legislation* (Sept. 3, 2015), www.ncsl.org/research/civil-and-criminal-justice/2015-state-rfra-legislation.aspx; National Conference of State Legislatures, *2016 State Religious Freedom Restoration Legislation* (Apr. 5, 2016), www.ncsl.org/research/civil-and-criminal-justice/2016-state-religious-freedom-restoration-act-legislation.aspx.

[13] *See, e.g.*, Eric Bradner, *Arkansas Governor Signs Amended "Religious Freedom" Measure*, CNN(Apr. 2, 2015), www.cnn.com/2015/03/31/politics/arkansas-religious-freedom-anti-lgbt-bill/.

[14] *See, e.g.*, Sandhya Somashekhar, *Georgia Governor Vetoes Religious Freedom Bill Criticized as Anti-Gay*, WASH. POST (Mar. 28, 2016), www.washingtonpost.com/news/post-nation/wp/2016/03/28/georgia-governor-to-veto-religious-freedom-bill-criticized-as-anti-gay/?utm_term=.85a716f3c87e.

[15] *See* Adams, Chapter 21, this volume.

So how should a court determine whether a law has imposed a burden on religious exercise that is substantial? Can claims of attenuated complicity in conduct believed by plaintiffs to be sinful satisfy RFRA's standard?

There are twin pitfalls to avoid. On the one hand, the Establishment Clause is typically understood to prohibit courts from investigating matters of religion and theology; so evaluating the theological substantiality of a law's burden on a person's religious exercise would seem to be off limits. On the other hand, RFRA requires courts to determine not only whether a burden exists, but also whether that burden is substantial. And, therefore, courts cannot simply defer to the assertions of a litigant without conducting the statutorily required inquiry of a burden's substantiality.

To avoid these twin pitfalls, this chapter argues that in order to determine whether a burden is substantial, courts must examine the substantiality of the *civil penalties triggered by religious exercise*. By focusing on civil penalties – as opposed to the substantiality of religious or theological burdens – courts can avoid Establishment Clause concerns, while still enforcing the threshold inquiry required by RFRA. In this way, courts can avoid a judicial inquiry into theology when deciding RFRA's threshold substantial burden question, while still ensuring that RFRA's protections are not granted simply on the say-so of claimants who assert that the burdens they have experienced are substantial.

This chapter proceeds in four sections. Section I considers the current controversies over the substantial burden standard, focusing largely on the mandate litigation. Section II then recounts various forms of substantial-burden skepticism – that is, judicial and legislative criticism of the substantial burden standard as a doctrinal vehicle for protecting religious liberty. Section III provides a framework for evaluating substantial burdens. Finally, Section IV considers some hard cases for the substantial burden standard articulated in this chapter.

I THE CURRENT DEBATE OVER SUBSTANTIAL BURDENS

The concept of "burden" has long been at the center of litigation over religious accommodations.[16] It first surfaced as a passing comment in the Supreme Court's 1961 opinion *Braunfeld v. Brown*,[17] in which Orthodox Jewish merchants argued that Pennsylvania's Sunday-closing law violated their free

[16] *See* Ira C. Lupu, *Where Rights Begin: The Problem of Burdens on the Free Exercise of Religion*, 102 HARV. L. REV. 933, 937–42 (1989).

[17] 366 U.S. 599, 606 (1961).

exercise rights.[18] The Sunday-closing laws significantly disadvantaged them, they said, because, in keeping with Jewish law, they also closed their stores on Saturday.[19] The Supreme Court rejected their claim, explaining that the law simply made "their religious beliefs more expensive."[20] But the Court noted in passing that government may not impose an incidental and indirect burden on religious conduct where "the State may accomplish its purpose by means which do not impose such a burden."[21]

This nascent concept of "burden" famously erupted into full bloom in the Supreme Court's 1963 decision, *Sherbert v. Verner*.[22] There, a Seventh-day Adventist was terminated for refusing to work on Saturday and was denied unemployment benefits. Finding in favor of the former employee, the Court made the substantial-burden standard an explicit centerpiece of its free exercise doctrine,[23] holding that a law may not impose an "incidental burden on the Free Exercise of appellant's religion," unless that burden can be justified by a "compelling state interest."[24]

The Court further entrenched the substantial burden framework in *Wisconsin v. Yoder*, holding that Wisconsin's compulsory education law infringed on the free exercise rights of Amish parents who, in accordance with their religious beliefs, refused to send their children to public school beyond eighth grade.[25] The Court echoed its decision in *Sherbert*: "A regulation neutral on its face may, in its application, nonetheless offend the constitutional requirement for governmental neutrality if it unduly burdens the Free Exercise of religion."[26] This concept of burden animated the Court's Free Exercise decisions in numerous subsequent cases.[27]

The centrality of the burden concept in free exercise doctrine waned in the 1980s,[28] before being dispatched in the Supreme Court's landmark decision, *Employment Division v. Smith*.[29] In *Smith*, the Supreme Court rejected the notion that an incidental burden on a person's religious exercise could trigger a free exercise claim; so long as a law is "neutral" and "generally applicable," it could not violate the Free Exercise Clause even where the law incidentally imposed a burden on religious conduct.[30]

[18] 366 U.S. 599, 601–602, 606 (1961); *see also supra* note 16, at 939.
[19] Braunfeld, *supra* note 17, at 602. [20] *Id.* at 605. [21] *Id.* at 607.
[22] Sherbert v. Verner, 374 U.S. 398 (1963). [23] *Id.* at 403. [24] *Id.*
[25] Wisconsin v. Yoder, 406 U.S. 205, 235–36 (1972).
[26] *Id.* at 220 (citing Sherbert, *supra* note 22, at 409).
[27] *See, e.g.*, Bob Jones Univ. v. United States, 461 U.S. 574, 603 (1983); United States v. Lee, 455 U.S. 252, 257–58 (1982); Thomas v. Review Bd., Ind. Emp't. Sec. Div., 450 U.S. 707, 717–18 (1981).
[28] *See, e.g.*, Lyng v. Nw. Indian Cemetery Prot. Ass'n, 485 U.S. 439, 451 (1988); Bowen v. Roy, 476 U.S. 693, 699–700 (1986).
[29] Smith, *supra* note 1. [30] *Id.* at 878–80.

In response, Congress blunted the impact of *Smith* by enacting RFRA, which once again placed "burden" – or, more specifically, "substantial burden" – at the center of religious accommodation doctrine. Thus, RFRA sought to restore free exercise protections to the pre-*Smith* standard, providing that "[g]overnment shall not substantially burden a person's exercise of religion even if the burden results from a rule of general applicability," unless that burden was the "least restrictive means of furthering a compelling government interest."[31] While the Supreme Court limited RFRA's application to federal laws, twenty-one states have enacted state RFRAs and others have court decisions interpreting their state free exercise provisions to require a similar result,[32] ensuring that the concept of "substantial burden" remains at the center of the religious accommodation enterprise.

The substantial burden inquiry, however, has also frequently proven to be the most difficult doctrinal hurdle for plaintiffs. Indeed, courts have long maintained significant skepticism of substantial-burden claims. Whether under the pre-*Smith* interpretation of the Free Exercise Clause or the post-RFRA standard for evaluating religious accommodation claims, courts have consistently questioned whether claimants seeking religious accommodations have truly experienced a *substantial* burden on their religious exercise.[33]

The most recent iteration of this substantial-burden skepticism emerged in the context of the mandate. Pursuant to the guidelines promulgated by the Department of Health and Human Services ("HHS"),[34] covered insurance plans must include "[a]ll Food and Drug Administration approved contraceptive methods, sterilization procedures, and patient education and counseling for all women with reproductive capacity."[35] The final rules issued by HHS exempted "religious employers," but not for-profit companies.[36]

31 42 U.S.C. § 2000bb–1(a) & (b) (2012). 32 *See* Adams, Chapter 21, this volume.

33 *See* James E. Ryan, *Smith and the Religious Freedom Restoration Act: An Iconoclastic Assessment*, 78 Va. L. Rev. 1407, 1416 (1992) (noting that even pre-*Smith*, "the Free Exercise claimant faced something of a Catch-22. In order to demonstrate a burden, the government … interference … had to be significant enough [to] potentially 'coerce' the adherent to abandon her faith. Yet such extensive … would almost always signify that the government had a compelling interest in the law or practice in question"); Ira C. Lupu, *The Failure of RFRA*, 20 U. Ark. Little Rock L. Rev. 575, 594 (1998) (showing that "a stunningly high proportion of all RFRA claims decided on the merits prior to *Boerne* involved rejection of claims as presenting insubstantial burdens").

34 The ACA required that covered health insurance plans provide "preventative care" for women in accordance with guidelines promulgated by the Health Resources and Services Administration, an agency of HHS. 42 U.S.C. § 300gg-13(a)(4) (2012, 2016).

35 *Women's Preventative Services Guidelines*, Health Resources and Services Admin., www.hrsa.gov/womensguidelines/. These guidelines were subsequently incorporated into HHS's final rules. *See* Group Health Plans and Health Insurance Issuers Relating to Coverage of Preventive Services Under the Patient, 76 Fed. Reg. 46623 (Aug. 3, 2011) (codified at 45 C.F.R. § 147.130 (2011, 2017)).

36 45 C.F.R. § 147.131 (2014, 2017).

In response to the guidelines, numerous Christian institutions filed suit, arguing that complying with the mandate would require them to violate their religious consciences.[37] This wave of lawsuits fell into two broad categories. The first wave included for-profit companies that argued that the government's refusal to extend its exemption beyond the category of nonprofits violated their rights under the federal RFRA. In 2014, this claim made its way before the Supreme Court. The specific case before the Court considered the claims of three closely held for-profit corporations: Hobby Lobby, an arts-and-crafts chain; Mardel, a chain of bookstores selling Christian books and products; and Conestoga Woods, a custom cabinet manufacturer. These corporations objected to providing insurance coverage for four of twenty contraceptives mandated under the ACA.[38]

The Supreme Court found in favor of these three plaintiffs, holding that the mandate substantially burdened the companies' religious exercise and was not the least restrictive means for ensuring employees received cost-free contraception.[39] The Court argued that government could extend the exemption crafted for nonprofit companies to for-profit companies as well, thereby ensuring that employees received cost-free contraception without burdening their employers' religious commitments.[40]

In perhaps the key holding of the decision, the Supreme Court concluded that the plaintiffs had demonstrated that the application of the mandate would constitute a substantial burden. Given the implications of this holding, the Court provided extensive analysis of the question, outlining a three-tiered argument supporting its conclusion that the mandate imposed a substantial burden on the employers.

First, the Court held that the cost to the employers of refusing to provide contraception insurance would be $100 a day per employee, leaving Hobby Lobby with an annual $475 million bill, Conestoga Woods with an annual bill of $33 million, and Mardel with an annual $15 million bill.[41] Such costs, explained the Court, clearly constituted a substantial burden.[42]

Critics, however, had argued that this conclusion was flawed. Employers could simply eliminate their employee healthcare plan completely, avoiding the $100 per day, per employee penalty.[43] In the second step of its argument,

[37] For up-to-date information on the range of lawsuits over the mandate, see *HHS Mandate Information Central*, THE BECKET FUND FOR RELIGIOUS LIBERTY, www.becketfund.org/hhsinformationcentral/.

[38] Hobby Lobby, *supra* note 4, at 2764–66. [39] *Id.* at 2779, 2782, 2785. [40] *Id.* at 2782–84.

[41] *Id.* at 2775–76. [42] *Id.*

[43] Marty Lederman, *Hobby Lobby Part III – There is No "Employer Mandate,"* BALKINAZATION BLOG (Dec. 18, 2013), balkin.blogspot.com/2013/12/hobby-lobby-part-iiitheres-no-employer.html.

the Court responded by noting that if the employers dropped their employee healthcare plan completely – avoiding the mandate – they would face costly penalties of $2,000 per year, per employee. Thus, the Court concluded that, regardless of which alternative these employers selected, they would face a substantial burden imposed by the ACA. [44]

The government, however, contended that even if the employers' religious exercise triggered significant penalties, the claim that it imposed a substantial burden was still flawed. The reason: the injuries caused by the mandate should not be considered "cognizable . . . where the relationship between the claimed injury and the challenged governmental action is too attenuated."[45] Thus, the fact that the employer provided insurance coverage for contraception was several causal steps removed from the conduct violating the employer's religious convictions – the destruction of an embryo.[46] This causal break, argued the government, undermined the claim that the burden imposed on employers could be *substantial*.

The Court disagreed, advancing a third argument supporting its conclusion that the mandate imposed a substantial burden. The First Amendment prohibits judicial inquiry into the theological grounds for the professed substantial burden, the Court noted,[47] and determining whether the employers' asserted burden was substantial implicated the types of questions that the First Amendment prohibited. Accordingly, the Court concluded that the only constitutionally permissible inquiry into the employers' beliefs was as to whether those beliefs were sincerely held – and the Court noted no party disputed that they were.[48] The Court held that the mandate posed a substantial burden, as employers would face significant financial penalties for failing to provide insurance for contraception, a step that violated a sincerely held religious belief.

Justice Ruth Bader Ginsburg harshly criticized the majority's conclusion that the mandate imposed a substantial burden. Relying on pre-*Smith* Supreme Court decisions, Justice Ginsburg contended that "beliefs, however deeply held, do not suffice to sustain a RFRA claim"; a court must still determine whether a plaintiff's "religious exercise is substantially burdened."[49] Justice Ginsburg argued that the majority's holding that the

[44] Hobby Lobby, *supra* note 4, at 2776–77. *But see* Lederman, *supra* note 43.

[45] Brief for Petitioners at 32, Hobby Lobby Stores, Inc., 134 S. Ct. 2751 (2014) *supra* note 4, (No. 13–354), www.becketfund.org/wp-content/uploads/2014/03/SG-Merits-Brief-Hobby-Lobby.pdf.

[46] Hobby Lobby, *supra* note 4, at 2777. [47] *Id.* at 2778–79. [48] *Id.* at 2779.

[49] *Id.* at 2798 (Ginsburg, J., dissenting) (quoting Kaemmerling v. Lappin, 553 F.3d 669, 679 (D.C. Cir. 2008)).

mandate imposed a substantial burden failed both because it failed to determine whether the employers truly experienced a burden that was *substantial* and, relatedly, because it failed to take into account the attenuated relationship between the mandate's requirements and the actual conduct that the employers found religiously objectionable. That attenuation, Justice Ginsburg concluded, undermined any claim that the burden was, in reality, substantial.

Notwithstanding *Hobby Lobby*, the battle over defining substantial burdens in the mandate context was far from over. In the wake of the Court's decision in *Hobby Lobby*, the government amended its regulations to exempt from the mandate both nonprofit and closely held, for-profit entities that "hold[] [themselves] out as [] religious organization[s]."[50] Unlike core religious organizations such as churches and their auxiliaries,[51] initially these nonprofits and closely held, for-profit entities had to self-certify to qualify for this exemption by filling out Form 700 and sending the form to their respective insurers and or third-party administrators.[52] However, many nonprofit companies objected; filling out Form 700 still made them complicit in the eventual provision of contraception. Therefore, they contended that filling out the form constituted a substantial burden on their religious exercise, violating RFRA's protections.[53]

By and large, the federal courts of appeals roundly rejected this claim, concluding that the requirement to fill out Form 700 could not be considered a "substantial burden." For example, the DC Circuit concluded that

> the challenged regulations do not impose a substantial burden on Plaintiffs' religious exercise under RFRA. All Plaintiffs must do to opt out is express what they believe and seek what they want via a letter or two-page form. That bit of paperwork is more straightforward and minimal than many that are staples of nonprofit organizations' compliance with law in the modern administrative state.[54]

Other federal courts of appeals reached similar decisions.[55]

50 45 C.F.R. § 147.131(b) (2017).

51 *Id.* § 147.131(a) (incorporating the definition from 26 U.S.C. § 6033(a)(3)(A)(i) (2012)).

52 If the entity is self-insured, it can provide Form 700 to the third-party administrator of its health plan. 45 C.F.R. § 147.131(c)(1)(i).

53 For an up-to-date list of cases filed by nonprofits over the self-certification process, see *HHS Mandate Information Central*, *supra* note 37.

54 Priests for Life v. U.S. Dep't of Health & Human Servs., 772 F.3d 229, 237 (D.C. Cir. 2014).

55 Geneva Coll. v. Sec'y U.S. Dep't of Health & Human Servs., 778 F.3d 422, 442 (3d Cir. 2015) ("[C]an the submission of the self-certification form, which relieves the appellees of any connection to the provision of the objected-to contraceptive services, really impose a 'substantial' burden on the appellees' Free Exercise of religion? We think not . . .. [W]here the actual provision of contraceptive coverage is by a third party, the burden is not merely attenuated at the outset but totally disconnected from the appellees."); Mich. Catholic

The Supreme Court, without ruling on the merits, initially indicated it might be receptive to claims that filling out Form 700 might constitute a substantial burden.[56] The Court issued an injunction in favor of Wheaton College, not requiring it to submit Form 700 to the third-party administrator of its health plan.[57] Instead, Wheaton College could simply "inform[] the Secretary of [HHS] in writing that it is a nonprofit organization that holds itself out as religious and has religious objections to providing coverage for contraceptive services."[58] The government subsequently amended its regulations to allow religious organizations to self-certify by sending Form 700 directly to the government.[59]

Justice Sonia Sotomayor harshly criticized the majority's grant of the injunction, ridiculing the conclusion that filling out and filing Form 700 could constitute a substantial burden: "Let me be absolutely clear: I do not doubt that Wheaton genuinely believes that signing the self-certification form is contrary to its religious beliefs. But *thinking* one's religious beliefs are substantially burdened – no matter how sincere or genuine that belief may be – does not make it so."[60] Wheaton, Justice Sotomayor argued, was mistaken about the legal import of its role in providing contraceptive coverage: "[T]he obligation to provide contraceptive services . . . arises not from the filing of the form but from the underlying law and regulations."[61] For Justice Sotomayor, because filling out Form 700 did not trigger the underlying legal obligation, it was not possible for the requirement to self-certify to constitute a substantial burden. To claim it was a substantial burden was to misunderstand the way the mandate accommodation worked.

After the *Wheaton* injunction, the Eighth Circuit – breaking with the other federal courts of appeals to rule on the issue – held that RFRA protects nonprofit companies that refuse to submit Form 700 because the self-certification requirement does constitute a substantial burden.[62]

Conference & Catholic Family Servs. v. Burwell, 755 F.3d 372, 388 (6th Cir. 2014) ("The government's imposition of an independent obligation on a third party does not impose a substantial burden on the appellants' exercise of religion . . . . [T]he Government's instruction to insurance issuers and third-party administrators to provide contraceptive coverage does not force the appellants to provide, pay for, and/or facilitate access to the coverage."); *see also* Univ. of Notre Dame v. Burwell, 786 F.3d 606, 613–16 (7th Cir. 2015).

56 *See, e.g.*, Univ. of Notre Dame v. Burwell, 135 S. Ct. 1528, 1528 (2015) (granting certiorari, vacating the appellate court's decision, and remanding for further consideration); Wheaton Coll. v. Burwell, 134 S. Ct. 2806, 2807 (2014) (issuing an injunction against requirement that petitioner use Form 700).

57 Wheaton Coll., *supra* note 56, at 2806. 58 *Id.*

59 *See* Coverage of Certain Preventive Services Under the Affordable Care Act, 80 Fed. Reg. 41, 322–23 (July 14, 2015) (to be codified at 45 C.F.R. pt. 147).

60 Wheaton Coll., *supra* note 56, at 2812 (Sotomayor, J., dissenting). 61 *Id.* at 2813.

62 *See, e.g.*, Sharpe Holdings, Inc. v. U.S. Dep't of Health & Human Servs., 801 F.3d 927, 936–37 (8th Cir. 2015).

In light of the circuit split, the Supreme Court granted certiorari, ostensibly putting the definition of substantial burden front and center on its docket.[63] However, left with only eight justices after Justice Antonin Scalia's death, the Court chose to vacate the nonprofit cases and remand to the federal courts of appeals, postponing resolution of the substantial burden question.[64] In an extraordinary step, the Court strongly signaled its desire for the parties to compromise: "The parties on remand should be afforded an opportunity to arrive at an approach going forward that accommodates petitioners' religious exercise while at the same time ensuring that women covered by petitioners' health plans 'receive full and equal health coverage, including contraceptive coverage.'"[65] While laudable, the Court's decision left the substantial burden question unanswered. Not surprisingly, the Court has already been petitioned in yet another case centered on this question[66] and is likely to continue receiving such petitions until it provides some clarifications on the substantial burden question. And all this brings us back to our initial question: how should we determine which burdens are, for RFRA purposes, *substantial*?

II SUBSTANTIAL-BURDEN SKEPTICISM

Substantial-burden skepticism permeated both free exercise as well as RFRA doctrine long before the recent mandate litigation. In the 1980s, in the years preceding *Smith*, the Supreme Court issued two decisions – *Bowen v. Roy* and *Lyng v. Northwest Indian Cemetery Protective Association* – that cast significant doubt on the viability of the substantial-burden doctrine.

In *Bowen*, the Court addressed a free exercise claim about whether state welfare agencies could require recipients of certain welfare benefits to first provide the social security numbers of all participants, including children.[67] According to one participant's parents, procuring a social security number for their child would "'rob the spirit' of his daughter and prevent her from attaining greater spiritual power."[68] The Court rejected the claim, arguing that the plaintiffs had failed to demonstrate a substantial burden on their religious exercise; absent this, their claim, pre-*Smith*, would fail. The majority opinion first argued that "[t]he Free Exercise Clause simply cannot be understood to require the Government to conduct its own internal affairs in ways that comport with the religious beliefs of particular citizens."[69]

[63] *See* Order Granting Certiorari, Zubik v. Burwell, 136 S. Ct. 444 (Nov. 6, 2015) (No. 14–1418).
[64] Zubik v. Burwell, 136 S. Ct. 1557 (2016). [65] *Id.* at 1560.
[66] *See* Petition for Cert., Sterling v. United States (Dec. 23, 2016), www.caaflog.com/wp-content/uploads/Sterling-Cert-Petition.pdf.
[67] Bowen v. Roy, 476 U.S. 693, 695 (1986). [68] *Id.* at 696. [69] *Id.* at 699.

But in Part III of Justice Warren Burger's opinion, which was, it should be noted, only joined by Justices William Rehnquist and Lewis Powell, the Court expressed even deeper skepticism of expanding the category of substantial burdens: "[T]he Court has steadfastly maintained that claims of religious conviction do not automatically entitle a person to fix unilaterally the conditions and terms of dealings with the Government. Not all burdens on religion are unconstitutional."[70] Expanding the category of what qualified as a substantial burden would be untenable due to the broad range of government-provided benefits:

> Governments today grant a broad range of benefits; inescapably at the same time the administration of complex programs requires certain conditions and restrictions. Although in some situations a mechanism for individual consideration will be created, a policy decision by a government that it wishes to treat all applicants alike and that it does not wish to become involved in case-by-case inquiries into the genuineness of each religious objection to such condition or restrictions is entitled to substantial deference.[71]

These concerns generated strong skepticism of the substantial-burden doctrine and whether laws that substantially burdened religion should be subjected to the rigors of strict scrutiny. Foreshadowing *Smith*, *Bowen* argued that "[i]n the enforcement of a facially neutral and uniformly applicable requirement for the administration of welfare programs," the government's regulations should not be subjected to strict scrutiny.[72]

Similar skepticism of substantial burdens emerged in *Lyng*. There the Court addressed claims that government construction through a national forest would substantially burden the religion of three Native American tribes that had been using the forest for religious purposes.[73] The Court rejected these claims, relying heavily on *Bowen*. The Court compared the issue in *Bowen* to that in *Lyng* – noting that in neither of the cases "would the affected individuals be coerced by the Government's action into violating their religious beliefs" – and leveraged this parallel in concluding that only government regulations that coerced individuals to act in a manner contrary to their faiths would constitute the type of substantial burden that would thereby trigger strict scrutiny analysis.[74] Imposing a coercion test on the category of substantial burdens represented somewhat of a turn in free exercise doctrine and therefore, not surprisingly, raised the ire of the dissent.[75]

70 *Id.* at 702. 71 *Id.* at 707. 72 *Id.*

73 Lyng v. Nw. Indian Cemetery Protective Ass'n, 485 U.S. 439, 441–42 (1988). 74 *Id.* at 449.

75 *Id.* at 468 (Brennan, J., dissenting) ("Ultimately, the Court's coercion test turns on a distinction between governmental actions that compel affirmative conduct inconsistent

This growing substantial-burden skepticism culminated with the Court's decision in *Employment Division v. Smith*, where the Court eliminated the need to interrogate what burdens qualified as legally relevant. But with the enactment of RFRA in 1993, courts once again were required to determine when a government regulation "substantially burden[ed] a person's exercise of religion."[76]

However, many federal courts expressed a new version of substantial-burden skepticism by advancing a narrow interpretation of RFRA's provisions that limited the category of what qualified as a substantial burden. Thus, some federal courts held that a burden would be deemed substantial only if the burden implicated central tenets of the plaintiff's faith.[77] Other courts – channelling *Bowen* and *Lyng* – interpreted substantial burdens as those that compelled conduct that violated a plaintiff's faith.[78] And yet others combined the centrality and the compulsion standards, using both to limit the category of substantial burdens.[79] To be sure, some federal courts eschewed this substantial-burden skepticism – holding that burdens could be substantial so long as the conduct in question was simply religiously motivated[80] – but this expansive approach to the substantial-burden inquiry was very much in the minority.[81]

As it did after *Smith*, Congress responded to the wave of judicial limitations on substantial burdens by revising RFRA.[82] RFRA now incorporates a definition of "exercise of religion" that includes "any exercise of religion, whether or not compelled by, or central to, a system of religious belief."[83] Accordingly, RFRA currently prohibits any substantial burden on religious exercise irrespective of whether religiously motivated conduct is religiously compelled or central to the person's faith commitments.

with religious belief, and those governmental actions that prevent conduct consistent with religious belief. In my view, such a distinction is without constitutional significance."). Justice Brennan proposed an inquiry into whether the burden implicated a central tenet of the faith. *Id.* at 474.

76 42 U.S.C. § 2000bb–1(b) (2012).

77 *See, e.g.*, Thiry v. Carlson, 78 F.3d 1491 (10th Cir. 1996); Abdur-Rahman v. Mich. Dep't of Corr., 65 F.3d 489 (6th Cir. 1995); Werner v. McCotter, 49 F.3d 1476, 1480 (10th Cir. 1995).

78 *See, e.g.*, Goodall v. Stafford Cnty. Sch. Bd., 60 F.3d 168 (4th Cir. 1995); Cheffer v. Reno, 55 F.3d 1517 (11th Cir. 1995).

79 *See, e.g.*, Small v. Lehman, 98 F.3d 762, 767–68 (3d Cir. 1996); Hicks v. Garner, 69 F.3d 22 (5th Cir. 1995); Bryant v. Gomez, 46 F.3d 948, 949 (9th Cir. 1995).

80 *See, e.g.*, Jolly v. Coughlin, 76 F.3d 468, 476–77 (2d Cir. 1996).

81 Steven C. Seeger, *Restoring Rights to Rites: The Religious Motivation Test and the Religious Freedom Restoration Act*, 95 MICH. L. REV. 1472, 1473 (1997).

82 *See* H.R. REP. NO. 106–219, at 13 (1999).

83 42 U.S.C. § 2000bb-2(4) (2012). *Id.* at § 2000bb–1(b); *id.* § 2000cc-5(7)(A).

The mandate litigation has triggered another round of substantial-burden skepticism, with skeptics contending that various nonprofits have pressed the definition of substantial burden too far.[84] Some argue courts cannot simply defer to the assertion of claimants that they have experienced a substantial burden.[85] When courts refuse to evaluate how much of a religious burden is being imposed by the law, critics argue, they give deference to RFRA claimants Congress did not intend. Others focus on RFRA's text; courts, they say, are required by the statute to evaluate substantiality and thereby differentiate between different degrees of substantiality when applying RFRA.[86] Thus, judicial failure to interrogate the religious implications of a law – and the extent of burden imposed – is to fail apply RFRA's terms.

These arguments boil down to one claim: we cannot simply treat all religious burdens equally. The purpose of RFRA was to protect against *substantial* burdens; insubstantial burdens are not sufficiently worrisome to justify a mandatory religious exemption. Thus, courts must differentiate between substantial and insubstantial burdens if RFRA is to serve its filtering function of protecting only against more egregious impositions on religious exercise. Restricting RFRA protections to substantial burdens means that courts must draw lines between impositions that have greater theological significance and impositions with less.

Such arguments have superficial allure. Still, this sort of a line drawing within the category of substantial burdens would be a grave error. Interrogating the religious substantiality of conduct on a theological metric runs afoul of core Establishment Clause prohibitions.[87] As the Supreme Court noted in *Thomas v. Review Board*, "it is not for us to say

84 *See, e.g.*, Univ. of Notre Dame v. Burwell, 786 F.3d 606 (7th Cir. 2015); Geneva Coll. v. Sec'y of U.S. Dep't of Health & Human Servs., 778 F.3d 422 (3d Cir. 2015); Priests for Life v. U.S. Dep't of Health & Human Servs, 772 F.3d 229 (D.C. Cir. 2014); Mich. Catholic Conference Servs. v. Burwell, 755 F.3d 372 (6th Cir. 2014).

85 *See, e.g.*, Abner S. Greene, *Religious Freedom and (Other) Civil Liberties: Is There a Middle Ground?*, 9 Harv. L. & Pol'y Rev. 161, 180 (2015); Samuel J. Levine, A *Critique of Hobby Lobby and the Supreme Court's Hands-Off Approach to Religion*, 91 Notre Dame L. Rev. Online 26, 31 (2015).

86 *See, e.g.*, Caroline Mala Corbin, *Closing Statement: Sincere Is Not Substantial and a Corporation Is Not an Orchestra*, 161 U. Pa. L. Rev. Online 278, 279 (2013) [hereinafter *Closing Statement*].

87 In contrast to government allocation of legal benefits and burdens pursuant to RFRA on the basis of a theological evaluation of substantiality, I have argued elsewhere that the Establishment Clause does not prohibit courts from adjudicating private law disputes between private litigants simply because those disputes implicate religious questions. *See* Michael A. Helfand, *Litigating Religion*, 93 B.U. L. Rev. 493 (2013) (arguing courts are, in principle, both sufficiently competent and constitutionally authorized to resolve such cases).

that the line [petitioner] drew was an unreasonable one. Courts should not undertake to dissect religious beliefs . . . because his beliefs are not articulated with the clarity and precision that a more sophisticated person might employ."[88]

Both advocates and critics of religious accommodations agreed upon this constitutional boundary in the past. The Supreme Court in *Smith* rejected an interpretation of the First Amendment mandating exemptions from facially neutral and generally applicable laws, precisely because line drawing between degrees of theological impact was not a constitutionally permissible inquiry for courts: "What principle of law or logic can be brought to bear to contradict a believer's assertion that a particular act is 'central' to his personal faith? Judging the centrality of different religious practices is akin to the unacceptable 'business of evaluating the relative merits of differing religious claims.'"[89] This skepticism of theological line drawing motivated Congress to clarify the substantial burden inquiry: "the burdened religious activity need not be compulsory or central to a religious belief system as a condition for the claim."[90]

Importantly, interpreting RFRA to require an inquiry into the theological substantiality of legal burdens would likely yield gross inequalities in application. Courts are predisposed to favoring religious majorities, whose religious practices are more well known and respected; the religious practices of religious minorities are more obscure.[91] Under a regime where courts evaluate the theological substantiality of religious burdens, the impact of laws on religious minorities is likely to be underestimated and underappreciated, unfairly circumscribing RFRA's protections.[92] As I note in Chapter 2 of this

88 Thomas v. Review Bd., Ind. Emp't. Sec. Div., 450 U.S. 707, 715 (1981).

89 Smith, *supra* note 1, at 887 (quoting United States v. Lee, 455 U.S. 252, 263 n.2 (1982) (Stevens, J., concurring)).

90 H.R. Rep. No. 106–219, at 13 (1999). It is worth noting that newly appointed Supreme Court Associate Justice Neil Gorsuch emphasized this point while sitting on the Tenth Circuit in his decision *Yellowbear v. Lampert* – a decision that explores the concept of substantial burden under RFRA's parallel statute, the Religious Land Use and Institutionalized Persons Act: "Just as civil courts lack any warrant to decide the truth of a religion, in RLUIPA Congress made plain that we also lack any license to decide the relative value of a particular exercise to a religion. That job would risk in the attempt not only many mistakes – given our lack of any comparative expertise when it comes to religious teachings, perhaps especially the teachings of less familiar religions – but also favoritism for religions found to possess a greater number of 'central' and 'compelled' tenets." 741 F.3d 48, 54 (10th Cir. 2014).

91 As an example, religious liberty claims advanced by Muslims in the United States have far lower success rates. *See* Gregory C. Sisk & Michael Heise, *Muslims and Religious Liberty in the Era of 9/11: Empirical Evidence from the Federal Courts*, 98 Iowa L. Rev. 231, 235–36, 260 (2012).

92 *Id.*

volume, such a result would be the height of irony, as it would invert RFRA's core commitment to protecting religious minorities.[93] As the Supreme Court emphasized "[r]epeatedly and in many different contexts ... courts must not presume to determine ... the plausibility of a religious claim."[94] To do so would amount to government allocating legal burdens on the basis of which religious claims it found more appealing, more important – and potentially more in keeping with its own notions of morality and ethics.[95]

To meet these constitutional challenges, some substantial-burden skeptics have tried to reformulate RFRA's substantial-burden inquiry. Recognizing that "rationality or plausibility to secular or other outsiders is irrelevant,"[96] Professor Frederick Gedicks explains "what matters is not whether *the court* finds a claimant's understanding of theological consequences credible, but whether *the claimant* does."[97] Gedicks, however, believes that courts can still evaluate the theological substantiality of a claim when it comes to cases of complicity – such as the claims advanced by nonprofits refusing to comply with the government's self-certification process via Form 700 implicated in the mandate cases – by "enlist[ing] common law tort principles as secular sources for measuring the substantiality of burdens on religion in the religious nonprofit cases."[98]

Courts, argues Gedicks, could apply the tort requirement of factual causation – for example, the factual causation requirement used in products liability cases – to determine whether the asserted connection between the self-certification process and the actual use of contraception gave rise to a substantial burden. In so doing, courts could evaluate whether the theological claim of causation could satisfy the law's general requirements for factual causation, thereby – according to Gedicks – differentiating between degrees of substantiality without engaging in a constitutionally prohibited theological inquiry.[99]

The problem with Gedicks's proposed solution is that imposing a secular framework of causation misses the entire object of RFRA. The question is not,

93 *See, e.g.*, Helfand, Chapter 2, this volume. 94 Smith, *supra* note 1, at 887.

95 Several authors have argued that either moral norms or secular legal norms – instead of the claimant's internal theology – should guide courts when determining the substantiality of a burden. *See, e.g.*, Amy J. Sepinwall, *Conscience and Complicity: Assessing Pleas for Religious Exemptions in* Hobby Lobby's *Wake*, 82 U. Chi. L. Rev. 1897, 1933 (2015) (arguing that "The state need not have a role in discovering and promoting moral truth, and by the lights of some versions of liberalism it should not have such a role .... But it does need to have a role in policing empirical truth, at least in the areas where it is permitted to regulate"); Frederick Mark Gedicks, *"Substantial" Burdens: How Courts May (and Why They Must) Judge Burdens on Religion Under RFRA*, 85 Geo. Wash. L. Rev.94 (2017).

96 Gedicks, *supra* note 95, at 130. 97 *Id.* at 130–31. 98 *Id.* at 28, 28–34. 99 *Id.*

as Gedicks acknowledges, whether the religious claim satisfies legal requirements of causation. Religionists perceive obligations that frequently do not track notions of liability under prevailing legal standards. It ought to be irrelevant for RFRA purposes whether a claim for religious accommodation rests on a theory of causation that would fail under standard tort principles. Consider again Gedicks's framing of his approach; the key is not "whether *the court* finds a claimant's understanding of theological consequences credible, but whether *the claimant* does."[100] Thus, a court cannot reject the religionist's experience of a substantial burden simply because that experience would be insubstantial if evaluated against prevailing legal standards. To do so would be to take the court's understanding of religious obligations as dispositive over and above the claimant's understanding. More fundamentally, that type of analysis violates the strictures of the Establishment Clause.

True, rejecting such attempts to massage tensions between the Establishment Clause and RFRA's substantial-burden inquiry leaves a problem: RFRA does require courts to evaluate the substantiality of a burden. If the Establishment Clause prohibits evaluating the theological substantiality of such burdens – prohibiting, in turn, the divvying of RFRA protections on the basis of theological substantiality determinations – then what should we make of RFRA's substantial-burden requirement? If only *substantial* burdens trigger RFRA's religious liberty protections, then how should we apply that standard? Is RFRA a statute that fails on its own terms? The answer is no: RFRA does not need to fail on its own terms. The next section explains why, using a more complete picture of substantial burden analysis.

III STRUCTURE OF BURDEN ANALYSIS

Substantial-burden skeptics paint a box that RFRA, they say, cannot escape. RFRA's protections are, by its terms, only available where the law imposes a *substantial* burden. But if courts cannot evaluate a law's theological impact on religious exercise, how can courts determine whether a burden is truly substantial?

This argument moves too quickly, ignoring the full structure of a substantial-burden claim. Let's start with the text of RFRA: "Government shall not substantially burden a person's exercise of religion."[101] Claims of substantial burden must, of course, be sincere; without sincerity, no claim under RFRA can go forward.[102] RFRA's text provides little guidance regarding

[100] *Id.* at 27–28. [101] 42 U.S.C. § 2000bb-1(a) (2012).

[102] Hobby Lobby, *supra* note 4, at 2774 n.28 ("To qualify for RFRA's protection, an asserted belief must be 'sincere[.]'").

the definition of "substantial."[103] As a pure conceptual matter, what "substantial" means is open to at least two types of questions.

The first is simply a question of *degree*: how "substantial" must a burden be in order to qualify under RFRA? To answer this question, a court must engage in standard judicial line drawing, which – while difficult – does not pose any fundamental challenges to the structure of a substantial-burden inquiry. Put differently, employing some metric, courts will determine when the burden has crossed the line from being insubstantial to substantial. This is what courts do.

The second question is far more fundamental: what *type* of burden qualifies as a substantial burden? Put differently, what is the metric courts should use when evaluating whether a burden is substantial? In theory, one way to do so is by investigating the importance or centrality of a particular religious practice within the grand scheme of a claimant's religious theology or doctrine to determine whether burdening that practice would be theologically substantial. As Section II has shown, doing so in the context of RFRA would run afoul of fundamental Establishment Clause principles, drawing courts into impermissible questions of theology.

More fruitful to the substantial-burden inquiry would be for courts to consider whether, by engaging in religious exercise, persons will be subject to some sort of civil penalty. Sometimes, a penalty takes the form of an additional cost or tax for engaging in governmentally regulated conduct.[104] Other times, the civil penalty may be a sanction for noncompliance with a governmental rule. However the civil penalty is framed, if penalties follow for engaging in prohibited religious exercise, a court could evaluate how substantial those penalties are. Consequently, having a stiff penalty for engaging in religious exercise – whether framed as a tax or a sanction – might constitute a substantial burden *if* that penalty is judicially determined to be sufficiently significant and that penalty is triggered by engaging in religious exercise.

To appreciate the distinction between the two approaches described, consider the following example. Imagine if Congress enacted a law similar to the proposed, and failed, 2011 San Francisco circumcision ban discussed by Rassbach, in Chapter 7 of this volume. The ban prohibited the "circumcis[ion] ... of the foreskin, testicles, or penis of another person who has not attained the age of 18 years."[105] As the penalty for engaging in the religious

103 *See, e.g.*, Dorf, *supra* note 3, at 1213–14 (noting that *Sherbert* "provides little guidance for the substantiality inquiry," while *Yoder* is "equally unilluminating").

104 *See* Adams, Chapter 21, this volume.

105 *See* Matthew Hess, *San Francisco MGM Bill*, MGMBILL.ORG, www.mgmbill.org/san-francisco-mgm-bill.html.

ritual of circumcision, the ban proposed a penalty of "a fine not to exceed $1,000" and/or "imprisonment in the County Jail for a period not to exceed one year."[106] Now if Congress were to enact such a law, its survival would quite possibly hinge on whether the law violated RFRA.[107] And employing RFRA as a defense, a claimant would first need to establish that the law *substantially* burdened his religious exercise.

One way of expressing the substantiality of the burden would involve evaluating the importance of circumcision in both Jewish and Islamic theology – and how failure to circumcise a male child might thereby *substantially* burden the parent's exercise of religion. Another way of establishing the burden's substantiality would require evaluating whether a fine of $1,000 and/or being imprisoned for a up to a year is a sufficiently grave sanction and therefore a *substantial* burden on a person's religious exercise.[108]

Here, a court has two different metrics for determining whether a burden is substantial. The first focuses on the substantiality of the theological obligation; the second focuses on the civil consequences triggered by the relevant religious exercise. Importantly, not only does each inquiry focus on a different metric of substantiality, but each has different underlying objectives. The purpose of focusing on the theological or religious substantiality of a burden is to ensure that not all religious burdens allow individuals to avoid the demands of otherwise valid laws. On this interpretation, the purpose of RFRA is to ensure that certain forms of religious exercise – those that are particularly important to an individual's theology or religious worldview – are shielded from legal burdens. RFRA, on this logic, should not provide protection against laws that restrict less important forms of religious exercise, those that are not particularly important as a matter of religious practice or theological commitment. As to circumcision bans, we might conclude that a law prohibiting the circumcision of male minors presents a substantial burden, but only because of the ritual's importance to certain religious groups. Laws prohibiting or taxing other, less central forms of religious exercise might not be deemed by a court to be sufficiently significant to qualify as a substantial burden.

106 *Id.*

107 *But see* Order Granting Writ of Mandate at 3, Jewish Community Relations Council of San Francisco v. Arntz, Case No. CPF-11–511-370 (San Francisco County Superior Court, Apr. 6, 2012) (holding, in the alternative, that the proposed San Francisco Circumcision Ban violated even the post-*Smith* interpretation of the Free Exercise Clause).

108 One could also interpret RFRA to require a court to engage in both forms of analysis as well. *See* Ira Lupu & Robert Tuttle, *Symposium: Religious Questions and Saving Constructions*, SCOTUSBLOG (Feb. 18, 2014), www.scotusblog.com/2014/02/symposium-religious-questions-and-saving-constructions/ (contending there are "two measures of substantiality, not just one").

Focusing on the substantiality of the civil penalty for engaging in religious exercise achieves a very different purpose. Focusing exclusively on the substantiality of a civil penalty provides protection to all forms of religious practice, regardless of their internal religious significance, but it does so only where the costs imposed by the law for engaging in those practices are too high. On this interpretation, RFRA would first require a claimant to demonstrate that a sincerely held religious belief required him to engage in a practice that was being burdened by the law. After satisfying that threshold showing, RFRA would still tolerate the imposition of civil costs, penalties, or sanctions on religious practice so long as those costs were not substantial. One can think of this as expressing the idea that religious individuals can be expected to absorb some minimal costs for their religious observances, just not costs that will price them out of the practice[109] – what the Court has described elsewhere as simply making "the practice of their religious beliefs more expensive."[110] Therefore, with the circumcision ban, a court might conclude that a $1,000 penalty and/or imprisonment for a year would qualify as a substantial penalty for noncompliance. If the law, however, simply required the payment of a $1 penalty, a court might conclude that the law did not substantially burden religious practice.[111]

Because there are two methods and metrics for evaluating substantiality, concluding that courts cannot evaluate the theological or religious substantiality of a burden does not mean – at least in the typical run of cases[112] – that there is no alternative metric available for courts to evaluate the substantiality of a burden. Courts can evaluate substantiality by examining whether a person's religious exercise will trigger significant civil taxes or sanctions, thereby imposing a substantial burden on that religious exercise.

The current litigation over Form 700 and the ACA's process of self-certification provides an ideal case study. Motivated by the Establishment

109 Professor Chad Flanders presents an alternative justification for what he describes as the "bare burden" requirement. Chad Flanders, *Insubstantial Burdens* *16 (June 2015), ssrn.com/abstract=2727423 (arguing "the plaintiff has to show that something the government is doing is putting pressure on her to change or modify her religious beliefs"). Underlying Flanders's framework is an argument that RFRA aims to prevent government from using civil sanctions to modify or manipulate religious behavior. And without imposing a burden on religious exercise, there would be no worry of government pressuring theological modifications.

110 Braunfeld, *supra* note 17, at 605.

111 *But see* Greene, *supra* note 85 ("[I]t cannot be the case that the amount of the penalty or tax determines what constitutes a substantial burden on religious exercise. Otherwise, we might say that a statute imposing a nominal penalty or tax (say, a dollar) doesn't constitute a substantial burden on religious exercise, even though the operative legal burden does so."). Greene does not elaborate.

112 For some cases that deviate from the typical pattern, *see supra* Section IV.B.

Clause argument outlined earlier, a court might avoid evaluating how theologically substantial the burden of filling out Form 700 might be for the plaintiffs,[113] concluding that distinguishing between different degrees of theological substantiality would constitute the type of impermissible religious inquiry prohibited by the First Amendment.

But reaching that conclusion would not resolve the substantial-burden inquiry. A court would then have to determine whether the plaintiff's religious exercise would incur substantial civil penalties. If plaintiffs could refuse self-certifying – and refuse to provide insurance that included the mandated contraceptive coverage – without significant civil penalties, then there would be no substantial burden on their religious exercise. They could simply flout the legal requirements, paying a nominal fee that a court could, in its judgment, conclude was not substantial.[114]

As this illustration shows, arguments that see prohibiting judicial inquiry into the theological substantiality of burdens as tantamount to either deferring to plaintiffs' assertions or ignoring RFRA's requirement to assess the substantiality of the asserted burden miss the mark. To assess substantiality, courts should determine whether engaging in religious exercise will, in fact, lead to imposition of civil penalties that are substantial. By engaging in that focused inquiry, courts can avoid wholesale deference to plaintiffs' assertions without abdicating their statutory obligations under RFRA.

To be sure, the Supreme Court has been far from consistent in identifying the appropriate metric – whether theological or civil – for its substantial-burden inquiry. Even in the two cases singled out in RFRA as representing the "compelling interest test" embodied by RFRA[115] – *Sherbert v. Verner*[116] and *Wisconsin v. Yoder*[117] – the Court appeared to move in opposite directions when it came to assessing substantial burdens.[118]

In *Sherbert*, the Court evaluated the substantial burden imposed on the plaintiff not by considering the theological import of observing the Sabbath, but by examining the unemployment benefits she lost:

> The ruling forces her to choose between following the precepts of her religion and forfeiting benefits, on the one hand, and abandoning one of the precepts

[113] *See supra* notes 87–95 and accompanying text.

[114] The imposition of a nominal civil sanction could trigger Establishment Clause considerations, especially if making a denominational preference. *See, e.g.*, Larson v. Valente, 456 U.S. 228 (1982).

[115] 42 U.S.C. § 2000bb(b)(1) (2012). [116] Sherbert v. Verner, 374 U.S. 398 (1963).

[117] Wisconsin v. Yoder, 406 U.S. 205 (1972).

[118] *See, e.g.*, Dorf, *supra* note 3, 1213–14 (noting that *Sherbert* "provides little guidance for the substantiality inquiry," while *Yoder* is "equally unilluminating").

> of her religion in order to accept work, on the other hand. Governmental imposition of such a choice puts the same kind of burden upon the Free Exercise of religion as would a fine imposed against appellant for her Saturday worship.[119]

By contrast, *Yoder* seemed to explore the question of substantial burden by focusing on the theological implications of the compulsory education law for the Amish community:

> The conclusion is inescapable that secondary schooling, by exposing Amish children to worldly influences in terms of attitudes, goals, and values contrary to beliefs, and by substantially interfering with the religious development of the Amish child and his integration into the way of life of the Amish faith community at the crucial adolescent stage of development, contravenes the basic religious tenets and practice of the Amish faith, both as to the parent and the child.[120]

The *Yoder* Court did not, however, evaluate whether the $5 fine for failing to abide by the state's compulsory education law constituted a substantial burden.[121]

The Court's inconsistent treatment of the "which metric" question is not the only challenge for focusing judicial inquiry on the civil costs of religious exercise. Evaluating the substantiality of civil costs, even as it avoids theological questions, can be quite dicey. First, it requires some judicial line drawing, which – while a typical task for courts – can present borderline cases where outcomes can feel arbitrary.[122]

119 Sherbert, *supra* note 116, at 404. In other cases, the Court also focused much of its substantial burden inquiry on the civil costs triggered by the religious exercise in question. *See, e.g.*, Jimmy Swaggart Ministries v. Bd. of Equalization, 493 U.S. 378, 391 (1990) ("The only burden on appellant is the claimed reduction in income."); Hernandez v. Comm'r, 490 U.S. 680, 699 (1989) ("Any burden imposed on auditing . . . derives solely from the fact that, as a result of the deduction denial, adherents have less money."). But even in those cases, inquiry into theological substantiality also crept into the Court's opinions. *See* Jimmy Swaggart Ministries v. Bd. of Equalization, 493 U.S. 378, 391 (1990) (rejecting the petitioner's claims because "appellant's religious beliefs do not forbid payment of the sales and use tax"); Hernandez v. Comm'r of Internal Revenue, 490 U.S. 680, 699 (1989) ("Neither the payment nor the receipt of taxes is forbidden by the Scientology faith generally, and Scientology does not proscribe the payment of taxes in connection with auditing or training sessions specifically.").

120 Yoder, *supra* note 117, at 218; *see also* Ira C. Lupu, Hobby Lobby *and the Dubious Enterprise of Religious Exemptions*, 38 HARV. J.L. GENDER 35, 81–82 (2015).

121 *See* Lupu & Tuttle, *supra* note 109.

122 Flanders has argued to the contrary, worrying that line drawing when it comes to civil costs also entails "a judgment about that person's religion, or at least her relationship to it: what kinds of pressures might make her go against what her religion says, and how serious those

Moreover, courts – when assessing the substantiality of civil costs also have to provide a methodological framework for assessing civil substantiality. They can take the perspective of the particular plaintiff; they can also take a "reasonable person" perspective – and that choice may generate different outcomes. Thus, focusing the substantiality inquiry on the civil costs for religious exercise answers some questions but also raises others.[123]

These inconsistencies and challenges highlight that identifying and applying the appropriate metric for the substantial-burden inquiry has long been a matter of deep judicial confusion. If, however, we are to identify a methodology that avoids both simply deferring to the assertions of plaintiffs as well as the Establishment Clause violations entailed in a theological assessment of burdens, then focusing on the substantiality of civil costs for religious exercise provides a workable solution. In the standard run of cases – from *Sherbert* and *Yoder* through *Hobby Lobby* and *Zubik* – courts can apply RFRA's framework by evaluating the substantiality of the civil impact of laws, as opposed to the theological substantiality of particular religious observances and doctrines. And in so doing, they can ensure that RFRA protects against the substantial burdening of religious exercise – unless, of course, doing so is the least restrictive means to achieving a compelling government interest.

IV HARD CASES

In the standard run of cases, courts can apply this version of the substantial-burden inquiry without much fanfare. Courts will have to draw lines between different degrees of substantiality of course. But the line drawing and methodological questions discussed earlier are well within the competency and authority of judges. Focusing the substantial-burden inquiry on the civil costs triggered by religious exercise ensures neither that courts get mired in Establishment Clause concerns nor that their inquiry simply rubber-stamps

pressures have to be before she bends or breaks." Flanders, *supra* note 110, at *14. While true, this argument goes a bit far given that courts can engage in the civil substantiality inquiry without violating the Establishment Clause. Flanders recognizes this, but still contends: "Even if we can analytically separate religious and secular burdens … maybe our respect for religious freedom should extend to deferring to when a plaintiff says that there is substantial secular cost at play as well." *Id.* While understandable, the problem with Flanders' conclusion is that it would leave courts without any real mechanism to assess the substantiality of burdens on religious exercise, rendering a provision of RFRA a nullity.

123 For more on this distinction, see Michael A. Helfand, *Identifying Substantial Burdens*, 2016 ILL. L. REV. 1771, 1796–97 (2016).

the plaintiff's assertion of substantiality, abdicating judicial responsibility under RFRA.

Not all cases, however, follow this standard blueprint. This section considers two hard questions for the substantial-burden doctrine, each of which helps illuminate the outer edges of the RFRA standard.

A *Substantial Burden Claims Predicated on "False" Beliefs*

One challenge of focusing solely on the civil consequences for engaging in religious exercise is that doing so would seemingly allow parties to allege burdens on the basis of obviously false factual claims. Thus, if courts avoid evaluating the internal theological logic of a substantial burden claim, parties seeking religious accommodations can claim laws impose a substantial burden in ways that fly in the face of conventional scientific knowledge.

For example, in the mandate context, Professor Caroline Corbin has argued that courts cannot ignore science,[124] emphasizing that "[p]eople are entitled to their own religious beliefs but not to their own facts. Blatant distortions of science ought to be rejected outright."[125] Corbin contends it is scientifically implausible to conclude that the contraceptives at stake in the *Hobby Lobby* litigation cause an abortion and, therefore, to claim that the mandate substantially burdens religious exercise cannot be a substantial burden because it is predicated on a falsehood.[126] That debate over science permeates Part II of this volume.[127]

Similarly, Professor Amy Sepinwall contends courts cannot grant religious accommodation claims on the basis of scientifically false assertions.[128] To do so "would commit us to a life of irrationality."[129] Refusing to credit these claims is justified because, while the state should not have a role in discovering or promoting moral truth, it "does need to have a role in policing empirical truth, at least in the areas in which it is permitted to regulate."[130] For both

124 Corbin, *Closing Statement*, *supra* note 86, at 280.

125 Caroline Mala Corbin, *Abortion Distortions*, 71 WASH. & LEE L. REV. 1175, 1177 (2014).

126 Like Rienzi, Chapter 4, this volume, Hobby Lobby argued, citing FDA labeling, that the contraceptives in question could prevent uterine implantation of a fertilized egg, which it believed to be the equivalent of an abortion. *See* Brief for Respondents at 5 n.2, Sebelius v. Hobby Lobby Stores, Inc. 723 F.3d 1114 (10th Cir. 2013) (No. 13–354), www.becketfund.org/wp-content/uploads/2014/02/13%96354-bs.pdf.

127 See Rienzi, Chapter 4, this volume; Goodwin, Chapter 3, this volume.

128 *See* Sepinwall, *supra* note 95. 129 *Id.*

130 *Id.* at 1932–33. *See also* Leslie C. Griffin, *A Tractor Is Not a Gun, Even If You Sincerely Believe It Is*, HAMILTON AND GRIFFIN ON RIGHTS (May 18, 2014), http://hamilton-griffin.com/a-tractor-is-not-a-gun-even-if-you-sincerely-believe-it-is/.

Corbin and Sepinwall, courts must reject RFRA claims where the religious claimant is simply wrong about the impact the law will actually have on his or her religious belief and, therefore, religious exercise.

But why should this be so? The entire enterprise of religious accommodations is predicated on providing some degree of protection to religious exercise from the imposition of substantial burdens. The religious beliefs that motivate religious practices quite often do not meet scientific standards of truth. The practices are, in the end, motivated by faith in a variety of propositions. And the assumptions underlying these practices often entail faith commitments to facts about the universe that are motivated by religious belief.

Whether it is a claim about the existence of God or when life begins, the fact that a predicate of the substantial burden claim is deemed by science to be false or deeply problematic should not – on its own – lead to the claim's rejection. Religion, by its very nature, generates faith-based claims – as opposed to evidence-based claims – about the world.

This fundamental feature of religion led Professor Brian Leiter to conclude that religious beliefs, "in virtue of being based on 'faith,' are insulated from ordinary standards of evidence and rational justification, the ones we employ in both common sense and in science."[131] The very nature of religion, Leiter says, requires the embracing of assertions that do not satisfy standard scientific methods of proof. Because of this quality, the Supreme Court has concluded that the truth or falsity of a theological claim cannot be the basis for allocating legal burdens – to do so would be to impose legal burdens on the basis of an inquiry that is "beyond the ken of mortals."[132] If we protect some subset of conduct motivated by sincerely held religious beliefs, then part of what we protect are faith-based claims about the world that do not accord with science.

That being said, there are cases where the admixture of religious belief and empirical fact raises more complicated questions. Consider, for example, the following hypothetical – posed by Judge Judith Rogers during oral argument – which tweaks the facts of *Thomas v. Review Board*. There, the Supreme Court addressed the claims of a Jehovah's Witness who objected to working for a company that produced sheet metal for weapons. But what if the Court had found that "the munitions factory for which [he] worked was not supplying arms for the war, that in fact it was supplying gadgets for tractors used on

[131] Brian Leiter, Why Tolerate Religion? 34 (2012). For a critique, see Michael W. McConnell, *Why Protect Religious Freedom?* 123 Yale L.J. 770 (2013).

[132] United States v. Ballard, 322 U.S. 78, 87 (1944) (describing these inquiries as "beyond the ken of mortals").

farms? Could the Court have examined whether his statement about what his employer was doing was correct?"[133]

In such a case, granting the factual assertions of the claimant would seem absurd. Should courts say that, in a case where the claimant erroneously contended – based upon, for example, his own skepticism of the government's assertion – that the metal was being used for munitions that he could maintain a bona fide claim of a substantial burden? What makes this case different is that the claimant maintains a factual belief about the world that is not motivated by faith; it comes instead from a personal skepticism stemming from secular considerations. Maybe these kinds of factual claims should not themselves be granted the same deference, motivated by Establishment Clause worries, that religiously motivated factual claims are granted.

As a first pass at factually misguided claims, the requirement of sincerity will typically afford a viable judicial response. What makes these kinds of claims absurd is not so much the claimant's factual error, but that it is highly implausible that the claimant – faced with the actual facts – can still maintain the sincerity of his claim that he is being substantially burdened. Indeed, as religious accommodation claims assume facts that are increasingly outlandish – veering further and further away from commonly held scientific truths – courts might reasonably begin to wonder whether the claimant is truly sincere. Thus, faced with empirical evidence demonstrating that the metal in question is not being used for munitions, it becomes increasingly hard to believe the claimant is sincere in his assertion that working in the factory substantially burdens his religious exercise.

Thus, in most cases involving RFRA claims predicated on secularly motivated factually false claims, courts can respond not with substantial-burden skepticism, but a searching examination of sincerity.[134] Courts can interrogate the sincerity of religious beliefs in order to ensure that the constitutional and statutory protections afforded religion are not being abused by fraudulent claimants. And, as a result, the more considerations courts can incorporate into their sincerity analysis, the better able they are to serve as gatekeepers, ensuring the overall integrity of a religious accommodations regime.

Still, a robust examination of sincerity – while resolving many cases – does not fully address the fundamental problem. At least in theory, cases remain where a court is completely convinced that a claimant sincerely believes,

133 *See* Griffin, *supra* note 131.

134 *See also* Gedicks, *supra* note 95, at 131 n.173 ("Secular inconsistency might function as a proxy for insincerity. This only underlines, however, the dangers of the sincerity inquiry, which too often functions as a proxy for the unreasonableness of minority and otherwise unfamiliar religious practices.").

based upon secular considerations, a scientifically false fact at the root of a RFRA claim. Thus, for example, a claimant might truly believe – for non-religious reasons – that his factory is using metal for munitions even as the evidence suggests otherwise. In such circumstances, how should the court address a claim that working in the factory substantially burdens religious exercise because the claimant religiously objects to participating in war? A court might simply conclude that there cannot be a substantial burden in such a case because as a factual matter, the claimant is *not, in reality*, participating in the war effort. In such circumstances, a court might embrace a version of the view that "[p]eople are entitled to their own religious beliefs but not to their own facts."[135]

But dispatching claims on purely factual grounds discounts the consequences of the interaction between a claimant's religious beliefs and factual commitments. Imagine again an RFRA claim predicated on the erroneous fact that a factory is producing munitions – when it is really just producing farm equipment. The court, by telling the claimant he is simply wrong about the existence of a substantial burden, does nothing to alleviate the claimant's religious predicament. In the end, because of the claimant's unique – and erroneous – factual views about the world, he still believes that he is being placed on the horns of a dilemma: engage in religiously prohibited conduct or lose a significant government benefit, his job and unemployment insurance. At bottom, even though the claimant's view is a function of a secularly motivated factual belief, the result is a dilemma that leaves the claimant with the *experience of a substantial burden* even if based on a sincerely held secular mistake.

RFRA, to be sure, only protects substantial burdens on religious exercise. It tells us precious little about whether it does so because it wants to alleviate only factually correct substantial burdens or because it is based upon a normative commitment that religious individuals should be protected from dilemmas that force them, at least as they see the world, from choosing between religious exercise and some government benefit or sanction. It is plausible for a court to construe RFRA to grant some degree of protection against the *experience* of a substantial burden on religious exercise – and not just *evidence* of a substantial burden on religious exercise. And if a court were to take such a view, concluding that scientific error should not *per se* undermine claims of substantial burden would seem wholly justified; to do so, a court might conclude, would miss the way in which religious claimants often experience substantial burdens on their religious practice, even as science encourages them to view the world otherwise.

[135] Corbin, *Abortion Distortions*, *supra* note 126, at 1177.

B Substantial Burden Claims Where No Civil Cost Is Present

As noted earlier, in the general run of cases, courts can interrogate the substantial burden of a law by considering not its theological substantiality, but the substantiality of the tax, penalty, or sanction triggered by the religious exercise. But not all burdens have sanctions attached. Consider again the facts of *Lyng*, where the government constructed a road through a national forest used for religious purposes by three Native American tribes.[136] This chapter has shown that the Court should avoid assessing the theological substantiality of petitioners' claims. Evaluating the burden's substantiality by examining the road's impact on the religious life of the three Native American tribes would violate core Establishment Clause concerns.

So how should a court assess substantiality in *Lyng*? Unlike most cases, *Lyng*'s facts do not raise any civil cost for the court to examine to determine whether a new road constituted a substantial burden. In *Lyng*, the question was not about the constitutionality of a particular cost, tax, or sanction; it was whether the government had the authority to execute on plans for a road. The tribes' religious exercise would not trigger some penalty that could be evaluated for substantiality: either the government would build the road or it would not. Plainly, cases like *Lyng* raise a significant question: how can a court apply the substantial burden framework if there is no applicable civil cost, tax, or sanction to evaluate?

One way to proceed is to simply discard the substantial-burden inquiry as an unworkable doctrinal framework. This appears to have been the tactic adopted by the Supreme Court in *Lyng*. In rejecting the tribes' claims, the Court did not evaluate the burden's substantiality but concluded that petitioners' claims failed because they were not being "coerced by the Government's action into violating their religious beliefs."[137] The Court chose to focus on the presence of coercion, and not the substantiality of the burden. Not surprisingly, discarding the pre-*Smith* substantial-burden framework opened *Lyng* majority's opinion to criticism from both the dissent and legal scholars.[138]

What the critics failed to acknowledge is that *Lyng* did not lend itself to the standard application of the substantial-burden doctrine. The majority emphasized this point, quoting *Bowen v. Roy*: "[t]he Free Exercise Clause … does

136 Lyng v. Nw. Indian Cemetery Prot. Ass'n, 485 U.S. 439 (1988). 137 *Id.* at 449.

138 *Id.* at 468 (Brennan, J. dissenting); Ira C. Lupu, *Where Rights Begin: The Problem of Burdens on the Free Exercise of Religion*, 102 Harv. L. Rev. 933, 964 (1989) (describing *Lyng*'s coercion-based approach to burdens as "both murky … and dangerously narrow"); James E. Ryan, Note, Smith *and the Religious Freedom Restoration Act: An Iconoclastic Assessment*, 78 Va. L. Rev. 1407, 1415–16 (1992).

not afford an individual a right to dictate the conduct of the Government's internal procedures."[139] At its core, the Court's problem was the lack of a civil penalty to evaluate for substantiality. The Court was – in essence – being asked to give the petitioners the authority to dictate the terms of government policy. In most cases, accommodating religious practice would not dictate government policy; the government would have to bend its policy only where claimants complained of a *substantial* burden. But without a penalty in question, the claim in *Lyng* was one of the uncommon cases where claimants were directly telling the government what to do if the claim was credited. The Court could not assess the theological substantiality because of the Establishment Clause and it could not evaluate the substantiality of the civil penalty because there was nothing to evaluate.

Given the challenge *Lyng* posed to the substantial-burden framework, it is not surprising that the Court's decision in *Smith* followed shortly thereafter. If courts cannot assess the substantiality of theological burdens, then the only way to assess substantiality is to evaluate the civil penalties of the given religious exercise. But *Lyng* – and other cases like it[140] – seemed to present scenarios where there was no civil penalty to evaluate. The *Lyng* Court responded by ignoring the substantial-burden framework in light of the case's unique facts. *Smith* later extended this lesson, discarding the framework in its entirety.

Should we embrace the lesson of *Lyng* and conclude that RFRA made a mistake in resuscitating the substantial-burden framework? While presenting something of a puzzle, there are good reasons to think that discarding the substantial-burden framework would be a mistake. To see why, consider the following.

Imagine, as in *Holt v. Hobbs*,[141] a prison prohibited all inmates from growing a beard of any length, notwithstanding any religious commitments requiring beards. And imagine that failure to comply subjected the inmate to three months in solitary confinement. If an inmate were to claim that the law imposed a substantial burden, a court might reason as follows: while we cannot assess the theological substantiality of the burden, surely imposing

[139] Lyng, *supra* note 136, at 448 (quoting Bowen v. Roy, 476 U.S. 693, 699–700 (1986)).

[140] Many prison cases filed by inmates pursuant to Religious Land Use and Institutionalized Persons Act follow *Lyng*'s pattern. In many such cases, the prison simply prevents certain religious activity or conduct as opposed to placing a high cost for engaging in the activity. *See, e.g.*, Taylor G. Stout, *The Costs of Religious Accommodations in Prison*, 96 VA. L. REV. 1201, 1209–14 (2010) (detailing restrictions on religious exercise predicated on security concerns).

[141] *See* Holt v. Hobbs, 135 S. Ct. 853 (2015).

three months in solitary confinement on the inmate constitutes a substantial penalty triggered by the religious exercise.[142]

Now imagine a parallel case where a prison prohibits inmates from growing a beard. However, instead of placing violators in solitary confinement, any inmate growing a beard would simply be rendered unconscious by guards, who would shave the beard. Assuming the process of shaving did not inflict any pain or discomfort, this second case presents a *Lyng*-like problem. The no-beard rule does not present any civil cost that can be evaluated for substantiality. Violations result in removal of the beard. Thus, because a court cannot evaluate the theological substantiality of growing the beard, then there would appear to be nothing for the court to evaluate. And yet, it would also seem that the burden on the inmate in this second case is more severe than the first case; actually removing the beard seems like a greater burden then putting a person in solitary confinement for growing the beard.

These hypothetical cases capture a key justification underpinning the substantial-burden framework. A law imposes a substantial burden because it leaves the aggrieved party with limited options for engaging in religious exercise. In a case of a substantial burden, the only option that remains to engage in religious exercise is to incur some sort of significant civil sanction, tax, or penalty. And in leaving only such an option, the law has thereby imposed a substantial burden triggered by religious exercise. In cases such as *Lyng* – or the hypothetical shaved inmate – the law has imposed an even more significant burden on religious exercise. Instead of providing an option to engage in religious exercise and then endure a significant sanction, tax, or penalty, the law refuses even that option.

Such laws – whether they be building a road or shaving an inmate – ought to be understood as constituting a substantial burden. Those laws leave a person in a position that is even worse than enduring a substantial burden; they are actually *coercing* a person into *not* engaging in religious exercise.[143] Thus, the intuition at the core of the substantial burden framework should be reformulated as follows: *notwithstanding government regulation, can a person still engage in religious exercise while only enduring an insubstantial civil burden?* In cases where government coerces a person's failure to engage in religious

[142] *Cf.* Barack Obama, *Why We Must Rethink Solitary Confinement*, Wash. Post (Jan. 25, 2016), www.washingtonpost.com/opinions/barack-obama-why-we-must-rethink-solitary-confinement/2016/01/25/29a361f2-c384-11e5-8965-0607e0e265ce_story.html.

[143] Justice William Brennan understood this well, calling a distinction between "governmental actions that compel affirmative conduct inconsistent with religious belief, and . . . governmental actions that prevent conduct consistent with religious belief . . . a distinction is without constitutional significance." Lyng, *supra* note 136, at 468 (Brennan, J., dissenting).

exercise, such laws therefore should constitute a substantial burden – both under the Court's pre-*Smith* doctrine as well as the Court's current RFRA framework.[144]

This conclusion is of particular importance given current litigation over the mandate and Form 700. [145] The substantial-burden skepticism at the heart of *Lyng* has been deployed by courts to reject claims that the self-certification process violates RFRA.[146] For example, the Tenth Circuit cited *Lyng* for the following proposition: "Pre-*Smith* case law and RFRA's legislative history underscore that religious exercise is not substantially burdened merely because the Government spends its money or arranges its own affairs in ways that plaintiffs find objectionable."[147] Leveraging *Lyng* in this context raises two distinct problems. First, *Lyng* mistakenly diagnosed the subset of cases where a government policy made certain forms of religious exercise impossible; those cases should have qualified as a substantial burden because the petitioners could not have chosen to engage in the relevant religious exercise *and* accept some insubstantial civil burden as a consequence. The government foreclosed the possibility of engaging in the relevant religious exercise under any circumstance.

Second, *Lyng*'s invocation in the mandate context ignores *Lyng*'s unique challenge to the substantial-burden framework. *Lyng* represents the height of substantial-burden skepticism because the government's action presented no obvious civil penalty to evaluate for civil substantiality. Recognizing the unique challenge of *Lyng* strongly counsels against invoking its skepticism of the substantial-burden framework in a case where there is a civil cost to evaluate for substantiality; in the context of Form 700 and the mandate's self-

144 Flanders, based on his "bare burden" requirement, *see infra* note 110, has reached the opposite conclusion, arguing that in cases like *Lyng*, a plaintiff "cannot say the government is burdening her just because the government has done something that makes the practice of her beliefs more difficult: it has to be doing something to her, where she is being put to a choice where that choice involves some secular costs." Id. at *16. As noted earlier, Flanders's claim assumes that the reason why RFRA prohibits burdening religious practice is that government should not be using civil sanctions to modify or manipulate religious behavior. However, as noted here, RFRA might be justified on a completely different principle: a view that individuals should be able to engage in religious exercise while only enduring an insubstantial civil burden. And on such an account, the facts in *Lyng* – and the making of certain religious exercise – present an even stronger case than mere civil sanction for finding a substantial burden; making religious exercise, on such an account, is far worse than making it difficult.

145 *See supra* notes 50–66 and accompanying text.

146 Geneva Coll. v. Sec'y U.S. Dep't of Health and Human Servs., 778 F.3d 422, 435–36 (3d Cir. 2015); Univ. of Notre Dame v. Sebelius, 743 F.3d 547, 552 (7th Cir. 2014).

147 Little Sisters of the Poor Home for the Aged v. Burwell, 794 F.3d 1151, 1193 (10th Cir. 2015).

certification process, the civil penalties for noncompliance provide an obvious opportunity to consider whether the regulation imposes a substantial civil cost triggered by religious exercise.[148] These cases, in no way, fall into the *Lyng* category.

Criticizing *Lyng* – and its misuse – does raise one final question: does allowing petitioners to successfully assert such claims "afford an individual a right to dictate the conduct of the Government's internal procedures"?[149] The correct answer here is to rely on RFRA's strict scrutiny framework to do its work. Petitioners can assert RFRA claims that contend various government policies – from building roads to issuing social security numbers – substantially burden their religious exercise. So long as these petitioners cannot simply engage in that religious exercise by enduring *insubstantial* burdens, their claims should go forward. Such claims will not succeed if the specific government regulation is the least restrictive means for accomplishing a compelling government interest.[150] If courts reject the worries expressed by the Court in *Lyng* – and allow such claims to constitute substantial burdens – they may need to recalibrate the compelling government interest standard to credit instances where the government must implement a policy effectively and uniformly.[151]

Such a recalibration – which amounts to lowering the bar for what constitutes a compelling government interest – animated the Supreme Court's decision in *United States v. Lee*.[152] There, the Court upheld the constitutionality of Social Security taxes over a free exercise challenge because of the compelling government interest at stake: "The tax system could not function if denominations were allowed to challenge the tax system because tax payments were spent in a manner that violates their religious belief."[153] Instead of taking a narrow approach to the compelling government interest inquiry, the Court looked at the overall impact some free exercise claims might have on the effective functioning of a government program. This broader approach accounts for concerns about free exercise claims interfering with the government's internal procedures; it takes this worry into account not by discarding the substantial-burden inquiry, but by incorporating that important concern into the compelling government interest inquiry.

148 *See supra* notes 50–66 and accompanying text.

149 Lyng, *supra* note 136, at 448 (quoting Bowen v. Roy, 476 U.S. 693, 699–700 (1986)).

150 42 U.S.C. § 2000bb–1(b) (2012).

151 For more on the need to lower the bar for what qualifies as a compelling government interest, *see* Michael A. Helfand, *Religious Institutionalism, Implied Consent, and the Value of Voluntarism*, 88 S. CAL. L. REV. 539, 578–84 (2015).

152 United States v. Lee, 455 U.S. 252 (1982).

153 *Id.* at 260.

Broadening the reach of the compelling government interest category ensures that substantial-burden claims will not overreach and interfere with important government policies. Because these limitations would be directly tied to the importance of a government policy, systems that require even-handed application would not be undermined by an avalanche of religious exemptions. In this approach, the limitations on substantial-burden claims come not from judicial attempts to ignore the degree of constraints imposed on religious claimants, but from the importance of the government policies themselves. Put succinctly, it amounts to endorsing the Court's approach to compelling government interests in *Lee* over the Court's missteps in *Lyng*.

V CONCLUSION

Undoubtedly, RFRA's substantial-burden standard is meant to distinguish between those burdens on religious exercise worthy of legal protection and those that are not. Its role, however, as doctrinal gatekeeper has been greatly imperiled by all the uncertainty associated with its interpretation and application. This chapter provides a workable framework for assessing the substantiality of burdens, ensuring that courts can appropriately identify those burdens on religious exercise that RFRA prohibits. This standard both gives real teeth to the substantial-burden inquiry without leading courts to place legal burdens under RFRA on the plaintiff on the basis of theological assessments. Courts should apply RFRA by assessing the substantiality of the civil penalties triggered by religious exercise. This ensures that individuals and institutions will not be forced to endure significant costs, taxes, or sanctions in the pursuit of religiously motivated conduct. At the same time, where laws impose insubstantial civil costs, taxes, or sanctions on religiously motivated conduct, individuals and institutions – absent other countervailing constitutional concerns – will be expected to shoulder those minimal burdens. In contemporary debates over the appropriate scope of religious liberty protections, courts using this framework can give meaning to RFRA's terms – providing meaningful religious liberty protections without allowing those protections to run roughshod over other implicated interests.

7

Coming Soon to a Court Near You

Male Circumcision in Religious Families in Europe and the United States

Eric Rassbach

Deputy General Counsel at the Becket Fund for Religious Liberty

During the 2009 American Academy of Pediatrics ("AAP") annual convention in Washington, DC, a group of protesters gathered at the Convention Center. Frequent protests are one of the peculiarities of Washington, along with traffic-gnarling motorcades and fifteen kinds of federal security agencies.[1] However, this protest was different. It was at the Convention Center, not the usual location for protests – the National Mall, Lincoln Memorial, and White House are far more popular venues. Moreover, while politicians are common targets of D.C. protesters, pediatricians are rarely so.

Who protests against pediatricians? One can understand protesting against lawyers, given that the power to sue can be the power to destroy. But pediatricians do not reflexively spark the public's ire. What could pediatricians possibly have done to make the protesters so angry? As this chapter's title intimates, the AAP's position on circumcising male children rankled the protesters.[2] Specifically, the protesters wanted the AAP to object to male circumcision, rather than allowing pediatricians who perform circumcisions to remain in good standing within the AAP.[3]

The protesters were "intactivists," the name those who wish to ban child male circumcision have given themselves.[4] In 2009, the intactivist movement firmly occupied the fringe; today it is a much more influential group with the potential

[1] *Federal Law Enforcement*, Bureau of Justice Statistics, www.bjs.gov/index.cfm?ty=tp&tid=74. A federal agency has truly arrived once it has its own police force.

[2] *See Task Force on Circumcision, Am. Acad. of Pediatrics, Circumcision Pol. Statement*, 130 PEDIATRICS 686 (Sept. 2012).

[3] Dan Bollinger, *Intactivists Protest AAP National Conference in Washington, DC*, INT'L COALITION OF GENITAL INTEGRITY (Oct. 12, 2009), www.icgi.org/2009/10/intactivists-protest-at-aap-national-conference-in-washington-dc/.

[4] *See, e.g., About Us*, INTACT AMERICA, www.intactamerica.org/aboutus (providing website of leading anti-male-circumcision organization describing members as "intactivists").

for enormous impact on religious liberty. The intactivist movement has gathered visible steam over the past decade, with a proliferation of new nonprofit organizations and a significant infusion of funds.[5] Intactivists also enjoy significant support within the legal academy, with faculty developing legal and medical ethical arguments to ban the circumcision of male children.[6] Governmental bodies, both courts and others, have begun to engage the issue.

So, why is the issue of male circumcision as a religious practice coming to the fore in both Europe and the United States? And why is it so important?

Emerging debates over circumcision are a harbinger of new conflicts between religious people and governments across the West. The long-uncontroversial practice of religiously motivated circumcision of male children will soon become an issue that religious liberty advocates, scholars, and eventually judges must consider. The social and legal movement against circumcision, if it continues to grow, will inevitably have significant repercussions for the religious liberty of two specific minority religious groups: Jews and Muslims. If unchallenged, it will also end up having significant effects on religious liberty for all faith groups.

How this development will affect the law of religious liberty and the law of the family deserves much thought. Indeed, the issue of circumcision of male children has already been litigated in European courts; sooner or later, this issue will end up in U.S. courts, too.

Section I of this chapter discusses, at a fairly high level of generality, the main religious practices in question – those from the Jewish and Muslim communities. Section II canvasses the past development of the law in this area, including recent developments of pro- and anti-circumcision activity in Europe. Sections III and IV then discuss how the law and politics concerning male circumcision in religious communities are likely to develop in the future, with particular attention to how the current wave of anti-immigrant sentiment in Europe and the United States could affect those developments. This discussion also explores how religious liberty law and family law might intersect, resulting in greater restrictions on religious circumcision of male children. Finally, Section V contrasts how protections for religious practice abroad are far narrower than in the U.S., with the result that multiple constitutional grounds exist in the U.S. to protect this important act of

5 Mark Joseph Stern, *How Circumcision Broke the Internet*, SLATE (Sept. 18, 2013), www.slate.com/articles/health_and_science/medical_examiner/2013/09/intactivists_online_a_fringe_group_turned_the_internet_against_circumcision.html.

6 *See, e.g.*, J. S. Svoboda, Robert S. Van Howe, & James G. Dwyer, *Informed Consent for Neonatal Circumcision: An Ethical and Legal Conundrum*, 17 J. CONTEMP. HEALTH L. & POL'Y 61, 61 (2000).

religious identity and belief. Section V uses the question of religiously motivated male circumcision as a heuristic for whether particular normative conceptions of the law of religious liberty and of family law make sense.[7]

I THE PRACTICE OF RELIGIOUSLY MOTIVATED MALE CIRCUMCISION

Religiously motivated male circumcision is a practice common in Judaism and Islam.[8] In most streams of Judaism, male circumcision, or *brit milah*, is performed on the eighth day after birth.[9] The practice is meant to keep the covenant (*brit*) between God and Abraham and his descendants, as described in the Book of Genesis:

> This is My covenant, which ye shall keep, between Me and you and thy seed after thee: every male among you shall be circumcised. And ye shall be circumcised in the flesh of your foreskin; and it shall be a token of a covenant betwixt Me and you. And he that is eight days old shall be circumcised among you, every male throughout your generations, he that is born in the house, or bought with money of any foreigner, that is not of thy seed. He that is born in thy house, and he that is bought with thy money, must needs be circumcised; and My covenant shall be in your flesh for an everlasting covenant. And the uncircumcised male who is not circumcised in the flesh of his foreskin, that soul shall be cut off from his people; he hath broken My covenant.[10]

7 This chapter is also not about the relatively noncontroversial practice of adult circumcision, nor is it about the practice – most widespread in English-speaking countries – of secular infant circumcision. This chapter does not address the various forms of female genital mutilation. Use of the term "female circumcision" is both inaccurate and, ultimately, a rhetorical tactic. Although intactivists and others frequently link the two practices, they are quite different. Of course, at a high level of generality both involve cutting the genitals, but that arbitrary commonality does not reflect the fundamental difference between mutilation and circumcision. Each practice should be considered on its own, alongside other modifications of the body, including tattoos, nose rings, ritual scarring, and the like. In April 2017, the United States initiated what appears to be the first-ever prosecution under the anti–female genital mutilation statute, 18 U.S.C. § 116; the defendant is a doctor accused of allegedly performing one form of female genital mutilation. *See* United States v. Nagarwala, No. 2:17-cr-20274-BAF-DRG (E.D. Mich., complaint sworn April 12, 2017).

8 In addition to Jewish and Muslim male circumcision practices, some animist groups in Africa, Asia, and Oceania also engage in circumcision; no circumcision-related cases in the U.S. or Europe appear to involve these groups. *See* Andrea Wilcken et al., *Traditional Male Circumcision in Eastern and Southern Africa: A Systematic Review of Prevalence and Complications*, 88 Bulletin of the World Health Organization 907 (2010), www.who.int/bulletin/volumes/88/12/09-072975/en/.

9 Sara E. Karesh & Mitchell M. Hurvitz, *Brit Milah*, in Encyclopedia of Judaism, 70-71 (2005).

10 *Genesis* 17:10-14 (Jewish Publication Society 1917).

In Judaism, the circumcision operation is typically performed by a trained circumciser or *mohel*.[11]

In Islam, the practice is known as *khitan*. Not described in the Quran, the *khitan* is instead set forth in several *hadith* or collected prophetic traditions.[12] There is no specific age set for circumcision, and it varies across different Islamic cultures from seven days after birth to puberty.[13] Doctrinally, the practice centers on purification rather than denoting a covenantal relationship; there is no Islamic counterpart to the Jewish *mohel*.[14]

For many Jews and Muslims, the issue of circumcision is one of basic religious identity. Being circumcised serves as a physical reminder of one's belonging to the faith community, especially important when the faith community is in the minority. For many, circumcision also denotes willingness to sacrifice for one's faith. Jews have a long history of suffering punishment at the hands of government authorities for engaging in circumcision.[15] Muslims have also experienced suppression of their identities through suppression of this religious practice.[16]

II DEVELOPMENTS IN THE LAW OF RELIGIOUSLY MOTIVATED MALE CIRCUMCISION

Although historical examples of circumcision being suppressed are legion, for much of the West's recent history the practice of circumcision has been free from government interference. Indeed, for much of the past century, male circumcision for secular reasons was almost universal within the U.S. and, to a lesser degree, other English-speaking societies.[17] However, in recent years a series of events on both sides of the Atlantic have moved the dial between

11 Karesh & Hurvitz, *supra* note 9.

12 Juan E. Campo, *Circumcision*, in ENCYCLOPEDIA OF ISLAM 139 (2009). 13 *Id.* 14 *Id.*

15 Aryeh Tuchman, *Circumcision*, in 1 ANTISEMITISM: A HISTORICAL ENCYCLOPEDIA OF PREJUDICE AND PERSECUTION 128 (Richard S. Levy, ed., 2005). Perhaps the most famous example was the complete ban on circumcision imposed by the Ptolemaic king Antiochus IV Epiphanes. *Id.* During Hellenistic times, government and social disapproval of the Jewish practice of circumcision was so great that many Jewish men would make painful attempts to "reverse" circumcision.

16 *See, e.g.*, Ali Eminov, TURKISH AND OTHER MUSLIM MINORITIES IN BULGARIA 60-61 (Routledge 1997) (describing Communist-era Bulgarian ban on circumcision designed to suppress Muslim religious identity).

17 World Health Organization, et al., *Male Circumcision: Global Trends and Determinants of Prevalence, Safety and Acceptability* (2007), whqlibdoc.who.int/publications/2007/978924159 6169_eng.pdf. For a review of circumcision practices across the world, *see* World Health Organization, et al., *Neonatal and Child Male Circumcision: A Global Review* (2010), www .who.int/hiv/pub/malecircumcision/neonatal_child_MC_UNAIDS.pdf.

tolerance and suppression of circumcision decidedly in the direction of suppression.

In Europe, the most prominent example of this trend came in a 2012 German appellate court's decision in a case involving a four-year-old Muslim boy's circumcision.[18] The doctor – who was also Muslim – carried out the circumcision at the request of the boy's parents. A few days later, the parents took the boy to the emergency room, concerned that the wound was still bleeding.[19] The state prosecutor then brought charges against the doctor who performed the circumcision, claiming that he violated the German Criminal Code by assaulting another person with a dangerous tool and harming his health.[20] The state district court found the parents' consent to perform the circumcision valid, and the doctor's performance of the circumcision justified, because of the religious reasons for the procedure.[21] Circumcision, the district court pointed out, was "a traditional ritual method for the documentation of cultural and religious belonging to the Muslim life community";[22] allowing the circumcision eliminated an incipient risk of the child's stigmatization.[23]

The North Rhine-Westphalia state intermediate appellate court reversed, holding that the parents' consent was invalid and the doctor's performance of the circumcision unjustified, because the child's right to bodily integrity under the German constitution outweighed the religious wishes of the parents.[24] In particular, the appellate court held that the child's welfare could not validate the parents' consent or justify the doctor's actions.[25] However, the court held that although the doctor violated the law, he acted with unavoidable ignorance of the law in this area and was therefore excused from criminal liability.[26] The practical effect of this ruling was to

18 Landgericht Köln, 151 Ns 169/11, Urteil (May 7, 2012), www.justiz.nrw.de/nrwe/lgs/koeln/lg_koeln/j2012/151_Ns_169_11_Urteil_20120507.html.

19 *Id.*

20 *Id.* ("*mittels eines gefährlichen Werkzeugs körperlich misshandelt und an der Gesundheit geschädigt*"). In America, the analogous crime would be assault with a deadly weapon.

21 *See* Amtsgericht Köln, Abteilung 528, 528 Ds 30/11 (Sep. 21, 2011), www.justiz.nrw.de/nrwe/ag_koeln/j2011/528_Ds_30_11_Urteil_20110921.html.

22 *Id.* ("*traditionell-rituelle Handlungsweise zur Dokumentation der kulturellen und religiösen Zugehörigkeit zur muslimischen Lebensgemeinschaft*").

23 *Id.* ("*Damit wird zugleich einer drohenden Stigmatisierung des Kindes entgegengewirkt.*").

24 Landgericht Köln, 151 Ns 169/11, Urteil (May 7, 2012) (relying in part on Grundgesetz für die Bundesrepublik Deutschland [Grundgesetz][GG][Basic Law], BGBl. 2(2) (Ger.)) (construing "*KÖRPERLICHE UNVERSEHRTHEIT*"). Ironically, this provision of the German Constitution dates to postwar Germany, when it was promulgated in part as a reaction to the atrocities performed by Josef Mengele and other Nazi physicians against Jewish victims.

25 *Id.* (discussing "*Kindeswohl*"). 26 *Id.*

treat male circumcision – prospectively – as criminal assault with a deadly weapon.

The Cologne *Landgericht*'s decision unleashed immediate outrage from Jewish and Muslim groups in Germany.[27] However, the decision also garnered praise from legal academics who have long advocated for a prohibition on religiously motivated male circumcision. The leading German legal academic advocating for a ban on religiously motivated male circumcision is Professor Holm Putzke of the University of Passau, cited in the decision. Shortly after the appellate court's decision Professor Putzke praised it. It "earned applause" for treating the "archaic ritual" as a criminal act, framing the ultimate issue as "how much religiously motivated violence against children a society is ready to tolerate."[28]

The decision unleashed a debate. Later that year, the German Bundestag enacted a provision of the Civil Code that allows parents to consent to certain male circumcisions, including those performed by a *mohel*, in the first six months of a child's life.[29] The legislation was strenuously opposed by anti-circumcision academics, but also by the largest German pediatric association, which has long characterized circumcision for nonmedical reasons as unethical.[30] The German pediatric association instead supported a bill that would allow male circumcision only after the boy was fourteen years old and capable of consent.[31]

Ultimately, the law enacted by the Bundestag rendered the German appellate court's decision nugatory. That decision acted as a domino, however, opening a space for other European critics of religiously motivated male circumcision to jump into. Shortly after the German decision, hospitals in parts of Austria and Switzerland ceased providing religious

[27] *See, e.g.*, *Muslim and Jewish Groups Denounce German Circumcision Ruling*, BBC (Jul. 12, 2012), www.bbc.com/news/world-europe-18807040.

[28] Holm Putzke, *LG Köln Fällt Wegweisendes Urteil: Religiöse Beschneidungen von Jungen Verboten*, Legal Tribune Online (June 26, 2012), www.lto.de/recht/hintergruende/h/wegweisendes-urteil-religioese-beschneidungen-von-jungen-verboten/.

[29] Bürgerliches Gesetzbuch [BGB][Civil Code], Dec. 20, 2012, § 1631d.

[30] *Rituelle Beschneidungen bei Minderjährigen-Kinder-und Jugendärzte Fordern: Allein das Recht eines Kindes auf körperliche Unversehrtheit Zählt*, BVKJ (July 17, 2012), www.bvkj.de/bvkj-news/pressemitteilungen/news/article/rituelle-beschneidungen-bei-minderjaehrigen-kinder-und-jugendaerzte-fordern-allein-das-recht-ein/ ("Ritual circumcisions of minors – child and adolescent doctors urge: solely the right of a child to bodily integrity counts").

[31] *Pressemeldung des Berufsverbandes der Kinder-und Jugendärzte (BVKJ) zum Franktionsübergreifenden Gesetzentwurf zur Rituellen Beschneidungen bei Jungen: Gesetzentwurf Entspricht Kindeswohl!*, BVKJ (Nov. 11, 2012), www.bvkj.de/bvkj-news/pressemitteilungen/news/article/pressemeldung-des-berufsverbandes-der-kinder-und-jugendaerzte-bvkj-zum-franktionsuebergreifenden/.

circumcision.[32] The Jewish Hospital of Berlin temporarily suspended its circumcision practice because of "the lack of legal clarity."[33] In Norway, the Ombudsman for Children, a government official, stated that religious circumcision should be replaced with a bloodless rite.[34]

Although less institutional support exists in the U.S. than in Europe, the U.S. too has seen burgeoning efforts to ban or restrict religiously motivated male circumcision. Beginning in 2006, there have been ongoing efforts in Massachusetts to enact the Massachusetts State Prohibition of Genital Mutilation Act.[35] The proposed act has never made it out of committee but received a public committee hearing in 2010.[36]

In 2011, a proposed San Francisco ballot measure would have criminalized the performance of male circumcision within the city limits.[37] Proposed by a group known as "MGMbill.org," Matthew Hess, one of the group's leaders, drafted the ballot measure. Hess also authored a comic book series called "Foreskin Man," in which a blonde-haired, blue-eyed superhero fights off villains, such as "Monster Mohel," who seek to circumcise boys.[38] The comic books are laden with stereotypical anti-Semitic tropes.[39]

After receiving the requisite number of signatures, the San Francisco measure initially was placed on the ballot. However, a California superior court upheld a challenge to the ballot measure in *Jewish Community Relations*

32 Associated Press, *Hospitals in Austria and Switzerland Suspend Circumcision*, GUARDIAN (July 25, 2012), www.theguardian.com/world/2012/jul/25/hospitals-in-austria-and-switzerland-suspend-circumcision.

33 Ofer Aderet, *Berlin Jewish Hospital to Cease Circumcisions After German Court Ruling*, HAARETZ (June 30, 2012), www.haaretz.com/jewish/news/berlin-jewish-hospital-to-cease-circumcisions-after-german-court-ruling-1.447850.

34 JTA, *Replace Circumcision With Symbolic Ritual, Says Norwegian Children's Watchdog*, HAARETZ (Aug. 7, 2012), www.haaretz.com/jewish/news/replace-circumcision-with-symbolic-ritual-says-norwegian-children-s-watchdog-1.456443. This statement was followed the next year by a joint statement of the Ombudsmen for Children of Norway, Sweden, Denmark, Finland, Iceland, and Greenland taking the position that male circumcision for religious reasons should be forbidden for minors. *See* Joint Statement, Nordic Ombudsmen for Children and Pediatric Experts, *Let the Boys Decide on Circumcision* (Sept. 30, 2013), www.crin.org/en/library/news-archive/male-circumcision-nordic-ombudspersons-seek-ban-non-therapeutic-male.

35 *See, e.g.*, S.Bill 1777, 186th Gen. Ct. (Mass. 2009), malegislature.gov/Bills/186/Senate/S1777.

36 *Law Proposed to Ban Circumcision in Massachusetts*, CROWN HEIGHTS INFO (Feb. 22, 2010), crownheights.info/jewish-news/24606/law-proposed-to-ban-circumcision-in-massachusetts/.

37 Committee for Parental Choice and Religious Freedom, *Proposed Ban*, stopcircban.com/pr oposedban/ (proposing to amend the San Francisco Police Code to make it "unlawful to circumcise, excise, cut, or mutilate the whole or any part of the foreskin, testicles, or penis of another person who has not attained the age of 18 years").

38 *Foreskin Man*, MGMBILL.org, www.mgmbill.org/foreskin-man.html.

39 *Id.*

Council of San Francisco v. Arntz. The measure was invalid as a matter of law because, if enacted, it would conflict with the California Business and Professions Code allowing circumcision.[40] In 2011, activists proposed a similar ballot measure in Santa Monica. After significant public pressure was directed toward the ballot measure's proponent, it was abandoned.[41]

After the public debate surrounding both the San Francisco and Santa Monica proposed ballot measures, in 2011, the California Legislature in the Health and Safety Code prohibited California municipalities from adopting any rules that prohibit or restrict male circumcision.[42] Under the law, medical and "affiliative" interests justify the practice of male circumcision.[43]

The issue of religiously motivated male circumcision practices made headlines in New York City in *Central Rabbinical Congress of the United States and Canada v. New York City Department of Health and Mental Hygiene*.[44] The New York City Department of Health and Mental Hygiene ("Department") issued a rule regulating *metzitzah b'peh*, the use of oral suction by the *mohel* to clean the post-circumcision wound.[45] This ancient practice is common among some streams of Hasidic Judaism, including several with adherents living in New York City. The Department concluded that the practice could spread the herpes simplex virus to infants and then began public awareness efforts and eventually issued regulations governing the practice.[46] In an effort to counteract the dangers it perceived, the Department required *mohels* to have the child's parents fill out a form that contradicted the *mohels'* beliefs. Failure to comply would result in a financial penalty.[47]

A group of *mohels* and rabbis sued in federal court, arguing that the regulation violated their rights to the free exercise of religion and freedom of speech. The federal district court ruled against them for two main reasons. First, the court held that the Department's rule was neutral and generally applicable, and therefore it did not trigger strict scrutiny under the Free Exercise Clause of the First Amendment of the U.S. Constitution, as

40 Jewish Comty. Rel. Council of S.F. v. Arntz, 2012 WL 11891474 (Cal. Super. Ct.) (citing San Diego v. Dunkl, 86 Cal. App.4th 384, 389 (Cal. Ct. App. 2001)).

41 *See* Jennifer Medina, *In Santa Monica, Circumcision Opponent Abandons Efforts*, N.Y. Times (June 7, 2011), www.nytimes.com/2011/06/08/us/08circumcise.html.

42 *See* Cal. Health & Safety Code § 125850 (b) ("No city, county, or city and county ordinance, regulation, or administrative action shall prohibit or restrict the practice of male circumcision, or the exercise of a parent's authority to have a child circumcised.").

43 Cal. Health & Safety Code § 125850 (a)(1).

44 Cent. Rabbinical Cong. of the U.S. and Can.v. N.Y.C. Dep't. of Health and Mental Hygiene, 763 F.3d 183 (2d Cir. 2014).

45 *Id.* at 185. 46 *Id.* 47 *Id.* at 186.

Helfand explains elsewhere in this volume.[48] Second, the court concluded that the City's enlisting of the *mohels* to spread the City's message – with which the *mohels* strongly disagreed – did not trigger strict scrutiny review under the Free Speech Clause of the First Amendment. Applying the more deferential rational basis review, the district court upheld the City's regulation.[49]

After the rabbis appealed, the U.S. Court of Appeals for the Second Circuit reversed.[50] Adopting an argument advanced in an amicus brief that Stanford Law School Professor (and former Tenth Circuit Judge) Michael McConnell submitted together with the Becket Fund for Religious Liberty, the Second Circuit held that the City's regulation was not neutral because it singled out a particular Orthodox Jewish practice for regulation.[51] By targeting a particular practice and a particular religion, the City triggered strict scrutiny rather than rational basis review.[52] Subjecting the City's actions to strict scrutiny did not mean that the City would ultimately lose since the public health can qualify as a compelling governmental interest.[53] It did mean, though, that the district court had to reevaluate the facts under that more demanding standard.[54] On remand, the City settled the case with the plaintiff rabbis and *mohels*, agreeing to repeal the regulation.[55]

This trend line shows that the practice of religiously motivated male circumcision is already under some pressure in the U.S., particularly in urban coastal areas, although far less than in Europe today.

III THE FUTURE OF THE LAW OF MALE CIRCUMCISION AS A RELIGIOUS PRACTICE

Perhaps as important as the developments synopsized in Section II are the long-term trends affecting the law surrounding the religious practice of circumcising male children in Europe and the U.S. In both Europe and the U.S., academics are likely to press the issue even more. In Europe, one should expect significant ongoing pressure put on the practice of religiously motivated male circumcision. The statement of the Ombudsmen for Children of the Nordic countries signals strong institutional support for the supposition

48 Cent. Rabbinical Cong. of the U.S. and Can.v. N.Y.C. Dep't. of Health and Mental Hygiene, No. 12 CIV. 7590 (NRB), 2013 WL 126399 at *30 (S.D.N.Y. 2013) *vacated and remanded*, 763 F.3d 183 (2d Cir. 2014). *See generally* Helfand, this volume.

49 *Id.* at *22. 50 Cent. Rabbinical Cong., *supra* note 44, at 186. 51 *Id.* at 194. 52 *Id.*

53 *Id.* at 198. 54 *Id.*

55 Michael M. Grynbaum, *New York City Health Board Repeals Rule on Consent Forms for Circumcision Ritual*, N.Y. Times (Sep. 9, 2015), www.nytimes.com/2015/09/10/nyregion/new-york-city-health-board-repeals-rule-on-consent-forms-for-circumcision-ritual.html.

that international human rights law simply forbids this religious practice.[56] It does not, although many reflexively assume it does.[57]

The main pediatric medical associations in northern Europe also support bans or severe restrictions on male circumcisions. For example, after the AAP took a pro-circumcision position in a 2012 policy statement, representatives of pediatric medical associations from Austria, the Czech Republic, Denmark, Estonia, Finland, France, Germany, Iceland, Ireland, Latvia, Lithuania, the Netherlands, Norway, Poland, Sweden, and the United Kingdom published a counterstatement in *Pediatrics*, AAP's official journal.[58] The piece contended that AAP's supportive position was the outlier among Western pediatric associations and unsupported by the relevant medical literature[59] – a point that is much disputed, as reports published by the World Health Organization and the Centers for Disease Control and Prevention show.[60]

Perhaps, most importantly, Professor Putzke and like-minded legal academics will continue to criticize the German circumcision law and look for ways to undermine it, possibly through a test case challenging the circumcision accommodation within the Civil Code under the German constitution. They are actively making the case in legal circles.[61]

In the U.S., circumcision of male children for religious reasons follows different patterns, making immediate opposition from institutional actors less likely Circumcision is practiced by a far greater percentage of the population than in Europe.[62] That fact alone makes institutions less likely to declare themselves opposed to circumcision.

However, over the long term, secular circumcision rates in the U.S. are likely to fall even further than they have over the past decade.[63] If circumcision becomes a minority practice, it will be even more closely associated with

[56] Joint Statement, *supra* note 34. [57] *Id.*

[58] *See* Morton Frisch et al., *Cultural Bias in the AAP's 2012 Technical Rep. and Pol. Statement on Male Circumcision*, 131 PEDIATRICS 796 (2013), pediatrics.aappublications.org/content/pediatrics/131/4/796.full.pdf.

[59] *See id.*

[60] Christopher Ingraham, *Americans Truly Are Exceptional – At Least When it Comes to Circumcision*, WASH. POST (May 26, 2015), www.washingtonpost.com/news/wonk/wp/2015/05/26/americans-truly-are-exceptional-at-least-when-it-comes-to-circumcision/?utm_term=.d7f7d1f7eaa7.

[61] *See, e.g.*, Reinhard Merkel & Holm Putzke, *After Cologne: Male Circumcision and the Law. Parental Right, Religious Liberty or Criminal Assault?*, 39 J. MED. ETHICS 444 (2013); Holm Putzke, *Das Beschneidungsgesetz (§ 1631d BGB) – Fauler Kompromiss und Fatales Signal*, *in* 161 MONATSSCHRIFT KINDERHEILKUNDE 950-51 (2013).

[62] Cordelia Hebblethwaite, *Circumcision, The Ultimate Parenting Dilemma*, BBC (Aug. 21, 2012), www.bbc.com/news/magazine-19072761.

[63] *See* Ingraham *supra* note 60 (presenting CDC data).

religious minority groups, specifically Jews and Muslims.[64] That will in turn enable increased legal, political, and social pressure from intactivists.

In the near term, the more likely source of change in American law lies elsewhere. Changes are underway in other areas of law that affect the nexus of health, religious freedom, and family law. In particular, the law of children's rights in the context of abortion, contraception, cosmetic surgery, tattoos, or other procedures involving children's bodies may well spill over to, and be a source of incidental restrictions on, male circumcision in religious communities.

For example, law professors who support abortion have vocally opposed proposed laws requiring parental consent to abortion. Professor B. Jessie Hill has argued that the idea of "bodily integrity" as a constitutional right under the Fourteenth Amendment ought to be read more expansively to trump even parents' interaction with their children.[65] In this framing, a child's right to bodily integrity, understood as a right to consent to abortion without parental consent, would counteract parental rights to have a say in a child's abortion.[66] Notably, although Professor Hill discusses circumcision, she does not advance the bodily integrity model as barring parents from circumcising their sons for religious reasons.

Taken to its extreme, the anti-parentalist school of family law would eliminate parental rights altogether. Samantha Godwin, a research fellow at Yale Law School, has challenged the very existence of parental rights – including, but not limited to, parental rights concerning religious upbringing. In "Against Parental Rights," she writes:

> But to enable parents to compel unwilling children to engage in religious practices, attend church, or receive religious education makes sense from a secular perspective only if we wish to vindicate the parents' interests in propagating their belief system. It does not make sense that inculcation into

[64] Some have pointed to the example of the United Kingdom in this regard, where circumcision was once strongly promoted by medical institutions, particularly during the Victorian era. However, during the post–World War II period, the National Health Service refused to cover circumcision as medically necessary, and circumcision rates fell off rapidly. *See supra* note 62.

[65] B. Jessie Hill, *Constituting Children's Bodily Integrity*, 64 DUKE L.J. 1295, 1297–1301 (2015). The U.S. Constitution makes no reference to "bodily integrity," but the Supreme Court has referred to it as a right variously protected under the Fourth Amendment and the Due Process Clause of the Fourteenth Amendment.

[66] *Id.* at 1355–61 (proposing suite of lawsuits minors could bring against their parents regarding issues concerning bodily integrity).

> that belief system is itself in the child's own best interests. Such parental power is a privilege or prerogative of the parent, not a matter of the child's interests.[67]

Obviously, if the government were given power to prevent parents from transmitting their faith to their children, religious minorities might be eliminated rather quickly. Religious minority groups face challenges as it is in transmitting their faith to younger generations even without government interference; under a legal regime that erases parents' role in child-rearing, it would be almost impossible.[68] In this conception, State knows best, and Father and Mother should stay out of it.[69]

The key intersection between opposition to circumcision with the anti-parentalist school lies in the concept of the best interests of the child (in German, the "welfare of the child" or *Kindeswohl*). The most important feature here of the "best interests of the child standard" is its threshold inquiry – at what point do courts (abetted by legal changes wrought by advocacy groups, law professors, and attorneys) get to displace parents and make the best interests decision instead of the parents? As Offit (Chapter 12, this volume) and Wilson and Sanders (Chapter 13, this volume) point out, the decisions parents make sometimes have heart-wrenching costs for children,[70] but society risks a grave threat to the religious identities of children – and faith communities – when it too readily supplants parents.

For the German appeals court, the line is crossed before the point at which permanent bodily changes are made. Godwin would put all parent-child interaction on the state's side of the line; no area would be free from state control. For now, the AAP puts circumcision on the parents' side of the line. But if the AAP eventually follows the lead of other Western pediatric associations, the line might be drawn in a different place, leaving parents no say over the circumcision decision.

67 Samantha Godwin, *Against Parental Rights*, 47 COLUM. HUM. RTS. L. REV. 1, 27 (2015).

68 Godwin studiously avoids addressing how her proposed legal regime would affect Jews and Muslims. But the echoes of Antiochus IV Epiphanes, who sought to "exterminate [Judaism] by force," are unmistakable. *See* Louis Ginzberg, *Antiochus IV., Epiphanes*, JEWISH ENCYCLOPEDIA, www.jewishencyclopedia.com/articles/1589-antiochus-iv-epiphanes.

69 Godwin's "modest proposal" is for parents to rights with respect to their own children mirroring those possessed by public school teachers. *See* Godwin, *supra* note 67, at 81–82.

70 Offit, Chapter 12, this volume (discussing religious exemptions to medical neglect laws); Wilson & Sanders, Chapter 13, this volume (discussing faith healing and corporal punishment practices in insular religious communities).

As the next section explains, legal trends can assume an internal momentum that ends up forcing the issue, particularly when they unite with political factors.

IV CIRCUMCISION RESTRICTIONS AND ANTI-IMMIGRANT SENTIMENT

One of those political factors – anti-immigrant sentiment – cannot be ignored when predicting how circumcision restrictions will play out over the next few years in Europe and the U.S. This factor has become increasingly stronger in recent years in both Europe and the U.S.

In Europe, the link between restrictions on minority religious practices and anti-immigrant and anti-foreigner sentiment is already fairly clear. In the context of the refugee and immigration crisis racking Europe, opposition to culturally and religiously distinct practices such as circumcision provides a convenient mask for xenophobia – one can simply oppose practices associated with certain minorities – especially Muslims – without admitting to fear or hatred of a people.[71] This is a tried and true approach. Across northern Europe, some have opposed kosher and halal slaughter, on the basis of protecting animals against cruelty.[72] Government actions such as a recent "pork mandate" in Danish public schools seem directed specifically at disfavored religious groups, even though they are billed as protecting Danish "food culture."[73]

Supercharging this trend are the slew of violent Islamist terrorist attacks striking Europe in the past five years. As Uddin (Chapter 26, this volume) shows, the "burkini bans" that proliferated across French beach towns in the summer of 2016 were direct reactions to the Bastille Day Islamist terrorist attack in Nice that killed eighty-six people, not the claimed need to maintain "public order."[74]

[71] Alex Hobbs, *Circumcision, Legislation, and Anti-Semitism*, FOREIGN AFFAIRS REVIEW (Nov. 16, 2012), foreignaffairsreview.co.uk/2012/11/circumcision/.

[72] *See, e.g.*, Adam Withnall, *Denmark Bans Kosher and Halal Slaughter as Minister Says "Animal Rights Come Before Religion,"* INDEPENDENT (Feb. 18, 2014), www.independent.co.uk/news/world/europe/denmark-bans-halal-and-kosher-slaughter-as-minister-says-animal-rights-come-before-religion-9135580.html. As before, American law departs from its European counterparts, specifically defining kosher and halal slaughter – which involve severing the carotid arteries without previous stunning – as humane. *See* 7 U.S.C. § 1902(b) (2012); Shuja Shafi & Jonathan Arkush, *Jewish and Muslim Methods of Slaughter Prioritise Animal Welfare*, THE GUARDIAN (Mar. 6, 2014), www.theguardian.com/commentisfree/2014/mar/06/jewish-muslim-slaughter-animal-welfare-humane.

[73] *See* Dan Bilefsky, *Denmark's New Front in Debate Over Immigrants: Children's Lunches*, N.Y. TIMES (Jan. 20, 2016), nyti.ms/1nm7nlL.

[74] Uddin, Chapter 26, this volume.

It is, thus, not hard to imagine that a ban on male circumcision would be politically attractive to some. Such a ban would make life for disfavored religious minorities very difficult, but without appearing openly to be anti-Semitic or Islamophobic.

In some cases, politicians seem unconcerned about appearances. For example, a leading proponent of a ritual slaughter ban in the Netherlands, Geert Wilders of the *Partij Voor de Vrijheid* or Party for Freedom – a Dutch, right-wing populist party[75] – has made the link between excluding religious minorities and banning their religious practices explicit:

> Islam is the Trojan Horse in Europe. If we do not stop Islamification now, Eurabia and Netherabia will just be a matter of time. . . . I can report that [the Dutch] have had enough of burkas, headscarves, the ritual slaughter of animals, so-called honour revenge, blaring minarets, female circumcision, hymen restoration operations, abuse of homosexuals, Turkish and Arabic on the buses and trains as well as on town hall leaflets, halal meat at grocery shops and department stores, Sharia exams, the Finance Minister's Sharia mortgages, and the enormous overrepresentation of Muslims in the area of crime, including Moroccan street terrorists.[76]

In the March 2017 Netherlands national parliamentary elections, *Partij Voor de Vrijheid* became the second-largest party in the Dutch Parliament.[77]

Similarly, in France, Marine Le Pen of the Front National was for a time leading in the polls for the 2017 French presidential elections. Like Wilders, Le Pen is strongly opposed to ritual kosher and halal slaughter, and many other minority religious practices, including the wearing of religious symbols in public. In 2017, she stated that French Jews ought to be willing to stop wearing yarmulkes in public – a religious obligation for many Orthodox Jews – in order to show solidarity in the fight against radical Islam.[78] In her words, everyone would have to "sacrifice," though she never suggests that Christians forgo wearing small crosses in public. The question naturally

[75] Sebastiaan Faber, *Why the Dutch Are Drawn to Right-Wing Populist Geert Wilders*, THE NATION (Feb. 21, 2017), www.thenation.com/article/why-the-dutch-are-drawn-to-right-wing-populist-geert-wilders/.

[76] Geert Wilders, *Mr. Wilders's Contribution to the Parliamentary Debate on Islamic Activism*, PARTIJ VOOR DE VRIJHEID (Sep. 6, 2007), pvv.nl/index.php/7-nieuws/nieuws/464-mr-wilderss-contribution-to-the-parliamentary-debate-on-islamic-activism.html.

[77] Saju Daniel, *The Rise of the "Dutch Trump" Could Set a Chain Reaction in Europe*, WEEK (Feb. 18, 2017), www.theweek.in/news/world/the-rise-of-dutch-rump-could-set-chain-reaction-europe.html.

[78] *Marine Le Pen: French Jews Should Sacrifice Yarmulke in Struggle Against Radical Islam*, JEWISH TELEGRAPHIC AGENCY (Feb. 6, 2017), www.jta.org/2017/02/06/news-opinion/world/marine-le-pen-french-jews-should-sacrifice-yarmulke-in-struggle-against-radical-islam.

follows: where does the logic of "sacrifice" stop? Would French Jews need to "sacrifice" circumcision to be proper citizens with full rights?

Therefore, it seems probable that anti-immigrant politics sweeping the Netherlands and France will gain a toehold in other European countries, too, inevitably hastening measures designed to prohibit minority religious practices including circumcision.[79] Even though candidates such as Wilders and Le Pen have not yet become the political leaders of their countries, other parties have already moved closer to their positions in an effort to obtain votes.[80]

The U.S. has moved in Europe's direction with respect to its anti-immigrant sentiment. A few years ago, the contrast between the U.S and Europe was far greater. But anti-immigrant sentiment, particularly against Muslim immigrants, began rising in the U.S. as well, even before the 2016 election.[81] The election spurred a level of anti-immigrant and anti-Muslim invective that had not been seen in decades.[82] Presidential candidate Donald Trump repeatedly invoked a "Muslim ban" with respect to immigration; and the admission of refugees from the Syrian Civil War became a major campaign issue.[83]

After the election, President Trump's issuance of a controversial executive order on immigration sparked widespread protests and a spate of lawsuits before being enjoined, revoked, and replaced – leaving the exact scope of President Trump's policy concerning immigration in a great deal of

[79] *See German Far-right Party Calls for Ban on Minarets and Burqa*, GUARDIAN (May 1, 2016), www.theguardian.com/world/2016/may/01/german-far-right-party-ban-minarets-burqa-alternative-fur-deutschland (describing platform of Alternative für Deutschland party); Nick Cumming-Price & Steven Erlanger, *Swiss Ban Building of Minarets on Mosques*, N.Y. TIMES (Nov. 29, 2009), www.nytimes.com/2009/11/30/world/europe/30swiss.html.

[80] *See* Faber, *supra* note 76 (discussing a public letter published in the leading Dutch papers by Wilders's opponent as a "shrewd attempt . . . to fend off" Wilders by saying Muslims "should act normally, or get out").

[81] *Islamophobia: Understanding Anti-Muslim Sentiment in the West*, GALLUP, www.gallup.com/poll/157082/islamophobia-understanding-anti-muslim-sentiment-west.aspx. Views about immigration more generally follow a different pattern. *See, e.g.*, Aaron Blake, *Anti-Immigrant Sentiment is Down in the United States – Way Down*, WASH. POST (June 27, 2014), www.washingtonpost.com/news/the-fix/wp/2014/06/27/americans-were-for-immigration-before-they-were-against-it.

[82] Bill Scher, *Five Reasons For Liberals To Have Hope: As Unlikely As It May Seem After Trump's Win, There Are Signs That Brighter Days Await Democrats And Progressives*, POLITICO (Nov. 9, 2016) (reporting that in exit polls, 25% of voters supported deportation of undocumented immigrants versus 70%, who supported legalization).

[83] *See* Russell Berman, *The Presidential Candidates Debate Granting Asylum to Syrian Refugees*, ATLANTIC (Sep. 22, 2015), www.theatlantic.com/politics/archive/2015/09/the-syrian-refugee-crisis-and-the-2016-campaign/406513/.

flux.[84] What is certain is that his rise to the presidency is a sign that immigration – particularly Muslim immigration – has become a key part of the U.S. political discussion in a way it had not been for many years.[85] Whether hostility toward immigration results in opposition to minority religious practices associated with immigrants, including circumcision, remains to be seen. But the political factors are present in a way that they have not been in a long time.

V CIRCUMCISION RESTRICTIONS AND THE LAW OF RELIGIOUS LIBERTY

If the trends are moving in the wrong direction, with respect to both legal theory and politics, the question arises: what protections do religious liberty provisions afford against government restrictions on male circumcision as a religious practice? In Europe, precious little religious liberty law stands between Europe's Muslim and Jewish communities and various circumcision restrictions. What protections there are may come from European human rights law or individual countries' constitutions and laws. Neither would do much to prevent severe restrictions on circumcision, particularly if those restrictions enjoy strong political support.

Under Article 9 of the European Convention on Human Rights, every person has the "freedom, either alone or in community with others and in public or private, to manifest his religion or belief, in worship, teaching, practice and observance."[86] This right is subject to a public order exception.[87] It seems clear that prohibiting the observance of religiously motivated male circumcision would constitute interference with the ability of individual Muslims and Jews to manifest their religious beliefs. Yet, the

[84] *See* State of Hawaii v. Trump, 17-15589 (9th Cir. 2017), *appeal from* State of Hawaii v. Trump, 17-cv-00050 (D. Haw. 2017) (enjoining revised travel ban); Kartikay Mehrotra, *U.S. Seeks Quick Action to Unblock Trump Immigration Order*, BLOOMBERG POLITICS (Mar. 31, 2017), www.bloomberg.com/politics/articles/2017-03-31/u-s-seeks-quick-action-to-unblock-trump-immigration-order; Adam Liptak, *Trump Will Issue New Travel Order Instead of Fighting Case in Court*, N.Y. TIMES (Feb. 16, 2017), www.nytimes.com/2017/02/16/us/politics/travel-ban-muslim-ninth-circuit.html?mtrref=www.google.com&gwh=70A15E9A77306C621D40BFF48B43B285&gwt=pay (discussing the various problems President Trump's revoked order encountered).

[85] For a review of differing accounts of discussions leading to the Trump executive orders, see David Bernstein, *Fake News: Giuliani Admitted that Trump's Executive Order on Immigration is a "Muslim Ban,"* WASH. POST (Mar. 31, 2017), www.washingtonpost.com/news/volokh-conspiracy/wp/2017/03/31/fake-news-giuliani-admitted-that-trumps-executive-order-on-immigration-is-a-muslim-ban/?utm_term=.0f06aec4bb9a.

[86] EUROPEAN CONVENTION ON HUMAN RIGHTS, art. 9(1).

[87] *Id.*, art. 9(2).

European Court of Human Rights has held that there is no interference with a particular ritual as long as the ritual is available to the religious claimant *somewhere*.[88] In *Cha'are Shalom ve Tsedek v. France*, the Court held that although the inability of Orthodox Jews to obtain *glatt* kosher meat would interfere with the Article 9 right, the fact that French Orthodox Jews could obtain *glatt* kosher meat from Belgium despite a French ban on kosher slaughter meant that France had not truly interfered with the practice.[89] Taken to its extreme, the decision means that as long as religious circumcision could be gotten somewhere in Europe – or perhaps even outside it – no Article 9 right exists to observe the practice within one's own country of residence. The disproportionate impact on families of little means raises its own questions of fairness.

Furthermore, Article 9s "public order" exception might also come to bear. In *S.A.S. v. France*, the European Court of Human Rights upheld France's burka ban law.[90] As Uddin chronicles at length (Chapter 26), the Court held that the public order exception justified the ban on wearing the burka – which veils the face as well as the body – because the law was aimed at the "preservation of the conditions of 'living together' as an element of the 'protection of the rights and freedoms of others.'"[91] Compounding matters is the broad "margin of appreciation" afforded to individual countries, making it more likely that their laws are sustained against challenge.[92] Criticized by many scholars, including Uddin, the flexible application of the public order exception means that socially disfavored religious practices may not find much protection in Strasbourg.[93]

National laws are unlikely to provide much additional succor. While the French *Conseil d'État* struck down a number of burkini bans in 2016, the courts upheld the burka bans.[94] Further, French courts upheld a number of other laws directed at religious practices, such as a ban on wearing "ostensible" religious symbols at state schools.[95] It is not clear that future restrictions on religiously motivated male circumcision would be treated any differently by the French courts.

88 Cha'are Shalom ve Tsedek v. France, 2000-VII Eur. Ct. H.R. § 83. 89 *Id.*

90 *See S.A.S. v. France*, 2014-III Eur. Ct. H.R. 1. 91 *Id.* at § 157.

92 George Letsas, *Two Concepts of the Margin of Appreciation*, 26 Oxf. J. Leg. Stud. 705 (2006), doi.org/10.1093/ojls/gql030.

93 *See* Uddin, Chapter 26, this volume, for more discussion of burka bans. 94 *Id.*

95 Loi 2004-228 du 15 mars 2004 sur les signes religieux dans les écoles publiques françaises [Law 2004-228 of Mar. 15, 2004 on Religious Symbols in French Public Schools], Journal Officiel de la République Française [J.O][Official Gazette of France], Mar. 17, 2004, p. 5190.

The situation in other European countries would necessarily vary. It seems clear, though, that in many European jurisdictions, a determined national parliament could severely restrict religiously motivated male circumcision without being overruled by a court.

In the U.S., religious liberty law would operate more protectively. Ever since *Pierce v. Society of Sisters*, the U.S. Supreme Court has recognized the right of parents to give their children a religious upbringing.[96] In addition, government actions that burden a religious exercise, such as the religious practice of circumcising males, would be subject to a host of other constitutional and civil rights laws. In particular, a law or regulation that – intentionally or unintentionally – singles out religiously motivated male circumcision for differential treatment would quickly run afoul of the Free Exercise Clause of the First Amendment to the U.S. Constitution, as Helfand explains elsewhere in this volume.[97] Similarly, any restrictions on circumcision – particularly if linked to any intentional targeting – might also raise questions under the Establishment Clause of the First Amendment by creating a denominational preference.[98] Aside from those protections, the Equal Protection Clause, the Due Process Clause, state constitutional provisions, and federal and state Religious Freedom Restoration Acts would inevitably be invoked against restrictions on religiously motivated male circumcision.[99] Those claims would have a strong likelihood of success.

That is not to say that restrictions on circumcision would not have their defenders, especially within the legal academy. Some scholars have argued that religious liberty rights should be read to protect individual claims over against the free exercise rights of the group; some argue that group religious rights simply do not exist.[100] In both camps, the existence of any "third-party harms" automatically negates a religious freedom right, a claim Goodwin

96 Pierce v. Soc. of Sisters, 268 U.S. 510 (1925).

97 *See* Helfand, this volume; Church of the Lukumi Babalu Aye, Inc. v. Hialeah, 508 U.S. 520 (1993) (applying Free Exercise Clause).

98 *See* Larson v. Valente, 456 U.S. 228 (1982) (striking under the Establishment Clause a state law exempting religious groups that receive more than 50% of their funding from member donations from duty to register with the state under its charitable solicitations act as creating a denominational preference).

99 *See, e.g.*, Burwell v. Hobby Lobby Stores, Inc., 134 S. Ct. 2751 (2014) (applying Religious Freedom Restoration Act); Adams, Chapter 21, this volume (listing state RFRAs).

100 *See, e.g.*, Leslie C. Griffin, *The Sins of Hosanna-Tabor*, 88 IND. L.J. 981, 983 (2013); Richard Schragger & Micah Schwartzman, *Against Religious Institutionalism*, 99 VA. L. REV. 917, 965 (2013) ("attributing human rights to institutions poses a potential danger to individual human rights"). *But see* INT'L COVENANT ON CIVIL AND POLITICAL RIGHTS, Art. 18(1) ("Everyone shall have the right to freedom of thought, conscience and religion. This right shall include freedom to have or to adopt a religion or belief of his choice, and freedom,

(Chapter 3) and Lipper (Chapter 5) make elsewhere in this volume.[101] The necessary corollary of this approach is that religiously motivated circumcision of male infants would not be protected by the First Amendment or a federal or state Religious Freedom Restoration Acts, because the free exercise rights of the group – the family – and the group's decision makers – the parents – could not be asserted with respect to the third party – the infant boy. Were a governmental entity of any sort to decide that circumcision harms infants, then it could ban circumcision without constitutional or statutory consequence.

Ultimately, this thin conception of religious liberty ought to be condemned. Very few constitutional protections create no externalities to others. Freedom of speech, as one example, protects the right to say extremely hurtful things even when it causes harm to third parties.[102] In the end, treating third-party harms as an impervious boundary around fundamental rights goes too far.

Which theories of religious liberty hold sway within the U.S. will also depend in large part on the composition of the Supreme Court when it decides a circumcision case. In April 2017, Neil Gorsuch was confirmed as an Associate Justice of the Supreme Court. Given his record on cases involving religious liberty claims, many observers expect him to be a proponent of a robust form of religious liberty.[103] Far harder to discern will be the effects of other possible changes in the Court's personnel over the coming years, but each such change will be important to the law of religious liberty.

In sum, U.S. courts are far more likely than European courts to interpose a bar to restrictions on religiously motivated male circumcision. But given the trend lines in both the academy and in public discourse, no outcome is certain.

VI RELIGIOUSLY MOTIVATED MALE CIRCUMCISION AS A HEURISTIC

This chapter offers many more questions than answers. However, it would be prudent for advocates, scholars, and judges to begin considering these questions now, before the time for answers is upon us. In particular, legal thinkers

either individually *or in community with others* and in public or private, to manifest his religion or belief in worship, observance, practice and teaching.") (emphasis added).

101 Goodwin, Chapter 3, this volume; Lipper, Chapter 5, this volume.

102 *See, e.g.*, Snyder v. Phelps, 562 U.S. 443 (2011) (prohibiting damages for speech that caused emotional distress to a third party).

103 *See, e.g.*, Michael McConnell, *Neil Gorsuch: An Eloquent Intellectual*, Hoover Inst. (Feb. 6, 2017), www.hoover.org/research/neil-gorsuch-eloquent-intellectual.

should use the question of the permissibility of government prohibitions on religiously motivated circumcision of male infants as a heuristic for evaluating different visions of family law and the law of religious liberty.

For example, if one is considering – in court, in class, or in public discourse – a vision of family law that places relatively low value on parental rights, then one should decide whether that vision would result in allowing governments to ban religiously motivated male circumcision, over presumably low-value, parental objections. Similarly, if one adopts a view of religious freedom that downplays the collective aspect of religious exercise, then one must be prepared to articulate why a collective entity – the family – would have any religious exercise at stake when seeking religious circumcision for an infant boy. Put another way, it is precisely because government bans on religiously motivated male circumcision are so obviously an overreach that hypothesized bans provide a useful test of normative theories of the law of religious freedom or the law of the family.

VII CONCLUSION

The trend lines show that religiously motivated male circumcision is likely to be litigated, adjudicated, and regulated in America and Europe increasingly over the next decade. The trends challenge the intuition of many Americans that "It Can't Happen Here."[104] Human history demonstrates that it is not unthinkable that circumcision would ever be challenged in the U.S. as violating positive law and basic principles of human rights. The American exceptionalism that fosters the notion that the U.S. is immune to this feature of human history is supported only the fact that it has not happened on a great scale yet.

Judges, scholars, and advocates ought to consider the question of male circumcision as a religious practice now – both as a coming necessity and because it provides a useful test for any normative theory of religious freedom or family prerogative. If recent political history in the U.S. has proven anything, it is that those who care about the religious practices of Jewish and Muslim Americans should not be complacent about the issue of religiously motivated male circumcision but should work hard to protect it now because protecting it expands freedom for all of us.

[104] *See* SINCLAIR LEWIS, IT CAN'T HAPPEN HERE (1935).

PART III

RELIGIOUS CLAIMS IN CHILDREARING

8

The Easiest Accommodation

Abandoning Other People's Children to Their Parents' Religious Views

James G. Dwyer

Arthur B. Hanson Professor of Law, William & Mary Law School

A right to religious accommodation was in the United States an invention of the Warren Court in the 1960s.[1] Before that time, Protestant Christian America manifested *some* but not a great deal of solicitude, without judicial compulsion, for religious minority norms and practices that conflicted with existing legal regulations.[2] U.S. Supreme Court decisions transforming the First Amendment Free Exercise Clause from a protection principally for worship and nondiscrimination against those who worship into a fairly strong basis for demanding exemption from generally applicable laws – that is, for special benefits and privileges–were one manifestation of the general societal challenge to traditional ortho doxies and distributions of power in the 1960s and 1970s. Those decisions essentially made free exercise claims equivalent to fundamental liberty substantive due process claims, triggering heightened judicial review. The Court made clear that even unintentional state imposition of burdens on religious practice, incidental to some religiously neutral regulation of general applicability, would require greater justification than state imposition of burdens on nonreligious, non-fundamental liberties or interests. The state would have to show that imposing the legal requirement on all, without exemption for religious objectors, was necessary to serve a compelling state interest.[3]

[1] *See* Melissa Murray, *Accommodating Nonmarriage*, 88 S. Cal. L. Rev. 661, 685 (2015).

[2] *See* Michael W. McConnell, John H. Garvey, & Thomas C. Berg, Religion and the Constitution 86–102 (2d ed. 2006) (discussing the history of religious accommodation in America).

[3] *See* James G. Dwyer, *Parents' Religion and Children's Welfare: Debunking the Doctrine of Parents' Rights*, 82 Cal. L. Rev. 1371, 1447 (1994). Michael Helfand's assertion that free exercise strict scrutiny before *Employment Division v. Smith* was more deferential to the state

The Court later retreated from this expansion of constitutional entitlement, in its 1990 decision *Employment Division v. Smith*.[4] This decision deflated the Free Exercise Clause to an equal protection right for religious minorities, once again guarding only against being singled out for unfavorable treatment. However, Congress and more than twenty state legislatures then substituted a legislative entitlement to accommodation, in some form of Religious Freedom Restoration Act ("RFRA"). Such statutes generally require legislatures to grant an exemption to legal requirements when they substantially burden a person's exercise of religion, unless the requirement is the least restrictive means of serving a compelling state interest.[5] The precise scope of this accommodation entitlement in federal and state laws is now a source of ongoing controversy.[6]

Initially, the most sympathetic cases for accommodation were ones pitting the state against a religiously observant individual member of a minority religion in situations where the state seemingly had little at stake. A prime example is states' barring unemployment benefits for individuals fired for refusing to work on religious days. Today, the most intractable conflicts over accommodation involve direct conflicts among private parties. Many arise because of federal or state laws requiring private businesses to provide certain benefits to employees or to refrain from discrimination on certain bases in hiring or providing services. Those legal commands conflict with the religious convictions of some business owners. The Supreme Court's decision in *Hobby Lobby v. Burwell*,[7] interpreting the federal RFRA as entitling even a secular, for-profit company an exemption from certain employment laws, sent shock

than strict scrutiny under other constitutional provisions might be true, but his basis for saying so is flawed. Basing a comparative assessment simply on the percentage of cases in which the state prevailed, without taking into account the numerous factors that distinguish legal challenges to state action in different doctrinal areas, is primitive armchair social science.

4 Emp't Div. v. Smith, 494 U.S. 872 (1990).

5 *See* 42 U.S.C. § 2000bb-1; (2012); Introduction, this volume (listing states).

6 Contrary to Michael Helfand's suggestion elsewhere in this volume, RFRAs do not prescribe a balancing. When things are balanced, the weight on one side is compared to the weight on the other side to determine the outcome based on which is weightier. Under the federal and typical state RFRAs, so long as the private interest a state law or other action thwarts exceeds the threshold standard of "substantial," a standard the *Hobby Lobby* decision interpreted to be very low, it is thereafter irrelevant to the outcome how strong that interest is. Whether the interest just barely passes the low "substantial" threshold or is truly monumental and far surpassing that threshold, the demand on the state is the same – namely, to show that the state action in question is necessary to serve a compelling state interest. Thus, even if the state action is necessary to serve an important state interest that is clearly weightier than the private interest at stake, if a court decides that the state interest – though important – does not reach that ultimate constitutional standard of "compelling," the private interest prevails. That is not balancing.

7 Burwell v. Hobby Lobby, Inc., 134 S. Ct. 2751 (2014).

waves through America. It seemed to signal that the legal system would side with religious interests in a very broad range of ideological clashes among private parties. Greatest consternation has arisen over the potential impact on women and sexual minorities.

Yet, one subset of situations pitting the religious beliefs and practices of some private individuals against the interests of other private individuals has produced little public controversy, even though it has given rise to the most enduring and robust legal accommodations for religious dissenters: many statutes aimed at protecting the welfare of children exempt parents who have religious objections to the legal duties they impose. As a result of these pervasive parental religious exemptions, the government in the U.S. and elsewhere has largely abandoned children to the ideological idiosyncrasies of parents, most troublingly in the realms of healthcare and education.

This chapter first summarizes the current state of the law governing conflicts between parental religious beliefs and state-imposed norms in the realms of medical care and education. It then explains why the *Hobby Lobby* decision will have no impact on religious childrearing, in large part because states had already, by statute and without judicial compulsion, bestowed on parents extraordinary legal power over basic aspects of children's well-being. Lastly, it argues that the state's extreme deference to parents' religious beliefs is paradoxical and, worse, immoral.

I CURRENT ACCOMMODATION OF DISSENTING PARENTS

Federal constitutional doctrine regarding parental free exercise rights actually accords religious-objector parents much less protection than most people assume. The Supreme Court has consistently stated that states are constitutionally free, regardless of parental religious beliefs, to restrict the liberty and child-rearing power of parents in order to further what the state views as children's well-being.[8] The Court's holdings clearly recognize the propriety of states' applying medical neglect laws equally to all parents, regardless of any religious objection some might have to medical care, and imposing substantial requirements for the content of instruction on private schools. Nevertheless, states have gratuitously conferred on parents who are religiously opposed to certain legal childrearing duties extraordinary power to control children's physical and cognitive growth. In effect, the state empowers such parents to

[8] *See* James G. Dwyer, *Equality Between Adults and Children: Its Meaning, Implications, and Opposition*, Mich. St. L. Rev. 1007, 1014 (2013).

waive children's statutory rights to healthcare and to what the state regards as an adequate education.

With respect to healthcare, the vast majority of U.S. states have, in their child protection laws, some form of religious exemption regarding the general requirement that parents secure professional medical attention for a child who is seriously ill or injured. Enacted at the insistence principally of the Christian Science Church, these statutory provisions preclude charges of neglect against parents who rely on prayer rather than doctors and hospitals.[9] This religious group urges followers to heal themselves and their children through prayer, rejecting mainstream medical profession expertise. In addition, the vast majority of states have religious exemptions in their laws mandating preventive testing and care for children – in particular, screening of newborns for genetic disorders and administration of childhood immunizations.[10] They grant these exemptions even though they clearly are not constitutionally required to do so.[11] A notable exception to this pervasive accommodation in the realm of physical well-being is the nationwide prohibition of female genital alteration, which makes no exception for parental religious conviction.[12]

With respect to education, all U.S. states leave private schools alone to do pretty much whatever they want with the children who attend them rather than a public school.[13] Most states also take this stance with respect to

9 *See* Offit, Chapter 12, this volume; Rita Swan, *On Statutes Depriving a Class of Children of Rights to Medical Care: Can This Discrimination Be Litigated?* 2 QUINNIPIAC HEALTH L.J. 73, 78–88 (1998).

10 *See* Offit, Chapter 12, this volume; Swan, *supra* note 9, at 76–78.

11 See Workman v. Mingo Cty. Bd. of Educ., 419 F. App'x 348, 353–55 (4th Cir. 2011) (reaching this conclusion and citing authorities for the same proposition in other jurisdictions).

12 *See, e.g.*, 18 U.S.C. § 116 (2012) (criminalizing "whoever knowingly circumcises, excises, or infibulates the whole or any part of the labia majora or labia minora or clitoris of another person who has not attained the age of 18 years" and stating that "no account shall be taken of the effect on the person on whom the operation is to be performed of any belief on the part of that person, or any other person, that the operation is required as a matter of custom or ritual"). Contrary to the unsupported assertion of Eric Rassbach, Chapter 7, this volume, there are variants of cultural female genital mutilation that are less severe than male circumcision yet absolutely prohibited in the U.S. *See, e.g.*, Sya Taha, *"A Tiny Cut": Female Circumcision in South East Asia*, THE ISLAMIC MONTHLY (Mar. 12, 2013). Rassbach is correct that the circumcision rate has dropped substantially in the U.S. in recent decades. And though he exaggerates the strength of anti-circumcision advocacy groups and of support for prohibition among legal scholars (I am, in fact, the only law professor he cites), it is plausible to suppose that in the not-too-distant future some states will begin to prohibit it absent medical necessity. If and when that occurs, legislators would be hard pressed to justify a religious exemption, given the absence of one in the previously mentioned criminal prohibitions of female genital alteration.

13 *See* James G. Dwyer, *No Accounting for School Vouchers*, 48 WAKE FOREST L. REV. 361, 363–64; James G. Dwyer, *The Children We Abandon: Religious Exemptions to Child Welfare*

homeschooling.[14] For the most part, this is not accomplished by explicit exemptions to otherwise universally applicable school regulations. Rather, it is accomplished by enacting education laws – and, in particular, laws about curriculum, assessment, and teacher qualifications – that apply in the first instance only to public schools.[15] These laws simply do not contemplate applying their requirements to any private schools, religious or secular, nor to homeschools.

Many states also accredit private schools, conditional upon accepting certain requirements and oversight. However, accreditation is voluntary on the part of the schools.[16] Some private schools do seek state accreditation, or accreditation by a private school organization approved by the state, because accreditation enhances their reputation in the market they serve. But, of course, the schools whose practices diverge most drastically from mainstream norms of education are precisely the ones that categorically reject state authority over childrearing. They are also the ones that might actually suffer in reputation among the parent population they serve if they have any involvement with state education officials.

The only types of regulations states apply universally to private schools, including religious schools, are those that apply also to non-educational businesses, such as building safety codes.[17] This is typically true even when states offer vouchers or other schemes of overt financial state support for religious schooling; the financial support is typically offered with no meaningful regulatory strings, even though these funding schemes could serve as an excellent mechanism for eliminating bad private schools or discouraging certain practices in private schools.[18] At most, voucher laws have imposed, as a condition for participation, a requirement that schools receiving state money not discriminate on the basis of race in admissions. This rather meaningless provision nevertheless made the Supreme Court think, when deciding the constitutionality of school voucher programs, that the state actually demands something in return for subsidizing private schools.[19] President Donald Trump's appointment of a strong voucher proponent as

and Educational Law as Denials of Equal Protection to Children of Religious Objectors, 74 N.C. L. REV. 1321, 1338, n.60 (1996).

14 *See* JAMES G. DWYER & SHAWN F. PETERS, HOMESCHOOLING: HISTORICAL AND PHILOSOPHICAL PERSPECTIVES (2018), chap. 3.

15 *See, e.g.*, ALA. CODE § 16–23-1, -8 (2016); N.Y. EDUC. LAW § 3001 (2006). *See also* Dwyer, *The Children We Abandon*, *supra* note 13.

16 *See, e.g.*, Dwyer, *supra* note 8, at 1338–39.

17 *See* Dwyer, *No Accounting for School Vouchers*, *supra* note 13.

18 *Id.* at 383–94.

19 *See* James G. Dwyer, *Funding Religion in a Post-Zelman World*, 5 GOV'T L. & POL'Y J. 11 (2003).

Secretary of Education, Betsy DeVos, portends a proliferation of no-strings-attached voucher programs. A small number of states do make modest efforts to check the educational progress of homeschooled students.[20] Most states, however, leave homeschools unsupervised, too – at least those operated by parents who claim to religiously homeschool.[21] Thus, the most important features of a school from a child-centered perspective – that is, what qualifications do the teachers have, the content of the curriculum, whether a school has incentives to provide a good education, and how teachers and administrators treat students – are almost entirely unregulated in the private school sector.[22]

Even if one stipulates that most private schooling is at least adequate, and that much of it is superior to the education provided in public schools in the same locale, there is no denying that a significant fraction of religious schools and homeschools in the U.S. are nonetheless grossly inadequate academically from the state's perspective. Some deliberately aim to stifle children's intellectual curiosity and to channel girls into conventional and severely limited social roles.[23] We simply do not know how prevalent this phenomenon is

[20] New York appears to make the most substantial effort. It requires homeschooling parents in the younger grades to submit a quarterly progress report and an annual assessment conducted by an outside evaluator approved by local school officials. Beginning with fifth grade, homeschooled students must take standardized tests every other year, and results are to be reported to the school district. If a school district concludes that the past year of homeschooling was inadequate, it gives the parents two years to improve, and only after three consecutive years of inadequacy could the state insist that the child attend a regular school. N.Y. COMP. CODES R. & REGS. TIT. 8, § 100.10. *See also* Jessica Huseman, *Small Group Goes to Great Lengths to Block Homeschooling Regulation*, PRO PUBLICA (Aug. 27, 2015), www.propublica.org/article/small-group-goes-great-lengths-to-block-homeschooling-regulation.

[21] *See* Jessica Huseman, *The Frightening Power of the Home-Schooling Lobby*, SLATE (Aug. 27, 2015), www.slate.com/articles/life/education/2015/08/home_school_legal_defense_association_how_a_home_schooling_group_fights.html; Kimberly A. Yuracko, *Education Off the Grid: Constitutional Constraints on Homeschooling*, 96 CAL. L. REV. 123, 130 (2008). In Virginia, state law establishes as a general rule for homeschooling that a parent must get approval from the local public school officials based on demonstration of an adequate curriculum and capacity to teach, and must show adequate academic progress after each year of homeschooling, but then pronounces that any parent who "by reason of bona fide religious training or belief is conscientiously opposed to attendance at school" is entirely exempted from any educational requirements whatsoever. VA. CODE ANN. § 22.1–254(B)(1) (2016).

[22] *See, e.g.*, U.S. Dep't of Educ., *State Regulation of Private Schools* (2009), www2.ed.gov/admins/comm/choice/regprivschl/regprivschl.pdf (listing state regulatory requirements for private schools).

[23] For examples of religious schools that are, in terms of the state's aims for children's education, troubling, see, for example, J.C. Blokhuis, *Book Review*, 8 THEORY & RES. EDUC. 322, 322–26 (2010) (reviewing ROBERT KUNZMAN, WRITE THESE LAWS ON YOUR CHILDREN: INSIDE THE WORLD OF CONSERVATIVE CHRISTIAN HOMESCHOOLING (2009)); Frances Patterson,

precisely because states have eschewed oversight and abandoned millions of children to whatever ideological inclinations their parents might have.

II THE IRRELEVANCE OF RELIGIOUS ACCOMMODATION MANDATES

As noted earlier, the Supreme Court no longer interprets the federal Constitution's First Amendment Free Exercise Clause as an accommodation mandate. But Congress and many state legislatures reinstituted such a mandate in RFRAs, which entitle individuals and many businesses and organizations to exemptions from generally applicable laws that substantially burden their religious practice unless the state can show that uniform application of a given law is necessary to serve a compelling state interest.[24] The federal act applies only to federal laws and regulations.[25] However, some state courts interpret their state RFRA, which applies to state laws and regulations, consistently with federal court interpretation of the federal law.[26] Thus, the Supreme Court's decision in *Hobby Lobby* has potentially far greater reach.

The specific dispute in *Hobby Lobby* arose in an employment-law context. The Patient Protection and Affordable Care Act of 2010 ("ACA") requires certain employers to provide their employees with health insurance that covers certain health services.[27] Some of those services were ones that some, including owners and operators of businesses, might deem immoral from a religious perspective. The case presented the Court with two basic questions: (1) do the protections of the federal RFRA extend to secular, for-profit, closely

With God on Their Side, RETHINKING SCHOOLS (Winter 2001/2002), www.rethinkingschools.org/special_reports/voucher_report/v_god162.shtml (describing extreme bias in religious schools' social studies textbooks); JAMES G. DWYER, RELIGIOUS SCHOOLS V. CHILDREN'S RIGHTS 16–44 (1998). For the view that "faith schools" are inherently indoctrinatory, *see generally* Michael Hand, *A Philosophical Objection to Faith Schools*, 1 THEORY & RES. EDUC. 89 (2003); Barbara Miner, *School Vouchers: A Threat to the Rights of Women and Gays*, RETHINKING SCHOOLS (Feb. 2002), www.rethinkingschools.org/special_reports/voucher_report/v_gay.shtml.

24 Hobby Lobby, *supra* note 7, at 2779 ("RFRA ... requires the Government to demonstrate that the compelling interest test is satisfied through application of the challenged law 'to the person' – the particular claimant whose sincere exercise of religion is being substantially burdened.") (quoting Gonzales v. O Centro Esp´ırita Beneficente Uniao do Vegetal, 546 U.S. 418, 430–31 (2006)).

25 City of Boerne v. Flores, 521 U.S. 507 (1997).

26 *See, e.g.*, Diggs v. Snyder, 775 N.E.2d 40, 44 (Ill. App. Ct. 2002); World Outreach Conference Ctr. v. City of Chicago, 591 F.3d 531, 533 (7th Cir. 2009) (internal citations omitted).

27 Patient Protection and Affordable Care Act, 42 U.S.C. § 18001 (2012).

held corporations, so that they have standing to assert a RFRA objection to a federal regulation of their operations; and (2) if so, does the federal RFRA require an exemption for such corporations from the ACA's mandate of coverage for contraceptives that sometimes may act as abortifacients,[28] if the owners of the corporations have religious beliefs that prohibit them from facilitating abortion.

The standing issue is not especially relevant to childrearing issues. Parents, as private individuals, clearly have free exercise rights and clearly have standing under federal and state RFRAs to complain that laws substantially burden their exercise of religion. Religious schools are generally operated by religious organizations, and they too clearly have standing under RFRAs.[29] However, how the *Hobby Lobby* Court answered the second question, as to when exemptions are required for persons who have RFRA standing, has implications for anyone asserting religious liberty claims, because the decision included general interpretations of the federal RFRA's scope and operation. Specifically, the Court adopted a minimalist conception of burden on religious freedom and a maximalist conception of least restrictive means.[30]

A *When Protecting One Person's Well-being Burdens Someone Else's Exercise of Religion*

Prior to *Hobby Lobby*, some lower federal courts interpreted the substantial burden threshold test of RFRA to require a showing that federal government action seriously impedes the ability to carry out an activity important to one's religion.[31] In 2000, Congress had amended RFRA to encompass "any exercise of religion, whether or not compelled by, or central to, a system of religious belief," but it had retained the term "substantial burden."[32] Childrearing as a whole is certainly important within most religions, even central, but not everything parents do in the course of raising children has great religious import, nor is every legal duty the state imposes on parents a significant obstacle to their complying with religious commands as to raising of children. This section examines what threshold showing of burden is required under

[28] For a review of evidence of whether mandated contraceptives ever act on the implantation site to disrupt an implanted embryo, see Goodwin, Chapter 3, this volume.

[29] *See* Office of Non-Public Education, *Statistics About Nonpublic Education in the United States* (Dec. 2, 2106), www2.ed.gov/about/offices/list/oii/nonpublic/statistics.html.

[30] See Goodwin, Chapter 3; Helfand, Chapter 2; Sepper, Chapter 1, this volume, for competing views of how to read the *Hobby Lobby* decision.

[31] *See* Alex J. Luchenitser, *A New Era of Inequality? Hobby Lobby and Religious Exemptions from Anti-Discrimination Laws*, 9 HARV. L. & POL'Y REV. 63, 67 (2015).

[32] *See* 42 U.S.C. § 2000bb–2(4); 42 U.S.C. § 2000cc–5(7)(A) (2012).

RFRA after the Supreme Court's *Hobby Lobby* decision and then considers its implication for religiously motivated parenting.

The Court in *Hobby Lobby* made clear that a burden triggering strict scrutiny can be "substantial" within the meaning of RFRA even if it relates to behavior at the fringes of a person's adherence to religious belief, and even if the burden is simply the imposition of a significant financial cost for adherence to one's faith regarding that peripheral activity. The Court treated as a substantial burden merely being required to provide another person with something (in this case, insurance coverage) that the recipient could (without the provider knowing it) use to engage in conduct the provider believes, as a matter of religious conviction, to be immoral. In other words, the decision renders presumptively unconstitutional the government's requiring or financially coercing a person to facilitate someone else's doing something of which the person disapproves because of his or her religious beliefs. In *Hobby Lobby*, the thing to be done was so far removed from the dissenters' own religious observance and study that the objecting employers were, for a substantial period of time, unaware of the phenomenon about which they complained – namely, that they themselves were providing insurance coverage that could facilitate use of abortifacients.[33]

The Court rejected the government's argument that the plaintiff employers' exercise of religion cannot be burdened by someone else's independently engaging in conduct the employers deem immoral.[34] It was sufficient to constitute a burden that one is required or financially pressured to participate in some way in behavior by other persons. Presumably, there must be some conceptual connection between what the religious objector is required to do and the immoral conduct, so one could not claim, for example, that minimum wage laws burden one's religion because some employees might use the extra wages to purchase alcohol or sexual services. Unfortunately, the Court left unclear how strong that connection must be.

A few things the Court clearly did not say are worth noting, because of their relevance to parenting: first, the Court never suggested RFRA empowers employers or anyone else to prevent other persons from receiving certain services or benefits simply because they have some relationship with the other persons. It was necessary for standing that federal law was affirmatively ordering employers to do something. If employers asked the government to prohibit their employees from using contraceptives that might be used as

33 For a review of how attenuated the objected-to act was from the objector's own action, *see* Sepper, Chapter 1, this volume.

34 Hobby Lobby, *supra* note 7, at 2777–78.

abortifacients, regardless of how they obtained those contraceptives, neither legislators nor courts would pay them any heed.[35] The notion of one person having a right to stop someone else from receiving some service *per se* is simply anathema. That point might seem too obvious to express, but it is generally forgotten when people think about childrearing. Second, the Court never suggested that a closely held corporation has a presumptive right to exemption from regulation if its owners' religious beliefs dictate that they completely reject the authority of the state to regulate their activity. That might seem the extreme conclusion to which the Court's subjective rendering of religious exercise leads; it might even be a core belief of some religious faith that one must not in any way recognize the authority of the state. But the Court itself certainly did not draw that conclusion, and it is inconceivable that it ever would. Third, and on the other hand, the Court never suggested that employers should simply go out of business if they do not approve of regulations to which they are subject; that a government imposition is just a condition on license to engage in voluntary activity does not weaken a RFRA claim. This, too, is significant for regulation of childrearing.

In addition to recognizing a broad scope for actions that can conflict with religious belief, the Court also suggested a capacious understanding of "substantiality." If a government action merely makes one's "practice of ... religious beliefs more expensive," even though it does not prevent such practice, it amounts to a burden that suffices to launch an RFRA objection.[36] The ACA did not, in fact, force employers such as Hobby Lobby to provide insurance coverage for contraceptives; it simply imposed a financial penalty if they refused to do so.[37]

What implications might these aspects of the Hobby Lobby analysis have for laws governing children's healthcare and education? First, it is significant that the Court treated as a burden of religious exercise merely being required or pressured to secure for some other person some service one opposes on religious grounds. This suggests courts should view as a burden on parents' religious exercise their having a legal duty to secure medical treatment or preventive care for a child, or their having to obtain or provide schooling of

[35] Indeed, it was implicit in the Court's least restrictive means analysis that government provision of abortifacients to employees of Hobby Lobby by some means other than employer-purchased healthcare would not infringe the religious rights of Hobby Lobby's owners. *Id.* at 2782–83.

[36] *Id.* at 2770. For a pair of competing views on how high the threshold test for substantial burdens should be, see Helfand, Chapter 2 and Sepper, Chapter 1, this volume.

[37] *Id.* at 2776.

a particular sort for a child, if their religion is opposed to medical care or to the sort of education the state prescribes.

Suppose, however, that child neglect laws, instead of stating a blanket religious exemption for parents religiously opposed to mainstream medicine or secular education, stated that any such parents could, instead of securing medical treatment or preventive care or secular schooling, simply notify the state that they cannot in good conscience participate in procuring such services. Upon such notification, social workers or school officials could step into the place of the parents, at no cost to the parents, and take the child from home to a doctor's office or hospital or school. The parents would simply have to stay out of the way. A question this would raise that *Hobby Lobby* does not implicitly answer is this: is requiring the parents to submit a notification itself a substantial burden on their religious exercise, if they think even that implicates them too much in their children receiving services to which the parents are religiously opposed?

As Elizabeth Sepper (Chapter 1, this volume) discusses, an analogous issue arose for courts after *Hobby Lobby*, as employers complained about even having to notify regulators or insurers of their religious objection to the contraceptive coverage mandate. One important fact that might distinguish the notification requirement from the procurement requirement is that the latter but not the former might be inherently contrary to religious commands. The Supreme Court will have to draw a line somewhere, either on the ground that required conduct is not inherently contrary to anyone's religious beliefs or that the required conduct is relatively costless. As Sepper notes, this will entail designating some such judgments as theological and therefore not fit for courts to make, and other such judgments as secular and a proper province for judges. But *Hobby Lobby* leaves unclear on what basis the Court will make such designations.

It is not even clear what the Court would say to RFRA claimants who assert that at the core of their religious faith lies a conviction that they must reject all state authority over how they conduct their business or raise their children, a position from which it would follow under RFRA that the state presumptively must exempt such persons from all laws. This might seem fanciful, but it is a position many parents and religious school operators have in fact asserted. Their religion might not have a specific proscription on teaching math to children, or on testing children's progress in math, or in the abstract on communicating the results of such testing. But their religion tells them to reject altogether the authority of the state in connection with child-rearing, and that is the foundation of their claiming a right against state imposition of a requirement that religious schools or homeschooling parents administer tests and report the results to the state. Another sort of limitless religious freedom claim was advanced by a West Virginia mother who, when refused an exemption from school immunization requirements for her child, asserted that her religion – though it said nothing about immunizations – instructed her to protect her child from harm and that she believed vaccinations would harm her child.[38]

The *Hobby Lobby* Court's treatment of a financial cost as satisfying the substantiality requirement is also relevant to childrearing. Some parents and religious school operators might say that accepting government oversight is not contrary to their religious beliefs, and the state's substantive requirements for teacher qualifications, curriculum content, and assessment are not inherently contrary to their religious beliefs, yet state regulation substantially burdens their exercise of religion simply because it makes their operation of a religious school or homeschool more expensive. Their religion instructs them to school their children separate from the mainstream and immersed in a religious environment, and the state would make that more costly by forcing them to hire credentialed teachers, to include certain subjects in their curriculum, or to administer certain assessments. Unless perhaps the government provided payments to cover all compliance costs, then those costs themselves could constitute the substantial burden on religious exercise, even though they are costs born by all schools, whether secular or religious, and even if the requirements are not inherently contrary to any religious belief. With respect to medical care, the costs for parents of procuring care themselves would include provider charges and transportation expenses, which can certainly be significant. Simply calling a social service agency hotline to report a child's injury or illness, so a social worker can pick up and transport the child, on the other hand, would presumably be virtually costless (assuming the government would not demand reimbursement from parents for agency expenses).

Of course, what religious-objector parents really want is not freedom from participation in a course of events whereby their children receive some service the parents regard as anathema, nor to avoid the expenses that compliance with child welfare laws might entail for them. What they really want is power over their children's lives. They want to be able to control all the inputs into their children's minds and bodies. It would not be enough for them to be able simply to stand aside, wash their hands of the matter, and protect their purses. They have an intense desire to ensure that no one does anything regarding the children in their custody that is contrary to what their religion tells them is

38 *See* Workman v. Mingo Cty. Sch., 667 F. Supp. 2d 679, 684 (S.D.W. Va. 2009).

proper for children. And this kind of power *per se* over the life of other persons – what we might call "other-determining power" – is, as noted earlier, something to which *Hobby Lobby* simply does not speak.

The Supreme Court's First Amendment doctrine, on the other hand, has addressed such claims to other-determining power. On rare occasion such claims have arisen even outside the context of parents' raising minor offspring; in those cases the Court has flatly rejected the claim, holding that individuals simply have no right to determine what happens to other people. In the Nancy Cruzan case, for example, parents asserted a free exercise right to decide whether their adult daughter in a persistent vegetative state would continue to receive life-sustaining treatment. The Court's denial of this claim was not based on a determination that controlling others' lives is not central to anyone's religious practice, nor on a determination that denial of such a power is an insubstantial burden on religious exercise. Rather, it was based on an implicit premise that other-determining power is different from both self-determining power and liberty, and simply not included within what the Free Exercise Clause confers on individuals. The Court in Cruzan treated the parents' claim as a category error, as resting on a misunderstanding of what individual rights are or are for.[39] Only the incompetent adult offspring herself had any rights at stake with respect to her own medical treatment, the Court stated, even though she was not capable of directly exercising any rights.[40] A proxy decision maker can exercise rights for a non-autonomous person, on the basis of "substituted judgment" or "best interests."[41]

Undoubtedly, the Court would say the same if a pro-life advocate asserted a free exercise right to prevent women from having abortions. Such a purpose might be central to the advocate's religious beliefs. And the state's denying that power and deploying police to prevent the advocate from attempting physically to stop women from entering abortion facilities surely would be a substantial burden on that belief. But the Court would say, under the Free Exercise Clause and presumably under RFRA as well, that the advocate's religious freedom claim never even gets off the ground, never triggers a burden of justification for the state, because what we mean by "a person's exercise of religion" is self-determining power and freedom from being forced affirmatively to do things contrary to one's faith. Either as a conceptual matter or as

39 Cruzan by Cruzan v. Dir., Missouri Dep't of Health, 497 U.S. 261, 286 (1990) ("If the State were required by the United States Constitution to repose a right of 'substituted judgment' with anyone, the Cruzans would surely qualify. But we do not think the Due Process Clause requires the State to repose judgment on these matters with anyone but the patient herself.").

40 *Id.* 41 *See* James G. Dwyer, The Relationship Rights of Children 206–08 (2006).

a matter of lawmakers' intent, a person's exercise of religion within the meaning of the Free Exercise Clause or of RFRA simply does not include other-determining power.

And yet, in child-rearing contexts, the Court has treated the right of religious exercise under the Free Exercise Clause as encompassing an other-determining power. The prime example is *Wisconsin v. Yoder*,[42] in which the Court considered application of a state compulsory education law to Amish children past the eighth grade. The Court held that requiring those children to attend a school violated a religious right – not a right of the children, but a right of their parents. The state law was phrased in terms of a parental obligation to do something – namely, to undertake the necessary practical steps to have a child enrolled. And the parents were fined for not doing so. But neither the parents nor the Court so much as hinted that the state might avoid constitutional restriction simply by removing the parents from the equation, by finding a way to get the adolescents in a school without their parents' involvement. Surely it would not have satisfied the parents or the Court if Wisconsin had offered to send someone to the homes of the Amish families to transport their adolescent children to a school, or if Wisconsin had only imposed on parents a negative duty not to interfere with their children's departure from the home. Instead, the Court treated merely being disempowered from preventing another person from being exposed to certain ideas constituted a burden on exercise of religion that triggers judicial review of state action. Ultimately, it was an other-determining power, not a personal liberty, at stake for the Amish parents. Yet, the Court found state denial of that power a substantial burden on religious exercise.[43]

The Court has not had occasion to carry over to RFRA interpretation this anomalous treatment of parental claims to other-determining power, but there is no reason to suppose it would not. Even if it did not do so, after *Hobby Lobby* it might nevertheless find colorable under RFRA a parental objection to having to participate in or bear costs for something the state mandates in connection with child welfare, as explained earlier. Some state courts applying state RFRAs have appeared to assume that parental objections to child welfare laws do fall within the ambit of those acts.[44] Thus, courts applying the federal RFRA or a state RFRA with similar language to

42 Wisconsin v. Yoder, 406 U.S. 205 (1972). 43 *Id.* at 235.

44 *See, e.g., Cf.* State v. Crank, 468 S.W.3d 15, 31 (Tenn. 2015) (holding that the state's RFRA did not apply to a religious child neglect case because the neglect occurred prior to its enactment); *In re* L.H., 2014 IL App (1st) 133252-U, ¶ 48 (2014) (holding that a trial court order against a parent that she must "help 'establish a support system outside of the church ministry' for her children" "did not substantially burden [the mother]'s free exercise of religion").

a new set of legal mandates regarding healthcare or religious schooling presumably would apply strict scrutiny if a parent or school operator objected on religious grounds.[45]

B The State Should Win Anyway

In interpreting the state's burden of justification under RFRA, *Hobby Lobby* also signaled a stance highly protective of religious claimants. To establish a compelling government interest, the state must show that "the *marginal interest* in enforcing" its law as to "*the particular claimant* whose sincere exercise of religion is being substantially burdened" is a compelling one.[46] Thus, it is not sufficient to show a government program or legal mandate on the whole serves a compelling state interest. Instead, the government must show that exempting any particular individual or business would undermine a compelling state interest. Moreover, even if the state establishes that a compelling interest is at stake in every individual case, it must meet a least restrictive means test for serving that interest that is "exceptionally demanding."[47]

The Court expressed serious doubts that the government had a compelling interest in "guaranteeing cost-free access to the four challenged contraceptive methods" and might have rejected the federal government's position on that ground, except that it found it easier to do so on the basis of the least restrictive means requirement.[48] Concretely, the Court decided that RFRA can require the government to spend money in order to accomplish by other means the aims it is pursuing through the challenged law – in that case, by ensuring that employees of the religious-objector employer could obtain contraceptives by some avenue other than the employer-purchased health insurance policy.

However, although the Court adopted a quite rigorous approach to RFRA's version of strict scrutiny, several specific kinds of state laws that protect child welfare should survive even that version of strict scrutiny, for example: (1) a law imposing on *all* parents a duty to secure medical care for a sick or injured child (or to at least notify medical professionals or a state child welfare office of the child's duress and to refrain from interference with others' efforts to secure treatment);[49] (2) a law requiring metabolic screening of *all* newborns and the more important vaccinations for older children; (3) a law prohibiting

[45] For competing views on how rigorous strict scrutiny under RFRA is, see Helfand, Chapter 2 and Sepper, Chapter 1, this volume.

[46] Hobby Lobby, *supra* note 7, at 2779 (emphasis added). [47] *Id.* at 2780. [48] *Id.*

[49] For a review of such laws, see Offit, Chapter 12 and Wilson & Sanders, Chapter 13, this volume.

amputation of any child's genital tissue absent medical necessity; (4) a law prohibiting vicious beating of a child;[50] and (5) a law imposing on private schools and homeschoolers meaningful curricular requirements, assessments to enforce those requirements, and norms of gender equality and intellectual freedom. With each, the state aim is to protect important aspects of children's well-being – their interests in health, physical integrity, development toward autonomy, or preparation for a wide range of careers consistent with their native abilities. State and federal courts, including the U.S. Supreme Court, have consistently held that furthering children's health, welfare, and cognitive development is a compelling state interest.[51]

Moreover, it is difficult to imagine what less restrictive means might exist to accomplish the particular aim of ensuring children receive proper healthcare, remain physically intact, and develop into adults who can assume the mantle of productive citizenship. Especially in a legal environment that enables parents to isolate their children from the outside world, parents may be the only persons aware of a child's serious illness or injury.[52] Metabolic screening at a child's birth is the only way to catch some inherited diseases before they cause serious harm and unvaccinated children are clearly at higher risk of contracting communicable diseases than they would be if vaccinated.[53] Amputation of genital tissue and vicious beatings are either allowed or they are not. Significantly, parents have routinely lost when they asserted a free exercise right to exemption from children's healthcare laws, even when courts applied strict scrutiny.[54]

Regarding schooling, it is not as if offering remedial education to adults can make up for those persons' having endured a grossly deficient or subordinating elementary and secondary education. If schools and parents object to

50 *Cf.* Emma Green, *Religious Freedom Doesn't Protect Child Abuse*, THE ATLANTIC MONTHLY (Sep. 2, 2016) (reporting the case of a mother in Indiana who asserted the state's new RFRA as a defense to child abuse charges after she beat her seven-year-old son with a coat hanger, leaving thirty-six bruises).

51 *See* Yoder, *supra* note 42, at 213–14 (discussing the high deference given to states' power over education).

52 *See* Offit, Chapter 12, this volume, for a discussion of the unique vantage point of healthcare providers.

53 For instance, a rare metabolic disorder caused by an enzyme deficiency, PKU, may cause mental retardation, delayed speech, and other abnormalities if undetected and not treated with diet. Every U.S. state tests for PKU at birth, although the vast majority permit parents to opt out. *See* Offit, Chapter 12, this volume; Karen L. Hellekson, *Practice Guidelines: NIH Consensus Statement on Phenylketonuria*, 63 AM. FAM. PHYSICIAN 1430 (Apr. 1, 2001), www.aafp.org/afp/2001/0401/p1430.html.

54 *See* Allan J. Jacobs, *Do Belief Exemptions to Compulsory Vaccination Programs Violate the Fourteenth Amendment?* 42 U. MEM. L. REV. 73, 84–87 (2011).

standardized testing, it seems unlikely they would consent to some other form of government assessment of student progress, such as interviews and portfolio reviews. If the objection is to particular curricular material or test questions that are not really essential to students' intellectual growth, then schools and parents might demand accommodation in the form of exemption just from those specific aspects. Yet the kinds of teachings to which religious objections are most commonly raised are generally not inconsequential from a secular child welfare perspective – for example, sex education and evolution. Without sex education, young people might make life-altering mistakes; without exposure to sound scientific ideas, young people may find it difficult to pursue higher education in some scientific fields.[55]

But suppose a mandated critical-thinking curriculum or a question on standardized tests incorporated a same-sex relationship into the situation to be analyzed. The Court's strong rendering of least restrictive means might mean the state must devise alternatives for religious schools that deem such a relationship unfit for any discussion other than condemnation. From a child-centered perspective, that is not so troubling. Of course, a young person who is gay and attending a religious school could benefit from curriculum or testing that presents same-sex relationships as normal or in a positive light. In that environment, though, the presentation is likely to trigger negative comments from teachers, and it might be better for all students if the school is accommodated – especially if that makes the school willing to accept a new mandate that improves the education it provides.

This hypothetical scenario of new state regulations governing private schooling, though, is quite unrealistic. Unless and until religious schooling visibly threatens state interests or the well-being of outsiders (e.g., by fomenting violent rebellion), state and federal legislators will undoubtedly remain heedless of what effect religious schooling is having on the well-being of schoolchildren. At most, some Americans object to use of public money, through some form of voucher scheme, for illiberal or grossly inadequate schooling. But even when their own pocketbooks are affected, not enough people show concern about what goes on in religious schools or homeschools to induce legislators to attempt to regulate or oversee those schools. Americans

55 Guttmacher Institute, *State Laws and Policies: Sex and HIV Education* (Mar. 1, 2017), www.guttmacher.org/state-policy/explore/sex-and-hiv-education?gclid=CI_msNzrvdICFYS1wAod2SwPoQ (reporting that less than half of the states, twenty-four, mandate sex education); Chris Kirk, *Thousands of Schools in States Across the Country Can Use Taxpayer Money to Cast Doubt on Basic Science*, SLATE (Jan. 26, 2014), www.slate.com/articles/health_and_science/science/2014/01/creationism_in_public_schools_mapped_where_tax_money_supports_alternatives.html.

appear to care even less when children suffer and die from communicable diseases or injuries because of parental religious objections to medical care, unless those children carry diseases into the general population.[56]

III EXPLAINING OUR EXTREME EMPOWERMENT OF PARENTS

The question naturally arises: if states could make medical child neglect laws universal and could impose meaningful regulations on the content of education in all nonpublic forms of schooling, with mandatory assessments to ensure compliance, and could prohibit harmful schooling practices in the private realm – without running afoul of the constitutional and statutory limitations described earlier – why do they not do so? Why does the state empower some parents to deprive their children of medical attention that the overwhelming majority of people think children need? Why does the state empower some parents to deprive children of the sort of education that, from the state's perspective and from the perspective of the vast majority of people in this country, children should have and instead force children to experience intellectually stifling, psychologically abusive, and subordinating treatment? In other words, why does the typical American implicitly say: "If parents have a religious reason for doing so, they should be free to do to a child in their custody things that I think are very bad for the child"?

One part of the explanation in the schooling context is probably a lack of public awareness. The image people generally have of religious schools is positive. The only awareness of religious schools that people typically have is of schools that are either operated by their own ideological community or highly visible in the community and thus likely to be operating in a way that triggers scant criticism. Similarly, the homeschoolers one is likely to be aware of are either within one's circle of friends and family or actively involved in community activities (and therefore more mainstream).

But a less visible world of religious schooling and homeschooling exists that the vast majority of Americans would likely find quite disturbing if they only knew about it. This world has receded from view because the religious schools and homeschoolers whose practices are most divergent from the norm have

[56] Linda Carroll, *Should Vaccines be Mandatory? New California Law Sparks Debate*, TODAY (Jun. 30, 2015), www.today.com/health/should-vaccines-be-mandatory-new-california-law-sparks-debate-t29441 (discussing the debate in state legislatures over "more than 70 vaccine-related laws" after the Disneyland measles outbreak).

been quite reclusive for the past few decades.[57] These communities turned inward in part because ethnographic work done on their schools in the 1970s and 1980s painted a quite negative picture of them.[58] Further, there have been almost no court battles over regulation of private schools in recent decades precisely because states gave up on trying to regulate them.[59] In addition to ignorance, certain widespread attitudes and misconceptions underlie the absence of public demand for legal protection of religious dissenters' children, as the subsections that follow explain.

A *Attitudinal Obstacles to Legal Protection of Children's Well-being*

First, a great number of Americans believe parents have a fundamental constitutional and moral right to control their children's lives. This thick notion of parental entitlement is a relatively modern notion, not much evident in the colonial era, but it is nevertheless pervasive. There is a strong anti-statist element to this belief, but even for private citizens to comment on another person's childrearing practices is rather taboo in our society. Implicit in this reticence to question another's parenting is denigration of the child to the status of property or appendage of parents, such that people in fact view parenting as a form of self-determination. Parenting becomes nothing more than adults exerting sovereignty over their own lives, rather than control over another distinct person's life. True, the prevailing orthodoxy in academia and in the legal system is that children are distinct persons with rights of their own.[60] But even highly educated liberals tend to view child-rearing legal issues through an adult-focused lens. They perceive conflicts over regulation of childrearing as pitting the state against the family. The family, they believe, is a unitary entity represented solely and fully by the expressed wishes of the adults.[61]

57 For a discussion of the difficulties facing legislatures attempting to change practices within insular communities, *see* Wilson & Sanders, Chapter 13, this volume.

58 For a summary of ethnographic work on religious schools, *see* Dwyer & Peters, *supra* note 14, at 7–44. For observations of homeschools, *see* Huseman, *supra* note 20; Kunzman, *supra* note 23, 43–87; Mitchell L. Stevens, Kingdom of Children: Culture and Controversy in the Homeschooling Movement 104–05 (2001).

59 Homeschoolers lobbying success has been more in the news in recent years. *See, e.g.*, Motoko Rich, *Home Schooling: More Pupils, Less Regulation*, N.Y. Times (Jan. 4, 2015). That success makes litigation less necessary or attractive.

60 For a recent review, *see* Pamela Laufer-Ukeles, *The Relational Rights of Children*, 48 Conn. L. Rev. 741 (2016).

61 *See* James G. Dwyer, *Changing the Conversation About Children's Education*, in NOMOS XLIII: Moral and Political Education (Stephen Macedo & Yael Tami eds., 2001).

A more benign reason that most people are indifferent to religiously motivated educational neglect is the pervasive but false belief that nonphysical forms of abuse or neglect are less consequential for children. The reality is that what parents do to children's minds generally has the greatest impact on their life prospects. Even when parents inflict physical or sexual abuse, the greater harm in the long run is, in most cases, the psychological rather than the physical impact.[62] Broken bones and cigarette burns heal. However, children's perceptions of how they are viewed by their parents remains in their minds long after. Additionally, the kinds of schooling of concern here can undermine children's self-respect and intellectual development to such an extent that they will never be able to have the sort of flourishing lives as adults that would otherwise have been possible for them.[63]

Relatedly, there is the "parents know best" mantra that pervades public discussion of childrearing.[64] Not only is this assertion entirely lacking in empirical support in connection with certain aspects of children's lives, including education and medical care that require an extensive amount of knowledge and training that cannot be derived simply from daily interactions with a child, it is also completely beside the point. The disparity between what parents who assert religious child-rearing rights want in terms of physical care or schooling for children in their custody and what the state wants has nothing to do with knowledge. It arises from a conflict of values and of aims for the children's lives. It is not as if parents who want their children subjected to fundamentalist indoctrination are saying, "I know my daughter especially well, and I know that she's just the sort of person for whom gender subordination is right." Or "Sure, critical thinking is good for some kids, but my Johnny's personality is such that this is not good for him; he really thrives when we punish him for independent thinking." Some parents who demand a right to homeschool however they see fit are saying: "We reject the values of autonomy and gender equality that the liberal state endorses, and we think all children would be better off if they received the type of schooling we are seeking for our children."

62 The impact of abuse extends to altering the structure of the brain itself as protective measure. For a review, *see* Christine M. Heim et al., *Decreased Cortical Representation of Genital Somatosensory Field After Childhood Sexual Abuse*, 170 Am. J. Psychiatry 616 (June 1, 2013).

63 For the latest review by the U.S. Department of Education of homeschooling in the United States, *see* Jeremy Redford et al., National Center for Education Statistics, Homeschooling in the United States: 2012 (Nov. 2016).

64 *See, e.g.*, Stephen Gilles, *A Parentalist Manifesto*, 63 U. Chi. L. Rev. 937 (1996); Kunzman, *supra* note 23, at 123.

A misconception closely related to the parents know best mantra is the belief that studies have shown private schools are better than public schools and so the state has no reason to oversee private schools.[65] Some comparative studies of test scores show that average test scores for children attending religious schools or being homeschooled are similar to or even higher than those for public school students.[66] Even highly educated people will allude to such studies as an explanation for not pushing for robust regulation of the private school sector. Perhaps the boosters can be forgiven for being unaware that private schools are not required to administer standardized tests. Thus, the studies report results only for those who voluntarily choose to administer standardized tests. In the parlance of empirical research, this creates a selection bias, yielding a disproportionately favorable, but unrepresentative set of test takers. Furthermore, even if the studies showed a higher average for all private schools, an average can mask wide disparities within a population and, therefore, instances of grossly deficient performance. Averages for a sector are, in fact, useless to policy reasoning. Nothing can turn on average figures. Imagine a state education department director announcing that public schools in a given state have no problems because the state average test scores for students are at the national average on a nationally normed test. No one would take such a claim seriously. It is astonishing how quickly people are contented with the condition of private schools when comparative studies of average test score results are cited.

This contentment likely reflects simple selfish indifference. A reality affecting all aspects of child welfare law is that people are generally not concerned about the well-being of "other people's children," just as they are generally unconcerned about other people in general. Unless and until children subjected to illiberal, indoctrinatory, or subordinating schooling threaten our own interests in immediate and evident ways, we do not care. And people generally do not think about the long-term consequences for society of a segment of the youth population not receiving preventive healthcare or receiving illiberal indoctrination.

At the extreme of selfishness, adults whose own children or grandchildren are receiving a high-quality education that prepares them to succeed in mainstream society might actually, perhaps subconsciously, be happy that other

65 *See, e.g.*, Michael Godsey, *Why I'm a Public-School Teacher But a Private-School Parent: It's Not Selling Out; It's Buying In*, The Atlantic (Mar. 4, 2015), www.theatlantic.com/education/archive/2015/03/why-im-a-public-school-teacher-but-a-private-school-parent/386797/.

66 *See, e.g.*, Kunzman, *supra* note 23, at 97, 126; Stevens, *supra* note 58, at 13.

people's children are disadvantaged by educational deprivation. Inadequate education for some only improves the ability of better-educated children to enjoy greater comparative success. Perhaps there is even a darker disposition in the hearts and subconscious of many people: an affirmative animosity toward groups viewed, because of difference in religion or class or race, as "The Other," and especially toward their unformed, unruly children. Perhaps most Americans do not want children of parents who are fundamentalist Christian or Muslim integrating into mainstream society. They might prefer that these children remain intellectually hobbled and cloistered, as long as they are not trained for insurrection.

In addition, and relatedly, there is an aversion to confronting ideological extremists unless absolutely necessary. Religious groups that absolutely reject any state authority to oversee the way they raise "their" children are frightening to the rest of us, so that, even if those in the mainstream do not apply the parents know best mantra to those seen as extremists, they are unwilling to express or mobilize opposition to what the extremists do with children. Many religious fundamentalists view themselves as perpetually at war with mainstream society and the state, and some are prepared to take up arms in order to win that war.[67] At the least, mainstream society may be sufficiently worried that fundamentalists might engage in violence that it chooses to cower in the face of angry protests – all the more so as terrorism occupies the minds of all of us.[68]

For their part, state officials perceive little or nothing for them to lose politically by exempting religious objectors. They see only headaches to gain by trying to impose regulations on belligerent fundamentalist religious groups prepared to take up arms to defend their view of parental sovereignty over children's upbringing.[69] Unless parental choices visibly threaten state interests or the well-being of outsiders (e.g., by fomenting violent rebellion), state and federal legislators will undoubtedly remain heedless of what effect religious schooling is having on the well-being of children enrolled in them. At most, sufficient numbers object to use of public money, through some form of voucher scheme, for illiberal or grossly inadequate schooling, so that legislators in some states have rejected pressure to institute voucher programs. Yet voucher programs have proliferated.

[67] *See* KUNZMAN, *supra* note 23, at 32. [68] *Cf.* Huseman, *supra* note 20.

[69] *See* Motoko Rich, *Home Schooling: More Pupils, Less Regulation*, N.Y. TIMES (Jan. 4, 2015), www.nytimes.com/2015/01/05/education/home-schooling-more-pupils-less-regulation.html?_r=0&mtrref=www.google.com&gwh=02A11304582DA400734E466FB43FC318&gwt=pay&assetType=nyt_now; Huseman, *supra* note 20; DWYER, *supra* note 23, at 8–13 and 45–61.

B Fundamental Misconceptions

Also at work are some very basic misunderstandings about the state's posture relative to children and about the duties each of us owes to children. In particular, there is a widespread belief that when parents are free legally to do whatever they want to children, this represents state inaction. The state is choosing to leave private citizens alone – something that in a liberal society is presumptively proper for the state to do. This belief is absolutely false.

People become legal parents of a child in the first instance because the state makes them such. The fact that states everywhere choose to confer initial legal parent status automatically to biological parents of newborn children makes it seem so natural that the state's role in creating legal parentage becomes invisible. But, it is in fact only because a state statute dictates that a child's first legal mother is the birth mother and a child's first legal father is the man presumed to be the biological father that procreators come to have legal status and state-protected custody of the children they create. The state is just as responsible for formation of this legal relationship as it is in the case of adoption. With adoption, we have no trouble seeing the state's crucial role in creating legal ties between parent and child, and citizens are more inclined to hold the state accountable for bad choices among potential parents. Further, the role of legal parent is a meaningless one, except insofar as the state acts further to invest it with various liberties and powers as to the child in the legal relationship – liberties and powers that no other persons possess.[70]

It is necessary that the state create legal parent-child relationships and that it invest legal parents with some liberties and powers. By so doing, children can receive the care the state thinks necessary. But the necessity of investing liberties and powers does not excuse the state from imbuing the wrong persons with authority or giving them authority of an inappropriate degree (i.e., too little or too much). And when parents demand that they be able to decide what sort of schooling children receive, what they are asking is not at all to be left alone by the state. Rather they are asking for the state to give them even greater legal power over children than the state is otherwise inclined to give.

If the state conferred similar other-determining rights on husbands over wives, or guardians over incompetent adults, empowering the one to deny the other benefits and to inflict physical harms, we would not have trouble seeing the state's role in harms suffered by the wives or incompetent adults, and we would demand justification from the state for its doing this. It would not be said that the state was simply leaving married couples alone if a law empowered

70 *See* Dwyer, The Relationship Rights of Children *supra* note 41, at 62–67.

husbands to decide whether, when, and where their wives would receive formal education – as once occurred in Anglo-American society and still occurs in some Muslim societies.[71] Instead, it would be clear that the state was intervening in private life in an extraordinary way that requires justification. Of course, there is justification for the state investing legal parents with substantial decision-making power regarding children's upbringing. However, the power states currently accord legal parents with respect to children's education – which effectively denies them a secular education and subjects them to subordination-promoting indoctrination – cannot possibly be justified on child welfare grounds, neither can empowering parents to deny children necessary medical attention, as Offit (Chapter 12, this volume) so poignantly demonstrates. It is therefore essential for people to recognize that the state acts affirmatively in enabling parents legally to harm children and to insist that the state either give strong and legitimate justification for this enabling or instead withdraw all parental power that is inconsistent with what the state views as children's best interests.

Relatedly, there is a widespread misconception about the responsibility each of us bears as citizens for the fate of children whose parents, under current law, act to deny children the sort of education that promotes the children's autonomy, gives the children an open future, and treats them with equal respect. As citizens we are responsible for the fate of these children because we are the electorate that legislators represent when they pass laws. Our acquiescence plays a causal role in the fate of these children, just as the acquiescence of most whites in the face of Jim Crow laws made them complicit.[72] Anyone who is aware of what is happening to some children and of the role that the laws in their state play in that, yet does not object to their state representatives, is complicit in the denial of equal educational opportunity to those children.

It is especially troubling that scholars of religious liberty would devote so much attention to relatively effete and arcane concerns, such as the desire of a closely held corporation's owners to be exempt from a law requiring them to provide certain sorts of healthcare coverage to employees, yet remain utterly indifferent to the much greater threat to religious liberty that certain forms of

[71] Such laws used to exist in Anglo-American society, and still do in some Muslim societies. *See Women and Islam*, Oxford Islamic Studies Online, www.oxfordislamicstudies.com/article/opr/t125/e2510 (discussing the education of Muslim women).

[72] Judith Goldstein, *The Presence of the Past: Confronting the Nazi State and Jim Crow*, in Humanity in Action: Collected Essays and Talks (2014) ("Without the complicity of almost the entire white South – through every level of the society – the system could not have survived decade after decade.").

religious schooling and homeschooling represent.[73] This is itself evidence that adults in general and academics specifically are adult centered in their moral outlook, and insufficiently attentive to the moral claims of children. The point here is not that the concerns of Hobby Lobby's owners are insubstantial; any conscientious person would be upset to discover they were facilitating what they regard as murder. The point is, rather, that what we are collectively doing to some children is profoundly wrong, by empowering their parents to prevent them from receiving needed medical care, or to deny them an adequate education, and, instead, subject them to autonomy-thwarting and potentially psychologically abusive indoctrination.

IV CONCLUSION

The most serious incursions on religious liberty in America today are being inflicted on children by parents and private school operators, using power that the state has given them. It is long past time to hold the state, which is simply an agent for the electorate, accountable for enabling this.

[73] Hobby Lobby, *supra* note 7.

9

Marriage Agreements and Religious Family Life

Brian H. Bix

Frederick W. Thomas Professor of Law and Philosophy, University of Minnesota

The challenge posed by religion to family law generally, and to marriage agreements in particular, is not that different from the challenge religion poses elsewhere to law (and, more generally, to society):[1] applicable legal standards should strive to be both neutral and accommodating relative to the views and requirements of religion.[2] Religious preferences and practices should not be treated any worse than other preferences and practices, but in

[1] In this chapter, "marriage agreement" encompasses three kinds of legal agreements entered into by spouses or those about to become spouses: premarital agreements, marital agreements, and separation agreements. Subcategories of each will be discussed when they are the focus of analysis.

This chapter will not cover the regulation of agreements between never-married parents, though many of the issues and legal responses would likely be similar. For a review of agreements between never-married parents, *see* Weiner, Chapter 11, this volume. This chapter also will not cover "covenant marriage" – meaning marital statuses offered in three states in which both parties agree to premarital counseling and heightened hurdles to exit; neither will it address efforts to enforce covenant marriage terms or a covenant-marriage-like agreement in a state that does not provide that status. *See* ARIZ. REV. STAT. ANN. §§ 25–901 to 25–906 (2017) (covenant marriage statute); ARK. CODE ANN. §§ 9-11-801 to 9-11-811 (2015 & Supp. 2017) (same); LA. REV. STAT. ANN. §§ 9:272 to 9:276 (2008 & Supp. 2017) (same); Blackburn v. Blackburn, 180 So. 3d 16 (Ala. Civ. App. 2015) (refusing to enforce Louisiana covenant marriage contract); *cf.* Brian H. Bix, *Choice of Law and Marriage: A Proposal*, 36 FAM. L.Q. 255, 262–271 (2002) (urging greater ability of spouses to opt into other states' marriage laws, including covenant marriage laws).

[2] For a legislator's account of the challenges to balancing competing interests in a diverse populous, *see* Adams, Chapter 21, this volume. For a primer on the Supreme Court's jurisprudence around neutral rules of general applicability satisfying constitution free exercise guarantees, *see* Helfand, Chapters 2 & 6, this volume; Sepper, Chapter 1, this volume.

Some commentators have complained that some areas of family law are not neutral, in the sense that the law *favors* religion and the religious, at least when the religious beliefs and practices in question are conventional ones. *See* Dwyer, Chapter 8, this volume; Rassbach, Chapter 7, this volume. Whether the law does (or should) favor religion and the religious in custody matters is addressed in part by Brinig, Chapter 10, this volume, but is beyond the scope of this chapter.

some cases, accommodating religious preferences and practices properly may entail some stretching of the usual standards.[3]

Beyond issues of neutrality and accommodation, the intersection of marriage agreements and religion also raises an additional set of issues relating to First Amendment entanglement with religion and the free exercise of religion.[4] For example, parties to a marital agreement may agree to resolve disputes before a religious arbitrator, panel, or court. Also, parties to a premarital or separation agreement may agree to actions that have religious significance – such as performing certain religious activities with a child or giving a spouse a Jewish or Islamic religious divorce.[5] The parties may agree to raise children under a certain religion or in certain religious ways. In such cases, the question arises whether court enforcement of such provisions implicates entanglement with religion or improper constraint of a parent's free exercise of religion.[6]

3 A real question arises about when "accommodation" becomes "preference," which is beyond the scope of this chapter. This question may arise in custody contests, when a practice that stems from a parent's sincere religious belief may also harm the child. *See* Offit, Chapter 12, this volume (discussing state intervention in families whose religious beliefs preclude them from providing their children with vaccinations and other medical treatments); Wilson & Sanders, Chapter 13, this volume (discussing concern in the context of corporal punishment). If the court does *not* use the practice as a reason to give custody to the other parent, is that a legitimate accommodation or an improper special preferential treatment? Compare Quiner v. Quiner, 59 Cal. Rptr. 503 (Cal. App. 1967) (reversing custody award to father based on mother's religious belief in "separation" and its effects on their child) with Leppert v. Leppert, 519 N.W.2d 287 (N.D. 1994) (reversing grant of custody to mother, whose religious practices were held to be harmful to children). As noted, religious parents may harm children when their beliefs lead them to refuse medical aid, giving rise to questions of the parent's capacity to parent. *See* Offit, Chapter 12, this volume; Wilson & Sanders, Chapter 13, this volume; George L. Blum, Annotation, *Religion as a Factor in Child Custody Cases*, 124 A.L.R. 5TH 203 (2004) (discussing whether and when courts can use religious matters as a reason for awarding custody to a particular parent); *see also* Johnson v. Johnson 564 P.2d 71 (Alaska 1978) (determining that it would be improper to base the custody decision solely on religion, even when the mother was an orthodox Jehovah's Witness who would refuse some forms of medical treatment).

4 *See* U.S. Const. amend. I; Lemon v. Kurtzman, 403 U.S. 602, 612 (1971) (stating government action must not "foster an excessive government entanglement with religion" (internal quotation marks and citation omitted)); *see also* Kent Greenawalt, *Religious Law and Civil Law: Using Secular to Assure Observance of Practices with Religious Significance*, 71 S. CAL. L. REV. 781 (1998) (considering entanglement issues when secular law is used to enforce religious standards or religious practices).

5 For an argument that providing a Jewish religious divorce (a *get*) is "not a sacerdotal or religious act," *see* J. David Bleich, *A Proposal to Withhold Divorce Decrees on Grounds of Equity*, 5 INT'L J. JURIS. FAM. 215, 216 (2014).

6 *See, e.g.*, in Soleimani v. Soleimani, No. 11CV4668, 2012 WL 3729939 (Kan. Dist. Ct. 2012) (refusing to enforce an Islamic *mahr* provision in part because of entanglement with religion); Avitzur v. Avitzur, 58 N.Y.2d 446 N.E.2d 136 (1983) (concluding enforcement of Jewish *ketubah* does not violate the First Amendment); Aflalo v. Aflalo, 685 A.2d 523 (N.J. 1996) (finding order

Here, the issue is *not* whether parties should be able to order their lives on these matters through express agreements. Spouses and other partners are free, within the quite broad boundaries of criminal law and social welfare legislation, to live as they individually or collectively see fit, including living according to religious principles, raising their children according to those same principles, and agreeing to act similarly in the future. And, of course, spouses are free to continue to abide by those agreements and understandings even after their marriage has ended. Legal issues generally only arise (a) when one party no longer wishes to abide by an agreement, and the other party seeks government (court) help in enforcing the agreement; and (b) when the agreement purports to bind a court (e.g., by choosing a particular forum for dispute resolution).

Ultimately, the question is *when* the state will offer its assistance for enforcement, or at least its recognition of purported changes in legal status. Consequently, the analysis, as with the enforcement of contracts generally, will normally be about when it is beneficial to enforce particular agreements, or particular kinds or categories of agreements. Inevitably, these sorts of evaluations will sometimes involve lawmakers, judges, and commentators in speculation they may not be competent to make, or at least require them to evaluate consequences for which there is nowhere near enough data available.[7] Still, recommendations need to be offered, because decisions need to be made.

This chapter looks at the way courts treat religious provisions in marriage agreements and evaluates whether those rules and standards should be changed. Section I offers an overview of current rules and practices regarding marriage agreements and religious provisions within such agreements. Section II reflects on general values and concerns, offering some conclusions regarding what approach courts and legislatures *should* take toward religious provisions in marriage agreements.

compelling husband to grant wife a *get* would violate husband's free exercise of religion); *In re* Marriage of Goldman, 554 N.E.2d 1016 (Ill. App. 1990) (court order requiring husband to obtain a *get* did not violate husband's First Amendment rights); *cf.* Lang v. Levi, 16 A.3d 980 (Md. 2011)(upholding Jewish arbitration decision after refusing to evaluate arbitration decision for First Amendment reasons). For a discussion of religious entanglement as it relates to protections under RFRA, see Helfand, Chapter 2, this volume; for a discussion of parents' decision to circumcise their children, as a religious choice, and the implications of such a decision, *see* Rassbach, Chapter 7, this volume.

7 Useful information would include whether the parties to the agreement would make or would have made the same decisions about marriage and children even if related agreements were not enforceable, or were enforceable only on different terms; what effects enforcement would have on these couples and their children; and what effects enforcement or non-enforcement would have on other couples and families, and on society generally. As noted *infra* Section I, such information is rarely, if ever, available.

I CURRENT RULES AND PRACTICES

This section offers brief summaries of the three main forms of marriage agreements – premarital agreements, marital agreements, and separation agreements – considering first their general legal treatment, and then looking at issues relating to agreement provisions touching on religion.

A *Premarital Agreements*

Premarital agreements (also known as "prenuptial agreements" and "antenuptial agreements") are agreements entered into before a marriage to alter what would otherwise be the rights of the spouses in case of divorce or the death of one spouse. This section provides an overview of how the legal system has viewed premarital agreements and also examines two types of premarital agreements, *ketubahs* and *mahr* provisions, that are specific to Judaism and Islam, respectively.

1 Legal Treatment of Premarital Agreements Generally

Until the 1970s, premarital agreements (at least, their divorce-focused provisions[8]) were considered unenforceable because they were contrary to public policy.[9] The justifications for the refusal to enforce terms usually included that spouses (and spouses-to-be) had no power to alter the legal "status" terms of marriage, and that provisions that reduced either party's obligations upon divorce improperly encouraged divorce.[10] Marriage was considered a social good in which society had as much interest as the spouses, making it partly

8 Historically, courts had been more willing to enforce premarital agreement provisions that governed the rights of a spouse upon the other's death. The ability of a wife to waive her right to dower goes back many centuries, to the English Statute of Uses, 27 Hen. VIII, c. 10, § 6 (1535).

9 For a brief overview of the history of the legal treatment of premarital agreements, *see* Brian Bix, *Bargaining in the Shadow of Love: The Enforcement of Premarital Agreements and How We Think About Marriage*, 40 Wm. & Mary L. Rev. 145, 148–58 (1998); *see also* Linda J. Ravdin, Premarital Agreements: Drafting and Negotiation 6–9 (ABA, 2011); Brett R. Turner & Laura W. Morgan, Attacking and Defending Marital Agreements 361–65 (2nd ed., ABA, 2012).

10 Even after premarital agreements became generally enforceable, courts occasionally refused enforcement on the basis that the agreement unduly encouraged divorce. *See In re* Marriage of Noghrey, 169 Cal. App. 3d 326, 331 (Cal. Ct. App. 1985) (refusing enforcement of payment provision in a *ketubah*, commenting: "The prospect of receiving a house and a minimum of $500,000 by obtaining [a] no-fault divorce … would menace the marriage of the best intentioned spouse"); *In re* Marriage of Dajani, 204 Cal. App. 3d 1387 (Cal. Ct. App. 1988) (following *Noghrey* in refusing enforcement of delayed *mahr* payment as "encouraging profiteering by divorce" (internal quotation marks and citation omitted)).

for that reason inappropriate for spouses (or those about to become spouses) to alter the legal terms of their marriage, especially in a way that might directly or indirectly encourage the dissolution of that marriage.[11]

During the 1970s, at roughly the same time that most states were adopting no-fault divorce as either the exclusive grounds for divorce or as an alternative to fault grounds for divorce, almost every state also began to permit enforcement of at least some premarital agreements through judicial or legislative mechanisms. Premarital agreements are now enforceable in all states, though some states subject them to more stringent procedural and substantive fairness requirements than those imposed upon conventional commercial agreements. In states that impose higher standards for substantive fairness, this more stringent inquiry reviews circumstances at the time the agreement was entered; a minority of states also add a second requirement that the agreement must be adjudicated as being fair at the time of enforcement.[12]

2 *Ketubahs*

Under Jewish religious law, men are allowed to divorce their wives by giving them a religious document called a "*get*," but women have no power to divorce their husbands.[13] A wife who has not received a *get* from her husband, even if the two have received a divorce from a civil court, is labeled as an "*Agunah*" – meaning she is still bound to her husband. According to Orthodox Judaism, she cannot marry someone else; if she does, and the couple has children, those children will be considered illegitimate and will be excluded from the community.[14]

[11] *See, e.g.*, Lester v. Lester, 87 N.Y.S.2d 517, 519 (Dom. Rel. Ct. 1949) ("The state and the community are interested in and concerned with the institution which marriage creates."). This view was sometimes taken to extremes under the old fault-divorce regime. *See, e.g.*, Rankin v. Rankin, 124 A.2d 639, 644 (Pa. 1956) ("The fact that married people do not get along well together does not justify a divorce. Testimony which proves merely an unhappy union, the parties being high strung temperamentally and unsuited to each other, ... is insufficient to sustain a decree [of divorce]."). On the topic generally of society's interest in the marriages of its citizens, *see* Brian H. Bix, *State of the Union: The States' Interest in the Marital Status of Their Citizens*, 55 U. Miami L. Rev. 1 (2000).

[12] For an overview and case citations relating to fairness reviews at the time of execution and at the time of enforcement, *see* Ravdin, *supra* note 9, at 69–77.

[13] For information on the Jewish laws of marriage and divorce, *see, e.g.*, Michael J. Broyde, *New York's Regulation of Jewish Marriage: Covenant, Contract, or Statute*, *in* Marriage and Divorce in a Multicultural Context 138–63 (Joel A. Nichols, ed., Cambridge, 2012).

[14] Naftali Silberberg, *The Agunah*, Chabad.org, www.chabad.org/library/article_cdo/aid/613084/jewish/The-Agunah.htm.

To avoid potential problems around the issue of divorce, some Jewish couples have placed provisions in the traditional ritual marriage "contract," the "*ketubah*." Some couples agree that the husband will provide a *get* to his wife if either seeks a civil divorce, agreeing to pay a penalty until such time as he provides the *get*.[15] Some agree to bring disputes relating to the marriage to a Jewish arbitration panel ("*Bet Din*"), which would then have the power (under appropriate conditions, defined by Jewish law) to order the husband to give his wife a *get*.[16] In New York State, statutes, promulgated with the support and assistance of the Orthodox Jewish community have the purpose and effect of pressuring Orthodox Jewish men to provide their wives with a *get* if and when either spouse files for divorce, by using the threat of withholding civil divorce (if the husband had been the one to file for civil divorce) or an unfavorable property division (if it had been the wife who filed).[17]

3 *Mahr* Provisions

Under Islamic religious law, marriage is a contract – not just metaphorically, but literally so: the spouses-to-be must sign a written contract. A standard part of this contract is a promised payment from the husband to the wife, known as *mahr*.[18] It is normal practice for the payment to be divided, with a smaller portion given at the time of marriage, and the larger portion, sometimes called the "delayed *mahr*," potentially due at the time of divorce, depending on the nature of the divorce. If the husband divorces his wife by way of simple announcement, or *talaq*, then the delayed *mahr* must be paid.[19] According to some sources, the delayed *mahr* is also due if the wife divorces the husband

15 *E.g.*, Light v. Light, 55 Conn. L. Rep. 145 (Conn. Sup. Ct. 2012) (enforcing agreement under which husband agreed to pay $100 per day from the date of the couple's separation until he provided her with a *get*).

16 For an excellent general discussion of the use of arbitration provisions by religious parties to have disputes resolved in accordance with religious law, *see* Michael A. Helfand, *Arbitration's Counter-Narrative: The Religious Arbitration Paradigm*, 124 YALE L.J. 2994, 3014–22 (2015). For premarital agreement forms provided by the Beth Din of America, *see Prenup Forms*, BETH DIN OF AMERICA, www.theprenup.org/prenupforms.html.

17 *See* N.Y. *Dom. Rel.* §§ 253, 256 Part B(5)(H); Broyde, *supra* note 13. These provisions are written in neutral terms and, thus also help Muslim wives force their husbands to give them Islamic religious divorces.

18 This practice is also sometimes called "*sadaq*."

19 *See* Robin Fretwell Wilson, *The Perils of Privatized Marriage*, *in* MARRIAGE AND DIVORCE IN A MULTI-CULTURAL CONTEXT: RECONSIDERING THE BOUNDARIES OF CIVIL LAW AND RELIGION 253 (Joel A. Nichols, ed., Cambridge, 2011).

because of the husband's bad behavior, but not if the wife initiates the divorce on grounds other than the husband's fault.[20]

A relatively small number of American cases have considered the legal enforcement of the provisions for delayed *mahr* payments. In these cases, the husband usually claims that the *mahr* obligation supplants any other financial obligations, such as property division or alimony he might owe at or after divorce, although sometimes the litigation is brought by the wife, attempting to enforce the payment provision. Courts often focus on whether the *mahr* agreements meet procedural requirements imposed on all premarital agreements[21] or on contracts generally.[22] Some courts explore whether enforcing *mahr* provisions is consistent with the constitutional separation of church and state.[23] But few courts seem to ask the basic interpretive question: was the *mahr* provision intended to supplant, rather than supplement, the default financial terms the state sets for divorcing couples?[24] Did the couple mean for this to be the exclusive remedy at divorce? The point is that if the *mahr* provision is *not* intended to waive the wife's rights to property division and alimony, there is a strong argument that it need not meet the special procedural and substantive requirements imposed on premarital agreements.[25] It would, of course, still be subject to standard contract doctrines, such as unconscionability.[26]

20 *See, e.g.*, Abed Awad, *Court Enforces Mahr Provision in Muslim Marriage Contract*, HG.ORG, www.hg.org/article.asp?id=23753.

21 *See, e.g.*, Zawahiri v. Alwattar, No. 07AP-925, 2008 WL 2698679 (Ohio App. 2008) (holding *mahr* agreement unenforceable under criteria applicable to premarital agreements); *see also* Nathan Oman, *Bargaining in the Shadow of God's Law: Islamic "Mahr" Contracts and the Perils of Legal Specialization* 45 WAKE FOREST L. REV. 579 (2010) (arguing that the *mahr* provision is a unique feature of Islamic law that has no analog in the legal treatment of premarital agreements and therefore should not be treated like premarital agreements).

22 *See, e.g., In re* Marriage of Obaidi and Qayoum, 226 P.3d 787 (Wash. App. 2010), rev. denied, 238 P.3d 503 (Wash. 2010) (holding *mahr* agreement unenforceable due to general contract law principles, in particular, duress and no meeting of the minds).

23 *See* Soleimani, *supra* note 6.

24 *See* Unif. Premarital and Marital Agreements Act § 2 cmt., 9C U.L.A. 12, 16–17 (Supp. 2015) [hereinafter, UPMAA] (suggesting that *mahr* provisions should not be subject to the rules covering premarital and marital agreements, because they "were not intended to affect the parties' existing legal rights and obligations upon divorce or death"); Brian H. Bix, *Mahr Agreements: Contracting in the Shadow of Family Law (and Religious Law) – A Comment on Oman's Article*, 1 WAKE FOREST L. REV. ONLINE 61 (2011), http://lawreview.law.wfu.edu/articles/.

25 For reasons for this special case, *see* Brian Bix, *The ALI Principles and Agreements: Seeking a Balance Between Status and Contract, in* RECONCEIVING THE FAMILY: CRITIQUE ON THE AMERICAN LAW INSTITUTE'S PRINCIPLES OF THE LAW OF FAMILY DISSOLUTION (Robin Fretwell Wilson, ed., 2006).

26 *See* UPMAA; Oman, *supra* note 21, at 603 ("[T]o the extent that bargaining over the *mahr* presents special concerns, the general law of contracts provides better tools for policing abuse than does the UPAA . . . . [T]he common law doctrines of duress and undue influence are

4 Other Provisions Relating to Religion

Generally, premarital agreements are only enforced to the extent that they touch on the financial obligations of the parties *inter se* – that is, rights against each other, including property division and alimony obligations.[27] Even within the category of purely financial obligations, agreements to restrict child support obligations are normally unenforceable.[28] Provisions in premarital agreements that purport to regulate the religious behavior of the spouses during or after marriage,[29] or the religious upbringing of the children of the marriage, would generally be unenforceable, because (among other reasons) they fall far outside the limited set of topics for enforceable contracting.[30] There are exceptions, however. The recently enacted Illinois Marriage and Dissolution of Marriage Act ("IMDMA") is one example; it directs courts at divorce to allocate responsibility for a child's religious upbringing according to "any express or implied agreement between the parents."[31]

B Marital Agreements

Marital agreements are agreements entered into between spouses during their marriage before divorce is imminent, with the purpose of modifying the rights

specifically designed to allow parties to escape their obligations entered into as a result of high-pressure tactics by intimates.").

27 *See, e.g.*, Unif. Premarital Agreement Act § 3(a), 9C U.L.A. 25, 43 (2001 & Supp. 2017) (listing acceptable subjects for premarital agreement) [hereinafter, UPAA].

28 *See, e.g.*, UPAA § 3(b), 9C U.L.A. at 43 ("The right of a child to support may not be adversely affected by a premarital agreement."); UPMAA, § 10(b)(1), 9C U.L.A. at 27 ("A term in a premarital agreement or marital agreement is not enforceable to the extent that it ... adversely affects a child's right to support.").

29 Additionally, agreements that purport to regulate the behavior of spouses during the intact marriage, even when the agreements are made during the marriage (not before the marriage, as with premarital agreements), are generally unenforceable, under the principle of "family privacy." *See, e.g.*, McGuire v. McGuire, 157 Neb. 226 (1953) (refusing to decide dispute over the degree of support due between spouses).

30 *See, e.g.*, *In re* Marriage of Nuechterlein, 587 N.E.2d 21, 22 (Ill. App. 1992) (refusing to enforce provision in premarital agreement on religious upbringing of children); *see generally* Jocelyn E. Strauber, *A Deal Is a Deal: Antenuptial Agreements Regarding the Religious Upbringing of Children Should Be Enforceable*, 47 Duke L. J. 971, 984 (1998) ("Courts are remarkably consistent in their refusal to effectuate antenuptial religious upbringing agreements."). Professor Strauber goes on to argue that such provisions *should* be enforced, for reasons roughly similar to those discussed in Section II, *infra*. There are a handful of cases, mostly from many decades ago, where the court enforced a premarital agreement provision regarding religious upbringing. *See* Martin Weiss & Robert Abramoff, *The Enforceability of Religious Upbringing Agreements*, 25 John Marshall L. Rev. 655, 667–68 (1992) (citing and summarizing three cases prior to 1950 where courts enforced such provisions).

31 750 Ill. Comp. Stat. 5/602.5(b)(3)(A) (Supp. 2017).

of the spouses upon divorce or at the death of one of the spouses. This section provides an overview of the different legal standards states use when reviewing marital agreements and then examines specifically whether religious provisions within marital agreements are held to different standards.

1 Legal Treatment of Marital Agreements Generally

The legal treatment of marital agreements is the least certain and least uniform of the three kinds of marital agreements discussed in this chapter.[32] Many states have no statutes or case law expressly setting the legal standard governing marital agreements. Other states, by statute or case law, have held marital agreements to be subject to the same standards as premarital agreements.[33] Still other states, by statute or case law, have held marital agreements to higher/stricter standards than premarital agreements.[34] At least one state holds all marital agreements to be unenforceable.[35] A few states treat differently and more favorably a subcategory of marital agreements that falls under the rubric of "reconciliation agreements" – agreements in which a wronged party agrees to stay in the marriage in return for greater rights or benefits.[36]

2 Provisions Relating to Religion

The issues for marital agreement provisions relating to religion are likely to have similar outcomes as the premarital agreement provisions relating to religion discussed in Section I.A. This is assuming that the marital agreement in question otherwise meets whatever standards the state has set for enforcement of marital agreements generally.

There is one important legal twist to keep in mind. Some couples choose to have both civil and religious marriage ceremonies.[37] If the religious ceremony is held after the civil ceremony – even if only a day or two after – any marriage contract signed in connection with the religious marriage may be treated as a marital contract rather than a premarital contract. In states where marital

32 *See generally* Sean Hannon Williams, *Postnuptial Agreements*, Wis. L. Rev. 827 (2007).

33 *See, e.g.*, D'Aston v. D'Aston, 808 P.2d 111, 112–113 (Utah Ct. App. 1990); Va. Code Ann. § 20–155 (2016 & Supp. 2017).

34 *See, e.g.*, Minn. Stat. Ann. § 519.11, subd. 1a (Supp. 2017); Ansin v. Craven-Ansin, 929 N.E.2d 955, 961–964 (Mass. 2010); Bedrick v. Bedrick, 17 A.3d 17, 23–25 (Conn. 2011).

35 Ohio Rev. Code Ann. § 3103.06 (2015 & Supp. 2017).

36 *See, e.g.*, Pacelli v. Pacelli, 725 A.2d 56 (N.J. Super. A.D. 1999) (discussing the category of "reconciliation agreements").

37 *See* Wilson, Chapter 16, this volume.

contracts are treated with greater suspicion and less deference than premarital contracts, the difference in treatment by courts can be significant.[38]

C Separation Agreements

Separation agreements, also called "marital settlement agreements" in some jurisdictions, are agreements entered into when divorce is imminent – frequently after one of the parties has filed a petition for divorce. Although courts generally tend to encourage parties to settle their divorce-related disputes through separation agreements, when the provisions concern religious matters, courts may be more hesitant to enforce the parties' chosen terms.

1 Legal Treatment of Separation Agreements Generally

In contrast to premarital agreements and marital agreements – indeed, in contrast to most agreements in the domestic relations area[39] – courts and family law doctrine support and encourage separation agreements. By setting such terms as property division, alimony, child custody, and child support by mutual agreement of the parties rather than by judicial imposition (after trial), separation agreements save on family court resources, reduce the animosity of divorce proceedings, and arrive at dissolution terms with which the parties are more likely to comply (because they helped to select them).[40]

Doctrinally, courts are supposed to treat terms relating to the purely financial obligations between the parties (e.g., property division and alimony) more deferentially than they treat terms relating to children (e.g., custody and child support); however, by most accounts, judges tend simply to rubber stamp their approval of separation agreements, without significant scrutiny of any of the provisions.[41] Invalidation of a previously entered separation agreement on grounds of unfair terms or unfair process is rare, but it does occur.[42]

38 *See, e.g.*, S.B. v. W.A., 959 N.Y.S.2d 802, 820–21 (N.Y. Sup. Ct. 2012).

39 *See, e.g.*, Brian H. Bix, *Agreements in American Family Law*, 4 Int'l J. Juris. Fam. 115 (2013) [hereinafter, Bix, *Agreements*].

40 *See generally* Brian H. Bix, *Domestic Agreements*, 35 Hofstra L. Rev. 1753 (2006).

41 *See, e.g.*, Unif. Marriage and Divorce Act § 306(b), 9A (Part I), U.L.A. 159, 249 (1998 & Supp. 2017) (restating general law on separation agreements). *See generally* Turner & Morgan, *supra* note 9, at 65–176 (discussing standards and cases on challenges to validity of separation agreements).

42 *See, e.g.*, Brennan-Duffy v. Duffy, 804 N.Y.S.2d 399, 400 (App. Div. 2005) ("An agreement will not be overturned merely because, in retrospect, some of its provisions were improvident or one-sided or because a party had a change of heart." (internal quotation marks and citations omitted)); *In re* Marriage of Thornhill, 200 P.3d 1083 (Colo. App. 2008) (finding property agreement unconscionable due to a combination of procedural and substantive factors).

2 Provisions Relating to Religion

The most common provisions relating to religion in separation agreements involve the divorcing spouses setting guidelines regarding the religious upbringing of their children: whether the children are to go to a parochial school, whether they are to attend religious services (and of which kind), whether they are to follow certain religious practices and restrictions, and so on.[43] Such provisions tend to result when the parents are of different religious faiths or different levels of observance, and one parent is trying to prevent the other from (in the first parent's perspective) undermining a particular religious upbringing earlier agreed upon.

Without express agreements on the subject, courts are reluctant to interfere with the religious practices of parents or any religious training or exposure the parents offer their children.[44] Most courts take a hands-off approach even if there has been an agreed-upon provision on the topic in a separation agreement; a few courts, however, especially in New York, have been willing to enforce religious upbringing provisions in separation agreements.[45]

II REFLECTIONS AND PRESCRIPTIONS

One reason for the past and present resistance to enforcing premarital and marital agreements is that they undermine one understanding of the spirit and purpose of marriage and family. That idea is one of the household and the

43 See generally Brinig, Chapter 10, this volume; Dwyer, Chapter 8, this volume.

44 *See, e.g.*, Zummo v. Zummo, 547 A.2d 1130, 1155 (Pa. Super. 1990) (overturning restrictions on father's exercise of religion with children over mother's claim that children suffered stress, which court found would be an insufficient ground for restraint of religious exercise unless "the stress experienced is unproductively severe"). For one of the rare cases finding that the heightened standard of "severe harm" had been met, justifying restrictions on parental religious actions with a child, *see* Kendall v. Kendall, 687 N.E.2d 1228 (Mass. 1997) (describing conflict between parents over religious upbringing of children who self-identified as Jewish, in which a fundamentalist Christian father who believed that anyone who did not accept Christ would go to hell, who had removed his son's peyas or sidelocks, which are often worn by Orthodox Jewish males, and who wished to "indoctrinate the ... children into his faith").

45 *See* Weiss & Abramoff, *supra* note 30, at 668–72; *see, e.g.*, Perlstein v. Perlstein, 429 N.Y.S.2d 896 (N.Y. A.D. 1981) (reinstating father's challenge to mother's custody based on mother's violation of separation agreement provision requiring that the child be raised in a household that followed Jewish dietary laws); Spring v. Glawon, 454 N.Y.S.2d 140 (N.Y. A.D. 1982) (finding religious upbringing provision violated by child being sent to parochial school); Smith v. Smith, 17 Fam. L. Rep. (BNA) 1024 (N.Y. Fam. Ct. 1990) (discussing agreement that child would be raised in the Catholic faith). *See also* Brinig, Chapter 10, this volume (indicating a correlation between couples specifying religious upbringing in the divorce agreement and lower rates of reported domestic violence, but noting the possibility of selection effects).

family as a unit, a unit in which society generally has an interest separate from the interests of the parties involved.[46] When marriages usually ended only upon the death of a spouse, it was easier to think of the interests of individual spouses as always being subordinate to the interests of the family or household as a unit, and subordinate, of course, also to the general interests of society – in this case, societal interests in marital and family stability. With divorce now more or less available on demand, it is clear that society recognizes rights and interests of individual spouses that often differ from those of the family or household generally. And if the interests of individual spouses are to be recognized separate from family interests, it is a small step to enforcing spousal agreements affecting marital rights and duties. With less social pressure on all individuals to marry[47] and less insistence that those who are married stay married, it is no surprise that we are also collectively more tolerant of parties choosing (through marital agreements) the terms on which they will marry or the terms on which they will stay married.

A parallel but different tension operates when religion is the topic of marital agreements. On one hand, religious communities have an interest in the recognition and protection of their rules and practices – which are protected by allowing parties to opt into the use of religious decision-making bodies, and, to a lesser extent, by allowing parties to make binding agreements regarding the religious upbringing of their children. On the other hand, there is an interest in protecting the rights of individuals from the claims of religious groups, and an overlapping, constitutionally grounded claim in preventing the use of the government as an enforcement mechanism for the interests of religious groups against individuals. There are also general concerns about whether enforcing agreements might sometimes be less a matter of enforcing mutually entered commitments and more a matter of an imposition on the weaker party or exploitation by the stronger party.[48]

These tensions are felt in the cases dealing with religious provisions of marital agreements. There is clearly a value to allowing religious parties, by express agreement, to have aspects of their domestic lives subject to the rules of their religious community.[49] Moreover, it can be beneficial to allow parties to

46 For a history of coverture and the legal treatment of spouses as a single unit, *see* Kar, Chapter 15, this volume.

47 *See, e.g.*, Weiner, Chapter 11, this volume; Wendy Wang & Kim Parker, *Record Share of Americans Have Never Married*, Pew Research Ctr. (Sept. 24, 2014), www.pewsocialtrends.org/2014/09/24/record-share-of-americans-have-never-married/.

48 For power imbalances in some communities, *see* Offit, Chapter 12, this volume; Strassberg, Chapter 18, this volume; Weiner, Chapter 11, this volume.

49 As Wilson notes, Chapter 16, this volume, religious marriage encourages stable and collaborative relationships, which are protective against domestic violence.

make binding commitments on matters relating to religion – something many couples seek to do, as Brinig shows empirically (Chapter 10, this volume). As just one example, one can think of partners of different faiths, where one partner would be unwilling – or far less willing – to go forward with having and raising children as a couple without an enforceable commitment that the child be raised in a particular faith. To have such provisions be unenforceable is to make it less likely that interfaith couples will be willing to have and raise children together.[50]

Another question is to what extent society should allow couples to opt out of the local and secular legal system and into a different, religious legal system? In a recent case, *Ofer v. Sirota*,[51] a New York court enforced a premarital agreement provision that made any divorce litigation subject to the jurisdiction of an Israeli court, over one party's objection that the standards that would be applied in Israeli courts would be religious standards.[52] By contrast, in an earlier case, In re *Marriage of Shaban*, a provision in a premarital agreement that indicated that the property rights of the parties were to be governed by Islamic law was held to be too vague to be enforced.[53]

Issues about opting into religious rules and institutions parallel questions about choice of law provisions, on one hand, and matters of comity, on the other. With choice of law, parties are generally allowed to choose the law of another state or another country to govern their agreements. However, this power to choose another law is restricted in two ways: first, by standard conflict of laws principles, which hold that the chosen law should not be applied if it would be contrary to the strongly held public policy of the jurisdiction with the strongest connection to the agreement; and second, on some topics, parties may chose only the law of a jurisdiction with some connection to the underlying matter.[54] Courts have generally enforced choice of law provisions in

[50] *See* Bix, *Domestic Agreements* (making a similar point about the enforcement of co-parenting agreements among same-sex couples at a time when marriage was not an alternative option for most same-sex couples).

[51] Ofer v. Sirota, 984 N.Y.S.2d 312 (N.Y. App. Div. 2014).

[52] In Israel, as in Kenya, India, and South Africa, the primary family law applied is that of the religion of the couple. For a review of the Israeli system, see Yefet & Barzilay, Chapter 25, this volume.

[53] *In re* Marriage of Shaban, 105 Cal. Rptr.2d 863 (Cal. Ct. App. 2001) (holding that such vague terms violate the Statute of Frauds requirement that terms be in writing).

[54] Restatement (Second) of Conflict of Laws § 187 (1971). Under the Uniform Commercial Code, only the law of a state with some connection to the transaction can be chosen – indeed, an effort to remove this restriction in the revised Article 1 process found no support in adopting state legislatures. *See* Unif. Commercial Code § 1–301 (2001); Jack M. Graves, *Party Autonomy in Choice of Commercial Law: The Failure of Revised U.C.C. § 1–301 and a Proposal for Broader Reform* 60 Seton Hall L. Rev. 59 (2005).

marriage agreements (at least in premarital agreements), where one or both parties had a connection to the state whose law was chosen.[55] The issue of comity arises when a party wants to enforce the judgment of a court from another country.[56] Judgments from other countries are generally to be recognized if they are the product of legal processes that are fundamentally fair, and are not grounded on rules or principles contrary to the strong public policy of the forum where recognition is sought.[57]

In general, Americans live in a multicultural, globalized world, where law and society do and should work to accommodate different normative systems – whether that be the (foreign) legal system in which a marriage agreement was entered, a legal or religious rule system chosen by the parties to govern their agreement, or a set of religious obligations to which the spouses consider themselves subject.[58] As the number of interfaith relationships increases, the need for accommodations for different normative systems becomes more important.[59] The efforts to find a process and structure for appropriate and,

Under the *Restatement of Conflict of Laws*, there must either be a connection between the transaction and the state whose law was chosen, or some other legitimate reason for choosing the state (e.g., the choice of Delaware for corporate law, or New York for executive compensation – in both cases because the law in those areas is well developed in those states). RESTATEMENT (SECOND) OF CONFLICT OF LAWS § 187. In *The Hague Principles on Choice of Law for International Contracts*, there are no restrictions on the states whose law can be chosen. THE HAGUE PRINCIPLES ON CHOICE OF LAW IN INTERNATIONAL COMMERCIAL CONTRACTS, art. 2 (2015).

55 *See also* UPMAA § 4(1) (enforcing choice of law if jurisdiction chosen "has a significant relationship to the agreement or either party and the designated law is not contrary to a fundamental public policy"); UPAA, § 3(a)(7), at 43 (naming "choice of law" as permissible topic for premarital agreement to cover).

56 When the judgment comes from another state in the United States, this is usually covered by either the Full Faith and Credit Clause of the United States Constitution, U.S. CONST. art. IV, or by federal law, *e.g.*, Full Faith and Credit for Child Support Orders Act, 28 U.S.C. § 1738B (2012 & Supp. 2016).

57 *See generally* Hessel E. Yntema, *The Comity Doctrine*, 65 MICH. L. REV. 9 (1966).

58 On a constrained and regulated pluralism within American family law, *see, e.g.*, Ann Lacquer Estin, *Embracing Tradition: Pluralism in American Family Law*, 63 MD. L. REV. 540 (2004); Ayelet Shachar, *Privatizing Diversity: A Cautionary Tale from Religious Arbitration in Family Law*, 9 THEORETICAL INQUIRIES IN LAW 573 (2008); Ann Laquer Estin, *Foreign and Religious Law: Comity, Contract, and the Constitution*, 41 PEPPERDINE L. REV. 1029 (2014) [hereinafter Estin, *Foreign and Religious*]; Brian H. Bix, *Pluralism and Decentralization in Marriage Regulation*, in MARRIAGE AND DIVORCE IN MULTI-CULTURAL CONTEXT: MULTI-TIERED MARRIAGE AND THE BOUNDARIES OF CIVIL LAW AND RELIGION 60–77 (Joel A. Nichols, ed., Cambridge, 2011).

59 Pew Research Center, *Religious Switching and Intermarriage* in AMERICA'S CHANGING RELIGIOUS LANDSCAPE (2015), www.pewforum.org/2015/05/12/chapter-2-religious-switching-and-intermarriage/#interfaith-marriage-commonplace. Interfaith marriages often entail increased marital conflict. To combat this, it may be helpful to develop rules or systems to regulate that conflict. *See* Darren Sharkat, *Religious Intermarriage in the United States:*

thus, limited recognition of this diversity and pluralism continue. At the same time, there have also been, in a handful of places, some generally misguided and misinformed populist pushback, instructing courts not to enforce foreign law generally, or Shari'a Law in particular.[60] More legitimate are the limits that will inevitably result from balancing pluralism and party autonomy. For example, religious standards should be recognized and enforced, but within the usual limits of strongly held public policies – which include minimal due process and protection of vulnerable parties – and the safeguarding of the interests of third parties, particularly children.

Of course, one should not overstate what can be concluded *generally* about religious provisions in marriage agreements. Agreements in family law are treated in quite different ways, in part because of the sharply different contexts and the varying values, fears, and objectives involved in different types of agreements.[61] For example, while premarital agreements raise issues of bounded rationality, marital agreements raise questions of coercion. Further, issues about government entanglement often conflict with issues of religious freedom, for example, when a court is asked to order a spouse or former spouse to act according to some religious dictate. Each of these concerns in turn may overlap with concerns about judicial supervision of best interests of the child, when the religious matter is the current and future religious activities or training of children. Finally, the general encouragement for parties to settle their own affairs under a separation agreement is in tension with the court's supervisory role – under which the court is both to ensure basic fairness between the ex-spouses and to protect children's interests.

CONCLUSION

The trend toward greater enforcement of marriage agreements reflects a tension in government policy between wanting to reinforce the family unit and wanting to protect individual interests and individual liberty. Questions regarding the enforcement of religious provisions in these agreements involve negotiating the same sorts of tensions – group interests versus individual interests, protecting commitments versus protecting liberty – with the additional complications created by the First Amendment objectives of free exercise and nonentanglement.

Trends, Patterns, and Predictors, 33 Soc. Sci. Research 606 (2004), www.sciencedirect.com /science/article/pii/S0049089X0300084X.

60 *See, e.g.*, Estin, *Foreign and Religious*, *supra* note 58, at 1030–32.

61 *See, e.g.*, Brian H. Bix, *Private Ordering and Family Law*, 23 J. Am. Acad. Matrimonial Law 249 (2010); Bix, *Domestic Agreements*, *supra* note 39.

Contract law in general is a balance: increasing autonomy by allowing parties to enter binding commitments that can be enforced in court, while creating many limits on both procedure and substance – to deal with misrepresentation, duress, unconscionability, limits on what damages can be agreed to, public policy, and so on. With provisions about religion in marriage agreements, further questions of balance arise along with those that come with all agreements. There is hope that a balance can be drawn that gives room for party choice and religious pluralism, while also setting minimal standards, providing exit opportunities, and minimizing exploitation and oppression.

10

Religious Parents Who Divorce

Margaret F. Brinig

Fritz Duda Family Chair in Law, The Notre Dame Law School

Even though adherence to organized religion is becoming less common for Americans,[1] religion remains important for many in the United States. This chapter sets out to show some of the effects of religion on a particular group of vulnerable Americans – those going through the divorce process, as they self-identify, not through surveys but through divorce pleadings and parenting agreements.[2] While some will rely more on faith during such difficult times, whatever stigma around divorce remains for divorcing parents may cause

[1] *New Pew Research Center Study Examines America's Changing Religious Landscape*, PEW RESEARCH CTR. (May 12, 2015), www.pewforum.org/2015/05/12/new-pew-research-center-study-examines-americas-changing-religious-landscape/ [hereinafter *Pew Study*] (stating that the percentage of Americans identifying as Christians dropped 8.2 percentage points in seven years to 70.8%, while those identifying as *unaffiliated* rose 6.7 percentage points to 22.8%).

[2] Questions of how to measure religious affiliation, whose religious needs within a family should be considered, and how to identify the causes for the decline in adherence are beyond the scope of this chapter. On the various methods used to measure religious affiliation, Pew uses nationally representative survey data, as do other datasets frequently used by academics. Some data comes from religious organizations themselves (through church membership rolls, baptisms, funerals and marriages, offering envelopes, etc.). The U.S. Census does not collect such data. *See Pew Study*, *supra* note 1, at n.5. Some studies measure the importance of religion in respondents' lives, the frequency of attendance at services or meetings of religious groups, or reliance on daily prayer or the Bible. *See, e.g.*, SUSAN CRAWFORD SULLIVAN, LIVING FAITH: EVERYDAY RELIGION AND MOTHERS IN POVERTY 27–28 (2011); Wilson, Chapter 16, this volume (reviewing findings and structure of studies of religiously married couples). This chapter will also not consider whose religious needs should be considered within a family. For more on this, *see* Margaret F. Brinig, *Children's Beliefs and Family Law*, 58 EMORY L.J. 55 (2008). Finally, identifying the causes for the decline in adherence to religion is also beyond the scope of this chapter. Declines have been seen in most Christian religious denominations and all regions of the country. *Pew Study*, *supra* note 1. They are particularly acute in the Catholic Church, which accounts for a plurality of the shifting of one faith to another, and among young, non-Hispanic white people, who are far more likely to be in the unaffiliated group. A number of publications suggest that formal affiliation may be far less common among unmarried, poor families. *See, e.g.*, SULLIVAN, *supra*; KATHRYN EDIN & TIMOTHY J. SULLIVAN, DOING THE BEST I CAN: FATHERHOOD IN THE INNER CITY (2013);

others to withdraw from church affiliation, particularly when they seek to remarry.[3] Other work has shown that when both spouses are similarly religious, they are less likely to divorce.[4] Of course, some couples quarrel about religion during their marriages, and differences either in religiosity or religious preference may add to the discord in the marriage that eventually culminates in divorce.[5] A prior study based upon data from Iowa showed that when religious couples did divorce, they tended to, more than others, indicate fault-based reasons for the divorce, even when a fault basis could not be used to any legal advantage, and to litigate rather than settle divorce-related issues.[6]

This chapter draws upon divorce pleadings and other records to show how indications of religion, or disaffiliation, that appear in parenting agreements and orders affect the course of the divorce proceedings and any legal activities over the five years following the divorce filing. Some of the apparent findings are normative, but most are merely descriptive and some may be correlative rather than caused by the indicated concern about religion. While parenting plans are accepted by courts only when they are in the best interests of the child, at least in theory, the child's *independent* religious needs were never mentioned in the files analyzed for this chapter. Instead the parents' religious practices and affiliation drove the court's understanding of what the couple could achieve for their children following dissolution. The data is consistent with more religious parents trying to make the best of what they understand is not ideal for their children.

I THE STUDY AND DATA

Despite the constitutional decisions over who may marry and how much autonomy parents have in the family discussed throughout this volume,

W. Bradford Wilcox & Nicholas H. Wolfinger, *Then Comes Marriage? Religion, Race and Marriage in Urban America*, 36 Soc. Sci. Res. 569 (2007).

3 *See, e.g.*, Paul H. DeGraff & Mattije Kalmijn, *Alternative Routes in the Remarriage Market*, 81 Soc. Forces 1459, 1466, 1488–89 (2003) (suggesting that religiosity pulls two ways, since people are less apt to cohabit if religious and, therefore, more likely to marry; prior studies are inconsistent but show Catholics less apt to remarry).

4 *See, e.g.*, Linda J. Waite & Evelyn L. Lehrer. *The Benefits from Marriage and Religion in the United States: A Comparative Analysis*, 29 Pop. & Dev. Rev. 255, 256 (2003); Wilson, Chapter 16, this volume (reviewing studies of religiosity and stability in marriages).

5 Some literature suggests that it is difference in religiosity rather than different denominations that causes stress. *See, e.g.*, Paul A. Nakonezy, Robert D. Shull, & Joseph Lee Rodgers, *The Effect of No-Fault Divorce Law on the Divorce Rates Across the 50 States and Its Relation to Income, Education and Religiosity*, 57 J. Marriage & Fam. 477 (1995).

6 Margaret F. Brinig, *Unhappy Contracts: The Case of Divorce*, 1 Rev. L. & Econ. 241 (2005) [hereinafter Brinig, *Unhappy Contracts*].

family law largely remains the province of the states.[7] To understand the law in practice, it is necessary to examine the law within a specific jurisdiction.

Several criteria informed the choice of the particular jurisdictions analyzed here. First, it was important to examine a "modern" statute – one that confronts post-separation parental roles in terms of parenting time. Second, and relatedly, this study sought to examine a state with established parenting guidelines propounded by the judiciary to give additional guidance to judges making decisions about parenting time. Given the first criterion, this study looked for states with substantial experience with shared parenting, which would likely be above average in the fraction of shared parenting awards, since this would minimize a selection effect into shared custody that might yield a misleading snapshot.[8] Lastly, this study sought states that afforded access to electronic records. This required that the counties involved keep electronic records of not only judicial activity but also scanned documents such as pleadings, reports of various kinds, motions, decisions and orders of judges and mediators, and more. Two states ultimately emerged from these criteria: Arizona and Indiana.

An Arizona law in place at the beginning of this study typifies the rules in many states "friendly" to shared parenting.[9] The state progressively moved in 2010[10] and again in 2012[11] toward mandating equal parenting time for all

7 *See generally* RECONCEIVING THE FAMILY: CRITIQUE ON THE AMERICAN LAW INSTITUTE'S PRINCIPLES OF THE LAW OF FAMILY DISSOLUTION (Robin Fretwell Wilson, ed., 2006).

8 A selection effect occurs when the characteristics of a sample are both related to the phenomenon under study *and* to behavior or characteristics that make the phenomenon more or less likely to occur. *See, e.g.*, Scott Stanley, *Selection and Science: Cohabitation Research as the Example*, SLIDING VS. DECIDING: SCOTT STANLEY'S BLOG (Aug. 6, 2011), slidingvsdeciding.blogspot.com/2011/08/selection-and-science-cohabitation.html. In this context, a selection effect might account for observed differences in outcomes if those seeking custody in the context of a divorce have a characteristic that is both related to the behavior being investigated (in this case, co-parenting) but also more associated with the probability of a party seeking or receiving a co-parenting arrangement. If, for example, those who come from families in which their parents divorced are more likely to seek co-parenting arrangements and those arrangements yield better or worse outcomes on any metric (less conflict, for example), a selection effect may explain the outcome – namely, that adult children of divorced couples will have less conflict when co-parenting, rather than co-parenting leading to less conflict post-divorce. By selecting jurisdictions that channel [nearly all] couples into co-parenting arrangements, the possibility of selection effects accounting for observed outcomes decreases.

9 ARIZ. REV. STAT. ANN. § 25–403.01 (2016).

10 *Id.*, amended by Laws 2010, Ch. 186, § 2.

11 *Id.*, amended by Laws 2012, Ch. 309, § 8 (effective Jan. 1, 2013).

separating couples consistent with the best interests of the child.[12] Even in 2007, Arizona as a whole had more equal parenting than most other jurisdictions; Maricopa County, the most populous in the state, led the way, driving the state-level results.[13]

The Court Administrator in Maricopa County, Arizona, sent a complete list of intake files from eight weeks in January, February, April, and September 2008. The list identified not only file names and the type of action involved but also the names of parties, their addresses (where available), their counsel (or whether, like most couples, they were self-representing, or "*pro per*" as it is called in Arizona), and very often their dates of birth. From these, files were randomly selected, representing specific types of actions, with the results shown in Table 10.1.

This chapter largely deals with the first category shown in Table 10.1 – dissolutions, or divorces with children, using the 363 cases from Maricopa County, Arizona, which encompasses Phoenix; together with another 322 from Pima County, Arizona, which encompasses Tucson; and another 310 from counties scattered across Indiana.

It examines two kinds of court data. The first, publicly available online,[14] simply lists transactions with the clerk's office dealing with the file. The second

[12] ARIZ. REV. STAT. ANN. § 25–403.02 (2016) now includes in part: "Consistent with the child's best interests in § 25–403 and §§ 25–403.03, 25–403.04 and 25–403.05, the court shall adopt a parenting plan that provides for both parents to share legal decision making regarding their child and that maximizes their respective parenting time. The court shall not prefer a parent's proposed plan because of the parent's or child's gender."

[13] Rates of shared time are very state specific. Arizona in 2007 had 15% equal custody, and another 19% with at least 116 shared days. Jane Venohr & Rasa Kaunelis, DENVER: CENTER FOR POLICY RESEARCH, ARIZONA CHILD SUPPORT GUIDELINE REVIEW: ANALYSIS OF CASE FILE DATA (Dec. 2, 2008), www.azcourts.gov/Portals/74/CSGRC/repository/2009-CaseFileRev.pdf. By contrast, in 2006, North Carolina had 15.3% of equal parenting cases with at least 123 days of parenting time, or 33% of all days shared. *See* Suzanne Reynolds, Ralph Peoples, & Catherine Harris, *Back to the Future: An Empirical Study of Child Custody Outcomes*, 85 N.C. L. REV. 1629, 1667 (2007). Oregon, in 2002, had 32% of its cases result in joint custody cases. MARGARET F. BRINIG, LAW, FAMILY AND COMMUNITY: SUPPORTING THE COVENANT 89, Fig. 2.1 (2010). Wisconsin had 43.8% with at least 30% parenting time in 2007. Judi Bartfeld, UNIVERSITY OF WISCONSIN INSTITUTE ON POVERTY, SHARED PLACEMENT: AN OVERVIEW OF PREVALENCE, TRENDS, ECONOMIC IMPLICATIONS, AND IMPACTS ON CHILD WELL-BEING (2011). Washington in 2007 had 16% equal time awarded and another 18% where parents shared more than 35% of time with children. Thomas George, OLYMPIA: WASHINGTON STATE CENTER FOR COURT RESEARCH, RESIDENTIAL TIME SUMMARY REPORTS FILED IN WASHINGTON JULY 2007–MARCH 2008, www.courts.wa.gov/subsite/wsccr/docs/ResidentialTimeSummaryReport2008.pdf.

[14] *See Public Access to Family Court Case Information*, JUDICIAL BRANCH OF ARIZ., MARICOPA COUNTY, www.superiorcourt.maricopa.gov/docket/FamilyCourtCases/; *Record*

TABLE 10.1 *Types of Cases in Maricopa County, Arizona, Sample*

	Frequency	Percentage	Valid Percentage	Cumulative Percentage
Dissolution with children	363	58.5	58.5	58.5
Dissolution without children	51	8.2	8.2	66.8
Legal separation	7	1.1	1.1	67.9
Custody	43	6.9	6.9	74.8
Protective order	1	.2	.2	75.0
Support	155	25.0	25.0	100.0
Total	620	100.0	100.0	

kind of data was obtained after receiving institutional review board approval, which is necessary for research involving humans, and giving assurances that individual records would be kept confidential. Such records included actual documents, such as pleadings and other motions, letters, reports, orders, and so forth, involved with each selected file. More specifically, it included petitions for divorce or custody, known as complaints, and answers (or motions and responses), reports by child coordinators or of drug testing, completed parental worksheets for child support, parenting plans whether joint or sole, orders dealing with motions or protective orders, and final dissolution orders.

The documents yielded a trove of demographic information. The complaint (or petition) typically included names and birth dates of parents and any children, the date of marriage (if the parties were married), addresses, occupations of the parents, what property was owned by the couple and how the petitioner wanted it split, what parenting time was asked for, and whether the petitioner asked for spousal support or child support. It also indicated which party was bringing the action (father or mother) and whether there had been or currently was domestic violence in the relationship.[15] The answer

Search, Office of the Clerk of the Superior Court, www.agave.cosc.pima.gov/home.asp?Include=pages/record_search.htm; Mycase.IN.gov, public.courts.in.gov/mycase/#/vw/Search; Lake County, Indiana, www.lakecountyin.org/portal/media-type/html/user/anon/page/online-docket.

[15] The Arizona complaint forms contained checkboxes for domestic violence. For example, in the consent decree packet, the form to be signed by the judge indicates as follows:

A. Domestic Violence has not occurred between the parties; OR

B. Domestic Violence has occurred between the parties, but:

1. It was mutual (committed by both parties), (see A.R.S. § 25–403.03 (D))

OR

2. It is otherwise still in the best interests of the minor child(ren) to grant joint or sole legal decision making (joint or sole custody) to a parent who has committed domestic violence because: (EXPLAIN).

corroborated or sometimes corrected the details found in the complaint, asking for the same or different relief. The child support worksheets at the time of the dissolution or other order identified which parent was the primary custodial parent, the amount of each parent's monthly income, whether either was responsible for additional or court-ordered support for another child, whether the child was older than age twelve or had extraordinary expenses, who was ordered to pay child support, the parenting time for the noncustodial parent (calculated by totaling the number of days or partial days), and whether the amount was adjusted because it exceeded the amount needed for self-support (which was $775 monthly in 2008).[16]

Some cases involved requests for custody evaluations or mediation, actions involving protective orders together with the results of any protective order hearings, and motions post-dissolution to increase or decrease child support or parenting time or to enforce one or both. The motions were accompanied by supporting reasons, which were frequently referred to by the court in resolving them. The divorce decrees or parenting orders incorporated any agreements of the parties. These usually included parenting plans and sometimes property settlement agreements. Stand-alone support orders included reasons for deviating from the amounts calculated on the worksheet (the state child support guideline amounts). All of these alleged or found facts were carefully coded.

The Arizona child support guidelines explicitly define how to count days or partial days for parenting time.[17] Once the total is determined, a table in the

Consent Decree for Divorce or Legal Separation for a Non-Covenant Marriage, Superior Court of Arizona in Maricopa County, www.superiorcourt.maricopa.gov/sscDocs/packets/dr7.pdf. *See also* Douglas W. Allen & Margaret F. Brinig, *Child Support Guidelines: The Good, the Bad, and the Ugly*, 45 Fam. L. Q. 135 (2011).

16 Arizona follows the "income shares" model for awarding child support, which seeks to award support as if the child lived with both parents in an intact relationship, an amount split pro-rata between the parents based on their relative incomes. *See Child Support Guideline Models By State*, National Conference on State Legislatures (June 9, 2016) www.ncsl.org/research/human-services/guideline-models-by-state.aspx.

After arriving at the basic child support amount, Arizona courts evaluate the amount to ensure that the noncustodial parent can "maintain at least a minimum standard of living" while paying the court-ordered award. *See* Arizona Child Support Guidelines, Adopted by the Arizona Supreme Court (2015) 14, des.az.gov/sites/default/files/2015CSGuidelinesRED.pdf.

17 In 2007, the courts operated under guidelines adopted in 2005. *See* Arizona Child Support Guidelines, Adopted by the Arizona Supreme Court [2005 Guidelines], at 10 (effective Jan. 1, 2006). The State adopted new guidelines in 2011 and again in 2015, which govern today. *See* Arizona Child Support Guidelines, Adopted by the Arizona Supreme Court, at 11 (effective June 1, 2011), amended by Exec. Order 2011–46, www.azcourts.gov/portals/31/guidesched10072011.pdf. The 2011 guidelines have since been replaced with new guidelines effective 2015. *See* Arizona Child Support Guidelines, Adopted

guidelines reveals what percentage of the obligation should be reduced to obtain preliminary child support owed.[18] For example, the traditional, or "basic," parenting plan would be for the child to spend every other weekend and one evening during the week, plus split holidays and two weeks in the summer with the non-primary parent. While many parents use a software calculator (obtainable as a free download) for this, the "basic" plan would net to 82 days, which results in a 10.5% reduction in the support that would otherwise have been awarded.[19] As the Guidelines explain, this adjustment reflects the reality that when a child is with the non-primary parent, "a portion of the costs for children normally expended by the custodial parent shifts to the noncustodial parent."[20] A separate table in the Guidelines – Appendix B – equates the total support obligation borne by (or imputed to) each parent when parenting time is equal.[21]

The study captured two additional jurisdictions by replicating the process used with Maricopa, including the relative proportion of case types, first in Pima County, Arizona, and then in Indiana. Obtaining the Indiana records required gaining a court order from the Indiana Supreme Court, and then drawing on five counties scattered around the state to permit consideration of different demographics: urban and rural, prosperous and poor, racially diverse, and homogeneous or not.[22] In each case, the study examined records for the same months in 2008 noted earlier but found smaller numbers of unmarried couples in Indiana. Table 10.2 presents demographics for each state and shows populations that share educational levels and similar household incomes if differing racially and by relationship status.

However, while Arizona and Indiana both use child custody and child support guidelines, Indiana's guidelines suggest meaningful contact with both parents based upon the age of the child – with (more/less) contact for teens suggested, for example, rather than "maximum contact with both." The difference is not semantic only: there is far less equally shared parenting

BY THE ARIZONA SUPREME COURT (2015), des.az.gov/sites/default/files/2015CSGuidelinesRED.pdf.

18 *Id.* at 11.

19 The 82 days results from 52 days (every other weekend or 2×26) + 13 days (for one mid-week evening a week, calculated as .25×52 under a formula from the Guidelines) + 5 days (for holidays) + 12 days (two weeks in for summer, less the weekend already counted).

20 *See* ARIZONA CHILD SUPPORT GUIDELINES, ADOPTED BY THE ARIZONA SUPREME COURT (2015) 10, des.az.gov/sites/default/files/2015CSGuidelinesRED.pdf.

21 *Id.* at App. A. The simplest way of thinking about this is to subtract the smaller amount due from each parent from the larger one and divide by two.

22 The counties are Lake (Gary and Crown Point), Marion (Indianapolis), Monroe (Bloomington), Posey (Evansville), and St. Joseph (South Bend).

TABLE 10.2 *State Demographics*

	Arizona	Indiana
Hispanic population	29.3%	12.4%
Black population	4%	19%[a]
Already divorced	6%	15%
Foreign born	14%	6%
Median household income	$55,862	$42,714
High school graduates	78%	86%

[a] The percentages were 27.6% in Marion and 25.3% in Lake Counties.

time among divorcing Indiana couples than for comparable divorcing parents in Arizona. In Indiana, the bulk of orders reviewed set parenting days between 20 and 128 days per year, with a mean of 72.47 days. By contrast, in Arizona, most orders awarded between 47 and 163 days, with a mean of 105 days.

The two states compute child support differently when there is shared parenting, as well. In Arizona, the base amount is typically reduced by a "parenting time deduction" ranging from 1% to 48.6%. In Indiana, the base amount is first multiplied by 1.4, after which the reductions credit only variable costs of parenting, such as the amount spent on food when a child is present, as opposed to the fixed costs of parenting, including housing Furthermore, a finding of domestic violence in Arizona at the time data was collected would trigger a rebuttable presumption against shared custody,[23] while in Indiana – as it does in most other states[24] – it would preclude shared physical

[23] While joint decision making was generally not granted, a surprising number of would-be custodians in both states were apparently able to rebut the presumption. The relationship between a pre-decree domestic violence allegation and parenting time days showed a statistically insignificant (p<.304) difference: 107 days if there was no allegation to 99 days if there was. A statistically significant difference existed in the percentage of equal custody cases, however (19% of the time versus 12.5%, p<.10). In Indiana, the difference was 74 days if no domestic violence, and nearly 61 days if there was (p=.214). About half as much equal custody was indicated on the child support worksheets (.04 compared to .02 of the cases).

Even if not given legal decision making, typically parenting time (visitation) will be awarded under ARIZ. REV. STAT. ANN. § 25–403.01: "A parent who is not granted sole or joint legal decision making is entitled to reasonable parenting time to ensure that the minor child has substantial, frequent, meaningful and continuing contact with the parent unless the court finds, after a hearing, that parenting time would endanger the child's physical, mental, moral or emotional health."

[24] *See, e.g.*, ARK. CODE ANN. § 9–13-101(c)(2) (2015); IDAHO CODE ANN. § 320717B(5) (2016); MINN. STAT. § 518.17 subdiv. 2 (2015). *See generally* Leslie Joan Harris, *Failure to Protect From Exposure to Domestic Violence in Private Custody Contests*, 44 FAM. L.Q. 169 (2010).

TABLE 10.3 *Descriptive Statistics: Arizona & Indiana*

	Sample AZ/IN	Arizona Mean	Indiana[a] Mean
Joint legal custody	685/310	.540	.519
Pre-divorce protective order	685/310	.187	.119
Monthly gross income – mother	608/225	$2163.72	$2241.37
Monthly gross income – father	609/225	$3608.85	$3193.88
Spousal support to mother (amount)	101/12	$103.04	$1070.00
Days of parenting time	567/203	105.00	74.70
Mediator involved	685/310	.251	.210
Dissolution after default	685/310	.385	.123
Dissolution by consent decree	685/310	.336	.526
Dissolution after trial	685/310	.142	.077
Post-order protective order	685/310	.072	.035

[a] Indiana child support worksheets use weekly income; this column multiples amounts by 52 and divides by 12 to make them comparable.

custody, resulting in no parenting time.[25] Descriptive statistics from the divorces involving children from the two states appear in Table 10.3.

Importantly, both states recognize that religious upbringing of children may be a central consideration for some parents after their breakup. Both states provide a mechanism for recognizing the religious upbringing couples may wish to provide their children. Arizona does so by statute[26] as well as through specific entries on the forms for parenting plans provided by the various counties, which prompt parents to affirmatively consider what they would like to do. Maricopa County's form, for instance, directs filers to "Choose ONE":

H. Religious Education Arrangements (Choose ONE)

- Each parent may take the minor children to a church or place of worship of his or her choice during the time that the minor children is/are in his or her care.

[25] IND. CODE § 31–17-2–8 (7) (listing domestic violence as a factor that must be considered by judges, and suggesting supervised visitation in § 31–17-2–8.3); Jennifer L. Hardesty & Lawrence H. Ganong, *How Women Make Custody Decisions and Manage Co-Parenting with Abusive Former Husbands*, 23 J. SOC. & PERSONAL RELATIONSHIPS 543 (2006).

[26] ARIZ. STAT. ANN. § 25.403.02 provides in part (emphasis added):

C. Parenting plans shall include at least the following:

1. A designation of the legal decision making as joint or sole as defined in § 25–401.
2. Each parent's rights and responsibilities for the personal care of the child and for decisions in areas such as education, health care, and *religious training*.

- Both parents agree that the minor children may be instructed in the __________faith.
- Both parents agree that religious arrangements are not applicable to this plan.[27]

In the Arizona cases sampled, 39.6% (271 cases) checked one of the top two boxes, with 9.1% (62 cases) specifying denominations.

The Indiana child custody statute does not mandate parents' consideration of religious upbringing but allows them to make such provisions.[28] The forms for divorce and complaint available for *pro se* petitioners on the Indiana Supreme Court website do not include a religious upbringing clause, presumably since any arrangement will be determined by the custodial parent or parents in cases of shared legal custody.[29] However, some law firm–generated custody plans in the sample and certain popular forms do supply religious upbringing paragraphs.[30]

27 Superior Court of Ariz. in Maricopa County, at 4, www.superiorcourt.maricopa.gov/sscDocs/packets/drmv7fz.pdf. Pima County's form contained a similar checklist:

RELIGIOUS EDUCATION ARRANGEMENTS

- Each of us may take the child(ren) to a church or place of worship of our choice during the time that the child(ren) is/are with either of us.
- We agree that the child(ren) may be instructed in the ____________faith.
- Other religious issues:________________________________

Parenting Plan, Arizona Superior Court in Pima County, at 2, www.sc.pima.gov/Portals/0/Library/Child_Custody_&_Parenting_(PimaSC09).pdf.

28 "Custodian may determine child's upbringing
Sec. 17. (a) Except:

(1) *as otherwise agreed by the parties in writing* at the time of the custody order; and
(2) as provided in subsection (b);
the custodian may determine the child's upbringing, including the child's education, health care, *and religious training*.
(b) If the court finds after motion by a noncustodial parent that, in the absence of a specific limitation of the custodian's authority, the child's:
(1) physical health would be endangered; or
(2) emotional development would be significantly impaired;
the court may specifically limit the custodian's authority."

Ind. Code § 31-17-2-17 (emphasis added).

29 Custody has two aspects: residential time with children, often called physical custody, and legal decision making about major decisions in the child's life, called legal custody. *See generally* Carl Schneider and Margaret Brinig, Invitation to Family Law (American Casebook Series, 3rd ed. 2007). Under this umbrella, religious upbringing is to be decided by the parent with legal custody, or both parents if legal custody is held jointly (or at the time of the original decree).

30 *See, e.g.*, *Sample Parenting Plan*, Fathers Unite, www.fathersunite.org/Legal%20Templates%20and%20Help/sample_parenting_plan.html ("30. [T]hat religious training and theology of (your religious preference) be pursued by said children. Both Parents shall show, by

In the Indiana case file data, 11% (34) of the cases had parenting plans that provided for religion, with 4.8% (15) referencing specific denominations. Because online forms supplied by the counties did not include them, default divorces, which comprised 12% of the Indiana cases, did not address religious upbringing.

II THE FINDINGS

This section presents the findings that included religion as a statistically significant coefficient.[31] The state involved is included in each table's caption; the religious choice may have indicated a specific religion[32] or that the filings included a reference to either a specific or a general religious upbringing.[33] Findings are presented in the order that they appear in most cases.

A *Religion and Domestic Violence*

About 19% of the cases reviewed contained allegations of domestic violence. A great deal of literature on custody as well as on domestic violence documents the problems faced when separation is complicated by domestic violence.[34] Indeed, domestic violence frequently increases at the time of separation or divorce and often continues afterward.[35] One research strand reports on the advisability, or non-advisability, of mediation or other forms of alternative dispute

example, their support of their respective churches by ensuring that their children REGULARLY attend services and observe holidays.").

31 In one case only, this study also includes a state where it was not statistically significant but still positive. *See infra* Table 10.10.

32 The coding for this required a specific denomination.

33 This included a specific denomination, an indication of "Christian," or a requirement that the parents negotiate the religious upbringing or directed the selection to one parent.

34 For a summary of the literature, *see* Margaret F. Brinig, Leslie Drozd, & Loretta Frederick, *Perspectives on Joint Custody Parenting as Applied to Domestic Violence Cases*, 52 Fam. Ct. Rev. 272 (2014) [hereinafter Brinig et al., *Perspectives*].

35 *See, e.g.*, Demetrios N. Kyriacou et al., *Risk Factors for Injury to Women from Domestic Violence*, 341 New Eng. J. Med. 1892, 1894 (1999) (stating that having a former partner was the relationship variable that had the strongest association with injury from domestic violence – 3.5 times the risk of injury); Lisa G. Lerman, *The Decontextualization of Domestic Violence*, 83 Nw. J. Crim. L. & Criminology 217 (1992); Martha R. Mahoney, *EXIT: Power and the Idea of Leaving in Love, Work, and the Confirmation Hearings*, 65 S. Cal. L. Rev. 1283 (1992) [hereinafter Mahoney, *EXIT*]; Martha R. Mahoney, *Legal Images of Battered Women: Redefining the Issue of Separation*, 90 Mich. L. Rev. 1 (1991) [hereinafter Mahoney, *Legal Images*]. For a review, *see* Peter G. Jaffe, Janet R. Johnson, Claire V. Crooks, & Nicholas Bala, *Custody Disputes Involving Allegations of Domestic Violence: Toward A Differentiated Approach To Parenting Plans*, 46 Fam. Ct. Rev. 500 (2008), www.law.buffalo.edu/content/dam/law/restricted-assets/pdf/cle/161118/jaffe-1.pdf.

resolution when coercive control situations are involved.[36] Another considers how false allegations of domestic violence may be used strategically in divorce, and particularly custody, negotiations.[37] To the extent that the child is witness to it, or even a direct victim him- or herself, no researcher doubts the harm.[38]

This study coded cases as a zero unless there had been an allegation of domestic violence, either in the complaint or in a separate protective order petition. While the files reviewed contain information about whether a permanent order was issued by a court, whether a victim was hospitalized or received other treatment, or whether the court took notice of it and considered it during a divorce hearing, as it was in one case, the coding made no differentiation between the cases where domestic violence undoubtedly occurred and those in which it was simply alleged. Whether a party simply alleges domestic violence or it actually occurred, the mere mention of domestic violence usually indicates a high-conflict divorce.[39] In the binary logistic regression that follows in Table 10.4,[40] other variables included are those typically related to domestic violence because they indicate the relative power of the mothers. Substance abuse or mental illness was included because both characteristics are often associated with domestic violence.[41]

36 *See, e.g.*, Robert Emery, David Sbarra, & Tara Grover, *Divorce Mediation: Research and Reflections*, 43 FAM. CT. REV. 22 (2005) [hereinafter Emery, *Divorce Mediation*].

For a review of how state laws encouraging mediation respond to evidence of domestic violence, *see Mediation in Family Law Matters Where DV is Present*, COMMISSION ON DOMESTIC VIOLENCE, AMERICAN BAR ASSOCIATION (2008), www.americanbar.org/content/dam/aba/administrative/domestic_violence1/Charts/2014%20Mediation%20Statutory%20Chart.authcheckdam.pdf.

37 Douglas W. Allen & Margaret F. Brinig, *Do Joint Parenting Laws Make Any Difference*, 9 J. EMPIRICAL L. STUD. 304 (2011); Elizabeth S. Scott & Robert E. Emery, *Gender Politics and Child Custody: The Puzzling Persistence of the Best-Interest Standard*, 77 LAW & CONTEMP. PROBS. 69 (2014).

38 *See, e.g.*, ROBERT E. EMERY, RENEGOTIATING FAMILY RELATIONSHIPS 100 (2012) [hereinafter EMERY, RENEGOTIATING] ("Hundreds of studies show that parental conflict is toxic for children in divorce.").

39 Janet R. Johnston et al., *Allegations and Substantiations of Abuse in Custody-Disputing Families*, 43–2 FAM. CT. REV. 284–294, 284 (April 2005).

40 Binary logistic regression is a method for determining how a set of independent variables explains the variance, if any, of a dichotomous dependent variable. *See Using Logistic Regression in Research*, STATISTICS SOLUTIONS, www.statisticssolutions.com/using-logistic-regression-in-research/.

Here this analysis attempts to tease out how much of the variation in the presence or absence of domestic violence allegations in custody proceedings is explained by a given characteristic, such as mother's age or the question of central interest to this chapter, religiosity.

41 *See, e.g.*, Sabra Bushra et al., *Risk Factors for Severe Intimate Partner Violence and Violence-Related Injuries Among Women in India*, 54 WOMEN & HEALTH 281 (2014).

TABLE 10.4 *Pre-Divorce Protective Order Sought in Arizona Cases*[a]

Variables	B[b]	S.E.[c]	Sig.[d]	Exp(B)[e]
Mother's gross monthly income	.000	.000	.039	1.000
Age of mother at marriage	.028	.002	.155	1.028
Religion indicated	−.493	.243	.042	.610
Substance abuse or mental illness involved	1.753	.264	.000	5.770
Constant	−2.028	.506	.000	.132

[a] Cox & Snell R^2 =.088. Cox & Snell R^2 is a measure of how well data fits a model and whether a "model needs to be more complex, specifically, whether it needs additional nonlinearities and interactions to satisfactorily represent the data." *See* Paul Allison, *What's the Best R-Squared for Logistic Regression?* STATISTICAL HORIZONS (Feb. 13, 2013), statisticalhorizons.com/r2logistic.
[b] B signifies the Y intercept value – or the coefficient for the constant (also called the "intercept") in the null model. *See Logistic Regression, SPSS Annotated Output*, UCLA INSTITUTE FOR DIGITAL RESEARCH AND EDUCATION, stats.idre.ucla.edu/spss/output/logistic-regression/.
[c] S.E. or standard error estimates variability between the means when multiple samples are taken.
[d] Sig. represents statistical significance. When the value is less than .05, the null hypothesis that observed variation is random is rejected. *See Logistic Regression, SPSS Annotated Output*, UCLA INSTITUTE FOR DIGITAL RESEARCH AND EDUCATION, stats.idre.ucla.edu/spss/output/logistic-regression/ (May 5, 2017).
[e] The exponentiation of the B coefficient presents an odds ratio. When the value is less than 1.0, a group with the variable under inquiry is less likely to have an outcome. When the value is more than 1.0, a group with the variable is more likely to experience the outcome. *See Logistic Regression, SPSS Annotated Output*, UCLA INSTITUTE FOR DIGITAL RESEARCH AND EDUCATION, stats.idre.ucla.edu/spss/output/logistic-regression/.

As noted earlier, in about 19% of the cases, a party alleged domestic violence. As with many of the regressions that follow, the predicted equation does not explain a large share of the variance in the likelihood that violence was alleged. The families that indicated religion in the parenting plans were about 40% less likely than the whole group to seek protective orders, at a 95% confidence level ($p < .05$). This is shown in the far right column in Table 10.4 as an odds ratio of .61 – or 40% less than the whole population under consideration. Taking into consideration the rate of domestic violence allegations in all cases, this means that only 11% of those couples indicating a religious upbringing alleged domestic violence, holding other variables constant.[42] This, of course, does not mean that greater indications of religiosity *cause* less violence or cause a party not to allege violence more often.[43]

42 This number is arrived at by multiplying 19%, the rate of domestic violence allegations for the full sample, by .61, yielding 11.4%.

43 *But see, e.g.*, Christopher G. Ellison & Kristin Landerson, *Religious Involvement and Domestic Violence Among U.S. Couples*, 40 J. SCI. STUD. RELIGION 269 (2001) (finding inverse relationship between domestic violence and church attendance, using NSFH) [hereinafter

B Religion and "Fault" Divorce

None of the nearly 1,000 cases examined in the two states utilized a "fault" ground for divorce.[44] Nonetheless, 10% of all cases reviewed alleged various forms of substance abuse or mental illness, a factor relevant to custody issues. Evidence from another empirical study, one done in Johnson County, Iowa,[45] suggested that more religious couples would both wait longer to divorce and also do so more often only for serious reasons, rather than just general marital malaise.[46] This study tested the hypothesis that religious couples would wait longer to divorce or divorce only for serious reasons using allegations of substance abuse or mental illness contained in the file (Table 10.5).[47]

Adding additional factors that might predict the use of a fault divorce, such as age at marriage, did not add appreciably to the simple findings here. Indicated

Ellison & Landserson]; Christopher G. Ellison et al., *Race/Ethnicity, Religious Involvement, and Domestic Violence*, 13 VIOLENCE AGAINST WOMEN 1094 (2007) [hereinafter Ellison et al.] (finding less violence, especially among African American women). *But cf.* Claire M. Renzetti et al., *By the Grace of God: Religiosity, Religious Self-Regulation, and Perpetration of Intimate Partner Violence*, J. FAM. ISSUES 1 (2015) (showing that the noted finding depends upon the precise way religiosity is defined: religious self-regulation is most important in reducing likelihood of IPV perpetration). Skeptics of less violence might claim that the more religious wives would feel it their duty to be "corrected" by their husbands or might be more likely to fear reprisal and therefore not want to "make waves" by alleging it. *See, e.g.*, Nancy Nason-Clark, *Making the Sacred Safe: Woman Abuse and Communities of Faith*, 61 SOC. OF RELIGION 349, 358, 359, 364 (2000) (finding that women who inhabit very closed religious or ethnic communities are especially vulnerable when abused, though the incidence rates of that abuse may approximate those of other women).

44 IND. CODE § 31–15-2–3 (2016) allows divorces on grounds of irretrievable breakdown, insanity lasting at least two years, a felony conviction, and incurable impotence. All divorces in this sample were on the "irretrievable breakdown" ground. Arizona is a no-fault state using irretrievable breakdown under ARIZ. REV. STAT. ANN. § 25–912 (2015), except for covenant marriages, which need to show grounds as in ARIZ. REV. STAT. ANN. § 25–903 (2015). There were no cases decided under the covenant marriage statute in this sample.

45 Brinig, *Unhappy Contacts, supra* note 6, at 255, 266, Tbl. 3 (reporting that a religious couple's divorce is five times more likely to be due to revelations of abuse of a spouse or child or adultery).

46 *See, e.g.*, Wilson, Chapter 16, this volume; Paul R. Amato & Stacy J. Rogers, *A Longitudinal Study of Marital Problems and Subsequent Divorce*, 59 J. MARRIAGE & FAMILY 612, 614, 623, Tbl. 3 (1997) (finding that divorce is less common if the couple is religious); Annette Mahoney et al., *Religion in the Home in the 1980s and 1990s: A Meta-Analytic Review and Conceptual Analysis of Links Between Religion, Marriage, and Parenting*, 1 PSYCHOL. OF RELIGION & SPIRITUALITY 63, 71, Tbl. 4 (2008) (detailing studies connecting lower divorce history or delayed divorce to frequency of church attendance).

47 In many of the substance abuse cases, restrictions were placed on the alleged user meeting with the children, such as supervised visits or drug/alcohol testing. Many of the cases alleging mental illness called for evaluations of the parent and sometimes visitation only in a center where visitation could be supervised.

TABLE 10.5 *"Fault" Divorce: Drug, Alcohol, or Mental Illness Alleged in Indiana Cases*[a]

Variable	B	S.E.	Sig.	Exp(B)
Specific religion indicated	1.572	.764	.040	4.815
Length of marriage	−.079	.041	.052	.924
Constant	−1.590	.375	.000	204

[a] Cox & Snell R^2 =.026.

religion in pleadings or parenting plans was associated with a higher risk of being in the 10% of divorces that involved alcohol, drug abuse, or mental illness. That association was just outside the 95% confidence level (p=.052).

C Religion and Shared Parenting

Both Indiana and Arizona encourage shared or alternating custody. Indiana does so through the use of judicially sponsored parenting time guidelines,[48] while Arizona encourages such arrangements through statutes and norms particularly favorable to shared custody.[49] While only one study has directly looked at the effect of religion on shared parenting after dissolution,[50] the few studies suggesting that evangelical fathers spend more time with their children during marriage do shed some light on parenting by religious fathers.[51] The study presented here provides direct evidence that, at least where the parents have planned for the religious upbringing of their

48 *See* INDIANA COURT RULES, INDIANA PARENTING TIME GUIDELINES, § 1, at 1–2 (2013), www.indianadivorceblog.com/new-indiana-parenting-time-guidelines-2013/.

49 ARIZ. REV. STAT. ANN. § 25–403.02(B) (effective Jan. 1, 2013) ("Consistent with the child's best interests . . . the court shall adopt a parenting plan that provides for both parents to share legal decision making regarding their child and that maximizes their respective parenting time."); Venohr & Kaunelis, *supra* note 13 (reporting statistics on cases resulting in equal custody or a significant number of days shared); Tbl. 3 (reporting mean (average) number of shared days as 105 in Arizona, compared to 75 in Indiana).

50 Elizabeth Cooksey & Patricia H. Craig, *Parenting from a Distance: The Effects of Paternal Characteristics on Contact Between Fathers and Their Children*, 35 DEMOGRAPHY 187, 196, Tbl. 3 (1998) (using the National Survey of Families and Households dataset to examine the effects of religion on custody determinations and finding, contrary to authors' hypothesis, more religious fathers were not significantly more apt to visit with noncustodial children, while noncustodial fundamentalist Christian fathers were significantly *less* likely to have weekly phone conversations with their children).

51 *See* W. Bradford Wilcox, *Religious Convention and Paternal Involvement*, 64 J. MARRIAGE & FAM. 780 (2002); *see also* Martha Mahoney, *Religion in Families*, 72 J. MARRIAGE & FAM. 805 (2010).

TABLE 10.6 *Parenting Time Days in (Arizona)*[a]

	Unstandardized Coefficients		Standardized Coefficients	
Variables	B	Std. Error	Beta	Sig.
(Constant)	81.710	5.509		.000
Mother's monthly income	.003	.001	.115	.006
Father's monthly income	.001	.001	.077	.067
Consent dissolution	15.429	5.111	.128	.003
Religion indicated	16.421	4.820	.140	.001
Either has Hispanic surname	−11.487	5.687	−.083	.044

[a] R^2 (adj) = .079. R^2 denotes how well a line fits the data, while an adjusted R^2 adjusts for the number of variables in a model. *See Adjusted R²/Adjusted R-Squared: What Is It Used For?* STATISTICS HOW TO, www.statisticshowto.com/adjusted-r2/

children, they plan to and receive orders allowing them to spend more time with their children following divorce.

Tables 10.6 and 10.7 show linear regressions for both states and include other factors that would also predict time spent with children. For instance, a number of studies have reported a relationship between shared custody and parents' income, with wealthier parents seeking and receiving a greater share of time as noncustodial parents.[52] This study was able to code for Hispanic identity in Arizona, but not in Indiana, where there are far fewer Hispanics in the counties studied.[53] In both jurisdictions, whether the couple entered into a consent dissolution is included[54]: in such cases, by definition, both parents agree to a parenting plan and therefore may be more likely to feature shared

52 *See, e.g.*, Marygold S. Melli & Patricia R. Brown, *Exploring a New Family Form – The Shared Time Family*, 22 INT'L J. L. & POL'Y 231 (2008) (presenting data from Wisconsin); Bartfeld, *supra* note 13 (presenting data from Wisconsin). *See also* Reynolds, *supra* note 13 (presenting data from North Carolina); Heather Juby, Céline Le Bourdais, & Nicole Marcil-Gratton, *Sharing Roles, Sharing Custody? Couples' Characteristics and Children's Living Arrangements at Separation*, 67 J. MARR. & FAM. 157 (2005) (finding a similar relationship in Canada).

53 Ethnicity is important because it is possible that, with certain populations, social norms might run toward mother caretaking, and also because information about the real possibility of judges' ordering equal or substantially shared custody may not be effectively communicated to the Hispanic parents. As a result, Hispanic parents may be less likely to elect shared parenting. *See* Christine Linquist Nord & Nicholas Zill, 1 NON-CUSTODIAL PARENTS' PARTICIPATION IN THEIR CHILDREN'S LIVES: EVIDENCE FROM THE SURVEY OF INCOME AND PROGRAM PARTICIPATION 12 (1996), fatherhood.hhs.gov/SIPP/NonCusp1.htm.

54 In 28.8% of cases, the court entered a default dissolution – meaning that the defendant never entered an appearance, while in 13.5% of cases, the court entered a decree of dissolution following a trial.

TABLE 10.7 *Parenting Time Days in (Indiana)*[a]

	Unstandardized Coefficients		Standardized Coefficients	
Variables	B	Std. Error	Beta	Sig
(Constant)	45.004	7.681		.000
Father's weekly income	.009	.007	.087	.220
Consent dissolution	32.638	7.528	.299	.000
Religion indicated	28.354	11.265	.174	.013
Neither party represented	-10.225	8.812	-.078	.247

[a] R^2 (adj.) = .147.

parenting – and more likely to take into account religious upbringing because they had more detailed parenting plans.

In Indiana, the regression analysis also accounted for the presence of lawyers.[55] It is hypothesized that lawyers were more likely to encourage shared parenting because they would be aware of both the court-directed Indiana parenting guidelines and the empirical work done on shared parenting and its positive effects. Several cases from Indiana in which the parties were represented actually included the entire Guidelines in the file as copies of what they had mailed to their clients.

The results from both states indicate that parents who include religious upbringing in their parenting plans have significantly more equal parenting time, holding constant income and whether or not there was a consent decree. This result obtained in Arizona both for Hispanic and for non-Hispanic parents. In Indiana, indicating religion was associated with more shared parenting both for couples where one or both were represented by counsel and for couples without representation. The coefficients are large in both Tables 10.6 and 10.7: in Arizona, it is the largest standardized coefficient (.140, $p < .001$ in Table 10.6), meaning that it is the independent variable that exerts the greatest effect on the *dependent variable*, shared custody. Likewise, in Indiana, indicating religion was strongly correlated with shared parenting, second only to whether the decree resulted from mutual consent. In fact, indicating religion (.174, $p < .05$) exerted more than twice as large an effect as income, which did not reach statistical significance, as Table 10.7 shows.

55 At least one party was represented in about three-quarters of the cases in Indiana, 76.45%, but in only 23.55% of cases in Arizona.

TABLE 10.8 *Motions to Reduce Parenting Time in (Indiana)*[a]

	B	S.E.	Sig.	Exp(B)
Specific religion indicated	2.856	1.190	.016	17.398
Father's weekly income	−.003	.001	.015	.997
Days of parenting time	.014	.006	.020	1.015
Constant	−2.250	.744	.002	.105

[a] Cox & Snell R^2=.074.

D *Stability of Shared Parenting Decrees*

However, the fact that shared parenting is decreed by court order does not necessarily mean that the arrangement will be stable. This study found that religion plays a role after parenting plans are put in place. In fact, in Indiana, it was far more likely that there would be a motion by the primary custodial parent to reduce parenting time, for those couples indicating a specific religion in their parenting plans – holding constant the original number of parenting days, as Table 10.8 shows.[56]

Table 10.8 also shows that it was less likely that there would be a motion to reduce the noncustodial parent's parenting time when the father's weekly income was higher than average – a statistically significant finding.[57] But the likelihood of a motion to reduce time increased with the number of days of parenting time. The very large exponent (17.398) means that the risk of such motions, filed in nineteen cases or 6.1% of all cases reviewed, was increased seventeen-fold when the parenting plan indicated a specific religion.[58]

56 For a specific religion to be coded, a particular denomination needed to be mentioned, for example, Catholic, Jewish, Latter Day Saints (known colloquially as Mormons). Quite a few couples in Arizona in particular indicated they wanted the child raised "Christian." It is uncertain whether this request signified a desire to raise the children as Evangelical Protestant or whether it signaled a desire to rear them Christian compared to nonreligious. This request is coded as "general religion." Consequently, this coding rubric may have undercounted the number who should be counted in "specific religion indicated."

57 About 12% of the couples had fathers as primary parents. A motion to reduce parenting time in these cases would be to reduce the noncustodial mother's parenting time. The growing instability with more shared parenting seen in this study is in contrast to the stability found in Wisconsin. *See* Lawrence M. Berger et al., *The Stability of Child Physical Placements Following Divorce: Descriptive Evidence from Wisconsin*, 70 J. MARRIAGE & FAM. 273, 273 (2008).

58 Another way of showing the difference is to compare the means for filing such motions by the couples with and without specific religious indicators, though this method is slightly less elegant since it does not account for income or the days of parenting time. A test called

TABLE 10.9 *Likelihood of Reduction of Child Support for Emancipation in Arizona*[a]

Variable	B	S.E.	Sig.	Exp(B)
Number of children	.3869	.188	.050	1.446
Length of marriage	.009	.002	.000	1.009
Religion indicated	.931	.409	.023	2.537
Total child support ordered	.001	.000	.163	1.001
Constant	−5.842	.724	.000	.003

[a] Cox & Snell R^2 =.053.

E Religion, Lengthier Marriages, and Older Children

Tables 10.9 and 10.10 display the results of another binary logistic regression, this time exploring whether the parent paying child support moved to have responsibility for payment reduced when a child was legally emancipated – this might occur in families with multiple children after the first one "ages out" of being a legal child or it might take the form of a motion to eliminate child support altogether after an only child or the youngest child reaches the age of majority.[59] As we would expect, this was more likely to occur when divorcing couples had older children, that is, those reaching age nineteen during the first five years after the divorce was initiated in 2008.

It would also be expected to be more common when the amount paid was substantial or when the payor parent's income was higher: if an individual is paying a lot of money for child support, that person might be more inclined to seek to reduce it than if the order is small, making it not worth the trouble given the costs of filing. Additionally, if the parent has a higher income, that person is more likely to be represented and to be aware that he or she can get a reduction if income changes. It was less obvious before this study whether indications that parents wanted children to have religious upbringing should

an ANOVA, which stands for "analysis of variance" tests whether "means of two or more populations are equal." *See What is Anova*, MINITAB17 SUPPORT, support.minitab.com/en-us/minitab/17/topic-library/modeling-statistics/anova/basics/what-is-anova/. Here, an ANOVA with significance of p =.022 shows a mean of .054 for couples without and of .200 for couples with specific religion indicated – meaning that the means of the two groups are statistically significantly different.

59 *See* ARIZ. REV. STAT. ANN. §§ 25–320(F), 25–501(A) (2015); IND. CODE § 31–16-6–6 (2016).

TABLE 10.10 *Likelihood of Reduction of Child Support for Emancipation in Indiana*[a]

Variable	B	S.E.	Sig.	Exp(B)
Specific religion indicated	.920	.795	.247	2.510
Father's weekly income	.002	.000	.001	1.002
Length of marriage	.040	.037	.000	1.151
Constant	−5.446	.846	.000	.004

[a] Cox & Snell R^2 = .172. Differences reported in this table are statistically insignificant.

be related to requests to reduce or eliminate duties of support, and if so, in which direction.[60]

In Arizona, holding other factors constant, the fact that the parenting plan indicated religious upbringing was significantly (at $p<.05$) and positively related to a motion to reduce or eliminate child support because of emancipation. That is, more religious parents were more likely than nonreligious parents to file for emancipation-related reductions in child support obligations.

In Indiana, as Table 10.10 shows, religious upbringing never reached statistical significance in its relationship to whether a parent would seek to reduce or eliminate child support after the child reached majority, although the direction of the relationship was positive – even after some modifications of the model. One can only speculate why this is: it may be related to more religious parents' identification of child support as a positive relationship, or it may be seen as a particular duty connected with their identity as parents of minors.[61] By contrast, father's weekly income had a weak effect, albeit statistically significant, on the likelihood that the noncustodial parent would seek to change the child support obligation after a child reached adulthood.

III CONNECTIONS TO OTHER RESEARCH

This chapter is confined to divorcing couples with children who consider their religious upbringing. It does not consider the increasing proportion of

60 For example, if the parents were sending the children to private religious schools, as Dwyer, Chapter 8, this volume, discusses, the relationship between seeking religious upbringing and seeking to end support upon emancipation should be positive. It might be negative for more religious couples if noncustodial parents felt an obligation to be the providers of support, whatever the child's age. *See, e.g.*, W. BRADFORD WILCOX, SOFT PATRIARCHS NEW MEN: HOW CHRISTIANITY SHAPES FATHERS AND HUSBANDS (2004).

61 In Arizona, specific religion was correlated at $p<.05$ with enforcement actions for child support. When controls were included, however, statistical significance disappeared.

children whose parents never married; neither does it include same-sex married couples since neither state recognized same-sex marriage in 2008.[62] There may be significant differences in how each group resolves custody matters upon dissolution.[63]

Although the U.S. divorce rate has continued to fall since its peak in 1981 to about what it was in 1970,[64] as long as the birthrate remains constant, the rate of disputes involving children is likely to rise. The rate of marriage has decreased while coupling and childbearing have not, as Weiner shows (Chapter 11, this volume). Indeed, the unwed birthrate has increased dramatically since 1960; by 2010 it was about 40.3%.[65] In the U.S., unmarried couples are less stable than their married counterparts, even when couples

62 Neither state recognized same-sex marriage until October 2014. Baskin v. Bogan, 766 F.3d 648 (7th Cir. 2014); Connolly v. Jeanes, 73 F. Supp. 3d 1094 (D. Ariz. 2014).

Arizona allowed same-sex couples to adopt in 2015 by executive order signed by the Governor, although some gay couples did do step-parent adoptions consonant with Arizona's statutes before 2015. Alia Beard Rau & Yvonne Wingett Sanchez, *Ducey: Arizona Gay Couples Can Again Adopt, Foster Together*, AZCENTRAL (Apr. 22, 2015), www.azcentral.com/story/news/arizona/politics/2015/04/23/arizona-sex-couples-can-adopt-foster-together/26224297/; *Can Gay Couples Adopt in Arizona*, STUART & BLACKWELL, http://stuartandblackwell.com/can-gay-couples-adopt-arizona//. Indiana has allowed same-sex couples to do second parent adoptions since 2003 and to jointly adopt since 2006. *In re* Adoption of M.M.G.C., 785 N.E.2d 267 (Ind. Ct. App. 2003) (second parent adoption); *In re* Infant Girl W., 785 N.E.2d 267 (Ind. App. 2006) (joint adoption). *See generally Legal Recognition of LGBT Families*, NATIONAL CENTER FOR LESBIAN RIGHTS (2016), www.nclrights.org/wp-content/uploads/2013/07/Legal_Recognition_of_LGBT_Families.pdf.

63 *See, e.g.*, Marsha Kline Pruett & J. Herbie DiFonzo, *Closing the Gap: Research, Policy, Practice and Shared Parenting*, 52 FAM. CT. REV. 152, 168 (2014). Pruett and DiFonzo argue as to shared parenting that it is inappropriate to have a presumption that covers all situations when not enough is known to verify that the presumption will benefit almost all children and families. Presumptions appear in the law as a blunt instrument, yet we know very little empirically about how a presumption would apply to same-sex couples, nonbiological parents, never-married partners who had no significant partnership before having a child together, and so on.

64 *See, e.g.*, DANA ROTZ, WHY HAVE DIVORCE RATES FALLEN? THE ROLE OF WOMEN'S AGE AT MARRIAGE (2011), papers.ssrn.com/sol3/papers.cfm?abstract_id=1960017; Betsey Stevenson & Justin Wolfers, *Marriage and Divorce: Changes and Their Driving Forces*, 21 J. ECON. PERSP. 27 (2007); Claire Caine Miller, *The Divorce Surge is Over, But the Myth Lives On*, N.Y. TIMES (Dec. 21, 2014), www.nytimes.com/2014/12/02/upshot/the-divorce-surge-is-over-but-the-myth-lives-on.html.

65 Joyce A. Martin et al., *Births: Final Data for 2010*, 61 NAT'L VITAL STAT. REP. 1, Tbl. C (Aug. 28, 2012), www.cdc.gov/nchs/data/nvsr/nvsr61/nvsr61_01.pdf (showing the birth rates for unmarried women in the U.S. at 40.8% in 2010). *See* Joyce A. Martin, et al., *Births: Final Data for 2015*, 66 NAT'L VITAL STAT. REP. 1, 2 (Jan. 5, 2017), www.cdc.gov/nchs/data/nvsr/nvsr66/nvsr66_01.pdf (showing that "The percentage of births to unmarried women was stable at 40.3%.").

have children.[66] When unmarried parents with children separate, courts still must deal with custody and child support issues should the parents want to seek or enforce an order as to custody or child support – or for that matter, if one parent seeks to collect public assistance.[67] However, many unmarried couples negotiate informal arrangements including visitation and support without court intervention.[68] Some literature suggests that unmarried mothers may sometimes act as gatekeepers, requiring payments or in-kind support before allowing contact.[69] Despite these trends, new federal legislation encouraging voluntary parenting time arrangements when child support duties are established may increase the number of formal agreements over time.[70]

66 *See, e.g.*, Marcia J. Carlson, Sara S. McLanahan, & Jeanne Brooks-Gunn, *Coparenting and Nonresident Fathers' Involvement with Young Children After a Nonmarital Birth*, 45 DEMOGRAPHY 461, 461 (2008).

67 In the U.S., custody rules pertain not only for divorces but also for separating unmarried parents. In practice, far fewer separating unmarried parents currently have formal custody or child support orders. *See, e.g.*, Rebecca M. Ryan, Ariel Kalil, & Kathleen M. Ziol-Guest, *Longitudinal Patterns of Nonresident Fathers' Involvement: The Role of Resources and Relations*, 70 J. MARRIAGE & FAM. 962 (2008).

68 *See, e.g.*, EDIN & NELSON, DOING THE BEST I CAN: FATHERHOOD IN THE INNER CITY, *supra* note 2, at ch. 8 loc. 3616 of 5420 (presenting ethnographic work in which fathers say that good fathers should provide for their children, but first must provide for themselves and the families with whom they live, and then offer their nonresident children some portion of what remains); Lenna Nepomnyashy, *Child Support and Father-Child Contact: Testing Reciprocal Pathways*, 44 DEMOGRAPHY 93, 106 (2007) ("It is very likely that fathers who see their children but do not pay support through the formal system contribute to these children and to their mothers informally."). *See also* Karen Benjamin Guzzo, *Maternal Relationships and Nonresidential Father Visitation of Children Born Outside of Marriage*, 71 J. MARRIAGE & FAM. 632, 643 (2009) (reporting that black fathers were twice as likely to have seen their child at either follow-up interview compared to white fathers); Solangel Maldonado, *Deadbeat or Deadbroke: Redefining Child Support for Poor Fathers*, 39 U.C. DAVIS L. REV. 991, 995 (2006) (observing that in-kind child support is particularly evident among impoverished black fathers).

69 *See, e.g.*, Daniela Del Boca & Rocio Ribero, *The Effect of Child Support Policies on Visitations and Transfers*, 91 AM. ECON. REV. 130 (2001); Guzzo, *supra* note 70, at 639–43, Tbls. 2 & 3 (showing the association between a father's visitation and mother's subsequent relationships; fathers were also less likely to visit when they had different co-residential partners).

70 Preventing Sex Trafficking and Strengthening Families Act, Pub. L. No. 113–183, § 303, 128 Stat. 1919 (2014). For commentary, *compare* Jessica Pearson, *Establishing Parenting Time in Child Support Cases: New Opportunities and Challenges*, 53 FAM. CT. REV. 246 (2015) (suggesting strengths and problems), *with* Stacy Brustin & Lisa Vollendorf Maskin, *Paved with Good Intentions: Unintended Consequences of Federal Proposals to Integrate Child Support and Parenting Time*, 48 IND. L. REV. 803 (2015) (giving a more critical evaluation suggesting the new federal law may impede unmarried mothers from accepting financial support for families designed to help them achieve self-sufficiency, known as Temporary Assistance to Needy Families, because of concern about contact with fathers).

Largely in conjunction with the Fragile Families study of unmarried parents, a number of authors recently have written about unmarried parents, most of whom are financially disadvantaged. Professor Susan Sullivan, in her 2012 ethnographic study,[71] notes that many of the unmarried mothers she interviewed remained intensely personally religious, but they had largely eschewed formal organized religion and therefore church attendance. They sometimes reported to her that their move away from formal religion was because they felt judged or otherwise unwelcome at the churches they formally attended.[72]

Using the Fragile Families study, researcher Richard Petts found that when poor single mothers did attend religious services frequently, their children were less likely to display problem behaviors, and the mothers were more likely to be more involved with them and to have reduced parenting stress.[73] In another work,[74] Petts noted that the fathers in the Fragile Families study increased their religious participation in the year following the birth of their children, and most maintained the higher rate of religious participation throughout the early years of their child's life.[75]

Natalie Sheets, working with data from the Pew Forum on Religion and Public Life 2007 Religious Landscape Survey,[76] found weak differences between married mothers and single mothers in church attendance and becoming members of a congregation. Married mothers attended religious services once a week 6% more often than did single mothers but were only 2% more likely to be members of a congregation.[77] Single mothers indicated they "never" participated in social activities at their house of worship more often than did married mothers, and sent their children to Sunday school less often, but were equally likely to participate in prayer groups. Black mothers were more likely than other mothers to pray and read Scripture with their children outside religious services and to be members of a house of worship than other mothers.[78]

Data limitations prevent the extension of this literature appreciably by the findings presented in this chapter. In neither state were there enough

[71] Sullivan, *supra* note 2, chap.6.

[72] *Id.* at 156–57. This has also been shown to be true of men. *See* EDIN & NELSON, *supra* note 2 ("[T]ies to organized religion are rare among our men.").

[73] Richard J. Petts, *Single Mothers' Religious Participation and Early Childhood Behavior*, 74 J. MARRIAGE & FAM. 251, 262–63, Tbls. 3 & 4 (2012).

[74] Richard J. Petts, *Fathers' Religious Involvement and Early Childhood Behavior* (Fragile Families, Working Paper No. 2009–22-FF).

[75] *Id.* at 17.

[76] Natalie J. Sheets, Single Mothers and Religiosity (May 2014) (unpublished M.A. thesis, East Tennessee State University), dc.etsu.edu/etd/2356/.

[77] *Id.* at 17–18, Tbl. 1.

[78] *Id.* at 38–39, Tbl. 9.

unmarried parent custody actions or actions brought independent of marital dissolution to do much comparative work on indications of religiosity. In Arizona, where statutes required consideration of religious training – or lack thereof – in parenting plans, 43 cases involved unmarried parents seeking custody orders, and just under 35% of these indicated a general religious upbringing. Just under 10% specified a denomination. This indicates almost as much desire among these parents as among married couples to speak to the religious upbringing of their children. Among married couples, 39.6% specified a general religious upbringing; 9.1% specified a particular denomination or religion. Indiana has no requirement in its law about addressing this subject, making religious upbringing the province of the custodial parent absent agreement. There, of the ten custody cases, none involved any indication of religious upbringing.

CONCLUSION

Divorcing couples specifying religious upbringing in their parenting plans tended to be more affluent, come from lengthier marriages, settle cases more often before litigation, share custody more equally, and have less domestic violence reported either prior to or following divorce. Their divorces also seemed to be precipitated by serious marital breaches more often – their divorce petitions were more likely to indicate substance abuse or mental illness. These families were more likely to seek reductions of the noncustodial parent's time with the children in the years after a final decree, particularly when fathers were relatively poorer. The noncustodial (payor) parent was more likely to seek relief because one of the children reached emancipation age. In general, while the pattern is complex, these parents seem like good and thoughtful parents, divorcing only when they needed to and minimizing conflict that the children would see or experience.

11

Regulating the Relationship Between Parents
Moving Beyond Marriage and Custody Law

Merle H. Weiner

Philip H. Knight Professor of Law, and Faculty Director, Domestic Violence Clinic, University of Oregon School of Law

American family law does not impose legal obligations between individuals merely because they are parents of the same child. Consequently, large numbers of children born outside of marriage have parents with no family law structure at all regulating the parents' relationships to each other. The absence of legal obligations between parents triggered by parenthood, rather than marriage, creates problems. Many people reproduce without considering their ability to share parenting responsibilities with the other parent over the long term – that is, to have the sort of "team mentality" that benefits children. Also, during the romantic relationship parents do not necessarily coparent supportively or try to keep their romantic relationship going for their children's sake. Without a strong connection to each other grounded in parenthood itself, parents often do not act as a team devoted to their child's well-being after their romantic relationships end.[1] Children in dissolved families then face a host of disadvantages, including less contact with one of their parents, more poverty, and less social mobility.[2]

The absence of a legal structure triggered by parenthood affects children born into marital relationships too. After all, marriage frequently ends and children of divorce can be disadvantaged by their parents' refusal to act as a team.[3] These children, like their non-marital counterparts, often experience a range of hardships.[4] If spouses with children had an additional legal structure

[1] *See infra* Section I.

[2] Leonard M. Lopoo & Thomas DeLeire, *Family Structure and the Economic Wellbeing of Children in Youth and Adulthood*, 43 Soc. Sci. Res. 30 (2014); Sara McLanahan & Gary Sandefur, Growing Up with a Single Parent. What Hurts, What Helps (1994).

[3] *See infra* Section I.

[4] Lopoo & DeLeire, *supra* note 2; McLanahan & Sandefur, *supra* note 2.

grounded in parenthood itself – one that continued even after divorce and that had relevance also during the marriage – these couples and their children might also benefit.

Even if marriage by itself were sufficient to govern and guide relationships of parents who are also spouses, marriage is likely to apply to fewer couples in the future if demographic shifts away from membership in organized religion continue.[5] Religious couples are more likely to marry when pregnant than to cohabit,[6] as Brinig shows (Chapter 10, this volume). As a result, there may be an increase in the fraction of children whose parents lack meaningful social roles to govern their *inter se* relationships and lack legal remedies to address injustices at their breakups.[7]

The law governing child custody is not an adequate substitute for a legal structure that would guide the relationships of parents with a child in common.[8] While custody law can ensure children spend time with both parents, it cannot meaningfully foster the type of shared parenting that really benefits children. A supportive parenting relationship before breakup is the best predictor of one after, yet the substantive law of custody does little to encourage supportive behavior during the parents' romantic relationship. True, modern procedures accompanying custody adjudications encourage parents to act cooperatively after the romantic relationship ends, but the procedures often are "too little, too late" or unavailable to some couples. While advocates of joint custody claim it can provide the necessary framework for parental cooperation after breakup, this chapter argues that such a claim is premature. In fact, ordering joint custody for parents who lack a supportive relationship can prove extremely problematic.

5 *New Pew Research Center Study Examines America's Changing Religious Landscape*, PEW RES. CTR. (May 12, 2015), www.pewforum.org/2015/05/12/new-pew-research-center-study-examines-americas-changing-religious-landscape/ (noting that the percentage of Americans identifying as Christians dropped 8.2 percentage points in seven years to 70.6%, while those identifying as unaffiliated rose 6.7 percentage points to 22.8% and those identifying with non-Christian faiths rose 1.2% to 5.9%).

6 Jeremy E. Uecker & Charles E. Stokes, *Early Marriage in the United States*, 70 J. MARR. & FAM. 835 (2008); Evelyn Lehrer, *Religion as a Determinant of Economic and Demographic Behavior in the United States*, 30 POPULATION & DEVELOPMENT REV. 707 (2004); Paul H. DeGraff & Mattije Kalmijn, *Alternative Routes in the Remarriage Market*, 81 SOC. FORCES 1459, 1466, 1488–89 (2003) (suggesting that religiosity pulls two ways, since people are less apt to cohabit if they self-identify as religious and, therefore, more likely to marry, while prior studies, though inconsistent, tend to suggest Catholics are less apt to remarry).

7 *See* Hong, Chapter 14, this volume, for an argument that *Obergefell v. Hodges* creates an affirmative duty to support families despite older doctrines of family autonomy that shielded marital families from state intervention.

8 *See infra* Section II.B.

This gap in the law calls out for a new approach: a legal status governing all relationships of two people who share a child in common that would continue regardless of the status of the couple's romantic relationship.[9] This status would automatically impose direct legal obligations between the parents, typically upon the birth or adoption of a child[10] – that is, obligations toward each other. A new social role created by the status, that of "parent-partner," would help couples see themselves as "team child." Specifically, it would encourage people to do four things: (1) reproduce only with persons with whom they can have a strong, supportive relationship, (2) work together from the get-go to ensure the best life possible for their child, (3) keep their parent-partnership strong and supportive, and (4) maintain this orientation even after their romantic relationship breaks up. This new status should lead more couples to elect joint custody and thereby keep children connected to both parents, without the harmful effects of "strong" joint custody laws.[11]

While lawmakers could create such a legal structure without broad input, they should instead involve stakeholders in the process, including religious organizations. Such inclusiveness would allow lawmakers to benefit from the insights of faith communities, as Adams explains (Chapter 21, this volume), and to receive these communities' assistance during the law reform process. Members of organized religions care about families and family law, as illustrated by the work of the Church of Jesus Christ of Latter-day Saints. That church has sought protections against discrimination in hiring and housing for the LGBT community and has strenuously (if misguidedly) opposed the Equal Rights Amendment and same-sex marriage, as Eskridge shows (Chapter 23, this volume). These examples underline that religious stakeholders engage the political process to influence the legal regulation of the family.[12]

[9] *See infra* Section III.

[10] The status would apply to "legal" parents. Typically legal parenthood is established for marital children though presumptions. For non-marital children, the father typically establishes legal parenthood by signing and filing a voluntary acknowledgment of paternity, although he may become the legal father through a paternity action or through presumptions.

[11] "Strong" laws could come in different forms but would include laws that do not require the parents' agreement, presume joint physical custody is in a child's best interest, and make the parent in opposition rebut the presumption by showing the arrangement would endanger the child's physical health or significantly impair the child's emotional development. *See, e.g.*, Colorado Senate Bill 15-129, 70th Gen. Assembly (2015). *See also* text accompanying notes 91–95, *infra*.

In this volume, Wilson (Chapter 16) documents a growing chorus of voices advocating for a smaller role for government in marriage post-*Obergefell*, something Wilson fears will undercut the protective features of marriage. Here, changing the legal relationship of parents, whether married or unmarried, should shore up families, as Section II explains.

[12] *See* Eskridge, Chapter 23, this volume and Adams, Chapter 21, this volume (discussing the Church of Jesus Christ of Latter-day Saints' support of legislation protecting LGBT rights).

The support of religious organizations would also enhance the effectiveness of any new status. After all, "socially progressive to conservative religious groups across the globe offer people spiritual guidance about their decisions about dating, cohabitation, marriage, sexuality in relationships, childbearing, coparenting, and divorce."[13] Religion in fact appears to influence the formation of family relationships, the maintenance of them, and the changes to them when they become distressed.[14] For example, spiritual intimacy can positively impact the quality of the parents' relationship at the transition to parenthood – a time when relationships between parents often become strained.[15] The mechanisms that permit religion's influence are not totally understood, and more research is needed,[16] but they appear to be personal spirituality, the sanctification of the relationship, and the effects of relationships formed within religious communities (such as access to social resources).[17] Consequently, religious organizations could play a critical role after the enactment of a new status by reinforcing for their members the importance of a new social role and the expectations attached to it, and thereby contributing to its success.

Given the potential power of faith communities to influence people's experience of family, they must be seen as partners in any attempt to achieve legal and social change. Theologians might explore how religious doctrine supports a parent-partner status. In the Lutheran tradition, for example,

> [T]here isn't any scripture ... that talk[s] about the relationship between parents ... [yet Jesus] called attention to children, telling people they must serve them ... If two people create a child (by birth or adoption, etc.) they have created a new relationship and to break that relationship or dishonor the relationship between the child and its other parent, would truly be the

13 Annette Mahoney & Annmarie Cano, *Introduction to the Special Section on Religion and Spirituality in Family Life: Delving into Relational Spirituality for Couples*, 28 J. Fam. Psych. 583, 583 (2014).

14 Annette Mahoney, *Religion in Families, 1999–2009: A Relational Spirituality Framework*, 72 J. Marr. & Fam. 805, 807 (2010); W. Matthew Henderson et al., *The Role of Religion in Parenting Satisfaction and Parenting Stress Among Young Parents*, 57 The Sociological Q. 675, 675–79 (2016); Mark G. Lyon et al., *Influences on Father Involvement: Testing for Unique Contributions of Religion*, 25 J. Child Fam. Stud. 3247 (2016).

15 Katherine G. Kusner et al., *Sanctification of Marriage and Spiritual Intimacy Predicting Observed Marital Interactions Across the Transition to Parenthood*, 28 J. Fam. Psych. 604 (2014).

16 Mahoney & Cano, *supra* note 13, at 584 ("[M]ore research is needed on specific, malleable spiritual variables centered on relationships that may motivate couples to form and maintain well-functioning unions.").

17 *Id.*; Henderson, *supra* note 14, at 679.

> definition of sin . . . (sin being broken relationships, either between God and self; or self and others).[18]

Certainly religious institutions already support many of the critical ideas that the law does not adequately promote at present, but that a parent-partner status would: "Diverse faith traditions agree that family members should treat one another in ways that maintain the quality and stability of the family relationships they create. Endorsement of virtues, such as being loving, unselfish, committed, and ethical, cut across religions."[19] Because a legal status predicated on parenthood would promote the same values that religious organizations already endorse, they might embrace the creation of a legal status to govern the relationships of parents with a child in common. As described next, such a status would benefit children.

I PARENTS OFTEN DO NOT ACT LIKE A CHILD-FOCUSED TEAM AFTER BREAKING UP

Over the past sixty-five years or so, family demographics in the United States have changed dramatically. In 1960, 5% of children were born out of wedlock.[20] In 2016, that number was approximately 40%.[21] In 1960, the divorce rate was 2.2 divorces per 1000 population.[22] In 2014, the divorce rate was 3.2 divorces per 1000 population,[23] and it is much higher at some educational levels, and in some locations.[24] Non-marital parents break up at an even higher

18 Email from Pastor Sarah Schaffner, Pastor at Bethesda Lutheran Church to author (Dec. 9, 2015) (on file with author) (adding "[F]rom a Christian perspective . . . parents are forever to be connected following the birth of a child, because God created us for whole, life-giving relationships. We were created in God's image, and in God's essence, God is a God of relationships (we believe in the Trinity, three different expressions of the one God) . . . which means, we were created to be in relationships.").

19 Mahoney, *supra* note 14, at 813.

20 Carmen Solomon-Fears, Congressional Research Service, *Nonmarital Births: An Overview*, 13 Tbl. 1 (July 30, 2014).

21 *Births, Provisional Data for 2016*, CTRS. FOR DISEASE CONTROL & PREVENTION, Vital Statistics Rapid Release, www.cdc.gov/nchs/data/vsrr/report002.pdf.

22 Alexander A. Broel-Plateris, *Divorces – Analysis and Summary*, in III VITAL STATISTICS OF THE UNITED STATES 1960, at 33 (U.S. Dep't of Health, Education and Welfare 1964), www.cdc.gov/nchs/data/vsus/mgdv60_3.pdf.

23 *National Marriage and Divorce Rate Trends*, CTRS. FOR DISEASE CONTROL & PREVENTION, www.cdc.gov/nchs/nvss/marriage_divorce_tables.htm.

24 *See* Bureau of Labor Statistics, *Marriage and Divorce: Patterns by Gender, Race, and Educational Attainment*, MONTHLY LABOR REV. (Oct. 2013), www.bls.gov/opub/mlr/2013/article/marriage-and-divorce-patterns-by-gender-race-and-educational-attainment.htm (noting that for baby boomers, "over half of marriages of those who did not complete high

rate than marital parents.[25] Part of the explanation may be tied to the increase in interfaith relationships. While many people share the same faith with their partner, Americans increasingly marry across faith traditions.[26] Interfaith relationships are even more prevalent among unmarried couples.[27] Interfaith relationships tend to be less durable than marriages where both spouses share the same faith.[28] A couple's mismatch on religion may increase fighting, as one example.[29]

After parents end their romantic relationships, they frequently treat each other in ways that undermine their children's interests. Most parents who split are not "perfect pals," a term coined by family therapist Constance Ahrons.[30] The Stanford Custody Project found that only one-quarter of parents in their sample were cooperative eighteen months after separation.[31] One-third were very

school . . . ended in divorce compared with approximately 30 percent of marriages of college graduates"); *Tennessee County has Divorce Rate of Almost 90 Percent*, WNCN (Sept. 25, 2015), wncn.com/2015/09/25/tennessee-county-has-divorce-rate-of-almost-90-percent/ (reporting a divorce rate of 90%).

25 The Fragile Families and Child Wellbeing study found that approximately 50% of the unwed mothers in the Fragile Families study were cohabiting with the fathers at the time of birth, 33% were romantically involved, and 8% were friends. Only 9% had little or no contact. Sara McLanahan, Irwin Garfinkel, & Ronald B. Mincy, *Fragile Families, Welfare Reform and Marriage*, 10 THE BROOKINGS INST. 2 (2001). By a child's fifth birthday, only 39% of all couples were still romantically involved. Bendheim Thoman Ctr. for Research on Child Well-Being, *Parents' Relationship Status Five Years After a Non-marital Birth*, 39 FRAGILE FAMILIES RESEARCH BRIEF 1 (June 2007) (studying married, cohabitating, and dating couples).

26 Pew Research Center, *Religious Switching and Intermarriage*, in AMERICA'S CHANGING RELIGIOUS LANDSCAPE (2015), www.pewforum.org/2015/05/12/chapter-2-religious-switching-and-intermarriage/#interfaith-marriage-commonplace.

27 *Id.*

28 *See id.; see also* Darren E. Sherkat, *Religious Intermarriage in the United States: Trends, Patterns, and Predictors*, 33 SOC. SCI. RES. 606, 622 (2004), www.sciencedirect.com/science/article/pii/S0049089X0300084X ("Religious diversity within families has been shown to create a number of difficulties for marriages, leading to decreased marital satisfaction, increased spousal conflict, higher rates of divorce, and increases in domestic violence.").

29 Samuel L. Perry, *A Match in Heaven? Religion-Based Marriage Decisions, Marital Quality, and the Moderating Effects of Spouse's Religious Commitment*, 123 SOC. INDICATORS RES. 203, 223 (2015) (analyzing data from the 2006 Portraits of American Life Study and finding that "once respondents' personal religious affiliations, practices, beliefs, and other socio-demographic factors are controlled for, religion's influence on the marriage decision seems to relate to marital quality as an indicator of expectations that may either be (a) met by a religiously-committed spouse with attendant returns to marital quality, or (b) unmet by an irreligious spouse and associated with negative marital experiences").

30 Constance R. Ahrons, *Family Ties After Divorce: Long-Term Implications for Children*, 46 FAM. PROCESS 53, 58 (2007) (noting only 2.55% of ex-spouses were "perfect pals," or "very friendly ex-spouse couples" at the time of divorce, but that number increased to 10% twenty years after the divorce).

31 *See* ELEANOR E. MACCOBY & ROBERT H. MNOOKIN, DIVIDING THE CHILD: SOCIAL AND LEGAL DILEMMAS OF CUSTODY 248, 292 Tbl. 9.14 (1991).

conflicted, with minimal support and lots of hostility. Most parents practiced "disengaged" parenting by three years after separation. The Binuclear Family Study, which assessed the well-being of divorced families four times over a twenty-year period starting in 1979, found that less than half of the divorced parents could coparent effectively at the time of divorce.[32] Two well-respected researchers said, "[*M*]*any* former spouses . . . act as competitors, frequently creating situations in which one parent's success occurs at the expense of the other, rather than fostering win-win situations in which both parties benefit."[33]

A manifestation of this sad reality is the speed at which the smiling divorce "selfie" taken by Chris and Shannon Neuman went viral late in 2015. Shannon explained that she and her ex took the selfie because they had "respectfully, thoughtfully, and honourably ended [the] marriage in a way that will allow us to go forward as parenting-partners for our children."[34] Similarly, the *New York Times* undoubtedly published Lara Bazelon's *From Divorce, A Fractured Beauty* in 2015 because it described an oddity: a divorced couple vacationing together with their children.[35]

Many unmarried couples have suboptimal relationships after they break up, too. In Minnesota, "most" unmarried parents responding to a 2007 survey administered during their court proceedings "characterized their relationship with their coparents as 'less than warm.'"[36] Researcher Maureen Waller found that parents in fragile families frequently had a disengaged, conflicted, or mixed (high conflict, but cooperative parenting) style by the child's third

[32] Ahrons, *supra* note 30, at 58; Constance Ahrons, *Binuclear Family Study*, 1979-2000, HARVARD DATAVERSE (2007), dataverse.harvard.edu/dataset.xhtml?persistentId=hdl:1902.1/01921 (describing study methodology). *See also* Jessica Pearson & Nancy Theonnes, *Custody After Divorce: Demographic and Attitudinal Patterns*, 60 AMER. J. ORTHOPSYCHIAT. 233, 237 (1990) (finding that 30% of parents with sole custody, or joint legal custody combined with residential custody with the mother, said that it was either "impossible" to cooperate with an ex-spouse or it was something they "no longer attempted" three years after the divorce). These now-dated studies are still cited by professionals when they describe coparenting today. *See, e.g.*, Claire M. Kamp Dush, Letitia E. Kotila, & Sarah J. Schoope-Sullivan, *Predictors of Supportive Coparenting After Relationship Dissolution Among At-Risk Parents*, 25 J. OF FAM. PSYCHOL. 356, 357 (2011).

[33] Marsha Kline Pruett & Tracy Donsky, *Coparenting After Divorce: Paving Pathways for Parental Cooperation, Conflict Resolution and Redefined Family Roles, in* JAMES MCHALE AND KRISTIN LINDAHL, COPARENTING: A CONCEPTUAL AND CLINICAL EXAMINATION OF FAMILY SYSTEMS 231, 235 (2011) (emphasis added).

[34] Tess Koman, *These Parents Took a Smiling "Divorce Selfie" to Show Their Kids They'll Never Have to Choose*, COSMOPOLITAN (Sept. 2, 2015), www.cosmopolitan.com/sex-love/news/a45814/neumans-divorce-selfie/.

[35] Lara Bazelon, *From Divorce, A Fractured Beauty*, N.Y. TIMES (Sept. 24, 2015), www.nytimes.com/2015/09/27/fashion/from-divorce-a-fractured-beauty.html.

[36] Mary S. Marczak et al., *Co-Parent Court: A Problem Solving Court Model for Supporting Unmarried Parents*, 53 FAM. CT. REV. 267, 268 (2015).

birthday.[37] In the Fragile Families and Child Wellbeing study, three-fourths of the mothers who were not romantically involved with the fathers five years after their children's births described their relationships with the fathers as "fair, poor, or non-existent."[38] Only 12% called the quality of their relationship very good or excellent.[39]

Evidence from Australia suggests that parental relationships do not necessarily improve over time but can move in the opposite direction.[40] Twenty-six percent of parents who described their relationships after dissolution as positive when first surveyed reported five year later that they had become distant or negative. Almost 62% of couples whose relationships were distant at first survey stayed distant or grew worse over the next five years. Sixty-seven percent of parents with considerable conflict and fear at first survey remained distant or negative five years later. In addition, almost 60% of all mothers and fathers reported *less* frequent communication over a five-year period.[41]

The absence of a friendly, supportive relationship between parents after breakup harms their children. Many children lose contact with one parent, typically their fathers. In the Fragile Families population, only 43% of the children whose parents were no longer romantic had seen their fathers in the past month, and the likelihood of contact depended upon the nature of the parents' relationship.[42] Seventy-four percent of the fathers reported seeing the child in the past month if the parents remained friends, compared with only 17% of fathers who had no relationship at all with the mother.[43]

[37] Maureen Waller, *Cooperation, Conflict, or Disengagement? Coparenting Styles and Father Involvement in Fragile Families*, 51 FAM. PROCESS 325 (2012). Parents who are disengaged from each other have "limited interactions with each other, low levels of conflict around raising the child, but also low levels of mutual cooperation and support." *Id.* at 327 (citing a typology developed by Maccoby and Mnookin). Parents who are conflicted "remained engaged as coparents in highly antagonistic relationships." *Id.*

[38] FRAGILE FAMILIES RESEARCH BRIEF, *supra* note 25, at 2.

[39] *Id.*

[40] *See* Australian Institute of Family Studies, POST-SEPARATION PARENTING, PROPERTY, AND RELATIONSHIP DYNAMICS AFTER FIVE YEARS, at 15, Tbl. 3.1 (2014).

[41] *Id.* at 18–19 Fig. 3.3.

[42] FRAGILE FAMILIES RESEARCH BRIEF, *supra* note 25, at 2 Tbl. 1 (reporting results of five-year follow-up).

[43] *Id.* at 2. The rate of successful coparenting outside of a romantic relationship may differ by the parents' race, but nonresident non-marital fathers of all races arguably have too little contact with their children, especially over time. In one article, it was reported that black fathers saw their nine-year-old children 5.93 days per month, White fathers saw them 7.15 days per month, and Hispanic fathers saw them 2.67 days per month. Calvina Z. Ellerbe, Jerrett B. Jones, and Marcia J. Carlson, *Non-Resident Fathers' Involvement after a Nonmarital Birth: Exploring Differences by Race/Ethnicity*, FRAGILE FAMILIES WORKING PAPER (Aug. 2014), crcw .princeton.edu/workingpapers/WP14-07-FF.pdf.

Even children who maintain contact with both parents can be disadvantaged if their parents lack a supportive relationship. Children can be harmed by exposure to their parents' conflict,[44] or from their parents' uncoordinated interactions.[45] "Parallel parenting" – an arrangement that encourages the parents to disengage from each other while parenting – is now the most popular form of coparenting, even among cooperative parents.[46] While parallel parenting may work well for highly conflicted couples, it is not ideal for parents who are capable of having a supportive coparenting relationship. The sum of disengaged parents' efforts never becomes more than the individual parts. Parallel parenting can also burden children, especially when parental rules conflict.[47] In addition, parallel parenting can foster misperceptions between the parents, as parents "misperceive, misreport, and misinterpret the motive, and actions of each other," causing hostility and resentment.[48] The unsatisfying nature of parallel parenting is captured by the fact that those who parallel parent "are at particular risk" of disengaging over time "and becom[ing] absent fathers."[49]

Parents who have poor relationships with each other typically fail to exhibit the type of coparenting flexibility that is good for children, especially after a parent re-partners.[50] For example, a supportive coparent would allow the

44 Marsha Kline Pruett & Carrie Barker, *Joint Custody: A Judicious Choice for Families – But How, When, and Why? in* The Scientific Basis of Child Custody Decisions 417, 427 (2d ed. Robert M. Glatzer-Levy et al., eds., 2009) (noting that studies consistently find that parental conflict has deleterious effects for children). *But see* John H. Grych & Frank D. Fincham, *Marital Conflict and Children's Adjustment: A Cognitive-Contextual Framework*, 108 Psychol. Bull. 267, 267 (1990) (suggesting conflict is not always harmful).

45 Kari Adamsons & Kay Pasley, *Coparenting Following Divorce and Relationship Dissolution, in* Handbook of Divorce and Relationship Dissolution 241, 251 (Mark A. Fine & John H. Harvey, eds. 2006). *See also* Frank F. Furstenberg Jr. & Andrew J. Cherlin, Divided Families: What Happens to Children When Parents Part 17 (1991); Mary F. Whiteside, *The Parental Alliance Following Divorce: An Overview*, 24 J. Marital & Fam. Therapy 4, 17 (1998).

46 Adamsons & Pasley, *supra* note 45, at 251.

47 Furstenberg & Cherlin, *supra* note 45, at 41. *See also* Elizabeth Marquardt, *Between Two Worlds: The Inner Lives of Children of Divorce* (2005).

48 Furstenberg & Cherlin, *supra* note 45, at 41.

49 James P. McHale, *Shared Child Rearing in Nuclear, Fragile, and Kinship Family Systems: Evolution, Dilemmas, and Promise of a Coparenting Framework, in* Strengthening Couple Relationships for Optimal Child Development: Lessons from Research and Intervention 77, 83 (Marc S. Schulz et al., eds. 2010).

50 Liz Trinder, *Maternal Gate Closing and Gate Opening in Postdivorce Families*, 29 J. Fam. Issues 1298, 1320-21 (2008); Adamsons & Pasley, *supra* note 45, at 254 (citing studies); Maccoby & Mnookin, *supra* note 31, at 245. Re-partnering can also intensify parallel parenting. Furstenberg & Cherlin, *supra* note 45, at 41. *See generally* Carey E. Cooper et al., *Mothers' Partnership Instability and Coparenting Among Fragile Families*, 96 Social

child to attend a special event with the other parent even though the activity fell outside of normal visitation hours. While court orders (and their enforcement) can stop "gate closing,"[51] which "inhibit[s] parental involvement,"[52] court orders cannot require "gate opening." After all, the inflexible parent is typically complying with the court order. Yet the failure to be generous to the other parent can still cause the other parent to become hostile and disengaged.[53]

Parents with unsupportive relationships also find themselves more stressed and parenting less effectively.[54] They fail to use each other as a safety net; that is, they do not call each other to step in and take over when help is needed.[55] Also, such couples rarely work together to minimize economic disadvantages to their children from the breakup.[56] They do not pool resources, coordinate to achieve economies of scale, help each other take advantage of opportunities that will eventually inure to their child's benefit, or jointly build social capital in their child.[57] Parents typically pay less child support if they dislike the other parent.[58]

SCIENCE Q. 1103 (2015); Julia S. Goldberg & Marcia Carlson, *Patterns & Predictors of Coparenting After Unmarried Parents Part*, 29 J. FAM. PSYCHOLOGY 416, 424 (2015).

51 A court order will not always stop gate closing, however. *Cf.* Richard Neely, *The Primary Caretaker Parent Rule: Child Custody and the Dynamics of Greed*, 3 YALE L. & POL'Y REV. 168, 185 (1984) ("Mature parents can make a bad court order work superbly; immature parents can – and usually will – make even the best court order useless.").

52 Trinder, *supra* note 50, at 1299.

53 *See* Debra A. Madden-Derdich & Stacie A. Leonard, *Shared Experiences, Unique Realities: Formerly Married Mothers' and Fathers' Perceptions of Parenting and Custody After Divorce*, 51 FAM. REL. 37, 42 (2002); SANFORD L. BRAVER & DIANNE O'CONNELL, DIVORCED DADS: SHATTERING THE MYTHS 158, 175, 179 (1998).

54 *Cf.* Pearson & Theonnes, *supra* note 32, at 238–39 (noting that more parents without joint physical custody than those with it agreed with the statement, "I often feel overwhelmed by the amount of time and energy my children require"); Robert Bauserman, A *Meta-analysis of Parental Satisfaction, Adjustment, and Conflict in Joint Custody and Sole Custody Following Divorce*, 53 J. OF DIVORCE & REMARRIAGE 464, 477 (2012) (noting that in six studies mothers with joint custody "felt less parenting stress and burden than" mothers with sole custody).

55 James P. McHale & Karina Irace, *Coparenting in Diverse Family Systems, in* COPARENTING: A CONCEPTUAL AND CLINICAL EXAMINATION OF FAMILY SYSTEMS 15, 31–32 (James P. McHale & Kristin M. Lindahl, eds., 2011).

56 Robert I. Lerman, *Capabilities and Contributions of Unwed Fathers*, 20 FUTURE OF CHILDREN 79 (Fall 2010) ("[A]n improved relationship between parents is likely to increase fathers' contributions of money and time, thereby improving the capacity of parents to raise healthy children.").

57 For the importance of joint parental effort for building children's social capital, *see* Shelly Lundberg and Robert A. Pollak, *The Evolving Role of Marriage: 1950-2010*, 25 FUTURE OF CHILDREN 29 (2015).

58 *See* Lerman, *supra* note 56, at 64–65 (explaining that low-income unwed fathers who lose touch with their children and are disengaged from the mothers tend to pay less support, with "one-half to two-thirds of unwed fathers provid[ing] little or no financial support to their children"). Only 46% of parents due child support receive the entire amount. Almost 26%

In 2013, the Association of Family and Conciliation Courts sponsored an interdisciplinary think tank on shared custody, consisting of thirty-two family law experts from a wide range of disciplines, and noted the importance of mutual support. The group's first "Consensus Point" stated:

> Parents who collaborate in childrearing have a positive effect on their children's development and well-being. Parents who engage in protracted and/or severe conflict that includes rejecting or undermining the other parent have a negative impact. The potential for shared parenting is present for children regardless of the family structure in which they live, and represents a key protective factor in (a) helping children adjust to separation and divorce and (b) establishing an ongoing healthy family environment in which to rear children and facilitate high-quality parenting.[59]

As Section II shows, despite the importance of supportive parenting for children, the law does little to encourage it.

II MARRIAGE AND CUSTODY LAWS DO NOT ENCOURAGE SUPPORTIVE PARENTING

In 2015, Professor Marsha Garrison astutely noted that it is a "pressing issue" to determine

> how to maximize the chances that children will have the love, care and support of both parents; family law describes the legal grounds for divorce and provides rules for allocating the economic support and residential care of children, but it offers no guidance at all on whether and how to help parents achieve high-quality relationships that are less prone to separation or on how to cooperate effectively when separation does occur.[60]

Neither does the law encourage couples at an earlier juncture, such as the outset of the relationship or before having unprotected sex, to assess whether a potential mate would make a supportive coparent over the long term.

receive no payment. Divorced custodial parents tend to receive more than never married custodial parents. *See* Timothy Grail, *Custodial Mothers and Fathers and Their Child Support: 2013*, CURRENT POPULATION REPORTS 1, 3, 10 (Jan. 2016), www.census.gov/content/dam/Census/library/publications/2016/demo/P60-255.pdf.

59 Marsha Kline Pruett and J. Herbie DiFonzo, *Closing the Gap: Research, Policy, Practice and Shared Parenting: AFCC Think Tank Final Report*, 52 FAM. CT. REV. 152, 160 (2014).

60 Marsha Garrison, *President's Message*, INTERNATIONAL SOCIETY OF FAMILY LAW NEWSLETTER 1 (Fall 2015).

A Laws Governing the Parents' Relationship to Each Other

Marriage has been the primary legal structure that guides parents' *inter se* relationships, but marriage today seems insufficient for that task. Many children are born outside of marriage.[61] Moreover, marriage by itself does not promote a healthy and supportive coparenting relationship throughout a child's minority. Marriage does not even require a commitment to family, as it did historically.[62] Marriage today is about personal fulfillment and easy exit.[63] Most people do not think children make the parents' breakup less of an option.[64] Tellingly, married parents themselves usually cannot identify how the birth or adoption of their child changes their legal relationship to each other.

Nor are unmarried couples placed in a new legal or social role by virtue of their children's births. Even unwed parents who cohabit characterize their relationships as having "flexibility in roles and expectations," allowing easy exit, and lacking formal commitment.[65]

No law encourages parents who are in a romantic relationship, whether married or not, to be supportive coparents from the get-go, to maintain that orientation throughout their children's minority, and to engage in activities that will help their coparenting relationship succeed, such as hands-on parenting during the relationship and taking relationship classes before or shortly after becoming parents.[66] Hands-on, supportive coparenting during the romantic relationship, for example, makes it less likely that a couple will end their romantic relationship,[67] and more likely that they will embrace supportive coparenting if

[61] Robin Fretwell Wilson, *From Moynihan to Murphy Brown*, LAW & LIBERTY (Mar. 10, 2015), www.libertylawsite.org/liberty-forum/from-moynihan-to-murphy-brown/#sthash.uPZU5DmC.dpuf.

[62] Paul R. Amato, *Institutional, Companionate, and Individualistic Marriage*, *in* MARRIAGE AT THE CROSSROADS 107, 108–09, 119–20 (Marsha Garrison & Elizabeth S. Scott, eds., 2012).

[63] See Hong, Chapter 14, this volume, for a review of how marriage's purposes have shifted over time.

[64] PAUL TAYLOR, CARY FUNK, & APRIL CLARK, AS MARRIAGE AND PARENTHOOD DRIFT APART, PUBLIC IS CONCERNED ABOUT SOCIETAL IMPACT 1, 10 (2007) (about two-thirds of people surveyed said they believe divorce is the best option for children and adults if the married parents are unhappy).

[65] Joanna M. Reed, *Not Crossing the "Extra Line": How Cohabitors with Children View Their Unions*, 68 J. MARR. & FAM. 1117, 1127 (2006).

[66] *Cf.* James McHale, Maureen R. Waller, & Jessica Pearson, *Coparenting Interventions for Fragile Families: What Do We Know and Where Do We Need to Go Next*, 51 FAM. PROCESS 284, 302 (2012) (mentioning the importance of preventative efforts before or soon after a child's birth for creating "functional and healthy coparenting"); Caroline Christopher et al., *Marital Quality Over the Transition to Parenthood as a Predictor of Coparenting*, 24 CHILD FAM. STUD. 3636, 3648 (2015) (noting the critical importance of easing the transition to parenthood for marital fathers in order to develop a positive coparenting relationship).

[67] *See* Bryndl E. Hohmann-Marriott, *Father Involvement Ideals and the Union Transitions of Unmarried Parents*, 30 J. OF FAM. ISSUES 898, 915–16 (2009). *See also* KYLE PRUETT &

the romantic relationship ends.[68] Why? Because parents come to appreciate the value of teamwork to both their child and themselves. It allows each parent to gain competence, which is "an important factor in custody preferences" at the romantic relationship's end.[69] It allows the couple to continue an established pattern rather than initiate a new caregiving arrangement for the first time at breakup.[70] Because many families in religious communities tend to be role divided,[71] building a norm of hands-on parenting would increase the likelihood that these fathers would stay engaged if the parents break up and might reduce the chance of breakup altogether.

B Laws Governing Parents' Relationships with Their Children

Custody law encourages parents to act in certain ways toward each other but is unlikely to affect behavior during the romantic relationship. Parents are unlikely to envision a future custody dispute or know the details of custody law. Further, because the "best interest of the child" test is multifactored and indeterminate,[72] parents are not likely to change behaviors or heed particular normative rules, even if they know them. True, at least half the states have a friendly-parent provision, and all states recognize the relevance of domestic

Marsha Kline Pruett, Partnership Parenting: How Men and Women Parent Differently – Why It Helps Your Kids and Can Strengthen Your Marriage 13 (2009) ("A successful parenting partnership requires . . . sharing child-care responsibilities."). It is unknown, but possible, that a parent-partner status would also make it more likely for the couple to marry. The status, and the new social role, might increase love between the parties, improve the quality of their relationship, or encourage people to have children with those whom they would be more likely to marry. *See* Merle Weiner, A Parent-Partner Status for American Family Law 515–16 (2015).

68 Adamsons & Pasley, *supra* note 45, at 251 ("The quality and nature of the postdivorce coparental relationship is closely tied to that of the predivorce coparental relationship."); Julia S. Goldberg & Marcia J. Carlson, *Patterns & Predictors of Coparenting After Unmarried Parents Part*, 29 J. Fam. Psych. 416, 423 (2015); Susan Steinman, *The Experience of Children in Joint-Custody Arrangement: A Report of a Study*, 51 Amer. J. Orthopsychiat. 403, 407 (1981) (noting that most families in the study that agreed to share custody had "shared parenting during the marriage to a great extent"). *See also* Maccoby & Mnookin, *supra* note 31, at 279 (talking about the need to modify pre-divorce roles to affect post-divorce division of responsibilities); Solangel Maldonado, *Shared Parenting and Never-Married Parents*, 52 Fam. Ct. Rev. 632, 634 (2014) ("Parents who did not share parenting when they were romantically involved are unlikely to agree to share parenting when the relationship has ended.").

69 *See* Pruett & Barker, *supra* note 44, at 426.

70 Adamsons & Pasley, *supra* note 45, at 251.

71 Jennifer Glass & Leda E. Nath, *Religious Conservatism and Women's Market Behavior Following Marriage and Childbirth*, 68 J. Marr. & Fam. 611 (Aug. 2006).

72 Robert Mnookin, *Child Custody Revisited*, 77 L. & Contemp. Problems 249, 251 (2014).

violence to custody adjudication.[73] But these rules are unlikely to shape parental behavior during the romantic relationship for the aforementioned reasons.[74] Moreover, these particular provisions only tell parents to avoid certain egregious acts, not to engage in supportive acts. If anything, the custody rules signal that the parents owe each other little, that their obligations to each other are solely derivative of each parent's obligations to his or her child, and that any obligations arise only upon breakup. At best, this structure weakly regulates the adults' relationship to each other.

Some judges think that "joint custody provides a legal framework to support the parents to develop a cooperative parenting relationship."[75] In fact, most states now permit, and some promote, "joint custody," by making available joint legal and/or joint physical custody to both divorcing and unmarried couples.[76] Specifically, most states today authorize joint legal custody,[77]

[73] Linda D. Elrod, Child Custody Prac. & Proc. § 4:32 n.1 and § 4:27 (2015) (citing states with friendly-parent provisions). This provision disadvantages a parent in a custody contest if he or she is unwilling or unable to foster a relationship between the child and the other parent. *See, e.g.*, Or. Stat. Rev. 107.137(1)(f) (2013). Similarly, some courts accept evidence of "parental alienation" in determining the child's best interests. *See, e.g.*, Palazzolo v. Mire, 10 So. 3d 748, 774 (La. Ct. App. 4th Cir. 2009). Many states have a presumption that a perpetrator of violence should not be awarded custody. *See* J. Herbie DiFonzo, Kristin Pezzuti, Nicole Guliano, & Diana Rivkin, Joint Custody Laws and Policies in the Fifty states: A Summary Memorandum [hereafter DiFonzo Memo], at 31, www.masslegalservices.org/system/files/library/JtCiustodySummary%20Memo-5.pdf. Forty-eight states have statutory provisions that require states to take account of domestic violence. *See* Fernanda Rossi et al., *Intimate Partner Violence and Child Custody, in* Parenting Plan Evaluations 346, 346 (Leslie Drozd et al., 2d ed. 2016).

[74] In addition, the effect of the law may be diminished because, among other reasons, batterers know batterers get custody, *see* Rossi, *supra* note 73, at 346–47; they know the mother has issues too (often the result of the battering, however), *see* Peter G. Jaffe et al., *Custody Disputes Involving Allegations of Domestic Violence: Toward a Differentiated Approach to Parenting Plans*, 46 Fam. Ct. Rev. 500, 503 (2008); or they care more about maintaining control over their victim than the outcome of a future custody dispute.

[75] *See* Julie E. Artis & Andrew V. Krebe, *Family Law and Social Change: Judicial Views of Joint Custody, 1998–2011*, 40 L. & Soc. Inquiry 723, 737 (2015).

[76] June Carbone & Naomi Cahn, Marriage Markets: How Inequality Is Remaking the American Family 116 (2014); Pruett & DiFonzo, *supra* note 59, at 156. Child custody law has changed in other ways as the American family has changed. Thirty-three states now have marriage-neutral custody laws, applying the same custody law to married and unmarried children once the unwed father's paternity is established. *See Elaina Rose and Crystal Wong, But Who Will Get Billy? The Effect of Child Custody Laws on Marriage*, IZA Discussion Paper Series 14 (Nov. 2014).

[77] Center for the Study of Social Policy, State Polices that Work: Encouraging Strong Family Relationships, Policy Brief 6, 8 (2012). *See also* Donald T. Kramer, *Joint Custody, in* 1 Leg. Rts. Child Rev. 2d § 2:28 (2d ed. 2012).

although states differ in their preferences or presumptions for it,[78] and whether parents must agree to it.[79] Many states also have statutes with statements about the need for "frequent and continuing contact with both parents"[80] or that tell courts to "maximize the amount of time the child ... spend[s] with each parent," subject to various considerations.[81] Typically an award of joint physical custody must be in the child's best interest.[82]

These laws appear to have increased judges' acceptance of joint custody[83] and to have affected whether joint custody is awarded.[84] Couples now share legal and physical custody after breakup at greater rates than in the past, although at different rates for divorced and never-married couples. National data does not exist,[85] but data from Wisconsin shows high levels of joint legal custody for both marital and non-marital couples and increasing levels of shared physical custody, especially for divorced fathers.[86] Specifically, the

78 A good number have preferences or presumptions for it. *See* Kelly Alison Behre, *Digging Beneath the Equality Language: The Influence of the Fathers' Rights Movement on Intimate Partner Violence Public Policy Debates and Family Law Reform*, 21 Wm. & Mary J. Women & L. 525, 593 (2015) (citation omitted). Nonetheless, judges typically have discretion about whether to award joint legal custody and the paramount consideration remains the child's best interest. *See* DiFonzo Memo, *supra* note 73, at 10, 34.

79 Some states require parental agreement. *See* Cabot v. Cabot, 697 A.2d 697 A.2d 644, 649 (Vt. 1997) (interpreting Vt. Stat. § 665(a) (2015)). Other states do not require the parents to agree to joint custody if the arrangement is in the child's best interests. *See, e.g.*, Neb. Rev. Stat. § 42-364(3)(b) (2014); S.C. Code Ann. § 63-15-230(C) (2012); Tenn. Code Ann. § 36-6-101(a)(2)(A)(i) (2014).

80 *See, e.g.*, Cal. Fam. Code § 3020(b) (2015). *See also, e.g.*, Wash. Rev. Code Ann. § 26.09.187(3)(a) (2015).

81 *See, e.g.*, Wis. Stat. § 767.41(4)(a)(2) (2015).

82 Katharine Bartlett, *Prioritizing Past Caretaking in Child-Custody Decisionmaking*, 77 L. & Contemp. Probs. 29, 31 & n.10 (2014) (citing statutes).

83 Julie E. Artis & Andrew V. Krebe, *Family Law and Social Change: Judicial Views of Joint Custody, 1998-2011*, 40 L. & Soc. Inquiry 723, 734 Tbl. 2 (2015) (citing a study of Indiana trial court judges).

84 *Compare* Yigu Chen, *Does a Nonresident Parent Have the Right to Make Decisions for His Nonmarital Children?: Trends in Legal Custody Among Paternity Cases*, 51 Child. & Youth Serv. Rev. 55, 63 (2015) (noting the importance of social and legal change for the increase in joint legal custody awards) *with* Chien-Chung Huang et al., *Child Support Enforcement, Joint Legal Custody, and Parental Involvement*, 77 Soc. Serv. Rev. 255, 267 (2003) (suggesting joint custody legislation did not strongly impact parental decisions about joint custody, but demographic characteristics and state child support legislation and enforcement efforts did).

85 Maria Cancian et al., *Who Gets Custody Now? Dramatic Changes in Children's Living Arrangements After Divorce*, 51 Demography 1381, 1383 (2014).

86 In 1999, Wisconsin enacted a presumption that joint legal custody was in the best interests of the child. Wis. Stat. § 767.24(2)(am) (1999); 1999 Wis. Act 9 § 3054co. That still exists today. *See* Wis. Stat. § 767.41(2)(a) (2015). In the late 1990s, Wisconsin courts had the discretion to award joint physical custody even without the parents' agreement. Lawrence M. Berger et al., The Stability of Shared Child Physical Placements in Recent Cohorts

percentage of joint legal custody awarded in divorce cases rose from 18% in 1980 to 87% in 2001, and in paternity cases from approximately 2% in 1993 to 70% in 2009.[87] Shared physical custody rose from 7% in 1986 to 45% in 2008, and more of these shared cases were equal-residence custody rather than residence primarily with the mother.[88] Sole-mother physical custody now stands at only 46% among divorced parents.[89] The number of unmarried parents with equal-residence custody has climbed from less than 1% in 1996 to 13% in 2009, although 84% of the cases still are sole-mother physical custody.[90]

Reformers have recommended the adoption of "strong" joint custody laws to give both parents significant time with the child.[91] Proposals differ, but some recommendations involve a presumption that equal physical custody is in the best interest of the child, even if the parents do not agree.[92] Utah's new Shared Parenting Law is one type of strong law. Utah increased the presumptive minimum parenting time for children ages five to eighteen years old from 30% to approximately 40%, or 145 overnights a year.[93] The law allows a court to order this without parental agreement and even if the parties are not able to

OF DIVORCED WISCONSIN FAMILIES 32 (Inst. For Research on Poverty, Discussion Paper No. 1329-07, 2007), www.irp.wisc.edu/publications/dps/pdfs/dp132907.pdf. The law currently requires "a placement schedule that allows the child to have regularly occurring, meaningful periods of physical placement with each parent and that maximizes the amount of time the child may spend with each parent, taking into account geographic separation and accommodations for different households." WIS. STAT. § 767.41(4)(a)(2)(2015).

87 *See* BERGER ET AL., *supra* note 86, at 5–6; Chen, *supra* note 84.

88 Cancian, *supra* note 85, at 1382, 1387.

89 PATRICIA BROWN & STEVEN T. COOK, CHILDREN'S PLACEMENT ARRANGEMENTS IN DIVORCE AND PATERNITY CASES IN WISCONSIN Tbl. 2a (Institute for Research on Poverty: Univ. of Wisconsin, Madison, Working Paper, 2012). Divorced fathers received sole custody 9% of the time. Cancian, *supra* note 85, at 1387.

90 Chen, *supra* note 84, at 59.

91 *See* Richard A. Warshak, *Parenting by the Clock: The Best-Interest-of-the-Child-Standard, Judicial Discretion, and the American Law Institute's Approximation Approach*, 41 U. BALT. L. REV. 83, 112 (2011); Ashby Jones, *Big Shift Pushed in Custody Disputes; Some 20 States are Considering Changing Laws to Give Fathers More Rights to their Children After Divorce*, WALL ST. J. ONLINE (Apr. 16, 2015), www.wsj.com/articles/big-shift-pushed-in-custody-disputes-1429204977. *See also supra* note 11.

92 *See, e.g.*, National Parents Org., 2014 SHARED PARENTING REPORT CARD, nationalparentsorganization.org/docs/2014_Shared_Parenting_Report_Card%2011-10-2014.pdf (discussing "positive" and "negatives" of various state laws). *Cf.* Linda Nielsen, *Parenting Time and Shared Residential Custody: Ten Common Myths*, NEB. LAWYER, Jan./Feb. 2013, at 7; Clare Huntington, *Postmarital Family Law*, 67 STAN. L. REV. 167, 225 (2015).

93 UTAH CODE § 30-3-34 (1) (2015). The bill was promoted by the National Parents Organization of Utah. *See* Dan Deuel, *Shared Parenting Law Puts Utah at Forefront of Progress*, SALT LAKE TRIB. (May 30, 2015), www.sltrib.com/opinion/2563052-155/op-ed-shared-parenting-law-puts-utah . Until 2013, the National Parents Organization was called Fathers and Families. Ned Holstein,

communicate effectively regarding the child so long as the noncustodial parent demonstrates, among other things, active involvement in the child's life, broadly defined;[94] a "plan" to accomplish effective communications regarding the child; and the arrangement is in the child's best interest.[95]

To be clear, joint custody or shared custody laws are not designed to encourage shared parenting. Professor Kelly Behre observed that recent efforts to promote shared custody "sound like progressive attempts to encourage coparenting," but they are not.[96] Shared custody laws establish shared decision-making authority and a percentage of time that each parent gives physical care – the number of overnights often mentioned is "30–35 percent and above."[97] In contrast, "shared parenting," as psychologists define it, signifies "the support and solidarity between adults responsible for the joint care of children."[98] Shared parenting involves showing each other respect, exhibiting solidarity, trusting each other, collaborating, and avoiding hostility and competition.[99] There is "warmth and connection, affirmation, and validation."[100] The bottom line is mutual support: "[T]he key guideposts… are communicating regularly with one another about child-related issues and decisions and supporting one another's parenting efforts."[101] The parents strive to be a good team.[102] This description does *not* assume that each parent does half of the caregiving work or that each parent spends an equal amount of time with the child. It does mean, however, that the each parent strives to view the other as equally valuable:

Announcing: National Parents Organization, NATIONAL PARENTS ORGANIZATION (Apr. 25, 2013), nationalparentsorganization.org/newsletter/archive/enews-2013425.html. The bill passed both houses of the legislature with only one opposing vote. Danielle Downs, *Utah's New Shared Parenting Law in Effect*, DAILY HERALD (May 19, 2015), www.heraldextra.com/news/local/govt-and-politics/utah-s-new-shared-parenting-law-in-effect/article_a13a3657-1ee9-5232-80f5-f2731d68283d.html.

94 UTAH CODE § 30-3-34 (2)(a) & § 30-3-35.1(3) (2015) ("In determining whether a noncustodial parent has been actively involved in the child's life, the court shall consider: (a) demonstrated responsibility in caring for the child; (b) involvement in day care; (c) presence or volunteer efforts in the child's school and at extracurricular activities; (d) assistance with the child's homework; (e) involvement in preparation of meals, bath time, and bedtime for the child; (f) bonding with the child; and (g) any other factor the court considers relevant.").

95 UTAH CODE § 30-3-35.1(2)(b) & (d) (2015).

96 Behre, *supra* note 78, at 592–93.

97 Pruett & DiFonzo, *supra* note 59, at 154.

98 Pruett & Donsky, *supra* note 33, at 233.

99 *See* James P. McHale, *Assessing Coparenting*, *in* COPARENTING, A CONCEPTUAL AND CLINICAL EXAMINATION OF FAMILY SYSTEMS 156–58 (James P. McHale & Kristin M. Lindahl, eds. 2011); JAMES P. MCHALE, CHARTING THE BUMPY ROAD OF COPARENTHOOD: UNDERSTANDING THE CHALLENGES OF FAMILY LIFE 3–11 (2007).

100 *See* MCHALE, CHARTING THE BUMPY ROAD OF COPARENTHOOD, *supra* note 99, at 9.

101 *See Id.*

102 McHale, *Assessing Coparenting*, *supra* note 99, at 156–58; MCHALE, CHARTING THE BUMPY ROAD, note 99, at 3–11.

"[B]eing viewed as equally valuable, though necessarily not equal ... creates harmonious and effective coparenting."[103]

Supportive coparenting is arguably *more* important for children's adjustment after a parental breakup than any particular custody arrangement,[104] although some custody arrangements may have positive effects on the parent-child relationship.[105] Family therapist Constance Ahrons found "[n]o single factor contributed more to children's self-reports of well-being after divorce than the continuing relationship between their parents."[106] She proclaimed, "Children benefit when the relationship between their parents – whether married or divorced – is generally supportive and cooperative."[107] Director of the Joint Custody Project Susan Steinman studied families that had voluntarily adopted joint custody and found the following:

> The most crucial and beneficial components of joint custody for the children lie in the attitudes, values, and behavior of their parents. The cooperative and respectful relationship between the parents for the purpose of child-rearing, and each parent's support of the child's relationship with the other parent, seemed to be more significant in helping the children adjust to the divorce than making sure that the time the children spent with each parent was precisely equal.[108]

103 Pruett & Donsky, *supra* note 33, at 235; *See id.* at 233 (citing McHale). *See also* Pruett & Pruett, *supra* note 67 ("The point is not that each parent needs to take a turn making sandwiches, but, overall are they both committed parents doing the best they can to support one another as parents?").

104 Pearson & Theonnes, *supra* note 32, at 245 (noting custody categories did not matter much to children's adjustment, but children did better if the parents were cooperative, violence was absent, and the parents considered reconciliation at breakup); Pruett & Barker, *supra* note 44, at 446 ("Custody arrangements do not systematically affect parental cooperation or conflict, nor do cooperation and conflict perfectly correlate with joint custody outcomes."). *See also* Melinda Stafford Markham & Marilyn Coleman, *The Good, the Bad, and the Ugly: Divorced Mothers' Experiences with Coparenting*, 61 FAM. RELATIONS 586, 590, 597 (2012) (noting almost 50% of the couples with shared legal and physical custody in the sample had mothers who described the coparenting relationship as "continuously contentious" and concluding that "the goal should be maintaining cooperative coparenting relationships that focus on the well-being of the child" and not "shared physical custody").

105 Pruett & Barker, *supra* note 44, at 446 (noting joint legal and physical custody "leaves fathers feeling more satisfied after divorce, which has a positive effect on their involvement with their children over time").

106 Ahrons, *supra* note 30, at 58.

107 CONSTANCE AHRONS, THE GOOD DIVORCE: KEEPING YOUR FAMILY TOGETHER WHEN YOUR MARRIAGE COMES APART 126 (1994). *See also* June Carbone, *The Missing Piece of the Custody Puzzle: Creating a New Model of Parental Partnership*, 39 SANTA CLARA L. REV. 1091, 1095 (1999) ("[T]he parental model that produces the best outcomes for children is one of supportive partnership.").

108 Susan Steinman, *The Experience of Children in a Joint-Custody Arrangement: A Report of a Study*, 51 AMER. J. ORTHOPSYCHIAT. 403, 414 (1981).

Joint custody laws do not address how parents should act toward each other. Consequently, couples can share custody but still have relationships characterized by conflict, parallel parenting, and/or a lack of generosity.[109] But joint custody can be inappropriate when a couple lacks a supportive partnership. While a general consensus exists that children benefit when both parents agree to joint custody,[110] many believe that joint custody harms children when the parents have a high amount of conflict or are hostile and one parent rejects the arrangement.[111] Professors Robert Mnookin and Lewis Kornhauser noted that the imposition of joint custody creates "endless possibilities for antagonism between the parents, with predictably detrimental effects on the child's well-being."[112] Professor David Chambers suggested that joint custody provides "opportunities … for an angry parent to make life difficult for the other parent."[113] Professor McHale suggested that "[h]igh levels of father engagement can actually catalyze or amplify competitive and antagonistic co-parental dynamics in couple-distressed families."[114]

Shared custody makes domestic violence more probable[115] and can negatively impact children whose "mothers have safety concerns [or who] are stuck in the middle of high ongoing parental conflict."[116] Professor Margaret Brinig's research in Arizona demonstrated that courts do not always screen out as

109 *See* Pruett & Barker, *supra* note 44, at 446; *id.* at 422 ("It is possible for [joint physical custody] arrangements to result in separate, uncoordinated ('parallel') parenting rather than highly communicative, shared decision making."); *id.* at 426–27 (noting that mothers' attitudes matter to whether joint custody is successful).

110 Pruett & DiFonzo, *supra* note 59, at 154.

111 *See, e.g.*, Pruett & Barker, *supra* note 44, at 437–38, 440, 443; Janet R. Johnston, Marsha Kline, & Jeanne M. Tschann, *Ongoing Postdivorce Conflict: Effects on Children of Joint Custody and Frequent Access*, 59 Am. J. Orthopsychiatry 576, 578, 590 (1989). For concerns about strong joint custody laws, *see, e.g.*, Behre, *supra* note 78, at 593, 598–99; J. Herbie DiFonzo, *From the Rule of One to Shared Parenting: Custody Presumptions in Law and Policy*, 52 Fam. Ct. Rev. 214, 224 (2014); Pruett & Barker, *supra* note 44, at 443 ("Equal parenting time presumptions also take choice and voice out of children's hands … [D]ecisions do not take into account the child's needs.").

112 Robert H. Mnookin & Lewis Kornhauser, *Bargaining in the Shadow of the Law: The Case of Divorce*, 88 Yale L. J. 950, 980 (1979).

113 David L. Chambers, *Rethinking the Substantive Rules for Custody Disputes in Divorce*, 83 Mich. L. Rev. 477, 558 (1984).

114 McHale, *supra* note 49, at 82. *See also* Pruett & Barker, *supra* note 44, at 438 (citing studies).

115 Peter Jaffe, *A Presumption Against Shared Parenting for Family Court Litigants*, 52 Fam. Ct. Rev. 187, 189 (2014). *See generally* Gabrielle Davis, et al., *The Dangers of Presumptive Joint Physical Custody, The Battered Women's Justice Project* (2010), www.bwjp.org/files/bwjp/articles/Dangers_of_Presumptive_Joint_Physical_Custody.pdf, http://perma.cc/MKZ9-53GH (summarizing research on mandatory joint physical custody).

116 Bruce Smyth et al., *Legislating for Shared-Time Parenting After Parental Separation: Insights from Australia?* 7 Law & Contemp. Probs. 109, 141 (2014) (citations omitted).

ineligible for joint custody those couples with a history of domestic violence.[117] Reviewing the research about joint custody in California and Wisconsin, Professor June Carbone noted that "high conflict cases were *more*, not less, likely to result in joint physical custody awards."[118] Consequently, strong joint custody laws come with real risks.

Moreover, there is currently a lack of evidence that shared custody *causes* parents to coparent supportively, to cooperate more than other custody arrangements do, or to do anything other than parallel parent with little more.[119] To the extent couples with shared custody seem more cooperative or supportive than couples with different custody arrangements, it may be a function of selection effects – that is, a factor that makes cooperation more likely also makes couples more likely to choose shared custody.[120] Also unknown is whether strong joint custody laws affect coparenting behavior *during* the parents' romantic relationship negatively or positively, either by undermining shared parenting because cooperation is no longer a prerequisite to a joint award or by encouraging joint caregiving by signaling its desirability.[121] For those who believe court-ordered joint custody has

[117] *See* Margaret F. Brinig, *Substantive Parenting Arrangements in the USA: Unpacking the Policy Choices*, 27 CHILD & FAM. L. Q. 249, * 15 (2015) (discussing Arizona). *But see* Margaret F. Brinig, *Result Inequality in Family Law*, 48 AKRON L. REV. 1, 21 (2015) (discussing Indiana).

[118] Carbone speculated that judges used joint custody "to resolve otherwise intractable parental disputes," including for cases in which there was extreme distrust or domestic violence. Carbone, *supra* note 107, at 1091, 1116, 1119 (citing research by Maccoby & Mnookin as well as by Brown & Cook, Melli, and Cancian).

[119] *See, e.g.*, Markham & Coleman, *supra* note 104, at 590, 593 (finding that only women who wanted shared custody initially had shared custody relationships with the father that could be characterized as transitioning from "bad to better" over time, and that women who did not want shared custody had "continually contentious" relationships with the father when shared custody was ordered). Emery and Emery posited that "joint legal custody . . . leads to increased parental cooperation and postseparation involvement with children, while at the same time decreasing parental conflict." Robert E. Emery & Kimberly C. Emery, *Should Courts or Parents Make Child-Rearing Decisions?: Married Parents as a Paradigm for Parents Who Live Apart*, 43 WAKE FOREST L. REV. 365, 380 (2008). However, the studies cited by the authors do not entirely support that conclusion. *See* Judith Seltzer, *Legal Custody Arrangements and Children's Economic Welfare*, 96 AM. J. SOC. 895, 915 (1991) (noting that income level affects any association between joint legal custody and amount of child support awards or payments, and payment increases are small even when they occur); Huang, *supra* note 89 (noting joint custody arrangements produce more visitation and child support payments, although the support result is diluted over time to the point of statistical insignificance, and increased visitation does not necessarily promote children's well-being). Moreover, these studies examine joint legal custody. Shared physical custody may lead to different results.

[120] *See* Brinig, Chapter 10, this volume.

[121] Alternatively joint custody might have no effect on caregiving during the romantic relationship, or different effects at the end of the romantic relationship from other times, or different effects depending upon a parent's level of caregiving for the child.

a positive effect on supportive coparenting after breakup, that effect would probably be more likely or larger if the parents had a history of hands-on, supportive coparenting during their romantic relationship. The bottom line is simple: court-ordered joint custody cannot serve as a substitute for a structure that encourages supportive coparenting from the beginning of the child's life; it can cause harm when couples lack the ability or willingness to cooperate; and, it seems unnecessary when couples have a supportive relationship and can agree to share custody.

Is there a better approach than strong joint custody laws for involving both parents in their children's lives after breakup *and* encouraging their supportive coparenting relationships? Perhaps a structure that encouraged parents to have a supportive coparenting relationship from the get-go would result in more agreed-upon joint custody at breakup, and without the disadvantages of strong joint custody laws.

Such a structure might offer other benefits too, such as helping fathers who are unlikely to obtain joint custody regardless of the custody rules. For example, some low-income men are "hesitant" to go to court, in part because of their "prior dealings with the legal system."[122] The shortage of lawyers and financial assistance for legal services also hinders their access to the courts.[123] Even if low-income men are involved in custody adjudications, judges do not always award them joint custody because the arrangement may not be in their children's best interest.[124] Judges typically require the parents to be on good terms, the arrangement to be economically feasible, and both parents to be competent caregivers.[125] Consequently, some fathers' best hope for joint custody is to have good coparenting relationships with their children's mothers so that the mothers agree to that arrangement. In addition, for all couples

122 Solangel Maldonado, *Shared Parenting and Never-Married Parents*, 52 FAM. CT. REV. 632, 634 (2014).

123 *Id.* at 635.

124 Bartlett, *supra* note 82, at 31.

125 *See, e.g.*, Buttle v. Buttle, 196 P.3d 174, 183 (Wy. 2008) (finding the existence of effective communication and cooperative decision making essential to a joint custody award); Johnson v. Lewis, 870 A.3d 368, 376 (Super. Ct. Pa. 2005) (noting trial court's finding that father's current and future living arrangements were suitable and that parents could cooperate). *See, e.g.*, Pearson & Theonnes, *supra* note 32, at 237. In Wisconsin, "[d]emographic and economic characteristics" have led judges to award joint custody at very different rates to divorced and unmarried fathers. Brown & Cook, *supra* note 89, at 17.

Judicial discretion is unlikely ever to disappear. In the view of scholars participating in the 2013 interdisciplinary think tank on shared custody, "nuances" in the literature about probable success of coparent arrangements means that custody matters should be resolved either by "parental agreement or individualized judicial assessments rather than decisions premised on legal presumptions." Pruett & DiFonzo, *supra* note 59, at 162.

a parental agreement is preferable to a court-imposed arrangement because the legal process can be costly and invasive.[126]

New court procedures for custody adjudications encourage parental agreements and coparenting and make cooperative coparenting more likely, but they are not sufficient for structuring parents' relationship to each other. Courts today use a range of techniques to further cooperative coparenting, such as parenting plans,[127] mediation,[128] parenting coordinators,[129] parenting education,[130] and coparenting courts.[131] Other processes also further this end,

126 Stacy Brustin & Lisa Vollendorf Martin, *Paved with Good Intentions: Unintended Consequences of Federal Proposals to Integrate Child Support and Parenting Time*, 48 INDIANA L. REV. 803, 827 (2015) (noting that "[f]unneling families to court in the absence of conflict risks depleting family resources, generating conflict, and upending settled parenting arrangements . . . Child custody also can be invasive. Courts may direct social services officers to conduct studies of parents' residences or require parents to undergo psychological evaluation.").

127 About half of U.S. states require parenting plans that courts can then incorporate into final decrees. *See* Richard E. Miller, *Child Custody Cases in Vermont: What is the Best Interest of the Child?* 35 SUM VT. B. J. 30 (2009). *See also* DiFonzo Memo, *supra* note 73, at 4. For a discussion of the effect of parenting plans, *see* Marsha Kline Pruett, Rachel Ebling, and Philip A. Cowan, *Pathways from a U.S. Co-parenting Intervention to Legal Outcomes*, 25 INT'L J. OF L., POLICY, AND THE FAM. 24, 27–28 (2011).

128 *See* Brinig, *Substantive Parenting*, *supra* note 117, at 252 ("Many states mandate mediation in disputed custody cases, and the remainder allow it when the parents wish it or allow judges to refer even recalcitrant parents to it."). For a discussion of the effects of mediation, *see* Robert E. Emery et al., *Child Custody Mediation and Litigation: Custody, Contact, and Co-parenting, 12 Years After Initial Dispute Resolution*, 69 J. CONSULTING & CLINICAL PSYCHOL. 323 (2001).

129 "[P]arenting coordination is practiced in over 30 states, and some [eleven] states have passed parenting coordination statutes or court-ordered rules." Sophie B. Mashburn, *"Throwing the Baby Out with the Bathwater": Parenting Coordination and Pennsylvania's Decision to Eliminate its Use*, 2015 DISP. RESOL. 191, 192, 195 (2015). For a discussion of the effects of parenting coordinators, see Emery & Emery, *supra* note 119, at 380–81; Victoria M. Ho, *Parent Coordinators: An Effective New Tool in Resolving Parental Conflict in Divorce*, 74 FAMILY BAR J. 101 (June 2000); Joi T. Montiel, *Why and How Alabama Courts Should Use Parenting Coordination in Divorce Cases*, 72 ALA. LAWYER 300 (July 2011); Wilma J. Henry, Linda Fieldstone, & Kelly Bohac, *Parenting Coordination and Court Relitigation: A Case Study*, 47 FAM. CT. REV. 682, 689 (2009).

130 Forty-six states offer or require parenting classes for divorcing couples, ranging from four to twelve hours of curriculum. *See* William J. Doherty & Leah Ward Sears, *Second Chances: A Proposal to Reduce Unnecessary Divorce: Presented to U.S. State Legislatures* (Institute for American Values July 2011), at 6. These classes are often, but not always, required of unmarried couples, too. *See, e.g.*, UTAH CODE § 30-3-11.3(3), (4) (2015). For a discussion of the effects of parenting education, *see, e.g.*, Tamara A. Fackrell, Alan J. Hawkins, & Nicole M. Kay, *A Special Focus on Court-Affiliated Parent Education Programs: How Effective Are Court-Affiliated Divorcing Parents Education Programs? A Meta-Analytic Study*, 49 FAM. CT. REV. 107 (2011); Stephanie R. deLusé and Sanford L. Braver, *A Rigorous Quasi-Experimental Design to Evaluate the Causal Effect of a Mandatory Divorce Education Program*, 53 FAM. CT. REV. 66 (2015).

131 Hennipen County, Minnesota, developed an innovative coparenting court to adjudicate paternity for unmarried parents and provide "support and services to help unmarried parents

such as collaborative lawyering[132] and family group conferencing.[133] These various tools show promise, although success varies by program and by the measure of success.[134]

Of course, court processes can only benefit parents who use the courts, but not all parents do. In addition, some of the processes work best when the parents are represented by counsel, but not all parents are.[135] Moreover, despite the benefits of these processes, they do not reduce the risk of family breakup by encouraging parents at the beginning of their relationships to engage in hands-on parenting, to support each other's coparenting throughout their child's minority, and to have healthy high-quality relationships overall. Reducing the risk of family breakup is important because children can still experience harm from a parental breakup even when it is a "good breakup."[136] Additionally, these programs are not necessarily sufficient by themselves to establish *supportive* coparenting relationships, as the data about parental relationships post-breakup suggests.[137] These tools emerge very late in the process and are relatively minor interventions. Notably, the new procedures have not eliminated calls for strong joint custody laws, which suggests that couples are not agreeing to joint custody in numbers that render calls for

develop the skills and knowledge to be involved parents – both financially and emotionally – and to develop a healthy coparent relationship." Marczak, *supra* note 36, at 268. For a discussion of the effects of the coparenting court, *see id.* at 276 (discussing effect on fathers' child support payments).

132 Kimberly C. Emery & Robert E. Emery, *Who Knows What is Best for Children? Honoring Agreements and Contracts Between Parents Who Live Apart*, 77 L & Contemp. Probl. 151, 154, 162 (2014). *See also* Jane C. Murphy & Jana Singer, Divorced From Reality: Rethinking Family Dispute Resolution 137–38 (2015).

133 *See* Murphy & Singer, *supra* note 132, at 137 (recommending that the use of family group conferencing be expanded from child welfare cases to family law disputes).

134 *See, e.g.*, Fackrell, Hawkins, & Kay, *supra* note 130, at 113–14 (selecting five "umbrella" outcome measures and reporting much more apparent success from parental education at divorce on some measures, *e.g.*, improved parental well-being, than others, *e.g.*, relitigation rate). *See generally* Smyth et al., *supra* note 116, at 142 (citing Rae Kaspiew et al., Australian Inst. of Family Studies, Evaluation of the 2006 Family Law Reforms 90 (2009)) (finding approximately "two-thirds of separated parents reported 'friendly' or 'cooperative' relationships with each other a year or so after separation" and that was likely attributable to the fact that there was "child-sensitive dispute-resolution processes, supported when appropriate by legal and relationship services"); Pruett, Ebling, & Cowan, *supra* note 127, at 29, 37–38 (noting that "a hybrid form of ADR that combines elements of psychoeducational parenting classes, clinical intervention, mediation, and case management services, with collaborative input from legal and mental health professionals" increased mothers' support of fathers as fathers).

135 Murphy & Singer, *supra* note 132, at 69–71 (discussing challenges posed by "substantial numbers of unrepresented parties" for both adjudication and mediation).

136 Paul R. Amato, Jennifer B. Kane, & Spencer James, *Reconsidering the "Good Divorce,"* 60 Fam. Relations 511, 519–20 (2011).

137 *See* Section I *supra*.

reform unnecessary. In addition, reducing the need for these processes would be beneficial because they can be expensive.[138] Finally, these procedures would presumably work better – that is, more quickly and successfully – and become less necessary if parents enjoyed supportive coparenting relationships prior to their romantic relationships ending. Section III explains how the law might foster these types of relationships.

III THE CASE FOR LEGAL OBLIGATIONS BETWEEN THE PARENTS

Society should impose on parents a legal structure that obligates them to each other from the get-go, thereby setting social expectations for their relationship. Creating a new legal status for parents with children – the "parent-partner" status – would promote healthier parenting practices and encourage parents to consider the ramifications of becoming parents prior to having children.[139] The law would not only encourage parents to choose good partners with whom to have a child, but it would also encourage them to keep their romantic relationships strong and healthy, to share caregiving during the romantic relationship, and to act supportively if their romantic relationships ever end.

This parent-partner status would arise automatically, typically upon the birth or adoption of a child,[140] and would impose core obligations between the parents that last throughout their child's minority. The status could entail any number of *inter se* obligations, but five particular legal obligations seem like good candidates: a duty to aid one's parent-partner, a duty not to abuse one's parent-partner, a duty to engage in relationship work with one's parent-partner at the transition to parenthood and at the demise of the romantic relationship, a duty of fairness when contracting with one's parent-partner, and a duty to give care or share with one's parent-partner. Together, these legal obligations would convey society's expectations for parent-partnerships and reinforce the norms that make people successful coparents: flexibility, fondness, acceptance, togetherness, and empathy.[141] Apart from the status's potential to enhance the coparenting relationship during and after the romantic relationship, it would provide remedies for instances of injustice between the parents, such as when one parent freeloads off the other parent's caregiving labor.[142]

[138] Murphy and Singer report that the Australian Family Relationship Centers were the "biggest investment in Australian family law ever." MURPHY & SINGER, *supra* note 132, at 112.

[139] *See* WEINER, *supra* note 67 (arguing for the creation of a new legal status for parents with a child in common).

[140] *See supra* note 10.

[141] WEINER, *supra* note 67, at 136–38.

[142] *See, e.g., id.* at 413–17.

Because the status would only create legal obligations between the parents themselves, and not trigger any governmental or third-party benefits, marriage would remain an important social and religious institution. In addition, marriage would continue to have its own social and religious significance.

The parent-partner status would affect parental behavior through at least three mechanisms. First, specific legal obligations would guide people to engage in activities that promote healthy, supportive relationships.[143] For example, the obligation of "relationship work" would expand participation in the kinds of programs used by the federal government in its Responsible Fatherhood and Healthy Marriage initiatives.[144] Programs at the transition to parenthood can help couples keep the quality of their relationships steady.[145] The duty to engage in relationship work would also give parents a tool to involve a reluctant partner in reconciliation counseling or friendship counseling at the end of a relationship, perhaps even before a custody dispute ensued.[146] In addition, the obligation "to give care or share" should encourage both parents to be caregivers for the child during the romantic relationship because a parent who performed an unfairly disproportionate amount of the caregiving would have a claim for compensation. This remedy would give parents a financial incentive to share caregiving equally from the time of the child's birth.[147]

Second, the status – which is created by the amalgam of legal obligations – would in turn foster a new social role. At a child's birth or adoption, the parents would become both a "mom" or "dad" and "parent-partners." The parent-partner role would help define people's identities and guide their behavior.[148] The legal obligations would act as a floor for the type of behavior that society expects between parent-partners and would convey the expectation that the relationship is a supportive one. The status might even influence parents'

143 *Id.* at 329, 352.

144 *See* U.S. Gov't Accountability Office, GAO-08-1002, Healthy Marriage and Responsible Fatherhood Initiative 3, 7, Tbl. 1 (2008); *see also* Office of Family Assistance, An Office of the Administration for Children and Families, www.acf.hhs.gov/programs/ofa/programs/healthy-marriage/about (noting, however, that these federal programs reach fewer than 100,000 people a year).

145 Weiner, *supra* note 67, at 365–69 (citing research). Violating the obligation of relationship work would be remedied with mandatory participation in an informational session that describes the advantages of relationship work programs. *Id.* at 361.

146 A victim of domestic violence would be able to opt out of relationship work with her batterer. *See Weiner's Response to Concerns about the Parent-Partner Status*, Concurring Opinions, Nov. 1, 2015, at concurringopinions.com/archives/2015/11/weiners-response-to-comments-about-the-parent-partner-status.html.

147 Weiner, *supra* note 67, at 411 *et seq.*

148 *Id.* at 226–28 (discussing identity theory).

relationships in other ways, such as by promoting love between parent-partners.[149]

Third, new legal obligations and a new social role should deter reproduction by those, and with those, who are unwilling or unable to undertake the legal obligations and assume the accompanying social role. Those people should be deterred from having children. For example, if two people do not want the legal obligation to lend reasonable aid to the other parent if that parent is physically injured, then those people lack the type of healthy and supportive relationship that should precede conception or adoption. Religious organizations, among others, could disseminate and emphasize the moral message implicit in the status: it is wrong to have a child if both parties cannot commit to being supportive of each other during their child's minority.

To be clear, the creation of a new parent-partner status would not entail changes to the law of child custody, in part because that subject is politically treacherous.[150] Instead, the parent-partner status represents an effort to regulate parental relationships directly, which in turn should impact custody outcomes at the end of romantic relationships.

In fact, the status should make strong joint custody provisions both unnecessary and unwise. On the one hand, the new social role and strong normative messaging should increase the number of parents who gravitate voluntarily to joint custody. Not only would "friends, family members, counselors, lawyers, parent education programs … mediators," and religious leaders have told them at the time of separation to be "parents together forever" and work out their differences,[151] but they would have received that message even before conception and throughout their romantic relationship as a result of this new status.

On the other hand, the proposal would make unwise strong joint custody laws because an award of joint custody would more often be inappropriate. Parents unable to agree to joint custody would likely be high conflict or predisposed to high conflict and therefore would be unsuited for it.[152] They would likely have experienced domestic violence, mental health issues, or drug and alcohol problems.[153] By adopting a parent-partner status and by keeping the substantive custody rules focused on the best interests of the child, society can achieve both shared parenting and shared custody, but with fewer unintended and harmful effects.

149 This love may be passionate or compassionate. *Id.* at Chap. 8.A.

150 *Id.* at 509.

151 Jaffe, *supra* note 115, at 189.

152 *See also* Pruett & Barker, *supra* note 44, at 445 (citing studies).

153 Jaffe, *supra* note 122, at 189; Emery & Emery, *supra* note 119, at 382.

IV CONCLUSION

Children will be well served if society shapes their parents' relationships through laws that directly govern the relationship of two people with a child in common. By having parenthood trigger the legal obligations, society could deter ill-advised conception and encourage shared parenting. By structuring the law in this way, the debates about shared custody should be rendered obsolete. A parent-partner status would encourage shared parenting and shared custody. The legal status would reinforce strong religious beliefs that encourage collaboration[154] while also creating an expectation of collaboration for secular parents too. The ultimate winners from such a structure would be the children who see their parents' ties strengthened, both during the romantic relationship and after it ends. This is an outcome that religious organizations should embrace. It is one they can help advance.

[154] *See* Wilson, Chapter 16, this volume; Brinig, Chapter 10, this volume.

12

Bad Faith

When Religious Beliefs Imperil Children

Paul A. Offit, M.D

Maurice R. Hillman Professor of Vaccinology and Professor of Pediatrics, Perelman School of Medicine at the University of Pennsylvania, and Director of the Vaccine Education Center, The Children's Hospital of Philadelphia

Across the United States, parents are legally empowered to rely upon their religious beliefs and "faith healing" practices as an antidote to when their children contract preventable and treatable illnesses.[1] Legislatures have empowered these parents to ignore modern medicine when their children are sick, and to ignore modern medicine when it is time for their children to receive doctor-recommended vaccinations. As a result of legal exemptions for religious beliefs, these parents are permitted to allow their children to suffer at the hands of diseases that modern medicine all-but eradicated decades before.

This chapter describes cross currents in states' protection of children's health and their protections for religious liberty. States attempt to protect children in all families through laws requiring children to receive proper vaccination and medical treatment and by empowering judges to authorize needed care for children when parents will not. But state laws also permit parents to legally decline medical treatment for children on the basis of the parents' religious or personal beliefs. This chapter examines the history of religious and personal exemptions to medical neglect laws, which reach back decades to Hubert Humphrey–era legislation. Prompted by the federal government, states crafted special exemptions that persist today for religious

[1] This chapter is largely adapted from my talk at University of Illinois College of Law on April 6, 2015. It draws together evidence in Paul A. Offit, Bad Faith: When Religious Belief Undermines Modern Medicine (2015) [hereinafter Bad Faith] and Paul A. Offit, Deadly Choices: How the Anti-Vaccine Movement Threatens Us All (2012). In this chapter, citations at the beginning of paragraphs are for the material in the entire paragraph unless additional citation is given.

families electing not to treat their children with modern medicine. These laws continue to extract heart-wrenching costs for children.

To make real how religious beliefs are imperiling children, Section I documents the extraordinary medical advance the measles vaccine brought to the United States in 1963. That vaccine eradicated this deadly threat to Americans by 2000. Unfortunately, these gains faltered with the dug-in resistance by vaccine-hesitant parents and religious fundamentalists in the late 1980s, as a consequence creating a measles resurgence. Section II chronicles the spread of measles in one city, Philadelphia, the single hardest-hit city during the 1989–91 measles epidemic. In the winter of 1991, Philadelphia suffered one of the largest measles epidemics in its history; 1400 children were infected and 9 died.[2] Faith communities that refused to vaccinate and treat their children were at the epicenter of this crisis. Section III then chronicles the enactment of the legislation through fierce lobbying by religious groups, legislation that allows these inconceivable outcomes across the country.

As a result of such legislation across the country, the United States is now seeing resurgence of once-eradicated diseases, with often deadly results. Ultimately, this chapter concludes that religious exemptions to laws requiring medical treatment of children unnecessarily endanger children and communities, causing dramatic but largely preventable harms to children across the nation. We should no longer tolerate the resurgence of deadly diseases given the deadly results.

I A VICTORY OVER THE HORROR OF MEASLES

Sixty years ago, the mere mention of measles elicited reactions of terror and anxiety – for good reason.[3] Measles, a contagious disease, is caused by a virus and can spread through the air when persons infected with it sneeze or cough.[4] Measles starts as a fever and turns to a cough and then the infected person breaks out in a rash that spreads throughout the body. Prior to the vaccine's introduction in 1963, the virus caused between 3 and 4 million cases in the U.S.[5] That resulted in about 48,000 hospitalizations, and 500 deaths a year.

[2] Offit, Deadly Choices, *supra* note 1, at 112; *see also* Tamar Lewin, *Measles and Faith Combine in 5 Deaths in Philadelphia*, N.Y. Times (Feb. 16, 1991), www.nytimes.com/1991/02/16/us/measles-and-faith-combine-in-5-deaths-in-philadelphia.html?pagewanted=all.

[3] *See* Bad Faith, *supra* note 1, at 92–112.

[4] *Measles (Rubeola)*, Centers for Disease Control and Prevention (Oct. 19, 2015), www.cdc.gov/measles/cases-outbreaks.html.

[5] Bad Faith, *supra* note 1, at 93.

Before the vaccine, almost everyone in the U.S. was infected with measles by age 15. When people died – typically children – they died of dehydration, encephalitis (inflammation of the brain), or pneumonia.[6]

Then, in 1963, the measles vaccination was introduced. The vaccine worked. In only fifteen years, the number of measles-related hospitalizations decreased by half;[7] 1978 witnessed only 27,000 cases of measles. Optimistic that measles could be eliminated from the U.S., the Centers for Disease Control and Prevention ("CDC") launched the Measles Elimination Program with the goal to eliminate measles by 1982. In 1983, only 1500 cases were reported.[8] As measles became a preventable horror of the past, the terror associated with the disease slowly subsided.

But in the late 1980s and early 1990s, the measles virus roared back. A single case study, Philadelphia's, shows the magnitude and source of the renewed health threat facing Americans.

II HOW MEASLES SPREAD THROUGH PHILADELPHIA

Philadelphia experienced a powerful resurgence of measles in late 1989.[9] The 1991 measles outbreak started on April 20, 1989, at the Spectrum, a concert venue in Philadelphia. A teenager with a blotchy rash, who had recently returned from a trip to Spain, attended an R.E.M. concert at the Spectrum. A couple of weeks later, several other teenagers were sick. The measles virus had now entered Philadelphia.

By November 29, 1990, ninety-six children in Philadelphia had been infected with measles.[10] By December 7, that number rose to 124. By December 31, that number reached 258 and in December of 1990, an eighteen-month-old unimmunized boy died from measles pneumonia. That was the first measles-related death in Philadelphia in twenty years.

On May 21, 1990, a headline, "No Measly Problem," appeared in *The Philadelphia Inquirer*.[11] The somewhat comical title implied that measles is really no big deal. But it is a big deal, as Section I explained. On January 12, 1991, another child died. Both measles deaths occurred in unimmunized children.[12] The Philadelphia Health Commissioner, Dr. Robert Ross, recommended vaccination of all children and that the first dose of vaccine be given at six months of age. Seven weeks later, in March 1991, city health officials did

[6] *Measles (Rubeola): For Healthcare Professionals*, CENTERS FOR DISEASE CONTROL AND PREVENTION (Oct. 19, 2015), www.cdc.gov/measles/hcp/.

[7] *Id.* [8] BAD FAITH, *supra* note 1, at 93. [9] *Id.* at 92–93. [10] *Id.* at 93–94.

[11] *Id.* at 92–93; M. Schogol, *No Measley Problem*, PHILADELPHIA INQUIRER (May 21, 1990).

[12] BAD FAITH, *supra* note 1, at 94.

something that had never been done before, and has never been done since, as will be evident shortly.[13]

On January 16, 1991, Dr. Ross received an anonymous phone call from a woman whose daughter belongs to the Faith Tabernacle Church in North Philadelphia. The woman warned Dr. Ross that church members did not believe in medical care.[14] "No one had died yet," Dr. Ross said, "But for the first time we were worried that we might not hear about a case of measles until a church member calls the police or calls the coroner to pick up the body."

The Faith Tabernacle Church's doctrine instructs members to "believe that the Bible is opposed in all means of healing apart from God's way."[15] "If I go to God and ask him to heal my body," said church member Gordon Korn, "I can't go to a doctor for medicine. You either trust God or you trust man." The church's school, the Faith Tabernacle Congregation School, contained hundreds of children, none of whom were immunized, and none of whom would receive medical care if they got sick. The Faith Tabernacle Church is still alive and well in Philadelphia today; hundreds of children are still enrolled in its school.[16]

On February 7, 1991, Caryn Still, a nine-year-old girl, was pronounced dead from measles.[17] Caryn was a third grader at the Faith Tabernacle Congregation School. On February 10, Monika Johnson, Caryn's classmate, was also pronounced dead. Monika was one of eleven children in her home, all of whom were unimmunized. Monika's father taught at the school. "I feel very confident in my belief in the way I've raised my children," he said, "Monika is something that God has given us and now has taken away." After Caryn Still's death, Dr. Ross met with Reverend Charles Reinert, the pastor of Faith Tabernacle Church. "He was soft-spoken, the consummate gentleman," said Dr. Ross, "But he drove me nuts. We told him we needed to vaccinate everyone in the school but he said the families wouldn't let us do it."

Reverend Reinert was adamant that the families in the Faith Tabernacle Church would not vaccinate their children.[18] However, Reverend Reinert provided Dr. Ross a list of the names and addresses of children attending the Faith Tabernacle Congregation School. The school was closed but that

[13] *Id.* at 108, 110. [14] *Id.* at 94. [15] *Id.* at 95.

[16] David Meekle, *Understanding the Faith Tabernacle Congregation*, Reading Eagle (Feb. 4, 2017), www.readingeagle.com/news/article/understanding-the-faith-tabernacle-congregation.

[17] Bad Faith, *supra* note 1, at 94–95. [18] *Id.* at 95.

unfortunately did nothing to slow the epidemic about to sweep through the Faith Tabernacle Church community.

On February 12, 1991, Dr. Ross began calling families with children enrolled in the school.[19] After a dozen phone calls, Dr. Ross learned that 129 students had contracted measles in the previous month. Only two of the families called reported no cases of measles affecting their children. Dr. Ross learned that none of the families had used anti-pyretics to treat their children and, in fact, no parents reported owning a thermometer.

On February 13, 1991, the legal community and the public health community took their first legal step to combat the outbreak.[20] Dr. Ross obtained a court order to visit the families. The families refused to let him touch their children, but Dr. Ross was allowed to look through the door to see whether or not the children were having difficulty breathing and to check their mental state. "Most of the families had six, eight, ten, twelve kids because they did not believe in birth control," said Dr. Ross, "There were also a lot of kids who were physically or mentally disabled because they all had in-house deliveries. Even if the kids were born breech, they didn't do a C-section. It was like the old days." The children, however, appeared well: "These kids had the rash, they were lying in bed, but they were alert, conversant, and appeared well hydrated." Hydration matters, as noted earlier; Dr. Ross believed that those children were not suffering dehydration and were not suffering measles pneumonia. He pleaded with the parents to let him know if their children got any sicker.

On February 14, 1991, another child died.[21] The day before, police had been called to the home of Linette Milnes, who was pronounced dead shortly after they arrived. Although Linette did not attend Faith Tabernacle Church School, her sister did. Linette's seven brothers and sisters were all unimmunized. "When another kid turned up at the morgue I checked my list and realized [Linette] was on it," said Dr. Ross, "I had just called the mother and she told me her kids were fine! She lied to me!" It disappointed Dr. Ross that he could not trust the parents to tell him whether or not their children were getting sicker.

Dr. Ross realized he was not going to get accurate information from the children's parents so he took the only step left to him to save these children.[22] He referred the case to District Attorney Ron Castille, who considered filing criminal charges but demurred. "Unfortunately, when the parent is willing to risk the death of their children because of religious beliefs," said Castille, "It's unlikely that the threat of prosecution will in any way act as a deterrent."

[19] *Id.* at 97. [20] *Id.* at 97–98. [21] *Id.* at 98. [22] *Id.* at 98–101.

Dr. Ross decided to get a court order to allow him to physically examine the children. He enlisted residents at Children's Hospital of Philadelphia ("CHOP") and St. Christopher's Hospital for Children ("St. Christopher's") to go door-to-door and examine children. They entered homes and insisted on interacting with potentially infected children. Upon encountering a gravely ill child with parents who were refusing to administer modern medical treatment, the officials received on-the-spot court orders and sent the ill children to a hospital for care. These severe legal remedies curbed the full effects of the outbreak. "It was one of the more inspiring moments in my thirty years in healthcare," said Dr. Ross, "[Residents] are busy people, on call every third night, yet they were happy to do it."

On February 15, 1991, two more children died.[23] In the early morning of February 15, Nancy Evans, a five-year-old from North Central Philadelphia, died from measles. Nancy, however, was not a member of the Faith Tabernacle Church. She belonged to the First-Century Gospel Church, another faith healing group in Philadelphia. Today, both churches are very active and very big in the city of Philadelphia.[24] Sadly, Tina Louise Johnson, the thirteen-year-old sister of Monika Johnson, also died February 15, the same day as her sister's funeral. Neither Nancy Evans nor Tina Louise Johnson was taken to a doctor when their illnesses worsened.

At this point, five children had died in ten days.[25] Philadelphia was now in the midst of the worst measles epidemic in the U.S. since the vaccine was widely adopted. Health officials found 134 cases of measles among the 201 students who attend the Faith Tabernacle Congregation School. In the U.S., in 1991, about 1 in 1000 infected children died from measles. In some developing countries, the death rate can reach as high as 1 in 300. In Philadelphia, 4 of 150 children with measles who attended Faith Tabernacle Church died. This is a rate of 1 in 35, worse than any developing country at that same time. On February 15, 1991, the CDC sent a team to investigate this measles outbreak. The question facing the team was whether the strain of measles virus circulating in the city of Philadelphia was more virulent than strains circulating through the rest of the country. Dr. William Atkinson, then-head of CDC, found that the measles outbreak had nothing to do with the circulating strain and everything to do with the parents. The strain of measles in Philadelphia was not particularly virulent. Rather, the parents were failing to provide

23 *Id.* at 100–101.

24 Meekle, *supra* note 16; First Century Gospel Church – Philadelphia PA, USA, First Century Gospel Church (Apr. 20, 2017), www.fcgchurch.org/.

25 Bad Faith, *supra* note 1, at 101. *See also* Lewin, *supra* note 2.

adequate medical treatment to their children to prevent measles-related deaths. Dr. Atkinson found that children were dying because they were not getting intravenous fluids for severe dehydration or receiving supportive therapy such as oxygen for their pneumonia.

On February 18, 1991, Reverend Reinert of the Faith Tabernacle Church, for the first time, was willing to speak out.[26] Up until this point, he had remained silent. "The Devil has tried to put fear in people's hearts," he said, "Job was robbed of everything he had. As he went through the trial, he learned from it. There is no fear when you can see God on your side." Reverend Reinert saw the deaths of these children in his church as a test of his faith, a test he had every intention of passing. "It's drawing us all together," he said.

At this juncture, the authorities in Philadelphia took a third legal step.[27] They obtained a court order to hospitalize children who were critically ill. With the telephone number of a judge in hand, residents from CHOP and St. Christopher's examined children from the Faith Tabernacle Church against their parents' will and acquired court orders to treat children in dire need of medical attention. "It was like entering a time warp," said Mark Joffe, who headed St. Christopher's team, "With the exception of the fact that they stay at home and watch their children die from measles, they seemed like wonderful people."

Later that same day, February 18, 1991, the team was able to successfully hospitalize children who were identified as stricken with measles and in need of hospitalization.[28] The first child admitted via court order was Daniel Kirn, a four-year-old who had measles pneumonia. The healthcare worker insisted on admitting Daniel to the hospital. However, his parents "politely, but firmly, refuse[d]" to allow him to be treated. Dr. Ross called City Solicitor Charisse Lille, who called Family Court Judge Edward Summers, who issued an emergency order to hospitalize Daniel against his parents' will.[29] Later that day, a second child, two-year-old Bianca Carpena, was also hospitalized against her parents' wishes after a court order was obtained.

The Philadelphia measles epidemic was now at its peak. At CHOP, about eighty-two children were treated in the Emergency Department by mid-February of 1991 and twenty-eight were hospitalized.[30] By the time the epidemic ran its course, more than 200 children were seen, and 40 were hospitalized there. At St. Christopher's, 250 children were seen in the Emergency

[26] *Id.* at 101. [27] *Id.* at 100, 102. [28] *Id.* at 102.

[29] For a discussion of judicial bypasses authorizing medical care, *see* Wilson and Sanders, Chapter 13, this volume.

[30] Bad Faith, *supra* note 1, at 103.

Department with three children hospitalized every week. Dr. Ross and his team had visited 80 families and almost 500 children by this time. On February 19, 1991, a court order was granted to hospitalize two girls suffering from measles pneumonia. By this point, four children had been hospitalized under court order, but Dr. Ross correctly predicted that more measles deaths would happen in Philadelphia.

Philadelphia had become a feared destination.[31] Two schools near the city canceled trips due to fears of children contracting measles. In an attempt to quell the outbreak, the city printed 50,000 educational pamphlets on prevention and care for measles patients. The city was also vaccinating hundreds of schoolchildren every week. The Commonwealth of Pennsylvania sent $100,000 in federal funds to help Philadelphia in its efforts to combat measles. On February 27, 1991, Major Wilson Goode asked the City Solicitor's office to obtain a court order to forcibly vaccinate children, even if their parents did not want them to be vaccinated for religious reasons.[32] Before examining how this radical step affected the arc of the epidemic, it is important to review the State's power to compel its citizens to receive medical services for the public good.

III COMPULSORY VACCINATIONS AND RELIGIOUS LIBERTY

The U.S. Supreme Court has interpreted the U.S. Constitution to allow a state to compel its citizens to be vaccinated and to enact health regulations in the interest of public health.[33] One can think of such mandatory vaccination policies as requests that you receive a vaccination, backed up by a threat of a social cost or expense should you decline. The Supreme Court limited the permissible exercise of this police power by a state through a few key decisions.[34]

[31] *Id.* at 104–05.

[32] *Id.* at 107; Anders Kelto, *Why a Court Once Ordered Kids Vaccinated Against Their Parents' Will*, NPR (Feb. 19, 2015) www.npr.org/sections/health-shots/2015/02/19/386040745/why-a-court-once-ordered-kids-vaccinated-against-their-parents-will; H. Goldman & S. Fitzgerald, *City Will Seek Court Order for Measles Shot*, PHILADELPHIA INQUIRER (Feb. 28, 1991).

[33] *See* Jacobson v. Massachusetts, 197 U.S. 11, 22 (1905) (holding that states may enforce mandatory vaccination laws).

[34] BAD FAITH, *supra* note 1, at 105–07. *See also* Lawrence O. Gostin, Jacobson v Massachusetts at 100 *Years: Police Power and Civil Liberties in Tension*, 95 AM J PUBLIC HEALTH 576, 576 (2005) ("In affirming Massachusetts' compulsory vaccination law [in *Jacobson v. Massachusetts*], the Court established a floor of constitutional protections that consists of 4 standards: necessity, reasonable means, proportionality, and harm avoidance.").

The landmark case holding compulsory vaccinations constitutional is *Jacobson v. Massachusetts*.[35] The case was brought in 1905, after two major outbreaks of smallpox in Cambridge, Massachusetts, left 270 people dead.[36] In an effort to stop the spread of the disease in the city, the Cambridge Board of Health adopted a regulation that required all citizens to receive the smallpox vaccination or pay a $5.00 fine.[37] Lutheran minister Henning Jacobson chose neither option, claiming that such a policy was an infringement of his personal liberties.[38] Specifically, Jacobson claimed, "vaccination does not tend to prevent smallpox, but tends to bring about other diseases, and that it does much harm, with no good."[39]

On his challenge to the constitutionality of the policy, the Court held that the policy had a real and substantial relation to the protection of the public health.[40] The Court stood by its long-standing position that state policies or regulations that limit personal freedom or cause personal sacrifice may be enacted when there is a benefit to the public health, morals, or safety.[41] Writing for the majority, Justice John Marshall Harlan said:

> The liberty secured by the Constitution of the United States does not import an absolute right ... to be ... wholly freed from restraint. There are manifold restraints to which every person is necessarily subject for the common good ... Society based on the rule that each one is a law unto himself would soon be confronted with disorder and anarchy.[42]

The holding in *Jacobson* marks a judicial shift toward ensuring states have the ability to protect the health and safety of their citizens.[43] *Jacobson* did not specifically address the religious concerns held by many anti-vaxers, but it left a legacy of social welfare philosophy as it relates to the exercise of police power.[44] Justice Harlan's test permits the state to use any reasonable means necessary, proportional to the risk to public safety and welfare, to avoid harm to the general public.[45] Thus, the legacy of *Jacobson* permits state intervention when disease outbreaks occur, including mandating the administration of vaccines.

Seventeen years after *Jacobson*, the Court was confronted with another challenge to compelled vaccination in *Zucht v. King*.[46] Rosalyn Zucht was expelled from Brackenridge High School in San Antonio, Texas, for refusing

[35] *See* Lawrence O. Gostin & Katrina A. Pagonis, Jacobson v. Massachusetts: *The Police Power and Civil Liberties in Tension, in* HEALTH LAW AND BIOETHICS: CASES IN CONTEXT 163, 163 (Sandra H. Johnson, Joan H. Krause, Richard S. Saver, & Robin Fretwell Wilson, eds., 2009) (describing *Jacobson* as the "foundational judicial decision in public health law") [hereinafter *Police Power*].

[36] Jacobson, *supra* note 33, at 22; *Police Power*, *supra* note 35, at 163.

[37] Jacobson, *supra* note 33, at 21. [38] *Id.* [39] *Id.* at 34. [40] *Id.* [41] *Id.* [42] *Id.* at 22.

[43] *Police Power*, *supra* note 35, at 163. [44] *Id.* [45] *Id.* at 579.

[46] BAD FAITH, *supra* note 1, at 106; Zucht v. King, 260 U.S. 174 (1922).

a smallpox vaccine.[47] There was no smallpox epidemic when Zucht challenged the vaccination scheme, but the Court invoked *Jacobson*'s holding.[48] The Court unanimously granted states the broad authority to impose health regulations and held that such a requirement was legal and part of the broad discretion of state police power that is required for the protection of public health.[49]

One final case, *Prince v. Massachusetts*, discusses vaccinations in part although it was a child labor law case, as Wilson and Sanders discuss at length in Chapter 13, this volume.[50] Sarah Prince wanted to take her niece to distribute pamphlets on the streets of Brockton, Massachusetts, relatively late at night, a violation of child labor laws.[51] She ultimately took her case to the Supreme Court to see whether or not her religious belief – to be able to distribute pamphlets on behalf of Jehovah's Witnesses – trumped child labor laws. The Court found her religious beliefs did not trump state child labor laws, citing the legality of compulsory vaccination policies as support for its decision:[52]

> [A parent or guardian] cannot claim freedom from compulsory vaccination for the child more than for himself on religious grounds. The right to practice religion freely does not include liberty to expose the community or the child to communicable disease or the latter to ill health or death. The State has a wide range of power for limiting parental freedom and authority in things affecting the child's welfare; and that this includes, to some extent, matters of conscience and religious conviction.[53]

The Court reasoned, "[p]arents may be free to become martyrs themselves. But it does not follow they are free, in identical circumstances, to make martyrs of their children before they have reached the age of full and legal discretion when they can make that choice for themselves."[54]

But the Court reaffirmed the general authority of parents in making decisions for children:

> It is cardinal with us that the custody, care and nurture of the child reside first in the parents, whose primary function and freedom include preparation for obligations the state can neither supply nor hinder. And it is in recognition of this that these decisions have respected the private realm of family life which the state cannot enter.[55]

Yet, the Court made clear that "the family itself is not beyond regulation in the public interest, as against a claim of religious liberty."[56]

[47] Zucht, *supra* note 46, at 175. [48] Bad Faith, *supra* note 1, at 106.
[49] Zucht, *supra* note 46, at 177. [50] Prince, v. Massachusetts, 321 U.S. 158 (1944).
[51] Bad Faith, *supra* note 1, at 154–55. [52] Prince, *supra* note 50, at 159. [53] *Id.*
[54] *Id.* at 170. [55] *Id.* at 166. [56] *Id.*

In instances of necessity or in an effort to broadly protect public health and safety, it is legally acceptable for a state to exercise its police power to protect its citizens.[57] As long as a policy does not arbitrarily target a single group of individuals and is broadly applied, the policy withstands constitutional validity.

A *Mandatory versus Compulsory Vaccination*

There is a difference between a mandatory vaccination and a compulsory vaccination.[58] A mandatory vaccination asks a person to get vaccinated and if he or she chooses not to get vaccinated, some sort of societal price may be imposed. In the case of Henning Jacobson, pay a fine; in the case of Rosalyn Zucht, get kicked out of school; and in the case of a hospital worker, perhaps to be unable to work at the hospital without vaccination. A compulsory vaccination occurs when a person is pinned down and vaccinated whether or not he or she wants to be vaccinated. The U.S. military has compulsory vaccination, but no one is forced to join the military.

Mandatory vaccination policies are most commonly encountered by citizens in a school setting. As of 2014, every state and the District of Columbia had laws requiring all children entering school to receive vaccinations that meet state-specific immunization requirements.[59] These policies date back to the 1970s, though their establishment is premised on the Supreme Court's decision in 1922 in *Zucht v. King*.[60]

The CDC currently recommends that children receive fifty-one doses of sixteen vaccines before age 18.[61] Most states mandate that children receive twenty-nine doses of nine vaccines to enter kindergarten, and some are required to receive multiple doses of thirteen vaccines.[62]

B *Exemptions to State-Mandated Vaccinations*

Although there is no constitutional right to refuse vaccines, state legislators need not require vaccinations. Further, a state may allow exemptions to its own mandatory vaccination scheme via exemptions for citizens to decline

57 For a discussion of this line of cases, *see* Bad Faith, *supra* note 1, at 154–60.

58 *Id.* at 107, 105–11.

59 Jared P. Cole & Kathleen S. Swendiman, *Mandatory Vaccinations: Precedent and Current Laws*, Congressional Research Service 2 (May 21, 2014).

60 *Id.*

61 *Recommended Immunization Schedule for Children and Adolescents Aged 18 Years or Younger*, Centers for Disease Control and Prevention (Oct. 19, 2015), www.cdc.gov/vaccines/schedules/downloads/child/0-18yrs-child-combined-schedule.pdf.

62 *Id.*

otherwise mandated treatment for medical, religious, or personal belief reasons.[63] As Figure 12.1 shows, many states have done just that. Figure 12.1 shows the states that allow parents not to vaccinate their children based on the parents' religious or philosophical beliefs.[64]

Exemptions are a state issue and, invariably, a political one.[65] The landmark cases allowing states to adopt mandatory vaccination policies burdened citizens who held sincere religious beliefs against vaccination. However, religious believers were unable to win constitutional challenges against these schemes because the state had a legitimate interest in the welfare of its citizens, and no person was being discriminated against based upon religion, because persons of all religions were asked to receive vaccinations. Consequently, parents with bona fide religious beliefs against vaccinating their children could be compelled to vaccinate against their wishes.

But that changed – at least, the thinking changed – because of something that happened in the New York State Assembly in 1966.[66] In that year, New York State was considering a bill requiring a polio vaccine for school entry. That bill passed by a vote of 150–2; the two dissenting votes were cast because the bill excluded parents whose religion forbade vaccinations. These votes were the direct result of the lobbying efforts of one particular religious group that specifically stated that no one should be vaccinated. In 1972, *Maier v. Besser* became the key case that took advantage of the two dissenters in the New York Legislature in 1966 and created liberal religious exemptions to states' mandatory vaccination laws. William Maier successfully claimed that a New York State law that required his sons to be vaccinated in order to attend public school violated that his First Amendment rights.[67] Maier, a Christian Scientist, was granted a permanent injunction to allow him to prove the genuineness of his religious beliefs and to permit the children to remain in school while his case was pending trial.[68]

While *Maier v. Besser* did not establish a constitutional right to refuse state-mandated vaccinations on religious grounds, it did create a cascading set of state legislation creating religious and philosophical exemptions to state-mandated vaccination. As a consequence, forty-seven states have religious or philosophical

[63] *Id.*

[64] Map adapted from *Vaccine Requirements vs. Federal Vaccine Recommendations*, NAT'L VACCINE INFO. CTR. (2016), www.nvic.org/Vaccine-Laws/federal-recommendations-vs-state-vaccine-laws.aspx. Not all jurisdictions express the exemption in terms of religious accommodations – examples include DC and Louisiana. Exemptions for philosophical reasons in those jurisdictions would accommodate religious objections to vaccinations.

[65] *See* Adams, Chapter 21, this volume. [66] BAD FAITH, *supra* note 1, at 106.

[67] Maier v. Besser, 73 Misc. 2d 241 (N.Y. Sup. Ct. 1972). [68] *Id.*

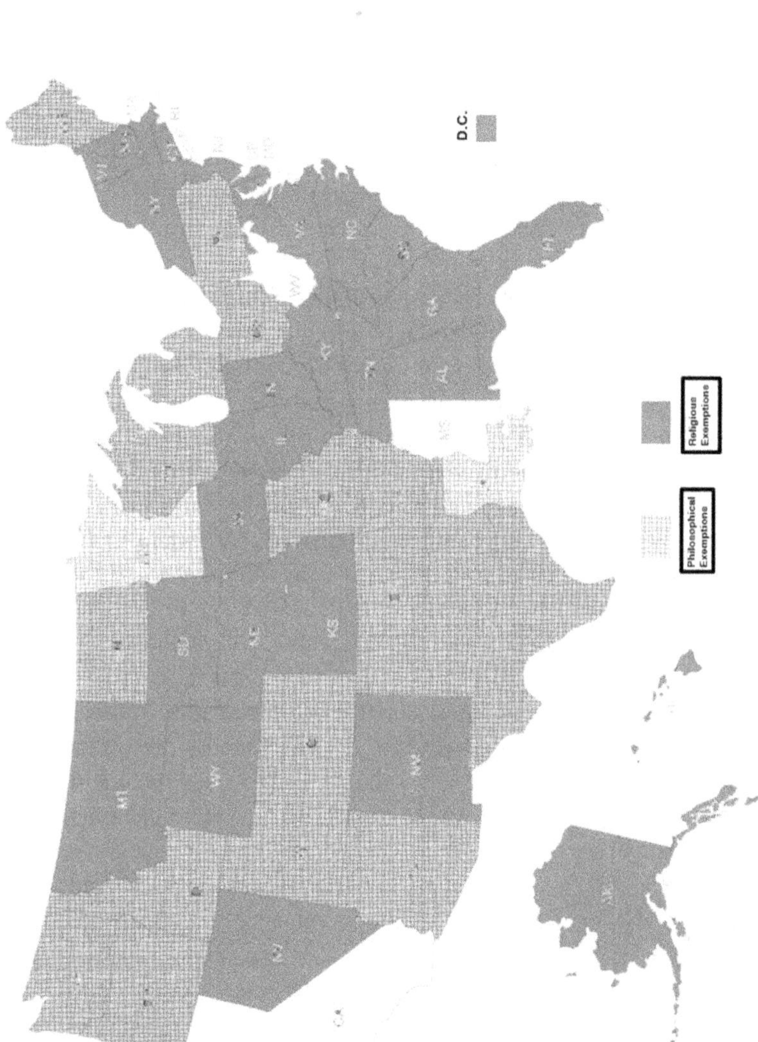

FIGURE 12.1 Exemptions to Mandatory Vaccination Laws

exemptions, as Figure 12.1 shows. Only California, Mississippi, and West Virginia do not have a religious or philosophical exemption, although each allows for a medical exemption.[69] Medical exemptions may be granted with proper documentation from a doctor or other certified healthcare provider.[70] Religious and personal belief exemptions, however, are not as rigid in their application.

C Consequences of Statutory Exemptions Extend Beyond Vaccinations

Medical neglect is considered a category of child abuse that must be examined under state statutes prohibiting child abuse and neglect. In recent decades, state legislatures carved out exceptions if a religious reason motivates parents to make choices that would otherwise constitute medical neglect. This definition of when something counts as medical neglect was developed through legislation enacted over the past century, with the influence of the religious individuals who played a part in the enactment.[71]

Throughout the first part of the 21st century, when a parent practiced medical neglect toward a child, the child was immediately removed from the home and sent to foster care.[72] The parent, meanwhile, was sent to jail.[73] This clear-cut understanding of medical neglect as it relates to child abuse changed in the early 1970s because of the enactment of Hubert Humphrey's Child Abuse Prevention and Treatment Act ("CAPTA").[74]

The establishment of CAPTA was done to protect all children.[75] Enacted during the Nixon Administration, two prominent Christian Scientists in Nixon's administration realized that an uncomfortable light was about to be shined on their religion, Christian Science, because Christian Scientists practice medical neglect. They pray instead of giving insulin for diabetes; they pray instead of giving antibiotics for meningitis. And so, these members of the Administration said to the states, "You cannot receive any federal funds unless you have, on your states' books, a law that states that you have a religious exemption to child abuse and neglect laws." Such exemptions allowed individuals to refuse to comply with statutory regulations – that is, types of required medical care – if the noncomplying individual could provide a religious basis for the refusal.[76]

The Christian Scientists' efforts were successful. In 1973, the law passed with the incorporation of religious exemptions.[77] Under CAPTA, medical

[69] *Vaccine Requirements vs. Federal Vaccine Recommendations*, NAT'L VACCINE INFO. CTR. (2016), www.nvic.org/Vaccine-Laws/federal-recommendations-vs-state-vaccine-laws.aspx.

[70] *Id.* [71] BAD FAITH, *supra* note 1, at 168–71.

[72] *Child Abuse*, ENCYCLOPEDIA BRITANNICA (2016), www.britannica.com/topic/child-abuse.

[73] *Id.* [74] *See* 42 U.S.C. § 5101 (2012). [75] BAD FAITH, *supra* note 1, at 167–71. [76] *Id.*

[77] *See* 42 U.S.C. § 5101 (2012).

neglect constitutes a form of child abuse, but if the parent taking the action cites a religious reason for his or her choices, the parent is not liable for the harms caused to the child. A few months after CAPTA's enactment, those two Christian Scientists went to jail for their role in the Watergate scandal. One was Nixon's Chief of Staff, Bob Haldeman; the other was his Chief of Domestic Policy Advisor John Ehrlichman.

Figure 12.2 shows states that allow religious exemptions to medical neglect laws that would otherwise punish parents' failure to provide adequate medical care for their children.[78] To this day, thirty-four states and the District of Columbia have laws in place that exempt parents from liability for acting with medical neglect toward their child if they have a religious basis for their choices.[79] Seventeen states have religious exemptions to felony charges.[80] Perhaps the most onerous religious defenses in the U.S. are those to manslaughter or negligent homicide.[81] Other states have variations on exemptions from criminal charges, but religious exemptions may successfully allow parents to evade liability for their neglectful actions, leaving affected children in these unvaccinated communities still severely harmed.

D The Rise of Faith Healing Religions

Faith healing religions believe in the power of faith in lieu of modern medical treatments or preventative care. About twenty such religions exist across the U.S., the largest of which is Christian Science.[82] The Jehovah's Witnesses, who do not practice faith healing but believe that their children should not get a blood transfusion even if life saving, illustrate that medical neglect is not

78 Map adapted from Aleksandra Sandstrom, *Most States Allow Religious Exemptions from Child Abuse and Neglect Laws*, Pew Research Center (Aug. 12, 2016), www.pewresearch.org/fact-tank/2016/08/12/most-states-allow-religious-exemptions-from-child-abuse-and-neglect-laws/; *Religious Defenses in State Penal Codes*, Children's Healthcare is a Legal Duty, Inc., http://childrenshealthcare.org/wp-content/uploads/2014/07/State-exemptions-criminal2.pdf (showing homicide and manslaughter exemptions).

79 Sandstrom, *supra* note 78.

80 *Religious Defenses in State Penal Codes*, Children's Healthcare is a Legal Duty, Inc., http://childrenshealthcare.org/wp-content/uploads/2014/07/State-exemptions-criminal2.pdf.

81 *See* Figure 12.2. West Virginia and Arkansas have religious defenses to homicide. No state has a religious defense within the manslaughter statute, but laws of five states, Idaho, Iowa, Ohio, Louisiana, and Mississippi, in effect have a religious defense to manslaughter because their prosecutors must prove that a lesser crime has been committed in order to prove a manslaughter charge and those states have religious defenses to the only other crimes that could be charged for medical neglect.

82 Jerry A. Coyne, *Faith Healing Kills Children*, Slate (May 21, 2015), www.slate.com/articles/health_and_science/medical_examiner/2015/05/religious_exemptions_from_medical_care_faith_healing_kills_children.html.

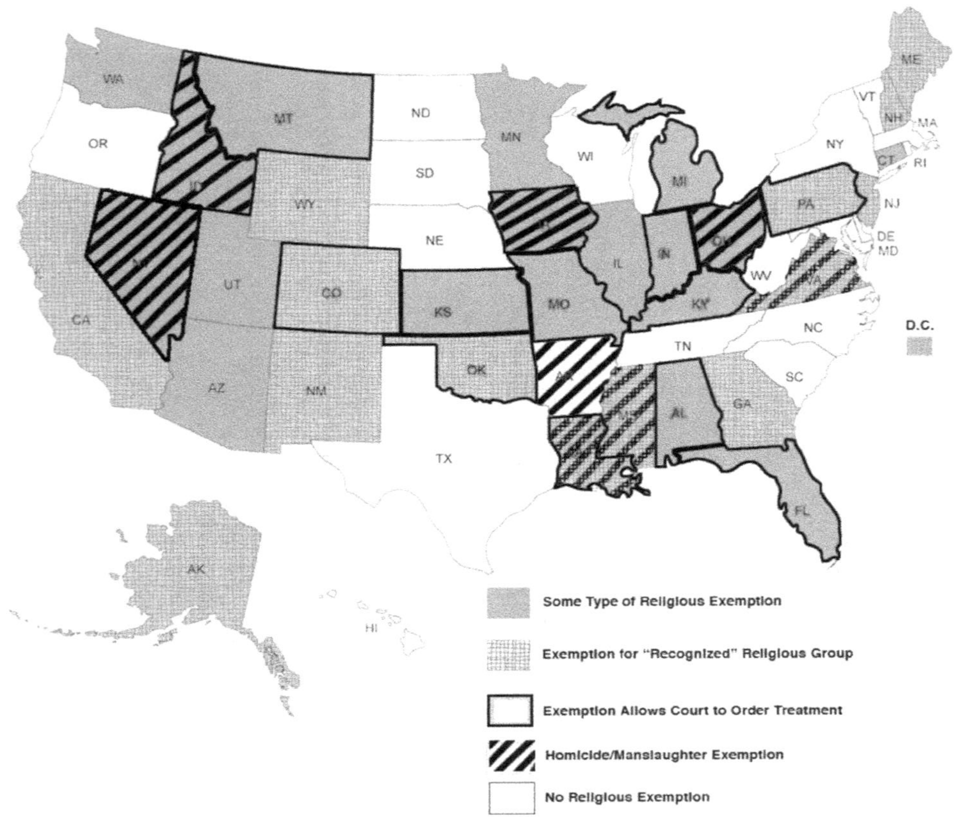

FIGURE 12.2 Exemptions to Medical Neglect Laws

isolated to faith healing communities.[83] It is logical to ask why parents follow the directives of these religions when doing so jeopardizes the health and safety of their child. This question is particularly pronounced when parents refuse lifesaving medical care to a child in desperate need. When asked why they do so, these parents will often say a single, simple, line: "Jesus was my doctor."

Independent of belief in the existence of a supreme being – or independent of belief that Jesus was the son of God, or that the Gospels, which were written decades after Jesus died, are in any way an accurate reflection of what Jesus did or said – one has to be impressed with the figure described in the four Gospels as Jesus of Nazareth.[84] At the time Jesus lived, child abuse was the prime vice of the Roman Empire. Abandonment was common; infanticide was common. Children were property and treated like slaves, as if they did not matter. This is evidenced by Hippocrates, who lived about 400 years before Jesus. He talked endlessly about how one can reasonably interact with parents, the ethics of interacting with patients, but he never mentioned children because children did not matter.[85] Jesus of Nazareth is portrayed as someone who cared about children. He believed that children were human, that children had souls and therefore could go to heaven: "Suffer little children, and forbid them not, to come unto me: for of such is the kingdom of heaven."[86] A great deal of the Gospel of Matthew is dedicated to children, "And the King shall answer and say unto them, Verily I say unto you, Inasmuch as ye have done *it* unto one of the least of these my brethren, ye have done *it* unto me."[87]

Religion has been beneficially intertwined with medicine throughout history. Constantine, the first Christian emperor of Rome in A.D. 315, passed the first basic law protecting children against abuse.[88] Six years later, he was the first to pass a law establishing welfare to protect children in poverty from being sold. Prior to the modern legislation, religion had a positive and profound impact on the way in which children were cared for. Several years later, Constantine was the first to pass a law protecting them from poverty, which formed the base for Christian relief societies for the next 1800 years. Early monasteries had both inpatient and outpatient facilities that formed a prototype for modern-day hospitals.

83 Bad Faith, *supra* note 1, at 158–60. 84 *Id.* at 113–28. 85 *Id.* at 125–26.

86 Matthew 19:14 (King James version). 87 Matthew 25:40 (King James version).

88 Bad Faith, *supra* note 1, at 127; Rachel Marie Stone, *What One of the Anti-Vaccination Movement's Least Favorite Doctors Discovered about Jesus*, Wash. Post (Apr. 13, 2015), www.washingtonpost.com/news/acts-of-faith/wp/2015/04/13/what-one-of-the-anti-vaccination-movements-least-favorite-doctors-discovered-about-jesus/.

Mary Baker Eddy founded Christian Science in 1875.[89] Her book, *Science and Health with Key to the Scriptures*, enumerated the beliefs of the religion to followers and became a leading source of Christian Science information. Eddy believed that illness was a spiritual, not physical, disorder, and that diseases should be treated with prayer, rather than medicines or surgeries. As she says in *Science and Health*, "[w]e have smallpox because others have it. But mortal mind, not matter contains and carries the infection." To Eddy, diseases did not exist but were merely a perception imposed upon yourself. Any problem causing a particular malady was simply created from individual's perception. So if a man had a boil, the man merely perceived himself to have a boil.[90] He did not really have a boil, because God was perfect and God made man in his image, and therefore man was perfect. The reason that the man perceived himself to have a boil was that he was not close enough to God. He had to pray to get closer to God, and as he prayed and prayed and prayed, his boil would disappear. Such perception derives from the individual's distance from God, and consequently Eddy believed that prayer to bring you closer to God would serve as the quickest remedy.

To Eddy's credit, Christian Science was one of the fastest-growing religions in the 1800s because medical remedies were not nearly as successful as modern treatments in 1875.[91] In Eddy's time, there was a smallpox vaccine, quinine to treat malaria, ether and chloroform were used as general anesthetics, but the list of cutting-edge treatment options ended there.[92] There were cathartics, leeches, corrosives, and emetics.[93] Common trope said that old doctors let you die, while solutions from new doctors killed you.[94] Eddy managed these concerns by putting ownership of the solution into the hands of the common man: through the ability to heal by prayer.

89 Bad Faith, *supra* note 1, at 2–5, 10, 21, 30–31, 41; *Christian Science*, Encyclopedia Britannica (2016), www.britannica.com/topic/Christian-Science; Ingrid Peschke, *Women's History Month: Mary Baker Eddy's Commitment to Health*, Huffington Post (Mar. 4, 2014), www.huffingtonpost.com/ingrid-peschke/womens-history-month-mary_b_4892042.html.

90 Bad Faith, *supra* note 1, at 4.

91 *Id.* at 5; Robert F. Reilly, *Medical and Surgical Care During the American Civil War, 1861–1865*, 29 Proc. Bayl. Univ. Med. Cent. 138, 139 (Apr. 2016).

92 *Id.* 93 Bad Faith, *supra* note 1, at 5.

94 *See, e.g.*, Erika Schwartz, *Don't Let Your Doctor Kill You*, U.S. News & World Report (Apr. 6, 2016), http://health.usnews.com/health-news/patient-advice/articles/2016%9604-06/dont-let-your-doctor-kill-you ("In my 40 years of practicing medicine, I have witnessed the disintegration of individualized care and the demise of the doctor-patient relationship as subspecialties and advanced technologies have changed the landscape and priorities in health care.").

IV MANDATORY VACCINATION PLAN TO CURB PHILADELPHIA'S 1991 MEASLES OUTBREAK

At the time that the measles outbreak occurred in 1991, Pennsylvania had a religious exemption to vaccination that had been on the books for about ten years.[95] So when Reverend Reinert said, "I have a religious claim to not vaccinate," he was right. That did not stop the city from seeking a court order to forcibly vaccinate children within the Faith Tabernacle Church community, however.

Reverend Reinert appealed to the Pennsylvania chapter of the American Civil Liberties Union ("ACLU") to represent him and the Faith Tabernacle Church families. The ACLU declined to help these parents. There was a panic in Philadelphia: hospital workers were pulling child after child dead from their home and people were scared they were going to catch measles and potentially suffer the consequences. "There is certainly a free exercise of religious claim by the parents," said Deborah Leavy of the Philadelphia chapter of the ACLU, "but there is also a competing claim that parents don't have the right to martyr their children." Thus, echoing the words of that 1944 *Prince v. Massachusetts* case, "I don't think we've walked away from our principles here." On March 4, 1991, Judge Summers ordered city officials to disregard Pennsylvania state rules allowing religious exemptions to mandatory vaccination.[96] Jerome Balter represented the parents of Faith Tabernacle Church children. He protested State Superior Court Judge Vincent Cirillo's decision. "Their healing is dependent on their faith," he said, "They believe that's the right thing to do for their children." The judge ruled in favor of the city, so Balter took the case to the Pennsylvania Superior Court of Appeals.

Tragedy struck during the appeals hearing.[97] Shawn Lacy, a public defender, was appointed as an advocate, to represent the children of the Faith Tabernacle Church. As Judge Cirillo was hearing the appeal, he noticed a pained expression on Lacy's face. "Are you ill?" he asked. Lacy had just been handed a note concerning a twenty-month-old boy, James Jones, whose parents were members of Faith Tabernacle Church. James had died of measles encephalitis at 9:30 the morning of the hearing. James was the fifth child from the Faith Tabernacle Church to die since Caryn Still on February 7. News of James's death set the tone for the remainder of the hearing. Balter argued that parents were now willing to allow sick children to be admitted to the hospital, but they still refused to be vaccinated, thus

[95] Bad Faith, *supra* note 1, at 108. [96] *Id.* at 110. [97] *Id.* at 110–11.

implying the treatment is as good as prevention. Within an hour, Judge Cirillo rejected Balter's arguments.

On March 5, 1991, this headline appeared in *The Philadelphia Inquirer*: "Judge Permits City to Vaccinate Objectors" as Judge Cirillo upheld Judge Summers's compulsory vaccination order and ordered six children be vaccinated.[98] On March 15, 1991, Judge Summers ordered a second round of compulsory vaccinations for children of the Faith Tabernacle Congregation School and the parents did not fight the order. "I recall we lined the children up and gave the immunizations, and many of the parents were actually weeping," Dr. Ross said.[99] By the time the vaccines were administered, the measles outbreak was subsiding and only nine children from the church were vaccinated.

In June of 1991, the measles epidemic slowed significantly. "Typically, measles is a disease of the late winter and early spring," said Robert Levenson, director of Philadelphia's Division of Disease Control, "When the warm weather comes, the cases disappear." Reverend Reinert interpreted those events differently. He focused on the children in his church who had survived the infection without medical care; Reverend Reinert said, "We believe God has provided his faithfulness."[100]

On December 3, 1992, Dr. Atkinson and coworkers from the CDC reported their findings from this outbreak among Faith Tabernacle Church members: 486 people were infected and 6 died.[101] As the virus then spread from the epicenter of those two churches into the surrounding community, among non-church members 938 people were infected and 3 died. All nine deaths were those of children. The attack rate in church members was about 1000-fold greater than in the surrounding community.

V THE NEED FOR CRUSADERS AGAINST FAITH HEALING

I was a young physician at CHOP during the 1991 Philadelphia measles outbreak. I just wondered where was the church? Why didn't it stand up and say "this isn't us," "these aren't Christian things to do" – that would have really helped. It puts one in mind of a quote from W. H. Auden's *The Shield of Achilles*: "[W]hen all the mass and majesty of the world, when all that carries weight and always weighed the same, lay in the hands of others; they were

[98] *Id.* at 111; H. Goldman, *Judge Permits City to Vaccinate Objectors*, PHILADELPHIA INQUIRER (Mar. 5, 1991).

[99] Kelto, *supra* note 32. [100] BAD FAITH, *supra* note 1, at 112. [101] *Id.* at 112.

small and could not hope for help, and no help came." And that's what I felt like here.

At the time Anthony Bevilacqua had been promoted from Archbishop of Philadelphia to Cardinal; he was an important voice in our city.[102] In a perfect world, he would have made clear that allowing one's child to die when the death is completely preventable is not a "Christian thing to do" – and made this point publicly. That did not happen.

But another voice emerged that would prove far more significant for child protection in the U.S., Rita Swan. Rita Swan was born and raised a Christian Scientist and was taught to believe in the medicinal power of faith healing.[103] In 1977, her sixteen-month-old son Matthew contracted bacterial meningitis. He was unvaccinated, in line with the beliefs of the Christian Scientists, and Rita and her husband refused to administer modern medical care because such actions did not conform to their religious beliefs. Instead, she prayed for the twelve days it took Matthew to die. And then after he died, she had an epiphany, and she said, "I've been duped. I need to learn about this."[104]

She had earned a PhD in English from Vanderbilt University, writing her thesis on Percy Shelley and British Romantic poetry.[105] Her husband, also a Christian Scientist, had gotten his PhD in mathematics from Vanderbilt University. When asked how she could let this happen to her son, she said what many faith healers say: "I was treating him. I was treating him by prayer." But she said, "You don't realize how little I knew about medicine. I didn't know what a thermometer was, I didn't know that a fever meant infection, so just because I was an expert in British Romantic poetry and my husband an expert in differential equations, doesn't mean I know anything about this."[106]

She accepted her role in the outcome of her son's death; instead of continuing to stand behind her religious beliefs, she began to educate herself on faith healing communities.[107] She did something no faith healer does: she said "I let this happen. I did this."[108] It was not the usual "It was God's will" passive position; it was "I did this." She went on the *Phil Donahue Show*, which was a popular TV show at the time, and basically declared a major religion as a fraud, or, in her words, "a fragile magic."[109] Rita quickly began to question

[102] Douglas Martin, *Anthony J. Bevilacqua, Retired Cardinal of Philadelphia, Dies at* 88, N.Y. Times (Feb. 1, 2012), www.nytimes.com/2012/02/02/us/anthony-j-bevilacqua-retired-cardinal-in-philadelphia-dies-at-88.html.

[103] Bad Faith, *supra* note 1, at 1, 6–18; Children's Healthcare Is a Legal Duty, Inc. *Victims of Religion-Based Medical Neglect* (2016), http://childrenshealthcare.org/?page_id=132.

[104] Bad Faith, *supra* note 1, at 19–21. [105] *Id.* at 7. [106] *Id.* at 20–21, 29.

[107] *Id.* at 177–78. [108] *Id.* at 21. [109] *Id.* at 179.

her religious community and the safety of their faith healing practices since Matthew's death and began investigating the practices of faith healing.[110]

Rita has begun a public campaign and organization called Children's Healthcare is a Legal Duty ("CHILD").[111] The organization seeks to fight against proponents of faith healing and protect the safety of all children. Rita travels across the country to tell her and Matthew's story and now works tirelessly in efforts to overturn laws that allow for religious exemptions.[112]

Rita Swan relentlessly goes from state to state speaking out against faith healing. To say she is the biggest pain in the butt for Christian Scientists out there is an understatement. She is out there trying to overturn those laws that allow religious exemptions, to try and put spades of dirt into a hole that will never be filled. She let her son die: "There is no peace for me; there is no angle of repose; I will just have to do this for the rest of my life."

An analogy to Rita Swan's story can be found in M. Night Shyamalan's 2004 movie *The Village*, which tells the story of an insular community united by fear. Several Philadelphians decide to create a 19th-century farming community in rural Pennsylvania after they are brought together by the murder of a loved one. Solace, they believe, can be found by retreating into the past, isolating the community from a world they fear. The elders create mythical monsters, hiding in the woods, referred to as "the things of which we do not speak." The monsters will not bother the villagers, as long as the villagers do not enter the woods. As a consequence, no one enters or leaves the village.

Then something happens that the elders did not anticipate: a young man is stabbed. Infection develops and the only way to save him is with antibiotics. Unfortunately, the community has been created to mimic the late 1800s, a time before antibiotics. Knowing the monsters are a hoax, the elders allow one of the residents, a young woman, to travel through the woods and get the antibiotics they need. They pick her because she is blind, hoping that when she returns, she will not have realized the wealth of lifesaving technologies on the other side.

Religions that ask the fathers to act against love, compassion, and reason use a similar tactic. Rita Swan was afraid to oppose her church and see a doctor because her church believed that doctors want "[t]o dethrone God, and are therefore evil."[113] If she had sought out modern medicine, she would have been forced to confront that evil and, worse, the anger of God.[114] But Rita

110 *Id.* at 177–94.

111 *Id.* at 180–83; Children's Healthcare Is a Legal Duty, Inc., *About CHILD*, (2016), http://childrenshealthcare.org/?page_id=28.

112 *Id.* 113 BAD FAITH, *supra* note 1, at 197. 114 *Id.* at 7–17.

Swan was not blind. She crossed the woods and entered Wayne State University Medical Library and understood how she could have treated her son's illness.[115] There was no going back, even if it meant ostracism from a community she had known all her life, even if it meant challenging her notion of God.

Swan's break with her church came when she realized that no god would ask a parent to let a child die in his name. Swan explained:

> I believe that the Sabbath was made for man and not man for the Sabbath. That's what Jesus said, so I think religion has to work. It has to bless people, and if it doesn't, if it causes pain, if it justifies cruelty, then it's something I don't want any part of. I think we have to be explicit in rejecting things that are cruel and unjust, whether they're religious or not. Religion has to serve the good of humanity.[116]

Not the other way around.

VI CONCLUSION

Religions teach us to care about our children, to keep them out of harm's way. A religious exemption to child abuse and neglect laws, therefore, is a contradiction of terms.[117] States that provide civil immunity from child neglect laws and criminal defense from child abuse laws to parents allow for the willful deprivation of lifesaving treatment to children on the basis of religious objection. It is time to rethink the state's solicitude's for such beliefs.

115 *Id.* at 177–78. 116 *Id.* at 197.

117 Paul A. Offit, *What Would Jesus Do About Measles?* N.Y. TIMES (Feb. 12, 1991), www.nytimes.com/2015/02/10/opinion/what-would-jesus-do-about-measles.html?emc=eta1&_r=0#permid=14090580.

13

By Faith Alone
When Religious Beliefs and Child Welfare Collide

Robin Fretwell Wilson

Roger and Stephany Joslin Professor of Law, University of Illinois College of Law

Shaakirrah R. Sanders

Associate Professor of Law, University of Idaho College of Law

In 2016, a Myanmarese immigrant who had received political asylum in the United States invoked Indiana's newly enacted Religious Freedom Restoration Act ("RFRA") after being charged with battery for leaving thirty-six bruises and marks on her son's back; she had disciplined him with a coat hanger to save his soul.[1] She claimed both a cultural and a religious defense. Seventeen months before, Texas authorities arrested and indicted Minnesota Vikings running back Adrian Peterson for "whooping" his son with a small tree branch, sparking a national debate over how harshly parents should discipline children.[2] During the deluge of publicity, Peterson explained that he was trying to teach his son right from wrong, exactly as his parents had done in East Texas. Six months before, in the heart of Philadelphia, eight-month-old Brandon Schaible died from a treatable infection because his parents refused to give him antibiotics. Brandon's parents believe "prayer offered in faith will make the sick person well," even though Brandon's older brother had also died of pneumonia that the Schaibles also treated through prayer.[3]

As this chapter shows, these stories have more in common than they are different. How to discipline one's child, like the decision to treat "by faith alone," sometimes runs deep in religious and cultural belief systems. The state's regulation of childrearing not only impacts the parent's liberty, but also a community's ability to hold onto its identity and transmit norms. Too often,

[1] *See* Section III.D *infra*. [2] *Id.*

[3] Eliana Dockterman, *Faith-Healing Parents Jailed After Second Child's Death*, Time (Feb. 19, 2014), http://time.com/8750/faith-healing-parents-jailed-after-second-childs-death/; James 5:14–15 (New International Version) ("Is anyone among you sick? Let them call the elders of the church to pray over them and anoint them with oil in the name of the Lord. And the prayer offered in faith will make the sick person well.").

the state's solicitude for parental autonomy dictates the child's fate. This chapter explores the limits of the broad and constitutionally recognized grant of parental power and documents the veritable kaleidoscope of exemptions for practices that expose children to real and present harm.

Parents in the U.S. generally have the right to raise and rear their children in the manner they see fit. Yet parental rights intersect with and are sometimes restrained by states' power to legislate and regulate for the general welfare of their citizens, including children who lack the wherewithal to protect themselves from illness or abuse by others. In their *parens patriae* role, states stand in the shoes of parents, safeguarding children even when a parent's "religion or conscience"[4] prevents them from doing so.

Standard wisdom holds that government protections of the parent-child relationship reflect a deep respect for religious liberty and individual autonomy. But as this chapter shows, these practices are deeply important to maintaining cultural identity, too. States credit parents' philosophical objections to modern medicine, not just their religious ones. Some take into account cultural reasons for corporal punishment; the majority give parents latitude to physically discipline in neutral terms, without referencing religious beliefs. States cast broad envelopes of discretion around childrearing, in part because of a general agnosticism about which childrearing practices produce the best outcomes for children.

Section I of this chapter reviews the constitutional parameters of the parent-child relationship, which help map the boundaries of parents' parental rights and free exercise of religion when their children might be harmed by the parents' beliefs and actions. It discusses four cases often invoked as proof of thick parental rights to the care, custody, and control of minor children and dependents – *Meyer v. Nebraska*, *Pierce v. Society of the Sisters of the Holy Names of Jesus & Mary*, *Prince v. Massachusetts*, and *Wisconsin v. Yoder*.[5] The section shows that the U.S. Supreme Court brackets parental authority derived from the Constitution: parents may not harm their children.

Section II evaluates the degree of harm to children that results from corporal punishment and faith healing. It presents a schism in views among social scientists about whether corporal punishment always harms children and shows that ethnic and cultural identity can moderate the experiences and effects of physical discipline. Section II then examines the few studies of faith healing

4 Prince v. Massachusetts, 321 U.S. 158, 166–67, 169 (1944).

5 Meyer v. Nebraska, 262 U.S. 390 (1923); Pierce v. Society of the Sisters of the Holy Names of Jesus & Mary, 268 U.S. 510 (1925); Prince, *supra* note 4; Wisconsin v. Yoder, 406 U.S. 205, 230–234 (1972).

practices and shows that the overwhelming majority of children who have died as a result suffered from wholly treatable ailments.

Section III shows the degree of respect for parental autonomy, religion, and cultural practices reflected in state statutes that otherwise require parents to secure needed medical treatment for and to not abuse or neglect their children. As this section and Appendix 1 show, faith healing and corporal punishment laws define the fault lines between parental freedom and child abuse and neglect in each state. Section III then shows that states compensate for the latitude given to parents by charging adults in the community as mandatory reporters of child abuse and by authorizing judges to consent to needed treatment. This section provides descriptions of the law that have been sorely missing in the national discussion of these questions.

Using a single state, Idaho, as a case study, Section IV illustrates how a state's regulation of child abuse, medical neglect, involuntary manslaughter, and lesser crimes operates to confer on parents in Idaho effective immunity from civil sanction when they act "by faith alone." This overlapping statutory scheme has proven hard to reform, even as children continue to die. This is so, in part, because lawmakers are unsure whether attempts to constrain parental choices would ensure that children receive necessary medical care – or would instead backfire, pushing communities and families further from the law. Rather than only prosecuting parents, we conclude that strengthening linkages between the outside world and insular communities holds great promise for protecting children from harm at the hands of their parents.

I CONSTITUTIONAL PARAMETERS OF THE PARENT-CHILD RELATIONSHIP

There is a "play in the joints"[6] between "the private realm of family life" and the state's exercise of police powers that leaves both children unprotected *and* parents at risk of second-guessing by the state. A quadrangle of cases establishing parental rights to rear children does not give parents unfettered discretion, however.

Meyer v. Nebraska represents the earliest announcement of parental rights grounded in the U.S. Constitution. *Meyer* considered a Nebraska law prohibiting public and private schools from teaching children any language other than English before the eighth grade.[7] Like so many laws today, Nebraska did not adopt a blanket ban[8] – it allowed the teaching of "ancient" or "dead"

6 Locke v. Davey, 540 U.S. 712, 718–19 (2004). 7 Meyer, *supra* note 5, at 396–97.

8 See Rienzi, Chapter 4, this volume, for a discussion of employers "grandfathered" out of the contraceptive coverage mandate.

languages, including Latin, Greek, and Hebrew.[9] But schools could not instruct students in German, French, Spanish, Italian, and any other "alien speech."[10] Robert Meyer violated the law when he taught German to a ten-year-old student at a Zionist parochial school. He faced a thirty-day jail sentence and a $25 to $100 fine.[11]

The *Meyer* Court wedged the "natural duty" of parents to choose a suitable education for minor children under the heading of parental autonomy.[12] Writing for the *Meyer* majority, Justice James McReynolds included religious worship and childrearing among the categories of constitutional parental liberty interests.[13] McReynolds asked whether Nebraska properly exercised its constitutional police powers, which Nebraska claimed were to foster American ideals by establishing English as "the mother tongue" for all children within the state.[14] McReynolds acknowledged the allure of establishing a "homogeneous people with American ideals" given the atrocities of World War I.[15] But Nebraska's exercise of its police powers ultimately amounted to using a "prohibited means" to promote a "desirable end."[16]

Meyer shows how states can overstep both the "letter and spirit" of the U.S. Constitution.[17] Practically, Nebraska's ban on modern language courses left "complete freedom as to other matters" and showed a preference for ancient or dead languages.[18] That preference proved fatal when Nebraska failed to show how knowledge of any foreign language harmed a child's health, morals, or understanding of citizenship.[19] Nor could Nebraska demonstrate that knowledge of a modern foreign language posed a danger to national security.[20]

Meyer demonstrates how laws, even well-intentioned ones, can intrude on questions reserved to parents. "[P]roficiency in a foreign language seldom comes to one not instructed at an early age," intruding on a parent's right to decide a child's education.[21] Nebraska also encroached on the teacher's right to choose a profession: German teachers would have fewer choices if Nebraska's ban stayed in place.[22] In an early framing of now-familiar substantive due process and equal protection doctrines, the *Meyer* Court declared "the protection of the Constitution extends to all, to those who speak other languages as well as to those born with English on the tongue."[23]

While *Meyer* struck down the law at issue, the Court did not question Nebraska's ability to override parental choices on educational matters that further the safety and morals of school-aged children.[24] States could "compel

9 Meyer, *supra* note 5, at 400–01. 10 *Id.* at 401. 11 *Id.* at 396–97. 12 *Id.* at 400.
13 *Id.* at 399. 14 *Id.* at 398. 15 *Id.* at 402. 16 *Id.* at 401. 17 *Id.* at 402.
18 *Id.* at 403. 19 *Id.* at 401–03. 20 *Id.* at 403. 21 *Id.* 22 *Id.*, at 400. 23 *Id.* at 401.
24 *Id.* at 402.

attendance" at school.[25] States could also require that *all* schools "give instruction in English," even if states could not selectively ban the teaching of other languages without more evidence.[26]

Like *Meyer*, the second case in this foursome, *Pierce v. Society of the Sisters of the Holy Names of Jesus & Mary*, also turned on whether the State reasonably exercised its police powers. Oregon required parents to send their eight-to sixteen-year-old children to a public school; the "manifest purpose" was to increase public school attendance.[27] Again, Justice McReynolds wrote for the majority.

Oregon, McReynolds concluded in *Pierce*, failed to show that a private school education was inherently harmful to children. Children are not "a mere creature of the state."[28] Oregon intruded on the "liberty of parents and guardians to direct the upbringing and education of children under their control."[29] Oregon's law also diminished the profitability and value of private schools, especially that of the military academies and orphanages that challenged the statute.[30] Thus, while states may generally impose educational requirements, states cannot demand a standardized education only in public schools.[31]

While *Meyer* stood on both substantive due process and equal protection grounds, *Pierce* firmly established substantive due process as the substrate of parental rights. In both cases, the states showed no harm from the prohibited activity – the teaching of modern foreign languages or a private school education. Nor did Nebraska and Oregon point to particular circumstances or emergencies that demanded such extreme measures.

The third case, *Prince v. Massachusetts*, occupies the space at the intersection of "parental right[s] as secured by the due process clause," "freedom of religion under the First Amendment," and state authority to intrude on such rights.[32] There, Sarah Prince and her nine-year-old niece, who was in Prince's legal custody, distributed religious periodicals on the streets of Brockton, Massachusetts.[33] They asked for a five-cent donation for each periodical, implicating a Massachusetts labor law that applied to boys under twelve and girls under eighteen.[34] Because both were ordained ministers in the Jehovah's Witness faith, both Prince and her niece claimed a religious duty to leaflet.[35]

At first blush, *Prince* presents just "another episode in the conflict between Jehovah's Witnesses and state authority."[36] Yet, swirling in *Prince* are questions not only of the rights of religious communities and individuals poised against the State but also of the rights of families and children and the state's role in

[25] *Id.* [26] *Id.* [27] Pierce, *supra* note 5, at 530–31. [28] *Id.* at 534. [29] *Id.* at 535.
[30] *Id.* at 531–34. [31] *Id.* at 535. [32] Prince, *supra* note 4, at 164. [33] *Id.* at 161.
[34] *Id.* at 160–61. [35] *Id.* at 161–64. [36] *Id.* at 159.

protecting children.[37] Here, a parent's right to teach her children the tenets and practices of her chosen faith overlap with a child's independent right to observe and "preach the gospel."[38]

Prince articulated the cardinal rule "that the custody, care and nurture of the child reside first in the parents," a "private realm of family life" that states must respect.[39] But the state can act to safeguard children from abuse and to give children the opportunity to grow into free, independent, and well-developed citizens.[40]

Turning to whether Massachusetts sufficiently rationalized the need for child labor restrictions,[41] *Prince* identified "the crippling effects of child employment" as an appropriate evil justifying the exercise of police power.[42] *Prince* established "psychological or physical injury" to children as a baseline for deciding when an action that would be protected free exercise for an adult properly becomes a subject for the state's concern for protecting children.[43] "The zealous though lawful exercise" of religious liberty "may and at times does create situations ... wholly inappropriate for children, especially of tender years, to face."[44] That which is "permissible for adults ... may not be so for children."[45]

Prince recognizes that the state "as *parens patriae*" may act "to guard the general interest in youth's well being," even if the parent's view is premised on "religion or conscience."[46] The rights of religion and parenthood do not prevent the state from requiring "compulsory vaccination" or protecting children from communicable disease, ill health, or death.[47] The *Prince* Court explained: "Parents may be free to become martyrs themselves. But it does not follow that they are free, in identical circumstances, to make martyrs of their children before they have reached the age of full and legal discretion when they can make that choice for themselves."[48] While *Prince* cautioned that religious training and indoctrination of children will continue to receive constitutional protection from state intervention that exceeds the state's police power[49] – and that the state should use delicacy when balancing parental control and state authority[50] – it painted outer boundaries of a parent's prerogatives, whether or not religiously motivated.

Dwyer (Chapter 8, this volume) critiques the fourth case, *Wisconsin v. Yoder*,[51] which he argues accorded religious parents, and religious communities, significant autonomy in a contest with the state over what best serves a child's welfare. In *Yoder*, Amish families challenged application of a

[37] *Id.* at 164. [38] *Id.* [39] *Id.* at 166. [40] *Id.* at 165. [41] *Id.* at 167. [42] *Id.* at 168.
[43] *Id.* at 169–70. [44] *Id.* [45] *Id.* at 169. [46] *Id.* at 166–67, 169. [47] *Id.* at 166–67.
[48] *Id.* at 170. [49] *Id.* [50] *Id.* at 165. [51] Yoder, *supra* note 5, at 230–234.

Wisconsin law that required all children to attend school until age sixteen; the Amish believed children should be educated only through eighth grade.[52] The Court stressed how additional years of education would interfere with the Amish's community-preserving strategy. The Wisconsin law, it noted, "takes [youth] away from their community, physically and emotionally, during the crucial and formative adolescent period of life." State-supported high school could not, "in curriculum or social environment ... impart the values promoted by Amish society."[53] A key witness testified that compulsory high school attendance might result in great psychological harm to Amish children because of the conflicts it would produce.[54] That same witness opined that such conflicts might hasten the destruction of the Old Order Amish church community as it existed in the U.S. at that time.[55]

As in *Meyer, Pierce*, and *Prince*, *Yoder* recognized that states may act against parents' wishes to safeguard child welfare. But the Amish "introduced persuasive evidence undermining" Wisconsin's argument that additional education advanced "the welfare of the child and society as a whole."[56] Specifically, "foregoing one, or at most two, additional years of compulsory education will not impair the physical or mental health of the child, or result in an inability to be self-supporting or to discharge the duties and responsibilities of citizenship, or in any other way materially detract from the welfare of society."[57]

Dwyer argues that the thrust of *Yoder* is to give Amish parents an "other-determining power," not a personal liberty – that is, *Yoder* allows believers not only to decide questions of their own fate but also those of their children. Yet, *Meyer, Pierce, Prince*, and *Yoder* all articulate a no-harm-to-children principle for the basis of the State's ability to supervise the choices parents make for children. In some instances, the government makes the needed showing; in others, such as *Yoder*, it does not.

Next, this chapter briefly reviews the evidence of harm to children from two specific practices that are bound up with religious identity, both for individual believers and for religious communities: corporal punishment and faith healing. This chapter demonstrates the differing views among social scientists that corporal punishment always harms children and shows that ethnic and cultural identity moderates the experiences and effects of physical discipline. It also examines the few studies of faith healing practices and shows that the overwhelming majority of children who have died suffered from wholly treatable ailments.

[52] Yoder, *supra* note 5, at 207. [53] *Id.* at 211–12. [54] *Id.* at 212. [55] *Id.* [56] *Id.* at 234.
[57] *Id.*

II THE EVIDENCE OF HARM TO CHILDREN FROM CERTAIN RELIGIOUS CHILDREARING PRACTICES

The balancing of religious liberty, family autonomy, and individual rights is nowhere more difficult than when a child's life or welfare hangs in the balance. Recently, a national discussion has erupted about how some parents parent. Adrian Peterson's indictment on charges of reckless or negligent injury to a child for "whopping" his son surfaced questions about the propriety of spanking and even harsher physical discipline.[58] As child deaths from faith healing continue to mount in parts of the country, including in Idaho, both citizens and policy makers are revisiting the wisdom of shielding parents from state oversight.

This section briefly presents empirical evidence about each practice, evaluating in particular when decisions about rearing children carry a substantial risk to those children.

A *Distinguishing Between Spanking and Use of Excessive Force*

As Section III will show, corporal punishment is allowed, to varying degrees, in forty-four of fifty states and the District of Columbia as exceptions to laws prohibiting the physical abuse of children. But how parents should discipline a child, and if they should use physical discipline at all, remains a divisive matter. Some believe in physical discipline to instill valuable lessons in a child, as vignettes that follow later illustrate. Others say parents should never spank a child, arguing for verbal discipline instead.

Whatever the reason for the use of discipline, a mottled snapshot has emerged about the possibility of harm from corporal punishment. Perhaps the most well-known work on corporal punishment and its effect on children comes from Murray Straus and Richard Gelles's seminal 1985 book, based on thirty-minute interviews of more than 6000 American families.[59] The authors would later say they found an astonishing prevalence of parental violence toward children: "each year a minimum of 1.7 million children are severely assaulted by their parents and ... an additional 5.4 million children are hit with objects."[60] Importantly, Straus defined corporal punishment as "the use

58 Ben Goessling & Darren Rovell, *Adrian Peterson Booked, Released*, ESPN.COM (September 14, 2014), www.espn.com/nfl/story/_/id/11514522/adrian-peterson-minnesota-vikings-indicted-chi ld-case; Offit, Chapter 12, this volume; Section IV *infra*.

59 Richard Gelles & Murray A. Straus, PHYSICAL VIOLENCE IN AMERICAN FAMILIES (1985).

60 Murray A. Straus & Carrie L. Yodanis, *Corporal Punishment by Parents: Implications for Primary Prevention of Assaults on Spouses and Children*, 2 U. CHI. L. SCH. ROUNDTABLE 35 (1995).

of physical force with the intention of causing [bodily] pain, but not injury, for purposes of correction or control of the child's behavior."[61] Straus gave as examples "spanking on the buttocks, hand slapping, shoving, grabbing or squeezing hard, ear twisting, pinching, and putting hot sauce or soap on a child's tongue (for example, for cursing)."[62]

Over time, social scientists would catalog the effects of corporal punishment to include increased depression, suicide, criminal behavior, participation in domestic violence, criminality, and delinquency.[63] For example, Straus and another colleague reported that those who experienced corporal punishment showed "restricted development of cognitive ability."[64] Summarizing this body of work in 2012, Straus concluded that when parents spank their children, "over the long term, there are greater odds that your child could become everything you don't want your child to become – an abuser, a depressed person, a person with temper-control issues. There is even evidence that children who are spanked end up with lower IQs."[65] Many, Straus included, attributed acceptance of corporal punishment in the U.S. to religious beliefs[66] – with some basis, as we show later.

To say Straus and Gelles have been influential across the world would be an understatement. The Council of Europe recommended legal prohibitions on corporal punishment and thirty-one European nations followed suit.[67] Some read the United Nations Convention on the Rights of the Child ("CRC"), to which the U.S. is not a signatory, to prohibit corporal punishment.[68] The CRC has sparked a movement to eradicate all corporal punishment, inside the home and outside: "50 [UN] states have prohibited all corporal punishment of

61 Murray A. Straus, Beating the Devil Out of Them: Corporal Punishment in American Families and Its Effects in Children 4 (2001).

62 Murray A. Straus, *Prevalence, Societal Causes, and Trends in Corporal Punishment by Parents in Worldwide Perspective*, 73 L. & Contemporary Problems 1, 1–2 (2010).

63 *See* Leonard P. Edwards, *Corporal Punishment and the Legal System*, 36 Santa Clara L. Rev. 983, 992–993 (1996).

64 Murray A. Straus & Mallie J. Paschall, *Corporal Punishment by Mothers and Development of Children's Cognitive Ability: A Longitudinal Study of Two Nationally Representative Age Cohorts*, 18 J. Aggression, Maltreatment & Trauma 459 (2009).

65 Bryan Marquard, *Dr. Murray A. Straus, 89; UNH Researcher Studied Violence*, Boston Globe (May 26, 2016), www.bostonglobe.com/metro/2016/05/26/murray-straus-unh-researcher-who-led-groundbreaking-studies-corporal-punishment-domestic-violence-dies/RlmWltvNGe5I5TfUQFq1NM/story.html.

66 *See* Straus, *supra* note 61.

67 Council of Europe, *Corporal Punishment*, www.coe.int/en/web/children/corporal-punishment.

68 Convention on the Rights of the Child, article 19, www.ohchr.org/EN/ProfessionalInterest/Pages/CRC.aspx.

children, including in the family home, 56 others have 'expressed a commitment to full prohibition.'"[69]

Nonetheless, in recent years, social scientists have collected in meta-analyses, analyzed, and summarized scientific studies of corporal punishment and its effects, a systematic review that allows for meaningful comparisons across studies.[70] Together, these studies show that the severity of corporal punishment's effects may not be nearly as great as Straus and Gelles originally posited. For instance, a recent meta-analysis of forty-six published studies found "a trivial to small, but generally significant relationship between the use of spanking and [corporal punishment] and long-term negative outcomes."[71] How researchers defined corporal punishment mattered greatly.[72]

Another meta-analysis looked at seventy-one studies, mostly from the U.S., conducted between 1961 and 2000 and capturing data from 47,751 people.[73] It found that most studies typically parse spanking from corporal punishment: studies characterized the former as "a mild open-handed strike to the buttocks or extremities," while the latter is defined as a "more severe use of physical punishments, such as striking the face, hitting with an object or shaking or pushing a child."[74] Even as to the latter, across studies researchers reported only "small negative behavioral and emotional effects of corporal punishment and almost no effect of such punishment on cognition."[75] Where researchers separated out the effects of spanking itself, spanking correlated with less severe effects than other forms of corporal punishment.[76]

Whether child aggression correlates with physical discipline may be a function of and moderated by the culture within which children find themselves. For example, Duke University professor Kenneth Dodge posits a biopsychosocial model of adolescents who chronically engage in conduct problems.[77] The notion is that biological dispositions and the contexts in which children grow up may influence early development of adolescent chronic conduct problems.[78] But this risk is moderated by the child's

69 *Id.*

70 A meta-analysis is a review of available literature addressing a specific research question, to assess what the body of data, rather than a single study, demonstrates.

71 Christopher J. Ferguson, *Spanking, Corporal Punishment and Negative Long-Term Outcomes: A Meta-Analytic Review of Longitudinal Studies*, 33 Clinical Psychology Rev. 196, 204 (2013).

72 *Id.* at 197.

73 Elizabeth Oddone Paolucci & Claudio Violato, *A Meta-Analysis of the Published Research on the Affective, Cognitive, and Behavioral Effects of Corporal Punishment*, 138 J. of Psychology 197 (2004).

74 Ferguson, *supra* note 71, at 197. 75 *Id.* 76 *Id.* 77 *Id.* 78 *Id.*

experiences with parents, peers, and social institutions, which can add to that risk or mediate it.[79]

The effects of spanking may differ by ethnic status, too. Researchers speculate that "the link between physical punishment and child aggression may be culturally specific."[80] So, while physical discipline correlated with higher externalizing scores for European-American children, they did not for other children.[81] A demographic profile correlates with use of spanking:

> A large body of studies has indicated that spanking is more likely to be used by parents who are younger, less educated, of lower income, single, and/or are more depressed and stressed. Studies have also indicated that spanking is most commonly used by parents who were themselves spanked, who live in the South, and/or who identify themselves as conservative Christians.[82]

Racial differences also appear to exist. African American parents reportedly spank their toddlers "more than their White counterparts."[83]

Spanking's most ardent supporters crop up among self-identified "born-again Christians," African Americans, people in the South, Black women, and men. In a national survey, researchers at the University of Chicago asked individuals if it is "sometimes necessary to discipline a child with a good, hard spanking."[84] Across all groups, seven in ten Americans approved of spanking

79 Kenneth A. Dodge & Gregory S. Pettit, A *Biopsychosocial Model of the Development of Chronic Conduct Problems in Adolescence*, 39 Dev. Psychol. 349 (2003).

80 Kirby Deater-Deckard, Kenneth A. Dodge, John E. Bates, & Gregory S Pettit, *Physical Discipline among African American and European American Mothers: Links to Children's Externalizing Behaviors*, 32 Dev. Psychol. 1065 (1996).

81 *Id.*

82 Lisa J. Berlin et al., *Correlates and Consequences of Spanking and Verbal Punishment for Low-Income White, African American, and Mexican American Toddlers*, 80 Child Dev. 1403, 1404 (2009).

83 *Id. See also* Jennifer E. Lansford, *The Special Problem of Cultural Differences in Effects of Corporal Punishment*, 73 L. & Contemporary Problems 89 (2010) (reviewing research suggesting different outcomes for corporal punishment based on culture); LaShaun Williams, *Spanking Is Part of Black Culture*, N.Y. Times (Aug. 14, 2011), www.nytimes.com/roomfordebate/2011/08/14/is-spanking-a-black-and-white-issue/spanking-is-part-of-black-culture?module=ArrowsNav&contentCollection=undefined&action=keypress&region=FixedLeft&pgtype=undefined.

84 Harry Enten, *Americans' Opinions On Spanking Vary By Party, Race, Region And Religion*, Five Thirty Eight (Sep. 15, 2014), http://fivethirtyeight.com/datalab/americans-opinions-on-spanking-vary-by-party-race-region-and-religion/. *See also GSS 1972–2014 Cumulative Datafile*, Survey Documentation and Analysis, http://sda.berkeley.edu/sdaweb/analysis/?dataset=gss14; *Favor Spanking to Discipline Child*, GSS Data Explorer, https://gssdataexplorer.norc.org/variables/646/vshow (giving four possible answers: strongly agree, agree, disagree, or strongly disagree).

sometimes.[85] This fraction has been remarkably stable since it was first measured in 1986, although the fraction of supporters ebbed in the late 1980s and 1990s before rebounding in later years.[86]

Religious, cultural, racial, regional, and political differences correlate with support for spanking as a way to discipline children. Eighty percent of born-again Christians supported spanking, 15% more than among non-born-again Christians, of whom 65% supported it. Geographically, people in the South (about 80%) are about 17% more likely to support spanking than people from the Northeast (about 63%), 5% higher than for people from the Midwest (about 75%) and 10% higher than people in the West (about 70%). Republicans are more likely than Democrats or independents to support spanking. Age, however, did not matter much. Millennials are "slightly more supportive than their elders," although the difference is not statistically significant.[87]

Racial differences emerged, too. More than 80% of African Americans support spanking, versus 71% of Whites.[88] Within groups, differences appear by gender, too. Eighty-one percent of Black women reported agreement with spanking a child versus 62% of White women and 62% of Hispanic women.[89] Eighty percent of Black men agreed with spanking a child, compared to a slightly lower percentage of White men (76%) and Hispanic men (73%).

Still, spanking is associated with religious beliefs for good reason. Many who engage in corporal punishment invoke Bible verses to ground that choice, as the case described in the Introduction and Section III.D makes clear. Further, as Figure 13.1 shows, only the adherents of Judaism disagreed with spanking more often than they agreed, while self-identified Catholics, Protestants, and those in other faith traditions all supported spanking by margins of roughly two to one. True, 61% of those who claimed no religious affiliation also supported spanking, but the influence of faith was statistically significant.

85 Scott Clement, *Millennials Like to Spank Their Kids Just as Much as Their Parents Did*, WASH. POST (Mar. 5, 2015), www.washingtonpost.com/news/wonk/wp/2015/03/05/millennials-like-to-spank-their-kids-just-as-much-as-their-parents-did/.

86 *Id.* 87 *Id.* 88 *Id.*

89 *Percentage of Adults Who Agree that it is Sometimes Necessary to Give a Child a "Good Hard Spanking," by Race and Hispanic Origin, and Sex: 2014*, CHILD TRENDS, www.childtrends.org/wp-content/uploads/2012/10/51_fig2.jpg. Church groups that have engaged in corporal punishment have been prosecuted. *See* Trisha Renaud, *House of Prayer Case Becomes Forum on Corporal Punishment, Daily Report* (Fulton County GA) (Oct. 14, 2002) (describing prosecution of members of one small African American church for corporal punishment – which stemmed from the "church's self-proclaimed battle to strengthen its families" – reigniting "a long-standing cultural debate about the discipline of children and corporal punishment").

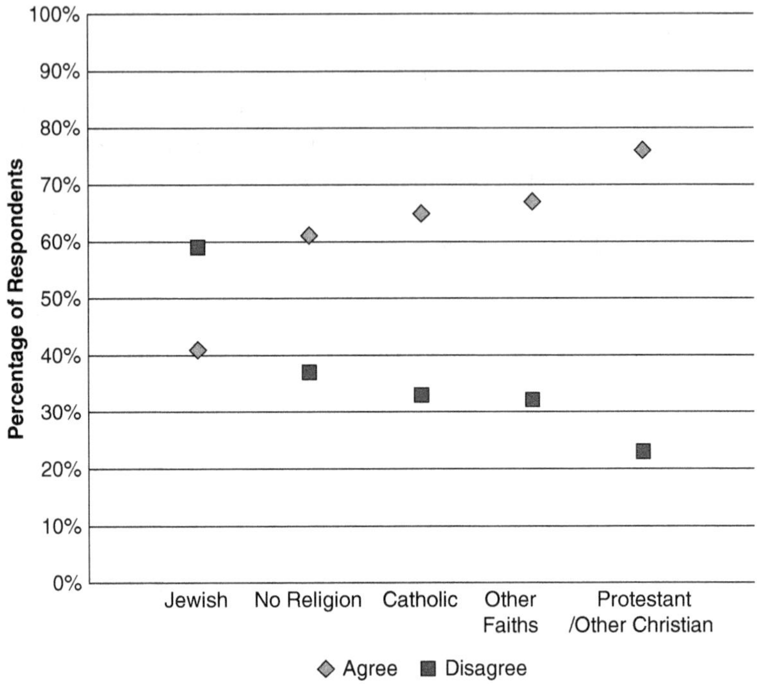

FIGURE 13.1 Agreement with Spanking by Religion

B Treating Children by Faith Alone Leads to Preventable Deaths

While corporal punishment may not have the health effects on the scale originally feared by Gelles and Straus, faith healing has been shown to be extremely dangerous and even deadly for children. Faith healing religions believe that the use of prayer and other spiritual means are all that are necessary when one is sick, as Offit poignantly chronicles (Chapter 12, this volume). Because religious fundamentalists who practice faith healing often live in insular communities, it is difficult to measure – other than by media accounts or anecdote – how often parents engage in faith healing or whether it results in *avoidable* harms.

A 1998 national study by Seth Asser and Rita Swan published in the peer-reviewed *Pediatrics* remains the leading study of the scale of preventable deaths.[90] (Rita Swan's heroic transformation from a mother who prayed over her child until his death from spinal bacterial meningitis to arguably the most

90 Seth M. Asser & Rita Swan, *Child Fatalities From Religion-Motivated Medical Neglect*, 101 PEDIATRICS 625, 625–29 (1998).

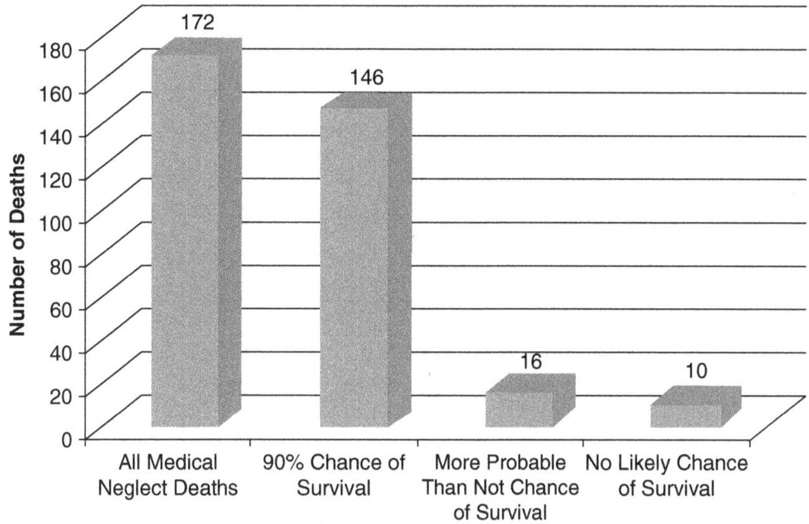

FIGURE 13.2 Deaths of Children in Faith Healing Homes

influential crusader against medical neglect exemptions in the U.S. is also chronicled by Offit.) Asser and Swan reviewed 172 child deaths in the U.S. from 1975 to 1995 in which faith healing parents denied their children medical care.[91] As Figure 13.2 shows, of the 172 children who died, 146 had a 90% chance of survival if treated using modern medicine.

For sixteen children, the prognosis was not as clear: they likely would have survived if treated with modern medicine. But for 10 of the 172 children, or slightly more than 5%, the child would likely have died even if the parents had used modern medicine to treat their condition.

Whether a child's death is in fact preventable varies dramatically with the underlying condition. For children who have cancer, the prognosis often is not good, whatever means parents choose. But among those children who died of non-cancer-related illnesses, the results are especially sobering, as Figure 13.3 shows. Of the 172 children, 98 died from a condition other than cancer. Of those 98, medical care likely would have been futile only for 2 children, less than 2%. Ninety-two children had an excellent prognosis for survival, four others had a reasonable chance of survival.

This study did not capture later deaths from medical illnesses of seventy-eight children in Oregon or of twelve children in Idaho belonging to the Followers of Christ Church, a group profiled in Section IV. While information is not

[91] *Id.*

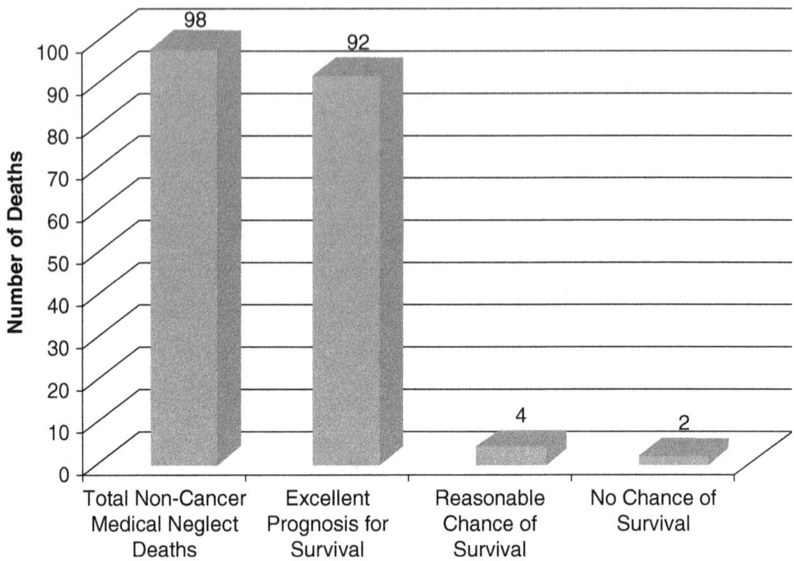

FIGURE 13.3 Deaths by Selected Characteristics

available on whether modern medicine could have saved the children who died in Idaho, it appears that twenty-one of the seventy-eight children in Oregon, or roughly 26%, "could have lived if they had received medical treatment."[92]

The distinction between preventable and unavoidable deaths matters to the state's police power, as Section I shows. It is the ability to prevent a child's death that vests the State with the power to override a parent's religious conviction to avoid harm to a child. Yet we continue to see wholly preventable deaths.

Consider the case of Brandon Schaible. Two decades after a measles epidemic raged through fundamentalist religious communities in Philadelphia,[93] seven-month-old Brandon died in his home from treatable pneumonia.[94] Brandon's parents, Herbert and Catherine, attended First-Century Gospel Church, a group that believes "prayer offered in faith will make the sick person well."[95] His parents had refused to administer antibiotics

92 Richard A. Hughes, *The Death of Children by Faith-Based Medical Neglect*, 20 J. L. & REL. 247 (2004).

93 Offit, Chapter 12, this volume.

94 Dockterman, *supra* note 3; David Usborne, *U.S. "Faith Healers" Sent to Prison for Death of Second Sick Child*, INDEPENDENT (Feb. 20, 2014), www.independent.co.uk/news/world/americas/us-faith-healers-sent-to-prison-for-death-of-second-sick-child-9142463.html.

95 James 5:14–15, *supra* note 3.

to save their young son. Pronounced dead on April 13, 2013, Brandon suffered for several days before succumbing.

Four years earlier, the Schaibles had lost another child to pneumonia after a treatment regimen of only prayer; they received probation, one term of which was to seek medical care for any child who became sick. This time, authorities charged the Schaibles with involuntary manslaughter and child endangerment. The parents pleaded no contest to third-degree murder. Sentencing the Schaibles to time behind bars, presiding Judge Benjamin Lerner told the couple, "You've killed two of your children ... not God, not your church, not religious devotion – you."

Next, this chapter shows that the choice the Schaibles made to "treat" by prayer alone is authorized by state laws across much of the country.[96] In most states, a respect for parental autonomy, for religion, and for cultural practices overwhelms the general requirement that parents must secure needed medical treatment for children and not abuse or neglect them. Section III discusses how faith healing and corporal punishment laws define the fault lines between parental freedom and child abuse and neglect in each state. States compensate for the latitude given to parents by naming all or some adults in the community as mandatory reporters of child abuse and by authorizing judges to consent to needed treatment.

III STATE LAWS GIVE WIDE SWATH TO RELIGIOUS AND CULTURAL PRACTICES

Faith healing and corporal punishment operate at the edge between parental freedom and child abuse and neglect. As the cases examined in Section I show, states have the power to safeguard children. Yet most states do not use that power; instead, they provide a buffer for many parental choices about how to raise children. While corporal punishment laws are generally not keyed to religious belief *per se*, they reflect a healthy respect for cultural and ethnic diversity. Statutory protections for faith healing, by contrast, are geared explicitly to religious belief, although philosophical objections to vaccination are also given credence.

A *Religious and Cultural Underpinnings of the Law*

The discretion given to faith healing is anchored to respect for religious belief by its very terms. As Offit (Chapter 12, this volume) shows, these laws have their

96 *See* Section III *infra.*

genesis in protecting the actions of fundamentalist religious believers, reaching back to the influence of Christian Scientists in the Nixon Administration. Although some states credit a parent's philosophical objections to vaccination, generally when it comes to treatment of illness, the discretion accorded parents is expressly for religious objections.[97]

Corporal punishment laws generally do not tie protections for parental choices as to discipline to the parent's religious beliefs *per se*. But some are anchored to religious liberty expressly. Indiana's law specifically references religious beliefs: "This chapter does not do any of the following: (1) Limit the right of a parent, guardian, or custodian of a child to use reasonable corporal punishment when disciplining the child. (2) Limit the lawful practice or teaching of religious beliefs."[98] However, the majority of state statutes draw boundaries around permitted corporal punishment without invoking religious belief.

All but two states include emotional factors in their definitions of child abuse.[99] Six states – Kentucky, Minnesota, Oregon, South Dakota, Tennessee, and Wyoming – consider the child's "culture" in cases of alleged emotional abuse.[100] Colorado takes into account the "culture" in which the child is enmeshed when investigating *any* form of child abuse: "In all cases, those investigating reports of child abuse shall take into account accepted child-rearing practices of the culture in which the child participates including, but not limited to, accepted work-related practices of agricultural communities."[101]

B The Degree of Discretion Accorded Parents

Every state by statute draws a line between permissible childrearing behavior and acts that constitute abuse of children. This section first identifies and locates critical provisions in the law of the fifty states on corporal punishment. It then extends Offit's analysis of medical neglect laws to examine mechanisms that states have instituted to safeguard children, notwithstanding exemptions for the religious or philosophical beliefs of parents.

97 Offit, Chapter 12, Figure 12.1, this volume. 98 Ind. Code Ann. § 31–34-1–15 (2016).

99 U.S. Department of Health and Human Services, Administration for Children and Families, Children's Bureau, *Definitions of Child Abuse and Neglect*, Child Welfare Information Gateway 4 (April 2016), www.childwelfare.gov/pubPDFs/define.pdf.

100 Ky. Rev. Stat. Ann. § 600.020 (West 2015); Minn. Stat. Ann. § 626.556 (2015); Or. Rev. Stat. Ann. § 419B.005 (2015); S.D. Codified Laws § 26-8A-2 (2015); Tenn. Code Ann. § 37–1-602 (2015); Wyo. Stat. Ann. § 14–3-202 (2015).

101 Colo. Rev. Stat. Ann. § 19–1-103 (2014).

1 The Laws of Child Physical Abuse

As Figure 13.4 and the Appendix 1 show, states locate the outer boundary of permissible discipline in different places. Just six states follow the Straus and Gelles view: any willful act that causes harm, physical injury, or pain constitutes abuse of a child, period.[102] In Massachusetts, for example, "abuse" encompasses "the willful infliction of injury, unreasonable confinement, intimidation, including verbal or mental abuse, or punishment with resulting *physical harm, pain* or mental anguish or assault and battery; provided, however, that verbal or mental abuse shall require a knowing and willful act directed at a specific person."[103]

By contrast, the overwhelming majority of states place a wide range of disciplinary behaviors outside the scope of prohibited child abuse. Thirty-three states and the District of Columbia allow the use of "reasonable" or "not excessive" force.[104] Colorado law expressly permits "A parent, guardian, or other person entrusted with the care and supervision of a minor [to] use *reasonable and appropriate physical force* upon the minor ... when and to the extent it is *reasonably necessary* and appropriate to maintain discipline or promote the welfare of the minor."[105] Note that the choice to discipline the child at all must be a reasonable one. In a variant on this formulation, the District of Columbia permits "[p]arents [to] use force as long as it is not excessive," but treats "excessive corporal punishment" as child abuse.[106]

In eight states, discipline slips over from permitted behavior to prohibited child abuse when it poses substantial risk of death or serious injury to a child.[107] Consider Kentucky, which treats as "justifiable" a parent's "physical force ... upon another person" in her care when she "believes that the force used is necessary to promote the welfare of a minor" and "is not designed to cause or known to create a *substantial risk of causing death, serious physical injury, disfigurement, extreme pain, or extreme mental distress*."[108]

102 *See* Appendix 1 (listing Delaware, Florida, Iowa, Massachusetts, North Carolina, and Vermont).

103 Mass. Gen. Laws ch. 111, § 72F (2016).

104 *See* Appendix 1 (listing Alabama, Arizona, Arkansas, California, Colorado, Connecticut, District of Columbia, Georgia, Idaho, Indiana, Kansas, Louisiana, Maine, Maryland, Minnesota, Mississippi, Missouri, Montana, Nevada, New Hampshire, New Jersey, New Mexico, Ohio, Oklahoma, Oregon, Rhode Island, South Dakota, Tennessee, Utah, Virginia, Washington, West Virginia, Wisconsin, and Wyoming).

105 Colo. Rev. Stat. 18–1-703 (2014) (emphasis added).

106 D.C. Code § 16–2351 (2015).

107 *See* Appendix 1 (listing Hawaii, Illinois, Kentucky, Michigan, North Dakota, Pennsylvania, and South Carolina).

108 Ky. Rev. Stat. § 503.110 (West 2015) (emphasis added).

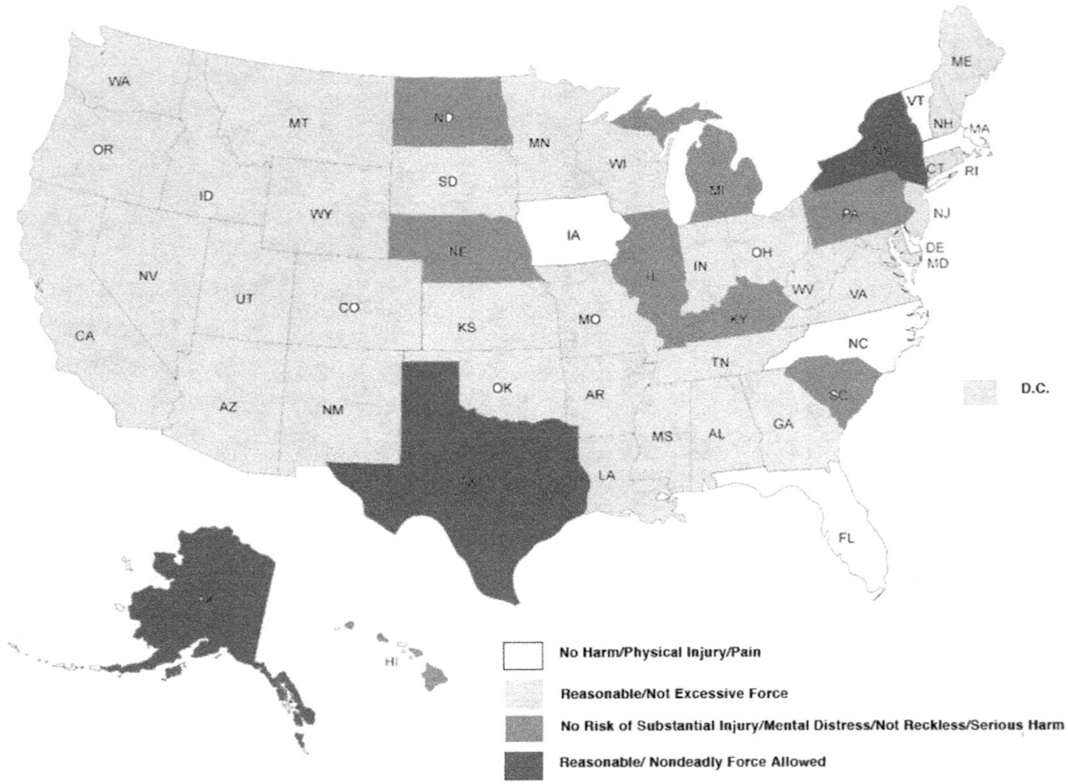

FIGURE 13.4 State Standards for Reasonable Discipline

Three states prohibit the use only of deadly force.[109] For example, New York expressly permits "[a] parent, guardian or other person entrusted with the care and supervision of a person under the age of twenty-one [to] use physical force, but *not deadly physical force*, upon such person when and to the extent that he reasonably believes it necessary to maintain discipline or to promote the welfare of such person."[110] As before, the parent disciplining the child must still be reasonable in the choice.

Altogether, forty-four states and the District of Columbia permit corporal punishment by parents. Some specifically contemplate the need to "safeguard" a child's welfare by preventing or punishing the child's misconduct.[111] Many, including Missouri, draw a sharp line between "spanking" and other acts: "Discipline including *spanking*, administered in a *reasonable* manner, shall not be construed to be abuse."[112]

Sometimes faith-driven concessions carry over to the religious education children receive in preschool or primary and secondary schools. Four states expressly carve out religiously affiliated day care centers, exempting them from laws banning corporal punishment.[113] Sixteen states waive certain health and safety standards required of non-religiously affiliated day care programs.[114]

2 The Laws of Medical Neglect

As Offit shows (Chapter 12, this volume), states make one set of rules about vaccination and another set of rules about needed medical treatment. As to the former, all but three states retain religious exemptions for childhood vaccination and school immunizations when the parent has a religious objection. Some give the same treatment to a parent's philosophical objection.

As to the duty to secure needed medical treatment for a child, the country remains a checkerboard. Eight states give parents a religious defense to negligent homicide, manslaughter, and capital murder when a child dies as a result of faith healing.[115] Seventeen states have religious exemptions for

109 *See* Appendix 1 (listing Alaska, New York, and Texas).

110 N.Y. Penal Law § 35.10 (McKinney 2016).

111 Neb. Rev. Stat. § 28–1413 (emphasis added).

112 Mo. Rev. Stat. § 210.110 (2015) (emphasis added).

113 Amanda Marcotte, *Religious Exemptions Kill: Church Day Care Deaths and Injuries Show the Dangers of Expanding the Privileges into Law*, Salon (Apr. 16, 2016), www.salon.com/2016/04/16/religious_exemptions_kill_church_day_care_deaths_and_injuries_show_the_dangers_of_expanding_the_privileges_into_law/.

114 *Id.*

115 *See* Offit, Chapter 12, this volume. *See also* Kirtlan G. Naylor, *Child Deaths in Idaho 2013: A Report of Finding by the Idaho Child Fatality Review Team*, Idaho Child Fatality

parents to child endangerment or neglect charges, acts that would otherwise be a felony.[116] Sixteen states make no religious allowances.

These laws provide immunity to parents from child neglect and child abuse laws.[117] The exemptions also may undermine a state's legitimate interest in the well-being of its most vulnerable citizens. The weighing of competing interests here would seem easy in one sense. On one side the child has the most significant of fundamental rights at stake, her life.[118] On the other are parents' interests in parenting, in privacy and autonomy from the state, and in transmitting and norming their child's values. Whether the child's right is seen as fundamental or whether the parents' rights have constitutional import as religious values or through the parent-child relationship may not matter much in the end – the state will surely have a compelling government interest in safeguarding a child's life when parents will not. The next subsection probes whether there are less restrictive ways to protect children.[119]

C Mechanisms to Protect Children

States use two important devices to mute the risk to children: mandatory duties to report and judicial authorization of needed treatment.

1 The State's Eyes and Ears

All fifty states and the District of Columbia statutorily require certain persons and institutions to report suspected child abuse or neglect.[120] As Figure 13.5 shows, mandatory reporters typically include people who have frequent contact with children: doctors, teachers, and clergy. One can think of mandatory

Review Team (May 2016), http://idcartf.org/ckfinder/userfiles/files/annual%20report%20child%20deaths%202013-may2016.pdf.

116 Offit, Chapter 12, this volume; *Religious Defenses In State Penal Codes*, Children's Healthcare is a Legal Duty, Inc., http://childrenshealthcare.org/wp-content/uploads/2014/07/State-exemptions-criminal2.pdf. It is not atypical for parents facing prosecution for child abuse to plead to a lesser charge. *Accord* Dinkler v. State, 699 SE 2d 541 (Ga. App. 2010) (concluding that although trial court should have instructed jury about the lesser-included charge of battery in a child abuse prosecution, "[i]n light of the overwhelming evidence of the commission of the greater offense … the failure to give the battery charge was harmless error").

117 *See* Jerry A. Coyne, *Faith Healing Kills Children*, Slate (May 21, 2015), www.slate.com/articles/health_and_science/medical_examiner/2015/05/religious_exemptions_from_medical_care_faith_healing_kills_children.html.

118 *Id.* 119 *See* Part I of this volume.

120 *Mandatory Reporters of Child Abuse and Neglect*, Children's Bureau (2016), www.childwelfare.gov/pubPDFs/manda.pdf#page=2&view=Reporting by other persons.

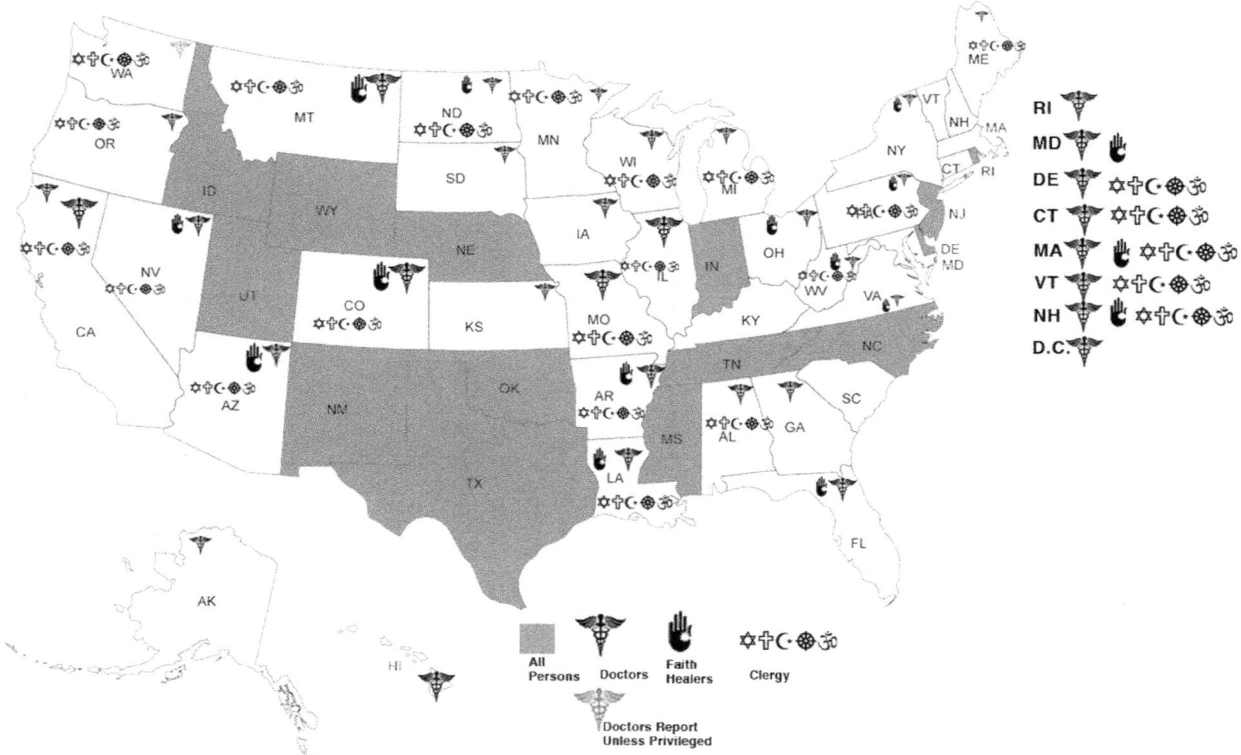

FIGURE 13.5 State Reporting Requirements
Source: *Adapted from Mandatory Reporters, supra* note 120.

reporters as the first line of defense for children neglected or abused by parents or others.

Several states, including Tennessee, specifically require Christian Science practitioners and faith healers to report suspected neglect, in addition to clergy.[121] Other states, including Idaho, impose reporting requirements on anyone who has reason to believe a child has been abused.[122] Some states extend duties to the clergy, although a subset of states treat information gained through confession differently, requiring no report.[123]

Although a powerful safeguard for most children, children in insular communities are effectively shut off from the state's eyes and ears. These communities are secluded, often homeschool their children, and may never be exposed to professionals with reporting duties, other than perhaps clergy and faith healers themselves.[124] Just consider whether church leaders and faith healers are likely to report a practice that they are urging parents to follow. Section IV discusses how difficult it is to change behavior within tight-knit communities.

2 Overriding Parental Wishes Through Judicial Authorization of Treatment

The judicial bypass is a mechanism that allows a state to intervene to authorize needed care for a child in need. One can think of it as the state defining *ex ante* when it has a compelling interest to override parental wishes and when it does not. Sixteen states authorize the court to order needed medical treatment for the child when the parents will not.[125]

A judicial bypass works in tandem with the background law around treatment duties. As Figure 13.6 shows, sixteen states give no religious exemptions

[121] *Id.*; TENN. CODE ANN. §§ 37–1-403; 37–1-605 (2015).

[122] IDAHO CODE § 16–1605 (2016) ("[A]ny person who has reason to believe that a child has been abuse, abandoned, or neglected is required to report.").

[123] New Hampshire, North Carolina, Oklahoma, Rhode Island, Texas, and West Virginia do not recognize the clergy-penitent privilege as grounds for failure to report child abuse. *Mandatory Reporters, supra* note 120.

[124] Dwyer, Chapter 8, this volume.

[125] ALA. CODE § 26–14-7.2 (2016); COLO. REV. STAT. § 19–3-103 (1993); FLA. ANN. STAT. § 39.01 (2016); IDAHO CODE ANN. § 16–1602 (2016); IND. CODE ANN. § 31–34-1–14 (1997); IOWA CODE ANN. § 232.68 (2016); KAN. STAT. ANN. § 38–2202 (2016); KY. REV. STAT. ANN. § 600.020 (2016); LA. CHILD. CODE ART. 603 (2015); MICH. COMP. LAWS ANN. § 722.634 (1975); MO. ANN. STAT. § 210.115 (2016); MONT. CODE ANN. § 41–3-102 (2013); NEV. REV. STAT. ANN § 432B.020(2) (2004); OHIO REV. STAT. ANN. § 2151.03(B) (2006); OKLA. STAT. ANN. TIT. 10A § 1-1-105 (2016); 23 PA STAT AND CONST. STAT. ANN. § 6304 (2015); *see generally* U.S. Department of Health and Human Services, Administration for Children and Families, Children's Bureau, *Definitions of Child Abuse and Neglect*, CHILD WELFARE INFORMATION GATEWAY 4 (Apr. 2016), www.childwelfare.gov/pubPDFs/define.pdf.

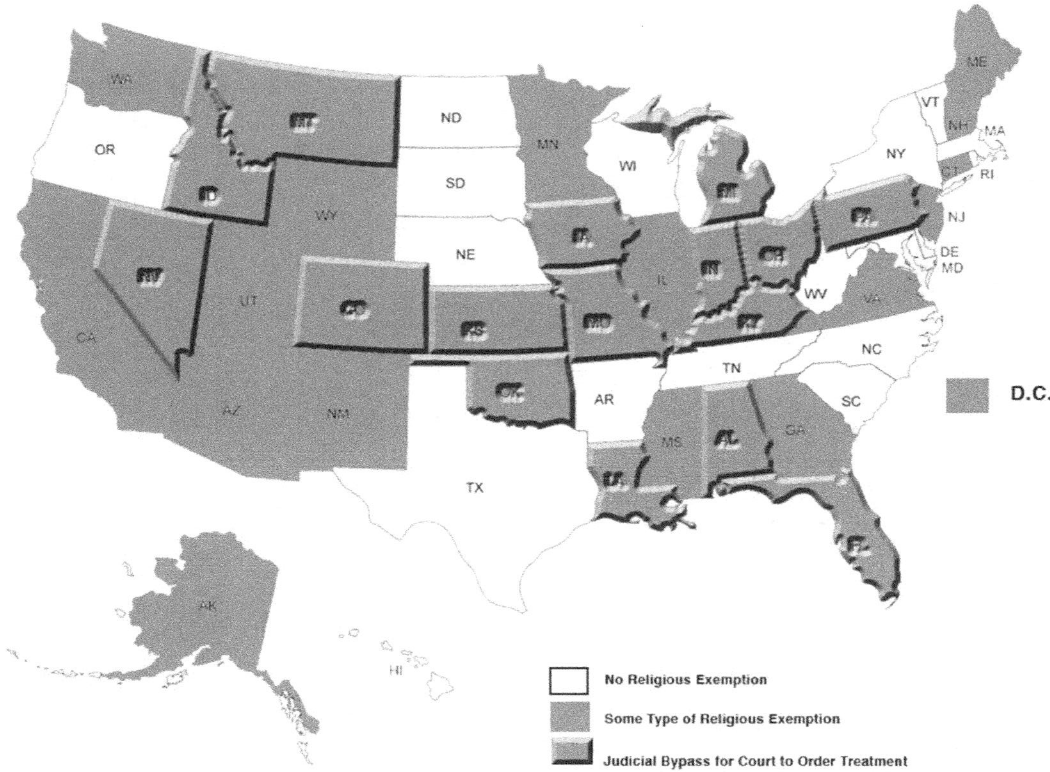

FIGURE 13.6 State Faith-Healing Exemptions

Source: *Adapted from U.S. Department of Health and Human Services, Administration for Children and Families, Children's Bureau,* Definitions of Child Abuse and Neglect, *Child Welfare Information Gateway* 4 (Apr. 2016), *www.childwelfare.gov/pubPDFs/define.pdf.*

to duties to treat children in need of medical attention, so a bypass mechanism would not be needed.[126] The remaining thirty-four states and the District of Columbia give some type of religious exemption.[127] Of these, states are nearly split on authorizing a judge to order needed care for the child over the parent's objection – sixteen states do; seventeen states do not.[128] In the latter states, the parent's refusal becomes the last word, potentially ending the child's life.

Importantly, a judicial bypass can keep children alive while honoring a parent's religious belief not to accept modern medicine. When children suffer from a treatable disease, having a judge authorize needed treatment can save a child's life.

Consider Alexandru Radita, a fifteen-year-old Canadian boy who died from untreated diabetes and starvation.[129] Found wearing a diaper in a closet, Alexandru, then just thirty-seven pounds, was so emaciated that he appeared mummified.[130] Alexandru's mother and father claimed as a defense to murder charges that it was against their religious beliefs to seek medical treatment from doctors; they were commanded to use prayer to heal. Alexandru's parents knew he, one of eight children, was diabetic and that medical attention would help him. After his parents failed to treat his diabetes at age five, Alexandru was hospitalized, removed from their care, and placed into foster care. Tragically

126 *See* Figure 13.6 (listing Arkansas, Delaware, Hawaii, Maryland, Massachusetts, Nebraska, New York, North Carolina, North Dakota, Oregon, Rhode Island, South Carolina, South Dakota, Tennessee, Texas, West Virginia, Wisconsin, and Vermont); Offit, Chapter 12, this volume.

127 *See* Figure 13.6 (listing Alabama, Alaska, Arizona, California, Colorado, Connecticut, District of Columbia, Florida, Georgia, Idaho, Illinois, Indiana, Iowa, Kansas, Kentucky, Louisiana, Maine, Michigan, Minnesota, Mississippi, Missouri, Montana, Nevada, New Hampshire, New Jersey, New Mexico, Ohio, Oklahoma, Pennsylvania, Utah, Virginia, Washington, and Wyoming); Offit, Chapter 12, this volume.

128 *See* Figure 13.6 (showing judicial bypass in Alabama, Colorado, Florida, Idaho, Indiana, Iowa, Kansas, Kentucky, Louisiana, Michigan, Missouri, Montana, Nevada, Ohio, Oklahoma, and Pennsylvania; and no bypass in Alaska, Arizona, Colorado, Connecticut, District of Columbia, Georgia, Illinois, Maine, Minnesota, Mississippi, New Hampshire, New Jersey, New Mexico, Utah, Virginia, Washington, and Wyoming); *see also* Offit, Chapter 12, this volume; Alexandra Sandstrom, *Most States Allow Religious Exemptions from Child Abuse and Neglect Laws*, PEW RES. CTR. (Aug. 12, 2016). www.pewresearch .org/fact-tank/2016/08/12/most-states-allow-religious-exemptions-from-child-abuse-and-negl ect-laws/.

129 *See* Bill Graveland, *Alexandru Radita Trial Verdict: Parents Found Guilty Of Killing Diabetic Son*, HUFFINGTON POST (Feb. 24, 2017), www.huffingtonpost.ca/2017/02/24/alexandru-radita-trial-verdict_n_14993442.html.

130 Bill Graveland, *"They Knew He Was Dying" Parents Guilty of 1st-Degree Murder in Son's Death*, OTTAWA CITIZEN (Feb. 24, 2017), www.ottawacitizen.com/health/verdict+expected+calgary+murder+trial+parents+diabetic+sons/12981497/story.html.

for Alexandru, he was later reunited with his parents, as are many children who are removed from their families.

Alexandru's death reveals gaping holes in society's safeguards for protecting children. When his family moved from one province to another, Alexandru slipped from state oversight. This means that if the Canadian province where he died had permitted judicial bypass, there was no opportunity for a judge to intervene because the state had lost track of Alexandru. It was in no position to keep him alive.

So, too, with Brandon Schaible, whose preventable death was described in the Introduction to this chapter. Brandon died of treatable pneumonia when his parents refused to administer antibiotics to the seven-month-old.[131] Brandon's parents were enmeshed in a community that would have had a mandatory reporter, such as a teacher, healthcare worker, or pastor, among others designated as mandatory reporters under Pennsylvania law.[132] If state officials had been made aware of Brandon's medical situation, the state's judicial bypass provision would have allowed a judge to authorize care when Brandon's parents would not.[133] But no one knew of Brandon's distress until it was too late.

In Brandon's case, the Commonwealth had good reason to take proactive steps to ensure his welfare. One of Brandon's siblings had died under similar circumstances years before; the attorneys involved had asked the court to mandate supervision by a Department of Human Services caseworker, but that request was denied in favor of supervision by a probation officer.[134] That substitution meant that caseworkers versed in neglect and abuse would not be periodically monitoring the Schaibles, watching if Brandon needed help.

Now, when the probability of the child's survival is low and a family chooses prayer or spiritual means, judicial authorization of medical treatment would needlessly tread on religious beliefs. This places a premium on good predictive judgments by doctors and, by extension judges, about whether treatment can, in fact, benefit a child. When it would not, courts, and the state, should continue to allow the family to care for their child by faith alone.

131 Dockterman, *supra* note 3; Usborne, *supra* note 94.

132 *Mandatory Reporters*, *supra* note 120.

133 U.S. Department of Health and Human Services, Administration for Children and Families, Children's Bureau, *Definitions of Child Abuse and Neglect*, Child Welfare Information Gateway 4 (Apr. 2016), www.childwelfare.gov/pubPDFs/define.pdf.

134 Maryclaire Dale, *Philadelphia Parents Herbert, Catherine Schaible Sentenced in Son's "Prayer Death,"* WPVI-TV (Feb. 19, 2014), http://6abc.com/archive/9437462/.

D Cultural and Religious Influences on Parenting

Two recent cases illustrate how parental discipline straddles religious, ethnic, and cultural lines, and how parents' views are deeply engrained as a result of the parents' own upbringing. As Section II showed, corporal punishment is not confined to religious fundamentalists but is a multiethnic and multicultural practice, too. That overlap complicates whether and how the state should regulate the parent-child relationship. Quite simply, unless these practices harm children, regulating them may be tantamount to stamping out practices core to a community's identity, much as Rassbach (Chapter 7, this volume) explains as to male circumcision practices.

Consider Khin Par Thaing, the political asylum refugee from Myanmar living in Indiana described in the Introduction, who was charged in 2016 with child abuse after striking her seven-year-old son on his back with a coat hanger as punishment for fighting with his sister.[135] A teacher spotted welts and bruises on the boy's back and reported Thaing. An examination revealed thirty-six bruises or marks across his back, thighs, and left arm. According to court documents, Thaing hit her son with the coat hanger before telling him to kneel and pray for God's mercy. Indiana authorities charged her with felony battery. Thaing cited both her religious beliefs about childrearing and Myanmarese cultural norms, invoking a cultural defense as well as a legal defense using Indiana's state RFRA.

In Myanmar, it is quite common for parents to use a rod to correct children's behavior.[136] For Thaing, a parent who "spares the rod, spoils the child," that is, a parent should not "withhold discipline from a child; if you strike him with a rod, he will not die. If you strike him with the rod, you will save his soul from Sheol," the "subterranean place of the dead."[137] Thaing ultimately pleaded guilty to battery and was sentenced to a year of probation.[138]

Thaing is far from the only parent to face criminal charges for using physical punishment with children. National Football League ("NFL") player Adrian

[135] *See* Vic Ryckaert, *Son Had 36 Bruises. Mom Quoted the Bible as Defenses*, INDY STAR (Aug. 31, 2016), www.citationmachine.net/bibliographies/194258414?new=true.

[136] *Woman Uses Indiana Religious Objections Law in Defense Against Child Abuse Charges*, CHICAGO TRIBUNE (Aug. 31, 2016), www.chicagotribune.com/news/local/breaking/ct-woman-uses-indiana-religious-objections-law-in-defense-against-child-abuse-charges-20160831-story.html.

[137] Mark Taylor, *Executed God: The Way of the Cross in Lockdown America*, 1 RUTGERS J. L. & RELIG. 1 (1999) (giving Hebrew meaning for *Sheol*).

[138] Kristine Guerra, *Ind. Woman Who Used "Religious Freedom" Law as Defense for Beating Son Gets Probation*, CHICAGO TRIBUNE (Oct. 30, 2016), www.chicagotribune.com/suburbs/post-tribune/news/ct-religious-freedom-law-beating-defense-20161030-story.html.

Peterson made national headlines in 2014 for disciplining his four-year-old son with a tree branch or "switch" after the boy pushed his sibling off a scooter at Peterson's Texas home.[139] That switch somehow wrapped around the boy's genitals unbeknownst to Peterson.[140] The discipline left lacerations on the child's legs, arms, and head.[141] While Texas allows parents to use reasonable force when physically disciplining their child, Texas prosecutors thought Peterson's decision to "whoop" the child with a small branch was excessive.[142] Peterson was indicted by a grand jury for "recklessly or by criminal negligence caus[ing] bodily injury"; he maintained his innocence and no intentional wrongdoing.[143]

Both Thaing's and Peterson's cases demonstrate the range of norms with regard to the types of allowable physical punishment for children. Peterson admitted to hitting his son with a branch but disputed it was excessive force.[144] He claimed a kind of cultural defense based on geography: using a switch to discipline his son is what "he experienced as a child growing up in East Texas."[145] Disciplining his son would help the boy, he believed: "I could have been one of those kids that was lost in the streets without the discipline instilled in me by my parents and other relatives. . . . My goal is always to teach my son right from wrong and that's what I tried to do that day."[146] Peterson also emphasized the pain he felt as a father and said he will "reevaluate how I discipline my son going forward."[147]

Peterson's case also demonstrates how good-faith explanations of why a parent would use physical punishment can be complicated by institutional interests. While the criminal case was pending, the NFL suspended Peterson from playing for the Minnesota Vikings.[148] Although the suspension came

139 Eliott C. McLaughlin & Steve Almasy, *Adrian Peterson: Not a Child Abuser, But Sorry About "Hurt I Have Brought" to Son*, CNN (Sep. 17, 2014), www.cnn.com/2014/09/15/us/adrian-peterson-child-abuse-charges/.

140 *Id.* 141 *Id.* 142 *See* Appendix 1; McLaughlin & Almasy, *supra* note 139.

143 McLaughlin & Almasy, *supra* note 139; Tom Pelissero, *Adrian Peterson: "I Won't Ever Use a Switch Again,"* USA Today Sports (Nov. 20, 2014), www.usatoday.com/story/sports/nfl/vikings/2014/11/20/adrian-peterson-roger-goodell-child-abuse-switch-minnesota-vikings/70025476/.

144 McLaughlin & Almasy, *supra* note 139. 145 *Id.*

146 Jeff Gray, *Peterson Apologizes, Says He's Not a Child Abuser*, SBNation.com (Sep. 15, 2014), www.sbnation.com/nfl/2014/9/15/6153477/adrian-peterson-statement-child-abuse-arrest.

147 *Id.* (quoting Peterson as saying, "I am someone that disciplined his child and did not intend to cause him any injury . . . No one can understand the hurt that I feel for my son and for the harm I caused him.").

148 Bernie Augustine, *Adrian Peterson: Child Abuse Suspension Was Unfair*, N.Y. Daily News (Sept. 8, 2016), www.nydailynews.com/sports/football/adrian-peterson-child-abuse-suspension-unfair-article-1.2783232.

with pay, Peterson missed almost the entire 2014 season; he was reinstated in April 2015.[149] Ultimately, as part of a plea deal, Peterson pleaded no contest to a lesser misdemeanor of reckless assault, resolving his felony child abuse case.[150] Under the deal, Peterson avoided jail time, paid a $4,000 fine and court costs, and completed eighty hours of community service.

Peterson's treatment may seem extraordinary, reflecting the hot spotlight of national media attention and fame. Examined against one state's – Idaho's – regulation of the parent-child relationship, Peterson's sanction for his treatment of his son pales in comparison.

This chapter next examines how, in Idaho, parental religious exemptions to child abuse, medical neglect, involuntary manslaughter, and lesser crimes operate to confer on parents in Idaho effective immunity from civil sanction when they act "by faith alone." Idaho's overlapping statutory scheme has proven hard to reform, even as children continue to die. This is so, in part, because Idaho lawmakers are unsure whether attempts to constrain parental choices would backfire, pushing faith healers, and the children the state wants to protect, further from the law.

IV A COMPLEX INTERPLAY OF STATE LAWS SHIELD PARENTAL DECISIONS: IDAHO AS A CASE STUDY

Despite the state's clear police power to protect children when their parents will not, real-world considerations hamstring the state's protective role – not least of which is a workable strategy for influencing insular communities. Here, Idaho provides an important case study.

A *The Shield Frustrating Child Protection*

Idaho has erected a shield around parental decisions. Like the majority of the country, Idaho allows not only religious opposition but also philosophical opposition to vaccinating one's child.[151] As Offit shows (Chapter 12, this volume), this means that common ailments including measles can rage through faith communities where every child is unprotected.

More troubling, Idaho shields parents from prosecution when a child dies from curable or preventable diseases. In fact, Idaho arguably provides greater

149 *Id.*

150 Eric Prisbell & Brent Schrotenboer, *Adrian Peterson Avoids Jail Time in Child Abuse Case*, USA TODAY (Nov. 4, 2014), www.usatoday.com/story/sports/nfl/vikings/2014/11/04/adrian-peterson-minnesota-vikings-child-abuse-plea-deal-misdemeanor/18466197/.

151 IDAHO CODE § 39–4802 (2016).

insulation for treating children "by faith alone" than any state in the country. Idaho exempts faith healing from its ordinary child abuse and neglect structure, as many states do.[152] By a circuitous route, that decision erects a legal defense if a child dies as a result of faith healing.

Idaho generally imposes a duty on parents to protect the health and safety of children:

> At all times the health and safety of the child shall be the primary concern. Each child coming within the purview of this chapter shall receive, preferably in his own home, the care, guidance, and control that will promote his welfare and the best interest of the state of Idaho.[153]

Idaho bans both medical neglect and the infliction of pain or mental suffering.[154] A person charged with the care of a child who "willfully causes or permits any child to suffer, or ... permits the ... health of such child to be injured, or willfully ... permits such child to be ... endangered, is punishable by imprisonment" for "not less than one year nor more than ten years."[155]

However, Idaho exempts from the definition of abuse "treatment by prayers through spiritual means in lieu of medical treatment"[156] or "treatment by prayer or spiritual means alone."[157] To avail oneself of the exemption, one must be a member of a "bona fide religious denomination that relies exclusively on this form of treatment."[158] When abuse or neglect results in a child's death, this would ordinarily be involuntary manslaughter,[159] that is, "the unlawful killing of a human being ... in the perpetration of or attempt to perpetrate any unlawful act."[160] The state has the burden of proof to show that an unlawful act occurred.

By its very terms, faith healing is not an unlawful act in Idaho. This means that if a death results because parents chose to treat by faith alone, rather than using modern medical interventions, the parents cannot be convicted of involuntary manslaughter and many other crimes, even if a child's ailment was curable or her death preventable. Because the needed unlawful act is lacking, parents who engage in faith healing are effectively immune from prosecution.

152 Idaho Code § 18–1501(4) (2016); Figure 13.6 *supra*.

153 Idaho Code § 16–1601 (2016). Idaho's goal is not to remove children from the home but rather to provide children services in their own home, ensuring child welfare without infringing on the parent-child relationship.

154 Idaho Code § 16–1602(31) (2016). 155 Idaho Code § 18–1501 (1) (2016).

156 Idaho Code § 16–1602(31) (2016). 157 Idaho Code § 18–1501(4) (2016).

158 Idaho Code § 16–1627(3) (2016). 159 Idaho Code § 18–4006 (2016). 160 *Id.*

Perhaps as devastating for child protection, the state's judicial bypass mechanism must take into consideration parental religious beliefs.[161] State law directs "[t]he court [to] take into consideration any treatment being given the child by prayer through spiritual means alone, if the child or his parent, guardian or legal custodian are adherents of a bona fide religious denomination that relies exclusively on it."[162]

Together, Idaho's statutes conspire to undermine the state's legitimate interest in the well-being of its most vulnerable citizens. Remarkably, Idaho's statutes insulating faith healing have not faced a state or federal court challenge in more than three decades.[163]

Today, this is a very real issue in Idaho, one of the nation's most rural states. Idaho has effectively become a haven for faith healing communities, including the Followers of Christ Church, a faith healing "nondenominational congregation with roots in the 19th-century Pentecostal movement."[164] The effects of Idaho law are easily seen today in Canyon County, Idaho, home to the Followers of Christ.[165] Canyon County's Sheriff Kieran Donahue estimates there have been three deaths in the four months spanning from December 2016 to March 2017.[166] In one cemetery alone, more than 200 of the 592 graves contain minor children.[167]

161 IDAHO CODE § 16–1627 (2016) ("(1) At any time whether or not a child is under the authority of the court, the court may authorize medical or surgical care for a child when: . . . A physician informs the court orally or in writing that in his professional opinion, the life of the child would be greatly endangered without certain treatment and the parent, guardian or other custodian refuses or fails to consent . . . In making its order under subsection (1) of this section, the court shall take into consideration any treatment being given the child by prayer through spiritual means alone, if the child or his parent, guardian or legal custodian are adherents of a bona fide religious denomination that relies exclusively on this form of treatment in lieu of medical treatment.").

162 IDAHO CODE § 16–1627(3) (2016).

163 Robert Ehlert, *"Unshackled" Former Idaho Supreme Court Justice Jim Jones Undaunted by His Cancer Diagnosis*, IDAHO STATESMAN (Feb. 24, 2017), www.idahostatesman.com/opinion/opn-columns-blogs/robert-ehlert/article134782399.html.

164 Jessica Bruder & Dana Tims, *Parents Plead Not Guilty in Deaths*, WASH. POST (Apr. 5, 2008), www.washingtonpost.com/wp-dyn/content/article/2008/04/04/AR2008040403314.html.

165 Dan Tilkin, *Oregon Woman Fights Idaho Faith Healing Laws*, KOIN 6 (Jan. 21, 2016), http://koin.com/2016/01/21/oregon-woman-fights-idaho-faith-healing-laws/.

166 Karen Lehr, *Canyon County Sheriff Urging Lawmakers to Make Change to Faith Healing Laws in Idaho*, KIVI 6 (Feb. 3, 2017), www.kivitv.com/news/canyon-county-sheriff-urging-lawmakers-to-make-change-to-faith-healing-laws-in-idaho.

167 *Religious Defenses In State Penal Codes*, CHILDREN'S HEALTHCARE IS A LEGAL DUTY, INC., http://childrenshealthcare.org/wp-content/uploads/2014/07/State-exemptions-criminal2.pdf.

As Section II showed, not all deaths from childhood illness are preventable. But something seems terribly amiss in Idaho. A task force established by the Governor of Idaho to examine faith healing deaths tallied child graves in the Followers of Christ's cemetery in Canyon County. By its estimate, between 2002 and 2011, the number of child deaths in that community was ten times the rate of child deaths in the rest of Idaho.[168]

A granular review shows many deaths were, in fact, preventable. The Idaho Child Fatality Review Team reported in 2013 that "five deaths of infants less than a month old were preventable had they received medical treatment."[169] Three years later, a task force reported two more child deaths occurred "under circumstances where medical care would have prevented death."[170]

Accounts from individuals who have since left the Followers of Christ reinforce this view. Linda Martin, a former Follower of Christ who has family still active in the church, grew up in Idaho.[171] Throughout Martin's life, many of the children in her family died from treatable illnesses and diseases, ranging from untreated diabetes to bronchial pneumonia; the "prayer and anointing with oil" she now "believe[s] is medical neglect."[172]

Because of the shield of immunity around faith healing, prosecutors simply do not file charges after a child dies. At least one coroner will not do autopsies on deceased children because the law requires autopsies only when a crime is suspected.[173] Like the affirmative steps to deceive authorities during Philadelphia's measles outbreak chronicled by Offit, Donahue says that in Canyon County evidence sometimes has been altered by the time law enforcement arrives.[174] For example, a child's clothing may be changed or the child's body swaddled in a blanket or some other type of fabric.[175] Donahue became a major proponent of change after he realized the difficulty of investigating child deaths in the Followers of Christ community.[176]

168 Lehr, *supra* note 166. 169 *Id.* 170 *Id.*

171 Betsy Russell, *Former Church Member: "The Way These Kids Die is Inhumane,"* SPOKESMAN REVIEW (Aug. 4, 2016), www.spokesman.com/blogs/boise/2016/aug/04/former-church-member-way-these-kids-die-inhumane/. *See also* Linda Martin, *Idaho Faith Healing Testimony, Idaho Legislative Interim Committee Meeting,* YOUTUBE (Aug. 4, 2016), www.youtube.com/watch?v=P9N9Gyrzb8o.

172 Russell, *supra* note 172.

173 A *Repeal Bill,* IDAHO CHILDREN, idahochildren.org/a-bill-to-repeal/.

174 Lehr, *supra* note 166.

175 *Id. See also* Nigel Duara, *An Idaho Sheriff's Daunting Battle to Investigate When Children of a Faith-Healing Sect Die,* L.A. TIMES (Apr. 18, 2017), www.latimes.com/nation/la-na-idaho-children-20170418-story.html.

176 *Id.*

Exemptions can have a far-reaching impact on the steps taken by state actors charged with protecting children. Child caseworkers and other officials often believe they cannot intervene to protect a child even when they suspect physical or psychological illness. As Asser and Swan reported in their seminal study of child deaths across the U.S., "[b]elieving they were powerless in the face of the parents' wishes, some teachers ignored obvious symptoms and sent lessons home to bedridden children. Some social workers and law enforcement officers allowed parents to decline examinations of children reported to be ill."[177] Although *Prince* limits itself to its facts,[178] there can be no doubt that Idaho's cascading religious accommodations frustrate the overall goal of protecting children.

B Better Protecting Idaho's Children

Tolerance is a hard value to credit when children are dying in droves. Yet reforming Idaho law to be more protective has proven challenging. To prevent child deaths "whenever possible," Donahue urged Idaho lawmakers to repeal the "by faith alone" exemption from abuse and neglect, collapsing the shield around faith healing.[179] Canyon County's Coroner Vicki DeGues-Morris urged caution, however. A repeal, she believes, will not lead to a "change of lifestyle." Quite the contrary, the Followers of Christ and other fundamentalist groups could "go underground," masking even more child deaths.[180] The rugged remoteness of the Idaho's landscape and the privacy such an environment affords lend credence to this concern. If communities close in on themselves further, it will become increasingly difficult to learn whether or when a child is in need of medical attention from the State. The State must have eyes and ears in the community in order to spot children who need State intervention.

On February 21, 2017, recently retired Idaho Supreme Court Chief Justice Jim Jones urged the repeal of Idaho's faith healing exemption. Jones implored "the Legislature to stand up for our children" by requiring that they receive basic healthcare.[181] Idaho has "numerous protections for children without religious exemptions – marital age, child labor, ability to contract, and the like," he noted.[182] While adults can "decide to forgo medical intervention for themselves for religious reasons, that is their prerogative ... the state has an

177 Asser and Swan, *supra* note 90, at 628. 178 *Prince*, 321 U.S. at 171.

179 Lehr, *supra* note 166. 180 *Id.*

181 Jim Jones, *Does the Right to Life End at Birth for Some Kids?*, Spokesman Review (Feb. 21, 2017), http://media.spokesman.com/documents/2017/02/Jones-faith-healing-oped.pdf.

182 *Id.*

interest in safeguarding the health and safety of minors who cannot speak for themselves."[183] "Unshackled," Jones felt compelled to "speak up" about this "injustice."[184] For Jones, "the right to have basic life-saving healthcare trumps [parental and religious] protections."[185]

In the 2017 term, Idaho Senator Dan Johnson introduced Senate Bill 1182, which would have allowed judges to intervene in faith healing cases and stripped out the limitation to members of a "bona fide religious denomination."[186] Senate Bill 1182 would have replaced the "by faith alone" concept with a test similar to Idaho's state RFRA, permitting the state to override religious beliefs when a compelling state interest requires intervention, although it must do so by the least restrictive means. The sponsor sought "a balance between protecting children and honoring parents' free exercise of religion under the First Amendment."[187]

The floor debate on Senate Bill 1182 crystalized the difficulty in finding a line between respecting the religious freedom of parents and fulfilling the state's duty to protect children. For then-Senate Majority Leader Bart Davis, who supported the bill, a core weakness of Idaho's religious exemption is the following:

> God expects people to "use all the tools available to us. And until those children can make that decision for themselves, the government in my opinion has a compelling government purpose, in its least restrictive means possible, a duty to protect the lives of children."[188]

Still, Senator Davis expressed disbelief at the notion of repealing the religious exemptions for parents without replacing it with *some* accommodation:

> I heard a lot of opposition to the bill because it doesn't go far enough, that we need to repeal the shield protection . . . . I can't get that bill passed, I don't believe I can . . . . I've been here for a while and I know kinda how to count votes; that bill will not pass.[189]

Senator Michelle Stennett, who opposed the bill, summarized her opposition succinctly: Senate Bill 1182 "muddies parental rights . . . . This doesn't solve any of that, this just makes more conflict."[190]

183 *Id.* 184 Ehlert, *supra* note 163. 185 *Id.* 186 *Id.*

187 Betsy Russell, *Johnson on Faith Healing Bill: "Not Sure if it Changes a Whole Lot,"* Spokesman Review (Mar. 20, 2017), www.spokesman.com/blogs/boise/2017/mar/20/johnson-his-faith-healing-bill-not-sure-it-really-changes-whole-lot/.

188 Betsy Russell, *Senate Panel Narrowly Backs Controversial Faith-Healing Bill*, Spokesman Review (Mar. 20, 2017), www.spokesman.com/blogs/boise/2017/mar/20/senate-panel-narrowly-backs-controversial-faith-healing-bill/.

189 *Id.* 190 *Id.*

The Idaho Senate voted to kill the faith healing amendment on the Senate floor.[191] Despite the fact that senators voted more than two-to-one against it, Senate Bill 1182 signaled an important and credible attempt by the Idaho legislature to carve back the shield around faith healing in Idaho.[192] To the extent that Senate Bill 1182 would have allowed Idaho judges to intervene in faith healing cases, its passage would have alleviated the human costs to children animating decisions such as *Prince*.

Senate Bill 1182 would also have stripped the protection for faith healing parents from civil and criminal charges. This is facially appealing. But a hard question remains whether criminal penalties would sufficiently protect children in communities like the Followers of Christ. Alexandru's case gives reason to doubt whether removing the exemption from prosecution will alone keep children safe. Families can always leave a particular location. After Alexandru was removed by social workers and later returned to his parents, Alexandru's family moved from one province in Canada to another; Alexandru fell off the state's radar.[193]

Neighboring Oregon's legislature was more successful than Idaho's when it removed its faith healing exemption in 1999.[194] After Oregon changed its law in 1998, not a single death occurred among the Followers of Christ for a three-year period, some believe out of fear of prosecution.[195] But that interruption turned out to be a hiatus, not a change in practice or beliefs. Instead, child deaths in Oregon's faith healing communities have come back in full force. At this writing, Oregon officials brought murder charges against the parents of a twin girl, Ginnifer, who died hours after birth in the couple's home as "dozens of people from the faith-healing Followers of Christ Church gathered at the

191 Betsy Russell, *Canyon Sheriff: "In My County Alone I've Had 3 Deaths in the Last 4 months, One Yesterday,"* SPOKESMAN REVIEW (Mar. 20, 2017), www.spokesman.com/blogs/boise/2017/mar/20/canyon-sheriff-my-county-alone-ive-had-3-deaths-last-4-months-one-yesterday/ (reporting that Senate Bill 1182 passed the State Affairs Committee by a 5–4 vote but failed on the Senate floor by 11 to 24).

192 Betsy Russell, *Senate Kills Faith Healing Bill on 11–24 Vote*, SPOKESMAN REVIEW (Mar. 21, 2017), www.spokesman.com/blogs/boise/2017/mar/21/senate-kills-faith-healing-bill-11–24-vote/.

193 *Calgary 1st-Degree Murder Trial Delayed for Parents in Diabetic Teen's Death*, CBC NEWS (Sep. 12, 2016), www.cbc.ca/news/canada/calgary/alex-radita-murder-trial-parents-resume-1.3758122.

194 Isolde Raferty, *Changes in Oregon Law Put Faith-Healing Parents on Trial*, N.Y. TIMES (May 29, 2011), www.nytimes.com/2011/05/30/us/30followers.html?mcubz=0; *see also* Everton Bailey Jr., *Followers of Christ Parents Charged With Murder in Death of Premature Twin Baby*, OREGON LIVE (June 5, 2017), www.oregonlive.com/oregon-city/index.ssf/2017/06/followers_of_christ_parents_of.html.

195 *See* Hughes, *supra* note 92, and accompanying text.

house."[196] Ginnifer "died from complications of prematurity … her lungs hadn't developed enough to work on their own," Oregon's State Medical Examiner said in an affidavit; "the death was preventable if Baby Ginnifer had been given the medical care available in a hospital neonatal intensive care unit."[197]

At one point, one of the two authors of this chapter believed that prosecuting parents for faith healing would save children from avoidable deaths.[198] But the ability to escape legal regulation by moving, as Alexandru's parents did, drives home the limits of the law. Indeed, some believe Oregon's decision to eliminate the faith healing exemption led members of the Followers of Christ to move to Idaho, where they have resumed faith healing.[199] True, if Idaho removed its religious exemption, there may be few places left in the U.S. where faith healing communities could go, as Figures 13.5 and 13.6 show. But the fact that faith healing practices continue in Oregon after the state has jailed Followers, including the sister and brother-in-law of Ginnifer's mother for the death of the couple's infant, shows how entrenched faith healing is in these communities.

Despite Senate Bill 1182s failure, it represents an important step in the right direction for Idaho. Removing the specific protection for treatment "by faith alone" would permit Idaho's RFRA to kick in. RFRA's balancing framework would acknowledge the importance of the parents' religious liberty, without dismissing the child's right to life. Like the federal and state RFRAs discussed extensively in this volume, Idaho's RFRA requires the state to defer to religious practices unless a compelling state interest requires intervention.[200] It declares the "[f]ree exercise of religion is a fundamental right."[201] Idaho's RFRA allows the state to substantially burden religious practices only when "[e]ssential to further a compelling governmental interest" and accomplished by the "[l]east restrictive means of furthering that compelling governmental interest."[202] Once a burden is shown, Idaho, not individual believers, has the burden to show that Idaho's "means" are sufficiently related to its "ends."[203] The challenged state action would enjoy no presumption; instead, the presumption would weigh against the application of state law.

196 *See* Bailey, *supra* note 194. 197 *Id.*

198 *See* Robin Fretwell Wilson, *The Perils of Privatized Marriage, in* MARRIAGE AND DIVORCE IN A MULTI-CULTURAL CONTEXT: RECONSIDERING THE BOUNDARIES OF CIVIL LAW AND RELIGION 253, 260 (Joel A. Nichols, ed., 2011).

199 Bill Dentzer, *Religious Freedom or Medical Neglect? Idaho Lawmakers Take Up Faith-Healing Exemption*, IDAHO STATESMAN (Jul. 29, 2016), www.idahostatesman.com/news/politics-government/state-politics/article92784987.html ("Some say that more members have moved to Idaho from neighboring Oregon in the years since Idaho's neighbor to the west eliminated faith-healing exemptions from its criminal statutes.").

200 *Id.* 201 *See generally* IDAHO CODE § 73-402 (2016). 202 *Id.* 203 *Id.*

What would that mean for faith healing practices? Removing the "by faith alone" provision would not mean the State could override every decision regarding a child's illness. On at least one dimension, whether a child's death could be prevented with timely medical intervention, the State would bear the burden of showing that stepping into the parents' shoes was warranted. Honoring parental preferences, including those based on faith, harms no one if the outcome would not change.

If Idaho removed the "by faith alone" provision, state authorities would have more opportunities to be at the bedside of a child in need of protection. This, of course, requires that mandatory reporters – who, in Idaho, include everyone – actually report. Once alerted, state officials would be equipped to seek judicial overrides when a child's life could be saved. Capitalizing on that opportunity may require greater efforts to encourage reporting, however.

In sum, faith healing practices and corporal punishment both reveal the limits of the law to reach into communities that are insular and remote. The failure to regulate fosters tangible and heart-wrenching harm for children. While it is hard to know whether any given child's illness is treatable or whether that child's death could be prevented, this fact places a premium on evaluating children. This mean that the State must gain the trust of isolated and insular communities in order to know a child is in need.

V CONCLUSION

At the intersection of parental rights and child protection lie the issues of faith healing in response to treatable and nontreatable illnesses and the use of corporal punishment as a means to "save a child's soul" and to "teach him right from wrong." States may wield their police power against a "parent's claim to control of the child" when harm to children is likely to result, even if parents claim religious or cultural reasons for placing their children at risk. Despite the authority to protect children, states prize – and protect – to different degrees a family's autonomy to make decisions about how to discipline children or heal them "by faith alone." Although parents' choices to physically discipline children have become a focus of national debate after Adrian Peterson's prosecution for disciplining his child, evidence is mixed that corporal punishment leaves significant lasting impacts on children.

The insulation for faith healing or treatment by spiritual means is a different matter. Tragic cases of children dying at the hands of their parents flout the no-harm principle that bounds both religious liberty and parental rights. What empirical evidence there is suggests that had states intervened, hundreds of children's deaths could have been averted. Patently, an adult who does not want to receive treatment for religious reasons, or no reason at all, should be able to do so.[204] But when a child would benefit from treatment, states should rethink their reflexive respect for parental autonomy, religion, and cultural practices.

Even as child graves continue to pile up in Idaho, however, lawmakers struggle with how to reach into insular communities and better protect children. Erasing the virtual immunity from prosecution for parents in Idaho after a child dies for a common, treatable ailment seems unlikely, without more, to save children's lives. More bridges must be built to reach into communities that treat "by faith alone."

204 Cruzan v. Dir., Mo. Dep't of Health, 497 U.S. 261 (1990) (assuming a right to refuse medical treatment, but holding the state has authority to enact procedural safeguards to protect persons lacking capacity to make their wishes known personally).

PART IV

RETHINKING MARRIAGE AFTER OBERGEFELL

14

After *Obergefell*

Locating the Contemporary State Interest in Marriage

Kari E. Hong

Assistant Professor of Law, Boston College Law School

During the forty-year debate over the merits of same-sex marriage, ideological rhetoric over the value of marriage was neatly divided. Conservative scholars lauded the institution of marriage and warned that its demise (whether through same-sex couples, divorce, or single motherhood) would exact lasting damage on families and society.[1] Many notable liberal scholars pivoted away from the sanctity of marriage, instead calling for support for the parent-child relationship.[2] In June 2015, *Obergefell v. Hodges* unequivocally established that same-sex couples have a fundamental right to marry.[3] Although the decision is a landmark case for LGBT equality, *Obergefell* did not resolve the underlying debate over the continuing purpose of the government (or "the State" or "state interest" as alternative nomenclatures) remaining involved in the institution of marriage.

Until *Obergefell*, a traditional pro-marriage ideology was used to justify laws limiting marriage to straight/heterosexual couples and the entrenched sexism of traditional marriages. Inside and outside courthouses, those who opposed same-sex marriage often did so by citing to inflammatory and faulty studies that suggested the most notable injury to a child – criminal activity for the boys, sexual promiscuity and adult poverty for the girls, and a heightened risk of child molestation for both – arose exclusively from not having proper

[1] *See generally* George Dent Jr., *Traditional Marriage: Still Worth Defending*, 18 BYU J. PUB. L. 419, 428–30 (2004); Maggie Gallagher, *Keynote Address: The Case for the Future of Marriage*, 17 REGENT U. L. REV. 185, 186 (2005); Lynn D. Wardle, *The Disintegration of Families and Children's Right to Their Parents*, 10 AVE MARIA L. REV. 1, 2–3 (2011).

[2] *See, e.g.*, Martha Albertson Fineman, *Why Marriage?*, 9 VA. J. SOC. POL'Y & L. 239, 244–45 (2001); Katherine M. Franke, *Longing for Loving*, 76 FORDHAM L. REV. 2685, 2686 (2008); Nancy D. Polikoff, *For the Sake of All Children: Opponents and Supporters of Same-Sex Marriage Both Miss the Mark*, 8 N.Y. CITY L. REV. 573, 573 (2005).

[3] Obergefell v. Hodges, 135 S. Ct. 2584, 2604 (2015).

gendered parent figures in the home.[4] The evidence upon which these assertions were made – and vigorously defended by state attorneys general in courtrooms – has now been discredited.[5] Moreover, marriage evolved from an institution simply heralded for its alleged timelessness to a more practical mechanism that provided tangible benefits to those individuals within it, as Kar (Chapter 15, this volume) shows.

Although a consensus has emerged that defenders of traditional marriage were normatively wrong in penalizing individuals who – by choice or circumstances – opted for other family structures over traditional marriage, this chapter asks what if the defenders of traditional marriage are in fact absolutely right in asserting that there is something of great value in the institution of marriage?

This chapter begins with the assumption that there is something special in, or about, marriage. But unlike those who used marriage to demarcate morality, and often assign superiority to those within the institution, this chapter argues that the *Obergefell* decision illuminates how for citizens who enter into marriages, their relationship to the *State* is what can become quite transformative. American law has – and American values have – a mythical and actual embrace of privacy as a valued and near-inviolable right. The belief that American citizens have a zone of privacy, a right to remain free from government intervention, has captured the imagination of both liberals and conservatives when embracing the rights to abortion, family planning, and gun ownership.

However, instead of recognizing the harm that the State can have when intruding on a citizen's fundamental right, *Obergefell* is predicated upon a recognition that some harms – such as humiliation – are inflicted when the State *fails* to intervene and recognize a same-sex couple (and their child) as a family. In a pointed exchange between Justice Anthony Kennedy's majority opinion and Justice John Roberts's dissent, Justice Roberts criticizes *Obergefell*'s new formulation of privacy that recognizes that when a citizen

4 For an overview of the arguments raised and criticisms of the proffered evidence, *see* Kari E. Hong, *Parens Patri(Archy): Adoption, Eugenics, and Same-Sex Couples*, 40 CAL. W. L. REV. 1, 9 (2003). For a review of the limitations of available evidence, *see* David J. Eggebeen, *What Can We Learn from Studies of Children Raised by Gay or Lesbian Parents?* 41 SOC. SCI. RES. 775 (2012).

5 *See generally* Perry v. Schwarzenegger, 704 F. Supp. 2d 921, 991–95, 997–1003 (N.D. Cal. 2010) (making eighty findings of fact after a twelve-day trial with nineteen witnesses that no compelling state interest justified denying same-sex couples the right to marry), *vacated on other grounds and remanded sub nom*, Hollingsworth v. Perry, 133 S. Ct. 2652, 186 L. Ed. 2d 768 (2013); *see also* Courtney G. Joslin, *Marriage, Biology, and Federal Benefits*, 98 IOWA L. REV. 1467, 1470 (2013).

is in a marriage, the State is empowered to provide affirmative rights and protections to those within in (instead of simply the guarantee to be let alone). *Obergefell*'s remarkable anointment of privacy as a guarantor of rights is a major departure from the position widely accepted before 2000, and this chapter asks how this newly minted right – or "Obergefell's sword" as phrased by Justice Roberts – might be applied to families in which some members are U.S. citizens and some are not. Section I explores how, in the past forty years, the State's purpose in supporting marriage began as a societal interest in procreation but was fundamentally redefined to be an individual right to self-determination. Prior to *Griswold v. Connecticut*'s privacy protections, the fifty states policed sex that occurred both inside and outside of marriages.[6]

Even as the scaffolding around the criminalization of sex fell, the state interest in marriage was largely unarticulated until the 2003 *Goodridge v. Department of Public Health* decision.[7] The first case to affirmatively extend protections to same-sex couples, the *Goodridge* court no longer claimed that marriage was a hallowed institution that perpetuated civilization. Instead, the private event of falling in love aggregated into a larger public project. Specifically, the intimate decision of choosing – or not choosing – a permanent, loving partnership with another person became a critical act of self-realization. And when chosen, those who elected to marry shared a common humanity with the larger population that had made the same choice.

Section II turns to a central question: whether there is something different and unique that marriage offers to its participants. Sex, procreation, and companionship have been defined as the legal essentials of a marital relationship.[8] In an effort to articulate an intangible, transcendent value of marriage, this section looks at three cases involving an elderly citizen seeking a wife to immigrate even though they are no longer interested in having sex, a prisoner's wife who was denied her request to be impregnated with his sperm, and a widow asking for the government to grant her deceased husband's request to have her move to the United States with legal status. These cases involve situations in which the purported essentials of marriage – sex, procreation, companionship, and for a widow, even a spouse – are not just absent but impossible to come into existence. Nonetheless, the courts were moved by the compelling and unique facts arising in each situation in which one spouse asked the government to honor the marriages, despite the

6 *See* Griswold v. Connecticut, 381 U.S. 479 (1965).

7 *See* Goodridge v. Dep't of Pub. Health, 440 Mass. 309 (2003).

8 For a religious case that marriage has transformative power, *see* Kar, Chapter 15, this volume.

formalistic deficiencies. The judges' defense of these formally deficient, yet still compelling, marriages shows that whatever it is that makes us cry at weddings is likely *Goodridge*'s insight that our common humanity – the dreams, hopes, and comforts we seek in our own private marriage – are in fact shared intangible values that society affirms in each new marriage.

Section III also proposes a tangible state interest in contemporary marriage: marriage as right conferring, creating a new relationship between the citizen and the Liberal State. In a fascinating exchange between the *Obergefell's* majority and Chief Justice John Roberts's dissent, Justice Roberts criticizes the majority for fashioning from a line of privacy cases a new right that had been previously unknown. Instead of a right to be let alone, Justice Roberts contends, the majority in *Obergefell* confers an affirmative protection to couples who were not harmed by any affirmative government intrusion, deprivation, or seizure. Justice Roberts's critique is on point: *Obergefell*'s represents a means by which individuals can newly obtain government benefits instead of being merely protected from government harm – in other words, marriage goes from being a shield against government intrusion into one's relationship into a sword for securing benefits.

Section IV ends with a call to rethink the concept of constitutional privacy and considers embracing government intrusions into personal affairs. This embrace in the immigration context may provide more protections than leaving citizens to fend for themselves.

I THE LEGAL PURPOSE OF MARRIAGE AND THE MOVE FROM PROCREATION TO LIBERTY

Much credit must be given to activists for the lesbian, gay, bisexual, and transgender ("LGBT") community who advocated for marriage equality.[9] However, *Obergefell* should not be seen as proof that Americans have fully embraced LGBT equality.[10] Rather, the extension of marriage to same-sex couples arose from the fact that, over the past forty years, most straight people had come to internalize a redefined view that marriage served a purpose that was much more than procreation.

[9] *See, e.g.*, Molly Ball, *How Gay Marriage Became A Constitutional Right*, ATLANTIC (July 1, 2015), www.theatlantic.com/politics/archive/2015/07/gay-marriage-supreme-court-politics-activism/397052/.

[10] *See generally* Adams, Chapter 21, this volume, for state-by-state breakdown of LGBT non-discrimination protections in public accommodations; Chris Isidore, *How Businesses Can Still Discriminate Against LGBT People*, CNN MONEY (June 26, 2015), money.cnn.com/2015/06/26/news/companies/lgbt-discrimination/.

A *Marriage Was the Exclusive Institution in Which Procreative Sex Was Permitted, and Supposed, to Occur*

Although comical to some when said out loud today, procreation's centrality to marriage – as it was understood fifty years ago – was correct as a descriptive legal statement. In actuality, however, procreation has never been confined to marriage. Children have been born out of wedlock ever since there was wedlock.[11] Today, in the U.S., approximately 40% of births occur outside of marriage.[12] However, until the 1960s, the fifty states marshaled their police powers to confine legal sex to marriage and to ensure that any sex that occurred in a marriage was procreative.

1 Sex Outside of Marriage Criminalized as Fornication, Adultery, and Rape

Sex outside of marriage was criminalized, punished as either the crime of fornication, that is, sex between unmarried adults, or the crime of adultery, sex between two adults and one person was married to another – in some states one or the other was a felony, in others, a misdemeanor.[13] In these prosecutions, a person's marital status was a critical element of the crime. When relevant, defendants routinely cited their own or their partner's marital status as a defense to the charged crimes.[14]

In contemporary rape law, marriage continues to divide sex acts into those that are legal and those that are not. The crime of statutory rape (sex between an adult and a minor) persists as a status crime, not requiring *mens rea*.[15] The fact that such an offense is a strict liability crime makes its only potential

[11] *See generally* Elisabetta Povoledo, *In Search for Killer, DNA Sweep Exposes Intimate Family Secrets in Italy*, N.Y. TIMES (July 26, 2014), www.nytimes.com/2014/07/27/world/europe/in-search-for-killer-dna-sweep-exposes-intimate-family-secrets-in-italy.html?_r=0 (discussing how, to find the killer of a child, "investigators embarked on the country's largest DNA dragnet, taking genetic samples from nearly 22,000 people. . . . [T]he DNA testing also revealed something unknown even to the suspect's family: that he was the illegitimate son of a man who had died in 1999").

[12] The most recent statistics from the Centers for Disease Control and Prevention are that unmarried women account for 40.3% of all births in the U.S. *See Unmarried Childbearing*, CDC FASTSTATS, www.cdc.gov/nchs/fastats/unmarried-childbearing.htm.

[13] *See generally* Hopgood v. State, 76 Ga. App. 240, 241 (1947).

[14] *Id.* at 242.

[15] "A majority of states make statutory rape a strict liability offense with respect to the child's age. This principle results in some prosecutions in which the intercourse is undisputedly consensual and the child is nearly the age of consent, with the defendant reasonably believing her to be of lawful age." CRUMP, ET AL., CRIMINAL LAW: CASES, STATUTES, AND LAWYERING STRATEGIES 356 (3d ed. 2013).

defense – marriage – an even more remarkable exception.[16] The crime of rape between adults also remains defined by marriage. Although the marital rape exception has been formally abolished, marriage reduces the seriousness of the offense and lengths of punishment.[17] As evident in rape law, marriage still casts a long shadow in the definition of contemporary sex crimes.

2 Criminalizing Cohabitation and Specific Types of Marriages

Illicit cohabitation – the crime of people of opposite sex living together – was also criminalized. These statutes gained popularity after the Civil War as a means to harass interracial relationships and members of the Church of Jesus Christ of Latter-day Saints.[18] Despite their nefarious origins, by the 1960s the majority of states had enacted them and used them against all cohabitating couples.[19]

Between 1800 and 1967, forty states criminalized interracial marriages in some form or another.[20] The state interest in banning these relationships

[16] Quintero-Salazar v. Keisler, 506 F.3d 688, 693–94 (9th Cir. 2007).

[17] Since 1993, the marital rape exception has been formally abolished in all fifty states as offering blanket immunity. *See* Michelle J. Anderson, *Marital Immunity, Intimate Relationships, and Improper Inferences: A New Law on Sexual Offenses by Intimates*, 54 HASTINGS L.J.1465, 1521 (2003). Some states still treat marriage differently, however. *See* Jessica Klarfeld, A *Striking Disconnect: Marital Rape Law's Failure to Keep up With Domestic Violence Law*, 48 AM. CR. L.R. 1819 (2011) (noting that "[a]lthough every state legislature has formally abolished its marital rape exemption, reminders of the exemption still remain in the statutory law of several states," in the form of "decreased sentences for the accused, proof of force and/or resistance, and shorter time frames by which a woman has to report a rape by her husband, ultimately making spousal rape more difficult to prosecute"). California, for instance, has separate statutes for rape of a non-spouse, Section 261, and rape of a spouse, Section 262. CAL. PENAL CODE §§ 261, 262 (West 2013). Under Section 262, the rape "of a person who is the spouse of the perpetrator" requires differently-defined conduct to constitute rape. *Id.* at § 262. Moreover, penalties under Section 262 include "probation, fines" for punishment whereas Section 261 offenses are punished with prison. *Id.* at §§ 261, 262.

[18] *See generally* Brown v. Buhman, 947 F. Supp. 2d 1170, 1193 (D. Utah 2013) (striking down Utah's cohabitation law as impermissibly vague); United States v. Higgerson, 46 F. 750, 751 (C.C.D. Idaho 1891); RANDALL KENNEDY, INTERRACIAL INTIMACIES: SEX, MARRIAGE, IDENTITY, AND ADOPTION 70–91 (Pantheon Books ed. 2003). In 1882, unlawful cohabitation became a crime in the U.S. with the enactment of the Edmunds Act. *See* Erin P. B. Zasada, *Civil Rights-Rights Protected and Discrimination Prohibited: Living in Sin in North Dakota? Not Under My Lease*, North Dakota Fair Housing Council, Inc. v. Peterson, 2001 *Nd* 81, 625 N.W.*2d* 551 *(2001)*, 78 N.D. L. REV. 539, 541 (2002).

[19] Margaret M. Mahoney, *Forces Shaping the Law of Cohabitation for Opposite Sex Couples*, 7 J. L. & FAM. STUD. 135, 141 (2005).

[20] For a full review, *see* Kreis, Chapter 22, this volume. Every state whose Black population exceeded 5% passed anti-miscegenation laws targeting Black and White couples. *See* Leti Volpp, *American Mestizo: Filipinos and Antimiscegenation Laws in California*, 33 U.C.

revolved around procreation and specifically preventing the birth of children from these unions.[21]

3 "Unnatural" Sex and Contraception

Marriage was never a license to engage in any type of sex. Sodomy – even when consensual – was criminalized as unnatural sex.[22] Further, although it was not illegal for married couples to use contraception, it was illegal for doctors – and others – to advise, counsel, and provide information and contraception to married couples.[23]

B Legal Purpose of Marriage as Procreation Sealed Fate of Early Marriage Equality Cases

This history shaped the pre-*Obergefell* lines of marriage cases. *Baker v. Nelson* was the first case to challenge a state clerk's decision not to issue a marriage license to a gay couple, in that case, two men.[24] In 1971, law in Minnesota expressly limited marriage to members of the opposite sex. The Minnesota Supreme Court nonetheless dismissed any statutory ambiguity on the grounds that it was "unrealistic" to think the drafters intended marriage to extend to people of the same sex.[25] The plaintiffs raised a second argument – that denial implicated a host of federal constitutional protections including freedom of speech and of association – on which the Minnesota Supreme Court was equally dismissive. In explaining that the right to marry was limited to heterosexual individuals, the Minnesota Supreme Court observed – in the most

DAVIS L. REV. 795, 833–38 (2000). On the West Coast, states passed anti-miscegenation laws targeting the Chinese, Japanese, Filipino, and Southeast Asian populations. *See id.*

21 *See* State v. Jackson, 80 Mo. 175, 179 (1883) ("It is stated as a well authenticated fact that if the issue of a black man and a white woman, and a white man and a black woman, intermarry, they cannot possibly have any progeny, and such a fact sufficiently justifies those laws which forbid the intermarriage of blacks and whites, laying out of view other sufficient grounds for such enactments.").

22 Cohen v. Cohen, 200 Misc. 19, 103 N.Y.S.2d 426, 427 (N.Y. Sup. Ct. 1951) (introducing husband's sodomy conviction as a means of receiving a divorce based on adultery in divorce proceeding).

23 *See, e.g.*, Buxton v. Ullman, 147 Conn. 48, 58 (1959) (upholding a law preventing use of contraception by married couples because "the greater good would be served by leaving the statutes as they are"). *But see* Griswold, *supra* note 6,. at 485–86 (overturning laws prohibiting usage of contraceptives because they concern "a relationship lying within the zone of privacy created by several fundamental constitutional guarantees").

24 Baker v. Nelson, 291 Minn. 310, 311 (1971), *appeal dismissed "for want of a substantial federal question" in* Baker v. Nelson, 93 S. Ct. 37 (1972).

25 Baker, *supra* note 24, at 311.

cursory manner – that "[t]he institution of marriage as a union of man and woman, uniquely involving the procreation and rearing of children within a family, is as old as the book of Genesis."[26]

It is a mistake to write off *Baker v. Nelson*'s citation to procreation as outdated antigay discrimination. To the contrary, what is notable is that procreation was presented as such an obvious, central, and defining aspect of marriage that no further explanation – or citation outside of the Book of Genesis – was needed.[27]

Baker v. Nelson's assumption that marriage could only exist with the promise of procreation was not confined to heterosexuality. To the contrary, *Loving v. Virginia*, which was decided four years earlier, reinforced the purpose of marriage to be procreation.[28] In explaining the value of marriage, the U.S. Supreme Court noted that marriage was "fundamental to our very existence and survival."[29] This phrase was not intended to be hyperbole. Rather, the Supreme Court supports "our very existence," with a citation to *Skinner v. Oklahoma*, the case that ended the State's ability to sterilize its citizens.[30] Procreation becomes an essential element of marriage, as marriage is the exclusive means by which the species propagates itself. The unassailable axiom is that marriage exists for producing children, and without marriage, no more children would be born.

Viewed with contemporary eyes, this centrality of procreation to marriage seems confusing and dated. But in 1967 (the date of *Loving*) and 1971 (the date of *Baker*), society was continuing to police, and still criminalize, sex outside of marriage. In this context, procreation as a – if not *the* – defining state interest in marriage was quite rational and reasoned.

C *From* Goodridge *to* Windsor: *Rethinking the Primary Purpose of Marriage*

In the history of social change, it is easy for observers to be reductive in their thinking, to trace shifts from one Supreme Court decision to another. Lost in this method is the fact that progress usually is not usually made in full, steady

26 *Id.* at 312.

27 The irony, of course, is that Genesis is not the place to find models of happy monogamous heterosexual pairings. Rather, fathers of the Judeo-Christian religion – Abraham, David, Jacob – were in adulterous, bigamous, and polygamous relationships. Genesis 16:1–16, 29; 1 Chronicles 3. *See* Kar, Chapter 15, this volume, for an exegesis of passages on marriage and homosexuality.

28 Loving v. Virginia, 388 U.S. 1, 12 (1967).

29 *Id.* at 12.

30 Skinner v. Oklahoma, 316 U.S. 535, 542 (1942).

strides. To the contrary, state courts show the fits and starts that occur as society grapples with the collateral issues that legal equality ushers in.[31]

Obergefell will most certainly be published in casebooks covering marriage equality for lesbian and gay individuals.[32] However, the *Obergefell* decision was not the first decision to recognize how society's view of marriage has changed. Rather, it was the 2003 decision, *Goodridge v. Massachusetts*, a decision from a decade earlier, that changed the social zeitgeist around marriage.

In 2003, *Goodridge* made history as the first state court case that fully and forcefully extended marriage to same-sex couples.[33] Unique to *Goodridge*, the Massachusetts Supreme Judicial Court did not ask whether gay and lesbian couples could be excluded from marriage.[34] In so doing, the decision avoided the pitfalls of prior decisions that noted the historical absence of these relationships or were mired in the contemporary moral condemnation of gay people.[35]

Instead, *Goodridge*'s starting point was that, "[s]imply put, the government creates civil marriage."[36] *Goodridge*'s deft turn reframed the question from a same-sex couple, as plaintiffs, asking for an exception to the long-standing history of civilization to, rather, examining what was the purpose of marriage

[31] By way of example, *Loving v. Virginia* is usually invoked as the case that ended the country's ban on anti-miscegenation laws. But nineteen years earlier – in 1948 – the California Supreme Court was the first to strike down an anti-miscegenation law – six years before the Supreme Court ended segregation as a violation of equal protection in Brown v. Board of Education. *See* Perez v. Lippold, 32 Cal. 2d 711, 729 (1948). For an excellent discussion on how *Perez* had a more robust discussion of the harms of anti-miscegenation laws than what is found in *Loving*, *see* R. A. Lenhardt, *Beyond Analogy*: Perez v. Sharp, *Antimiscegenation Law, and the Fight for Same-Sex Marriage*, 96 CAL. L. REV. 839, 844–45 (2008).

[32] *See* WALTER WADLINGTON, RAYMOND C. O'BRIEN, & ROBIN FRETWELL WILSON, DOMESTIC RELATIONS: CASES AND MATERIALS (8th ed., 2017).

[33] In 1993, Hawaii became the first state to have its judiciary suggest that the denial of marriage to same-sex couples might deprive them of equal protection under the law. Baehr v. Lewin, 74 Haw. 530, 559 (1993). In 1998, Hawaii's voters undid the judicial ruling by amending their constitution to bar such unions. In 1999, Vermont became the first state to expressly declare that the denial of marriage to same-sex couples violated Vermont's "Common Benefits Clause," a state provision that operated as a more robust form of the federal Equal Protection Clause. *See* Baker v. State, 170 Vt. 194, 202 (1999). However, this court decision too was diluted by the legislature that refused to extend marriage to same-sex couples. *See* Liz Halloran, *How Vermont's "Civil" War Fueled the Gay Marriage Movement*, NPR (Mar. 23, 2013), www.npr.org/2013/03/27/174651233/how-vermonts-civil-war-fueled-the-gay-marriage-movement.

[34] Goodridge, *supra* note 7, at 320.

[35] Andersen v. King Cnty., 158 Wash.2d 1, 44 (2006); Hernandez v. Robles, 7 N.Y.3d 338, 362 (2006); Baehr, 74 Haw. at 553, *as clarified on reconsideration*.

[36] Goodridge, *supra* note 7, at 321.

for everyone. In answering this question, *Goodridge* made three notable contributions to the framing of the marriage debate.

First, *Goodridge* enumerated the hundreds of private and social advantages that the State conferred on those who married.[37] *Goodridge* squarely defended marriage as a public institution that was properly defined by state government, taking marriage outside of the moral and religious debates of the day.[38]

Second, *Goodridge* redefined the personal commitment to marriage, stating that "the decision whether and whom to marry is among life's momentous acts of self-definition."[39] Instead of presenting marriage as the linchpin that perpetuates the human race, the court centered marriage on the seemingly much more modest act of falling in love with another: a choice that some people made, and others did not.

Third, *Goodridge* reimagined how the institution of marriage contributed to society: "[I]t fulfills yearnings for security, safe haven, and connection that express our common humanity."[40] Of note, a person's most intimate act of falling in love contributed to a larger public purpose. The seemingly personal decision to marry was no longer unique or private. Rather, *how* a person celebrated his or her private love with another became a public act in which one formed a public identity. The public impact of such a decision permitted one's identity as a married person to then become a currency that was shared with the others who made the same choice. The State's election to formally recognize this choice both validated it and let others recognize what they shared with a fellow citizen.

The state interest in marriage no longer hewed to an exclusively heterosexual function of procreation or perpetuating the species. Instead, the right to marry became fundamental because it permitted someone to partake in the full range of human experience. Those who choose to marry share a means of publicly expressing their inclusion in the larger community, which gives dignity by virtue of being included.[41] Gay men and lesbians were no longer excluded from the biological function of procreation. To the contrary, a gay man's or lesbian's act of falling in love with another became a recognized trait, forming an invitation to the previously exiled into an invited, included

37 *Id.* at 322. For a review of some benefits associated with marriage, *see* Wilson, Chapter 16, this volume.

38 In 2003, no mainstream religious organizations supported same-sex marriage. Robert P. Jones, *Religious Americans Support Gay Marriage*, ATLANTIC (Apr. 28, 2015), www.theatlantic.com/politics/archive/2015/04/religious-americans-support-gay-marriage/391646/.

39 Goodridge, *supra* note 7, at 322. 40 *Id.*

41 For criticisms of elevating this purpose as the reason for marriage, *see* Michael Cobb, *The Supreme Court's Lonely Hearts Club*, N.Y. TIMES (June 30, 2015), www.nytimes.com/2015/06/30/opinion/the-supreme-courts-lonely-hearts-club.html.

community.[42] In a remarkable shift, *Goodridge* transformed the position of the plaintiffs from gay and lesbian outsiders – whose sexual orientation marked them as different and morally suspect – to insiders who mirrored and enhanced the values of the sizable number of Americans who married or, at least, wanted to marry.[43]

In today's world, outside of the legal arena, procreation no longer resonates as the primary purpose of marriage. Sex outside of marriage has been decriminalized, as this section showed. Young people, even those who self-identify as religious, no longer save themselves for marriage.[44] Those who do are treated as a curiosity, befitting reality TV shows.[45]

In short, gay people were not granted marriage rights because of a shift in gender roles in heterosexual marriages or because of an embrace of a larger LGBT equality movement alone.[46] Rather, straight people no longer required

42 After Goodridge's redefinition of the marriage debate in 2003, some states raced to reject that vision, not embrace it. From 2004 to 2012, forty-one states amended state laws and constitutions to prevent their courts from following Massachusetts. *See* Robin Fretwell Wilson, *A Marriage of Necessity: Same-Sex Marriage and Religious Liberty Protections*, 64(3) Case Western Law Review 1161 (2014) (giving state-by-state breakdown of the amendments); Tim Grieve, *Bush's War Over Gay Marriage*, Salon (Feb. 26, 2004), www.salon.com/2004/02/26/gay_marriage_15/.

43 The project of transforming gay and lesbian couples from outsiders to insiders is not without its criticisms, given that it keeps in place rewards for those who choose to marry and penalties for those who do not. The concern arises that life circumstances, class differences, and economic insecurity often will shape the decision to marry rather than any decision relating to fitness or character. For a valuable critique, *see* Weiner, Chapter 11, this volume. In addition, for years, feminist scholars have been questioning the value in maintaining this system that ultimately penalizes the children of unmarried couples. *See* Fineman, *supra* note 2, at 244–45; Polikoff, *supra* note 2, at 573; Claire Huntington, Failure to Flourish: How Law Undermines Family Relationships (2014).

44 In Gallup polls, those who found it "morally acceptable" for unmarried men and women to have sex increased from 53% in 2001 to 68% in 2015. Those who found it "morally acceptable" to give birth outside of marriage also rose from 42% in 2001 to 61% in 2015. *Marriage*, Gallup, www.gallup.com/poll/117328/marriage.aspx. *See generally* John Blake, *Why Young Christians Aren't Waiting Anymore*, CNN (Sept. 27, 2011), religion.blogs.cnn.com/2011/09/27/why-young-christians-arent-waiting-anymore/.

45 *See The Virgin Diaries* (MTV) (depicting, in a reality show, young people saving their virginity for ethical or religious reasons); 19 *Kids and Counting* (TLC) (depicting, in a recently cancelled reality show, a conservative Christian family that did not use birth control and did not permit their children to engage in sexual activity before marriage).

46 For a fascinating account of one legislator's evolution of the question of same-sex marriage and the need for LGBT nondiscrimination protections, *see* Adams, Chapter 21, this volume. For an empirical examination of the role played by protections for religious dissenters in states that voluntarily embraced same-sex marriage, *see* Robin Fretwell Wilson, *A Marriage of Necessity: Same-Sex Marriage and Religious Liberty Protections*, 64 Case Western Law Review 1161 (2014).

procreation to bring value to a marital relationship.[47] It is precisely this shift in the societal understanding of marriage that allowed marriage to be logically – and legally – extended to same-sex couples in a seamless manner.

II SEARCHING FOR A TRANSCENDENT STATE INTEREST IN MARRIAGE

The forty-year debate over the merits of same-sex marriage was marked with an ideological divide over the virtues of marriage as an institution. Conservative scholars lauded the institution of marriage while many liberal scholars were skeptical of the emphasis on and importance of marriage.[48]

A *Something Special About Marriage?*

Now that marriage is divorced from the debate over rights for lesbian and gay citizens – some would say from nefarious attempts to divest lesbian and gay couples of their rights – new conversations have begun regarding the value of marriage *qua* marriage. Marriage is different from other relationships in two notable ways.

First, there is a postmodern, formalist function to marriage. When the State of California gave every single of the 1000-plus legal rights and benefits to same-sex couples that it gave to opposite-sex couples,[49] the omission of one single word – the word marriage – mattered. The U.S. Court of Appeals for the Ninth Circuit observed that a constitutional right may even attach to "the extraordinary significance of the official

47 Nicholas DiDomizio, *11 Brutally Honest Reasons Why Millennials Don't Want Kids*, MIC (July 30, 2015), mic.com/articles/123051/why-millennials-dont-want-kids#.Uqm8n1hQH. *See supra* note 44.

48 *See supra* note 2 and accompanying text. *But see* MARRIAGE AT THE CROSSROADS (Marsha Garrison & Elizabeth Scott eds., 2012) (discussing aspects of policy that promote marital and non-marital families).

49 CAL. FAM. CODE § 297.5 (West 2004) ("Registered domestic partners shall have the same rights, protections, and benefits, and shall be subject to the same responsibilities, obligations, and duties under law, whether they derive from statutes, administrative regulations, court rules, government policies, common law, or any other provisions or sources of law, as are granted to and imposed upon spouses."); Mitchell L. Engler & Edward D. Stein, *Not Too Separate or Unequal: Marriage Penalty Relief After* Obergefell, 91 WASH. L. REV. 1073, 1080 n. 26 (2016) (listing citations to more than 1000 federal rights and New York's calculation of more than 1300 state rights that attach to marriage). Goodridge, *supra* note 7, at 323 ("The benefits accessible only by way of a marriage license are enormous, touching nearly every aspect of life and death. The department states that 'hundreds of statutes' are related to marriage and to marital benefits.").

designation of 'marriage.'"[50] Writing for the majority, Judge Stephen Reinhardt observed that "[a] rose by any other name may smell as sweet, but to the couple desiring to enter into a committed lifelong relationship, a marriage by the name of 'registered domestic partnership' does not."[51] Even as many dispute the primacy that the law accords to marriage, there is growing scholarship that contends that the act of marriage itself, the formalization of a private relationship into something larger, does indeed create something larger that cannot be replicated in other relationships.[52]

Second, others have started to excavate and name the intangible benefits that may arise from marriage.[53] That said, an inquiry into the intangible benefits would be a tangled one at best. There exists a century's worth of cases recognizing various values that marriage has had in the lives of its citizens. Traditionally, those benefits have been conferred to only one party, most specifically husbands rather than wives.[54] Nonetheless, there have been notable moments when courts have recognized some transcendent values in marriage that provide desirable benefits in contemporary times.

B *Seeking a Transcendent, Intangible Benefit in Marriage*

Three cases where procreation, sex, and companionship are not just absent but impossible help isolate an intangible benefit uniquely arising from marriage: a shared common humanity that demands the support of the state. First, consider a case in which procreation was barred. In 2002, in *Gerber v. Hickman*, a prisoner brought a claim under 42 U.S.C. § 1983 asking the warden to give him permission to send through the mail a vial of sperm to his wife so that she could attempt to have his child with medical assistance.[55] The *en banc* court upheld the warden's denial over the fiery dissent of Judge

[50] Perry v. Brown, 671 F.3d 1052, 1078 (9th Cir. 2012) *vacated and remanded sub nom*, Hollingsworth v. Perry, 133 S. Ct. 2652 (2013).

[51] *Id.*

[52] *Compare* Weiner, Chapter 11, this volume, *with* Kar, Chapter 15, this volume, and Rebecca Aviel, A *New Formalism for Family Law*, 55 WM. & MARY L. REV. 2003, 2009–10 (2014) (discussing the transformative effects of formalizing relationships such as marriage). *See* Wilson, Chapter 16, this volume, for a critique of efforts to substitute for marriage a state-recognized civil union.

[53] *See* MARTHA M. ERTMAN, LOVE'S PROMISES: HOW FORMAL AND INFORMAL CONTRACTS SHAPE ALL KINDS OF FAMILIES (2015).

[54] *See generally* Kar, Chapter 15, this volume (discussing coverture); Borelli v. Brusseau, 12 Cal. App. 4th 647, 651 (1993).

[55] Gerber v. Hickman, 291 F.3d 617, 619 (9th Cir. 2002) (en banc). 42 U.S.C. § 1983 provides a remedy when a person, acting under the color of state law, denies another person his or her constitutional rights.

Alex Kozinski, who took the majority to task the holding that "the right to procreate is inconsistent with incarceration."[56] Judge Kozinski cited state regulations that permit prisoners to potentially procreate when conjugal visits are granted. His dissent, however, is more powerful as a means to question what goods marriage can provide to parties who are permanently separated because of one spouse's life imprisonment. These are couples who cannot share lives in the way that those living together do, but can marriage nonetheless serve some important good?

Consider a second case in which sex is wholly absent. In *Matter of Peterson*, in 1964, a fifty-six-year-old American citizen met a forty-nine-year-old woman who was a citizen of Iran.[57] The husband, a widower, and the wife, who had an adult daughter from her first marriage, first met when the wife answered an ad placed by the husband, which indicated he was looking for a housekeeper, with marriage as a potential result. They in fact married. When the husband applied for his wife's green card – which allows the holder to live permanently in the U.S. subject to certain rules, such as not committing a crime[58] – the federal Immigration and Naturalization Service agency initially deemed the application fraudulent; it cited as proof the couple's initial meeting, and their admission that they sleep in separate bedrooms and have not, and will not, engage in sexual intercourse. On appeal, the Board of Immigration Appeals ("BIA") – an agency that currently is known for interpretations of immigration law that will result in deportations more often than relief[59] – reversed. The BIA

56 In employing humor in a way that only Judge Kozinski can, he criticizes the penological interests in the five steps that would be involved in the prisoner's request. Gerber, 291 F.3d at 629 (Kozinski, J., dissenting).

57 Matter of Peterson, 12 I. & N. Dec. 663, 664 (BIA 1968).

58 *Rights and Responsibilities of a Green Card Holder (Permanent Resident)*, U.S. Citizenship & Immigration Services (July 15, 2015), www.uscis.gov/green-card/after-green-card-granted/rights-and-responsibilities-permanent-resident/rights-and-responsibilities-green-card-holder-permanent-resident.

59 Kari E. Hong, *Removing Citizens: Parenthood, Immigration Courts, and Derivative Citizenship*, 28 Geo. Immigr. L.J. 277, 337, 339 (2014) ("Akin to the appointment of immigration judges, all members of the BIA are appointed by the Attorney General and are employees of the Department of Justice. As mentioned before, in 2002, the board members were purged if they had viewpoints that differed from Attorney General John Ashcroft's prosecutorial agenda. No curative regulation or statute to protect existing BIA members from a similar employment purge has been enacted. . . . In October 2002, the BIA denied alien claims at a rate of 59%. One year after Attorney General Ashcroft's reforms [to fire board members who issued decisions favorable to noncitizens] were introduced, the denial rate climbed to 86%. By 2005, the denial rate rose to 94%. Today, the denial rate is at 93%. Unlike criminal appeals that have a similarly high denial rate, the denial rate is not the result of the cases lacking legal or factual errors. To the contrary, of the cases that are appealed to the federal courts, approximately up to 11% to 21% of the BIA cases are found to have reversible errors.").

did not detail how and why. But it noted with sympathy that the husband was a widower in genuine need of a housekeeper. In a conclusory manner, the BIA found that "[t]he reasons for the marriage appear to be far sounder than exist for most marriages."[60]

The most obvious shared insight from *Gerber* and *Peterson* is that companionship is an aspect to marriage that the State recognizes and values. The State's protection of companionate marriages benefits its citizens and society at large. True, some cynically would say such thinned-down marriages serve as private welfare; more optimistically others would see them as a means by which the State may encourage the pursuit of happiness to its citizenry.

But the third case, *Freeman v. Gonzales*, prevents companionship from being the only available answer to the question of the state interest in contemporary marriage.[61] Under U.S. immigration laws, citizens are allowed to bring their spouses to the country and give them lawful permanent residence.[62] This is more than settled practice and policy; it is a defining hallmark of the U.S. immigration system.[63]

In 1997, Congress enacted a confusing provision regulating what happens when a citizen spouse dies during the other spouse's petition process. A circuit split arose, with *Freeman* among the courts that defended the statutory interpretation that authorized immigration to proceed – specifically, that when a citizen dies, his or her surviving spouse can enter and live in the US: "Under the express terms of the statute, rs. Freeman qualified as the *spouse* of a U.S. citizen when she and her husband petitioned for adjustment of status, and absent a clear statutory provision voiding her spousal status upon her husband's untimely death, she remains a *surviving* spouse."[64] In 2009, President Obama signed a law firmly establishing that the *Freeman* rule will be uniformly applied.[65] As a result, when a citizen dies, his or her surviving spouse – a foreigner who is a citizen from another country – can now enter and live in the U.S., a coveted privilege conferred only to the spouses, children, and parents of citizens. This profound change in immigration law follows from recognizing that the benefits

60 Matter of Peterson, 12 I. & N. Dec. 663, 664 (BIA 1968).

61 *See* Freeman v. Gonzales, 444 F.3d 1031 (9th Cir. 2006).

62 Immigration and Nationality Act ("INA"), 8 U.S.C. § 1153 (2012).

63 Two-thirds of lawful immigration occurs through family relationships with citizens or other lawful permanent residents. INA § 203; Jacquellena Carrero, *The Immigration Line: Who's on It and For How Long*, NBC Latino (Apr. 11, 2013), http://nbclatino.com/2013/04/11/the-immigration-line-whos-on-it-and-for-how-long/.

64 Freeman, *supra* note 61, at 1039–40.

65 Dept. of Homeland Security Appropriations Act of 2010, Pub. L. No. 111–83.

of marriage do not vanish after death. Unlike many immigration rights that are under attack by the Trump Administration, extending protection to the surviving spouses of citizens currently is not one.[66]

Together, these three cases survey instances when sex, procreation, companionship are not just missing, but completely impossible in the marital relationship. In *Freeman*, the couple itself no longer existed after one spouse died. These cases are significant because usually, when these essentials are absent, the State will not recognize a formal relationship. Most states expressly define consummation as an essential statutory element of the marriage.[67] For most everyone but the Petersons, the federal government will require consummation as proof that a marriage is not fraudulent when conferring immigration benefits.[68] The vast majority of states require both people to be present and alive for a marriage to be recognized.[69]

Peterson, *Gerber*'s dissent, and *Freeman* defied these general rules. Interestingly, judges defended the marital relationship – and their exceptions to the general rule – without being able to name what precisely it is about the marriage relationship that compels such sympathy. Whether it be a platonic companionship, economic security, a caretaking function, an ideal, or even posthumous identity, marriage is providing important benefits society has yet to easily articulate. Nonetheless, as much as these cases do not conclusively name what merits the State's solicitude, they signal a trailhead, a path that is worthy to undertake to identify and articulate what that intangible aspect of marriage is. As these cases show and as *Obergefell* affirmed, something intangible and of value exists in marriage. Like the impulse to cry at weddings, these three marriages remind us of our common humanity.

66 *See* Kari Hong, *The Costs of Trumped-Up Immigration Enforcement*, 2017 CARDOZO L. REV. 119, https://papers.ssrn.com/sol3/papers.cfm?abstract_id=2957888 (summarizing the emphasis of Trump's immigration policies that relate to enforcement efforts in arresting, detaining, and deporting millions).

67 *See generally* Edwards v. Edwards, 188 Ga. App. 821 (1988); GA. CODE ANN. § 19–3-1 (West 2016).

68 Both statutes and case law state that consummation is not required to prove the existence of a valid marriage. *See* Matter of M, 7 I & N. Dec 601 (BIA 1957). Nonetheless, in immigration proceedings, citizens and noncitizens are often required to answer questions about their sex lives. *See* Adi v. United States, 498 F.Appx. 478, 482 (6th Cir. 2012). Individual immigration officers will find a marriage invalid in the absence of convincing evidence as to consummation. *See* Nina Bernstein, *Do You Take This Immigrant?*, N.Y. TIMES (June 11, 2010), www.nytimes.com/2010/06/13/nyregion/13fraud.html?pagewanted=all.

69 *See generally* Andrea B. Carroll, *Reviving Proxy Marriage*, 76 BROOK. L. REV. 455, 457 (2011) (noting that only five states recognize proxy marriages, and "nearly all in an exceptionally narrow context involving military personnel").

III THE COUNTERINTUITIVE LIBERAL STATE INTEREST IN CONTEMPORARY MARRIAGE

Contemporary marriage offers an important opportunity for citizens to redefine their relationship to the Liberal State. The State has a role to protect those who cannot otherwise fend for themselves – a doctrine known as *parens patriae*, the same authority the modern State uses to protect the vulnerable, most often children and the mentally incompetent.[70] When the State intervenes for the purpose of protecting the vulnerable, the vast majority of Americans see state involvement as a normative good.[71]

Asking the State to lend additional support to married couples – who today have the most resources and protections,[72] is a counterintuitive, if not morally questionable project. In today's society, it is the unmarried people, especially those with children, who face the vulnerabilities that arise from a lack of legal protections and economic insecurity.[73] A number of scholars have persuasively noted disadvantages – and at times, harms – that the institution of marriage can perpetuate – Martha Fineman and Clare Huntington among the most persuasive voices. Like Weiner (Chapter 11, this volume), they call for reforms to support nonmarital family units.[74] Although there is a need to protect and benefit all families, including those outside of marriage, it is important that the State continue to support and be the guarantor of affirmative benefits for those who do opt for marriage.

70 *Parens patriae* empowers the State to confer "protection for those unable to care for themselves." BLACK'S LAW DICTIONARY 1114 (6th ed. 1990); *see also* Sarah Abramowicz, Note, *English Child Custody Law, 1600–1839: The Origins of Judicial Intervention in Paternal Custody*, 99 COLUM. L. REV. 1344, 1346–47 (1999).

71 *See generally* Michael Levenson, *Baker Says State Will Review DCF Handling of Auburn Child*, BOSTON GLOBE (Aug. 17, 2015), www.bostonglobe.com/metro/2015/08/17/baker-says-state-will-review-dcf-handling-auburn-child/AayI1VaDx8Ouq4sVrvIFwK/story.html.

72 Allison Linn, *Why Married People Tend to Be Wealthier: It's Complicated*, TODAY (Feb. 13, 2013), www.today.com/money/why-married-people-tend-be-wealthier-its-complicated-1C8364877; Erez Aloni, *Married People Tend to Be Wealthier – So Why Give Them Tax Breaks?*, GUARDIAN (Nov. 9, 2015), www.theguardian.com/commentisfree/2015/nov/09/married-people-wealthier-why-give-them-tax-breaks.

73 *See* Weiner, Chapter 11, this volume, for a compelling case that additional duties should attach outside marriage.

74 *See* CLARE HUNTINGTON, FAILURE TO FLOURISH: HOW LAW UNDERMINES FAMILY RELATIONSHIP (2014); MARTHA ALBERTSON FINEMAN, THE NEUTERED MOTHER, THE SEXUAL FAMILY AND OTHER TWENTIETH CENTURY TRAGEDIES (1995).

A Privacy as the Fundamental Right to Be Let Alone

As a preliminary matter, it is important to revisit one key assumption about marriage's value: that the right to be let alone that marriage historically conferred is an essential protection to citizens and democracy. It is an understatement to contend that privacy is a valued commodity in the U.S. As Justice Louis Brandeis articulated 100 years ago, the Founders "sought to protect Americans in their beliefs, their thoughts, their emotions and their sensations. They conferred, as against the government, the right to be let alone – the most comprehensive of rights and the right most valued by civilized men."[75]

From a citizen's right to control his home and destiny, American life has been imbued with a sense that an individual's right to privacy is a precondition to achieving essential freedoms and liberties.[76] The First, Second, Fourth, Fifth, Ninth, and Tenth Amendments reinforce the idea that the right to be let alone – or left alone, in more modern terms – from the State remains a vital, contemporary protection Americans receive from our democratic institutions.

In family law, privacy also has been embraced as an expansive, dynamic doctrine, preventing the State from intruding upon familial decisions relating to procreation, abortion, childrearing, education, and family formation.[77] Privacy also anchors respect for childrearing, as Wilson and Sanders show (Chapter 13, this volume). Family scholars have robustly critiqued the conditional nature of these protections. Functional families are "let alone by the State" because the State provides few rights between the parties or "*inter se* rights." A family that possesses either a man or money (preferably both) may raise its children with as much confusion and chaos as it pleases – whether for religious reasons or otherwise – as privacy shields inquiries and intrusion by the State – at least when childrearing practices fall short of abuse and neglect.[78] Ironically, the State's absence from these relationships may be far more impactful than religious exemptions given by the law for childrearing, schooling, and vaccination, all of which may negatively impact children but

75 Olmstead v. United States, 277 U.S. 438, 478–79 (1928) (Brandeis, J., dissenting) (dissenting from a decision upholding the government's collection of evidence by wiretapping). *See also* Samuel D. Warren & Louis D. Brandeis, *The Right to Privacy*, 4 Harv. L. Rev. 193, 205 (1890) (articulating the "right to be left alone" in tort contexts).

76 *See* Alexander de Tocqueville, I Democracy in America 244–47 (1825).

77 *See* Planned Parenthood of Southeastern Pennsylvania v. Casey, 505 U.S. 833 (1992) (discussing abortion); Michael H. v. Gerald D., 491 U.S. 110 (1989) (discussing family formation); Moore v. East Cleveland, 431 U.S. 484 (1977) (discussing what counts as a family); Griswold, *supra* note 6 (discussing procreation).

78 *See generally* John DeWitt Gregory, Peter N. Swisher, & Robin Fretwell Wilson, Understanding Family Law, § 7.09 (4th ed., 2013).

where religious believers often have to show proof to trigger the protection.[79] In this respect, the vacuum carved out by the law is arguably more profound than any impact that a legal right imposes.

By contrast, what Martha Fineman has called "public families" – families that are (unfairly) marked as inadequate or inferior – are subject to state "regulation, supervision, and control."[80] The disruption of divorce, poverty, and abuse invites – and sometimes compels – the State to intervene.[81] But short of these triggering events, these families are left without protection against overreach within the family.

Underlying these criticisms is the unspoken assumption that a family's right to be let alone is ultimately a desired station to which all families normatively should belong and from which all members benefit. However, this privacy carries significant costs for children who are subject to parental abuse via lack of state intervention, as Offit (Chapter 12) and Wilson and Sanders (Chapter 13) show in this volume.

But query whether state intervention is in fact the problem. What if it is underlying biases – rather than a family's public status – that sort out some families for regulation and not others? Stated another way, what if the problem of regulating, policing, and punishing public families arises from the biases that seek to make couples and children conform to a normative ideal, not the vehicle of state intervention by itself?

B Obergefell's *Sword: Rethinking State Harm as Arising from No State Intervention*

Much has been written about the triad of *Griswold*, *Eisenstadt*, and *Roe v. Wade*,[82] which are known for paving the path that resulted in a right to privacy giving a person a shield from state powers that would otherwise limit the right to plan and birth children. But the right to privacy has taken on new qualities in the marriage equality movement. Beginning in *Lawrence v. Texas*, the right to be let

79 *See* Offit, Chapter 12, this volume; Dwyer, Chapter 8, this volume; Wilson & Sanders, Chapter 13, this volume.

80 Fineman, *supra* note 74, at 177–78.

81 *See generally* Hodge v. Jones, 31 F.3d 157, 168 (4th Cir. 1994) (upholding a right for a state to maintain a record of suspected child abusers because a parent's claim of familial privacy does not override the state interest in protecting children); Khiara M. Bridges, *Privacy Rights and Public Families*, 34 Harv. J. L. & Gender 113, 118–19 (2011).

82 Griswold, *supra* note 6 (finding a privacy right for married couples to use contraceptives); Eisenstadt v. Baird, 405 U.S. 438, 453 (1972) (finding an equal protection right for single individuals to use contraceptives); Roe v. Wade, 410 U.S. 113 (1973) (grounding a right to abortion in privacy).

alone emerged as a key reason in protecting same-sex individuals. The Supreme Court could have evaluated the sodomy laws at issue under the Equal Protection Clause; indeed, that is exactly what Justice Sandra Day O'Connor's concurrence argued would have been the proper analysis. But the majority opinion, authored by Justice Kennedy took a different tack. Instead of asking which rights gay and lesbian individuals should be given, the *Lawrence* majority framed the issue as a privacy case in which the right to be let alone was the vehicle that resulted in equality. *Lawrence* begins with the precise pronouncement that "[l]iberty protects the person from unwarranted government intrusions into a dwelling or other private places. In our tradition, the State is not omnipresent in the home."[83] This predicate formulation of privacy – not equality – resulted in abolishing state laws that criminalized what is otherwise consensual, intimacy between adults described in Section I. In a fascinating and significant decision, twelve years later, *Obergefell* cited to *Lawrence* a dozen times to support its reasoning and result that marriage is a fundamental right that must be opened to same-sex couples.[84]

Importantly, *Obergefell* articulated a new intrusion of the state, which is *not* regulating or punishing private choices. The harm inflicted on those from whom marriage is withheld is "the imprimatur of the State itself on an exclusion that soon demeans or stigmatizes those whose own liberty is then denied."[85] Privacy no longer is a carved-out realm or a space apart from the State's views in which individuals may order their lives in peace. Rather, Justice Kennedy articulates a privacy right that demands that the State remove itself from public expressions that inflict humiliation and stigmatization onto others. In defending this rule, Justice Kennedy lists the plaintiffs by name and invokes the unique harm they will face if the decision resulted in a different outcome – a surviving spouse would not be able to bury his husband, mothers would not be able to protect their children, a veteran would not be able to receive the protection for which he risked his life for the sake of others.[86] In so doing, Justice Kennedy makes clear that there is no longer a neutrality that arises from not intervening. Rather, the State then must arbitrate values and affirmatively protect those who are vulnerable to nonlegal and intangible injuries: "The Nation's courts are open to injured individuals who come to them to vindicate their own direct, personal stake in our basic charter."[87] The State suddenly becomes a guarantor of affirmative benefits.[88]

83 Lawrence v. Texas, 539 U.S. 558, 562 (2003).

84 Obergefell, *supra* note 3, at 2600 (Roberts, J., dissenting). 85 *Id.* 86 *Id.* at 2606.

87 *Id.* at 2605.

88 This is not to say older cases have rejected such a role. For example, in the controversial case of *DeShaney v. Winnebago County*, the Supreme Court found no state liability when a child was

In his dissenting opinion, Justice Roberts strongly objects to *Obergefell*'s new definition of privacy. In objecting to the majority's conclusion that recognition of same-sex marriage is required by the U.S. Constitution, Justice Roberts observes that "[n]either *Lawrence* nor any other precedent in the privacy line of cases supports the right that petitioners assert here."[89] Justice Roberts notes that

> [u]nlike criminal laws banning contraceptives and sodomy, the marriage laws at issue here *involve no government intrusion*. They create no crime and impose no punishment. Same-sex couples remain free to live together, to engage in intimate conduct, and to raise their families as they see fit. No one is "condemned to live in loneliness" by the laws challenged in these cases – no one.[90]

Justice Roberts affirms that "the laws [limiting marriage to opposite-sex couples] in no way interfere with the 'right to be let alone.'"[91] Emphasizing the perceived break that *Obergefell* makes from prior precedent, he contends: "petitioners do not seek privacy. Quite the opposite, they seek public recognition of their relationships, along with corresponding government benefits. Our cases have consistently refused to allow litigants to convert the shield provided by constitutional liberties into a sword to demand positive entitlements from the State."[92]

Yet, *Obergefell* posits the right to marry. Justice Roberts is right: for the first time, the privacy doctrine is no longer a means to let people alone. The harm imposed on same-sex couples by the State is not the harm envisioned by Justice Louis Brandeis. It was not an unwanted intervention in the sacred realm that caused injury, but, rather, the State's *lack of intervention* that inflicted the harm on the couple. Under the guise of privacy, State intervention then becomes a powerful tool to obtain needed benefits and protections. *Obergefell* indeed acted as a sword.

C *Extending* Obergefell's *Sword Beyond Marriage*

State intervention in marriage can be a means to open more families to constructive regulation by the State. As Wiener argues (Chapter 11, this volume), this is good public policy. For many, arguing for more state intervention is counterintuitive. Why would anyone want to invite the State into his or her personal affairs, casting judgments on what he or she should or should

not taken into state custody, even though a state social worker had feared for the child's life if he remained with his father at home. 489 U.S. 189 (1989).

89 *Id.* 90 *Id.* (emphasis added). 91 *Id.* 92 *Id.*

not be doing? But the reality is that in many private families, individuals who are fully functioning need the benefits of state intervention that currently the State only provides to families receiving public financial assistance. These "public families" are subject to government policing and supervision, which is often helpful to those families. In some instances, state intervention is the only means to mute harms facing married couples. Witte (Chapter 17, this volume) and Strassberg (Chapter 18, this volume) discuss the need for state regulation of polygamy, despite religious claims that polygamy should be a private matter. Here, immigration provides a second concrete example of the utility of the State's intervention in families.

A case decided eleven days before *Obergefell*, a decision about the constitutional protections afforded to a citizen married to a foreigner, illustrates how *Obergell's* sword may be the only means to remedy specific harms in the immigration context – absent specific positive law, as Adams explains (Chapter 21, this volume). In *Kerry v. Din*, Mrs. Din, a U.S. citizen, petitioned for her husband to join her in the U.S.[93] When a noncitizen is in the U.S., the agency formerly known as the Immigration and Naturalization Service ("INS") adjudicates that request.[94] When the noncitizen is outside of the country, such as Mr. Din, the citizen family members file paper work with the U.S. consulate's adjudicate, asking the officer to grant their relative permission to enter the U.S. and reside lawfully once there. In *Kerry v. Din*, the consular officer denied the citizen wife's request in which she asked for her husband to receive an entry visa and ultimately a green card based on their marriage.[95] The consular officer claimed that the husband was not admissible to the U.S. because he was involved in or promoted terrorism. No further reason was given. Under the immigration rules, no review of a consular decision is permitted.[96] The non-reviewability of an action by a consular

93 Kerry v. Din, 135 S. Ct. 2128, 2132 (2015).

94 In 2003, Congress abolished the Immigration and Naturalization Service ("INS") and replaced it with the U.S. Citizen Immigration Services (USCIS), which is responsible for adjudicating such matters as family petitions, green card applications, and naturalization applications, and the Immigration and Customs Enforcement agency ("ICE"), which is tasked with immigration enforcement matters. Congress abolished the INS – and its Deciding Service Officers – in 2003. *See* 6 U.S.C. § 291 (2012). *See also* Garcia-Guerrero v. Holder, 544 F. App'x 752, 753 (9th Cir. 2013) (citing 6 U.S.C. § 291).

95 Kerry, *supra* note 93, at 2132.

96 *See* Cardenas v. United States, 826 F.3d 1164, 1170 (9th Cir. 2016) (upholding consular non-reviewability doctrine involving a decision denying a husband the chance to join his citizen wife in the United States due to the consular officer's belief that he might engage in unlawful activity in the future); *but see* Rivas v. Napolitano, 714 F.3d 1108, 1111 (9th Cir. 2013) (noting two exceptions to the consular non-reviewability doctrine and holding one existed in the case before it).

officer is a problematic policy. News reports – and criminal dockets – contain brazen examples of corrupt consular officers, profiting handsomely without the benefit of immediate oversight.[97]

Writing for the majority, the late Justice Antonin Scalia dismissed out of hand the dissent's call for a constitutional recognition for Mrs. Din to live with her spouse in the US: "Nothing in the cases Din cites establishes a free-floating and categorical liberty interest in marriage (or any other formulation Din offers) sufficient to trigger constitutional protection whenever a regulation in any way touches upon an aspect of the marital relationship."[98] Din's request to know the reasons why the federal government would not let a spouse enter the country, Justice Scalia urged, is not akin to the State's exercise of authority in the form of "dispossess[ion] of property, [being] thrown in jail, or even executed."[99]

But Mrs. Din was seeking more than simply a right to live with her husband anywhere in the world. Mrs. Din was seeking the right to know the basis for a decision that denied her request to live with her husband in the U.S. She further was asking that if any factual or legal mistake was made, that she have an opportunity to correct it. Most often, notice and opportunity to be heard are dismissed as merely procedural rights. For those whose lives are fundamentally altered by government decisions, being left in the dark – with the confusion and doubts over the process – is often much more painful than the closure that comes from a final decision. In this respect procedural rights regarding how a government joins or separates family members from citizens quickly elevate into potent and powerful means by which citizens are or are not treated with fairness.

In the actual Supreme Court case, the Din family did not receive any protection from being let alone. The precise harm the Dins were seeking to remedy – an opportunity to review whether the government official made a mistake when finding the husband inadmissible – was unavailable because of the State's lack of power to review the consular decision. Mrs. Din's marriage diminished in stature and operation because of the lack of engagement by the State, not the State's intrusion. This decision was reached because the legal issue was framed as whether a foreigner had a right to know why he was not let into the country.[100]

[97] Calvin Godfrey, *U.S. Consulate Officers Gone Wild*, VICE (Sept. 4, 2013), www.vice.com/read/the-corrupt-secrets-of-the-american-consulate (reporting on the arrest of a consular officer who netted $10 million in a fraudulent visa scheme).

[98] Kerry, *supra* note 93, at 2135 (coming to a 5–4 decision). [99] *Id.* at 2133.

[100] *See* Zadvydas v. Davis, 533 U.S. 678, 689 (2001) (commenting on Congress's plenary powers to shape immigration law); Juliet Stumpf, *The Crimmigation Crisis: Immigrants, Crime, and Sovereign Power*, 56 AM. U. LAW REV. 367, 392–93 (2006).

By contrast, Mrs. Din could have very much used *Obergefell*'s sword – which came into existence eleven days after her decision – to ensure that her marriage – and the attendant right to choose to marry a specific person – received the affirmative rights of notice and fair process from the federal government. *Obergefell* thus offers the possibility that a citizen's marriage is a legal status to which heightened protections will attach.

Reimagining the legal question in *Din* from being a foreigner's right to know why he was excluded into a citizen's right to be treated fairly by her government is not a naïve project. In the Travel Ban case, this very same re-imagination is what took place in the first and second Ninth Circuit decisions that enjoined enforcement of the order. On January 27, 2017, President Donald Trump issued an executive order that banned the entry of any national of seven Muslim-majority countries from entering into the U.S.[101] The impact of the order was "immediate and widespread," resulting in the cancellation of thousands of visas, Immigration and Customs Enforcement ("ICE") detaining people at airports, and airlines not permitting others to board planes.[102] A federal district court in the State of Washington enjoined the order on a preliminary basis, and the Ninth Circuit upheld the decision. Before getting to the merits, on March 6, 2017, the White House revoked the first order and issued what it called a more measured and considered executive order, limiting the entry to nationals of six (instead of seven) Muslim-majority countries, excluding lawful permanent residents from the order, and excluding anyone who had already received a visa to the United States.[103] A federal district court in Hawaii enjoined that one as well.[104]

In the first order, the Ninth Circuit had held that the States of Washington, Hawaii, and Minnesota had standing to challenge the Travel Ban due to the harm that the states' universities encountered when some of their "students, scholars, and faculty" were not permitted to return to their studies, jobs, or research projects.[105] In the second order, the federal district court also recognized the harm that a U.S. citizen, named Dr. Ismail Elshikh, encountered when his mother-in-law was not allowed to enter the U.S.

Dr. Elshikh is a U.S. citizen, resident of Hawaii, and an imam at a mosque. His wife is from Syria and their young children are also U.S. citizens.[106] Dr. Elshikh's mother-in-law is a Syrian national who has visited the family in Hawaii. At that time, she had no visa, so that under the executive order, she would be forever barred from visiting her citizen grandchildren at their home.

[101] Washington v. Trump, 847 F.3d 1151, 1157 (9th Cir. 2017). [102] *Id.*
[103] Hawai'i v. Trump, 2017 WL 1011673, at *1 (D. Haw. 2017). [104] *Id.*
[105] Washington, *supra* note 101, at 1159–60. [106] Hawai'i, *supra* note 103, at *9.

Of note, Dr. Elshikh was permitted to challenge the executive order not out of any showing of economic harm but based on the humiliation arising from citizen grandchildren not being able to have their grandmother visit. This is *Obergefell*'s sword in operation – the initial harm of family separation came from the federal government mistakenly arguing that an elderly Syrian woman had no right to visit the U.S. Initially, it had an argument. This Syrian woman had no legal status and no existing visa to visit. But this framing of the problem was found to be the incorrect one because modern immigration is not able to divide the world into "us" and "them" when so many of "them" are in fact the mothers, fathers, spouses, children, and in this case grandchildren of those of us rightfully in this country. The cure for what was a wrongful separation was not found in the traditional right of privacy that let citizens be let alone. Rather, the cure arose from active and affirmative State intervention – in the form of a federal district court – recognizing that citizen grandchildren had a right to be visited by grandmothers, irrespective of the religion the grandmother followed.

Obergefell's sword then might be a welcomed means to reimagine immigration as no longer a question of foreign policy but of family formation. International travel and the Internet have transformed modern immigration in the U.S. No longer simply being intact families emigrating together from their foreign homelands, the ease of international travel has increased the number of citizens who wish to marry or parent someone born abroad: "The rise of cross-border relationships prevents immigration law from being the exclusive arm of foreign policy that it was in the twentieth century. Immigration policies can no longer categorically exclude aliens when such exclusion infringes on a citizen's right to marry or parent the alien."[107] It seems quite appropriate that family institutions are in the middle of the legal transformation that must follow to mirror the changes around us.

IV CONCLUSION

This chapter has been an attempt to ask questions too long neglected. Starting with the premise that marriage can provide unique and desirable value, it articulates what precisely such value may be. The answer to that question most likely includes recognition that the old shield of privacy – the right to be let alone – may have outlived its usefulness. At a minimum, there are specific contexts in which the involvement of the State in personal affairs of spouses is

[107] Kari E. Hong, *Famigration (Fam-Imm): The Next Frontier in Immigration Law*, 100 VA. L. REV. ONLINE 63, 64 (2014).

precisely the needed salve for an otherwise irreparable and irremediable injury. For this reason, the lasting impact of *Obergefell* may not be its recognition of same-sex marriage in the face of religious dissent. To the contrary, if Justice Roberts's dissent is correct, *Obergefell*'s sword may be the precise remedy for which many citizens – who are vulnerable to the harms arising from the lack of state intervention – have been waiting.

15

Transformational Marriage

The Religious Case for Supporting Same-Sex Marriage

Robin Bradley Kar

Professor of Law and Philosophy, University of Illinois College of Law

When the Supreme Court found a constitutional right to same-sex marriage in *Obergefell v. Hodges*,[1] it settled a legal question for the nation. In the view of many, it nevertheless deepened a preexisting culture war over the role of religion in family life. Some conservative writers now argue that *Obergefell* requires an enduring response from the Religious Right, which is national in scale and modeled on the pro-life movement. If that were to occur, *Obergefell* may end up functioning like *Roe v. Wade*[2] – that is, as a central and seemingly intractable source of political, cultural, and legal division in the United States for many years to come.

Though the term "culture war" can be used in many ways, it derives from the German "Kulturkampf," which originally referred to a conflict between religious and secular authorities in 19th-century Germany.[3] The conflict was over how much authority the Church and its official religious doctrines should have in shaping matters of law and public policy. Some doubt whether all contemporary religious objections to same-sex marriage are genuinely religious, as opposed to political, but this chapter takes the religious dimensions of

Special thanks for helpful input or conversations on these topics from Helen Alvaré, Greg Caramenico, Stephanie Coontz, William Eskridge, Margareth Etienne, Robert Gagnon, Aziz Huq, Andrew Koppelman, Sarah Lawsky, Douglas Laycock, Brian Leiter, Jason Mazzone, William Miller, Melissa Murray, Douglas NeJaime, Benjamin Paulsen, Michael Perry, Michael Pollack, Margaret Jane Radin, Richard Ross, Jennifer Rothman, Paul Schmitt, Larry Solum, Geoffrey Stone, Helga Varden, Tobias Barrington Wolff, Robin Fretwell Wilson, Ekow Yankah, and Karin Yefet.

1 135 S. Ct. 2584 (2015).

2 *See, e.g.*, Ryan T. Anderson, Truth Overruled: The Future of Marriage and Religious Freedom 8 (2015) ("Everything the pro-life movement did needs to be done again, now on this new frontier of marriage.").

3 William N. Eskridge Jr., A *Jurisprudence of "Coming Out": Religion, Homosexuality, and Collisions of Liberty and Equality* 106 Yale L. J. 2411, 2414 (1997).

the debate seriously. It therefore uses the term "culture war" in its original sense to refer to a conflict over the appropriate role of religious as opposed to secular values to decide the appropriate contours of legal and social institutions like marriage.

Given this definition, *Obergefell* clearly holds a central place in contemporary culture wars over religion in family life. Many view *Obergefell* as a major attack on religious definitions of marriage. *Obergefell*'s position in the culture wars nevertheless depends on a particular understanding of the case. On this view, *Obergefell* represents just the latest in a long series of triumphs of secular-progressive values – including privacy, individual liberty, and equal treatment of lesbian, gay, bisexual, and transgender ("LGBT") persons – over Judeo-Christian religious values, which until recently shaped Western family life and intimacy for millennia. Other recent developments commonly thought to fit this pattern of encroaching secularism include the passage of no-fault divorce statutes throughout the nation in the 1970s, the expansion of legal rights to cohabitation prior to marriage, the decriminalization of sodomy for consenting adults in the privacy of their homes, the establishment of legal rights to view pornography in the privacy of one's home, the announcement of legal rights to information about and access to contraception, and *Roe v. Wade* itself.[4] All these developments occurred over the past half century and were hotly contested by many who view the conflicts as pitting religious against secular values. Conflicts between religious and secular values can be incredibly divisive and persistent. Whether *Obergefell* has the same long-term trajectory as *Roe* is likely to depend, in part, on how strongly the public continues to view the decision as a simple triumph for secularism in a culture war.

The standard view of *Obergefell* has undeniable appeal for people on all sides of the political and religious spectrum. It fits *Obergefell* into a well-recognized pattern of historical developments in family law, which have dominated many people's political attention over the past half century. Because *Obergefell* grants the legal right to same-sex marriage to members of the LGBT community, it can look like a mere late consequence of the sexual revolution of the 1960s, which led to the expansion of many earlier LGBT rights. Many people also have psychological reasons to be invested in the standard view. People who prefer secular-progressive values may well enjoy a

[4] Denese Ashbaugh Vlosky & Pamela A. Monroe, *The Effective Dates of No-Fault Divorce Laws in the 50 States*, 51 FAM. RELATIONS 317, 322–23 (2002); Weiner, Chapter 11, this volume; Stanley v. Georgia, 294 U.S. 557, 568 (1969) ("States retain broad power to regulate obscenity; that power simply does not extend to mere possession by the individual in the privacy of his own home."); Griswold v. Connecticut, 381 U.S. 479, 486 (1965); Lawrence v. Texas, 539 U.S. 558, 585 (2003); Roe v. Wade, 410 U.S. 113, 166 (1973).

sense of secular triumph. Religious conservatives who dislike the decision can still welcome the standard view of it as confirming their perception that religious family values are under attack from all sides. They can thus cite the standard view as a rallying cry in that larger fight.

Still, before the standard view becomes too deeply entrenched in the public consciousness, one should ask whether it offers the best way to understand *Obergefell*. This chapter argues that it does not. There are good reasons to reject, or at least significantly complicate, the view that *Obergefell* represents a simple triumph of secularism in a culture war. *Obergefell* is also the result of a recent and major, but less well studied, expansion in the religious and spiritual functions of marriage. This expansion came with the historical rise of what this chapter calls "transformational marriage." Transformational marriage is a social institution that serves as a vehicle for the maturation of early romantic desire into the psychological capacities needed to break free from the bondage of self and attain greater personal communion with the totality of life – or with God or the divine – however one conceives of these. Transformational marriage can help people achieve certain psychological transformations needed to live joyfully and well come what may, and to identify and contribute better to the common good.

These are values that people from many different faiths and non-observant people can all endorse.[5] Yet the values have a distinctive quality, which warrants calling them "religious" or "spiritual" in at least one recognizable sense of these words: the values do not depend on any particular states of affairs about the world but rather add value to life come what may.[6] If given sufficient social, legal, and pastoral support, same-sex marriage of the transformational variety has this underappreciated religious and spiritual potential. Even if same-sex marriage reflects a break in Western tradition, these facts should

[5] Hence, even though the concept of a transformational marriage will be distilled from Pope Francis's writings, the value of transformational marriage is in no way limited to people of any particular denomination or religious belief. Indeed, for reasons to be explained, see Section II, *infra*, even agnostics or atheists can acknowledge the value of transformational marriage. This chapter thus seeks to articulate a route to what John Rawls would call an "overlapping consensus" on the value of transformational marriage. *See* John Rawls, *The Idea of an Overlapping Consensus*, 7 Oxford Journal of Legal Studies No. 1, (Spring, 1987). Rawls defines an "overlapping consensus" as a consensus that is "affirmed by the opposing religious, philosophical and moral doctrines likely to thrive over generations in a more or less just constitutional democracy . . .." *Id.* at 1.

[6] Section II, *infra*, explains why transformational marriages can produce values of just this kind, regardless of a person's religious beliefs or affiliations – and, indeed, whether a person has any particular religious beliefs or affiliations at all.

complicate the way that committed religious observers respond to same-sex marriage and perceive its place the contemporary culture wars.

To set the stage for these arguments, Section I explains why so many people-including Senator Orrin Hatch in the introduction to this volume-currently assume that *Obergefell* reflects a simple triumph of secularism. It identifies harmful consequences of the assumption for people on all sides of the contemporary same-sex marriage debate. The problems all arise from assuming an intractable conflict between Judeo-Christian religious values and contemporary same-sex marriage. Whether this conflict is real depends on what the religious and spiritual functions of contemporary marriage are. Section II addresses this topic through a close reading of Pope Francis's recent writings on love and marriage. Contrary to what many marriage traditionalists assume, the religious and spiritual functions of marriage began to evolve in the West in the 17th and 18th centuries. This period, culminating in the middle 20th century, witnessed the historical rise of transformational marriage as a social institution, which in turn depended on widespread cultural acceptance of a fundamental link between romantic love, personal choice, intimate satisfaction, and marriage. Section II describes these historical developments and observes that the value of transformational marriage is non-parochial. It has a type of value that religious observers from many faiths and non-observant people can all endorse as having a special kind of value that is not merely material.

Section III explains why a better understanding of these historical developments should complicate contemporary debates over same-sex marriage. With the rise of transformational marriage, there are now identifiable religious and spiritual costs to opposing access to transformational marriage to any capable persons, including people who can only fall into the most comprehensive, romantic forms of love with people of the same sex. Section IV, finally, discusses whether these religious and spiritual costs should be borne because there are countervailing religious reasons to condemn all same-sex marriages, including of the transformational variety. Traditional definitions of marriage provide little guidance on this question because transformational marriage is itself a recently emergent historical phenomenon. There are, however, a number of well-known scriptural passages within the Judeo-Christian tradition that many currently cite as grounds to oppose same-sex marriage. Section IV discusses these passages and explains why they do not plausibly condemn same-sex marriage of a transformational variety.

In short, the relationship between *Obergefell* and the place of religion, spirituality and religious liberty in family life is nowhere near as simple as many currently presume in Judeo-Christian society. Nor is the relationship set in stone. One reason to stress these points early and widely is to divert

Obergefell from *Roe*'s divisive trajectory. Debates over same-sex marriage need not and should not become a permanent fixture in the culture wars between religious and secular values.

I *OBERGEFELL* AS SECULAR TRIUMPH?

The common wisdom around *Obergefell* is that it reflects just the latest in a recent series of secular triumphs over religious values in family life. When a case appears to fit a well-known historical pattern that involves major public controversy, it can be easy to overlook its special and distinguishing features. Before questioning the standard view of *Obergefell*, it will help to explain why so many people find it compelling. Fleshing out the standard view will clarify its harmful consequences for people on all sides of the current debate – regardless of whether *Obergefell* remains good law. These facts should motivate the usefulness of a critical reappraisal of the standard view.

One initial reason for the standard view, noted earlier, is that the past half century witnessed a sea change in the domestic relations laws governing family life, reproduction, parenting, and sexual and intimate expression. These changes often appear to reflect a triumph of secular over religious values, and many of the people and organizations that were on opposite sides of these earlier debates found themselves on opposite sides of the same-sex marriage debate.[7] Circumstances of passionate contestation are not, however, the best for producing judicious and well-tempered understandings of major historical, legal, cultural or religious and spiritual developments.

A second reason for the standard view is that many currently perceive the conflict between same-sex marriage and Judeo-Christian religious views to be particularly egregious – even when compared to other supposed triumphs of secularism in the contemporary culture wars. This perception arises from the fact that homosexual conduct was considered inherently sinful for much of Judeo-Christian history,[8] whereas marriage, a sacrament. In both the Old and

[7] For example, the American Civil Liberties Union and Lambda Legal have been active on the so-called "secular" side of many of these legal developments, actively opposed by the Family Research Council, which is often perceived as seeking to protect "religious" values. *See, e.g.*, *ACLU Demands PA School District Stop Use of Internet Filters*, American Civil Liberties Union (Feb. 27, 2013), www.aclu.org/news/aclu-demands-pa-school-district-stop-use-discrimi natory-internet-filters.

[8] *See* Robert A. J. Gagnon, The Bible and Homosexual Practice: Text and Hermeneutics (2001) (suggesting that this view is supported by both Scripture and two millennia of church tradition); *see also* Witte, Chapter 17, this volume, for a detailed historical account charting the evolution of early Christian teachings on homosexual unions and relations and how these teachings slowly influenced Roman law relating to homosexuality.

New Testaments, marriage is used as the central metaphor for the ideal covenantal relationships between both God and his creations and Jesus and the Church.[9] Hence, for many religious conservatives – who may be willing to tolerate the legal permission of sexual conduct they presume sinful but not physically harmful to others – the legalization of same-sex *marriage* is a bridge too far to cross. Taking this further step seems to them to devalue the religious and sacramental nature of marriage.

Third, while homosexual relationships and conduct have been documented across the globe and in every era, many consider the legalization of same-sex marriage to reflect a novel development, which runs contrary to millennia of global tradition. Chief Justice John Roberts expressed this view by charging the majority in *Obergefell* with "ordering the transformation of a social institution that has formed the basis of human society for millennia, for the Kalahari Bushmen and the Han Chinese, the Carthaginians and the Aztecs."[10]

The world historical record is more complex than this. Historians and anthropologists of marriage have been unable to develop a single definition of marriage, which identifies a social institution with common features vital in every human society.[11] If one views marriage to include any long-term intimate relationship with sexual and emotional components receiving legal or other significant social recognition, then same-sex marriages do appear in the historical and ethnographic record.[12] The evidence of same-sex marriage in Judeo-Christian history is more controversial.[13] Some of the controversy derives from semantics. Debates over how to construe the evidence are complicated by the fact that – as Professor Douglas Laycock observes – marriage in Judeo-Christian history has traditionally combined "a personal relationship, a legal relationship, *and a religious* relationship."[14] For religious

9 *See* Witte, Chapter 17, this volume; EUGENE BOROWITZ, EXPLORING JEWISH ETHICS: PAPERS ON COVENANT RESPONSIBILITY 256 (1990).

10 Obergefell, *supra* note 1, at 2612 (Roberts, C.J., dissenting).

11 *See* STEPHANIE COONTZ, MARRIAGE, A HISTORY: HOW LOVE CONQUERED MARRIAGE 24–33 (2006). This is not to say that there are not institutions with overlapping features that have proven vital in every human society and might all be considered cases of "marriage," without a common core.

12 *See id.* at 2 ("[S]ame-sex marriage, though rare, has been sanctioned in some cultures under certain conditions.").

13 *See* Witte, Chapter 17, this volume. John Boswell has offered compelling historical evidence of same-sex unions within the Judeo-Christian tradition during medieval Europe. *See* JOHN BOSWELL, SAME-SEX UNIONS IN PREMODERN EUROPE (1994). Whether these unions were *marriages* is still debated. *See, e.g.*, Lutz Kaelber, *Review: Same-Sex Unions in Premodern Europe, by John Boswell*, 24 CONTEMP. SOC. 367, 367–68 (1995).

14 Douglas Laycock, *Religious Liberty and the Culture Wars*, 2014 U. ILL. L. REV. 839, 848 (2014) (emphasis added).

conservatives who see same-sex marriage as an attack on Judeo-Christian values, the fact that some non–Judeo-Christian societies have given legal or other significant social support to some same-sex intimate relationships is therefore beside the point. To them, the real point is that Judeo-Christian religious values, which they interpret to limit marriages to comprehensive unions between men and women, are (or at least should be) considered intrinsic aspects of marriage, as they have for millennia in the West until recently.

Still, complexities such as these explain why many people currently assume that contemporary debates over same-sex marriage necessarily implicate questions about the appropriate role of religion in family life. Given long-standing religious views on the sanctity of marriage and sinfulness of homosexual conduct in the West, many people on both sides of the current debate simply assume that concerns for religious liberty must lie primarily on one side of the debate.[15] Laycock therefore suggests that many who endorse same-sex marriage tend to fall on the "secular side" of the debate and see "the legal relationship, or the committed personal relationship between the spouses, as primary," whereas many committed religious observers tend to "see the religious relationship as primary."[16] Laycock sees the former (which he often refers to as the "secular side") as objecting to the role of religion in policing the boundaries of a legal institution such as marriage. He sees the latter (which often refers to as the "traditional religious" side) as objecting to the state's authority to "interfere[] with the sacred" by recasting an institution as secular, which they see as fundamentally religious in nature.[17]

This way of framing debates over same-sex marriage preceded *Obergefell*, but it would be naïve to think this assumed framing matters less now just because *Obergefell* settled the legal question by finding a constitutional right to same-sex marriage in the U.S. The standard view of this case as a move in a secular-religious culture war is still proving harmful in at least three ways.

First, when *Obergefell* is viewed as a win for secularism, the decision sparks a range of more local and particularized conflicts. These conflicts presume that rights to same-sex marriage and rights to religious liberty are inherently antagonistic. For example, citing religious conscience, some governmental workers, most famously Kentucky clerk Kim Davis, refused to issue civil

[15] Laycock observes that "[b]oth supporters and opponents agree that same-sex marriage poses serious religious liberty issues." *Id.*

[16] *Id.*

[17] *Id.* For emerging efforts post-Obergefell to unwind civil and religious understandings of marriage in the U.S., see Wilson, Chapter 16, this volume.

marriage licenses to all couples or, sometimes, only to same-sex couples.[18] Some businesses refuse to offer their goods or services to same-sex couples as they marry, citing religious objections[19] — an issue that has just now found its way to the Supreme Court and will likely be decided by the time this goes to print.[20] Other emerging conflicts relate to the rental of commercial and even religious premises for same-sex weddings, whether religious universities should acknowledge the existence of same-sex marriages for married student housing or other purposes, and the like.[21] Same-sex couples encountering reactions like these from committed religious observers often perceive them to be hostile, demeaning, and discriminatory. Religious observers often counter that they are merely trying to exercise their sincere religious beliefs. Litigation often ensues.

Conflicts like these have the potential to harm not only the dignitary and material interests of same-sex couples but also legal protections for religious liberty. This is because the First Amendment's Free Exercise Clause offers very little protection to religiously motivated conduct when laws are neutral and generally applicable, as PART I of this volume shows.[22] Neither same-sex marriage recognition nor statutes protecting LGBT people from discrimination target specific religions. Still, under democratically passed Religious Freedom Restoration Acts ("RFRAs"), citizens can claim religious exemptions from generally applicable laws if the laws "substantially burden" their exercise of religion and fail to further a "compelling governmental interest" in the

[18] *See* Adams, Chapter 21, this volume; Robin Fretwell Wilson, *"Getting the Government Out of Marriage" Post* Obergefell: *The Ill-Considered Consequences of Transforming the State's Relationship to Marriage*, 4 U. ILL. L REV. 1445, 1454 (2016).

[19] *See, e.g.*, Erik Eckholm, *Colorado Court Rules Against Baker Who Refused to Serve Same-Sex Couples*, N.Y. TIMES (Aug. 13, 2015), www.nytimes.com/2015/08/14/us/colorado-court-rules-against-baker-who-refused-to-serve-same-sex-couples.html; Mark Joseph Stern, Washington Supreme Court Rules Against Florist Who Refused to Serve Same-Sex Couple, Slate (Feb. 16, 2017), www.slate.com/blogs/outward/2017/02/16/washington_supreme_court_rules_against_anti_gay_florist.html.

[20] See, Masterpiece Cakeshop, Ltd. v. Colorado Civil Rights Commission, Supreme Court Docket No. 16-111, OT 2017 (cert granted to determine whether applying Colorado's public accommodations law to compel Christian baker to create wedding cake for same-sex wedding, which contains expressions inconsistent with sincerely held religious beliefs about marriage, violates religious liberty or free speech clauses of the First Amendment).

[21] *See generally* SAME-SEX MARRIAGE AND RELIGIOUS LIBERTY: EMERGING CONFLICTS (Douglas Laycock, Anthony Picarello Jr., & Robin Fretwell Wilson, eds., 2008); Douglas Nejaime & Reva B. Siegel, *Conscience Wars: Complicity-Based Conscience Claims in Religion and Politics*, 124 YALE L.J. 2516, 2561–63 (2015).

[22] *See* PART I, this volume (discussing Emp't Div., Dep't of Human Res. of Oregon v. Smith, 494 U.S. 872, 890 (1990)).

"least restrictive manner."[23] Questions over the religious liberty implications of the constitutional right to same-sex marriage have thus begun to morph into debates over how narrowly or broadly to construe federal and state RFRAs.[24] Not surprisingly, political groups are now mobilizing to expand or repeal various RFRAs.[25] Because RFRA's are non-constitutional in origin, continued conflicts over same-sex marriage may hasten popular movements to cabin statutory protections for religious liberty in the U.S. That risk to religious liberty is as real as the risk to the dignitary and material interests of LGBT people. Neither risk can be wished way because neither gay and lesbian people nor people with deeply held religious convictions are going anywhere anytime soon.

Second, if reactions to *Roe* are any indication, political efforts to overturn *Obergefell* modeled on the pro-life movement may prove incredibly costly, divisive, and damaging to democratic deliberation – often with little real legal payoff.[26] Mobilization efforts to overturn hot button constitutional cases can increase polarization and cultural division, while creating focal points that undermine people's capacities to reach more nuanced democratic compromises where there is still legal room.[27] Before *Obergefell*, some worried that deciding the legality of same-sex marriage as a matter of constitutional law might create similar patterns of controversy.[28] Yet *Roe*, despite decades of controversy and some limitations on scope, remains essentially good law.[29] There is little reason to think that *Obergefell* will be overturned either.

23 *See, e.g.*, Religious Freedom Restoration Act, 42 U.S.C. § 2000bb-1(1) to (b) (2012). States have enacted parallel RFRAs, sometimes with differences. *See* Adams, Chapter 21, this volume. For an argument that RFRAs give religious proponents of polygamy the possibility to make claims, *see* Strassberg, Chapter 18, this volume.

24 *See, e.g.*, Nejaime & Siegel, *supra* note 22, at 2518–22; Emma Green, *Can States Protect LGBT Rights Without Compromising Religious Freedom?* THE ATLANTIC (Jan. 16, 2016), www.theatlantic.com/politics/archive/2016/01/lgbt-discrimination-protection-states-religion/422730/.

25 *See, e.g.*, Daniel O. Conkle, *Repealing RFRA Would Be a Step Backward for Indiana*, INDYSTAR (Jan. 30, 2016), www.indystar.com/story/opinion/readers/2016/01/30/repealing-rfra-would-step-backward-indiana/79567190/; Michael C. Dorf, *Arizona and Other States Consider Expanding Freedom to Discriminate*, VERDICT (Feb. 25, 2014), https://verdict.justia.com/2014/02/25/arizona-states-consider-expanding-religious-freedom-discriminate.

26 Some argue that too much overt focus on overturning or protecting *Roe* has undermined values of people on both sides. *See, e.g.*, Cass Sunstein, *Three Civil Rights Fallacies*, 79 CAL. L. REV. 751, 766–67 (1991); Mary Ziegler, *Beyond Backlash: Legal History, Polarization, and Roe v. Wade*, 71 WASH. & LEE L. REV. 969, 971 (2014).

27 *See* Adams, Chapter 21, this volume, for a legislator's views.

28 *See* Kreis, Chapter 22, this volume; Emily Bazelon, *Backlash Whiplash: Is Justice Ginsburg Right That Roe v. Wade Should Make the Court Cautious About Gay Marriage?*, SLATE (Mat 14, 2013), www.slate.com/articles/news_and_politics/jurisprudence/2013/05/justice_ginsburg_and_roe_v_wade_caution_for_gay_marriage.html.

29 *See* Whole Woman's Health v. Hellerstedt, 136 S. Ct. 2292, 2309, 2320 (2016).

When it comes to constitutional decisions such as *Roe* and *Obergefell*, hot button questions can also motivate "single-issue voters, [creating a] system [that] incentivizes politicians to refrain from enacting meaningful change to address interest on both sides of these conflicts for fear of losing these vote-drawing issues."[30] In this volume, Adams (Chapter 21, this volume) charts the complex political constraints that state lawmakers now face when trying to enact laws responsive to concerns of both the LGBT and faith communities. These political constraints often arise from viewing *Obergefell* as a simple case of secular triumph in a secular-religious culture war.

Finally, going beyond the law, questions about the appropriate atttitudes for religious observers to take to LGBT persons and same-sex marriage are creating significant social divisions within Christian denominations and between committed religious observers and non-observant people. Robert Gagnon notes that "[n]o other issue has so consumed mainline denominations for the past thirty years or holds greater potential for splitting these denominations."[31] As Wilson shows (Chapter 16, this volume), many with deeply held religious views have responded to *Obergefell* by forgoing state-sanctioned marriage altogether and arguing that others should too – a move that Wilson believes would be self-defeating, harming both their marriages and the marriage culture they prize.[32] Despite *Obergefell*, the continued opposition of some Christian denominations to same-sex marriage and homosexual conduct is similarly causing many gay and lesbian people and their supporters to feel alienated by religion and spirituality.[33] Hostile attitudes toward same-sex marriage are now a cause of rising secularism, not a remedy.

The standard view of *Obergefell* paints the decision as taking sides in a larger conflict between secular and religious values. Under that construal, the decision is bound to fuel conflicts that are divisive and intractable. The next section begins to point a way out of these problems, by reflecting on whether

30 Luke T. Harrington, *Trump and the Consequences of Being a Single Issue Voter*, Christ and Pop Culture (June 29, 2016), https://christandpopculture.com/trump-and-the-consequences-of-being-a-single-issue-voter/.

31 Robert A. J. Gagnon, *The Bible and Homosexual Practice: Key Issues*, in Dan O. Via & Robert A. J. Gagnon, Homosexuality and the Bible: Two Views, at 40; *see also, e.g.*, James V. Brownson, Bible, Gender, Sexuality: Reframingthe Church's Debate on Same-Sex Relationships 3 (2013).

32 Wilson, Chapter 16, this volume.

33 *See generally* Matthew Vines, God and the Gay Christian (2015); Daniel Cox et al., *A Shifting Landscape: A Decade of Change in American Attitudes About Same-Sex Marriage and LGBT Issues*, PRRI (Feb. 26, 2014), www.prri.org/research/2014-lgbt-survey/ (reporting that the roughly 25% of Americans who left their childhood religion did so in response to "negative teachings about or treatment of gay and lesbian people").

the assumed conflict between religious and secular values over same-sex marriage can be overcome with a better understand of the religious and spiritual functions of marriage.

II THE HISTORICAL RISE OF TRANSFORMATIONAL MARRIAGE

Before assuming that there is an ineliminable conflict between same-sex marriage and the religious and spiritual functions of marriage, one should presumably get clear on what those religious and spiritual functions are. Many people in the U.S. who currently oppose same-sex marriage on religious grounds assume that marriage has always had a fixed definition and core set of religious and spiritual functions within Judeo-Christian tradition. The religious and spiritual functions of Judeo-Christian marriage have not, however, always been static. Neither has the social institution of marriage remained fixed even in the West. Pope Francis cautions that "neither today's society nor that to which we are progressing allow an uncritical survival of older forms and models" of marriage.[34]

In the spirit of Pope Francis's comment, this section highlights a dramatic but underappreciated historical transformation in the religious and spiritual functions of marriage within the West. To establish the religious bona fides of these developments, which began in the 17th to 18th centuries, I draw on Pope Francis's 2016 *Amoris Laetitia* ("On Love in the Family") to distil the concept of a *transformational marriage*. Transformational marriage is a social institution that – with the right social, legal, pastoral, or other religious and spiritual support – aims to transform early romantic passion into the more mature capacities of love needed to achieve greater personal communion with the totality of life – or God or the divine – however one defines these concepts. Though the concept of a transformational marriage will be drawn from Pope Francis's writings, its value is not parochial. For reasons to be explained, its value can be accepted by religious observers of many different faiths as well as by people who are not religiously observant.

The historical development of transformational marriage is nevertheless something with genuine religious and spiritual significance. It is not the mere result of a culture war, judicial activism or rising secularism. Later sections will suggest that a better understanding of the historical emergence of transformational marriage will have implications for the appropriate religious

[34] Pope Francis, *Amoris Laetitia: On Love in the Family* § 32 (2016) [hereinafter *Amoris Laetitia*] [all ensuing references are to section numbers].

attitudes to take to same-sex marriage. The purpose of this section is more preliminary. It is to describe the historical emergence of transformational marriage with respect to opposite-sex couples – including its distinctive features, its distinctive value, and its expanded religious and spiritual potentials.

Let us therefore start with Pope Francis's writings. Writing in the 21st century, Pope Francis describes what he considers to be the modern religious and spiritual ideal with respect to how love and marriage should relate. In this ideal, romantic love, personal choice, and marriage are essentially linked. "Romantic love" refers here to a love that combines deep emotional and sexual attachment to another person with spiritual recognition of the other as having intrinsic and unconditional value. To suggest these links, Pope Francis says that "[m]arriage is … a friendship marked by passion."[35] He explains that "[d]esires, feelings, emotions, what the ancients called 'the passions', all have an important place in married life."[36] But he does not view marriage as a mere vehicle for the hedonistic satisfaction of these passions because he also says that "[t]he aesthetic experience of love is expressed in that 'gaze' which contemplates other persons as ends in themselves, even if they are infirm, elderly or physically unattractive."[37]

Pope Francis distinguishes marital love from mere "friendship, filial devotion or devotion to a cause"[38] – all of which involve passions but lack an erotic dimension. Unlike some early Christian theologians, he insists that the erotic dimensions of marriage "must be seen as a gift from God that enriches the relationship of the spouses" – not merely "a permissible evil or a burden to be tolerated for the good of the family."[39] But he resists any reduction of the purpose of erotic passion to that of biological reproduction, noting that "'marriage was not instituted solely for the procreation of children' but also that mutual love 'might be properly expressed, that it should grow and mature.'"[40] If appropriately tamed, erotic passion holds the seeds of spiritual regard for another as having intrinsic and unconditional value.

To contemporary ears, it might seem uncontroversial to link romantic love, personal choice, and marriage. The historical record suggests, however, that this link is very new. For most of recorded human history, both inside and outside the Judeo-Christian world, marriage served primarily as a political or practical arrangement, binding extended families into broader social and

35 *Id.* at § 125. 36 *Id.* at § 143. 37 *Id.* at § 128. 38 *Id.* at § 142. 39 *Id.* at § 152.

40 *Id.* at § 125 (quoting SECOND VATICAN ECUMENICAL COUNCIL, Pastoral Constitution on the Church in the Modern World *Gaudieum et Spes*, 50).

economic coalitions.[41] Spouses often had no choice with respect to whom they married – let alone the ability to choose out of love. Even when personal choice figured in a decision, it often played a secondary role to the choices of elders.[42] For most of Judeo-Christian history, romantic love was rarely a cause of marriage and – apparently – often in scarce supply.[43] In some periods, romantic love existed primarily outside of marriage.[44]

In addition, many traditional societies viewed romantic love to be both irrational and antisocial.[45] Romantic love can produce profound ecstasy but also deep suffering and obsessive, unhealthy attention. Especially early on or when people are young, many find these passions hard to embed in a life of sufficient stability and responsibility. Thus, many traditional societies viewed romantic love as a potential threat to people's abilities to shoulder other important moral, legal, social, religious, and even parental and marital obligations.[46]

Ironically, some key aspects of what many now call "traditional marriage" are therefore actually quite recent – and even revolutionary – when compared with the larger historical record of marital experience. The view that romantic love, personal choice, and marriage should be linked began to emerge in the West only in the 17th to 18th centuries.[47] By the mid-20th century, this wide-spread consensus contained a greater acceptance of both more egalitarian gender norms and the value of sexual fulfillment within marriage.[48] As more women entered into the workplace in the 1960s, and many families began to function better with two "breadwinners" instead of one, older assumptions that men and women occupy fundamentally different spheres began to dissipate, and marriages became even more egalitarian and less role-circumscribed by sex or gender.[49] By the time Pope Francis penned *Amoris Laetitia* in 2016, these historical transformations were far advanced, if not complete. In the U.S. and many parts of the West, most people simply assume now that there should be some link between marriage and romantic love, personal choice, sexual fulfilment and more equality of respect and division of labor between partners.[50]

In *Amoris Laetitia*, Pope Francis applauds all these developments as responding to a standing religious and ethical demand to grow in love and respect for the inherent dignity of all persons.[51] Unlike most "marriage traditionalists," however, Pope Francis does not ignore the much longer history of traditional concerns with romantic love in marriage. He explicitly notes them,

[41] *See* Coontz, *supra* note 11, at 6. [42] *Id.* at 7. [43] *Id.* [44] *Id.* [45] *Id.* at 15–23, 15.
[46] *Id.* at 16. [47] *Id.* at 145–46. [48] *See id.* at 196–246. [49] *See id.* at 247–81.
[50] *See id.* [51] *Amoris Laetitia*, *supra* note 35, at §§ 33 & 54.

concerned that "[m]any tend to remain in the early stages of their affective and sexual life."[52] Rather than condemning romantic love for its destructive potential, Pope Francis sees in it the seeds of spiritual regard for another as having intrinsic and unconditional value. This fact allows the contemporary institution of marriage to serve an expanded and powerful transformational function.

More specifically, Pope Francis suggests, "the grace of the sacrament of marriage is intended before all else 'to *perfect* the couple's love.'"[53] He describes the love that is to be perfected in highly contemporary terms, as "an 'affective union' . . . which combines the warmth of friendship and erotic passion, and endures long after emotions and passions subside."[54] Pope Francis sees a moral and spiritual role for sexual expression in these ideal, love-based relationships when "[s]exuality is not a [mere] means of gratification or entertainment; [but also] an interpersonal language wherein the other is taken seriously, in his or her sacred and inviolable dignity."[55] But untamed erotic passion can remain selfish and narcissistic in aim, and Pope Francis is clear that "[n]arcissism makes people incapable of looking beyond themselves, beyond their own desires and needs."[56] The sacrament of marriage is therefore intended, above all else, to give these passions a "vocation" – to infuse them into something with greater and less selfish purpose.[57] Unions that involve transformed passions such as these offer some of the most comprehensive and valuable affective unions that people can develop in life.

So how might romantic love be channeled to help people develop their love of God or personal communion with the divine, or their sense of unity with the totality of life, however they understand these concepts? And why might romantic love – which is so peculiarly comprehensive for so many people – be so critical for the development of so many? Pope Francis's point is not that transformations out of the self happen automatically whenever two people fall into romantic love. Otherwise the sacrament of relationships, and social and pastoral support for relationships, would not be needed. Nor does Pope Francis mean that marriage automatically turns the heart away from the self and toward the divine simply by being outwardly solemnized. Otherwise Pope Francis would not need to outline the many types of pastoral and social support needed for contemporary love-based relationships to serve a transformative function.

52 *Id.* at § 41.
53 *Id.* at § 89 (emphasis added) (quoting Catechism of the Catholic Church, 1641).
54 *Id.* at § 120 (quoting Thomas Aquinas, SUMMA THEOLOGIAE II–II, q. 27, art. 2).
55 *Id.* at § 151. 56 *Id.* at § 39. 57 *Id.* § 72.

To understand Pope Francis's point, one must instead examine the ideal love that he posits to be the spiritual aim of these love-based relationships. Rooting his discussion in 1 Corinthians 13:4–7,[58] Pope Francis says that ideal love requires patience: "We encounter problems whenever we think that relationships or people ought to be perfect, or when we put ourselves at the centre and expect things to turn out our way."[59] Ideal love is also kind, "ever ready to be of assistance,"[60] and thus helps people "experience the happiness of giving."[61] Ideal love is neither jealous nor envious and "has no room for discomfiture at another person's good fortune." It "values the other person's achievements"[62] and "does not see him or her as a threat."[63] Ideal love is inconsistent with boastfulness: "Those who love not only refrain from speaking too much about themselves, but are focused on others; they do not need to be the centre of attention."[64] Hence, "[i]n family life, the logic of domination and competition about who is the most intelligent or powerful destroys love."[65]

Because ideal "[l]ove abhors making others suffer," its "actions, words and gestures are pleasing and not abrasive or rigid."[66] Ideal "love is not rude or impolite; it is not harsh."[67] To the contrary, "[t]hose who love are capable of speaking words of comfort, strength, consolation and encouragement."[68] Ideal love also motivates people to be generous, and is neither irritable nor resentful.[69] When there is "a hidden irritation that sets us on edge where others are concerned, as if they were troublesome or threatening and thus to be avoided," that psychological tendency, which is often related to narcissism, can undermine love and cause "hurt and alienation."[70] Instead of letting resentment "take root in our hearts," love should practice forgiveness and not blame others for problems."[71] By growing in our capacities for love and self-acceptance, individuals can learn to "live with our limitations, and even to forgive ourselves, in order to have this same attitude towards others."[72]

Of course, given the human condition, love necessarily "coexists with imperfection."[73] Ideal love should therefore "limit[] judgment, checking the impulse to issue a firm and ruthless condemnation ..."[74] Instead of responding to every perceived defect in character or a relationship, partners should find "joy in the happiness of others" and rejoice in their well-being.[75] Hence,

[58] 1 Corinthians 13:4-7 ("Love is patient, love is kind; love does not envy or boast; it is not arrogant or rude. It does not insist on its own way; it is not irritable or resentful; it does not rejoice at wrongdoing, but rejoices with the truth. Love bears all things, believes all things, hopes all things, endures all things.") (English Standard Version).

[59] *Amoris Laetitia*, *supra* note 35, at § 92. [60] *Id.* at § 93. [61] *Id.* at § 94. [62] *Id.* at § 97.

[63] *Id.* [64] *Id.* at § 97. [65] *Id.* at § 98. [66] *Id.* at § 99. [67] *Id.* [68] *Id.* at § 100.

[69] *Id.* at §§ 101–04. [70] *Id.* at § 103. [71] *Id.* at §§ 106–08. [72] *Id.* at § 107.

[73] *Id.* at § 113. [74] *Id.* at § 112. [75] *Id.* at § 110.

"[m]arried couples joined by love speak well of each other; they try to show their spouse's good side, not their weakness and faults."[76]

Romantic love can be challenging because it draws people together with different interests, desires, and views about how the world and its inhabitants ought to be. No two people's individual wills are ever in perfect harmony, which means that partners who seek to perfect their love must learn to set aside their own wills at times. To perfect such a union, the goal cannot be to win a contest of wills at all times because – as Pope Francis emphasizes – love "does not try to control, possess and dominate everything."[77] It can be a confident love: "we do not have to control the other person, to follow their every step lest they escape our grip."[78] Individuals must learn the joys that come with placing their individual wills in the service of a greater community of interests out of deep emotional attachment, so that the couple begins to identify with something that transcends each private self. At bottom, transformational marriage develops the capacity to break free of the self and a life aimed at narrow individual interests.

Submerging one's personal will to a greater community of interests, born from an emotionally laden sense of unity with something greater than oneself, is precisely what is needed to accept the inevitable conflicts between one's individual will and reality – or God's will (to speak in theological terms). Couples who grow toward these ideals can experience attitudes of acceptance in life that sustain them in the face of life's greatest difficulties.[79] This can help people develop greater capacities for patience and abilities to act in ways that place principles over immediate pleasure, even in circumstances of adversity or when self-will is thwarted. Capacities such as these can help people "show[] a certain dogged heroism, a power to resist every negative current, an irrepressible commitment to goodness."[80]

For all of these reasons, the religious and spiritual functions of marriage go well beyond the personal and legal elements of intimate relationships. When a transformational love-based relationship helps a couple perfect their romantic love, it can foster a "mutual concern," which is less focused on the self and "'brings together the human and the divine,' for it is filled with the love of God."[81] Hence, according to Pope Francis, "marital spirituality is a spirituality of the bond, in which divine love dwells."[82] Though it is not the only path, Pope Francis emphasizes that "[a] positive experience of family communion is

76 *Id.* at § 113. 77 *Id.* at § 115. 78 *Id.* 79 *Id.* at §§ 116–17. 80 *Id.* at § 118.

81 *Id.* at § 315 (quoting SECOND VATICAN ECUMENICAL COUNCIL, Pastoral Constitution on the Church in the Modern World *Gaudium et Spes*, 49).

82 *Id.*

a *true* path to daily sanctification and mystical growth, a means for deeper union with God."[83]

Though the concept of a transformational marriage has been distilled from Pope Francis's writings, its value is not parochial. It is not ultimately a Catholic or even just a Christian idea. Nor is its value even necessarily limited to love-based relationships that are outwardly solemnized as "marriages". Instead, one can think of transformational marriage as a social institution that aims to produce a classic "conversion" experience, which shapes a person's total reaction to life. As will now be shown, conversion experiences through transformational love can be described in purely secular and non-denominational terms. The experiences nevertheless have a special type of value, which some might term "religious" or "spiritual," but can be accepted by religious and non-religious people alike.

In his seminal work, *The Varieties of Religious Experience*, William James – one of the greatest psychologists of all time – uses the term "conversion" to describe the psychological experiences of people who claim greater personal communion with the divine.[84] James defines the "divine" as that which "overarches" and "envelops" all that is real and possible: "from [it] there is no escape."[85] Hence, the experience of greater personal communion with the divine cannot be expressed in terms of any particular representative belief[86] – even a belief in God, if construed as a representative belief. Instead, conversion experiences bring new attitudes toward the totality of life and toward everything real or imaginable. James then suggests that personal "[r]eligion, whatever it is, is a man's total reaction upon life."[87] But he does not say conversion experiences must involve attachment to any particular religious institutions or acceptance of any particular religious beliefs. In today's language, it may cause less confusion to call these personal experiences "spiritual" rather than "religious transformations."

James then points to examples of the conversion experience in every part of the world historical record, among people of every imaginable denomination, and, indeed, among people who disclaim belief in God and religion altogether. Despite numerous variations, "[t]he most characteristic of all the elements of the conversion [experience] is the ecstasy of the happiness

83 *Id.* at § 316 (emphasis added).

84 William James, The Varieties of Religious Experience Lects. IX–X (2d ed. 1902).

85 *Id.* at 34.

86 A representative belief is one that aims to represent some particular state of affairs that is real or imagined. Given how James defines the "divine," it cannot be represented in this way and so cannot be the object of a mere representative belief.

87 *Id.* at 35.

produced."[88] Empirically, these experiences follow a typical pattern, which affects people in similar ways:

> Their experience of self somehow was enlarged to embrace the other. They moved away from self-centeredness, toward consciousness of and concern for the world around them. They also reported less need for approval from others and a greater sense of acceptance of themselves and other people. They evidenced little need to persuade others of the truth of what had been revealed to them, for they themselves knew it with surety. In some deep sense, they became more mature, secure, and settled people.[89]

Conversion experiences can have value for people of many denominations – and, indeed, for people who claim to be agnostic or atheistic but seek a greater experience of harmony and identification with the totality of life.

Though the term "conversion" is often associated with "religious conversion," one should not get lost in semantics. In a highly pluralistic society like ours, with so many good but imperfect people with every variety of view, religious terminology often obscures more than it illuminates. Regardless of one's particular "religious" beliefs or lack thereof, everyone should be able to agree that there is a distinction between values that depend on some particular state of affairs (and can thus often be pursued or thwarted) and values that do not. Conversion experiences add a source of value to people's lives come what may – and hence regardless of what particular things, real or imaginable, come to pass. Committed religious observers will tend to think of this as a specifically "religious" source of value, but others will prefer to think of it as "spiritual" or just "unconditional." Regardless, conversion experiences depend on a personal shift in psychological orientation, so that one begins to identify less with the self and more fundamentally with a wider community of interests.

Transformational marriages are not the only route to conversion experiences. Still, romantic love has a peculiar comprehensiveness and emotional power, which can pull people together and motivate them to overcome major differences, bringing them out of the self. Romantic love focuses people on the particularity of another person, which can be especially important for some aspects of people's support and moral and spiritual development. Many people think that morality can be reduced to simple conformity with general rules. Pope Francis says, however, that while

88 *Id.* at 258.

89 William R. Miller, *The Phenomenon of Quantum Change*, 60 J. Clinical Psychol. 453, 459 (2004).

"general rules set forth a good which can never be disregarded or neglected,"[90] it is "not enough simply to apply moral laws to those living in 'irregular' situations, as if they were stones to throw at people's lives."[91] This is because general rules "in their formulation . . . cannot provide absolutely for all particular situations."[92] When people idolize general rules, without asking how well each application respects the inherent dignity of every person in his or her concrete particularity, these attitudes – according to Pope Francis – can "bespeak the closed heart of one used to hiding behind the Church's teachings, 'sitting on the chair of Moses and judging at times with superiority and superficiality difficult cases and wounded families.'"[93]

In addition, people who seek greater personal communion with the divine or to develop and contribute their special gifts to contribute to the good "often respond as best they can . . . amid their limitations, [and] are capable of carrying out their own discernment in complex situations."[94] Pope Francis thus urges that the Church's proper mission is to "form consciences, not to replace them."[95] One can easily see how transformational love-based relationships could play a critical role in promoting this process in relation to the concrete particularities of many people's lives. Transformational love is spiritual sustenance.

Given these facts, personal growth through romantic love with another person may well be one of the most powerful contemporary vehicles for helping many people develop their special gifts, both personal and moral. Pope Francis makes a similar remark about the importance of particularity when discussing the Christian duty to be fruitful in marriage. He says:

> We also do well to remember that procreation and adoption are not the only ways of experiencing the fruitfulness of love. Even large families are called to make their mark on society, finding other expressions of fruitfulness that in some way prolong the love that sustains them. Christian families should never forget that "faith does not remove us from the world, but draws us more deeply into it . . . Each of us, in fact, has a *special* role in preparing for the coming of God's kingdom in our world."[96]

[90] *Amoris Laetitia*, *supra* note 35, at § 304. [91] *Id.* at § 305. [92] *Id.* at § 304.

[93] *Id.* at § 304 (quoting the *Address for the Conclusion of the Fourteenth Ordinary General Assembly of the Synod of Bishops* (Oct. 24, 2015): *L'Osservatore Romano*, October 26–27, 2015, p. 13.

[94] *Id.* at § 37. [95] *Id.* [96] *Id.* at § 181 (quoting *Relatio Finalis* 2015, 65) (emphasis added).

Another reason that transformational love-based relationships are so potentially powerful for people's moral and spiritual development is that they create the needed space for the loving support and development of people's special spiritual gifts and moral capacities.

III IMPLICATIONS OF TRANSFORMATIONAL MARRIAGE FOR SAME-SEX MARRIAGE

The last section discussed the recent historical emergence of transformational marriage for opposite-sex couples but did not yet address the implications of these developments for religious attitudes toward contemporary same-sex marriage and love-based relationships. In *Amoris Laetitia*, Pope Francis does nothing to disturb traditional Catholic teachings about marriage being between a man and a woman.[97] Yet, nowhere in Pope Francis's moving account of transformational love's ability to bring individuals in their particularity closer to God (or to the divine), and to shape people in the image of God's unconditional love, is the transformational capacity of romantic love limited to those who can procreate. This should be clear from Pope Francis's discussions of infertile couples. Pope Francis says, "[e]ven in cases where, despite the intense desire of the spouses, there are no children, marriage still retains its character of being a *whole* manner and communion of life."[98] Given the historical rise of transformational marriage, there are now religious and spiritual costs to preventing people who can only fall into deep romantic love with people of the same sex from developing similar whole manners and communions of life.

Closer attention to the historical rise of transformational marriage should, in fact, complicate contemporary religious and cultural debates over same-sex marriage several ways. It should be clearer that many contemporary debates assume an overly narrow set of options. In *What Is Marriage? Man and*

[97] *Id.* at § 251 (observing that the Synod Fathers have not found religious grounds to place "proposals to place unions between homosexual persons on the same level as marriage") (quoting submissions from the Synod Fathers). It is worth noting, however, that their central concern seemed to be that they would find it unacceptable "that local Churches should be subjected to pressure in this matter and that international bodies should make financial aid to poor countries dependent on the introduction of laws to establish 'marriage' between persons of the same sex." *Id.* (quoting *Relatio Finalis* 2015; cf. Congregation for the Doctrine of the Faith, *Considerations Regarding Proposals to Give Legal Recognition to Unions between Homosexual Persons* (June 3, 2003), 4). That concern will not arise if local Churches or religious observers, in their own consciences and with the aid of thoughts like those developed in this chapter, begin to comprehend marriage more expansively.

[98] *Id.* at § 178 (emphasis added).

Woman: A Defense, Sherif Girgis, Ryan T. Anderson, and Robert P. George present what is widely considered the most cogent, non-theological defense of marriage as limited to man and a woman.[99] Their defense depends on reducing the debate to a competition between two – and only two – views of marriage. The first, which they call "conjugal marriage," they define as "a bodily as well as an emotional and spiritual bond, distinguished thus by its comprehensiveness, which is, like all love, effusive."[100] The second, which they call "revisionist marriage," they define as "in essence, a loving emotional bond, one distinguished by its intensity – a bond that needn't point beyond the partners, in which fidelity is ultimately subject to one's desires."[101]

Girgis et al. then argue that marriage has traditionally been (and ought to remain) more than just an intense emotional bond, subject to one's desires. They argue that the only cogent way to distinguish the comprehensiveness of traditional marriage from such intense emotional bonds is to recognize that heterosexual sex is naturally ordered to reproduction.[102] Heterosexual sex, they contend, thus possesses a natural function that goes beyond the couple's needs and desires, warranting social support for the permanence of heterosexual marriages. In this account, same-sex relationships are, by contrast, rooted in mere sexual or emotional attractions, which are wholly subject to one's desires. This account overlooks the many heterosexual couples who adopt or use assisted conception and fails to distinguish same-sex couples who form families by the same methods.[103] This account also fails to recognize that opposite-sex couples who reproduce biologically need not live a psychological life that is shaped by more than their mere desires.

More fundamentally, the Girgis et al. account obscures the fact that transformational marriage represents a third conception of marriage, which is recently emergent and serves functions that do not fit neatly into either of their assumed categories. Transformational marriage and related love-based relationships aim to transform youthful romantic desire into a more ideal form of love that points increasingly beyond itself. Because it aims to perfect a couple's love and bring each partner increasingly out of the self, it is not merely subject to their desires. But the aim of the transformation is in no way reducible to mere biological reproduction either (or even to marriage reconceived as the vehicle for childrearing). Rather, transformational marriage's

99 GIRGIS ET AL., WHAT IS MARRIAGE?: MAN AND WOMAN: A DEFENSE 1 (2012).

100 *Id.* (italics omitted). 101 *Id.* at 1–2. 102 *Id.* at 26.

103 Obergefell, *supra* note 1, at 2600. In 2011, the U.S. Census Bureau found that ("[o]ut of the 594,000 same-sex couple households, 115,000 reported having children"). U.S. Census Bureau, *Same Sex Couple Households*, Report No. ACSBR/10-03 (Sep. 2011), www.census.gov/library/publications/2011/acs/acsbr10-03.html.

great potential, in the words of Pope Francis, is to help resist the "cultural decline that fails to promote love or self-giving."[104] That decline permits people to "treat affective relationships the way we treat material objects and the environment: everything is disposable; everyone uses and throws away, takes and breaks, exploits and squeezes to the last drop. Then, goodbye."[105] Some resistance to same-sex marriage causes that very denigration of love and its transformative potential.

While many factors explain this cultural decline, Pope Francis confesses that the Church is partly responsible. He says that "[w]e [*i.e.*, Christians and the Church] need a healthy dose of self-criticism," and "need to be humble and realistic, acknowledging that at times the way we present our Christian beliefs and treat other people has helped contribute to today's problematic situation."[106] He thereby models the type of humble self-reflection and confession of past wrongs that lies at the core of true Christian routes to spiritual growth and development.

With respect to marriage, he says that the Church has "often present[ed] marriage in such a way that its unitive meaning, its call to grow in love and its ideal of mutual assistance are overshadowed by an almost exclusive insistence on the duty of procreation." In addition, the Church has

> [a]t times . . . proposed a far too abstract and almost artificial theological ideal of marriage, far removed from the concrete situations and practical possibilities of real families. This excessive idealization, especially when we have failed to inspire trust in God's grace, has not helped to make marriage more desirable or attractive, but quite the opposite.[107]

This excessive idealization has, in other words, alienated many people – especially when it is combined with insufficient empathy for the real facts, experiences and dilemmas that people face in love and family life. It has thus compromised the Church's ability to maintain the ideals of love and marriage in the face of "the growing danger represented by an extreme individualism . . ., leading in some cases to the idea that one's personality is shaped by his or her desires, which are considered absolute."[108] Given the rise of transformational marriage and other supported love-based relationships for many, there is now a danger that religious opposition to same-sex marriage of a transformational variety may promote just these same problems for same-sex couples who seek to grow in their deepest capacities for love. It does not help to claim that their capacities for love are the mere product of intense

[104] *Amoris Laetitia*, *supra* note 35, at § 39. [105] *Id.* [106] *Id.* at § 36. [107] *Id.*

[108] *Id.* at § 33 (quoting *Relatio Synodi* 2014, 5).

emotional feelings or hedonism, incapable of further growth or depth, and wholly subject to their desires.

In addition, nothing about how the social institution of transformational marriage has been described so far limits the expanded religious and spiritual potential of transformational marriage to people who can fall into deep romantic love with someone of the opposite sex. Gay and lesbian couples, like straight couples, can draw strength from transformational marriages and love-based relationships, and the nurturing of selfless love. Like Pope Francis's homily to marriage, studies of married couples show that marriage can foster a happiness that is separate and apart from a person's baseline outlook on life[109] – thus adding value to their lives that is not dependent on any real or imaginable states of affairs. Also, "[t]he role of friendship within marriage" matters greatly to marriage's benefits: "Those who consider their spouse or partner to be their best friend get about twice as much life satisfaction from marriage as others."[110] But the deeper moral and spiritual point is that this satisfaction comes in part from widening one's sense of identification beyond the limits of the self, with someone with whom one has fallen into romantic love, especially when supported by a larger community.

Once again, the question thus arises whether religious opposition to contemporary same-sex marriage (and LGBT love-based relationships more generally) contributes to the very culture of "extreme individualism," "loneliness," and materialism that Pope Francis seeks to combat.[111] Transformational marriage offers a powerful salve for "one symptom of the great poverty of contemporary culture," which is "loneliness, arising from the absence of God [or a personal connection with some conception of what James calls the 'divine'] in a person's life and the fragility of relationships."[112]

The transformational dimensions of contemporary love-based relationships are fragile and not always easily accessible or sustainable. Contemporary marriage is, in fact, fragile in part *because* of some of the very same features that give it its transformative potential: that is, because it is now widely assumed that marriage should be freely chosen, entered into out of romantic love, and offer one of the primary relationships in which people can develop personally and morally and find greater emotional, spiritual, and intimate

109 *See* Claire Cain Miller, *Study Finds More Reasons to Get and Stay Married*, N.Y. Times (Jan. 8, 2015), www.nytimes.com/2015/01/08/upshot/study-finds-more-reasons-to-get-and-stay-married.html?_r=0.

110 *Id.* (also finding the effect "as strong for people who lived together but weren't married").

111 *Amoris Laetitia, supra* note 35, at § 43 (quoting *Relatio Synodi* 2014, 6) at § 43 (quoting *Relatio Synodi* 2014, 6).

112 *Id.*

fulfilment.[113] For love-based relationships to serve transformative functions, they therefore need more social, legal, religious, and other forms of informal and communal support than in most other historical periods.[114] It does not help this cause to insist that the recent legalization of same-sex marriage is a purely secular development, with no religious or spiritual potential.

Given the recent historical rise of transformational marriage, there are now identifiable – if still widely underappreciated – religious and spiritual costs to opposing same-sex marriages of the transformational variety.

IV POSSIBLE SCRIPTURAL OBJECTIONS

It is unclear why Pope Francis has not yet traced out the implications described in the last section of the historical rise of transformational marriage for the Church's official stance toward contemporary same-sex marriage. One reason may be that the specifically religious or spiritual dimensions of the historical shifts that produced transformational marriage have not yet been widely recognized. Though there is now widespread consensus that love-based marriage is a recent historical development in the West,[115] the religious and spiritual – as opposed to merely secular – causes and significance of these historical developments are rarely noted in debates over same-sex marriage or marriage equality.

That these developments are often assumed to be unrelated, thus obscuring the religious and spiritual potential of these developments for all people, can be seen in the reactions of some Supreme Court Justices to same-sex marriage. In his dissent to *United States v. Windsor*, for example, Justice Alito acknowledges the historical consensus that love-based marriages are a recent phenomenon in the West. He cites that historical consensus to point out that "the gradual ascendance of the idea that romantic love is a prerequisite to marriage ... [has] had far reaching consequences," which would have been impossible

[113] *See* COONTZ, *supra* note 11, at 307 (observing that the modern revolution, which led to love becoming "the main reason for marriage" has had – by virtue of that fact – "negative as well as positive implications for the stability of marriage as an institution").

[114] Cf., e.g., *Amoris Laetitia*, *supra* note 35, at §§ 32 (noting the need for support from social structures), 37 (noting the need for changing religious understandings to offer more helpful support), 207 (noting the role of Christian and presumably other religious and secular communities to support engaged couples as they grow in love), 229 (noting the use of parishes, movements, schools, and other Church institutions to supporting families) (noting the importance of groups of families that support other families), 236 (noting the importance of support from relatives, friends, and sometimes even outside help and professional assistance).

[115] COONTZ, *supra* note 11, at 145–246.

to foresee as the cultural changes were emerging.[116] Both there and in his dissent to *Obergefell*, however, Justice Alito then argues against the legalization of same-sex marriage in part because he views it as a new and *unrelated* cultural intervention, which might have similarly unpredictable results.[117] In interpreting the historical record in this way, Justice Alito misses the fact that the legalization of same-sex marriage is itself one of the results of the larger historical developments that he cites toward a love-based social institution of marriage and other intimate relationships.

When it comes to seeing the potential religious and spiritual significance of rights for LGBT people and couples, Justice Scalia's attitudes suggest a similarly limited imagination. In response to *Romer v. Evans*, which held that the Constitution forbids the singling out of homosexual intimate conduct for disfavorable treatment, Justice Scalia famously suggested that "[t]he Court has mistaken a Kulturkampf [a religious-cultural war] for a fit of spite." In assuming that these debates can be reduced to a conflict between religious and secular values, however, Justice Scalia himself mistook developments with religious and spiritual significance for a *mere* Kulturkampf.

Mistakes like these can be cured by a fuller appreciation of the historical emergence and nature of transformational marriage, and its implications for contemporary same-sex marriage. There is, however, another possible basis for objecting to same-sex marriage, which many sincere religious observers cite. For many Christian observers, even if there are now weighty religious and spiritual costs associated with opposing same-sex marriage, as prior sections suggest, these costs cannot be considered from a religious standpoint if Scripture rules out all same-sex sexual conduct in a clear and weighty enough manner. This would be the case if Scripture were to deem homosexual conduct intrinsically sinful, regardless of motive, romantic attachment, the forms of marriage that are culturally available, and the place of the conduct in a person's personal and spiritual development. The idea that homosexual conduct is intrinsically sinful has a long history within Judeo-Christian tradition. This premise may therefore help explain why Pope Francis and other committed religious observers – like Justices Alito and Scalia – have not yet recognized the religious and spiritual considerations that now favor more religious support of same-sex marriages of a transformational variety marriage.

This section thus turns to questions of Scripture and its proper interpretation. There is already a large secondary literature that examines the scriptural verses that might lead one to conclude that homosexual conduct is

116 133 S. Ct. 2675, 2715 (2013) (Alito, J., dissenting).

117 *Id.*; *see also* Obergefell, *supra* note 1, at 2641–2643 (Alito, J., dissenting).

intrinsically and universally sinful. This literature suggests that the relevant passages are reasonably susceptible to more than one interpretation.[118] It would be hard to improve on these interpretive debates when the verses are considered in isolation. Still, the secondary literature has not yet considered how the historical emergence of transformative marriage might affect the underlying interpretive questions. The purpose of this section is to cure that defect. Upon close examination, there is very little plausible scriptural support for condemning same-sex marriage or love-based relationships of a transformational variety.

The two most cited scriptural grounds for the view that homosexual conduct is universally and intrinsically sinful come from the Book of Leviticus in the Old Testament. One says: "You shall not lie with a male as one lies with a female; it is an abomination."[119] The other: "If there is a man who lies with a male as those who lie with a woman, both of them have committed a detestable act."[120] These passages undoubtedly ruled out homosexual conduct for the early tribes of Israel – with whatever force should have attached to general rules of this kind. The passages address conduct, however, not same-sex desire or romantic attachment. They did so in a context where marriage was still largely a practical arrangement, and there was no widespread acceptance of a critical link between romantic love, personal choice, intimate satisfaction, and marriage. Populations were small enough at the time that there was neither a term for homosexuality (as a sexual *orientation*) nor any widespread understanding that some small percentage of people can only fall into romantic love with people of the same sex.[121]

In addition, for every Levitical rule, there is always a further interpretive question about its scope and contemporary application. No Christian society has considered all Levitical rules – which include many complex and arcane dietary restrictions and rituals – to be universally applicable. This is not because Christian societies lack respect for the word of God or think people can just pick and choose which Levitical rules to obey. It is because – according to the literal words of the Old Testament –

118 For useful synopsis, *see* VIA & GAGNON, *supra* note 31, *Compare also* GAGNON, *supra* note 8, *with* BROWNSTONE, *supra* note 31 and VINES, *supra* note 33.

119 Lev. 18:22, New American Standard Bible.

120 Lev. 20:13, New American Standard Bible.

121 *See, e.g.*, VIA & GAGNON, *supra* note 118, at 15 (noting that "the generally held belief of the ancient world" was "that there was only one sexual nature, what we would call a heterosexual nature"); *but see also id.* (acknowledging that "in certain – perhaps small – circles in the ancient Mediterranean world there was some awareness of a homosexual disposition or orientation").

Levitical rules are part of a particular covenant God made with the People of Israel and their physical descendants.[122] Hence, the Old Testament *itself* suggests that there is always a further interpretive question whether specific Levitical rules apply to people who are not descended from the People of Israel and so are not literal parties to this local covenant. Most Christians fall into this category.

Underlining the significance of this distinction, the Old Testament contains noteworthy depictions of people not belonging to the Mosaic covenant who worship God in exemplary ways while breaching Mosaic requirements. Consider Abraham – who lived long before the Levitical Code was given to Moses. Abraham is one of the primary founders of the Judeo-Christian tradition of monotheism and considered an exemplary follower of God within not only Christianity but also Judaism and Islam. Abraham was, however, willing to sacrifice his child to God, even though Mosaic law explicitly prohibits child sacrifice.[123] Or consider Jacob – whose name was changed to Israel but lived before the Mosaic covenant was established.[124] When Jacob had his first conversion experience, he worshipped God using a *massabeh* stone, which Mosaic law prohibits as a form of idolatry.[125] Jacob's actions are nevertheless represented as expressing true devotion to God, not a breach of his commands, and Jacob is considered an exemplary follower of God within not only Christianity but also Judaism and Islam.

This differential treatment of persons outside the Mosaic covenant extended even to sexual conduct that might otherwise be considered illicit. Mosaic law clearly states that "[n]o one is to approach any close relative to have sexual relations."[126] Yet Lot's two daughters, who were saved from God's destruction of Sodom and Gomorrah, have sexual intercourse with their father just after the cities' destruction.[127] Had Lot and his daughters been descended from the tribes of Israel, this would have breached Mosaic law. But Lot's daughters were not. Instead of condemning these sexual activities as contrary

[122] *See, e.g.*, Exodus 10:5–6.

[123] Genesis 22:1–19; Leviticus 18:21. Abraham was the father of Isaac, who was the father of Jacob. Matthew 1:2. Jacob's lineage established the twelve tribes of Israel, Exodus 1:1–5, with Moses's birth occurring in Exodus 2 and the Ten Commandments delivered in Exodus 20, beginning Mosaic law. Abraham was following God's instructions in this case, but this shows that God's instructions can differ within and outside a covenant.

[124] *See* Genesis 32:28 ("Then [God] said, 'Your name shall no more be called Jacob, but Israel, for you have striven with God and with men, and have prevailed.'").

[125] *See* James Kugel, How to Read the Bible: A Guide to Scripture, Then and Now 152–63 (2007).

[126] Leviticus 18:6, New International Version.

[127] Genesis 19:30–38.

to God's commands, the Old Testament depicts the resulting children as establishing two tribes worthy of continued existence.[128]

Facts like these highlight that one original purpose of Mosaic law was to create a clear set of behavioral rules to distinguish outward forms of worship that were monotheistic in aim from the polytheistic forms of worship that dominated in all neighboring ancient societies at the time. The sections of Leviticus that deal with illicit sexual conduct make this distinguishing function clear in the introduction by saying: "You must not do as they do in Egypt, where you used to live, and you must not do as they do in the land of Canaan, where I am bringing you. Do not follow their practices."[129] This distinguishing function was presumably especially important when monotheism was first coming into the human experience of religion and when people needed some way to show they were seeking to worship something that could not be represented as any mere idol.

It is therefore noteworthy that Mosaic law offers the most general and extreme condemnation of homosexual conduct found in any known ancient Near Eastern legal or social code.[130] Homosexual conduct existed throughout the ancient Near East, often as parts of pagan cult rituals[131] but was nowhere condemned as harshly or generally as in Mosaic law.[132] These facts suggest that the Levitical rules against homosexual conduct served at least in part a distinguishing function, by prohibiting members of the Tribes of Israel from engaging in certain polytheistic and highly sexualized forms of worship that were once common in neighboring regions.[133] Given the limited application of Mosaic law to people within the Mosaic covenant, there is nothing in the bare text of Leviticus that could establish that homosexual conduct is intrinsically and universally sinful apart from that covenant and its local purposes.

The Old Testament contains only one other passage that might plausibly suggest that homosexual conduct is sinful apart from the Mosaic covenant. This is the story of Sodom and Gomorrah.[134] According to this story, long before the Mosaic covenant, God heard that the people of Sodom and

[128] *Id.* at 37–38. [129] Leviticus 18:2–3; *see* Kugel, *supra* note 126, at 261.

[130] *See, e.g.*, GAGNON, *supra* note 8, at 56; David F. Greenberg & Marcia H. Bystryn, *Christian Intolerance of Homosexuality*, 88 AM. J. SOC. 515, 520 (1982).

[131] *See generally* Tom Horner, JONATHAN LOVED DAVID: HOMOSEXUALITY IN BIBLICAL TIMES (1978); *see also* Gagnon, *supra* note 9, at 100.

[132] *See, e.g.*, GAGNON, *supra* note 8, at 56; Greenberg & Bystryn, *supra* note 131, at 520.

[133] *See* BROWNSON, *supra* note 31, at 42.

[134] A passage in Judges repeats many similar features of the story of Sodom and Gomorrah, including a threat of homosexual rape. *See* Judges 19:22–25. This story arose, however, after the emergence of Mosaic law. The person threatened is a Levite, *see id.* at 19:1, the people doing the threatening are Benjaminites, *see id.* at 16. Because all of these people were members of the tribes of Israel, all were subject to the literal requirements of Mosaic law.

Gomorrah were "wicked" and sent two angels to see if this was true.[135] Lot, an immigrant to the cities, housed the angels on the outskirts of the towns and treated them with great hospitality and reverence. The male citizens of the towns nevertheless came forth and sought to rape the angels.[136] That unsuccessful attempt gave God sufficient evidence that these people were indeed "wicked," and the Bible says that God destroyed both cities and their inhabitants as a result.[137]

Most contemporary interpreters of this story ask whether the sin committed by the people of Sodom and Gomorrah consisted of (1) a breach of ancient conventions of hospitality, (2) an attempted homosexual gang rape, or (3) attempted homosexual conduct without more.[138] Mosaic law's prohibiting homosexual conduct has led some to favor the third interpretation.[139] Yet, Mosaic law did not apply to the people of Sodom and Gomorrah because they were not descended from the people of Israel – thus making this line of reasoning circular if meant to establish the universal and intrinsic sinfulness of homosexual conduct. That the Old Testament represents Lot and his daughters as explicitly breaching some of the Mosaic rules relating to sexual conduct, just after being saved from the destruction of Sodom and Gomorrah, tells the reader that that the Mosaic rules relating to sexual conduct do not necessarily apply to people who are outside the scope of this local covenant.

But then what was the "wickedness" described in the story of Sodom and Gommorah? Though rarely noticed, when contemporary debates focus on only the three interpretive options under discussion, they fail to identify *any* command from God that applied to the people of Sodom and Gomorrah that they breached. This interpretive problem could be addressed, on the other hand, by recognizing that according to the Bible, God's covenant with Noah – who is represented as the precursor of all living humans – was fully applicable to all people, including the inhabitants of Sodom and Gomorrah. God's standing command to all people, which already appears in his covenant with Noah and his descendants, is to worship him and only him as God – an injunction that remains central throughout all of the Abrahamic religions.

[135] Genesis 19:1. [136] Genesis 19:5. [137] Genesis 1:13–25.

[138] *See, e.g.*, JOSH BOSWELL, CHRISTIANITY, SOCIAL TOLERANCE, AND HOMOSEXUALITY 93 (1980).

[139] *See, e.g.*, GAGNON, *supra* note 8.

This leads to a better and more clearly biblically based interpretation of the sin in the story of Sodom and Gomorrah. In many parts of the Old Testament, God speaks to people through angels who are his messengers. Though rarely noticed, these angels take the form of ordinary humans who speak in ordinary human language, not the otherworldly, winged creatures of Hollywood.[140] The noted biblical scholar James Kugel observes that consistently, the Old Testament thus describes people who encounter angels as initially in a "state of confusion," which causes them to see the angels as ordinary people.[141] This confusion typically "goes on for a while, and then somehow, it suddenly dawns on the humans that they are actually talking to an angel, at which time they fall to the ground in reverence."[142] This is an act of reverence of God: they worship God by taking the words of God's messengers' to reveal his purposes. Lot engaged in just such acts of reverence upon seeing the angels. The men of Sodom and Gomorrah, by contrast, sought to rape the angels and thus failed to recognize God's messengers as messengers or worthy of any special reverence. In doing so, they disregarded a clear command from God to all people: to worship God.

This construal of the sin in the story of Sodom and Gomorrah is better rooted in the biblical text as a whole. On this construal, however, there is nothing to suggest that homosexual conduct is universally and intrinsically sinful apart from the Mosaic covenant and its local purposes. Hence, contrary to currently popular belief among many committed religious observers nothing in the Old Testament establishes that homosexual conduct is universally or intrinsically sinful.

For Christians, what to make of Mosaic prohibitions of homosexual conduct is further problematized by Jesus's complex relationship to Mosaic law. When discussing the Torah, which means Law, and the Jewish prophetic scriptures, Jesus says: "Do not think I have come to abolish the Law or the Prophets; I have come not come to abolish them but to fulfill them."[143] Yet in numerous instances in the Gospels, Jesus breaks the letter of Mosaic law. For example, Mosaic law says that lepers are ritually impure[144] and requires specific rituals before they can return into the Jewish community.[145] Jesus, however, sees a leper and renders him spiritually pure without those ritual processes.[146] Mosaic law also restricted certain foods, which – if ingested – would defile a person.[147] But Jesus says, "it is not what goes into the mouth that

[140] Kugel, *supra* note 126, at 110. [141] *Id.* [142] *Id.* [143] Matthew 5:17.

[144] Jonathan Klawans, *Concepts of Purity in the Bible*, *in* THE JEWISH STUDY BIBLE 1998, 1999 (2d ed. 2014).

[145] Leviticus 14:1–56. [146] Matthew 8:1–4. [147] *See, e.g.*, Leviticus 11:1–12.

defiles a person, but what comes out of the mouth."[148] He explains, "what comes out of the mouth proceeds from the heart, and this is what defiles a person" because "out of the heart come evil thoughts."[149] A third example: Mosaic law requires that Jews treat the Sabbath as a day of rest, but Jesus says his disciples are guiltless when they pluck heads of grain and eat on the Sabbath "[f]or the Son of Man is Lord of the Sabbath."[150] Jesus explains that "the Sabbath was made for man, not man for the Sabbath."[151] There are many other examples – so many, in fact, that this is one of the central and most persistent themes of the Gospels.

By consistently breaking the letter of Mosaic law while insisting he was fulfilling God's law in spirit, Jesus sought to emphasize a distinction between the letter and spirit of the law.[152] In Paul's words: "[O]ur sufficiency is from God, who made us sufficient to be ministers of a new covenant [through Christ], not of the letter but of the Spirit. For the letter kills, but the Spirit gives life."[153] By separating the spirit of God's law from its literal scope and content, Jesus offered a new and more inclusive covenant that allowed all people – Jews and Gentiles alike – access to the kingdom of God.[154]

Here, the most important point to notice is that Jesus describes the essence, or spirit, of God's new covenant in terms of love. When asked what God's greatest commandment is, Jesus says that there are two on which "all the Law and the Prophets hang."[155] The first is "love the Lord your God with all your heart and all your soul and with all your mind."[156] Because every person is an equal creation of God, the second just follows from the first: "Love your neighbor as yourself."[157] True, different groups can develop more particular traditions, conventions, interpretations, or rituals to express their love of God and one another – some more detailed than others. But it is these two commandments that truly bind all people as spiritual children of God, and hence the fundamental *spiritual* test for all rules and their applications must be in terms of how well they promote the development of ideal love and greater personal communion with God, the divine, or

148 Matthew 15:11, English Standard Version. 149 Matthew 15:18–19.

150 Compare Leviticus 23:3 with Matthew 12:8 and Luke 6:5. 151 Mark 2:27.

152 *See, e.g.*, 2 Corinthians 3:1–18.

153 *See* Matthew 19: 16–30 (discussing the rich young man who followed the Ten Commandments but when asking Jesus how to enter the Kingdom of Heaven, Jesus replied, "sell what you possess and give to the poor, and you will have treasure in heaven; and come, follow me," to which the young man went away sad for he had great possessions).

154 Acts 13:26, New International Version ("Fellow children of Abraham and you God-fearing Gentiles, it is to us that this message of salvation has been sent.").

155 Matthew 22:40, New International Version.

156 Matthew 22:37, New International Version. 157 Matthew 22:38.

the totality of life – including all of God's creations, considered as deserving of equal respect and dignity. To place the letter over the spirit of any contingent law, however generally stated and perceived by the limited human mind, is thus to kill the spirit of God's law. That was Jesus's essential message, and the same risk occurs whenever people idolize particular historical interpretations of God's word in ways that prevent the deepening of its revealed meaning in context.

If, however, the essence and spirit of God's law is love, then it breaches the spirit – if not the letter – of God's law to oppose access to transformational marriage to any person.[158] The function of transformational marriage is to help people who fall into romantic love learn to outgrow the self and perfect their capacities for love. At its best, transformational love offers a powerful route to outgrowing a narrow identification with the self and one's narrow desires.

This does not mean, of course, that every form of same-sex sexual conduct (or opposite-sex sexual conduct) will be transformational. Obviously, that is not the case. Still, Jesus, however, never condemned same-sex desire or homosexual conduct himself. This is a striking omission if romantic love among people of the same sex were intrinsically and universally sinful in his view, even if embedded in relationships and social institutions that seek to help people perfect their love. There are, in fact, only three passages in the New Testament that condemn homosexual conduct of any form. All of the condemnations appear in the writings of only one of Jesus's apostles Paul (who was not one of his personally chosen twelve), and only in the context of letters to three specific communities that were dealing with culturally local problems. This is an equally striking fact when it is remembered that Jesus sent his twelve personally chosen apostles to all ends of the earth to spread his message. In any event, as will now be shown, none of the relevant passages from Paul to these three local audiences condemns same-sex conduct or love-based relationships with transformative potential.

The first passage arises in Paul's letter to the Romans, where he describes people not naturally inclined to engage in homosexual conduct, who *because of a prior attachment to idolatry* "gave up natural relations with women and were consumed with passion for one another, men committing shameless acts with men and receiving in their own persons the due penalty of their error."[159] Paul says these people "exchanged the truth about God for a lie and worshiped and served the creature rather than the Creator," as a

158 *See* Witte, Chapter 17, this volume; Strassberg, Chapter 18, this volume, for arguments against polygamous marriages.

159 Romans 1:26–27.

result of which "God gave them up to dishonorable passions."[160] But these passions appear to have involved a mixture of idolatry, sexual profligacy outside of marriage, and sexual activities that lack transformative aim. The condemned behaviour is also represented as *caused* by idolatry, and aimed at worshipping the created over the creator, not as part of a course of development out of the self to achieve a closer sense of communion with the totality of life. Even while describing these idolatrous forms of same-sex sexual conduct, Paul cautions his audience not to "judge another [for these acts]; for in passing judgment upon him you condemn yourself, because you, the judge, are doing the very same things [presumably, engaging in equally weighty sins, but of condemnation]."[161] That Paul described a particular orgiastic practice among polytheistic Romans as harmful to these people's spiritual development does nothing to undermine the powerful religious and spiritual potential of transformative love-based relationships for same-sex couples today.

The second relevant passage comes from 1 Corinthians 6:9 and is repeated with some minor alterations in 1 Timothy 1:10, which provides the third relevant passage. In these passages, the terms "malakoi" and "arsenokoitai" appear in a list of people who will "not enter into God's kingdom."[162] The meanings of these terms are highly contested.[163] Brownson identifies some of the open issues in interpreting these terms:

> In 1 *Corinthians* 6:9, the words translated in the NRSV [New Revised Standard Version] as "male prostitute" (*arsenokoites*) and "sodomote" (*malakos*) carry with them a number of interpretive problems. The word *arsenokoites*, for example, does not occur in any extrabiblical Greek texts that are prior to or contemporaneous with other contemporary or earlier texts ... Boswell ... argu[es] that the word [*arsenokoites*] refers to male prostitutes – without any particular homosexual connotation. Robin Scroggs, by contrast, emphasizes the link between both of these terms (*arsenokoites* and *malakos*) and the Greek practice of pederasty, the sexual use of younger boys (*malakoi*) by older men (*arsenokoitai*). Dale Martin suggests that we cannot know much more about the word *arsenokoites* than that it refers to some kind of sexual abuse or exploitation.[164]

160 *Id.*

161 "[S]ame things" should not be read as suggesting that everyone engaged in homosexual conduct but as failing to acknowledge God perfectly, itself a sin.

162 1 Cor. 6:9–11; *see also* 1 Timothy 1:10 (referring to arsenokatoi).

163 For discussions of interpretive difficulties, *compare* Gagnon, *supra* note 8 *with* Brownson, *supra* note 31, at ch. 3.

164 Brownson, *supra* note 31, at ch. 3.

But exploitive sexual conduct fails to show adequate regard for another as having unconditional value and inherent dignity. Conduct of this kind thus lacks the religious and spiritual potential of sexual conduct within a transformative marriage, and nothing in these passages clearly and universally condemns same-sex conduct with transformative potential.

Hence, the only three New Testament passages that condemn homosexual conduct of any kind appear to condemn homosexual conduct motivated by idolatry, profligacy, violence, exploitation, hedonism, or lack of reverence for God and the transformative potential of romantic love. No passage clearly condemns same-sex unions apart from these ills.

Consistent with these facts, intolerance of homosexuality was not even widespread in early Christianity.[165] Researchers David Greenberg and Marcia Bystryn suggest that this intolerance began to emerge only in the 3rd century AD, as part of a broader set of radical ascetic developments in the ancient Near East.[166] Some Christian sects became so extreme at that time that they required self-castration or complete sexual abstinence (even within marriage) as a condition of church membership. These views were later replaced with a policy "accepting sexuality only within marriage."[167] This early policy helped "reconcile[] the public demand for asceticism and personal purity with the necessities of organizational survival."[168] Still, the original target of these ascetic ideals was not homosexuality *per se* but rather pleasure of any form, even within marriage.[169] St. Augustine typified this view by suggesting that "any married person who requested sex for pleasure, rather than procreation, [committed] a venial sin."[170]

The Church has now abandoned that radical ascetic ideal.[171] That rejection came with a growing cultural acceptance of a link between romantic love, personal choice, intimate fulfillment, and marriage. In the 21st century, Pope Benedict XVI therefore explained (with some revisionism) that the Church's official teaching never really meant to reject "*eros as such*, but rather declared war on a warped and destructive form of it, because this counterfeit divinization of *eros* . . . actually strips it of divine significance and dehumanizes it."[172] Pope Francis echoes his predecessor. He says that the search for pleasure, especially when it "becomes obsessive," can hold "us in thrall and keep us

165 *See* Greenberg & Bystryn, *supra* note 131. 166 *Id.* at 524. 167 *Id.* 168 *Id.*

169 *Id.* at 525.

170 Mary E. Becker, *The Politics of Women's Wrongs and the Bill of "Rights": A Bicentennial Perspective*, 59 U. Chi. L. Rev. 453, 467 (1992).

171 *See supra* notes 33–185 and accompanying text.

172 Encyclical Letter *Deus Caritas Est* (Dec. 25, 2005) 3: AAS (2006), 220 (quoted in *Amoris Laetitia*, *supra* note 35, at § 148).

from experiencing other satisfactions" – namely, the *joy* that love, when perfected, can bring to people's lives.[173] He distinguishes narcissistic and obsessive forms of erotic desire from erotic desire itself. Rather than dismissing erotic desire altogether, Pope Francis seeks to transform it. He recognize its spiritual importance enough, in fact, to insist that "a love lacking either pleasure or passion is insufficient to symbolize the union of the human heart with God: 'All the mystics have affirmed that supernatural love and heavenly love find the symbols which they seek in marital love, rather than in friendship, filial devotion or devotion to a cause'"[174] – precisely because of the "totality" of romantic love.[175]

This moving portrayal of transformational love-based relationships tees up the question: why then should a committed religious observer, who is sincerely concerned with the spiritual development of all people, oppose the transformational potential of marriage for people who can only fall into romantic love with someone of the same sex? Yes, Judeo-Christian marriage has traditionally been limited to a comprehensive union between a man and a woman.[176] But the great bulk of that history occurred before the modern rise of transformational marriage, which are love-based, non-hierarchical and less divided by gender roles than in this prior history. Given the historical rise of transformational marriage – with its expanded religious and spiritual functions and its greater ties to personal choice and emotional and intimate growth and fulfilment – the religious and spiritual costs of opposing same-sex marriage are now clear. The scriptural passages that have traditionally served as grounds for religious opposition to same-sex marriage are, by contrast, sparse, ambiguous, and not plausibly applicable to same-sex marriages of a transformational variety.

At the very minimum, Scripture is sufficiently open to conflicting interpretations on the issues most critical to understanding the religious and spiritual significance of same-sex marriage. It follows that however contestants have traditionally understood same-sex marriage, debates over these legal and social developments cannot be understood in terms of a mere win for secularism in a culture war. There are now genuine religious and spiritual concerns (including concerns for religious liberty and freedom of conscience) on both sides of the debate – however dimly the fact has been perceived by most. Those who support the religious liberty and freedom of conscience for all persons

173 *Amoris Laetitia, supra* note 35, at § 126.

174 *Id.* at § 142 (quoting A. Sertillanges, *L'Amour chrétien*, Paris, 1920, 174).

175 *Id.* quoting A. Sertillanges, *L'Amour chrétien*, Paris, 1920, 174).

176 Witte, Chapter 17, this volume.

should therefore support gay and lesbian couples who attempt to place their own personal religious, moral, spiritual, and conscientious convictions into practice by seeking to perfect their love-based relationships.

V CONCLUSION

Whenever an age-old institution like marriage evolves in ways that appear new, it is natural to worry that change may involve a loss of something valuable. It is also easy – though not always valid – to move from the long pedigree of a religious tradition to the conclusion that every feature must have timeless religious value. But that is not true. Christian theology distinguishes between the letter and the spirit of Scripture and religious tradition. It also allows for the historical unfolding of Scripture's revealed meaning. Hence, when encountering novel historical developments and trying to understand whether their primary significance is religious or secular, religious and spiritual significance unreflective reliance on tradition can sometimes prove detrimental to a deeper understanding of Scripture's revealed meaning in context.

For a concrete example, which might serve as a template for the changes in religious understanding recommended here consider Pope Francis's discussion of Ephesians 5:22. This passage relates to Christian conceptions of marriage that were once traditional and instructs women to "be subject to your husbands."[177] For millennia until at least the 19th century, many Christian societies interpreted this passage to support a patriarchal form marriage. By the time John Stuart Mill published *The Subjection of Women* in 1869, patriarchal forms of marriage had prevailed for so long, and in so many societies, that many assumed "[t]he subjection of women to men is a universal custom, so any departure from it quite naturally appears unnatural!"[178] For millennia, this reading of Ephesians lent purportedly "religious" support to certain features of the law that contributed to women's subjection and inequality – including the rights of husbands to engage in chastisement to coerce obedience to their will and limited rights for women to own property or contract.

Rather than simply accepting those age-old interpretations of Ephesians however, Pope Francis suggests that this passage "mirrors the cultural categories of the time," whereas "our concern is not with its cultural matrix but with the *revealed* message that it conveys."[179] Elsewhere, he observes that "[h]istory is burdened by the excesses of patriarchal cultures that considered

[177] Ephesians 5:22. [178] John Stuart Mill, The Subjection of Women 8 (1869).
[179] *Amoris Laetitia, supra* note 35, at § 156 (emphasis added).

women inferior ....”[180] To understand the revealed message of this passage, Pope Francis suggests reading Ephesians 5:22 along with Ephesians 5:21, which says: “Be subject to one another.”[181] Rather than justifying long-standing traditions of patriarchal marriage, which were once supported by Christian tradition for millennia, he reads these combined passages as “actually concerned with encouraging everyone to overcome a complacent individualism and to be constantly mindful of others.”[182]

This reading is clearly more consistent with Christ’s central aim and message. Promoting this aim is precisely the function that transformational marriage, and other love-based relationships, can now serve for both heterosexual and homosexual couples alike. Changes in religious understandings like these are thus some of the very same ones that counsel in favor of expanded social and religious support for same-sex marriages and relationships of a transformational variety. Gay and lesbian couples who seek to marry do not seek to enter into the hierarchical marriages of the past, which were chosen by others, were not love-based, and required one partner to lose her right to own property and contract while being placed into a position of legal submission to the other. They seek to participate in the more egalitarian and love-based marriages of the present, which now have new and expanded transformative potential.

Historical developments toward deeper understandings of Scripture’s revealed meaning in context, which upset long traditions of prior interpretation, are rare. But given the natural limitations humans face, they are not isolated, and when they occur, they often have poignant religious, moral and spiritual significance. In *A Church that Can and Cannot Change: The Development of Catholic Moral Teaching*, Judge John T. Noonan Jr. documents three such examples that prove this point. He shows that Church teachings have developed over time to better capture Scripture’s revealed meanings on (1) the permissibility of slavery (once assumed for millennia to be permissible features of human society but now thought to violate the inherent dignity of all persons); (2) the permissibility of some forms of commercial exchange and credit that in involve interest (once deemed to be inherently exploitative and usurious for millennia but now accepted *within measure* as central and permissible aspect of modern market exchange that can aid human prosperity and economic development); and (3) the value of religious tolerance and freedom of conscience (once denied for millennia but now widely accepted among Christians of most denominations and

180 *Id.* at § 54. 181 *Id.* at § 156. 182 *Id.*

people of many other faiths).[183] The upshot of this chapter is that a similar development – with similar moral and spiritual poignancy – is warranted with respect to religious attitudes toward same-sex marriage. Generations from now, the moral, spiritual, and religious obviousness of this transformation should be as clear as in these other cases just mentioned.

Hence, a richer understanding of the expanded religious and spiritual functions – or *spirit* – of transformational marriage can help reorient religious discussions of same-sex marriage from whom to exclude from love's transformative potential, based on the letter of outworn traditions, to how to perfect a living and breathing love-based institution to make it more appealing, stable, and fulfilling for all. By rejecting an outworn interpretatoin of these debates as part of a culture war, which closes the hearts and empathy of people on all sides of the debate, new life and spirit can be breathed into the institution path of love and the institution of marriage. As Pope Francis laments in a related context, the Church has too often "wast[ed] pastoral energy on denouncing a decadent world without being proactive in proposing ways of finding true happiness."[184] To make contemporary marriage and families more attractive and a greater source of joy and moral and spiritual growth for more people – something that secular and religious communities can both support – committed religious observers and religious institutions should focus more attention on how to support the maturation of romantic love and less on whom to exclude from love's transformative potential. Cases like *Obergefell* need not – and should not – become a permanently divisive fixture in the culture wars between religious and secular values.

[183] *See* John T. Noonan, Jr., A Church That Can and Cannot Change: The Development of Catholic Moral Teaching (2005).

[184] *Amoris Laetitia*, *supra* note 35, at § 38.

16

Divorcing Marriage and the State Post-*Obergefell*

Robin Fretwell Wilson

Roger and Stephany Joslin Professor of Law, University of Illinois College of Law

The United States Supreme Court's landmark decision extending the right to marry to same-sex couples, *Obergefell v. Hodges*, turned a simmering dispute into a "raging inferno."[1] Chief Justice John Roberts, reading portions of his twenty-nine-page dissent from the bench for the first time in a decade-long tenure,[2] accused the majority of "an act of will, not legal judgment."[3] "People of faith," he said, "can take no comfort in the treatment they receive from the majority today."[4]

Collisions over same-sex marriage erupted almost immediately around the country – from Alabama, Louisiana, and North Carolina, to Ohio, Indiana, Oregon, and beyond.[5] Perhaps most infamous, elected county clerk Kim

[1] Greg Bluestein, *White House Contenders Pledge in Georgia that Gay Marriage Fight Will Go On*, AJC (July 10, 2015), http://politics.blog.ajc.com/2015/07/06/white-house-contenders-pledge-in-georgia-that-gay-marriage-fight-will-go-on/ (quoting then-candidate Texas Senator Ted Cruz).

As just two barometers, a Tennessee legislator proposed "a law that 'any court decision purporting to strike down natural marriage, including *Obergefell v. Hodges*, is unauthoritative, void, and of no effect'"; two South Carolina lawmakers proposed banning taxpayer funds and government salaries for "licensing and support of same-sex marriage." *Tennessee Bill Would Nullify Supreme Court's Gay "Marriage" Decision Statewide*, Life Site (Sept. 18, 2015, 6:47 PM), www.lifesitenews.com/news/tennessee-bill-would-nullify-supreme-courts-gay-marriage-decision-statewide; 2015 South Carolina House Bill No. 3022. Such measures would have no legal effect.

[2] Obergefell v. Hodges, 135 S. Ct. 2584, 2611–26 (2015); *Supreme Court Extends Gay Marriage Nationwide*, Chicago Tribune (June 26, 2015), www.chicagotribune.com/news/nationworld/ct-supreme-court-gay-marriage-20150626-story.html.

[3] Obergefell, *supra* note 2, at 2612. [4] *Id.* at 2626.

[5] *See* Victor Puente, *Casey County Clerk: Let People Buy Marriage Licenses Online*, WKYT (July 6, 2015), www.wkyt.com/home/headlines/Ky-Clerk-Let-people-buy-marriage-licenses-online-311820401.html; Nick Gass, *Same-Sex Marriages Still on Hold in Louisiana, Mississippi*, Politico (June 26, 2015), www.politico.com/story/2015/06/mississippi-gay-marriage-on-hold-supreme-court-ruling-119473; Rose Hackman, *Meet the Alabama Judges Who Refuse to Issue*

Davis shut down marriage to everyone in Rowan County, Kentucky, because issuing licenses to same-sex couples "would conflict with God's definition of marriage" and "would violate [her] conscience."[6] Federal District Court Judge David Bunning broke the impasse, jailing Davis and instructing her deputies to issue licenses or go to jail, too.[7]

Like Davis, some faith leaders distanced themselves from the new public meaning of marriage. More than 700 religious figures signed a pledge "to disengage civil and Christian marriage," saying they would "no longer serve as agents of the state in marriage."[8] In their view, "to continue with church practices that intertwine government marriage with Christian marriage will implicate the Church in a false definition of marriage."[9] The impulse to withdraw religious marriage from the public sphere is part of a larger movement by some believers to retreat from civil culture and develop instead intentional orthodox communities of believers.[10]

Faced with deep unease over the public meaning of marriage, commentators – and increasingly, legislators – have latched onto a seductively simple solution to the conflicts erupting around same-sex marriage: "[G]et the government out of the marriage business, altogether."[11] U.S. Senator Rand Paul said in *Time Magazine* that "the government should not prevent people from making contracts but that does not mean that the government must confer a special imprimatur upon a new definition of marriage. Perhaps the time has come to examine whether or not governmental recognition of marriage is a good idea."[12]

Marriage Licenses – Gay or Straight, GUARDIAN (July 12, 2015), www.theguardian.com/us-news/2015/jul/12/alabama-judges-gay-marriage-licenses; *McCrory Vetoes NC Religious Objection Bill on Gay Marriage*, ABC 11 & ASSOCIATED PRESS (May 29, 2015), http://abc11.com/politics/mccrory-vetoes-nc-religious-objection-bill-on-gay-marriage/746406/.

6 Abby Ohlheiser, *Kentucky Clerk Kim Davis on Gay Marriage Licenses: "It is a Heaven or Hell Decision,"* WASH. POST (Sept. 1, 2015), www.washingtonpost.com/news/acts-of-faith/wp/2015/09/01/kentucky-clerk-kim-davis-on-gay-marriage-licenses-it-is-a-heaven-or-hell-decision/.

7 *Kentucky Clerk Kim Davis Ordered to Jail for Refusing Marriage Licenses to Gay Couples*, ABC7 (Sept. 3, 2015), www.abc-7.com/story/29944148/kentucky-clerk-gets-jail-time-for-failing-to-issue-same-sex-marriage-licenses.

8 Ephraim Radner & Christopher Seitz, *The Marriage Pledge*, FIRST THINGS, www.firstthings.com/marriage-pledge; *see also* Bryan Cones, *It's Time to Separate Church and State Marriages*, U.S. CATHOLIC, Feb. 2014, at 40–43.

9 Radner & Seitz, *supra* note 8.

10 *See* ROD DREHER, THE BENEDICT OPTION: A STRATEGY FOR CHRISTIANS IN A POST-CHRISTIAN NATION (2017).

11 Keith Ablow, *When It Comes to Marriage, Government Should Divorce Itself*, FOX NEWS (Mar. 27, 2013), www.foxnews.com/opinion/2013/03/27/when-it-comes-to-marriage-government-should-divorce-itself.html.

12 *Rand Paul: Government Should Get Out of the Marriage Business Altogether*, TIME (June 28, 2015), http://time.com/3939374/rand-paul-gay-marriage-supreme-court/.

Legislators, however, have advanced quite different conceptions of what it would mean to "end marriage."[13] Bills in Oklahoma, Michigan, and Utah would shift responsibility for issuing marriage licenses to "churches of any denomination, even a notary public,"[14] in order to insulate religious objectors from having to "accept ... marriage" in its current form or "reject [one's] own beliefs regarding [marriage]."[15] A Tennessee legislator argued that Tennessee should return to common law marriage, saying that marriage clerks "don't answer to the Supreme Court."[16] Alabama and Indiana legislators would eliminate marriage licenses altogether in favor of marriage contracts. Seeing marriage as "simply a contract between two people," Indiana Representative Jim Lucas would require "a signed contract, witnessed by two other[s] ... to legally wed."[17] A "big fan of simplicity," Lucas believes that "[b]y taking state government out of marriage," churches cannot "be forced to perform or recognize something that goes against their religious beliefs."[18] Lucas's bill would also "eliminate[] a 'Kim Davis' situation."[19]

Despite the possibility of muting the impact on religious dissenters with well-drawn statutory protection as Utah Senator Stuart Adams argues elsewhere in this volume (Chapter 21), the dangerous idea of radically transforming the State's relationship to marriage has taken hold. This chapter examines these emerging attempts to solve clashes over same-sex marriage by divorcing marriage from the State. It critiques specific proposals to limit state-sponsored marriage. Section I briefly reviews notions for "ending marriage" cropping up in statehouses and public debate. Section II links these proposals to, ironically, older more left-

13 Michael A. Lindenberger, *A Gay-Marriage Solution: End Marriage?* Time (Mar. 16, 2009), http://content.time.com/time/nation/article/0,8599,1885190,00.html?xid=rss-mostpopularemail.3.

14 Chris Jones, *Utah Legislator Working on Bill to Get State Out of Marriage Business*, KUTV.com (June 26, 2015), http://kutv.com/news/local/utah-legislator-working-on-bill-to-get-state-out-of-marriage-business.

15 Cheryl Wetzstein, *Oklahoma Bill Abolishes State Marriage Licenses: Couples Would Need Clergy or Notary to Process New Certificates*, Wash. Times (Mar. 11, 2015), www.washingtontimes.com/news/2015/mar/11/oklahoma-bill-abolishes-state-marriage-licenses/?page=all.

16 Tracy Kornet, *TN Legislator Wants State to Stop Issuing All Marriage Licenses*, WSMV.com (Jan. 12, 2016, 9:51 PM), www.wsmv.com/story/30850413/tn-legislator-wants-state-to-stop-issuing-all-marriage-licenses.

17 H.B. 1163, 120th Gen. Assemb., 2d Reg. Sess. (Ind. 2017) (referred to Judiciary Committee); Stephanie Wang, *Lawmaker Proposes an End to Indiana Marriage Licenses*, Indy Star (Jan. 7, 2016, 6:59 PM), www.indystar.com/story/news/politics/2016/01/07/lawmaker-get-government-out-marriage/78364598/ (discussing 2016 bill, H.B. 1041).

18 January Rutherford, *Seymour Lawmaker's Bill Gets Government out of Marriage*, Vincennes Sun-Commercial (Indiana) (Jan. 19, 2016).

19 *Id.*

leaning claims that society should "abolish marriage." Section III arrays proposals to divorce marriage from the State on a continuum from weaker to stronger claims – from the idea that society should simply redub civil marriages as civil unions to the idea that the State should only enforce parties' contractual agreements, rather than specifying rights and obligations that attach when a couple marries. A radical transformation of the State's relationship to marriage, whatever form that may take, risks disturbing the delicate web of norms around marriage – norms of faithfulness, permanence, emotional and financial interdependence, and physical security. This section suggests that these norms are reinforced when religious couples participate in the institution now known as "marriage."

After probing the general proposition that society should transform the State's relationship to marriage, this chapter explores concerns raised by specific legislative proposals to back-walk the State's regulation of marriage. It asks, what happens to the millions of Americans who have relied upon the State's existing structure if proposals to divorce marriage from the State become law? It explores practical questions – will other states or the federal government recognize the "marriages" of couples who privately contract after the State backs away from marriage? Will couples in this newly privatized status qualify for the social benefits attached to marital status? If the new privatized marriages take the form of a contract, will couples have the foresight, discipline, and, most significantly, roughly equal bargaining power to arrive at fair agreements governing the financial and domestic aspects of their relationship? Can couples contract their way into the cocoon of protections for marriage that give it unique privacy and intimacy, such as the right not to testify against one another or share marital confidences?

Section IV ultimately concludes that society should be loath to unwind the religious and civil dimensions of marriage since the consequences are difficult to predict and may be profound.

I A DANGEROUS IDEA TAKES HOLD

Every state in America "still comingles religious and civil marriage."[20] As Professor Harry Krause notes, "The law requires a civil license but allows a (civil or) *religious* pronouncement to be the last word in formalizing the marriage."[21] In all fifty states, marriage by a religious figure brings into

[20] Harry Krause, *Marriage for the New Millennium: Heterosexual, Same-Sex – Or Not at All?* 34 FAM. L.Q. 271, 283 (2001) (emphasis in original).

[21] *Id.*

existence a civil marriage regulated by the State.[22] It is a crime or regulatory violation for religious figures not to record a marriage they have solemnized.[23] So while it is possible to have a civil marriage without a religious ceremony, it is impossible to enter into a religious-only marriage in the United States.[24]

As the "keystone of the Nation's social order," married couples are preferred in such matters as the following:

> [T]axation; inheritance and property rights; rules of intestate succession; spousal privilege in the law of evidence; hospital access; medical decision-making authority; adoption rights; the rights and benefits of survivors; birth and death certificates; professional ethics rules; campaign finance restrictions; workers' compensation benefits; health insurance; and child custody, support, and visitation rules.[25]

Indeed, "1,138 [federal] benefits, rights and protections" flow to married couples.[26] States have also privileged married couples in "many facets of the [State's] legal and social order."[27] Marriage law does more than dictate rights and obligations between the two spouses – it creates rights against third parties, requiring others to respect a spouse's "power to make medical decisions," and entitling spouses "to public benefits, such as family leave or social security."[28]

In the months preceding *Obergefell*, religious figures had begun to rethink the role religion plays in civil marriage. Latching onto an idea that has been around for decades, more than 700 pastors, imams, priests, and others pledged in *First Things* to "no longer serve as agents of the state in marriage."[29] In order to separate "civil marriage from religious marriage," pledge signers would instruct their parishioners "to seek civil marriage separately from their church-related vows and blessings."[30] Not every religious figure believes it is necessary

22 *See, e.g.*, S.B. 296, 61st Leg., Gen. Sess. (Utah 2015) (naming ministers, imams, and other religious figures as authorized celebrants of marriage).

23 *See* TEX. FAM. CODE ANN. § 2.206 (West 2015) (misdemeanor not to file license). IND. CODE ANN. §§ 31-11-11-8, 34-28-5-4 (West 2015) (infraction punishable by fine).

24 Couples may immigrate to the United States whose relationships would not be recognized as civil marriages if entered into here, such as those in polygamous marriages. *See* Witte, Chapter 17, this volume, and Strassberg, Chapter 18, this volume, for critiques of the norms around polygamy.

25 Obergefell, *supra* note 2, at 2601.

26 *Federal Right and Protections Granted to Married Couples*, MASSEQUALITY, www.massequality.org/content/federal-rights-and-protections-granted-married-couples.

27 Obergefell, *supra* note 2, at 2590.

28 Gregg Strauss, *Why the State Cannot "Abolish Marriage": A Partial Defense of Legal Marriage*, 91 IND. L.J. 1261, 1265 (2015).

29 Radner & Seitz, *supra* note 8. *See* Bryan Cones, *It's Time to Separate Church and State Marriages*, U.S. CATHOLIC, Feb. 2014, at 40–43.

30 Radner & Seitz, *supra* note 8.

to take such a radical step, that "not officiating at unions that are not gospel-qualified" would suffice.[31] Still, one in four pastors and one in three Americans think that a sharp break between religious marriage and state regulation is a good idea.[32]

Earlier, author and commentator George Weigel of the Ethics and Public Policy Center argued that the Catholic Church should "pre-emptively withdraw from the civil marriage business, its clergy declining to act as agents of government in witnessing marriages for purposes of state law."[33] This fracturing would challenge "the state (and the culture) by underscoring that what the state means by 'marriage' and what Catholics mean by 'marriage' are radically different, and that what the state means by 'marriage' is wrong."[34]

Since *Obergefell*, the notion that the deep divide over marriage should be solved by getting the government out of marriage has gotten significant traction with legislators. Senator Paul argued, "[t]he 14th Amendment does not command the government endorsement … conveyed by the word 'marriage,'" so society can reexamine the government's role in marriage.[35] For Paul, government's role should be limited to enforcing contracts that couples write to govern their own relations. A growing set of state legislators also believes "the best way to protect marriage is to divorce marriage from government."[36] Texas State Representative David Simpson wants to "get [Texas] out of the business of licensing marriage"[37] because "the federal government usurp[ed] our authority here in Texas to regulate and respect this institution."[38] Instead, "clergy members would issue marriage licenses."[39]

31 Ruth Moon, *Should Pastors Stop Signing Civil Marriage Certificates?* Christianity Today (Jan. 26, 2015), www.christianitytoday.com/ct/2015/januaryfebruary/should-pastors-stop-signing-civil-marriage-certificates.html?share=ReueLRxknZy/6QU%20onpbIVAhWRRo%20pkv (quoting Russell Moore, president of the Ethics & Religious Liberty Commission of the Southern Baptist Convention).

32 *Id.* (reporting on Fall 2015 survey of 2000 Americans and 1000 senior Protestant pastors); Bob Smietana, *Religious Weddings Should Not Be Connected to the State's Definition and Recognition of Marriage*, LifeWay Research (Dec. 2, 2014), www.lifewayresearch.com/2014/12/02/most-americans-say-the-state-should-not-define-marriage/.

33 George Weigel, *The Crisis of a Second Obama Administration*, First Things (Nov. 14, 2012), www.firstthings.com/web-exclusives/2012/11/the-crisis-of-a-second-obama-administration.

34 *Id.*

35 Carlos Santoscoy, *Rand Paul Reacts to Supreme Court Ruling: Let's Do Away with Civil Marriage*, On Top (June 29, 2015), www.ontopmag.com/article.aspx?id=21134&MediaType=1&Category=26.

36 Risa Morris, *East Texas Legislator Asks Governor for Special Session About Marriage*, CBS19.tv (June 29, 2015), www.cbs19.tv/story/29436201/east-texas-legislator-asks-governor-for-special-session-about-marriage.

37 *Id.* 38 *Id.* 39 *Id.*

Sharing this view, lawmakers have begun to put pen to paper. Indiana Representative Lucas reintroduced his measure in Indiana. Missouri Republican Representative T.J. Berry filed a 336-page bill in the 2017 legislative session that would "treat[] everybody the exact same way . . . leaving space for people to believe what they believe outside of government."[40] Under the proposal, Missouri would no longer recognize marriage but would recognize only domestic unions for straight and gay couples.[41] Marriage would be an exclusively religious institution, with no legal effect. Berry's proposal would grandfather existing marriages into domestic partnerships but going forward, this status would become the exclusive province of the State; couples are free to have religious marriage ceremonies, or civil ones for that matter, but that proceeding "shall have no legal effect upon the validity of the contract of domestic union."[42] For Berry, the severing of the ties between religious marriage and the State's regulation "would get back to government being in its role and religion being in its role. . . . Marriage has been, through history going back thousands of years, a religious ceremony not a governmental ceremony."[43]

A number of commentators and scholars believe that Missouri's approach is the right "fix": the State should create a new status with a new label other than marriage that would unlock the benefits presently reserved for married couples.[44] Like Representative Berry's bill, marriages would become a private matter, giving "religious organizations [the ability] to set their own rules regarding who could marry."[45] Advocates contend that government recognition of civil unions or domestic partnerships would reduce "the unnecessary and sometimes ugly intensity of current public debate."[46] As Section II shows, this post-*Obergefell* narrative taps into criticisms of marriage that previously garnered little mainstream attention.

II RECASTING A VINTAGE IDEA

Rattling around long before *Obergefell* have been criticisms of marriage as a dated, patriarchal institution that it is wildly unfair to use to confer benefits

40 Summer Ballentine, *A Lawmaker's Solution for Marriage Debate: Remove the State*, AP NEWS (Dec. 30, 2016), https://apnews.com/efcdc917b4d04b2ba05126c7557d1bf2/lawmakers-solution-marriage-debate-remove-state.

41 H.B. 62, 99th Gen. Assemb., 1st Reg. Sess. (Mo. 2017).

42 *Id.* at 451.125.1(5). Out-of-state marriages would be treated as domestic partnerships. *Id.* at 451.125.1(7).

43 Alisa Nelson, *Missouri Legislator Says His Bill Would Defuse Some Controversy in Gay Weddings Resolution*, MISSOURINET (Dec. 1, 2016), www.missourinet.com/2016/12/01/missouri-legislator-says-his-bill-would-diffuse-some-controversy-in-gay-weddings-resolution/.

44 *See* Section III.B.3. 45 STEPHEN MACEDO, JUST MARRIED 121 (2015). 46 *Id.* at 120.

upon families. As this section shows, critiques have long called for marriage to be abolished.

Professor Krause argues that the "close association of marriage and religion" in our country's history is a thing of the past:

> [O]nce upon a time not long ago, marriage was a near-mandatory institution. "Family" was the all but inevitable consequence of marriage, and the unacceptability of women in the marketplace limited women to family roles. Then it made sense to deal with marriage and family as one unitary concept – even if there was the occasional infertile couple, or the occasional female professional.[47]

To successfully adapt "civil regulation of marriage and the family" to society's current needs, Krause believes, "we must start by separating civil marriage from our continuing romance with religious images of 'marriage' as ... a natural virtue."[48] A state's interest in adults' relationships should be guided by a single consideration: "[W]hat does this or that union do for society, and what rights and rules should society provide in return?"[49] Part and parcel of this "pragmatic, rational approach" is for the State to extend "social benefits and privileges" to a given status, however triggered, leaving "sentiment, religion, love and romanticism ... to the personal sphere."[50] Elsewhere in this volume, Weiner (Chapter 11) argues that society should leave state-supported marriage in place but build up duties outside marriage to reflect the reality of non-marital co-parenting.

Those who would "abolish marriage" entirely advance three distinct reasons: "favoring marriage discriminates against cohabitants and single people," the "state has no legitimate reason to define the terms of intimate relationships[,] and marriage law is an ineffective means to protect children and caregivers."[51] For instance, Professor Paula Ettelbrick laments the "cruel punishment of families in crisis who don't fit the [marriage] mold."[52] She argues that "families are actually strengthened when we expand our view of 'The Family' because our policies have greater reach to support the value of families."[53] In part, Ettelbrick's claim rests on the notion that non-marital partners are "no less committed to seeing their loved one through an illness or financial crisis than

47 Harry Krause, *Marriage for the New Millennium: Heterosexual, Same-Sex – Or Not at All?* 34 FAM. L .Q. 271, 284 (2001).

48 *Id.* at 283–84. 49 *Id.* 50 *Id.* at 276, 284.

51 Strauss, *supra* note 28, at 1263 (summarizing arguments).

52 Paula Ettelbrick, *Domestic Partnerships, Civil Unions, or Marriage; One Size Does Not Fit All*, 64 ALB. L. REV. 905, 909 (2001).

53 *Id.* at 912.

spouses."[54] Ettelbrick urges the State to "provide economic and legal supports to a wider range of families, and stop stigmatizing any family structure that is not packed neatly into the marriage or biological parent box."[55] As appealing as the push for marriage equality was, it "incorporated the politics of preference for marriage as the centerpiece of family,"[56] threatening to wipe out substantial and important progress in recognizing a broader conception of what constitutes a family – and therefore what should be encouraged and supported by the State.[57]

Although Ettelbrick appears to contemplate multiple institutions receiving state support, not just marriage alone, others, such as Professor Martha Fineman, contend that as long as marriage exists in any scheme of state support, "[i]t will continue to occupy a privileged status and be posited as the ideal, defining other intimate entities as deviant."[58] Echoing Fineman, Professor Nancy Polikoff believes that recognition of same-sex marriage "valorizes the current institution," one she sees as "grossly hierarchical" and "gendered."[59] By "mimic[king] the worst of mainstream society," the same-sex marriage movement failed to reach for "a truly transformative model of family for all people." For Scholars like Fineman and Polikoff, support for marriage must be scuttled.

Some question the utility of marriage as "a bright line to identify those couples whose intimacy is presumed to be deserving of such protection."[60] Professor Patricia Cain argues the State should seek to protect couples who "demonstrate personal commitment to a shared life" through private contracts, not public status.[61] For Cain, marriage can be "abolished so long as intimacy, a negative liberty, is protected."[62] Of course, the current tax system would have to be changed to make benefits available on some basis other than marital status, as Cain acknowledges.[63] But in a world without marriage, couples could formalize their commitment to each other through private contracts, much as Indiana Representative Lucas envisions.

54 *Id.* at 909. 55 *Id.* at 912. 56 *Id.* 57 *Id.*

58 Martha Fineman, The Neutered Mother, the Sexual Family, and Other Twentieth Century Tragedies 234–35 (1995) (arguing the State should support the "mother-child dyad" as the core, legally privileged, family connection).

59 Nancy Polikoff, *We Will Get What We Ask For: Why Legalizing Gay and Lesbian Marriage Will Not "Dismantle the Legal Structure of Gender in Every Marriage,"* 79 Va. L. Rev. 1535, 1536, 1541 (1993).

60 Patricia Cain, *Imagine There's No Marriage*, 16 Quinnipac L. Rev. 27, 42 (1996).

61 *Id.* at 43. 62 *Id.* at 30.

63 *Id.* at 49. Among other things, Professor Cain notes that tying benefits to marital status undercuts a couple's right to privacy if they must prove the legitimacy of their relationship to receive the benefit. *Id.*

Thus, in Cain's conception, couples could contract as to property rights, support rights, children, or other items of concern to them, as Bix (Chapter 9, this volume) and Brinig (Chapter 10, this volume) both show couples do after divorce. Cain sees this as advantageous because "[n]ot all relationships are the same. Customized agreements that reflect the reasonable expectations of the parties make it easier for the couple to live up to those expectations."[64] Breach of contract would become the exclusive remedy, obviating the need for marriage and divorce law.[65]

Social progressives are not the only ones to advocate for limiting the State's role in marriage before *Obergefell*. Religious leaders have long expressed concern about the melding of religious and civil marriage. In 1880, Pope Leo XXIII issued an encyclical on "Christian marriage," warning that shared authority over marriage invades what is properly an ecclesiatical sphere.[66] Shared authority is troubling because "when the Church exercises any [power over marriage], [men] think that she acts either by favor of the civil authority or to its injury," when matrimony should be the "subject of the [Church's] jurisdiction."[67] Men, Pope Leo contended, will "endeavor to deprive [marriage] of all holiness, and so bring it within the contracted sphere of those rights which, having been instituted by man, are ruled and administered by the civil jurisprudence of the community."[68]

Some modern scholars echo this view. Shortly after the country's first same-sex marriage decision, *Goodridge v. Department of Public Health*[69] in 2009, Professor Daniel Crane urged a return to religion of exclusive control over the social phenomenon known as marriage. Religious authorities should want this, he contended, because it would protect their autonomy from the State.[70] Crane believes religious communities should prepare standard-form religious agreements that believers can use to reflect their religious understandings of marriage, bounded only by "minimal norms of [a] liberal democratic society."[71]

Professor Edward Zelinsky advocates for a "multiplicity of contractual regimes" that couples can enter into instead of marriage, which will better

[64] Cain, *supra* note 60, at 43. [65] *See id.*

[66] Letter from Pope Leo XIII to the Patriarchs, Primates, Archbishops, and Bishops of the Catholic World in Grace and Communion with the Apostolic See (Feb. 10, 1880), http://w2.vatican.va/content/leo-xiii/en/encyclicals/documents/hf_l-xiii_enc_10021880_arcanum.html.

[67] *Id.* [68] *Id.* [69] 798 N.E.2d 941 (Mass. 2003).

[70] Daniel A. Crane, A *"Judeo-Christian" Argument for Privatizing Marriage*, 27 CARDOZO L. REV. 1221, 1250 (2006).

[71] *Id.* at 1254.

"satisfy their most intimate consumer preferences."[72] The State can eliminate marriage as a status because "as a practical matter, rules . . . governing married couples [with respect to parentage, custody, immigration, inheritance, and other matters] increasingly apply outside of marriage."[73] Further, marriage carries not just benefits but disadvantages that "penalize marriage."[74] Because family law has long permitted spouses to privately order their affairs using prenuptial agreements, Zelinsky believes couples will be better served with tailor-made arrangements: "People will feel more committed to domestic arrangements that they have affirmatively chosen."[75] Zelinsky would not invalidate agreements "except upon very compelling grounds," for example, to protect minor children.[76]

For everyday people, the notion that the government should get out of the marriage business holds commonsense appeal. It has become commonplace on blogs and social media to see sentiments such as these: "Marriage is truely [sic] a religious ceremony, o[f] no concern to the civil government."[77]

III WHAT IS WRONG WITH GETTING THE GOVERNMENT OUT OF MARRIAGE

Transforming the State's relationship to marriage – whether by substituting a customized legally recognized contract for marriage's off-the-rack benefits or by shifting the State's largesse to something other than marriage – risks disturbing not only the complicated structure of benefits tied to marriage, with unintended consequences. It risks disturbing the web of healthy norms surrounding marriage.

A *What Is Wrong with the Overarching Idea*

As a society, we are in far too deep to unwind the civil and religious aspects of marriage. Radically transforming the State's relationship to marriage would raise thorny questions about the benefits now accorded to married couples in Social Security, tax, immigration, employee benefits, healthcare, and many other dimensions.[78] Getting the government out of marriage is not as "simple

[72] Edward A. Zelinsky, *Deregulating Marriage: The Pro-Marriage Case for Abolishing Civil Marriage*, 27 CARDOZO L. REV. 1161, 1164, 1215 (2006).

[73] *Id.* at 1163. [74] *Id.* at 1207-08. [75] *Id.* at 1184, 1164. [76] *Id.* at 1184.

[77] *See generally* Robin Fretwell Wilson, *"Getting Government Out of Marriage" Post* Obergefell: *The Ill-Considered Consequences of Transforming the State's Relationship to Marriage*, 2016(4) ILL. L. REV. 101 (2016) (tracing this sentiment on internet forums and blogs).

[78] *See supra* note 26.

as waving a magic wand": it would complicate "things like spousal privilege"; entail "remov[ing] probate courts and divorce courts . . . put[ting matters] back in the hands of the church"; and require "completely reform[ing the] tax code and tax law" tied to "marital status" – in other words, countless changes because "[t]he state's regulation of marriage is older and far more embedded than even the welfare state itself."[79]

Legislative proposals for back-walking the State's regulation of marriage uniformly overlook the millions of Americans who have married or aspire to marry. In 2014, a total of 2,140,272 couples in America were married,[80] representing a slim majority, 44%, of all adults.[81] Although younger Americans are delaying marriage and the fraction of never-married individuals has more than doubled since 1960,[82] 85% of all Americans "will marry at least once."[83] Of those marriages, 50% to 60% "will last until death."[84] Thus, marriage remains the primary vehicle for protecting individuals against hardship and vulnerability within the family. Even if we collectively would not accord significant state support to marriage if deciding the question today, proposals to transform the State's relationship to marriage have not explained whether or how the proposal would treat couples who married believing that "marriage" provided all of the needed protections.[85]

Legislative proposals for divorcing the State from marriage also fail to consider whether other states, the federal government, and private parties would accord the same rights to contracts between parties or domestic partnerships as they do to marriage. An entire scaffolding of societal benefits rests on marital status, including entitlement to spousal benefits from employers; the ability to participate in Social Security as a result of a spouse's work history, file

79 Steve Deace, *Laissez Faire Marriage*, Western Journalism (March 21, 2013), www.westernjournalism.com/laissez-faire-marriage/?utm_source%3DTwitter%26utm_medium%3DPostSideSharingButtons%26utm_content%3D2016-12-29%26utm_campaign%3Dwebsitesharingbuttons.

80 The marriage rate in 2014 of 6.9 marriages per 1000 people represents a decrease from 8.2 marriages per 1000 people in 2000. *See National Marriage and Divorce Rate Trends*, CDC (Nov. 23, 2015), www.cdc.gov/nchs/nvss/marriage_divorce_tables.htm.

81 Frank Newport & Joy Wilke, *Most in U.S. Want Marriage, But Its Importance Has Declined*, Gallup (Aug. 2, 2013), www.gallup.com/poll/163802/marriage-importance-dropped.aspx.

82 Wendy Want & Kim Parker, *Chapter 2: Trends in the Share of Never-Married Americans and a Look Forward*, Pew Research Center (Sept. 24, 2014), www.pewsocialtrends.org/2014/09/24/chapter-2-trends-in-the-share-of-never-married-americans-and-a-look-forward/.

83 *See* Ron L. Deal, *Marriage, Family, & Stepfamily Statistics*, SmartStepfamilies, www.smartstepfamilies.com/view/statistics.

84 Strauss, *supra* note 28, at 1266.

85 "Marriage," when used in quotes, means the legal status regulated by the State, to which benefits and obligations attach.

taxes jointly, or hold property jointly; and thousands of sundry benefits attached to marriage.[86]

Just as important, forcing couples to contract or enter domestic partnerships may put at risk the recognition of the relationship by other states. Many couples marry in one state and later move to another.[87] State laws address what a couple must do to avail themselves of the second state's marriage and divorce laws. But if a couple began in Missouri and Indiana and contracted or entered a domestic partnership, it is unclear whether a later state would have the jurisdiction to decide rights between the couple, or at death, or the desire to do so.

Equally problematic, many protections attached to marriage apply during the pendency of the relationship, shielding spouses, for example, generally from testifying against each other or sharing marital confidences.[88] Absent such protections, adults in an intimate relationship occupy more of an arm's length relationship and cannot freely and securely share their deepest concerns.

Proposals to substitute contract for status overlook the value of off-the-rack rules that couples assume through the simple act of marrying. "Intimate relationships involve rights and expectations that deserve legal protection" but are hard to enforce "without imposing status norms on couples. Marital status offers a way to manage this tension."[89] For this reason,

> The state cannot simply get out of the marriage business. As long as intimates can bring legal claims against one another in tort, contract, or equity, the law must determine who has obligations, how those obligations arise, how they change, and what their default content will be – and these legal rules will be tailored to the nature of our relationships. If a state abolished intimate-relationship licenses, then private law would refashion ad hoc categories of intimate status.[90]

Society has seen fundamental transformations in "marriage" before. More recently, "no fault divorce brought a huge change to the meaning of civil

[86] GAO-04-353R – Defense of Marriage Act: Update to Prior Report; Morgan Quinn, *What's Cheaper: Marriage or Domestic Partnership?* GoBankingRates (Feb. 4, 2015), www.gobankingrates.com/personal-finance/whats-cheapermarriage-domestic-partnership/#.VqAi5D94fhM.mailto.

[87] Obergefell, *supra* note 2, at 2607–08; Tom Oldham, *Marital Property Rights of Mobile Spouses When They Divorce in the United States*, 42 Fam. L.Q. 263 (2008).

[88] *See* Walter Wadlington, Raymond C. O'Brien, & Robin Fretwell Wilson, Domestic Relations: Cases and Materials 189 (7th ed. 2013); Trammel v. U.S., 445 U.S. 40 (1980).

[89] Strauss, *supra* note 28, at 1310.

[90] *Id.* at 1287–88.

marriage," although not one as great as the elimination of coverture.[91] A lively debate continues to rage about whether no-fault divorce made it more likely people would in fact divorce.[92] Social conservatives seeking to alter the relationship between marriage and the State generally see no-fault divorce as wreaking havoc on the institution of marriage.[93] Whatever one thinks about cleaving apart gender and marriage[94] – as *Obergefell* does – proposals to get the government out of marriage would work a far greater change than eliminating gender from the legal meaning of marriage. Just as significantly, marriage carries with it a set of positive norms that may be disrupted by a radical restructuring of the State's relationship to marriage.

1 Marriage Is Regulated by Norms as Well as Law

Two notable changes have occurred to marriage in the past century – both of which offer a caution to those urging the State to back away from marriage. At the end of the 19th century, Married Women Property Acts eradicated coverture, the system by which a woman's legal identity melded into her husband's upon marriage, meaning she could not contract, sue or be sued, or hold property.[95] Ending coverture helped to hasten a conception of marriage as a "relationship between two spouses with equal rights and equal duties."[96] Although the change did not precipitate marriage's demise, the social understanding of marriage changed.

However one thinks about different genders as a prerequisite to legal marriage,[97] proposals to get the government out of marriage would likely disrupt settled meanings of marriage today. Marriage encourages positive norms

[91] Douglas Laycock, *The Campaign Against Religious Liberty*, *in* The Rise of Corporate Religious Liberty 243 (Micah Jacob Schwartzman et al. eds., 2016).

[92] Leora Friedberg, *Did Unilateral Divorce Raise Divorce Rates? Evidence from Panel Data*, 88 Am. Econ. Rev. 608–27 (1998); Jonathan Gruber, *Is Making Divorce Easier Bad for Children? The Long-Run Implications of Unilateral Divorce*, 22 J. of Lab. Econ. 799, 799 (2004).

[93] Scott Keyes, *Conservatives Aren't Just Fighting Same-Sex Marriage. They're Also Trying to Stop Divorce*, Wash. Post (Apr. 11, 2014), www.washingtonpost.com/opinions/conservatives-arent-just-fighting-same-sex-marriage-theyre-also-trying-to-stop-divorce/2014/04/11/5f649bd6-bf48-11e3-bcec-b71ee10e9bc3_story.html?utm_term=.39f261c106d8.

[94] *See, e.g.*, Eugene Volokh, *Same-Sex Marriage and Slippery Slopes*, 33 Hofstra L. Rev. 1155 (2006); Macedo, *supra* note 45; Robert P. George, Sherif Girgis, & Ryan T. Anderson, *The Argument Against Gay Marriage: And Why it Doesn't Fail*, Pub. Discourse (Dec. 17, 2010), www.thepublicdiscourse.com/2010/12/2217/.

[95] Martha M. Ertman, *Private Ordering Under the ALI Principles: As Natural as Status*, *in* Reconceiving the Family: Critique on the American Law Institute's Principles of the Law of Family Dissolution 284, 295 (Robin Fretwell Wilson. ed. 2006).

[96] Laycock, *supra* note 91, at 243.

[97] *See* Kar, Chapter 15, this volume, for competing views.

that may be disrupted by a radical restructuring of the State's relationship to marriage.

Most Americans "think marriage should be monogamous and [they] want it to last for life."[98] Marriage signifies "an obligation to be faithful, to give and receive help in times of sickness, and to endure hardships. . . . Society enforces these ideals both formally and informally."[99] The "tangle of overlapping moral norms" around marriage includes "sexual fidelity, emotional fidelity, economic support (including financial and domestic services), emotional support, and relationship maintenance."[100]

Norms, or societal rules that govern and enforce "collective behaviors *outside of the law*,"[101] "operate over and are 'somehow accepted within' particular groups or communities."[102] Group members treat norms as "general requirements,"[103] even though they are neither recorded nor static.[104]

The law plays an important role in shaping and reinforcing norms, over and above the "effect created by its [formal] sanctions."[105] Laws can "provide unmistakable evidence of a consensus," unifying a group around a new idea.[106] But laws can also undercut social norms. Whether the law has an impact depends on how many people feel a certain way about the subject the

98 Sara McDougall, *Polygamy and Western History: Book Review*, 17 J. of Politics, Religion and Ideology 312 (2016) (reviewing John Witte, The Western Case for Monogamy Over Polygamy, at xvii, 531(2015)).

99 Marriage and Family: Perspectives and Complexities 306 (H. Elizabeth Peters & Claire M. Kamp Dush, eds., 2009); *see also* Elizabeth S. Scott & Robert E. Scott, *Marriage as Relational Contract*, 84 Va. L. Rev. 1225, 1289 (1998) ("[M]arriage is subject to many tangible social conventions that announce and reinforce the parties' commitment. Beyond this, behavior in marriage is subject to long-standing societal expectations that tend to constrain the parties' freedom and influence them toward trustworthiness, fidelity, honesty, and altruism.").

100 Gregg Strauss, *Why the State Cannot "Abolish Marriage": A Partial Defense of Legal Marriage*, 91 Ind. L.J. 1261, 1301 (2015); *see also* Elizabeth S. Scott, *The Legal Construction of Norms: Social Norms and the Legal Regulation of Marriage*, 86 Va. L. Rev. 1901, 1910 (2000) ("[M]arital norms encourage sexual fidelity, openness, emotional sharing, and altruism.").

101 Stephen R. Galoob & Adam Hill, *Norms, Attitudes, and Compliance*, 50 Tulsa L. Rev. 613, 614, 619 (2015) (quoting Geoffrey Brennan et al., Explaining Norms 3(2013)) (quotations omitted).

102 *Id.* Classic examples of norms include the general expectation that one should keep a promise.

103 Galoob & Hill, *supra* note 101, at 614.

104 Or indeed, formally recordable at all. *See* Eric A. Posner, *Law, Economics, and Inefficient Norms*, 144 U. Pa. L. Rev. 1697, 1713 (1996).

105 Richard H. McAdams, *An Attitudinal Theory of Expressive Law*, 79 Or. L. Rev. 339, 339 (2000); Richard H. McAdams, *The Origin, Development, and Regulation of Norms*, 96 Mich. L. Rev. 338, 391 (1997).

106 McAdams, *Origin*, *supra* note 105, at 402.

law is regulating.[107] The risk here is that transforming the State's relationship to marriage will fray the tissue of norms surrounding marriage.

2 Marriage May Benefit from the Participation of Religious Couples

Despite the withering criticisms of marriage described in Section II, married couples who self-identify as religious may strengthen the norms around marriage. In one study of 4587 married couples, those who attended church regularly had "the lowest risk of divorce" even after controlling for other demographic factors.[108] This finding is not isolated. Reviewing ninety-four studies of religion and marital or parental functioning published in journals since 1980, and using meta-analytic techniques to summarize key quantitative findings across seventy-eight studies, Professor Annette Mahoney and colleagues found "greater religiousness appeared to decrease the risk of divorce" in multiple national surveys.[109] Additionally, "couples belonging to the same denomination or faith tradition" experienced a "better marital adjustment."[110]

To be sure, religious believers may struggle with conflicting beliefs: a sense of duty to remain bound, arrayed against the belief that God would also want them to be "happy," which may not be possible were they to remain married.[111] Further, religious observance is not an inoculant against

[107] Eric A. Posner, *Symbols, Signals, and Social Norms in Politics and the Law*, 27 J. Legal Stud. 765, 789 (1998) (discussing the "impact of laws on various equilibria").

[108] Vaughn R. A. Call & Tim B. Heaton, *Religious Influence on Marital Stability*, 36 J. Sci. Study Religion 383 (1997) (using panel data from the National Survey of Families and Households). Conversely, "differences in patterns of religious attendance between spouses create problems for a marriage that cannot be explained by the demographic composition of other aspects of the marriage included in this analysis." *Id.* at 387–88. The reasons why church attendance exerts this positive effect may differ for men and women. Call and Heaton found that the wife's views of marital commitment and non-marital sex were more important to marital stability than the husband's. *Id.*

[109] Annette Mahoney et al., *Religion in the Home in the 1980s and 1990s: Meta-Analytic Review and Conceptual Analysis of Links Between Religion, Marriage, and Parenting*, 15 J. Fam. Psych. 559, 560 (2001); *see also* The National Marriage Project, The State of Our Unions: Marriage in America 2012, at 72, www.stateofourunions.org/2012/SOOU2012.pdf; Deal, *supra* note 83. Findings of increased marital stability may reflect delayed divorce. Luiza Y. W. Chan & Tim B. Heaton, *Demographic Determinants of Delayed Divorce*, 13 J. of Divorce 97, 102 (1989).

[110] Annette Mahoney et al., *Marriage and the Spiritual Realm: The Role of Proximal and Distal Religious Constructs in Marital Functioning*, 13 J. Fam. Psychology 321, 321 (1999).

[111] *See* Steven M. Harris, *How Faith Influences Divorce Decisions*, Institute For Family Studies (March 13, 2017), https://ifstudies.org/blog/how-faith-influences-divorce-decisions.

divorce.[112] Still, these findings suggest that religious marriages contribute to marriage's overall stability.[113]

Religious couples are happier in their marriages, too.[114] When marriage and religion are integrated, couples perceive greater benefits from being married, report less conflict, engage in more verbal collaboration with each other and less "verbal aggression and stalemate"; they have "greater global marital adjustment."[115] Married couples who pray together report better relationships.[116]

True, engaging in "more joint religious activities" may make couples more satisfied by virtue of time spent together.[117] Shared expectations "for the marital relationship" because both have a "relationship with God" may foster intimacy in the marriage that explains these results.[118] Couples say they "sojourn" together.[119] Shared commitment appears to be explanatory, too.[120] Professor Samuel Perry found that religion influenced marital quality positively when the spouses share a commitment to religion, but negatively when one spouse is religious and the other is not.[121] Across dozens of studies, "greater religiousness ... facilitate[s] marital functioning," although the effects are "small."[122] The benefits do not disappear among the most religious couples.[123]

Children benefit, too. Individual studies find that "greater parental religiousness relates to more positive parenting and better child

[112] *See* Brinig, Chapter 10, this volume; Bix, Chapter 9, this volume.

[113] In some religious groups, earlier and more frequent child bearing occurs, lowering income and increasing divorce risk. Jennifer Glass & Philip Levchak, *Red States, Blue States, and Divorce: Understanding the Impact of Conservative Protestantism on Regional Variation in Divorce Rates*, 119 AM. J. SOC. 1002, 1008–09 (2014).

[114] Rachel Lile Colbert, Scale Development of the Religious Marital Factor Measure (Mar. 13, 2007) (unpublished Psy.D dissertation, Regent University), gradworks.umi.com/32/56/3256899.html (online questionnaire). Although positive for both genders, religiosity may influence men and women differently. *See, e.g.*, Gary L. Hansen, *The Effect of Religiosity on Factors Predicting Martial Adjustment*, 50 SOC. PSYCHOL. Q. 264, 265 (1987).

[115] Mahoney et al., *supra* note 110.

[116] Christopher G. Ellison et al., *The Couple That Prays Together: Race and Ethnicity, Religion, and Relationship Quality Among Working-Age Adults*, 72 J. MARRIAGE FAM. 963, 963 (2010).

[117] Mahoney et al., *supra* note 110, at 333. [118] Colbert, *supra* note 114. [119] *Id.*

[120] *See generally* Christopher G. Ellison & Kristin L. Anderson, *Religious Involvement and Domestic Violence Among U.S. Couples*, 40 J. SCI. STUDY RELIGION 269, 273–74 (2001).

[121] Samuel L. Perry, *A Match in Heaven? Religion-Based Marriage Decisions, Marital Quality, and the Moderating Effects of Spouse's Religious Commitment*, 123 SOC. INDICATORS RES. 203, 223 (2015).

[122] Mahoney et al., *supra* note 110, at 560.

[123] *See* Margaret R. Wilson & Erik E. Filsinger, *Religiosity and Marital Adjustment: Multidimensional Interrelationships*, 48 J. MARRIAGE & FAM. 147 (1986).

adjustment."[124] A review of the literature concluded that "[b]eing married and being involved in religious activities are generally associated with positive effects in several areas, including physical and mental health, economic outcomes, and the process of raising children."[125]

Religious couples experience less violence. This "inverse association between religious attendance and abuse persists" after controlling for the degree of social support and integration, substance and alcohol abuse, depression and low self-esteem.[126] The positive effect of church attendance "is stronger for African American men and women and for Hispanic men," groups that otherwise "experience elevated risk."[127] It is not surprising that married religious couples would experience "far-reaching, positive effects": marriage and religion "influence similar domains of life" and act through pathways that share "important parallels."[128]

But religiosity is not a panacea against unhappiness or dysfunction.[129] Some studies report mixed results, for example, that "religiosity" improved marital satisfaction among "less neurotic husbands," but not "more neurotic" ones.[130]

Religiosity has its costs. It can increase marital dependency – that is, believing that one's life would shatter or "be worse should the marriage end," especially for more fundamentalist believers.[131] It may discourage help seeking, isolating spouses in dysfunctional relationships.[132]

Nonetheless, across large groups, those who are religiously married have marriages that function positively along a number of dimensions. They are, on

124 Annette Mahoney et al., *Religion in the Home in the 1980s and 1990s: Meta-Analytic Review and Conceptual Analysis of Links Between Religion, Marriage, and Parenting*, 15 J. FAM. PSYCHOL. 559, 560 (2001).

125 Linda J. Waite & Evelyn L. Lehrer, *The Benefits from Marriage and Religion in the United States: A Comparative Analysis*, 29 POPULATION DEV. REV. 255, 255–56 (2003).

126 For men, the "protective effect" against domestic violence occurs only for those who attend church weekly, but not less frequently; for women, church attendance, however frequent, correlated with less violence. Christopher G. Ellison & Kristin L. Anderson, *Religious Involvement and Domestic Violence Among U.S. Couples*, 40 J. SCI. STUDY RELIGION 269, 273–74 (2001).

127 Christopher Ellison et al., *Race/Ethnicity, Religious Involvement, and Domestic Violence*, 13 VIOLENCE AGAINST WOMEN 1094, 1100 (2007).

128 Waite & Lehrer, *supra* note 125, at 255–56.

129 *See* Kieran T. Sullivan, *Understanding the Relationship Between Religiosity and Marriage: An Investigation of the Immediate and Longitudinal Effects of Religiosity on Newlywed Couples*, 15 J. FAM. PSYCHOL. 610 (2001). *See also* Offit, Chapter 12, this volume; Wilson and Sanders, Chapter 13, this volume.

130 Sullivan, *supra* note 129.

131 John Wilson & Marc Musick, *Religion and Marital Dependency*, 35 J. SCI. STUDY RELIGION 30, 32, 39 (1996) (reporting more marital dependency among more conservative Protestant denominations).

132 Sullivan, *supra* note 129.

balance, happier than nonreligious married couples, less likely to divorce, more collaborative, and more faithful, and less likely to report domestic violence, even after controlling for other demographic factors. This empirical snapshot, although far from perfect,[133] illuminates precisely what is at stake if religious marriage somehow withdraws from the public sphere.

3 How Would Transforming the Government's Relationship to Marriage Disturb Marriage Norms?

Indiana Representative Lucas's contractual model, like Missouri Representative Berry's shift to domestic partnerships and academic proposals described below, would sever the relationship between religious marriage and the state-recognized union. In neither instance would religious marriage solemnization cause the state-recognized union to spring into existence. The religious marriage would now become separable from the state-supported union.

Cleaving apart what has always been intertwined aspects of marriage – civil and religious – carries the risk that the norms and understandings surrounding marriage become torn or frayed. How would this occur? It would not occur if people who enter the state-sponsored union, by contract or registration as a partnership, still understand it to be marriage – and if the same fraction of people continue to embrace that state-sponsored union, whatever it is called, *and* also religiously marry. There would then be no reason to worry about altering the norms and legal understandings around marriage. The title would change, and little else.

If, however, people entering the new state-sponsored union come over time to see it as something wholly distinct from marriage as society now understands it, then different norms governing that union may develop. Indeed, longtime marriage critics have argued for something other than "marriage" precisely to shed patriarchy and other negative norms they ascribe to marriage.[134] There is no assurance that the security, satisfaction, and safety many enjoy in their marriages will carry over to this new union. Moreover, if couples can contract for some but not all the protective features associated with marriage now, there is every reason to believe norms around the union would change.

133 Donald H. Baucom, *Religion and the Science of Relationships: Is a Happy Marriage Possible?* 15 J. Fam. Psychol. 652 (2001) (arguing for more specific hypotheses and study of mechanisms).

134 *See* Fineman, *supra* note 58; Polikoff, *supra* note 59.

Religious marriage is shoring up the marriage culture through long-term, stable, monogamous relationships in which both parties are physically secure. As a part of the broader marriage culture, religious marriage increases the fraction of well-functioning marriages among all married couples, reinforcing the norms associated with the cultural status known as "marriage" for everyone.

Substituting a different substrate for state benefits changes the relative attractiveness of marriage to some couples and may affect the number of couples who ultimately marry. It is an article of faith that the benefits accorded to couples when they assume the mantle of marriage "channels" couples into that status.[135] By no longer privileging all marriages, including religious ones, society impoverishes the cluster of goods that motivates couples to marry. True, religious couples have independent reasons to continue to marry (such as the belief that God sanctifies the relationship or because they are pressured, or encouraged, by their religious community) – in which case, they may continue to share in norms around "marriage." Less religious couples may not share those reasons, however, with fewer participating in the positive norms around marriage.

Unwinding the civil and religious aspects of marriage would harm not only the marriage culture but religious marriages, too. If religious adherents never take an additional step to ensure their marriages have civil effects, they would lose out on the valuable protections. While religiously married couples benefit from a religious experience of marriage, none of the studies previously mentioned show that religious marriages function well *only* because of religious commitments. The civil regulation of marriages likely reinforces religious norms of permanence and sharing. Civil exit rules increase the transaction cost of divorce and force sharing of marital property or one's income through property division and alimony rules. This may encourage struggling religious couples to work on their relationships. In other words, the difficulty of civil exit strengthens marriage.[136]

A retreat of religious marriage from the public sphere also risks affecting the social signal marriage sends. The *First Things* pledge to solemnize religious

[135] Carl E. Schneider, *The Channeling Function in Family Law*, 20 Hofstra L. Rev. 495 (1992).

[136] *Cf.* Sarah W. Whitton et al., *Attitudes Toward Divorce, Commitment, and Divorce Proneness in First Marriages and Remarriages*, J. Marriage & Family 276 (2013) (observing that the easier it is to exit a relationship, the more often people will do so, "making the marriage more fragile"). Religious communities may also lose an important entrance into the couple's life – the religious wedding – which can help bind couples more strongly to a religious faith community.

marriages but refuse to assist with civil effects places a burden on those who religiously marry to take additional steps to enter the state-supported union, with its attendant benefits and protections.[137] And so, too, does Representative Berry's proposal to change Missouri's existing regulation of marriage. If couples religiously marry but never cement the state-recognized union, the subset of religious-only marriages, which empirically are stronger relationships, may diverge from, and be seen as distinct from, the set of civil relationships. Put another way, what was once conceived of as a single thing – marriage – will increasingly be seen as two distinct categories, which may or may not share a single set of norms.

Indeed, it would be quite remarkable if basic parameters of the new state-recognized union did not diverge from those associated now with marriage. Just as one cannot turn over a glass of ice water and expect only the water to come out, leaving the ice behind, severing the state-recognized union from religious marriage assumes the two aspects can be divorced without losing religion's positive influence on the civil relationship.

While it is true that some countries long ago stripped religious authorities of the power to bind couples with legal effect, leaving "marriage" entirely to civil authorities, political leaders such as Germany's Bismarck rationalized the State's monopoly over marriage as increasing its power over religion and individual citizens – outcomes that many would find problematic.[138] Moreover, in countries where civil authorities exercise exclusive control over marriage, a significantly smaller fraction of citizens conduct their intimate relationships within marriage.[139] Countless differences between these cultures and their legal systems may account for differences in how couples

[137] Some people marry for the romantic cache. *See* STATE OF OUR UNIONS, *supra* note 111. If marriage is divorced from the State, some couples may marry for the romantic meaning, if not the religious import despite available alternatives, but may enter only religious marriages, not the benefit-conferring civil status.

[138] *See* Heiner de Wall & Andreas Gestrich, *Constitutional Complexity and Confessional Diversity*, *in* THE DYNAMICS OF RELIGIOUS REFORM IN NORTHERN EUROPE, 1780–1920: POLITICAL AND LEGAL PERSPECTIVES 149, 174–80 (Keith Robbins ed., 2010).

[139] *See* Laurie DeRose et al., *Family Instability and Early Childhood Health in the Developing World*, WORLD FAMILY MAP 14–16 (2014), worldfamilymap.ifstudies.org/2014/articles/family-instability-and-early-childhood-health (reporting highest levels of cohabitation in Europe and Latin America); Omar G. Encarnación, *Why Latin American Courts Favor Gay Rights*, N.Y. TIMES (Jan. 29, 2014), www.nytimes.com/roomfordebate/2014/01/29/why-is-latin-america-so-progressive-on-gay-rights (describing Latin America's system of civil marriage only); Jonathan Luxmoore, *European Countries Distinguish Between Religious, Civil Marriages*, NAT'L CATHOLIC REP. (Apr. 15, 2015), www.ncronline.org/news/global/european-countries-distinguish-between-religious-civil-marriages (describing separation of civil and religious marriage in Europe).

structure, and the State regulates, intimate relationships – but the increasing irrelevancy of marriage in these countries should give current proponents pause.

The social cues signaling one is married may change, as well. Today, religious marriage and civil marriage are outwardly indistinguishable to the public because married couples, whether religious or not, usually signal their commitment by wearing wedding rings or otherwise informing the world of their status.[140] Indiana Representative Lucas's proposal to "get the government out of marriage" effectively erases the status now known as civil marriage, substituting a private contractual regime. Individuals who contract may or may not continue to outwardly declare themselves married. If they do not declare themselves as married, one would expect over time that different norms would develop around contractual, intimate relationships. Couples who previously may have married civilly increasingly may not share, or buy into, many norms now associated with marriage.

In short, whether one erases the civil status now known as "marriage" – or leaves the civil part to mere contract – there is the risk that fewer Americans will participate in relationships with the protective features of religious marriage. Overall, the religious marriage culture would suffer by becoming more isolated and less germane.

Society should care about this outcome if fewer children are raised in households that benefit from protective norms, including long-term stability, faithfulness, and less domestic violence.[141] As with many things affecting the family, the gravest impact may fall on the most vulnerable Americans. Professor Helen Alvaré, an adviser to Pope Benedict XVI's Pontifical Council for the Laity, believes those who would suffer most from the change would be "the poor, new immigrants and racial minorities."[142] Alvaré argues that "[t]he last thing [the vulnerable] need is for religious people, and religious institutions – who have and practice a thick form of marital commitment, with a long history of overlap with civil marriage – to abandon the public square by

[140] The wearing of rings by both sexes has changed with time, with 80% of men wearing wedding rings after World War II, versus 15% "at the end of the Great Depression." Eric V. Copage, *Without This Ring, I Thee Wed*, N.Y. TIMES, Apr. 15, 2011, at ST14. Some committed non-marital couples wear rings, including gay couples who were once locked out of marriage, to signal permanence and commitment. Stephanie Hallett, *Gay Engagement: Which Etiquette Rules Apply?* HUFFINGTON POST (Dec. 08, 2011), www.huffingtonpost.com/2011/12/08/gay-engagement-rules_n_1132852.html.

[141] *See* Weiner, Chapter 11, this volume, for an empirical snapshot of parenting outside marriage.

[142] Brian Fraga, *Separating Religious and Civil Marriage*, OUR SUNDAY VISITOR (June 6, 2012), www.osv.com/OSVNewsweekly/ByIssue/Article/TabId/735/ArtMID/13636/ArticleID/8611/Separating-religious-and-civil-marriage.aspx.

removing the witness of marriage which we solemnize and practice as faithful, permanent and oriented to children."[143]

B Critiquing Individual Proposals to Get the Government Out of Marriage

Many of the notions for getting the government out of the marriage business are critically "short on substance."[144] This section critiques the variants on this idea.

1 First Proposal: Retrenching Religious Marriage from Civil Solemnization

One conception of getting the government out of the marriage business is for religious adherents to withdraw their marriages from the public realm. For proponents, foisting back onto the government the sole authority for civil solemnization avoids complicity with same-sex marriage.[145] The *First Things* pledge would accomplish this separation by solemnizing religious marriages but refusing to memorialize the civil marriage with state officials; the couple would have to seek a civil marriage separately.[146] The primary risk: the couple religiously marries but never takes the second step of civilly marrying – missing out on the State's legal protections.

Of course, religious believers could "be married first in a civil ceremony and then, if they so choose, have the marriage blessed by the Church in a religious ceremony."[147] The risk here is that couples civilly marry but may never bother to marry religiously. Some religious communities may not perceive this as a loss if the couple was never likely to participate in the community of believers. Presumably, however, solemnizing a marriage religiously is an

[143] *Id.*

[144] Stella Morabito, 5 *Questions For Libertarians Who Support Privatizing Marriage*, FEDERALIST (July 28, 2015), thefederalist.com/2015/07/28/5-questions-for-libertarians-who-support-privatizing-marriage/.

[145] *See* Shikha Dalmia, *Privatizing Marriage is a Terrible Idea*, REASON.COM (July 21, 2015), reason.com/archives/2015/07/21/privatizing-marriage-is-a-terrible-idea; *see also supra* notes 8 and 11.

[146] George J. Marlin, *After* Obergefell: *What is to be Done?* CATHOLIC THING (Aug. 8, 2015), www.thecatholicthing.org/2015/08/08/after-obergefell-what-is-to-be-done/ (speculating that the government will strip religion "of its powers to represent the state in marriage" if religious figures "stand[] [their] ground" and refuse to solemnize same-sex marriage).

[147] *Id.*

important introduction to a faith community, opening the possibility that the couple becomes more active in the faith.

Collapsing religious marriage with civil marriage is a good thing: society wants religious marriages to have civil effects. Without civil effects, religious adherents will be stranded in the position of mere cohabitants under the law, leaving them with inadequate remedies.[148] In such a scheme, traditionally vulnerable dependents, such as women and children, lose. Even if child support is adequate, children suffer when their custodial parent, usually the mother, experiences severe financial strain.

To see the cataclysmic effect that a failure to secure marriage's civil incidents could have for women, one need look no farther than the eighty-five Shari'a courts operating throughout Great Britain.[149] As members of insular communities, many women who appear before these courts have religious marriages, but not civilly recognized ones. Such a system leaves women with no recourse other than the Shari'a court for dissolution of the marriage.

Under the school of Islamic law most often applied, the *Hanafi* school, the norms governing property division, spousal maintenance, and custody sharply depart from what would happen under British law if these women civilly divorced, resulting in outcomes that in the U.S. would be against public policy. For instance, fathers receive custody of male children older than age seven and female children older than age nine upon divorce, without consideration of the child's best interests.[150] Men are entitled to divorce by unilateral proclamation, but a woman must satisfy certain requirements to end her marriage – not least of which is that she must sometimes buy her way out by paying back the *mahr* – a payment received by her for marrying – or by forfeiting the right to any deferred *mahr* that would otherwise be due.[151] Women do not receive an equitable share of property acquired during the marriage and titled in the man's name, and receive alimony only for several months following divorce, known as the "*iddat* period."[152] Not surprisingly, under British law, these women would receive considerably more protection,

[148] *See* Weiner, Chapter 11, this volume. In states recognizing common law marriage, vulnerable parties may become married by virtue of co-residence, agreement to be bound, and holding out as married; in that case, they would receive full marriage remedies. *See* John DeWitt Gregory, Peter N. Swisher, & Robin Fretwell Wilson, Understanding Family Law 36–38 (4th ed. 2013).

[149] Robin Fretwell Wilson, *The Perils of Privatized Marriage*, *in* Marriage and Divorce in a Multi-Cultural Context: Reconsidering the Boundaries of Civil Law and Religion (Joel A. Nichols ed., 2011).

[150] Robin Fretwell Wilson, *Privatizing Family Law in the Name of Religion*, 18 Wm. & Mary Bill Rts. J. 925, Fig. 1 (2010).

[151] *Id.* at Fig. 2. (discussing procedural hurdles to divorce for women).

[152] *Id.*

including equitable division of the couple's assets, and alimony if the wife is unable to provide for herself.[153] Although an extreme example, when religious marriages have no civil effects, vulnerable parties may be left destitute and without access to their children.

Equally unconscionable results can occur upon a spouse's death. This is so because civil marriage provides important protections after death. Consider one hypothetical: a couple has two sons and one daughter; after the husband passes away, his wife, children, and both of his parents survive him. If British law governed the outcome in this case, the woman would receive 100% of her husband's estate upon his death. In the absence of a civilly recognized marriage, the outcome under the *Hanafi* school of Islamic law is starkly different: the widow now receives a mere 12.5% of her husband's estate.[154] Compounding the woman's plight, many families in Great Britain ignore duties under Islamic law to care for divorced or widowed relatives, foisting the widow onto the social safety net rather than caring for her themselves.[155] Outside of civilly recognized marriage, the State does not have many tools to fix such unconscionable outcomes.

Of course, not all religious understandings will be as harsh as those described here. Moreover, some religious believers may seek to do right by an ex-spouse or widow, although they may be defeated in doing so by religious norms – for example, by Islamic rules limiting who can be named in a will.[156]

Educating religious adherents to civilly bind themselves before or after religiously marrying is a possibility. The insularity of some religious communities will pose a challenge to such efforts, as might countervailing advice from other community members or religious leaders themselves.[157] Indeed, many religious communities that now see civil marriage as tainted likely would advise congregants to avoid what they see as the "black stain" of civil marriage post *Obergefell*.

2 Second Proposal: Scrapping State Support for Marriage in Favor of Enforcing Contracts

U.S. Senator Paul and Indiana Representative Lucas propose abolishing state-sponsored marriage, leaving couples to contract for rights and obligations in the relationship. Indiana House Bill 1163, now before the legislature for a second year, would eliminate the State's off-the-rack regulation

[153] *Id.* at 930. [154] *Id.* at 945. [155] *Id.* at 947. [156] *See id.*

[157] *See* Offit, Chapter 12, this volume; Wilson & Sanders, Chapter 13, this volume (discussing role of faith leaders).

of marriage, relying instead on couples to memorialize their own agreements for the relationship under Indiana contract law.[158] Age limits and other constraints that now apply to marriage would govern the ability to contract, dissolution would "happen through the courts," and contract terms that would now be void in marital agreements would still be void.[159] Couples could contract around duties of support after a marriage, but not during it; they could decide not to share property; but contract terms that would imperil a child's support or welfare would not be allowed.[160] Lucas believes House Bill 1163 to be "an all-around win" and marriage "wouldn't change."[161]

It is simply implausible that a couple's relationship left to contract would substantively arrive at agreements that approximate the status of being married. Couples are unlikely to bargain for all the duties between spouses under civil law, if for no other reasons than a lack of knowledge or power. Would they know enough to require confidentiality of communications or certain property distribution upon death?[162]

When the State sets the terms of the relationship, it makes the benefits and risks easier to assume; permitting couples to privately set the terms of their relationship eliminates this channelling function of marriage.[163] Arguably, there are "social benefits to the way the state has structured marriage – such as the benefits that might come from the guarantee of an equal, or near-equal, division of marital resources upon divorce – benefits that might be lost if parties are allowed to alter the state-supplied terms."[164]

Equally troubling, couples rarely sign contracts now to privately order their marital affairs.[165] Cohabitants also rarely enter into agreements, and when they do, the agreements "rarely meet traditional standards for enforceable contracts."[166] While "all but two American jurisdictions will enforce express cohabitation contracts," some "states limit enforcement to express or written contracts, out of the same pragmatic concerns that underlie statutes of frauds,

158 Wang, *supra* note 17. 159 *Id.*

160 H.B. 1163, 120th Gen. Assemb., 2d Reg. Sess. (Ind. 2017). 161 Wang, *supra* note 17.

162 *See supra* note 150 (discussing protections upon death).

163 Carl E. Schneider & Margaret F. Brinig, An Invitation to Family Law: Principles, Process and Perspectives 157 (1996).

164 *See* Brian H. Bix, *The ALI Principles and Agreements: Seeking a Balance Between Status and Contract*, *in* Reconceiving the Family: Critique on the American Law Institute's Principles of the Law of Family Dissolution 380 (Robin Fretwell Wilson ed., 2006).

165 *See* Brian Bix, *Bargaining in the Shadow of Love: The Enforcement of Premarital Agreements And How We Think About Marriage*, 40 Wm. & Mary L. Rev. 145 (1998). There is a dearth of empirical studies of whether couples enter agreements, however. Merle Weiner, A Parent-Partner Status for American Family Law 396–97 (2015).

166 Strauss, *supra* note 28, at 1296.

such as the ease of false allegations, the lengthiness of court battles, and the difficulty of determining precise terms."[167] Some things that couples may well value and would contract for, such as sexual access or fidelity, cannot form the basis for an enforceable agreement, jeopardizing enforcement of other bargained-for exchanges around property, duties of support, or financial interdependence.[168]

A purely contractual regime raises concerns about the bargaining power and capability of the parties.[169] Bargaining for protections is fraught with pitfalls: "[I]t is hard to think clearly about the financial terms of the end of a romantic relationship when one is at an early period of the relationship."[170] Overly optimistic soon-to-be newlyweds may view their relationship through "rose-colored glasses," discounting the possibility that they will ever break up.[171] Although slightly less than 50% of first marriages end in divorce, 100% of engaged couples say they will not.[172] Any bargain reached is only valid if there is full disclosure.[173] Finally, most couples "slide into" cohabiting, and many slide from cohabiting into marriage; there often is no natural opportunity to reach express agreements before entering the relationship.[174]

Reducing the social understanding around marriage to whatever terms a couple can agree to skips an important step: solemnization of the relationship.[175] Whether by a civil authority or a religious figure, solemnization helps drive home the significance of marriage – something the State quite rightly wishes to reinforce.

167 *Id.* at 1278.

168 American Law Institute's Principles of the Law of Family Dissolution Ch. 1 (2000) (recommending non-enforcement of any term that would introduce fault); *In re* Mehren, 118 Cal. App. 4th 1167, 1171 (Cal. Ct. App. 2004); Diosdado v. Diosdado, 97 Cal. App. 4th 470, 496–97 (Cal. Ct. App. 2002); *Unif. Premarital and Marital Agreements Act*, Nat'l Conference of Comm'rs on Uniform State Laws § 10(b)(3) (2012), www.uniformlaws.org/shared/docs/premarital%20and%20marital%20agreements/2012_pmaa_final.pdf (making unenforceable a term that purports to modify the grounds for a court-decreed separation or marital dissolution) [hereinafter UPMAA].

169 Carol Sanger, *A Case for Civil Marriage*, 27 Cardozo L. Rev. 1311, 1312 (2006).

170 *See* Bix, *supra* note 166, at 379 (discussing "bounded rationality").

171 *Social Indicators of Marital Health & Well-Being*, State of Our Unions (Aug. 27, 2016), www.stateofourunions.org/2011/social_indicators.php#divorce.

172 Sanger, *supra* note 169. 173 *See* UPMAA § 9(d).

174 Jeffry H. Larson & Thomas B. Holman, *Premarital Predictors of Marital Quality and Stability*, 43 Fam. Rel. 13, 13 (1994); W. Bradford Wilcox, *Men and Women Often Expect Different Things when They Move in Together*, Atlantic (July 8, 2013), www.theatlantic.com/sexes/archive/2013/07/men-and-women-often-expect-different-things-when-they-move-in-together/277571/.

175 *Indiana Marriage Laws*, Universal Life Church Monastery, www.themonastery.org/wedding-laws/Indiana.

Couples may gloss over significant differences in how committed each person is to the relationship.[176] Even if they set pen to paper, offer and acceptance would be thoroughly unromantic:

> Intimate partners would have to make offers regarding financial, homemaking, caretaking, and domestic services. They would need to place an economic value on their contributions to the relationship and bargain for services in return. Consider, first, what is required for intimate partners to enter binding contracts for economic services such as domestic or wage labor. The first hurdle is formation – offer, acceptance, and consideration. Where are the offer and the acceptance? Intimate partners rarely make explicit arrangements for dividing economic services, and even when they do, their arrangements fluctuate. … [Many] cohabitants may decide to move in together and make agreements about rent or bills, but they rarely negotiate chores.[177]

Couples will inevitably overlook important questions because they simply do not know enough about the duties and obligations that marital status would impose or address in order to contract for similar terms. Consequently, the law will have to supply significant legal gap fillers.[178]

Because couples likely will not write down their understandings, most litigated "agreements will be implied-in-fact contracts for which the court infers the parties' promises from their conduct."[179] Yet, implied-in-fact contracts may not provide more relief. A court may decide that the services were "rendered gratuitously," warranting no compensation after the fact.[180] Few states are willing to force repayment by one partner for the domestic services of the other.[181]

In the absence of a contract, the weaker earning party will not have access to remedies, unless the background law that currently governs cohabitating relationships changes.[182] Equitable remedies are unlikely to provide an adequate backstop. As Professor Gregg Strauss notes, cohabitants can seek

> restitution for money or services contributed to the other's property or business, but cohabitants typically fail to recover money or services that "can be characterized as part of the ordinary give-and-take of a shared life," such as domestic chores or living expenses. Even if one cohabitant contributed more

176 Michael Pollard & Kathleen Mullan Harris, *Cohabitation and Marriage Intensity: Consolidation, Intimacy, and Commitment*, RAND (2013), www.rand.org/content/dam/rand/pubs/working_papers/WR1000/WR1001/RAND_WR1001.pdf.

177 Strauss, *supra* note 28, at 1294. 178 Sanger, *supra* note 169.

179 Strauss, *supra* note 28, at 1293. 180 *Id.* at 1279. 181 *Id.* at 1279.

182 *See* Bix, Chapter 9, this volume.

to the couple's domestic life, courts assume that the couple received a mutual benefit and refuse (as in marriage) to balance their relationship ledgers.[183]

Children may also "be harmed by the enforcement of certain ... agreements."[184] For example, an agreement between adults may adversely affect a child's right to support. Absent thick notions of state law public policy constraints on such terms,[185] a purely contractual regime may jeopardize the interests and well-being of children.

For religious couples in particular, a purely contractual regime is likely to be unsatisfactory. Contractual terms restricting divorce to "fault" grounds such as infidelity, or deciding dispositively who would receive custody of any children, would be against public policy and unenforceable.[186]

A contractual regime may encourage tallying by each party, rather than norms of sharing that foster give and take: "Each [spouse] would have an incentive to keep track of who pays for dinner, cleans the dishes, or mows the lawn. They need an accurate tally, both because nonperformance can justify a future demand for compensation and because sufficient nonperformance can be a material breach that justifies ending the relationship and seeking damages."[187]

Apart from the limits of contract, marriage as a status shields families from oversight.[188] "Abolishing state-recognized marriage would actually separate family members in the eyes of the law," erasing marital benefits like the presumption of paternity for married husbands or the family's "veil of privacy."[189] While scholars have been critical of family privacy since it can

183 Strauss, *supra* note 28, at 1282–83. Moreover, "before a court can decide whether it is unjust for the defendant to retain benefits from the relationship, the court must make judgments about the level and type of commitment in the relationship." *Id.* at 1297. Even if restitution became "generally available for intimate parties ... restitution law openly relies on moral judgments about the nature of our relationships." *Id.* at 1296.

184 *See* Bix, *supra* note 164, at 380 (describing how pre-marital agreements affect women and children).

185 If courts police the agreement between cohabitants for substantive and procedural unfairness, the law will introduce "status norms on couples" at the back end, instead of at the front end when the couple decides to marry. Strauss, *supra* note 28, at 1310. Couples will necessarily have less notice of what those norms will be.

186 Mehren, *supra* note 168.

187 Strauss, *supra* note 28, at 1295. Moreover, when a partner "falls short, the other would have an incentive to insist on prompt performance; otherwise, a court might later interpret his acquiescence as a rescission of the original arrangement." *Id.*

188 *See* McGuire v. McGuire, 59 N.W.2d 336 (Neb. 1955) (refusing to intervene in dispute between spouses over financial support beyond "necessaries"). Refusing to police choices during intact relationships, of course, leaves the weaker spouse without remedies other than divorce.

189 *Id.*

enable domestic violence, the State's noninterventionist stance does provide families the autonomy to structure their own relationships.[190] Privacy and autonomy from the State are two goods that libertarians including Rand should be especially loathe to disturb since doing away with the status of marriage may increase government involvement in people's personal lives.[191]

3 Third Proposal: Redubbing "Marriage" as "Domestic Partnership"

After Judge Vaughn Walker released his opinion in *Perry v. Schwarzenegger*,[192] invalidating Proposition 8, a number of prominent voices called for the "end [of] marriage[]." *Time Magazine*, for example, proposed:

> [G]ive gay and straight couples alike the same license, a certificate confirming them as a family, and call it a civil union – anything, really, other than marriage. For people who feel the word *marriage* is important, the next stop after the courthouse could be the church, where they could bless their union with all the religious ceremony they wanted. Religions would lose nothing of their role in sanctioning the kinds of unions that they find in keeping with their tenets. And for nonbelievers and those who find the word *marriage* less important, the civil-union license issued by the state would be all they needed to unlock [marriage's] benefits.[193]

Professors Richard H. Thaler and Cass R. Sunstein have advocated a "freedom expanding" approach: substitute "civil union" for the word "marriage" across all laws. Civil unions would become the only "legally recognized domestic partnership";[194] marriages "would be strictly private matters, performed by religious and other private organizations [eliminating] the same one-size-fits all arrangement of state marriage."[195]

190 For a pair of competing views on the value of family autonomy, *see* LEE E. TEITELBAUM, FAMILY HISTORY AND FAMILY LAW (1985) and BRUCE C. HAFEN, THE FAMILY AS ENTITY (1989).

191 *See* Dalmia, *supra* note 145; Jason Kuznicki, *Marriage Against the State Toward a New View of Civil Marriage*, CATO POLICY ANALYSIS, Jan. 12, 2011, http://object.cato.org/sites/cato.org/files/pubs/pdf/PA671.pdf.

192 704 F. Supp. 2d 921 (N.D. Cal. 2010), http://documents.nytimes.com/us-district-court-decision-perry-v-schwarzenegger.

193 Lindenberger, *supra* note 13.

194 MACEDO, *supra* note 45, at 120; RICHARD H. THALER & CASS R. SUNSTEIN, NUDGE: IMPROVING DECISIONS ABOUT HEALTH, WEALTH, AND HAPPINESS (2009).

195 MACEDO, *supra* note 45 (describing THALER & SUNSTEIN, *supra* note 194). Professor Robin West has advanced a related proposal that differs in a crucial respect: civil unions and marriages would exist "side by side." ROBIN WEST, MARRIAGE, SEXUALITY, AND GENDER 315 (2007). Entering into a civil union would entitle a couple "to the state's support, including those

The struggle over who owns marriage – religion or the State – has its genesis in the "enormous array of benefits"[196] the State uses to channel couples into marriage.[197] It is murky whether the federal government will continue to treat registered domestic partners as they do married spouses now that *Obergefell* has opened marriage to everyone, gay or straight, since equal treatment in taxes and other matters was driven by the patent unfairness of gay couples being able to marry – and treated as married – in some states and not others.[198] In any event, nothing compels a state to accord the benefits of marriage to couples who enter into other statuses elsewhere.[199]

Concerned about eliminating the "dichotomy between single and married [that] does not do justice to what people might choose," Thaler and Sunstein seek to "end the state monopoly on ... marriage [because it] gives public authorities the sole power to confer official legitimacy, a stamp of approval of immense importance."[200] For them, it is far more preferable for "religious organizations to set their own rules regarding who could marry."[201] In this scheme, only private institutions, not the State, would recognize something called "marriage."[202]

First published in 2008, Thaler and Sunstein's minimalist vision has taken on greater relevance since *Obergefell*.[203] Politically, redubbing marriages as civil unions would likely be seen as "a form of leveling down."[204] To the extent that any redubbing reflects animus, it would be constitutionally suspect.[205]

Professor Steven Macedo wonders whether society can now "drop the term" marriage, as Missouri Representative Berry proposes, since the Supreme Court decided the marriage question on due process grounds as a fundamental

supports states now bestow upon married couples." Even though both statuses would coexist, civil unions "would be understood to be the ordinary, normal, accepted means by which the state involves itself in family life," becoming "the norm *over time*."

As Maryland debated its same-sex marriage legislation, one legislator introduced a measure to recognize civil unions, along with marriage, as a way to resolve the religious issues around marriage. 2008 Md. Laws HB1112.

196 Thaler & Sunstein, *supra* note 194. 197 Schneider & Brinig, *supra* note 163, at 157.

198 Heidi L. Brady & Robin Fretwell Wilson, *The Precarious Status of Domestic Partnerships in a Post-*Obergefell *World*, 24 Elder Law Journal 49 (2016).

199 Steve Sanders, *Is the Full Faith and Credit Clause Still "Irrelevant" to Same-Sex Marriage?: Toward a Reconsideration of the Conventional Wisdom*, 89 Ind. L.J. 95, 96 (2016).

200 Macedo, *supra* note 45; Thaler & Sunstein, *supra* note 194. 201 *Id.* 202 *Id.*

203 Obergefell, *supra* note 2. 204 Macedo, *supra* note 45.

205 Some read Justice Kennedy's opinion in *Obergefell*, though at times "difficult to follow," as saying a civil union granting the same set of rights and responsibilities to all married couples would not be constitutionally suspect – so long as the dropping of the term "marriage" was not based on animus toward same-sex couples. *See* Kenji Yoshino, A *New Birth of Freedom?:* Obergefell v. Hodges, 129 Harv. L. Rev. 173–74 (2015).

right.[206] One reading of *Obergefell* may be that the State cannot withdraw the civil status known as marriage.[207] A second is that if the State has a civil status known as marriage, it must be open to lesbian and gay couples, but governments need not give tangible benefits to marriages at all.[208]

Finally, to the extent that this renaming would remove the requirement that an authorized celebrant must solemnize the civil status, the significance of the choice to enter a civil union may be lost on the couple.[209] And as noted earlier, renaming the supported status risks disturbing the web of understandings around marriage. Reacting to Representative Berry's proposal, Missouri Catholic Conference Executive Director Mike Hoey asked, "If you replace marriage with domestic union, will people still take [marriage] as seriously?"[210]

IV CONCLUSION

In the firestorm ignited by *Obergefell*, some want to allay the concerns of religious objectors by distancing the State from the institution of marriage. Not only would a breach between the State and marriage fail to materially resolve the religious liberty tensions Senator Adams catalogues (Chapter 21, this volume), but it also threatens to diminish the institution of marriage for the religious and secular alike. Every predictive judgment is that divorcing marriage from the State would be self-defeating. An unwinding would likely mean that fewer people of faith would channel into state-recognized unions, shearing those couples of the powerful protections and benefits the State provides.

206 *Id.*

207 In concluding that "[i]t demeans gays and lesbians for the State to lock them out of a central institution of the Nation's society," the Court noted that marriage has long been "a great public institution, giving character to our whole civil polity," that it is a "keystone of the Nation's social order," and that "[s]tates have contributed to the fundamental character of marriage by placing it at the center of many facets of the legal and social order." Obergefell, *supra* note 2, at 2590, 2601–02. Although "the state itself makes marriage all the more precious by the significance it attaches to it," it is unclear whether the State can withdraw the "respected status and material benefits [it bestows] on married couples." *Id.* at 2601–02; *id.* at 2613 (Roberts, C.J., dissenting).

208 *See* Obergefell, *supra* note 2. In other passages, the Court's decision reads much more narrowly. "The Constitution, however, does not permit the State to bar same-sex couples from marriage on the same terms as accorded to couples of the opposite sex." *Id.* at 2607. Indeed, the Court explicitly acknowledged that states are "free to vary the benefits they confer on all married couples," which presumably would encompass extending no benefits at all. *Id.* at 2601.

209 *Indiana Marriage Laws*, UNIVERSAL LIFE CHURCH MONASTERY, www.themonastery.org/wedding-laws/indiana.

210 Ballentine, *supra* note 40.

Further, the norms around marriage are delicate and complicated, creating the need to proceed with caution. An unwinding risks a disruption of those norms by altering the cultural fabric of the institution – potentially making *all* marriages, both civil and religious, less beneficial for participants. Ironically, the chorus of voices calling for the government to "get out of marriage" have latched onto a vintage idea long pursued by critics of marriage, who see it as patriarchal and oppressive. The idea had no takers then, and it should not now. A far more measured course would provide thick protections for people to live out their faith convictions about marriage, while ensuring that marriage as a civil institution remains as beneficial as it is now.[211]

[211] *See* Adams, Chapter 21, this volume.

17

Why No Polygamy

John Witte, Jr.

Robert W. Woodruff Professor of Law; McDonald Distinguished Professor; and Director, Center for the Study of Law and Religion, Emory University School of Law

A century and a half ago, Mormons made international headlines by claiming a First Amendment right to practice polygamy,[1] despite criminal laws against it. In four cases from 1879 to 1890, the United States Supreme Court firmly rejected their claims.[2] Part of the Court's argument was historical: the common law has always defined marriage as monogamous, and to change those rules "would be a return to barbarism."[3] Part of the argument was prudential: religious liberty can never become a license to violate general criminal laws lest chaos ensue. And part of the argument was sociological: monogamous marriage "is the cornerstone of civilization," and it cannot be touched without upending our whole culture.[4] These millennium-old prohibitions on polygamy are still the law of the land today – not only in America, but also in 121 of the world's 198 nations, including all of Europe and Latin America, as well as Russia, China, Japan, and much of India.[5]

This chapter is distilled from my book, John Witte, Jr., The Western Case for Monogamy Over Polygamy (2015) and used herein with the publisher's permission.

1 I am using the term "polygamy" colloquially to include both polygyny (one man with two or more wives) and polyamory (one woman with two or more husbands). Classically, the term "polygamy" covered all manner of other forms of plural union, too, some of which had their own distinct names. For an overview of the shifting and confusing terminology, *see* the Appendix in John Witte, Jr., The Western Case for Monogamy Over Polygamy (2015), 27–33.

2 Late Corp. of the Church of Jesus Christ of Latter-Day Saints v. United States, 136 U.S. 1, 66 (1890); Davis v. Beason, 133 U.S. 333, 374 (1890); Murphy v. Ramsey, 114 U.S. 15, 35 (1885); Reynolds v. United States, 98 U.S. 145, 162 (1879).

3 Late Corp., 136 U.S. at 49.

4 *Cf.* Davis v. Beason, *supra* note 2, at 345 (discussing the "basis of the idea of the family, as consisting in and springing from the union for life of one man and one woman in the holy estate of matrimony; the sure foundation of all that is stable and noble in our civilization").

5 Witte, *supra* note 1, at 8–21.

The question of polygamy is back in the headlines today in America and other Western lands. Fundamentalist Mormons and various Muslim, Hmong, and other emigres from Asia, Africa, and the Middle East are pressing new arguments to practice polygamy on grounds of religious freedom and the right to cultural self-determination. Various liberal scholars have now joined their cause, pressing arguments of sexual liberty, equality, and autonomy.[6] Traditional criminal prohibitions against adultery, abortion, contraception, and sodomy, they argue, have all been struck down. Criminal prohibitions against polygamy must be repealed, too. Same-sex marriage is now constitutionally protected in twenty-three Western nations and counting. Polygamous marriages must now be allowed as well.

The first cases challenging the constitutionality of anti-polygamy laws have been filed in North America and Europe. The first rounds of public debate about the legality of polygamy have appeared in Western newspapers, journals, and social media, with many writers favoring polygamy. The first wave of popular media portrayals of good polygamous families has now broken with shows such as *Big Love* and *Sister Wives*, stoking the cultural imagination and sympathy much as *Ozzie and Harriet* and *Little House on the Prairie* did for prior generations. Just as same-sex marriage advocates moved first to decriminalize sodomy and then pressed for the recognition of same-sex marriage, so pro-polygamy advocates aim first to repeal traditional criminal laws against polygamy and then to include polygamy among the marriage options recognized by the state.[7]

The traditional Western arguments against polygamy and same-sex unions, however, are strikingly different. Same-sex relations were regarded as unnatural and immoral sexual taboos that violated biblical norms.[8] Polygamy was regarded as a harm crime that victimizes wives and children, correlates with other crimes and abuses, and threatens good citizenship and political stability. Same-sex opposition was largely Christian in inspiration, opposition that has now faded with the church's waning political influence in the West.[9] Anti-polygamy laws had pre-Christian origins and post-Christian logics that now serve to enhance rather than erode fundamental liberties.

6 *See* Strassberg, Chapter 18, this volume, for a detailed account of claims.

7 *See* Ronald C. Den Otter, In Defense of Plural Marriage (2015); Mark A. Goldfeder, Legalizing Plural Marriage: The Next Frontier in Family Law (2017).

8 *See* Section I *infra*.

9 *See "Nones" on the Rise*, Pew Research Center (Oct. 9, 2012), www.pewforum.org/2012/10/09/nones-on-the-rise/ (explaining that one in five Americans now "do not identify with any religion," a category shorthanded as "nones," while one in three adults under age 30 self-identify as "nones").

Because these legal arguments are so different, I submit that Western nations can responsibly hold the line against polygamy, even if they choose to accept same-sex marriage and its accompanying norms of sexual liberty, domestic autonomy, and nondiscrimination. I reject ideological arguments, pro and con, that anti-polygamy laws are a form of traditional Christian morality. I reject slippery slope arguments, from the right and the left, that acceptance of same-sex marriage must inevitably lead to acceptance of polygamous marriage. And I reject arguments from domestic and international sources that religious freedom norms command the accommodation, if not validation, of religious polygamists. The West may and should politely say "No" to polygamy.

I BIBLICAL AND LEGAL ARGUMENTS

The Western case against same-sex relations was (and for some still is) based on the Bible. Mosaic law commanded firmly: "You shall not lie with a male as with a woman; it is an abomination"; "If a man lies with a male as with a woman, both of them have committed an abomination; they shall both be put to death."[10] The Apostle Paul declared ominously that "the wrath of God is revealed from heaven against all ungodliness and wickedness," including specifically the acts of "sodomites," "sexual perverts," and others who succumbed to "dishonorable passions": "women [who] exchanged natural relations for unnatural, and the men [who] likewise gave up natural relations with women and were consumed with passion for one another, men committing shameless acts with men."[11] While some modern scholars see ambiguity in these passages,[12] the Christian tradition until recently treated these texts as a clear condemnation of same-sex activities and unions, let alone marriages.[13]

It was thus the church, not the state, that led the first campaigns against same-sex activities and unions in the Western tradition. The early canons of the church prohibited sodomy, buggery, transvestism, and other stated forms of "fornication" and "perversion," spiritually punishing such sins and excommunicating recalcitrant sexual sinners. These prohibitions became more

[10] Leviticus 18:22; 20:13 (using Revised Standard unless otherwise indicated).

[11] Romans 1:18–19, 24–27; 1 Corinthians 6:9–10; 1 Timothy 1:10.

[12] *See, e.g.*, AUTHORIZING MARRIAGE: CANON, TRADITION, AND CRITIQUE IN THE BLESSING OF SAME-SEX UNIONS (Mark D. Jordan et al., eds., 2006); William Stacy Johnson, A TIME TO EMBRACE: SAME-GENDER RELATIONSHIPS IN RELIGION, LAW, AND POLITICS (2d ed., 2012).

[13] JAMES A. BRUNDAGE, LAW, SEX, AND CHRISTIAN SOCIETY IN MEDIEVAL EUROPE 57, 73–74, 147–49 (1987).

detailed and severe in the Germanic penitential literature that followed, and even more so in high medieval canon laws and scholastic texts.[14] Sex between men was singled out as a particularly vile form of "unnatural" sin, even more so if it involved a cleric.[15] While a few church leaders may have winked at occasional same-sex relationships and even quietly blessed a few of them in special liturgies,[16] one cannot rewrite this history by anecdote. The overwhelming teaching and practice of the historical Christian church was to condemn same-sex relations.

Roman law, for its first 1000 years, allowed same-sex acts and relationships – though only heterosexual couples of the proper class could contract valid marriages and produce heritable children.[17] It was only after the 4th-century Christian conversion of Emperor Constantine that these biblically based norms against homosexual activities slowly soaked into Roman law. By the 6th century, the Christian Roman Emperor Justinian called sex between men an "abominable," "abhor[rent]," "diabolical," and "reprehensible vice" that is so "contrary to nature" that the practice is "not committed [even] by beasts."[18] Since the biblical days of Sodom, Justinian declared, such "impious and criminal acts" and "filthy practices" have brought "the wrath of God" unto any community that countenanced them. "[S]evere measures" were thus needed to stamp out these acts for good. This classic Christian condemnation of sodomy and same-sex activities was echoed and elaborated in the civil law, canon law, and common law traditions thereafter. By the 12th and 13th centuries, church and state courts worked together to mete out severe punishment against convicted sodomists, including death by burning, beheading, or hanging (by their testicles and penises, no less!) for egregious offenders.[19]

By marked contrast to same-sex relations, not a single command against polygamy appears in the Bible. Mosaic law, in fact, contemplated polygamy in cases of seduction, enslavement, poverty, famine, or premature death of one's married brother, and it made special provision for the maintenance and

14 *Id.* at 103–75, 300–24. 15 *Id.* at 212–14, 313–14, 398–400, 534–35.

16 *See, e.g.*, John Boswell, Same Sex Unions in Premodern Europe (1994); Mark D. Jordan, Blessing Same-Sex Unions: The Perils of Queer Romance and the Confusions of Christian Marriage (2005).

17 Remnants of this structure exist today in countries such as Israel, which commit marriage to the exclusive authority of religious communities but will recognize same-sex marriages entered into outside Israel. *See* Yefet and Barzilay, Chapter 25, this volume.

18 Justinian's Institutes 1.10, 4. 18.4 (Paul Krüger ed., Peter Birks and Grant McLeod trans., 1987); Justinian's Novels 12.1; 77.1; 89.12.5; 141.1 (Fred H. Blume trans., unpub. ca. 1952).

19 Brundage, *supra* note 13, at 397–401, 472–74.

inheritance of multiple wives and their children in those cases.[20] More than two dozen polygamists appear in the Hebrew Bible.[21] Almost all of them were good and faithful kings, judges, or aristocrats, and not one of them was punished for practicing polygamy *per se*. While the New Testament condemned a wide range of sexual practices of the Jewish, Greek, and Roman cultures of the day, it, too, was silent on polygamy, save for its special rules that a bishop or deacon had to be "the husband of one wife" and a deaconess "the wife of one husband."[22] The laity were commanded to "flee fornication,"[23] but in all the long New Testament lists of sexual sins illustrating what "fornication" means, not a word appears about polygamy.

Accordingly, the Christian church, for its first 1000 years, said and did rather little about polygamy, though the practice persisted among some first-millennium Jews, 7th- through 10th-century Muslims, and various Indigenous groups in the Middle East, Africa, and Asia. A few early Church Fathers called polygamy a dangerous betrayal of the natural ideals of marriage as a creation of "two in one flesh."[24] Others criticized the spousal rivalries and family unrest of biblical and contemporary polygamists.[25] But in the 5th century, the preeminent Western Church Father St. Augustine called polygamy a perfectly natural form of sexual interaction and an efficient means of procreation.[26] The Old Testament polygamists, said Augustine, committed no offense "against nature, custom, or law."[27] By the same token, the early canon law of the church said virtually nothing against polygamy. Only a few cryptic canons on point have survived from the first millennium, and they called for polygamists in the church to be punished at the same level as petty thieves would be.[28]

It was the state, not the church, that always led the Western campaign against polygamy. Indeed, half a millennium before the advent of Christianity, both Greek and Roman laws treated polygamy as a form of "barbar[ism]" and domestic "tyranny" that violated the natural human need for pair-bonding.[29]

20 Exodus 21:1–2, 22:16–17; Leviticus 20:10, 20–22; Deuteronomy 17:17, 21:7–16; 22:22–29; 1 Kings 11:4; Isaiah 4:1, 13:12; Ruth 4:5–6, 13–21.

21 WITTE, *supra* note 1, at 36, 44.

22 1 Timothy 3:2–5; 5:9.

23 1 Corinthians 6:18 (King James Version).

24 Genesis 2:24; Matthew 19:5; 1 Corinthians 6:16; Ephesians 5:31.

25 WITTE, *supra* note 1, at 98–99, 107–08, 125–27.

26 *Id.* at 88–93.

27 AUGUSTINE, CONTRA FAUSTUM, 21.47, (Philip Schaff, ed. Nicene and Post-Nicene Fathers, repr. ed. 1989), 4:289–90; ST. AUGUSTINE: TREATISES ON MARRIAGE AND OTHER SUBJECTS, 33–34, 49–51 (Roy J. Deferrari, ed., Charles T. Wilcox et al. trans., 1955).

28 WITTE, *supra* note 1, at 114–21.

29 *See* Walter Scheidel, *Monogamy and Polygyny*, *in* A COMPANION TO FAMILIES IN THE GREEK AND ROMAN WORLDS, 108, 111 (Beryl Rawson, ed., 2011).

"Love is born into every human being," Plato wrote famously; "it calls back the halves of our original nature together; it tries to make one out of two and heal the wound of human nature."[30] In extension of these monogamous ideas, early Roman laws also banned a man from having a wife and a concubine at the same time, even if they lived in separate households or cities.[31] By the 3rd century A.D., the pre-Christian Roman emperors declared polygamy to be a crime of infamy whose punishment gradually escalated under their imperial successors. Polygamy was declared a capital crime in the 9th century, and so it remained in much of the West until the 19th century. With the exception of medieval England, it was the state courts of the West that, for nearly two millennia, took the lead on punishing polygamy.

It was only in the 12th and 13th centuries, after the medieval church developed a robust sacramental theology and canon law of monogamous marriage, that it came to condemn polygamy clearly as a heretical violation of the exclusive and enduring marital sacrament.[32] It was only then that the church courts – and for a time the Inquisition – joined the state courts in punishing polygamists. And it was only then that polygamy was made a formidable "boundary marker" between true Christians of the West and various Jews, Muslims, Asians, Africans, heretics, and free thinkers who preached or practiced polygamy.

But even then the Christian tradition wavered in its opposition to polygamy. Late medieval Catholic luminaries such as Cardinal Cajetan, reaching back to Augustine, said that polygamy was a "perfectly natural" option in cases of personal or political necessity.[33] Sixteenth-century Protestants such as Martin Luther went back to the Bible and ultimately considered consensual polygamy to be a better biblical option than brazen adultery or no-fault divorce to resolve hard cases of friction inside marriage.[34] The biblical texts on polygamy also led a few early modern Christian communities including the Anabaptists in Münster to experiment with biblical polygamy anew.[35] It also led a few free thinkers such as Bernard Ochino, John Milton, and Martin Madan to suggest further that allowing polygamy might be a better way to end prostitution, rape, fornication, concubinage, adultery, and bastardy than insisting on monogamy alone.[36]

30 Plato: Symposium, 25–31 (Alexander Nehamas & Paul Woodruff trans., 1989).

31 Krüger, *supra* note 18, at 5.26.1. 32 Witte, *supra* note 1, at 144–95.

33 Dennis Doherty, The Sexual Doctrine of Cardinal Cajetan 233–34 (1966).

34 Witte, *supra* note 1, at 205–18.

35 *See* John Cairncross, After Polygamy was Made a Sin 1–33 (1974).

36 Bernardino Ochino, A Dialog on Polygamy: Originally Written in Italian by Bernardino Ochino (Don Milton ed., 2009); Leo Miller, John Milton Among the Polygamophiles 20–21, 45–46, 205–08 (1974); Martin Madan, Thelyphthora; or,

It was only when the Council of Trent in 1563 issued its final confirmation of the sacramentality of monogamous marriage and its forceful anathema on the heresy of polygamy that this internal speculation about polygamy finally ended in Catholic circles.[37] In turn, it was only when Protestants came to treat marriage systematically as a divine covenant modeled on God's exclusive relationship with his elect – or as a "little commonwealth" at the foundation of the commonwealths of church and state – that Protestants had the theological machinery needed to declare anew that monogamy was the only valid form of marriage. Marriage, early modern Catholics and Protestants together now clearly said, was created as an enduring and exclusive "two in one flesh" union, rooted in the natural order of creation and modeled on the mysterious relationship of God and his elect, Christ and his church. Early modern Western states responded by reconfirming their traditional capital laws against polygamy and strengthening their prosecution and punishment of polygamists.

"So what!" a modern skeptic might well say to all this history. So what if, two plus millennia ago, sodomy happened to be born a biblical sin and polygamy a Roman crime? So what if the first-millennium church took the lead in punishing sodomy, and the first-millennium state took the lead in punishing polygamy? So what if it took until the High Middle Ages or even the Reformation era for church and state to align forces coherently in condemning and punishing both sodomy and polygamy? The reality is that for at least half a millennium the Christian church and the Christian state together branded sodomy and polygamy as unnatural sins and crimes, and together they condemned and punished as sexually deviant anyone who felt naturally drawn to same-sex or plural unions. Under the hot, bright lights of modern constitutional liberty, these centuries-old sex "crimes" look equally problematic to the modern skeptic. Since consensual sodomy and same-sex marriages are now constitutionally protected, consensual polygamy and other forms of polyamorous union should be protected, too. Clever reconstruction of the variant ancient pedigrees of these purported crimes avails us little today. Dusty historical arguments about what is natural and unnatural just are not good enough anymore, the modern skeptic concludes.

A Treatise on Female Ruin, in its Causes, Effects, Consequences, Prevention, and Remedy (Don Milton ed., 1781).

37 Witte, *supra* note 1, at 218–20, 285–90.

II ARGUMENTS FROM NATURE

There are striking differences, however, between the traditional natural arguments against same-sex unions and those against polygamous unions. The heart of the traditional natural argument against same-sex relations was that they are by nature "non-generative." However consensual and loving, same-sex intimacy simply cannot produce a child, which is the ultimate end and good of sexual intercourse, the tradition has long taught. And having a child is essential for the preservation of the human race and for the perpetuation of one's own family name, business, identity, memory, and more. Like every other animal, Aristotle put it three centuries before Christ, a "male and female must unite for the reproduction of the species," and humans are thus born with "the natural impulse ... to leave behind them something of the same nature as themselves."[38] Same-sex partners simply cannot procreate together, rendering their sexual intimacy unnatural.

Moreover, the traditional natural argument added, "even the beasts" do not engage in same-sex activities, despite their lack of reason and conscience.[39] Many animals do kill and eat each other; take each other's homes, food, mates, and offspring; and ignore other creatures in peril, even those of their own species. All of this violates basic natural laws of homicide, theft, adultery, family, and charity that humans have discovered and learned to implement through the use of their reason and conscience. But even the beasts, following natural instincts alone, know that same-sex activities are unnatural, even repulsive. If even the beasts instinctually know better, the traditional argument went, even the most irrational and irresponsible humans should also know that same-sex desires, relations, and activities are unnatural.

Finally, the human sexual body itself reflects what is natural, the tradition taught. A penis can slide into a vagina easily and comfortably during love-making, while anal penetration requires artificial lubrication and often causes pain. Vaginal intercourse can bring intense orgasmic pleasure to both parties in a way that oral sex cannot, absent simultaneous masturbation and spilling of seed by the other party. Face-to-face missionary vaginal sex brings the couple's whole bodies more closely together in intimacy than any other sexual positions. We might blush or roll our eyes at these distinctions today, using our imaginations or the Internet to find exceptions and counterexamples. But, historically, those differences between male-female and same-sex intimacy

[38] THE POLITICS OF ARISTOTLE, 1.2.2. (Ernest Baker, ed. & trans. 1972).

[39] NOV. 141.1 (A.D. 559). A modern debate swirls around whether animals "can be gay." John Mooallem, *Can Animals Be Gay?* N.Y. TIMES MAGAZINE (March 31, 2010), www.nytimes.com/2010/04/04/magazine/04animals-t.html.

were taken as important evidence that the natural end or telos of the human sexual body was for straight sex, not gay or lesbian sex.

All of these traditional natural arguments against same-sex relations are seriously disputed today, and their erosion has helped topple traditional Western laws against same-sex partners. But none of these traditional natural arguments applies to polygamy, in particular polygyny. Procreation is not only possible but is enhanced by having multiple wives rather than one. Polygyny is not only known in nature but is the predominant form of reproduction in most animals, including more than 95% of all higher primates.[40] Pairing birds, voles, and a few other animals are the monogamous exception. The human body is not only capable of having multiple sex partners but also allows a man to impregnate several women in a night, though a woman can have only one pregnancy at a time no matter how many men she takes into her bed. That's why Augustine and many later Western sages thought that only polygyny (one husband, multiple wives), not polyandry (one wife, multiple husbands), was a "natural" form of procreation. And that's why the current erosion of the traditional natural argument against same-sex relations has little bearing on the Western case against polygamy.

The traditional natural argument against polygamy was of a different order. Nearly eight centuries ago, the great Dominican scholar Thomas Aquinas summed up what was, and what would continue to be, a commonplace of Western thought and law. Human beings, Aquinas argued, are distinct among animals in having perennial sex drives rather than annual mating seasons. They produce vulnerable babies who need the support of both their mother and father for a long time in order to survive and thrive. Women bond naturally with children; men do so only if they are certain of their paternity. Exclusive and enduring monogamous unions are the only way that humans can at once have regular sex, paternal certainty, and mutual caretaking for their young children. Humans have thus learned by natural inclination and hard experience to the contrary to develop enduring pair-bonding strategies as the most effective means of reproduction, child-rearing, and community formation.[41]

By contrast, polyandry is naturally unjust to children, Aquinas continued. If a woman has sex with several husbands, it removes the likelihood that any child born to that woman will clearly belong to any one husband. That will

[40] Melvin Konner, The Evolution of Childhood: Relations, Emotion, Mind 452–62 (2010).

[41] St. Thomas Aquinas, Summa Contra Gentiles, III–II, ch. 123 (Vernon J. Bourke trans., 1975) [hereafter SCG]; Thomas Aquinas, Summa Theologica (Fathers of the English Dominican Province, trans. 1948), Supp. q. 41, art. 1; q. 65, arts. 1–5; q. 67, art. 1.

undermine paternal certainty and, consequently, paternal investment in their children's care.[42] The children are thus more likely to suffer from chronic neglect and deprivation, and the wife will be overburdened trying to care for them and trying to tend to her multiple husbands and their disproportionate sexual needs at once. Polygyny is similarly unjust to wives and children. It does not necessarily erode paternal certainty. So long as his multiple wives are faithful to him alone, a man can be assured of being the father of any children born in his household. But this requires a man to pen up his wives like livestock, isolating them from other males even as his own energies are dissipated over the several women gathered in the household. It places half-siblings in competition for every scrap of food, shelter, and paternal attention and sets their mothers against each other and especially against rival stepchildren in the household.[43] This is not "an association of equals, but, instead, a sort of slavery on the part of the wife," said Aquinas.[44] It betrays the fundamental requirements of fidelity and mutuality of husband and wife, of the undivided and undiluted love and friendship that become a proper marriage. Polygamy is thus unnatural, unjust, and unfair, Aquinas concluded. It violates the natural law.

Later Catholic and Protestant writers argued that polygamy violates not only natural law but also natural rights. Calvinist jurist Theodore Beza put this argument clearly nearly five centuries ago. Beza took the Ten Commandments of the Bible to be the best summary of natural law, but he saw parallel commands in many other formulations of natural law. He argued that polygamy violates the commandments against adultery, theft, false testimony, and coveting all at once. Polygamy is a form of adultery that breaches a man's duty to be faithful to his first wife alone. It is a form of theft that breaches his duty to provide sufficient material support for his wife and their children even after his death. It is a form of false witness that breaches his duty to honor his promise of marital fidelity. And it is a form of coveting that breaches a man's duty not to lust after his female neighbor.[45]

Each of these natural duties about fidelity, property, honesty, and respect for others rooted in the Decalogue has correlative natural rights that polygamy

[42] For a review of empirical studies around certainty of paternity, *see* Robin Fretwell Wilson, *Evaluating Marriage: Does Marriage Matter to the Nurturing of Children?*, 42 San Diego Law Review 847 (2005); Jeffrey Rosenberg & W. Bradford Wilcox, *The Importance of Fathers in the Healthy Development of Children*, U.S. Department of Health and Human Services (2006), www.childwelfare.gov/pubPDFs/fatherhood.pdf.

[43] For a review of empirical evidence about polygamy's harms, *see* Strassberg, Chapter 18, this volume.

[44] SCG, *supra* note 41, at III–II, ch. 123.4.

[45] Theodore Beza, Tractatio de Polygamia 12–40 (1587).

also breaches, Beza continued.[46] Polygamy breaches the first wife's natural rights to marital fidelity and trust, to ongoing marital property and material security, and to contractual expectations and reliance on her husband's fidelity to the marriage contract. It breaches the children's natural rights to proper support and inheritance and to the undiluted care, nurture, and education of their father and mother together. And it breaches a neighbor's rights to have an equal opportunity to marry without having most of the eligible women hoarded in one harem or having the neighbor's own wife or daughters subject to the covetous privations of a powerful polygamous neighbor. Polygamy was thus doubly unnatural, Beza concluded – a violation of natural law and natural rights alike.

Liberal philosophers and common law jurists from the 17th century onward drew directly on these traditional natural law and natural rights arguments against polygamy, even while they supported the legal disestablishment of Christianity. Most liberals posited natural rights as "inherent" in human nature or the state of nature rather than commanded in the Bible or the order of creation. But they came to the same conclusion as earlier Christians that polygamy violated the natural rights and liberties especially of women and children. Seventeenth-century English philosopher John Locke, for example, regarded polygamy as a violation of the natural-born equality of men and women, as well as the natural rights of children to be properly nurtured and fully supported by both their mother and father until they were emancipated.[47] For Locke, the natural laws favoring monogamy trumped religious arguments for polygamy, and he would allow no religious liberty exemptions from criminal prohibitions on polygamy. A century later, leading common law jurist William Blackstone condemned polygamy as a "singularly barbaric" violation of the reciprocal natural rights and duties of husbands and wives and parents and children, which no modern civilization could countenance.[48] To Blackstone, polygamy was a grave offense against public health and public order.

Eighteenth-century women's rights advocate Mary Wollstonecraft castigated polygamy for privileging men and degrading women, forcing them to compete with other women, especially the more nubile and fertile young

[46] *Id.*; John Witte, Jr., The Reformation of Rights: Law, Religion, and Human Rights in Early Modern Calvinism 81–142 (2007).

[47] John Locke, Two Treatises of Government, 165–66, 287–91, 318–19, 341, 350–51 (Peter Laslett ed., 1988) (1690); John Locke: A Letter Concerning Toleration and Other Writings 69, 84, 105–11 (Mark Goldie ed., 2010).

[48] William Blackstone, Commentaries on the Laws of England 1.15.1–I.16.3; 4.13 (1765).

women whom their husbands would inevitably drag home to replace them when they grew barren or lost their good looks. A woman is not just a temporary object of beauty or a dispensable channel of procreation, Wollstonecraft insisted. A woman is a full citizen who must be given the right, education, and opportunity to choose her own public and private vocations and to enjoy her natural-born liberty and equality within her own monogamous home if she chooses to marry.[49] Marriage must be structured as a "dyadic friendship."[50] Scottish philosophers Henry Home, David Hume, and Adam Smith argued that polygamy would breed tyrannical patriarchy or servile submissiveness in children, depending on their and their mother's place in the polygamous home. Children of polygamy simply cannot learn the healthy balances of authority and liberty, equality and respect, and property and responsibility that they need to survive, let alone thrive. For these Scottish sages and the many 19th-century American writers who echoed them, this was no way to treat the natural rights of the child.[51]

"So what!" – a modern skeptic again might say to all this talk about natural law, natural justice, or natural rights. Traditional "natural" arguments against polygamy are no more convincing than traditional biblical arguments. After all, modern philosophers and linguists have made clear that "nature" talk is just a thin and movable cover for the imposition of underlying religious and cultural preferences and prejudices. They have proved that "irrefutable" principles of reason or "objective" facts of nature are always conditioned by a community's levels of socialization and scientific knowledge. They have shown that "self-evident" truths are only temporary normative stopping points in endlessly evolving cultures.[52]

Take the naturalist argument for exclusive and enduring heterosexual marriages that Thomas Aquinas introduced and nearly eight centuries of Western jurists and philosophers thereafter repeated. Today, genetic testing has made paternity much easier to establish. Contraceptives have made extramarital sex much safer to pursue. Artificial reproductive technology, adoption, and surrogacy (and maybe cloning soon) have made reproduction readily available to men and women, straights and gays, single and married, couples or communes. And the welfare state is there to help all these parents if they or

49 Mary Wollstonecraft, A Vindication of the Rights of Woman 63, 100, 103, 106 133, 141 (Janet Todd ed., 2d ed., 2008).

50 Eileen Hunt Botting, Wollstonecraft, Mill and Women's Human Rights 57 (2016).

51 Witte, *supra* note 1, at 372–80, 416–41.

52 For a critical review, *see* Don S. Browning, *A Natural Law Theory of Marriage*, 46 Zygon 733, 733–760 (2011).

their children have need.[53] What Aquinas took as objective "natural" conditions about human sexuality and heterosexual pair-bonding strategies of reproduction were, in fact, conditioned by the level of science, economy, and politics of his day. As the conditions changed, domestic arrangements have changed, too. LGBT advocates have used this evolutionary insight to open the door to same-sex equality and marriage.[54] Polygamy advocates can and must do the same, the argument goes.

Shifting the discourse from natural law to natural rights arguments against polygamy only compounds the problem, this skeptical argument continues. Plainly, natural rights – or "universal human rights," as we now call them – are also cultural constructs. They are rooted in and reflective of the values and beliefs of the Western cultures that first named and used them. Theodore Beza and other early modern Christians were at least honest in rooting these natural rights firmly in the Bible and the order of creation. But post-Christian liberals have rooted these rights in the shifting sands of human nature and the state of nature. Jeremy Bentham was perhaps a bit too harsh in calling all this "nonsense upon stilts."[55] But the reality is that human rights are just normative totems of a community's ideals, procedural means to enforce a favored set of social and institutional relationships. Calling these rights "natural" or "human" does not change the reality that most purportedly "universal" human rights in vogue today are principally Western (Christian) constructions of value and belief. They have little salience or cogency in polygamous communities around the world that have chosen to reject rights talk, or at least Western formulations of human rights.

III HARM ARGUMENTS

But even if we reject the validity of human rights, we cannot deny the reality of human wrongs. Even if we reject the capacity of the state to prohibit fault, we cannot deny the state the power to punish harm. And even if a global human rights campaign against polygamy might be out, a Western insistence on maintaining monogamy is still apt. The most enduring argument in the

[53] Often the state finds it easier to pursue polygamists for child support or other crimes than for polygamy itself. Of ten prosecutions in a decade, six "involved defendants who were also prosecuted for crimes other than bigamy, such as criminal non-support, unlawful sexual conduct with a minor, forcible sex abuse, marriage license fraud, and insurance fraud." Brown v. Buhman, 822 F.3d 1151, 1158 (10th Cir. 2016).

[54] For commentary on state legislative responses around same-sex marriage and nondiscrimination protections for LGBT persons, *see* Adams, Chapter 21, this volume.

[55] Nonsense Upon Stilts: Bentham, Burke and Marx on the Rights of Man 2:46, 53 (Jeremy Waldron, ed., 1987).

Western tradition is that polygamy is too often the cause, consequence, or corollary of harm, especially to the most vulnerable populations. And that argument about the harms of polygamy still has power today.

Some 1800 years ago, ancient Jewish Rabbis and early Church Fathers alike warned that polygamy was "trouble,"[56] even when practiced by the most noble and God-fearing men and women. Think of Abraham with Sarah and Hagar, Jacob with Rachel and Leah, Elkanah with Hannah and Peninnah.[57] All of these biblical households suffered bitter rivalries between the wives; bitter disputes among their children over inheritance and political succession; deadly competition among half-siblings that ultimately escalated to incest, adultery, kidnapping, enslavement, banishment, and more. Think of the great King David who lustfully murdered Bathsheba's husband to add Bathsheba to his already ample harem.[58] Or think of King Solomon with his thousand wives and concubines who led him into idolatry, and whose children ended up raping, abducting, and killing one another, precipitating civil war in ancient Israel.[59]

Some 800 years ago, William of Auvergne and other observers of Middle Eastern Muslim polygamy argued that the "bent love" of polygamy was inevitably harmful. Women are harmed because they are reduced to rival slaves within the household, exploited for sex with an increasingly sterile and distracted husband, sometimes deprived of the children they do produce, and forced to make do for themselves and their children with too few resources as other women and children are added to the household against their wishes. Children are harmed because their chances of birth and survival are diminished by their calculating fathers who might contracept, abort, smother, or sell them, and by their mothers who sometimes lack the resources, support, and protection to bring them to term, let alone to adulthood. Men are harmed because they do not have the time, energy, or resources to support their polygamous households and because their minds and hearts cannot rest if they are always on the lookout for another woman to add to their harems or for another dangerous man who will abduct his women. And societies are harmed because polygamy results in too many unattached men who become menaces to public order and morality. Finally, polygamy creates too many ad hoc seats of domestic power that are based on sheer numbers rather than on legitimate political succession or election.[60]

56 The Hebrew word for a co-wife (*tzarah*) literally means "trouble." *See* Michael J. Broyde, *Jewish Law and the Abandonment of Marriage, in* MARRIAGE, SEX, AND FAMILY IN JUDAISM 88–89 (Michael J. Broyde & Michael Ausubel, eds., 2005).

57 Genesis 16:1–6; 29:15–30; 1 Samuel 1:1–8. 58 2 Samuel 11:27. 59 1 Kings 11:1–6.

60 GUILIELMI ALVERNI OPERA OMNIA, 1:512–28 (repr. ed., Frankfurt am Main: G.m.b.H., 1963); PETER BILLER, THE MEASURE OF MULTITUDE: POPULATION IN MEDIEVAL THOUGHT 60–88 (2000).

Some 500 years ago, European critics of the Anabaptist town of Münster documented the harms done when religious leaders gained power over an isolated polygamous community.[61] There, a group of young men, giddy with lust and theocratic pretensions, combined charisma, brutality, and biblical platitudes to force a gullible Christian community to adopt their utopian vision of polygamy. Old couples were forced to end their marriages and start again. Young girls and women were coerced into premature and unwanted marriages; even little prepubescent girls were fair game and were literally raped to death. Husbands collected wives like spiritual trophies, measuring their faith by the size of their harems and nurseries. Wives were used and then spurned when they were pregnant or nursing or when the next wife was added to the harem. Polygamous households were filled with bickering wives and children, who were then cowed into silence with threats of the sword. Wives who still objected, or who rejected their husband's sexual advances to protest the unwanted polygamy, were summarily executed. Community dissenters and critics of these utopian excesses faced the sword as well.

Some 150 years ago, American critics of Mormon polygamy found much the same thing on the Western frontier.[62] First, they charged, polygamy harmed young girls who were too often tricked, coerced, or commanded to enter spiritual marriages with older men and had too little education and too few means of escape when they were inevitably neglected or replaced by another favorite wife. Their plight was exacerbated by the practice of unilateral male divorce that allowed men to banish wives who failed to fall in line or who no longer offered children, labor, support, or sex. Second, polygamy licensed and encouraged male lust for sex and power. It induced inevitable restlessness on the part of some males to add more women to their harems. It invited inevitable repression and ostracism of rival males eager to find a wife or lover among the scant supply of women who were left to them. It favored marriage by the richest and most powerful, not necessarily the fittest and most virtuous, males of the community. Third, polygamy created religious power structures that rivaled the legitimate power of the state. Church leaders slowly gained control of the property, economy, and workforce. They compelled their congregants, workers, and family members to support their polygamous policies and to vote for new officials who would do the same. The new officials colluded to create laws and policies favoring polygamy and to suborn the perjury and contempt of those polygamists who were sought by the authorities. And when government officials sought to restore legal and moral order in the territory, these communities confronted them with boycotts, guns, riots, and

[61] Cairncross, *supra* note 35, at 1–33. [62] WITTE, *supra* note 1, at 429–39.

violence. This simply could not be countenanced in a democratic land dedicated to the separation of church and state.[63]

Today, observers of polygamous communities scattered about the West point to similar problems of higher than average incidences of arranged, coerced, and underage marriages of young girls to older men; rape and statutory rape; wife and child abuse; social and educational deprivation of women and children in polygamous households; abuse and ostracism of young boys and poorer men who compete for fewer brides; rampant social welfare abuses by oversized polygamous families; social isolation of polygamous communities; and dangerous conflations of religious and political authority.[64] Outside of the West, most polygamous cultures are rural, poor, and uneducated. They exist in low-technology and labor-intensive economies that require many children to do the work and that feature low survival rates among these children. Or they are part of powerful political and religious families in traditional tribal settings, Muslim settings, or both. But regardless of "whether it is practiced in a Western democracy or sub-Saharan Africa, polygamy produces harmful effects that ripple throughout a society," Brown University political scientist Rose McDermott concludes after a thorough cross-cultural study of polygamy in more than 170 countries.[65] All these polygamous communities suffer from increased levels of physical and sexual abuse against women, increased rates of maternal mortality, shortened female life expectancy, lower levels of education for girls and boys, lower levels of equality for women, higher levels of discrimination against women, increased rates of female genital mutilation, increased rates of trafficking in women, and decreased levels of civil and political liberties for all citizens.

The Western legal tradition has thus long regarded polygamy as a *malum in se* offense – something "evil in itself." Other *malum in se* offenses today include slavery, sex trafficking, prostitution, indentured servitude, obscenity, bestiality, incest, sex with children, self-mutilation, organ-selling, cannibalism, and more. Polygamy is usually regarded as less egregious than some other offenses on this list. But, like other *malum in se* offenses, polygamy is too often the cause, consequence, or corollary of other wrongdoing. That someone wants to engage in these activities voluntarily for reasons of religion, bravery, custom, or autonomy makes no difference. That other cultures past and

63 For a pair of views on the modern boundaries of free exercise in the United States, *see* Helfand, Chapter 2, this volume; Sepper, Chapter 1, this volume.

64 Strassberg, Chapter 18, this volume; Julia Chamberlin & Amos N. Guiora, *Polygamy: Not "Big Love" But Significant Harm*, 35 WOMEN'S RIGHTS L. REP. 144, 171–85 (2014).

65 Rose McDermott & Jonathan Cowden, *Polygyny and Violence Against Women*, 64 EMORY L.J. 1767 (2015).

present allow such activities makes no difference. That these activities do not necessarily cause harm in every case also makes no difference. For nearly two millennia, the Western legal tradition has included polygamy among the crimes that are inherently wrong because polygamy routinizes patriarchy, deprecates women, jeopardizes consent, fractures fidelity, divides loyalty, dilutes devotion, fosters inequity, promotes rivalry, foments lust, condones adultery, harms children, and more – not in every case, to be sure, but in enough cases to make the practice of polygamy too risky to condone as a viable legal family structure.

Furthermore, allowing religious polygamy as an exception to the rules is even more dangerous, the Western tradition has concluded, because it will make some churches, mosques, tribes, and temples a law unto themselves.[66] It is notable that no religious community in the West today regards polygamy as an absolute religious requirement.[67] For the faithful, it is a custom not a command, an option not an obligation. It is also notable that some Western communities that once preached and practiced polygamy, namely, Jews and Mormons, have now renounced the practice. It is even more notable that polygamy is shrinking in the Muslim world, even though fifty-three of the fifty-five Muslim-majority nations today still allow the practice. More conservative schools of Islamic jurisprudence, particularly the Wahhabi and Hanafi schools, do allow for a limited right to practice polygamy for men of ample means. This has persisted in some Islamic communities to this day, both in Muslim-majority lands and in dispersed Muslim communities throughout the world, including in the West. In Muslim lands and communities that follow the more liberal teachings of the Malaki and Shaf'i schools of jurisprudence, however, polygamy is typically an unpopular and shrinking domestic practice, particularly for families in urban settings and more developed cultures. A number of Muslim jurists within these schools have been openly critical of the practice because of concern for the treatment of women and children.

But even if polygamy were religiously favored or obligatory, modern Western constitutional laws still empower states to prohibit behavior that the states consider harmful or dangerous.[68] Again, some religious communities and their members might well thrive with the freedom to practice polygamy. But, inevitably, closed repressive and isolated regimes, such as Anabaptist Münster in the 16th century or the Fundamentalist Mormon

[66] Reynolds, *supra* note 2, at 167.

[67] *See* Azizah Y. Al-Hibri, and Raja' M. El Habti, *Islam*, *in* Sex, Marriage, and Family in World Religions, 150–225 (Don S. Browning, M. Christian Green, and John Witte, Jr. eds., 2006).

[68] Adams, Chapter 21, this volume; Helfand, Chapter 2, this volume.

communities in thinly populated regions of western Mexico, America, and Canada today[69] will also emerge – with underage girls duped or coerced into sex and marriages with older men, with women and children trapped in sectarian communities with no realistic access to help or protection from the state, and no real legal recourse against a religious community that is following its own rules. The West prizes liberty, equality, and consent too highly to court such a risk.

"So what!" a skeptic might argue for the final time. Monogamous households are filled with many ugly harms, too: wife and child abuse, deprivation and abandonment of children, wastrel habits, welfare abuses, and, sadly, so much more.[70] That has not led to the abolition of monogamy but only to the closer policing and punishment of each harm as it occurs. Why not do the same here? If polygamy really does cause or correlate with various harms, why not just punish those harms when they occur?[71] If polygamous wives or children really do suffer from increased levels of abuse, neglect, or deprivation, why not give them model contracts with strong, built-in protections for the vulnerable that are scrupulously enforced, a possibility Bix (Chapter 9, this volume) explores. If religious leaders really do subvert due process, why not let polygamous parties just litigate their claims in state courts? If religious communities really do isolate their members at the risk of abuse, why not make polygamy more mainstream, transparent, and accountable. If *Big Love* and *Sister Wives* can make the polygamous family work, why can't everyone else be given a fair chance?

IV SYMBOLIC AND EDUCATIONAL ARGUMENTS

"Bad cases make bad law," a familiar legal dictum holds, and that is the case here. The compelling case for the lawfulness of polygamy is when three or more well-educated parties – similar in wealth, ability, and opportunity, with eyes and doors wide open – choose to enter into a polygamous union. They

69 Modern Polygamy in the United States: Historical, Cultural, and Legal Issues xvi, 163–84 (Cardell K. Jacobson and Lara Burton, eds., 2011) (giving map of Fundamentalist Latter-day Saints communities); Martha Bailey and Amy J. Kaufman, Polygamy in the Monogamous World: Multicultural Challenges for Western Law and Policy 69–132 (2010).

70 *See generally* Rachel Kidman, *Child Marriage and Intimate Partner Violence: A Comparative Study of 34 Countries*, Int. J. Epidemiology (Oct. 12, 2016), https://academic.oup.com/ije/article-abstract/doi/10.1093/ije/dyw225/2417355/Child-marriage-and-intimate-partner-violence-a?redirectedFrom=fulltext.

71 *See* similar argument in State v. Holm, 137 P.3d 726, 758 (Utah 2006) (Durham, J., concurring and dissenting).

can calculate and negotiate the costs and benefits and the advantages and disadvantages of their pending plural union. They can protect themselves through prenuptial and postnuptial contracts and through their own independent means.[72] They can hire lawyers, accountants, private investigators, and security guards to help them if their partners betray or endanger them or their children. And they can hit the airwaves and social media to elicit sympathy and action if the state authorities do not respond quickly or fully enough. For these exceptional parties, a state's criminal prohibition against polygamy hardly seems necessary.

But general criminal prohibitions against polygamy are designed not for the exceptional case, but for the typical case. And throughout Western history and still today, a typical case of polygamy too often involves vulnerable parties who do not have the knowledge, resources, or connections to engage in the kind of self-protection and self-help available to the families depicted on *Big Love* or *Sister Wives*.[73] Every Western state has general laws on the books against wife and child abuse; coerced marriage and statutory rape of young girls; deprivation of food, shelter, and education of children; welfare abuse; and more. The reality, however, is that, in action, these laws have provided far too little support and protection for these vulnerable populations, especially as state administrative agencies face shrinking budgets, dwindling personnel, and political disincentives to prosecute.

But these traditional criminal laws against polygamy are more than just prudential prophylactics against harm. They also play an important symbolic and teaching function that the state and its family laws still have in our lives. Historically, in the West, the laws against polygamy were part of a broader set of family laws designed to support the classical Western ideal that the monogamous family was the most primal and essential institution of Western society and culture. Aristotle and the Roman Stoics called the union of husband and wife, and parent and child, the "foundation of the polis" and "the private font of public virtue."[74] The Church Fathers and medieval Catholics called the

[72] *See* Bix, Chapter 9, this volume, for a discussion of the extent to which parties can contract on questions related to child welfare. For a recent decision granting custody to three adults using existing law of custody, based on the parties' decision to "create this unique relationship" between a legally married couple and a downstairs neighbor, *see* Dawn M. v. Michael M., 2017 NY Slip Op 27073 (N.Y. Sup. Ct, Suffolk Cty., 2017).

[73] *See* State v. Holm, *supra* note 71, as one example (describing religious marriage of sixteen-year-old girl to thirty-two-year-old man legally married to the girl's sister, which led to the girl giving birth to one child before eighteen and another three months after she turned eighteen, for which the man was tried and convicted of two counts of unlawful sexual conduct with a sixteen- or seventeen-year-old and one count of bigamy, all third-degree felonies).

[74] *See* John Witte, Jr., From Sacrament to Contract: Marriage, Religion, and Law in the Western Tradition (2d ed., 2012).

monogamous household the "seedbed" of the city, "the sacramental force that welds Christian society together." Early modern Protestants and Anglo-American common lawyers called the stable household a "little church"; a "little commonwealth"; the first school of love and justice, nurture and education, charity and citizenship. John Locke and the Enlightenment philosophers called monogamous marriage "the first society" to be formed as men and women moved from the state of nature to an organized society dedicated to the rule of law and the protection of natural rights. All these traditional metaphors taught a certain vision of the good life and the good society, with monogamous marriage at its core.

For all of our new cultural emphasis on liberty and autonomy, and for all our current wariness about totalitarian power, Western society still looks to the law to promote private and public "health, safety, and welfare" and to discourage activities and relationships that harm them. The state has shrunk the traditional ideals of sex, marriage, and family life that it teaches, and modern family law systems have moved away from many of the absolute "thou shalt" and "thou shalt not" commands of the past, as well as the harsh measures used to enforce them. But still, in the "soft law" between these two clear commands, the modern state still does its teaching work, "nudging" its citizens in one direction or another. The state does not require its citizens to get married, but it does "nudge" in that direction: it provides state marital licenses, tax and Social Security benefits, spousal evidentiary and healthcare privileges, and hundreds of additional federal and state benefits and incentives.[75] In turn, while the state rarely prosecutes polygamy *per se*, it still nudges strongly against polygamy by providing it with no funding, facilitation, licenses, or support, and threatening prosecution when polygamy is combined with other harms and crimes.

V CONCLUSION

All Western nations to date have held the line against polygamy, even if they have accepted sexual liberty and same-sex marriage. They should continue to do so. Polygamy causes or correlates with too many harms to women, children, men, and society. It defies the natural family form that the Western classical, Christian, and liberal tradition has defended for 2500 years. It ignores the conclusions of modern evolutionists that pair-bonding is part of the "deep

[75] *See* Wilson, Chapter 16, this volume (canvassing legal incidents of marriage); Obergefell v. Hodges, 135 S. Ct. 2584 (2015) (listing benefits associated with marriage); United States v. Windsor, 133 S. Ct. 2675 (2013) (same).

structure"[76] of human reproduction that humans have developed as their best strategy for long-term survival and success.

But let's face it: the argument for polygamy is and always has been primarily about a small group of men seeking the social, moral, and legal imprimatur to have and to hold sundry females at once. However, plenty of empirical evidence shows that historically and today, most men and almost all women are instinctively attracted to single partner intimacy for the long term, especially when children are involved, and instinctively repulsed and angered if forced to share their bed with a third party. Despite our wide cultural acceptance of sexual liberty in the West, sexual infidelity still breaks marriage and intimate relationships more than any other single cause.[77]

For the West to maintain its traditional stance against polygamy does not mean that it needs to trade in the ugly rhetoric that has historically attended this stance. We do not have to posit narratives of moral progress that brand polygamists as "barbarians" and "savages" and polygamy as "odious among the northern and western nations."[78] We do not have to say that the West is more "advanced" than the rest because of its monogamy. We do not have to repeat the haughty and xenophobic arguments used by Graeco-Roman writers against their imperial subjects, by early Christians against Jews and Muslims, by early modern Europeans against New World natives, or by 19th-century Americans against emancipated slaves, Native Americans, Asian workers, or traditional Mormons, all of whom practiced polygamy. The West can now simply and politely say to the polygamist who bangs on its door seeking admission or permission to practice polygamy: "No thank you; we don't do that here," and close the door firmly.

76 Bernard Chapais, Primeval Kinship: How Pair-Bonding Gave Birth to Human Society 10 (2008).

77 *Divorce in America: Who Wants Out and Why?* Austin Institute (Apr. 9, 2014), www.austin-institute.org/research/divorce-in-america/ (listing "infidelity by either partner" as the "most-cited reason[] for wanting a divorce").

78 Reynolds, *supra* note 2, at 164.

18

Scrutinizing Polygamy Under Religious Freedom Restoration Acts

Maura Irene Strassberg

Professor of Law, Drake University Law School

Fundamentalist Mormons and others practice religious polygamy today in scattered communities in the United States. Both in the U.S. and globally, polygamy almost exclusively takes the form of polygyny – one husband with multiple wives – and not polyandry – one wife with multiple husbands.[1]

Predicated on the religious practices of a fundamentalist group ("FLDS") that splintered off from the Church of Jesus Christ of the Latter-day Saints or Mormon Church and other polygamous groups, legal challenges to laws criminalizing polygamy have long relied on free exercise arguments, with little success.[2] This is so because polygamy laws are generally viewed as neutral laws of general applicability, satisfying the low bar for free exercise under the First Amendment announced in *Employment Division v. Smith*, the governing standard today.[3]

Of course, state constitutions sometimes provide greater protection for free exercise of religion than the First Amendment does after *Smith*, as

[1] This chapter refers to polygyny, not polyandry, when discussing polygamy. It does not address polyamory, an entirely different practice that may or may not be encompassed by criminal polygamy laws. *See* Maura I. Strassberg, *The Challenge of Post-Modern Polygamy: Considering Polyamory*, 31 Capital U. L. Rev. 439 (2003).

[2] *See, e.g.*, Reynolds v. United States, 98 U.S. 145 (1879); Potter v. Murray City, 760 F.2d 1065, (10th Cir. 1985); State v. Green, 99 P.3d 820, 830 (Utah 2004); State v. Holm, 137 P.3d 726. 743–44 (Utah 2006). *But see* Brown v. Buhman, 947 F.Supp.2d 1170 (D. Utah 2013) (finding Utah's bigamy statute neither neutral nor generally applicable and holding that it failed strict scrutiny), *vacated by* Brown v. Buhman, 822 F.3d 1151 (2016) (finding case moot due to prosecutor's policy not to prosecute absent collateral crimes, as well as because of plaintiff's move to Nevada). *Compare* Maura I. Strassberg, *Scrutinizing Polygamy: Utah's Brown v. Buhman and British Columbia's Reference Re: Section* 293, 64 Emory L. J. 1815 (2015) (arguing that Utah's bigamy law was neutral and generally applicable but that it could survive strict scrutiny).

[3] 494 U.S. 872 (1990). *See* Helfand, Chapter 2, this volume, and Sepper, Chapter 1, this volume, for competing views on how protective Smith is of religious practice.

Adams shows (Chapter 21, this volume). Moreover, laws burdening religious beliefs and practices may be tested for whether the burden is necessary under state statutes mirroring the federal Religious Freedom Restoration Act ("RFRA"), the statute at the heart of *Burwell v. Hobby Lobby*.[4] Congress enacted RFRA to require the federal government to show proof that its laws and policies do not substantially burden religious belief or practice or, if they do, they "further[] . . . a compelling government interest . . . [accomplished by] the least restrictive means."[5] RFRA has had little effect on polygamy challenges because the federal RFRA does not bind the states.[6]

Far more germane to a state's ability to police and punish polygamy are the state laws in twenty-one states that mirror the federal RFRA ("state RFRAs"). These laws greatly increase the likelihood that laws criminalizing polygamy will be subject to strict scrutiny in the future. Some RFRAs by their very terms apply only to challenges to civil laws, not criminal ones.[7] Moreover, as statutes, state RFRAs cannot trump state constitutional provisions expressly prohibiting polygamy[8] or limiting marriage to "*one* man and *one* woman

[4] 42 U.S. § 2000bb-1(b) (2012); Burwell v. Hobby Lobby Stores, Inc., 134 S. Ct. 2751 (2014) (finding requirements that closely held for-profit corporations cover certain contraceptive drugs and devices that their owners believe end a human life violated RFRA because less restrictive means existed to serve the government's desired end of providing women contraceptive coverage at no cost to them).

[5] Hobby Lobby, *supra* note 4, at 2760–61 (describing the enactment of RFRA as an attempt to reinstate the far less deferential, pre-Smith test in Sherbert v. Verner, 374 U.S. 398 (1963)).

[6] City of Boerne v. Flores, 521 U.S. 507, 534–537 (1997) (finding application of RFRA to state actions exceeded Congress's authority). Conceivably, the federal RFRA may apply to the Congressional Enabling Acts that admitted Utah, Arizona, New Mexico, and Oklahoma into the Union because each conditioned entrance on forever prohibiting polygamy in the state's constitution. However, RFRA would be of value only if a state attempted to strip the polygamy prohibition out of its constitution by amendment. In this scenario, the Enabling Act would constitute the federal action imposing a burden on religion. But the chances of a state taking this unprecedented step are remote. Significant change in attitude toward polygamy would have to occur in such a state (*see* Witte, Chapter 17, this volume), followed by considerable legislative and constitutional reform.

[7] Pennsylvania's RFRA does not apply to "any criminal offense," PA. STAT. TIT. 71, § 2406(b)(1), meaning that its bigamy offense, 18 PA. C.S.A. § 4301, which covers polygamy, would not be subject to strict scrutiny under its RFRA. Pennsylvania's constitution gives heightened scrutiny to religious exercise, as many states with state RFRAs do. *See* Commonwealth v. Stewart, 690 A.2d 195 (Pa. 1997) (rejecting diocese's claim to withhold documents in litigation but requiring that government actions that substantially burden religion serve a compelling state interest in the least restrictive way possible); Adams, Chapter 21, this volume.

[8] Ariz. Const., art. 20, § 2; Idaho Const., art. I, § 4; New Mexico Const., art. XXI, § 1; Okla. Const., art. I, § I-2; Utah Const., art. III, § 1.

only" or "*a* man and *a* woman"[9] – these laws do not bar same-sex marriages after *Obergefell v. Hodges*, but they would bar polygamous marriages.

Given these constitutional bars on polygamy, only five of the twenty-one state RFRAs could be deployed to challenge a state's criminalization of polygamy. In these states, courts would subject to strict scrutiny the state's criminal polygamy bans and laws limiting marriage to two people only.[10] And this is where the U.S. Supreme Court's decision in *Hobby Lobby*[11] may play a role in eroding the bulwark against polygamy that state laws have erected. Importantly, state courts often look to federal law when interpreting state RFRAs.[12] Thus, *Hobby Lobby* may *guide* state courts attempting mini-RFRA strict scrutiny.

The significance of *Hobby Lobby* primarily arises out of its new gloss on evaluating whether a state's purpose is compelling and whether the state's method of achieving that purpose represents the least restrictive alternative under RFRA. On compelling interest, the *Hobby Lobby* majority assumed for the sake of argument that the government had a compelling interest in providing free access to the four contraceptive methods required as essential health benefits under the Patient Protection and Affordable Care Act ("ACA").[13] But that was not the question to be asked under RFRA, the Supreme Court explained. Instead, RFRA's "'more focused' [compelling interest] inquiry"[14] asks whether the government can show a compelling interest in not providing a religious exemption to Hobby Lobby and similar

9 Ala. Const. art. I, § 36.03; Alaska Const. art. I, § 25; Ariz. Const. art. XXX, § 1; Ark. Const. amend. LXXXIII, § 1; Colo. Const. art. II, § 31; Fla. Const. art. I, § 27; Idaho Const. art. III, § 28; Kan. Const. art. XV, § 16; Ky. Const. § 233a; La. Const. art. XII, § 15; Mich. Const. art. I, § 25; Miss. Const. art. XIV, § 263A; Mo. Const. art. I, § 33; Mont. Const. art. XIII, § 7; Neb. Const. art. I, § 29; Nev. Const. art. I, § 21; N.C. Const. art. XIV, § 6; N.D. Const. art. XI, § 28; Ohio Const. art. XV, § 11; Okla. Const. art. II, § 35; Or. Const. art. XV, § 5a; S.C. Const. art. XVII, § 15; S.D. Const. art. XXI, § 9; Tenn. Const. art. XI, § 18; Tex. Const. art. I, § 32; Utah Const. art. I, § 29; Va. Const. art. I, § 15-A; Wis. Const. art. XIII, § 13.

10 The remaining states are Alabama, Illinois, Indiana, Connecticut, and Rhode Island. Ala. Const. art. I, § 36.03; CONN. GEN. STAT. § 46b-20a (2009); 750 ILL. COMP. STAT. § 5/201 (2014); R.I. GEN. LAWS § 15-1-5 (2013).

11 134 S. Ct. 2751, 2785.

12 Diggs v. Snyder, 775 N.E.2d 40, 44 (Ill. App. 2002); *see* World Outreach Conference Ctr. v. City of Chicago, 591 F.3d 531, 533 (7th Cir. 2009) (internal citations omitted).

13 *Id.* at 2780; Patient Protection and Affordable Care Act, Pub. L No. 111–148, 124 Stat 119 (2010), amended by Health Care and Education Reconciliation Act of 2010, Pub. L No. 111–152, 124 Stat 1029.

14 *Id.* (quoting Gonzalez v. O Centro Espirita Beneficente Uniao do Vegetal (O Centro), 546 U.S. 418, 430 (2006)) (holding that criminalizing sacramental use of *hoasca* violated RFRA absent a showing that compelling state interests were served by restricting this particular use).

closely held for-profit corporations substantially burdened by the regulations requiring contraceptive coverage ("mandate").[15]

Hobby Lobby also suggested that a viable less restrictive alternative to the mandates was for the government to "assume the cost of providing the four contraceptives" itself.[16] The broader significance of the Court's suggestion might be, as Justice Ruth Bader Ginsberg articulates in her dissent, that courts should consider a wider scope of less restrictive government actions, even if such actions might less effectively further the government's interests.[17]

Applying *Hobby Lobby*'s framework to the claim for exemption by religious polygamists reveals difficulties in using this test not previously encountered in RFRA cases. To date, the government's compelling interest in preventing polygamy has largely followed the reasoning of its 1879 case, *Reynolds v. United States*,[18] which relied on openly racist attitudes and 19th-century political theory to enforce a federal prohibition of polygamy in the territories.[19] Because the modern Court continues to cite *Reynolds* as good law,[20] there has been little reason to develop a deeper, more contextualized understanding of polygamy's harms.

In addition, recent constitutional polygamy cases have only involved Mormon polygamists. New state justifications for criminalizing polygamy rest on limited law enforcement experience with isolated polygamous communities and on anecdotal critiques and exposés by ex-community members.[21] As a result, no American court has articulated precisely what the state's

[15] Hobby Lobby, *supra* note 4, at 2779 (observing that "it is arguable that there are features of ACA that support th[e] view" "that HHS has not shown that the mandate serves a compelling government interest").

[16] *Id.* at 2780.

[17] *Id.* at 2803 (Ginsburg, J., dissenting) (arguing that requiring women to separately access a government program to provide contraceptives free of charge would undermine the ACA's purpose to provide preventive care services with "minimal logistical and administrative obstacles") (quoting 78 Fed. Reg. 29888).

[18] Reynolds, *supra* note 2. (holding that free exercise did not protect religious polygamy from criminal prosecution).

[19] The Morrill Act, ch. 126, § 1, 12 Stat. 501. 501 (1862) (repealed 1910) (criminalizing polygamy in the territories).

[20] *See, e.g.*, Church of the Lukumi Babalu Aye, Inc. v. City of Hialeah, 508 U.S. 520 (1993) (citing Reynolds for the proposition that "a social harm may have been a legitimate concern of government for reasons quite apart from discrimination" against religion); Bob Jones Univ. v. U.S., 461 U.S. 574, 604 (1983) (citing Reynolds as one of a few cases where government interests were "so compelling as to allow even regulations prohibiting religiously based conduct").

[21] *See, e.g.*, Potter v. Murray City, 760 F.2d 1065 (10th Cir. 1985); State v. Green, 99 P.3d 820, 830 (Utah 2004); Holm, *supra* note 2, at 743–44; Brown v. Buhman, 947 F.Supp.2d 1170 (D. Utah 2013).

justifications for criminalizing polygamy are, based on contemporary social scientific evidence of polygamy's consequences.

This chapter remedies this deficit. It presents evidence relied upon in a 2011 Canadian case, *Reference re: Section 293 of the Criminal Code of Canada* ("*Reference*"),[22] to uphold the constitutionality of Canada's criminal polygamy law. This chapter suggests that *Reference*'s analysis of polygamy's harmful effects can provide American courts with the particularized compelling state purposes needed to uphold criminal bans in the face of challenges under state RFRAs.

Turning to the least restrictive means prong, it may be argued that state governments already have a less restrictive way of deterring polygamy in place: states can simply refuse to legally recognize polygamous marriages. While nonrecognition lacks the teeth that criminal penalties have for deterring the practice and is presumably less effective at deterring polygamy than criminal sanctions, it could be the less restrictive, albeit less efficient, alternative, opening the door to polygamy in RFRA cases.

I CRIMINALIZING POLYGAMY SUBSTANTIALLY BURDENS RELIGIOUS PRACTICE

Under RFRA and state RFRAs, strict scrutiny is triggered by a government action that places a substantial burden on the exercise of religion, as Helfand (Chapter 6, this volume) explains. Polygamy is a religious practice for Fundamentalist Mormons. To understand how, it is necessary to know something about Mormon theology. In that faith tradition, all human beings are God's embodied spirit children whose life on earth is an opportunity to grow worthy of returning to God's celestial kingdom.[23] The most worthy humans can achieve "exaltation,"[24] or eternal life in the celestial kingdom, which is the highest degree of glory after death[25] and the ultimate religious goal for all

[22] 2011 BCSC 1588 (Can.).

[23] The First Presidency and Council of the Twelve Apostles of the Church of Jesus Christ of Latter-day Saints, *The Family: A Proclamation To The World*, The Church of Jesus Christ of Latter-day Saints (Sep. 23, 1995), www.lds.org/topics/family-proclamation?lang=eng&cid=PA0414-02 ("In the premortal realm, spirit sons and daughters knew and worshipped God as their Eternal Father and accepted His plan by which His children could obtain a physical body and gain earthly experience to progress toward perfection and ultimately realize their divine destiny as heirs of eternal life.").

[24] *Eternal Life*, The Church of Jesus Christ of Latter-day Saints, www.lds.org/topics/eternal-life?lang=eng ("Eternal life, or exaltation, is to live in God's presence.").

[25] *Celestial Kingdom*, The Church of Jesus Christ of Latter-day Saints, www.lds.org/topics/celestial-kingdom?lang=eng&query=celestial+Kingdom (describing the celestial kingdom as "[t]he highest of the three degrees or kingdoms of glory in heaven").

Mormons, both mainstream and fundamentalist.[26] Exaltation is limited to those who "remain[] faithful to the ordinances and covenants of the temple."[27] This includes entering into a marriage sanctioned and conducted by the church,[28] known as a "celestial marriage."[29]

Polygamy increases the number of progeny a man can have. For the early Mormons, it served as a way to ensure that more of God's spirit children awaiting embodiment by birth would be born to Mormon fathers in Mormon homes, where they would have the opportunity to become exalted and enter the kingdom of their heavenly father, God.[30] For Fundamentalist Mormons, polygamous marriages are the only marriages that are celestial and offer the possibility of eternal life.[31] For those holding these beliefs, the only way to enter the celestial kingdom is to serve God by maximizing the number of children born to the limited number of men who can achieve exaltation (righteous Fundamentalist men). To deny a Fundamentalist Mormon the opportunity to enter into

[26] Here, "mainstream" refers to the Mormon Church, which the vast majority of Mormons follow today; that group largely stopped performing polygamous marriages in 1890 and began excommunicating those who continued the practice in 1904. *The Manifesto and the End of Plural Marriage*, THE CHURCH OF JESUS CHRIST OF LATTER-DAY SAINTS, www.lds.org/topics/the-manifesto-and-the-end-of-plural-marriage?lang=eng. "Fundamentalist" refers to sects that broke from the LDS after the Manifesto, which ended plural marriage in the Mormon Church, *id.*; the FDLS view polygamy as the only form of "celestial marriage."

[27] Russell M. Nelson, *Salvation and Exaltation*, THE CHURCH OF JESUS CHRIST OF LATTER-DAY SAINTS, www.lds.org/general-conference/2008/04/salvation-and-exaltation?lang=eng&query=women+exaltation.

[28] *See* Doctrines and Covenants 131:1–4 ("And in order to obtain the highest, a man must enter into this order of the priesthood [meaning the new and everlasting covenant of marriage]; And if he does not, he cannot obtain it.").

[29] Russell M. Nelson, *Celestial Marriage*, THE CHURCH OF JESUS CHRIST OF LATTER-DAY SAINTS, www.lds.org/general-conference/2008/10/celestial-marriage?lang=eng ("A temple marriage is also called a celestial marriage.").

[30] *Plural Marriage and Families in Early Utah*, THE CHURCH OF JESUS CHRIST OF LATTER-DAY SAINTS, www.lds.org/topics/plural-marriage-and-families-in-early-utah?lang=eng ("The Book of Mormon identifies one reason for God to command [plural marriage]: to increase the number of children born in the gospel covenant in order to 'raise up seed unto [the Lord]' (Jacob 2:30).").

[31] *Is Plural Marriage Required for Exaltation?* MORMON FUNDAMENTALISM, www.mormonfundamentalism.com/archive/NEWFILES/IsPMRequiredToday.htm ("Modern polygamists . . . assert[] that plural marriage is always required [and] [t]hat . . . God has always expected His people to practice polygamy or suffer eternal consequences"). *See also* Janet Bennion, *Women of Principle: Female Networking, in* CONTEMPORARY MORMON POLYGYNY 151–52 (1998) (describing fundamentalist Mormon beliefs that plural marriage is essential to receive "the highest rewards" and, especially for women, failure to enter into plural marriage can result in "losing their place in the kingdom," "damnation," or losing their "exaltation") (hereafter, Bennion, *Women of Principle*).

polygamous marriage is, therefore, to prevent both service to God and access to their own exaltation.[32]

Statutes criminalizing polygamy put individuals with these beliefs to a hard choice. They can choose to avoid polygamy, thereby giving up the possibility of exaltation/eternal life. Alternatively, they can practice their religion under the threat of criminal conviction,[33] using strategies to avoid such prosecution. Some polygamous families have left the country altogether.[34] Those who have stayed in mainstream society have either imposed extreme secrecy on family members or have kept each subfamily (a wife and her children) widely separated to avoid suspicion.[35] Others have moved to isolated homogenous communities where there is no one to report them to the authorities.[36] Each of these strategies has its own negative psychic, economic, and social consequences. These consequences are without doubt a substantial burden on religious practice required by RFRA and the state RFRAs.[37]

II THE COMPELLING STATE INTEREST IN PREVENTING POLYGAMY

If a RFRA challenge is brought against state criminal polygamy laws, states defending them must show that such laws serve a compelling state interest. While the state interests discussed in *Reynolds* – such as harms to a monogamous society and the avoidance of political despotism – may suffer from not having laid an adequate foundation, contemporary state interests in protecting women and children from abuse also need a foundation, not mere assertion. That lack of foundation ultimately doomed defenses of traditional-only marriage in *Obergefell*.[38] As this section shows, the *Reference* court detailed an evidentiary basis for the view that harms result from polygamy, to both individuals within polygamous groups and society in

32 *Id.*

33 Dorothy Allred Solomon, Daughter of the Saints 156–57 (2003) (daughter of Apostolic United Brethren sect leader Rulon Allred describes her father's imprisonment in 1945).

34 *Id.* at 78–79 (describing an attempt to set up a colony for Mormon polygamists in 1890), 104–12 (describing the hardships endured in Mexico until they were forced to leave by the Mexican revolution), 165–70 (describing how Rulon Allred moved his polygamous family to Mexico in 1947 to avoid violating his probation and returning to prison), 191–95 (describing how the families with children born after Rulon Allred's prison term had to go to Mexico to avoid incriminating their father).

35 *Id.* at 177, 204–11 (describing the scattering of wives and children to different states to avoid further prosecution in 1955).

36 Janet Bennion, Polygamy in Primetime: Media, Gender and Politics in Mormon Fundamentalism 27–28 (2012).

37 *Cf.* Reference, 2011 BCSC ¶¶ 1091–93 (holding that the Canadian law burdens religion).

38 Hong, Chapter 14, this volume.

general. However, questions remain as to whether the state has a compelling interest that warrants a no exemption for religious polygamists stance.

A *Reynolds v. U.S.*

The discussion of polygamy's harms in *Reynolds* is confined to two paragraphs in the decision. It begins with a blatantly racist disparagement of polygamy, that polygamy has "always been odious among the northern and western nations of Europe, and, until the establishment of the Mormon Church, was almost exclusively a feature of the life of Asiatic and of African people."[39] Later, in *Late Corp. of The Church of Jesus Christ of Latter-day Saints v. United States*,[40] the Court would describe polygamy as "a return to barbarism" and "contrary to the spirit of Christianity, and of the civilization which Christianity has produced in the western world."[41] The modern polygamy case *Brown v. Buhman* properly characterized these statements as an example of "Orientalism"[42] – that is, an appeal to the racial and moral superiority of the West over the Orient. That tinge of racism led the district court to dismiss the government's justifications for criminalizing polygamy as inconsistent with the Supreme Court's modern "religious freedom, due process, [and] equal protection" jurisprudence.[43]

1 Harm to Society

There is, however, more to the critique of polygamy in *Reynolds* than *Brown* gives credit for, as this section shows. As argued in more depth elsewhere,[44]

39 98 U.S. at 164.

40 136 U.S. 1 (1890) (upholding the revocation of the church's corporate charter and the seizure of its property due to its promotion of polygamy).

41 *Id.* at 49. For a review of primary sources, *see* Witte, Chapter 17, this volume (noting that Roman law also classified polygamy as barbaric).

42 947 F.Supp. 3d at 1182–83 (describing what Professor Edward Said called "Orientalism," a 19th-century ideology of "Western superiority and Oriental inferiority," and attributing the decision in *Reynolds* to that ideology).

43 *Id.* at 1188–89 (suggesting that it would have found *Reynolds* "no longer . . . good law" but for the continued citation of *Reynolds* by both the Supreme Court and the U.S. Court of Appeals for the Tenth Circuit).

44 *See* Maura I. Strassberg, *Scrutinizing Polygamy*, 64 Emory L. J.1815,1822–27 (2015) (arguing that while *Reynolds* identified two state interests, it concluded, but did not show, that prohibition of polygamy was essential to achieving those interests); Maura I. Strassberg, *Distinctions of Form or Substance: Monogamy, Polygamy and Same-Sex Marriage*, 75 N.C. L. Rev. 1501, 1515–37 (1997) (discussing the connection made between polygamy and despotism in *Reynolds* and tracing it back to the work of Francis Lieber and G.W.F. Hegel).

two potentially viable state interests can be found in the brief *Reynolds* discussion. The first interest is in avoiding harm to an otherwise monogamous society, the U.S. The Court described society as "built" upon marriage, and polygamy as "an offense against society," but it failed to explain how polygamy would "disturb the social condition" of the monogamous society around it.[45] Contemporary courts addressing constitutional challenges to criminalization of polygamy have echoed this state interest in monogamous marriage as a crucial building block of society,[46] but they also failed to explain how polygamy is harmful to American society.

As the recently resolved legal battle over same-sex marriage demonstrates, more is required to show a compelling state interest sufficient to impair a fundamental right. While the right at issue in *Obergefell v. Hodges* was a fundamental right to marriage itself,[47] rather than the statutorily protected free exercise of religion that would undergird RFRA-based polygamy challenges, the general requirement of a compelling state interest in both analyses is the same. In *Obergefell*, the States argued that same-sex marriage would harm the institution of marriage for opposite-sex couples by allowing same-sex partners to marry; fewer opposite-sex partners would choose to marry because marriage would no longer be primarily about natural procreation.[48] The Court did not address whether maximizing the number of opposite-sex partners who marry was actually a compelling state interest. Indeed, it did not even use the words "compelling state interest." Rather, the majority focused on the States' failure to show that opposite-sex couples would be less likely to marry if same-sex marriages were recognized, describing the argument as "counterintuitive"[49] and "wholly illogical,"[50] presumably informed by the jurisdiction's own personal experiences either as members of an opposite-sex married couple and/or as observers of the opposite-sex couples around them.

The lack of "a foundation for the conclusion that allowing same-sex marriage will cause the harmful outcomes they describe"[51] was fatal to the States'

45 Reynolds, *supra* note 2, at 166.

46 *See, e.g.*, Potter v. Murray City, 760 F.2d 1065, 1070 (10th Cir. 1985) ("[m]onogamy is . . . the bedrock upon which our culture is built"); State v. Green, 99 P.3d 820, 830 (Utah 2004) (describing "the State's interest in regulating marriage as an important social unit"); Holm, *supra* note 2, at 743–44 ("Our State's commitment to monogamous unions is a recognition that decisions made by individuals as to how to structure even the most personal of relationships are capable of dramatically affecting public life."). *Compare* Obergefell v. Hodges, 135 S. Ct. 2584, 2590 (2015) ("[T]his Court's cases and the Nation's traditions make clear that marriage is a keystone of our social order.").

47 Obergefell, *supra* note 46, at 2604. 48 *Id.* at 2606. 49 *Id.* at 2607.

50 *Id.* (quoting Kitchen v. Herbert, 755 F.3d 1193, 1223 (10th Cir. 2014)).

51 Obergefell, *supra* note 46, at 2607.

attempt to continue prohibiting same-sex marriage. At the same time, the States did at least identify a specific harmful outcome they were trying to avoid: decreased participation in marriage by procreation-capable, sexually involved opposite-sex couples. Neither *Reynolds* nor subsequent cases specify what polygamy's claimed harmful effects on "society" are. Nor are such harms intuitively obvious. Without more specifics as to what these harms are, it is impossible to evaluate the foundation for the claim that polygamy causes them. Consequently, as thus far developed by American case law, a state interest in avoiding harm to society visited upon it by polygamy likely would not suffice as a compelling state interest.

2 Monogamy Is the Foundation of Liberal Democracy

The second state interest *Reynolds* suggested concerns the political consequences of different forms of marriage: a society built on polygamy will have different fundamental political principles than a society built upon monogamy.[52] More specifically, the *Reynolds* Court stated, polygamy is the natural foundation of political despotism, while monogamy is antithetical to such despotism.[53] Given the Court's understanding that marriage shapes the very political principles that inform governmental structure, *Reynolds* concluded that "there cannot be a doubt that . . . it is within the legitimate scope of the power of every civil government to determine whether polygamy or monogamy shall be the law of social life under its dominion,"[54] unless that power is "restricted by some form of constitution."[55]

Certainly, the need to preserve our non-despotic government would seem to be both a specific and compelling state interest. However, the link between this interest and criminalizing polygamy is far from clear. The Court's conclusion rested upon the writing of Professor Francis Lieber, a 19th-century intellectual who is considered the "founder of American political science"[56]

52 Reynolds, *supra* note 18, at 165–66 ("In fact, according as monogamous or polygamous marriages are allowed, do we find the principles on which the government of the people, to a greater or less extent, rests.").

53 *Id.* at 166 ("[P]olygamy leads to the patriarchal principle, and which, when applied to large communities, fetters the people in stationary despotism, while that principle cannot long exist in connection with monogamy."). *See* Witte, Chapter 17, this volume (tracing the secular ban on polygamy back to the pre-Christian Roman Empire and describing the ban as necessary to avoid tyranny, among other reasons).

54 Reynolds, *supra* note 18, at 166. 55 *Id.*

56 Brown, *supra* note 42, at 1187 (quoting Edwin Brown Firmage & Richard Collin Mangrum, Zion in the Courts: A Legal History of The Church of Jesus Christ of Latter-day Saints 155 (1988) (internal quotation mark omitted)).

but would be considered by modern social scientists to be a political or anthropological philosopher.[57] However, scholarly attempts to connect monogamy to the emergence of democracy, and ultimately gender equality, remain more speculative than empirical, as the *Reference* court noted.[58] In the absence of empirical evidence that polygamy is incompatible with democracy, this interest, which would be compelling if established, may suffer from a "foundation" problem similar to the states' argument in *Obergefell*. Absent more, it is not likely to survive strict scrutiny.

B Contemporary American Justifications: Protecting Women and Children from Abuse

More recent polygamy decisions identify one specific harm the avoidance of which would certainly qualify as a compelling state interest: protecting women and children from crimes such as "incest, sexual assault, statutory rape, and failure to pay child support."[59] In *State v. Green*, the Utah Supreme Court found that these crimes "often coincide[d]" with polygamy,[60] that polygamy "provides a favorable environment in which crimes of physical and sexual abuse can thrive," and that "the closed nature of polygamous communities makes obtaining evidence of and prosecuting these crimes challenging."[61] However, in both *Green* and a subsequent polygamy case, *State v. Holm*, the Utah Supreme Court found the avoidance of such crimes as a state interest sufficient to reject constitutional challenges to polygamy's criminalization – in both, the level of scrutiny applied was no more than

57 Maura I. Strassberg, *Distinctions of Form or Substance*, 75 N.C. L. Rev. 1501, 1515–36, 1547–56 (1997) (arguing that Lieber was strongly influenced by and derivative of Georg W. F. Hegel's social and political philosophy and providing a modern Hegelian analysis of monogamous marriage as a foundation of liberal democracy that is consistent with modern American political principles of gender and sexual orientation equality).

58 Maura I. Strassberg, *Scrutinizing Polygamy*, 64 Emory L. J. 1815, 1827–28 (2015) (detailing the testimony on the relationship between monogamy and the development of egalitarian democracy and suggesting that this theory would not be sufficient for strict scrutiny).

59 Green, *supra* note 46, at 830; Holm, *supra* note 46, at 744. *See also* Maura I. Strassberg, *The Crime of Polygamy*, 12 Temple Pol. & Civ. Rts. L. Rev. 353, 369–75, 377–89, 407–11 (2003) (arguing that polygamy is the foundation for "insular and theocratically governed communities" that "shelter criminal abuse of other community members from government observation and sanction").

60 Green, *supra* note 46, at 830.

61 *Id.* (quoting Richard A. Vazquez, Note, *The Practice of Polygamy: Legitimate Free Exercise of Religion or Legitimate Public Menace? Revisiting Reynolds in Light of Modern Constitutional Jurisprudence*, 5 N.Y.U. J. Legis. & Pub. Pol'y 225, 243 (2001) (internal quotation marks omitted)).

rational basis.[62] The evidence of a causal connection between polygamy in general and these crimes was largely anecdotal in nature and limited to polygamy as practiced by Fundamentalist Mormons in the Western U.S.[63] Yet it sufficed under rational basis scrutiny to turn back a constitutional challenge.

In contrast, when these state interests were subjected to strict scrutiny in the recently vacated case of *Brown v. Buhman*, the level of scrutiny triggered by RFRA, the court found a paucity of evidence showing "a causal relationship or even a strong correlation between the practice of polygamy . . . and the offenses of 'incest, sexual assault, statutory rape, and failure to pay child support.'"[64] In essence, *Brown* concludes that there is a lack of "foundation" for the claim that polygamy leads to abuse of women and children – fatal deficits in the state's case of a compelling state interest.

What sort of foundation for this claim is currently available? Three major polygamous Mormon sects operate in the U.S., as well as numerous small groups and independent families.[65] Much of the recent negative publicity about polygamy has concerned Warren Jeffs and the Fundamentalist FLDS communities he has shaped and established, such as the Yearning

62 Green, *supra* note 46, at 830; Holm, *supra* note 46, at 744–5.

63 *See, e.g.*, Green, *supra* note 46, at 830 (convicting man of criminal nonsupport and rape of a child in addition to polygamy and citing State v. Kingston, 46 P.3d 761 (Utah Ct. App. 2002), which affirmed the conviction of a polygamist for incest and sexual conduct with a 16-year old); Holm, 1*supra* note 46, at 730, 744 (affirming conviction for polygamous marriage and unlawful sexual conduct with a minor). *See also* Bennion, Polygamy in Primetime, *supra* note 36, at 214–15 (describing the now defunct anti-polygamy website Tapestry Against Polygamy and its accounts of systematic incest, sexual abuse, rape, statutory rape, beatings, and financial exploitation and control); Brent W. Jeffs & Maia Salavitz, Lost Boy 67–69 (2009) (describing his rape at age five by his uncle, Warren Jeffs, prior to the latter's leadership of the FLDS); Flora Jessops & Paul R. T. Brown, Church of Lies (2009) (detailing a woman's molestation and rape by her father and numerous escape attempts while growing up in the FLDS); Carolyn Jessop & Laura Palmer, Escape (2008) (Jessop's escape with eight children from a coerced and abusive FLDS polygamous marriage); Elissa Wall & Lisa Pulitzer, Stolen Innocence: My Story of Growing Up in a Polygamous Sect, Becoming a Teenage Bride, and Breaking Free of Warren Jeffs (2009) (giving autobiography of FLDS woman who was coerced at age fourteen to marry her cousin and later became the center of the criminal case against Warren Jeffs).

64 947 F.Supp. 3d at 1120 (quoting Holm, *supra* note 46, at 775) (Durham, C.J., dissenting)), vacated 822 F.3d 1151 (2016) (vacating as moot district court holding that aspects of Utah's polygamy law selectively targeted religious practice and failed free exercise strict scrutiny).

65 Janet Bennion, *History, Culture, and Variability of Mormon Schismatic Groups*, *in* Modern Polygamy in the United States: Historical, Cultural and Legal Issues 102–07 (Cardell Jacobson & Lara Burton eds., Oxford 2011).

for Zion ("YFZ") Ranch in Texas and the town of Short Creek, Utah.[66] The FLDS is the second-largest of the three major polygamous Mormon sects that operate in the U.S.[67] More than anecdotal evidence connects FLDS polygamy and statutory rape. The Texas raid on the YFZ Ranch led to convictions of ten FLDS men, including Jeffs, for having sex with their underage plural wives,[68] with another eleven convictions of men from other FLDS communities.[69] The Kingstons, another smaller sect, are "known for the large number of underage marriages they perform, the highest number of incestuous marriages, and the highest natural birth rate of any of the fundamentalist Mormon groups."[70] Only two convictions have

66 Kelly McLaughlin, *Warren Jeffs' Ranch on Sale for $20m*, DAILY MAIL (June 25, 2015), www.dailymail.co.uk/news/article-3143747/Texas-authorities-left-care-Yearning-Zion-Ranch-belonged-Fundamentalist-Church-Jesus-Christ-Day-Saints.html.

67 *Id.* at 103–04 (estimating the FLDS to have 8000 members as of 2008).

68 *See, e.g.*, Warren Steed Jeffs v. State, 2012 WL 1068797, at *1 (Tex. App. 2012) (FLDS prophet Warren Jeffs convicted of aggravated sexual assault of a child and sexual assault of a child); Raymond Merril Jessop v. State, 368 S.W. 3d 653, 664–65 (Texas App. 2012) (holding the evidence of a thirty-two-year-old's celestial marriage to a fifteen-year-old girl followed by the birth a child shown genetically to be the husband's child when the girl was sixteen sufficed to prove the elements of sexual assault of a child); Abram Harker Jeffs v. State, 2012 WL 1660612 (Tex App. 2012) (convicting thirty-four-year-old man of sexual assault of a child for marriage to fourteen-year-old girl who had his child at age sixteen); Lehi Barlow Jeffs v. State, 2012 WL 601846 at *1 (Tex. App. 2012) (affirming conviction for sexual assault on a child); Keate v. State, 2012 WL 896200 (Tex. App. 2012) (convicting fifty-three-year-old of sexual assault on a child for marriage to fifteen-year-old girl who had his child at age sixteen); Emack v. State, 354 W.S.3d 828, 834–839 (Tex. App. 2011) (sexual assault of a child and bigamy); Matthew Waller, *Progress: FLDS Prosecutions, Plea Deals Keep Courts Busy*, SAN ANGELO STANDARD-TIMES (Feb. 26, 2011), archive.gosanangelo.com/news/progress-flds-prosecutions-plea-deals-keep-courts-busy-ep-439993463–356927951.html (describing the conviction of Merril Leroy Jessop for sexual assault of a fifteen-year-old child, a plea by Lehi Barlow Jeffs to bigamy, and the conviction after trial of FLDS member Keith William Dutson of sexual assault of a fifteen-year-old); Matthew Waller, *Sect Member Gets 7 Years*, SAN ANGELO STANDARD-TIMES (Nov. 1, 2011), archive.gosanangelo.com/news/sect-member-gets-7-years-ep-439580408-356557311.html (reporting Leroy Johnson Steed pled "no contest to two counts of bigamy and one count of child sexual assault" involving a sixteen-year-old).

69 Holm, *supra* note 21, at 730, 749. For the ten 2005 cases, see Janet Bennion, *History, Culture, and Variability of Mormon Schismatic Groups*, *in* MODERN POLYGAMY IN THE UNITED STATES: HISTORICAL, CULTURAL AND LEGAL ISSUES 116 (Cardell Jacobson & Lara Burton eds., Oxford 2011). Importantly, sexual abuse was likely underreported. *See* David Kelly & Gary Cohn, *Blind Eye to Culture of Abuse*, L.A. TIMES (May 12, 2006), www.latimes.com/news/la-na-sect12may12-story.html#page=2 (recounting the story of a sexual abuse victim who "never once considered going to the police," the polygamist police chief's failure to report 20–25 child sex abuse cases, and light jail sentences for perpetrators, such as thirteen days for a repeated sexual abuse of five daughters between the ages of twelve and nineteen, and thirty days for molestation of a four-year-old).

70 BENNION, POLYGAMY IN PRIME TIME, *supra* note 36, at 40.

stuck.[71] The Apostolic United Brethren ("AUB"), the largest polygamist Mormon sect, which reportedly boasts about 10,000 members,[72] has had only one conviction since 2000.[73] True, in the 1990s four highly placed leaders of the AUB were accused, and in some cases convicted, of child molestation.[74] Twenty-three other cases of incest during the 1990s in an 800-person AUB community in Montana went unreported to the police.[75] In addition, outside the three main sects, there has been only one sexual abuse conviction of an "independent" Mormon polygamist.[76] With less community connections and oversight, these independent families, which comprise almost 40% of fundamentalist Mormons who either live in or believe in polygamy,[77] may be fertile ground for abuse. Still, it will be extremely difficult to assess its frequency.

For anthropologist Janet Bennion, who has observed polygamous family life in the AUB and in the LeBaron sect in Mexico, it is the criminalization of polygamy itself that makes abuse more likely by motivating polygamists to locate in isolated rural environments where women are less able to leave or

71 State v. Kingston, 46 P.3d 761 (Utah App. 2002) (affirming the conviction of David Ortell Kingston for incest and sexual conduct with a minor for marrying his sixteen-year-old niece); Linda Thomson, *Kingston Pleads Guilty to Incest Charge*, Deseret News (Oct. 31, 2003), www.deseretnews.com/article/525034698/Kingston-pleads-guilty-to-incest-charge.html?pg=all (Jeremy Ortell Kingston pled guilty to incest for marriage to his fifteen-year-old first cousin).

72 Bennion, *supra* note 69.

73 *Utah Mother Sentence for Sexual Abuse of Daughters*, KSL (Mar. 21, 2003), www.ksl.com/?nid=148&sid=91382 (describing the conviction of Gustavo Palacios for sexually abusing his two stepdaughters and the conviction of the children's mother, his wife, for encouraging the abuse, for which she received a lenient sentence from the judge due to the mother's own sexual abuse as a child in a polygamous family). *See infra* note 74 (naming Cherval or Shevroll Palacios, whose real name was Gustavo, as a member of the AUB Priesthood Council).

74 Janet Bennion, "*Abbas Raptus: Exploring Factors that Contribute to the Sexual Abuse of Females in Rural Mormon Fundamentalist Communities*," Forum on Public Policy: A Journal of the Oxford Round Table, at 10–13 (Fall 2007), www.forumonpublicpolicy.com/archive06/bennion.pdf (naming John Jay, Joe Thompson, and Cherval Palacios); Joseph B. Thompson, Mormon Fundamentalism, www.mormonfundamentalism.com/ChartLinks/AUB.htm ("Within the Priesthood Council over the past decade, several members were accused of child molestation causing the release of Joseph Thompson in 1994 (Thompson was the last Council member called in 1952 by Joseph Musser), George Maycock in 1998, and Shevroll Palacios in 2002.").

75 Bennion, *Abbas Raptus*, *supra* note 74, at 7.

76 Green, *supra* note 46. *See* Bennion, Polygamy in Prime Time, *supra* note 36, at 107 (describing Tom Green as an "unaffiliated independent polygamist").

77 *Survey Finds Increase in Polygamous Communities*, KSL (Sep. 28, 2009), www.ksl.com/?sid=8093904 (finding that 15,000 out of then estimated 38,000 were independents not affiliated with any of the organized sects).

find supportive law enforcement.[78] Bennion also argues that the practice of fundamentalist polygamy should not be equated with the abuses found in the FLDS and the Kingstons.[79] Well-functioning families and communities, she says, can be found within the "rich diversity of polygamist lifestyles."[80] In particular, she notes that the "AUB is currently considered by law officials to be one of the more 'progressive' groups"[81] – in recent years, it has formally repudiated both underage and arranged marriages, become more open to law enforcement, emphasized that "child and spousal abuse and incest [were] serious sins," and encouraged "victims ... to report the incidents to the police."[82] Unfortunately, whether or not the AUB is truly practicing polygamy free of these abuses will only be known decades from now, when the children of today are adults who can freely report any intra-familial childhood abuse.[83] Even Bennion agrees that her observations of polygamy do not provide the final answer to the connection between polygamy and abuse and that "a thorough investigation of polygamy must be made to clarify whether only a few miscreants are guilty of abuse or all polygamous families contain abuse."[84]

Preventing child sexual abuse would likely be a compelling state interest if a sufficient connection to polygamy can be shown. The problem remains whether existing evidence is sufficient to establish a compelling state interest in *criminalizing* Fundamentalist Mormon polygamy, let alone all practices of polygamy. Because the U.S. Supreme Court has little experience evaluating empirical evidence to establish compelling state interests, it is impossible to know what might or might not be sufficient to create the foundation between harms such as child sexual abuse and the conduct targeted by state law.

78 Bennion, Polygamy in Prime Time, *supra* note 36, at 16 ("it is my belief that forcing polygamous families to the fringes of society facilitates instances of abuse taking place outside the watchful eye of law enforcement"). *See also infra* Section II.D.2.a.

79 Bennion, *supra* note 69 (protesting "the attempts made by the government to enact policies against entire communities ... [without taking into account] the variability and complexity in Mormon fundamentalism").

80 Bennion, Polygamy in Prime Time, *supra* note 36, at 8–9 (describing "a happy little polygamous, self-sustained community whose members lived contentedly off the grid" with "many examples of female autonomy, achievement, and contentment"); Bennion, *supra* note 69.

81 Bennion, *supra* note 69.

82 Bennion, Polygamy in Prime Time, *supra* note 36, at 36–37.

83 *Polygamy Group Launches Investigation of Its Leader after His Daughter – Star of TLC's "My Five Wives" – Claims He Molested Her When She was 12*, Daily Mail (Dec. 4, 2014), www.dailymail.co.uk/news/article-2859686/Polygamy-group-investigates-abuse-allegations.html (recounting allegations of the current AUB leader's daughter, Lynn Thompson, that her father molested her more than twenty years before).

84 *Id.* at 16.

C The *Reference* Account of the Harms of Polygamy

Reference grounded its examination of harms in empirical as well as anecdotal evidence. Before discussing the specific harms of polygamy detailed by the *Reference* court, the evidentiary significance of the court's findings should be noted.

1 The Evidentiary Basis of *Reference*'s Findings

After forty-two days of hearings, ninety affidavits and expert reports, and "Brandeis Brief materials . . . comprise[d of] several hundred legal and social science articles, books and DVDs,"[85] the British Columbia Supreme Court, a trial-level court, issued a 228-page opinion in *Reference* setting out the psychological, sociological, economic, and political impacts of polygamy worldwide. The court held that these harms were sufficient to justify criminalization, despite the resulting infringements on liberty and freedom of religion guaranteed by the Canadian Charter of Rights and Freedoms.[86] The *Reference* court's finding that polygamy is harmful to "women, children and to society"[87] was largely grounded on the testimony of three expert witnesses: an evolutionary psychologist whose testimony was based on "an extensive review of the academic literature on polygyny in the sciences and social sciences";[88] an economist who was an expert in the economic effects of polygyny;[89] and a political scientist who conducted a statistical analysis using a unique 172-country dataset with ten years of data about women and children and the countries themselves.[90] *Reference* found that there was a "remarkable convergence of the evidence"[91] at every possible level of analysis, "from high level predictions based on human evolutionary psychology, to the recurring harms identified in intra-cultural and cross-cultural studies, to the 'on the ground' evidence of polygyny in contemporary North America."[92] All show

85 2011 BCSC 1588 at 2–3, ¶¶ 28, 32. 86 *Id.* ¶ 1359.

87 Reference, 2011 BCSC 1588, ¶ 1331.

88 *Id.* ¶ 495, 496 (noting that Dr. Joseph Henrich "was qualified as an expert in psychology, particularly evolutionary psychology, in economics and in anthropology, as well as in the interdisciplinary field of culture, cognition and co-evolution").

89 *Id.* ¶ 588 (referring to Dr. Shoshana Grossbard, Professor of Economics at San Diego State University).

90 *Id.* ¶¶ 580, 609–15 (noting that Dr. Rose McDermott, Professor of Political Science at Brown University "also holds an M.A. in Experimental Social Psychology from Stanford University" and describing the WomanStats Project Database and another database). *See also* Rose McDermott & Jonathan Cowden, *Polygyny and Violence Against Women*, 64 Emory L.J. 1767 (2015).

91 *Id.* ¶ 492. 92 *Id.*

that polygyny is harmful and that "the harms of polygyny do not depend upon a particular regional, religious or cultural context. They can be generalized, and they can be expected to occur wherever polygyny exists."[93]

2 The Harms of Polygamy

As this subsection shows, the *Reference* court found that polygamy's harms extend to men, women, and children within polygamous communities and threaten society in general – harms that doubtless would qualify as compelling state interests to avoid.

A HARMS TO INDIVIDUALS One harm of polygamy stems from simple arithmetic: "when some men are able to have multiple wives simultaneously, other men will be unable to find wives."[94] *Reference* illustrated this as follows:

> Imagine a society of 40 adults, 20 males and 20 females ... Suppose those 20 males vary from the unemployed high-school drop outs to CEOs, or billionaires ... Let's assume that the twelve men with the highest status marry 12 of the 20 women in monogamous marriages. Then, the top five men (25% of the population) all take a second wife, and the top two (10%) take a third wife. Finally, the top guy takes a fourth wife. This means that of all marriages, 58% are monogamous. Only men in the to[p] [sic] 10% of status or wealth married more than two women. The most wives anyone has is four. The degree of polygynous marriage is not extreme in cross-cultural perspective ... but it creates a pool of unmarried men equal to 40% of the male population.[95]

Indeed, in the real world, "polygyny causes the proportion of young unmarried men [to unmarried women] to be high, up to a ratio of 150 men to 100 women."[96] Unmarried men are likely to be low status.[97]

Another consequence of this arithmetic is greater competition among men for wives than is found in monogamous communities. This competition results in women getting married at younger and younger ages.[98] Early marriage has the effect of depressing the socioeconomic advancement of polygynous wives, as they receive less education, have lower literacy levels, and participate in the labor market less.[99] In addition, in polygynous marriages, a greater number of

93 *Id.* ¶ 624. 94 *Id.* ¶ 505. 95 *Id.*¶ 505 (omissions in original). 96 *Id.* ¶ 586.

97 *Id.* ¶ 500, 505, 555.

98 *Id.* ¶ 779. See also para. 499 (noting that woman are more likely to "marry[] before age 18, or be[] 'promised' in marriage prior to age 18").

99 *Id.* ¶¶ 621, 784, 622, 789, 533.

children are born to each wife as compared to women in monogamous marriages.[100] The combination of early marriage and increased pregnancies negatively impacts the health of polygynous wives, who experience an increased likelihood of dying in childbirth and a shortened lifespan.[101] Polygyny further adds the stresses of "co-wife conflict," insufficient financial support, marital dissatisfaction and issues of self-esteem, and "higher rates of depressive disorders and other mental health issues."[102]

This competition also leads to increased control of women by men as women come to be perceived as valuable commodities[103]: "men (as fathers, husbands and brothers) ... seek to exercise more control over the choices of women, increasing gender inequality and undermining female autonomy and rights. This is exacerbated by larger age disparities between husbands and wives."[104] Effects of this control and commodification include higher fertility arising from a lack of reproductive autonomy, less divorce and more domestic violence, genital mutilation and sex trafficking, and "discrimination under the law."[105]

Overall, children do not fare as well in polygynous families either because men's ability to invest temporally, emotionally, and monetarily in their offspring recedes as the number of their wives and offspring increase.[106] Furthermore, the competition for wives motivates men to direct their resources toward the acquisition of more wives rather than to the support of existing wives and children.[107] Harms to children found by the court include the following:

> [H]igher infant mortality ... more emotional, behavioural and physical problems, as well as lower educational achievement ... [arising out of] higher levels of conflict, emotional stress and tension in polygynous families ... inability of fathers to give sufficient affection and disciplinary attention to all of their children [and] enhanced risk of psychological and physical abuse and neglect.[108]

For young men and boys, "[t]he sex ratio imbalance inherent in polygyny means that young men are forced out of polygamous communities to sustain

[100] *Id.* ¶ 621. [101] *Id.* ¶ 782.

[102] *Id.* ¶¶ 584, 782; *see also id.* ¶¶ 603, 607–08, 696, 699–700, 780.

[103] *Id.* ¶ 532. *See also* para. 322 (describing how allowing FLDS women to decide whom they would marry resulted in thirteen-year-old girls choosing the youngest suitors, which prevented church leaders from obtaining further young wives which led in the 1950s to a policy of church-controlled marriages, ensuring that church leaders would get the wives they wanted).

[104] *Id.* ¶ 779. [105] *Id.* ¶¶ 621, 782, 532–33, 584, 621, 622.

[106] *See* Witte, Chapter 17, this volume. [107] Reference ¶322, 532.

[108] *Id.* ¶ 783; *see also id.* ¶ 603.

the ability of senior men to accumulate more wives. These young men and boys often receive limited education ... few life skills and little social support."[109] The lower education levels associated with polygyny for men – and women, as noted earlier – means that when they do enter the labor force, their level of employment will be low as well.[110]

B HARMS TO SOCIETY *Reference* also identified ways in which polygamy negatively impacts society more broadly. For the reasons outlined in Section I.B.2.a, polygynous societies will have greater levels of familial poverty.[111] When basic needs are not met, the human resources that societies need to grow are not available; the resulting lack of growth can foster a more authoritarian government in order to avoid the political instability arising from poverty and lack of opportunity.[112] In fact, economic modeling of the impact of imposing monogamy on highly polygynous states showed an increase in per capita gross domestic product ("GDP").[113] Further, "[s]tates with higher levels of polygyny display fewer political rights and civil liberties for both men and women than those with less polygyny."[114]

At the same time, in a society with such commodification of women, the high cost of marriage pushes the many men who are unmarried due to scant resources and prospects "to take substantial risks so they can eventually participate in the mating and marriage market."[115] These risks can take the form of increased antisocial behaviors, such as violence and crime, which are in fact statistically more prevalent in polygamous societies.[116] "States with higher levels of polygyny [also] spend more money per capita on defence [sic], particularly on arms expenditures,"[117] which in turn reduces resources available for "domestic infrastructure and projects geared toward health and education."[118] One legal expert who testified in *Reference*, Dr. Joseph Henrich, speculated that polygamy may promote military aggression[119] for a number of reasons – for example, to exclude outside men from the already competitive marriage market, to expand the marriage market by bringing women in from outside, or to externalize the antisocial behavior of unmarried men and reduce their numbers.[120]

A final harm of polygamy concerns the potential impact of a legitimated practice of polygamy on monogamous marriage. The *Reference* court found that monogamy provides benefits that are not provided by polygamy:

109 *Id.* ¶ 785. 110 *Id.* ¶ 586. 111 *Id.* ¶ 787. 112 Reference, 2011 BCSC 1588, ¶ 787.
113 *Id.* ¶ 535. 114 *Id.* ¶ 621. 115 *Id.* ¶ 505. 116 *Id.* ¶¶ 499, 507–16, 587, 787.
117 *Id.* ¶ 621. 118 *Id.* ¶ 790. 119 *Id.* ¶¶ 534, 536. 120 *Id.* ¶ 536.

> [E]xclusive and enduring monogamous marriage is the best way to ensure paternal certainty and joint parental investment in children. It best ensures that men and women are treated with equal dignity and respect, and that husbands and wives (or same-sex couples), and parents and children, provide each other with mutual support, protection and edification through their lifetimes.[121]

If the practice of polygamy were to increase because it was decriminalized, fewer monogamous marriages presumably would follow, and the benefits of monogamy would decrease, increasing the harms of polygamy.

Of course, some individuals who do not marry monogamously might choose to marry polygamously, so that more polygamy does not lead to less monogamy. However, experience teaches otherwise. Relying in part on France's experience, which saw its polygamous population swell during the forty-to-fifty-year period it allowed immigrants to continue the practice,[122] the *Reference* court found that polygamy's decriminalization would in fact increase polygamy at the expense of monogamy.[123] First, it would increase immigration by polygamists to Canada.[124] Second, it would free citizens with polygamous backgrounds, whether cultural or religious, to reinstate the practice.[125] This might include immigrant citizens and their children with pre-immigration familiarity or involvement in polygamy, as well as a sizeable portion of the mainstream Mormon church that continues to believe that polygamy is required by God when legal conditions make it possible. Third, decriminalization would remove a brake on a natural propensity of humans "towards a polygynous mating system."[126] Finally, the population of people raised in polygamous families would grow at a more rapid rate than that of people raised in monogamous families, simply because polygamous unions produce more children. Across time, the number of people who are more likely to choose polygamous marriage will dwarf those who would prefer monogamous marriage.[127] Even if polygamy never completely replaces monogamy, a significant population of polygamous families would produce the social impacts described earlier, affecting even those in monogamous families.

[121] *Id.* ¶ 884.

[122] *Id.* ¶ 562–64 (noting France changed its immigration policy after the polygamous population swelled to 200,000 and was marked by "co-wife competition, spousal neglect and coercion into marriage at a young age," and overcrowding of living quarters due to inability to afford separate living quarters in an industrialized economy).

[123] *Cf.* Potter v. Murray City, 585 F. Supp. 1126, 1139–40 (D. Utah 1984) (arguing that if polygamy were decriminalized, and perhaps even legally recognized, it would be difficult to contain).

[124] Reference, 2011 BCSC 1588, ¶¶ 555, 557, 558, 560, 567–68, 570, 573, 1317.

[125] *Id.* ¶¶ 309, 559, 575. [126] *Id.* ¶¶ 500–501, 555, 556, 575, 1304. [127] *Id.* ¶¶ 555, 621, 649.

The specific harms to society resulting from polygamy identified by the *Reference* court raise the next question: whether avoiding these harms is sufficiently important to be a compelling state interest. If providing cost-free access to contraception can be assumed to be a compelling state purpose in *Hobby Lobby*, it is difficult to imagine that avoiding the much greater lack of reproductive autonomy that comes from the polygamous commodification of women – along with all the other negative health, educational, economic, and legal consequences for women and children described earlier – would not be a compelling state interest. In addition, avoiding the broader social impacts of an increased practice of polygamy, which could include economic stagnation, more authoritarian government, and greater military aggression, should qualify as compelling state interests.

D *Would Exempting Religious Polygamists from Criminal Penalties Produce the* Reference *Harms?*

Once compelling state interests have been identified, to burden the religious practice RFRA requires a showing that the burden is necessary in order to serve the compelling state interest.[128] This is easier to do when the law is uniformly applied, with no exemptions at all.[129]

1 Underenforcement as an Exemption to the Criminalization of Polygamy

In the context of an RFRA challenge to criminal polygamy laws, the government could easily show that criminal polygamy laws do not have any statutory

[128] O Centro, *supra* note 14, at 445–46.

[129] *See, e.g.*, United States v. Lee, 455 U.S. 252, 260 (1982) (finding, under pre-Smith First Amendment strict scrutiny, that "the tax system could not function if denominations were allowed to challenge the tax system because tax payments were spent in a manner that violates their religious belief"); O Centro, *supra* note 14, at 431–34 (concluding waiver authority for the Attorney General within the Controlled Substances Act plus codification and expansion of a long-standing exemption for peyote use to all "members of every recognized Indian Tribe," rebutted government arguments that the law's effectiveness to protect public health and safety would be undercut if not uniformly applied); Hobby Lobby, *supra* note 4, at 2764 (noting that since more than one-third of 149 million employees with employer-sponsored health insurance received coverage through grandfathered plans that did not have to provide contraceptive coverage under the ACA, and that an additional 34 million employees worked for small employers not covered by the ACA, the government could not claim that only uniform application of the contraceptive mandate was essential to protecting women's health and providing gender equity).

exceptions. However, criminal polygamy laws are rarely enforced.[130] In many states, this is probably because polygamous marriages are not licensed; therefore, polygamous marriages rarely come to the attention of law enforcement. However, in states with large fundamentalist FLDS Mormon populations that live in homogenous, relatively isolated communities, law enforcement is well aware that certain communities practice polygamy.[131]

Choosing not to enforce a law is a matter of prosecutorial discretion. Indeed, Utah law enforcement officials now have a policy that they do not prosecute religious polygamists unless there is a marriage involving a minor or there is evidence of an associated crime, such as domestic/child abuse or statutory rape.[132] Could this lack of enforcement be viewed as the equivalent of an exemption from the law, undercutting the state's claim of a compelling state purpose for criminalizing religious polygamists? In *Brown v. Buhman*, the district court found that selective prosecution "alone supports the 'conclusion that a blanket criminal prohibition on religious polygamous unions is not necessary to further the state's interests, and suggests that a more narrowly tailored law would be just as effective.'"[133]

However, selective prosecution of religious polygamists may actually reflect prosecutorial issues unique to polygamy. These prosecutions often require the state to take custody of the children. For religious reasons, many polygamous wives will have as many children as they can. Prosecuting even one polygamous father, and possibly his wives as well, means leaving many children without one or more parents. Enforcing the law against an entire polygamous community just multiplies this disruption. During the 1953 law enforcement action against the polygamous town of Short Creek, Arizona took custody of 236 children.[134] Similarly, the 2008 action against the YFZ Ranch in Texas resulted in 468 children being taken into state custody.[135] Aside from being

[130] *See, e.g.*, Brown v. Buhman, 947 F. Supp.2d at 1178 (D. Utah 2013), vacated 822 F.3d 1151 (2016).

[131] *Id.* [132] *Id.* at 1179.

[133] *Id.* at 1217 (quoting Holm, *supra* note 46, at 775) (Durham, C.J., dissenting in part) (holding that Utah's selective prosecution was one of several indications that the law was not generally applicable, thus justifying free exercise strict scrutiny under Church of the Lukumi Babalu Aye, Inc. v. City of Hialeah, 508 U.S. 520 (1993), which held that city ordinances that effectively prohibited ritual slaughter of animals for religious purposes, while allowing other kinds of animal killing and slaughter through specific exemptions, were not operationally neutral or generally applicable, subjecting the ordinances to strict scrutiny).

[134] Bennion, Polygamy in Primetime, *supra* note 36, at 27.

[135] *In re* Texas Department of Family and Protective Services, 255 S.W.3d 613, 613 (Tex. 2008) (holding that a polygamous culture was an insufficient basis for a grant of emergency custody over all 468 children living at the YFZ ranch).

very expensive for the state,[136] there is considerable potential for psychological harm to the children. Also, media images of children being torn from their mothers' arms can make the public more sympathetic to polygamists than law enforcement.[137]

Furthermore, liberalized social attitudes toward sexuality and legal recognition of same-sex sexual relations and marriage – combined with a lack of understanding of the broad social reasons for criminalizing polygamy – has led both the public and the legal community to question whether criminalization of polygamy is still constitutional.[138] Prosecutors are not immune to these public perceptions, particularly those who hold elected positions.[139] Limiting prosecution of polygamists to cases involving abuse of women or children – such as in cases involving statutory rape of underage brides, coerced marriages, or domestic violence, as Utah has done[140] – puts the prosecution on the side of individuals the public can easily recognize as victims needing assistance. However, the fact that prosecuting polygamists is uniquely difficult, both practically and politically, does not mean under-enforcement operates as a legislative exemption undercutting the purposes of the law.

2 Would Exempting Religious Polygamists Still Cause Harm?

The fact that no exceptions have been made expressly in criminal polygamy laws does not mean that none could be made without frustrating the

136 Mark Shurtleff, *Religion and Non-State Governance: Warren Jeffs and the FLDS*, 2010 Utah L. Rev. 115, 120–21 (2010) (quoting Utah Attorney General as stating, "I don't have the resources to put you all in prison and take away all your kids, thousands and thousands of children. Texas couldn't handle five hundred; we couldn't handle tens of thousands.").

137 Brent W. Jeffs & Maia Salavitz, Lost Boy 207 (2009) (describing how "images of chastely dressed women and weeping toddlers" arising out of the Short Creek and YFZ raids created negative publicity).

138 Lawrence v. Texas, 539 U.S. 558, 575 (2003) (striking Texas criminal sodomy ban which applied only to persons of the same sex as unconstitutional); Obergefell, *supra* note 46 (holding prohibitions against and nonrecognition of same-sex marriage unconstitutional); Romer v. Evans, 517 U.S. 620, 648–52 (1996) (Scalia, J., dissenting) (predicting that legal normalization of homosexuality would make continued prosecution of polygamy potentially problematic); Obergefell, *supra* note 46, at 2621 (Roberts, C.J., dissenting).

139 Debra Weyermann, *FLDS Continues Abusive Polygamist Practices in Utah and Arizona*, High Country News (June 18, 2012), www.hcn.org/issues/44.10/flds-continues-abusive-polygamist-practices-in-utah-and-arizona?b_start:int=1#body (quoting David Leavitt, who prosecuted Green for bigamy and child rape and lost reelection bid shortly thereafter, as saying this prosecution "cost me my job").

140 Shurtleff, *supra* note 136, at 121 ("But you cannot commit crimes against women and children, or we will prosecute you.").

compelling purpose of such statutes. The necessity of uniformity can only be proven by "scrutiniz[ing] the asserted harm of granting specific exemptions to [these] particular religious claimants."[141] There are two potential ways for the criminalization of religious polygamy to survive this particularized scrutiny: first, show that the practice of polygamy does produce the identified harms within the population of religious practitioners, and second, show that allowing religious polygamy will inflict these harms on the non-polygamous public. This section recaps some of the harms *Reference* established, asking how the state's regulation and *refusal to exempt* people of faith are necessary to achieve the state's goals.

A HARM TO THE RELIGIOUSLY POLYGAMOUS Determining whether the religiously polygamous would suffer the *Reference* harms if allowed to practice polygamy is complicated by one stark reality: not every individual in every polygamous family will suffer these harms. The harms to individuals in *Reference* relied upon statistical analyses of conglomerated polygamous populations. A statistic showing that polygamous wives marry at a younger age than monogamous wives would not mean that all polygamous wives marry at a younger age; some individuals will still marry at a more mature age; although across large groups, fewer will do so.

Moreover, for every *Reference* harm, there will be anecdotal evidence that supports it and anecdotal evidence that does not. Indeed, the *Reference* court was presented with academic studies of FLDS fundamentalist Mormon polygamists showing more than one highly functional family well supported by the husband, with apparently healthy psychological adjustment of children, educational success by both wives and children, and female autonomy in and outside the home.[142] The court also reviewed academic studies and clinical treatment accounts of abuse, curtailed and limited education, difficulty adjusting to mainstream society, health and mental health problems, and extreme control of all facets of life by husbands and fathers.[143]

141 O Centro, *supra* note 14, at 1220, 1224 (finding that the government did not meet its burden of showing that the use of *hoaca* by church members was either dangerous to the health of those who used it under church supervision or posed a threat that the substance would be diverted to the general public).

142 Reference, 2011 BSCS ¶749 (referring to studies by Bennion, Ginat & Altman, and Campbell).

143 *Id.* at 2011 BSCS ¶¶ 654–64 (recounting the testimony of sociologists Stephen Kent and Timothy Dunfield, and clinical psychologist Lawrence Beall, who treated thirty patients who had left polygamous communities).

Insider accounts confirm that both types of families exist within the universe of polygamous families. Testimony in *Reference* emphasized the positive aspects of polygamous family life, which for children included "camaraderie and bond, a richness of people, an 'unloneliness,'" parties, participation in sports, and no experience of abuse, and for wives included "[r]ich relationships among sister wives[, g]reater autonomy . . . [, e]xpanded support networks," as well as masters and professional degrees.[144] The court heard testimony and journalistic accounts of the negative aspects of polygamous family life, including lack of parental attention from a father with nineteen wives and seventy-five children, arranged marriages of younger women to much older men, conflicts among co-wives and abuse of other wives' children, sexual abuse within the family, depression and nervous breakdowns of wives, undereducation and expulsion of excess boys from their families and communities, training children to be obedient and subservient, training girls to believe their life's purpose is to have children, cross-border trafficking of children for marriage and discipline between the U.S. and Canada, devaluation of education, lack of reproductive control, inequality of women, separation of boys and girls, and dominance of favorite wives.[145]

It is unclear how the Supreme Court would deal with a complex and nonuniform experience of harm within the population that would potentially be exempted. If the Court in *Hobby Lobby* had not assumed the presence of a compelling state interest, this issue would have arisen there. While the individual owners of the corporations would have benefited from stepping aside from the mandate, their women employees and female dependents of their employees – some of whom would *not* have shared the owners' religious beliefs – would have benefited by the cost-free access to such contraceptive methods, which they ultimately received under the Court's resolution of the case. A similar issue of how widespread the benefit need be existed in the background of *Wisconsin v. Yoder*;[146] the Court could avoid the question because the record showed no conflict between Amish parents and their children, and the children were not a party to the litigation.[147] As a result, the *Yoder* Court did not have to consider the "possible competing interests of parents, children, and the State" that would arise if there were Amish children

144 *See, e.g.*, Reference, 2011 BCSC ¶¶ 683, 690–91. 145 *Id.* 649, 667–74.

146 406 U.S. 205, 218, 231 (1972) (finding the requirement of public education through age sixteen for Amish adolescents severely burdened the free exercise of both the "Amish community" and individual Amish parents and children, while failing to advance the self-sufficiency of Amish children or their preparation for citizenship). *See* Wilson & Sanders, Chapter 13, this volume, for a detailed discussion of *Yoder*.

147 *Id.* at 231–32; *see supra* note 146.

who wished to attend high school but were prevented from doing so by their parents. Elsewhere in this volume, Offit (Chapter 12), Dwyer (Chapter 8), and Wilson & Sanders (Chapter 13) paint poignant portraits of instances where the interests of parents and their children collide. Prior Supreme Court precedent involving strict scrutiny simply leaves unclear what amount of harm must exist to the class seeking a religious exemption to show that a compelling state interest in applying its laws exists.

A second potential obstacle to showing that a religious exemption would result in harm to religious polygamists arises from the nature of the data underlying the 172-country statistical analysis relied upon by *Reference*. That analysis compared data from countries where polygamy is legal or tolerated to data from countries, such as Canada and the U.S., where only monogamy is legal. What was not available is data showing specific outcomes for all religiously polygamous persons living in various American states.[148] This critique was raised but dismissed in *Reference* for three reasons: the statistical analysis had addressed this by controlling for GDP;[149] there was specific statistical evidence from the Canadian FLDS polygamous community of Bountiful showing higher than expected numbers of teen births,[150] a greater age difference between parents,[151] significant teen births to women who had been born in American FLDS communities,[152] and lower educational outcomes for secondary and post-secondary enrollment; and the "congruity ... in the dangers of polygamy found in the African and Middle Eastern based empirical studies ..., those predicted by ... [the 172-country statistical] work, and those found 'on the ground' and anecdotally in North America."[153]

An additional concern, raised in *Reference*, is that the criminalization of polygamy, rather than polygamy itself, may be responsible for the harms anecdotally reported to arise from FLDS polygamy.[154] Making polygamy a crime requires polygamous families to hide their status by extreme secrecy[155] or by developing geographically isolated polygamous communities. Both strategies create a particularly conducive environment for

148 *Id.* ¶¶ 641.

149 *Id.* ¶¶ 618, 642 (finding that the statistically significant correlations between polygyny and negative outcomes that persisted after controlling for GDP provided meaningful information about polygyny itself).

150 *Id.* ¶¶ 711–23. 151 *Id.*¶ 722. 152 *Id.* ¶¶ 724–25. 153 *Id.* ¶ 643.

154 *Id.* ¶ 598 (recounting the testimony of Professor Angela Campbell that "criminalized polygamy gives rise to insularity, and that women in such communities may be more vulnerable to abuse").

155 Dorothy Allred Solomon, Daughter of the Saints: Growing Up in Polygamy 326 (2003).

abusers.[156] Again, the congruity between statistical evidence on the outcomes of polygamy in countries where it is allowed and the statistical and anecdotal evidence coming from Canada and the U.S. convinced the *Reference* court that polygamy itself causes the most problematic negative outcomes, not its criminalization.

When Chief Justice John Roberts described RFRA scrutiny in *Hobby Lobby* as evaluating "the marginal interest in enforcing the [law]"[157] against religious practitioners, he did not explain what amount of harm avoided would satisfy the state's burden – or how conflicting evidence of harm would impact the court's conclusion. Here, the question becomes how much evidence is needed that polygamy is responsible for harms to its practitioners. Should either of these issues be viewed as undermining claims for a compelling state interest in protecting polygamists from these harms, the weight of the scrutiny would shift to the necessity of protecting the non-polygamous public from the harms of polygamy, taken up next.

B. HARMS TO THE NON-POLYGAMOUS PUBLIC RFRA scrutiny can also be satisfied by showing that exempting religious polygamists from criminal polygamy laws would impose polygamy's harms on other Americans – namely, the monogamous public and society in general. The *Reference* court found that decriminalization of polygamy would expand the practice in Canada "non-trivially,"[158] increasing its resulting in individual and social harms and decreasing monogamy's individual and social benefits.[159] Would an exemption for religious polygamists in the U.S. have the same effect?

An initially small polygamous population naturally increases fairly rapidly. Indeed, in the 125 years since the mainstream LDS church stopped polygamy, a small group of holdout fundamentalists has produced an American population of somewhere between 21,000 and 50,000 individuals who view polygamy as a religious mandate.[160] While conversion in the FLDS and other fundamentalist belief systems has contributed to this growth, 75% of that population is estimated to have been born into fundamentalist communities.[161] Given that this growth occurred while polygamy

156 *See id.* at 18. ("[T]he secrecy imposed by an illegal lifestyle further undermines individual development, increasing the likelihood of abuse and exploitation."); Reference, 2011 BCSC ¶ 310.

157 Hobby Lobby, *supra* note 4, at 2779. 158 Reference, 2011 BCSC ¶ 576. 159 *Id.* ¶ 885.

160 D. Michael Quinn, *Plural Marriage and Mormon Fundamentalism*, 31 DIALOGUE 1, 23 (Summer 1998).

161 *Id.*

was criminalized, it seems likely that providing a religious exemption from criminal prosecution would accelerate this population's growth.

A much greater expansion of polygamy could come from mainstream LDS church members reverting to polygamy. Today, there are more than 6 million American LDS members,[162] and 15 million LDS members worldwide as of 2014.[163] The LDS church instructs that while polygamy was a divinely mandated practice during the church's early years, that mandate was subsequently suspended.[164] Decriminalization could be interpreted as a sign by some members or even leaders of a new divine mandate for polygamy's return.[165]

In addition, 2.7 million American Muslims[166] might seek a religious exemption for polygamy.[167] The Muslim population in the U.S. is expected to more than double in the next forty years.[168] An unknown number of American Wiccans might assert similar claims, as the *Reference* court noted.[169] Add to this the potential religious liberty claims of Christian fundamentalists such as Preacher Don Milton, who views polygamy as the divinely ordained way for

162 Newsroom, *Facts and Statistics: United States*, THE CHURCH OF JESUS CHRIST OF LATTER-DAY SAINTS, www.mormonnewsroom.org/facts-and-statistics/country/united-states (6,466,267 American church members).

163 Newsroom, *Worldwide Statistics*, THE CHURCH OF JESUS CHRIST OF LATTER-DAY SAINTS, www.mormonnewsroom.org/facts-and-statistics (15,372,337 church members worldwide).

164 *Plural Marriage and Families in Early Utah*, THE CHURCH OF JESUS CHRIST OF LATTER-DAY SAINTS, www.lds.org/topics/plural-marriage-and-families-in-early-utah?lang=eng.

165 *See* Zoe Mintz, *Utah Polygamy Ban Reversal "Bad News" for LDS Church: Mormon Scholar*, INTERNATIONAL BUSINESS TIMES, August 29, 2014, www.ibtimes.com/utah-polygamy-ban-reversal-bad-news-lds-church-mormon-scholar-1673848%20 (suggesting that the decriminalization of polygamy in Utah resulting from *Brown* will pressure the LDS church to accept polygamy or encourage LDS members to affiliate with polygamous Mormon sects).

166 *Religious Composition by Country, 2010–2050*, PEW RESEARCH CENTER (Apr. 2, 2015), www.pewforum.org/2015/04/02/religious-projection-table/. *See also* Barbara Bradley Hagerty, *Some Muslims in U.S. Quietly Engage in Polygamy*, NPR (May 27, 2008), www.npr.org/templates/story/story.php?storyId=90857818 (noting that academic estimates for the number of Muslims living in polygamous families in the U.S. ranged from 50,000 to 100,000).

167 2011 BCSC at ¶ 243 (noting that Qur'an 4:3 – "If you fear that you will not be just to the orphans, then marry women of your choosing, either a second, third, or fourth" – "has been interpreted as providing men with a license to marry up to four wives as long as they treat those wives justly").

168 *The Future of World Religions: Population Growth Projections 2010-2050*, PEW RESEARCH CENTER (Apr. 2, 2015), www.pewforum.org/2015/04/02/religious-projections-2010-2050/ (projecting that Muslims will grow from 0.9% of the U.S. population in 2010 to 2.1% in 2050).

169 *Estimates of the Number of Wiccans in the U.S.*, RELIGIOUS TOLERANCE, www.religioustolerance.org/estimated-number-of-wiccans-in-the-united-states-4.htm (gathering estimates from 1972 through 2008, which range enormously from a few hundred thousand to several million adherents); 2011 BCSC ¶ 1092(c) (explaining that for Wiccans, "all forms of consensual sexual and emotional ties that adults freely enter into are sacred, or at a minimum, are potentially routes to an encounter with the sacred"). *See* Kar, Chapter 15, this volume, for a similar account of marriage as bringing one closer to God, using Christian texts.

men to satisfy their "God given desires,"[170] and one can imagine a flood of claims.

Indeed, given the ease by which religious bases for polygamy can be identified, the natural propensity toward polygamy may push additional individuals to find a way to take advantage of a potential RFRA religious exemption.[171] As the district court judge in *Potter v. Murray City* noted in 1984:

> It would be the height of naiveté to suppose that the lawful practice of polygamy thus could be limited to those of the plaintiff's faith, leaving aside the problem of the false assertion of religious motivation for physical gratification. The gate would be open by the developing trend of decision to everyone who might desire more than one wife at a time on the basis of his own particular religious belief.[172]

It may also be the case that nonreligious, morally based claims to polygamy would have to be given the same exemption under Equal Protection or Establishment Clauses.[173] In geographic portions of the U.S., and in certain ethnic groups, single women outnumber marriageable men – with polygamy being proposed or tried as a solution.[174]

In short, an exemption under RFRA for religious polygamists could also result in some part of today's monogamous public favoring polygamy instead, a risk the *Reference* court assessed as "non-trivial."[175] This would bring with it polygamy's considerable negative impacts on society, including more familial

[170] Don Milton, *Christianpolygamy.com*, Christian Polygamy, http://christianpolygamy.com/ (finding permission for polygamy in the Bible at Isaiah 4:1, King James Version). *See* Kar, Chapter 15, this volume, for other Biblical references to marriage, including polygamous marriages.

[171] 2011 BCSC ¶ 555, 575 (noting that evolutionary biology suggests that human beings have a natural tendency toward polygyny).

[172] Potter v. Murray City, 585. F. Supp. 1126, 1139 (D. Utah 1984), *affirmed* Potter v. Murray City, 760 F.2d 1065 (10th Cir. 1985).

[173] *Cf.* March For Life v. Burwell, 128 F. Supp. 3d 116 (D.D.C. 2015) (holding that refusing to provide to a secular nonprofit organization the accommodation extended to religious employers who objected to the mandate when the secular organization was morally opposed to abortion and employed persons universally opposed to such contraception violated equal protection).

[174] Lauren Kay, *Why NYC Women Should Consider Flying Across the Country to Find Men*, Huffington Post (Mar. 4, 2014), www.huffingtonpost.com/lauren-kay/why-nyc-women-should-consider-flying-across-the-country-to-find-men_b_4894602.html (describing New York City as having 150,000 more single women than men); Barbara Bradley Hagerty, *Philly's Black Muslims Increasingly Turn to Polygamy*, NPR (May 28, 2008), www.npr.org/templates/story/story.php?storyId=90886407 (reporting on single African American Muslim women who reluctantly turn to polygamy due to a shortage of marriageable African American men caused by incarceration and AIDS).

[175] Reference, 2011 BCSC ¶ 576.

poverty, less educated citizens, lower GDP, less political stability, increased gender inequality, more authoritarian government, and increased antisocial behaviors and military aggression. The social impact of more families being deprived of the benefits of monogamy, together with a less favorable marriage market for all men – both uncontestable consequences of decriminalizing polygamy – should be sufficient to show that the state has a more than "marginal interest" in criminalizing polygamy. Although the *Reynolds* court did not make clear what it meant when it remarked that even "an exceptional colony of polygamists under exceptional leadership" would eventually "disturb the social condition of the people who surround it,"[176] the *Reference* decision shows precisely in what ways decriminalized polygamy would negatively impact American society today.

III IS CRIMINALIZING POLYGAMY THE LEAST RESTRICTIVE MEANS OF AVOIDING ITS HARMS?

RFRA also requires that the means chosen by the state, criminalization, be "the least restrictive means of furthering that compelling governmental interest."[177] This requires one to consider whether there is another way to deter polygamy, both in populations that do and do not currently practice it.

The *Reference* court concluded that Canada's law easily survived a similar analysis.[178] It found that existing criminal statutes targeting statutory rape, child abuse, and domestic violence could not address the wide range of both individual and social harms that arise from polygamy.[179] Since "the positive objective of the measure [is] the protection and preservation of monogamous marriage," there is "no alternative to the outright prohibition of that which is fundamentally anathema to the institution."[180] Put differently, there is no less restrictive means to control polygamy than a law that targets polygamy itself.

Of course, some would contend that a less burdensome and equally effective alternative to criminalizing polygamy already exists on the books: refusing to legally recognize more than one marriage. However, as discussed earlier,[181] decriminalization would likely provide a significant boost to the practice of polygamy among several distinct American populations. Furthermore, it may be difficult to explain why polygamous relationships are not so harmful as to be criminalized, but too harmful to be recognized – particularly in the face of

176 Reynolds, *supra* note 18, at 166. 177 § 2000bb-1(b)(2).

178 Reference, 2011 BCSC ¶¶ 1299–1300 (applying the "minimal impairment" test: "the law must be carefully tailored so that rights are impaired no more than necessary" (quoting Alberta v. Hutterian Brethren of Wilson Colony, 2009 SCC 37, ¶¶ 53–54)).

179 *Id.* ¶ 1194. 180 *Id.* ¶ 1343. 181 *See supra* Section II.D.1.

actual wives and children whose legal status to their husband/father hangs in the balance. As the Supreme Court noted in *Reynolds*, "out of [marriage's] fruits spring social relations and social obligations and duties, with which government is necessarily required to deal."[182] Legal nonrecognition of polygamous marriage is not an alternative to criminalization if decriminalization will likely lead to legal recognition.

IV CONCLUSION

This chapter has considered both the complexities of applying RFRA's strict scrutiny to laws criminalizing polygamy and the impact a modern and empirical understanding of polygamy's harms provided by *Reference* might have on this scrutiny. Avoiding the *Reference* harms would be a compelling state interest for criminalizing polygamy. Yet, whether global empirical evidence is sufficient to create the necessary link between polygamy and these harms is a difficult question – there is no statistical data on the outcomes of polygamous Americans and no data on the negative impacts of criminalization itself.

Also unclear is whether decriminalization for religious practitioners will result in a non-trivial growth in the polygamous population in the U.S., and whether the prediction that it would is sufficiently convincing. Without such evidence, the state may not be able to show a compelling state interest in not exempting religious practitioners and that no less restrictive alternative to criminalization exists. For example, legal nonrecognition of polygamous marriages itself may be sufficiently effective to keep polygamy in check. However, if same-sex marriage serves as a guide, then decriminalization may lead to legal recognition. Legal nonrecognition would then be an entirely ineffective alternative.

What would all of this mean for polygamy's legal future? If these harms can be shown, state criminal polygamy laws might survive the strict scrutiny required by state RFRAs.

[182] Reynolds, *supra* note 18, at 165.

PART V

RELIGIOUS CLAIMS AT THE END OF LIFE

19

Religion and Advance Medical Directives

Formulation and Enforcement Implications

Richard L. Kaplan

Guy Raymond Jones Chair in Law, University of Illinois College of Law

Since the mid-1970s, patients in the United States have sought various mechanisms for registering their medical treatment preferences when they are unable to communicate those preferences directly. Such documents are typically described as "advance medical directives" and come in two general forms: (1) living wills, which set forth certain limitations on treatment regimens in specific circumstances; and (2) healthcare proxies, which designate some named individual to make any treatment decisions required, usually with little or no specific guidelines in the document itself. At this point, every state has authorized one or both of these types of advance directives, and most of the state-by-state variations are relatively minor.[1] These documents are devices to reflect a patient's values when she cannot speak for herself – whether religious commitments involving end-of-life care, as Cahn and Ziettlow explore (Chapter 20, this volume), or more secular values.

That said, certain key aspects of advance medical directives underlay any serious consideration of their uses and limitations. First, these documents must be prepared while a person still has legal capacity, even though they take effect only when that person is unable to make and communicate medical treatment decisions.[2] Second, these documents can be changed or even terminated as long as the person who made them has decisional capacity.[3]

[1] *See, e.g.*, Lawrence A. Frolik & Richard L. Kaplan, Elder Law in a Nutshell 28–44 (6th ed. 2014).

[2] *Id.* at 31; *see also Living Wills and Health Care Proxies*, Harvard Health Publications (July 1, 2005), www.health.harvard.edu/staying-healthy/living-wills-and-health-care-proxies (noting that "[a]s long as [a patient is] able to make and communicate [his or her] decisions, [the patient's] word supersedes anything [the patient has] written or said to others").

[3] Frolik & Kaplan, *supra* note 1, at 39; *see also Advanced Directives*, Am. Cancer Soc'y, www.cancer.org/acs/groups/cid/documents/webcontent/002016-pdf.pdf ("Once you make an advance directive, you may change or revoke it … at any time while you are competent to do so.").

Third, these documents have no effect on any future medical decisions if their maker has the legal capacity to make those decisions directly.[4] For example, assume that a person with a terminal illness wants some medical treatment and can communicate that decision. The fact that this person executed a living will indicating that such treatment should not be provided does not preclude this person from now receiving the treatment in question. Healthcare directives, in other words, fill the void in medical decision making when a patient cannot make such decisions but are limited to that particular situation.

Beyond these rather fundamental parameters, a thorough examination of advance medical directives would entail analyzing particular state-to-state differences dealing with an intriguing constellation of issues, such as the availability of standard forms on various websites, document execution variations (e.g., notarization versus witnesses), limitations on allowable proxies (e.g., attending physician) or witnesses (e.g., legatees and beneficiaries under intestate succession statutes), accessibility of executed forms in various medical settings, portability from one state to another, and the like.[5] In keeping with the focus of this volume on religious claims across a person's life, however, this chapter focuses instead on the role that religion plays in the formulation and enforcement of advance medical directives. Section I considers religiously oriented advance medical directives, Section II then addresses the impact of physicians' religious views on advance medical directives, and Section III analyzes the enforcement problems that arise when religion combines with political aspirations. Section IV concludes.

I RELIGIOUS ADVANCE DIRECTIVES

As noted earlier, the two general types of advance medical directives are very different documents. A living will is a relatively brief declaration that in certain specific situations – often terminal illness or permanent unconsciousness – death-delaying procedures should not be continued.[6] These directives respond directly to many people's fears of being "hooked up to machines" that serve only to maintain some semblance of biological life that the person

[4] Frolik & Kaplan, *supra* note 1, at 31; *see also* Am. Cancer Soc'y, *supra* note 3 ("An advance directive will not affect the type or quality of your care while you can voice your own decisions. It only comes into play when you can't.").

[5] *See generally* Charles P. Sabatino, *The Evolution of Health Care Advance Planning Law and Policy*, 88 Milbank Q. 211, 219–21 (2010) (discussing different state requirements for advance medical directives).

[6] *Id.* at 212.

making the document would deem unacceptable if there is little realistic hope for recovery or improvement. States employ slightly different definitions for the medical conditions that activate living wills, as well as the scope of treatments and medical "procedures" that may not be commenced or continued pursuant to the living will. But the key point is that living wills are relatively straightforward instruments that address a fairly narrow set of circumstances and make no pretense of covering every possible situation that might arise in the future, especially in light of ever-developing medical interventions and discoveries.

In contrast, healthcare proxies or healthcare powers of attorney, as they are often styled, generally provide no guidance about what medical treatments are desired; instead, they simply designate an all-purpose decision maker to assess the medical situation as it arises and, in consultation with the treating physician, to make whatever medical treatment decisions are required. Some healthcare proxy documents include highly generalized imprecations, such as "continue life at all costs," but most simply indicate who should be asked about what treatments are desired and establish no real criteria for the designee to follow. Often, there is an expectation that the designee will consider the document maker's own values and objectives in making medical decisions, but the document usually contains no guidelines that inhibit the flexibility the designee has, and that is the intended result.

Against this inexorably legal backdrop, many religious organizations have attempted to graft religious values onto one or both of the general advance medical directive formats. These modifications incorporate religious teachings or provide guidance to ensure that decisions being made on behalf of incapacitated adherents comply with the religious imperatives that those persons would undoubtedly have followed if they could make those decisions themselves. In addition, some religiously affiliated medical institutions, especially hospitals and nursing homes, may impose restrictions on the scope of permissible medical decisions to take account of their religious teachings and strictures.[7] As one astute commentator noted, there is an essential tension between (1) the empowerment of the individual that advance medical directives seek to enable and (2) the goal of many religions to ensure compliance with their principles and edicts.[8] Further, he observed that "[t]he general public has focused primarily on using advance directives to ensure that life-

7 *See* Michael A. Grodin, *Religious Advance Directives: The Convergence of Law, Religion, Medicine, and Public Health*, 83 Am. J. Pub. Health 899, 902 (1993).

8 *Id.* at 900. For a discussion of the role of ethical directives in religiously affiliated hospitals, *see* Goodwin, Chapter 3, this volume.

support technologies are either discontinued or not initiated [while m]any religious groups . . . are equally concerned about undertreatment in the form of premature withdrawal, denial, or withholding of desired life-support technologies."[9]

To that end, some religious organizations have fashioned advance medical directives that state explicitly which medical treatments must be provided in specific clinical situations. These instructions sometimes seem inherently contradictory. For example, a directive created by the Catholic Health Association Affirmation of Life provides that "ethically extraordinary treatment," which it defines as "treatment that does not offer a reasonable hope of benefit" should not be provided[10] but then states that "[n]o treatment should be used with the intention of shortening my life."[11] Similarly, a Roman Catholic Health Care Proxy requires that the document maker be given "food and water to sustain my life, including when provided by artificial means [when] I am reasonably expected to live if given food and water," but the designated agent may discontinue such treatments "when they no longer provide reasonable hope of prolonging my life."[12]

Other religiously oriented documents set up standards that may be difficult to apply in particular situations. For example, a group representing Orthodox Jewish rabbis has developed a healthcare proxy that directs all medical decisions "be made pursuant to Jewish law and custom as determined in accordance with Orthodox interpretation and tradition."[13] To this end, the form directs the designated agent to consult with a named Orthodox rabbi and "to comply with his halachic decisions."[14] It also provides for an alternate named Orthodox rabbi in case the first named rabbi is "unable, unwilling or unavailable to provide such consultation and guidance."[15] Similarly, the Roman Catholic Health Care Proxy previously referenced directs the designated agent to make decisions that "are consistent with *authentic* Roman Catholic ethical, moral and religious principles,"[16] though it does not specify how or by whom the authenticity of such principles is to be determined.[17]

9 *Id.* 10 *See id.* (internal quotations omitted). 11 *See id.* (internal quotations omitted).

12 Mass. Catholic Conference, Roman Catholic Health Care Proxy 2, http://catholicbenefits.org/PDF/health/Catholic_Health_Care_Proxy_form.pdf.

13 Rabbinical Council of Am., Halachic Health Care Proxy: Proxy and Directive With Respect to Health Care Decisions and Post-Mortem Decisions 3, www.rabbis.org/pdfs/FINAL_Revised_Halachic_Health_Care_Proxy.pdf.

14 *Id.* at 3, ¶ 3. 15 *Id.* at 4.

16 *See* Mass. Catholic Conference, *supra* note 12, at 2 (emphasis added).

17 *Id.*; *see also* Faroque A. Khan, *Religious Teachings and Reflections on Advance Directive – Religious Values and Legal Dilemmas in Bioethics: An Islamic Perspective*, 30 Fordham Urb.

The inevitable result of such provisions to incorporate religious doctrine is to limit the discretion of the designated proxy to make medically optimal decisions in any particular clinical situation.[18] To be sure, death and dying are tough circumstances to contemplate in the best of situations, and the prospect of facing these issues without the ability to communicate or otherwise direct one's care makes this context even more unsettling. Incorporating religious imperatives may well provide some degree of comfort and general assurance to makers of advance medical directives, and these imperatives might even encourage certain individuals to undertake the difficult process of discussing their treatment preferences and memorializing their decisions in such directives. These are real benefits that should not be denied or trivialized.

At the same time, however, introducing religious perspectives into a setting that is already fraught with emotions and misgivings might further complicate the task of healthcare professionals who must apply these directives in specific contexts. As the previously referenced commentator observed, "when faced with catastrophic illness, family and friends may have varied rescue fantasies, fears of loss, or past experiences that significantly affect their interpretations. And a religiously informed advance directive may be given yet a different interpretation by the hospital chaplain and personal clergy."[19] Accordingly, he concludes, "[t]he use of specific religious language in advance directives may be more likely to confuse than to enlighten."[20] Indeed, how can it be otherwise?

Rather than explicitly incorporating religious views or doctrine in advance medical directives, individuals would be better advised to carefully consider their choice of designated decision maker and select someone whose religious outlook mirrors theirs.[21] As Cahn and Ziettlow show (Chapter 20, this volume), religious values of the designated decision maker often drive decision making for the patient, placing a premium on carefully selecting one's decision maker.[22] This approach accomplishes much, if not most, of what some religiously oriented advance medical directives try to provide, without introducing additional administrative uncertainties.

L.J. 267, 271 (2002) ("Advance directives are permitted as long as the efforts are sincere and the intentions are to abide by Islamic rules and follow the commands of Allah.").

18 Grodin, *supra* note 7, at 901–02. 19 *Id.* at 901. 20 *Id.* at 902.

21 *Cf.* 755 Ill. Comp. Stat. 40/20(b)(1) (2016) (providing that decision makers who are designated statutorily rather than in an advance medical directive should consider "the patient's personal, philosophical, *religious* and moral beliefs and ethical values relative to the purpose of life, sickness, medical procedures, suffering, and death") (emphasis added).

22 *See* Cahn & Ziettlow, Chapter 20, this volume.

II RELIGIOUS VIEWS OF TREATING PHYSICIANS

One of the principal purposes of advance medical directives is to stimulate discussions about end-of-life treatment preferences between a patient and that person's physician or physicians.[23] But a key variable that is usually overlooked in fashioning this paradigm is the religious views of the physician(s). This omission is important because those views might affect what treatment options are discussed during these critical planning sessions. An important study published in one of the leading U.S. medical journals, *The New England Journal of Medicine*, explored how the religious views of physicians may shape patient interactions regarding "controversial clinical practices."[24] This study focused on three such practices, the first of which is especially pertinent to this chapter – namely, administering terminal sedation to dying patients.[25] The other two controversial practices, incidentally, were providing abortion after contraception failed and prescribing birth control to adolescent patients without a parent's approval.[26]

As a general matter, the results of this study were fairly reassuring: 63% of the physicians who responded to the mail-in survey believe that "it [would] be ethical . . . to plainly describe to the patient why he or she objects to the requested procedure," but 86% believe that doctors "have an obligation to present all possible options to the patient, including information about obtaining the requested procedure," and 71% believe that "physician[s] have an obligation to refer the patient to someone who does not object to the requested procedure."[27] A later national survey of primary care physicians by two of the same researchers found that "[a] substantial minority of physicians [42%] do not believe there is ever a professional obligation to do

[23] *See, e.g.*, Ezekiel J. Emanuel & Linda L. Emanuel, *Four Models of the Physician-Patient Relationship*, 267 JAMA 2221, 2222 (1992); Timothy E. Quill & Howard Brody, *Physician Recommendations and Patient Autonomy: Finding a Balance Between Physician Power and Patient Choice*, 125 ANNALS INTERNAL MED. 763, 765 (1996); David C. Thomasma, *Beyond Medial Paternalism and Patient Autonomy: A Model of Physician Conscience for the Physician-Patient Relationship*, 98 ANNALS INTERNAL MED. 243, 246 (1983).

[24] Farr A. Curlin et al., *Religion, Conscience, and Controversial Clinical Practices*, 356 NEW ENG. J. MED. 593, 594–95 (2007).

[25] *Id.* at 595. [26] *Id.*

[27] *Id.* at 597. At least in the context of physician-assisted suicide, state legislators have insulated physicians from a duty not only to hasten a patient's death but also from liability for "*refusing to inform a patient* regarding his or her rights under this part, and not referring an individual to a physician who participates in activities authorized under this part." CAL. HEALTH & SAFETY CODE § 443.15 (West 2016).

For a rich exchange over whether referral duties constitute a substantial burden on religious objectors or should be nonnegotiable duties of healthcare providers, *see* Goodwin, Chapter 3, this volume; Riezi, Chapter 3, this volume; Helfand, Chapter 6, this volume.

something they personally believe is wrong."[28] But in a recent essay, Ezekiel Emanuel, the prominent bioethicist, contended that "[i]n a professional context, personal religious convictions are *secondary*" and that "[b]y entering a health care profession, the person assumes a professional obligation to place the well-being and rights of patients at the center of professional practice."[29] Doing otherwise, he asserted, should be considered "unethical."[30]

In any case, whether a surveyed physician has a personal objection to a particular clinical practice does influence attitudes about his or her professional duties. Physicians who object to terminal sedation are more likely than non-objecting physicians (69% versus 62%, $p = 0.11$) to say physicians may describe their moral objections and more inclined (89% versus 78%, $p = .001$) to say all physicians must disclose all possible options, and much less likely (58% versus 75%) to say physicians are obligated to refer the patient to other clinicians.[31] Be that as it may, only 17% of physicians object to terminal sedation versus 52% who object to abortion due to failed contraception and 42% who object to prescribing birth control to adolescents without parental consent.[32] Consequently, the role of physicians' personal objections may be less consequential in the context of terminal sedation than with the other two procedures simply because such objections are less common.

Nevertheless, a closer look at the survey results reveals important differences depending upon a physician's "intrinsic religiosity," frequency of attendance at religious services, and to a lesser degree, his or her personal religious affiliation. This study defined the somewhat vague criterion of "intrinsic religiosity" as "the extent to which a person embraces his or her religion as the 'master motive' that guides and gives meaning to his or her life."[33] This characteristic was assessed by asking survey respondents whether they agreed with the following two statements:

a. "I try hard to carry my religious beliefs over into all my other dealings in life."
b. "My whole approach to life is based on my religion."[34]

If a physician agreed with both statements, that person was categorized as having "high" intrinsic religiosity. Agreeing with only one statement

[28] Ryan E. Lawrence & Farr A. Curlin, *Physicians' Beliefs About Conscience In Medicine: A National Survey*, 84 ACAD. MED. 1276, 1276 (2009).

[29] Ronit Y. Stahl & Ezekiel J. Emanuel, *Physicians, Not Conscripts – Conscientious Objection in Health Care*, 376 NEW ENG. J. MED. 1380, 1382 (2017) (emphasis supplied).

[30] *Id.* at 1384. [31] Curlin, *supra* note 24, at 599, Tbl. 3. [32] *Id.* at 596, Tbl. 1.

[33] *Id.* at 595. [34] *Id.*

TABLE 19.1 *Percentage of Responding Physicians Who Agree*

	Intrinsic Religiosity		
Course of Action	Never	Once	Twice or More
Physicians may describe their moral objections	56	62	73
Physicians are obligated to disclose all possible options	92	84	81
Physicians are obligated to refer the patient	82	73	56

constituted "moderate" intrinsic religiosity, and disagreeing with both statements categorized the respondent as having "low" intrinsic religiosity.[35]

The percentage of physicians who agreed with the proffered responses for the three controversial clinical practices according to the intrinsic religiosity of those physicians is summarized in Table 19.1.[36]

As might be expected, the higher the intrinsic religiosity, the more likely the physician believed it is appropriate for physicians to describe their personal moral objections, the less likely that the physician believed all physicians must disclose alternative approaches, and *significantly* less likely that the physician responded that all physicians must refer the patient to some other healthcare provider who might be willing to comply with the requested clinical practice.

The second criterion – namely, frequency of attendance at religious services – was determined on a monthly basis. The percentage of physicians who agreed with the proffered responses for the three controversial clinical practices according to this measure of religious commitment is summarized in Table 19.2.[37]

Again as might be expected, the greater the degree of religious commitment, at least as measured by regular attendance at religious services, the more likely the physician believed it is appropriate for physicians to describe their personal moral objections, the less likely that the physician believed physicians must disclose alternative approaches, and *significantly* less likely that physician would refer the patient to some other healthcare provider who might be willing to comply with the requested clinical practice.

Finally, this study classified the responses according to the religion of the responding physician, and those results are shown in Table 19.3.[38]

This time, the results are less conclusive, other than the expected result that those physicians who did not identify with any religious affiliation were less likely to say physicians may describe their personal moral objections, more

35 *Id.* 36 Information adapted by author. *Id.* at 598, Tbl. 3. 37 *Id.* at Tbl. 3. 38 *Id.*

TABLE 19.2 *Percentage of Physicians Who Agree*

	Monthly Attendance at Religious Services		
Course of Action	Never	Once	Twice or More
Physicians may describe their moral objections	51	59	71
Physicians are obligated to disclose all possible options	94	89	82
Physicians are obligated to refer the patient	84	79	60

TABLE 19.3 *Percentage of Physicians Who Would*

Religion	Describe Objections	Disclose Options	Refer Patient
Protestant	70	86	65
Catholic	63	79	66
Jewish	56	93	80
Other (Buddhist, Hindu, Mormon, Muslim, etc.)[a]	63	89	71
None	52	92	88

[a] *See* Farr A. Curlin et al., *Religion, Conscience, and Controversial Clinical Practices*, 356 New Eng. J. Med. 593, 595 (2007).

likely to believe physicians must disclose alternative approaches, and more likely to believe that physicians must refer the patient to some other healthcare provider who might be willing to comply with the requested clinical practice. To be sure, the "Other" category includes individuals from very different religious traditions, and the label "Protestant" may similarly be unduly broad.

In any case, this study shows that physicians' personal religious affiliations and commitments might affect the flow of information that patients receive – an extraordinarily important facet of the advance medical directive paradigm and a critical component of end-of life care planning generally. That fact alone may have implications for whether physicians fulfill their duty to secure a patient's informed consent, as that duty encompasses the duty to disclose alternatives to the proposed course of treatment.[39] Moreover, as the study's authors noted in analyzing the study's results:

[39] For a review of these duties, *see* Robin Fretwell Wilson, *The Promise of Informed Consent, in* Oxford Handbook Of American Health Law (Glenn Cohen, Allison Hoffman, & William Sage, eds., 2016).

> [Patients] should know that many physicians do not believe they are obligated to disclose information about or provide referrals for legal yet controversial treatments . . . . Patients may not have ready access to information about physicians' religious characteristics and moral convictions. Thus, if patients are concerned about certain interventions . . . they should ask their doctors ahead of time whether they will discuss such options.[40]

Given America's increasing ethnic and religious diversity, the personal religious views of physicians are likely to become a more important consideration in the years ahead.[41]

Moreover, such religious views are given particular salience by the laws that authorize advance medical directives. These statutes typically include so-called conscience clauses that allow physicians to not follow a patient's medical directive for any reason, which would include religious objections. For example, the Illinois law on living wills provides the following:

> If the physician is unwilling to comply with [the medical directive's] provisions, the physician shall promptly so advise the declarant. If the . . . patient is able, it is the patient's responsibility to initiate the transfer to another physician of the patient's choosing. If the . . . patient is at any time not able to initiate the transfer, then the attending physician shall without delay notify the person with the highest priority, as set forth in this section, who is available, able, and willing to make arrangements for the transfer of the patient and the appropriate medical records to another physician for the effectuation of the patient's declaration.[42]

The persons authorized in this section to transfer a patient to a willing physician are first, anyone with authority to make such arrangements, the patient's court-appointed guardian, and then "any member of the patient's family."[43]

Similarly worded provisions apply in the context of healthcare powers of attorney[44] and healthcare surrogacy statutes.[45] The Illinois surrogacy statute, in fact, specifically references a healthcare provider's "personal views or beliefs or his or her conscience" and applies to the full panoply of such providers, including "physicians, nurses, health care facilities, and any employee, officer, director, agent, or person under contract with such a person."[46] In other words,

40 Curlin, *supra* note 24, at 597.

41 *America's Changing Religious Landscape*, PEW RESEARCH CENTER (May 12, 2015), www.pewforum.org/2015/05/12/americas-changing-religious-landscape/; Anthony Daniel Perez & Charles Hirschman, *The Changing Racial and Ethnic Composition of the U.S. Population: Emerging American Identities*, 35 POPULATION AND DEV. REV. 1 (2009).

42 755 ILL. COMP. STAT. 35/3(d) (2016).

43 *Id.*

44 755 ILL. COMP. STAT. 45/4–7(b) (2016).

45 755 ILL. COMP. STAT. 40/35 (2016).

46 *See* 755 ILL. COMP. STAT. 40/10 (2016) (defining "health care provider").

the religious outlooks and values of healthcare providers may affect the information flow that is so critical to the functioning of advance medical directives, but those religious outlooks and values are not legally preferenced over those of their patients.[47]

III RELIGIOUSLY FRAMED ENFORCEMENT CHALLENGES

Advance medical directives respond to several independent phenomena, including the incredible development of new medical technologies and therapies that extend biological life, the fear of healthcare providers facing malpractice claims for not doing "everything possible," the effect of third-party payment mechanisms that reduce the role of cost as a limiting consideration, and the like. But the history of such directives is also inexorably linked with the specter of family-wrenching litigation over unwanted medical care at the end of life.

The famous *In re Quinlan* case spawned the growth of hospital ethics committees and state statutes that authorized living wills to document end-of-life medical treatment preferences when a patient cannot communicate those preferences directly.[48] The U.S. Supreme Court's landmark decision involving Nancy Cruzan similarly prompted states to authorize healthcare proxy documents to enable citizens to designate a substitute decision maker in advance, as well as healthcare surrogacy statutes that provide a prioritized listing of medical decision makers for those who did not prepare advance medical directives themselves.[49] The federal government similarly responded to the *Cruzan* litigation with the Patient Self-Determination Act, which requires that adult patients who are admitted to a hospital or nursing home be provided with their state's advance medical directive forms.[50] The clear thrust of these legislative changes was to encourage patients to memorialize

47 Illinois recently amended its Health Care Right of Conscience Act, 745 ILL. COMP. STAT. 70/2 (2016), to require facilities to adopt written protocols governing access to care and information to ensure that conscience-based objections do not impair patients' health and to explain how patient healthcare services will be facilitated. *See* Illinois Public Act 99–0690 (Senate Bill 1564), http://ilga.gov/legislation/BillStatus.asp?DocNum=1564&GAID=13&DocTypeID=SB&LegID=88256&SessionID=88&SpecSess=&Session=&GA=99.

48 355 A.2d 647 (N.J.), cert. denied, 429 U.S. 92 (1976).

49 *See* Cruzan v. Dir., Mo. Dep't of Health, 497 U.S. 261 (1990); Am. Bar Ass'n, Comm'n on Law & Aging, Default Surrogate Consent Statutes, AM. BAR ASS'N COMM'N ON LAW & AGING, www.americanbar.org/content/dam/aba/administrative/law_aging/2014_default_surrogate_consent_statutes.authcheckdam.pdf (June 2014).

50 Omnibus Budget Reconciliation Act of 1990, Pub. L. No. 101–508, §§ 4206, 4751, 104 Stat. 1388, 1388–115, 1388–204 (codified at 42 U.S.C. §§ 1395cc(f), 1396a(w)) (2012).

their end-of-life care preferences in such directives in lieu of heart-wrenching litigation of these sensitive issues.

To be sure, advance medical directives do not completely forestall the prospect of such litigation, but much of their appeal is that, barring someone petitioning the court to establish a formal guardianship, these documents should be largely self-executing. Such expectations, however, were seriously challenged a decade ago when certain religious communities disrupted the enforcement of advance medical directives even though they did not change the ultimate result. That episode also showed that religion can be particularly disruptive when politically ambitious public officials make common cause with religious adherents.

Terri Schiavo was a twenty-seven-year-old woman who lost consciousness briefly in 1990 and lapsed into a persistent vegetative state from which she never recovered. Like most young people, she did not have an advance medical directive, but Florida's healthcare surrogacy statute designated her husband, Michael, as her healthcare proxy and he sought to have her feeding tube removed.[51] Her parents sought to intervene and were able to enlist various conservative politicians and religious organizations on their behalf.[52] During the ensuing litigation, it emerged that the Catholic Church (Terri Schiavo was Catholic) at the time Terri lapsed into unconsciousness considered withholding artificial nutrition acceptable in certain cases.[53] Nevertheless, a papal statement on life-sustaining treatment issued fourteen years after Terri lapsed into a persistent vegetative state also entered into the discussion.[54] This sorry tale consumed seven years of litigation before twenty judges,[55] as well as a special statute passed by the Florida Legislature that authorized then-Governor Jeb Bush to order the reinsertion of Terri's feeding tube, which he did.[56]

51 *In re* Guardianship of Schiavo, 851 So.2d 182, 187 (Fla. Dist. Ct. App. 2003).

52 *See* David D. Kirkpatrick & Sheryl G. Stolberg, *How Family's Cause Reached the Halls of Congress: Network of Christians Rallied to Case of Florida Woman*, N.Y. TIMES, March 22, 2005, www.ncbi.nlm.nih.gov/labs/articles/15838972/.

53 There is strong consensus around this distinction, as now–Supreme Court Justice Neil M. Gorsuch has noted in his work probing common suppositions that physician-assisted suicide should be legal. Neil M. Gorsuch, *A Reply to Raymond Tallis on the Legalization of Assisted Suicide and Euthanasia*, 28 J. LEGAL MED. 327, 331 (noting his agreement with a prominent advocate of assisted suicide that "refusals of treatment should be permitted").

54 *See* Lindsay A. Hampson & Ezekiel J. Emanuel, *The Prognosis for Changes in End-Of-Life Care After the Schiavo Case*, 24 HEALTH AFFAIRS 972, 974 (2005).

55 George J. Annas, *"Culture of Life" Politics at the Bedside – The Case of Terri Schiavo*, 352 NEW ENG. J. MED. 1710, 1710 (2005).

56 *Id.* at 1712.

That statute was subsequently declared unconstitutional by the Florida Supreme Court.[57]

Even Governor Bush's brother, then-President George W. Bush, became involved in this case. President Bush encouraged the U.S. Congress to take up Terri Schiavo's case and flew back to the nation's capital to sign emergency legislation that was enacted on her behalf. The U.S. Senate actually met in a special emergency session on a Sunday (!) during its spring recess to pass a law that applied only to Terri Schiavo.[58] This legislation did not change any of the underlying applicable statutes regarding advance medical directives or healthcare surrogacy; it merely provided that a federal district court had jurisdiction to hear any claim "relating to the withholding or withdrawal of food, fluids, or medical treatment necessary to sustain [Terri Schiavo's] life."[59] It further provided that any "parent of Theresa Marie Schiavo shall have standing to bring a suit under this Act."[60] This federal legislation cautioned that "[n]othing in this Act shall be construed to create substantive rights not otherwise secured"[61] by existing law and that this new law did not "constitute a precedent with respect to future legislation, including the provision of private relief bills."[62] In the end, Terri's husband prevailed in every court that dealt with the case and eventually had Terri's feeding tube withdrawn.[63]

Nevertheless, the entire episode raises questions about the ultimate enforceability of advance medical directives and whether executing such directives is worth the effort entailed if religious considerations can so disrupt their effectuation. A much less publicized but similarly revealing case involved a man named Hugh Finn in Virginia. As the attorneys who represented Mr. Finn reported, lawyers should be alert to possible misuse of religious perspectives, especially when conflicts arise between a family's priest and the local Catholic parish.[64] In this case as well, the ability of politicians to mobilize local faith communities can lead to extended litigation and considerable expense.

To that end, it is extremely important to note that following the Schiavo case, no new laws or other changes in advance medical directives were made.[65] In other words, the underlying law was clear, but religion – especially

[57] Bush v. Schiavo, 885 So. 2d 321, 337 (Fla. 2004).

[58] Relief of the Parents of Theresa Marie Schiavo, Pub. L. No. 109–3, 119 Stat. 15 (2005).

[59] *Id.* § 1, 119 Stat. at 15. [60] *Id.* § 2, 119 Stat. at 15. [61] *Id.* § 5, 119 Stat. at 16.

[62] *Id.* § 7, 119 Stat. at 16. [63] Schiavo, *supra* note 57, at 337.

[64] *See* M. Gary Eakes & Alex L. Moschella, *Two Cases that Never Should Have Happened: The Misuse of Religious Doctrine in Cases Concerning the Withdrawal of Artificial Life Prolonging Medical Treatment*, NAELA [Nat'l Acad. Elder L. Att'ys] Q., Summer 1999, at 4–5, 7–8.

[65] Hampson & Emanuel, *supra* note 54, at 975; Annas, *supra* note 55, at 1714.

when combined with politics – can seriously interfere with the operation of these directives, a troubling prospect that remains unabated to this day.

IV CONCLUSION

Advance medical directives seek to empower individuals to determine their medical treatment preferences whey they have lost the fundamental ability to make those preferences known. Religious concerns can never be completely disentangled from a subject as inherently personal as one's medical care near the end of life, but such concerns have the potential to erode the efficacy of advance medical directives by (1) complicating the communicative function of these directives and (2) introducing additional, perhaps preemptive, considerations when family members have differing religious outlooks. While some religious concerns can be addressed through careful selection of a designated medical decision maker, enforcement problems are much less easily accommodated and remain an issue affecting the ultimate utility of advance medical directives.

20

Personal Religious Identity at the End of Life

Naomi Cahn

Harold H. Greene Professor of Law, George Washington University Law School

Amy Ziettlow

Pastor of Holy Cross Lutheran Church (ELCA) & former COO of Hospice of Baton Rouge

The actual practice of end-of-life decision making typically occurs in private, in hospital, or under hospice care, with family members often working together to determine, and then effectuate, the patient's wishes. That's what happened for Keith, a participant in a study we conducted about how adult children care for their seriously ill parents.

Keith's father was dying. Keith was the oldest son, but he was emotionally estranged from his father. So were all of Keith's siblings. But as Keith's father lay comatose in a hospital bed, everyone, including Keith's aunts and his full and half-siblings, agreed that Keith should serve as his father's decision maker. The hospital physician informed Keith of his father's prognosis, explaining that there was nothing more that could be done to revive him. The medical staff waited for Keith's directive for whether to remove life-sustaining measures. Here's Keith's description of how he made his decision:

> I prayed on it. "You know, Lord, 6:00, it's going to be your will" . . . And I did learn death come when God decides – designated it to come, not when we want to. I was talking to [my dad]. I was holding his hand, telling him I love him, and kissed him before the doctor pulled the plug.

We use Keith's story as an opportunity for an inquiry into the role of religion and spirituality in end-of-life care,[1] a time when religious beliefs may

[1] Defining spirituality and contrasting it to religion is a complex endeavor. *See, e.g.*, BRUCE LEDEWITZ, AMERICAN RELIGIOUS DEMOCRACY: COMING TO TERMS WITH THE END OF SECULAR POLITICS 156 (2007); Hugo Kamya, *Engaging Spirituality in Family Conflict: Witnessing to Hope and Dialogue*, 26 J. AM. ACAD. MATRIMONIAL LAW 15, 18 (2013); *see also* United States v. Seeger, 380 U.S. 163, 174 (1965) (labeling "the task of discerning

profoundly affect individuals' choices about treatment. To ground this inquiry, the chapter relies on the experiences of actual decision makers. As shown in both this chapter and Professor Richard Kaplan's contribution (Chapter 19, this volume), religion is an influence on choices of family members[2] as well as institutions' provision of care.[3]

While not explicitly acknowledged by Keith, his specific choices on behalf of his father fit into a broader framing of medical care in the United States where medicine and religion have historically been closely intertwined: consider practices ranging from healing rites to exorcisms, and the role of religious orders in operating hospitals from medieval times to the present.[4] Most medical schools offer courses on spirituality and health, even though many healthcare professionals feel uncomfortable discussing these issues.[5] Most patients want some form of spiritual care, and with end-of-life decision making, religious affiliation plays a determining factor.[6]

Section I of this chapter first discusses the legal grounding for surrogates' decisions, and it then considers hospice care, showing that the law supports an individual's choices concerning the desired impact (or nonimpact) of

the intent of Congress in using the phrase 'Supreme Being' a complex one" that is not "made the easier by the richness and variety of spiritual life in our country").

2 *See* Kaplan, Chapter 19, this volume.

3 Hobby Lobby concerned the impact of the federal Religious Freedom Restoration Act ("RFRA") on a private, closely held for-profit corporation. *See generally* Helfand, Chapter 2, this volume; Sepper, Chapter 1, this volume; Ira C. Lupu, *Moving Targets:* Obergefell, Hobby Lobby, *and the Future of LGBT Rights*, 7 Ala. Civ. Rts & Civ. Lib. L. Rev. 1 (2015) (discussing goals of RFRA). State constitutions and state RFRAs may also have consequences for end-of-life care, as Adams explains, Chapter 21, this volume, but those consequences are beyond the scope of this chapter.

4 Stacey A. Tovino, *Hospital Chaplaincy Under the HIPAA Privacy Rule: Health Care or "Just Visiting the Sick?"* 2 Ind. Health L. Rev. 51, 59 (2005); *see* Robin Fretwell Wilson, *Essay: The Limits of Conscience: Moral Clashes over Deeply Divisive Healthcare Procedures*, 34 Am. J.L. & Med. 41, 41 (2008).

5 Laura Landro, *Health Matters: Medicine's Growing Spirituality*, Wall St. J. (Dec. 8, 2013), www.wsj.com/articles/SB10001424052702304854804579236053907496062; Michael J. Balboni, *Nurse and Physician Barriers to Spiritual Care Provision at the End of Life*, 48 J. Pain & Symptom Mgmt. 400 (2014), projects.iq.harvard.edu/files/rshm/files/barriers.pdf; Vyjeyanthi S. Periyakoil et al., *No Easy Talk: A Mixed Methods Study of Doctor Reported Barriers to Conducting Effective End-of-Life Conversations with Diverse Patients*, PLOS One, (Apr. 22, 2015), journals.plos.org/plosone/article?id=10.1371/journal.pone.0122321#pone.0122321 (citing religio-spiritual beliefs as one of the top barriers physicians name to having end-of-life conversations).

6 *See, e.g.*, Sarah R. Alcorn, *"If God Wanted Me Yesterday, I Wouldn't Be Here Today": Religious and Spiritual Themes in Patients' Experiences of Advanced Cancer*, 13 J. Palliative Med. 581 (2010). Surrogates draw support and comfort from their religious beliefs. *See also Views on End-of-Life Medical Treatments*, Pew Research Center (Nov. 21, 2013), www.pewforum.org/2013/11/21/views-on-end-of-life-medical-treatments/.

religious beliefs and practices. Section II shows how these laws are interpreted and lived, specifically in how surrogates handle end-of-life decision making, based on empirical data obtained directly through in-depth interviews with those who have experienced the death of their parents.[7] We find that surrogates use religion to guide them in determining what the patient would have wanted, as well as to support them through this decision as they move forward. Section III speculates on the potential effect of *Burwell v. Hobby Lobby* on religious expression at the end of life.[8] Our goal is to show how the legal system both supports individualized expressions of religion but also has the ability to complicate those expressions.

I PUBLIC ROLE OF RELIGION AND SPIRITUALITY

Recognizing and reinforcing the preference of most American patients to include a discussion of spiritual issues as part of their care,[9] the law provides support for such integration. In this section, we explore two ways in which the law acknowledges the impact of religion on end-of-life issues.

A *State Guidance on Surrogate Decision Making*

Written directives provide guidance when a patient is unable to make her own healthcare choices, offering a structure for surrogate decision makers. Despite the many reasons for advanced care planning, most people have not done so; they do not have any of their preferences about end-of-life decision making in writing, and they have not even spoken with family members or their doctors about their wishes.[10] Surveys report that among severely or terminally ill patients, fewer than 50% have an advance directive in their medical

[7] All names and identifying characteristics of study participants have been changed to protect their privacy.

[8] Burwell v. Hobby Lobby Stores, Inc., 134 S. Ct. 2751 (2014). Notwithstanding the ubiquity of state statutes directing that surrogate decision makers consider religious or moral beliefs, the legal issues involving end-of-life care and religion have been studied little. For an early article, *see* Kathleen M. Boozang, *An Intimate Passing: Restoring the Role of Family and Religion in Dying*, 58 U. PITT. L. REV. 549 (1997). Of course, the impact of religion on other healthcare issues has received more attention, as PART II of the volume shows.

[9] Stacey A. Tovino, *Hospital Chaplaincy Under the HIPAA Privacy Rule: Health Care of "Just Visiting the Sick?"* 2 IND. HEALTH L. REV. 51, 51 (2005); *see supra* note 5.

[10] J. M. Clements, *Patient Perceptions on the Use of Advance Directives and Life Prolonging Technology*, 26 AM. J. HOSPITAL PALLIATIVE CARE 270 (2009), www.ncbi.nlm.nih.gov/pubmed/19229067. "Of 306 participants, 77 (25.2%) had a durable power of attorney and 45 (14.7%) had living wills. Of these, 226 (73.9%) responded that it was important to make healthcare wishes known to their doctor. Only 36 (15.9%) had done so. A total of 266

record,[11] as do only 28% of home healthcare patients.[12] By contrast, as patients become more involved with healthcare professionals, they become increasingly likely to have an advance directive: 65% of nursing home residents and 88% of hospice care patients have filled out an advance directive.[13]

Most U.S. adults (78%) say that a family member should be allowed to make end-of-life decisions on behalf of a loved one who is unable to communicate her decisions.[14] Designating a trusted family member, who either shares or is aware of the patient's religious beliefs and affiliations and knows to what extent the patient's religious identity should dictate healthcare decisions, can ensure maximum respect for the patient's beliefs.[15] Indeed, the law affirms this intuition by designating family members as the preferred surrogates, who can also function as advocates for the patient in cases where the medical professional or institution follows religious mandates that are the patient's.

In the absence of patient-completed directives, surrogates draw on a wide variety of other tools, both formal and informal. States generally have laws that establish a hierarchy of default healthcare decision makers for any medical decision that must be made while the person is incapacitated. Under these statutes, spouses, sometimes along with recognized domestic partners, are generally listed first. For example, Louisiana law sets out a list of people who can authorize surgical or medical treatment, with priority given to the individual herself, then a court-appointed guardian, followed by family members: a spouse who is not legally separated from the patient, an adult child, the patient's parents, the patient's siblings, then other relatives.[16] If there are no family members who can act, Louisiana authorizes an "adult friend," someone who is familiar with the patient's wishes, to act; absent this, among others, an interdisciplinary team of professionals may decide matters for the patient, even though they may have beliefs that differ from those of the patient.[17] The surrogate is then charged with making the best decision for the incapacitated person.[18]

(86.9%) believed it was important to discuss healthcare wishes with their family and only 160 (60.1%) had done so." *Id.*

[11] Centers for Disease Control and Prevention. *Advance Care Planning: Ensuring Your Wishes Are Known and Honored If You Are Unable to Speak for Yourself, Critical Issue Brief* (2012), www.cdc.gov/aging/pdf/advanced-care-planning-critical-issue-brief.pdf.

[12] *See* Clements, *supra* note 10. [13] *Id.* [14] *Id.* at 61.

[15] *See* Kaplan, Chapter 19, this volume. [16] La. Rev. Stat. Ann. § 40:1299.53 (2015).

[17] *Id.* On the impact of physicians' moral beliefs on patient care, *see* Kaplan, Chapter 19, this volume.

[18] *See* Shana Wynn, *Decisions by Surrogates: An Overview of Surrogate Consent Laws in the United States*, 36 Bifocal 10, 13 (2014). For a guide, *see* Am. Bar Assoc. Comm'n on Aging, *Making Medical Decisions for Someone Else: A How-To Guide*, (2009), www.americanbar.org

End-of-life decision making by surrogates raises a set of distinct issues. The parameters of the decisions states authorize surrogates to make – including whether an individual can choose to end life-sustaining treatment and what rights her surrogate has to make the choice on her behalf – have been framed by numerous high-profile court cases over the past few decades. While a competent person has a constitutionally protected liberty interest in refusing unwanted medical treatment, when another seeks to act on an incapacitated person's behalf, the interests of additional third parties come into play.[19] Indeed, in discussing the Terri Schiavo case in Chapter 20, this volume, Kaplan indicates how religion can complicate, and may even frustrate, surrogate decision making. To promote a strong public interest in life, many states require clear and convincing evidence for withdrawal of life support, preferring prolonging life as a default. The burden of proof in other states might be the lesser one of a preponderance of the evidence.[20] As a constitutional matter, no state is required to authorize medical aid-in-dying (also referred to as physician-assisted suicide or death), although some do.[21] These states place significant guardrails around the practice to avoid harm and to ensure that patients decide free from coercion.[22] Indeed, in those states that permit the practice, the individual must be mentally competent; this is not an option for a surrogate.

States differ on the substantive standard for how the surrogate must establish what should happen with the patient. Some states requires surrogates to act in the patient's best interests; others use "substituted judgment," a standard based on what the patient would choose if she could speak on

/content/dam/aba/administrative/law_aging/2011/2011_aging_bk_proxy_guide_gen .authcheckdam.pdf.

19 Cruzan v. Dir., Mo. Dep't of Health, 497 U.S. 261 (1990); Judith D. Moran, *Schiavo and Its Implications for the Family Justice System*, 46 FAM. CT. REV. 297, 301 (2008).

20 *See* Lois Shepherd, *The End of End-of-Life Law*, 92 N.C. L. REV. 1693, 1702–04 (2014). The Louisiana statute does not specify the applicable standard for making a substituted judgment. *See* LA. REV. STAT. ANN. § 40:1299.58.1 et seq. (2015). In a few states, surrogates are permitted to make decisions based on the patient's best interests. Shepherd, *id.*, at 1702. *See* Section II.B.2 for further discussion of best interests.

21 Vacco v. Quill, 521 U.S. 793 (1997); Washington v. Glucksberg, 521 U.S. 702 (1997); CAL. HEALTH & SAFETY CODE § 443.1, et seq. (2016); COL. REV. STAT. § 25-48-101, et seq. (2014); D.C. ACT 21-577, sec. 11 (2015); OR. REV. STAT. 127.800 § 1.01, et seq. (2015); 18 VT. STAT. ANN. § 5281, et seq. (2015); WASH. REV. CODE §70.245.010, et seq. (2015).

22 Considerable attention has been given to how Justice Neil Gorsuch's addition to the Court is likely to affect constitutional jurisprudence on this and other questions. With medical aid in dying, it seems likely that Justice Gorsuch would not find a constitutional right to the assistance of others to ending one's life. *See* Neil M. Gorsuch, *The Right to Assisted Suicide and Euthanasia*, 23 HARV. J. L. & PUB. POL'Y. 599 (2000).

her own behalf.[23] Some states have developed a hybrid that allows the surrogate to exercise substituted judgment when the patient's wishes are known but to make a decision in the patient's best interests where these wishes are unknown. Courts consider a variety of written and oral evidence if the surrogate's decision is challenged, such as any information about the patient's preferences, her religious beliefs, and other matters. Relatively few cases involving religion and surrogate decision making appear in court.[24] When they do, they typically have two elements: first, family members with conflicting opinions and, second, inadequate documentation (of the patient's wishes).[25]

States may explicitly require, as part of a substituted judgment standard, that the surrogate act after considering the patient's religious and ethical beliefs.[26] And courts have used the patient's religion – or lack thereof – as a guiding factor. Legal conflicts have been resolved by measuring the fervency and frequency of an individual's historically documented religious practices, such as membership in a congregation, frequency of attendance at worship services, and observance of religious holidays, as supporting evidence for whether the religious beliefs of the individual should be taken into consideration.[27]

B Hospice

Beyond its support for surrogates using religion as a factor in their decision making, the law provides additional recognition that spirituality plays an

23 Lawrence A. Frolik & Linda S. Whitton, *The UPC Substituted Judgment/Best Interest Standard for Guardian Decisions: A Proposal for Reform*, 45 U. MICH. J.L. REFORM 739 (2012); Nina A. Kohn & Jeremy A. Blumenthal, *Designating Health Care Decisionmakers for Patients Without Advance Directives: A Psychological Critique*, 42 GA. L. REV. 979, 986 (2008) (describing hybrid approach); *see, e.g.*, UNIFORM HEALTH CARE DECISIONS ACT § 5(f), § 2 (e). Indiana, for example, uses a best interest approach. IND. CODE ANN. § 16–36-1–5(d) (2015). While some states explicitly set out the appropriate standard, others, such as Louisiana, are silent.

24 For some of the more high-profile cases, *see* Kaplan, Chapter 19, this volume.

25 Stanley A. Terman, *It Isn't Easy Being Pink: Potential Problems with POLST Paradigm Forms*, 36 HAMLINE L. REV. 177, 183–84 (2013).

26 For example, New York's statutes provides, "After consultation with a licensed physician, the agent shall make health care decisions: (a) in accordance with the principal's wishes, including the principal's religious and moral beliefs." N.Y. PUB. HEALTH § 2982(2) (2015). The Uniform Health Care Decisions Act requires that the surrogate consider the principal's "personal values." UHCDA § 5(f). Guardianship law may require similar considerations. *See, e.g.*, MINN. STAT. ANN. § 524.5–313 (2015) ("The guardian shall not consent to any medical care for the ward which violates the known conscientious, religious, or moral belief of the ward.").

27 *See infra*. For specific examples of court cases, *see* Naomi Cahn and Amy Ziettlow, *Religion and End of Life Decision-Making*, 1713 U. ILL. L. J. (2016).

important role in end-of-life decision making through the Medicare Hospice Benefit. Over the past thirty years, end-of-life care has become increasingly associated with hospice.[28] Under current Medicare rules, hospice care has been limited to beneficiaries whose doctors determine that they have fewer than six months to live, and who agree not to pursue any further life-prolonging treatment related to their disease.[29] The hospice philosophy of care acknowledges that pain can be physical, emotional, financial, relational, *and* spiritual;[30] thus hospice organizations utilize an interdisciplinary group of specially trained providers, such as nurses, social workers, and chaplains.[31] The National Hospice and Palliative Care Organization uses an illustration to describe the hospice team, with the patient and family in the center and professional team members surrounding them.[32] Spiritual counselors stand on equal footing with physicians, social workers, and other professionals; all are legally obligated to promote the patient's right to self-determination, which includes refusal of any service.[33]

Medicare sets out two specific requirements concerning spirituality.[34] First, it requires that hospice units assess a patient's spiritual needs and provide "spiritual counseling."[35] While the nature of the spiritual assessment is not

[28] For a brief history of the hospice movement in the U.S., *see* Nat'l Hospice & Palliative Care Org., *History of Hospice Care*, www.nhpco.org/history-hospice-care. The National Hospice and Palliative Care Organization estimates that more than 1.5 million patients are served by hospice each year. *See* Nat'l Hospice & Palliative Care Org., *NHPCO's Facts and Figures: Hospice Care in America, 2014 Edition* (2014), www.nhpco.org/sites/default/files/public/Statistics_Research/2014_Facts_Figures.pdf [hereinafter NHPCO Facts and Figures 2014].

[29] *See* Kathy Cerminara, *Pandora's Dismay: Eliminating Coverage-related Barriers to Hospice Care*, 11 Fl. Coastal L. Rev. 107 (2010); Ctrs. for Medicare and Medicaid Servs., *Medicare Hospice Payment Reform: A Review of the Literature* 7 (2014), www.cms.gov/Medicare/Medicare-Fee-for-Service-Payment/Hospice/Downloads/MedicareHospicePaymentReformLiteratureReview2013Update.pdf.

[30] *Id.*

[31] *See, e.g.*, Cerminara, *supra* note 29; Ryan A. Walsh, Note, *A Matter of Life, Death, and Children: The Patient Protection and Affordable Care Act Section 2302 and A Shifting Legal Paradigm*, 86 S. Cal. L. Rev. 1119, 1123 (2013); Steven R. Connor, Hospice and Palliative Care: The Essential Guide (2d ed. 2009).

[32] NHPCO Facts and Figures 2014. [33] 42 C.F.R. § 418.52 (2017).

[34] The Medicaid hospice benefit is an optional state plan that tends to follow the conditions of participation for Medicare and mirrors Medicare's interdisciplinary team requirements, which must include "at least one pastoral or other counselor." 42 U.S.C. § 1395x(dd)(2)(B)(i)(2012). Most states offer hospice coverage under Medicaid. *See* Hospice Directory, *Paying for Hospice: Medicare/Medicaid/More Options*, www.hospicedirectory.org/cm/about/paying.

[35] 42 C.F.R. § 418.54 (2017); 42 C.F.R. § 418.64 (d)(3)(2017). Hospices are required to offer counseling services, which consist of bereavement counseling, dietary counseling, and spiritual counseling. *Id.*

explicitly defined in the applicable regulations, the notice of proposed rule-making that preceded the final rule explained that such assessments "should not be solely related to religious affiliation (or lack thereof)." Instead, they should instead be broader and "might focus on a patient's sense of peace, purpose, beliefs, etc., but may not be warranted for all patients, particularly if they already have an available spiritual/emotional support system."[36] Second, the interdisciplinary hospice group must include a "pastoral or other counselor,"[37] who is an employee of the hospice.

Government support for such spiritual counseling may be seen by some as "legally questionable" under the Establishment Clause.[38] Nonetheless, courts have repeatedly found that the Establishment Clause does not forbid chaplains in the legislature,[39] in the military,[40] or in prisons.[41] The mechanism of funding hospice chaplaincy provides some insulation from Establishment Clause claims. First, the government is not paying the hospice chaplains but is requiring their presence, and the government is providing per patient Medicare reimbursement – a kind of voucher, beneficiary choice funding, somewhat akin to the school voucher system already upheld by the Supreme Court.[42] Second, the chaplains are private, not public, employees, so not directly analogous to military and prisons settings,

36 Medicare and Medicaid Programs: Hospice Conditions of Participation, 73 Fed. Reg. 32088–01 (June 5, 2008) [hereinafter Hospice Conditions of Participation].

37 42 C.F.R. Sec. 418.56(a)(iv) (2017); *see* Elaine Wittenberg-Lyles et al., *Communication Dynamics in Hospice Teams: Understanding the Role of the Chaplain in Interdisciplinary Team Collaboration*, 11 J. PALLIATIVE MED. 1330, 1330 (2008). More than half of hospice chaplains serve as professional volunteers, receiving no payment. *Id.* at 1330. In 2001, the National Hospice and Palliative Care Organization developed voluntary recommendations for hospice chaplains' qualifications and practices. *Id.* In 2004, the Council for Collaboration, composed of American and Canadian professional certification bodies for pastoral care, developed common standards for professional chaplains, although many (40%) do not have clinical pastoral counseling training. *Id.* at 1334.

38 *See, e.g.*, Malyon v. Pierce County, 935 P.2d 1272 (Wash. 1997) (en banc) (upholding sheriff department's voluntary chaplaincy service against challenges that public support violated the Establishment Clause); Mary Jean Dolan, *Government-Sponsored Chaplains and Crisis: Walking the Fine Line in Disaster Response and Daily Life*, 35 HASTINGS CONST. L. Q. 505, 507 (2008) (noting the paucity of decisions challenging the constitutionality of publicly supported chaplains).

39 *E.g.*, Marsh v. Chambers, 463 U.S. 783 (1983); Engel v. Vitale, 370 U.S. 421, 437 n. 1 (1962) (Douglas, J., concurring); *see also* Christopher C. Lund, *Legislative Prayer and the Secret Costs of Religious Endorsements*, 94 MINN. L. REV. 972, 997 (2010).

40 Katcoff v. Marsh, 755 F.2d 223 (2nd Cir. 1985); SECULAR POLITICS, *supra* note 1; Ira C. Lupu & Robert W. Tuttle, *Instruments of Accommodation: The Military Chaplaincy and the Constitution*, 110 W. VA. L. REV. 89 (2007).

41 *See, e.g.*, Rudd v. Ray, 248 N.W.2d 125 (Iowa 1976).

42 Zelman v. Simmons-Harris, 536 U.S. 639 (2002).

in which the government is hiring a chaplain and directly paying the salary. Third, however, hospice *is* akin to the military and prisons in the sense of confinement and immobility; the patient is dying and cannot readily go to her own spiritual counselor outside the facility. On the other hand, the patient or her guardian is permitted to reject spiritual counseling, and this non-coercive quality is important to insulating against First Amendment and statutory challenges.[43]

The law clearly states its parameters and aims for supporting spiritual expression in healthcare and at the end of life. However, we wondered how people accessed religious beliefs and practices in end-of-life care. Does the law ratify or channel behavior?[44] We conducted semi-structured qualitative interviews to find out.

II THE LAW IN EVERYDAY END-OF-LIFE

Using interviews from the Homeward Bound[45] study, this section looks at how decision makers actually used religion when facing two critical decisions related to death: the choice to enroll in hospice care and the choice to withdraw life support.

A *The Study*

Relatively few studies have been conducted concerning how surrogate decisions are actually made at the bedside.[46] Our qualitative research involved interviews with grown children who either served as a surrogate or who observed the role of another family member who functioned as the surrogate.[47] One-third of the deceased parent figures needed surrogate decision makers because of their

43 As discussed *infra*, a patient may not experience hospice chaplaincy as non-coercive.

44 *See* ROBERT ELLICKSON, ORDER WITHOUT LAW: HOW NEIGHBORS SETTLE DISPUTES (1994); Carl Schneider, *The Channelling Function in Family Law*, 20 HOFSTRA L. REV. 495 (1992). For a related discussion of norms and laws shaping behavior in marriages, *see* Wilson, Chapter 16, this volume.

45 *See* AMY ZIETTLOW & NAOMI CAHN, HOMEWARD BOUND (2017).

46 Most of our knowledge of surrogate decision making comes from either bioethical studies or litigation related to specific medical cases. *See* Maria J. Silveira et al., *Advance Directives and Outcomes of Surrogate Decision Making Before Death*, 362 NEW ENG. J. MED. 1211–18 (2010). Reported cases, of course, represent an extremely small set of actual conflicts.

47 For further description of the study, *see* Naomi Cahn & Amy Ziettlow, *Making Things Fair: An Empirical Study of How People Approach the Wealth Transmission System*, 22 ELDER L.J. 325 (2015); Amy Ziettlow & Naomi Cahn, *The Honor Commandment: Law, Religion and the Challenge of Elder Care*, 30 J. L. & RELIG. 229 (2015).

incapacity,[48] a statistic that echoes national studies showing that 40% of patients admitted to a medical care facility are unable to direct their own treatment.[49] Excluding three individuals who indicated the existence of a Do Not Resuscitate ("DNR") order, none of those interviewed mentioned the completion of an advance care planning document or accessing one. The scheduling of the interviews a year after the death of the decedent gave the surrogates ample time to reflect on their choices, as well as to repress painful memories and rationalize self-interested decisions.

The respondents' religious upbringing, their families' religious history, and their current religious beliefs and practices formed a core part of the interview.[50] As Figure 20.1 shows, no study participants identified themselves as having been raised outside of the Christian faith, and virtually all continued to identify themselves as Christians.[51] This number is higher than the general U.S. population, as well as that of Baton Rouge, Louisiana.[52] Within the Christian traditions represented, the majority were nondenominational and evangelical Protestant Christians, which may have shaped their approach to end-of-life decision making.[53] The relative homogeneity of the study population and their greater religiosity may limit what we can surmise about religious traditions generally and their intersection with medical decision making. Regardless of intensity or lack of diversity, however, the study population

[48] Thirteen of the deceased had decisions made for them by their spouse. Seven of the deceased had decisions made for them by their grown child; two of those grown children included the significant other of their parent, who did not share in the decision-making role.

[49] V. Raymont et al., *Prevalence of Mental Incapacity in Medical Inpatients and Associated Risk Factors: Cross-Sectional Study*, 364 LANCET 1421 (2004).

[50] The interviews were semi-structured, and the explanation of time of death and the decisions preceding that moment emerged naturally in the narrative. The semi-structured interviews included questions about religious upbringing, the religious history of their families, and their current religious beliefs and practices.

[51] In terms of religious affiliation, nationally, about 70% of Americans identify as Christian. *America's Changing Religious Landscape*, PEW RESEARCH CENTER (May 12, 2015), www.pewforum.org/2015/05/12/americas-changing-religious-landscape/.

[52] Clifford Grammich, et al., 2010 *U.S. Religion Census*, Religious Congregations & Membership Study Association of Statisticians of American Religious Bodies (2012); Dale E. Jones et al., *Congregations and Membership in the United States* 2000, GLENMARY RESEARCH CENTER (2002), www.city-data.com/county/religion/East-Baton-Rouge-Parish-LA.html#ixzz4eczx2HSW.

[53] *See* Wendy S. Goffe, *Conform Health Care Directive to Client's Religious Views – Part 1*, 39 EST. PLAN. 19 (2012), for an overview of religious views related to withholding life-sustaining treatment. *See also Religious Groups' Views on End of Life Issues*, PEW RES. CENTER (Nov. 21, 2013), www.pewforum.org/2013/11/21/religious-groups-views-on-end-of-life-issues/, for an overview of additional end-of-life issues.

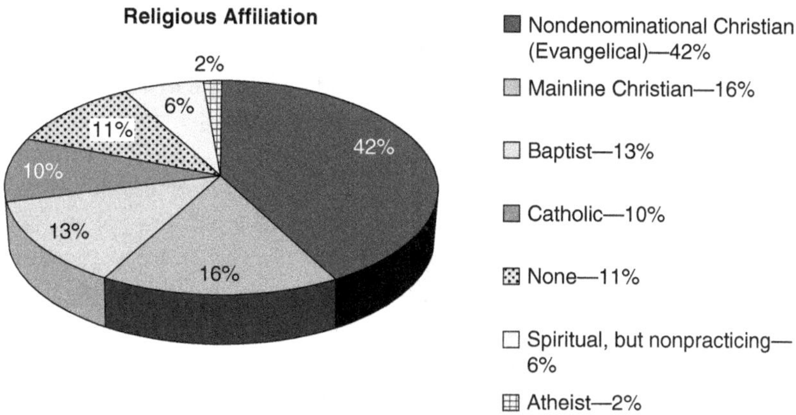

FIGURE 20.1 Religious Affiliation of Study Participants

allows us to analyze the professional or corporate interference in individual religious reasoning and practice.

B Actual Practices

Even before they faced questions of ending life, almost all participants mentioned that religious beliefs had affected their feelings of responsibility toward their parents.[54] Respondents also discussed early in the interview their faith background as children and how their religious beliefs and practices had evolved in relation to the religious affiliation of their parents. As the parent's illness progressed and joint decisions between the parent and family members were made concerning treatment options, the parent included religious beliefs as reason or justification, in instances of conflict, for a particular course of care. Despite disagreement, the family complied with the medical choices of the parent. In joint decisions, the expressed religious beliefs of the parent played a salient role. However, once the parents were incapacitated, their religious beliefs played a less prominent role in what decisions were made, while the religious beliefs and practices of the surrogate assumed more prominence. Unlike the drama played out in high-profile cases, such as *Schiavo* and *Cruzan*, the families themselves worked through end-of-life decision making, prompted by medical staff. Internal family conflicts caused

[54] Indeed, the biblical Honor Commandment ("Honor your father and your mother, that your days may be long upon the land which the LORD your God is giving you") is supported in a variety of secular laws. Ziettlow & Cahn, *supra* note 47. Fifty-five of the sixty-three interviewees spoke of their religious beliefs and practices as informing the care provided.

problems within the families, but no surrogate felt the need to vindicate a specific choice through legal means. The resentments did come "home" later, in fights about funeral arrangements and distribution of assets.[55]

What we found is that, in practice, medical professionals honored the religious framing used by surrogate decision makers as well as the time needed by the decision maker to engage in religious practices that would inform their healthcare decision.[56] Medical professionals did not evaluate the salience or sincerity of the religious beliefs or measure the frequency or fervency of the historical religious practices, deferring to – and respecting – the surrogate decision makers. In this section, we begin by explaining how religion affected the decision to stop curative treatments and to enroll in hospice care. We then analyze what role religion played in informing the surrogate decision to withdraw life support.

1 Hospice

Of the fifty-eight deaths of parents in the study, one-quarter occurred in hospice care, either at home or in a hospice inpatient facility. Religion guided families in their decision to enter hospice, religion supported parents and families while under hospice care, and hospice care providers assisted individuals in completing advanced care documents, such as a DNR order.

Most of the parents were mentally competent during the discussion concerning admission to hospice, and many called on their religious beliefs for guidance. Parents and families expressed that the parent's or the surrogate's choice fell under God's providence or that God's presence guided the parent or the surrogate to make a choice in the dying person's best interest. The individuals or families did not directly refer to theological or biblical texts or seek direct guidance from religious professionals as a way to confirm or support their interpretation of "God's will."[57] For example, Wanda's mother, Laurie Ann, said that "it was time" for her to stop aggressively treating her lung cancer and that God gave her peace about entering hospice care, even though Wanda believed, "If you can fight, you fight." Ultimately, Wanda deferred to her mother's beliefs.

[55] *See* Ziettlow & Cahn, *supra* note 47.

[56] Medical professionals played a key role in instigating when a choice needed to be made, with doctors forcing choices concerning hospice and life support, and nurses providing information and support.

[57] Given that more than 50% of the respondents could be considered nondenomination/evangelical and Baptist Christians, this focus on the individual's authority to both access and interpret divine "will" did not surprise us.

Once admitted to hospice care, Katie's mother completed DNR paperwork. A few days before her death, Katie's mother had a stroke and was taken to a hospital emergency room, where her DNR order trumped the religious beliefs of her daughter. Katie's evangelical background led her to believe that medical interventions should be sought at all costs as a way to allow God to do a miracle. When Katie and her sister arrived in the emergency room, they had to make a decision about how the doctors should proceed in treating their mother; the existence of the DNR circumvented the ongoing tensions and arguments between the daughters over seeking or discontinuing curative care. As was true for other families in which there was formal documentation of the parent's choices, for Katie even relatively simple advance care planning (such as the DNR) helped the family members set aside their own preferences, religiously based or otherwise, and focus on the wishes of their loved one.

After their parent had been admitted to hospice care, study participants also noted that they felt that hospice care itself provided spiritual support.[58] They were not surprised when a hospice chaplain made routine visits as a member of the care team. Chaplains also arrived when a crisis or death occurred and offered a "non-anxious presence."[59]

2 Surrogate Decision Making

Surrogate decision makers in the study faced a number of health-related decisions concerning treatment interventions. While they were not surprised that choices needed to be made, few respondents had formal advance planning documents at their disposal. Consequently, default rules came into play. No one referred to the law explicitly when it came to designating a decision maker or to making decisions, so the surrogate generally assumed responsibility informally, but without challenge. Notwithstanding the legal emphasis on patient autonomy and decision making, the religious beliefs of the incapacitated parent were rarely mentioned or specifically considered in making choices to withdraw life support. Instead, the surrogate's own religious beliefs and practices played an important role in the decision to remove life support measures. Indeed, this reality, explored further later (and confirmed anecdotally by the authors' experiences outside of the

58 Only several interviewees mentioned the role of a chaplain in hospice care explicitly. This may be due, in part, to a short length of stay in hospice because of the acute nature of the admitting diagnosis.

59 Interview with Katie (Feb. 16, 2012); interview with Phillip (Apr. 24, 2012).

study), provides confirmation of the significance of the designated decision maker.[60]

In this section we focus specifically on the respondents and families who made a decision about withdrawing life support measures for the parent on the parent's behalf. Most respondents used the idiom "pull the plug" to describe this decision.[61] Religion came into play in two ways. First, the religious beliefs of the surrogate concerning the goals of medical care, their varying understandings of the role of "God's will"[62] in the decision at hand, and an understanding of life after death informed their comprehension of the parent's best interests. Second, the religious practices of the surrogate served as a form of support for discerning what decision to make.

I RELIGIOUS BELIEFS When major decisions about medical treatments were faced, families drew upon their faith beliefs to discern what was in the best interest of the incapacitated parent. The key question respondents sought to answer when deciding to remove life support measures concerned the best interests of the incapacitated loved one.[63] Religious beliefs and practices figured prominently in this assessment, even though respondents did not refer to specific doctrinal statements or theological texts to support their own or their loved one's religious beliefs relating to when life ends.[64] This surprised us, considering contentious public debates about when life begins and when life ends frequently draw on formal theological writings.[65]

Many surrogates shared a common theological belief in the concept of mercy, understood to be an unmerited gift of kindness or compassion, and in a merciful God who would be present to relieve suffering.[66] Overall, suffering

60 Kaplan's analysis of medical professionals reinforces this observation. *See* Kaplan, Chapter 19, this volume.

61 Six of the sixty-three interviewed faced the decision to remove life support.

62 *See* Kaplan, Chapter 19, this volume, on the differing interpretations of "God's will."

63 While the law often expects a decision based on "substituted judgment," where that is not known, the surrogate is instructed to use a best interest standard. *See supra* notes 20, 23, 24.

64 For example, they did not explicitly reference a historical creed, a scriptural commentary, a papal encyclical, or Halakhah.

65 *See, e.g.*, Sandra H. Johnson, *Quinlan and Cruzan: Beyond the Symbols*, *in* HEALTH LAW AND BIOETHICS: CASES IN CONTEXT (Sandra H. Johnson, Joan H. Krause, Richard S. Saver, & Robin Fretwell Wilson, eds., 2009). In 2014, these issues resurfaced when teenager Jahi McMath in California and mother Marlise Munoz in Texas were both deemed brain dead. *See* Daniel B. Wood & Gloria Goodale, *When Does Life End? Two Emotional Cases Probe the Complexities*, CHRISTIAN SCI. MONITOR (Jan. 19, 2014), www.csmonitor.com/USA/Justice/2014/0119/When-does-life-end-Two-emotional-cases-probe-the-complexities.

66 Although participants did not necessarily use the word "mercy," that word, as religiously interpreted, accords with the words they did use. For example, Courtney talked at length about her prayers and hopes – how she wanted God to cure her mother, then she just wanted

was not viewed as holding spiritual merit or as something to be endured for the sake of spiritual purification. Respondents sought to relieve suffering without hastening death. Up until the point of withdrawing life support, respondents spoke of a cure as in the best interest of their loved one. Their prayers and hopes focused on a full recovery from illness or injury. However, once hospice care entered the picture, hopes shifted from a cure to a merciful, pain-free life until death. For example, when Sam's mother came home, where she received hospice care, Sam said that his family prayed, asking God "please just show mercy." Framing his family's decision theologically – using the term "mercy" – helped Sam understand the goals for his mother's care at the end of her life, especially when his family faced the decision of not inserting a feeding tube and determined that it would be an extraordinary treatment. When all medical interventions could not return his mother to full health, they could still hope for a peaceful, pain-free death.

As surrogates considered the best interests of their parent, many respondents framed the choice of withdrawing life support interventions as "putting it in God's hands." As was true for Keith, whose story opened this chapter, belief in God's providence and control became a comfort after he made the decision about withdrawing his father's life support. From the perspective of the surrogate decision maker, beliefs about God's control of life's length tended to predominate in such statements as "it was a God thing," "God's plan," "God took her," "God planned it," "God does things for a reason," or "if God brings you to it, God will bring you through it." A year after the death, a pronounced sense of God's providence gave comfort to most respondents and allowed them to justify their decision to themselves and to any family members who doubted the decision. Making a decision was easier if it was not ultimately theirs to make.

This faith in providence reflects religiosity, on the one hand. But it can also be seen as allowing religion to serve as the denial of agency by those who are acting, and as a reflection of the psychic discomfort we all feel when asked to make a life or death decision regarding a loved one. Believing that one lacks agency, that God is in control, lessens the internal struggle but does not erase it. Moreover, most respondents did not have access to a living will that explicitly communicated the parent's wishes concerning life-sustaining treatment. For those respondents who did believe they knew what their mother or

to have God keep her alive when a cure was no longer possible. When she saw that her mother was in pain and that the tumors and cancer that would end her life were the very thing causing her pain and that the medicines could only hold pain at bay so long, her prayer changed to asking God to let her mom be pain free and then die.

father wanted, based on either brief conversations during the hospitalization or through a DNR order, they expressed trust in God's presence with them through the experience, without having to use God's will as justification for making a difficult decision.

II RELIGIOUS PRACTICES In addition to their religious beliefs, engaging in religious practices helped surrogates make a decision. Medical professionals did not heavily influence the specific choices made by a surrogate beyond presenting the available treatment options. Doctors acted to force the choice; nurses provided information and focus after a decision was made. The doctors offered a diagnosis and presented options for treatment or removing treatment. For example, doctors were the ones who said, "It's time to call hospice." When asked about what advice they might offer physicians, interviewees stressed that they appreciated the doctors who were honest and direct with them about the prognosis and the seriousness of the illness. A year after the death, they spoke highly of those doctors who "didn't sugarcoat things" and "didn't speak over our heads, but told us clearly what to expect." No one interviewed mentioned being aware of the religious beliefs of their medical provider, hospital system, or hospice organization.[67]

In contrast to the instigating role of doctors, nurses asked instrumental questions and responded with directive statements related to providing hands-on care. The nurses helped the family members understand what making a particular decision meant regarding withdrawal of treatment or admission to hospice, and then with interpreting the signs and symptoms of the end of life as they unfolded. Nurses were the ones who told families that death was near. They encouraged family members to "talk to their" loved one; they taught families about the dying process, telling them that "hearing is the last sense to go." Because end-of-life decision making involved highly emotional stakes, the nurses provided a useful grounding that helped family members focus on what the patient needed. They especially appreciated when the nursing staff allowed a large group of family members to visit, despite being cramped in the room and a little loud, or when a nurse allowed a son to stay after the intensive care unit ("ICU") visiting hours the night his father died. Nurses were "people who care."

67 The two major hospital systems in Baton Rouge are both religiously affiliated. Our Lady of the Lake is Roman Catholic and Baton Rouge General is Baptist. Many of the hospice organizations appear to be religiously affiliated based on name: St. Joseph's Hospice, Trinity Hospice, In His Hands Hospice, Hospice Compassus, and so on. The only nonprofit hospice provider has the least religious name: The Hospice of Baton Rouge.

a Prayer When the end of a parent's life approached, participants engaged in personal and collective prayer.[68] At the moment of the decision, personal prayer enabled participants to believe that God was present, giving them strength to make the choice. Medical professionals did not interfere when respondents engaged in prayer as a way to guide their decision and hospital chaplains served to facilitate prayer. Keith told the doctors and his family that he needed to go home and "pray on it" before he could make a decision. His prayers focused on asking God to affirm his decision to remove life support. When Keith arrived at the hospital the next day, the hospital chaplain visited and offered to pray with him. Again, he found a quiet place to be alone at the hospital and prayed, "You know, Lord, 6:00, it's going to be your will. Whatever you decided to do is already decided." Keith then felt that he could let his father go, to be "where God wants him to be."

Nancy also assumed the role of surrogate decision maker for her single mother. She consulted with her two brothers, her father, as well as her mother's second ex-husband (her brothers' father), and her mother's current boyfriend of more than ten years. Balancing all their opinions, combined with the heaviness of the decision, led Nancy to pray, "Please God, just take her, because I do not want to have to make the decision to take my mom off life support." When the medical team gave Nancy and her family a 72-hour window to observe her mother's condition for signs of improvement before withdrawing life support, she especially appreciated that her mother's priest, a good friend of the family, came to visit, pray with the family, administer "last rites," and agreed to conduct the funeral service. That window of time allowed Nancy to come to peace with the decision to withdraw life support measures.

b Pastoral Care from a Clergy Member While many of the surrogates drew on their own religious practices and beliefs, some of the respondents also called upon a clergy person for spiritual help. For some, like Nancy, it was the parent's clergy member who visited. Nancy, a Methodist, spoke to her pastor for guidance, but he did not visit. Nancy believed that her mother, as a practicing Catholic, would want her priest to visit to conduct the rites and rituals that Catholics find meaningful at the end of life.

Other clergypersons who visited the hospital served as the pastor for the whole family. For Peter, Pastor Frank (his minister as well as his father's) supported the families' decision making. Peter and his family wanted Pastor

68 The relative religious homogeneity of the study population and their greater religiosity provide insight, of course, only into their experiences.

Frank to be in the ICU with them as they made the decision to remove his father, Leonard, from life support. Although Pastor Frank did not refer directly to the religious beliefs of Peter's father (at least Peter did not recall him doing so), his presence and tacit support of the decision to remove life support gave Peter's decision theological affirmation. Pastor Frank helped the family say good-bye and then stayed with the family until Leonard died. Peter explained that the pastor's counsel was critical to allowing his family to sort through all of their complex emotions to reach the result his father would have wanted.

No one in our research mentioned the faith background of the parent, explicitly, in informing their pull the plug decision, whereas they were acutely aware of the influence of their own religious background. On the one hand, this omission may tell us that the religious beliefs and practices of the implicated parent did not register during the time of crisis.[69] On the other hand, perhaps because the interviews occurred a year after the death and the respondent came to talk about his or her experience, interviewees may have emphasized their own religious beliefs and practices during the interview.

Regardless of why, while the law often directs that surrogates use a substituted judgment rule for patients unable to make their own decisions, surrogates drew on their own religious beliefs and practices; those religious beliefs supported their determinations of what was in their parents' best interests when they could not use substituted judgment. Ultimately, the narratives show that people did not believe that their religious beliefs or practices were silly or burdensome, they did not believe that their religious integrity was questioned, and they did not feel pressure to espouse a certain belief or practice by hospital or hospice chaplains, or any physicians or nurses.

III RECOMMENDATIONS CONCERNING END-OF-LIFE DECISION MAKING (IN THE SHADOW OF *HOBBY LOBBY*)

So how does *Hobby Lobby*[70] play into this? At its core, *Hobby Lobby* considered a government action that objecting employers, organized as for-profit closely held corporations, said imposed a substantial burden on their religious liberty under the Religious Freedom Restoration Act. Our qualitative research

69 This interpretation seems unfortunate considering our culture's high value for substituted judgment and the expressed relief of those respondents who did know the choices of their parent and were able to follow those choices rather than their own.

70 Hobby Lobby, *supra* note 2, at 2761.

shows the significance of religion, and how it weaves its way into the experiences of individuals and families facing the end of life. No one in our qualitative interviews was aware of the religious beliefs of the hospice or healthcare organization caring for their loved one.[71] All respondents assumed that their decision making would trump those of the institutional provider and those of the physician for that matter. At the same time, respondents tempered their beliefs about the appropriate end-of-life decision based on their own religious identity.

Because spirituality can play such an important role in end-of-life decision making,[72] legal institutions can take numerous steps to respect the individual's core beliefs. *Hobby Lobby* might be interpreted to protect an institution's religious perspective at the expense of quality end-of-life care that honors the individual's religiously based choices.[73] To prevent *Hobby Lobby*, or other statutory protections for conscience such as those described by Adams (Chapter 21, this volume), from interfering with a patient's chosen end-of-life care, the law can develop better approaches that support the individual's decision making, regardless of the entity providing care. This can be done by providing more structure at the time of execution of advance directives, providing more structure to surrogates who are making decisions, and providing more training to personnel who are present at the time of advance directive – and surrogate – decision making.

As a foundational issue, our study shows the need for more families to engage in end-of-life conversations that address preferences for care, including their religious and moral beliefs about such care – and for those conversations to be documented through advance medical directives. The instances when a patient's choices were followed, even when in conflict with the wishes of the surrogate, happened when the individual completed an advance directive that became a physician's order.[74]

Transforming one's wishes into a legal and medical order was a critical component to others' honoring the choices of the patient. The legal pieces are in place to foster such documentation, and numerous organizations provide

[71] As noted earlier, the two main hospital systems in Baton Rouge, Louisiana, are Our Lady of the Lake (Roman Catholic) and Baton Rouge General (Baptist).

[72] *See* Nancy Berlinger et al., The Hastings Center Guidelines for Decisions on Life-Sustaining Treatment and Care Near the End of Life 149–50 (Oxford University Press 2013).

[73] For competing views on whether institutions, including nonprofit organizations, should be able to assert conscience claims in the healthcare context, *see* Parts I and II of this volume.

[74] *See* Cahn & Ziettlow, *Making Things Fair*, *supra* note 47, at 339; Erik K. Fromme et al., *Association Between Physician Orders for Life-Sustaining Treatment for Scope of Treatment and In-Hospital Death in Oregon*, 62 J. Am. Geriatrics Soc. 1246 (2014).

easily accessible tools,[75] but still the conversations are often quite difficult for both families *and* professionals.[76] Yet, as Kaplan suggests (Chapter 19, this volume), the best way of protecting a patient's wishes, including religiously based preferences, is to appoint a surrogate who understands the patient's beliefs.

First, to comply with Medicare and Medicaid, hospitals, hospices, and other medical service institutions must provide information, in writing, to each patient about her right to have an advance directive, and the hospital's approach to respecting that directive.[77] Given, as Kaplan (Chapter 19, this volume) describes, that religiosity may affect how physicians approach patient care at end of life, allowing patients to state, in advance, their preferences is critical to shaping their own care.[78] The patients can, if competent, verbalize their wishes during treatment, or through advance directives, and thus define how their religious identity will shape what they want or do not want in medical treatment when they are no longer competent. Legally appointed surrogates or surrogates by default – family members – are extensions of the patient, literally, the patient's agent, and best practice is when they make choices in line with the known or imagined or historically defined wishes of the patient (in many instances, surrogates define what their loved one would wish as "they would choose what is in their best interest").

Our research shows what that looks like in practice; our research also shows that, where family members have weaker identity ties (such as to a stepparent), those ties may be strengthened by shared religious identity or practice. Having a religious figure as a surrogate also falls into this category because such a surrogate will not only make sure that religious doctrine is followed, but also in faiths with no religiously defined decisions (i.e., there is no such thing as a "Lutheran healthcare decision" in the way that there is a "Catholic healthcare decision"), the religious leader is simply someone, like family, who hopefully knows the patient well and can accurately imagine what she would want.

Second, since 2016, Medicare has provided reimbursement for visits between a physician or nurse practitioner and the patient and any family or friends the patient would like to include to discuss advance care planning.[79] These discussions can occur at a time of acute illness or during an annual

75 *E.g.*, Aging with Dignity, *Five Wishes* (2015), www.agingwithdignity.org/five-wishes; The Conversation Project, http://theconversationproject.org/.

76 *See, e.g.*, Harry L. Anderson et al., *End-of-Life Conversations at Dinner*, aahpm.org/uploads/microsites/Abstracts_2015/End-of-Life_Conversations_at_Dinner.pdf.

77 42 U.S.C. § 1395cc(f)(1)(2012).

78 *See* Kaplan Chapter 19, this volume, n.18.

79 80 Fed. Reg. 41686 (July 15, 2015), www.regulations.gov/document?D=CMS-2015–0081-0002.

wellness visit, thereby allowing such discussions to become more routine.[80] Third, service providers are required to offer education for their own staff and the community on issues relating to advance directives.[81]

As part of these efforts, medical personnel who work with an individual to fill out advance medical directives, or other indications of a patient's wishes, such as a Physician Order for Life-Sustaining Treatment ("POLST"), should explicitly ask about, and then explore the impact of, any relevant spiritual beliefs as part of a standard procedure for filling out the forms.[82] Clergy and faith communities could themselves undertake to provide more education and discussion concerning end-of-life planning, although, as Kaplan (Chapter 19, this volume) notes, the goal is to ensure identification and compliance with the patient's own belief system, if any. Indeed, notwithstanding Americans' increasing turn away from religious observance, religious affiliation remains high, and spirituality is growing.[83] Consequently, end-of-life discussion and integration with spiritual beliefs remain important.

An additional issue concerns maintaining the status quo with respect to the Hospice Medicare Benefit, a benefit that predates the Patient Protection and Affordable Care Act and presumably will remain, whatever happens with healthcare reform during the Trump Administration.[84] Spiritual counseling should continue to be a core service on par with physicians, registered nurses, and social workers. As non-hospice-related palliative care programs proliferate in hospital settings, and the shift to hospice as a predominately for-profit industry continues, the temptation may arise to eliminate spiritual counseling as a required service. The hospice therapeutic model of spiritual counseling

80 80 Fed. Reg. 41686; *see, e.g.*, CMS, *Frequently Asked Questions about Billing the Physician Fee Schedule for Advance Care Planning Services* (2016), www.cms.gov/Medicare/Medicare-Fee-for-Service-Payment/PhysicianFeeSched/Downloads/FAQ-Advance-Care-Planning.pdf; Charles P. Sabatino, *Summary of Center for Medicare and Medicaid Services (CMS) Rule for Covering Cost of Advance Care Planning Services*, 37 Bifocal 19 (2015); Kaiser Family Foundation, *10 FAQs: Medicare's Role in End-of-Life Care* (Nov. 2015), http://kff.org/medicare/fact-sheet/10-faqs-medicares-role-in-end-of-life-care/.

81 42 U.S.C. § 1395cc(f)(1)(E) (2012).

82 *See* Terman, *supra* note 25, at 187–88 (offering specific suggestions on options that clinicians can present). A POLST is a "system that identifies patients' wishes regarding medical treatment and communicates and respects them by creating portable medical orders." *See* National POLST Paradigm, http://polst.org/about-the-national-polst-paradigm/what-is-polst/.

83 *U.S. Public Becoming Less Religious*, Pew Res. Center (Nov. 3, 2015), www.pewforum.org/2015/11/03/u-s-public-becoming-less-religious/.

84 *The Medicare Hospice Benefit*, National Hospice and Palliative Care Organization (Oct. 2015), www.nhpco.org/sites/default/files/public/communications/Outreach/The_Medicare_Hospice_Benefit.pdf; Robert Pear, Thomas Kaplan, and Maggie Haberman, *In Major Defeat for Trump, Push to Repeal Health Law Fails*, N.Y. Times (March 24, 2017), www.nytimes.com/2017/03/24/us/politics/health-care-affordable-care-act.html.

reflects best practice in end-of-life care, and it echoes what laypeople expect when a loved one dies in a hospital setting, or in hospice care in a variety of care settings.

Hospice aims to facilitate the full expression of spiritual beliefs, as well as practices that support the beliefs of the individual patient and family members. The religious or areligious beliefs of the individual hospice practitioner or hospice organization should yield to respect for a patient's choices. In *Hobby Lobby* terms, the compelling government interest should be in preserving patient autonomy, a right the Supreme Court has "assume[d]" patients have.[85]

V CONCLUSION

End-of-life care draws on ethics, and those ethics are shaped by many forces outside the law, including religion and spiritual beliefs. Indeed, based on our study participants, religion profoundly affects end-of-life decision making on a personal level, providing guidance and comfort to patients and to the surrogates who make decisions on their behalf. The law appropriately supported the religious-based reasoning; on the other hand, in the absence of either formal or informal advance direction, notwithstanding the legal emphasis on patient autonomy, surrogates generally made decisions in accord with their own religious beliefs, although these typically aligned with the patient's.

As advances in medical technology and practice expand our ability to extend life, an increasing number of individuals and families will need to make nuanced decisions about when that technology is no longer curative or no longer accords with the individual's definition of life. Protecting the personal religious beliefs and practices of those patients and families will be tantamount to ensuring they have access to a critical source of guidance and encouragement during those liminal times between life and death.

85 Cruzan, *supra* note 19, at 279 (1990) ("[F]or purposes of this case, we assume that the United States Constitution would grant a competent person a constitutionally protected right to refuse lifesaving hydration and nutrition."). Importantly, Justice Gorsuch seems ill-inclined to disturb this deference to competent patients. *See* Neil Gorsuch, *A Reply to Raymond Tallis on the Legalization of Assisted Suicide and Euthenasia*, 28 J. LEGAL MED. 327, 331 (2007), http://tandfonline.com/doi/full/10.1080/01947640701554468?scroll=top&needAccess=true& (indicating his agreement that "refusals of treatment should be permitted").

PART VI

SHAPING THE LEGAL CULTURE OF THE FAMILY

21

Taking Colliding Trains Off a Collision Path

Lessons from the Utah Compromise for Civil Society

J. Stuart Adams

Senate Majority Whip, Utah State Senate

With a new presidential administration, the United States Supreme Court's momentous decision in *Obergefell v. Hodges*[1] still settling in, and continuing skirmishes over the religious liberty of people who believe in traditional marriage, there is a palpable sense of uncertainty about whether tensions between gay rights and religious liberty will ever subside.[2] A majority of the country finds itself now where Utah found itself months before *Obergefell*, with a new civil right handed down by court decision – in Utah's case, courtesy of *Kitchen v. Herbert*, which struck the amendment in our state constitution limiting marriage to one man and one woman.[3] Like a majority of the country, Utah had no positive statutory law assisting Utahns in navigating the predictable questions that would arise – questions such as whether people authorized to marry persons under state law must marry everyone who asks; how would the state discharge its duty to provide access to marriage for everyone who otherwise qualified; whether religious people would be able to speak in favor of traditional marriage without fearing legal repercussions and faith communities could support those in traditional marriages through religious counseling and marriage retreats? For Utah, the second-most religious state in America, these were more than academic questions.[4]

1 135 S. Ct. 2584 (2015).

2 For one exchange capturing crosscurrents, *see* Chapters 14–16, 22–24.

3 UTAH CONST. art. I, § 29 ("[Marriage]: (1) Marriage consists only of the legal union between a man and a woman. (2) No other domestic union, however denominated, may be recognized as a marriage or given the same or substantially equivalent legal effect."); Kitchen v. Herbert, 961 F. Supp. 2d 1181 (D. Utah 2013) (invalidating Section 29 as violating the Due Process and Equal Protection Clauses), *aff'd*, 755 F.3d 1193 (10th Cir. 2014).

4 Mark A. Kellner, *Utah is Second Most-Religious State, Mississippi Ranks First and Vermont Last*, DESERET NEWS (Feb. 5, 2014), www.deseretnews.com/article/865595683/Utah-is-second-most-religious-state-Mississippi-ranks-first-and-Vermont-last.html.

As the majority whip in the Utah Senate, I was tasked with carrying the bill that would answer as-yet unanswered questions. Now, if that was all Utah's legislation sought to do, what became known as the Utah Compromise would have been little different from many bills I have carried – for example, deciding whether to apply the onerous local regulations applicable to taxis to a new, disruptive technology such as Uber.[5]

But the legislation that Utah enacted after the courts gave us same-sex marriage did something far more challenging: it sought to give rights to *two* communities that are often pitted against each other – people of faith and the lesbian, gay, bisexual, and transgender ("LGBT") community – in a law that would be enduring and would bring a sense of peace, security, and respect to all Utahns.

This chapter charts the evolution of Utah's marriage and nondiscrimination law, from a constitutional amendment barring same-sex marriage and halting attempts to enact nondiscrimination protections to a two-bill package.[6] That package protected the full LGBT community from discrimination in housing and hiring while cementing more protections around marriage than any other state in America.[7] It shows that in times of great social change, people naturally look to legislators to take colliding trains off a collision course. It also shows that when legislatures have not acted, a vacuum results that places pressure on courts to decide competing rights – without all the advantages of the legislative process, such as hearings or the opportunity for multiple stakeholders to weigh in. In the end, it is incumbent upon legislators to flesh out how best to balance rights given the state's body of preexisting law, the needs of its citizens, and the character of the state's commitment to equality, liberty, religious freedom, and other values we hold dear.

I UTAH'S COLLIDING TRAINS

The saga over same-sex marriage unfolded in Utah much as it has in most of the country. In 2015, we received a mandate from the courts to issue marriage

5 Michelle L. Price, *Bill Before Utah Governor to Regulate Ride-Hailing Companies*, KSL (Mar. 27, 2015), www.ksl.com/?nid=757&sid=33985428; 2015 Utah S.B. 294, https://le.utah.gov/~2015/bills/static/SB0294.html.

6 Some include a third bill, House Bill 447, that required schools to excuse children from instruction related to sexuality unless parents specifically opted in; 2015 Utah HB 44, https://le.utah.gov/~2015/bills/static/HB0447.html. Analysis of this law is beyond the scope of this chapter.

7 Robin Fretwell Wilson, *Bargaining for Religious Accommodations: Same-Sex Marriage and LGBT Rights After Hobby Lobby*, *in* The Rise of Corporate Religious Liberty 265–68 (Micah Schwartzman, Chad Flanders, Zoë Robinson, eds., 2016).

licenses to same-sex couples with no positive law surrounding it.[8] At the time, only twenty-one states and the District of Columbia banned discrimination based on sexual orientation or gender identity.[9] Three of these states offered partial protections for gay individuals only.[10]

Some states had statutory protections around marriage – which many people, in Utah and elsewhere, see as sacred[11] – because those states had enacted laws recognizing same-sex marriage.[12] Much of the country was otherwise a blank slate about how to proceed. Some had statutes saying religious burdens would be subject to heightened scrutiny; others subjected infringements on gay rights to heightened scrutiny. And perhaps most confusing, some did both in their laws.

At the state level, Utah had no law to assist us: it had neither a Religious Freedom Restoration Act ("RFRA") nor heightened scrutiny of religious burdens in its constitution, and still does not.[13] And at the time, it did not protect the LGBT community from discrimination of any kind in state law.

As Figure 21.1 details, six states today follow this pattern.[14] But most speak to religious protections or LGBT rights. Some states give special protection to religious believers through constitutional guarantees *and* state RFRAs.[15] Some give heightened protection only in their state constitutions,[16] others only through a RFRA.[17] Eleven give protections to the LGBT community but make no general concessions for religious practice.[18] A number give special

8 Kitchen, *supra* note 3.

9 *See* Appendix 2 (listing California, Colorado, Connecticut, Delaware, District of Columbia, Hawaii, Illinois, Iowa, Maine, Maryland, Massachusetts, Minnesota, Nevada, New Hampshire, New Jersey, New Mexico, New York, Oregon, Rhode Island, Vermont, Washington, and Wisconsin).

10 *See* Appendix 2 (listing New Hampshire, New York, and Wisconsin).

11 Introduction, this volume.

12 Robin Fretwell Wilson, *When Governments Insulate Dissenters from Social Change: What Hobby Lobby and Abortion Conscience Clauses Teach About Specific Exemptions*, 48 U.C. Davis L. Rev. 703 (2014).

13 *See* Appendix 2 for a list of states in this category (listing California, Colorado, Delaware, District of Columbia, Georgia, Iowa, Maryland, Nebraska, Nevada, New Hampshire, New Jersey, North Dakota, Oregon, Utah, Vermont, West Virginia, and Wyoming).

14 *See* Appendix 2 (listing Georgia, Nebraska, North Dakota, South Dakota, West Virginia, and Wyoming).

15 *See* Appendix 2 (listing Arkansas, Indiana, Kansas, Mississippi, Pennsylvania, and Virginia).

16 *See* Appendix 2 (listing Alaska, Hawaii, Maine, Massachusetts, Michigan, Minnesota, Montana, New York, North Carolina, Ohio, Washington, and Wisconsin).

17 *See* Appendix 2 (listing Alabama, Arizona, Connecticut, Florida, Idaho, Illinois, Kentucky, Louisiana, Missouri, New Mexico, Oklahoma, Rhode Island, South Carolina, and Texas).

18 *See* Appendix 2 (listing California, Colorado, Delaware, District of Columbia, Iowa, Maryland, New Hampshire, New Jersey, Oregon, Utah, and Vermont).

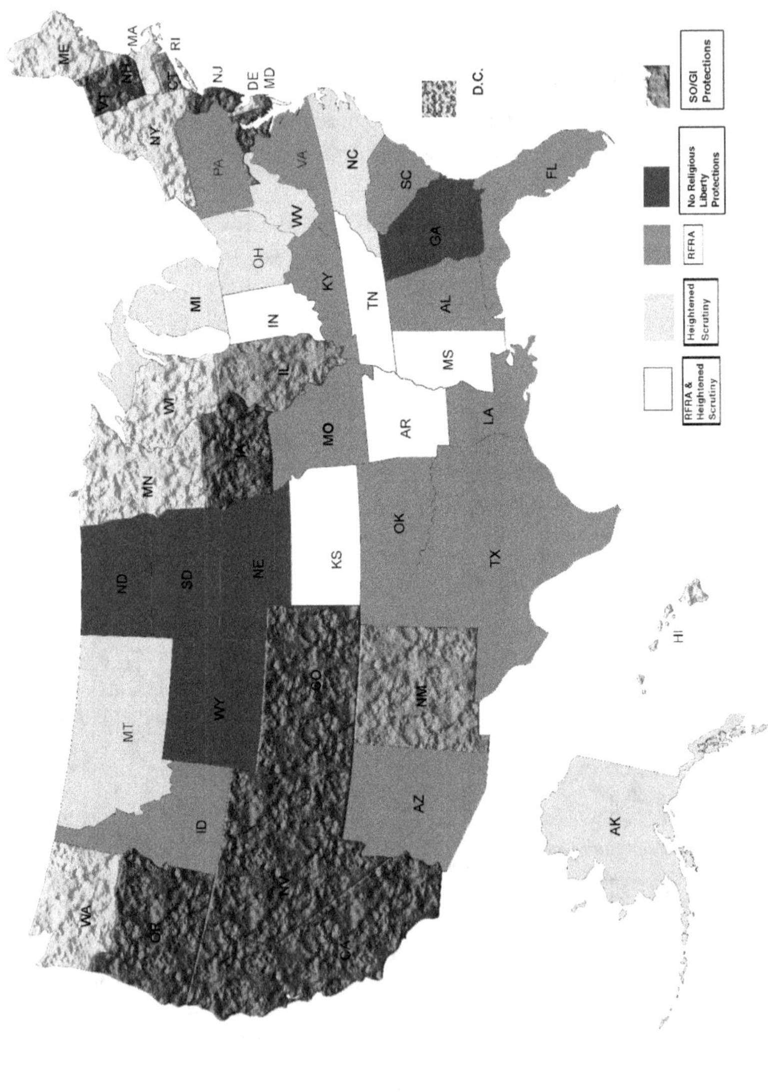

FIGURE 21.1 State Religious Liberty and Discrimination Protections

protections for religious practice and protect LGBT persons from discrimination.[19]

We concluded quickly that a RFRA would not give sufficient answers to what should happen post-*Kitchen* around marriage, for two reasons. First, at that point in 2015, no state or federal RFRA had ever been successfully invoked as to a nondiscrimination claim, despite twenty-three years of history.[20] Indeed, to my knowledge, it has happened only once since, in August 2016, to dismiss a hiring discrimination claim brought by a transgender woman against a funeral home that had fired her after she transitioned. The owners of the funeral home claimed their religious beliefs precluded being represented by a transgender employee.[21] Commentators believe that the dismissal will be overturned; oral argument in the case is scheduled for October 2017.[22] By contrast, "specific" protections for religious exercise give the courts greater clarity about what should happen when disputes arise and are more likely to be enforced.[23]

Second, Utah faced this question shortly after Arizona's attempt to revise its existing RFRA sparked boycotts and significantly damaged the state's image in many quarters.[24] In large measure, the pushback resulted

19 *See* Appendix 2 (listing Connecticut, Hawaii, Illinois, Maine, Massachusetts, Minnesota, New Mexico, New York, Rhode Island, Washington, and Wisconsin).

20 The "T-shirt" case, which applied RFRA as a defense to a nondiscrimination ordinance in a suit against a printer for refusing to print a t-shirt for a gay pride festival saying "Lexington Pride Festival 2012," rested in part on a factual finding of no discrimination. *See* Lexington-Fayette Urban County Human Rights Commission v. Hands On Originals, No. 2015-CA -000745 (Ky. App. 2017), https://s3.amazonaws.com/becketnewsite/Hands-on-Originals-ruling .pdf (the lead opinion ruled the county discrimination ordinance did not reach speech, a concurring opinion argued RFRA prevented liability, and the dissent argued that the printer did discriminate). The printer had consistently refused to print materials for "adult entertainment products and establishments," as well as shirts with profanity or that mocked religion. *Id.* at 3 (slip op.).

21 EEOC v. R.G. & G.R. Harris Funeral Homes, Inc., Case No. 14–13710 (E.D. Mich. 2016); *see also* German Lopez, *How Indiana's Religious Freedom Law Sparked a Battle Over LGBT Rights*, Vox, Apr. 2, 2015, www.vox.com/2015/3/31/8319493/indiana-rfra-lgbt (citing Professor Douglas Laycock).

22 German Lopez, *For First Time, Court Opens Door to Anti-LGBTQ Discrimination Through Religious Freedom Law*, Vox, Aug. 20, 2016, www.vox.com/2016/8/20/12558034/religious-freedom-lgbtq-discrimination-michigan ("Legal experts have also repeatedly told me that religious freedom laws like RFRAs shouldn't and don't allow discrimination, because the government does have a compelling interest to prevent anti-LGBTQ discrimination.") (citing Professors Douglas Laycock and Josh Blackman); EEOC v. R.G. & G.R. Harris Funeral Homes, Inc., Case No. 16-2424 (6th Cir 2017).

23 *See* Wilson, *supra* note 12.

24 Libby Hill, *Some Call it Religious Freedom, Others Call it Anti-Gay. Here's a Look at the Battle in Some States*, L.A. Times, Apr. 5, 2016, www.latimes.com/entertainment/la-et-states-antigay -battle-20160325-snap-htmlstory.html.

from statements religious stakeholders made during the debate – to the effect that "we need RFRA to stave off gay rights."[25] That misunderstanding tarnished RFRA, which can give faith communities latitude to do good work and protect religious minorities from government overreach.[26] But after Arizona, enacting RFRAs has become politically costly.[27] During the same session in which Utah enacted its two-bill package, an RFRA-type bill was introduced but failed to advance in the Senate.[28]

When *Kitchen* came down, Utah had swirling controversy around gay rights and religious liberty. Questions began almost immediately about the rights of gay couples to marry. Who would marry them? Utah law did not create a duty for anyone to marry heterosexual couples, let alone gay couples.[29] Members of the media asked Governor Gary Herbert if he would perform marriages for same-sex couples. He said he would not.[30] When asked the same question, Speaker of the Utah House of Representatives Greg Hughes said, "You know what? I don't have a problem with it."[31] Who exactly would be the marrying official of last resort turned out to be only one of many questions we would resolve in our new law.

25 Juliet Eilperin, *After Veto in Arizona, Conservatives Vow to Fight for Religious Liberties*, WASH. POST (Feb. 27, 2014), www.washingtonpost.com/politics/after-veto-in-arizona-conservatives-vow-to-fight-for-religious-liberties/2014/02/27/4e0f877a-9fcb-11e3-b8d8-94577ff66b28_story.html?utm_term=.136252f8c27f&wpisrc=nl_cuzheads (describing RFRA supporters as saying "that religious-liberty legislation is the best way to stave off a rapid shift in favor of gay rights").

26 Bill Bowden, *Religious Freedom Law Lets Couple Provide Soup*, ARKANSAS ONLINE (Feb. 26, 2016), http://m.arkansasonline.com/news/2016/feb/16/religious-freedom-law-lets-couple-provi/#/; Holt v. Hobbs, 135 S. Ct. 853 (2015) (permitting Muslim inmate to wear a beard as a religious observance under a generalized protection like RFRA known as the Religious Land Use and Institutionalized Persons Act). For competing views on RFRA's merits, *see* PARTS I and II of this volume.

27 *See* Emma Margolin, *Did Indiana and Arkansas Kill "Religious Freedom" for Everyone Else?* MSNBC (Apr. 3, 2015), www.msnbc.com/msnbc/did-indiana-and-arkansas-kill-religious-freedom-everyone-else (discussing boycotts in Indiana, Arkansas, and Georgia); Robert King, *RFRA: Boycotts, Bans and A Growing Backlash*, INDY STAR (Apr. 2, 2015), www.indystar.com/story/news/politics/2015/04/01/rfra-boycotts-bans-growing-backlash/70810178/.

28 2015 Utah H.B. 322, https://le.utah.gov/~2015/bills/static/HB0322.html.

29 Utah law did not create a duty for anyone to marry heterosexual couples, yet alone gay couples, until the Utah Compromise. *See* UTAH CODE § 30–1-6 (2016).

30 Ben Winslow, *Utah's Governor Says He Would Not Marry Same-Sex Couples*, FOX 13 (Feb. 12, 2015), http://fox13now.com/2015/02/12/utahs-governor-says-he-would-not-marry-same-sex-couples/.

31 *Id.*

II MARRIAGE LAW AND LGBT ORDINANCES BEFORE *KITCHEN*

In November 2004, Utah added thirty-four words to its Constitution affirming that Utah would recognize as a marriage only the union of a man and a woman.[32] Utah was one of eleven states that passed similar ballot amendments that year on the heels of *Goodridge v. Department of Public Health*.[33] At the time, I served in the Utah State House of Representatives and stood locked arms with my colleagues as we passed that constitutional amendment. I believed the amendment went to the core of values I and other Utahns consider most dear: family, sexuality, my religious beliefs. We believed we had protected and bullet-proofed traditional marriage.

Not long after, beginning in 2008, a small contingent of mostly Democratic legislators began pushing for legislation that would provide nondiscrimination protections in housing and employment to LGBT persons. For the next three years, they introduced a bill in the House that received no traction.[34]

During that same period, however, Utah municipalities began enacting nondiscrimination ordinances in earnest. Salt Lake City moved first, in 2010.[35] By the beginning of 2015, eleven cities and towns and three Utah counties had passed local employment and housing nondiscrimination protections for the LGBT community.[36] None protected against discrimination based on gender identity. This patchwork of local rules created inconsistencies between jurisdictions.

32 Utah Const. art. I, § 29, *held unconstitutional by* Kitchen v. Herbert, 755 F.3d 1193 (10th Cir. 2014). Section 29 reads: "[Marriage]: (1) Marriage consists only of the legal union between a man and a woman. (2) No other domestic union, however denominated, may be recognized as a marriage or given the same or substantially equivalent legal effect."

33 798 N.E.2d 941 (Mass. 2003); James Dao, *Same-Sex Marriage Issues Key to Some G.O.P. Races*, N.Y. Times (November 4, 2014), www.nytimes.com/2004/11/04/politics/campaign/04gay.html ?_r=0 (reporting passage by "overwhelming" margins, "clearly receiving support from Democrats and independents as well as Republicans").

34 *See* 2009 Utah H.B. 267, https://le.utah.gov/~2009/bills/static/HB0267.html; 2010 Utah H.B. 305, https://le.utah.gov/~2010/bills/static/HB0305.html; 2011 Utah S.B. 148, https://le.utah.gov /~2011/bills/static/SB0148.html.

35 *See* Salt Lake City Ordinance No. 63 (2009), www.slcdocs.com/ODHR/ord63employment .pdf; Rosemary Winters, *Legislature May Let SLC's Gay-rights Measures Stand*, Salt Lake Trib. (Jan. 11, 2010), http://archive.sltrib.com/story.php?ref=/news/ci_14154767 ("In November, Salt Lake City passed two ordinances – the first of their kind in Utah – that ban housing and employment discrimination based on sexual orientation and gender identity.").

36 *See* Equality Utah, *Housing and Workplace Discrimination in Utah* 15 (Jan. 2011), www .equalityutah.org/resources/reports-publications/nondiscrimination/6-discriminationinutah-report-equalityutah/file; Human Rights Campaign, *Cities and Counties with Non-Discrimination Ordinances that Include Gender Identity*, www.hrc.org/resources/cities-and-counties-with-non-discrimination-ordinances-that-include-gender (Salt Lake City, Logan,

Because they were written before *Kitchen*, the ordinances could not have included specific protections around traditional marriage, even though the municipalities included categorical exemptions for religious employers.[37]

After Salt Lake City enacted its municipal nondiscrimination ordinance in 2010, a statewide nondiscrimination bill was again introduced in the House.[38] In 2011, Senator Ben McAdams introduced Senate Bill 148 but it effectively died without a hearing.[39] In 2012, the Business and Labor Committee tabled Senate Bill 5l introduced by Senator McAdams.[40] In 2013, Senator McAdams was elected mayor of Salt Lake County and the idea acquired a new Republican sponsor, Senator Stephen Urquhart; the Rules Committee released the bill, which was heard by the Senate Economic Development and Workforce Services, a standing committee, which sent it to the Senate floor for consideration.[41] The bill was never debated on the floor and died.

Nine months after the 2013 session adjourned, on December 20, 2013, Judge Robert Shelby handed down *Kitchen*.[42] There was significant tension on both sides. Some Utahns wanted to secede from the union.[43] Others believed that *Kitchen* was a harbinger of even more successes. In 2014, Senator Urquhart again introduced nondiscrimination protections in the form of Senate Bill 100.[44] Frustrated by the lack of progress, in February LGBT supporters taped "blue notes" – blue sheets of paper on which messages from constituents are sent to legislators who are on the floor – to the Senate chamber doors Martin Luther–style, demanding that SB 100 be heard in committee.[45] They blocked

Grand County, Ogden, West Valley City, Alta, Harrisville, Midvale, Moab, Murray, Salt Lake County, Springdale, Summit County, Taylorsville, West Valley, and Park City).

37 Salt Lake City Ordinance No. 63 (2009), www.slcdocs.com/ODHR/ord63employment.pdf (exempting "a religious organization" and expressive associations under Boy Scouts of America v. Dale, 530 U.S. 640 (2000)).

38 2010 Utah H.B. 305, https://le.utah.gov/~2010/bills/static/HB0305.html.

39 2011 Utah S.B. 148, https://le.utah.gov/~2011/bills/static/SB0148.html. It was held by the Rules Committee and not heard elsewhere.

40 2012 Utah S.B.51, https://le.utah.gov/~2012/bills/static/SB0051.html.

41 S.B. 262, 60th Leg., Gen. Sess. (Utah 2013), https://le.utah.gov/~2013/bills/static/SB0262.html.

42 Kitchen, 961 F. Supp. 2d 1181.

43 *How Utah's Compromise Could Serve As A Model For Other States*, NPR (June 1, 2016), www.npr.org/2016/06/01/480247305/how-the-utah-compromise-could-serve-as-a-model-law-for-other-states.

44 2014 Utah S.B. 100, https://le.utah.gov/~2014/bills/static/SB0100.html.

45 Bob Henline, *"Operation Blue Note" Underway at Utah State Capitol*. Q SALT LAKE MAG., (Feb. 3, 2014), http://gaysaltlake.com/news/2014/02/03/operation-blue-note-underway-utah-state-capitol/#Q5GJOaUGHpKrD24m.99; Dennis Romboy and Lisa R. Roache, *Protesters Arrested After Blocking Senate Committee Room*, KSL (Feb. 10, 2014), www.ksl.com/?nid=148&sid=28668522.

entrances to committee rooms and the Governor's office; thirteen arrests were made.

As Section I noted, Judge Shelby's decision gave no guidance about how to implement such a fundamental shift in state policy, nor did it provide protections for those who adhere to a traditional view of marriage or have strongly held religious beliefs. The State immediately filed an appeal of the marriage decision to the U.S. Court of Appeals for the Tenth Circuit.[46] Judge Shelby declined to stay his decision, an order appealed all the way to the Supreme Court, which ordered the stay.[47] As the appeal percolated through the Tenth Circuit, our legislative leadership, despite great social pressure, subsequently held all legislation that would have addressed either religious liberties or nondiscrimination throughout the 2014 session; we believed we should wait for the Tenth Circuit to provide some much-needed clarity. On June 25, 2014, the Tenth Circuit affirmed Judge Shelby's ruling.[48] The stay remained in place. Then on November 4, the U.S. Supreme Court denied cert in *Herbert v. Kitchen* and the stay was lifted.[49] Gay couples began marrying.[50]

Before proceeding, an observation about courts is in order. For communities that feel on the outside looking in, courts can be important agents of change, as Kreis (Chapter 22, this volume), Eskridge (Chapter 23, this volume), and others show in this volume. Yet the recognition of new civil rights by courts almost always creates as many new questions as are laid to rest by the decision. Nowhere was that more true than with same-sex marriage after *Kitchen*. Legislatures are where all citizens can be heard, whether their interests are directly implicated by a restriction the state is imposing, as was true of the LGBT community in *Kitchen* and *Obergefell*, or they simply care deeply about the state, its citizens, and their welfare. With a raft of unanswered questions, the Legislature had to step in and fill the gap.

Utah has the shortest legislative session of any state in the country – a mere forty-five calendar days[51] – and during those seven weeks we meet only during the thirty-three regular working days. Many legislators were frustrated by the

46 Lee Davidson, *Utah Legislators May Rewrite State Law on Gay Marriage*, SALT LAKE TRIB. (Oct. 6, 2014), www.sltrib.com/news/1676687-155/marriage-state-court-issues-gay-law.

47 Brooke Adams & Lindsay Whitehurst, *Supreme Court Halts Utah Gay Marriages Pending Appeal*, SALT LAKE TRIB. (Jan. 7, 2014), http://archive.sltrib.com/story.php?ref=/sltrib/news/57357406-78/court-utah-state-stay.html.csp.

48 Kitchen v. Herbert, 755 F.3d 1193 (10th Cir. 2014).

49 135 S. Ct. 265 (2014).

50 Dennis Romboy, *Same-Sex Marriage Now Legal in Utah*, DESERET NEWS (Oct. 6, 2014), www.deseretnews.com/article/865612522/Same-sex-marriage-stay-lifted-in-Utah-marriage-licenses-issued-in-Salt-Lake-City.html.

51 *See* Michelle L. Price, *Utah Legislature Enters Final Days of Session*, DAILY HERALD (Mar. 11, 2013), www.heraldextra.com/news/local/govt-and-politics/legislature/utah-legislature-enters-final-days-of-session/article_731181ca-8a7f-11e2-a291-0019bb2963f4.html.

loss of the state's defense of Utah's constitutional ban. There was word that the LGBT nondiscrimination bill would be put to the floor in the upcoming legislative session; most gave it little hope of passage. Several proposals for religious liberty legislation were expected, too. With both types of bills moving down the tracks, we were headed for a different kind of wreck.

III AN UNPRECEDENTED REQUEST FOR AN ALTERNATIVE TO INTOLERANCE

Against this backdrop, something unprecedented happened. On the second day of the session, the Church of Jesus Christ of Latter-day Saints ("LDS"), sometimes called the Mormon Church, held a press conference.[52] It requested that the Utah Legislature find a way to combine protections for religious liberty and nondiscrimination protections in employment and housing.[53]

Elder Jeffrey R. Holland, a member of the Church's governing Quorum of the Twelve Apostles, finished the press conference with a call for "an alternative to the rhetoric and intolerance that for too long [have] come to characterize national debate:" "We must find ways to show respect for others whose beliefs, values and behaviors differ from ours while never being forced to deny or abandon our own beliefs, values and behaviors in the process."[54] The LDS Church urged the Legislature to follow one overarching principle: "fairness for all" – that is, an "approach that balances religious freedom protections with reasonable safeguards for LGBT people – specifically in areas of housing, employment and public transportation, which are not available in many parts of the country."[55]

While some, including Eskridge (Chapter 23, this volume), may see this as a shift in positions, it is encompassed within one of the Church's fundamental

[52] Press Release, The Church of Jesus Christ of Latter-day Saints, Transcript of News Conference on Religious Freedom and Nondiscrimination (Jan. 27, 2015), www.mormonnewsroom.org/article/publicstatement-on-religious-freedom-and-nondiscrimination.

[53] *Id.*

[54] *Id.* He also said: "Every citizen's rights are best guarded when each person and group guards for others those rights they wish guarded for themselves. Today we have spelled out the Church's concerns about the erosion of religious liberties, while at the same time calling for fairness for all people." *Id.*

[55] Press Release, The Church of Jesus Christ of Latter-day Saints, Transcript of News Conference on Religious Freedom and Nondiscrimination (Jan. 27, 2015), www.mormonnewsroom.org/article/publicstatement-on-religious-freedom-and-nondiscrimination (statement of Elder Dallin H. Oaks in transcript of a news conference held January 27, 2015, that included three members of the governing Twelve Apostles and one woman leader of the Church).

beliefs: "We claim the privilege of worshiping Almighty God according to the dictates of our own conscience, and allow all men the same privilege, let them worship how, where, or what they may."[56] As Section V explains, we put this principle into law, creating a space for everyone – whether or not involved in a religious organization – to act according to individual conscience dictates without legal risk. To say the LDS Church's announcement generated a tectonic shift in the dialogue would be an understatement.[57]

In keeping with the LDS Church's request, Senator Urquhart, I, and others sought to produce legislation that would provide protection for all stakeholders. The concepts of fairness, equality, and respect are far easier to articulate in conversation than to define legally. Our goal was to capture the meaning of these words in the Utah State statute.

With the LGBT rights advocates arrayed on one side – groups including Equality Utah, the American Civil Liberties Union of Utah, National Association for the Advancement of Colored People Utah, and the Human Rights Campaign – and conservative religious communities, a majority of Utah legislators, and their constituents on the other, it appeared converting those concepts into a workable law, that all could agree upon, might be impossible. Indeed, most believed it simply could not happen, certainly not within the thirty-one days to go.

Judicial rulings, particularly around heated social conflicts, create winners and losers – one side's perspective emerges victorious over the other's. The legislative process has the advantage of negotiation and compromise; it can temper absolutes while allowing both sides in a dispute to share in the gains and losses. The Legislature knew there would be many challenges in

[56] The Church of Jesus Christ of Latter-day Saints, *Articles of Faith*, www.mormon.org/beliefs/articles-of-faith.

[57] The LDS Church emphasizes that it has not changed its fundamental tenets as to marriage, which remains a union between a man and a woman. *See* Interview between Michael Otterson and Elder D. Todd Christofferson, *Church Provides Context on Handbook Changes Affecting Same-Sex Marriages* (Nov. 6, 2015), www.mormonnewsroom.org/article/handbook-changes-same-sex-marriages-elder-christofferson. However, individuals with same-gender attraction are to be treated courteously and respectfully. Several weeks after the signing of the bills, the LDS Church made a significant donation to a food bank dedicated exclusively to helping homeless LGBT youth. As Senator Jim Dabakis, Utah's only openly gay legislator said, "[a]lthough the LDS Church and the LGBTQ community do not agree on everything, this is yet another link in a continuing relationship of respect and civility." Jennifer Dobner, *Mormon Church Makes First-Time Donation to Utah Pride Center Youth Program*, SALT LAKE TRIB. (July 1, 2015), www.sltrib.com/home/2687980-155/mormon-church-makes-first-time-donation-to.

combining nondiscrimination provisions and protections for religious liberty into a single piece of legislation. Bringing all the stakeholders to the table – and keeping them there – while we reduced these complicated concepts to a workable compromise was a formidable challenge.

Yet, the time limitation proved an advantage. Such a short time places everyone under immense pressure, but it also focuses stakeholders on finding an acceptable balance. A few weeks into the session, the editor of this volume, Robin Fretwell Wilson, visited Utah to speak at a conference. The *Deseret News* ran a profile on her visit.[58] Well versed in the nuances of accommodating religious liberty while providing sufficient protection to members of LGBT communities,[59] I asked my staff to contact her. Professor Wilson agreed to help with the initial bill drafting and then generously volunteered her time and expertise until the legislative session ended to assist with the arduous process of drafting, negotiating, redrafting, and renegotiating. Our efforts would not have been successful without her involvement or that of Professor Cliff Rosky of the University of Utah's College of Law, an influential voice within Equality Utah;[60] representatives of the LDS Church; and our own legislative counsel. Remarkably, with a mere ten days left in the session, it appeared that we had created a congenial foundation. By that time, one week remained in the session, we had found common ground.

IV THE ELEMENTS OF COMMON RESPECT

SB 296 and 297 together have come to be known as the Utah Compromise. We were guided in drafting the two bills by a number of principles.

Meet Each Side's Needs Even if We Cannot Accommodate All Their Wants

The Utah Compromise gives the LGBT community more protections than it expressly had in New York law at the time.[61] Senate Bill 296, the Employment

58 Dennis Romboy, *Illinois Professor Could Help Utah Draft Religious Liberty, Nondiscrimination Bill*, DESERET NEWS (Feb 25, 2015), www.deseretnews.com/article/865622845/Illinois-professor-could-help-Utah-draft-religious-liberty-nondiscrimination-bill.html?pg=all.

59 SAME-SEX MARRIAGE AND RELIGIOUS LIBERTY: EMERGING CONFLICTS (Douglas Laycock, Anthony R. Picarello, & Robin Fretwell Wilson, eds., 2008).

60 *See e.g.*, Clifford J. Rosky, Perry v. Schwarzenegger *and the Future of Same-Sex Marriage Law*, 53 ARIZ. L. REV. 913 (2011).

61 For instance, New York law does not expressly cover transgender individuals. *See* Office of N.Y. State Office of the Attorney Gen. Eric T. Schneiderman, *The Sexual Orientation Non-Discrimination Act (SONDA)*, www.ag.ny.gov/civil-rights/sonda-brochure.

and Housing Anti-discrimination Amendments, modified Utah's Anti-discrimination Act and the Utah Fair Housing Act by protecting the full LGBT community from discrimination in housing and employment.[62] The inclusion of not only sexual orientation but also gender identity as illicit grounds for hiring or housing decisions puts Utah on a short list of states that have granted these protections.[63] Incidentally, the law did not cover the thorny issue of public accommodations, such as wedding vendors, because no municipal law had reached so far.

Including the transgender population in the scope of protections was not an easy or insignificant accomplishment in a deeply conservative and religious state.[64] But inclusion of the full LGBT community was a must-have for Equality Utah and others. Their inclusion proved very positive as it resolved for Utah many issues much of the rest of the country still struggles with.

On the other side, we recognized the exceptional character and function of faith communities in our society. It was important to leave religious organizations, religious schools, and religiously affiliated entities free to order their employment affairs and housing arrangements according to the dictates of their respective faith traditions.[65] For this reason, as I explain later, SB 296 maintained Utah's existing carve-out of religious entities in employment but expanded it to include religious primary and secondary schools, as well as a group in Utah that plays a significant role in the development of our children, the Boy Scouts of America ("BSA").[66] SB 296 carries forward and extends somewhat similar carve-outs in housing context, too.[67]

[62] S.B. 296, 61th Leg., Gen. Sess. (Utah 2015), http://le.utah.gov/~2015/bills/ static/SB0296.html; UTAH CODE ANN. § 34A-5-106 (2015).

[63] *See* Appendix 2.

[64] *See, e.g., supra* note 4; Philip Bump, *America's Reddest and Bluest Places*, WASH. POST (Dec. 4, 2014), www.washingtonpost.com/news/the-fix/wp/2014/12/04/americas-reddest-and-bluest-places.

[65] Not only is this sound public policy, but some of these provisions may be required by the religion clauses of the First Amendment. U.S. CONST. amend. I; *see* Hosanna-Tabor Evangelical Lutheran Church & Sch. v. E.E.O.C., 132 S. Ct. 694 (2012).

[66] UTAH CODE ANN. §§ 34A-5-102(i), 57-21-2(1), 57-21-3(b) (2015).

[67] UTAH CODE ANN. § 57-21-3 (4) (2015) ("(4) (a) (i) Unless membership in a religion is restricted by race, color, sex, or national origin, this chapter does not prohibit an entity described in Subsection (4)(a)(ii) from:

(A) limiting the sale, rental, or occupancy of a dwelling or temporary or permanent residence facility the entity owns or operates for primarily noncommercial purposes to persons of the same religion; or

(B) giving preference to persons of the same religion when selling, renting, or selecting occupants for a dwelling, or a temporary or permanent residence facility, the entity owns or operates for primarily noncommercial purposes).

At the same time, we were cognizant of the need not to roll back at-will employment or to hobble employers unduly. Under SB 296, employers have a duty to ensure that the gender-based needs of all employees for the use of restrooms and other facilities are reasonably accommodated.[68] But employers control the environment and tenor of the workplace through the creation of reasonable dress and grooming standards and reasonable policies that preserve "sex-specific facilities, including restrooms, shower facilities and dressing facilities."[69] This permits them to respect the privacy of transgendered employees and their coworkers, which can be implemented by means as simple and affordable as locked stalls or a lock on an individualized restroom door.

Leave Existing Law in Place as Much as Possible

We realized early on that creating a whole new set of rights and obligations only as to sexual orientation and gender identity might create unintended consequences. We feared we would inadvertently fail to replicate something from existing law in a new, separate chapter. Having all the duties around nondiscrimination in a single body of Utah law proved important to the LGBT community, as well.[70]

(ii) The following entities are entitled to the exemptions described in Subsection (4)(a)(i):

(A) a religious organization, association, or society; or
(B) a nonprofit institution or organization operated, supervised, or controlled by or in conjunction with a religious organization, association, or society.

(b) (i) This chapter does not prohibit an entity described in Subsection (4)(b)(ii) from:

(A) limiting the sale, rental, or occupancy of a dwelling, or a temporary or permanent residence facility, the entity owns or operates to persons of a particular religion, sex, sexual orientation, or gender identity; or
(B) giving preference to persons of a particular religion, sex, sexual orientation, or gender identity when selling, renting, or selecting occupants for a dwelling, or a temporary or permanent residence facility, the entity owns or operates.

(ii) The following entities are entitled to the exemptions described in Subsection (4)(b)(i):

(A) an entity described in Subsection (4)(a)(ii); and
(B) a person who owns a dwelling, or a temporary or permanent residence facility, that is under contract with an entity described in Subsection (4)(a)(ii)."

68 *Id.* § 34A-5-110. 69 *Id.* § 34A-5-109.

70 Zack Ford, *Utah Bill Would Ban LGBT Discrimination, With Some Big Exceptions*, THINK PROGRESS (Mar. 6, 2015), https://thinkprogress.org/utah-bill-would-ban-lgbt-discrimination-with-some-big-exceptions-767990f9a9fc.

The existing scaffolding of Utah's law seemed a good place to begin. Before SB 296 and 297, Utah's nondiscrimination law protected Utahns from discrimination in housing and hiring of the basis of race, sex, color, national origin, religion, age, and disability.[71] Our nondiscrimination statute always left religious organizations to the side, through a categorical set-aside. In our preexisting hiring provisions, for example, our law specified that "'[e]mployer' does not include, (A) a religious organization or association; (B) a religious corporation sole; or (C) any corporation or association constituting a wholly owned subsidiary or agency of any religious organization or association or religious corporation sole."[72] In practice this meant that the LDS Church was not regulated, and neither were wholly owned subsidiaries such as religious schools.[73]

SB 296 also maintained the fifteen-employee threshold for discrimination claims under the law,[74] ensuring that Utah's numerous small family-run businesses could manage their workplaces according to their values and needs without governmental interference. This structural protection allows Utah's vibrant family-run enterprises to operate nimbly. True, it permits them to follow their faith commitments when operating their business, but for many, this is secondary to hiring family members without fear of government reprisal, as they could before SB 296.

Some have argued that Utah should have provided more protections to religious employers, by increasing the number of employees a business could have and remain outside the nondiscrimination structure.[75] That, however, would have meant rolling back current protections against discrimination for people of color or other protected classes, unsettling long-held understandings of who was protected by the laws. Care was taken not to disturb preexisting protections for religious liberty, too. We instructed courts not to interpret SB 296 "to infringe upon the freedom of expressive association or the free exercise of religion protected by the First Amendment of the United States Constitution and Article I, Sections 1, 4, and 15 of the Utah Constitution."[76]

[71] Utah Code § 34A-5-104 (2015).

[72] Utah Code § 34A-5-102(1)(i)(ii)(A)-(C) (2015). *See* later for additions to these existing categorical exclusions.

[73] Id. [74] Utah Code § 34A-5-102(a)(i)(D).

[75] Andrew T. Walker & Russell Moore, *Is Utah's LGBT-Religious Liberty Bill Good Policy?*, Ethics & Religious Liberty Commission of the Southern Baptist Convention (Mar. 6, 2015), http://erlc.com/resource-library/articles/is-utahs-lgbt-religious-liberty-bill-good-policy (describing the fifteen employees as an "arbitrary threshold").

[76] Utah Code § 34A-5-111 (2016).

Give Clarity About What Duties Are Owed and When

A legislator quickly learns – as do students of the law – that definitions do a lot of the important work in statutes and policy making generally. One definition would prove especially thorny and central to reaching an accord between religious stakeholders, the LGBT community, social conservatives, and employers and landlords: the definition of gender identity.

We believed a medically objective definition was needed to provide as much clarity about when duties and protections were triggered as possible. We agreed on the following definition for gender identity drawn from the medical community:

> "Gender identity" has the meaning provided in the [American Psychiatric Association's] Diagnostic and Statistical Manual (DSM-5). A person's gender identity can be shown by providing evidence, including, but not limited to, medical history, care or treatment of the gender identity, consistent and uniform assertion of the gender identity, or other evidence that the gender identity is sincerely held, part of a person's core identity, and not being asserted for an improper purpose.[77]

The condition must continue and be treated for at least six months. By requiring documentation, employers and landlords receive an important safeguard against fraudulent claims. Transgender renters and employees gain valuable protections against discrimination in employment and housing.

Some might dismiss the clarity we built in as an unwarranted burden, having to provide a doctor's note. We adapted the documentation requirement from Connecticut and other states with a longer history of protecting transgendered individuals.[78] Like Justice Louis Brandeis's laboratories of experimentation, we sought consciously to benefit from the experience of legislators across the country about what works.

77 *Id.* § 34A-5-102(k). For a person to be diagnosed with gender dysphoria under the DSM-5, there must be a marked difference between the individual's expressed or experienced gender and the gender others would assign him or her, and it must continue for at least six months. In children, the desire to be of the other gender must be present and verbalized. This condition causes clinically significant distress or impairment in social, occupational, or other important areas of functioning. Gender dysphoria is manifested in a variety of ways, including strong desires to be treated as another gender or to be rid of one's sex characteristics, or a strong conviction that one has feelings and reactions typical of the other gender. *See* American Psychiatric Association, *Gender Dysphoria Fact Sheet* (2013), www.psychiatry.org/File%20Library/Psychiatrists/Practice/DSM/APA_DSM-5-Gender-Dysphoria.pdf.

78 Conn. Gen. Stat. Ann. § 46a-51 (West 2016). *See also* Del. Code Ann. tit. 19, § 710 (2014).

Take Care Not to Disturb the Faith Character of Faith Communities

Before the law was amended in 2015, Utah's nondiscrimination statute never reached certain religious organizations, a structure that reflects the significant role of faith in Utah's culture. This structure does not "exempt" religious actors from the law so much as leave them to the side, separating society into secular and sectarian spheres. Much of the work done in SB 296 and 297 carries forward that model of separate spheres. It retained the categorical set-aside for certain religious groups but added additional detail:

> "Employer" does not include (A) a religious organization, a religious corporation sole, a religious association, a religious society, a religious educational institution, or a religious leader, when that individual is acting in the capacity of a religious leader; (B) any corporation or association constituting an affiliate, a wholly owned subsidiary, or an agency of any religious organization, religious corporation sole, religious association, or religious society; or (C) the Boy Scouts of America or its councils, chapters, or subsidiaries.[79]

We also carried forward the discretion in hiring when a characteristic is a bona fide occupational qualification.[80]

Let me say a word about carving out religious primary and secondary schools and the Boy Scouts of America by name. Utah's existing protections omitted Utah's freestanding religious educational schools. These schools number in the dozens and include not just schools associated with the LDS Church but also those in the Catholic, Baptist, and Evangelical traditions.[81]

79 *Id.* "Religious leader" is defined as "an individual who is associated with, and is an authorized representative of, a religious organization or association or a religious corporation sole, including a member of clergy, a minister, a pastor, a priest, a rabbi, an imam, or a spiritual advisor." UTAH CODE § 34A-5-102 (1)(s) (2016).

80 UTAH CODE § 34A-5-106(3)(a)(i) (2016) ("(3) (a) It is not a discriminatory or prohibited employment practice: (i) for an employer to hire and employ an employee, for an employment agency to classify or refer for employment an individual, for a labor organization to classify its membership or to classify or refer for employment an individual, or for an employer, labor organization, or joint labor-management committee controlling an apprenticeship or other training or retraining program to admit or employ an individual in the program on the basis of religion, sex, pregnancy, childbirth, or pregnancy-related conditions, age, national origin, disability, sexual orientation, or gender identity in those certain instances when religion, sex, pregnancy, childbirth or pregnancy-related conditions, age, if the individual is 40 years of age or older, national origin, disability, sexual orientation, or gender identity is a bona fide occupational qualification reasonably necessary to the normal operation of that particular business or enterprise.").

81 Robin Fretwell Wilson, *SB296 Comes in the American Tradition of Live and Let Live*, SALT LAKE TRIB. (Mar. 9, 2017, 9:44 PM), www.sltrib.com/opinion/2255002-155/op-ed-sb296-

Thus, nondenominational religious schools received insulation even if not owned or directed by a specific church. K-12 education plays an important role for many families concerned about the moral and religious training of children.

And so with the Boy Scouts, which are part of the DNA of Utah. The LDS Church was the first institutional sponsor of the Boy Scouts of America in 1913, a time when there was great cultural suspicion about the LDS Church; the BSA's willingness to partner with the Church was appreciated.[82] In 2015, "more than 430,000 of the BSA's roughly 2.6 million Boy Scouts belonged to units sponsored by the LDS Church, making it by far the largest charter in the country."[83] At the end of 2008, the *Salt Lake Tribune* reported that 197,000 Utah youths participated in scouting and 91,000 people across the State volunteered.[84]

The division of secular and sectarian occurred in the housing context, too.[85] As Professor Wilson observed at the time:

> SB296 accomplishes a balancing act between nondiscrimination protections and religious liberties by placing faith groups outside the bounds of state dictates. Thus, existing law simply exempts religious sole corporations, like the LDS Church, giving them much-needed autonomy. Existing law also leaves aside wholly-owned corporations, the classic example of which is Brigham Young University.[86]

comes-in-the-american; UTAH CODE ANN. § 34A-5-106(3)(a)(ii) (2016). Specifically, SB 296 omits

"(ii) ... a school, college, university, or other educational institution to hire and employ an employee of a particular religion if:

(A) the school, college, university, or other educational institution is, in whole or in substantial part, owned, supported, controlled, or managed by a particular religious corporation, association, or society; or

(B) the curriculum of the school, college, university, or other educational institution is directed toward the propagation of a particular religion."

82 *A Century of Scouting in the Church*, ENSIGN (Oct. 2013), www.lds.org/ensign/2013/10/a-century-of-scouting-in-the-church?lang=eng.

83 Scott Taylor & Ben Lockhart, *Boy Scouts of America Announces That It Will Allow Transgender Youth in Boys-Only Program*, DESERET NEWS (Jan. 30, 2017), www.deseretnews.com/article/865672207/Boy-Scouts-of-America-says-it-will-allow-transgender-youth-in-boys-only-program.html.

84 Kristen Moulton, *From Great Britain to Great Basin: A Brief Look at History of Scouting*, SALT LAKE TRIB. (Feb. 10, 2010), http://archive.sltrib.com/article.php?id=14464125&itype=NGPSID.

85 *See supra* note 67.

86 Wilson, *supra* note 81.

Recognize the Dual Nature of Marriage as Civil and Religious

In addition to categorically setting aside religious groups and protecting speech about marriage, family, and sexuality in SB 296, SB 297, Protections For Religious Expression And Beliefs About Marriage, Family Or Sexuality, protected specific practices related to marriage.[87] It borrowed from the states that voluntarily enacted same-sex marriage by statute or initiative.[88] Like those states, we protected the decision not to solemnize, host, or facilitate a particular marriage if doing so would violate a sincerely held religious belief, gave step-offs for the clergy, allowed religious groups that do religious counseling to support marriages decide for themselves who could participate in such counseling, and protected all the covered entities from civil lawsuits and coercion by the government.[89] And like those states, we have ironclad assurances to religious groups that availed themselves of these protections that their tax-exempt status would not be disturbed because they acted on their beliefs on marriage and sexuality.[90]

But we added innovations to reflect Utah's specific traditions and needs. We assured religious groups that government could not strip their ability to perform recognized marriages if a group or official exercised prerogatives not to perform certain marriages based on the tenets of their faith.[91]

We protected speech in a nonreligious setting because religious figures in the LDS tradition often are businesspeople who also hold religious office. That dual identity sets up LDS people for punishment by secular authorities for disfavored positions through, for example, loss of one's professional license – we forestalled such results.[92]

87 S.B. 297, 61th Leg., Gen. Sess. (Utah 2015), http://le.utah.gov/~2015/bills/static/SB0297.html.

88 2012 Md. HB 438 (approved by referendum); R.I. Gen. Laws Ann. § 15-3-6.1 (2015); N.H. Rev. Stat. Ann. § 457:37 (2015); Minn. Stat. Ann. § 363A.26 (2015); Conn. Gen. Stat. § 46b-22b 2016); D.C. Code § 46-406 (2015); N.Y. Dom. Rel. Law § 11 (2016); Wash. Rev. Code § 26.04.010 (2015); 18 Vt. Stat. Ann. § 5144(b) (2015); Haw. Rev. Stat. § 572 -D (2015); 750 Ill. Comp. Stat. 5/209 (2010); Del. Code Ann. tit. 13 § 106 (2014); Me. Rev. Stat. tit. 19-A, § 655 (2015).

89 S.B. 297, 61th Leg., Gen. Sess. (Utah 2015), http://le.utah.gov/~2015/bills/static/SB0297.html, statutes in *supra* note 78.

90 Utah Code Ann. § 63G-20-102(1)(b)(i) (2016). Forbidden government retaliation actions include: "impos[ition of] a formal penalty on, fines, disciplines, discriminat[ion] against, deni[al of] the rights of den[ial of] benefits to, or deni[al of] tax-exempt status of a person." *Id.* § 63G-20-102(1)(b)(i).

91 *Id.* § 63G-20-201(2).

92 2015 Utah S.B. 297, https://le.utah.gov/~2015/bills/static/SB0297.html.

We avoided the entire Kim Davis problem,[93] too. Before the legislation, county clerks, including the Governor and Speaker of the House, had the authority to solemnize marriages but no legal duty to do so.[94] SB 297 created a legal duty under Utah law for the first time for someone to provide solemnization services to qualifying couples. Specifically, the bill amended Utah law to require that county clerks in all twenty-nine counties in Utah ensure solemnization services are available to every couple that makes a request and has the legal right to marry.[95]

But we provided a mechanism that avoided needless crises of conscience. The innovation: the county clerk's office could designate any "willing" celebrant, whether a worker in the office or someone outside the office, in the community, who is willing to perform marriages for all who ask. Offices might select someone outside the office for a variety of reasons: scheduling issues, religious beliefs, and so on. Should no one be willing, the elected county clerk would be the party required to perform the new duty placed upon the office by SB 297.

Whatever method used, every clerk's office must provide immediate service to all couples, gay or straight.[96] And there could be no retaliation from the clerk's office or any other branch of government if an employee exercised the choice not to solemnize any marriage – and no one need know that any county employee had any objection to marrying anyone.[97] This means government

93 *See* Robin Fretwell Wilson, *"Getting the Government Out of Marriage" Post Obergefell: The Ill-Considered Consequences of Transforming the State's Relationship to Marriage* 1445 U. Ill. L. Rev (2016).

94 *See* Dennis Romboy, *County Clerks in Utah Poring over New Law on Access to Marriage Ceremonies*, Deseret News (Apr. 15, 2015), www.deseretnews.com/article/865626791/County-clerks-in-Utah-poring-over-new-law-on-access-to-marriage-ceremonies.html?pg=all.

95 Utah Code Ann. § 17-20-4(1) & (2) (2016).

96 *Id.*

97 *Id.* § 63G-20-102 (1). A clerk in the county in which I reside has opted not to perform marriages. As a result, when a couple comes to the office and requests a marriage license, they are given a list of those in the county who have agreed to marry everyone. The clerk has indicated to me most couples are relieved to have the list and contact information. Everyone is treated identically. Contrast this experience with reactions in other states to the mandate. In Tennessee, every clerk in one office resigned rather than perform marriages contrary to their beliefs. Tyler Whetstone, *Decatur County Clerk, Employees Resign Over Same-Sex Ruling*, Jackson Sun (July 1, 2015), www.jacksonsun.com/story/news/politics/2015/07/01/decatur-county-clerk-employees-resign-over-same-sex-ruling/29579785/. A clerk in Arkansas resigned overnight after twenty-four years of service. *Arkansas County Clerk to Resign Over Same-Sex Marriage*, CBS News (June 29, 2015), www.cbsnews.com/news/arkansas-county-clerk-to-resign-over-same-sex-marriage/. In Texas, a clerk who was given the mandate to perform a marriage that she did not believe in also made the extreme choice to leave her job. *County Clerk in East Texas Resigns Over Gay Marriage Ruling*, Wash. Times (July 10, 2015), www.washingtontimes.com/news/2015/jul/10/county-clerk-in-east-texas-resigns-over-gay-marria/. At time of writing, instances where individuals are being forced to give up lifetime

workers would not be forced to violate their consciences *and* LGBT people would be treated like everyone else, receiving seamless access to marriage. We instituted a win-win where both sides were treated with respect.

Give Everyone as Much Liberty as Possible Without Infringing Other Values

A hallmark of the Utah Compromise was its emphasis on individual liberties. At a time of great division and fear about the place of traditional values in our culture, we were especially concerned to permit Utahns to continue to speak about their religious and moral commitments. As before, our guiding principle of fairness for all meant that protections for speech needed to extend to all, whether the speaker held a traditional view or a more progressive one.

SB 296 protected employees from discrimination based on their expression within the workplace about matters of marriage, family, and sexuality. Specifically, employees may express their "religious or moral beliefs and commitments in the workplace in a reasonable, non-disruptive, and non-harassing way on equal terms with similar types of expression of beliefs or commitments allowed by the employer in the workplace,"[98] so long as the employees' expression is not "in direct conflict with the essential business-related interests of the employer."[99] Recognizing that business-oriented goals are paramount in such an environment, we merely leveled the playing field when employers allow any speech on non-work matters.

This protection extended outside the workplace, too. Employers may not discharge, demote, terminate, or refuse to hire any person or retaliate against, harass, or discriminate in matters of compensation or in terms, privileges, and conditions of employment against any person otherwise qualified, for lawful expression *outside the workplace* regarding the person's religious, political, or personal convictions, including convictions about marriage, family, or sexuality.[100] So, whether employees attend a pro-life rally or a gay-pride parade on the weekend, they cannot be fired or reprimanded at work on Monday morning for such actions.[101]

careers or violate deeply held religious convictions are still commonplace. Utah's legislative solution allowed it to avoid such tragedies.

98 UTAH CODE ANN. § 34A-5-112.

99 *Id.* 100 *Id.* (emphasis added).

101 Numerous examples exist of intolerance toward speech about religious or traditional values in the workplace and public arena. A Newport Beach City Councilman faced a possible formal reprimand for an email criticizing same-sex marriage. Hanna Fry, *No Censure for Newport Beach Councilman over Anti-Gay Marriage Remarks*, L.A. TIMES (Aug. 15, 2015), www

Disagreement on these matters will not disappear overnight, if ever. In our democratic society, deliberation free of government interference is of the utmost importance; people must remain free to believe and speak on those topics, whatever view they hold, without fear of government retaliation or censure.

Involve Everyone and Listen Earnestly

The Utah process was so effective because it did what legislators should be doing: getting stakeholders across the spectrum to find constructive solutions. Here, we assembled and consulted business groups, LGBT advocacy groups, and religious groups, asking them for advice on how best to craft nondiscrimination laws with appropriate religious allowances.

We sat down with members of Utah's LGBT community; we sat down with social conservatives; we sat down with business interests. Many were familiar to us as seasoned advocates at the statehouse; others were people we had never met, especially some in the LGBT community. We listened to stories they shared of feeling like outcasts and second-class citizens. Putting a human face to legislative needs changed the tenor of the discussion. And for those who expressed concerns about religious liberty, as I did, we felt listened to and respected, too. That effort is not only best done legislatively; it can only be done legislatively.

End Divisiveness with an Enduring Compact

Finally, the measures in SB 296 reflected "the Legislature's balancing of competing interests."[102] We preempted local law to the extent it was inconsistent with the balancing we reached at the state level.[103] We tied the fate of

.latimes.com/local/lanow/la-me-ln-no-censure-for-councilman-over-anti-gay-marriage-remarks-20150812-story.html. Ford Motor Company fired an engineer via voicemail for disagreeing with the company's support of GLOBE, a separate organization that promotes LGBT inclusivity in the workplace. His expression of his religious convictions, he was told, was "discrimination in and of itself and that's not something that we can protect." Kate Abbey-Lambertz, *Ford Worker Fired for Anti-Gay Comment Sues For Religious Discrimination*, Huffington Post (July 14, 2015), www.huffingtonpost.com/entry/thomas-banks-ford-lawsuit_55a42530e4b0a47ac15d2669. Craig James, a former running back for the New England Patriots, was an ESPN pundit who quit in 2012 to run as a candidate for a U.S. Senate seat in Texas. After an unsuccessful bid, he was later hired by Fox Sports Southwest only to be fired days later for comments he had made opposing same-sex marriage while on the campaign trail. *Sportscaster Sues Fox Sports, Saying He Was Fired for Religious Views Against Gay Marriage*, Religion News Service (Aug. 4, 2015), www.religionnews.com/2015/08/04/sports caster-sues-fox-sports-saying-he-was-fired-for-religious-views-against-gay-marriage/.

[102] Utah Code Ann. § 34A-5-102.7.

[103] Utah Code Ann. § 57-21-2.5.

protections for both sides to each other through a non-severability clause. Thus, if any part of the bill were found to be invalid by a court, the remainder of the bill would be "rendered without effect and void."[104]

Although rarely deployed, this measure keeps both sides honest – no one is incentivized to agree to protections for the other side only to later undo concessions through litigation. Though unusual in Utah's code, the addition of a non-severability provision assured stakeholders that the bargain arrived at would not be revisited, permitting groups to move on.

V A TRANSFORMATION IN VIEW

As humans, our natural impulse is to assume that one person's rights come at another's expense. We can be selfish; we sometimes reflexively desire to restrict the ability for anyone to exist who does not agree with us. When I stood lock-armed in the House with colleagues to constitutionally limit marriage to one man and one woman, I thought I was protecting my faith. With *Goodridge* just handed down, challenging our views of marriage as a heterosexual institution, I thought it was best to restrict other people's ability to have rights in order to protect my own.

After going through this process, a light went on. I thought to myself, "I am a Christian and I believe in the New Testament and loving your neighbor and trying to be compassionate and tolerant and follow Christian principles." I realized that by looking out for and trying to do good by those who may not agree with me, trying to be respectful of other people and trying to love my neighbor, I am living my religion. These good, Christian religious principles are ones that we ought to not just talk about; we ought to actually live by and act on. Utah's landmark law does just that. I believe by following these principles I am not only protecting my beliefs, I am now living my religious beliefs. As I have become more compassionate and tolerant, I am getting respect back from others. Far better, I have learned, is to do the hard work Utah did: to ask how we can secure rights for everyone.[105]

This transformation in views can be hard to make. The label "Utah Compromise" does not help. Like most Utahns, I have deep-seated religious beliefs. And like many of my colleagues in the Utah Legislature, I am a very

104 *Id.* § 57-21-2.7.

105 *How Utah's Compromise Could Serve As A Model For Other States*, NPR (June 1, 2016) www.npr.org/2016/06/01/480247305/how-the-utah-compromise-could-serve-as-a-model-law-for-other-states.

conservative legislator. Some in my state rankle at the term "Utah Compromise," which the media attached to the law. Like them, my religious principles are not in any way, shape, or form compromisable. But nothing in this landmark legislation forces anyone to change any doctrine or beliefs. Quite the contrary, we protected religious organizations to maintain their doctrines and beliefs.

VI CONCLUSION

If there is one lesson from Utah's experience around marriage and LGBT rights, it is this: it is important to find a statutory solution before judicial rulings are made. In a pluralistic society, with differing views about the great questions facing us, there is a better way than litigating. Legislating rather than litigating gives us the ability to find common ground.

When *Kitchen* and *Obergefell* declared marriage to be a fundamental right for same-sex couples, they left unresolved important questions about discrimination and the scope of Utah's and the nation's civil rights laws. They left unresolved core questions about religion's role in civil society. Striving for "fairness for all" offered us a way to protect the LGBT community while cementing protections for the religious community.

In the end, none of the stakeholders got everything they wanted from the Utah legislation, but everyone gained specific and very significant statutory protections that a court could not deliver. And Utah experienced none of the rancor and public ire felt by Indiana, Arkansas, or Arizona.[106] The result is a less costly, more enforceable, and *more decent* legal regime in which we can coexist, true to who we are and respecting others for who they are – a clear win-win.

[106] David Blankenhorn, *A Way Forward for LGBT and Religious Liberty Rights*, TIME (Aug. 10, 2015), http://time.com/3989228/gay-marriage-lgbt-religious-liberty-rights/; Editorial, *Religious Freedom Is Guaranteed by the Constitution. There's No Reason to Sacrifice the Liberties of Others*, AZ CENTRAL (Mar. 31, 2015), www.azcentral.com/story/opinion/editorial/2015/03/31/indiana-take-lesson-tolerance-utah/70748856/.

22

Family Law and Civil Rights Movements

Examining the Influence of Courts and Legislatures on Racial and Sexual Orientation Equality

Anthony Michael Kreis

Visiting Assistant Professor of Law, Chicago-Kent College of Law

Past may be prologue when it comes to matters of the family. This chapter explores the iterative conversations taking place between courts and legislatures on questions of who can form a family. Although our common wisdom about the gains made on tearing down bans on interracial marriage and gay marriage emanated from the courts, this chapter shows that changes in access to marriage based on race and sexual orientation came from an evolving dialogue between courts and state legislators. As Americans continue to debate other contentious issues including the constitutionality of the death penalty, anti-transgender policies, polygamy, and reproductive freedom, it is important to examine how legal rights arise from social movements and through political institutions.

In 1952, William Rehnquist authored a memo on the constitutionality of segregated schools while a United States Supreme Court clerk to Justice Robert H. Jackson. Entitled *A Random Thought on the Segregation Cases*, the memo evaluated the Supreme Court's historical efficacy in shaping social attitudes and influencing political dynamics. Rehnquist concluded that "[o]ne hundred and fifty years of attempts on the part of this Court to protect minority rights of any kind – whether those of business, slaveholders, or Jehovah's Witnesses – have been sloughed off, and crept silently to rest."[1]

Rehnquist's dim view diverges from the romantic, and common, narratives of the judiciary rising above the political brawl to vindicate minority rights.[2] Despite running against the cultural grain, the memo's institutional analysis

[1] *Memorandum Signed "WHR," A Random Thought on the Segregation Cases* (1952), reprinted in *Nomination of Justice William Hubbs Rehnquist to be Chief Justice of the United States: Hearings Before the S. Comm. on the Judiciary*, 99th Cong., 2d Sess. (1986), www.gpo.gov/fdsys/pkg/GPO-CHRG-REHNQUIST/pdf/GPO-CHRG-REHNQUIST-4-16-6.pdf.

[2] *See, e.g.*, Douglas Laycock, *Constitutional Theory Matters*, 65 TEX. L. REV. 767, 770 (1987) ("[T]heories [of judicial review generally] recognize that democracy generally protects the

squares with substantial research findings that courts cannot effectively produce social change.[3]

The tension between the normative and empirical understandings of courts and social change was at the fore in the U.S. Court of Appeals for the Sixth Circuit's decision upholding the state constitutional bans on same-sex marriage of four states. Waxing philosophical on the limits of judicial review, the Sixth Circuit concluded the entitlement of same-sex couples to marry was ill suited for judicial resolution.[4] Judge Jeffrey Sutton's majority opinion echoed Rehnquist's 1952 memo: "For all of the power that comes with the authority to interpret the United States Constitution, the federal courts have no long-lasting capacity to change what people think and believe about new social questions."[5]

Dissenting on the three-judge panel, Judge Martha Daughtrey praised counter-majoritarian courts and made much to do about the extensive judicial role in advancing same-sex marriage:

> [A]s it turns out, legalization of same-sex marriage in the "nineteen states and the District of Columbia" mentioned by the majority was not uniformly the result of popular vote or legislative enactment. Nine states now permit same-sex marriage because of *judicial* decisions ... In addition, another 16 states have been or soon will be added to the list, by virtue of the Supreme Court's denial of *certiorari* [in federal appellate decisions overturning state same-sex marriage bans]. Moreover, the 35 states that are now positioned to recognize

majority from government abuse but does much less to protect minorities and individuals from government abuse. Our Constitution addresses this problem by creating judicially enforceable constitutional rights, most of which are stated in broad terms."); Martin H. Redish, *Advocacy of Unlawful Conduct and the First Amendment: In Defense of Clear and Present Danger*, 70 CAL. L. REV. 1159, 1186 (1982) ("Ultimately, if there is to be any protection against the courts becoming imbued with a 'mob' psychology in time of crisis, it is the nation's long tradition of judicial independence and widespread recognition of the role of the courts as protectors of minority rights against majoritarian oppression.").

3 *See* Robert Kagan, *A Consequential Court: The U.S. Supreme Court in the Twentieth Century in* CONSEQUENTIAL COURTS: JUDICIAL ROLES IN GLOBAL PERSPECTIVE (Diana Kapiszewski, Gordon Silverstein & Robert A. Kagan, eds.) 199 (2013) ("To many political scientists ... the Court's actual influence is an unsettled empirical and theoretical question."); Gerald N. Rosenberg, *Courting Disaster: Looking for Change in all the Wrong Places*, 54 DRAKE L. REV. 879 (2005) ("To rely on litigation rather than political mobilization, as difficult as it may be, misunderstands both the limits of courts and the lessons of history. It substitutes symbols for substance and clouds our vision with a naive and romantic belief in the triumph of rights over politics.").

4 DeBoer v. Snyder, 772 F.3d 388, 395 (6th Cir. 2014) (upholding bans in Michigan, Kentucky, Tennessee, and Ohio and observing: "This is a case about change – and how best to handle it under the United States Constitution. From the vantage point of 2014, it would now seem, the question is not whether American law will allow gay couples to marry; it is when and how that will happen.").

5 *Id.* at 417.

same-sex marriage are comparable to the 34 states that permitted interracial marriage when the Supreme Court decided *Loving*. If the majority in this case is waiting for a tipping point, it seems to have arrived.[6]

Judge Sutton's and Judge Daughtrey's colloquy on family law history, tipping points, judicial restraint, and capacity to change minds suffers from a glaring analytical weakness. Neither opinion develops a comparative analysis of family law's evolution on the question of same-sex marriage and its evolution on interracial marriage.[7] Indeed, both Sixth Circuit opinions leave two questions unanswered: how did family law develop in the crucial twenty years prior to *Loving v. Virginia*, and how does the historical record square with our understandings of courts' role in the evolution of family life?

Examining past developments around marriage and family can help with the questions looming on the horizon: whether to recognize polygamous families; whether and what remedies non-marital families should have available to them; and who should speak for family members on important questions such as medical care or end-of-life decisions.

Section I describes the law of interracial marriage in the U.S. before *Loving v. Virginia* to set context for assessing the role of courts versus legislatures in effecting social change and more expansive understandings of family. Section II describes the groundbreaking litigation to constitutionalize interracial marriage rights, beginning with a pivotal decision from the California Supreme Court, *Perez v. Sharp*, which struck California's interracial marriage ban. Section III describes the impact of decisions by state courts on efforts to mobilize legislators to enact legislation affirming the right of interracial couples to marry. Section IV documents the successful legislative efforts to remove most interracial marriage bans in the states before *Loving*. Section V then takes up the same-sex marriage debate and offers thoughts on its relevance to questions in family law that remain contested, such as reproductive rights and polygamy.

I ANTI-MISCEGENATION AND AMERICAN LAW

Law and custom in the Americas dating to the Colonial period prohibited interracial marriage. In the early 17th-century, Virginia enforced unwritten

6 *Id.* at 40 (Daughtrey, J., dissenting).

7 Judicial involvement in matters of the family is no historical anomaly. *See* Mark E. Brandon, States of Union: Family and Change in the American Constitutional Order (2013) (exploring the history of courts shaping family law through constitutional jurisprudence).

miscegenation prohibitions punishable by public whippings and religious penance.[8] By 1691, Virginia codified the proscription.[9] Virginia's early interracial marriage ban was soon followed by bans in Maryland, Delaware, Massachusetts, and North Carolina prior to 1725 – jumpstarting a trend that continued throughout the antebellum era.[10]

Outlawing interracial marriage remained commonplace in the early 20th century.[11] Of the forty-eight contiguous states, only Minnesota, Wisconsin, New York, New Jersey, Vermont, and Connecticut never enacted an anti-miscegenation law.[12] Between 1780 and 1887, eleven states repealed interracial marriage prohibitions.[13] No interracial marriage laws were repealed between 1888 and the California Supreme Court's 1948 decision in *Perez v. Sharp*, which held that California's anti-miscegenation law contravened the Fourteenth Amendment's equal protection guarantee.[14]

Until *Perez*, no U.S. court ever held that anti-miscegenation statutes violated equal protection principles.[15] At that point in time, nineteen years before the U.S. Supreme Court decided *Loving v. Virginia*, twenty-nine states prohibited interracial marriages, six in the state's constitution.[16] However, in the fifteen years immediately preceding *Loving*, fourteen states would repeal their statutory bans.[17]

During this period of liberalization, the U.S. Supreme Court had opportunities to strike down anti-miscegenation laws. After *Brown v. Board of Education*, the justices were wary of tackling anti-miscegenation laws and dodged the issue. Justice Felix Frankfurter, for example, feared a firestorm would erupt if the Court struck a blow to miscegenation prohibitions and

[8] Walter Wadlington, *The Loving Case: Virginia's Anti-Miscegenation Statute in Historical Perspective*, 52 VA. L. REV. 1189, 1191 (1966).

[9] *Id.* at 1191–92. [10] Perez v. Sharp, 198 P.2d 17, 38–39 (1948).

[11] Loving v. Virginia, 388 U.S. 1, 6 n. 5 (1967).

[12] PETER WALLENSTEIN, TELL THE COURT I LOVE MY WIFE: RACE, MARRIAGE, AND THE LAW – AN AMERICAN HISTORY 253 (2004).

[13] *Id.* at 136. [14] *Id.*

[15] Perez, *supra* note 10, at 41 (Shenk, J., dissenting) ("[Interracial marriage bans] have never been declared unconstitutional by any court in the land although frequently they have been under attack."); *see also* Alfred Avins, *Anti-Miscegenation Laws and the Fourteenth Amendment: The Original Intent*, 52 VA. L. REV. 1224, 1224 (1966) ("[Interracial marriage prohibitions] have been upheld as constitutional by every appellate court which has considered the point, with the single exception of the Supreme Court of California, which split four-to-three on the question.").

[16] *See* ALA. CONST. art. 4, § 102 (repealed 2000); FLA. CONST. of 1885 art. 16, § 24; MISS. CONST. art. 14, § 263 (repealed 1987); N.C. CONST. of 1868, art. XIV, § 8 (repealed 1971); S.C. CONST. art. 3, § 33 (repealed 1999); TENN. CONST. art. 11, § 14 (repealed 1978).

[17] American Civil Liberties Union, *The Lead Up to Loving* www.aclu.org/other/map-leadup-loving.

worked to steer the Court away from the marriage issue altogether.[18] A challenge to Virginia's miscegenation statute reached the Court in the 1955 case *Naim v. Naim*.[19] The Court, however, evaded the merits through a series of procedural maneuvers. With the nation reeling over *Brown* and the implementation of school integration, Justice Tom Clark urged restraint, saying "[o]ne bombshell at a time is enough."[20]

Judicial overreach was on others' minds, too. The National Association for the Advancement of Colored People ("NAACP") expressed little appetite to dismantle interracial cohabitation and marriage restrictions immediately after *Brown*, at least publicly. In a *U.S. News and World Report* interview, the NAACP's Executive Secretary Walter White said the organization had no plans to test marriage laws.[21] While the NAACP publicly approached anti-miscegenation litigation with caution, others, including the Japanese American Citizens League and certain Native American tribes, were actively dismantling anti-miscegenation laws in the West.[22]

In 1964, the Supreme Court had another opportunity to definitively end marriage discrimination but opted for a scalpel over an axe in *McLaughlin v. Florida*. There, the Court held Florida's criminalization of interracial cohabitation failed under the Equal Protection Clause of the Fourteenth Amendment[23] but declined to address the intertwined restriction of interracial marriage.

While the liberalization of racially restrictive state marriage laws pre-*Loving* is noteworthy, the shift cannot be attributed to a swell in public opinion favoring interracial marriages. In 1958, less than ten years before *Loving*, only 4% of Americans approved of interracial marriages.[24] A year after

[18] *See* Morton J. Horwitz, The Warren Court and the Pursuit of Justice 50 (1998) ("Justice Frankfurter devoted considerable energy to throwing procedural roadblocks in the way of deciding whether *Brown* extended to overturning anti-miscegenation laws."); Bruce Ackerman, 3 We the People: The Civil Rights Revolution 289 (2014) (acknowledging Justice Frankfurter's resistance to deciding anti-miscegenation cases for fear of undermining *Brown*'s implementation).

[19] Naim v. Naim, 197 Va. 80 (1955), *vacated*, 350 U.S. 891 (1955) and *adhered to*, 197 Va. 734 (1956). *See also* Richard Delgado, Naim v. Naim, 12 Nev. L.J. 525 (2012) (providing an in-depth case history).

[20] Walter F. Murphy, Elements of Judicial Strategy 193 (1964).

[21] *The Supreme Court Ruling*, Lincoln Evening Journal, May 25, 1954, at 6.

[22] *See* Peggy Pascoe, What Comes Naturally: Miscegenation Law and the Making of Race in America 224 (2009).

[23] McLaughlin v. Florida, 379 U.S. 184 (1964).

[24] Joseph Carroll, *Most Americans Approve of Interracial Marriages*, Gallup (Aug. 16, 2007), www.gallup.com/poll/28417/most-americans-approve-interracial-marriages.aspx. In the 1965 poll, 48% of Americans supported criminalization of interracial relationships, while 46% disapproved. *Id.*

Loving in 1968, Americans' approval of interracial marriages rose significantly to 20% but still represented only one in five Americans surveyed.[25]

II CONSTITUTIONALIZING INTERRACIAL FAMILIES

In 1948, Section 69 of the California Civil Code prohibited white persons from marrying a "Negro, Mulatto, Mongolian or member of the Malay race."[26] California's anti-miscegenation law first appeared in the Civil Code in 1872.[27] However, its first iteration only prohibited marriages between white persons and persons of African ancestry.[28] California later expanded the law's scope twice, in 1901 and 1933, to cover persons of Asian and Pacific Islander dissent, respectively.[29]

Nearly fifteen years after the last amendment, in 1948, a Los Angeles County clerk denied Andrea Perez and Sylvester Davis a marriage license. Perez, who was white, and Davis, who was black, filed a constitutional challenge to Section Code 69.[30] As Roman Catholics, they claimed the racially restrictive marriage laws impermissibly abridged their religious freedom because the Catholic Church would marry them but for the state marriage ban.[31] A divided 4–3 court struck down the statute. However, the California Supreme Court did not embrace the religious liberty claim.[32]

In the court's plurality opinion, Justice Roger Traynor reiterated that the "regulation of marriage is considered a proper function of the state" and, foreshadowing *Employment Division v. Smith* decades later,[33] observed that marriage regulations are valid even if "such a law might inhibit the free exercise of certain religious practices."[34] Squarely focused on whether California law comported with the Fourteenth Amendment of the U.S. Constitution, Justice Traynor explained:

> A state law prohibiting members of one race from marrying members of another race is not designed to meet a clear and present peril arising out of an emergency. In the absence of an emergency the state clearly cannot base a law impairing fundamental rights of individuals on general assumptions as

[25] *Id.* [26] *See* Perez, *supra* note 10, at 712. [27] *Id.* [28] *Id.* [29] *Id* at 713. [30] *Id.*

[31] *Id.*

[32] Chief Justice Phil Gibson and Justice Jesse Carter joined Justice Roger Traynor's plurality opinion to void the statute on equal protection grounds. Justice Douglas Edmonds concurred in the judgment but reasoned that the anti-miscegenation law was an unconstitutional impingement on religious free exercise.

[33] *See* Helfand, Chapter 2, this volume, and Sepper, Chapter 1, this volume, for a discussion of Employment Division v. Smith and the latitude given to states to regulate for general welfare even when a neutral law burdens religious practice.

[34] *Id.*

> to traits of racial groups. It has been said that ... Section 60 does not discriminate against any racial group, since it applies alike to all persons whether Caucasian, Negro, or members of any other race. The decisive question, however, is not whether different races, each considered as a group, are equally treated. The right to marry is the right of individuals, not of racial groups. The equal protection clause of the United States Constitution does not refer to rights of the Negro race, the Caucasian race, or any other race, but to the rights of individuals.[35]

The three dissenting justices also dismissed the couple's religious liberty claim. Writing for the dissenters, Justice John Shenk parsed marriage into its civil and religious components – which some are doing today after *Obergefell v. Hodges* to remedy perceived conflicts with religious values, as Wilson (Chapter 16, this volume) shows. Though marriage holds religious meanings, Justice Shenk reasoned that ultimately it is a civil institution and that "the community at large has an interest in the maintenance of its integrity and purity."[36] Thus, if marriage law "bears a substantial relationship to the health, safety, morals or some other phase of the general welfare of the people of this state, it would not be invalid because incidentally in conflict with the conduct and practice of a particular religious group."[37]

Only Justice Douglas Edmonds, who provided the fourth concurring vote to strike down California's interracial marriage ban, anchored his decision to religious liberty. He maintained that since the state failed to demonstrate how interracial marriages posed a clear and present peril to society, it could not withstand a free exercise challenge.[38] The legality of interracial marriages in other large states including Illinois, New York, and Pennsylvania, Edmonds said, undermined any plausible argument that multiracial families threatened social welfare.[39] Even though six members of the seven-member court rejected the couple's religious liberty claim out-of-hand, the free exercise claim was dispositive of the outcome in *Perez*.

Widely reported in newspapers nationally and in California,[40] the decision was not necessarily the last word. The statute's defenders could file a petition for a rehearing with the California Supreme Court or an appeal with the U.S. Supreme Court. Los Angeles officials petitioned for a rehearing; the California Supreme Court rejected it without comment.[41] Los Angeles

[35] *Id.* at 20 (internal citations omitted). [36] *Id.* at 37 (Shenk, J., dissenting). [37] *Id.*

[38] *Id.* 35 (Edmonds, J., concurring). [39] *Id.*

[40] *See, e.g.*, Lawrence E. Davies, *Mixed Marriages Upheld By Court*, N.Y. TIMES, Oct. 2, 1948, at 13.

[41] *State High Court Stands By Mixed Marriage Ruling*, MODESTO BEE & NEWS HERALD, Oct. 29, 1948, at 9.

officials proceeded to instruct the marriage clerk to disregard the now-invalidated racial restrictions and issue marriage licenses to couples who otherwise qualified to marry.[42] Other counties followed in short order.[43] Ironically, the California legislature did not formally repeal the statute for more than a decade, despite halting attempts to do so.[44]

Perez reverberated in Oregon. In 1950, Governor Douglas McKay convened a conference on the status of Oregon's Native American population. Members of the Klamath Tribe[45] formally requested the Governor to endorse the repeal of Oregon's anti-miscegenation law. In a memo analyzing the ban's legality, Oregon's Attorney General George Neuner wrote:

> I have perused the statutes of neighboring states and have found no such discriminatory restriction against Indians of more than half blood, but did find a similar statute with the reference to other races. The Supreme Court of the State of California in 1948 declared this statute invalid in that the law is discriminatory and irrational and unconstitutionally restricts not only religious liberty but the liberty to marry as well.[46]

Given *Perez* and the Oregon Supreme Court's leanings, the Attorney General predicted "it is not beyond the realm of possibility that if the Oregon sections were brought before a similar constitutional test they would meet with the same fate."[47]

As the Oregon Senate considered a repeal, the *Oregon Statesman* commented on its editorial page that "the [S]upreme [C]ourt of California on Oct. 1, 1948, handed down a decision declaring the miscegenation provisions of the California civil code unconstitutional."[48] The *Oregon Statesman* reprinted an Associated Press summary of the *Perez* decision and advised:

> This was a California case, to be sure, but it sets a precedent which courts of other states may well follow. It is safe to venture that the Oregon court would, after its decision in an alien land case, opinion by Justice Rossman, invalidating restrictive statutes on holding of lands by certain classes of aliens …

42 *End of Racial Bill Stands*, N.Y. TIMES, Nov. 2, 1948, at 32.

43 *White, Filipino Get Marriage License*, BAKERSFIELD CALIFORNIAN (San Francisco, Cal.), Nov. 11, 1948, at 1; *Japanese Girl Weds Army Captain*, SANTA CRUZ SENTINAL NEWS (Oakland, Cal.), Dec. 19, 1948, at 1.

44 Julian Beck, *Sacramento News Letter*, VAN NUYS NEWS, May 24, 1951, at 5-D; *State Senate Refuses to Repeal Invalid Interracial Marriage Law*, SAN BERNARDINO CTY. SUN, May 15, 1951, at 1.

45 *Interracial Marriage Ban Gains Favor*, OR. STATESMAN (Salem), Mar. 13, 1951, at 3.

46 Anthony Kreis, *Marriage Demosprudence*, 2016 ILL. L. REV. 1679, 1691.

47 *Id.*

48 *California Court Ruled Marriage Ban Invalid*, OR. STATESMAN (Salem), Feb. 16, 1951, at 4.

> In view of the court decision in California ... the legislature in this state might as well wipe off the statutes banning intermarriage of races.[49]

As the legislative process unfolded, legislators adopted the opinions of the Oregon Attorney General and the *Oregon Statesman*. Senator Phillip Hitchcock told the Senate Chamber that the anti-miscegenation statute was "a disgrace to the state of Oregon, which violates the constitution and the laws of God."[50] One co-sponsor of the bill, Senator Warren Gill, said that while he was agonistic on the merits of interracial marriages, it was nevertheless a "personal right."[51] The Senate passed the repeal bill 21 to 7.[52] The House approved the bill with only four dissenting votes.[53]

There is no evidence that the Klamath Tribe initiated its request for removing racial barriers in marrying the person of one's choice because of the *Perez* decision, yet Oregon's political process benefited from it. Repeal proponents significantly relied on *Perez*. Lawmakers' prediction that the Oregon courts would follow California's lead was a well-reasoned calculation given the Oregon Supreme Court's equal protection analysis in the Alien Land Act case noted in the previous quote. Thus, courts of last resort in both California and Oregon legitimized the repeal campaign, even if they did not induce action on the part of those who supported the repeal.

III LITIGATION AND LEGISLATIVE RESPONSES

Other states took a different path to the repeal of their interracial marriage bans, trying first to succeed legislatively before reverting to the courts. Nevada's statute regulating miscegenation originated with its territorial government in 1861 but was untouched until 1953.[54] Republican Assemblyman George Hawes introduced legislation in January of that year to repeal the ban.[55] Hawes was inspired by the hardship endured by a friend of Japanese descent whose daughter could not legally marry an ethnically Greek man under Nevada law.[56]

Hawes's efforts were initially successful in the Democratic-controlled Assembly, where his bill passed 39–9.[57] However, his bill was met with

49 *Id.* 50 *Id.* 51 *Id.*

52 John H. White, *Boost in Dependent Exemptions Passes*, OR. STATESMAN (Salem), Apr. 13, 1951, at 1.

53 *Id.*

54 Phillip I. Earl, *Nevada's Miscegenation Laws and the Marriage of Mr. And Mrs. Harry Bridges*, 37, NEV. HIST. SOC. Q. 1, 7 (1994).

55 *Id.* 56 *Id.* 57 *Bill Would O.K. Mixed Marriages*, NEVADA STATE J., Mar. 18, 1953, at 2.

hostility in the Republican-held Senate and in his home district.[58] The Senate contemplated maintaining the ban on black-white marriages while scrapping the remaining restrictions, but the bill died in the Senate.[59] A 1955 bill met a similar fate.[60]

In 1956, Democratic Assemblyman Oscar Jepson introduced repeal legislation.[61] His effort was a remarkable failure – the Assembly's Judiciary Committee did not recommend passage of the repeal bill, but it was permitted to proceed to a floor vote where the Assembly killed it 33–10.[62]

A fourth push, in 1957, also failed in the Assembly, despite having four lead sponsors.[63] One of those sponsors, Gene Evans, reportedly took interest in a repeal measure after hearing about an Elko County clerk denying an interracial couple a marriage license.[64] This prompted a conversation between Assemblyman Evans, Elko County District Attorney Grant Sawyer, and local judge Taylor Wines, who encouraged Evans to introduce legislation.[65] The resulting bill died in committee, never receiving a floor vote.[66]

On December 9, 1959, Harry Bridges and Noriko Sawada applied for a marriage license in Reno, Nevada. Clerk Viola Given refused to give them a license, saying "It's against the law."[67] Given explained that though Sawada was a natural born citizen, her Japanese ancestry rendered her ineligible to marry Bridges, who was white. "It is not a matter of where you were born. It's the blood. It's against the law here," she explained to the couple.[68] Bridges and Sawada appealed to the head clerk for the county in which Reno is situated, Washoe, who again rejected their application for a marriage license for want of appropriate racial qualifications.[69]

The couple and their attorney, Samuel Francovich, filed a lawsuit challenging the constitutionality of Nevada's interracial marriage ban.[70] Judge Wines scheduled a hearing for the following afternoon.[71] According to media accounts, the courtroom was "packed" with "newsmen, photographers, lawyers and spectators."[72]

At the hearing, Francovich urged Judge Wines to follow the California Supreme Court's lead.[73] The district attorney pushed back – marriage was social policy and should not be constitutionalized: "The right to regulate marriage ceremonies has been a power of the individual states since the

58 *See* Earl, *supra* note 54, at 7.
59 *Inter-Race Weddings Win House Approval*, NEVADA STATE J., Mar. 18, 1958, at 6. 60 *Id.*
61 *See* Earl, *supra* note 54, at 8. 62 *Id.* 63 *Id.* 64 *Id.* 65 *Id.* 66 *Id.*
67 *Nevada Won't Allow Bridges to Marry Nisei*, N.Y. TIMES, Dec. 10, 1958, at 28. 68 *Id.*
69 *Id.* 70 *Id.* 71 *Id.*
72 Robert Mount, *Law Overturned; Bridges Weds*, NEV. ST. J., Dec. 11, 1958, at 1.
73 *Id.* at 6.

beginning of time. The state must be able to set an age limit, regulate the legal disposition and who can legally perform the ceremony."[74]

Another attorney for the couple, Bruce Roberts, retorted by invoking the standoff fomented by Arkansas Governor Orval Faubus when he sought to block public school integration in Little Rock.[75] Roberts told the court, "[n]o laws within a state can be unreasonable or discriminatory. The right to marry is an individual right, not a group or racial right."[76]

Judge Wines issued no written opinion but said that *Perez* was correctly decided and that he could "see no evil which would justify the state interfering with the freedom of an individual to marry."[77] Wines issued an order compelling the county clerk to issue a license. Bridges and Sawada married later that day.[78] The county attorney pledged to appeal to the Nevada Supreme Court but the Nevada Legislature would intervene to end his plans.[79]

The local Reno paper's editorial board praised Judge Wines:

> Few persons, certainly, can doubt the law, long since declared unconstitutional in California, has any merit. Even if there is doubt in some minds that "all men are created equal" the law makes Nevada look ridiculous. This state prides itself on being a great western frontier of freedom. Gambling is legal, liquor is sold around the clock, and marriages (of the same race) can be performed in minutes.[80]

For the local editorial board, the nearly century-old law lacked legal merit. Query, however, whether the opposition was as thin as the paper portrayed. The paper's own later reporting suggested that the public reaction was not lopsidedly in favor of Wines's ruling.[81] Moreover, the "few persons" whom the paper purported to take the interracial marriage ban seriously were seemingly overrepresented in the state legislature given legislators' resistance to repeal legislation.

The Nevada Supreme Court never weighed in on the constitutionality of Nevada's law. Less than a month after Judge Wines's order, legislation was again introduced in the Nevada House to repeal the statute.[82] The media linked the need for legislation to the Bridges' litigation:

74 *Id.* 75 *Id.* 76 *Id.* 77 *Id.* 78 *Id.*

79 *Bars Still Up Against Mixed Race Marriage*, Reno Evening Gazette, Dec. 13, 1958, at 1.

80 *State on Miscegenation Gets Some Rude Treatment*, Nev. St. J., Dec. 11, 1958, at 14.

81 *Inter-Race Bill Offered*, Nev. St. J., Jan. 22, 1959, at 2 ("The marriage set up a clamor among Nevada residents, many opposed to the verdict handed down by Judge Taylor Wines, and many hailing the decision as a major advancement of civil rights."). *See also*, Earl, *supra* note 54, at 13–15.

82 *Id.*

> The bill was introduced in the Senate Jan. 21 by the judiciary committee and is considered an outgrowth of the successful battle waged last fall by union leader Harry Bridges to wed a pretty Nisei secretary in Reno. After a much-publicized, two-day wrangle with sympathetic authorities, the district court ordered a marriage license issued to the longshoreman leader and his American-born Japanese fiancé.[83]

In a staggering turnaround, the repeal bill passed the Nevada Senate 17 to 0 and the Assembly 32 to 5.[84] Only one member of the Assembly took to the floor to denounce the legislation. Nevada Governor Grant Sawyer signed the bill with little apparent fanfare.[85]

The historical evidence does not suggest that *Perez* mobilized actors in the political process to begin a campaign to repeal the exclusionary marriage laws. Personal connections and experiences motivated a handful of Nevada legislators to rid the state code of its ban on interracial marriage. The intervening order from Judge Wines in December 1958 was a significant event that undergirded the shift in dynamics between 1957 and 1959.

Like Nevada, Arizona first adopted its anti-miscegenation law prior to statehood, a law upheld by the Arizona Supreme Court in 1942.[86] More than ten years later, Henry Oyama and his fiancée Mary Ann Jordan re-litigated the ban's legality. Oyama, who was of Japanese descent, and Jordan, a Caucasian, asked the court to invalidate the statute as violating their constitutional rights to religious freedom, due process, and equal protection under the law.[87] The couple did not wait long for a decision; District Court Judge Herbert F. Krucker ruled in their favor within an hour of the hearing.[88]

County Attorney Henry Ackerman appealed the decision to the Arizona Supreme Court – with the hope the court would affirm Judge Krucker's ruling with statewide effect.[89] "This is one suit I hope to lose," he told the media.[90]

Finality would prove far off. The Chief Justice of the Arizona Supreme Court told reporters that it would likely be a year before the court would hear the appeal.[91] In the interim, talk of repealing the territorial-era marriage laws

[83] *Interracial Marriage Ban Dropped as Bill Is Signed*, Reno Evening Gazette, Mar. 18, 1959, at 18.

[84] Earl, *supra* note 54, at 15. [85] *See id.* [86] State v. Pass, 59 Ariz. 16 (1942).

[87] *Couple File Suit Against Race Law*, Tucson Daily Citizen, Dec. 11, 1959, at 1. [88] *Id.*

[89] *Couple Happily Wed As Racial Bars Fall*, The Ariz. Republic, Dec. 29, 1959, at 1 ("A superior court ruling has no effect upon the law. Only the supreme court has that authority. That's why we are anxious to get this before it for final determination of its constitutionality.").

[90] *Kruker Rules Couple May Wed, Law Unconstitutional*, Tucson Daily Citizen, Dec. 23, 1959, at 1.

[91] *Marriage Case Appeal Dismissed*, Tucson Daily Citizen, May 5, 1962, at 52.

sprung up. For example, a student group at the University of Arizona held a panel discussion on the topic. One panelist, political science professor Richard Burke, who favored legislative repeal, pointed out that the issue had never received serious attention in state legislative debate.[92] Another panelist, attorney Frank Barry, was skeptical of deferring to the legislative process: in his view, the law was unconstitutional – and courts had a duty to overturn it.[93]

A month after Judge Krucker's decision, Pima Senator David Wine filed a bill to codify the ruling. Senator Wine told the *Tucson Daily Citizen*, "The introduction of this bill is the direct result of the Oyama situation in Tucson. Judge Krucker ruled that the miscegenation statute is unconstitutional. Now, the statute should be erased."[94] Support came quickly from organized interests. The Arizona Civil Liberties Union endorsed Wine's legislation, stating that passage of the bill would mean "the people of this state realize that such a law is not only unconstitutional but un-American in spirit."[95]

Wines's legislation made no headway in 1960. The litigation pressed on though, through late 1960 and early 1961. Judge Krucker for a second time struck down the interracial marriage ban, this time as applied to Caesar Lee and Hazel Grimmwood.[96] On March 10, 1961, Superior Court Judge Lee Garrett joined Judge Krucker, striking down the interracial marriage ban for a third time, compelling the local marriage clerk to issue a marriage license to Harold Merchant and Mary Beth Lynn.[97]

On January 5, 1962, two Democrats and two Republicans introduced a repeal bill a little over a month before oral arguments were set to be heard at the Arizona Supreme Court.[98] The repeal legislation successfully passed the House by a margin of 71 to 6 and the Senate 20 to 6.[99]

In Arizona, courts did not have the last word. However, the litigation that immediately preceded legislative action mattered. Consider historian Peggy Pascoe's assessment:

92 *Interracial Marriage Law Repeal Asked*, ARIZ. REPUBLIC, Dec. 11, 1959, at 13 ("because of the committee system in our state legislature it has never come up for discussion on the floor as far as I know").

93 *Id.*

94 *Miscegenation Repeal Introduced By Wines*, TUCSON DAILY CITIZEN, Jan. 12. 1969, at 15.

95 *Marriage Bill Backed*, ARIZ. REPUBLIC, Jan. 17, 1960, at 4.

96 *Judge Clears Path For 2nd Inter-Racial Marriage*, TUCSON DAILY CITIZEN, Nov. 12, 1960, at 11.

97 *Racial Marriage Ban Again Fails Court Test*, TUCSON DAILY CITIZEN, Mar. 10, 1961, at 3.

98 *Inter-racial Ban Measure's Target*, ARIZ. DAILY SUN, Jan 15, 1962, at 1; Pascoe, *supra* note 22, at 240.

99 *Id.*

> Although the [Japanese American Citizens League] has discussed repealing Arizona's marriage as early as 1955, it was the ACLU's decision in 1958 to take the *Oyama* case to court, which generated a burst of publicity about the denial of a marriage license to a Japanese American man and a White woman, that provided the catalyst for Arizona's repeal. When the Arizona Supreme Court took its time issuing a decision in the case, the state branch of the ACLU grew impatient with the courtroom strategy and used the *Oyama* example as a rallying point to get the Arizona legislators to consider repealing the law.[100]

In Arizona, much like neighboring Nevada, state court judges provided much needed momentum to overcome the institutional inertia working against legislation to end race discrimination in marriage.

IV LEGISLATIVE CAMPAIGNS

Between 1953 and 1965, Montana, North Dakota, Colorado, South Dakota, Idaho, Utah, Nebraska, Indiana, and Wyoming also repealed racial marriage prerequisites – all without the threat of litigation. In the absence of judicial intervention, what motivated legislators in these states to reexamine the role of race in marriage law?

In Montana, war brides drove the debate. Scott Pfohl, a Montana repeal proponent, said that the repeal was necessary because "servicemen are intermarrying with other races all over the world."[101] Further, Pfohl told legislators, "The present law creates conflict in the future because children of mixed marriages are not considered legitimate in Montana."[102] Similarly, the lead sponsor on Montana's 1953 repeal, Representative Leo Graybill, reported to the Anti-Defamation League that the bill's success was owed to military spouses:

> The repealer went through with little opposition due, of course, to the fact that many of our soldiers have come back to Montana with Japanese wives. The Legislature recognized that it seemed silly that we would disinherit such a wife, who, in many instances, had been well received by the local community to which the soldier returned.[103]

100 Pascoe, *supra* note 22, at 240.

101 *House Names Probers for Prison, Industrial School and Hospital*, BILLINGS GAZETTE, Jan. 10, 1953, at 1.

102 *Id.*

103 Letter from Leo Graybill, Member of the Montana General Assembly to Sol Rabkib, Anti-Defamation League, Mar. 3, 1953.

Utah ended racially restrictive marriage laws, hedging off a coordinated effort to litigate. Utah's 1888 marriage law was never tested on the merits in court.[104] However, throughout the early 1960s, the ACLU actively looked for test plaintiffs. Salt Lake City area officials were eager to help. The county attorney's office urged the ACLU to file litigation against the state's marriage law.[105] When potential plaintiffs presented to the county clerk's office, the county clerk referred them to the ACLU.[106] On the legislative front, the county clerk predicted advocates could "easily repeal the provision outlawing marriages between white people … and oriental and malays … [but] could not change the law forbidding marriages between white people and negroes."[107]

The clerk's political calculus underestimated legislators' willingness to act. After the Utah Senate passed the measure in January 1963 by a margin of 17 to 7, the Utah House passed a repeal measure 52 to 6 on March 13, 1963.[108] As in other states, the arguments in favor and against were varied. Representative Ray Harding urged repeal because the existing statute improperly interfered with individual rights. Representative J. M. Smith, who represented Salt Lake City, feared the legislation would result in a loss of heritage.[109] Smith said, "It appears we really have no problem except to whether we should allow the marriage of blacks and whites … I would not want to sell my heritage or the heritage of my posterity."[110]

Other members said repeal was the only way to avoid litigation, resolve legal ambiguity, and address interstate recognition problems. The "chief justification" for the legislation, one member said, was to redress the denial of death benefits and inheritance to interracial families.[111] Another representative clarified that his support for repeal was not an endorsement of interracial relationships; it was necessitated by other states. "I think that any marriages between races should be discouraged, but in view of the fact that some of these things are legalized in other states and then they come here to live, I vote aye," he said.[112]

104 Plaintiffs in one case tried to contest the constitutionality of the miscegenation law in the Utah courts, but the resolution turned on the state's anti-bigamy law. *See* Thomas v. Children's Aid Soc. of Ogden, 12 Utah 2d 235, 239 (1961) ("Having determined … that the purported marriage was void, it follows the trial court's decision must be sustained and we need not, therefore, concern ourselves with our miscegenation statute … the constitutionality of which is questioned by plaintiffs.").

105 Pascoe, *supra* note 22, at 240–41. 106 *Id.*

107 *Id.* (giving account of a local ACLU attorney). 108 *Id.*

109 *Utah*, OGDEN STANDARD-EXAMINER, Mar. 14, 1963, at 2A.

110 Utah State Legislature, *House Floor Proceedings*, Mar. 13, 1963 (on file with author).

111 *Id.* 112 *Id.*

The representative who delivered the longest floor speech told the House that the law could not meet constitutional muster:

> The Supreme Court of the United States has struck down [in *McLaughlin v. Florida*] milder miscegenation statutes than this, and regardless of what your ultimate belief is, if you want to see the Supreme Court of the United States strike this one down, then vote against this bill . . . [W]e should pass this bill as it stands, it's a good bill, and not force this before the United States Supreme Court.[113]

Subsequently, Governor George Dewey Clyde signed the legislation into law ending Utah's eighty-four-year-old prohibition on interracial marriages.

Attempts to repeal Nebraska's marriage laws prior to 1963 failed, often in committee. Though a proposal to strike the law successfully navigated the legislature in 1895, Governor Silas Holcomb vetoed it.[114] The legislature's apparent lack of animus toward racial minorities was short lived. In 1913, the scope of Nebraska's law was expanded from prohibiting black-white intermarriage to also banning marriages between white people and persons of Japanese or Chinese ancestry.[115]

In the early 1960s, the law received renewed attention. Nebraska Governor Robert Crosby's Committee on Human Rights was tasked with studying the issue. In late 1962, some churches in Lincoln fought the statute. At a meeting of the Lincoln Council of Churches, members discussed the interracial marriage ban, predicting that the courts would strike it down, if challenged.[116]

When a repeal measure was introduced in 1963, a pro-repeal victory seemed likely. Repeal proponents focused on the susceptibility of Nebraska's law to judicial invalidation. As the *Lincoln Star* reported, "This year, widespread support of the bill to erase the prohibition is anticipated. Opponents of the marriage ban say it is discriminatory and probably unconstitutional."[117] The bill passed the Judiciary Committee by the narrowest of margins – 4 to 3.[118] The committee heard from nineteen proponents of the legislation. The *Lincoln Evening Journal* summed up their testimony:

> Arguments put forth by religious leaders took generally the same line. The speakers said there is no basis for the allegation that inter-racial marriage will result in a "biological deterioration" of the white race. They said the

[113] *Id.* [114] *Vetoed by Holcomb*, North Platte Semi-Weekly Trib., Apr. 12, 1895, at 3.

[115] Neb. Rev. Stat. § 44–103; 42–328; 42–117 (1949).

[116] *Dr. White: State Interracial Marriage Ban "Not Christian,"* Lincoln Star, Nov. 17, 1961, at 24.

[117] *Marriage Bill Hearing Monday*, Lincoln Star, Feb. 24, 1963, at 13.

[118] *Bill Will Lift Bar on Race*, Omaha World-Herald, Feb. 26, 1963, at 8m.

> present law is prejudicial, unconstitutional, contrary to the will of God, an infringement on civil rights and the "shame of all Christians."[119]

Supporters of the ban on interracial marriage offered religious justifications for maintaining the status quo. "God made man different colors and he intended for him to stay that way," said Omaha attorney Roy Harropp. Theodore Fitch of Council Bluffs offered similar testimony, telling the committee that whites who married non-whites risked divine vengeance.[120] One opponent testified that the legislation was part of a "Communist plot."[121] On March 27, 1963, the unicameral legislature approved the measure on final passage 29 to 12 and was signed into law soon thereafter.[122]

Wyoming was the second-to-last state outside the South to eliminate the state ban on interracial marriages. As historian Roger Hardaway described the repeal, the legislature acted, knowing the end of Wyoming's interracial marriage ban was a *fait accompli*:

> Many legislators realized that the time was not far off when the United States Supreme Court would rule that all miscegenation statutes were unconstitutional. Consequently, in the 1965 session of the Wyoming State Legislature, several members introduced a bill to repeal Wyoming's miscegenation law because they believed it to be unconstitutional. The repeal measure faced some opposition but passed the House of Representatives on January 19 by the vote of 51–8, and the Senate on January 25 by the vote of 21–3. Governor Clifford Hansen signed the bill on January 27, 1965, bringing the legal history of miscegenation in Wyoming to an abrupt end.[123]

Similar developments unfolded in another non-Southern state, Indiana. In 1964, the Indiana Civil Rights Commission, charged with reviewing state civil rights laws, recommended repeal of the state's anti-miscegenation law to the legislature. Chairman Harold Hatcher reported that a majority of the commission believed that the statute "should not be on the books" and predicted that if the legislation was not repealed it could be invalidated "by a court ruling that it was unconstitutional."[124]

In January 1965, Indianapolis Representative Russell Dean introduced legislation to put the interracial marriage ban to bed. In addition to

[119] *Marriage Bill Gets Response*, LINCOLN EVENING J. & NEB. ST. J., Feb. 26, 1963, at 8.

[120] *Id.* [121] *Id.*

[122] *Interracial Marriage Ban Repeal Bill OKd*, LINCOLN EVENING JOURNAL AND NEBRASKA STATE JOURNAL, Mar. 27, 1963, at 8.

[123] Roger D. Hardaway, *Prohibiting Interracial Marriage: Miscegenation Laws in Wyoming*, 52 ANNALS OF WYO. 55 (1980).

[124] *ICRC Seeks Miscegenation Law Repeal*, ANDERSON HERALD, Feb. 20, 1964, at 19.

emphasizing that Indiana and Wyoming were the last non-Southern states with such laws,[125] Dean pointed out that a definitive ruling on Indiana's law was not far off:

> Under the equal protection clause of the 14th-Amendment to the Federal Constitution, the Anti-Miscegenation laws are untenable. Indiana should remove this morally and legally indefensible blot from its record by repealing the Anti-Miscegenation law without further delay.[126]

At least one large pro-repeal organization made the case that the statute could not withstand judicial scrutiny. In a formal statement endorsing Representative Dean's bill, the Indiana Council of Churches cited Justice Potter Stewart's concurring opinion in *McLaughlin v. Florida* to support its position.[127] At the House Judiciary Committee, testimony in support of the measure was offered by the Vice Chairman of the Indiana Conference on Civil Rights, a representative of the Indiana Council of Churches, and a Butler University history professor. No one appeared at the committee hearing to speak in opposition.[128] The House Judiciary Committee unanimously recommended repeal of Indiana's interracial marriage ban.[129] The Indiana House voted 73 to 5 for repeal.[130]

Despite the election of a new progressive governor, the repeal measure surprised some because of the state's deep ties to racially regressive politics. The *New York Times* reported at the time: "Indiana . . . has been famous for its conservative isolationist politics . . .. In the early nineteen-twenties, the Ku Klux Klan ran the state for a while. Last May Gov. George Wallace, the avowed segregationist from Alabama, got almost 30% of the Presidential Primary Democratic vote."[131]

Wyoming and Indiana were among the last states to successfully end racial requirements for marital eligibility. Outlier Border States that had laws intact when *Loving* was decided did not go unchallenged, however. Legislation was

[125] *Rep. R.J. Dean Authors Bill to Abolish Law*, Indianapolis Recorder, Jan. 16, 1965, at 1.

[126] *Id.* at 6.

[127] *Council Urges Miscegenation Repeal Also*, Indianapolis Recorder, Jan. 16, 1965, at 1 ("A STATEMENT released by the council's department of Legislation and Civil Affairs quoted the words of Supreme Court Justice Potter Stewart: 'I cannot conceive of a valid legislation purpose under our Constitution for a state law which makes the color of a person's skin the test of whether his conduct is a criminal offense.'").

[128] *State's Mixed Marriage Ban Heads for Repeal*, Kokomo Morning Times, Jan. 21, 1965, at 3.

[129] *Panel Votes Race-Law Repeal*, N.Y. Times, Jan. 21, 1965, at 39

[130] Austin C. Wehrwein, *Branigan in Quest of New Indiana*, N.Y. Times, Feb. 7, 1965, at 52.

[131] *Id.*

introduced in Kentucky,[132] Missouri, Texas,[133] Virginia, and West Virginia to repeal race-based marriage laws. Some of these states saw significant movement behind the legislation, most visibly in Missouri and West Virginia.[134]

V SAME-SEX COUPLES AND THE EVOLVING FAMILY

Justice Louis Brandeis's description of states as "laboratories of democracy" continues to be an apt description of public policy development in our federal system.[135] Indeed, contemporary debates on a range of issues benefit from federalism as lawmakers look across the country for guidance on public policy – states looking at one another, and the federal government looks at the states for promising approaches. The yields of policy diffusion extend beyond discretionary programs. Indeed, echoing Eskridge's (Chapter 23, this volume) description of a dialectical process that fueled a deeper appreciation within the Mormon community on LGBT rights, interracial relationship recognition advanced through a combination of litigation, legislation, and grassroots efforts. That trinity explains not only interracial marriage recognition, but it is also the story of the same-sex marriage movement.[136]

As with interracial marriage, early same-sex marriage litigation failed to secure full marriage rights for same-sex couples. Promising lawsuits for same-sex couples in Hawaii and Alaska were thwarted by state constitutional amendments. As Eskridge (Chapter 23, this volume) shows, voters amended the Hawaii Constitution to permit a statutory same-sex marriage ban,[137] while Alaskans amended their state constitution to forbid same-sex nuptials outright.[138] The first judicial decision to require the state to recognize same-

[132] Kentucky State Representative Arthur Johnson introduced an equal marriage bill in February 1964. *See*, *Miscegenation Law Repeal Asked*, MIDDLESBORO DAILY NEWS, Feb. 20, 1964, at 2.

[133] Pascoe, *supra* note 22, at 290. [134] *See* Kreis, *supra* note 46, at 1708–09.

[135] New State Ice Co. v. Liebmann, 285 U.S. 262, 311 (1932) (Brandeis, J., dissenting) (Experimentation "is one of the happy incidents of the federal system that a single courageous state may, if its citizens choose, serve as a laboratory; and try novel social and economic experiments without risk to the rest of the country").

[136] For an extensive evaluation of early same-sex marriage legislation, *see* Anthony Michael Kreis, *Marriage Equality in State and Nation*, 22 WM. & MARY BILL RTS. J. 747 (2014).

[137] HAW. CONST. ART. 1, § 23 (West 2015) ("The legislature shall have the power to reserve marriage to opposite-sex couples.").

[138] ALASKA CONST. ART. I, § 25 ("To be valid or recognized in this State, a marriage may exist only between one man and one woman."). The amendment was invalidated in 2014. Hamby v. Parnell, 2014 WL 5089399, at *12 (D. Alaska, Oct. 12, 2014) ("This Court finds that Alaska's same-sex marriage laws violate the Due Process and Equal Protection Clauses of the Fourteenth Amendment.").

sex relationships occurred in Vermont in 1999 – but gave a less-than-satisfying victory to hopeful couples. The Vermont Supreme Court compelled the Vermont legislature to provide the tangible benefits of marriage to same-sex couples but did not mandate full marriage rights.[139]

The Massachusetts Supreme Judicial Court in a historic decision, *Goodridge v. Department of Public Health*, extended the freedom to marry to same-sex couples.[140] But New Jersey's Supreme Court declined to follow that approach in 2006, requiring instead that "same-sex couples must be afforded on equal terms the same rights and benefits enjoyed by married opposite-sex couples."[141] The courts of last resort in Connecticut,[142] Iowa,[143] and California[144] recognized equal marriage rights for same-sex couples in their respective state constitutions.

All along the path to *Obergefell*, with victories also came losses. As in New Jersey, courts in Maryland, New York, and Washington upheld statutory same-sex marriage bans.[145] Undeterred by the setbacks, same-sex marriage advocates successively pushed legislation through each of those states.[146]

Between the historic 2004 *Goodridge* decision and the 2013 U.S. Supreme Court decision striking down the Defense of Marriage Act,[147] many

139 Baker v. State, 170 Vt. 194, 224 (1999) ("[P]laintiffs are entitled under Chapter I, Article 7, of the Vermont Constitution to obtain the same benefits and protections afforded by Vermont law to married opposite-sex couples.").

140 Goodridge v. Dep't of Pub. Health, 440 Mass. 309, 344 (2003) ("We declare that barring an individual from the protections, benefits, and obligations of civil marriage solely because that person would marry a person of the same sex violates the Massachusetts Constitution.").

141 Lewis v. Harris, 188 N.J. 415, 457 (2006) (construing the equal protection guarantee of Article I, Paragraph 1 of the New Jersey Constitution).

142 Kerrigan v. Comm'r of Pub. Health, 289 Conn. 135 (2008) (ruling Connecticut's civil union statute violated the state constitutional equal protection guarantee).

143 Varnum v. Brien, 763 N.W.2d 862 (Iowa 2009) (extending marriage rights to same-sex couples under the Iowa Constitution).

144 *In re* Marriage Cases, 43 Cal. 4th 757 (2008) (holding California's domestic partnership law failed to provide equal rights to same-sex couples).

145 Conaway v. Deane, 401 Md. 219 (2007) (upholding Maryland law prohibiting two persons of the same-sex from marrying); Hernandez v. Robles, 7 N.Y.3d 338 (2006) (upholding New York law limiting marriage rights between two persons of the opposite sex); Andersen v. King Cty., 158 Wash. 2d 1 (2006) (affirming the constitutionality of Washington law's limitation of marriage rights to heterosexual couples).

146 N.Y. Dom. Rel. Law § 10-a (McKinney) (2011) ("A marriage that is otherwise valid shall be valid regardless of whether the parties to the marriage are of the same or different sex."); Md. Code Ann., Fam. Law § 2–201 (West, 2006) ("Only a marriage between two individuals who are not otherwise prohibited from marrying is valid in this State."); Wash. Rev. Code Ann. § 26.04.010 (West, 2006) ("Marriage is a civil contract between two persons who have each attained the age of eighteen years, and who are otherwise capable.").

147 United States v. Windsor, 133 S. Ct. 2675 (2013).

jurisdictions joined the marriage equality fold – some by legislation, some by judicial intervention, and some by referenda.[148]

Like the debates over anti-miscegenation laws, legislative deliberations featured personal stories, expressions of religious conviction, and policy. But, as was the case in the 1950s and 1960s, constitutional tradition and history significantly undergirded the legislative movement. Some legislators in Vermont, for example, rejected civil unions in favor of equal marriage in 2009, drawing parallels between the state's failure to provide marriage rights and separate-and-unequal segregated schools before *Brown v. Board of Education*.

After a conservative wave gave Republicans control of the New Hampshire General Court in 2010, some legislators hoped to capitalize on the new majorities and repeal the Granite State's 2009 same-sex marriage law.[149] Invoking lessons from litigation over California's vacillation between same-sex marriage recognition and prohibition, many New Hampshire legislators reasoned that the state could not revoke a right once granted, tracking the same rationale adopted by the Ninth Circuit's decision voiding Proposition 8.[150] Legislators looking to enact same-sex marriage also contemplated case law from the civil rights era, including *Griswold* and *Loving*, other states' legislation, and contemporary judicial decisions addressing same-sex marriage.

Much like the legislative debates throughout the 1950s and 1960s concerning race and marriage, the political dialogue over equal marriage rights for same-sex couples was colored by religious themes. The first states to enact same-sex marriage recognition statutes crafted nuanced laws that recognized same-sex marriage and protections for religious objectors.[151] Legislators took great care to assess the relationship between same-sex marriage legislation, preexisting nondiscrimination law, and constitutional values to balance marriage equality legislation with religious liberty rights. In doing so, each of the early equal marriage states provided greater protections for religious objectors than constitutionally required.

148 Anthony Kreis and Robin Fretwell Wilson, *Embracing Compromise: Marriage Equality and Religious Liberty in the Political Process*, 15 Georgetown University Journal of Gender and the Law 485 (2014).

149 *See id.*

150 Perry v. Brown, 671 F.3d 1052, 1063 (9th Cir. 2012), vacated and remanded sub nom. Hollingsworth v. Perry, 133 S. Ct. 2652 (2013) ("Proposition 8 serves no purpose, and has no effect, other than to lessen the status and human dignity of gays and lesbians in California, and to officially reclassify their relationships and families as inferior to those of opposite-sex couples.").

151 *See Marriage Equality in State and Nation*, 22 Wm. & Mary Bill Rts. J. 747 (2014) (describing early legislative debates and the impact of debate of religious values and protections for religious objectors).

The historical evidence reveals a similar pattern throughout the 1950s and early 1960s between the California Supreme Court's decision in *Perez* and the final resolution of the constitutional question in *Loving*. Throughout this period, dialectic collaboration between judicial actors, political branches, civil rights groups, religious organizations, and individual citizens fueled the diffusion of policy between states and the expansion of family law rights.

VI CONCLUSION

From this history, we can draw a number of lessons. As a threshold matter, overstating the impact of judicial actors in eradicating race-based marriage bans is a trap to be avoided. Indeed, the regularity with which courts dodged anti-miscegenation litigation and offered churlish rejections of interracial couples' constitutional claims belies the claim that courts are the primary engine of marriage law reform. Still, while courts did not provide the final nail in the coffin for most state miscegenation prohibitions, popular history accounts fail to fully capture the degree of judicial influence. This glossing over of courts may have occurred for two reasons. First, trial court decisions were unpublished, and, second, legislatures intervened during the appellate process. Moreover, scholars have not extensively examined legislators' motivations to end race-conscious family laws, many of which were jurisprudential in nature.

Ultimately, the era of marriage law liberalization pre-*Loving* was more dynamic, much like the years preceding *Obergefell*, than a cursory examination of the period might suggest. A careful examination of these two periods undercuts the critique that courts cannot help produce social reform. Courts have had a legitimate and profound influence in shaping the meaning of family – a role that surely will continue as states grapple with the entitlement of other families to the thick protections given to marriage.

23

Latter-Day Constitutionalism
Sexuality, Gender, and Mormons

William N. Eskridge, Jr.
John A. Garver Professor of Jurisprudence, Yale Law School

On March 12, 2015, Utah Governor Gary Herbert signed the Antidiscrimination and Religious Freedom Amendments into the state nondiscrimination code.[1] The 2015 Amendments add sexual orientation and gender identity to the list of personal traits that cannot be the basis for employment discrimination, but with allowances for employers to require reasonable dress standards and sex-specific facilities, and for employees to engage in some religious expression within the workplace.[2] The 2015 Amendments also prohibit such discrimination in housing, but with exemptions as well.

Why would one of the nation's most politically conservative, religiously strict, business-friendly states add new nondiscrimination protections for lesbian, gay, bisexual, and transgender ("LGBT") persons? Ironically, the inspiration for this surprising legislative move was the Church of Jesus Christ of the Latter-day Saints ("LDS"), also known as the Mormon Church – a highly traditionalist faith. This chapter explores how this Church's theology of the family has influenced American public law, which in turn has transformed the LDS Church. That conversation between secular norms and sectarian ones serves as a profound challenge to the notion that protections for religious beliefs freeze norms in place.[3]

1 SB 296, 2015 Gen. Sess. (Utah 2015), amending various provisions in UTAH CODE §§ 34A & 57 (West 2015).

2 For a detailed description of how Utah balanced nondiscrimination protections for the full LGBT community with protections for faith communities and individual religious believers, *see* Adams, Chapter 21, this volume.

3 For a view that religious liberty protections wall faith traditions off from change, *see* Marci A. Hamilton, *The Religious Liberty Shell Game Needs to End Now Before the Civil Rights of Women and LGBTQ Recede into History*, VERDICT (Jan. 24, 2017), verdict.justia.com/2017/01/24/religious-liberty-shell-game-needs-end-now-civil-rights-women-lgbtq-recede-history.

I THE MORMON THEOLOGY OF THE FAMILY

The family is, theologically, more important to Mormon religious doctrine and practice than it is to almost any other faith tradition. As summarized in the important LDS document *The Family: A Proclamation to the World*, all human beings are created in the image of God, but deeply gendered: "Gender is an essential characteristic of individual premortal, mortal, and eternal identity and purpose."[4] Thus, human beings have a premortal existence, as "sons and daughters," with "God as their Eternal Father." After birth, these persons are supposed to live their mortal lives in obedience to God's plan for them. God's central commandment is "for His children to multiply and replenish the earth" through "the sacred powers of procreation … employed only between man and woman, lawfully wedded as husband and wife." Hence, "family is ordained of God. Marriage between man and woman is essential to His eternal plan." Indeed, Mormons believe that marriage on earth parallels the heavenly union between God the Father and God the Mother; the Mother in Heaven is a belief distinctive to LDS faith.[5]

The eternal plan entails a gendered division of labor within the marital family: "By divine design, fathers are to preside over their families in love and righteousness and are responsible to provide the necessities of life and protection for their families. Mothers are primarily responsible for the nurture of their children."[6] This admonition does not entirely prohibit wives from working outside the home and husbands from helping raise the children, but it does seem to discourage arrangements where the wife is the sole breadwinner, while the husband remains at home and assumes primary responsibility for child care and housekeeping. Once a champion of plural marriages, the LDS Church now endorses fidelity within a monogamous marriage as an "eternal truth."[7]

A strict reading of the Mormon theology of the family is in tension with social change, fueled by the changing status and economic role of women.

4 The First Presidency and Council of the Twelve Apostles of the Church of Jesus Christ of Latter-day Saints, *The Family: A Proclamation to the World* ¶ 2 (Sept. 23, 1995), www.lds.org/topics/family-proclamation?lang=eng&old=true (hereinafter PROCLAMATION). In this chapter, all the quoted material in a paragraph is given in a single pinpoint cite where first used, unless noted.

5 *See* The Church of Jesus Christ of Latter-day Saints, *Mother in Heaven* (2015), www.lds.org/topics/mother-in-heaven?lang=eng&old=true; TERRYL L. GIVENS, WRESTLING THE ANGEL: THE FOUNDATIONS OF MORMON THOUGHT: COSMOS, GOD, HUMANITY 106–12, 274–79 (2014).

6 PROCLAMATION ¶ 7.

7 *See, e.g.*, Eugene England, *On Fidelity, Polygamy, and Celestial Marriage*, 20 DIALOGUE: A JOURNAL OF MORMON THEOLOGY 138, 147–53 (1987).

Since World War II, American women have found jobs outside the home, engaged in sexual activities earlier in their lives, and have delayed and increasingly declined marriage and bearing children.[8] Consequently, the marriage rate has steadily declined and the number of children born outside of marriage has increased, with divorce rates persistently high by historical standards. These trends have contributed to a conception of marriage as more individualized, more hedonic, and less gendered than is contemplated by the relatively communitarian Mormon model.[9] At the same time that marriage has moved away from its traditional procreative function for many Americans, lesbians and gay men have moved out of the closet and into family structures resembling modern marriage, including civil unions and domestic partnerships, and have raised children together.[10]

Since the 1960s, American family law has changed as well. Most states have decriminalized consensual sex outside of procreative marriage; legalized and regulated sexual cohabitation; removed penalties against non-marital children; opened up civil marriage to more couples (including lesbian and gay couples everywhere); passed laws allowing no-fault, relatively easy divorce; and eliminated many gendered features of alimony and child support law.[11]

By the mid-1970s, the Salt Lake City leadership of the LDS Church – the First Presidency (consisting of the President and two Counselors), the Quorum of the Twelve Apostles (from which the First Presidency is drawn), and the Presidency of the Seventy (the next level) – recognized that social and legal trends were at odds with the Mormon theology of the family.[12] Nonetheless, Mormons have not retreated from their traditional theology of the family;[13] instead, they have engaged in political activism on a national level. Latter-day constitutionalism is the process by which Mormons have engaged in democratic activism aimed at entrenching LDS family values in national and state constitutional law.

[8] Claudia Goldin, *The Quiet Revolution that Transformed Women's Employment, Education, and Family*, NBER Working Papers Series #11953 at 15–24 (Jan. 2006), www.nber.org/papers/w11953.pdf.

[9] Andrew J. Cherlin, The Marriage-Go-Round: The State of Marriage and the Family in America Today 87–115 (2009); Andrew J. Cherlin, *Deinstitutionalization of American Marriage*, 66 J. Marriage & Fam. 848, 851 (2004).

[10] For a review of statuses outside marriage, *see* Weiner, Chapter 11, this volume.

[11] William N. Eskridge Jr., *Family Law Pluralism: The Guided-Choice Regime of Menus, Default Rules, and Override Rules*, 100 Geo. L.J. 1881 (2012); Obergefell v. Hodges, 135 S. Ct. 2584 (2015).

[12] O. Kendall White Jr., *Overt and Covert Policies: The Mormon Church's Anti-ERA Campaign in Virginia*, 19 Va. Soc. Sci. J. 11–16 (1984).

[13] Letter from LDS First Presidency to Members of the LDS Church, "Standards of Morality and Fidelity" (Nov. 14, 1991).

II LATTER-DAY CONSTITUTIONALISM TO PRESERVE THE "TRADITIONAL FAMILY"

The parents of Latter-day constitutionalism were Spencer W. Kimball, the LDS President (1973–85), and Gordon Hinckley, the founding chair of the LDS Special Affairs Committee (1974–81), a Counselor in the First Presidency (1981–95), and finally President (1995–2008). Working within the consensus-oriented structure of LDS decision making, these leaders committed the Church to a highly influential opposition to two of the great constitutional debates of the past century – equal rights for women and marriage equality for LGBT persons.

As this section shows, LDS opposition to the Equal Rights Amendment ("ERA"), premised on its concern for the family, sealed the fate of the ERA. Like that large-scale effort, on September 23, 1995, President Hinckley issued the important church document *The Family: A Proclamation*, "warn[ing] that the disintegration of the family will bring upon individuals, communities, and nations the calamities foretold by ancient and modern prophets" and calling upon "responsible citizens and officers of government everywhere to promote those measures designed to maintain and strengthen the family as the fundamental unit of society."[14] Mormon activism achieved a series of popular constitutional triumphs – defeating the proposed ERA and overturning gay marriage in California.

A *LDS Opposition to the Equal Rights Amendment*

Congress voted in favor of the ERA and sent the amendment on to the states for ratification on March 22, 1972. By the end of 1973, thirty states had ratified the ERA, closing in on the thirty-eight needed to add the ERA to the United States Constitution. Utah's legislature seemed poised to ratify the ERA in early 1975, which would have continued the amendment's cascade into the law of the land. Or so its supporters expected.

In 1975, the proposed amendment hit a roadblock. Only three states ratified the ERA after Montana (1974), and five that had ratified the ERA later voted to rescind their ratification.[15] Utah never did ratify, nor did neighboring Nevada –

[14] PROCLAMATION ¶ 8–9.

[15] *See generally* THOMAS H. NEALE, CONG. RES. SERV., R42979, THE PROPOSED EQUAL RIGHTS AMENDMENT: CONTEMPORARY RATIFICATION ISSUES 9 (2013), www.equalrightsamendment.org/misc/CRS%20ERA%20report%204-8-14.pdf.

states with significant Mormon populations.[16] The decisive variable was LDS mobilization. Advised by Hinckley's Special Affairs Committee, Spencer Kimball's First Presidency devoted unprecedented resources to a national constitutional effort.[17]

The LDS leadership was persuaded that the ERA would contribute to a national culture hostile to the Mormon theology of the family. As the official LDS First Presidency's statement on the ERA put it in 1980, a general concern was that "[o]ur Creator has especially suited fathers and mothers, through physical and emotional differences, to fulfill their particular parental responsibilities," and any legal development "that could blur those roles gives cause for concern."[18] Specifically, "[c]ourt and administrative interpretations of the ERA could endanger time-honored moral values by challenging laws that have safeguarded the family and afforded women necessary protections and exemptions."[19]

The Church expressed specific concerns with the ERA, too. First, "[a]ny reasonable chance for reversing the accelerating trend of courts to grant abortion on demand would probably be eliminated."[20] Second, "passage of the ERA could extend legal protection to same-sex lesbian and homosexual marriages, giving legal sanction to the rearing of children in such homes."[21] Because the ERA barred any state discrimination "on account of sex," it might require states to marry man-*man* couples if they married man-*woman* couples.[22] Third, "the ERA could make it more difficult for wives and mothers to remain at home because it could require the removal of legal requirements that make a husband responsible for the support of his wife and children." If the ERA opened up jobs (including those in the armed forces) to women, there would be "[g]reat pressure" for women "not to marry or have children and to join or remain in the labor force."

16 For a granular look at the geographic distribution of faith groups in the United States, *see* Pew Center for Religion and Family Life, Religious Landscape Study, www.pewforum.org/religious-landscape-study/.

17 *See* Rex E. Lee, A Lawyer Looks at the Equal Rights Amendment (1980); D. Michael Quinn, *The LDS Church's Campaign Against the Equal Rights Amendment*, 20 J. Mormon Hist. 85–155 (1994); Neil J. Young, *"The ERA Is a Moral Issue": The Mormon Church, LDS Women, and the Defeat of the Equal Rights Amendment*, 59 Am. Q. 623 (2007).

18 Spencer W. Kimball et al., *The Church and the Proposed Equal Rights Amendment: A Moral Issue*, Ensign (March 1980), www.lds.org/ensign/1980/03/the-church-and-the-proposed-equal-rights-amendment-a-moral-issue?lang=eng.

19 *Id.* 20 *Id.*

21 *Id.* (discussing the testimony before the Senate Judiciary Committee of Harvard law professor Paul A. Freund linking the ERA with constitutionally required gay marriage).

22 Andrew Koppelman, *Why Discrimination Against Lesbians and Gay Men Is Sex Discrimination*, 65 N.Y.U. L. Rev. 137 (1994).

The Utah Legislature was poised to ratify the ERA when its session began in January 1975; almost half of its members were on record in support. But the day before the session commenced, an editorial in the LDS-owned *Deseret News* objected to the proposed constitutional amendment as "dangerous."[23] Mormons understood the editorial to represent the views of the First Presidency. When the legislature voted on February 18, 1975, the ERA was handily defeated, 21–54.[24]

Even with the Utah rout, the ERA's ratification count stood at thirty-four states by April 1975, with just four more needed for passage – that margin would shrink to only three after Indiana ratified it on January 24, 1977.[25] Next up was Nevada, where opponents held up ERA ratification pending the results of a 1978 voter referendum. Polls showed a close vote, with pro-ERA forces having an edge – until the LDS Church mobilized in opposition. Under the guidance of Elder Hinckley's Special Affairs Committee, local leaders held a meeting for 2000 married LDS members in vote-rich Las Vegas the weekend before the referendum.[26] These rank-and-file Mormons were warned that the ERA would undermine the family and require unisex bathrooms and women to serve in the armed forces. Fired up, these volunteers canvassed door-to-door to persuade co-religionists and neighbors to turn out against the amendment – as they did on election day, defeating the ERA by a 2 to 1 margin.[27]

Virginia and Missouri were battlegrounds in 1978–79. Even though these states had modest Mormon populations, the LDS leadership team mobilized resources to help defeat ratification efforts there as well. Coordinated by the Special Affairs Committee, lay bishops and stake leaders formed the Missouri Citizens Council and the Virginia Citizens Coalition (as well as local coalitions) to oppose ratification.[28] Ward bishops solicited contributions for

[23] Editorial, *Equal Rights Amendment*, DESERET NEWS, Jan. 11, 1975 at 16.

[24] D. MICHAEL QUINN, THE MORMON HIERARCHY: ORIGINS OF POWER 377 (1994).

[25] *See generally* James T. Richardson, *The "Old Right" in Action: Mormon and Catholic Involvement in an Equal Rights Amendment Referendum*, *in* NEW CHRISTIAN POLITICS 213, 215, 222 (David G. Bromley & Anson Shupe eds., 1984).

[26] Laura Myers, *Mormon Voters Lean Toward Romney, Regardless of Party Affiliation*, LAS VEGAS REV. J. (Sept. 4, 2012).

[27] Young, *supra* note 17.

[28] Linda Sillitoe, *Church Politics and Sonia Johnson: The Central Conundrum*, SUNSTONE, Jan.-Feb. 1980, at 35–40.

The LDS church organizes the faithful into local congregations known "wards" (in areas where there are few members, the local congregation might be called a "branch"). The Church of Jesus Christ of Latter-day Saints, *Wards*, www.mormonnewsroom.org/article/ward. Wards and branches make up "stakes," typically comprising five to twelve wards or branches and similar to a Catholic diocese. The Church of Jesus Christ of Latter-day Saints, *Stake*, www.mormonnewsroom.org/article/stake.

anti-ERA groups from congregations, sought signatures for anti-ERA petitions in ward lobbies, offered church buildings for anti-ERA meetings, published tens of thousands of pamphlets ("Equality Yes, ERA No"), and personally "called" several thousand Mormon women to serve as the ground troops for the campaign.[29] Owing in part to LDS grassroots efforts, ratification failed in both states.

Mormon grassroots activists (especially women) were also involved in the successful campaigns to defeat the ERA in Illinois, Florida, and North Carolina. Although LDS involvement may not have been decisive in any of the three or Virginia, it was certainly decisive in Utah, Nevada, and possibly Missouri.

B *Mormons and the "Homosexual Agenda"*

LGBT persons were also demanding equal treatment in the 1970s. The "homosexual agenda," as opponents derided it, sought to repeal or nullify consensual sodomy laws, to secure protection against discrimination, and (in a distant third place) to win the right to marry.[30] In an internal LDS document entitled *Principles to Govern Possible Public Statement on Legislation Affecting Rights of Homosexuals* dated August 1984 ("*Principles*"), Elder Dallin Oaks laid out a proposed church stance on each of the issues raised by LGBT rights supporters.[31]

1 Sodomy Laws

Elder Oaks observed that most sex-based sins condemned by the Church are either not the subject of the criminal law (e.g., fornication) or are crimes but almost never prosecuted (e.g., adultery). Accordingly, the *Principles* suggested that LDS leaders steer clear of debates over the continued criminalization of consensual sodomy. Concerned that the Church not be seen as singling out

[29] When one is "called," he or she is asked to do a specific service in the church, which can be declined. Though it is not required, there is an expectation that, unless circumstances prevent it, a member in good standing would accept a call to serve. The Church of Jesus Christ of Latter-day Saints, *Lay Leadership: Volunteer Ministry of the Church*, www.mormonnewsroom.org/article/mormon-lay-ministry.

[30] *See generally* William N. Eskridge, Jr., Dishonorable Passions: Sodomy Law in America, 1861–2003 (2008), at 194–201.

[31] Dallin H. Oaks, Principles to Govern Possible Public Statement on Legislation Affecting Rights of Homosexuals (Aug. 7, 1984). All citations in this section are to the Principles unless otherwise noted.

"homosexuals," Elder Oaks urged the LDS leadership not to support laws that target only homosexual (versus heterosexual and homosexual) sodomy.

2 Nondiscrimination Laws

Although laws protecting homosexuals against discrimination might be said to "promote homosexuality," the *Principles* urged restraint. "The best strategy to oppose further anti-discrimination legislation protecting homosexuals is to propose well-reasoned exceptions rather than to oppose such legislation across the board," including the ability to exclude homosexual from jobs or positions involving minors: "Parents who prefer and a society which prefers male-female marriages and procreation should be able to insist on teachers and youth leaders who will teach (or at least not contradict) those values."

When the Boy Scouts of America ("BSA") (heavily populated with LDS-sponsored scouts) later took a public position against gay scoutmasters, it closely hewed to Elder Oaks's *Principles*. "We believe," BSA announced in 1991, "that homosexual conduct is inconsistent with the requirements in the Scout Oath that a Scout be morally straight and in the Scout Law that the Scout be clean in word and deed, and that homosexuals do not provide a desirable role model for Scouts."[32] In the 1984 *Principles*, Elder Oaks had suggested that exclusion of homosexuals from youth-oriented positions "should be explained, with careful emphasis on the bad effects of homosexual practices (not homosexuals) and the need – for the good of society – to protect youth from homosexual proselytizing and role models among their teachers and counselors."

3 Homosexual Marriages

"[I]n religious terms, homosexual 'marriages' would be a devilish perversion of the procreative purposes of God and the earth life He has granted His children. Homosexual relations are wholly deviant to the procreative purpose of sexual relations. Homosexual marriages are wholly deviant to the patriarchal family." However, the *Principles* urged the Church not to oppose "homosexual marriages" on sectarian grounds, such as depopulation. The primary argument should be "defense of the family." In particular, the "legal rights conferred on marriage partners are granted in consideration of the procreative purpose and effects of a marriage between a man and a woman."

[32] Boy Scouts of America, Position Statement on Homosexuality (June 1991); *see* Boy Scouts of Am. v. Dale, 530 U.S. 640, 659 (2000).

C Latter-Day Constitutionalism and Same-Sex Marriage Ballot Initiatives

In *Baehr v. Lewin*, the Hawaii Supreme Court ruled in 1993 that Hawaii's exclusion of same-sex couples from civil marriage required heightened scrutiny under the state's ERA – precisely the same inference reached by LDS leaders about the national ERA.[33] The court remanded the case for trial to see if Hawaii could meet the ERA's exacting standard. For the next five years, Hawaii's judicial and political process debated whether to recognize lesbian and gay relationships as marriages – as other states debated what to do if Hawaii did so. Consistent with *Principles*, the LDS First Presidency, effectively led by that point by then–First Counselor Gordon Hinckley, assumed a leadership position to nip this development of recognizing same-sex marriage in the bud, just as Hinckley's Special Affairs Committee had helped kill the ERA.

On February 1, 1994, just months after *Baehr*, the First Presidency issued a call to action. Because the gendered, procreative family "offers the best hope for avoiding many of the ills that afflict society," the Church encouraged members "to appeal to legislators, judges, and other government officials to preserve the purposes and sanctity of marriage between a man and a woman, and to reject all efforts to give legal authorization or other official approval or support to marriages between persons of the same gender."[34]

Immediately after Hinckley assumed his position as LDS President in 1995, he issued the *Proclamation* and made an initial commitment of $500,000 to political efforts against "same-gender marriage" in Hawaii.[35] Responding to a lobbying and public relations campaign orchestrated behind the scenes by the LDS Church, Hawaii's legislature in 1997 voted to put a state constitutional amendment to the voters in the November 1998 election; the amendment would allow the legislature to limit marriage to one man, one woman.[36] Operating in coalition with the Catholic Church, the LDS Church financed much of the campaign in support of the constitutional amendment. At the same time, the Church was coordinating with other family values groups to fund and staff similar grassroots initiatives in Alaska and California.[37]

33 Baehr v. Lewin, 852 P.2d 44, 67 (Haw. 1993).

34 LDS First Presidency, Same Gender Marriages (Feb. 1, 1994), *reprinted in* ENSIGN (Apr. 1994).

35 Letter from Loren C. Dunn to Elder Neal A. Maxwell (Oct. 31, 1995).

36 *See generally* David Orgon Coolidge, *The Hawai'i Marriage Amendment: Its Origins, Meaning and Fate* 22 U. HAW. L. REV. 19 (2000).

37 Letter from Lynn D. Wardle, Professor, J. Reuben Clark Law School to Elder Marlin K. Jensen, Chair SGM Comm., Presidency of the Seventy, et al. (Oct. 19, 1998).

With vast LDS support, the Hawaii marriage amendment won with 69% of the vote and was added to the state constitution.[38] The same day, Alaska voters amended their state constitution to bar same-sex marriages by a similar lopsided margin. The Church then focused on California. As it had done in opposing the ERA, the LDS leadership channeled money, intellectual and legal support, and grassroots volunteers to support Proposition 22, an initiative proposed by state Senator Pete Knight to bar same-sex marriages in California's code. In May 1999, the LDS leadership sent a series of letters to California stakes and members, imploring them to get involved in the nascent campaign for Proposition 22, but also avoiding direct LDS handling of contributions or publicity for the initiative.[39] At the October 1999 General Conference of the Church, President Hinckley rallied all Mormons to support Proposition 22, an event that sparked local LDS congregations to devote church buildings and resources to advancing this cause. In early 2000, church pressure for members to contribute money and time to the initiative grew more intense. With the help of Mormon money and volunteers, Proposition 22 prevailed with the voters by a whopping 61%–39% margin on March 7, 2000.

On May 5, 2008, the California Supreme Court invalidated Proposition 22 as inconsistent with the equality guarantees of the California Constitution.[40] A family values coalition, Protect Marriage, had already collected most of the signatures it would need to place on the November 2008 ballot what would become Proposition 8 to amend the state constitution to limit civil marriage to a man and a woman. Between June and November 2008, the LDS leadership in Salt Lake City and in many local California stakes and wards devoted more money, energy, and excitement to Proposition 8 than any religious group has ever devoted to a ballot measure in American history.[41] Although President Hinckley died in January 2008, the reconstituted First Presidency carried on the constitutional campaign vigorously.

In letters from the First Presidency read by all California LDS wards in June and July 2008, Mormons were urged to support Proposition 8 with their votes,

38 *See* Office of Elections, State of Hawaii, Hawaii General Election 1998, http://files.hawaii.gov/elections/files/results/1998/general/histatewide.pdf. For citations to each state constitutional marriage amendment and the margin by which it was adopted, *see* Robin Fretwell Wilson, *A Marriage of Necessity: Same-Sex Marriage and Religious Liberty Protections*, 64 Case Western Law Review 1161 (2014).

39 Letter from John B. Dickson, John M. Madsen, & Cecil O. Samuelson North America West First Presidency, to California Latter-Day Saints (May 11, 1999); Letter from Elder Douglas L. Callister, Area Authority, to California Stake Presidents (May 20, 1999).

40 *In re* Marriage Cases, 183 P.3d 384 (Cal. 2008).

41 Jesse McKinley & Kirk Johnson, *Mormons Tipped Scale in Ban on Gay Marriage*, N.Y. Times (Nov. 14, 2008), www.nytimes.com/2008/11/15/us/politics/15marriage.html.

their canvassing, and their monetary contributions.[42] In a conference call with all of the presidents of LDS California stakes, Apostle Russell Ballard analogized Proposition 8 as the Gettysburg (the single most important battle of the Civil War) for the culture war over same-sex marriage.[43] If supporters of traditional marriage could "hold" California, that might snuff out the possibility of gay marriage expanding beyond Massachusetts. Contributions from Mormons poured into the coffers of ProtectMarriage.com, ultimately amounting to at least half of the more than $40 million raised and spent in support of Proposition 8.[44] More important was the massive grassroots effort. On October 8, Apostle Ballard and other members of the LDS leadership broadcast by satellite their inspirational words to LDS congregations all over California.[45] Ballard asked that each Mormon congregation call upon thirty of its members to donate four hours a week to the Proposition 8 campaign, urged all young married couples to blog and text-message their support for Proposition 8 to all their friends, and announced a new website with materials that the faithful could distribute to get out the truth about Proposition 8.

The website PreservingMarriage.org elaborated upon the LDS philosophy of the family. One man, one woman marriage is not only a "divine institution" but is also one that has been foundational for every society.[46] Marriage's transhistorical purpose has been "to preserve and foster the institution most central to rearing children and teaching them the moral values of civilization." While LGBT parents may rear children successfully, this LDS-sponsored website maintained that "gender differentiated parenting" is uniquely useful to a child's healthy development. In light of the "close links that have long existed between marriage, procreation, gender, and parenting," same-sex

42 The first such missive was the Letter from the LDS First Presidency, *Preserving Traditional Marriage and Strengthening Families* (read to all California LDS congregations on June 29, 2008).

43 An apostle in the LDS Church is a priesthood office in the Church and a calling to serve full time as a Church leader for the rest of one's life. The president of the Church his two Counselors and the Quorum of the Twelve Apostles are the highest governing body of the church and all have the office of apostle. It is not used as a title by members; they are called "elder" or "president" depending on their role. The Church of Jesus Christ of Latter-day Saints, *Apostle*, www.mormonnewsroom.org/article/apostle.

44 The Church of Jesus Christ of Latter-day Saints, Newsroom, *Church Clarifies Proposition 8 Filing, Corrects Erroneous News Reports* (Feb. 2, 2009), www.mormonnewsroom.org/article/church-clarifies-proposition-8-filing-corrects-erroneous-news-reports.

45 *See* Veronique de Turenne, *Southern California – This Just In*, L.A. TIMES (Oct. 9, 2008).

46 The Church of Jesus Christ of Latter-day Saints, Newsroom, *The Divine Institution of Marriage* (2008), www.mormonnewsroom.org/article/the-divine-institution-of-marriage. The Church still describes marriage in these terms. *See* The Church of Jesus Christ of Latter-day Saints, Newsroom, *The Divine Institution of Marriage*, www.mormonnewsroom.org/article/the-divine-institution-of-marriage.

marriage is not just another individual right but is "a far-reaching redefinition of the very nature of marriage itself."

The Church's argumentation in favor of Proposition 8 was broader than that which the Church had deployed in past constitutional marriage campaigns. The website's new emphasis was that gay marriage was a threat to religious liberty. Thus, in some states, Catholic Charities had been "forced" to abandon its adoption services in the face of demands that it place children in lesbian and gay households. Churches might lose their tax exemptions, wedding photographers might be subject to lawsuits, and parents might have no way to prevent their children from being taught that gay marriage is just as good as straight marriage.[47]

An LDS-inspired pamphlet "Six Consequences If Proposition 8 Fails" argued in August 2008 that if the state constitution were not amended to restore the traditional definition of marriage (1) children in public schools would have to be taught that same-sex marriage is just as good as traditional marriage, (2) churches might lose their tax-exempt status if they refuse to perform same-sex marriages, (3) religious adoption agencies would be prodded to give up their policy of placing children in homes with one mother and one father, (4) religious schools might have to open their married student housing to same-sex couples, (5) ministers preaching against same-sex marriage could be charged with hate speech, and (6) everyone would have to pay for the many lawsuits engendered by same-sex marriage advocates.[48] These were speculative but heartfelt fears harbored by many religious groups and families.

In the last month of the campaign, "Yes-on-8" commercials emphasized these religious liberty threats posed by marriage equality. Tens of thousands of Mormon volunteers made these arguments in the door-to-door and telephone canvassing that intensified in the weeks leading up to the vote. Fueled by last-minute donations from wealthy Mormon supporters, "Yes-on-8" saturated the airwaves with new ads in the waning days of the campaign. Due in large part to an impressive get-out-the-vote campaign by Mormon volunteers, on top of previous LDS contributions, Proposition 8 won a decisive 52%–48% victory on November 4, 2008.[49]

Proposition 8 was the Church's last great hurrah in the marriage equality debate. Within two years, Proposition 8 would be nullified by a federal

47 The present-day discussion of marriage also cites these instances under a discussion of "How Would Same-Sex Marriage Affect Religious Freedom?" *Divine Institution of Marriage*, *supra* note 46.

48 *Six Consequences If Proposition 8 Fails*, Prop 8 Blog (Aug. 24, 2008), http://prop8savingmarriage.blogspot.com/2008/08/six-consequences-if-proposition-8-fails.html.

49 *See* McKinley & Johnson, *supra* note 41.

district court, whose judgment ultimately withstood appellate challenges because of a procedural technicality, that the challengers did not have standing to bring suit.[50] Three years later, on December 20, 2013, federal District Judge Robert Shelby ordered Utah to issue marriage licenses to same-sex couples.[51] Although the U.S. Supreme Court stayed Judge Shelby's order on January 6, 2014,[52] thousands of lesbian and gay couples were married in Utah before the Supreme Court's action. When the Supreme Court denied further review on October 6, 2014, Utah's Governor Gary Herbert again ordered marriage licenses to be issued.[53] Ultimately, the U.S. Supreme Court followed Judge Shelby when it ruled, in *Obergefell v. Hodges*,[54] that state marriage exclusions unconstitutionally deprive same-sex couples of their fundamental right to marry.

III LESSONS SUGGESTED BY LATTER-DAY CONSTITUTIONALISM FOR AMERICAN INDIVIDUAL RIGHTS LAW

Many lessons can be drawn from the experience of Latter-day constitutionalism. There are lessons for the nature of American constitutionalism, for the evolution of religious faiths, and for the less-gendered future of the family.

A *Our Democratic-Pluralist Constitution*

Academics tend to believe that the evolution of American constitutional law has been strongly influenced by social movements advancing civil rights for people of color, for women, for people with disabilities, for gun owners, and for sexual and gender minorities.[55] The relationship between social movements and constitutional law is incomplete, however, without considering the important role of the traditional family values ("TFV") movement, brilliantly exemplified and deployed by Latter-day constitutionalism.

50 Perry v. Schwarzenegger, 704 F. Supp. 2d 921, 927 (N.D. Cal. 2010).

51 Kitchen v. Herbert, 961 F. Supp. 2d 1181 (D. Utah 2013).

52 Herbert v. Kitchen, 134 S. Ct. 893 (2014).

53 Dennis Romboy, *A Year Later, a Look at the Utah Decision on Same-Sex Marriage That "Shocked the Nation,"* Deseret News (Dec. 19, 2014), www.deseretnews.com/article/865618112/A-year-later-a-look-at-the-Utah-decision-on-same-sex-marriage-that-shocked-the-nation.html.

54 135 S. Ct. 2584 (2015).

55 William N. Eskridge, Jr., *Some Effects of Identity-Based Social Movements on Constitutional Law in the Twentieth Century*, 100 Mich. L. Rev. 2062 (2002); Reva B. Siegel, *Dead or Alive: Originalism as Popular Constitutionalism in* Heller, 122 Harv. L. Rev. 191 (2008).

For example, the feminist campaign for the ERA was thwarted by Mrs. Phyllis Schlafly and STOP ERA, who were able to reframe the debate as one about what legal structure best suited the genuine interests of women and the country.[56] With a focus on the family and a skeptical view about what erasing all gender discriminations would mean for the welfare of children, Latter-day constitutionalism reinforced the normative vision of STOP ERA and helped frame constitutional law after the ERA failed.

Starting in 1976, the Supreme Court recognized sex as a quasi-suspect classification and created a framework for sweeping away state sex discrimination that denied women equal opportunities for equal citizenship, such as jury duty.[57] This framework responded to the strong public support for throwing out laws that excluded women from opportunities because of stereotypes. Indeed, the LDS First Presidency's statement opposing the ERA repeatedly endorsed the norm that women should have equal opportunities.[58] Latter-day constitutionalism made a contribution to issues it did *not* contest, as well as to issues the Church vigorously contested. Thus, the Supreme Court's sex discrimination jurisprudence bowed to the strongest concerns raised by STOP ERA and by the LDS First Presidency, namely, concerns that sex equality might force women to serve in the military, states to recognize gay marriages, and governments to repeal special protections for women.[59] Thus, in the ten years the country was debating the ERA, a Supreme Court that struck down sex discrimination laws denying women equal life opportunities also rejected equal protection challenges to government prohibitions of same-sex marriage;[60] to women's ineligibility for draft registration;[61] and to laws rationally designed to protect women's interests, especially their interests in pregnancy and family.[62]

This dialectic illustrates how constitutional norms are typically the result of conflict as well as consensus among social groups, in a normative contest for

56 *See* Reva B. Siegel, *Constitutional Culture, Social Movement Conflict and Constitutional Change: The Case of the De Facto ERA*, 94 Calif. L. Rev. 1323, 1389–1403 (2006) (detailing Mrs. Schlafly's philosophy and her ERA critique).

57 While the ERA was in play, the Supreme Court left open the level of scrutiny for sex-based classifications. *See* Frontiero v. Richardson, 411 U.S. 677 (1973). After the ERA's chances receded, the Court subjected sex-based classifications to heightened but not strict scrutiny in Craig v. Boren, 429 U.S. 190 (1976).

58 Kimball et al., *supra* note 18 ("The Church is firmly committed to equal rights for women.").

59 Eskridge, *supra* note 55, at 2138; Siegel, *supra* note 56, at 1403.

60 Baker v. Nelson, 409 U.S. 810 (1972). 61 Rostker v. Goldberg, 453 U.S. 57 (1981).

62 Califano v. Webster, 430 U.S. 313 (1977) (upholding gendered Social Security provision because it advantaged women); *see also* Michael M. v. Superior Court, 450 U.S. 464 (1981) (upholding a state law making sex with an underage female, but not a male, statutory rape).

Americans' allegiance in our constitutional culture. This understanding of constitutionalism is rooted in democratic pluralism. Our society consists of many social groups, and one role of government is to mediate group conflict and to integrate new social groups into our constitutional culture – without alienating existing social groups. As reflected in Latter-day constitutionalism, the Religion Clauses of the First Amendment are the constitutional model.[63] The Free Exercise Clause bars the government from persecuting minority religions, and the Establishment Clause bars majority religions from using government to entrench their advantage. One consequence of the Religion Clauses has been a rich religious pluralism in this country – and it is to America's credit that the Mormons, long disparaged by mainstream Christian faiths, have been able to flourish here and, now, to form alliances with denominations once their enemies.

This democratic-pluralist Constitution played out productively and democratically in the same-sex marriage debate. Marriage equality was not a viable constitutional aspiration until LGBT Americans not only formed political and legal organizations to assert their equality rights but also secured many allies in the straight population. It is no coincidence that the Supreme Court handed down *Obergefell* only after both the President Barack Obama and the Supreme Court had concluded that the Defense of Marriage Act was unconstitutional (with virtually no public backlash) *and* only after decisive majorities of the American people supported that move *and* only after thirty-six states were already handing out marriage licenses (Figure 23.1). In short, *Obergefell* was not possible without extensive public deliberation in hundreds of governmental forums – from state courtrooms to state and local legislatures and state ballot boxes to government agencies to the White House itself.

A central LDS concern was that gay marriage would dissolve the connection among marriage, self-sacrifice, and responsible childrearing. This was a serious claim – and one that impelled a close look at what happened to families after Massachusetts and other states recognized same-sex marriage.[64] That marriage itself has not taken a hit, while thousands of LGBT families (including many with children) have flourished, has been an important learning curve for the country. As Strassberg (Chapter 18, this volume) argues,

63 William N. Eskridge, Jr., *A Jurisprudence of "Coming Out": Religion, Homosexuality, and Collisions of Liberty and Equality in American Public Law*, 106 YALE L. J. 2411 (1997).

64 *See* The Church of Jesus Christ of Latter-day Saints, Newsroom, *The Divine Institution of Marriage* (2008), www.mormonnewsroom.org/article/the-divine-institution-of-marriage; Weiner, Chapter 11, this volume.

FIGURE 23.1 Marriage Recognition on the Eve of *Obergefell*, June 25, 2015

concerns for the status of women and children may play out differently in the movement to recognize plural families.

Moreover, deliberation ought not mean that society picks a winner and kicks the losers to the curb. A notable feature of Justice Anthony Kennedy's opinion for the *Obergefell* Court was its engagement with the norms reflected in Latter-day constitutionalism. The centerpiece of the Court's opinion was its discussion of *why* marriage is fundamental. Consistent with the Mormon theology of the family, the Court painted marriage as essential for individual flourishing, for personal interconnection, for the welfare of children, and for the good of society.[65] Except for its disregard of gender differentiation (admittedly, a big "except" for those who oppose same-sex marriage), this opinion largely reflects and tries to build upon a LDS vision of the family and family values.

Even though it settled the issue of marriage equality, *Obergefell* explicitly opened up new issues for ongoing constitutional debate; the Court contemplated a continuation of the social deliberative process. In its *amicus* brief in *Obergefell*, lawyers for the LDS Church worried that marriage equality for sexual minorities would mean losses of liberty for religious minorities.[66] Nothing in marriage equality for same-sex couples, Justice Kennedy advised, prevents people of faith from continuing to recognize only one-man, one-woman marriages. Indeed, the First Amendment affirmatively protects the freedom of religious organizations and persons "to teach the principles that are so fulfilling and so central to their lives and faiths" and to advocate and live "the family structure they have so long revered."[67] As Utah Senate Majority Whip Stuart Adams (Chapter 21, this volume) explains, legislators, rather than courts, are tasked with finding a space for religious dissenters to continue to live out their convictions about marriage, family, and sexuality, free from concern about social punishment. This assurance did not satisfy the dissenting Justices. Yet, Justice Kennedy was the fifth vote to recognize the LDS-affiliated Boy Scouts' First Amendment right to exclude gay people from positions of trust, suggesting that both communities should have the ability to be who they are.[68]

65 *Obergefell*, *supra* note 54, at 2597–2602.

66 *Id.*, Brief of Major Religious Organizations as *Amici Curiae* in Support of Respondents at 12–39, (No. 14–556 et al.), 2015 WL 1534341.

67 Obergefell, *supra* note 54, at 2607; *e.g.*, Hosanna-Tabor Evangelical Lutheran Church and Sch. v. EEOC, 132 S. Ct. 694 (2012) (protecting churches against application of nondiscrimination laws to "ministerial" personnel).

68 Boy Scouts of America v. Dale, 530 U.S. 640 (2000).

The same pluralist impulse reflected in *Obergefell* is also reflected in Utah's landmark 2015 law that protected both the liberties of LGBT people and those of traditionalists, a pair of bills colloquially known as the Utah Compromise.[69] The Utah Compromise is a model for future "red state" nondiscrimination laws. Senator Adams (Chapter 21, this volume) explains why similar laws are achievable in other red states and provide the best way for ending the perpetual culture war over gay rights.

B Constitutionalism and the Evolution of Faith

A central reason the LDS Church became involved with the ERA and marriage equality debates was that its leadership feared that standing by and allowing the ERA and gay marriage to sweep the nation would lead to a sea change in the culture that would undermine the Mormons' gendered theology of the family. There was good reason for the leadership to suppose this might be the case – and the best example came during the Church's involvement in the ERA debate.

In the 19th century, LDS theology disparaged persons of African descent and other persons of color. On February 13, 1849, LDS President Brigham Young announced a Revelation from the Lord that even free persons of African descent could not be Mormon priests nor could they be allowed in the holy parts of the Temple or have their marriages "sealed" within the Temple.[70] In 1852, Young, by then the Governor of Utah, invoked Scripture to legalize slavery for persons of African or Indian descent.[71]

These race-based teachings of the Church later became inconsistent with public attitudes in the post-1945 civil rights era – and they had an effect on LDS leaders, including Presidents David McKay (1951–70) and Spencer Kimball (1973–85). In 1963, on the eve of the March on Washington, the Church endorsed "full civil equality for all of God's children."[72] The First Presidency was more precise in 1969: "Negro[es]" should enjoy "full

69 2015 Utah SB 296; 2015 Utah SB 297. The Utah Legislature also passed a third bill about public education that some Utahns group together with the SB 296 and 297 as part of the Utah Compromise, 2015 HB 447.

70 Newell G. Bringhurst, Saints, Slaves, and Blacks: The Changing Place of Black People Within Mormonism 97–99 (1981).

71 Newell G. Bringhurst, *The Mormons and Slavery – A Closer Look*, 50 Pac. Hist. Rev. 329 (1981); Lester E. Bush Jr., *Mormonism's Negro Doctrine: A Historical Overview*, 8 Dialogue 54, 65–75 (Spring 1973).

72 *See* Bush, *supra* note 71, at 92.

Constitutional privileges," though "matters of faith, conscience, and theology are not within the purview of the civil law."[73]

On June 8, 1978, President Kimball, his Counselors, and the Quorum of the Twelve Apostles announced a new Revelation: God did *not* approve of the exclusion of persons of African descent from Mormon priesthood and Temple privileges.[74] The LDS leadership's official explanation makes it apparent that core Mormon doctrine evolved in parallel with America's constitutional culture.[75] It is noteworthy that once a public consensus formed against overt racial exclusions, revealed doctrine of the LDS leadership reversed course after 129 years.

Given the responsiveness of the LDS Church to evolving public attitudes toward racial exclusions, the *Obergefell* dissenters had a valid point about the coercive nature of constitutional culture. The dissenters feared that the constitutional culture that now accepts marriage equality for sexual and gender minorities is one that will pressure supporters of traditional marriage into conformity, much as some may read the Church's change in doctrine about race as LDS leaders being pressured into conformity with the constitutional culture of racial equality in the 1970s. The process of pressuring religious dissenters into changing their views has already commenced and will in fact proceed along the lines suggested by the *Obergefell* dissenters.[76] The transformation of religious practice and doctrine proceeds because of both external (constitutional culture) and internal (people within the Church) pressure.

Consider the LDS Church's support for Proposition 8, which created big rifts within the Church and Mormon families.[77] Meeting with California congregations outraged over the Church's arguments in the "Yes-on-8" campaign, Elder Marlin Jensen, the official LDS historian, tearfully apologized – something virtually unheard of in LDS history. In 2012, the Church created its own website, Mormonsandgays.org, which seeks to provide support for and

73 Statement of the First Presidency, Dec. 15, 1969, reprinted in CHURCH NEWS, Jan. 10, 1970, at 12.

74 ARMAND L. MAUSS, ALL ABRAHAM'S CHILDREN: CHANGING MORMON CONCEPTIONS OF RACE AND LINEAGE 231–36 (2003); Edward L. Kimball, *Spencer W. Kimball and the Revelation on Priesthood*, 47 BYU STUDIES ISSUE 2, at 40–59 (2008) (providing account of the evolving views held by President Kimball, the author's father).

75 Church of Jesus Christ of Latter-day Saints, *Race and the Priesthood* (Dec. 6, 2013), www.lds.org/topics/race-and-the-priesthood?lang=eng&_r=1 (viewed May 30, 2016).

76 Obergefell, *supra* note 54, at 2625–2626 (Roberts, C.J., dissenting).

77 *See* Stephanie Mencimer, *Mormon Church Abandons Its Crusade Against Gay Marriage*, MOTHER JONES (Apr. 12, 2013), www.motherjones.com/politics/2013/04/prop-8-mormons-gay-marriage-shift. (chronicling a family rift and quoting Matt Lawrence).

dialogue with gay Mormons. That the Church would even use the word "gays" rather than "persons afflicted with same-gender attraction," its long-preferred terminology, may be further evidence of a thaw.

On the other hand, the LDS Church has reaffirmed its commitment to traditional marriage. In early November 2015, within months of *Obergefell*, the Church revised its internal Handbook of Instruction to inform local congregations and their leaders that the now-legal "same-gender" marriages constitute an "apostasy" in violation of God's Word and that children raised in "same-gender" households cannot be baptized in the Church; youth aged eighteen years and older can be baptized only if they "disavow" their parents' apostasy.[78] This was an odd church response to marriage equality, in part because it was not the product of a deliberative process and consensus among the LDS leadership. More important, the Handbook's counsel that same-gender marriages are "apostasy" is quite striking: when a Mormon commits an "apostasy," such as same-sex marriage, he or she is subject to a mandatory disciplinary council; if a Mormon commits a "major transgression," such as attempted murder, rape, or spousal abuse, the Handbook blandly says that a disciplinary council "may be necessary." Is a committed relationship morally worse than murder or rape? Finally, the new handbook language threatens to encourage strife within lesbian and gay families and seems to punish children for the "apostasy" of their parents. Hundreds of Mormons have resigned their Church membership over this issue.[79]

Even as the Church struggles with issues of tolerance within its membership, it has taken a bold step in support of nondiscrimination in the public sphere in the form of the Utah Compromise.[80] Part of the Church's motivation was to address backlash for its aggressive support for Proposition 8.[81] In the wake of nasty Proposition 8 demonstrations, LDS leaders opened a discreet dialogue with Equality Utah, the umbrella LGBT rights group.[82] When Salt Lake City's Council in 2009 adopted an ordinance barring sexual orientation

78 *See* Jennifer Dobner, *New Mormon Policy Makes Apostates of Married Same-Sex Couples, Bars Children from Rites*, Salt Lake Trib. (Nov. 5, 2015).

79 Rich Kane, *Hundreds Rally Against New Mormon Policy; Many File Forms to Quit the Faith*, Salt Lake Trib. (Nov. 14, 2015), www.sltrib.com/home/3178894–155/hundreds-rally-against-new-mormon-policy.

80 Dennis Romboy, *LDS Church, LGBT Advocates Back Anti-Discrimination, Religious Rights Bill*, Deseret News (Mar. 4, 2015, 12:00 PM), www.deseretnews.com/article/865623399/Utah-lawmakers-unveil-anti-discrimination-religious-rights-legislation.html.

81 Jessica Garrison & Joanna Lin, *Prop. 8 Protesters Target Mormon Temple in Westwood*, L.A. Times (Nov. 7, 2008).

82 Jennifer Dobner, *Little-Known History Behind Utah's LGBT Nondiscrimination Law Recounted*, Salt Lake Trib. (Mar. 16, 2015).

discrimination in housing and employment, the Church was on board. It characterized the new ordinance as "fair and reasonable and [it] does not do violence to the institution of marriage," a surprisingly warm reception.[83] With these encouraging words from the LDS leadership, nineteen Utah municipalities adopted nondiscrimination ordinances modeled on the Salt Lake City one.[84] Gay-friendly legislators proposed statewide measures prohibiting sexual orientation discrimination in employment and services. In 2013, Republican Senator Steve Urquhart became the chief sponsor.[85] In 2014, Urquhart reintroduced the legislation and arranged a series of meetings among legislators, staff members, lesbian and gay families, and representatives of Equality Utah. While only a few legislators attended these meetings, they were transformed by them. One powerful Mormon Republican representative recalls learning how "these families looked just so much like my family – parents expressing their love for their children."[86] Other legislators learned from media attention and from conversations with their own children that LGBT persons were persecuted by bigots, sometimes turned out of their homes, and subject to pervasive employment and housing discrimination.

On January 22, 2015, a representative of the LDS Public Affairs Committee contacted the Utah Senate leadership, alerting them that the Church was prepared to endorse nondiscrimination legislation. At a press conference on January 27, 2015, Elders Dallin Oaks, Jeffrey Holland, and Todd Christofferson, as well as Sister Neill Marriott (Second Counselor of the LDS Young Women General Presidency), announced their support for state and federal legislation barring job and housing discrimination because of sexual orientation or gender identity, provided there are sufficient allowances for religious liberty.[87] The public endorsement by prominent LDS leaders made it much more likely that state nondiscrimination legislation would be enacted – so long as it contained sufficient allowances for religious freedom – a process in which Professor Robin Fretwell Wilson was instrumental. Negotiations between Equality Utah, the LGBT group, and Republican legislators also included discussions with LDS

83 Aaron Falk & Scott Taylor, *Mormon Church Supports Salt Lake City's Protections for Gay Rights*, Deseret News (Nov. 11, 2009), www.deseretnews.com/article/705343621/Mormon-church-supports-Salt-Lake-Citys-protections-for-gay-rights.html.

84 *See* Adams, Chapter 21, this volume.

85 Ben Winslow, *LGBT Non-Discrimination Bill Dies in the Legislature*, Fox13 (Mar. 11, 2013), http://fox13now.com/2013/03/11/lgbt-non-discrimination-bill-dies-in-the-legislature/.

86 Source on file with author.

87 *Transcript of News Conference on Religious Freedom and Nondiscrimination*, Newsroom (Jan. 27, 2015), www.mormonnewsroom.org/article/publicstatement-on-religious-freedom-and-nondiscrimination.

leaders and representatives. At one or two points, the Church broke logjams by encouraging the legislators to accommodate LGBT concerns.

For the most remarkable example, an early draft of SB 296, the nondiscrimination bill, would have created a special, separate set of protections for sexual and gender minorities, as well as a special, separate set of religious conscience allowances.[88] This was normal red state politics. Equality Utah insisted that this "separate but not equal" approach was not acceptable – and LDS leaders as well as academic experts quietly backed them up. The Utah Senate leadership immediately revised the bill to integrate sexual orientation and gender identity into the state's existing nondiscrimination statute.

Under ferocious time pressure, the GOP leadership, LDS officials, and Equality Utah worked out all of the points of dispute, as Senator Adams (Chapter 21, this volume) details. On March 12, 2015, Utah Governor Gary Herbert signed SB 296, the Antidiscrimination and Religious Freedom Amendments into the state nondiscrimination code.[89] Protections for religious conscience in a parallel bill were signed into law more quietly, in the Governor's office on March 20, 2015.[90] Together, the two measures, now law, combine job and housing protections for sexual and gender minorities with liberal allowances for religious persons and institutions. Although vigorously criticized by less-compromising supporters of traditional marriage and of LGBT rights, the 2015 legislation has largely been hailed on both sides as a step forward.[91]

Notwithstanding these remarkable developments, no one is saying that the Mormon theology of the gendered family has changed. Indeed, the June 29, 2015, Letter from the First Presidency, responding to *Obergefell*, explicitly reaffirmed the precepts contained in President Hinckley's *Proclamation*.[92] Will the Church ever soften its doctrine on LGBT families?

88 The discussion in text is based upon the author's telephone interviews with key players in the 2015 legislative negotiations.

89 SB 296, 61st Leg., Gen. Sess. (Utah 2015). The Governor also signed SB 297, which created a structure for marriage licenses that allowed local officials to opt out of these duties for conscience reasons.

90 Ben Winslow, *Governor Signs Bill Letting Clerks Opt Out of Same-Sex Marriages on Religious Grounds*, Fox 13 (Mar. 20, 2015), fox13now.com/2015/03/20/governor-signs-bill-letting-clerks-opt-out-of-same-sex-marriages-on-religious-grounds/.

91 *See* Jay Michaelson, *A Great Utah Compromise on LGBT Equality? There's No Such Thing*, Daily Beast (Mar. 13, 2015), www.thedailybeast.com/articles/2015/03/13/a-great-utah-compromise-on-lgbt-equality-there-s-no-such-thing.html; *The Utah Compromise: Needlessly Surrendering Freedom*, Alliance Defending Freedom, http://flfamily.org/wp-content/uploads/2016/02/Utah-Compromise-Needlessly-Surrendering-Freedom-ADF.pdf.

92 The Church of Jesus Christ of Latter-day Saints Press Release, *Church Leaders Counsel Members After Supreme Court Same-Sex Marriage Decision* (Jun. 30, 2015), www.mormon

As documented by Mormon historians such as Lester Bush, official doctrinal reaffirmations over many decades do not necessarily entrench doctrine in the LDS Church.[93] President Spencer Kimball's son reports that a primary reason for abandoning the Church's race-based exclusions was that the "American conscience was awakened to the centuries of injustice against blacks; the balance had tipped socially against racism and toward egalitarianism."[94] This kind of reason suggests a parallel between the rise and decline of Mormon race-based exclusions and the rise and possible decline of Mormon gender-based exclusions.

Most Mormons do not see much of a parallel. From their perspective, the Church's previous doctrines on racial exclusion were far from central to the LDS faith, while the gendered theology of the family is central to Mormon cosmology. In the longer term, however, one can imagine a more subtle doctrinal adjustment if social acceptance of LGBT families and marriages becomes entrenched.

Consider the Church's advice to single-parent families. Rather than condemning them as "apostates" whose lifestyles must be "disavowed," the Church says this: "Because of a variety of circumstances, including death, divorce, and separation, many Church members find themselves in single-parent families. Regardless of their family situation, all Church members are entitled to receive all the blessings of the gospel of Jesus Christ."[95] To be sure, the traditional LDS advice to women who become pregnant outside of wedlock is, first, to marry the father and, failing that, to arrange an adoption.[96] But the LDS Handbook invites unwed mothers to join the Relief Society, the association for Mormon women, and to participate in religious activities.[97] In 2012, Elder David Baxter, who was raised by a single mother, admonished local congregations to focus on the well-being of the single-parent family – the mother and the children – rather than pronouncing judgments on these children of God.[98] If the number of same-sex

newsroom.org/article/top-church-leaders-counsel-members-after-supreme-court-same-sex-marriage-decision.

93 Bush, *supra* note 71. 94 Kimball, *supra* note 74.

95 The Church of Jesus Christ of Latter-day Saints, *Single-Parent Families* (2006), www.lds.org/topics/single-parent-families?lang=eng&old=true.

96 LDS Family Services, *Adoption and the Unwed Mother*, ENSIGN (Feb. 2002) (summarizing LDS policy, reaffirmed by the First Presidency in 1998).

97 The Church of Jesus Christ of Latter-day Saints, HANDBOOK 2: ADMINISTERING THE CHURCH at 10.12.4 (2010), www.lds.org/handbook/handbook-2-administering-the-church/young-women/10.12.4?lang=eng#1012.

98 *See* Jane Edwards, *Has the LDS Church Changed Its Policy on Adoption?*, FIRST MOTHER FORUM (Sept. 29, 2013), www.firstmotherforum.com/2013/09/has-lds-church-changed-its-policies-on.html.

married Mormons proliferates and if those couples raise children responsibly and lovingly, it would be surprising if these families were not accepted by local Mormon congregations and tolerated by Salt Lake City.

Is there not another path that the Church might follow? In the wake of *Roe v. Wade*, some faith traditions (including the Mormons) became *more* dogmatically critical of abortions.[99] Might the LDS Church double down on issues of gender and sexuality? Might the Mormons expand the new handbook policy that treats "same-gender" marriages as "apostasy" to cleanse the Church entirely of openly gay persons or families? Such a strategy would be inconsistent with the sociology of a religion that is highly evangelical and cosmopolitan. Specifically, an exclusionary strategy would founder upon the phenomenon of "pop up homosexuals," or Mormon children who unexpectedly turn out to be LGBT. Such children are not going to become straight because their Church tells them this is God's sexual orientation, and many of those children will want families of their own. If these children are driven from the Church, their devout parents and siblings might leave as well. Disenchantment will deepen if young straight Mormons have friends, teachers, mentors, and relatives who are LGBT and come to see their Church as bigoted or cruel to people they love.

That LGBT people are popping up everywhere creates a big contrast between gay marriage and abortion.[100] At the same time that women choosing abortion have been retreating into the closet, gay Mormons and Mormon women working outside the home have been coming out of their closets. The more the Church is populated with wives working outside the home, husbands doing domestic work, and lesbian and gay congregants together with their extended families, the more internal pressure the Church will feel to soften doctrine. In this regard, the Church is no different from other faith traditions.[101]

99 Maggie Gallagher, *DOMA Ruling: Echoes of Roe v. Wade*, L.A. Times (June 27, 2013), http://articles.latimes.com/2013/jun/27/opinion/la-oe-gallagher-prop8-ruling-20130627; Alexander Dushku, *Culture, Law, and Religious Liberty*, BYU Magazine (Fall 2015), https://magazine.byu.edu/article/culture-law-and-religious-liberty/.

100 Michael C. Dorf, *"Shout Your Abortion" Movement Raises Questions About the "Coming Out" Analogy*, Verdict (Oct. 7, 2015), https://verdict.justia.com/2015/10/07/shout-your-abortion-movement-raises-questions-about-the-coming-out-analogy; Brief of Amicus Curiae Lambda Legal Defense and Education Fund, Inc., Whole Women's Health v. Hellerstedt, 136 S. Ct. 2292 (2016), www.lambdalegal.org/in-court/legal-docs/wwh_tx_20160104_amicus.

101 Pew Research Center, *Knowing Gays and Lesbians, Religious Conflicts, Beliefs about Homosexuality* (June 8, 2015), www.people-press.org/2015/06/08/section-2-knowing-gays-and-lesbians-religious-conflicts-beliefs-about-homosexuality/.

C Family and Constitutionalism

The most important lesson from the foregoing case study involves the relationship between the American family and our constitutional culture. Latter-day constitutionalism makes the family central to religious belief and to public constitutional culture. "Family" as a governance structure saturates American constitutionalism.

For example, "family" is famously at the center of our national understanding of the right to privacy – which protects marriage, parental rights, childrearing and education, contraception, abortion, and even sodomy.[102] The civil rights movement did not win complete formal equality under the Constitution until *Loving v. Virginia* ended state bans on interracial marriage,[103] and the gay rights movement won its greatest constitutional victory in *Obergefell*. With *Obergefell*, family also assumes a central place in the Court's jurisprudence of equal liberty.[104] Within this framework, Justice Kennedy situates "marriage" as central rather than fading: marriage for LGBT people, just as for straight people, is the choice Americans make that seeks to advance their possibilities for individual flourishing, for interpersonal connection, and for raising children.[105] Although Latter-day constitutionalism vigorously opposed the holding of *Obergefell*, much of its discussion about the governance values of marriage could have been penned by Mormon theologians.

Latter-day constitutionalism makes clear that equal citizenship for women is all about family in a deep and pervasive way. From a liberal point of view, the deepest roots of sexism stem from the gendered marital role of women as childbearing and domestic, and liberals read the Court's sex discrimination jurisprudence as assuring women freedom to structure their familial relationships. From this vantage, contraception and abortion are properly equal protection as well as liberty issues.[106] From the LDS point of view, in contrast, women's, or anybody's, equal citizenship does not allow them to take a human life, nor ought the Equal Protection Clause be interpreted to encourage women to avoid their familial destiny (i.e., procreative marriage).

Similarly, Latter-day constitutionalism reveals ways in which the First Amendment pervasively involves conceptions of the family. Today, the Free

[102] Ken Gormley, *One Hundred Years of Privacy*, 1992 Wis. L. Rev. 1335 (1992).

[103] For an insightful review of the pressures that result in Loving v. Virginia, *see* Kreis, Chapter 22, this volume.

[104] Obergefell, *supra* note 54, at 2593. [105] *Id.* at 2598–2602.

[106] Ruth Bader Ginsburg, *Some Thoughts on Autonomy and Equality in Relation to Roe v. Wade*, 63 N.C. L. Rev. 375 (1985); Goodwin, Chapter 3, this volume; Lipper, Chapter 5, this volume.

Exercise Clause's protection for religious minorities, such as the Mormons, often involves the minority's understanding of the family.[107] *Obergefell* assured religious parents believing traditional marriage is the only valid form of family that they would have every right to raise their children in their faith tradition. Do the First Amendment, the Due Process Clause, and federal or state Religious Freedom Restoration Acts *also* provide constitutional or statutory protection for parents who want to shield their children from public school instruction inconsistent with their denomination's theology of the family? This hard question is taken up across this volume.[108] Latter-day constitutionalism also enables us to apprehend Justice Samuel Alito's concerns in the gay marriage cases: nationwide marriage equality will defeat or marginalize traditionalist parents' different understanding of family because their children will see flourishing LGBT families in the media, in their communities, and in the classroom.

The best illustration of the First Amendment implications of Latter-day constitutionalism is *Boy Scouts of America v. Dale*,[109] where the Supreme Court overturned a state nondiscrimination law challenge to the Boy Scouts' LDS-inspired exclusion of gay scoutmasters. *Dale* is the Court's leading case on the First Amendment's right of expressive association – and it is centrally a case involving parental concerns about gay role models for their children – the LDS concern. But even *Dale* is a cautionary tale. In the wake of the Boy Scouts' constitutional victory, the organization faced an escalating social backlash, both within local troops and from outside scouting. In July 2015, the Boy Scouts voted to allow openly gay scoutmasters, but with local sponsoring organizations controlling those appointments.[110] The LDS Church and the Roman Catholic Church sponsor the largest number of local scout troops, and both have tentatively gone along with the local option compromise.[111]

The centrality of family to American constitutionalism is even deeper. To liberals, what is most striking about the Mormon theology of the family is its gendered feature – but to Mormons themselves what is most striking (after its divine inspiration) is its communitarian feature, the emphasis on each spouse's dedication of her and his energies to advancing the human race by

107 *E.g.*, Wisconsin v. Yoder, 406 U.S. 205 (1972).

108 *See, for example*, Dwyer, Chapter 8, this volume.

109 530 U.S. 640 (2000).

110 Todd Leopold, *Boy Scouts Change Policy on Gay Leaders*, CNN (July 28, 2015), www.cnn.com/2015/07/27/us/boy-scouts-gay-leaders-feat/.

111 Tad Walch, *LDS Church Will Continue Boy Scout Program*, Deseret News, Aug. 26, 2015, www.deseretnews.com/article/865635368/LDS-Church-will-continue-Boy-Scout-program.html.

procreation and then advancing the interests of their children through constant self-sacrifice.[112] Each perspective on the LDS theology of the family provides deep insights about larger constitutional issues.

Start with the liberal perspective. Latter-day constitutionalism reveals, more starkly than most other constitutional discourses, the interaction of sexuality, gender, and the law. Recall Elder Oaks's central theological objection to marriage equality for LGBT persons in 1984: "Homosexual marriages are wholly deviant to the patriarchal family."[113] From a liberal point of view, this is an argument *in favor of* marriage equality, a point suggested by *Obergefell*'s linkage of gay people's freedom to marry with the feminist critique of traditional marriage rules, such as coverture, and with the Court's sex discrimination jurisprudence.[114] The Mormon theology of the family makes clear that the stakes of the marriage equality debate involve *both* sexuality *and* gender – and that the two features are related. That is, a deep normative objection to homosexual intimacy is that it is intrinsically non-procreative and is inconsistent with the supposed centrality of gender differentiation to intimate relationships (and beyond).[115]

Looking forward, gay and lesbian persons or groups will be challenging discriminatory policies under the Equal Protection Clause. Although its holding rests upon the fundamental right to marry, *Obergefell* will be cited in support of heightened scrutiny for sexual orientation classifications.[116] LGBT advocates should simultaneously make a pitch that most discriminations affecting this group are also sex discriminations, the argument for LGBT rights that has now been accepted by the EEOC as the grounds for interpreting Title VII to bar job discrimination against gay as well as transgender employees.[117] It appears that the Trump Administration is trying to walk back policies

[112] Obergefell, *supra* note 54, at 2630 (Scalia, J., dissenting) (adverting to the liberty-sacrificing features of marriage).

[113] Oaks, PRINCIPLES, *supra* note 31, at 18.

[114] Obergefell, *supra* note 54, at 2595–96, 2603–04; Nan D. Hunter, *Marriage, Law, and Gender: A Feminist Inquiry*, 1 LAW & SEXUALITY 9 (1991) (describing coverture, which is the legal doctrine that treated a woman's property as her husband's while married).

[115] On the links between homophobia and sexism, *see* Adrienne Rich, *Compulsory Heterosexuality and Lesbian Existence, reprinted in* BLOOD, BREAD, AND POETRY: SELECTED PROSE 23–75 (1986).

[116] *See* Henderson v. Adams, Case No. 1:15-cv-00220 (S.D. Ind. 2016); Board of Education of the Highland Local School District v. U.S. Dept. of Education, Case No. 2:16-CV-524 (S.D. Ohio 2016).

[117] Macy v. Holder, EEOC Doc. 0120120821, 2012 WL 1435995 (2012) (gender identity as sex discrimination); Complainant v. McHugh, EEOC DOC 0120133395, 2015 WL 1607756 (2015) (sexual orientation as sex discrimination).

developed in the Obama Administration extending sex discrimination bans to encompass sexual orientation and gender identity.[118]

A further lesson of Latter-day constitutionalism is that a great deal of post-*Obergefell* discrimination now will be *relational*: public as well as private employers and other institutions will be said to discriminate by not recognizing same-sex relationships on the same terms as they recognize different-sex relationships.[119] Thus, the LDS's Brigham Young University does not offer married student housing to same-sex married couples (including couples married in Utah), though it does offer university housing to different-sex married couples and to single lesbian and gay students.[120] So the discrimination is not that gay people cannot secure student housing – but is instead that gay students in a same-sex marriage cannot secure such housing under circumstances where straight married students can. This discrimination does not violate the new Utah nondiscrimination statute, which exempts student housing from its coverage[121] – but it might violate Title IX, a federal statute barring universities receiving federal funds from discriminating on account of sex, depending on how capaciously courts interpret the protection given to religious universities under Title IX to follow its "religious tenets."[122]

In contrast, consider the Church's communitarian perspective. Although resting on Scripture, the LDS theology offers a vision of marriage and family grounded in public policy.[123] The Mormon theory of the family is rooted in the norm of self-sacrifice for the benefit of others. Backed up by religious, social, and state sanctions, marriage is a commitment mechanism, whereby the spouses each give up personal freedoms to create a public good – procreation that perpetuates the human race, and then rearing the procreated children in an environment that provides a time-tested good structure for them.[124] Contrary to the Supreme Court's depiction of a right to marry as resting upon

118 *See* Kevin McGowan, *Will Trump Administration Retreat on LGBT Protections?*, Daily Labor Report, BNA (Feb. 16, 2017), www.bna.com/trump-administration-retreat-n57982083898/.

119 Douglas NeJaime, *Marriage Inequality: Same-Sex Relationships, Religious Exemptions, and the Production of Sexual Orientation Discrimination*, 100 Calif. L. Rev. 1169 (2012).

120 Barbara Christiansen, *BYU Doesn't Anticipate Changes from Same-Sex Marriage Ruling*, Daily Herald (June 26, 2015).

121 Utah Code Ann. § 57-21-5 (West 2015).

122 *See generally* Robin Fretwell Wilson, *Squaring Faith and Sexuality in Religious Institutions: The Unique Challenge of Sports*, 34 Law and Inequality: A Journal of Theory and Practice 385 (2016) (reviewing scope of protections under Title IX and cases construing them).

123 *See* United States v. Windsor, 133 S. Ct. 2675, 2711 (2013) (Alito, J., dissenting).

124 The Church of Jesus Christ of Latter-day Saints, Newsroom, *The Divine Institution of Marriage*, www.mormonnewsroom.org/article/the-divine-institution-of-marriage.

and enhancing *freedom* and *liberty*, the Mormon theory of marriage rests upon *responsibility* and *duty* and is liberty sacrificing. As Wilson (Chapter 16, this volume) shows empirically, many religiously married couples approach marriage as a source of obligation, but one that brings them closer to God and is, for them, protective and more satisfying. "Marriage" cannot be understood without apprehending both the liberal view and the communitarian view.

The Mormons' communitarian focus on *virtuous families* stands in striking contrast to *Obergefell*'s individualist focus on *hedonic families* formed to maximize spousal happiness. Thus, the deep LDS critique of Justice Kennedy's *Obergefell* opinion is that its focus on individual liberty is wrong; the essential point of marriage is not so much libertarian as it is liberty sacrificing. As the four states defending constitutional marriage bans in *Obergefell* argued, the reason they vest marriage with so many benefits and rewards, as well as limits on spousal liberties, is that procreative marriage serves society in a big way.[125] An underemphasized feature of the LDS theology is the notion that gendered marriage contributes to the possibility of unselfish, liberty-denying conduct on the part of spouses in ways that nongendered marriage does not.

It is hard to credit this claim when the lesbian and gay couples who have sought the right to marry have been models of self-sacrifice and community building. For example, April DeBoer and Jayne Rowse, the Michigan couple in *Obergefell*, are raising five adopted children in a female household that is the epitome of the virtuous family.[126] Gender differentiation is not the big variable that makes virtuous, nurturing families more likely. Education and wealth are more likely to be key variables for the flourishing of a stable marriage or family unit, although role-divided families are sometimes less fragile than others.[127] As with most issues of family law, however, the empirical evidence is far from conclusive that the Mormon view is wrong – and LDS-dominated Utah codifies the precepts of traditional marriage more than almost any other state, and it enjoys a flourishing family culture.[128]

125 Brief of Respondents, Tanco v. Haslam, No. 14-562 at 38-39 (2015); Brief for the Respondents, Bourke v. Beshear, No. 14-574 at 29-30 (2015).

126 Obergefell, *supra* note 54.

127 Naomi Cahn & June Carbone, Red Families v. Blue Families: Legal Polarization and the Creation of Culture (2010); W. Bradford Wilcox & Nicholas Zill, *Red State Families: Better than We Knew* Am. Enter. Inst. (June 11, 2015); W. Bradford Wilcox, *Unequal, Unfair, and Unhappy: The 3 Biggest Myths About Marriage Today*, The Atlantic (June 3, 2013), www.theatlantic.com/sexes/archive/2013/06/unequal-unfair-and-unhappy-the-3-biggest-myths-about-marriage-today/276468/.

128 *See 2017 Family Prosperity Index*, Family Prosperity Initiative (Feb. 16, 2017), familyprosperity.org/blog/2017/02/2017-family-prosperity-index (Utah is number one state for family well-being).

Latter-day constitutionalism poses a set of empirical questions that might be explored in the wake of *Obergefell*. As a statistical matter, does marriage equality "cause" increases in non-marital births and child rearing? Does it have a deleterious effect on the levels of commitment and self-sacrifice of parents to their children? If marriage equality really does impose a communitarian cost upon American families, Latter-day constitutionalism ought to propound new policy initiatives, such as some form of covenant marriage.[129] And American legislators and judges ought to be attentive not only to new initiatives but also to the consequences for the family of feel-good legislation to "get the government out of marriage" after *Obergefell*.[130]

CONCLUSION

Ultimately, the agenda for Latter-day constitutionalism in the post-*Obergefell* era ought to be how to improve the family-based setting for the benefit of children, hard questions engaged by Weiner (Chapter 11, this volume) and others elsewhere in this volume. If marriage is the best setting, how might more couples be persuaded to get married and to raise children in a marital setting? If it is not the best setting, how does the state protect families as it finds them? What policy strategy helps lower rates of dissolution so children spend more of their lives with two committed parents? If Latter-day constitutionalism makes genuine progress on these issues, America needs to listen.

129 Three states – Arkansas, Arizona, and Louisiana – recognize a form of marriage known as "covenant marriage." Mark Baer, *The Problem With Covenant Marriages And Fault-Based Divorce*, Huffington Post Blog (Nov. 6, 2014, 6:05 PM), www.huffingtonpost.com/mark-baer/the-problem-with-covenant_b_6110600.html. Covenant marriages require couples to undergo premarital counseling and restrict the grounds for divorce to what is essentially fault-grounds, eliminating many common reasons for divorce, such as emotional and financial abuse. "For example, 'in Arkansas, a couple may seek divorce only for the following reasons: (1) Adultery by the other spouse; (2) Commission of a felony or other infamous crime by the other spouse; and (3) Physical or sexual abuse of the spouse or of a child of either spouse.'" While proponents see covenant marriage as a way to stabilize marriage, few people have elected the additional obligations after it became available. Katherine Shaw Spaht, *Postmodern Marriage As Seen Through the Lens of the ALI's "Compensatory Payments" in* Reconceiving the Family 249, 265 (Robin Fretwell Wilson ed., 2006).

130 *See* Wilson, Chapter 16, this volume (charting the introduction of such measures in statehouses across America).

PART VII

INTERNATIONAL PERSPECTIVES

24

The Future of Marriage in Secular Societies

Patrick N. Parkinson

Professor of Law, University of Sydney

In the United States, and around the world, the relationship between religion and government continues to be hotly debated, as the opening chapters of this volume illustrate.[1] To the extent that the traditional view of marriage as being between a man and a woman reflects religious beliefs and values, those values no longer hold as much sway in the public square as they once did.

It is typical of U.S. constitutional law, so dominated as it is by the rhetoric of individual and minority group rights, that these major decisions on the relationship of law and religion rely upon a rights discourse. In *Obergefell v. Hodges*, the U.S. Supreme Court did not seek to redefine a fundamental social institution, but rather to insist that intimate personal relationships between two persons of the same gender could not be excluded from eligibility for the status of marriage, with all the attendant support the state gives marriage.[2] In the process, though, marriage law came to no longer reflect a still-prevailing Judeo-Christian understanding of the institution.[3] The emergence of a right to same-sex marriage across the country as a consequence of *Obergefell v. Hodges*[4] brought about a complete divorce of Church and State in one of the few areas where there was, until some years ago, common ground.[5]

1 *See* Helfand, Chapter 2, this volume; Sepper, Chapter 1, this volume; Goodwin, Chapter 3, this volume; Rienzi, Chapter 4, this volume.

2 Obergefell v. Hodges, 135 S. Ct. 2584 (2015) (holding that "[u]nder the Constitution, same-sex couples seek in marriage the same legal treatment as opposite-sex couples, and it would disparage their choices and diminish their personhood to deny them this right").

3 *See* Introduction, this volume (showing that a slim majority of Americans still believe marriage is a fundamentally religious institution).

4 *See* Adams, Chapter 21, this volume.

5 Because same-sex marriage was recognized nowhere in the United States until 2003, and nowhere in the world before 2001, religious views of marriage and civil ones aligned. *See* Goodridge v. Department of Public Health, 798 N.E.2d 941 (Mass. 2003); Nancy G. Maxwell, *Opening Civil Marriage to Same-Gender Couples: A Netherlands-United States Comparison*, 18 Ariz. J. Int'l & Comp. L. 141, 157 (2001).

This could be seen as an aspect of the process of secularization in which government policy is based on "public," "neutral," or "secular" reasons rather than the "comprehensive doctrines" of particular religious and nonreligious worldviews.[6] In the modern secular state, if there is a value system or core set of beliefs, it is often to be found in human rights jurisprudence rather than a shared cultural or religious heritage.

There has been a similar secularization of marriage as a matter of constitutional law in Australia, but this has occurred as a consequence of a fundamental redefinition of marriage, rather than beliefs about human rights or equality before the law. In the Australian Constitution, the federal Parliament has the power to make laws concerning marriage.[7] At the time the Constitution was enacted, the English common law defined marriage in terms of Christian teaching. That definition was given in a famous judgment of Sir James Wilde (who later became Lord Penzance) in the 1866 case of *Hyde v Hyde and Woodmansee*.[8] The case concerned the validity of a potentially polygamous marriage entered into by members of the Mormon faith. The judge held that such a marriage would not be recognized in the English common law. Marriage, he said, is "a union for life of one man and one woman to the exclusion of all others, as understood in Christendom."[9] That left no room for polygamy. It also did not allow for same-sex marriage, although such a union could hardly have been in contemplation at the time.

Australia's High Court, the ultimate court of appeal, held in 2013 that this definition does not apply to the word "marriage" in the federal Constitution.[10] The Court observed that marriage had had different meanings and characteristics at different stages of history and in different cultures, and that marriage in some cultures involved polygamy. The Court wrote: "The status of marriage, the social institution which that status reflects, and

6 John Rawls, Political Liberalism (2005); *see also* David Oppenheimer, Alvaro Oliveira, & Aaron Blumenthal, *Religiosity and Same-Sex Marriage in the United States and Europe* 32 Berkeley J. Int'l L. 195 (2014) (discussing secularism and support for same-sex marriage).

7 Australian Constitution s.51(xxi).

8 Hyde v. Hyde and Woodmansee, (1866) L.R. 1 P. & D. 130.

9 *Id.* at 133.

10 Commonwealth v. Australian Capital Territory (2013) 250 CLR 441 (Austl.). The issue arose because the Australian Capital Territory ("ACT"), where Canberra is located, enacted a law allowing for same-sex marriage. The High Court had to determine whether doing so was inconsistent with the federal Marriage Act 1961. The High Court held, unanimously, that it was inconsistent and therefore invalid. It decided that because the word "marriage" in the Constitution could be interpreted to allow for same-sex marriage, the ACT's law intruded onto a field that was exclusive to the federal Parliament.

the rights and obligations which attach to that status never have been, and are not now, immutable."[11]

The Court offered a new and secular definition of marriage for the purposes of constitutional law that allows for both same-sex marriage and polygamy:

> Once it is accepted that "marriage" can include polygamous marriages, it becomes evident that the juristic concept of "marriage" cannot be confined to a union having the characteristics described in *Hyde v Hyde* and other nineteenth century cases. Rather, "marriage" is to be understood in [Section]51(xxi) of the Constitution as referring to a consensual union formed between natural persons in accordance with legally prescribed requirements which is not only a union the law recognises as intended to endure and be terminable only in accordance with law but also a union to which the law accords a status affecting and defining mutual rights and obligations.[12]

The decision did not introduce same-sex marriage in Australia. Instead, it established that, should the federal Parliament choose to do so, it *could* enact a law for same-sex marriage or to recognize polygamy and that this power to legislate was exclusive to the federal Parliament. In doing so, the decision made it clear that the secular constitution was not constrained by a Judeo-Christian worldview. The Parliament has now passed a same-sex marriage law.

Can marriage survive this divorce from its Judeo-Christian meaning? Asking this is not the same as asking whether marriage can survive same-sex marriage. The arguments on whether allowing same-sex marriage will have any effect on heterosexual unions have raged for some time.[13] This chapter seeks to explore a much broader question, of which the recognition of same-sex marriage is just a part – can marriage, in the form we know it, survive its conceptual separation from its religious and cultural roots? In a secularized world, will the entry into and exit from marriage continue to be regulated by law other than in terms of maintaining an evidentiary record of relationships?[14]

[11] *Id.* at 456. [12] *Id.* at 461.

[13] *See, e.g.*, Lynn Wardle, *Is Marriage Obsolete?* 10 MICH. J. GENDER & L. 189 (2003); M. V. Lee Badgett, *Will Providing Marriage Rights to Same-Sex Couples Undermine Heterosexual Marriage?* 1 SEXUALITY RESEARCH & SOC. POL'Y 1 (2004); Mircea Trandafir, *The Effect of Same-Sex Marriage Laws on Different-Sex Marriage: Evidence From The Netherlands*, 51 DEMOGRAPHY 317 (2014).

[14] The merits of this have been argued elsewhere. *See* Eric Clive, *Marriage: An Unnecessary Legal Concept? in* MARRIAGE AND COHABITATION IN CONTEMPORARY SOCIETIES 71 (J. Eekelaar & S.N. Katz eds., 1980). For essays debating the abolition of the status of marriage entirely, *see* MARRIAGE PROPOSALS: QUESTIONING A LEGAL STATUS (Anita Bernstein ed., 2006).

I LEGAL MARRIAGE AND THE RISE OF INFORMAL COHABITATION

Putting aside those jurisdictions that retain a notion of "common law marriage,"[15] the distinction between legal (*de jure*) marriage and informal cohabitation around the Western world rests on four differences. First, legal marriage requires a celebrant who witnesses the couple's exchange of promises and pronounces them to be married at the conclusion of that exchange. Second, legal marriage requires registration of that union in the jurisdiction's official records. Third, to formally terminate a legal marriage, a State official – almost invariably a judge or someone acting on behalf of the court – must pronounce a divorce. Fourth, most jurisdictions recognize differences in terms of the incidents or legal effects of legal marriage as opposed to informal cohabitation. These may include differences in the division of property after the marriage breakdown, maintenance or alimony obligations, and rights *vis-à-vis* the state that are consequent upon marital status (such as survivor benefits for spouses) that have not been extended to informal cohabitation.

A *The Demise of Legal Marriage*

Legal marriage, once the only accepted context for sexual relations and the raising of children in Western countries, has long ceased to be central to people's sexual or reproductive lives in many parts of the world.[16] Although marriage remains the most common form of couple relationship within Western and Northern Europe, the gap between marriage and cohabitation as a family form is narrowing. Figures from 2006 show that in France, 26% of adults between ages 18 and 49 were cohabiting, while 39% were married. In Sweden, 25% were cohabiting and 37% were married.[17] In the United Kingdom in 2011, 22% of adults aged 20 to 34 were cohabiting, while 32% were married.[18]

In the U.S., marriage is increasingly stratified by reference to educational level. The percentage of adults aged 25 to 60 with four years of high school education but no college education in first marriages fell from 73% in the

[15] *See* Section III.E *infra* for a discussion of common-law marriage.

[16] Ron Lesthaeghe, *The Unfolding Story of the Second Demographic Transition*, 36 POP. & DEV. REV. 211 (2010).

[17] Child Trends, *World Family Map, 2014: Mapping Family Change and Child Wellbeing Outcomes* 15 (2014), worldfamilymap.org/2014/wp-content/uploads/2014/04/WFM-2014-Final-LoResWeb.pdf.

[18] *Id.*

1970s to 45% in the 2000s, a 28% decline.[19] While rates of marriage have declined for people of all educational levels, the rate of decline has been least among college-educated people, a "marriage gap" that compounds the effects of less education and income.[20]

Perhaps the lowest rates of marriage are in Latin America, where "consensual unions" have long been common in indigenous and poor communities.[21] In recent years, the practice has spread to the middle and upper classes.[22] In the Dominican Republic, Panama, Honduras, Nicaragua, Peru, Colombia, and Uruguay, the proportion of consensual unions is higher than for marriages among women in partnerships aged 15 to 49.[23]

B Childrearing Outside Marriage

Not only has there been a decline in marriage as the basis for an intimate adult relationship, it has also ceased to be the dominant context for childrearing. In 2013, nearly 41% of all births in the U.S. were outside of marriage, with some demographic groups recording even higher rates of non-marital births.[24] Figures show that 71.5% of all births to African American mothers were non-marital, as were 53.2% of all births to Hispanic mothers.[25] In many parts of Europe, rates of non-marital births are also high. Indeed, in the European Union, the share of non-marital births has been on the rise in recent years in almost every member state.[26] In some countries, the majority of live births are outside marriage. In 2011, for example, Estonia (59.7%), Slovenia (56.8%), Bulgaria (56.1%), France (55.8%), and Sweden (54.3%) all witnessed a majority of births occurring outside marriage, while in Belgium the figure was

[19] THE STATE OF OUR UNIONS, WHEN MARRIAGE DISAPPEARS: THE NEW MIDDLE AMERICA 21 (Bradley Wilcox & Elizabeth Marquardt eds., 2010).

[20] *Id.*; Leah Ward Sears, *Brennan Lecture: The "Marriage Gap": A Case For Strengthening Marriage in the 21st Century*, 82 N.Y.U L. REV. 1243 (2007).

[21] Teresa Castro-Martín, *Consensual Unions in Latin America: Persistence of a Dual Nuptiality System*, 33 J. COMP. FAM. STUD. 35 (2002).

[22] Benoît Laplante et al., *Childbearing within Marriage and Consensual Union in Latin America, 1980–2010*, 41 POP. & DEV. REV. 85 (2015).

[23] *Id.* at 88.

[24] U.S. Dept. Health & Hum. Servs., NATIONAL VITAL STATISTICS REPORTS 64(1), *Births: Final Data for 2013*, www.cdc.gov/nchs/data/nvsr/nvsr64/nvsr64_01.pdf.

[25] *Id.*

[26] *Europe in Figures – Eurostat Yearbook 2011: Population*, EUROSTAT (Dec. 19, 2011), ec.europa .eu/eurostat/en/web/products-statistical-books/-/CH_02_2011.

50.0%.[27] The highest rate of non-marital births in Europe is in Iceland at 65% of all births.[28]

More than half of these non-marital births across Europe are in cohabiting unions, although there are significant variations between countries.[29] Moreover, many children are being born to single mothers outside of any cohabiting relationship. For example, in Ireland 35% of all births occur outside marriage. Of these, nearly half (45%) are to single mothers without the other parent in the home – comprising nearly 16% of all Irish births.[30] This fraction mirrors the figure in Britain.[31] In the U.S., between 2006 and 2010, 24% of first births were to women who were neither married nor cohabiting.[32] While many in the same-sex–attracted community have placed a very high value on the legal right to marry[33] – whether or not they choose this status for themselves – marriage has become increasingly irrelevant to the intimate partnerships of heterosexual couples.[34] In part, this reflects the very trends that have led many countries to accept same-sex marriage. Marriage is being redefined in secular Western societies through the prism of individualism,[35] just as it was in *Obergefell v. Hodges*. The historic Judeo-Christian consensus has been that marriage has a religious and cultural meaning that transcends personal choice. That is, it is not enough that two people choose to join in an intimate partnership. In traditional Christian teaching, they must, of course, be of different genders and be old enough to enter into matrimony; but they must also accept a partnership that is sexually exclusive and, in principle, for life. Thus, while in Judeo-Christian thought, a marriage is to be freely entered,

27 *EU Employment and Social Situation Quarterly Review: March 2013 Special Supplement on Demographic Trends*, EUR. COM. (2013), http://ec.europa.eu/eurostat/documents/3217494/5775829/KE-BH-13-0S2-EN.PDF/e99e7095-df33-42ee-9429-626e04ddec11.

28 *See supra* note 26. 29 *Id.* 30 *Id.*

31 Office of National Statistics, *Statistical Bulletin: Live Births in England and Wales by Characteristics of Mother 1*, U.K. OFFICE NAT'L STATS. (2012), www.ons.gov.uk/peoplepopulationandcommunity/birthsdeathsandmarriages/livebirths/bulletins/livebirthsinenglandandwalesbycharacteristicsofmother1/previousReleases.

32 U.S. Dept. Health & Hum. Servs., (2012), *Fertility of Men and Women Aged 15–44 Years in the United States: National Survey of Family Growth, 2006–2010*, 51 NATIONAL HEALTH STATISTICS REPORTS 9, www.cdc.gov/nchs/data/nhsr/nhsr051.pdf.

33 Suzanne Goldberg, *Why Marriage? in* MARRIAGE AT THE CROSSROADS: LAW, POLICY, AND THE BRAVE NEW WORLD OF TWENTY-FIRST-CENTURY FAMILIES 224 (Marsha Garrison & Elizabeth Scott, eds., 2012).

34 Kathleen Kiernan, *The Rise of Cohabitation and Childbearing Outside Marriage in Western Europe*, 15 INT. J. L. POL. FAM. 1 (2001); ANNE BARLOW ET AL., COHABITATION, MARRIAGE AND THE LAW: SOCIAL CHANGE AND LEGAL REFORM IN THE 21ST CENTURY (2005).

35 Paul Amato, *Institutional, Companionate, and Individualistic Marriages, in* MARRIAGE AT THE CROSSROADS: LAW, POLICY, AND THE BRAVE NEW WORLD OF TWENTY-FIRST-CENTURY FAMILIES 107 (Marsha Garrison & Elizabeth Scott eds., 2012).

the rights and obligations to which marriage gives rise are externally derived from religious values. Understood this way, marriage has typically offered only a standard form contract on a take-it or leave-it basis concerning the duration and exclusivity of the commitment.

Over time, the terms of that contract have progressively weakened.[36] The exclusivity of the marital relationship used to be enforced by criminal prohibitions on adultery, which was also a ground for divorce. Criminal offences based on adultery have all but disappeared in liberal democracies, and in many countries divorce is now a unilateral choice that may be exercised by a party to a marriage without attribution of blame.[37] Additionally, over time the idea that marriage is to be lasting has been seriously compromised by the ease with which a divorce may be obtained. The law no longer provides support for the standard form contract regarding duration and exclusivity.

What, then, is the future of marriage? In answering this question, it is important to differentiate between marriage as a religious and cultural tradition and marriage as a legal institution. There is no reason to believe that marriage, as a religious tradition, will not continue; for, at least among adherents to Judaism, Christianity, and Islam, a public and religiously sanctioned marriage remains important. To the extent that religion and culture are closely intertwined, many will also marry because it is a cultural expectation – even if they are not themselves deeply religious.[38] People will still commit to each other and will register their marriages if required by law.

But what about secular forms of marriage that are not reflective of a particular religious or cultural tradition? The demise of marriage and the increase in the number of children born outside marriage across Europe and North America suggest that among those who do not have strong religious and cultural reasons to marry, legal marriage is already declining rapidly as a cultural norm.

II RELIGIOUS HERITAGE AND THE NEED FOR A CELEBRANT

One major feature that distinguishes legal marriage from informal cohabitation in the formation of the relationship is the need for a celebrant to pronounce the couple as married. A private exchange of vows, even before

[36] Mary Ann Glendon, The New Family and the New Property (1981).

[37] *See* Carl Schneider, *Moral Discourse and the Transformation of American Family Law*, 83 Mich. L. Rev. 1803, 118 (1985) (discussing legal and moral shifts in U.S. family law).

[38] Wilson, Chapter 16, this volume (arguing that civilly married couples benefit from the continued overlap between civil and religious marriage, which reinforces positive norms around marriage, including monogamy and fidelity).

hundreds of witnesses at a large and expensive ceremony, does not suffice to marry the couple unless there is a state-authorized celebrant in whose presence those vows are exchanged.[39]

Why is this? And can, or should, such a requirement survive secularization? Is there any rational basis for why weddings should involve the government at all, other than for registration? Does the government have any legitimate interest in being present at the wedding ceremony? In practical terms, the government has no role to play in religious weddings, other than licensing marriages and imposing various requirements that are preliminary to the celebration. Is there any reason why there should be a state-directed celebrant for civil marriages?

As will be seen, the only explanation for having a celebrant is that it is a secular imitation of Christian tradition, especially as it developed around the 12th century onward in Europe. This notion of marriage as a public event with a celebrant who represents God does not have a pre-Christian history, nor does its plagiarized secular counterpart: a wedding conducted by a state official.

A Marriage in Roman Law

In Roman law, marriage was based only on consent – the consent of the couple, and the consent of a paterfamilias. As Professor Susan Treggiari explains:

> The essential characteristic of Roman marriage was the consent of each partner. (If there was a paterfamilias, his consent at the initiation of the marriage was also required: for a daughter his consent might be assumed unless he evidently dissented.) Consent was signified at the beginning of a marriage. There was no prescribed form of words or action or written contract which had to be used at all weddings. Nor did any priest or public official act as president or witness of a ceremony.[40]

No religious figure, lawyer, or public official was involved in divorce either, and no public record was kept of divorce.[41] Professor Max Rheinstein has aptly described marriage, in Roman and Greek thought, as "a secular affair,

[39] Adams, Chapter 21, this volume (discussing solemnization by authorized celebrants under state law).

[40] Susan Treggiari, *Divorce Roman Style: How Easy and How Frequent Was It? in* MARRIAGE, DIVORCE AND CHILDREN IN ANCIENT ROME 32–33 (Beryl Rawson ed., 1991); *see also* H. F. JOLOWICZ, HISTORICAL INTRODUCTION TO THE STUDY OF ROMAN LAW 113 (2d ed. 1967).

[41] Treggiari, *supra* note 40, at 36; LEAGE'S ROMAN PRIVATE LAW 98–114 (A. M. Pritchard, ed., 3d ed. 1967).

a contract, that, like any other, was concluded by the consent of the parties and that could be terminated even more easily than a commercial contract, namely, by the will of just one of the participants."[42] That is not to say that marriage was entirely without ceremony. There might well have been some ritual ceremony of crossing the threshold, and gifts might have been presented.[43]

Through the influence of the Church, marriage was gradually transformed from a secular affair to a sacred institution, but its evolution from private agreement to religious sacrament was a very slow one, as the next subsection shows.

B Canon Law Rules of Marriage

Through Christian influences, marriage eventually came to be seen as indissoluble, and the Church itself asserted jurisdiction in matrimonial matters.[44] In Church law, as applied throughout those parts of Europe under the spiritual governance of Rome prior to the Reformation, marriage was seen as a matter of private contract. The basic rules were formulated by Pope Alexander III (1159–81), who synthesized the canon law rules. Marriage could be entered into by consent through *verba de praesenti* – that is, words uttered by each of the parties evincing a present intent to marry – or *verba de futuro subsequente copula* – a promise to marry in the future that was consummated by sexual intercourse. The minimum age for capacity to marry was fourteen for boys and twelve for girls. From a theological perspective, capacity and consent were all that were required to make the marriage valid.[45]

However, canon law drew a distinction between the requirements for the validity of a marriage and the evidence needed to prove the existence of a marriage. That proof, provided by having witnesses, was needed for a great variety of reasons – in the event of a dispute between the parties about whether there was a marriage; in the event of some uncertainty affecting, for example, the legitimacy of children, property rights, or inheritance issues; and as the

42 Max Rheinstein, Marriage Stability, Divorce, and the Law 2 (1972).

43 Mary Ann Glendon, The Transformation of Family Law 17 (1989) [hereinafter Glendon, Transformation]; *See also* John Witte, From Sacrament to Contract: Marriage, Religion, and Law in the Western Tradition (2d ed. 2012).

44 Glendon, Transformation, *supra* note 43, at 23–31.

45 Charles Donahue, *The Canon Law on the Formation of Marriage and Social Practice in the Later Middle Ages*, J. Fam. Hist. 144 (1983).

precondition for ecclesiastical courts to be able to punish adultery and other moral wrongs.[46]

Pope Innocent III decreed in the 13th century that two persons witness the exchange of consents.[47] The Church encouraged a form of wedding that included a priestly blessing and nuptial mass.[48] Clandestine marriages were, at various times and places, strongly discouraged; indeed, penalties might be applied.[49] A marriage that was not entered into in the presence of a priest might be regarded as illicit, and the parties would need to do penance.[50]

C The Need for a Celebrant

Eventually, the position came to be established that a marriage required formalities that went beyond private consent. In countries with a Roman Catholic heritage, this development can be traced to the Decree Tametsi of the Council of Trent, promulgated in 1563. The Church therein decreed that, for a marriage to be valid, there needed to be three witnesses, one of whom had to be the parish priest of one of the parties; and there had to be an announcement about the prospective marriage beforehand, known as "publishing the banns of marriage."[51] The notion that a marriage could be contracted by *verba de praesenti* in private survived these reforms to some extent, but only as a form of contract to marry. If proven, the ecclesiastical courts would order the couple to solemnize their marriage in Church.[52]

The requirement for a celebrant also came to be established in Protestant countries in the 16th century. One of the major concerns that led to strict regulation of marriages was a concern about clandestine marriages, entered

46 These courts were often called the "bawdy courts" because their jurisdiction was to police bastardy and sexual immorality. *See* Eleanor Fox & Martin Ingram, *Bridewell, Bawdy Courts and Bastardy in Early Seventeenth-century London*, *in* COHABITATION AND NON-MARITAL BIRTHS IN ENGLAND AND WALES, 1600–2012 (Rebecca Probert ed., 2014).

47 LAWRENCE STONE, ROAD TO DIVORCE 52 (1990).

48 Donahue, *supra* note 45, at 146.

49 In the 12th century, for example, Pope Alexander III excommunicated those who contracted clandestine marriages. *See* John De Reeper, *The History and Application of Canon 1098*, 14 THE JURIST 148, 153–54 (1954).

50 Richard H. Helmolz, *Recurrent Patterns of Family Law*, 8 HARV. J. L. & PUB. POL. 175, 178 (1985).

51 While the Decree Tametsi established the need for a priestly celebrant in countries where Roman Catholicism was the religion of the State, this rule was not universal. It was not applicable for Catholics in Protestant lands, where priests might not be available. For these believers, marriage remained a private and consensual union without the need for witnesses. De Reeper, *supra* note 49, at 155–58.

52 Rebecca Probert, *Common Law Marriage: Myths and Misunderstandings*, 20 CHILD & FAM. L. Q. 1 (2008).

into without parental consent. These marriages provided a means for unscrupulous suitors to gain access to a family's wealth as a consequence of the property rights that attached upon marriage. Martin Luther, in particular, railed against clandestine marriages for this reason, and in some Protestant cities in what is now modern Germany and Switzerland, the presence of a minister was made mandatory, as was parental consent.[53]

In England, reforms to clamp down on clandestine marriages entered into without parental consent were not enacted until Lord Hardwicke's Act, 1753. This law provided that a marriage was null and void unless it was preceded by reading aloud the banns for three consecutive Sundays in church, or there was an official license. The marriage had to be carried out publicly in a church or chapel by a regular Anglican clergyman and had to take place within prescribed daylight hours.[54] It was also essential for the marriage's validity that it be recorded in a parish register, which was signed by the bride and groom, the officiating clergyman, and at least two witnesses. Provision was made for Jews and Quakers to marry according to the rites of their own faiths, but it was only many years later that Catholics and nonconformists[55] had an option to marry other than in the Church of England.[56]

D The Emergence of Civil Marriage

In England, civil marriage was first introduced by legislation in 1836, which allowed for a civil form of marriage ceremony before a registrar.[57] This offered an option for people not affiliated with one of the faiths to solemnize their marriages.

In France, compulsory civil marriage had been introduced much earlier. As Professor Lloyd Bonfield observes, long before the French Revolution the monarchy sought to exercise control over the process by which couples entered into marriage. Consequently, by the time of the French Revolution, "considerable secularization of the law concerning marriage formation had already been undertaken."[58] The Revolution continued this process of

[53] GLENDON, TRANSFORMATION, *supra* note 43, at 29.

[54] STONE, ROAD TO DIVORCE, *supra* note 47, at 123.

[55] The term "nonconformist" refers to Protestant religious groups other than the Church of England. At various stages these included Methodists and Baptists.

[56] STEPHEN CRETNEY, FAMILY LAW IN THE TWENTIETH CENTURY: A HISTORY 4–12 (2003); PETER BROMLEY, FAMILY LAW 34–52 (1987).

[57] Marriage Act 1836 (England and Wales).

[58] *See* Lloyd Bonfield, *European Family Law*, *in* THE HISTORY OF THE EUROPEAN FAMILY: FAMILY LIFE IN THE LONG NINETEENTH CENTURY (1789–1913) 109, 128 (David Kertzer & Marzio Barbagli eds., 2002).

wresting control of marriage from the Church. France made civil ceremonies mandatory by means of a revolutionary decree on September 20, 1792.[59] The law denied all legal effect to religious weddings.[60] The Napoleonic Code of 1804 included these provisions for compulsory civil ceremonies. This model spread through much of Europe, in some countries as an alternative to religious ceremonies, and in others, such as Germany, as the only form of legal marriage.[61] In France and Germany, the civil ceremony had to precede a religious ceremony.[62] Many countries of Continental Europe retain that requirement.[63]

A society in which a secular wedding ceremony was compulsory needed to imbue it with meaning, and this the French did – by imitating the sacred. The leading French scholar Jean Carbonnier wrote of French marriage law that "[e]ven though secularized, marriage has a sort of religious gravity which is peculiar to it . . . a gravity based on the idea that man's binding himself until death is an aspect of his intimation of mortality and his struggle against the ephemeral nature of existence."[64] Professor Mary Ann Glendon has written of the French system that "marriage formation law in France seems to be part and parcel of the country's civil religion."[65] Secular law borrowed from religion the idea of a celebrant and a ceremony and adopted the religious terms and conditions of what marriage meant – a union of a man and a woman, 'til death do them part.

Thus, the option of civil marriage developed as an imitation of religious marriage. Just as ministers or priests solemnized religious marriages and pronounced a couple to be husband and wife, the State, represented by a government official, fulfilled this function for those seeking a secular wedding. In either instance, the marriage required an authorized celebrant representing either divine or human authority.

E Marriage in a Secular Society

It is questionable how much this idea of marriage as requiring solemnization by a person holding religious or secular authority has survived secularization

59 GLENDON, TRANSFORMATION, *supra* note 43, at 33. 60 *Id.* at 71.

61 *Ehegesetz* [Marriage Act], Feb. 20, 1946, BGB III at 404–1, § 11 (Ger.); Bonfield, *supra* note 58.

62 GLENDON, TRANSFORMATION, *supra* note 43, at 71, 73.

63 *See generally* Dagmar Coester-Waltjen & Michael Coester, Formation of Marriage, in 4 International Encyclopedia of Comparative Law: Persons and Family § 3–102 (Aleck Chloros et al., eds., 2007).

64 JEAN CARBONNIER, FLEXIBLE DROIT – TEXTES POUR UNE SOCIOLOGIE DU DROIT SANS RIGUEUR 137 (1971), English translation in Glendon, TRANSFORMATION, *supra* note 43, at 72.

65 GLENDON, TRANSFORMATION, *supra* note 43, at 72.

or will survive it into the future. Two major developments have occurred in recent years that might signal the demise of this notion of marriage. The first is the decline in the insistence that if a marriage is not solemnized in the presence of God's representative, it must instead be solemnized in the presence of the State's representative. The second is the blurring of the distinction between formal marriage and cohabitation. These developments can be seen if one considers the options for relationship formation in five of the great cities of the world: Amsterdam, London, Edinburgh, Melbourne, and Washington, DC.

III A TALE OF FIVE CITIES

Alex and Chris are in love. They are a young professional couple with options for employment in a number of the great cities of the world. At the commencement of the couple's partnership, their options for family formation depend greatly on which city they choose to live in.

A *Amsterdam*

If Alex and Chris live in Amsterdam, they have two choices for formalizing their relationship that have almost identical legal effects. Marriage in the Netherlands, as in other countries of Continental Europe, requires a civil ceremony conducted by an official of the town hall or equivalent.[66] Indeed, it is illegal to conduct a religious ceremony of marriage unless the civil ceremony has occurred first.[67]

However, Alex and Chris do not actually have to marry at all to have a formalized legal partnership. The Netherlands introduced the idea of a "registered partnership" in 1998 as an alternative for same-sex couples, to whom marriage was not available at the time.[68] When marriage was made available to same-sex couples in 2001, the registered partnership became more or less redundant. It is, however, still a registered, legal form of cohabitation. There is practically no difference in legal effect between a marriage and

[66] Article 1.63 of the Burgerlijk Wetboek (Dutch Civil Code) provides: "The marriage shall be contracted in public in the town hall before the Registrar of Civil Status in the presence of at least two and at the most four adult witnesses." BW, art. 1.63.

[67] Article 1.68 of the of the Burgerlijk Wetboek (Dutch Civil Code) provides: "No religious ceremonies may take place before the parties have shown to the foreman of the religious service that the marriage has been contracted before a Registrar of Civil Status." BW, art. 1.68.

[68] Wendy Schrama, *Registered Partnership in the Netherlands*, 13 INT. J. L. POL. & FAM. 315 (1999). The Netherlands recognized same-sex marriage in 2001, the first country to do so. *See supra* note 5.

a registered partnership, and a registered partnership is open to both heterosexual and same-sex couples.[69] Effectively, then, these represent alternative, but equivalent, forms of registering a domestic, intimate partnership with the State.

If Alex and Chris choose to live together informally outside marriage or a registered partnership, their legal position will be very different.[70] Dutch law does not provide a property-sharing regime similar to marriage for couples in informal *de facto* relationships. There is, therefore, a clear choice to be made between a registered relationship and an unregistered one.

B London

If Alex and Chris live in London, they have a bewildering smorgasbord of options. They may choose to marry, but their choice of ceremony depends to a great extent on their religious affiliation, or lack thereof. Whether or not they are devoutly religious, they have a legal right to marry in any Church of England church, in which case notice of the marriage is given by the reading of banns in church for three weeks prior to the marriage. A marriage that takes place in accordance with the rituals of the Church of England will, without more requirements, qualify as a marriage. This is also the case if the couple goes through a Jewish or Quaker wedding, but not if they marry in a Baptist or Catholic church. If they choose to marry in any other religious tradition apart from that of Anglican, Jewish, or Quaker religious traditions, then their marriage will be valid only if it is contracted in a building that is registered as a "place of meeting for religious worship."[71]

The validity of their marriage is subject also to compliance with certain additional formalities such as the presence of an "authorized person," who is normally a religious leader within that faith tradition. Additionally, the marriage must be registered with the superintendent registrar.[72] This rather strange set of requirements, differing from one religious tradition to another, reflects the gradual evolution of marriage law from the time of Lord Hardwicke's Act in 1753 and onward.

[69] Wendy Schrama, *Reforms in Dutch Family Law During the Course of 2001: Increased Pluriformity and Complexity, in* International Survey of Family Law 2002 at 277 (Andrew Baiham ed., 2002).

[70] Masha Antokolskaia, *Economic Consequences of Informal Heterosexual Cohabitation from a Comparative Perspective: Respect Parties' Autonomy or Protection of the Weaker Party?, in* Liber Amicorum Walter Pintens (Alain-Laurent Verbeke ed., 2012).

[71] Places of Worship Registration Act, 1855, 15 & 16 Vict., c. 36, § 2 (Eng.).

[72] *Id.* at § 10.

If Alex and Chris do not want a religious ceremony, they can have a civil marriage. This ceremony must be a secular one and can take place either in a registry office or on any other premises that have been approved for the purpose by the local authority.[73] Also, a superintendent registrar, registrar, and two witnesses must be present at the ceremony and a prescribed form of words must be used.[74]

The echoes of Lord Hardwicke's Act remain in the notice requirements. Anyone who does not marry in accordance with the Church of England practices (which still require the banns of marriage to be read for three weeks prior to the wedding) is required to give notice of the intended marriage at a registry office.[75] The law provides for various other civil preliminaries for ceremonies other than those conducted by the Church of England.[76] Thus, in England Alex and Chris will have a choice between a Church of England ceremony as of right, a secular ceremony as of right, and various other kinds of religious ceremony if the religious celebrant is willing to perform it.

In English law, it follows that God's approval is sufficient if the marriage takes place in a Church of England ceremony. God's approval is almost sufficient for Quakers and Jews also, but they need a marriage license and to give notice to the Registrar first. Once these formalities are fulfilled, the wedding ceremony alone is sufficient for the couple to be married in the eyes of the State.[77] The approval of both God and the State is needed for a Catholic, Baptist, Methodist, Muslim, Hindu, or other faith-based wedding to be valid in English law. The marriage ceremony alone, even after satisfaction of prior formalities,[78] is insufficient to ensure that the couple is married in the eyes of the State. The couple must have a license and give notice, and in addition they must marry in a building registered as a place of worship and subsequently register the marriage.[79] Only when all these demands of Caesar have been satisfied, will they be married in the eyes of the State and God.

[73] MARRIAGE ACT 1949, 12, 13 & 14 Geo. 6, c. 76, §§ 46A, 46B (Eng.) [74] *Id.* at § 17.

[75] *Id.*at §§ 5, 27. [76] *Id.* at §§ 53–57. [77] *Id.* at § 26.

[78] *Id.* In the Islamic tradition, marriage is formed through contract rather than solemnization by a religious figure. *See* Nate Oman, *How to Judge Shari'a Contracts: A Guide to Islamic Marriage Contracts in American Courts*, 2011 UTAH LAW REV. 287 (2011). If the marriage is not registered in law, Muslim women may be left without the legal protections accorded to a civilly recognized marriage, creating pressure on "Sharia courts" to resolve couples' financial and custodial arrangements when dissolving their marriages religiously, *See* Robin Fretwell Wilson, *The Perils of Privatized Marriage, in* MARRIAGE AND DIVORCE IN A MULTI-CULTURAL CONTEXT: RECONSIDERING THE BOUNDARIES OF CIVIL LAW AND RELIGION 267 (Joel A. Nichols, ed., 2011), https://papers.ssrn.com/sol3/papers.cfm?abstract_id=2016231.

[79] MARRIAGE ACT, *supra* note 73, § 27.

The requirement that the building be registered as a place of worship causes particular difficulties in circumstances where the religious community fails to apply for registration of the building or is unaware of the need to do so.[80] The consequence is that the marriage, while valid in accordance with the religious traditions of the couple and in the eyes of family and community, is not valid in the eyes of the State.

On the other hand, the State's approval is sufficient for a civil ceremony, in which the State is represented by an official registrar. God is not permitted to take part.[81] In short, English law provides the options of God without a license, God with a license, God with a license and registration, and a license and registration without God. No explanation can be given for this except history.

If Alex and Chris are a same-sex couple, their options are more limited. They cannot be married in the Church of England, for the compromise between secularism and faith concerning gay marriage was to ensure that the Church of England could not be required, contrary to its official doctrinal position, to conduct marriage ceremonies for same-sex couples.[82] Other faith communities were given the option to conduct same-sex weddings in a registered building if the appropriate authorities applied for registration to do so.[83] An option that remains open to Alex and Chris, as a same-sex couple, is to enter into a civil partnership, which carries all the same consequences as marriage.[84] Unlike in the Netherlands, heterosexual couples do not have this option.[85]

It is reasonable to ask why there are such differences in the law governing different faith communities. Why does the State need to insist that the building be registered for certain kinds of marriages? And why is it that celebrants must either be religious leaders or state-employed officials? The position is rather different just north of the border in Scotland.[86]

C Edinburgh

If Alex and Chris live in Edinburgh, they may choose a religious marriage or a civil marriage.[87] However, the concept of a "religion" has been extended to

80 John Eekelaar, *Marriage – A Modest Proposal*, 43 FAM. L. 82 (2013).

81 MARRIAGE ACT, *supra* note 73, at § 17.

82 MARRIAGE (SAME SEX COUPLES) ACT, 2013, c. 30, § 1 (Eng.). 83 *Id.* at § 2.

84 CIVIL PARTNERSHIP ACT, 2004, c. 33 (Eng.).

85 *Id.* at § 3. This restriction has been challenged as constituting discrimination against heterosexual couples, but so far without success. Steinfeld & Anor v. The Secretary of State for Education [2017] EWCA Civ 81.

86 Scotland has long had a different tradition of family law than England, reflected in different marriage laws. D. W. R. Brand, *The Marriage Law of Scotland*, 25 QUIS CUSTODIET 178 (1969).

87 MARRIAGE (SCOTLAND) ACT, 1977, c. 15 (Scot.).

other belief systems that are not actually religious. In particular, the practice emerged in 2005 for leaders of a humanist society also to be allowed to solemnize marriages.[88] As a consequence, whereas the legislation itself referred to "religious marriages" as opposed to civil ones, the phrase "religious and belief marriages" came to be used in official documents.[89] This usage gained statutory recognition only in 2014.[90] The humanist celebrations are now reportedly the third-largest category of weddings after those performed in the Church of Scotland and civil marriages.[91] In 2010, there were more humanist weddings than Catholic marriage ceremonies in Scotland.[92] As in England, same-sex couples can marry in Scotland.[93]

D Melbourne

If Alex and Chris begin their family life in Melbourne, they have a range of options for formalizing their relationship as well. They may choose a religious wedding, get married in a registry office, or purchase the services of a private marriage celebrant. By authorizing private marriage celebrants, Australia has partially privatized the solemnization of marriages. The celebrant need not be a state official who pronounces the couple duly married. It is enough that the celebrant is someone who has been authorized by the government to perform weddings.[94] Being a secular celebrant is a professional occupation or business.

If Alex and Chris do not want to marry then there may be other options. In Melbourne, as in many other parts of the country such as in Queensland,[95] Alex and Chris can enter into a "registered relationship."[96] A registered relationship, which is open to heterosexual or same-sex couples, has the same

88 This authority resulted from a temporary authorization under section 12 of the Marriage (Scotland) Act 1977. The Humanist Society Scotland says of itself that it includes "atheists and agnostics who make sense of the world using reason, experience and shared human values." *About Humanism*, HUMANIST SOCIETY SCOTLAND, www.humanism-scotland.org.uk/. They seek to make the best of the one life they have by creating meaning and purpose for themselves, individually and together. *Id.*

89 Citizens Advice Scotland, *Advice for Scotland: Getting Married*, CITIZENS ADVICE SCOTLAND, www.citizensadvice.org.uk/scotland/relationships/living-together-marriage-and-civil-partnership-s/getting-married-s/.

90 Marriage and Civil Partnership (Scotland) Act 2014.

91 John Eekelaar, Marriage and Religion 9 (May 2014) (paper given at Economic & Social Research Council seminar).

92 Mike Wade, *More Humanist Weddings Will Outstrip the Kirk*, TIMES (Apr. 23, 2015), www.thetimes.co.uk/tto/news/uk/scotland/article4419931.ece.

93 Marriage and Civil Partnerships Act 2014 (Scotland).

94 *Becoming a Marriage Celebrant*, AUSTL. ATT. GEN. DEPT., www.ag.gov.au/FamiliesAndMarriage/Marriage/Pages/Becomingamarriagecelebrant.aspx.

95 Registered Relationships Act 2011 (Qld) (Austl).

96 Relationships Act 2008 (Vic) (Austl).

effects as marriage for the purposes of the law of that jurisdiction.[97] In federal law, the relationship will be treated as a "*de facto* relationship."[98]

Being treated as a *de facto* relationship makes little difference though in terms of the legal consequences of their relationship. While both registration and marriage are options for Alex and Chris to formalise their relationship, they will be treated as married just by living together – at least for some period of time. There is now almost no difference at all between being married and living in a *de facto* relationship in any area of state or federal law. The trajectory of law reform at both state and federal levels for more than twenty years has been to insert the words "or *de facto*" wherever the word "marriage" or "spouse" appears in legislation. Initially, this approach was taken to address the issues facing heterosexual couples who do not marry, and later the term "*de facto*" was extended to include same-sex couples.[99]

There are some legal consequences of living in a *de facto* relationship that require a minimum period of living together, for example, two years, or having a child.[100] However, once these thresholds are crossed, the *de facto* relationship carries exactly the same effects as marriage. In New Zealand, there has also been a substantial assimilation of the legal consequences of marriage with those of informal cohabitation.[101]

In Australia, then, whether Alex and Chris choose to marry, have a registered relationship, or live together as a couple without formalizing or registering their relationship, the effects are much the same.

E Washington, DC

If Alex and Chris live in Washington, DC, they can ask anyone to solemnize their marriage. Indeed, they may even solemnize it themselves. The Marriage Officiant Amendment Act 2013 amended the DC Code to provide that the following people may solemnize a marriage as long as they are at least eighteen years old: a judge or retired judge, the Clerk of the Court or such deputy clerks

97 For example, the Civil Unions Act provides: "A civil union is different to a marriage but is to be treated for all purposes under territory law in the same way as a marriage." Civil Unions Act 2012 (ACT) § 6(2) (Austl.).

98 Family Law Act 1975 § 4AA.

99 This process began with State and Territory laws in the late 1990s. In 2008, the federal Parliament passed omnibus legislation to equalize the legal position of same-sex couples throughout federal law: Same-Sex Relationships (Equal Treatment in Commonwealth Laws – General Law Reform) Act 2008.

100 Family Law Act 1975 § 4AA.

101 Bill Atkin, *The Legal World of Unmarried Couples: Reflections on "De Facto Relationships" in Recent New Zealand Legislation*, 39 VUWLR 793 (2008).

as are approved by the Chief Judge of the Court; a minister, priest, rabbi, or authorized person of any religious denomination or society; a civil celebrant (defined as a person of a secular or nonreligious organization who performs marriage ceremonies); a temporary officiant who is authorized by the Clerk of the Court to solemnize a particular wedding;[102] members of the City Council; the Mayor; or the parties to the marriage.[103]

The idea that parties can marry themselves is somewhat strange, but it is not unique to the country's capital. Such "self-uniting marriages" have their religious origins in the Quaker tradition and have long been possible in Pennsylvania.[104] Couples may marry themselves in Colorado as well.[105]

Further, DC broadly defines a religious denomination or society. The term "religious" is defined as including or pertaining to "a belief in a theological doctrine, a belief in and worship of a divine ruling power, a recognition of a supernatural power controlling man's destiny, or a devotion to some principle, strict fidelity or faithfulness, conscientiousness, pious affection, or attachment."[106] This goes far beyond the Scottish embrace of humanism as a religion. It is broad enough to include an organization or society that holds a belief in, or commitment to, almost anything.

The various ways in which Alex and Chris could get married do not exhaust their options. They may also enter a common-law marriage, which generally requires "present intent and agreement of the parties to enter into a matrimonial relationship," usually manifested with cohabitation and a public holding out as married.[107] In the U.S., eleven states in addition to the District of Columbia permit common-law marriages.[108] Like statutory marriages, common-law marriages may be dissolved only by annulment, divorce, or death.[109]

Outside statutory and common-law marriage, Alex and Chris may also enter into a registered domestic partnership, which in DC offers some but not all the benefits of marriage to both same-sex and heterosexual couples.[110] Registered partners receive hospital and nursing home visitation rights and, for people employed by DC after 1987, health insurance coverage just as spouses do.

[102] Allowing a temporary officiant to solemnize a marriage with authorization from the court gives a basis upon which a family friend could be authorized to officiate at the wedding.

[103] D.C. Code § 46–406 (2013). [104] *See* 23 Pa. Cons. Stat. § 1502 (2016).

[105] Colo. Rev. Stat. § 14-2-109 (2013). [106] D.C. Code § 46–406 (2013).

[107] *See* John DeWitt Gregory, Peter N. Swisher, & Robin Fretwell Wilson, Understanding Family Law § 2.05 (4th ed. 2013).

[108] *Id.* (listing Alabama, Colorado, Georgia (until 1997), Idaho, Iowa, Kansas, Montana, Ohio (until 1991), Oklahoma, Pennsylvania (until 2003), Rhode Island, South Carolina, Texas, Utah, and the District of Columbia).

[109] *Id.* [110] Health Care Benefits Expansion Act of 1992, D.C. Law 9–114.

Unlike DC, other states that voluntarily enacted same-sex marriage by statute offered partnered couples the opportunity to marry but then closed down the partnered status as an alternative to marriage.[111]

IV WHAT THEN IS MARRIAGE?

This brief survey of just five jurisdictions shows how confused the law of marriage is becoming in secularized societies. Civil marriage was only ever a pale imitation of the ritual and ceremony of the Church.[112] Most people wanted to be married in the eyes of God, but the State provided an alternative form of ceremony for those of a minority faith or no faith at all, and an alternative source of authority to the divine. The State had an official celebrant because the Church had an official celebrant – the priest or minister. Civil marriages gained a derivative sense of meaning and solemnity from the religious meaning of marriage as a covenant under God, and a sacrament.

There is no compelling justification – maybe no justification at all – for insisting on an official celebrant in a secular society other than to imitate the religious nature of marriage. And so in different ways, the modern law of marriage in various countries has drifted away from its former insistence that to be valid a marriage had to be solemnized either by Church or State.

Scottish law provides one illustration. The concept of a religious wedding in the law has now been extended to irreligious weddings by a practice of authorizing members of the Humanist Society to conduct weddings under the religious wedding provisions. The humanist celebrant stands in the shoes of neither God nor government. That begs the question: is there something about marriage that requires it to be solemnized by a State official or by someone with a worldview on the meaning of life and the origins of human existence?

If the humanist or atheist has no special authority for pronouncing a couple to be married, there may be some logic in the government simply licensing private individuals to be marriage celebrants, as in Australia. To be sure, they are authorized by the government, but they do not represent the government any more than the humanists in Scotland do. They are essentially running a private business under license from the State.

111 Heidi L. Brady & Robin Fretwell Wilson, *The Precarious Status of Domestic Partnerships in a Post-Obergefell World*, 24 ELDER LAW JOURNAL 101 (2016) (charting the repeal of marriage-like statuses after recognition of same-sex marriage).

112 *See* Wilson, Chapter 16, this volume. Pope Leo XXIII, for instance, believed that marriage authority rested solely with the church and that civil authority served only to "deprive [marriage] of all holiness" – a belief shared by many today.

And so there is a somewhat charming *reductio ad absurdum* logic in the law of Washington, DC, which provides that anyone can solemnize a particular marriage with authorization from the Clerk of the Court, or indeed that the parties can have their own do-it-yourself wedding and declare themselves to be married. Why not? In a secular worldview, there is a need for neither celebrant nor ceremony. As the High Court of Australia perceptively observed, there is no intrinsic reason why a wedding should not be very simple – just the exchange of promises before witnesses.[113]

Yet, if this is so, where is the boundary line between marriage and non-marriage? Is a registered partnership in the Netherlands really just a marriage by a different name? What about a registered relationship in Victoria, Australia? Is the intent involved in registering one's partnership with a government office materially different from the expression of intent that is necessary in Washington, DC, for someone to be married? In reality, all that Washington, DC, requires is that the parties obtain a license before making their private commitment to each other.

The law in Australia and certain other countries, including jurisdictions that recognize common-law marriage, raises a question whether people should be deemed married by the fact of cohabitation in an intimate domestic partnership. As Stephanie Coontz has observed, the wall separating marriage from non-marriage is breaking down.[114] Indeed, even as to common-law marriage, the "public holding out" is frequently supplied by cohabitation, the wearing of rings, and little more – although it technically requires agreement to be bound in marriage.[115] If the consequences of non-marriage are the same as for marriage, then what is marriage in civil law but a form of registration?

And if marriage is simply a form of registration that is sufficient (but not, in Australia, even necessary) to confer upon a couple the rights, privileges, and obligations of marriage, should divorce be anything more than a form of deregistration, with financial and parenting issues dealt with separately?[116] In practice, that is all divorce is in countries with unilateral no-fault divorce statutes, such as Australia. The divorce still goes through the court, but in

[113] Commonwealth v. Austl. Capital Territory (2013) 250 CLR 441, 462 (Austl.).

[114] Stephanie Coontz, *The World Historical Transformation of Marriage*, 66 J. MARR. & FAM. 974 (2004).

[115] *See* Gregory, Swisher, & Wilson, *supra* note 107; Crosson v. Crosson, 668 So. 2d 868 (Ala. Civ. App. 1995) (finding of "holding out" as married from being silent when introduced by a woman as her "husband" together with the filing of joint tax returns, a filing privilege reserved to married couples).

[116] For discussion, *see, e.g.*, Richard Ingleby, *Regulating the Termination of Marital Status: Is It Worth the Effort?* 17 MELB. U. L. REV. 671 (1990).

Australia, for example, divorces are pronounced by registrars – who are the equivalent to Clerks of the Court – in a quasi-administrative process. Issues concerning property division, maintenance, and parenting arrangements for children are dealt with separately from the divorce itself, with the consequence that a divorce is of no significance other than as a right to remarry.[117] In certain other countries, many divorces are dealt with by administrative process also.[118] In a secular society, which does not hold to the belief that the State has any role in keeping people together, why would divorce not become simply an administrative act of deregistration of a marriage?[119]

CONCLUSION

Can marriage survive secularization? Yes – in the same way that the echo of a distant voice reverberates around a canyon for sometime after the speaker has ceased to emit sound. Marriage has little meaning except insofar as it is rooted in history, faith, and culture. Marriage was not first of all a legal institution in any society of the world; it was grounded in culture, custom, and faith. To the extent that civil marriage derives its identity, meaning, and solemnity from being an echo of the sacred, it will surely not long survive secularization. It may be that it will develop its own identity within a secular culture. Sociologist Andrew Cherlin has observed that as marriage has become deinstitutionalized in American life, it has become more symbolically important, having "evolved from a marker of conformity to a marker of prestige."[120] It is perhaps evolving to become a capstone of a successful intimate domestic relationship, not the foundation stone.[121] This may explain the comparative strength of marriage among the most educated members of American society whose identity is partly defined by the world of work and who, to some extent at least, live out their private lives in public.[122]

117 Family Law Act 1975 § 49.

118 Katherina Boele-Woelki, et al., Principles of European Family Law Regarding Divorce and Maintenance between Former Spouses 20–21 (2004).

119 Britain's leading family law judge, Sir James Munby, has asked: "May the time not come when we should at least consider whether the process of divorce still needs to be subject to judicial supervision?" Sir James Munby, *21st Century Family Law*, The 2014 Michael Farmer Memorial Lecture, at 14, www.judiciary.gov.uk/wp-content/uploads/2014/10/munby-speech-bangor-10102014.pdf.

120 Andrew Cherlin, *The Deinstitutionalization of American Marriage*, 66 J. Marr. & Fam. 848 (2004).

121 Pamela Smock, *The Wax and Wane of Marriage: Prospects for Marriage in the 21st Century*, 66 J. Marr. & Fam. 966 (2004).

122 *See* Sears, *supra* note 20.

This may put a different perspective on the intense debates about same-sex marriage. For advocates of same-sex marriage, the goal has been to obtain access to a prestigious status, because marriage is the ultimate form of acceptance of the legitimacy and value of same-sex partnerships.[123] Opponents of same-sex marriage have sought to preserve the historic connection between the religious meaning of marriage and its secular meaning. In the U.S., as in many other countries, the former arguments have prevailed, but the opponents of same-sex marriage may prove to be right – that it is another steppingstone toward the eventual decline and fall of the idea of marriage as a civil institution.[124]

At the heart of the problem is not that same-sex couples can marry in many countries. The bigger problem is that the secular State is utterly unable to provide any convincing narrative about what marriage *is*. Yes, marriage is a commitment between two people made before family and friends, but that can happen without the regulatory infrastructure of marriage law. If once marriage was an enforceable contract or covenant, it is no longer in countries that allow for unilateral no-fault divorce without fault-based financial consequences.

Like an ancient civilization that loses its battle with the encroaching jungle, Western society is slowly returning to a pre-Christian state in which the ruins of a stable and healthy marriage culture,[125] deeply embedded in the soil of the Judeo-Christian tradition, are covered over with the dense leaves and tangled branches of secular confusion about what marriage really means. Civil marriage, divorced from its religious and cultural heritage, and no longer involving a commitment to a lifelong union, may end up being little more than the name that is given to an intimate domestic partnership that is registered with the State.

Will this mean the end of the wedding industry? Not at all. For the public commitment of one person to another, and the celebration of love, will long be popular. For some time to come, no doubt, marriage will continue to be a marker of prestige. Nor will secularization mean the complete end of marriage as we now understand it, for where it has deep religious and cultural

123 *See* M. V. Lee Badgett, *Social Inclusion and the Value of Marriage Equality in Massachusetts and the Netherlands*, 67 J. Soc. Issues 316 (2011).

124 *See* Maggie Gallagher, *(How) Will Gay Marriage Weaken Marriage as a Social Institution*, 2 U. St. Thomas L. J. 33 (2004). For the view that balanced legislation that protects both religious convictions around marriage and sexuality, while protecting the LGBT community from discrimination, can provide a bulwark for faith communities and their beliefs around traditional marriage, *see* Adams, Chapter 21, this volume.

125 For an empirical snapshot of marriage rates and their decline across time, *see* National Marriage Project, The State of Our Unions: Marriage in America 2012 (2012).

roots, marriage will continue to matter.[126] However, it will be only one of the accepted forms of intimate partnerships between two adults, with non-marital cohabitation and "living together apart" relationships also becoming established social institutions.[127]

What may not long survive secularization is nonreligious marriage in its traditional form, with the State providing an official celebrant and the law regulating the form of the exchange of promises. Marriage without a religious or cultural underpinning has no clear meaning or identity. The echo of the sacred is fading now, and, sooner or later, the canyon will lapse back into silence.

126 Wilson, Chapter 16, this volume.

127 Jan Trost, *The Social Institution of Marriage*, 41 J. Comp. Fam. Stud. 507 (2010) (describing the rise of LATs or couples who live together apart; that is, they do not cohabit but identify as in romantic, long-term committed relationships).

25

A Tale of Fragmentation and Intertwinement

The Sacred and the Secular Systems for Forming and Dissolving Marriages in Israel

Arianne Renan Barzilay

Assistant Professor of Law, University of Haifa Faculty of Law

Karin Carmit Yefet

Associate Professor of Law, University of Haifa Faculty of Law

I. INTRODUCTION

Few decisions in recent United States history have so sharply divided the American public as the Supreme Court's decision recognizing same-sex marriage in *Obergefell v. Hodges*.[1] For one part of the American public, a decision opening the legal marriage market to same-sex couples was a long-awaited cause for celebration. For many others, it represented such a sharp break with the nation's Judeo-Christian history as to be one of "the darkest hours" in the nation's history.[2] Outrage over the ruling by an "imperial court"[3] – "stealing," as Chief Justice John Roberts put it, a major social debate from the American people[4] – has fueled a hazardous movement – one that seeks to replace so-called judicial tyranny[5] with tyranny of a different form: religion. As Professor Wilson (Chapter 16, this volume) shows, in the wake of *Obergefell*, social conservatives and religious dissenters have been growingly

[1] Obergefell v. Hodges, 135 S. Ct. 2584 (2015).

[2] *See* Hunter Walker, *Ted Cruz says "Lawless" Supreme Court Rulings Have led to "Some of the Darkest 24 Hours in Our Nation's History,"* BUSINESS INSIDER (Jun. 26, 2015), www.businessinsider.com/cruz-supreme-court-rulings-mean-the-darkest-24-hours-in-history-2015–6 (quoting Texas Senator Ted Cruz). *See* Adams, Chapter 21, this volume; Wilson, Chapter 16, this volume, for additional reactions.

[3] Kathie Obradovich, Column: *Divorcing States From Marriage Would be Messy*, THE DES MOINES REGISTER (July 4, 2015), www.desmoinesregister.com/story/opinion/columnists/kathie-obradovich/caucus/2015/07/05/kathie-obradovich-sex-marriages/29702557/.

[4] Obergefell, *supra* note 1, at 2614 (Roberts, C.J., dissenting).

[5] Obradovich, *supra* note 3.

vocal about forcing the government "out of the marriage business altogether"[6] and separating "civil marriage from Christian marriage."[7]

This nascent project to unwind the state's relationship to marriage, especially marriage as it is religiously understood by some dissenters, manifests itself in legislative bills and the statements of public and religious figures. As Professor Wilson explicates, the movement takes two principal modern forms, each with its own set of risks and problems, both reflecting a desire to "protect" the institution of marriage.[8] In one form, the idea is for all couples, whether or not religiously devout, to formalize intimate relationships without civil solemnization or a civil status called marriage, using a purely contractarian model. In that contractual model, couples could give voice to religious principles or not, but the relationship captured in contract would be called a civil union, not marriage. By withdrawing marriage from the public realm, in those faith traditions that see marriage as one-man, one-woman unions, this approach preserves holy matrimony as a union untainted by same-sex couples. In a competing approach, the church-state struggle over who should lawfully control marriage, the church or the state, is resolved in favor of making marriage the sole province of religion, with the state regulating only a couple's civil union.[9] This approach differs from the first in relying on a state-regulated status to give content to the couple's duties and rights, rather than relying on contract. Both attempt to unwind civil effects from the religious institution called marriage. This chapter examines the ill effects of divorcing marriage from government oversight by drawing on the rich Israeli experimentation with a religious-based system of family law.

The Israeli vantage point surfaces the potential consequences of fragmenting marriage in the U.S. civil family law system. The overarching feature of Israeli modern family law is that it is not uniform, but rather *personal* in the sense that the law is contingent upon one's religious affiliation. Israel's current family law system grants jurisdiction to both religious and civil courts and is based on a mixture of both religious and secular doctrine, depending on the specific subject matter. As demonstrated later, Israel serves as a cautionary tale against the vision of marriage regulation now espoused by some social

[6] *Matt Bevin Urges Gov Beshear to Protect Constitutional Rights of County Clerks*, Matt Bevin For Governor, www.mattbevin.com/matt_bevin_urges_gov_beshear_to_protect_constitutional_rights_of_county_clerks (Dec. 7, 2015).

[7] Ephraim Radner & Christopher Seitz, *The Marriage Pledge*, First Things (Dec. 7, 2015), www.firstthings.com/marriage-pledge.

[8] Wilson, Chapter 16, this volume; Robin Fretwell Wilson, *Divorcing Marriage and the State Post* Obergefell: *The Ill-Considered Consequences of Unwinding Civil and Religious Marriage*, 2016 Illinois Law Review 101.

[9] *Id.*

conservatives. This chapter shows that even within what purports to be the pure province of religion, civil forces are at work and operating with surprising consequences.[10]

II. A FRAGMENTED YET INTERTWINED FAMILY LAW SYSTEM – THE RELIGIOUS TRIBUNALS AND THE CIVIL FAMILY COURTS

The intricate yet intriguing Israeli family law system is best described as both fragmented and intertwined, jurisdictionally and jurisprudentially.[11] This fragmentation is rooted in the Ottoman Empire's *Millet* system, under which family issues were religious matters.[12] Accordingly, religious minorities were granted autonomy in matters relating to personal status and were permitted to govern family affairs in their own religious tribunals, pursuant to their own religious codes – a system that persists not only in Israel, but also in India, Indonesia, Iraq, Ireland, Lebanon, Malaysia, and Pakistan.[13] For Jewish citizens, Rabbinical Courts applied Jewish law (known as *Halakha*),[14] while Christians self-governed in the Ecclesiastical Courts. Similarly, Muslims self-governed following Muslim Law in the Shari'a Courts. The Ottoman Empire controlled the region from the early 16th century until World War I, when the British Empire conquered the region and again adopted the *Millet* system, most importantly with regard to marriage, divorce, alimony, maintenance,

[10] Pinhas Shifman, *Family Law in Israel: The Struggle Between Religious and Secular Law*, 24 Israel L. Rev. 537, 537-38 (1990).

[11] This chapter does not purport to discuss all the details and developments regarding jurisdiction in family matters but will give an overview to explain how the Israeli system is both fragmented and intertwined.

[12] Zvi Triger, *Freedom From Religion in Israel: Civil Marriages and Cohabitation of Jews Enter the Rabbinical Courts*, 27 Israel Stud. Rev. 1 (2012); Ruth Halperin-Kaddari, Women in Israel, A State of Their Own 228 (2004).

[13] Josh Goodman, *Divine Judgment: Judicial Review of Religious Legal Systems in India and Israel*, 32 Hastings Int'l & Comp. L. Rev. 477 (2009); Daphna Hacker, *Religious Tribunals in Democratic States: Lessons from the Israeli Rabbinical Courts*, 27 J. L. & Religion 59 (2012); Adam S. Hofri-Winogradow, *A Plurality of Discontent: Legal Pluralism, Religious Adjudication and the State*, 26 J. Law & Relig. 101, 104 (2011). On the jurisdiction of religious courts in Iraq, Lebanon, Pakistan, and Malysia, *see* Islamic Family in a Changing World: A Global Resource Book 112, 127, 231–32, 269–70 (Abdullahi An-Naim ed., 2002). As to the extending jurisdiction of Islamic courts in Indonesia, *see* John R. Bowen, *Consensus and Suspicion: Judicial Reasoning and Social Change in an Indonesian Society 1960-1994*, 34 L. & Soc'y Rev. 97 (2000); Alfitri, *Expanding a Formal Role for Islamic Law in the Indonesian Legal System: The Case of Mu'amalat*, 23 J.L. & Religion 249 (2007–08).

[14] Moshe Chigier, *The Rabbinical Courts in the State of Israel*, 2 Isr. L. Rev. 147 (1967). *See also* Elimelech Westreich, *Jewish Judicial Autonomy in Nineteenth Century Jerusalem: Background, Jurisdiction, Structure*, 22 Jewish L. Ass'n. Stud. 303 (2012).

guardianship, succession, wills and legacies, legitimation, and the adoption of minors.[15] In 1922 by British mandate, various personal status matters, mainly those related to marriage and divorce, continued to be judged under the religious law applying to the parties involved.[16]

After Israel's establishment in 1948, its parliament, the Knesset, adopted the preexisting fragmented system with a few noteworthy modifications,[17] namely the statutory removal of adoption, inheritance, and wills and legacies from the default jurisdiction of the religious courts.[18] The Knesset also enacted secular statutory laws on issues of custody, property division, and adoption, which were to be adjudicated under civil law, not religious law, unless both parties agreed otherwise.[19] Importantly, the Knesset left marriage and divorce under the exclusive jurisdiction of the religious tribunals, where it remains today.[20] This is significantly different from the U.S. family law system, where alimony, custody, property distribution, and divorce all proceed within the civil context; this is true of marriage, too, even if marriage is also a religious sacrament for some. Today, Israel recognizes fourteen religious communities, each with its own religious tribunals for personal law: Rabbinical Courts in the Jewish community, Shari'a courts in Muslim communities, Druze courts in Druze communities, and various religious court services in the different Christian communities.[21] This institutional fragmentation carries important and substantial legal consequences, the most obvious being that different tribunals

15 Palestine Order in Council, 1922, § 51, 3 L.O.P. 2569 (1934) (Isr.) (dealing also with property of the legally incompetent or absent persons). *See also* Elimelech Westreich, *The Legal Activities of the Chief Rabbis During the Period of the British Mandate: A Response to the Zionist Challenge, in* A HUNDRED YEARS OF RELIGIOUS ZIONISM 83 (A. Sagi & D. Schwartz eds., 2003) (Heb.).

16 This structure was effected by the Palestine Order in Council. Triger, *supra* note 12; Ariel Rosen-Zvi, *Family and Inheritance Law, in* INTRODUCTION TO THE LAW OF ISRAEL 75, 75 (Amos Shapira & Keren C. De-Witt-Arar eds., 1995).

17 Ruth Zafran, *The "Jurisdiction Race" is Alive and Kicking – Rabbinical Courts Gain Power over Civil Family Courts*, 43 MISHPATIM 571, 575 (2013) (Heb.); PINHAS SHIFMAN, FAMILY LAW IN ISRAEL vol. 1 (2d ed., 1995); Rabbinical Courts Jurisdiction (Marriage and Divorce) Law, 5713-1953, S.H. No. 134 p. 165 (Isr.) [hereinafter Rabbinical Courts Law].

18 Parties can agree, nonetheless, to the religious tribunals' jurisdiction. *See* Adoption of Children Law, 5741-1981, SH No. 1028, p. 293 (Isr.); Inheritance Law 5725 – 1965, SH No. 446, p. 65 (Isr.).

19 Legal Capacity and Guardianship Law, 5722-1962, SH No. 380, p. 120 (Isr.); Adoption of Children Law, *id*; Spouses' Property Relations Law, 5733-1973, SH No. 712, p. 267; Rabbinical Courts Law, *supra* note 18, § 2. *See also* Shifman, *supra* note 18, at 29–32, Ben-Zion Shershevski, FAMILY LAW 8-9 (1993) (Heb.); Zafran, *supra* note 17, at 575.

20 Triger, *supra* note 12; and Rosen-Zvi, *supra* note 16, at 76–77.

21 Karin Carmit Yefet, *Israeli Family Law as a Civil-Religious Hybrid: A Cautionary Tale of Fatal Attraction*, 2016 U. ILL. L. REV. 1505.

decide and apply different rules to citizens based solely on their religious affiliation.

But the fragmentation is even more pervasive because alongside the differing laws of these communities runs a secular family law system, with civil courts open to all Israelis regardless of their religious affiliation.[22] These civil courts differ dramatically from their religious counterparts. For example, in Rabbinical tribunals, only men – ordained Orthodox Rabbis who often are not legally trained[23] – may serve as judges; in the secular, civil family courts, both men and women may preside over matters.[24] In other words, even within a single religious community, and even for an individual in a given case, two competing family law systems coexist in disharmony, with each having some exclusive and some concurrent jurisdiction over various aspects of family law. To make this concrete, consider a Jewish couple who has married and later divorces. Jurisdiction to dissolve the marriage rests exclusively with the Rabbinical Court. But matters of custody and property division will be heard in civil courts under civil law, unless both parties agreed to have those matters decided by the Rabbinical Court or, as we explain later, an issue is properly and in good-faith "attached" to a divorce suit in the Rabbinical Court.[25]

Consequently, a given couple seeking to resolve their divorce dispute may find their case fragmented, with the primary issue (whether a divorce should be granted) adjudicated before the Rabbinical tribunal, but some or all of the related matters (such as maintenance, custody, child support and education, and division of property) heard by the secular family Court.[26] Since related matters can be adjudicated in either the religious or the civil system,[27] jurisdiction over each related issue is a function of a "race to the courthouse," as the first party to file a claim on a specific related matter effectively chooses the forum.[28] The procedural question of whether related matters were

22 Today Family Courts Law 5755-1995, SH No. 1537, p. 393 (Isr.).

23 Zafran, *supra* note 17, at 627.

24 Ronen Shamir, Michal Shitrai, & Nelly Elias, *Religion, Feminism, and Professionalism*, 38 Jewish J. Soc. 73 (1997); Frances Raday, *On Equality*, *in* Women's Status in Law and Society 19 (Frances Raday, Carmel Shalev, & Michal Liban-Kobi eds., 1995) (Heb.); Triger, *supra* note 12.

25 Rabbinical Courts Law, *supra* note 17, § 3; Ariel Rosen-Zvi, *The Jurisdictional Race in Matters Connected with Divorce Suits and its Impact on Family Law*, 14 Tel-Aviv L. Rev 67 (1989); Daphna Hacker, *What's Different this Year? Families Law Between The Chaotic and the Harmonic*, 9 Haifa L. Rev. 13 (2015) (Heb.); CA 384/85 Ben-Yair v. Ben Yair 39(4) PD 775 (1986) (Isr.); CA 423/79 Tzabari v. Tzabari 35(4) PD 242 (1981) (Isr.); HCJ 787/14 Plonit v. Ploni (Oct. 26, 2015), Nevo Legal Database (by subscription, in Hebrew) (Isr.).

26 *See also* HCJ 5507/95 Amir v. Haifa District Rabbinical Court 50(3) PD 321 (1996) (Isr.).

27 The parties may, of course, also agree on the forum.

28 Halperin-Kaddari, *supra* note 12, at 233–34, 260. But see *infra* note 33.

"properly" attached is also jurisdictionally fragmented and can be decided by either the civil, family Court or the religious, Rabbinical tribunal depending upon which tribunal heard and adjudicated this preliminary issue first, subject to some oversight by the Supreme Court, as explained later.[29]

This crucial jurisdictional fragmentation has enabled a jurisprudential fragmentation, the implications of which will be explored in regard to Israel's majority Jewish population. In Israel, Orthodox Rabbinical Courts have exclusive jurisdiction over marriage (e.g., how and who one can marry in Israel) and divorce (e.g., how and when one can divorce) for all Jews living in Israel, regardless of the couple's subjective religious beliefs or lack thereof.[30] Rabbinical Courts apply Jewish law exclusively to questions of marriage and divorce, stripping individuals of the right to be free from religion but also resulting in a harsh violation of gender equality because Jewish law requires divorce to be given by men's consent, resulting in the ability to refuse divorce or use consent as leverage on matters such as custody or property dissolution.

Fragmentation can drive legal outcomes. The religious and civil tribunals not only apply different law but also can interpret the same law differently and apply different procedural and evidentiary rules. This might occur, for example, when a Rabbinical Court decides a matter of custody that would ordinarily be decided by a civil court – both courts would be guided by the same civil law but the two courts might interpret or apply it differently, leading to importantly different outcomes.

Because case outcomes can differ crucially depending on the forum of adjudication,[31] a litigant's ability to choose the forum becomes vital even when both bodies theoretically apply the same law.[32] This fact substantially motivates the race to the courthouse to the detriment of would-be litigants, who are incentivized to cement jurisdiction often at the cost of escalating their dispute rather than attempting reconciliation.[33]

29 HCJ 8497/00 Fyge-Felman v. Felman 57(2) PD 118 (2001) (Isr.); Zafran, *supra* note 17, at 602 (noting that the two court systems are obliged to "respect" the earliest decision and only in extreme circumstances in which there was a clear and basic error in the religious court's ruling as to the question of its own authority to adjudicate the related questions, the civil-family court may intervene and decide otherwise).

30 Rabbinical Courts Law, *supra* note 18. *See also* Halperin-Kaddari, *supra* note 12, at 233–34.

31 Zafran, *supra* note 17, at 577–82.

32 Rosen-Zvi, *supra* note 16; Halperin-Kaddari, *supra* note 12, at 233.

33 But note the recent Settlement of Litigation in Family Disputes (Provisional Measure) Law 5775-2014, SH No. 2485, p. 116 (Isr.), which enables a party to decide the forum without having to first submit a claim against his or her spouse, but rather by first submitting a request to settle the family dispute.

Overlaying this already complex system is Israel's Supreme Court. Despite fragmentation, religious tribunals and secular courts are both bound by the Supreme Court's decisions on jurisdictional questions. The Supreme Court also oversees the substantive rulings of the Rabbinical Courts to a limited degree.[34] More so than in the recent past, however, the Israeli Supreme Court is hesitant to interfere in the Rabbinical tribunals' rulings, except in extreme circumstances of *ultra vires* or a critical violation of natural justice principles.[35] Nonetheless, the Supreme Court's decisions have jurisprudentially intertwined the religious and the secular courts in two important ways.

First, religious tribunals are now obliged to apply secular civil law, including civil rights and constitutional principles, when adjudicating civil disputes, such as those regarding the dissolution of joint property, the interpretation of marital contracts, or questions of custody.[36] Starting in the 1990s, the Supreme Court began attempting to subject religious courts to the basic norms and principles that govern the civil legal system.[37] In the landmark case *Bavli v. Great Rabbinical Court*, the Israeli Supreme Court heard a petition as to the Great Rabbinical Court's ruling regarding the dissolution of property held by the divorcing couple, the Bavlis.[38] The Bavlis accumulated significant wealth throughout their marriage, largely held in Mr. Bavli's sole name by the time of their divorce. Mr. Bavli won the jurisdictional race by attaching the dissolution of property matter to the primary divorce case that he filed in Rabbinical Court, which then heard the couple's dispute over these funds. Mrs. Bavli argued before the Rabbinical Court that she was entitled to half of the marital property based on the civil community property rule, which treats assets accumulated in the course of marriage as shared property regardless of how formal title is held. The religious court, however, declined to apply the community property rule, instead granting Mrs. Bavli only her *Ktuba*, which as Bix (Chapter 9, this volume) explains, is a religious document that states how much money the husband owes a wife in case of divorce. The latter sum was far less than half of the funds in question. The Supreme Court reversed and remanded this decision, ruling that the Rabbinical tribunal was required to apply civil family law when deciding related civil matters and thus was bound by the civil rule of community property division.

34 Basic Law: Judiciary, § 15(c), 15(d)(4), SH No. 1110, p. 78, (1984) (Isr.).

35 Zafran, *supra* note 17, at 577, 591; Basic Law: Judiciary, *id.*

36 HCJ 1000/92 Bavli v. Great Rabbinical Court 48(2) PD 221 (1994) (Isr.); HCJ 3914/92 48(2) PD 491 (1994) (Isr.).

37 Halperin-Kaddari, *supra* note 12, at 234.

38 Bavli v. Great Rabbinical Court, *supra* note 37, at 227.

The Rabbinical tribunal, however, was unwilling to follow this order. No further ruling was issued, and the Bavlis eventually settled, to Mrs. Bavli's detriment. Today, some Rabbinical Courts still refuse to apply the civil community property rule, often harming women who are deprived of their legal share of marital property. Other Rabbinical Courts apply the secular rule but interpret it according to religious principles.[39] For example, they may treat female adultery as a reason to deviate from the rule of equal distribution when civil law does not.[40] Similar results can occur when Rabbinical tribunals interpret the "best interest of the child" standard in child custody cases and, unlike civil courts, grant ample consideration to religious observance, as well as to each parent's heterosexual orientation and sexual practices.[41]

Second, the legislature and the Supreme Court have obligated civil courts to apply religious law, typically in regard to issues concerning wife maintenance and child support, further intertwining religious and civil courts jurisprudentially.[42] As might be expected, civil courts interpret religious law differently than religious tribunals do. Wife maintenance is a case in point. Under Jewish law, a husband's obligation to support his wife ceases if she commits adultery. In religious courts, once a wife's adultery is admitted or proven, the husband is released from his obligation to support her. By contrast, civil courts interpret Jewish law and jurisprudence, *Halakha*, differently; specifically, in cases where the husband too has been adulterous, civil courts may grant the wife maintenance, especially if she has no other way of supporting herself.[43] In this intertwined system of religious and secular courts and religious and secular family law, the outcomes for families depend heavily on who is deciding and under what body of law. Nowhere is this more true than for questions surrounding marriage itself, as the next section illustrates.

39 Halperin-Kaddari, *supra* note 12, at 234; Zafran, *supra* note 17, at 580.

40 For a case in which the Rabbincal Court deprived an adulterous wife of property and the Rabbinical Court was later reprimanded by the Israeli Supreme Court, *see* HCJ 8929/06 Plonit v, Great Rabbinical Court, 63(1) PD 273 (2008).

41 HCJ 5227/97 David v. Great Rabbinical Court 55 (1) PD 453 (Isr.); *see also* File No. 922153/4 Rabbinical Court (Haifa) Ploni v. Plonit (Aug. 23, 2015), Daat Rabbinical Rulings Database (Heb.). For a discussion of the role of religion in child custody proceedings in the United States, *see* Brinig, Chapter 10, this volume; Bix, Chapter 9, this volume.

42 Family Law Amendment (Maintenance) Law 5719–1959, SH No. 276, p. 72 (Isr.).

43 Ruth Halperin-Kaddari, *Towards Concluding Civil Family Law – Israel Style*, 17 Bar-Ilan L. Stud. 105, 113–23 (2001) (Heb.); Ruth Halperin-Kaddari, *Wife Support: From Perception of Difference to Perception of [In] Equality*, 7 Haifa Stud. L. Governance 767 (2003) (Heb.).

III. THE CURIOUS CASE OF ISRAELI MARRIAGE LAW – A SCHEME FRAGMENTED AND INTERTWINED

No other area of legal regulation more clearly illustrates the fragmented yet intertwined nature of Israeli family law than marriage law itself. In theory, marriage is subject to the exclusive jurisdiction of religious courts and marriage law is the sole province of religious law. This section shows that it is within this very "sterilized" and exclusively religious zone of marriage that the most significant and surprising interactions between civil and religious law occur. Indeed, the civil law system has responded to the nominally exclusive religious authority by developing an "underground" set of civil alternatives to religiously defined marriage.

These "detours" around religious law are necessitated by Israel's legal system, in which the only way to achieve married status is to marry in accordance with the rules of one's recognized religion. As a result, Israeli law throws up roadblocks or "impediments" to marriage that would be flagrantly unconstitutional elsewhere.[44] Same-sex and interfaith marriages are both a legal impossibility in Israel, as is marriage between individuals who are affiliated with a religion not recognized in Israel, such as Protestants or those who were not born into a religious community, such as persons from a Communist nation.

In addition to these interreligious disqualifications from marriage, many marriage hopefuls are also blocked from marrying by *intra*-religious rules. The most notorious examples of this in Jewish religious law are that a "bastard" may marry only another bastard or a convert to Judaism,[45] and that a female divorcee may not marry her paramour or a descendant of the ancient Jewish priesthood caste, usually denominated by the common surnames of Cohen, Cahn, or Kahn.[46]

Of course, some individuals may technically be eligible to marry but reject marriage on ideological grounds. Consider the would-be spouse born to a religious faith as a matter of genetics and community who embraces atheism as a matter of subjective belief – he or she may wish to marry in a civil framework without the religious oversight of a system they have rejected.

[44] For a discussion of various restrictions on the right to marry under Jewish Orthodox law, *see* Yuval Merin, *The Right to Family Life and Civil Marriage Under International Law and Its Implementation in the State of Israel*, 28 B.C. Int'l & Comp. L. Rev. 79, 135-36 (2005).

[45] A child born to a woman as a result of an extramarital affair or as a result of an incestuous union is a bastard in Jewish law.

[46] Marc Galanter & Jayanth Krishnan, *Personal Law and Human Rights in India and Israel*, 34 Israel Law Rev. 101, 122-23 (2000).

Israel denies them this option. In Israel, there is no freedom from religion in the realm of marriage law. For these individuals, exercising the right to marry comes at the expense of their right to freedom of conscience.

Religious marriage resisters and marriage ineligibles have not suffered silently. Instead, they have responded to religious limitations by devising a series of informal alternatives to religious marriage. First, Israeli citizens increasingly employ the strategy of traveling outside Israel to marry civilly overseas. This option, by which civil-minded couples bypass religious marriage in favor of a civil marriage, is in a sense a reverse parallel to a recent phenomenon in the U.S., where Christian couples have begun to renounce sex-blind civil marriage in favor of religious marriage.[47] Second, some intrafaith couples may opt for a private ceremony in the absence of a state-recognized religious authority. Finally, some couples forgo the institution of marriage altogether in favor of non-marital cohabitation.

As the remainder of this section shows, the civil judiciary and to a lesser extent the legislature have taken steps to legitimize these informal marriage alternatives.[48] Though each fragmented detour to official, state-sanctioned religious marriage is accorded a varying degree of recognition by the state, each remains peculiarly subject to the authority and jurisprudence of religious courts and law. Accordingly, the scheme of civil alternatives to religious marriage continues the simultaneous fragmentation and intertwinement of the civil and religious systems.

A. *Civil Marriage Outside of Israel*

While performing a civil marriage ceremony is impossible on Israeli soil, tens of thousands of Israeli couples have been voting with their feet by traveling abroad to marry civilly outside of Israel's borders.[49] The Israeli civil legal system has not turned a blind eye to this civilian protest. Conscious of the inequities imposed by religious law, the civil judiciary has ensured that the state recognizes marriages performed abroad.

47 Wilson, *supra* note 8. The rationales, however, are distinct, as Israeli couples marrying civilly denounce religious authority, while Christian couples "divorcing the state" are attempting to enhance it.

48 As of 2010, Israeli law has begun providing marriage-ineligibles with no recognized religious community limited access to the institution of marriage by crafting a special form of legal union, "covenant partnership," available only if both members of the partnership are religiously unaffiliated. Covenant Partnership for the Religionless Law 5770–2010, SH No. 2235, p. 428 (Isr.). *See also* Merin, *supra* note 44, at 135 n.259.

49 Avishalom Westreich & Pinhas Shifman, A Civil Legal Framework For Marriage And Divorce In Israel 27 (Ruth Gavison ed., 2013) (Heb.).

Starting in the 1960s, case law compelled the state to register all marriages conducted overseas in the official Population Registry if the marriage is evidenced with a foreign marriage certificate.[50] In the famous *Funk-Schlesinger* case, registration served to establish a marriage alternative with legal effects. There, a Belgian Christian woman married an Israeli Jewish man in a civil marriage ceremony in Cyprus. When Israel's Minister of Interior refused to register the marriage on the grounds that Israeli law prohibited interfaith unions, the wife sought relief from the Israeli Supreme Court. The Court held that a registration official has no authority to decide status matters and is not competent to examine the validity of marriages.[51] To the contrary, a registration official's administrative power is limited to registering any items of information supported by authenticated public certificates unless they are manifestly false, which might occur if an adult sought to be registered as a child of tender years.[52]

As the Court saw it, registration in the Population Registry database served strictly statistical purposes, neither supplying any substantive rights to these couples nor constituting *prima facie* evidence of the correctness of the data encoded therein.[53] The Court took pains to stress that registration of foreign marriages is merely an administrative procedure that does not amount to recognition.

Nonetheless, registration effectively confers upon registered couples a range of civil benefits and burdens concomitant to an official marriage license in Israel.[54] For example, Mrs. Funk-Schlesinger, originally a foreigner, received her permanent resident status after she registered her marriage.[55] In other words, "registered" couples resemble "married couples" in their *de facto* legal status. In this way, the *Funk-Schlesinger* decision stoked a silent revolution, a substantive reform in procedural clothing.[56]

50 The first case to develop this strategy in the context of interfaith marriage was HCJ 143/62 Funk-Shlezinger v. Ministry of the Interior, 17 PD 230 (1963) (Isr.).

51 *Id.* at 252.

52 *Id.* at 243. *See also* HCJ 58/68, Shalit v. Minister of the Interior, 23(2) P.D. 477, 506-08 (1969).

53 *Id.* at 243–44.

54 Halperin-Kaddari, *supra* note 12, at 244; MENASHE SHAVA, THE PERSONAL STATUS LAW IN ISRAEL 586-87 (4th ed., 2001) (Heb.); Eitan Levontin, *A Tower Floating in the Air: Funk-Schlesinger and the Law of the Population Register*, 11 HAIFA STUD. L. GOVERNANCE 129, 154 (2007) (Heb.); Menashe Shava, *Civil Marriages Celebrated Abroad: Validity in Israel*, 9 TEL-AVIV U. STUD. L. 311, 321–22 (1989).

55 Levontin, *id.*, at 145–48.

56 *See* Rivka Weill, *The Power of Understatement in Judicial Decisions*, XXX ANNUAIRE INTERNATIONAL DE JUSTICE CONSTITUTIONNELLE 125 (2014), (observing that the force of the decision stems from the fact that the justices were able to successfully veil its revolutionary impact).

The revolutionary impact of *Funk-Schlesinger* has nowhere been more pronounced than with same-sex families. In 2006 in *Ben-Ari v. Director of Population Administration, Ministry of the Interior*, the Israeli Supreme Court followed *Funk-Schlesinger* to register same-sex marriages at a time when only 3% of jurisdictions around the globe recognized them.[57] *Ben-Ari* concerned five Israeli homosexual couples who married in Canada and challenged the Israeli legal system to extend the reach of *Funk-Schlesinger* to gay marriage.[58] When Israel's registration official refused their applications for registration, arguing that the applications were manifestly false because Israeli law does not recognize such marriages, the case went to the Supreme Court. Again, the Court sided with the couples. It ordered the official to register the couples as married, while repeatedly underscoring that its decision did not rule on the validity of same-sex marriages. Rhetorical denials notwithstanding, the *Ben-Ari* decision makes Israel the only country on earth to treat same-sex marriages as null and void if executed domestically, but valid if solemnized outside the country.[59]

Since judicially mandated formal registration has *de facto* equated civil marriages performed abroad under foreign law with religious marriages performed in Israel for legal purposes (e.g., for tax, evidentiary, or mortgage privileges), Israel's courts have skirted the legally and politically thorny question of the substantive validity of civil marriages performed outside Israel under conflict-of-law rules. Recently, however, courts have begun recognizing civil marriages performed outside Israel, at least for couples who were eligible to religiously marry in Israel.[60] Yet, the hardships visited upon couples are

57 HCJ 3045/05 Ben-Ari v. Director of Population Administration, Ministry of the Interior 61 (3) PD 537 (2006) (Heb.), after URL (translation). elyon1.court.gov.il/files_eng/05/450/030/a09/05 030450.a09.htm. (translation) *See* para. 10 of J. Rubinstein's opinion (describing the status of same-sex marriage around the world).

58 *See* Dan Yakir & Yonathan Berman, *Same-Sex Marriages: Is it Really Necessary? Is It Really Desirable?* 1 L. & Soc. Change 169, 172 (2008), who represented two of the homosexual couples.

59 Ben-Ari v. Director of Population Administration, Ministry of the Interior, *supra* note 57. *See, e.g.*, section 22 of CJ Emeritus Barak's opinion.

60 HCJ 2232/03 Plonit. v. Tel-Aviv-Jaffa Regional Rabbinical Court, 61(3) PD 496 (2006) (Isr.) (henceforth Noahides case) (the Court recognized the validity of overseas civil marriage conducted by an Israeli Jewish couple who were eligible to marry each other under Jewish law by virtue of the English choice of law rules), URL (translation). elyon1.court.gov.il/file s_eng/03/320/022/a16/03022320.a16.htm. *See* FA 9607/03 Ploni v. Plonit 61(3) PD 726 (Isr.), at p. 742 para 23 (stating *in obiter* the validity of interfaith marriages conducted abroad according to the American choice of law rule). For a useful overview, *see* Ayelet Blecher-Prigat, *A Basic Right to Marry: Israeli Style*, 47 Israel L. Rev 433, at 434 & n.7, 439–42 (2014). *See also* Yuval Merin, *Anglo-American Choice of Law and the Recognition of Foreign Same-Sex Marriages in Israel: On Religious Norms and Secular Reforms*, 36 Brook J. Int'l L. 509, 548 (2011).

legion. This system inflicts obvious economic discrimination because indigent couples cannot so easily travel abroad to marry.

Moreover, Israel's "underground" civil marriage system has splintered Israel's family law system even more. The religious system's monopoly on marriage within Israel's borders, together with the extraordinary judicial commitment to recognizing civil marriages outside Israel, has birthed three fragmented marital routes: state-recognized religious marriage, out-of-state opposite-sex civil marriage, and out-of-state same-sex civil marriage.

This splintering has deepened, not lessened, the intertwinement of Israel's civil and religious systems. Opposite-sex civil marriages performed outside of Israel and later registered in Israel remain trapped in the exclusive jurisdictional web of religious courts in matters of divorce.[61] That occurs because the state gives religious courts the jurisdiction to adjudicate the dissolution of marriages formed outside Israel, imposing religious divorce law on civil marriages. The absurdity is underscored by assigning couples married outside Israel to courts associated with one of Israel's fourteen recognized religions.[62] Thus, the dissolution of civil marriages of heterosexual Jewish couples is subject to the authority of Rabbinical Courts. The substantive law applied becomes a sort of a legal lottery that depends on the presiding rabbi's religious views of the concept of civil marriage.

In 2003, the Great Rabbinical Court notified the Supreme Court that Rabbinical Courts would not follow its usual cumbersome and strict divorce procedure for dissolving religious marriage to civil marriages. Instead, the Great Rabbinical Court crafted a special, quicker no-fault divorce procedure for those civil marriages solemnized by Gentile law, known as "Noahide" Marriage, a procedure that could be employed in special cases with no hope for matrimonial reconciliation.[63] The development of a procedure for Noahide marriages may have been offered to dissuade the Supreme Court from taking civil marriage out of the Rabbinical Courts' jurisdictional ambit.[64] However, the majority of Rabbinical Courts have declined to use this divorce shortcut, instead applying religious divorce law even to civilly married couples.[65]

61 It is noteworthy that usually Israeli couples who performed a civil marriage abroad cannot similarly obtain a decree of divorce abroad because of lengthy residency requirements.

62 Noahides case, *supra* note 60.

63 File No. 4276/63 Great Rabbinical Court H.Sh. v. H.Y. (Nov. 11. 2003), Daat Rabbinical Rulings Database (Heb.), which was followed by the Noahides case, *supra* note 60.

64 Amichai Radziner, *Indeed Rhetoric Only: A reply to Avishalom Westreich*, 6–7 Fam. L. 579, 580–81, 583 (2013–2014) (Heb.).

65 For the documentation of this trend, see Triger, *supra* note 12, at 2, 6–7 (2012); Westreich & Shifman, *supra* note 49, at 39. *But see* Avishalom Westreich, *Rhetoric and Substance "Came*

The ironies are many. Not only is religious law used to sever a civil marriage, but couples who married abroad find themselves, at divorce, subject to religious law, sometimes the very system a couple deliberately sought to escape. Further complicating matters, religious law governs marriage dissolution grounds, but not the legal consequences of divorce, such as the financial rights and spousal support obligations – after a recent Supreme Court decision,[66] these questions are under the exclusive jurisdiction of the secular family court system and so are governed by judge-made, women-friendlier civil family law.[67]

In contrast, same-sex civil marriages performed abroad completely escape the clutches of religious courts and the application of religious law, because religious courts have not acknowledged same-sex marriages. In this sense, gay couples are uniquely rewarded in Israel. All aspects of same-sex marriages are adjudicated in the secular family court, making questions of property division and spousal support for these couples subject to the more progressive civil statutory and decisional family law. Yet the issue of marital exit has proved challenging even for these couples. In a 2012 case, a homosexual Jewish couple married abroad and registered the marriage in Israel. When they later sought

Down Wrapped Together"? On Civil Marriage in Israel Following the Noahide Decision, 6–7 FAM. L. REV. 543 (2013–2014) (Heb.); Avishalom Westreich, *On the Law and Its Decisor: A Response to Amihai Radzyner*, 6–7 FAM. L. REV. 605 (2013–2014) (Heb.) (arguing that the Nohaide decision has had a significant impact on the Rabbincial approach toward civil marriage and divorce). The divorce processes for the religiously and civilly married do differ, however. While civilly married couples must still obtain a Jewish divorce decree known as a *get*, these couples receive a *get le-humra*, that is, a *get* issued as a precautionary measure, making the procedure more lenient. *See* Westreich & Shifman, *supra* note 49, at 38; Avishalom Westreich & Amichai Radziner, *Civil Marriage in Israel Following the Noahide Decision: A Debate*, 6-7 FAM. L. REV. 543 (2013–2014) (Heb.).

66 *See, e.g.*, Noahides case, *supra* note 60 (holding that the civil family court has exclusive jurisdiction over financial aspects of civil marriage). Israeli courts have developed a rich body of civil family law through reliance on contract, property, and tort doctrines. *See, e.g.*, LCA 8256/99 Plonit v. Ploni, 58(2) PD 213 (2004) (Isr.) (spousal support between the civilly married is governed by civil contractual principles with the amount and duration controlled by the principle of good faith); LFA 9607/03 Ploni v. Plonit (Nov. 29, 2006), Nevo Legal Database (by subscription, in Hebrew) (Isr.) (the term "spouse" in the Law of Succession includes overseas civil marriages that are valid where celebrated, and thus a civilly married wife is entitled to inherit half of her husband's estate); Blecher-Prigat, *supra* note 60, at 455. Some Rabbinical courts have interpreted the Noahides case as not depriving them of concurrent jurisdiction over the legal consequences of civil marriage. *See* Westreich, *Rhetoric*, *supra* note 65, at 564–73.

67 Occasionally, the Rabbinical Courts defy this division of authority and insist on assuming jurisdiction over collateral matters such as the economic consequences of the dissolution of civil marriages under their authority over appended matters. *See, e.g.*, File No. 764411/1 Rabbinical court (Netanya) (unpublished, 2010), as cited in Triger, *supra* note 12, at 7–8.

to divorce, they found themselves at a dead end.[68] Israel's Ministry of Interior refused to change the couple's marital status in the Population Registry to "divorced," and the Rabbinical Court refused to open a divorce file for the couple and suspended their case pending further internal consultation. Finally, the couple turned to the civil family court, asking it to hear the case in the face of the Rabbinical Court's refusal.

The civil court rose to the challenge. It found it inconceivable to register a couple's marriage but render their union indissoluble. That result, the Court noted, would violate the constitutional rights of homosexuals and betray the state's fundamental values of justice and equality.[69] The Court had little trouble finding the authority to adjudicate the matter. When a religious tribunal fails to recognize the very existence of same-sex marriage, the religious tribunal *ipso facto* deprives itself of jurisdiction to decide the union's validity. Authority to preside over the marriage's dissolution then transfers to the family court, which can grant a registered divorce by virtue of the couple's mutual consent to part ways.[70]

Because Israel lacks a statutory nonreligious divorce regime, however, the right of same-sex couples to exit a marriage remains within the discretion of each presiding family law judge. A judge, for example, may grant a speedy unilateral no-fault divorce, but a judge may also decline to adjudicate matters of divorce for same-sex couples altogether.[71] Thus, it remains to be seen what particular shape the grounds for divorce for same-sex marriages will take.

The inevitable conclusion is that the combination of a religious and civil law system that operates in tandem yields paradoxical and unexpected results: same-sex couples have won a privilege – civil dissolution of marriage – bestowed upon no other couple in Israel precisely because the religious system in Israel enjoys *de jure* exclusive power over marriage and divorce but renounces homosexual marriage as an impossibility.[72]

68 *See* FC (Tel-Aviv) 11264-09-12 The Plaintiffs v. Ministry of Interior (Nov. 21, 2012), Nevo Legal Database (by subscription, in Hebrew) (Isr.).

69 *Id. at* §§ 33–34.

70 *Id.*

71 In one case, a court granted the requisite divorce but claimed the decision should not be read as recognizing the validity of homosexual marriage. *See* MDC (Tel Aviv) 52224-11-13 In the Matter of Plonim (Dec. 8, 2013), Nevo Legal Database (by subscription, in Hebrew) (Isr.). In another case, a lesbian couple married in New York but failed to register the marriage in Israel. The court refused to provide a decree of dissolution of marriage because same-sex marriage is unrecognized in Israel but issued a declaratory judgment that both women were not married to each other. FC (Tel-Aviv) 56248-10-12 Plonit v. Almonit (Feb. 19, 2014), Nevo Legal Database (by subscription, in Hebrew) (Isr.).

72 Merin, *supra* note 60, at 556 ("Orthodox Judaism does not perceive same-sex marriage as a forbidden category – it is simply nonexistent.").

B. Private Religious Marriages

The second, less common alternative to official, state-recognized religious marriage is a private religious ceremony conducted in Israel according to Jewish religious tradition, but without fulfilling the state's requirements – say, for instance, by having a religious ceremony without an Orthodox Rabbi presiding to sanction it. This phenomenon of performing state-unsanctioned religious marriage in Israel has interesting parallels to what *First Things*, the religious intellectual magazine, envisions for believers in traditional marriage in the post-*Obergefell* era: that religious authorities would perform religious marriages without civil effects, leaving the parties to secure the state-supported civil status.[73]

In Israel two types of Israeli Jews may opt for the informal private marriage track. First, a very specific group of marriage-ineligible persons gravitates to private marriages because Jewish marriage in Israel is equated with and monopolized by Orthodoxy. Consequently, some Jewish couples are unable to marry under Orthodox Judaism – for example, a divorcee and her paramour or a male descendant of the *Cohen* family who seeks to marry a female divorcee – which considers such unions as sinful and prohibited *a priori* (but will treat those marriages as valid after the fact). Such marriage-ineligibles seize upon this odd understanding of the sinful-yet-valid marriage and bypass the official religious establishment by joining in marriage in a private religious ceremony performed without the blessing of any state-appointed Orthodox Rabbis. This private avenue is closed to interfaith or same-sex couples whose unions are void *ab initio* under Jewish law.[74]

The second group of privately married couples consists of conscientious objectors, usually non-Orthodox or "secular" Jewish couples who qualify to religiously marry but for ideological reasons refuse to submit to the formal Orthodox religious marriage recognized by Israel. These couples simply opt for private ceremonies solemnized without a Rabbi or presided over by an unofficial (non-Orthodox) Rabbi. Because the private ceremony still meets the scant technical requirements for a *Halakhic* marriage, it is valid under Jewish law, though sinful. While in theory the law gives the Rabbinical Courts sole jurisdictional authority to decide the validity of marriages of Jews, in practice civil and religious oversight is entangled. The Israeli Supreme Court has established jurisdiction over private religious marriages but differentiates

[73] Ephraim Radner & Christopher Seitz, *The Marriage Pledge*, FIRST THINGS (May 16, 2016), www.firstthings.com/marriage-pledge (as quoted in Wilson, *supra* note 8).

[74] *See, e.g.*, CA 373/72 Tapper v. State of Israel 28(2) PD 7 (1974) (Isr.) (a petition to recognize the private marriage of an interfaith couple, a Jewish man and a Christian woman, denied).

between the two types of privately formalized unions: it recognizes marriages of marriage-ineligible persons, even when the Rabbinical Court refuses to do so, while refusing to recognize private marriages of conscientious objectors.[75]

The rational for granting civil judicial relief only to marriage-ineligible couples and not to conscientious objectors is that those who are ineligible have no way of marrying officially under religious law because their unions are forbidden;[76] the second group *does* have the option of swallowing their ideological convictions for the sake of "public order."[77] Even in the case of marriage-ineligibles, however, when the civil law recognizes a religiously prohibited private marriage, that legal recognition is incomplete. A marriage-ineligible wife forfeits her right to spousal support as a consequence of her "sinful" marriage, putting her in an inferior position to wives in religion-approved marriages.[78]

Conscientious objectors reap none of the valuable benefits and protections attached to marriage by virtue of their private ceremony. The loss of the full panoply of rights and obligations attached to marriage as a status is a measurable deficit. If U.S. states adopt a post-*Obergefell* marital regime like that described by Wilson (Chapter 16, this volume), this legal fate may also await people of faith who religiously marry but either fail or refuse to cement the civil status of their union.

C. *The Institution of Non-marital Cohabitation*

The third way that civil courts have attempted to bust the religious monopoly on formal marriage is to legally recognize the informal institution of cohabitation, rendering it a legitimate civil alternative. This civilly created status is one of the most conspicuous products of Israel's secular family law. Progressive forces in the Knesset and the judiciary have elevated the formal status of "reputed spouses" to nearly equal that of married spouses in terms of both socioeconomic and symbolic rights. This ranges from property, maintenance,

75 *See, e.g.*, HCJ 29/71 Kedar v. The Regional Rabbinical Court of Tel Aviv-Jaffa 26(1) PD 608 (1972) (Isr.); HCJ 51/69 Rodnizki v. The Rabbinical Court 24(1) PD 707 (1969) (Isr.); HCJ 80/63 Gurfinkel v. Minister of Interior 17 PD 2048 (1963) (Isr.); CA 238/53 Cohen v. Attorney-General 8(4) PD 19 (1954) (Isr.); HCJ 47/82, The Foundation of the Israel Movement for Progressive Judaism v. The Minister of Religious Affairs 43(2) PD 661 (Isr.).

76 Importantly, private ceremony wives, while recognized as married, forfeit their rights to spousal support as a consequence of the "sinful" marriage. Shifman, *supra* note 18, at 325–43.

77 *See, e.g.*, CA 640/82 Cohen v. Attorney General, 39(2) PD 673 (Isr.); Rodnisky v. Rabbinical Court, *id.*

78 Shifman, *supra* note 18, at 325–43.

and inheritance entitlements to immigration rights on the same basis as married couples and surname privileges.[79]

A major motivating force behind the construction of cohabitation law as a substitute for religious marriage is the desire to circumvent harsh religious rules.[80] As Professor Shahar Lifshitz observed, "[i]n the Israeli legal and public discourse, the need to 'compensate' those unable to marry is presented, time and again, as justification for strengthening the institution of cohabitation."[81] While the impetus for recognition began with religious marriage-ineligibles, today more and more couples that are able to marry religiously are opting out of marriage and into cohabitation. Cohabitation is considered a viable alternative to marriage because cohabitating couples can receive most of the benefits enjoyed by married couples – with the notable exception of adopting children together and solemnization by the state.[82] This regime varies substantially from the U.S. where couples who forgo marriage also forgo nearly all social benefits attached to marital status, as Wiener (Chapter 11, this volume) illustrates.[83]

Israel's generous recognition of unmarried cohabitants extends to same-sex couples. Starting with the celebrated *El-Al Israel Airlines Ltd v. Danielowitz*, case in the 1990s, a watershed in gay rights in Israel, the Israeli Supreme Court has begun equalizing homosexual and heterosexual relationships.[84] Today, Israeli civil law treats sexual orientation as a suspect classification, so that distinctions based on sexual orientation receive strict judicial scrutiny.[85] As a consequence, homosexual couples get the same benefits and burdens vis-à-vis each other, the state, and third parties as

79 *See, e.g.*, the landmark case CA 2000/97 Lindorn v. Karnit – Road Accident Victims' Fund, 55(1) PD 12 (1999) (according cohabitants rights even without express legislative authority); HCJ 6068/94 Ella Nazri v. Population Registry, 49(5) PD 693 (1996) (holding that a cohabiting partner of a married man may change her surname to that of her partner, notwithstanding his wife's opposition). *See also* Shahar Lifshitz, *The External Rights of Cohabiting Couples in Israel*, 37 Israel L. Rev. 346 (2003/04); Blecher-Prigat, *supra* note 60, at 434, 443–44; Shahar Lifshitz, A *Potential Lesson from the Israeli Experience for the American Same-Sex Marriage Debate*, 22 BYU J. Pub. L. 359, 360, 372–74 (2008); Westreich & Shifman, *supra* note 49, at 32.

80 Westreich & Shifman, *supra* note 49, at 31–32. *See also* Shifman, supra note 10, at 541; Yakir & Berman, *supra* note 58, at 172; Daniel Friedman, *The Cohabitants in Israeli Law*, 3 Tel-Aviv Stud. L. 459, 483 (1973).

81 Lifshitz, *supra* note 79, at 365, 360.

82 Triger, *supra* note 12, at 4. 83 Wiener, Chapter 11, this volume.

84 HCJ 721/94 El-Al Israel Airlines Ltd v. Danielowitz, 48(5) PD 749 (1994), URL (translation). elyon1.court.gov.il/files_eng/94/210/007/Z01/94007210.z01.htm.

85 AdminA 343/09 The Open House in Jerusalem for Pride and Tolerance v. Jerusalem Municipality 64 920 PD 1 (2010).

their heterosexual counterparts.[86] These include pension rights and inheritance rights, as well as work benefits, social security and tax privileges, and immigration status.[87]

Not only have Israel's civil courts gone a long way to equalize the status of married couples and unmarried cohabitants; they have also increasingly relaxed the criteria for being treated as cohabitants.[88] The floor for legal cohabitation status is such that a married individual can simultaneously be married to one person and recognized as the cohabitant of an extramarital lover.[89] As before, this doctrinal peculiarity stems from a system in which civil and religious components are inextricably intertwined. Because marital exit under Jewish divorce law is strictly limited, some women are trapped in legal limbo indefinitely absent their husband's consent to a religious divorce.[90] The secular system created a civil alternative to divorce by recognizing the cohabiting relationships of married individuals who are unable to dissolve

86 Weill, *supra* note 56, at 8.

87 *See* El-Al Israel Airlines Ltd v. Danielowitz, *supra* note 84, at 767, para. 19 of CJ Barak's opinion (examining the status of homosexual couples in Israel). *See also* Merin, *supra* note 60, at 561. The main remaining difference between homosexual and heterosexual couples relates to parental rights. In this area of family life, the law treats same-sex couples not as cohabitants, but as single people. This is the case as to both adoption and surrogacy; neither avenue of becoming parents is available to gay couples. *See, e.g.*, HCJ 5771/12 Moshe v. The Board for Approval of Surrogacy Agreements (Sep. 10, 2014), Nevo Legal Database (by subscription, in Hebrew) (Isr.). *See also generally* Ruth Zafran, *More than One Mother: Determining Maternity for the Biological Child of a Female Same-Sex Couple – the Israeli View*, 9 GEO. J. GENDER & L. 115 (2008).

88 Courts have sometimes found legal cohabitation between couples who had lived together for as little as a few months, *see* EC (Tel Aviv) 3693/90 Amir v. Zager (Sep. 16, 1991), Takdin Legal Database (by subscription, in Hebrew) (Isr.), those residing with each other rather than in the same apartment in certain circumstances, *see* CA 79/83 Attorney General v. Shukran, 39(2) PD 690 (1985) (Isr.); EC 833/81 Meir v. Attorney General, 42(2) PM 428 (1982), those who maintain separate finances when other characteristics of the relationship are present, *see* CA 107/87 Alon v. Mendelson, 53(1) PD 431, 438 (1989), and even acknowledged non-monogamous relationships, *see* CA 4385/91 Salem v. Carmi, 51(1) PD 337 (1997).

89 The first case to establish this ruling is CA 384/61 State of Israel v. Fessler, 16(1) PD 102 (1962) (Isr.); HCJ 6068/94 Nazri v. Population Registry 49(5) PD 693 (1996) (Isr.). *See also* Ayelet Blecher-Prigat & Benjamin Shmueli, *The Interplay Between Tort Law and Religious Family Law: The Israeli Case*, 26 ARIZ. J. INT'L & COMP. L. 279, 299 (2009). For a critique that such decisions legitimize *de facto* bigamy, *see* SHAHAR LIFSHITZ, COHABITATION LAW IN ISRAEL FROM THE PERSPECTIVE OF A CIVIL LAW THEORY OF THE FAMILY 267–74 (2005) (Heb.).

90 For an analysis of Israeli divorce case law, *see, for example*, Karin Carmit Yefet, *Unchaining the Agunot: Enlisting the Israeli Constitution in the Service of Women's Marital Freedom*, 20 YALE JOURNAL OF LAW & FEMINISM 101 (2009) (showing that Jewish women's right to marital freedom may be strictly limited and dependent on the goodwill of their husbands to grant the *get*).

their religious marriages.[91] As a result, a woman denied divorce is *de facto* able to enter a quasi-marriage status in which her new union receives almost all the civil benefits and privileges attendant to formal marriage.[92] In other words, secular cohabitation law serves a dual function: a civil alternative to marriage for a single individual cohabitating with a partner, and a civil alternative to divorce for a married individual cohabitating with an extramarital partner. Thus, in Israel, cohabitants' remedies arise in part from status; in the U.S., cohabitants' remedies generally rest on contract or equity, but not on status.

Israel's well-developed body of civil cohabitation law intersects with religion in yet another way. In a nascent and deeply troubling trend, the Rabbinical Courts have begun to appropriate jurisdiction over cohabitants and to trap even the unmarried in the clutches of religious divorce law – despite Supreme Court precedent to the contrary.[93] For the Rabbinical Courts, sexual intercourse may create a valid marriage under Jewish law, known as "betrothal by cohabitation." In this emerging trend, cohabiting couples seeking to separate may find themselves subject to the full-fledged process to religiously divorce.[94] Ironically, then, cohabitants who purposely abstained from "walking down the (either civil or religious) aisle" may nonetheless be forced to seek a formal divorce to end their relationship.

IV. CONCLUSION

The system of compulsory religious marriage in Israel has given rise to a remarkable fragmentation in which several civil alternatives compete with "holy" matrimony in Israeli society. Although religious and civil family law systems are nominally separate and parallel, they are also paradoxically and inextricably intertwined. Heterosexual civil marriages in Israel are dissolved by religious tribunals applying religious law. By contrast, civil courts have exclusive jurisdiction over divorce for same-sex marriages, precisely because religious law denies the very existence of same-sex marriages. Simply put, a conservative religious law led civil law to develop more advanced and liberal results. But outside the case of same-sex marriage, civil alternatives to religious marriage remain subject to the strictures of religious law.

91 *See, e.g.*, Michael Shashar, Haim Cohn – Supreme Justice: Conversations With Michael Shashar 234 (1989) (Heb.); Shifman, *supra* note 10, at 551.

92 Yefet, *supra* note 22. According to religious law, children born of this union will be bastards and unable to marry non-bastards.

93 *See, e.g.*, HCJ 673/89 Meshulam v. The Great Rabbinical Court 45(5) PD 594 (1991) (Isr.).

94 Triger, *supra* note 12, at 2 & at 9–10, 13–14.

In this volume, Wilson (Chapter 16) demonstrates the effort in U.S. politics to divorce marriage from government. In one form, clergy members would issue marriage licenses instead of the state, shifting "greater responsibility to religious authorities, not less, entangling religion even more with civil marriage."[95]

We have shown that in Israel, affording religious authorities a monopoly over marriage not only threatens democratic notions of equality but also works a profound problematic entanglement of the religious and the secular. The lesson from the Israeli case is this: it is precisely the attempt to give religion a monopoly over marriage and divorce that paradoxically yields a fragmented-but-intertwined scheme. That family law structure breeds instability and subversion. The designation of marriage as a "pure" religious sphere, free of secular fingerprints, has proved not only unworkable – parallel civil routes have flourished – but ironically also damaging to the very values that social conservatives hold so dear: nonreligious marriage undermines not only religious marriage, but the need to marry at all.

[95] Wilson, *supra* note 8.

26

Religious Modesty for Women and Girls

A Comparative Analysis of Legal Protections in France and the United States

Asma T. Uddin

Director of Strategy for the Center for Islam and Religious Freedom

Siam is a thirty-four-year-old, third-generation French citizen from Toulouse. On Tuesday, August 16, 2016, she was on vacation with her mother, sister, and two children on the French Riviera at a beach in Bocca, Cannes. Siam was wearing a burkini – a combination of a tunic, leggings, and headscarf – as she lay on the beach with her children frolicking around her.[1]

So-named by the Lebanese-Australian inventor of the product, Aheda Zanetti, the burkini is mostly worn by conservative Muslim women, but it has also been utilized by women of other faiths preferring a modest swimsuit, or by women who prefer to limit sun exposure for aesthetic or medical reasons.[2]

At around 4:00 p.m., Siam was startled out of her comfortable repose when three policemen appeared above her.[3] Equipped with tear gas, they glared at her menacingly. "Are you aware of the burkini ban?" they asked.[4] Siam tried to explain that, while she had heard there was controversy about the burkini, she did not know there was a ban.[5] The policemen gave her the order detailing the ban and Siam realized that her outfit was not considered "proper beach attire."[6]

1 Alissa J. Rubin, *French "Burkini" Bans Provoke Backlash as Armed Police Confront Beachgoers*, N.Y. Times (Aug. 24, 2016), www.nytimes.com/2016/08/25/world/europe/france-burkini.html.

2 Mike Ives, *Burkini Inventor Says Sales Have Skyrocketed On Heels of Controversy*, N.Y. Times (Aug. 24, 2016), www.nytimes.com/2016/08/25/world/australia/burkini-ban-france-aheda-zanetti.html.

3 *Id.*

4 Laura Thouny, *Siam Verbalized on a Beach in Cannes Wearing a Simple Veil*, L'OBS (Aug. 23, 2016), tempsreel.nouvelobs.com/societe/20160822.OBS6680/siam-verbalisee-sur-une-plage-de-cannes-pour-port-d-un-simple-voile.html.

5 *Id.* 6 *Id.*

By this time, a crowd had gathered around to watch and jeer. The policemen told Siam to remove her burkini if she wanted to stay on the beach, and the crowd agreed, chanting "We are Catholic here." While some of the onlookers defended Siam, most began to hurl insults, telling her to "go back" where she came from and that everyone was "fed up with the fuss."[7]

In tears, Siam was forced to undress – right there, in front of everyone, in front of her own children. And if that was not humiliating enough, she was slapped with a fine for failing to comply with the ban.[8] "Because people who have nothing to do with my religion kill, I do not have the right to go to the beach," she cried, "Because they commit attacks, it deprives me of my rights . . . it is absurd!"[9]

In the weeks to follow, Siam found herself defensive about her hijab, or headscarf, and even a bit frightened.[10] For the first time ever, it dawned on her just how deeply some segments of the public disapproved of her religious dress.[11] Yes, the French government had previously banned headscarves and other "conspicuous religious symbols" in public schools and had outlawed the wearing of face veils, or burqas, in public places.[12] But the burkini ban reflected a whole new level of disapproval of Muslim dress.

The burkini ban was the source of great debate among the French public, government, and courts; it began in Cannes in July 2016 and spread to twenty-four towns at the time of this writing, primarily on the French Riviera.[13] Mayors of these towns justified the bans on the basis of public order, gender equality, and hygiene. In August 2016, the ban in Villenueve-Loubet on the Cote d'Azur was challenged in court and the French Council of State, the country's highest administrative court, ruled that the burkini ban was a "serious and manifestly illegal attack on fundamental freedoms." A number of mayors have refused to comply with the court's ruling, even though the decision was supposed to set a legal precedent for burkini bans throughout the

7 Rubin, *supra* note 1. 8 *Id.* 9 Thouny, *supra* note 4. 10 *Id.* 11 *Id.*

12 Loi 2004–228 du 15 mars 2004 encadrant, en application du principe de laïcité, le port de signes ou de tenues manifestant une appurtenance religieuse dans les écoles, collèges et lycées publics [Law 2004–228 of Mar. 15, 2004, concerning, as an application of the principle of the separation of church and state, the wearing of symbols or garb that show religious affiliation in public primary and secondary schools], JOURNAL OFFICIEL DE LA RÉPUBLIQUE FRANÇAISE [J.O.][OFFICIAL GAZETTE OF FRANCE], Mar. 17, 2004, p. 5190; Loi 2010–1192 du 11 octobre 2010 interdisant la dissimulation du visage dans l'espace public [Law 2010–1192 of Oct. 11, 2010 on prohibiting concealment of the face in public space], JOURNAL OFFICIEL DE LA RÉPUBLIQUE FRANÇAISE [J.O.][OFFICIAL GAZETTE OF FRANCE], Oct. 12, 2010, p. 18344.

13 Angelique Chrisafis, *Sadness, Anger and Fear: How Nice is Responding to the Burkini Ban*, GUARDIAN (Aug. 26, 2016), www.theguardian.com/world/2016/aug/26/nice-france-burkini-ban-response-after-bastille-day-truck-attack.

country.[14] Meanwhile, the public remains deeply divided. Some French citizens find it unfair and illegal to impose restrictions on women's clothing, while others find it important to maintain the traditional French identity – in both appearance and mind-set.[15]

The burkini ban fiasco captivated the globe for weeks, and once again raised questions about the scope and value of religious freedom, the extent to which countries differ in their religious accommodations, and the ways religion intersects with politics. This chapter examines these issues as they arise in the context of laws regulating religious modesty, with a special focus on France and the United States. The section on the U.S. includes considerations of religious modesty in communal spaces and healthcare, as well as political and social self-expression.

For many religious women (and men), modesty is an important virtue throughout their lives, and in multiple contexts. Religious modesty requires young girls to overcome bias and discrimination at school or while biking down the street, while their mothers confront the realities of finding religiously sensitive healthcare in a secular world or making difficult decisions while vacationing with their families at seaside resorts. Given the centrality of modesty to religious women's lives and identity, religious freedom protections must include robust protection for religious modesty.

I MODESTY IN FRANCE

The concept of *laïcité* – loosely translated as "secularity"[16] – has a long and storied history in France. Lawmakers and political leaders revere it as a cornerstone of the French republic and the "conception of the common good" that unifies the French people.[17] Yet, despite the continuous invocation and celebration of *laïcité*, the concept is ambiguous. For some scholars, "*[l]aïcité* certainly evokes the concepts of secularism and separation of religion and the state, but, like the term 'democracy,' it can have widely different meanings and applications … [I]n France,

14 Sheena McKenzie, *French Mayors Maintain Burkini Bans despite Court Ruling*, CNN (Aug. 29, 2016), www.cnn.com/2016/08/29/europe/french-mayors-refuse-lift-burkini-ban.

15 Chrisafis, *supra* note 13.

16 *English Translation of "Laïcité,"* COLLINS, www.collinsdictionary.com/dictionary/french-english/la%C3%AFcit%C3%A9.

17 T. Jeremy Gunn, *Religious Freedom and Laïcité: A Comparison of the United States and France*, 2004 B.Y.U. L. REV. 419 (2004).

laïcité often bears the connotation of the state protecting citizens from the excesses of religion."[18]

Other scholars use *laïcité* to describe a tension between religion and society that has a deep impact on religious exercise:

> Laïcité is a secular concept that "conveys . . . a profound suspicion" and "a somewhat tense attitude where religion is concerned." Rather than allowing the free exercise and expression of all religions, France has moved toward "fundamental secularism," where the government "denies religious conviction or belief any place for expression in the public realm." Laïcité has "functioned as a tool of coercive cultural uniformity . . . especially among immigrant populations" instead of as a means of multiculturalism.[19]

Laïcité, as a concept, was birthed in the years after the French Revolution of 1789, and it developed between 1879 and 1905 as a movement to separate two pillars of French society: government and religion.[20] The initial concept of *laïcité* was not about religious freedom; instead, it was primarily about suspicion and dislike toward the Roman Catholic Church.[21] The "Church opposed not just the Revolution's excess, but the Revolution itself. It supported repeated cycles of counterrevolution through most of the nineteenth century." Viewed "as opposed to the liberties of the people," the Church became "the subject of enmity, suspicion, and hostile regulation," resulting in "a very narrow view of religious liberty in French law and in French public opinion."[22] The government responded to the threat posed by the Church by taking steps to weaken religious organizations, such as passing laws to dissolve religious organizations, demanding that clergy and citizens choose between loyalty to their religion and loyalty to France, and generally creating a climate of hostility toward religion and religious practice.[23]

French secularism is not only a principle of identity and society, but also a legally enforceable principle that often serves as a justification for laws that are aimed at promoting public order or limiting certain freedoms. One reason the principle predominates French society so thoroughly is that the right to

[18] *Id.* at n.2 (explaining extensively the concept of Laïcité). *See also* Douglas Laycock, *Conference Introduction: American Religious Liberty, French Laïcité, and the Veil*, 49 J. Cath. Leg. Stud. 21, 51 (2010) (comments by Mark Movsesian) ("The problem is that most jurists in France don't know what laïcité and separation mean. There are at most ten professors of law who understand what these terms mean.").

[19] Shaira Nanwani, *The Burqa Ban: An Unreasonable Limitation on Religious Freedom or a Justifiable Restriction?* 25 Emory Int'l L. Rev. 1444 (2011).

[20] Gunn, *supra* note 17, at 432–33. [21] *Id.*

[22] Douglas Laycock, *Religious Liberty and the Culture Wars*, 3 U. Ill. L. Rev. 839, 865 (2014).

[23] Gunn, *supra* note 17, at 432–42.

free exercise of religion – while protected by French law – is not considered a right inherent to human beings (as it is, for example, in the U.S.). Rather, it is one of several "public freedoms" granted and limited by the government, at the government's discretion.[24]

This view of religious freedom is further reflected in France's approach to religious exemptions: there is no right to such exemptions; indeed, few exist in the law: "France can, and ... does, single out religion for discriminatory regulation. French school girls can wear a head scarf for fashion reasons, or medical reasons, or any other secular reason, but not for religious reasons."[25]

In this way, *laïcité* makes religion vulnerable to special governmental discrimination. Citizens must actively keep religion private and separate from their public lives. *Laïcité* leaves little room for physical religious observance outside the confines of one's home or one's church, temple, or mosque – while no laws ban all displays of religion in public, they are not encouraged. *Laïcité* pushes French citizens toward becoming the proverbial melting pot and assimilating with traditional French culture, in contrast to the American conception of the salad bowl, which allows citizens to maintain their cultural and religious identities:[26] "In the United States, religion and liberty [a]re perceived as natural allies; in France, religion and liberty [a]re perceived as natural enemies."[27] For religious believers who abide by religious dress codes – which necessarily are relevant largely in the public sphere – such strictures pose serious complications.

Indeed, *laïcité* as a justification for legislation regularly arises in relation to religious garb, with special attention paid to modest garb.[28] The connection between the two came to the forefront of French politics in December 2003, when President Jacques Chirac issued a decree creating the Stasi Commission (named for the Commission's chairman, Bernard Stasi) and charged it with "conducting an analysis of the application of the principle of *laïcité* in the Republic."[29] The Commission, after conducting its studies, made a number of

[24] "That which in other countries falls under the rubric of civil rights, in France falls under the rubric of public freedoms (libertés publiques). This is because, in France, one does not conceive of civil rights as natural rights that each individual can assert against the state, but as the natural right to enjoy freedoms defined and delimited exclusively by law. In this sense, rights are confused with freedoms, and freedoms are realized not against the state but by the state." Michel Troper, *French Secularism, or Laicite*, 21 CARDOZO L. REV. 1267, 1268 (2000).

[25] Laycock, *supra* note 22, at 864. [26] Nanwani, *supra* note 19.

[27] Laycock, *supra* note 22, at 865.

[28] Lina Ragep Powell, *The Constitutionality of France's Ban on the Burqa in Light of the European Convention's Arslan v. Turkey Decision on Religious Freedom*, 2013 WIS. INT'L L.J. 218.

[29] Gunn, *supra* note 17, at 462.

recommendations. These ranged from improving living standards in poorer communities to banning political symbols from schools and providing neutral learning environments. Only one recommendation was partially accepted and enacted, while all other recommendations were either rejected or ignored.[30] Less than one week after receiving the recommendations, Chirac proposed a law that would ban conspicuous religious clothing. In 2004, this proposal became law.[31]

As the remainder of this section explains, after the 2004 law, which called for a ban on headscarves and other religious symbols in public schools, came the 2011 ban on the burqa – a full-body covering that includes a face veil, worn by a small minority of Muslim women. The third most recent religious garb ban is the 2016 ban on the burkini, a modest swimsuit consisting of a tunic, pants, and head cover. Each of these bans is discussed next.

A *Religious Symbols Ban of 2004*

France's debate over headscarves followed a tortuous route. Initially, the headscarf took center stage in September 1989, when three Muslim girls were temporarily barred from school because of their headscarves.[32] A local newspaper picked up the story, igniting a media frenzy and national conversation across France about the headscarf and its place (or lack thereof) in French society and schools.[33] While some news stories expressed anger and indignation at the school's intervention in the students' private lives and religious beliefs, others wrote that the school had acted correctly because there was no place for the headscarf in French schools.[34] As a response, the Minister of Education, Lionel Jospin (who later became the prime minister of France in 1997) asked the Council of State to deliver a formal opinion about "[w]hether the wearing of religious clothing in public schools could be reconciled with the important French doctrine of *laïcité*."[35]

The Council of State issued a statement that *laïcité* was consistent with religious expression.[36] That 1989 ruling held that *laïcité* requires neutrality

[30] *Id.* at 462–63. [31] *Id.* at 463. [32] *Id.* at 454.

[33] Joan W. Scott, *Symptomatic Politics: The Banning of Islamic Head Scarves in Public Schools*, 23 FRENCH POLITICS, CULTURE & SOCIETY 106 (Winter 2005).

[34] *Id.* at 106–07. [35] Gunn, *supra* note 17, at 455.

[36] The opinion stated: "It results from the constitutional and legislative texts and from France's international engagements . . . that the principle of laïcité in public education, which is one of the elements of the laïcité of the state and of the neutrality of all of the public services, requires that education be dispensed with respect, on one hand, for this neutrality by the programs and teachers and, on the other hand, for the students' liberty of conscience . . . This freedom on the

and respect from schoolteachers and educational programs for students wishing to express their religious beliefs.[37] The court also held that students could wear religious clothing in schools as long as the religious symbols are not so "ostentatious" as to "constitute an act of intimidation, provocation, proselytizing, or propaganda; threaten the dignity and freedom of students or other members of the educational community" or disrupt the school's normal functioning.[38] Should there be any issues arising from such religious expression, each case should be investigated and decided accordingly by school officials.[39]

The 1989 headscarf ruling triggered a public outcry, with French citizens and lawmakers questioning whether the power of the Council of State had to be recalibrated, given what seemed to them its apparent lack of regard for the public interest.[40] This outcry suggested to some French legal scholars that the controversy was less about "high principles of a neutral republic education in public schools" and more about "a deeper unease about Islam."[41] According to these scholars, the law reflected French cultural sentiment about Muslim religious garb – particularly modest garb that opposed the highly fashionable French dress. This sentiment assumed that Muslim women who choose to wear religious garb prefer their Muslim identity to their French identity.[42] Those who believed this found the religious garb of Muslim women to be an affront to their country and society.

In the years following the Council of State's ruling, school officials filed lawsuits and the Minister of Education issued a number of directives that attempted to undermine the ruling.[43] The Council heard forty-nine lawsuits against Muslim girls who wore headscarves to school; of these, forty-one found in favor of the Muslim student.[44]

By 2003, it finally seemed as though all parties had accepted the Council's initial ruling. The conflicts had declined; when they did arise, they were not as sensational as before.[45] Unfortunately, this respite did not last long. Based on the Stasi Commission's recommendation to prohibit religious symbols in public schools, a law was passed in 2004 that banned all conspicuous religious

students' part includes the right to express and to manifest their religious beliefs inside educational establishments, [so long as such expression is done] with respect for pluralism and for the freedom of others, and without detracting from the [school's] educational activities [and] the content of [its] programs." Conseil d'État, Nov. 27, 1989, Stasi Commission Report.

37 Gunn, *supra* note 17, at 455.

38 Elisa T. Beller, *The Headscarf Affair: The Counseil d'Etat on the Role of Religion and Culture in French Society*, 39 TEX. INT'L L.J. 581 (2004).

39 Gunn, *supra* note 17, at 455. 40 *Id.* at 456. 41 *Id.* at 457. 42 *Id.* at 456–57.

43 *Id.* at 457. 44 *Id.* 45 *Id.* at 457–58.

symbols from school, including the headscarf.[46] The ban, an amendment to the French Code of Education,[47] stated:

> In schools, colleges, and public high schools, the wearing of signs or clothes by which pupils overtly manifest a religious affiliation is prohibited. The rules shall state that the implementation of a disciplinary procedure is preceded by a dialogue with the student.[48]

Private schools were left untouched by the ban.

The law itself is brief and generalized, but the Stasi Commission's report specified the religious symbols that would violate the rule – the Muslim headscarf, the Jewish yarmulke, and Christian crosses of such excessive size as to be ostensible and in violation of the law.[49] At the same time, the law specified as acceptable discreet pendants such as those of the cross, the Star of David, and the Hand of Fatima (worn primarily by Shi'a Muslims).[50]

Some scholars argued that although the law expressly aimed to promote *laïcité*, it had the unofficial goal of targeting Muslim girls' headscarves:[51]

> The [i]mpetus for the law clearly stemmed from controversy over Muslim girls wearing headscarves to school. President Chirac admitted there had never been a problem with Catholic students wearing crosses "obviously of an excessive dimension," and most Jewish students who wear skullcaps attend private Jewish schools. Thus, the formally "neutral" breadth of the 2004 law with its focus on the conspicuousness of any religious symbol masks the particular concern underlying the law.[52]

The French public by and large approved of the amendment. To many, the headscarf ban was seen as a measure protecting against the oppression of women. Right before the amendment was passed, sixty influential French women, including historian Elisabeth Badinter, Former Minister of Women's Rights Yvette Roudy, actress and singer Isabelle Adjani, and designer and writer Sonia Rykiel, signed and published a petition in the prominent fashion magazine, *Elle*, addressed to President Chirac.[53] The petitioners pushed to

46 *Id.* at 458–59. 47 Loi 2004–228, *supra* note 12.

48 *Id.* The title of the ban reflects its applicability to both, primary and secondary, schools ("Law #2004–228 of March 15, 2004, concerning, as an application of the principle of the separation of church and state, the wearing of symbols or garb which show religious affiliation in public primary and secondary schools.").

49 Beller, *supra* note 38. 50 *Id.*

51 Leti Volpp, *The Culture of Citizenship*, 8 THEORETICAL INQUIRIES L. 571 (2007).

52 *Id.* at 573–74.

53 *It Appealed Against the Veil*, L'OBS (Dec. 5, 2003), http://tempsreel.nouvelobs.com/societe/20031204.OBS0783/elle-lance-un-appel-contre-le-voile.html.

ban the headscarf from France as a "visible symbol of the submission of women."[54]

French suspicion of the headscarf runs deep:

> This suspicion . . . has often led to [sic] some to imagine, behind the behavior of some students, a concerted effort to subvert republican values. The reverberations of the headscarf issue in the media and in the political debate reveals a particularly French sensibility to Islam, which is not expressed in other major European countries with the same intensity.[55]

B Burqa Ban of 2011

The theme of preventing oppression against women by limiting modest religious garb came up in relation to the burqa, or "full veil," in 2009; an official ban followed in 2011.[56] In a speech on June 22, 2009, then-President Nicolas Sarkozy voiced his concerns about the burqa in his address to the French Parliament:[57]

> In our country, we cannot accept that women be prisoners behind a screen, cut off from all social life, deprived of all identity . . . The burqa is not a religious sign, it's a sign of subservience, a sign of debasement – I want to say it solemnly . . . It will not be welcome on the territory of the French Republic.[58]

The day after Sarkozy's speech, the French Parliament put together the Parliamentary Commission to Study the Wearing of the Full Veil in France. It tasked the Commission with investigating the burqa, its impact, and possible ways of limiting its public presence.[59] After a six-month investigation, including 211 interviews with witnesses and experts, the Commission published a report stating that the burqa was contrary to French values.[60]

In his statement about the report, Commission President M. Andre Guerin said:

> The report shows with precision how the wearing of the full veil infringes upon three principles that are included in the motto of the Republic: liberty, equality and fraternity. The full veil is an intolerable infringement on the freedom and the dignity of women. It is the denial of gender equality and of

[54] Volpp, *supra* note 51. [55] Gunn, *supra* note 17, at 457. [56] Nanwani, *supra* note 19.
[57] *Id.* at 1440.
[58] *Sarkozy: Burqas "Not Welcome" in France*, CBS News (June 22, 2009), www.cbsnews.com/news/sarkozy-burqas-not-welcome-in-france/.
[59] Nanwani, *supra* note 19, at 1441. [60] *Id.* at 1442.

> a mixed society. Finally, it is the will to exclude women from social life and the rejection of our common will to live together.[61]

The full veil, Geurin also said, reflects "Islamic fundamentalism."[62] Despite its findings, the Commission was unable to reach consensus on whether the full veil should be banned by law.

Then–Prime Minister Francois Fillon moved forward nonetheless, asking the French Council of State to issue a statement on the possibility of enacting a ban of the full veil.[63] The Council issued a statement, in March 2010, that while a ban on the full veil would violate fundamental rights and freedoms,[64] a restriction on face coverings generally could plausibly be justified on the basis of public security.[65]

The French National Assembly drafted a bill banning the burqa in May 2010.[66] Despite its previous cautions about encroaching on fundamental rights and freedoms, the Council of State endorsed the bill in October 2010, holding that the ban did not violate the French Constitution because it did not disproportionately prevent citizens from worshipping or exercising their religions in their places of worship.[67] Having passed the domestic legal test, the law was officially enacted on April 11, 2011, creating two offenses: (1) wearing a face-covering veil and (2) forcing someone to wear a face-covering veil.[68]

Known colloquially as the "burqa ban," the law provides the following:

> **Section 1**
>
> No one may, in public places, wear clothing that is designed to conceal the face.
>
> **Section 2**
>
> I. For the purposes of section 1 hereof, "public places" comprise the public highway and any places open to the public or assigned to a public service.
>
> II. The prohibition provided for in section 1 hereof shall not apply if the clothing is prescribed or authorised by primary or secondary legislation, if it is justified for health or occupational reasons, or if it is worn in the context of sports, festivities or artistic or traditional events.

[61] *France: Highlights of Parliamentary Report on the Wearing of the Full Veil (Burqa)*, Lib. of Cong., www.loc.gov/law/help/france-veil.php.

[62] *Id.* [63] *Id.*

[64] The fundamental rights and freedoms included "individual freedom, personal freedom, right to privacy, freedom of expression and freedom to manifest [one's] convictions, notably religious, and prohibition of any discrimination." Nanwani, *supra* note 19, at 1441.

[65] *Id.* at 1442. [66] *Id.* [67] *Id.* [68] *Id.* at 1431.

Section 3

Any breach of the prohibition laid down in section 1 hereof shall be punishable by a fine, at the rate applying to second-class petty offences (contraventions) [150 euros maximum].

An obligation to follow a citizenship course, as provided at paragraph 8 of Article 131–16 of the Criminal Code, may be imposed in addition to or instead of the payment of a fine.[69]

Section 4 of the law adds the following to the Criminal Code:

> Any person who forces one or more other persons to conceal their face, by threat, duress, coercion, abuse of authority or of office, on account of their gender, shall be liable to imprisonment for one year and a fine of 30,000 euros. Where the offence is committed against a minor, such punishment shall be increased to two years' imprisonment and a fine of 60,000 euros.[70]

Because the burqa ban does not specify a single prescribed punishment – it provides that a violation "is punishable by a fine [or] [t]he obligation to fulfill the citizenship course" – its enforcement has been arbitrary. Police are confused about which situations require punishment by fine or punishment by citizenship classes and have "warned that the law banning niqabs [or face veils][71] was 'infinitely difficult' to enforce and would not be a priority."[72]

The face veil has inspired government opposition outside of France, too. At the time of this writing, burqa bans in some form or another are in force in France, Belgium, Switzerland, Austria, and the Netherlands.[73] In the Netherlands, the burqa ban was proposed as an amendment to the Penal Code in 2007, which mentioned the niqab and burqa by name;[74] that

69 Loi 2010–192 *supra* note 12 (as translated and quoted in S.A.S. v. France, Eur. Ct. H.R., App. No. 4385/11, Judgment (July 1, 2014)).

70 *Id.*

71 In the various legal bans and related public discourse, the face veil is referred to as either "burqa" or "niqab."

72 Angelique Chrisafis, *French Veil Ban: First Woman Fined for Wearing Niqab*, GUARDIAN (Apr. 12, 2011), www.theguardian.com/world/2011/apr/12/french-veil-ban-woman-niqab-fined; *Niqab*, BBC, www.bbc.co.uk/religion/religions/islam/beliefs/niqab_1.shtml (defining niqab).

73 *Belgian Ban on Full Veils Comes into Force*, BBC NEWS (July 23, 2011), www.bbc.com/news/world-europe-14261921; *Burka Ban for Muslims Enforced in Switzerland with Fines as Much as £8,000*, TELEGRAPH (July 7, 2016), www.telegraph.co.uk/news/2016/07/07/burka-ban-for-muslims-enforced-in-switzerland-with-fines-of-up-t/; *Netherlands Approves Plans for Partial Niqab Ban*, AL JAZEERA (May 22, 2015), www.aljazeera.com/news/2015/05/netherlands-niqab-ban-partial-150522144420609.html.

74 The proposal was to "[a]mend the Penal Code in Connection with a Ban on Wearing of Burqas and Niqabs in the Public Space." Sally Pei, *Unveiling Inequality: Burqa Bans and*

amendment was abandoned when the Netherland's Council of State held that it would violate rights to free exercise of religion and nondiscrimination under the national constitution and the European Convention on Human Rights.[75] The failed 2007 attempt was followed by another bill in 2012, this one seeking to ban the face veil without explicitly mentioning the burqa and niqab.[76] That bill was rescinded in 2015, when the Dutch cabinet approved a partial burqa ban limited to schools, hospitals, and public transportation – that is, those "'specific situations where it is essential for people to be seen' or for security reasons."[77]

Unlike the narrow focus of the Netherland ban, the French ban remains broad – and the European Court of Human Rights has upheld that broadness. The European Court considered the French ban in *SAS v. France*, a case brought by a Muslim woman born in France who wore a burqa of her own volition.[78] While she did not wear the burqa at all times, she wanted personal discretion to wear it at her choosing as part of her religious observance. The applicant was thus in violation of France's burqa ban enacted in 2011. After exhausting all possible remedies in the French legal system, she applied to the European Court in 2011, arguing that the burqa ban violated Articles 8,[79] 9,[80] 10,[81] and

Nondiscrimination Jurisprudence at the European Court of Human Rights, 122 YALE L. J. 1089, 1091 (2013).

75 *Id.*

76 The 2012 bill was titled, "Proposal of Law, Establishing a General Ban on the Wearing of Face-Covering Clothing." *Id.*

77 *Netherlands Approves Plans for Partial Niqab Ban*, *supra* note 73.

78 S.A.S. v. France, Eur. Ct. H.R., App. No. 4385/11, Judgment (July 1, 2014).

79 "Right to respect for private and family life:

1. Everyone has the right to respect for his private and family life, his home and his correspondence.
2. There shall be no interference by a public authority with the exercise of this right except such as is in accordance with the law and is necessary in a democratic society in the interests of national security, public safety, or the economic wellbeing of the country, for the prevention of disorder or crime, for the protection of health or morals, or for the protection of the rights and freedoms of others." Eur. Conv. H.R., Art. 8, www.echr.coe.int/Documents/Convention_ENG.pdf.

80 *See* Conseil d'État, *supra* note 36.

81 "Freedom of Expression:

1. Everyone has the right to freedom of expression. This right shall include freedom to hold opinions and to receive and impart information and ideas without interference by public authorities and regardless of frontiers. This Article shall not prevent States from requiring the licensing of broadcasting, television, or cinema enterprises.
2. The Exercise of these freedoms, since it carries with it duties and responsibilities, may be subject to such formalities, conditions, restrictions, or penalties as prescribed by law and are necessary in a democratic society, in the interests of national security, territorial integrity or

14[82] of the European Convention of Human Rights. The court's Grand Chamber heard the case on November 27, 2013.[83]

The Grand Chamber dismissed the Article 8, 10, and 14 claims and focused largely on Article 9. Specifically, Article 9 provides the following:

> Everyone has the right to freedom of thought, conscience and religion; this right includes freedom to change his religion or belief and freedom, either alone or in community with others and in public or private, to manifest his religion or belief, in worship, teaching, practice and observance.[84]

These protections are subject to "such limitations as are prescribed by law and are necessary in a democratic society in the interests of public safety, for the protection of public order, health or morals, or for the protection of the rights and freedoms of others."[85]

Applying this provision – including the vague limitations just quoted – the Grand Chamber found that while the burqa ban violated the applicant's rights under Article 9, the violation was justified because it protected "the rights and freedoms of others."[86] The French government had argued that these "rights and freedoms of others" included "respect for gender equality, respect for human dignity, and respect for the minimum requirements of living together."[87] The Grand Chamber rejected the first two justifications but accepted the third.[88] More specifically, it accepted the government's argument that a face-concealing veil undermined the ability to "live together."[89] The government argued, and the Grand Chamber agreed, that the "face played a significant role in social interaction," and that facial concealment was a practice that "fundamentally call[s] into question the possibility of open interpersonal relationships."[90]

Acknowledging that the "living together" exception is broad and subject to abuse, the Grand Chamber undertook a necessity analysis, noting that "many

public safety, for the prevention of disorder or crime, for the protection of health or morals, for the protection of the reputation of rights of others, for preventing the disclosure of information received in confidence, or for maintaining the authority and impartiality of the judiciary." Eur. Conv. H.R., Art. 10, www.echr.coe.int/Documents/Convention_ENG.pdf.

82 "Prohibition of discrimination:

The enjoyment of the rights and freedoms set forth in this Convention shall be secured without discrimination on any ground such as sex, race, colour, language, religion political or other opinion, national or social origin, association with a national minority, property, birth, or other status." Eur. Conv. H.R., Art. 14, www.echr.coe.int/Documents/Convention_ENG.pdf.

83 Press Release, *French Ban on the Wearing in Public of Clothing Designed to Conceal One's Face Does Not Breach the Convention*, Eur. Conv. H.R. (Nov. 6, 2016), goo.gl/iDnWxB.

84 Eur. Conv. H.R., Art. 9, www.echr.coe.int/Documents/Convention_ENG.pdf. 85 *Id.*

86 *Supra* note 83. 87 *Id.* 88 *Id.* 89 *Id.* 90 *Id.*

national and international human rights bodies" found a blanket ban "disproportionate."[91] The Grand Chamber also noted that the burqa ban was enacted in a climate of anti-Muslim sentiment and risked legitimizing stereotypes and prejudice.

Despite these problems, the Grand Chamber upheld the ban because it limited only that garb that covered the face and did so because of facial concealment, not because of the religious significance of the face veil. Moreover, the sanctions were negligible at 150 euros and/or a citizenship class. Finally, the Grand Chamber concluded it was required to give wide deference to the French government as the democratically elected legislature that passed the ban.[92]

Two of the dissenting judges raised concerns about limiting fundamental rights on the "far-fetched and vague" notion of living together.[93] The two dissents also argued that facial concealment is not uniformly a barrier to social interaction – noting motorcycle helmets, carnival costumes, ski masks, and Internet and phone activity as examples of how an inability to see a person's face does not harm interpersonal connections.[94]

C Burkini Ban of 2016

The third and most recent religious garb ban was the prohibition of the burkini by more than thirty beach towns in France.[95] The burkini's creator, Zanetti, told the press that the burkini was never meant to be a political or religious symbol; Zanetti just wanted to provide women with another option for beachwear.[96]

The Cannes order detailing the burkini ban is typical of such bans:

> In a context where France and religious landmarks and spaces are currently being attacked, it is necessary to prevent any risk of disturbances (troubles, danger) to the public order (gatherings, confrontations, etc.) possibly created by ostentatiously religious affiliated bathing suits. Access to the beaches and bathing is prohibited from the date of this law until 8/31/2016 to anybody

[91] *Id.* [92] *Id.*; S.A.S. v. France, Eur. Ct. H.R., App. No. 4385/11, Judgment (July 1, 2014).

[93] Armin Steinbach, *Burqas and Bans: The Wearing of Religious Symbols Under the European Convention on Human Rights*, 4 CAMBRIDGE J. INT'L & COMP. L. 1 (2015).

[94] *Id.*

[95] *Cannes Bans Burkinis over Suspected Link to Radical Islamism*, BBC NEWS (Aug. 12, 2016), www.bbc.com/news/world-europe-37056742.

[96] Ives, *supra* note 2; *See also* Aheda Zanetti, *I Created the Burkini to Give Women Freedom, Not to Take it Away*, GUARDIAN (Aug. 24, 2016), www.theguardian.com/commentisfree/2016/aug/24/i-created-the-burkini-to-give-women-freedom-not-to-take-it-away.

> displaying an appearance going against respect for good morals and for the idea of laicity, hygienic rules, and rules of security to all in the public maritime space. In all public lower, middle and high schools, any signs or outfits ostentatiously showing any religious affiliation is prohibited.[97]

The rule cited public order, morality, secularism, hygiene, and safety as reasons for the ban.[98] Politicians also invoked gender equality. The Prime Minister of France, Manuel Vall, described the burkini as "part of a political project to enslave women," and "not compatible with the values of France."[99]

However, the political justification for the law quickly made apparent the predominance of the public order rationale.[100] The ban was a reaction to the terrorist attack in the French Riviera city of Nice on July 14, 2016.[101] The attack killed more than eighty people who had gathered at the seafront to watch fireworks celebrating Bastille Day. The attack put France on edge and aggravated the already rising apprehension toward the Muslim community, one of Europe's largest. The tension was further exacerbated when, only twelve days later, a priest in Burgundy was stabbed and killed by attackers who pledged allegiance to ISIS.[102] Four days after this attack, Cannes enacted the first of the burkini bans to alleviate tensions and maintain "public order."[103]

Theirry Migoule, the head of municipal services in Cannes, made clear the perceived connection of the burkini with terrorism: "We are not talking about banning the wearing of religious symbols on the beach … but ostentatious clothing which refers to an allegiance to terrorist movements which are at war with us."[104] David Lisnard, the Mayor of Cannes and one of the foremost critics of the burkini, labeled the burkini a sign of extremism.[105] Noting that

97 Translated from the French by Angela Wu Howard.

98 Aurelien Breeden & Lilia Blaise, *Cannes, Citing Security Risks, Bans Full-Body "Burkinis" From Its Beaches*, N.Y. Times (Aug. 12, 2016), www.nytimes.com/2016/08/13/world/europe/cannes-muslims-burkini-ban.html.

99 Agence-France Presse, *Mayor of Cannes Bans Burkinis on Resort's Beaches*, Guardian (Aug. 11, 2016), www.theguardian.com/world/2016/aug/11/cannes-mayor-bans-burqinis-beachwear-must-respect-secularism.

100 *Id.*

101 Cassandra Vinograd, *Cannes Mayor David Lisnard Bans Burkinis on City's Beaches*, NBC News (Aug. 12, 2016), www.nbcnews.com/news/world/cannes-mayor-david-lisnard-bans-burkinis-city-s-beaches-n628946.

102 *France: Priest Killed in ISIL-Linked Attack on Church*, Al Jazeera (July 26, 2016), www.aljazeera.com/news/2016/07/hostage-takers-northern-france-neutralised-160726090127273.html.

103 *Id.* 104 Agence-France Presse, *supra* note 99.

105 Marta Cooper, *Citing Terrorism, The French Mayor of Cannes has Banned Muslim Women from Wearing "Burkini" Swimwear*, Quartz (Aug. 12, 2016), qz.com/757070/citing-terrorism-the-french-mayor-of-cannes-has-banned-muslim-women-from-wearing-burkini-swimwear/.

the ban does not stop people from wearing veils, the Jewish kippah, or the cross, Lisnard said, "I simply forbid a uniform that is the symbol of Islamic extremism."[106]

In terms of the actual scope of the problem – the burkini ban, like the burqa ban before it, responded to an exaggerated phenomenon. All of the media and public attention the ban garnered would suggest that the burkini is prevalent on beaches along the French Riviera; yet, most mayors who have enacted the ban, such as Olivier Majewicz of Oye-Plage or Daniel Fasquelle of La-Touquet, have never seen a burkini on their towns' beaches.[107]

Without a clear definition of "beach dress ostentatiously manifesting a religious affiliation," the ban gave police extraordinary discretion in interpretation and enforcement. The mayors who enacted the ban not only failed to address this fundamental flaw in the law, but some, like Cannes' Lisnard, actually praised the police's overbroad enforcement of the ban.[108] Many of the women ticketed or accosted by police for wearing burkinis were actually swimming in pants and long-sleeved shirts, or wearing wetsuits or competition swimwear – all of which are permitted on beaches.[109]

Shortly after the ban was enacted, a number of human rights groups challenged the burkini bans in local courts, which subsequently ruled in favor of the bans.[110] The Human Rights League ("LDH") and the anti-Islamophobia Association ("CCIF") appealed to the Council of State, trying their case against the town of Villenueve Loubet.[111] As noted earlier, in late August 2016, the court decided in favor of the LDH and CCIF. Writing for the Council of State, three judges said that the ban "ha[d] dealt a serious and clearly illegal blow to fundamental liberties such as the freedom of movement, freedom of conscience and personal liberty."[112] The court found that to limit fundamental freedoms, there must be an

[106] *Id.*

[107] Alissa J. Rubin, *Fighting for the "Soul of France," More Towns Ban a Bathing Suit: The Burkini*, N.Y. TIMES (Aug. 17, 2016), www.nytimes.com/2016/08/18/world/europe/fighting-for-the-soul-of-france-more-towns-ban-a-bathing-suit-the-burkini.html.

[108] Angelique Chrisafis, *French Burkini Ban Row Escalates After Clothing Incident at Nice Beach*, GUARDIAN (AUG. 25, 2016), www.theguardian.com/world/2016/aug/24/french-burkini-ban-row-escalates-clothing-incident-woman-police-nice-beach.

[109] Rubin, *supra* note 1.

[110] Aurelin Breeden & Lillia Blaise, *Court Overturns "Burkini" Ban in French Town*, N.Y. TIMES (Aug. 26, 2016), www.nytimes.com/2016/08/27/world/europe/france-burkini-ban.html.

[111] *Id.*

[112] Lizzie Dearden, *Burkini Ban Suspended: French Court Declares Law Forbidding Swimwear Worn By Muslim Women "Clearly Illegal,"* INDEPENDENT (Aug. 26, 2016), www.independent.co.uk/news/world/europe/burkini-ban-french-france-court-suspends-rule-law-forbidding-swimwear-worn-muslim-women-seriously-a7211396.html.

adequate risk to public order and safety.[113] "[T]he outfits worn by some people to go swimming" did not pose such a risk to public order and safety, and, thus, the ban unlawfully restricted the freedom of those who wished to wear the burkini.[114]

While the ruling was meant to set a precedent for all of the towns that had enacted burkini bans,[115] a number of mayors have refused to repeal their bans.[116] Human rights groups including LDF and CCIF plan to file suit against each town that maintains its ban despite the ruling from the Council of State.[117]

D French Perceptions of Modesty

Section I started with an examination of *laïcité* and the ways it has been invoked to restrict Muslim religious garb. Beyond *laïcité*, scholars of French culture also note that the history of French colonization plays a significant role in shaping French treatment of religious garb and modesty.[118] France colonized a number of Muslim-majority countries – such as Algeria, Morocco, Egypt, and Tunisia.[119] For the French rulers, the headscarves and flowing cloaks worn by many Muslim women were seen as socially backward.[120] The relatively bland modest dress, mostly products of a religious dress code, was contrasted with the flexible, "fashionable" dress of many French women that emerged as a symbol of progressive, "superior" French culture. The contrast itself helped justify the colonization of Muslim Arabs as "lesser" people, and, over time, dress became connected to a conception of French cultural superiority.[121]

Intrinsic to this conception of modesty as socially backward is the idea that Muslim women in modest religious garb are oppressed.[122] It is argued that the dress is imposed on them by their male relatives or religious authorities, and even women who claim to wear it by choice are brainwashed into thinking they have agency.[123] As such, the government needs to step in and "save" these women by making it impossible for them to lawfully wear religious garb in public. If the women can blame the government, they will be free to dress in less modest ways.[124]

Of course, the logic is deeply flawed, since the government's solution to what it sees as coercion is to impose its own form of coercion – not just on

113 *Id.* 114 *Id.* 115 *Id.* 116 McKenzie, *supra* note 14. 117 *Id.*

118 Amanda Taub, *France's "Burkini" Bans Are About More Than Religion or Clothing*, N.Y. Times (Aug. 18, 2016), www.nytimes.com/2016/08/19/world/europe/frances-burkini-bans-are-about-more-than-religion-or-clothing.html.

119 *Id.* 120 *Id.* 121 *Id.* 122 Gunn, *supra* note 17. 123 *Id.* 124 *Id.*

Muslim women but on all women who wear such clothing for religious or entirely nonreligious reasons.[125] There is also no evidence that prohibiting religious garb in public helps women dress differently in public, as opposed to limiting their public movement altogether. In other words, for those women who may actually be coerced into wearing religious garb, their families may now force them to stay home because they are not allowed to wear the garb in public.

The bans are counterproductive in other ways, too. For example, regarding the burkini ban, critics have argued that it alienated and stigmatized innocent Muslims, a silly/nonsensical move if the purpose of the ban is to alleviate tension among the French people.[126] One critic, Nicolas Cadéne, the spokesman for the French Observatory on *Laïcité*, established in 2007 to define and apply *laïcité*, explained, "[d]uring crises, there are crises of passion, of looking to your own experiences, of retreating, of rising fear. One must not overreach in such a climate ... One should not exploit *laïcité* for partisan ends and to stigmatize people."[127]

Many of these seemingly obvious counterarguments to government bans on religious garb are taken as exactly that in the U.S. – obvious. But that does not entirely prevent the U.S. from its own thorny contestations with modesty. The next section examines some of the cases where these negotiations take place.

II MODESTY IN THE U.S.

The starting point for church-state relations in the U.S. is vastly different from that in France, and the law is responsible for that.[128] Certain cases under the Free Exercise Clause and the Religious Freedom Restoration Act require the government to demonstrate a compelling interest justifying its restriction on religious exercise – when a claimant can demonstrate that the government has placed a substantial burden on his or her sincerely held religious belief.[129] The government must also show that the restriction in question is the least restrictive means of achieving that compelling interest.

[125] Zanetti, *supra* note 96. [126] Rubin, *supra* note 107. [127] *Id.*

[128] While the constitutional language protecting religious freedom in the U.S. and France is remarkably similar, "from those common beginnings, France and the United States have come to opposing answers to almost every important question about religious liberty." Laycock, *supra* note 22, at 864.

[129] U.S. Const, amend. I; Religious Freedom Restoration Act, 42 U.S.C. § 2000bb (2012); Sherbert v. Verner, 374 U.S. 398 (1963). *See* Helfand, Chapter 2, this volume; Sepper, Chapter 1, this volume.

Together, these components are short handed as the strict scrutiny standard.[130]

The strict scrutiny standard has been successful in pushing back against many government encroachments on religious exercise.[131] Despite this protection, however, there are plenty of religious liberty challenges in the U.S., including some – albeit rare – to the right to wear religious garb in public. For example, Nebraska and Pennsylvania have laws preventing public school teachers from wearing religious garb while teaching.[132] A similar law in Oregon was only overturned in 2011.[133] The stated purpose of the laws is to maintain religious neutrality in the public school system, lest a public schoolteacher in religious garb influence a student or send the message that the government endorses a specific religion.[134] Notwithstanding this purported justification, the legitimacy of such laws is questionable; scholars have found evidence that the antireligious garb statutes were originally rooted in anti-Catholic animus, targeting Catholic nuns in particular.[135]

For example, the Pennsylvania law was enacted in the aftermath of an 1894 case decided by the Supreme Court of Pennsylvania, *Hysong et al. v. School District of Gallitzin Borough et al.*[136] The first time a teacher's right to wear religious garb in public schools was challenged, *Hysong* occurred at a time rife with anti-Catholic animus. Public schools taught Protestant religious beliefs and hired nuns on an as-needed basis to teach after hours. The plaintiff argued that permitting the nuns to teach in their garb, which included a habit, cross, and rosary beads, amounted to "sectarian" teaching, which was, at the time, a pejorative code word for Catholic influence. The court disagreed.[137]

Given the climate at the time, the *Hysong* decision was highly unpopular. The following year, the Pennsylvania legislature took action. The first state to prohibit religious garb in public schools, Pennsylvania enacted a religious garb statute that even today bans public school teachers from wearing "any dress, mark, emblem or insignia indicating . . . that such teacher is a member

[130] Sherbert, *supra* note 129. *But see* Helfand, Chapter 2, this volume (noting that the Sherbert-era cases applied something akin to intermediate scrutiny, at least sometimes).

[131] Helfand, Chapter 2, this volume; Rienzi, Chapter 4, this volume.

[132] 3 *States Still Ban Teachers' Religious Clothing*, NBC News (Sep. 2, 2009), www.nbcnews.com/id/32661080/ns/us_news-faith/t/states-still-ban-teachers-religious-clothing/#.WKIjbbHMzNw.

[133] Caitlin S. Kerr, *Teachers' Religious Garb As an Instrument for Globalization in Education*, 18 Ind. J. Global Legal Stud. 539, 550 (2011).

[134] *Id.* [135] *Id.*

[136] Hysong v. Sch. Dist. of Gallitzin Borough, 164 Pa. 629, 30 A. 482 (1894). [137] *Id.*

or adherent of any religious order, sect or denomination."[138] Public school administrators face a criminal penalty if they fail to suspend or fire a teacher wearing religious dress.[139]

While the Pennsylvania religious garb statute targeted nuns in public schools, more than 100 years after it was enacted, the law was enforced against a Muslim public school teacher, in 1990.[140] In *U.S. v. Board of Education for the School District of Philadelphia*, the U.S. Court of Appeals for the Third Circuit held against a Muslim public school teacher who wished to wear her Muslim headscarf in the classroom. The court reasoned that permitting the teacher, Alima Reardon, to wear a headscarf would place an undue burden on school administrators, because it would require the school district to violate the religious garb statute, which had passed constitutional muster and would require the school to take extra steps to ensure Reardon's clothing did not compromise the school's religious neutrality.[141]

Despite this disappointing holding, the fact remains that antireligious garb statutes – once common in the U.S. – are now on the books in only two states after Oregon's fell.[142] Further there is no evidence of enforcement of the ban in Nebraska, one of the two remaining states. Religious modesty has, of course, been contested in other spaces, though much of the debate has occurred in the media and other nonlegal spaces instead of in courts. The next subsections delve into some of these incidents.

A *Unique Challenges in Communal Spaces*

Communal spaces offer special challenges of balancing countervailing interests in access and modesty. One prominent set of incidents where modesty concerns have cropped up involves public swimming pools that choose to reserve hours for female swimmers only. In summer 2016, a Brooklyn public pool sparked controversy over its accommodation of women members of the predominantly Hasidic Jewish local community.[143] The Metropolitan Recreation Center's decades-long accommodation was challenged by an

138 Holly M. Bastian, *Religious Garb Statutes and Title VII: An Uneasy Coexistence*, 80 Geo. L.J. 211, 213 (1991).

139 *Id.*

140 United States v. Bd. of Educ. for Sch. Dist. of Philadelphia, 911 F.2d 882 (3d Cir. 1990).

141 *Id.*

142 Betsy Hammond, *Oregon Legislature Repeals Ban on Religious Dress in Public Schools*, Oregon Live (Feb. 23, 2010), www.oregonlive.com/politics/index.ssf/2010/02/oregon_legislature_repeals_ban.html.

143 Adam Chandler, *Who Should Public Swimming Pools Serve?* Atlantic (June 3, 2016), www.theatlantic.com/politics/archive/2016/06/public-pool-brooklyn/485489/.

anonymous complaint. The city responded first by rescinding the women-only swim hours, then later reinstating the hours and reaffirming the need to be "culturally sensitive."[144] The city's Parks Department pointed to other reasons for the gender segregation: "Histories of domestic and sexual abuse, as well as body image concerns – to which the city deemed women and girls primarily susceptible – were also considered."[145]

A *New York Times* editorial attacked the city's decision, claiming that during the gender-segregated pool hours, the public pool would be "temporarily unmoored from the laws of New York City and the Constitution, and commonly held principles of fairness and equal access."[146] In the newspaper's view, the religious accommodation reflected "a theocratic view of government services."[147]

Other media commentators disagreed. Yair Rosenberg of the Jewish American magazine *Tablet* pointed out the parallel between the *New York Times*'s position and that of well-known anti-Muslim activist Pamela Geller.[148] He explains in his piece that in October 2013, the city of St. Paul, Minnesota, began providing women-only swimming hours at its public YMCA pool. The purpose of the gender segregation was to permit young, mostly Somali Muslim women to learn how to swim without having to violate their religious and cultural beliefs. The accommodation included clearing out all other swimmers from the pool, locking the men's locker room, and providing female lifeguards. The city's police department also provided the girls transportation to the pool.

Rosenberg notes that the accommodation was celebrated in St. Paul, but some national commentators, including Geller, denounced the move as "creeping sharia," railing against accommodation of a "cultural norm" that was Somali, not American.[149] Geller wrote: "There are thousands of Islamic centers across the country – sharia swim belongs there, not in our public

144 *Hikind Announces Major Victory for Human Rights*, Dov Hikind NYS Assemblyman (May 26, 2016), http://dovhikind.com/news/hikind-announces-major-victory-for-human-rights?version=meter+at+0&module=meter.

145 Emma Whitford, *City Approves Women-Only Swimming Hours at Two Public Pools*, Gothamist (July 6, 2016), http://gothamist.com/2016/07/06/women_only_swim_hours_update.php.

146 Editorial Board, *Everybody into the Pool*, N.Y. Times (June 1, 2016), www.nytimes.com/2016/06/01/opinion/everybody-into-the-pool.html?_r=0.

147 *Id.*

148 Yair Rosenberg, *Should There Be Different Rules for Jews and Muslims at Public Pools?* Tablet Magazine (June 2, 2016), www.tabletmag.com/scroll/203984/does-the-new-york-times-think-there-should-be-different-rules-for-jews-and-muslims-at-public-pools.

149 *Id.*

pools." Rosenberg argues that by taking a similar position against pool accommodations in Brooklyn, the *New York Times* supported Geller-like bias. He also notes the prevalence of similar accommodations for Muslim women in numerous other venues, including public pools in San Diego and Seattle, and at pools and gyms at private U.S. universities such as Harvard, Princeton, and George Washington.

Beyond media commentary, American legal scholars also weighed in. Harvard University law professor Noah Feldman told Rosenberg that "[t]he laws are a constitutional accommodation of religion. And the NYC Human Rights law also allows for public policy accommodations; this qualifies [as constitutional]."[150] Eugene Volokh, a nationally known law professor at the University of California at Los Angeles, was less sure that accommodation was required but admitted that a plausible case could be made for the legality of the accommodation.

Conservative Muslim and Jewish beliefs about modesty have intersected with other forms of exercise in public. The Brooklyn swimming pool that continues to offer women-only swimming hours as an accommodation of its Orthodox Jewish community members used to share an avenue with a public bike lane that was subsequently removed in response to the Orthodox community's complaints about modesty.[151] The community complained that the bikers on the path "seemed 'more naked than clothed'" and that biking in general is "vulgar."[152] The Hasidic community moved to remove the bike lane to "protect the sensibilities of Hasidic men."[153]

B Culturally Respectful Healthcare

Exercise is only one healthful practice challenged by modesty concerns. Healthcare providers in the U.S. are expected to pay careful attention to "culturally competent care" – that is, to practice with "the knowledge and interpersonal skills that allow providers to understand, appreciate, and work

[150] *Id.* [151] Chandler, *supra* note 143.

[152] Ted Mann, *An Ultra-Orthodox Neighborhood Goes against Bikes*, WALL ST. J. (June 11, 2012), http://blogs.wsj.com/metropolis/2012/06/11/an-ultra-orthodox-neighborhood-goes-against-bikes/.

[153] Jonathan Turley, *Ultra-Orthodox Rabbi Bans Girls Older than Five From Riding Bikes as "Provocative,"* JONATHANTURLEY (June 8, 2016), https://jonathanturley.org/2016/06/08/ultra-orthodox-rabbi-bans-girls-older-than-five-from-riding-bikes-as-provocative/. A similar rationale was later used by a rabbi in Jerusalem to ban bike riding for girls ages five and older; the rabbi proclaimed that young girls riding bikes may prove too "provocative" for men watching them. *Id.*

with individuals from cultures other than their own."[154] While culturally sensitive healthcare has long been a practice in the U.S., only recently have providers begun to grapple with specific challenges posed by American Muslims, and Muslim women in particular.[155] Muslim women's healthcare beliefs include the following: "(1) [S]hame and honor principles, (2) modesty, (3) gender roles, (4) use of physical touch, (5) gender preferences of health care providers, and (6) spiritual beliefs that may influence the Muslim women's healthcare decisions."[156]

While not all Muslims have the same healthcare beliefs, "maintaining modesty is the 'overarching Islamic ethic'" when it comes to interaction between opposite sexes.[157] Culturally sensitive healthcare practices require the following when it comes to modesty health beliefs:[158]

- The woman should be cared for by a healthcare provider of the same sex, especially when it comes to maternity or gynecological care. If a female provider is not available, a female staffer or an adult relative of the patient should accompany the male provider.
- Clinical procedures that require uncovering body parts should be approached with care – only those parts that must be exposed should be, and the healthcare professional should seek permission before uncovering any portion of the body. Islamic law provisions differ on which parts of the body are permitted to be viewed by members of the opposite versus same sex – a concept termed "awrah."[159]
- Many conservative religious believers, Muslims included, believe that physical touch – including even handshaking – should not occur between men and women who are not related to each other by blood

154 *Cultural Sensitivity and Awareness in the Delivery of Healthcare*, AM. COLL. OBSTETRICS & GYNECOLOGISTS (May 2011), www.acog.org/Resources-And-Publications/Committee-Opinions/Committee-on-Health-Care-for-Underserved-Women/Cultural-Sensitivity-and-Awareness-in-the-Delivery-of-Health-Care.

155 Lori Maria Walton, Fatima Akram, & Ferdosi Hossain, *Health Beliefs of Muslim Women and Implications for Health Care Providers: Exploratory Study on the Health Beliefs of Muslim Women*, ONLINE J. HEALTH ETHICS (2014), aquila.usm.edu/cgi/viewcontent.cgi?article=1132&context=ojhe.

156 *Id.*

157 Ronni Caryn Rabin, *Respecting Muslim Patients' Needs*, N.Y. TIMES (Nov. 1, 2010), www.nytimes.com/2010/11/01/health/01patients.html.

158 G. Hussein Rassool, *Cultural Competence in Nursing Muslim Patients*, NURSING TIMES (Mar. 30, 2015), www.nursingtimes.net/roles/nurse-educators/cultural-competence-in-nursing-muslim-patients/5083725.article.

159 "The awrah, or parts of the body that are not to be exposed, differ depending on who else is present." Rabin, *supra* note 158.

or marriage (a concept termed "mahram").[160] Healthcare providers should be cognizant of this belief when engaging in care. Touch is, however, permitted when the care requires it.

- Some female Muslim patients may avoid making eye contact with a male healthcare professional out of concerns for modesty. Culturally sensitive care advises male healthcare providers not to interpret this reluctance as a sign of rejection or lack of trust.
- Muslim beliefs counsel against men and women being alone together unless they are related to each other by blood or marriage. One of the sayings of the Muslim Prophet Muhammad states that when an unrelated man and woman are together, Satan is the third party. "The laws prohibit not only adultery but 'proximity' to adultery."[161]
- Some scholars even suggest that hospitals "provide more modest hospital gowns or give patients the option of wearing their own clothing."[162]

Scholars specializing in culturally sensitive healthcare emphasize that while these modesty concerns are strict, they by no means require gender-segregated facilities.[163] They are simply ways of making a patient feel more comfortable. One physician shared a case study of a Muslim woman who underwent surgery. Prior to her operation, she told her doctor that she had to at least have her head covered when she was taken out of the operating room. When she awoke postsurgery, she found herself wearing only a hospital gown, with her head uncovered. She was incensed by the lack of sensitivity, vowing to never return to that hospital again.[164]

Another case study involved a Muslim woman who had fallen on her back and had been unable to use the bathroom for twenty-four hours. When she arrived at the emergency room in an ambulance, a female physician was not available and the patient refused to let the male doctor do a rectal exam due to modesty concerns.

C *Complex Motivations: Modesty as a Political or Fashion Statement*

Complicating the modesty analysis is a world racked time and again recently with terrorist attacks by people purporting to act in the name of Islam. Some incidents have involved female terrorists – and in the case of the 2015 attacks in

[160] This aspect of religious modesty recently made headlines when two Muslim schoolboys in Switzerland declined to shake hands with their female teachers. For a cogent analysis of the issue, *see* Jennifer Bryson, *Handshakes, Islam, and Religious Tolerance in the West*, PUBLIC DISCOURSE (Jan. 21, 2016), www.thepublicdiscourse.com/2016/06/17151/.

[161] *Id.* [162] *Id.* [163] *Id.* [164] *Id.*

San Bernardino, California, the female attacker was wearing a headscarf.[165] Inflammatory political and media rhetoric also often attribute such incidents to all Muslims or address the American Muslim community as either a danger that must be limited or a political tool that only serves to combat terrorism.[166]

Inevitably, then, the headscarf has taken on meanings beyond modesty. For some, it has become a symbol of extremism. Unfortunately, many Muslim women who wear it for modesty purposes increasingly face harassment and discrimination because of these other meanings attributed to the headscarf. In fact, 69% of women who wear a Muslim headscarf have experienced at least one incident of discrimination.[167] The incidents include everything from discrimination in hiring to physical and verbal attacks in schools and are attributable at least in part to the identifiable nature of Muslim religious garb.[168]

In the weeks after the 2016 presidential election, the Southern Poverty Law Center found that Muslim women who wear a headscarf were particularly vulnerable to harassment, intimidation, and assault.[169] In fact, the phenomenon of a "hijab grab" has become increasingly common.[170] A number of self-defense instructors now help train headscarf-wearing women to defend against attackers who physically grab their scarves. One recent incident occurred at San Jose University, where an attacker grabbed a student's hijab from behind, temporarily strangling her and causing her to fall.

With society attaching political import to the headscarf, it is no surprise that Muslim women themselves are more likely to embrace the headscarf as

165 Saeed Ahmed, *Who Were Syed Rizwan Farook and Tashfeen Malik?* CNN (Dec. 4, 2015), www.cnn.com/2015/12/03/us/syed-farook-tashfeen-malik-mass-shooting-profile/.

166 Wajahat Ali, *What We Saw in the Second Debate. Enter, Muslims*, N.Y. Times (Oct. 9, 2016), www.nytimes.com/interactive/projects/cp/opinion/clinton-trump-second-debate-election-2016/trump-is-the-student-who-didnt-do-the-reading (arguing that for Trump, "Muslims' only function is to 'report' crimes," whereas Clinton sees Muslims "as an instrument in the never-ending war on terror that has claimed the lives of thousands of innocent Muslims … [Muslims] are the 'eyes and ears' of an apparatus that sees us not as humans but as political props").

167 *Discrimination Against Muslim Women – Fact Sheet*, ACLU, www.aclu.org/other/discrimination-against-muslim-women-fact-sheet?redirect=religion-belief-womens-rights/discrimination-against-muslim-women-fact-sheet.

168 *Id.*

169 *Ten Days After: Harassment and Intimidation in the Aftermath of the Election*, S. Poverty L. Ctr. (Nov. 29, 2016), www.splcenter.org/20161129/ten-days-after-harassment-and-intimidation-aftermath-election.

170 Samantha Schmidt, *Hijab Grab' Defense: As Reports of Hate Crimes Spike Postelection, Muslim Women Turn to Self-Defense*, Wash. Post (Nov. 21, 2016), www.washingtonpost.com/news/morning-mix/wp/2016/11/21/hijab-grab-defense-as-reports-of-hate-crimes-spike-postelection-muslim-women-turn-to-self-defense/?utm_term=.46706266fd8f.

a political act, rather than (or in addition to) a reflection of modesty. For example, in an article for *Time.com* titled "American Hijab: Why My Scarf is a Sociopolitical Statement, Not a Symbol of My Religiosity," one woman writes:

> In spite of, or rather in response to, the negative portrayal of Muslims by those (Muslims and non-Muslims) who seek to define our narrative as one of barbaric killing and atrocity, women choose hijab – a piece of cloth that declares their identity as Muslims while simultaneously expressing their individual identity as smart, driven, successful, and independent. A simple yet powerful message. A way in which Muslim women can reclaim their narrative. In choosing to wear the hijab, American Muslim women reconstruct the narrative of Islam in America.[171]

Other Muslim women seeking to make a media splash have acknowledged that the headscarf visual is key:

> You have to wear a headscarf, of course, because the media's lazy perception of Muslim women – and the only visual they're keen to perpetuate – is that all of them wear headscarves … Then, of course, you have to be fashion-forward. Like, you need to wear a headscarf and show that you're still different, but you need to make them forget that you're different by mixing it with the perfect combination of Western trends to remind everyone that you're also the same.[172]

This latter point about acceptable hijab fashion reflects another increasingly common motivation for religious modesty: to make a fashion statement. In sharp contrast to the French conception of modesty as drab, Muslim women have initiated a phenomenon that while not limited to the U.S., is certainly present in the US: Instagram feeds and Facebook pages filled with pictures that seamlessly combine fashion, style, and modesty. These modest fashionistas intentionally or unintentionally make a point about choice that is often lost on governments and private entities that view modesty as oppressive.[173] That is, modesty can and often is embraced as a medium for

[171] Mariam Gomaa, *American Hijab: Why My Scarf is a Sociopolitical Statement, Not a Symbol of My Religiosity*, TIME (Nov. 11, 2014), http://time.com/3576827/american-hijab-scarf-sociopolitical-statement-religion.

[172] Amani Al-Khatahtbeh, *On Being the Media's Token Muslim Girl*, N.Y. MAGAZINE (Oct. 19, 2016), http://nymag.com/thecut/2016/10/amani-al-khatahtbeh-on-being-the-medias-token-muslim-girl.html.

[173] Reina Lewis & Asma T. Uddin, *What the Modest Movement Can Teach Every Woman About Choice*, REFINERY 29 (Nov. 10, 2016), www.refinery29.com/2016/11/129291/modest-dress-choice-muslim-women-clothing.

confident self-expression. Further amplifying these women's work are mainstream designers, who have taken the women's lead and launched entire fashion lines designed for the modest, mostly Muslim dresser.[174] Modesty in the modern world has become complex and politicized, and in the process, also become quite chic.

Complex motivations for modesty also complicate the legal protections afforded the headscarf. Political and social motivations are not protected under the religious freedom provisions of American law – those provisions are limited to acts rooted in sincerely held religious beliefs. Of course, it may be impossible to draw the line between where religious motivations end and secular ones start; after all, political or fashion motivations do not preclude religious ones. Religion, especially Islam, in the modern age is increasingly becoming politicized in many ways, religious modesty being just one of them.

CONCLUSION

This chapter explored religious modesty in a wide variety of contexts. In France, many of the religious modesty issues making global headlines and dominating public discourse are related to Muslim women and their dress choices. To many in France, Muslim women's dress choices fly in the face of all that is fashionable, modern, and empowered – a perception that makes it even more difficult to accord these religious choices proper legal protection.

In the U.S., popular discussions around modesty are far more varied. While still largely focused on dress, they also include questions of behavior, such as co-ed mingling in communal spaces and religiously sensitive healthcare. As compared to France, the U.S. not only offers stronger legal protections for religious modesty; it also allows religious women to express and explain modesty in multiple ways. Indeed, broader religious freedom protections pave the way for a deeper, more probing discourse about religious belief and exercise.

174 Asma Uddin, *Hijabi Fashionistas Show That Modesty Can be Beautiful*, ACCULTURATED (Mar. 10, 2016), http://acculturated.com/hijabi-fashionistas/.

APPENDIX 1

Fifty-State Survey of Corporal Punishment Laws

State	Classification	Statute
Alabama	Reasonable/Not Excessive Force	"May use reasonable and appropriate physical force upon the minor or incompetent person when and to the extent that he reasonably believes it necessary and appropriate to maintain discipline or to promote the welfare of the minor or incompetent person." ALA. § 13A-3–24 (2017)
Alaska	Reasonable/ Non-deadly Force	"When and to the extent reasonably necessary and appropriate to promote the welfare of the child or incompetent person, a parent, guardian, or other person entrusted with the care and supervision of a child under 18 years of age or an incompetent person may use reasonable and appropriate nondeadly force on that child or incompetent person." ALASKA STAT. § 11.81.430 (2016)
Arizona	Reasonable/Not Excessive Force	"A parent or guardian and a teacher or other person entrusted with the care and supervision of a minor or incompetent person may use reasonable and appropriate physical force upon the minor or incompetent person when and to the extent reasonably necessary and appropriate to maintain discipline." ARIZ. REV. STAT. ANN. § 13–403 (2017)
Arkansas	Reasonable/Not Excessive Force	"Physical discipline of a child when it is reasonable and moderate and is inflicted by a parent or guardian for purposes of restraining or correcting the child. There are certain acts that are specifically prohibited." ARK. REV. STAT. ANN. § 12–18–103 C(3)(i) (2017)

(cont.)

State	Classification	Statute
California	Reasonable/Not Excessive Force	"'[C]hild abuse' means a situation in which a child suffers ... [s]erious physical injury inflicted upon the child by other than accidental means." CAL. WELF. & INST. CODE § 300 (West 2017)
Colorado	Reasonable/Not Excessive Force	"A parent, guardian, or other person entrusted with the care and supervision of a minor or an incompetent person ... of a minor, may use reasonable and appropriate physical force upon the minor or incompetent person when and to the extent it is reasonably necessary and appropriate to maintain discipline or promote the welfare of the minor or incompetent person." COLO. REV. STAT. §§ 19–1-103; 19–3-103 (2016)
Connecticut	Reasonable/Not Excessive Force	"A parent, guardian or other person entrusted with the care and supervision of a minor or an incompetent person, except a person entrusted with the care and supervision of a minor ... may use reasonable physical force upon such minor or incompetent person when and to the extent that he reasonably believes such to be necessary to maintain discipline or to promote the welfare of such minor or incompetent person." CONN. GEN. STAT. § 53a-18 (2016)
Delaware	No Harm/ Physical Injury/Pain	"The force is used for the purpose of safeguarding or promoting the welfare of the child, including the prevention or punishment of misconduct; and the force used is intended to benefit the child, or for the special purposes. The size, age, condition of the child, location of the force and the strength and duration of the force shall be factors considered in determining whether the force used is reasonable and moderate." DEL. CODE ANN. tit. 11, § 468 (2017)
District of Columbia	Reasonable/Not Excessive Force	"Parents can use force as long as it is not excessive." "Child 'abuse' includes excessive corporal punishment." D.C. CODE § 16–2351 (2017)

(cont.)

State	Classification	Statute
Florida	No Harm/ Physical Injury/Pain	"Corporal discipline of a child by a parent or legal custodian for disciplinary purposes does not in itself constitute abuse when it does not result in harm to the child. Statute lists several things that may be considered excessive including broken bones, burns, and bites." FLA. STAT. § 39.01 (2016)
Georgia	Reasonable/Not Excessive Force	"The term 'family violence' shall not be deemed to include reasonable discipline administered by a parent to a child in the form of corporal punishment, restraint, or detention." GA. CODE ANN. § 19–7-5 (2016)
Hawaii	No Risk of Substantial Injury/ Mental Distress/Not Reckless/No Serious Harm	"The use of force upon or toward the person of another is justifiable [if] the force is employed with due regard for the age and size of the minor and is reasonably related to the purpose of safeguarding or promoting the welfare of the minor, including the prevention or punishment of the minor's misconduct; provided that there shall be a rebuttable presumption that the following types of force are not justifiable for purposes of this [paragraph]: throwing, kicking, burning, biting, cutting, striking with a closed fist, shaking a minor under three years of age, interfering with breathing, or threatening with a deadly weapon; and(b) The force used does not intentionally, knowingly, recklessly, or negligently create a risk of causing substantial bodily injury, disfigurement, extreme pain or mental distress, or neurological damage." HAW. REV. STAT. § 703–309 (2017)
Idaho	Reasonable/Not Excessive Force	Abuse includes physical cruelty in excess of that required for reasonable disciplinary purposes. IDAHO CODE § 16–1602 (2017)
Illinois	No Risk of Substantial Injury/ Mental Distress/Not Reckless/No	"'Abused child' means a child whose parent or immediate family member, or any person responsible for the child's welfare, or any individual residing in the same home as the child, or a paramour of the child's parent: (a) inflicts, causes to be inflicted, or allows to be inflicted upon such child physical injury, by

(cont.)

State	Classification	Statute
	Serious Harm	other than accidental means, which causes death, disfigurement, impairment of physical or emotional health, or loss or impairment of any bodily function; (b) creates a substantial risk of physical injury to such child by other than accidental means which would be likely to cause death, disfigurement, impairment of physical or emotional health, or loss or impairment of any bodily function." 325 ILL. COMP. STAT. 5/3 (2016)
Indiana	Reasonable/Not Excessive Force	Law does not limit right of parent/guardian/ custodian to use reasonable corporal punishment when disciplining a child. The statute on child abuse and neglect specifically exempts religion. "This Chapter does not limit the right of a parent, guardian, or custodian of a child to use reasonable corporal punishment when disciplining the child and does not limit the lawful practice or teaching of religious beliefs." IND. CODE ANN. §§ 31–34-1–15 (West 2017)
Iowa	No Harm/ Physical Injury/Pain	Child endangerment includes using unreasonable force, torture, or cruelty which results in physical injury, is intended to cause serious injury, or causes substantial mental or emotional harm. IOWA CODE § 726.6 (2017)
Kansas	Reasonable/Not Excessive Force	"Abuse of a child is knowingly: (1) Torturing or cruelly beating any child under the age of 18 years;(2) shaking any child under the age of 18 years which results in great bodily harm to the child; or (3) inflicting cruel and inhuman corporal punishment upon any child under the age of 18 years." KAN. STAT. ANN. § 21–5602 (2017)
Kentucky	No Risk of Substantial Injury/ Mental Distress/Not Reckless/No	"The use of physical force by a defendant upon another person is justifiable when the defendant is a parent, guardian, or other person entrusted with the care and supervision of a minor or an incompetent person or when the defendant is a teacher or other person entrusted with the care and supervision of a minor, for

(cont.)

State	Classification	Statute
	Serious Harm	a special purpose, and (a) The defendant believes that the force used is necessary to promote the welfare of a minor or mentally disabled person or, if the defendant's responsibility for the minor or mentally disabled person is for a special purpose, to further that special purpose or maintain reasonable discipline in a school, class, or other group; and(b) The force that is used is not designed to cause or known to create a substantial risk of causing death, serious physical injury, disfigurement, extreme pain, or extreme mental distress." Ky. Rev. Stat. Ann. § 503.110 (West 2017)
Louisiana	Reasonable/Not Excessive Force	Not considered child abuse if the injury resulted from what might be considered a reasonable exercise of discipline for the child's misbehavior. La. Civ. Code Ann. Art. 223 (2017)
Maine	Reasonable/Not Excessive Force	"A parent, foster parent, guardian or other similar person responsible for the long term general care and welfare of a child is justified in using a reasonable degree of force against that child when and to the extent that the person reasonably believes it necessary to prevent or punish the child's misconduct." Me. Rev Stat. Ann. tit. 17-A, § 106 (2017)
Maryland	Reasonable/Not Excessive Force	"Nothing in this subtitle shall be construed to prohibit reasonable punishment, including reasonable corporal punishment, in light of the age and condition of the child, from being performed by a parent or stepparent of the child." Md. Code Ann., Fam. Law § 4–501 (West 2017)
Massachusetts	No Harm/ Physical Injury/Pain	"'Abuse', the willful infliction of injury, unreasonable confinement, intimidation, including verbal or mental abuse, or punishment with resulting physical harm, pain or mental anguish or assault and battery; provided, however, that verbal or mental abuse shall require a knowing and willful act directed at a specific person." Mass. Ann. Laws ch. 111, § 72 F (West 2017)

(cont.)

State	Classification	Statute
Michigan	No Risk of Substantial Injury/ Mental Distress/Not Reckless/No Serious Harm	"This section does not prohibit a parent or guardian, or other person permitted by law or authorized by the parent or guardian, from taking steps to reasonably discipline a child, including the use of reasonable force." MICH. COMP. LAWS § 750.136b (2017)
Minnesota	Reasonable/Not Excessive Force	"A parent, legal guardian, or caretaker who, by an intentional act or a series of intentional acts with respect to a child, evidences unreasonable force or cruel discipline that is excessive under the circumstances is guilty of malicious punishment of a child." MINN. STAT. ANN. § 609.379 (West 2017)
Mississippi	Reasonable/Not Excessive Force	Abuse includes inflicting bodily harm. "'Bodily harm' means any bodily injury to a child and includes, but is not limited to, bruising, bleeding, lacerations, soft tissue swelling, and external or internal swelling of any body organ." MISS. CODE. ANN. § 97–5-39 (2017)
Missouri	Reasonable/Not Excessive Force	"Discipline including spanking, administered in a reasonable manner, shall not be construed to be abuse." MO. ANN. STAT. § 210.110 (West 2017)
Montana	Reasonable/Not Excessive Force	"A parent or an authorized agent of a parent or a guardian, master, or teacher is justified in the use of force that is reasonable and necessary to restrain or correct the person's child, ward, apprentice, or pupil." MONT. CODE ANN. § 45–3-107 (2017)
Nebraska	For Sake of Welfare/No Substantial Risk of Death, Serious Bodily Harm	"The use of force upon or toward the person of another is justifiable if: (1) The actor is the parent or guardian or other person similarly responsible for the general care and supervision of a minor or a person acting at the request of such parent, guardian, or other responsible person and: (a) Such force is used for the purpose of safeguarding or promoting the welfare of the minor, including the prevention or punishment of his or her misconduct; and

(cont.)

State	Classification	Statute
		(b) Such force used is not designed to cause or known to create a substantial risk of causing death, serious bodily harm, disfigurement, extreme pain or mental distress, or gross degradation." NEB. REV. STAT. § 28–1413 (2017)
Nevada	Reasonable/Not Excessive Force	"Excessive corporal punishment may result in physical or mental injury constituting abuse or neglect of a child under the provisions of this chapter." NEV. REV. STAT. § 128.013 (2017)
New Hampshire	Reasonable/Not Excessive Force	"A parent, guardian or other person responsible for the general care and welfare of a minor is justified in using force against such minor when and to the extent that he reasonably believes it necessary to prevent or punish such minor's misconduct." N.H. REV. STAT. ANN. § 627:6 (2017)
New Jersey	Reasonable/Not Excessive Force	"'Abused child' means a child under the age of 18 years whose parent, guardian, or other person having his custody and control (a) Inflicts or allows to be inflicted upon such child physical injury by other than accidental means which causes or creates a substantial risk of death, or serious or protracted disfigurement, or protracted impairment of physical or emotional health or protracted loss or impairment of the function of any bodily organ." N.J. STAT. ANN. § 2 C:3–8 (West 2017)
New Mexico	Reasonable/Not Excessive Force	"Abuse of a child consists of a person knowingly, intentionally or negligently, and without justifiable cause, causing or permitting a child to be: (1) placed in a situation that may endanger the child's life or health; (2) tortured, cruelly confined or cruelly punished." N.M. STAT. ANN. § 32A-4–2(B) (2017)
New York	Reasonable/ Nondeadly Force Allowed	"A parent, guardian or other person entrusted with the care and supervision of a person under the age of twenty-one or an incompetent person, and a teacher or other person entrusted with the care and supervision of a person under the age of twenty-one for a special purpose, may use

(cont.)

State	Classification	Statute
		physical force, but not deadly physical force, upon such person when and to the extent that he reasonably believes it necessary to maintain discipline or to promote the welfare of such person." N.Y. PENAL LAW § 35.10 (McKinney 2017)
North Carolina	No Harm/ Physical Injury/Pain	Abuse includes "Uses or allows to be used upon the juvenile cruel or grossly inappropriate procedures or cruel or grossly inappropriate devices to modify behavior." N.C. GEN. STAT. § 7B-101 (2017)
North Dakota	No Risk of Substantial Injury/ Mental Distress/Not Reckless/No Serious Harm	"A parent, guardian, or other person responsible for the care and supervision of a minor, or other person responsible for the care and supervision of a minor for a special purpose, or a person acting at the direction of any of the foregoing persons, may use reasonable force upon the minor for the purpose of safeguarding or promoting the minor's welfare, including prevention and punishment of the minor's misconduct, and the maintenance of proper discipline. The force may be used for this purpose, whether or not it is "necessary" as required by subsection 1 of section 12.1–05-07. The force used must not create a substantial risk of death, serious bodily injury, disfigurement, or gross degradation." N.D. CENT. CODE ANN. § 12.1–05-05 (2017)
Ohio	Reasonable/Not Excessive Force	"No person, who is the parent, guardian, custodian, person having custody or control, or person in loco parentis of a child under eighteen years of age or a mentally or physically handicapped child under twenty-one years of age, shall create a substantial risk to the health or safety of the child, by violating a duty of care, protection, or support. It is not a violation of a duty of care, protection, or support under this division when the parent, guardian, custodian, or person having custody or control of a child treats the physical or mental illness or defect of the child by spiritual means through prayer alone, in accordance with the tenets of a recognized religious body." OHIO REV. CODE ANN. § 2151.031 (2017)

(cont.)

State	Classification	Statute
Oklahoma	Reasonable/Not Excessive Force	Parents can use ordinary force as a means of discipline, including but not limited to spanking, switching, or paddling. OKLA. STAT. ANN. tit. 21, § 844 (West 2017)
Oregon	Reasonable/Not Excessive Force	"A parent, guardian or other person entrusted with the care and supervision of a minor or an incompetent person may use reasonable physical force upon such minor or incompetent person when and to the extent the person reasonably believes it necessary to maintain discipline or to promote the welfare of the minor or incompetent person." OR. REV. STAT. ANN. § 161.205 (2017)
Pennsylvania	No Risk of Substantial Injury/ Mental Distress/Not Reckless/No Serious Harm	"The use of force upon or toward the person of another is justifiable if: (1) The actor is the parent or guardian or other person similarly responsible for the general care and supervision of a minor or a person acting at the request of such parent, guardian or other responsible person and: (i) the force is used for the purpose of safeguarding or promoting the welfare of the minor, including the preventing or punishment of his misconduct; and (ii) the force used is not designed to cause or known to create a substantial risk of causing death, serious bodily injury, disfigurement, extreme pain or mental distress or gross degradation." 18 PA. CONS. STAT. § 509 (2017)
Rhode Island	Reasonable/Not Excessive Force	Any person who "inflicts upon a child serious bodily injury, shall be guilty of first degree child abuse." R.I. GEN. LAWS ANN. § 40–11-2 (2016)
South Carolina	No Risk of Substantial Injury/ Mental Distress/Not Reckless/No Serious Harm	Permits force if reasonable in manner and moderate in degree and it causes no permanent damage and is not reckless or grossly negligent. S.C. CODE ANN. § 63–7-20 (2017)

(cont.)

State	Classification	Statute
South Dakota	Reasonable/Not Excessive Force	"To use or attempt to use or offer to use force upon or toward the person of another is not unlawful if committed by a parent or the authorized agent of any parent, or by any guardian, teacher, or other school official, in the exercise of a lawful authority to restrain or correct the child, pupil, or ward and if restraint or correction has been rendered necessary by the misconduct of the child, pupil, or ward, or by the child's refusal to obey the lawful command of such parent, or authorized agent, guardian, teacher, or other school official, and the force used is reasonable in manner and moderate in degree." S.D. Codified Laws § 22–18-5 (2017)
Tennessee	Reasonable/Not Excessive Force	Abuse includes: "The risk must be of such a nature and degree that the failure to perceive it constitutes a gross deviation from the standard of care that an ordinary parent or legal custodian of a child eight (8) years of age or less would exercise under all the circumstances as viewed from the defendant's standpoint." Tenn. Code Ann. § 39–15-401 (2017)
Texas	Reasonable/ Nondeadly Force Allowed	"The use of force, but not deadly force, against a child younger than 18 years is justified: (1) if the actor is the child's parent or stepparent or is acting in loco parentis to the child; and (2) when and to the degree the actor reasonably believes the force is necessary to discipline the child or to safeguard or promote his welfare." Tex. Penal Code § 9.61 (2017)
Utah	Reasonable/Not Excessive Force	Use of force by a parent is justified when "when the actor's conduct is reasonable discipline of minors by parents, guardians, teachers, or other persons in loco parentis." Utah Code Ann. § 76–2-401 (West 2017)
Vermont	No Harm/ Physical Injury/Pain	"'Abused or neglected child' means a child whose physical health, psychological growth and development, or welfare is harmed or is at substantial risk of harm by the acts or omissions of his or her parent or other person responsible for the child's welfare." Vt. Stat. Ann. tit. 33 4912 (2017)

(cont.)

State	Classification	Statute
Virginia	Reasonable/Not Excessive Force	Abuse does not include physical pain, injury or discomfort caused by the use of incidental, minor or reasonable physical contact or other actions designed to maintain order and control as permitted in clause. VA. CODE ANN. § 18.2–57.2 (2016)
Washington	Reasonable/Not Excessive Force	"The physical discipline of a child is not unlawful when it is reasonable and moderate and is inflicted by a parent, teacher, or guardian for purposes of restraining or correcting the child. Any use of force on a child by any other person is unlawful unless it is reasonable and moderate and is authorized in advance by the child's parent or guardian for purposes of restraining or correcting the child." WASH. REV. CODE § 9A.16.100 (2017)
West Virginia	Reasonable/Not Excessive Force	Force must be reasonable and cannot be excessive. W. VA. CODE § 49–1-201 (2017)
Wisconsin	Reasonable/Not Excessive Force	"When the actor's conduct is reasonable discipline of a child by a person responsible for the child's welfare. Reasonable discipline may involve only such force as a reasonable person believes is necessary. It is never reasonable discipline to use force which is intended to cause great bodily harm or death or creates an unreasonable risk of great bodily harm or death." WIS. STAT. § 939.45 (2017)
Wyoming	Reasonable/Not Excessive Force	"'Abuse' means inflicting or causing physical or mental injury, harm or imminent danger to the physical or mental health or welfare of a child other than by accidental means, including abandonment, unless the abandonment is a relinquishment substantially in accordance with W.S. 14–11-101 through 14–11-109, excessive or unreasonable corporal punishment, malnutrition or substantial risk thereof by reason of intentional or unintentional neglect, and the commission or allowing the commission of a sexual offense against a child as defined by law." WYO. STAT. ANN. § 14–3-202 (2017)

APPENDIX 2

States with RFRAs, Heightened Scrutiny of Religious Claims, or Sexual Orientation/Gender Identity Laws

State	Religious Protections	Employment	Housing	Public Accommodations
Alabama	RFRA Only[1]			
Alaska	Heightened Scrutiny Only[2]			
Arizona	RFRA Only[3]			
Arkansas	RFRA and Heightened Scrutiny[4]			
California	No RFRA or Heightened Scrutiny	SOGI[5]	SOGI[6]	SOGI[7]
Colorado	No RFRA or Heightened Scrutiny	SOGI[8]	SOGI[9]	SOGI[10]
Connecticut	RFRA Only[11]	SOGI[12]	SOGI[13]	SOGI[14]

1 ALA. CONST. Art. I, § 3.01 (constitutional amendment).

2 Larson v. Cooper, 90 P.3d 125, 131–32 & n.31 (Alaska 2004); Swanner v. Anchorage Equal Rights Comm'n, 868 P.2d. 274 (Alaska 1994).

3 ARIZ. REV. STAT. ANN. § 41–1493.01, et seq. (2016).

4 ARK. CODE ANN. § 16–123–401, et seq. (2015); Gipson v. Brown, 749 S.W.2d 297 (Ark. 1988).

5 CAL. GOV'T CODE § 12920, 12940, and 12949 (West 2016); *see also* Assemb. 2601, 1991–1992 Calif. Leg. Reg. Sess. (Feb. 11, 1992); Assemb. 196, 2003–2004 Leg., Reg. Sess. (Cal. 2003) (enacted 2003, became effective Jan. 1, 2004).

6 CAL. GOV'T CODE § 1135 (West 2016). 7 CAL. CIVIL CODE § 51(b) (West 2016).

8 COLO. REV. STAT. § 24–34–402 (2014). *See also* Colorado Anti-Discrimination Act, S. 08–200, 2008 Leg., (Co. 2008).

9 COLO. REV. STAT. § 24–34–501 (2014). 10 COLO. REV. STAT. § 24–34–601 (2014).

11 CONN. GEN. STAT. § 52-571b (2013).

12 CONN. GEN. STAT. § 46a-60 (2009). *See also* An Act Concerning Discrimination on the Basis of Sexual Orientation, Pub. Acts No. 91–58 (Reg. Sess.) (codified as amended at CONN. GEN. STAT. § 46a-64c (2009)); An Act Concerning Discrimination, H.R. 6599, 2011 Leg., Reg. Sess. (Conn. 2011).

13 CONN. GEN. STAT. § 46a-64c (2016). 14 CONN. GEN. STAT. § 46a-63 (1) (2016).

(cont.)

State	Religious Protections	Employment	Housing	Public Accommodations
Delaware	No RFRA or Heightened Scrutiny	SOGI[15]	SOGI[16]	SOGI[17]
DC	No RFRA or Heightened Scrutiny	SOGI[18]	SOGI[19]	SOGI[20]
Florida	RFRA Only[21]			
Georgia	No RFRA or Heightened Scrutiny			
Hawaii	Heightened Scrutiny Only[22]	SOGI[23]	SOGI[24]	SOGI[25]
Idaho	RFRA Only[26]			
Illinois	RFRA Only[27]	SOGI[28]	SOGI[29]	SOGI[30]
Indiana	RFRA and Heightened Scrutiny[31]			

15 DEL. CODE ANN. tit. 19, § 711 (West 2014). *See also* An Act to Amend Titles 6, 9, 18, 19, 25, and 29 of the Delaware Code Relating to Discrimination in Employment, Public Works Contracting, Housing, Equal Accommodations and the Insurance Business, ch. 90, sec. 4, 77 DEL. LAWS 264 (2009) (codified as DEL. CODE ANN. tit. 6, § 4604 (West 2014)); Gender Identity Nondiscrimination Act, S. 97, 147th Gen. Assemb. (Del. 2013).

16 DEL. CODE ANN., tit. 6, § 4603 (West 2014). 17 DEL. CODE. tit. 6, § 4502(14) (2014).

18 D.C. CODE § 2–1402.11 (LexisNexis 2012). *See also* Human Rights Act of 1977, D.C. Law 2–38, title II, 24 D.C. Reg. 6038 (Dec. 13, 1977) (codified at D.C. CODE § 2–1402.21 (LexisNexis 2012)); Human Rights Clarifications Amendment Act of 2005, Council Bill 16–389 (D.C. 2005).

19 D.C. CODE § 2–1402.21 (LexisNexis 2015).

20 D.C. CODE § 2–1402.02(24) (LexisNexis 2015). 21 FLA. STAT. § 761.01, et seq. (2016).

22 Dedman v. Board, 740 P.2d 28 (Haw. 1987).

23 HAW. REV. STAT. § 378–2 (2015). Hawaii did enact a law in 2011 to clarify existing law with regard to sex discrimination on the basis of gender identity in employment. *See* A Bill for an Act Relating to Civil Rights, Act 76, sec. 3, 2006 Haw. Sess. Laws 214, 215 (codified as HAW. REV. STAT. § 489–3 (2015)); H.R. 546, 26th Leg. (Haw. 2011).

24 HAW. REV. STAT. § 515–3 (2015). 25 HAW. REV. STAT. § 489–2 (2015).

26 IDAHO CODE § 73–402, et seq. (2016); State v. Fluewelling, 249 P.3d 375, 378–79 (Idaho 2011).

27 775 ILL. COMP. STAT. 35/1, et seq. (2010).

28 775 ILL. COMP. STAT. 5/102(A) (2010). *See also* An Act Concerning Human Rights, Pub. Act No. 93–1078, art. 1, 2004 Ill. Laws 4837, 4838 (codified as 775 ILL. COMP. STAT. 5/102(A) (2010)).

29 775 ILL. COMP. STAT. 5/3–101 (2010). 30 775 ILL. COMP. STAT. 5/5–101(A) (2010).

31 IND. CODE § 34–13–9–1, et seq. (2016); City Chapel Evangelical Free Inc. v. City of South Bend, 744 N.E.2d 443, 445–51 (Ind. 2001); Church of Christ v. Metropolitan Board of Zoning Appeals, 371 N.E.2d 1331 (Ind. Ct. App. 1978).

(cont.)

State	Religious Protections	Employment	Housing	Public Accommodations
Iowa	No RFRA or Heightened Scrutiny	SOGI[32]	SOGI[33]	SOGI[34]
Kansas	RFRA and Heightened Scrutiny[35]			
Kentucky	RFRA Only[36]			
Louisiana	RFRA Only[37]			
Maine	Heightened Scrutiny Only[38]	SOGI[39]	SOGI[40]	SOGI[41]
Maryland	No RFRA or Heightened Scrutiny[42]	SOGI[43]	SOGI[44]	SOGI[45]
Massachusetts	Heightened Scrutiny Only[46]	SOGI[47]	SOGI[48]	SOGI[49]

[32] IOWA CODE § 216.2 (2016). *See also* An Act Relating to the Iowa Civil Rights Act and Discrimination Based Upon a Person's Sexual Orientation or Gender Identity, S. 427, 82d Gen. Assemb., Reg. Sess. § 1 (Iowa 2007).

[33] IOWA CODE § 216.8 (2016). [34] IOWA CODE § 216.2(13) (2016).

[35] KAN. STAT. ANN. § 60–5301, et seq. (2015); Lower v. Bd. of Dirs. of the Haskell Cnty. Cemetery Dist., 56 P.3d 235, 244–46 (Kan. 2002); State v. Evans, 796 P.2d 178 (Kan. Ct. App. 1990).

[36] KY. REV. STAT. ANN. § 446.350 (West 2015); Gingerich v. Commonwealth, 382 S.W.3d 835, 844 (Ky. 2012).

[37] LA. REV. STAT. ANN. § 13:5231, et seq. (2015).

[38] Foltin v. Roman Catholic Bishop, 871 A.2d 1208, 1227–30 (Me. 2005); Rupert v. Portland, 605 A.2d 63 (Me. 1992).

[39] 2005 Bill Text ME S.B. 413, PL 1993, c. 327 (effective June 29, 2005). *See also* P.L. 2005, c. 7, § 1 (Me. 2005).

[40] ME. REV. STAT. tit. 5, § 4582 (2015). [41] ME. REV. STAT. tit. 5, § 4553(8) (2015).

[42] Montrose Christian Sch. Corp. v. Walsh, 770 A.2d 111, 123 (Md. 2001).

[43] MD. CODE ANN., STATE GOV'T § 20–606 (West 2015). *See also* H.R. 51, ch. 120, sec. 3 2009 Md. Laws 540, 554 (codified at MD. CODE ANN., STATE GOV'T § 20–304 (West 2015)); Fairness for All Marylanders Act of 2014, 2014 Md. Legis. Serv. ch. 474 (West) (codified at MD. CODE ANN., STATE GOV'T § 20–101(e)).

[44] MD. CODE ANN., STATE GOV'T § 20–705 (West 2015).

[45] MD. CODE ANN., STATE GOV'T § 20–301 (West 2015).

[46] Rasheed v. Comm'r of Corr., 845 N.E.2d 296, 302–03, 308 (Mass. 2006); Attorney General v. Desilets, 636 N.E.2d 233 (Mass. 1994).

[47] MASS. GEN. LAWS, chap. 151B § 4 (2016). *See also* An Act Making It Unlawful to Discriminate on the Basis of Sexual Orientation, 1989 Mass. Acts 516; An Act Relative to Transgender Anti-Discrimination, S.735, 189th Gen. Ct. (Mass. 2016).

[48] MASS. GEN. LAWS, chap. 151B § 4 (2016).

[49] MASS. GEN. LAWS, chap. 151B, § 4(18) (2016).

(cont.)

State	Religious Protections	Employment	Housing	Public Accommodations
Michigan	Heightened Scrutiny Only[50]			
Minnesota	Heightened Scrutiny Only[51]	SOGI[52]	SOGI[53]	SOGI[54]
Mississippi	RFRA and Heightened Scrutiny[55]			
Missouri	RFRA Only[56]			
Montana	Heightened Scrutiny Only[57]			
Nebraska	No RFRA or Heightened Scrutiny[58]			
Nevada	No RFRA or Heightened Scrutiny	SOGI[59]	SOGI[60]	SOGI[61]
New Hampshire	No RFRA or Heightened Scrutiny[62]	SO[63]	SO[64]	SO[65]
New Jersey	No RFRA or Heightened Scrutiny	SOGI[66]	SOGI[67]	SOGI[68]

50 McCready v. Hoffius, 586 N.W.2d 723, 729 (Mich. 1998), vacated on other grounds, 593 N.W.2d 545 (Mich. 1999); Porth v Roman Catholic Diocese, 532 N.W.2d 195 (Mich. Ct. App. 1995).

51 Hill-Murray Federation of Teachers v. Hill-Murray High School, 487 N.W.2d 857 (Minn. 1992); State v. Hershberger, 462 N.W.2d 393, 396–99 (Minn. 1990).

52 Minn. Stat. Ann. § 363.08 subd. 2 (2015). *See also* H.R. 585, 2015 Sess., 89th Leg. (Minn. 2015).

53 Minn. Stat. Ann. § 363.09 (2015). 54 Minn. Stat. Ann. § 363A.03(34) (2015).

55 Miss. Code. Ann. § 11–61–1 (West 2015); *In re* Brown, 478 So. 2d 1033 (Miss. 1985).

56 Mo. Rev. Stat. § 1.302, et seq. (2015).

57 Davis v. The Church of Jesus Christ of Latter Day Saints, 852 P.2d 640 (Mont. 1993); St. John's Lutheran Church v. State Comp. Ins. Fund, 830 P.2d 1271, 1276–77 (Mont. 1992).

58 *In re* Interest of Anaya, 758 N.W.2d 10, 19 (Neb. 2008).

59 Nev. Rev. Stat. § 613.340 2015). *See also* Assemb. 311, 1999 Sess., 70th Leg. (Nev. 1999); Assemb. 211, 2011 Sess., 76th Leg. (Nev. 2011).

60 Nev. Rev. Stat. § 118.100 (2015). 61 Nev. Rev. Stat. § 651.050(3) (2015).

62 Appeal of Trotzer, 719 A.2d 584, 589 (N.H. 1998).

63 N.H. Rev. Stat. Ann. § 354-A:6 (2015). *See also* An Act Amending the Law Against Discrimination to Prohibit Discrimination on Account of a Person's Sexual Orientation, ch. 108, 1997 N.H. Laws 88, 92 (codified as N.H. Rev. Stat. § 354-A:10 (2015)).

64 N.H. Rev. Stat. § 354-A:10 (2015). 65 N.H. Rev. Stat. Ann. § 354-A:2(XIV) (2015).

66 N.J. Stat. Ann. § 10:5–4 (2015). 67 N.J. Stat. Ann. § 10:5–9.1 (2015).

68 N.J. Stat. Ann. § 10:5–5(l) (2015).

(cont.)

State	Religious Protections	Employment	Housing	Public Accommodations
New Mexico	RFRA Only[69]	SOGI[70]	SOGI[71]	SOGI[72]
New York	Heightened Scrutiny Only[73]	SO[74]	SO[75]	SO[76]
North Carolina	Heightened Scrutiny Only[77]			
North Dakota	No RFRA or Heightened Scrutiny			
Ohio	Heightened Scrutiny Only[78]			
Oklahoma	RFRA Only[79]			
Oregon	No RFRA or Heightened Scrutiny[80]	SOGI[81]	SOGI[82]	SOGI[83]
Pennsylvania	RFRA Only[84]			
Rhode Island	RFRA Only[85]	SOGI[86]	SOGI[87]	SOGI[88]

69 N.M. Stat. Ann. § 28–22–1, et seq. (2015).

70 N.M. Stat. Ann. § 28–1–7 (2015). *See also* An Act Relating to Human Rights, S. 28, 46th Leg., 1st Sess. (N.M. 2003).

71 N.M. Stat. Ann. § 28–1–7 (2015). 72 N.M. Stat. Ann. § 28–1–2(H) (2015).

73 Catholic Charities v. Serio, 859 N.E.2d 459, 465–68 (N.Y. 2006).

74 N.Y. Exec. Law §§ 291, 296(1)–(1-a) (McKinney 2016). *See also* Secs. 2, 7, §§ 291, 296(2) 2002 N.Y. Laws at 46, 48 (codified as amended at N.Y. Exec. Law §§ 291, 296(2) (McKinney 2016)). Courts have interpreted provisions of the Human Rights Laws to cover transgender people. *See also* Sexual Orientation Non-Discrimination Act of 2002, ch. 2, § 5, 2002 N.Y. Sess. Laws 48–56 (McKinney 2016).

75 N.Y. Exec. Law § 290 (McKinney 2016).

76 N.Y. Exec. Law § 292 & 296 (McKinney 2016).

77 Matter of Browning, 476 S.E.2d 465 (N.C. Ct. App. 1996).

78 Humphrey v. Lane, 728 N.E.2d 1039 (Ohio 2000).

79 Okla. Stat. tit., 51 § 251, et seq. (2015).

80 Meltebeke v. Bureau of Labor & Indus., 903 P.2d 351, 359–62 (Or. 1995).

81 Or. Rev. Stat. § 659A.403 (2015). *See also* The Oregon Equality Act of 2007, S. 2, 74th Leg., Reg. Sess. (Or. 2007).

82 Or. Rev. Stat. § 659A.421 (2015). 83 Or. Rev. Stat. § 659A.400 (2015).

84 Pa. Stat. tit. 71, § 2403, et seq. (2016).

85 R.I. Gen. Laws § 42–80.1–1, et seq. (West 2006).

86 R.I. Gen. Laws § 28–5–7 (West 2015). *See also* An Act Relating to Civil Rights, ch. 32, sec. 7, 1995 R.I. Pub. Laws 83 (codified as R.I. Gen. Laws Ann. § 11–24–2 (Supp. 2013)); An Act Relating to Civil Rights, H. 5920A, Gen. Assemb. (R.I. 2001).

87 R.I. Gen. Laws § 34–37–2.2 & 2.3 (West 2015). 88 R.I. Gen. Laws § 11–24–3 (2015).

(cont.)

State	Religious Protections	Employment	Housing	Public Accommodations
South Carolina	RFRA Only[89]			
South Dakota	No RFRA or Heightened Scrutiny			
Tennessee	RFRA and Heightened Scrutiny[90]			
Texas	RFRA Only[91]			
Utah	No RFRA or Heightened Scrutiny	SOGI[92]	SOGI[93]	
Vermont	No RFRA or Heightened Scrutiny	SOGI[94]	SOGI[95]	SOGI[96]
Virginia	RFRA Only[97]			
Washington	Heightened Scrutiny Only[98]	SOGI[99]	SOGI[100]	SOGI[101]
West Virginia	Heightened Scrutiny Only[102]			

89 S.C. Code. Ann. § 1–32–10, et seq. (2015).

90 Tenn. Code Ann. § 4–1–407 (West 2015); State ex rel. Swann v. Pack, 527 S.W.2d 99, 107 (Tenn. 1975); Wolf v. Sundquist, 955 S.W.2d 626 (Tenn. App. 1997); State v. Loudon, 857 S.W.2d 878 (Tenn. Crim. App. 1993).

91 Tex. Civ. Prac. & Rem. Code Ann. § 110.001, et seq. (2016).

92 2015 Utah Laws Ch. 13. 93 2015 Utah Laws Ch. 13.

94 Vt. Stat. Ann. tit. 21, § 495(a) (2014). *See also* An Act Relating to Discrimination on the Basis of Sexual Orientation, No. 135, 1992 Vt. Acts & Resolves 26, 30–31 (codified as Vt. Stat. Ann. tit. 9, § 4502(a) (Supp. 2013)); S. 0051, 2007–2008 Leg., Reg. Sess. (Vt. 2007). *See also* 1 V.S.A § 144; S. 51, 2007 Vt. Laws 41 (legislative history).

95 Vt. Stat. Ann. tit. 9, § 4503 (2015). 96 Vt. Stat. Ann. tit. 9, § 4501(1) (2015).

97 Va. Code Ann. § 57–2.02 (2015).

98 City of Woodlinville v. Northshore United Church of Christ, 211 P.3d 406, 410 (Wash. 2009); Munns v. Martin, 930 P.2d 318 (Wash. 1997).

99 Wash. Rev. Code § 49.60.180 (2015). *See also* An Act Relating to the Jurisdiction of the Washington Human Rights Commission, ch. 4, 2006 Wash. Sess. Laws 12 (codified as Wash. Rev. Code § 49.60.215 (2012)).

100 Wash. Rev. Code § 49.60.222 (2015). 101 Wash. Rev. Code § 49.60.040(2) (2015).

102 State v. Everly, 146 S.E.2d 705 (W.Va. 1966) (applying a standard of review that is unclear, but inconsistent with *Employment Division v. Smith*).

(cont.)

State	Religious Protections	Employment	Housing	Public Accommodations
Wisconsin	Heightened Scrutiny Only[103]	SO[104]	SO[105]	SO[106]
Wyoming	No RFRA or Heightened Scrutiny			

103 Coulee Catholic Schs. v. Labor & Indus. Review Comm'n, 768 N.W.2d 868, 884–87 (Wisc. 2009); State v. Miller, 549 N.W.2d 235 (Wis. 1996).

104 Wisc. Stat. § 111.36 (2015). *See also* An Act to Amend 15.04 (1) (G), 16.765 (1) and (2) (a), 21.35, 66.39 (13), 66.395 (2m), 66.40 (2m), 66.405 (2m), 66.43 (2m), 66.431 (3) (E) 2, 66.432 (1) and (2), 66.433 (3) (a) and (C) 1. B and (9), 101.22 (1), (Lm) (B), (2m) and (4n), 101.221 (1), 111.31 (1) to (3), 111.32 (5) (a), 111.70 (2), 111.81 (9) (B), 111.85 (1), 227.033 (1), 230.01 (2), 230.18, 234.29 and 942.04 (1) (a) to (C) and (3); And to Create 111.32 (4s) and (5) (I) of the Statutes, Relating to Prohibiting Discrimination Based Upon Sexual Orientation, Assemb. 70, 1981 Assemb. (Wis. 1982).

105 Wisc. Stat. § 106.50 (2015).

106 Wisc. Stat. § 106.52(1)(e)(1) (2015).

Statute Index

Case Index

Subject Index

www.ingramcontent.com/pod-product-compliance
Lightning Source LLC
LaVergne TN
LVHW052012200926
848481LV00005B/1469

* 9 7 8 1 1 0 8 4 0 5 5 0 8 *